A BIBLIOGRAPHY OF

JEWISH | EDUCATION

IN THE UNITED STATES

A BIBLIOGRAPHY OF
JEWISH EDUCATION
IN THE UNITED STATES

Compiled and Edited by   NORMAN DRACHLER

WAYNE STATE UNIVERSITY PRESS   DETROIT

In Association with   AMERICAN JEWISH ARCHIVES   CINCINNATI

Copyright ©1996 by Wayne State University Press, Detroit, Michigan 48201.

Library of Congress Cataloging-in-Publication Data

Drachler, Norman.
    A bibliography of Jewish education in the United States / compiled and edited by Norman Drachler.
    p.   cm.
    Includes index.
    ISBN 978-0-8143-4350-0 (alk. paper); 978-0-8143-4349-4 (ebook)
    1. Jews—Education—United States—Bibliography. 2. Jewish religious education—United States—Bibliography. I. American Jewish Archives. II. Title.
Z5814.J4D72 1996
[LC741]
016.2966'8—dc20   93-47221

DESIGNER | S. R. TENENBAUM

The publication of this volume in a freely accessible digital format has been made possible by a major grant from the National Endowment for the Humanities and the Mellon Foundation through their Humanities Open Book Program.

http://wsupress.wayne.edu/

This book is dedicated TO MY WIFE EVELYN
to the memory of my parents, ROSE AND ISRAEL DRACHLER
and to the memory of our daughter JUDITH DRACHLER HANDEL
1945–1983

Publication of this book was made possible by the generosity of the following foundations and funds:

THE BENARD L. MAAS FOUNDATION
THE ALAN AND SHARYL ACKERMAN FUND
THE SAMUEL AND JEAN FRANKEL FOUNDATION
THE MORRIS AND EMMA SCHAVER PUBLICATION FUND FOR JEWISH STUDIES
THE COHN FAMILY PHILANTHROPIC FUND
THE TAUBMAN FOUNDATION

CONTENTS

Foreword by Jacob R. Marcus and Abraham J. Peck x
Preface xii
Acknowledgments xv
Introduction to Sources xvii
Abbreviations xx

THE SCHOOLS 1

CHAPTER		
1	Types of Jewish Schools	7
2	Curriculum	10
3	Pedagogy	18
4	The Arts	30
5	Bar/Bat Mitzvah	41
6	The Bible	45
7	Early Childhood Education	54
8	Exceptional Children	60
9	Guidance	66
10	Hebrew	69
11	History	86
12	The Holocaust	97
13	School Library	104
14	Life Cycle of a Jew	107
15	Literature	119

16	Mitzvot/Values and Contemporary Issues 123
17	Textbooks 143
18	The High School 147
19	American Jewry and the Land of Israel 159
20	Day School 176
21	Yiddish Secular Schools 204
22	Higher Education 232

THE PROFESSION 243

CHAPTER 23	Administration 245
24	The Teacher 263
25	The Rabbi and Jewish Education 270
26	Conferences in Jewish Education, 1890–1988 274
27	Men and Women Who Influenced Jewish Education 287

COMMUNITY AND JEWISH EDUCATION 313

CHAPTER 28	Historical Background of Jewish Education 317
29	History of Jewish Education in the United States 335
30	The American Jewish Community 353
31	The Home and Jewish Education 379
32	Adult Education 390
33	The Woman's Role and Jewish Education 398
34	Sephardim and Jewish Education 405
35	Youth and Jewish Education 409
36	Camp 417
37	Local Sources for Jewish Education 422

PART IV

CRITERIA AND EVALUATION 517

CHAPTER		
38	Theology and Education	521
39	Religious Education	524
40	Philosophy of Jewish Education	533
41	Goals of Jewish Education	539
42	Research in Jewish Education	545
43	Change in Jewish Education	551
44	The Social Sciences and Jewish Education	559
45	Assessment	573
46	The Future of Jewish Education	597
47	Bibliographies of Jewish Education in Other Lands	600
48	Bibliographies of Jewish Education and Related Fields in the United States	603

Supplement 619 | *Index* 671

FOREWORD

Norman Drachler's bibliography of Jewish education in America is a most important book. The American Jewish Archives is delighted to be a copublisher of the volume because its intent is very much our intent.

Let us be more specific. The American Jewish Archives was founded in 1947 at a critical time in the history of the American Jewish community. The Holocaust had just recently devastated the thousand-year history of European Jewish communal existence. The Archives was created as one of the means by which American Jews and their leadership could begin to understand the history and development of the Jewish experience in this nation and in the Western Hemisphere. It was our hope that such an understanding would help American Jewry, now the best-educated Jewish community in history, face the awesome responsibility of preserving the continuity of Jewish life and learning.

In much the same way, Norman Drachler's book is being published at a time when American Jewry, indeed much of world Jewry, is faced with the realization that individual assimilation and a loss of Jewish identification (through intermarriage and a significant decrease in religious practice) have placed the Jewish people in a growing worldwide crisis of Jewish identity.

In such a crisis environment, many within the Jewish community have identified Jewish education, a major transmitter of Jewish identify, as potentially the single most effective antidote to this dilemma.

But in its present form Jewish education cannot serve this function. Certainly not where Jewish children view Jewish education until their thirteenth year (and hardly ever beyond) as something to endure and be liberated from with the celebration of one's bar or bat mitzvah. Certainly not where Jewish education remains a step-child in the budgeting priorities of Jewish communal life.

On the other hand, there has never been a more advantageous period in the history of American Jewish life for the rejuvenation of Jewish education. Over three hundred different institutions of higher learning in the United States offer one or more undergraduate courses in Jewish studies. Of these, at least forty offer a Judaic studies major and nearly thirty sponsor graduate programs.

We alluded earlier to a similarity between the intent of this book and that of the American Jewish Archives. It has always been our purpose to provide the researcher of the American Jewish experience with the most comprehensive set of materials available for his or her research project. Whether it was primary documentation in the form of letters, newspaper clippings, microfilms, or printed ephemera, we have always sought to satisfy each and every research need.

In much the same way, Norman Drachler has sought to provide the reader of this book with an abundance of selected materials on almost every conceivable area of Jewish education in America. Think of it—his bibliography includes over six hundred doctoral dissertations and over four hundred master's theses on Jewish education and related fields!

Beyond the simple abundance of listed items in this volume, there is also Drachler's determined effort to bring together the literature of the various ideologies in Jewish education, whether it be the Orthodox Talmud Torah, the Conservative or Reform Sunday School, or the growing number of non-Orthodox day schools. And in this book one has sources in Hebrew and Yiddish, reflecting the smaller but nevertheless important streams in American Jewish educational history.

In compiling this massive bibliography on American Jewish education Drachler has really presented the reader with a history of American Jewish life and identity. The history of American Jewry and its development is integrally tied to education—whether that education meant advancement and achievement on an individual level or the belief in public education (and the strict separation of religious and secular schooling) on a communal basis.

But, most important, Jewish education has sought to be the foundation stone of Jewish identity in America—whether it meant merging an American and a Jewish identity into one or (more recently) stressing the Jewish aspect. Isaac Leeser, no doubt the most important religious leader of early American Jewry, understood this as early as 1840. In commenting upon the success of the first Jewish Sunday school in America, founded in 1838 in Philadelphia by Rebecca Gratz, Leeser wrote, "it is the first duty of Israel to instill knowledge of divine things in the hearts of the young. . . . It is but seldom that so noble an aim has been sought after, begun solely for the glorification of our Maker and the well-being of his people."

This is still a noble aim a century and a half after it was first articulated. If the American Jewish Archives and this volume can advance that aim in some way, then our efforts will have borne fruit and satisfaction will be our greatest reward.

Jacob R. Marcus
Director, American Jewish Archives

Abraham J. Peck
Administrative Director, American Jewish Archives

PREFACE

During the early stages of Jewish settlement in America the synagogue generally assumed responsibility for the religious and educational needs of Jewish children. Up until about 1850 many, if not most, Jewish children received their Jewish and general education in a synagogue school or from a private tutor. As the Jewish population increased, particularly in the latter half of the nineteenth century, the majority of Jewish children entered the public schools. Synagogues continued their educational programs either on Sunday or after school hours, though some all-day schools continued offering both general and religious Jewish education.

In the first half of the twentieth century Jewish religious groups and some Jewish organizations adopted plans for Jewish education and established national commissions to foster and improve educational programs. Some cities introduced central agencies or bureaus in an effort to advance the quality of Jewish education at the local level. During this period national educational organizations were launched by lay leaders and educators concerned with setting higher standards for Jewish education. Teacher and principal organizations were founded on both the local and national level. Some professional organizations were based on ideological interests. These groups, in turn, published educational journals and textbooks, extending the scope of educational development.

Thus data about Jewish education in the United States is spread over a multitude of publications, education and general journals, synagogue histories, research reports, conference proceedings, bureau reports, and proceedings of various rabbinical conferences and national organizations. There are also Jewish yearbooks and psychological and sociological studies of Jewish life in America that include important articles and inquiries related to Jewish education. Because of this diffusion, there has long been a need for a comprehensive bibliography on Jewish education in the United States to acquaint the Jewish educator and the general reader with some of the primary sources and major works on Jewish education past and present.

There are, of course, many reasons to justify the publication of a bibliography on Jewish education. I wish to underscore two: the growth of the Jewish day school after World War II and the recent practice of many congregations to hire full-time educational directors. Both changes bring into Jewish education full-time professionals with the training and time to utilize Jewish sources for the improvement of the educational program. The growing involvement of thousands of university-educated lay volunteers on religious school boards and committees, as well as the expanded responsibilities of community Federations and national organizations in Jewish education offer additional incentives for the compilation of this bibliography. Lay leaders and educators need access to information that will assist them in decision making, research, and curriculum development.

A bibliography that brings together the literature of various ideologies in Jewish education would also be useful to university students working on dissertations in education. General history of education courses in most schools and colleges of education contain little information on Jewish education, and what little there is usually focuses on the ancient era. With the recent increase in Judaic departments in American colleges and universities, there will be a growing need for Jewish sources. This bibliography includes about six hundred doctoral dissertations and about four hundred master's theses on Jewish education and related fields. There is also a growing interest in local Jewish history. Chapter 37, Local Sources for Jewish Education, lists materials on the Jewish community at the state and local level.

This bibliography will also be useful to those concerned about how to transmit their religious, historical, and cultural values to their children. Those who reside in communities with extensive Judaica collections too often forget that the majority of Jewish educators work in communities where information about Judaica and Jewish education is very limited. In some instances, educators are not aware of the materials that do exist.

In compiling this volume, efforts were made to include all aspects of Jewish education, from preschool through secondary education, in the various types of schools in the United States. Included were entries from educational and general periodicals, yearbooks, books, proceedings, bibliographies, and encyclopedias that provided sufficient data for the reader to locate the source of the reference. Information about publications of the various central agencies in cities are from periodicals, histories of Jews in American cities, or publications by Jewish historical societies. In some instances where articles about schools reflecting a particular educational ideology were not found, textbooks issued by the organization were included.

To illustrate the diffusion of Jewish educational information, let us take the day school as an example. This volume records about seven hundred items on the Jewish day school in the United States. These entries consist of thirty-seven doctoral dissertations, ten master's theses, and fifty different periodicals. About four hundred items are from periodicals and the remaining entries are from books, proceedings, reports, and pamphlets. The vast majority were written in English, but there is also a rich literature in Hebrew, Yiddish, and Ladino on the day school.

As an educator I am grateful to the bibliographers of Jewish education whose publications are listed in this work. My classroom experience undoubtedly accounts for some of the categories included. I have followed the counsel of the late historian and rabbinic scholar Simha Assaf and included references related to Jewish education in the United States. The areas added, particularly the social sciences, are selective and I hope adequate to open related vistas for educators and community leaders concerned with Jewish education. Education is not a discipline that is isolated from the society in which it functions. As teacher, principal, or school board member, one needs awareness and understanding of the social forces that influence Jewish education in the United States.

In compiling this bibliography the prime focus was upon the anticipated audience of the volume, primarily teachers, principals, and educational lay leaders. Each part begins with a detailed table of contents, listing the subheadings under which materials are grouped in that part. Where the quantity of material warrants, topics are subdivided into materials prior to 1950 and materials after 1950. Most materials prior to 1900 are listed in chapter 29, History of Jewish Education in the United States.

Chapter 27, Men and Women Who Influenced Jewish Education, has been a particular concern. While I included what I found in the existing literature, I am aware that important educators have been omitted. Because it contributes to a better understanding of Jewish education, the material in this chapter, though incomplete, has been included nonetheless.

The section called "Gleanings" that appears at the end of most chapters, though not common in general bibliographies, is intended to give the insider greater awareness of some of the issues and problems that confront teachers, administrators, and lay leaders. For those outside the field, these gleanings may shed some light on the state of Jewish education in America—its goals, achievements, and problems.

ACKNOWLEDGMENTS

Compiling a bibliography is dependent upon the help and suggestions made by knowledgable individuals in the area of Jewish education. I was fortunate in finding many who were both supportive and helpful.

The publication of a bibliography on Jewish education in the United States by the American Jewish Archives and Wayne State University Press reflects the commitment of both institutions to the need for research in all aspects of America's cultural and religious life. My thanks and appreciation to Dr. Jacob R. Marcus and Dr. Abraham J. Peck of the American Jewish Archives and to Arthur B. Evans, Alice Nigoghosian, and Leonard N. Simons, longtime friend and benefactor of the Wayne State University Press, for their counsel and assistance.

Sol Drachler, my brother, has read the original and subsequent copies of the entire manuscript. His comments and suggestions have improved both the content and the organization of the bibliography. I am also very appreciative of his efforts in obtaining support for the publication.

Dr. Abraham P. Gannes has read the entire manuscript and improved on the Hebrew translations. He has also provided a great deal of material that has enriched the total manuscript. I am very grateful for his advice and support of the total project. I am indebted to Joseph M. Papo for the section on Sephardim, particularly for his research on the educational items from the Ladino press in America.

I am thankful to Rabbi Alexander M. Schindler and Rabbi Daniel B. Syme of the Union of American Hebrew Congregations for finding time in their busy schedules to review the early manuscript and to involve others in the needs of a comprehensive bibliography on Jewish education in the United States.

I want to acknowledge the following, who provided encouragement and help: Rabbi Sidney Akselrad of Congregation Beth Am; Dr. Shimon Frost and Dr. George Pollak at the Jewish Education Service of North America; Micha Falk Oppenheim, senior cataloger of the Library of The Jewish Theological Seminary of America; Barbara Leff, librarian of the Stephen S. Wise Temple; Hava Ben-Zvi, librarian of the Bureau of Jewish Education of Los Angeles; Sara S. Lee, director, HUC-JIR, Rhea Hirsch School of Education; Rabbi Samuel Joseph, HUC-JIR, of Cincinnati; Dr. Eduardo Rauch, co-director of Melton Research Center; Rabbi Yaakov Fruchter, director of publications, Torah Umesorah; Rabbi Stuart Kelman, executive director of the Jewish Agency of the Greater East Bay Area (San Francisco area);

ACKNOWLEDGMENTS

Dr. Alvin I. Schiff, executive vice president of the Board of Jewish Education of Greater New York; and Dr. William B. Brickman, emeritus professor of education, University of Pennsylvania, of blessed memory.

Several libraries have been very helpful in locating materials. My special thanks to the library of the Jewish Theological Seminary, the YIVO Institute for Jewish Research, the Judaica section of the New York Public Library, the libraries of the HUC-JIR in Cincinnati and Los Angeles, and the Jewish Community Library of San Francisco.

My thanks and appreciation also to the following Institutions that have provided financial aid for travel and research: Memorial Foundation for Jewish Culture, Dr. Jerry Hochbaum, executive director; The Paul and Jean Hanna Archival Collection on The Role of Education, Hoover Institute, Stanford University, Gerald A. Dorfman, senior fellow and curator.

INTRODUCTION TO SOURCES

A number of sources exist listing works on various aspects of Jewish education and related topics, sources that have proved invaluable in the preparation of this volume.

Efforts to document literature on Jewish education are not confined to this century. In his *Bibliography of Jewish Bibliographies* (Jerusalem, 1969), Shlomo Shunami cites Baruch Strassburger's *History of Jewish Education and Instruction,* published in Stuttgart, Germany, in 1885. Under various categories—pedagogy, the Bible, textbooks, Hebrew, prayer books for students, educational journals, textbooks, mathematics books in Hebrew, etc.—Strassburger lists items ranging from 1200 C.E. to 1885. The texts are generally listed in Hebrew with notes in German.

A major source for Jewish education in general and Jewish textbooks in particular is the four-volume study by Simha Assaf, *Sources for the History of Jewish Education* (H.) from the Middle Ages to 1840 (Jerusalem, 1942–45). Volume four lists 348 textbooks, including year, place of publication, and citations to his discussion of the texts.

The five-volume *Educational Encyclopedia* (H.) (Jerusalem, 1961–69), includes extensive bibliographies on Israel and other countries. The Institute of Contemporary Jewry of the Hebrew University of Jerusalem published in 1965 an annotated bibliography by Uriah Z. Engelman, *Jewish Education in Europe 1914–1962.* Another very important Israeli publication is *Kirjat Sefer* (H.), a bibliographical quarterly published since 1924. It includes a section on education in Israel and other countries. References from other countries are listed in the language of publication.

All educational journals published in the United States are, of course, important to the student of Jewish education. Two journals with the longest publication span and containing indexes are *Sheviley Hahinuch* (H.) and *Jewish Education,* both published by the Council for Jewish Education, formerly the National Council for Jewish Education. Back in 1928, Professor Samuel I. Feigin urged Jewish educators to provide supplementary bibliographies in their textbooks to broaden the teacher's knowledge of the subjects taught (*Sheviley Hahinuch* 3:3 (Fall 1928), 219–23).

The Union of American Hebrew Congregations, Commission on Jewish Education (with CCAR and NATE) currently publishes *Compass* (formerly *The Jewish Teacher,* 1933–88). The United Synagogue of America, CJE, publishes *Impact,* formerly *The Jewish School and Democracy* and *Synagogue School,* 1943–1988). These have indexes in various issues. Torah Umesorah's *Jewish Parent* (1948–77) is a journal on day school education.

INTRODUCTION TO SOURCES

The Jewish Education Service of North America, Inc., formerly American Association for Jewish Education, has published The Pedagogic Reporter since 1949 and has an index for its first thirty years. *Alternative Magazine* (Denver) has an index for the first eight years (1970–78). *Studies in Bibliography and Booklore,* published since 1953 by HUC-JIR, has several bibliographies on European Jewish education.

In 1964, the National Curriculum Research Institute of the AAJE and the University of Judaism, the Jewish Theological Seminary of America, published *Abstracts of Doctoral and Masters' Dissertations on Jewish Education and Related Areas,* compiled and edited by Frank Rosenthal with the assistance of Judah Pilch. In 1983, JESNA added *Doctoral Dissertations in Jewish Education, 1975–1982,* compiled by George Pollack. Between 1963 and 1975, Yivo—Institute for Jewish Research published eight monographs, *American Doctoral Dissertations and Masters Theses on Jewish Subjects,* edited by Phyllis Disenhouse and Witta Ravid. Yivo, both in Europe and the United States, has published in Yiddish several major bibliographical studies of Jewish education in Europe and North America.

A major bibliographic contribution to Jewish education by JESNA are several volumes of *Materials Resource Guide for Jewish Education,* developed by the Department of Pedagogic Services, Fradle Freidenreich, Director, and published by the Central Agency for Jewish Education, Miami. The bibliographies are annotated and contain data on numerous topics—social studies, literature, Jewish life, synagogue, prayer, liturgy, and so on—as well as an author index. The materials are organized along recommended age levels and contain a great deal of helpful information for teachers and administrators.

Eliezer R. Malachi and Ephim H. Jeshurin are two U.S. bibliographers who have devoted their energies to Jewish education. Their contributions appear frequently in various sections of this volume. In the *Jubilee Book of the Hebrew Teachers' Union of Greater New York* (H.), edited by Zevi Scharfstein (New York, 1944), Malachi published a bibliography "The Literature of Jewish Education in America." Organized under various educational classifications, it totals 729 entries. The *Hadoar* (H.) and various other Hebrew and Yiddish journals contain bibliographic articles by Malachi on Hebrew literature and education.

Ephim H. Jeshurin has devoted his efforts to Yiddish education in America and to modern Yiddish literature. His volume *One Hundred Years: Modern Yiddish Literature—Bibliography* (Y.) was published by the Education Committee of the Workmen's Circle in 1965. The bibliography consists of two major divisions: Yiddish Literature and Bibliography on the School Movement Educational Problems. Jeshurin's education bibliography has more than four thousand entries and is organized into nine sections. It also lists some educational items in English. The large number of items from Yiddish newspapers and journals is particularly valuable, since many of these periodicals are no longer being published and can be found only in a limited number of libraries.

Bibliographic works exist on four distinguished American Jewish educators. Abraham P. Gannes has edited and compiled two studies, one on Leo L. Honor and another on Alexander M. Dushkin. Each includes an introductory essay by Gannes, selected writings, and a bibliography of the works of each. A bibliography on Zevi Scharfstein, *Sefer Scharfstein: Jubilee Volume* (H.), edited by Zvulun Ravid, was published in Tel Aviv in 1970. It includes a bibliography of Scharfstein's writings compiled by Akivah Ben Ezra. The entries are listed chronologically under various categories. *Emanuel Gamoran: His Life and His Work,* edited by Samuel Grand and Mamie G. Gamoran, includes biographic materials, a selection of Gamoran's writings, and a bibliography of his works.

There are also several bibliographic volumes which include educational sections: *Bibliography of Jewish Social Studies* by Salo W. Baron, *An Index to Scientific Articles on American Jewish History* by Jacob R. Marcus, and *The Jewish Community in America* by

INTRODUCTION TO SOURCES

William W. Brickman. The state of California has enhanced the study of American Jewish History with three bibliographic volumes. *California Jewish History,* selected and annotated by Norton B. Stern (1967) is a descriptive bibliography from the Gold Rush to post-World War I. Sara G. Cogan's *The Jews of San Francisco and The Greater Bay Area, 1849–1919* (1973) and *The Jews of Los Angeles, 1849–1945* (1980), both annotated bibliographies, were published by the Western Jewish History Center, Judah L. Magnes Museum.

Children's literature has not received in the past the attention it merits. In the last fifty years teachers, parents, and children have benefited from articles in *The Jewish Book Annual* and various journals on books for children. Enid Davis's *A Comprehensive Guide to Children's Literature with a Jewish Theme,* published in 1981, is an important contribution to this field.

The following indexes and bibliographies were most helpful: *An Index to Jewish Periodicals,* edited by Miriam Leikind; *American Jewish History,* with its annual sections "Judaica Americana," compiled and annotated by Nathan M. Kaganoff, and "American Jewish Studies," compiled and annotated by Marc Lee Raphael; *The Jewish Book Annual,* which compiles annually new fiction and nonfiction books published in English, Hebrew, and Yiddish. The bibliographic works by Micha Falk Oppenheim were also of great help. To all the above, I am very grateful

It is encouraging to note the growing literature on the history of local communities, many studies sponsored by local Jewish Federations, and the rise of local historical societies. It is hoped these developments and the increasing numbers of Jewish studies programs in U.S. colleges and universities will provide increased opportunities for scholars to enhance our cultural needs, including Jewish education.

ABBREVIATIONS

AAJE	American Association for Jewish Education (now JESNA)
Act	Braverman, Libbie L., and Nathan Brilliant. *Activities in the Religious School.* N.Y.: UAHC, 1950
ADL	Anti-Defamation League of B'nai B'rith
Adult Jew Ed	*Adult Jewish Education* (National Academy for Adult Jewish Studies, USCJE)
AJ	Kohn, Eugene, ed. *American Jewry: The Tercentenary and After.* N.Y.: Reconstructionist Press, 1955.
AJA	*American Jewish Archives* (HUC-JIR)
AJC	American Jewish Committee
AJ Congress	American Jewish Congress
AJE	Halevi, Mordecai. *American Jewish Educators* (H.). 1972.
AJH	*American Jewish History* (American Jewish Historical Society).
AJHE	Pilch, Judah, ed. *A History of Jewish Education in the United States.* N.Y.: The National Curriculum Research Institute of the AAJE, 1969.
AJHQ	*American Jewish Historical Quarterly*
AJHS	American Jewish Historical Society
AJud	*American Judaism* (UAHC)
AJYB	*American Jewish Year Book* (annual). N.Y. and Phila.: AJC and JPS.
AM	*Alternative Magazine* (Alternatives in Jewish Religious Education). Denver.
ARE	Alternatives in Religious Education
ARIAN	Picker, Chaim, ed. *He Kindled a Light: In Memory of Shraga (Philip) Arian.* N.Y.: USCJE, 1976
ATJQ	Baron, Joseph L., ed. *A Treasury of Jewish Quotations.* A.L. Barnes, 1965.
A Zion	*American Zionist*
BAA	Shubow, Joseph S. *The Brandeis Avukah Annual of 1932.* N.Y.: Avukah, American Student Zionist Federation, 1932.
Baron	Blau, J.L., et al., eds. *Essays on Jewish Life and Thought: In Honor of Salo Wittmayer Baron.* N.Y.: Columbia U.P., 1959.
BJC	Kaminetsky, Joseph, and Murray J. Friedman. *Building Jewish Ethical Character.* N.Y.: TU, 1978.
BJE	Bureau of Jewish Education
BJR	Blau, Joseph L., ed. *Reform Judaism: A Historical Perspective.* N.Y.: CCAR, Ktav, 1973
BM	Katsh, Abraham I., ed. *Bar Mitzvah.* N.Y.: Shengold, 1955.
BYD	*Bleter far Yiddisher Derziung* (Y.). (World BJE)
CA	Gannes, Abraham P. *Central Community Agencies for Jewish Education.* Phila.: Dropsie College for Cognate Learning, 1954.
CAJ	Marcus, Jacob Rader. *The Colonial American Jew: 1492–1776.* Detroit: Wayne State U.P., 1979. 3 vols.

ABBREVIATIONS

CAJE	Coalition for the Advancement of Jewish Education
Cat 1	Siegel, Richard, Michael Strassfeld, and Sharon Strassfeld, eds. *The Jewish Catalog.* Phila.: JPS, 1973.
Cat 2	Strassfeld, Sharon, and Michael Strassfeld, eds. *The Second Jewish Catalog: Sources and Resources.* Phila.: JPS, 1976.
Cat 3	———. *The Third Jewish Catalog: Creating Community.* Phila.: JPS, 1980.
CCAR	Proceedings of Central Conference of American Rabbis of the UAHC
CCAR J	*Central Conference of American Rabbis Journal*
CCJE	Gamoran, Emmanuel. *Changing Conceptions in Jewish Education.* N.Y.: Macmillan, 1924. 2 vols.
CCS	Lang, Leon S. *A Curriculum for the Congregational School.* Phila.: BJE, Branch of the USA, 1951.
CE	*Culture and Education* (Y.). (Education Department, Workmen's Circle).
Chi Jew Forum	*Chicago Jewish Forum*
CHP	Rawidowicz, Simon, ed. *The Chicago Pinkas* (E., H.). Chicago: College of Jewish Studies, 1952.
CJCS	Council of Jewish Communal Service
CJE	Commission for Jewish Education
CJF	Council of Jewish Federation, Inc. (Formerly CJFWF, Council of Jewish Federations and Welfare Funds)
CJR	Landesman, Alter F. *A Curriculum for Jewish Religious Schools.* N.Y.: USA, 1922.
Cong M	*Congress Monthly* (American Jewish Congress). Formerly weekly and biweekly.
Con Jud	*Conservative Judaism* (RA)
CP	CJF Pulbication
CPA	Feldman, L.A., ed. *Changing Patterns in American Jewish Life.* N.Y.: JEC, 1958.
CYCO	Central Yiddish Culture Organization
DCS	Dropsie College Symposium, *The Goals of Jewish Education.* Phila.: Dropsie College, 1957.
DEC	Department of Education and Culture of the Jewish Agency
DER	Bass, H.B., ed. *Dertsiungs Entsiklopedie* Y.). N.Y.: World Jewish Congress, 1957–59. 3 vols.
DSSE	Department of Synagogue and School Extension of the UAHC
EAJ	Marcus, Jacob Rader. *Early American Jewry.* Phila.: JPS, 1951. 2 vols.
ECL	*Education and the Creative Life.* N.Y.: AAJE, 1957.
Ed As	Educators Assembly of the USA
Ed As	*Proceedings of the Jewish Educators Assembly of the USA*
Ed Enc	Buber, Martin, ed. *Educational Encyclopedia: Thesaurus of Jewish and General Education* (H.). Jerusalem: The Ministry of Education and the Bialik Institute, 1961–69. 5 vols.
EHZA	Meyer, Isidore S., ed. *Early History of Zionism in America.* N.Y.: AJHS and Theodore Herzl Foundation, 1958.
Enc Jud	Roth, Cecil, ed. *Encyclopaedia Judaica.* Jerusalem: 1972.
ERC	Educational Research Council of America
ES	Scharfstein, Zevi. *Education and Survival* (H.). N.Y. and Jerusalem: Shilo, 1947.
Ess	Marcus, Jacob Rader, ed. *Essays in American Jewish History.* Cincinnati: American Jewish Archives, 1958.
FAJ	Kaplan, Mordecai M. *The Future of the American Jew.* N.Y.: Macmillan, 1948.
FJCA	Sidorsky, David, ed. *The Future of the Jewish Community in America.* Institute of Human Relations Press/Basic Books, 1973.
For	*Jewish Daily Forward* (Jewish Forward Association). Formerly daily (Y.), now weekly (Y. and E.).
FPDE	Nardi, Noah, ed. *Fundamental Principles for Diaspora Education* (H.). Jerusalem: DEC, 1958.
Freiheit	*Morning Freiheit* (Y.). 1922–89. Daily, later weekly.
Friedland	Ribalow, M., ed. *H.A. Friedland Memorial Book* (H.). N.Y.: Histadruth Ivrith of America, 1940.
FSTC	Fox, Seymour, and Geraldine Rosenfield, eds. *From the Scholar to the Classroom.* N.Y.: MRC, 1977.

ABBREVIATIONS

GA	General Assembly of the CJF
Gamoran	Grand, Samuel, and Mamie G. Gamoran, eds. *Emanuel Gamoran, His Life and His Work*. N.Y.: Emanuel Gamoran Memorial Fund, 1979.
Gingold	*Pinchas Gingold Book* (Y., H., and E.). N.Y.: Pinchas Gingold Foundation of the National Committee of the Jewish Folk Schools, 1955.
GJE	Scharfstein, Zevi. *Great Hebrew Educators in the Last Centuries* (H.). Jerusalem: R. Moss, 1964.
GJP	Noveck, Simon, ed. *Great Jewish Personalities in Modern Times*. Clinton, Mass.: Colonial Press for the B'nai B'rith Department for Adult Jewish Education, 1960.
GJT	———. *Great Jewish Thinkers of the Twentieth Century*. Clinton, Mass.: Colonial Press for the B'nai B'rith Department for Adult Jewish Education, 1963.
GOH	Jung, Leo, ed. *Guardians of Our Heritage*. N.Y.: Bloch, 1958.
Golomb	Shtarkman, Moshe, ed. *Abraham Golomb Jubilee Book* (Y.). A. Golomb Jubilee Committee, Los Angeles YIVO, 1970.
Had Mag	*Hadassah Magazine* (Hadassah, Women's Zionist Organization of America). Formerly *Hadassah Newsletter*.
HDS	Kaminetsky, Joseph, ed. *Hebrew Day School Education*. N.Y.: TU and the National Society for Day School Education, 1970.
HUC m	*Hebrew Union College Monthly* (HUC-JIR)
HUC–JIR	Hebrew Union College-Jewish Institute of Religion
HYB	Patai, Raphael, ed. *Herzl Year Book*. N.Y.: Herzl Press.
IJL	Institute for Jewish Life. *Fellowship in Jewish Educational Leadership*. 1973.
IL	Nadel, Max, ed. *Integrative Learning: The Search for Unity in Jewish Day School Programs* (Proceedings of an invitational conference, May 15–17, 1978). N.Y.: AAJE.
Impact	*Impact* (USACJE). Formerly *Syn Sch*.
Intrater	Bennett, Alan D., ed. *Commitment in Honor of Aaron Intrater*. Cleveland, 1977.
IOT	Jung, Leo, ed. *Israel of Tomorrow*. N.Y.: Herald Square Press, 1946.
Issues	Katzoff, Louis, *issues in Jewish Education: A Study of the Philosophy of the Conservative Congregational Schools*. N.Y.: Ktav, 1949.
IWO	International Workers Orden-Orden Schools (later changed to Progressive Yiddish Schools)
JAC	Kaplan, Mordecai M. *Judaism as a Civilization*. N.Y.: Reconstructionist Press, 1957.
Jan 1	Janowsky, Oscar I., ed. *The American Jew: A Composite Portrait*. N.Y.: Harper & Bros., 1942.
Jan 2	———. *The American Jew: An Appraisal*. Phila.: JPS, 1964.
Jan 3	———. *The Education of American Jewish Teachers*. Boston: Philip W. Lown Center for Contemporary Jewish Studies/Beacon Press, 1967.
JAS	Sklare, Marshall, ed. *The Jew in American Society*. N.Y.: Behrman, 1974.
JAUA	Herscher, Uri D. *Jewish Agricultural Utopias in America, 1880–1910*. Detroit: Wayne State U.P., 1981.
JB	Scharfstein, Zevi, ed. *Jubilee Book of the Hebrew Teachers' Union of Greater New York* (H.). N.Y., 1944.
JBA	*Jewish Book Annual*. N.Y.: JWB-JBC.
JBC	Jewish Book Council
JCA	Sklare, Marshall, ed. *The Jewish Community in America*. N.Y.: Behrman, 1974.
JCC	Jewish Community Council
JDH	Blau, Joseph H., and Salo W. Baron. *The Jews of the United States: A Documentary History, 1790–1840*. Phila.: JPS, 1962. 3 vols.
JEC	Jewish Education Committee of Greater New York
JED	Rieger, E., ed. *Jewish Education in the Diaspora* (H.). Jerusalem: University Press, 1948.
JEDS	Cohn, Jack J. *Jewish Education in Democratic Society*. N.Y.: Reconstructionist Press, 1964.
JER	Kuselewitz, David, ed. *Jewish Education in Response to the Challenge of Our Times* (Conference May 10–12, 1957, IJE, DEC, AAJE). N.Y.: DEC of the Jewish Agency, 1957.

ABBREVIATIONS

JES	Sklare, Marshall, ed. *The Jews: Social Patterns of an American Group.* Glencoe, Ill.: Free Press, 1958.
JESNA	Jewish Education Service of North America
JEUS	Gartner, Lloyd P., ed. *Jewish Education in the United States: A Documentary History.* N.Y.: Teachers College Press, 1969.
Jew Digest	Jewish Digest
Jew Ed	Jewish Education (Council for Jewish Education). Formerly NCJE.
Jew Fron	Jewish Frontier (LZOA)
Jewish Teacher	*The Jewish Teacher* (Jewish Teachers Organization, N.Y.). 1916–1924.
Jew J Soc	Jewish Journal of Sociology (World Jewish Congress)
Jew Life	Jewish Life (UOJCA)
Jew Obs	Jewish Observer
Jew Parent	Jewish Parent (National Association of Hebrew Day School Parent Association, Torah Umesorah)
Jew Rev	Jewish Review
Jews	Finkelstein, Louis, ed. *The Jews: Their History, Culture, and Religion.* 3d ed. 4 vols. N.Y.: Harper & Bros., 1960.
Jew Spec	Jewish Spectator
Jew Teach	*The Jewish Teacher* (UAHC). Now *Compass.*
JI	Sklare, Marshall, and Joseph Greenblum. *Jewish Identity on the Suburban Frontier: A Study of Group Survival in the Open Society.* N.Y.: Basic Books, 1967. 2 vols.
JIS	Dinnerstein, Leonard, and Mary Dale Pallson, eds. *Jews in the South.* Baton Rouge: Louisiana State U.P., 1973.
J Jew Com Ser	Journal of Jewish Communal Service (Conference of Jewish Communal Service)
JJS	Pilch, Judah, and Meyer Ben Horin, eds. *Judaism and the Jewish School.* N.Y.: AAJE/Bloch, 1960.
JL	Jung, Leo, ed. *Jewish Leaders.* 1953.
JLUS	Gittler, Joseph B., ed. *Jewish Life in the United States: Perspectives from the Social Sciences.* N.Y.: New York U.P., 1981.
JMW	Fried, Jacob, ed. *Jews in the Modern World.* Twayne, 1962.
JNF	Jewish National Fund
JNWA	Jewish National Workers Alliance (later, Farband Labor Zionist Order, and now United Labor Zionist Organization). See LZOA.
JPH	Marcus, Audrey Freeman, and Raymond A. Zwerin. *The Jewish Principal's Handbook.* Denver: ARE, 1983.
JPPP	Abramovitch, R., et al., eds. *Jewish People Past and Present.* Jewish Encyclopedic Handbooks. 2 vols. 1948.
JPS	Jewish Publication Society of America
JQR	Jewish Quarterly Review (Dropsie College)
JSA	Chipkin, I.S., ed. *Jewish Schools in America.* N.Y.: AAJE, 1949.
JSD	Jewish School and Democracy (USACJE first journal). See *Impact*
JSS	Jewish Social Studies (Conference on Jewish Social Studies, Inc.)
JSSQ	Jewish Social Service Quarterly
JTH	Marcus, Audrey Friedman. *Jewish Teacher's Handbook.* Denver: ARE, 1980 and 1982. 2 vols.
JTI	Jewish Teachers' Institute of the JTSA
JTSA	Jewish Theological Seminary of America (also JTS)
Jud	Judaism (American Jewish Congress)
JUET	Hirsch, Samson Raphael. *Judaism, Eternal.* Trans. I. Grunfield. 2 vols.
JWB	Jewish Welfare Board (NJWB)
JWF	Jewish Welfare Federation of Detroit
Kaplan	Davis, Moshe, ed. *Jubilee Volume in Honor of M. M. Kaplan.* N.Y.: JTSA, 1953.
KP	Keeping Posted (UAHC, High School)
LJE	Chazan, Barry. *The Language of Jewish Education: Crisis and Hope in the Jewish School.* N.Y.: Hartmoore House, 1976.
Lown	Pilch, Judah, ed. *Philip W. Lown Jubilee Volume.* 1967.

ABBREVIATIONS

LZOA	Labor Zionist Organization of America (formerly, Farband Labor Zionist Order and JNWA. Now, Labor Zionist Alliance, uniting Poale Zion-United Labor Zionist Organization of America and American Habonim Association.
Marcus	Korn, Bertram W., ed. *A Bicentennial Festschrift for Jacob Rader Marcus.* N.Y.: AJHS, Ktav, 1976.
Mem	Marcus, Jacob R., ed. *Memoirs of American Jews.* Phila.: JPS, 1955. 3 vols.
Mid	*Midstream* (Theodor Herzl Foundation)
MJ	*Melton Journal* (The Melton Research Center for Jewish Education/JTSA). Formerly *MRCN.*
MJET	Weinstein, David, and Michael Yizhar, eds. *Modern Jewish Educational Thought* (E. and H.). Chicago: College of Jewish Studies, 1964.
MJH	*Michigan Jewish History* (Jewish Historical Society of Michigan)
MN	*Melton Notes*
MRC	The Melton Research Center for Jewish Education/JTSA
MRCN	*Melton Research Center Newletter.* Now *MJ.*
MTJE	Kurzweil, Zvi E. *Modern Trends in Jewish Education.* N.Y.: Yoseloff, 1964.
NAAJS	National Academy for Adult Jewish Studies, USCJE
Na'amat	Na'amat USA. The Women's Labor Zionist Organization of America (formerly, Pioneer Women)
NATE	National Association of Temple Educators of the UAHC
NATE	*Proceedings of the Annual Conference of the NATE, UAHC*
Nat Jew M	*National Jewish Monthly* (B'nai B'rith)
NCJE	National Council for Jewish Education (later, Council for Jewish Education, CJE)
NCJSS	National Conference of Jewish Social Service
NCJSW	National Conference of Jewish Social Workers
NCJW	National Council of Jewish Women
NCRI	National Curriculum Research Institute of the AAJE
NCTE	National Commission on Torah Education
NFTB	National Federation of Temple Brotherhoods (UAHC)
NFTS	National Federation of Temple Sisterhoods (UAHC)
NICD	National Institute for Curriculum Development
NICD	Schanin, Norman, and Walter I. Ackerman, eds. *New Insights into Curriculum Development.* Ed As, 1966.
NJCRAC	National Jewish Community Relations Advisory Council
NJWB	National Jewish Welfare Board (often JWB, Jewish Welfare Board)
Occ	*The Occident* (19th-century American Jewish periodical edited by Isaac Leeser)
OFFY	*Our First Fifty Years: The Sholem Aleichem Folk Institute* (E. and Y.). N.Y., 1972.
ORT	Organization for Rehabilitation through Training
PAJHS	Publications of the American Jewish Historical Society, 1892–1994
PB	*Pedagogic Bulletin* (AAJE/JESNA)
PDE	Nardi, Noah, ed. *Problems of Diaspora Education* (H.). Jerusalem: DEC of the Jewish Agency, 1961
Ped Rep	*The Pedagogic Reporter* (JESNA; formerly AAJE)
Penn	Penn, Ascher. *Judaism in America* (Y.). N.Y.: Judaism in America Library, 1958.
Phil	Pilch, Judah, ed. *Readings in Jewish Educational Philosophy.* N.Y.: NCRI and AAJE, 1962.
Pinkas	Rawidowicz, Simon, ed. *The Chicago Pinkas* (E. and H.). Issued on the 25th anniversary of the College of Jewish Studies. Chicago: TCJS, 1952.
Pio Woman	*The Pioneer Woman* (Na'amat USA, The Women's Labor Zionist Organization of America; formerly, Pioneer Women)
PJS	Cohen, Samuel M. *The Progressive Jewish School.* N.Y.: USA, 1932.
Pop	Robinson, Sophia M. *Population Studies.* N.Y.: Conference on Jewish Relations, 1943.
Post	Postal, Bernard, and Lionel Koppman. *A Jewish Tourist's Guide to the U.S.* Phila.: JPS, 1954.
Pro D	*Proletarishe Dertziung* (Y.) (IWO)
PYB	Udin, Sophie A., ed. *The Palestine Yearbook.* Vol. 1 Washington, D.C.: ZOA, 1945.

ABBREVIATIONS

RA	Rabbinical Assembly (JTSA, USA)
RA	*Proceedings of the Rabbinical Assembly* (USA)
RCA	Rabbinical Council of America
Rec	*The Record* (Jewish Historical Society of Greater Washington, D.C.)
Recon	*The Reconstruciionist* (Jewish Reconstructionist Foundation, Inc.)
Reg	*Jewish Education Register and Directory.* 7th ed. N.Y.: AAJE and JESNA, 1951–84.
Rel Ed	*Religious Education* (Religious Education Association)
RIJHN	*Rhode Island Jewish Historical Notes* (Rhode Island Jewish Historical Association)
RJ	*Reform Judaism* (UAHC)
RMJHN	*Rocky Mountain Jewish Historical Notes* (Rocky Mountain Jewish Historical Society)
RTHE	Eisenberg, Azriel, ed. *Readings in the Teaching of Hebrew.* N.Y., 1961.
RTJH	Eisenberg, Azriel, and Abraham Segal, eds. *Readings in the Teaching of Jewish History.* N.Y.: JEC of New York, 1955.
RTJP	Eisenberg, Azriel, ed. *Readings in the Teaching of Jewish Prayer.* 1964.
RTJS	Berger, Milton, Joel S. Geffen, and M. David Hoffman, eds. *Roads to Jewish Survival.* N.Y.: National Federation of Jewish Men's Clubs/Bloch, 1967.
SAFI	Sholem Aleichem Folk Institute Schools
S Alm	Novak, H. comp. *School Almanac* (Y).
SCA	Synagogue Council of America
Schappes	Schappes, Morris U., ed. *Documentary History of the Jews in the United States.* N.Y.: Citadel Press, 1950.
Scharfstein	Ravid, Z., ed. *Zevi Scharfstein Jubilee Volume* (H.). Tel Aviv: Scharfstein Jubilee Committee and Hebrew Teachers Union in Israel, 1970.
S Ed	Blumenfield, Samuel M. *Society and Education in American Judaism* (H.). 1965.
Sh Hah	*Sheviley Hahinuch* (H.) (Council for Jewish Education; formerly with the NCJE)
Shunami	Shunami, Shlomo. *Bibliography of Jewish Bibliographies* (H.). International list of bibliographies, references in language written. Jerusalem: The Magnes Press, Hebrew University, 1969.
Shu P	Pomerantz, I. Chaim, and Shloime Bercovich, eds. *Shul-Pinkes* (Y.). Chicago: SAFI, 1948.
SNE	Niger, Sh. *In the Struggle for a New Education* (Y.). N.Y.: Educational Department of the WC.
SPE	Lehrer, Leibush, ed. *Studies in Psychology and Education* (Y.). Vilna: Yiddish Scientific Institute.
Stu	*Studies in Jewish Education.* Ed. Chazan and Rosenak. Jerusalem, 1983–84. 3 vols.
SWJ	Malamut, Joseph I., ed. *Southwest Jewry.* Vol. 3. Los Angeles, 1957.
SWJT	*Southwest Jewish Teacher*
Syn Sch	*Synagogue School* (USA). Formerly *The Jewish Schools and Democracy;* now *Impact.*
Teen	Grad, Eli, ed. *The Teenager and Jewish Education.* N.Y.: Ed As of the USA, 1968.
Ten	Lipman, Eugene J., and Vorspan, Albert. *A Tale of Ten Cities: The Proceedings of a Colloquium.* N.Y.: UAHC, 1962.
TJU	Jick, Leon A., ed. *The Teaching of Judaica in American Universities: The Proceedings of a Colloquium.* N.Y.: Association for Jewish Studies/Ktav, 1979.
Touroff	Touroff, Nissan. *Evaluations: Problems of Culture and Education* (H.). N.Y.: Organization of Teachers in America and Histradruth Ivrith of America, 1947.
Trad	*Tradition* (RCA)
TST	Blumenfield, Samuel M. *Thou Shalt Teach.* Ed. Judah Pilch. 1973.
TU	Torah Umesorah Day Schools
UAHC	Union of American Hebrew Congregations
Un Syn Rev	*United Synagogue Review*
UOJCA	Union of Orthodox Jewish Congregations of America

ABBREVIATIONS

USA	United Synagogues of America
USCJE	United Synagogue Commission on Jewish Education
USWPA	United States Works Project Administration
WC	Workmen's Circle Schools
Wiseman	Dunsky, Shimshion, ed. *Shloime Wiseman Book* (E., Y., and H.). Montreal: Jewish Peoples Schools, 1961.
WSJH	*Western States Jewish History Quarterly* (Western States Jewish History Association)
WVJ	Shinedling, Abraham I. *West Virginia Jewry: Origins and History.* Phila., 1963. 3 vols.
YA	*Yivo Annual.* N.Y.: Jewish Scientific Institute.
YB	*Yivo Bleter* (Y.) (Yiddish Institute for Jewish Research). Vilna, 1931; N.Y., 1942.
YD	*Yiddishe Dertziung* (Y.) (Central Committee of Jewish Folk Schools, JNWA, LZOA)
Yesod	Scharfstein, Zevi, ed. *Fundamentals of Jewish Education in America* (H.). N.Y.: Teachers College of JTSA, 1947.
YK	*Yiddisher Kemfer* (LZOA). Formerly weekly, now monthly.
YKUF	Los Angeles Yiddish Writers Society of YKUF. *Writings on California, 1854–1954* (Y.). Jubilee edition. Los Angeles: Yiddish Culture Society, 1955.
WZO	World Zionist Organization
ZOA	Zionist Organization of America
Zuk	*Die Zukunft* (Y.) (World Yiddish Congress and CYCO). Monthly

THE SCHOOLS

PART I | THE SCHOOLS

CONTENTS

1 | TYPES OF JEWISH SCHOOLS 7
Schools 7
Gleanings 8

2 | CURRICULUM 10
Development and Assessment prior to 1950 10
Curricula prior to 1950 11
Development and Assessment since 1950 12
Curricula since 1950 14
Gleanings 15

3 | PEDAGOGY 18
Projects, Methods, and Concerns 18
Judaic Sources—Teaching the Texts (Selected) 21
Clubs and Extracurricular Artivities (Selected) 22
Games, Role-playing, and Learning (Selected) 23
Sex Education and the School (Selected) 23
Computers in the School 24
Education for New Immigrants 24
Cults, Drinking, Suicide, and Youth 25
Marriage, Divorce, and Intermarriage (Selected) 25
Bereavement in the Classroom 27
Gleanings 27

4 | THE ARTS 30
General (Selected) 30
Art in the Jewish School 31
Audio-Visual Aids 33
The Dance (Selected) 34
Drama—General (Selected) 35
Drama in the School 35
The School Assembly 36
Music—General (Selected) 37
Music in the School 37
Gleanings 39

PART I   THE SCHOOLS

5 | BAR/BAT MITVAH 41

Prior to 1950 41
Since 1950 41
Gleanings 43

6 | THE BIBLE 45

General (Selected) 45
Teaching the Bible prior to 1950 46
Teaching the Bible since 1950 47
Textbooks and Guides for Teachers prior to 1950 49
Textbooks, Workbooks, and Guides since 1950 50
Gleanings 50

7 | EARLY CHILDHOOD EDUCATION 54

Prior to 1950 54
Articles, Manuals, and Books since 1950 54
Literature for the Very Young (Selected) 57
Guides, Curricula, and Manuals prior to 1950 58
Guides, Curricula, and Manuals since 1950 58
Gleanings 59

8 | EXCEPTIONAL CHILDREN 60

Special Education 60
Gleanings 67

9 | GUIDANCE 66

In the School 66
Gleanings 67

10 | HEBREW 69

Hebrew in Jewish Life (Selected) 69
Methodology and Teaching Aids prior to 1950 70
Methodology and Teaching Aids since 1950 72
Basic Vocabulary Lists prior to 1950 76
Basic Vocabulary lists since 1950 76
Reading 76
Pronunciation 78
Assessment prior to 1950 78
Assessment since 1950 80
Testing and Evaluation 80
Hebrew in Public High Schools 81
Hebrew Textbooks prior to 1950 (Selected) 81
Hebrew Textbooks since 1950 81
Gleanings 82

11 | HISTORY 86

General History (Selected) 86
Prior to 1950 86

PART I   THE SCHOOLS

Since 1950 88
Social Studies 90
Texts, Readers, and Resources prior to 1950 (Selected) 91
Texts, Readers, and Resources since 1950 (Selected) 91
Gleanings 93

12 | THE HOLOCAUST 97

Background Materials (Selected) 97
Teaching and Commemoration 99
Texts and Literature for Students (Selected) 101
Gleanings 102

13 | SCHOOL LIBRARY 104

The Library 104
Gleanings 106

14 | LIFE CYCLE OF A JEW 107

Synagogue and Prayer—General (Selected) 107
Synagogue and Prayer in the Classroom 108
The Junior Congregation 110
Prayer Books, Guides, and Textbooks for Synagogue and Prayer 110
Holidays, Ceremonies, and Customs 112
Texts, Guides, and Books for Holidays, Ceremonies, and Customs 115
Gleanings 117

15 | LITERATURE 119

Juvenile Literature prior to 1950 119
Juvenile Literature since 1950 119
Periodicals for Children and Youth 121
Gleanings 122

16 | MITZVOT/VALUES AND CONTEMPORARY ISSUES 123

Prior to 1950 (Selected) 123
Since 1950 (Selected) 124
Transmitting Values in the Classroom prior to 1950 128
Transmitting Values in the Classroom since 1950 129
Keren Ami in the Classroom 135
Textbooks and Teacher Guides 135
Gleanings 137

17 | TEXTBOOKS 143

1900 to 1950 143
Since 1950 143
Gleanings 144

18 | THE HIGH SCHOOL 147

Prior to 1950 147
Since 1950 147

PART I   THE SCHOOLS

Curriculum and Pedagogy 149
Confirmation in the High School 152
Adolescence and Its Implications 153
Evaluation 154
Books, Mini Courses, and Texts (Selected) 155
Gleanings 156

19 | AMERICAN JEWRY AND THE LAND OF ISRAEL 159

Prior to 1948 (Selected) 159
Since 1948 (Selected) 161
Zion in the Classroom before 1948 163
Israel in the Classroom since 1948 164
Texts and Fiction prior to 1948 (Selected) 171
Elementary Textbooks and Workbooks since 1948 (Selected) 171
Secondary Textbooks, Guides, and Workbooks 172
Curricula, Units, Mini Courses, and Materials for Students and Teachers 172
Gleanings 173

20 | DAY SCHOOL 176

History 176
Types 176
Goals 177
The Debate 177
Growth and Development 179
Curriculum and Pedagogy 180
Programs for Exceptional Children 184
Integration of Curriculum 185
Organization and Administration 187
Professional Organizations 188
Parents and the Jewish Day School 188
Assessment 190
Values and Identity 194
Financial Support 196
Periodicals for Children and Youth 197
Texts and Guides 197
Gleanings 198

21 | YIDDISH SECULAR SCHOOLS 204

Background Materials (Selected) 204
History of Yiddish Secular Schools 205
Rationale 206
Curriculum—General 208
Language 208
Literature 210
Bible 211
Hebrew 211
History 212
Pedagogy and Related Programs 212
The Day School 214
Secondary Education 214
Tradition 215

PART I   THE SCHOOLS

Change 216
Textbooks 216
The Teacher 216
Higher Education and Teacher Training 217
Home and Education 218
On Consolidating Yiddish chools 219
Camps 219
Assessment prior to 1950 219
Assessment since 1950 222
Organizations Sponsoring Yiddish Education 225
Books for Children and Youth (Selected) 225
Periodicals for Youth (Selected) 226
Periodicals for Educators and Parents (Selected) 226
Textbooks, Readers, Workbooks, and Teacher Guides (Selected) 227
Gleanings 228

22 | HIGHER EDUCATION 232

Teacher Training prior to 1925 232
Teacher Training 1925–1950 232
Teacher Training since 1950 233
Jewish Institutions of Higher Learning prior to 1950 (Including Judaic Studies in General Colleges and Universities) 235
Jewish Institutions of Higher Learning since 1950 237
Gleanings 240

1 | TYPES OF JEWISH SCHOOLS

See also chapters 20 and 21

SCHOOLS

American Council for Judaism. *Working Curriculum and Statement of Objectives, School for Judaism.* 1956–57.

Barkan, Irving. "The Congregational Schools in American Jewish Education." *Jew Ed* 24 (Spring 1953): 19–22.

Benathan, Morris. *The Role of the Talmud Torah in Jewish Education in America.* The Jewish Library Series, no. 5. N.Y.: Herald Square Press, 1946.

Benson, Paulette. *Jewish Educational Movements: The Goals and the Differences.* A comparison of the stated educational goals of the four major North American Jewish movements. Master's project, HUC–JIR, 1978.

Chipkin, Israel S., ed. *Jewish Schools in America: A Description of Types of Jewish Schools in Jewish Communities in the United States and Canada.* N.Y.: AAJE, 1947.
    1. The Afternoon School
    Greenberg, Simon. "The Congregational School" (Three days a week), pp. 13–19.
    Mark, Yudel. "The Yiddish Schools" (Five and three days a week), pp. 20–27.
    Whiteman, Kalman. "The Talmud Torah School" (Five days a week), pp. 7–12.
    2. The All-Day School
    Azrieli, Shlomoh. "The Foundation School," pp. 36–43.
    Lookstein, Joseph H. "The Jewish Day School," pp. 28–35.
    3. Gamoran, Emanuel. "The Jewish Sunday School," pp. 44–49.

* Diskind, Zalman. *The Orthodox Congregational Hebrew School in the United States: A Study of its Background, Administration, Methods, and Outlook.* Dropsie U., 1974.

Gelbart, Gershon G. "Types of Jewish Schooling." *Reg* (1959): 1–4.

Greenstone, Julius H. "The Talmud Torah in America." *Jewish Teacher* 1 (Jan. 1916): 28–34.

Jewish Education 21 (Spring 1950)
    Bass, Hyman. "The Yiddish Schools," pp. 56–57.
    Gamoran, Emanuel. "The Union of American Hebrew Congregations," pp. 59–60.
    Kaminetsky, Joseph. "Torah Umesorah," pp. 58–59.
    Margolis, Isidor. "Mizrachi," pp. 54–55.
    Millgram, Abraham E. "The United Synagogue of America," pp. 57–58.

Kaminetsky, Joseph. "The Jewish Day Schools." *Phi Delta Kappa* (Dec. 1963): 141–44.

Nardi, Noah. "בתי התּ״ת באמריקה" (Talmud Torahs in America). *Sh Hah* (H.) 6 (Mar. 1946): 110–27. Also in *JSS* 8 (Apr. 1946): 51–74.

* Natelson, Herman. *The Talmud Torahs: A Study of the School, the Pupil, and the Home.* Fordham U., 1937. 214 pp.

1 TYPES OF JEWISH SCHOOLS

Penn, Ascher. „אמעריקען קאונסיל פאר דשודאאיזם גרינדעט אייגענע שולן" (The American Council for Judaism Establishes Its Own Schools). *Penn*, 401–12.

Schiff, Alvin I. "Types of Schools." In *The Jewish Day School in America*, 87–91. N.Y.: JEC Press, 1966.

Siegel, Morton, ed. "In Our School System." (USCJE) *Ped Rep* 21 (Dec. 1969): 1–5.

Union of American Hebrew Congregations, CJE. "In Our School System." *Ped Rep* 19 (Dec. 1967): 11–13.

GLEANINGS

Leeser, Isaac
Memorial On Sunday Schools, 1840
"As may easily be imagined, some prejudice was at first manifested by various persons, who fancied that they discovered an objectionable imitation of gentile practices in this undertaking, forgetting that it is the first duty of Israel to instil knowledge of divine things in the hearts of the young, and this institution was eminently calculated to bestow this necessary blessing alike upon rich and poor without fee or price. It is but seldom that so noble an aim has been sought after, begun solely for the glorification of our Maker and the well-being of his people; it is therefore gratifying to record, that this unfounded prejudice has nearly died away, and one cannot give a better evidence of the fact, that now fully one hundred children are enrolled."
JDH, 448.

The American Hebrew, May 14, 1880,
"We may distinctly state that the Sunday School movement among American Jews which commenced by Rebecca Gratz less than a half century ago, is but the legitimate expression of a deep instinct of the Jewish mind. Real nurseries of Judaism, the institution deserves earnest support of the community."

Quoted by Moshe Davis in *The Emergence of Conservative Judaism* (1963), 434.

Brickner, Barnett R.,
"If you go over the Conference yearbooks, you find a steady and continuous reference to the fact that this Conference urges upon its members and upon the Sunday schools of the country a more intensified form of Jewish education in the form of more time assigned to the work of Jewish education. What we should like to know is how are we to get more time for education for our schools? I do not think there is a rabbi in this Conference who is satisfied with the Sunday school, who is not willing to subscribe his name to the fact that the Sunday school has been, as far as the purposes of Reform Judaism are concerned, a failure. Why is it that we have not been able in our schools, with the conviction that we have on education, to put a week-day religious school in place of the Sunday school?"
CCAR 33 (1923), 340.

The Commission on Jewish Education—UAHC,
"Resolved: That this Commission in planning a detailed curriculum for the Jewish religious school of comprehensive scope, is unanimous in the conviction that a week-day session will have to be added to the present Sunday session in building up a system of religious education that shall be adequate to our needs. And this Commission urge upon the rabbinate and the congregations of this country that such an arrangement for additional instruction be adopted in our religious schools."
Quoted by Jacob B. Pollak in "The Union of American Hebrew Congregations and the Problem of Jewish Education," *Proceedings*, NCJSS (1926), 289.

Mark, Yudel,
"The Yiddish school was not built on tradition. It did not have any ready made examples. From the very beginning it was seeking its way. It was free from the burden of superfluous but it also did not have the benefit of established forms. It was, therefore, natural that in the course of the thirty-six years of its existence in

America it should have passed through a number of transmigrations."
Jew Ed 19 (Fall 1947), 31.

Honor, Leo L.,

"With the emergence of non-sectarian public schools, and with the change of attitude towards the Hebrew Language under the influence of Reform ideas, it was considered adequate to limit lessons in religious education to Saturday and Sunday mornings, or even to Sunday mornings only; consequently the all-day schools were given up."
The Jewish People, Past and Present (1948), 2:154.

Yefroikin, Zalman

"One of the newer manifestations in the sphere of Jewish education was the Yiddish secular school which made its appearance shortly before World War I, and which owed its inception principally to the Jewish socialist movement and the Jewish labor organizations. . . . By 1918 three distinct and recognizable tendencies had crystallized in the Yiddish school movement: the schools of the Jewish National Workers' Alliance, which changed its name from 'National—Radical' to 'Jewish Folk Schools'; the Sholem Aleichem Schools and the Workmen's Circle Schools. . . .

An additional change has manifested itself within the Yiddish secular school movement during recent years. The view that a Jewish national life could be possible without observance of a Jewish pattern . . . has been found erroneous; it has come to be recognized that to be a Jew it is necessary to live a Jewish life."
The Jewish People, Past and Present (1948), 2:144–48.

Axelrod, Herman C.,

"While the creation of a religious community outside the school is our ultimate objective, our immediate objective should be the formation of a religious community within the Yeshiva proper. Modern education speaks of the school as a miniature society. The Yeshiva, by its very nature, must become a miniature Torah-society in the full sense of the word. This means that it must concern itself with every aspect of child development both within and without the classroom. It means that we must plan a program of co-curricular or extra-curricular activities that will meet the needs and interests of our children and provide them with the opportunity for creative expression, social contact and religious inspiration."
HDS, p. 184.

Ackerman, Walter I.,

"When judged by even the least demanding standard of what it means to be an educated Jew, it is hard to avoid the feeling that the academic aspirations of the one-day-a-week school are either a colossal joke or an act of cynical pretentiousness."
Quoted in *The Second Jewish Catalog* (1976), 209.

2 CURRICULUM

For earlier period see chapter 29

Bugatch, Simon, William Chomsky, and Ben M. Edidin. "New Developments in the Jewish Curriculum." *Jew Ed* 17 (Nov. 1945): 13–21.

Chomsky, William. "The Curriculum for the New Jewish Weekday School." *Jew Ed* 5 (Jan.–Mar. 1933): 22–31.

Comins, Harry L. "An Experiment with an Activity Curriculum." *Jew Ed* 3 (Jan./Mar. 1931): 39–49.

———. "An Integrated Curriculum for the Jewish School." *Jew Ed* 4 (Apr./June 1932): 93–110.

Dushkin, Alexander M. "Content of the Curriculum of the Jewish School." *Jew Teach* 5 (Aug. 1923): 2–3.

Edelstein, Menachem M. „תכנית הלמודים והחמר מטעם ועד התכנית של אגודת המנהלים" (The Curriculum and Materials Prepared by the Principals Association's Curriculum Committee). *Sh Hah* (H.) 4 (Mar. 1944): 134–41.

———. „קביעת תכנית למודים בבית הספר העברי" (Determining a Curriculum in the Jewish School). *Sh Hah* (H.) 9 (Aug. 1949): 123–29.

Edidin, Ben M., Jacob S. Golub, and Samuel Dinin. "Re-evaluating Jewish School Curriculum." *Jew Ed* 11 (Jan. 1940): 200–212.

Eisenberg, I. L. (Azriel). "How To Write a Curriculum for a Jewish School." *Jew Ed*, 2 (June 1930): 90–95.

Emil, Charles. "A Problem Course in World Jewry." *Jew Teach* 13 (Nov. 1944): 1–7.

Epstein, A. „על החבור" (On Composition). *Sh Hah* (H.) (May–June 1939): 49–64.

Gamoran, Emanuel. "What Shall Our Curriculum Be?" *Jew Teach* 1 (June 1933): 1–9.

DEVELOPMENT AND ASSESSMENT PRIOR TO 1950

Gamoran, Emanuel. *Weekday Jewish Instruction*. Cincinnati: DSSE, 1928. 9 pp.

Glasner, Samuel. "Analysis of References to Jewish History, Religion, Ceremonies, and other Subjects of Jewish Religious School Instruction in Current Jewish Periodical Literature, as an Aid to Curriculum Construction." Master's thesis, HUC–JIR, 1936.

———. "A Study in the Curriculum of the Jewish School." *Jew Ed* 9 (Oct.–Dec. 1937): 153–62.

Glatstein, Harry N. "Historical Survey of the Curriculum of the Jewish School." Master's thesis, Temple U., 1932.

Goldman, I. M. "Let Us Search Our Ways." *Con Jud* 3 (Feb. 1947): 1–5.

Goldman, Lucille W. "Teaching Our Third Grade." *Jew Teach* 5 (Nov. 1936): 7–11.

Goldman, Yehuda. „פעולות כלליות של המחלקה" (General Classroom Activities). *Sh Hah* (H.) 4 (Dec. 1943): 39–42.

Golub, Jacob S. "Activity Curriculum for Sunday Schools." *Jew Ed* 14 (Jan./Mar. 1943): 146–50.

———. "A Curriculum for the Primary Grades." *Jew Ed* 3 (Jan./Mar. 1931): 49–55.

———. "Re-Evaluating Jewish School Curricula." *Jew Ed* (Jan. 1940): 200–212.

Golub, Jacob S., and Leo L. Honor. "Some Guiding Principles for the Jewish School of Tomorrow." *Jew Ed* 4 (Oct.–Dec. 1932): 150–62.

Goodman, Abram V., and Mrs. Abram V. Goodman. "Folklore in the Religious School." *Jew Teach* 4 (Nov. 1935), 8–14; 5 (Jan. 1936), 24–32.

Greenberg, Simon. "Educational Content in Terms of Contemporary Needs." *RA* (1941–44): 182–90. Also *Jew Ed* 15 (Jan. 1944): 70–74.

Kurzband, Toby K. "Enriching Our Curriculum with Science." *Jew Teach* 17: 3 (1949).

———. "Notes on a Life-Activity Curriculum." *Jew Ed* 3 (Oct.–Dec. 1931): 172–76.

Leibman, Moshe. "Jewish Values as a Basis for Curriculum Organization." *Jew Ed* 9 (Oct./Dec. 1937): 163–68.

———. "New Trends in Methodology in America and in Our Jewish Schools." *Sh Hah* (H.) 1 (1941): 15–29.

Levin, Mildred. "Jewish Children Write." *Jew Teach* 2 (June 1934): 15–17.

* Markowitz, Samuel H. *An Approach to a Curriculum of Religious Education for a Reform Jewish Community in the Middle West.* U. of Chicago, 1932. 194 pp. See *CCAR* 43 (1933): pp. 169–203.

Michlin, Michael. „שיעורים לדוגמא" (Model Lessons) On the teaching of calligraphy. *Sh Hah* (H.) 2 (1926): 49–53.

Mittleman, Jacob. "Pupil Activities" (Talmud Torah). *Jew Ed* 18 (Summer 1947): 31–37.

Nardi, Noah. „צורה ותכן בחנוך העברי" (Form and Substance in Hebrew Education). *Sh Hah* (H.) 2 (Oct. 1942): 247–53.

Pearlman, David W. "The Curriculum of a Congregational Hebrew School." *Jew Ed* 3 (Apr.–June 1931): 98–100.

Pollak, I. Sh. „אין שיעור בלי טעמא" (There is No Lesson Without 'Motivation'). *Sh Hah* (H.) 7 (1926): 39–45.

Ranson, Marius. "A Completely Departmentalized Religious School." *CCAR* 45 (1935): 432–57.

Rappaport, Israel B. "Some Essentials in the Reconstruction of the Jewish School Curriculum." *Jew Ed* 8 (Oct.–Dec. 1936): 141–46.

* Schwartz, Lawrence W., *Curriculum Development in a Reform Jewish School*. Columbia Un., 1942, 174pp.

Slominsky, J. D. "We Are Thankful." *Jew Teach* 10 (Nov. 1941): 14–19.

Stone, Anne. "Creative Self-Expression in the Religious School." *Jew Teach* 1 (1933): 11–15.

Strouse, Edith M. "Notes on a Reform Religious School" *Jew Ed* 6 (Apr./June 1934): 82–86.

Touroff, Nissan. „יסודות לתכנית-למודים בבית ספר עברי" (Principles for a Curriculum in the Hebrew School) *Sh Hah* (H.) 2 (1927): 1–9, 1–7.

Wolf, Ernest M. "Curriculum Trends in the Jewish Sunday School." *Recon* (June 28, 1946): 17–23.

Zlowe, Pauline. "In the Intermediate Grades." *Jew Teach* 6 (Nov. 1937): 15–17.

CURRICULA PRIOR TO 1950

Cohen, Samuel. *The Progressive Jewish School: An Integrated Activity Curriculum*. N.Y.: USA, 1932. 171 pp.

Commission on Jewish Education, UAHC. "The Curriculum of the Jewish Religious School" (Elementary and High School Departments) (2 sessions weekly). *CCAR* 33 (1923): 328–43.

Franzblau, Abraham. *Curriculum of the Jewish Religious School: Syllabus for Education*. Cincinnati: CJE of UAHC, 1935. 56 pp.

Frishberg, I. Z. *Curriculum for Talmud Torah.* Council of Orthodox Jewish Schools, 1943. 73pp.

———. "תכנית למודים כללית". (Tokhnit Limudim Kellalit) (H.). A general curriculum for the Hebrew school with a special section, "Zionism in the Past and Present." N.Y.: Mizrachi National Education Committee, 1946. 108 pp.

Gamoran, Emanuel. *A Curriculum for the Jewish Religious School: Course of Study 1 and 2.* Cincinnati: UAHC, 1937. (Revisions Annually).

Golub, Jacob S. *Tentative Outline of Curriculum for Sunday School.* N.Y.: JEC, 1944. 28 pp.

Hebrew Principals' Association. *Talmud Torah Curriculum.* N.Y.: JEC, 1941. 121 pp.

Jung, Leo, and Joseph Kaminetsky. *A Model Program for the Talmud Torah: A Handbook for Rabbis, Principals, Teachers, Officers, and Lay Members of the BJE.* N.Y.: UOJCA, 1942–43. 205 pp.

Landesman, Alter. *A Curriculum for Jewish Schools.* N.Y.: USA, 1922. 276 pp.

Lehman, E. H. *A Curriculum for the Jewish Religious School.* N.Y.: Bloch, 1910.

Merkos L'Inyonei Chinuch Inc. *Tokhnit Limudim* (H.). A curriculum. N.Y.: 1944.

Mizrachi Teachers Institute, *Curriculum.* (H.) With special emphasis on the land of Israel and Jewish nationalism. N.Y.: 1918–19.

Ruffman, Louis L. *Curriculum Outline for the Congregational School: Primary and Elementary Divisions.* USCJE, 1948. 47 pp.

Solomon, George. "A Review of Courses of Study and Methods in Use in Jewish Sunday Schools." *CCAR* 19 (1909): 388–400.

Vaad Haharedi. *Curriculum of Council of Jewish Orthodox Schools.* N.Y.: 1943. 73 pp.

DEVELOPMENT AND ASSESSMENT SINCE 1950

Ackerman, Walter I. *An Analysis of Selected Courses of Study of Conservative Congregational Schools.* N.Y.: MRC and JTS, 1968. See also *Jew Ed* 40 (Mar. 1970), 7–23, and (Summer 1970), 37–48.

———. "The Curriculum of the Conservative Congregational School." *Jew Ed* 48 (Summer 1980): 12–20.

———. "The New Curricula: Some Observations." *Con Jud* 32 (Fall 1978): 43–62.

———. "Toward a History of the Curriculum of the Conservative Congregational School." *Jew Ed* 46 (Spring 1980): 19–26.

Ackerman, Walter I., Elana Shohamy, J. West, and David Zisenwine. *A World Survey of Jewish Educational Curriculum: The State of the Art.* Tel Aviv: Tel Aviv University, Israel-Diaspora Institute, 1984.

Ariav, Tamar. "Learning from General Education: A Curriculum Perspective." *Ped Rep* 35 (Mar. 1984): 7–8.

———. "Curriculum Development and the Central Agency for Jewish Education." *Jew Ed* 54 (Fall 1986): 8–10, 27.

Bettman, Batia. "The Role of Faculty in Curriculum Development." *Ped Rep* 32 (Fall 1980): 25–26.

Bogot, Howard I. "Jewish Assertiveness." (Implementing the Curriculum) *Compass* 1 (Summer 1978): 12–14.

Braver, Joseph. "Formulating Educational Objectives in the Curriculum." *Impact* 35 (Summer 1977): 41–45.

Braver, Joseph, and Shimon Frost, eds. *New Directions in the Jewish School Curriculum, 1972 Yearbook.* N.Y.: Ed As, 1973.

Bridger, David. "Subject Matter and Themes of Primary Education." *Jew Ed* 28 (Winter 1957): 50–56.

Brown, Steven M. "Curriculum Development in the Jewish School." *Ped Rep* 32 (Fall 1980): 24–25.

*———. *Media, Materials, and Instruction in Jewish Religious Education.* Columbia U. Teachers College, 1975. 283 pp.

* Chorowsky, Joshua. *Generating a Theory of the Curriculum for the Jewish School.* Ohio State U., 1980. 165 pp.

Danziger, Harry K. "Towards a Course of Study for the Primary Grades in 'The Wonders of the Universe.'" Master's thesis, HUC–JIR, 1964.

Dinin, Samuel. "The Curriculum of the Jewish School." *AJYB* 63 (1962): 214–25.

Ende, George. "Requisites of Fair and Objective Criticism." A response to critics of *Curriculum Outline of the Congregational School*. *Syn Sch* 11 (Nov. 1952): 23–26.

Feinstein, Joseph H. "A Curriculum for the Midweek Hebrew School." *Jew Teach* 33 (Oct. 1964): 23–25.

Fox, Seymour, and Geraldine Rosenfield, eds. *From Scholar to the Classroom: Translating Jewish Tradition into Curriculum*. N.Y.: MRC-JE and JTS, 1977. 121 pp.

Freidenreich, Fradle Pomerantz. "Curriculum Development." *JPH*, 287–92.

Frost, Shimon. "Come Now and Let Us Reason Together." *Jew Ed* 47 (Winter 1979): 8–12.

Gertman, Stuart A. "The Language of Survival: Curriculum and Textbook." *CCAR J* (Summer 1977): 37–45.

Glasner, Samuel. "A Global Curriculum for Religious Education: Multiple Dimensions in the Curriculum of the Jewish School." *Ped Rep* 22 (Mar. 1971): 15.

———. "Multiple Conflicts in the Curriculum of the American Jewish Religious School." *Rel Ed* (July–Aug. 1961).

———. "Old-New Directions in the Jewish School Curriculum." *Jew Ed* 43 (Winter/Spring 1975): 33–37.

Goldin, Judah. "The Content of Jewish Education." *RA* (June 1953): 243–50.

* Gorin, Paul. *Towards Establishing a New Curriculum for the Reform Jewish Religious School*. HUC–JIR, 1956. 322 pp.

Hessel, Carolyn Starman. "National Educational Resource Center." *Ped Rep* 33 (Oct. 1982): 29–31.

Honor, Leo L. "Changing Approaches to Curriculum Development in the Supplemental Week Day Jewish School." *Jew Ed* 24 (Spring 1954): 12–21.

Kroman, Nathan. "A Theoretical Framework for the Jewish School Studies." *Jew Teach* (Oct. 1962).

Krug, Mark. "Observations on the New Curriculum for Conservative Congregational Schools." *Syn Sch* 11 (Sept. 1952): 21–25.

Kudan, Harold L. "Current Trends and Their Development in Christian Educational Curricula and Their Implications for the Reform Jewish Religious School. Master's thesis, HUC–JIR, 1959.

Kurzband, Toby K. "Creating a New Curriculum." *CCAR J* (Apr. 1957): 26–32.

———. "Curriculum Exchange." *Jew Teach* 33 (Feb. 1965).

Lakritz, William B. "A Curriculum for the Conservative Congregational School." *Syn Sch* 18 (June 1960).

———. "The School Curriculum." *NICD*.

* Lang, Leon S. *A Curriculum for the Congregational School*. Dropsie College, 1950. 190 pp.

Lukinsky, Joseph. "Let's Not Give Up Yet: A Response to the Menorah Curriculum." *Con Jud* 31 (Winter 1977): 87–92.

Margoshes, Samuel. "The Jewish School Curriculum." *The Day* (Dec. 20, 1959).

Melton Research Center. "Developing the Melton Curriculum." *MRCN* 7 (Fall 1977): 1–5.

"The Menorah Curriculum." *Con Jud* 31 (Winter 1977). A symposium on curriculum.

National Commission on Torah Education. "Should We Revise Our Curriculum?" *Ped Rep* 22 (Mar. 1971): 22.

Pilch, Judah. "The National Curriculum Research Institute." *Jew Ed* 37 (1967): 152–61.

Pollak, George. "Curriculum Development." *RA* (1975): 171–76.

Prystowsky, S. "Problems in Curriculum Facing Jewish Religious Schools." *Rel Ed* 62 (Sept.–Oct. 1962): 431–34.

Resnik, Reuben. "An Evaluation of the Curriculum Outline for the Congregational School." *Syn Sch* 11 (Sept. 1952): 19–20.

Ruffman, Louis L. "Curriculum Development and Pupil Achievement." *Jew Ed* 31 (Fall 1960): 25–35.

———. "The Organizing of Learning Experiences." In *Curriculum for the Congregational School*. CJE and USA, 1958. Also in *JJS*, 111–18.

Sacher, Byron, and Arthur Monsky. "A Change of Pace Program." 34 *Jew Teach* (Dec. 1965).

Schanin, Norman, and Walter Ackerman. *New Insights into Curriculum Development*. N.Y.: Ed As, 1966.

Schremer, Oded. "The Hidden Curriculum in Jewish Education" (H.). *Stu*, 51–92.

Schwartzman, Sylvan D. "Curriculum." *CCAR* 68 (1958): 154–56.

———. "A More Realistic Approach to Curriculum." *CCAR J* (Apr. 1957): 21–25.

———. "What's Happening with Our Curriculum?" *Jew Teach* 34 (Feb. 1966): 3–6.

Segal, Abraham. "The Curricula of the Reform Religious Schools." *CCAR J* (Apr. 1957): 5–12.

Skolnick, Irving. *A Guide to Curriculum Construction for the Religious School*. Chicago: College of Jewish Studies, 1969. 143 pp.

Slesinger, Zalmen. "Basic Considerations in Curriculum Building." *Ped Rep* 15 (June 1964): 11–14.

———. "Basic Problems in Curriculum Building." *Ped Rep* 11 (Mar. 1960) and 12 (Sept. 1960).

———. "Priorities in Jewish Learning—The Basic Issue in Curriculum Construction." *Jew Ed* 43 (Spring 1974): 5–13.

———. "Some Guidelines in Curriculum Building." *Ped Rep* 22 (Mar. 1971): 9.

———. "Toward a Program of Essential Learnings." *Ped Rep* 12 (Sept. 1960).

Spotts, Leon H. "Trends and Currents in Curriculum Development, 1930–1970." *Jew Ed* 40 (Spring 1971): 36–45.

Stern, Jay B. "The Menorah Curriculum." *Con Jud* 31 (Winter 1977): 82–86.

Sugarman, Alvin Marx. "Toward the Construction of a Curriculum for the First Grade of the Reform Religious School." Master's thesis, HUC–JIR 1971.

Toubin, Isaac. "The Right Hand's Cunning." *Jew Ed* 42 (Spring 1973): 44–47.

Weitzman, Alan G. "Toward a Course of Study in Jewish Symbols for the Primary Grades of the Reform Religious School." Master's thesis, HUC–JIR, 1960. 86 pp.

Wollman, Benjamin. "A Foundation Program and Jewish Education in the US." *Sh Hah* (H.) 14 (Fall 1954): 3–18.

Zisenwine, David W. "Curriculum Planning—How?" *Jew Ed* 43 (Winter–Spring 1975): 42–45.

———. "The Jewish Curriculum—A Local Approach." *Con Jud* 29 (Spring 1975): 64–73.

———. "Jewish Curriculum—A Matter of Culture." *Rel Ed* 70 (May–June 1975): 300–307.

* ———. *A Reconceptualization of Foundations for Curriculum Development in Jewish Education*. Ohio State U., 1974. 183 pp.

CURRICULA SINCE 1950

Baum, Eli, ed. *Curriculum Guide for Afternoon Religious Schools*. N.Y.: National Commission on Torah Education, 1979. 216 pp.

Borowitz, Eugene B., ed. *An Outline of the Curriculum of the Jewish Religious School*. N.Y.: CJE, UAHC, and CCAR, 1960–61. 85 pp.

Commission on Jewish Education of UAHC and CCAR. *Curriculum for the Jewish Religious School*. 1970.

Eisenberg, Azriel. *A Curriculum for Small Jewish Religious Schools*. N.Y.: USA. 214 pp.

Gamoran, Emanuel. *A Curriculum for the Jewish Religious School*. (For Two- and Three-Day-a-Week Schools) Course of Study. N.Y.: UAHC, 1952–53 and 1957–58. 57 pp.

———, ed. *Unit of Activity and Instruction*. (Junior and Senior High School) N.Y.: UAHC, 1956. 316 pp.

Lister, Rebecca. *Teachers' Syllabus for Grade Three*. N.Y.: UAHC, 1963. 235 pp.

Nemzoff, Samuel L. *Teacher's Syllabus for Grade Eight*. N.Y.: UAHC, 1964.

Pedagogic Reporter, September 1952. Contains a list of curricula. See also *Ped Rep* 8 (Sept. 1956): 5–8, 18.

Peskind, Steven J. "Toward a Curriculum for the First Grade of the Reform Religious School." Master's thesis, HUC–JIR, 1973.

Pins, Margot C. *Teacher's Syllabus for Grade Four*. N.Y.: UAHC, 1958.

Pollak, George, and Gerhard Lang. *Inventory of Curricular Subjects in Supplementary Jewish Schools.* JESNA Bulletin No. 51, Sept. 1981. 36 pp.

Pryzant, Nancy. "Lo Shinu et Shenam (They Have Not Changed Their Name): A Curriculum for the Reform One-Day-a-Week Religious School." Based upon research in secular education by Paul Hanna and John B. Lee, this course of study emphasizes thematic teaching, personal problem solving, use of original texts, and intellectual contact with Jewish sources. Master's project, HUC–JIR, 1978.

Rocky Mountain Curriculum Planning Workshop. *Le Havdil: To Make a Difference.* Lesson guides for the Jewish Religious School. Denver, 1972.

Ruffman, Louis L. *A Curriculum Outline for the Afternoon Jewish School.* N.Y.: USA, 1978.

———. *Curriculum Outline for the Congregational School.* N.Y.: USA, 1958, 1959. 278 pp.

———. *Curriculum Outline for the Congregational School. Part II: Junior High School Division.* N.Y.: USCJE, 1951. 60 pp.

Schindler, Alexander M., ed. *An Outline of the Curriculum.* N.Y.: CJE and UAHC, 1963–64. 76 pp.

Schwartzman, Sylvan D. *Toward a New Curriculum for the One-Day-a-Week Reform Jewish Religious School.* Cincinnati: HUC, 1955. 35 pp.

Stern, Jay B., ed. and comp. *A Curriculum for the Afternoon Jewish School.* N.Y.: USCJE, 1978.
  1. Mosenkis, Rebekkah K. Modern Hebrew.
  2. Siegel, Morton. History/Community.
  3. Stern, Jay B. Judaism—sources.
  4. Wachs, Saul P. Tefilah/Mitzvah.

Sussman, Leonard R. *Working Curricula and Weekly Guide with Syllabus from Kindergarten through the 12th Grade.* N.Y.: Religious Education Department, American Council for Judaism, 1957. 392 pp.

Union of American Hebrew Congregations. *An Outline of the Curriculum for the Jewish Religious School.* N.Y.: UAHC, Graded Textbook List, 1968, 1969.

The UAHC William and Frances Schuster Curriculum. *Guidelines for the Preschool Year, Guidelines for the Primary Years, Guidelines for the Intermediate Years, and Guidelines for the Junior High School Years.* 4 vols. N.Y.: UAHC, 1984.

Warschauer, Heinz. *Teachers' Syllabus for Grade Nine.* N.Y.: UAHC, 1961.

Weinstein, Barry L. "Toward the Construction of a Curriculum for the Second Grade of the Reform Religious School." Master's thesis, HUC–JIR, 1971.

GLEANINGS

The Commission on Jewish Education (UAHC) (1924),
"The curriculum of the Jewish Religious School . . . (should therefore) be so arranged as to awaken in the young the religious consciousness and to stimulate them to aid in building up the important institutions of Jewish life, such as the home, the synagogue, and the community."
Quoted in NCJSS Proceedings (1926), 284.

Frishberg, I. Z.,
"The content of education is a thing which stands forever and is not made to be changed according to the demands of time."
Tochnit Limudim (H.) 1946, p. 11. (Quoted by Irving H. Skolnick, *A Guide to Curriculum Construction for the Religious School* (1969), 5.

Hertz, Richard C.,
"The most obvious trend noted in this entire survey is the chaotic condition of the curriculum in Reform Jewish education. Standardization and uniformity are minimal when they should be maximal. Different subjects are taught with varying frequency and with an endless number of textbooks and teaching material. The only subjects which appear to be consistently taught are Hebrew, Jewish History, Current Events, Customs and Ceremonies, and the Bible."

The Education of the Jewish Child. UAHC (1953), 158–59.

Honor, Leo L.,
"The most important influence on curriculum development in the Jewish school emanates from the distinction made by American educators between 'course of study' and 'curriculum', and their defining the latter as "the total series of experiences in the school, or made possible through the school, or for which the school is responsible." This conception has not only affected the content taught and the method used in the Jewish school, but has led to the attempt to extend the influence of the school, and to the placing of emphasis upon parent education as part of the curriculum of the school."
JQR 45 (Apr. 1955), 495.

Schwartzman, Sylvan D.,
"What's Wrong With The Curriculum? (Reform)
1. It is based upon the theory, no longer tenable, that education consists principally of the transmission of factual information. . . .
2. Our curriculum focuses upon adult rather than child needs, and its content is in a large measure ill-suited to the intellectual and emotional maturity of children. . . .
3. The curriculum concentrates far too heavily upon the past. . . .
4. The meagerness of content in the earlier grades and the abundance of material for the later grades indicate another deficiency. . . .
5. The philosophy of Judaism which underlies our curriculum is clearly out of balance. Too heavily weighted in the direction of Jewish sociology. . . .
6. The present course of study is insufficiently oriented toward Reform. . . .
7. Because we make no provision for effective parent education as an integral part of our program, there is a wide gap between what the children are taught in the school and the Jewish practice of their parents. . . ."
Toward a New Curriculum for the One-Day-a-Week Religious School (1955), 6–9.

The Commission for Jewish Education (USA),
"The congregational school curriculum should include a broad range of subjects grouped within three major areas of instruction: Torah and the Hebrew language, Jewish living, and the Jewish people. The content of the curriculum must reflect the varying interests of Jewish life."
CJE, 1958.

Dushkin, Alexander M., and Uriah Z. Engelman,
"In the American setting of religious pluralism, in which the Jews are influenced by both Protestant and Catholic school experience, it is inevitable that the differentiation of curricula should be more varied than ever before in Jewish History. However, the uniquely Jewish common experience must be continued through community educational concern, in the direction of greater unity where possible, and of greater intensification in teaching the Hebraic character of our common literary historic culture."
Jewish Education in the United States (1959), 177.

Commission for the Study of Jewish Education in the United States,
"A National Curriculum Institute should be set up to concern itself continuously with the tasks involved in translating the general objectives of Jewish education into the realities of curriculum and teaching. The many possible functions of such a Curriculum Institute are suggested in connection with particular findings in the Study. It is projected as a national program for studying all aspects of the educational process as applied to Jewish schools, and for devising the necessary instruments and procedures toward translating general objectives into specific objectives and national norms of what schools can and should achieve in imparting Jewish knowledge as the basis for realizing all the other aims of Jewish education."
Summary Report, (5).

Bennett, Alan D.,
"Curriculum structure is integrally bound up with philosophy and goal. A consequence of liberal religion and the at-

tendant autonomy of its leaders and congregations is the lack of a uniform statement of objective. A variety of Reform Jewish educational aims receive varying degrees of emphasis and priority. It is therefore not surprising that curricula of Reform Jewish schools present a picture characterized by diversity of aims, multiplicity of courses of study, and seemingly endless lists of textbooks used for an astonishing range of grades."

Rel Ed (Jan.–Feb. 1963), 48.

Cohen, Jack J.,
"Seeing Torah as that which enhances the intellectual, moral and spiritual quality of Jewish life gives the modern Jew the breadth of perspective of a curriculum necessary to make the Jewish school a living center of culture....

The content of Jewish curriculum must be determined by the largest possible context. For the Jewish aspect of Jewish education that context is the living people. However, it is for the component groups within Jewry to argue forcefully and consistently for their philosophies of Judaism, they can neither influence nor appraise the thinking of the other denominations through a policy of comfortable isolation."

JEDS, 109, 116.

Melton Research Center,
"The development here being presented is a blending of classical and contemporary elements: Bible, prayer, Jewish history and thought, mitzvot, holidays, Hebrew language and contemporary Jewish life.

The grading of the curriculum is both vertical and horizontal. Vertical grading denotes the intellectual progression of each subject as the child grows and advances in school and becomes more receptive to conceptual aspects of the subject matter....

Horizontal grading coordinates the subjects taught in any one year."

"Developing the Melton Curriculum," *MRCN* 7 (Fall 1977), 3.

Baum, Eli, ed.,
"A. To design a program which enables Talmud Torah education to meet the religious needs and interests of our students for the last quarter of the Twentieth Century and well beyond.

B. To engender in our students a love, reverence, and appreciation of the Torah, halakha, and teachings which have enabled Judaism to survive, despite many adversities throughout the centuries—and despite many opportunities to assimilate to the majority culture and lose its identity."

Curriculum Guide for Afternoon Religious Schools (N.Y.: National Commission on Torah Education, 1979), 2.

3 PEDAGOGY

PROJECTS, METHODS, AND CONCERNS

Adelman, Martin D. "A Semantic Analysis in Jewish Education." Master's thesis, Ohio State U., 1962.

Ben-Shoham, Hannah. "Creating Environments for Jewish Learning." *AM* (Fall 1978).

Bogot, Howard. "Teaching for Concepts." *Jew Teach* 32 (Oct. 1963): 6–7.

Borovetz, Fran. "Motivation in Motion." Stories as motivators. *Compass* (Summer 1982): 12–13.

Botwinick, Moshe L. "Jewish Education in a Technological Age." *Ped Rep* 35 (Jan. 1985): 5–7.

Brennan, Alice M. "Problems of a Progressive Jewish School." *Jew Ed* 6 (Oct./Dec. 1934): 162–67.

Brenner, Anton. "Re-examining Readiness." *Ped Rep* 19 (Sept. 1967): 3–4.

Brichto, Mira. "Creative Thinking in the Classroom." *Jew Teach* 28 (May 1960): 18–19.

Brilliant, Nathan, and Libbie L. Braverman. *Activities in the Religious School*. N.Y.: UAHC, 1950.
   1. "Consecration and Confirmation," 200–224.
   2. "Contests," 165–73.
   3. "Recognition of Achievement—Honor and Awards," 174–83.

Brown, Sheldon S. "Do Report Cards Really Report?" Report cards or Conferences. *Syn Sch* 22 (Summer 1964): 24–28.

Brown, Steven M. "Competition or Cooperation: What Is Best for the Jewish School?" *MJ* 12 (Spring 1981): 7, 18.

Charish, Sharon. "Classroom Climate: Guidelines for the Effective Teacher." *Ped Rep* 35 (Oct. 1984): 5–6.

Chazan, Barry. "Beineinu: Tradition and Autonomy, the Paradox of Contemporary Jewish Education." *Con Jud* 35 (Spr. 1982), 55–65

———. "Indoctrination and Religious Education." In *LJE*, 57–76.

———. "In the Jewish Classroom." *Mid* 17 (Aug./Sept. 1971): 3–8.

Chomsky, William. דרכי הוראה ולמידה (Methods of Teaching and Learning) (H.). N.Y.: JEC, 1967. 207 pp.

* Cohen, Burton. *Criteria for Developing Curricular Proposals for the Teaching of Deliberation*. U. of Chicago, 1974.

———. "The Teaching of Deliberation in the Jewish School." *Stu* 2:122–35.

Cohen Jack J. "Content and Method." In *JEDS*, 96–116. See also "Education as Art and Science," 78–95.

———. "Indoctrination vs. Education." In *JEDS*, 64–77.

3 PEDAGOGY

Cohen, Mimi. "The Idea Store: Hints and Suggestions for the Jewish Educator." *MJ* 20 (Spring 1986): 28.

Cutter, William. "Reading and Leading: Two Impulses of Jewish Life." *Jew Ed* 52 (Winter 1984–85): 22–28.

Cutter, William, and Jack Dauber. "Confluent Education." *Ped Rep* 23 (June 1972): 14.

Davis, Moshe. "The Ladder of Jewish Education." *RA* (1947): 10–30.

Dorff, Elliot. "A Renewed Understanding of Mission and Method in Jewish Education." *Rel Ed* 70 (Fall 1984): 78–87.

Dorph, Sheldon A. "A Model for Jewish Education in America: Guidelines for the Restructuring of Conservative Congregational Education." In *Stu* 2:85–103.

Eisenberg, Azriel. "How to Begin a Lesson." *Syn Sch* 16 (Jan. 1948): 43–47.

Elkin, Harry. "Stimulating Pupil Initiative." *Sh Hah* (H.) 21 (Summer 1961).

Euster, Sandra D. "Piaget Goes to Sunday School." *Compass* 4 (Spring 1981): 8–9.

Feifer, Richard. "Programmed Instruction in the Jewish Religious School." An exploration of some of the principles of behavior modification as the basis of programmed instruction. Master's project, HUC–JIR, 1975.

———. "Programmed Instructional Module: Introduction to the Torah." A one-hour instructional program for Junior High school designed to teach the basic facts about the Torah. Includes Field test analysis and evaluation. Master's project, HUC–JIR, 1976.

Feldheim, Eric. "Religious School Chavurot." *Ped Rep* 22 (June 1971): 19.

Fields, Harvey J. *Modern Jewish Problems: A Teacher's Guide*. N.Y.: UAHC, c. 1966. 122 pp.

Fine, Jeanne. "Some Classroom Techniques for the Beginning Teacher." *Jew Teach* 19 (Nov. 1950): 1–9.

Fishman, Joshua. "How Long Should a Lesson Be?" *Syn Sch* 10 (1952): 5–9.

Franck, Isaac. "Oversimplification of Motivation." *JSS* 17 (July 1955): 195–99.

Frickles, Anita A., and Sharon G. Witkin. "Year Round Religious Education" (Summer Program). *Compass* 6 (Fall 1982): 15, 21.

Glasner, Samuel. "Silent Reading Method." *Jew Ed* 33 (Summer 1963): 231–34.

———. "A Teacher's Check-List for Lesson Planning." *Jew Teach* 24 (Nov. 1955): 5.

Golub, Jacob S. "Individuality and the System." *Jew Ed* 1 (Oct. 1929): 165–72. Also in *RTJH*, 119–26.

Gorodetzer, Phil. "Synagogue School Tours." *Syn Sch* 22 (1964).

Green, Kathy. "Toward Lesson Plans." *MJ* 21 (Winter 1987): 13, 29.

Gross, Morris B. *Learning Readiness in Two Jewish Groups*. N.Y.: Center for Urban Education, 1967. See also *Jew Ed* 39 (July 1967): 15–16.

Grossman, Louis. "Pedagogic Methods in the Sabbath School." *CCAR* 13 (1903): 173–83.

Hachen, David S. "Old-New Frontiers in Education." *Jew Teach* 33 (Oct. 1964): 1–2.

Henkin, Anne D. "Motivating Home Assignments." *Syn Sch* 18 (June 1959).

Ingall, Carol K. "Classroom Management: Two Workshop Models." *Ped Rep* 35 (Oct. 1984): 8–9.

———. "The Feminization of Jewish Education." *MJ* 22 (Fall 1987): 11.

Israel, Sherry. "Structured Experiences in Jewish Education." *Rel Ed* 76 (July/Aug. 1981): 403–15.

Isseroff, Sampson. "National Commission on Torah Education." *Ped Rep* 25 (Fall 1973): 23–26.

Joseph, Samuel K. "Breaking the Cycle: Inviting School Success." *Ped Rep* 35 (Oct. 1984): 1–3.

———. "Six Steps to Self-Responsibility." *Ped Rep* 36 (Nov. 1985): 6–7.

Kagan, Henry E. "Jewish Education of the Child." *Jew Teach* 33 (Dec. 1964): 19–20.

Karten, Esther. "Fun and Fluency." *AM* (Spring 1976).

Kirschenbaum, Aaron. "Students and Teachers: A Rabbinic Model." *Con Jud* 26 (Spring 1972): 20–32.

Kohanski, Alexander S. "Content of the Jewish School." *Jew Ed* 23 (Winter 1952): 60–62.

———. "Jewish Educational Content and the Jewish Child." *Recon* (Jan. 29, 1954): 25–28.

Kollin, Gilbert. "In Search of a Balance." *Con Jud* 23 (Spring 1969): 74–78.

Krieger, Leslie H. "Aiding the Unpopular Student: A Research Based Technique." *Jew Teach* 32 (Oct. 1963): 8–9.

Lakritz, William B. "Providing Meaningful Experiences for Our Children." *Syn Sch* 14 (Nov. 1955): 3–6.

Lang, Leon S. "Congregational Schools and Progressive Jewish Education." *RA* (1930–32): 140–47.

Lear, Elmer N. "The Committee Method in the Classroom." *Jew Ed* 24 (Spring 1953): 41.

Lee, Sara S. "Mediated Instruction: Utilizing Multiple Resources." A mediated instructional project which brings together 35 millimeter slides, audio-tape narratives, and teacher's guides. The two instructional packets deal with "The American Jewish Immigrant and His Role in the American Labor Movement" and "A Study of Moses and the Exodus from Egypt." Master's project, HUC–JIR, 1977.

Leos, Irving. "Sensitivity Training in Religious School." *Ped Rep* 22 (June 1971): 20.

Lipman, Matthew. "Thinking Skills in Religious Education." *Ped Rep* 35 (Mar. 1984): 25–29.

Lister, Louis. "Encounter, Inquiry and Discovery in Jewish Education." *Rel Ed* 67 (Nov./Dec. 1972): 435–39.

Lobman, Frances W. "Learning Styles." *Ped Rep* 34 (Mar. 1984): 30–32.

Lukinsky, Joseph. "Integration within Jewish Studies." *Jew Ed* 46 (Winter 1978): 39–41.

Lurie, Rose G. "The Repudiation of Essentials." *Jew Ed* 26 (Fall 1955): 47–51.

———. "Three Years' Experience with the Unit Approach." *Jew Ed* 22 (Winter–Spring 1951): 45–48.

Marcus, Audrey Friedman. "Building Lessons and Units." In *JTH*, 1:1–24.

———. "Classroom Management." In *JTH*, 1:165–71.

———. "Creative Teaching in the Jewish Religious School." The first four chapters of a handbook for Jewish religious school teachers, presenting practical teaching suggestions as well as resources. Master's project, HUC–JIR, 1976.

———. "Creative Writing." In *JTH*, 1:145–50.

———. "Designing and Teaching Mini-Courses and Short Units." In *JTH*, 2:23–32.

———. "Individualizing/Personalizing Instruction." In *JTH*, 1:33–46.

———. "Inquiry Teaching." In *JPH*, 49–62.

———. "Listening Skills, Lecture and Discussion." In *JTH*, 1:25–32.

———. "Resource Guide for Jewish Educators." In *JTH*, 1:189–204.

Marcus, Audrey Friedman, and Deborah Levy. "Classroom Learning Centers." In *JTH*, 47–61.

Marcuson, Isaac E. "The Use of the Story in Religious School Work." *CCAR* 24 (1914): 346–51.

Matek, Ord. "Planning in Classroom Management." *Jew Teach* 28 (Oct. 1959): 6–7.

Meyers, Lawrence, ed. *Teaching in the Jewish Religious School.* N.Y.: Department of Teacher Education, UAHC, 1967.

Millgram, Abraham E. "Implementing a Program of Intensive Jewish Education in the Congregational School." *Con Jud* 5 (June 1949): 1–9.

Morgenlander, Frances, and Lillie Rubee. "Do We Need A Lesson Plan?" *JEC Bulletin* 84 (Dec. 1952). Also in *RTJH*, 207–10.

Moskowitz, E. "Testing for Grouping." *Syn Sch* 21 (1963).

Moskowitz, Nachama. "Questions in the Classroom." *Compass* (Summer 1982): 7, 16–17.

Nadel, Max. "Improving Instruction." *Ped Rep* 32 (Sept. 1981): 29–31.

———. "What We Can Learn from General Education." *Ped Rep* 35 (Mar. 1984): 1–3.

Nardi, Noah. "Education in Discipline." *Ha-Hinnukh* (H.) 11 (1938): 373–82.

Pekarsky, Maurice. "The Challenge to Our Students." *Had Mag* (Nov. 1955).

Peri, Chaim. "Integration: The Overlooked Aspects." *Jew Ed* 46 (Winter 1978): 42–43.

Perry-Marx, Jeffrey A. "Teaching Jewish Concepts Through NLP." An introduction to the learning of concepts, with an emphasis on the application of the neurolinguistic programming (NLP) model to Jewish education. Master's project, HUC–JIR, 1984.

Pitlick, Sh. "החבור בבית הספר העברי", (Composition in the Hebrew School). *Sh Hah* (H.) 2 (1927): 34–40.

Resnick, Miriam Roher. "What Every Religious School Teacher Should Know about Child Development." *JTH* 2:1–9.

Rosen, Gladys. "Teaching About the Role of Women." *Ped Rep* 32 (Fall 1980): 27–30.

Rosenblatt, Howard B. "An Integrated Non-Karaitic Approach to Teaching Torah" (A model). In *IL*, 125–29.

Rosenthal, Ira D. "Publishing a Religious School Newspaper." *Jew Teach* 21 (Nov. 1952): 8–11.

Rosman, Steven M. "Process Thought and Jewish Education." *Rel Ed* 79 (Fall 1984): 601–12.

Rothman, Irving N. "Competency Based Learning Modules." *AM* (Fall 1976).

Schachter, Lifsa. "The Practicum: Jewish Education as Instruction." *Ped Rep* 33 (Oct. 1982): 16–17.

Schanin, Norman. "Toward a Theory of Jewish Instruction." *Recon* 30 (Nov. 27, 1964): 13–19.

Scharfstein, Zevi. "הכשדת הלבבות לחנוך עברי", (Preparing the Hearts for Jewish Education). In *ES*, 181–92. Also *JJS*, 137–43.

Schein, Jeffrey L., and Jacob J. Staub, eds. *Creative Jewish Education in Reconstructionist Perspective*. Phila.: Reconstructionist Rabbinical College Press and Rossel Books, 1985. 221 pp.

Schiff, Alvin I. "Vertical Articulation—A Necessary Concomitant of Growth in Learning in our School System." *Ped Rep* 20 (Dec. 1969): 27–30.

Schoem, David. "Improving School Climate in an Afternoon School." *Ped Rep* 35 (Oct. 1984): 20–21.

Segal, Abraham. "But What Does The Lord Require? The Challenge to Jewish Educators." *NATE* (1973), 6–15.

Seidenfeld, Morton A. "Meeting Individual Needs Through Jewish Education." *Jew Teach* 25 (May 1957): 3–6.

Sherman, Robert. "Creative Writing in the Judaic Studies Classroom." *Ped Rep* 36 (1985): 27–29.

Siegel, Morton. "The Value Centered Curriculum." *Impact* 35 (Summer 1977): 21–25.

Silverman, Jerry. "Chomsky Revisited: Emotional Training and the Building of Character in the Jewish School." *Jew Ed* 53 (Summer 1985): 40–43.

Slesinger, Zalmen. "Educational Technology: Promise or Peril." *Ped Rep* 19 (Sept. 1967).

———. "Education for Creativity." *Ped Rep* 13 (Sept. 1961).

Soref, Irwin I. "The New Instructional Technology—A Review." *Jew Ed* 32 (Spring 1962): 164–72.

Spiro, Jack D. "Toward a Conceptual Framework for Reform Jewish Education." *Compass* (Jan.–Feb. 1971).

Spotts, Leon H. "Montessori School for Jewish Education." *Syn Sch* 22 (Sept. 1964): 23–28.

Stein, Kenneth E. "Emotional Conditioning." *Jew Teach* 32 (Oct. 1963): 3–5

Stern, Suzanne C. "Teaching Kashrut by the Activity Method." *Syn Sch* 12 (Feb. 1954): 9–14.

Tannenbaum, A. *What General Education Might Contribute to Jewish Education*. Cleveland College of Jewish Studies. 1965.

Touroff, Nissan. "תעמולה וחנוך", (Propaganda and Education). *Sh Hah* (H.) 1 (1941): 3–14.

Wagner, Hilman. "Fifteen Ways to Improve Classroom Teaching/Learning." *Ped Rep* 35 (Oct. 1984): 3–4.

Wahl, Amiel. "Pedagogy Marches on: A contribution to American Jewish Folklore." *Jew Teach* 29 (Feb. 1961): 15–16.

Zisenwine, David. "Jewish Education an Opportunity Model." *Rel Ed* 75 (Sept./Oct. 1980): 558–62.

JUDAIC SOURCES—TEACHING THE TEXTS (SELECTED)

Bialik, M. L. *Gemara Mevoereth: Introductory Talmudic Textbook*. N.Y.: Mizrachi National Education Committee, c. 1950.

3
PEDAGOGY

Cook, Julian I. "The Historical Development of Pharisaism: A History Test for Teachers Utilizing Primary Sources." Master's thesis, HUC–JIR, 1972.

Dushkin, Alexander M. "The Sources of Jewish Religious Teaching." *Recon* (May 14, 1948): 9–15.

German, Joseph. "Original Rabbinic Sources: A Means of Learning Jewish Concepts." Master's thesis, HUC–JIR, 1975.

Glicksberg, Abraham A. "The Shulkhan Arukh on Jewish Education." *Jew Spec* 35 (Nov. 1970): 13–14.

Grishaver, Joel. "Beyond Bible Tales: Toward Teaching Text." In *JPH*, 69–85.

———. "Teaching Jewish Texts: Sources." *Ped Rep* 27 (Fall 1975): 21, 23–25.

Holtz, Barry W., ed. *Back to the Sources: Reading the Classic Jewish Texts*. N.Y.: Summit Books. 1984, 447pp.

———. "Midrash and Aggadah in the Classroom: Finding One's Way Through the Classroom Sources." *MJ* 13 (Winter 1982): 13, 15.

———. "Why Texts: Literature and Jewish Education." *Ped Rep* 36 (Jan. 1985): 17–19.

Kaunfer, Alvan. "Synectics: An Approach to Teaching Midrash." *MN* 11 (Fall 1980): 2–3.

Kirschenbaum, Aaron. "The Talmud and You." A series of four units. N.Y.: Hadassah Ed. Department, 1967.

Kraemer, David C. "Critical Aids to Teaching the Talmud." *Jew Ed* 49 (Spring 1981): 37–40.

Levine, Etan B. "Aggadah Reconsidered." *Jew Ed* 38 (Oct. 1968): 53–56.

Lewittes, Mordecai H. "Teaching Source Material." *Ped Rep* 30 (Winter 1979): 30.

Mirsky, Samuel K. "לדרכי הוראת הגמרה„ (Methods for Teaching Gemarrah). *Hinnukh* (H.) 1 (1936): 59–62.

Neusner, Jacob. *Learn Mishnah* (H. and E.). N.Y.: Behrman. 1978. 136 pp. Grades 5–6.

———. *Learn Talmud* (H. and E.). N.Y.: Behrman 1979. 167 pp. Grades 6–7.

Rosenfeld, Israel. *Gemora L'Maschilim*. (For beginners) N.Y.: TU, 1970. 123 pp.

Rossoff, Don. "The Midrashic Process." A ten-part mini-course for grades 10 and up which introduces the learner to the literature of the Midrash and to the unique process of midrashic thought. Master's project, HUC–JIR, 1979.

Shtrigler, Mordecai. "די קונסט פון לערנען„ אינעם אלט אידישן וועלט באנעם" (The Art of Learning in the Ancient Jewish World Outlook [Weltanschauung]) *For* (Y.), Dec. 14, 1975.

Siegel, Danny, comp. *Where Heaven and Earth Touch: An Anthology of the Midrash and Halacha*. Spring Valley, N.Y.: Town House Press, 1983. 52 pp.

Skaist, Solomon N. "The Place of Talmud in the Jewish School." *Jew Ed* 49 (Spring 1981): 34–36.

Soltes, M., ed. *Rashi Manual*. Phila.: NJWB, JEA of NYC, and the Associated Talmud Torahs of Philadelphia, c. 1940.

CLUBS AND EXTRACURRICULAR ACTIVITIES (SELECTED)

Blumenfield, Samuel M. "הקלוב' בבית„ הספר העברי" (The Club in the Jewish School). *Hinnukh* (H.) 1 (1937): 97–101.

Braverman, Libbie L. "Club Activities in the Religious School." (High School) *Jew Ed* (Jan./Mar. 1937): 20–25.

Brilliant, Nathan, and Libbie L. Braverman. "Club Activities in the Religious School." In *Act*, 36–54.

Cohen, Jack J. "Clubs in the Jewish School." *Syn Sch* 4 (Mar. 1946): 67–71.

Colodner, Solomon. "Coordinating the Hebrew Schools via Extra-Curricular Activities." *Jew Teach* 10 (Nov. 1941): 26–28.

Edidin, Ben M. "Suggestions for the Preparation of Club Program Materials." *Jew Ed* 3 (Apr./June, 1931): 87–91. See also *Sh Hah* (H.) 1 (1941): 23–31.

Essrig, Harry. "How a Peace Club Functions." *Jew Teach* 7 (Jan. 1939): 1–12.

Goldman, Yehudah. "המועדון לדרמתיות בבית„ הספר העברי" (The Dramatic Club in the Hebrew School). *Sh Hah* (H.) 4 (1946): 280–87.

Gursky, Samuel. "The Effect of Club Work on the Individual." *Jew Ed* 13 (Jan. 1942): 176–79, 193.

Kessler, Aharon. *The Club, the Leader, the Program*. N.Y.: Young Judea, 1945. 114 pp.

Rosenkranz, Samuel. "Workshops and Clubs in the Religious School." *Jew Teach* 25 (May 1957): 18–19.

Union of Orthodox Jewish Congregations of America. *Manual for Groups and Orthodox Youth Leaders*. N.Y.: c. 1942.

GAMES, ROLE-PLAYING, AND LEARNING (SELECTED)

Blaser, Elissa. *The Russian Jewry Simulation Game: Exodus*. N.Y.: Behrman, 1974.

Fisher, Phyllis J. *Mischakay—Games: For Jewish Holidays and Celebrations*. N.Y.: UAHC, 1984. 26 pp. (Experimental education)

Grishaver, Joel Lurie. "Games and Jewish Learning." In *JTH*, 1:63–71.

———. "The Pin Game: A Fantasy for Jewish Teachers." In *JTH*, 1:173–81.

Grishaver, Joel Lurie, Morley Feinstein, and Howard Wasserman. *The Jewish Values Game*. Denver: ARE, c. 1980. Grades 4–10.

Grollman, Earl. "Role Playing: Mixed Marriage.". *Jew Teach* 34 (Oct. 1965): 22–26.

Hurwich, Louis. "Hebrew Education Through Play." *Jew Ed* 10 (Jan./Mar. 1938): 35–40.

* Isaacs, Ronald H. *Affective and Cognitive Changes in Using Hebrew Language Games with Thirteen and Fourteen Year Old Students: An Exploratory Study*. Columbia U., 1979. 154 pp.

———. "The Impact of Language Games on Students' Hebrew Comprehension." *Jew Ed* 47 (Fall 1979): 37–43, 48.

Israel, Richard J. *Jewish Identity Games: A How-to-Do-It Book*. N.Y.: B'nai B'rith Hillel, 1978.

Kaunfer, Marcia. A Simulation Game on the Issues of Boundaries and Arab Refugees. N.Y.: NCRI of AAJE, 1970. Teacher Manual, 13 pp. Student Manual, 13 pp.

Kopin, Rita. *The Lively Jewish Classroom: Games and Activities for Learning*. Denver: ARE, 1980. 132 pp.

Kronish, Amy. "Arabs in Israel: A Simulation Game." *Compass* 21 (1972–73).

Lister, Rebecca, and Louis Lister. "Bible Games." *Jew Teach* 25 (Nov. 1956): 6–9.

Marcus, Audrey Friedman, ed. "Teaching with Simulation Games." In *JTH*, 2:43–52.

"Oneg Shabbat." Program and Games. *Syn Sch* 4 (Feb. 1946): 56–60.

Pitlick, Sh. "משחקי עזר בלמודים העברים" (Games as Teaching Aids in Hebrew Studies). *Sh Hah* (H.) 4 (1929): 240–46, 336–41.

Reikes, Vicki. "Educational Games in Supplementary Jewish Education." A presentation of some of the theory for the utilization of educational games. Master's project, HUC–JIR, 1978.

Rothman, Iris. "Games and Dances for Beginners' Hebrew." *Jew Teach* 23 (Nov. 1954): 11–12.

Schatz, Shirley. "Twenty-Six Games for Lower Grades." *SWJT* 7 (Spring/Summer 1975): 6.

Segal, Abraham. "Fun with the Siddur." *Syn Sch* 12 (1954): 19–24.

Siegman, Sarah M. "Games Children Should Play." *Ped Rep* 34 (Jan. 1983): 24–26.

Skolnik, Nachama. *Hebrew Games, Parts I and II*. N.Y.: UAHC, 1978.

Sperber, Matthew, comp. *Simulation Games Catalog*. N.Y.: N.Y. Federation of Temple Youth.

Troupp, Leonard B. "Simulation Games as a Point of Entry into Content," *Ped Rep* 32 (Winter 1981): 19–20.

Weintraub, Simkha. "SA! An Original Learning Game for the Melton Language Program." *MRCN* 10 (Summer 1979): 10–12.

SEX EDUCATION AND THE SCHOOL (SELECTED)

Baumblatt, Lori B. *Human Sexuality—A Jewish Response*. LA: HUC–JIR, Tartak Learning Center, 1984.

3 PEDAGOGY

Berman, Myron. "Sex and the Jewish Teenager." *Rel Ed* 65 (Sept./Oct. 1970): 415–21.

———. "Sex Education and the Religious School." *Syn Sch* 26 (Spring 1968): 4–9.

Borowitz, Eugene B. *Choosing a Sex Ethic: A Jewish Inquiry*. A guide for young people. N.Y.: Schocken, 1969. 182 pp.

Goldman, Norman Saul. "Redefining the Goals of Sex Education." *Jew Ed* 45 (Summer-Fall 1977): 24–32.

Kaplan, Harry. "The Sexual Revolution and Religious Education." *Rel Ed* 61 (Nov./Dec. 1966): 424–28.

Keeping Posted. *Teenage Sexuality*. Mini-Course, no. 840870. Leader's Edition, no. 840872.

Lamm, Norman. "The Role of the Synagogue in Sex Education." *News and Views* (Sept./Oct. 1967): 6. Part 2 Dec. 1967, Jan. 1968.

Maller, Allen S. "Sexual Standards of Jewish College Girls." *Jew Digest* 12 (Aug. 1967): 17–20.

Matt, Hershel J. "A Jewish Approach to Sex Education." *Ped Rep* 20 (Sept. 1968): 18–23.

Milgrom, J. "Sex and Family Life in the Bible." R. Patai, review. *Recon* 29 (Nov. 1, 1963): 28–30.

Nadel, Max. "Sex Education in the Jewish School." *Ped Rep* 37 (Fall 1986): 23–24.

Shapiro, M. S. "Sex Education and Jewish Education." *Jew Digest* 15 (Feb. 1970): 81.

Shusterman, Abraham. "Sex Education in the Religious School." *CCAR J* (Oct. 1959): 46–49.

Soloveichik, A. "Torah Tsnious (modesty) versus New Morality and Drugs." *Trad* 13 (Fall 1972).

Targan, Judith L. "Preparing a Curriculum: The Jew Views of the Body." Master's thesis, JTSA Teacher Institute, 1975.

COMPUTERS IN THE SCHOOL

Corre, A. D. "I Came to Learn." *Recon* 48 (Summer 1983): 24–27.

Gold, P.K. "Is Computer Aided Instruction the Best Way to Teach 5,000 Years of Jewish Tradition?" *Nat Jew M* 98 (Nov. 1983): 12–14.

Hollander, Ben. "Of Making the Soft Revolution Happen in Jewish Education." *Response* 5 (Fall 1971): 58–66.

Jaskoll, Ira L. "Computers in Jewish Education." *Ped Rep* 35 (Jan. 1984): 1–5.

———. "Guide to Jewish and Hebrew Software." *Compass* 8 (Spring 1985): 20–22.

Jordan, Cecile B. "Practical Helpful Advice." (Computers) *Compass* 8 (Spring 1985): 4–5, 16.

Joseph, Samuel K. "Technology as a Tool." (Computers for Jewish Education) *Compass* 8 (Spring 1985): 3–4, 17.

Matanky, Leonard A. "A Computer Department for Jewish Studies." *Ped Rep* 35 (Jan. 1984): 12–14.

Porath, Gerald. "Teaching the Bible with Computers." *Ped Rep* 30 (Spring 1979): 32–33.

Rosenbaum, Alan. "The Use of Computers in Contributing to a More Joyful School Atmosphere." *Ped Rep* 35 (Oct. 1984): 12–13.

Spiegler, S. "Responsa at the Touch of a Button." *J Jew Com Ser* 60 (Fall 1983): 77.

EDUCATION FOR NEW IMMIGRANTS

Bagali, Yona. *The Falashas of Ethiopia*. Council of Jewish Federations General Assembly, June 1979. 2 pp.

Blum, Deborah Cardozo. "Integration of Russian Jews in the Jewish Community: Bureau Responsibilities." *Jew Ed* 48 (Summer 1980): 34–37, 50.

Chesler, Evan. *The Russian Jewry Reader*. N.Y.: Behrman, 1974.

Council Publication. *Jewish Books in the Russian Language*. (Catalogue of more than 70 books translated into the Russian language). (May 7, 1980).

Efron, Benjamin. "Educational Implications of the Soviet Jews in the United States." *Ped Rep* 25 (Spring 1974): 1.

Fisher, Leon D. "Initial Experiences in Resettlement of Soviet Jews in the United States." *J Jew Com Ser* 51 (Spring 1975): 267–69.

Frankel, Edwin R. "Teaching Students Concern for Ethiopian Jews." *Ped Rep* 36 (Nov. 1985): 17–18.

Goodman, Jerry, and Sheila Woods. "Soviet Jewry: A Look Ahead." *Ped Rep* 25 (Spring 1974): 2.

Grossman, Henry. "Orientation of Russian and Israeli Students." *Ped Rep* 31 (Fall 1979).

"Jewish Family Education Program for Soviet Immigrants." *Ped Rep* 32 (Apr. 1981): 6–7.

Jewish Welfare Board. *Acculturation of Soviet Jewish Immigrants*. September 1982. 60 pp.

Kaplan, A. S. "Degreening the Greenhorns." *KP* 29 (Fall 1984): 14–15.

The Kohl Jewish Teacher Center. *Teaching the Soviet Child: A Handbook for Jewish Teachers*. Wilmette, Ill: June 1980.

* Kolodner, Anna. *The Socialization of Children of Concentration Camp Survivors*. Boston U., 1987.

Leslau, Wolf, ed. *The Black Jews of Ethiopia*. N.Y.: Schocken, 1951.

National Commission on Torah Education. "Teaching Units on Soviet Jewry." *Ped Rep* 22 (June 1971): 27.

Pollak, George. *The Financial and Educational Integration of the Russian Immigrant Jewish Student*. N.Y.: AAJE, 1979. 26 pp.

Porath, Jonathan D. "Ideas for a Soviet Jewry Course of Study." *Ped Rep* 25 (Spring 1974): 4.

Reichwald, Faye. *18 Lives*. (For students of English as a second language) N.Y.: FJP of N.Y. and BJE of N.Y., 1981. 256 pp.

"Resources for Teaching Soviet Jewry." *Ped Rep* 25 (Spring 1974): 10–14.

Spotts, Leon H. "Educating the Russian Immigrant: Challenge and Opportunity." *Jew Ed* 48 (Summer 1980): 21–23.

Stern, Ian. "A Curriculum for Teaching Ethiopian Jewry in a Hebrew High School." Master's thesis, HUC–JIR, 1978.

Ulanovsky, Lev. "Trying to Study and Teach Hebrew." (Written by a former Russian Jew) *Present Tense* 8 (Aut. 1980): 47–48.

West, C. T. "Adolescent Immigrants from the Soviet Union." *Jew Ed* 47 (Spring 1979): 27–32.

CULTS, DRINKING, SUICIDE, AND YOUTH

Andron, Sandy. "Our Gifted Teens and the Cults." *Ped Rep* 31 (Fall 1979): 37–38.

Daum, Annette, in cooperation with Balfour Brickner. *Missionary and Cult Movements*. N.Y.: UAHC, 1979. Grades 8–9.

Gordon, Sol. *When Living Hurts*. N.Y.: UAHC, Task Force on Youth Suicide, 1985.

Keeping Posted. *Teenage Drug Abuse*. Nos. 841000 and 841002.

———. *Teenage Suicide*. Nos. 840950 and 840952.

Landman, R. H. "Studies of Drinking in Jewish Culture: Drinking Patterns of Children and Adolescents Attending Religious Schools." *Quarterly J of Studies in Alcohol* 13 (1952): 87–94.

Levin, Alan J. "Teaching About Cults." *Compass* 4 (Summer 1981): 16–17, 27.

Schwartz, Lita Linzer. "Cults and the Vulnerability of Jewish Youth." *Jew Ed* 46 (Summer 1978): 23–26, 42.

Sigel, Gerald. *Jews and the Christian Missionary: A Response to Missionary Christianity*. N.Y.: Ktav, n.d. Grades 9–12

Union of American Hebrew Congregations, Task Force on Youth Suicide. *Youth Suicide Prevention: Programs and Resources for Congregations*. N.Y.: UAHC, 1985.

MARRIAGE, DIVORCE, AND INTERMARRIAGE (SELECTED)

Benson, Paulette, and Sherry Bissel. "Divorce in Jewish Life and Tradition." A 6–10 hour mini-course for grades 7–12 with accompanying leader's guide. Master's project, HUC–JIR, 1977.

3
PEDAGOGY

———. *Divorce in Jewish Life and Tradition.* Mini-course manual. Denver: ARE, 1977. 16 pp.

Children of Divorced Parent Households: Some Suggested Guidelines for Perspectives. N.Y.: UAHC, 1980.

Commission on Reform Jewish Outreach. *Guidelines for Outreach Education.* N.Y.: CRJO, CCAR, CJE, UAHC, and NATE, 1986.

———. *Times and Seasons: A Jewish Perspective for Intermarriage Couples.* N.Y.: Commission on Reform Jewish Outreach, CCAR, UAHC, 1987. 186 pp.

Cottle, Thomas. *Divorce and the Jewish Child.* N.Y.: AJC, 1981.

Friedman, Barry Roger. "Different People, Different Needs." (Intermarriage) *Compass* 8 (Fall 1984): 12–14, 21.

Friedman, Natalie, and Theresa F. Rogers. *Jewish Community and Children of Divorce: A Pilot Study of Perception and Response.* N.Y.: AJC, 1983. 32 pp.

Gittelsohn, Roland B. *Consecrated Unto Me.* N.Y.: UAHC, 1965.

———. *The Extra Dimension: A Jewish View of Marriage.* Rev. Ed. N.Y.: UAHC, 1983.

———. *My Beloved Is Mine: Judaism and Marriage.* N.Y.: UAHC, 1969. 320 pp.

Goodman, Philip, and Hannah Goodman. *The Jewish Marriage Anthology.* Phila.: JPS, 1965. 360 pp.

Grollman, Earl A. "Role-Playing: Mixed Marriage." *Jew Teach* 34 (Oct. 1965): 22–26.

Kadden, Bruce. "The Educator's Challenge." (Intermarriage) *Compass* 8 (Fall 1984): 20–21.

Keeping Posted. *Love, Marriage, Intermarriage.* Nos. 840280 and 840282.

———. *Divorce.* Nos. 840830 and 840832.

Kligfield, B. "Intermarriage: A Review of the Social Science Literature on the Subject." *CCAR J* (June 1960).

Kukoff, Lydia. *Choosing Judaism.* N.Y.: UAHC, 1981. 152 pp.

Lamm, Norman. *Hedge of Roses: Jewish Insights into Marriage and Married Life.* N.Y.: Feldheim, 1968.

Layman, Jonah. "Project Link: An Educational Outreach Program for the Mixed Married of the Conservative Movement." Master's thesis, JTS Department of Jewish Education, 1989.

Lehrer, Leibush. „אידישע דערציונג און נאך עפעס" (Jewish Education and Something More). (Intermarriage) *YK* (Y.) (Nov. 22, 1963).

Levinson, Maria H., and D. Levinson. "Jews Who Intermarry: Socio-Psychological Basis of Ethnic Identity and Change." *YA* 12 (1958–59): 103–30.

Lippman, Froma. "The Caring Family in the Face of Divorce." *Compass* 6 (Summer 1983): 10–11, 20.

Maller, Allen S. "The Get (Divorce) in the Modern Classroom: Facing up to Today's Single Parent Family." *Compass* 2 (Fall–Winter 1978): 7–9.

———. "Religious Education and Interfaith Marriage." *Ped Rep* 27 (Fall 1975): 29.

Mayer, Egon. *Children of Intermarriage: A Study of Identification and Family Life.* N.Y.: AJC, 1983.

———. *Intermarriage and the Jewish Future.* N.Y.: AJC, 1979. 33 pp.

Olitzky, Kerry M. "The Teacher's Challenge." (Intermarriage) *Compass* 8 (Fall 1984): 6–7, 16.

Rabinowitz, Stanley. *A Jewish View of Love and Marriage.* Washington D.C.: B'nai B'rith Orgnization, 1961. 48 pp.

Rosenthal, Ira A. "Marriage and the Family." (A high school unit) *Jew Teach* 18 (Jan. 1956): 6–11.

Roth, Shana. "Mixed Marriage: A Values Clarification Seminar for Jewish Professionals." An outline of a values clarification seminar for Jewish professionals who must contend with the reality of mixed marriage as an institutional concern. Master's project, HUC–JIR, 1983.

Salkowitz, Selig. "Toward a Course of Study for Young Adults in Preparation for Jewish Marriage." Master's thesis, HUC–JIR, 1954.

Schiff, Alvin I. "Intermarriage and Jewish Education." *Jew Ed* 47 (Summer 1979): 18–21.

Schwartz, Arnold. "Intermarriage in the United States." *AJYB* 71 (1970): 101–21.

Seltzer, Sanford. *Jews and Non-Jews Getting Married: A Look at Interfaith Marriage and Its Consequences for Jewish Survival.* N.Y.: UAHC, c. 1984.

Weinberg, Debora. "Children of Divorce: A Family Life Education Program for Children of Single Parent Families." A program designed to link the child's educational experience in the Jewish school and the role the family plays in supplementing this education at home. Master's project, HUC–JIR, 1981.

Wikler, Meir. "Preparation for Marriage: A Prevention for Divorce." *Jew Obs* (Jan. 1979): 9–13.

Zucker, David J. "Mixed Marriages: Discussion Group." *Compass* 8 (Fall 1984): 11, 19, 22.

Zwerin, Raymond A., and Audrey Friedman Marcus. *Marriage in Jewish Life and Tradition.* Denver: ARE, c. 1980. 29 pp.

BEREAVEMENT IN THE CLASSROOM

* Elkin, Joshua Charles. "An Exploration of Alternatives for Educating Jewish Adolescents to Dying, Death and Bereavement: A Pre-Deliberation Research Project." Columbia U. Teachers College, 1979.

Evans, Beth J. "Dealing with Tragedy in the Classroom." *Jew Ed* 49 (Summer 1981): 28–31.

Gertman, Stuart A., ed. *What Is the Answer?* N.Y.: UAHC, 1971.

Grollman, Earl A., ed. *Explaining Death to Children.* Boston: Beacon Press, 1967. 296 pp.

———. "The Way of Dialogue on Death Between Parents and Children." *Rel Ed* 69 (Mar./Apr. 1974): 198–206.

———. "Toward a Development of a Model Program of Instruction in Reform Jewish Life-Cycle Ceremonies for the Elementary Department of the Religious School (Death as the Model.)" Master's thesis, HUC–JIR, 1976.

Joseph, Samuel K. *A Time to Die: A Course on Death.* Seven Units for Third and Fourth Grade Students. N.Y.: UAHC, 1977. Experimental Edition.

Lamm, Maurice. *The Jewish Way in Death and Mourning.* N.Y.: Jonathan David, 1969.

Lasker, Arnold A. "When Children Face Bereavement." *Con Jud* 18 (Winter 1964): 53–58.

Lippman, Fromma. "Children and Death." *Compass* 8 (Winter 1986): 12–13, 17.

Marcus, Audrey Friedman, Sherry Bissel, and Karen S. Lipschutz. *Death, Burial and Mourning in the Jewish Tradition.* A student manual for grades 5–12. Master's project, HUC–JIR, 1976. 21 pp.

———. "Teaching About Death and Dying." *JPH*, 97–107.

Mersky, David. "A Teaching Unit on Death." *Compass* (Mar. 27, 1974).

Riemer, Jack. *Jewish Reflections on Death.* N.Y.: Schocken, 1974.

Schoenberg, Elliot S. "Jewish Education and Dying." *Rel Ed* 78 (Spring 1983): 210–16.

Schwartz, Celia. "I Took My Class to the Cemetery." *Syn Sch* 12 (Feb. 1954): 19–21.

Syme, Daniel B. *Death and Mourning.* (4 Parts) N.Y.: UAHC Press, c. 1990.

"A Time to Be Born—A Time to Die." *KP* 17 (Mar. 1972).

Wolowelsky, Joel B. "Death Education." *Ped Rep* 3 (Fall 1980): 32–33.

* ———. *Death Education in Religious High Schools.* New York U., 1979.

GLEANINGS

Krochmal, Nahman (1785–1840),

> "Even if a method were found at one time to be fruitful, it is quite possible that the same method would be worthless in teaching the members of a generation far removed from that age in time and character."
> Quoted in *Cat 2*, 209.

Golub, Jacob S., and Leo L. Honor,

> We have, in many instances, taught teachers to do better what they should not be doing at all."
> *Jew Ed* 4 (Oct.–Dec. 1932), 150.

3
PEDAGOGY

Cohen, Jack J.,

"As long as students are exposed to experiences that open vistas ignored in their denominational education, there will always be the chance that they will come to conclusions that are at variance with the narrow approach of their own formal schooling.

The wise educator understands that he can hide nothing from the minds of his students and therefore will go out of his way to anticipate as far as possible the many challenges to his own point of view that the students will ultimately confront. Needless to say, the anticipation must be made with fairness and sympathy. Jewish education has nothing to fear from a confrontation with the often-harsh reality surrounding the Jewish school; it has everything to fear from the present ostrichlike burying of the head in the sands of denominational confines."

JEDS, 77.

Cutter, William, and Jack Dauber.

"We are concerned with difficulties in combining the emotional presence of the teacher and student with the more academic and cognitive goals of education. Curriculum planners often either focus on specific behavioral objectives which overdetermine what a child receives, or are too concerned with presenting factual material and not with whether the child learns. In addition, education today finds itself on the threshold of a great technological revolution through which mechanical equipment will alter radically our teaching techniques.

While not opposed to teaching with behavioral objectives in mind, and certainly not to technology, it is our belief that 1) a teacher cannot teach values or cognitive data without himself undergoing basic changes as a teacher; 2) values and data come best through the emotional experience of the child; 3) values are best learned when there is a climate of support present in the class; values cannot be conveyed as if classroom had a homogeneous composition; 4)students will derive different values form the same experience and the teacher must be equipped to deal with that multiplicity of values; 5) technology can only be the handmaiden of human beings, and not the reverse; the greatest lesson for a Jewish teacher, a religious leader, or any teacher for that matter is to take personal risks and responsibility for those risks!"

Quoted by W. I. Ackerman, "The Present Moment in Jewish Education," in *JCA*, 275.

Gertman, Stuart A.,

"Educators were asked to indicate what method or methods were used in each grade. Multiple answers were given in most cases. Many respondents indicated that more than one method was used in each grade, and it is assumed that the choice of methods was based on the nature of the material they wished to convey....

Overwhelmingly, a traditional teaching method was employed in all grades through six. The use of traditional classroom was indicated almost three times as often as the next most popular method in each grade, and more than three times as often as all other methods. Beginning in the seventh grade, there is a sharp decline in the use of traditional classroom method that continues through the rest of the grades. By eighth grade the traditional classroom is indicated little more than half the time.

We find a similar pattern with regard to the open classroom. It is used most heavily in kindergarten and then declines steadily. It should be noted that at most the open classroom is used in only 32% of the schools.

Individualized learning appears most heavily in grades four through six, probably because the UAHC has developed individualized learning programs for these grades. This might indicate that if more such programs were developed for other grades, the use of this method might increase.

As would be expected, independent study program increase steadily from kindergarten through twelfth grade, probably because of the students' increased capacity for independent work as they grow older....

Confluent education is used most often in grades four through eight, though its philosophy is equally suited for younger and older grades."

And You Shall Teach Them Diligently: A Study of the Current State of Religious Instruction in the Reform Movement, 39.

Dorph, Gail Zaiman, and Victoria Koltun Kelman,

"The Melton Curriculum is an integrated program. In most schools a wide range of subjects is taught—Hebrew, Bible, holidays, customs and ceremonies, some prayers, some stories about Jewish heroes. But few, if any connections are drawn between these subjects. In our curriculum ethical values, prayers and festival celebrations are taught as part of a single course. The organizing principle of the curriculum is the idea of mitzvot."

Holidays, Mitzvot, Prayer, 3d ed., level alef, introduction (MRC, 1979, 1982), 4.

Omer-Man, Jonathan,

"Jewish religious education comprises a wide range of activities and processes. Many of these, and certainly those which receive the greatest attention, are concerned with the acquisition of basic information and skills. The student is taught the elements of Jewish history, Bible, the nature of Sabbath and Festivals, and some Hebrew; he or she is instructed in the prayer book, which prayers are read, and when and how to perform certain rituals. Furthermore, considerable efforts are invested in the development and cultivation of Jewish identity; . . . However, there is another aspect of the process of religious education that is, at least in essence, largely unaffected by modern technologies and psychological theories, for it is based on a human relationship of a unique kind. This is the teaching of the student how to become, to remain, and to develop as a religious person. . . . Such a religious consciousness or awareness can generally only be acquired by the student's identifying with a role model."

MJ 14 (Spring 1982): 3, 22.

4 THE ARTS

GENERAL (SELECTED)

Abner, Ira. *The Art of Judaic Needlework.* N.Y.: Scribner's, 1980.

"An Album of Paintings, Drawings and Sculpture by 60 Jewish Artists of America, Europe and Israel." *Menorah J* 37 (Summer 1949).

Ariel (quarterly) (H. or E.). Jerusalem.

"Art." In *Enc Jud* 3: 499–652.

Cohen, Boaz. "Art in Jewish Law." *Jud* 3 (Spring 1954): 165–76.

Eisenstein, Judith K. "The Arts in American Jewish Life." *Recon* 11 (Feb. 23, 1945).

Gordis, Robert, and Moshe Dawidowicz, eds. *Art in Judaism.* N.Y.: National Council on Art in Jewish Life and Judaism, 1975. 105 pp.

Gutmann, Joseph. *Beauty in Holiness: Studies in Jewish Ceremonial Arts and Customs.* N.Y.: Ktav, 1970.

———. *Jewish Ceremonial Art.* N.Y.: Yoseloff, 1968. 57 pp.

Halperin, Moses P. "Does It Look Like a Synagogue?" *Recon* 16 (Jan. 12, 1951): 18–22.

Heschel, Abraham J. "Symbolism and Jewish Faith." In *Religious Symbolism,* edited by F. Ernest Johnson. Port Washington, N.Y.: 1969.

Kampf, Avram. *Contemporary Synagogue Art: Developments in the United States, 1945–1965.* N.Y.: UAHC. 1976. Also Century, Mass.: Bergin and Garvey, 1984. 240 pp.

———. *Jewish Ceremonial Art and Religious Observance.* N.Y.: Abrams, 1980. 253 pp.

Kayser, Stephen S. "Defining Jewish Art" In *Mordecai M. Kaplan Jubilee Volume,* ed. Moshe Davis. N.Y.: JTSA, 457–68.

———, ed. *Jewish Ceremonial Art.* Phila.: JPS, 1955. 168 pp.

Kline, Alexander S. "Synagogue Architecture in America." *Recon* 18 (June 27, 1952): 21–28.

Landsberger, Franz. *History of Jewish Art.* Port Washington, N.Y.: Kennikat Press, 1973 (reprint of 1946 ed.). 369 pp.

Lewbin, Hyman J. *Rebirth of Jewish Art: The Unfolding of Jewish Art in the Nineteenth Century.* N.Y.: Shengold, 1974.

Lichtenstein, Isaac. „ייִדישע קונסט-און ייִדישער קינסטלער" (Jewish Art and the Jewish Artist). *Our Generation* (Y.) (Art Issue) (Nov.–Dec. 1962): 1–2.

"A List of Works by Jewish Artists in the United States (Aug. 1906–July 1907). *AJYB* (1907–8): 467–72.

Lozowick, Louis. "A Jewish Art School." (Exhibit by Jewish Educational Alliance Art School) *Menorah J* 10 (Nov.–Dec. 1924).

Lozowick, Louis. "The Jew in American Plastic Art." In *One Hundred Contemporary American Jewish Artists: Biographies, Credos, Re-*

productions (Y. and E.), ix–xv. N.Y.: YKUF, 1947.

Marks, Cara Goldberg. *Handbook of Hebrew Calligraphy: The ABCs of Alef-Bet*. Northville, N.J.: J. Aronson, 1990.

Mumford, Lewis. "Toward a Modern Synagogue Architecture." *Menorah J* (June 1925).

Narkiss, Bezalel. *Hebrew Illuminated Manuscripts*. Jerusalem and New York: Encyclopedia Judaica and Leon Amiel, 1969. 175 pp.

Podwal, Mark. *A Book of Hebrew Letters*. Phila.: JPS, 1978.

Raskin, Saul. "Three Dimensions for the Jewish Artist." *Jew Life* 18 (Feb. 1951).

Reifenberg, R. J. *Ancient Hebrew Arts*. N.Y.: Schocken, 1950. 171 pp.

Rockland, Mae Shafter. "Jewish Folk Art." In *Cat 2*, 320–28.

Rosenberg, Harold. "Is There a Jewish Art?" *Commentary* 42 (July 1966): 57–60.

Roth, Cecil, ed. *Jewish Art*. N.Y.: McGraw-Hill, 1961. 971 pp.

Rubenowitz, Mignon L. *Altars of My Father*. N.Y.: Women's League for Conservative Judaism.

Salpeter, H. "American Jews in Art." *Jew Life* 15 (Apr. 1958).

Schwartz, David. "Art and the Synagogue." *Recon* 16 (June 21, 1959): 16–20.

Schwartz, Shirley, ed. *Traveling Exhibitions: Perspectives on the Jewish Experience*. N.Y.: National Foundation for Jewish Culture, 1984. 104 pp.

Schwarz, Karl. *Jewish Artists of the 19th and 20th Centuries*. N.Y.: Philosophical Library, 1949. 273 pp.

Shrire, T. *Hebrew Magic Amulets: Their Decipherment and Interpretation*. N.Y.: 1982. 180 pp.

Werner, Alfred. "Art and the American Jew." In *Jan 2*, 235–44.

———. "Bezalel and Oholiab: The Design and Construction of the Ark." *Jew Life* 20 (Apr. 1953).

———. "Masters of Israeli Art." *Jew Life* 24 (Dec. 1956).

———. "Story of Jewish Art." In *JMW*, 2:328–55.

———. "Ghetto Graduates." *American* Art J (Nov. 1973).

Wigoder, Geoffrey, ed. *Jewish Art and Civilization*. 2 vols. N.Y.: Walker and Co., 1972.

Wischnitzer, Rachel. "Judaism and Art." In *Jews*, 1322–48.

———. *Synagogue Architecture in the United States: History and Interpretation*. Phila.: JPS, 1955. 204 pp.

———. "Jewish Art." In *JPPP*, 268–323.

———. "Jewish Art Books and Albums." In *JBA* (1952–53), 129–35.

Wischnitzer, Rachel, (Rachel Bernstein). "Books on Jewish Art." In *JBA* (1946–47), 64–69.

ART IN THE JEWISH SCHOOL

Abrahams, Edith, and Carol Tauben. *Integrating Arts and Crafts in the Jewish School: Vol. 1, Kindergarten to Second Grade*. N.Y.: Behrman, 1979.

Ackerman, Andrew S., and Judith C. Siegel. "A Museum in the School." In *JPH*.

Aron, Isa. "The Burgeoning World of Jewish Art." *Ped Rep* 36 (Jan. 1985): 5–7.

Azriel, Elyce Karen. "Bulletin Boards: An Effective Teaching Tool." In *JPH*, 11–15.

Berman, Nancy. "The Hanukkah Lamp as Related to Architecture: An Educational Slide-Tape." An educational slide-tape presentation tracing the changing artistic expression of the Hanukkah lamp in Western and Islamic art. Master's project, HUC–JIR, 1977.

Blatter, Janet, and Sybil Milton. *Art of the Holocaust*. N.Y.: Rutledge Press, 1981. Grades 7–12.

Bogot, Howard I. "Art is Not Extracurricular." In *JPH*, 311–13.

Bragman, Rae. *The Bulletin Board in the Jewish Religious School*. N.Y.: UAHC.

———. "The Bulletin Board in Religious Education." *Jew Teach* 21 (May 1953): 9–11.

4
THE ARTS

Brin, Ruth Esrig. *Let's Celebrate! 57 Jewish Holiday Crafts for Young Children.* Kar-Ben, 1977.

Buller, Rochelle. "How Art Can Be Used in Teaching Jewish Social Studies to Pre-Adolescents. Master's thesis, HUC–JIR, 1974.

Chipkin, Israel S. "The Role of Jewish Arts in Jewish Education." *Jew Ed* 23 (Fall 1952): 2–3.

Coen, R. N. "The Jewish School in Jewish Art." *Un Syn Rev* 25 (Summer 1972): 15.

Cohen, Jack J. "The Arts." In *JEDS*, 234–37.

Comins, Harry L., and R. Leaf. "Art-Crafts for the Jewish Child." *Jew Ed* 7 (Apr. 1935): 116.

Davis, Eli, and Elise Davis. *Jewish Folk Art over the Ages: A Collector's Choice.* Jerusalem: R. Mass, 1977. Grades 9 and up.

Fischman, Joyce, and Heidi Steinberger. *Let's Learn about Jewish Symbols Workbook.* N.Y.: UAHC, 1983. 64 pp.

Freund, Iser L. "Artcraft in the Religious School Curriculum." *CCAR* 44 (1934): 271–73.

Gezari, Temima. *Festival Crafts in the Jewish Center.* N.Y.: NJWB.

———. *Footprints and New Worlds: On the Teaching of Art.* N.Y.: Recon Press, 1957. 168 pp.

———. "The Role of Art in My Life and in Jewish Education." *Jew Ed* 51 (Fall 1983): 32–36.

———. "They Work Together Through Art." *Jew Ed* 23 (Fall 1952): 55–58, 71.

———. "Universal Aspects of Child Art." *Jew Ed* 22 (Winter–Spring 1951): 54–55, 111.

Ginsberg, Ruth. *Crafts for the Jewish Child.* N.Y.: Shulsinger Bros., 1976.

Glinert, Joan, and Lewis Glinert. "Building a Character: From the World of Puppets." *MJ* 20 (Spring 1986): 22.

———. "Jewish Puppetry: New Vistas for an Ancient Art. *MJ* 13 (Winter 1982): 8.

Grand, Samuel. "Introduction to the Flannel-graph." *Jew Teach* 20 (May 1952): 3–18.

Grand, Tamar. *Holiday-Craft Kit for the Jewish Child.* N.Y.: UAHC, 1981.

Green, Kathy. "The Uses and Abuses of Photography in Jewish Schools." *MJ* 15 (Winter 1983): 12–14.

Greenspan, Jay Seth. *Hebrew Calligraphy: A Step-by-Step Guide.* N.Y.: Schocken, 1980.

Herstein, Isabell Smith. "Using the Art Gallery in Jewish Education." *Compass* 6 (Fall 1982): 14, 20–21.

Katz, Harold E. "Jewish Education and the Arts: A Dilemma, Design for Jewish Survival." *Recon* 42 (Apr. 1976): 19–25.

Kohn, Therese. "Our Ancestors Build a Temple in Jerusalem." *Jew Teach* 12 (Nov. 1943): 10–16.

Koltun, Judy. "A 'Hands on' Museum." *Ped Rep* 36 (Jan. 1985): 8–9.

Kopin, Rita. "Teaching with Puppets." *JPH*, 17–28.

Kurzband, Toby K. "Art for the Jewish School Teacher." *Jew Ed* 19 (Spring 1948): 28–30, 44.

Levy, D., and L. Meyer. "Integrating Arts and Crafts." *Jew Teach* 29 (Feb. 1961): 3–5.

Neumann, Richard. "The Arts in Jewish Schools." *Jew Ed* 46 (Winter 1978): 44–46.

Shandler, Jeffrey. "Art and Religion: The Creative Process." *Compass* 6 (Summer 1983): 3–5, 21.

Sharon, Ruth. *Arts and Crafts the Year Round.* 2 vols. N.Y.: USCJE, 1965.

Siegman, Sarah M. "Jewish Art Education for the '80s." *Ped Rep* 32 (Winter 1981): 28–29.

Silverstein, Ruth. "The Feltogram in the Religious School." *Jew Teach* 23 (Nov. 1954): 12–15.

Snitzer, Lee H. "The Remaking of Halloween in a Jewish Setting." *Compass* 8 (Spring 1980): 12–15.

Springer, Josephine. *Arts and Crafts for Judaism: A Notebook for Teachers in Religious Schools.* N.Y.: American Council for Judaism, 1955.

Transfer Letters and Symbols. "Hebrew Transfer Letters," "Jewish Holiday Transfer Symbols," and "Synagogue Transfer Symbols." Denver: ARE.

Weinstone, Mrs. Howard. "Providing Meaningful Experiences Through the Arts." *Syn Sch* 14 (Nov. 1955): 25–28.

Wise, Syd. "A Creative Arts Program." *Ped Rep* 24 (Fall 1971): 20.

Zuckerman, Helen. "Art in the Religious School." *Jew Teach* 34 (Apr. 1966): 40–41.

———. "The Place of the Arts in the Primary Grades." *Jew Teach* 25: (May 1957): 9–11.

AUDIO-VISUAL AIDS

AAJE. *Films and Filmstrips for the Religious School*. N.Y.: AAJE.

———. *Jewish Audio Visual Review*. Films and filmstrips of Jewish content with description and evaluation. N.Y.

———. "Selected List of Audio Visual Materials for Teaching Brotherhood." *Ped Rep* 5 (Nov. 1953).

ADL Catalog (Audio-visual materials). N.Y.: ADL.

Altman, Sh. "Auditory Aid for the Jewish School." *Jew Ed* 1 (Winter/Spring 1951): 56–58.

"Audio-Visual Aids in the Teaching of Bible: A Bibliography." *Ped Rep* 9 (Jan. 1958); 10 (Nov. 1958).

"Audio-Visual Materials." *Ped Rep* (Mar. and June 1967).

"The Audio-Visual Scene" (Symposium). *AM* (Fall 1975).

Baum, Eli, ed. *Curriculum Guide for Afternoon Religious Schools*. (Contains extensive audio-visual bibliography.) N.Y.: National Commission on Torah Education, Yeshiva U., 1979.

Benderly, Shlomo. "Telecommunications: An Audio Visual Project." *Compass* 2 (Summer 1979): 4–6.

Berg, Esther L., and Florence B. Friedman. *Manual on Audio Visual Aids for the Jewish School*. N.Y.: AAJE, c. 1951. 32 pp.

A Guide to Feature and Documentary Films. Wash. D.C.: B'nai B'rith.

Bragman, Louis J. "Visual Aids in Jewish Education." *Jew Ed* 19 (Fall 1947): 45–48.

Bragman, Rae, ed. *A Year's Program of Audio Visual Units and Projects*. N.Y.: UAHC, 1959. 226 pp.

Catalogue of Audio Visual Materials. N.Y.: NJWB.

* Citron, Samuel J. *Audio-Visual Materials for Elementary Jewish Education in America: A Study in Light of Goals of Jewish Education, Jewish Cultural and Ideological Differences, and Accepted Educational Criteria*. New York U., 1963. 681 pp.

———. "Jewish Educators Speak out about Jewish Audio Visual Materials." *Jew Ed* 35 (Winter 1965): 106–11, 123.

Ehrmann, Eliezer. "Teaching with Slides." *Jew Teach* 21 Mar. 1953): 12–15.

———. "The Use of Audio-Visual Aids in the Social Studies." *Jew Ed* 26 (Fall 1955): 40–46.

Eisenberg, Azriel. *A Guide to Audio-Visual Aids in the Jewish School*. Cincinnati: UAHC, c. 1945. See also *Jew Teach* (Apr. 1945): 1–24.

———. "Toward a Film Strip Production Program." *Jew Ed* 25 (Summer 1954): 55–57.

———. "Visual Aids in Teaching Jewish History, Customs and Ceremonies." *Jew Teach* 3 (Nov. 1934): 1–6.

* Engel, Alvin David. *Single-Concept Instructional Film for Use in Jewish Religious Elementary Schools*. New York U., 1972.

Entin, Nathaniel A. "The Pre-Recorded Lesson." *Syn Sch* 17 (1959).

———. "Using the Overhead Projector." *Syn Sch* 25 (Spring 1967): 22–25.

Epstein, Seymour. "Videotape Recording and Jewish Schools." Master's thesis, Brandeis U., 1970.

Feldman, Abraham J. "Visual Aids to Religious Instruction." *CCAR* 32 (1922): 189–220.

Filmstrips and Films of Jewish Interest. N.Y.: Yeshiva U.

"Filmstrips, Visual Aid Charts and Related Materials." In *TU Catalog, 1985*, 18–62. N.Y.: TU, 1985.

Fish, Nathan. *Teaching with JEC Filmstrips*. N.Y.: JEC.

Gellert, Charles Lawrence. *A Guide to Motion Pictures on Jewish History in the National Ar-*

chives of the United States. Washington, D.C.: 1984. 123 pp.

Golub, Jacob S., and Zalmen Slesinger. *List of Recommended Films and Filmstrips*. N.Y.: AAJE, 1949.

Grand, Samuel. "Audio-Visual Aids—A Broader Perspective." *CCAR J* (Jan. 1954): 27–31.

———. *Audio-Visual Education in the Religious School*. N.Y.: UAHC, 1955. 64 pp.

———. "First Steps in Audio-Visual Education in the Jewish Religious School." *Jew Teach* 20 (Nov. 1951). See also 20 (Jan. 1952, Mar. 1952, and May 1952).

———. "Methods in Audio-Visual Education." *Jew Teach* 21 (Nov. 1952): 4–5.

Greenstone, Joseph. "החנוך החושני„ (Audio-Visual Education). *Sh Hah* (H.) 7 (June 1947): 120–26.

———. "The Use of Motion Pictures." *Jew Teach* 12 (1943).

Jaffa, Herbert. "Considerations in the Use of Audio-Visual Materials in Teaching Brotherhood." *Ped Rep* 7 (Jan. 1956).

Jewish Welfare Board. *Feature Films of Jewish Interest*. N.Y.: NJWB Lecture Bureau.

Kolatch, Arthur. "Audio Visual Aids." *Jew Teach* 10 (Jan. 1942): 10–18.

Kronish, Amy W. "Audio-Visual Overview." In *JTH*, 1:113–14.

Nadel, Max, ed. "Audio-Visual Materials." In *Teaching the Jewish Experience*, 71–78. N.Y.: AAJE, 1975.

National Council on Jewish Audio-Visual Materials, *The Jewish Audio-Visual Review*.

Siegel, Jonathan P. "Slides For Teaching: A Practical Guide." *Compass* 1 (Summer 1978): 15–16.

Siegel, Morton. "Youth Films." *Ped Rep* 32 (Fall 1980): 34.

Slesinger, Zalmen. *Audio-Visual Program Aids for the Jewish Festivals*. N.Y.: AAJE, 1958. 71 pp.

———. *Films and Filmstrips of Jewish Interest*. Series 1–6. N.Y.: National Council on Jewish Audio-Visual Service.

———. "The National Council on Jewish Audio-Visual Materials." *Reg* (1959), 26–27; *Reg* (1965), 42–43.

———. *Teaching Bible Through Audio-Visual Aids*. N.Y.: AAJE, 1961.

Soref, Irwin I. "Audio-Visual Aids in Jewish Education." *Jew Ed* 23 (Fall 1952): 5–6.

———. "Evaluation and Utilization of Audio-Visual Materials." *Ped Rep* 3 (Sept. 1951).

———. "דרכי הוראה ראי-קוליים„ (Teaching Methods of Audio-Visual Aids). *Sh Hah* (H.) 23 (Summer 1963): 202–12.

Strauss, Ruby G. "Mitzvah Movies." *AM* (Spring 1977).

Sussman, Eva. "Audio-Visual Aids in the Classroom." *Syn Sch* 12 (Feb. 1954): 15–18.

Syme, Daniel B. "The UAHC Television and Film Institute." *Ped Rep* 35 (Jan. 1984): 16.

Tarnor, Mrs. Norman. "Audio-Visual Aids in the Teaching of Hebrew." *Syn Sch* 17 (1959).

UAHC CJE. "Breakthrough in Audio Visual Education." *Ped Rep* 22 (June 1971): 19.

Zoreff, Ephraim. "יד להוראה ראי-קולות„ (Guide for Teaching Audio-Visual Aids). *Sh Hah* (H.) 12 (June 1952): 150–56.

THE DANCE (SELECTED)

Berk, Fred. *The Chasidic Dance*. N.Y.: UAHC and American Zionist Youth Foundation, 1975. 64 pp.

———. *The Jewish Dance: An Anthology of Articles*. N.Y.: Exposition, 1960. 46 pp.

———. *Ha Rikud: The Jewish Dance*. N.Y.: UAHC, 1972. Grades 9 and up.

Berk, Fred, and Dona Rosenblatt. "Dance." (Includes resources and bibliography) In *Cat 2*, 337–51.

Chochem, Corrine. *Jewish Holiday Dances*. N.Y.: Behrman, 1948.

"Dance." In *Enc Jud*, 5: 1262–74.

Delakova, K., and Fred Berk. *Dances of Palestine*. B'nai B'rith Hillel Foundation, 1947.

———. *Jewish Folk Dance Book*. N.Y.: NJWB, 1948.

Freehof, Florence. *Jews Are a Dancing People*. San Francisco: Stark-Rath Pub. Co., 1954. 71 pp.

Keeping Posted. *A Time to Mourn, A Time to Dance*. Nos. 840300 and 480302. Leader's edition.

Lapson, Dvorah. "Dance in the Jewish School." *Recon* (Dec. 1951). See also *Ped Rep* 3 (May 1952).

———. „הריקוד בבית הספר היהודי" (The Dance in the Jewish School). *Sh Hah* (H.) 12 (Mar. 1952): 94–100.

———. "They Dance Together." *Jew Ed* 23 (Fall 1952): 60–62.

Nateman, Evelyn. "Dance as a Classroom Technique for Teaching Bible, Siddur and Literature." In *JTH*, 95–104.

Rothman, Iris. "Games and Dances for Beginners' Hebrew." *Jew Teach* 23 (Nov. 1958): 11–12.

Vernon, Lisa. "Integrating Jewish Dance into the Religious School Curriculum." A series of lessons utilizing dance as reinforcement for learning or as a medium through which to introduce material. Master's project, HUC–JIR, 1977.

Vizonsky, Nathan. „רקודי עמנו וערכם בחנוך" (Dances of Our People and Their Educational Value). *Sh Hah* (H.) 5 (May 1945): 164–67.

———. "The Evolution of the Jewish Folk Dance." *Chicago Jewish Forum* (Fall 1954): 45–50.

———. *The Jewish Folk Dances—A Manual for Teachers and Leaders*. Chicago: American Hebrew Theatrical League, 1942. 59 pp.

Waxman, Shirley T. "Israeli Folk Dance." *Ped Rep* 31 (Spring 1980): 30–31.

DRAMA—GENERAL (SELECTED)

See also New York City

Ben Ari, Raikin. *Habima*. A famous Hebrew theatre group in Europe, America and Israel. Translated from the Hebrew by A. H. Gross and I. Soref. N.Y.: Yoseloff, 1957. 253 pp.

Citron, Samuel J. "Yiddish and Hebrew Drama." In *A History of Modern Drama*, edited by Barrett H. Clark and George Freedly, 601–38. N.Y.: D. Appleton-Century, 1947.

Cohen, Edward H., ed. *New Jewish Voices: Plays Produced by the Jewish Repertory Theatre*. Albany: State U. of New York Press, 1985.

Cohen, Sarah B., ed. *From Hester Street to Hollywood: The Jewish-American Stage and Screen*. Bloomington: Indiana U. Press, 1983.

Goren, B. „די געשיכטע פון אידישן טעאטער" (The History of Jewish Theater) (Y.). 2d ed. 2 vols. N.Y.: Maisel, 1923.

"Hebrew Drama." In *Enc Jud*, 6:193–207.

Kohansky, Mendel. *The Hebrew Theatre*. 1969.

DRAMA IN THE SCHOOL

Addison, Robert. "The Use of Drama in Teaching the Holocaust." *Ped Rep* 33 (Mar. 1982): 20–21.

Bridger, David. „דראמאטישע אויפפירונגען" On drama in the school—formal and informal. In *DER*, 3:168–74.

Brilliant, Nathan, and Libbie L. Braverman. *Religious Pageants for the Jewish School*. N.Y.: UAHC, 1951. 155 pp.

Citron, Samuel J. *Dramatics for Creative Teaching*. N.Y.: USCJE, 1961. 403 pp.

———. *Dramatics the Year Round*. N.Y.: USA–CJE, 1956. 654 pp.

———. "Socio-Drama in Teaching Bible." *Syn Sch* 16 (Mar. 1958): 19–20.

———. "They Live Together Through Dramatics." *Jew Ed* 23 (Fall 1952): 49–54.

———. "Two Projects in Educational Dramatics." *Jew Ed* 22 (Winter–Spring 1951): 49–53.

Cohen, Edward M., ed. *Plays of Jewish Interest*. (Resource Guide) N.Y.: National Foundation for Jewish Culture, 1982. 126 pp.

Cohen, Joan Freeman. "There's No Business Like . . . Creative Dramatics in the Classroom." *MJ* 13 (Winter 1982): 8, 14.

Dramatics for the Jewish Club Leader. N.Y.: Yeshiva U. Dept. of Youth Services, Div. of Communal Services.

Eisenstein, Ira (words), and Judith K. Eisenstein (music). *What is Torah?* (Cantata) N.Y.: Reconstructionist Foundation.

Gabriel, Michelle. *Jewish Plays for Jewish Days: Brief Holiday Plays for Ages 8–12.* Denver: ARE, 1978.

Gewirtz, Shimon. "Drama." *Ped Rep* 32 (Winter 1981): 27–28.

Hollander, Carl. "Role Playing in the Classroom." *AM* (Spring 1972).

Katz, David. "The Jewish Family Theatre." *Compass* 4 (Spring 1981): 16–17, 27.

Kessler, Harry. *Creative Dramatics for Young Judea Clubs.* N.Y.: National Young Judea, 1944.

Klein, Joyce. "Drama in the Jewish Classroom." In *JTH*, vol. 1.

Lipkin, Bela. *Creative Drama in the Hebrew School.* N.Y.: Bloch, 1978.

Mokdoni, A. "הערך החנוכי של התיאטרון„ (The Educational Value of the Theatre). *Sh Hah* (H.) 4 (1928): 19–26.

Miller, Lillian. "Dramatics in the Religious School." *Jew Teach* 9 (Jan. 1941): 17–22.

Nanus, Susan. *Five in One: Holiday Plays for Children.* N.Y.: UAHC, 1983. 45 pp.

Newman, Mordecai. "Drama." In *Cat 2*, 352–59. For High School Youth.

Rembrandt, Esther. "Educational Theatre in the Religious School." In *JTH*, 2: 69–77.

Schwardelson, Susan J. *Kadima Drama Manual.* N.Y.: USA, Dept. of Youth Activities.

Sugarman, Lillian. "The Children Write a Pageant." *Jew Teach* 9 (Apr. 1941): 18–20.

Wyenn, Than R. "How to Pepare a Play for the Jewish School." *Ped Rep* 36 (Jan. 1985).

———. "Teaching Language Through Creative Drama." *Syn Sch* 9 (Nov. 1950): 17–19.

THE SCHOOL ASSEMBLY

Assembly Playlets for Day Schools and Afternoon Schools. N.Y.: TU.

Belkin, Louis. "A Thanksgiving Assembly and Service." *Jew Teach* 10 (Nov. 1941): 1–5. For High School Students.

Bloom, David I. "Planning Meaningful Assemblies." *Syn Sch* 14 (May 1956): 15–16.

Brilliant, Nathan, and Libbie L. Braverman. "The Assembly." In *Act*, 104–16, 138–49.

———. "The Assembly." *Jew Teach* 3 (June 1935), 1–13; 4 (Nov. 1935), 15–25. For high school students, 4 (Jan. 1936), 28–37; 4 (Apr. 1936): 8–23.

———. *Religious Programs for the Jewish School.* Cincinnati: UAHC, c. 1941. 155 pp.

Cohen, Reba. "Assembly Programs." *Jew Teach* 10 (Jan. 1942); 11 (Jan. 1943), 27–30. (See also 10:2.)

Cohn, Morton J. "The Assembly as an Instrument in Religious Education." Master's thesis, HUC, 1934.

Fish, Nathan M. "Planning a School Sabbath Assembly." *Syn Sch* 11 (Apr. 1953): 10–13.

Ginsberg, Morris B. "Opening Day Assembly." *Jew Teach* 7 (June 1939): 22–24.

Gold, Charles H. "An Experiment in Thematic Unity in Assembly Programs." *Syn Sch* 21 (Mar. 1953).

Goldman, Sylvia. "The Assembly in the Religious School." *Jew Teach* 22 (Jan. 1954): 7–8.

Levinger, Elma Ehrlich. *Entertaining Programs for the Assembly.* Cincinnati: UAHC, 1930. 192 pp.

Lister, Louis, comp. and ed. *The Religious School Assembly Handbook.* N.Y.: UAHC, 1963.

Lurie, Rose G. "Assembly Program on Torah." *Syn Sch* 13 (Dec. 1954): 25–28.

Nudelman, Edward A. "The Jewish Sunday School Assembly." *Jew Teach* 2 (Nov. 1933): 1–9.

Ruffman, Louis L., and Ben M. Edidin. *The School Assembly.* N.Y.: JEC, 1953.

Sussman, Samuel, and Abraham Segal. *50 Assembly Programs for the Jewish School.* N.Y.: USCJE, 1948.

Weinberg, Werner. "The School Assembly." *Syn Sch* 17 (Sept. 1958): 25–26.

Zeligs, Dorothy E. "The Sunday School Assembly Problem in Religious Education." *Jew Teach* 1 (June 1933): 17–22.

MUSIC—GENERAL (SELECTED)

Altman, Shalom. *The Judean Songster*. N.Y.: Young Judea, 193?. 130 pp.

Binder, Abraham W. "Jewish Music." In *JPPP*, 3:324–76.

———, comp. and ed. *New Palestinian Folk Songs*. N.Y.: Bloch, 1933, 1935.

Bugatch, Samuel. *Songs of Our People: 300 Hebrew and Yiddish Songs*. N.Y.: Farband Book Publishing Association, 1952. 245 pp.

Carp, Bernard. *The Jewish Center Songster*. N.Y.: JWB.

Davidson, C. "A Quarter of a Century of Synagogue Music in America." *J of Synagogue Music* (Feb. 1969): 3–10.

Eisenstein, Judith K. *Heritage of Jewish Music*. N.Y.: UAHC.

———. "Music and the Jew." In *Jan 2*, 245–51.

Gerson-Kiwi, E. "The Legacy of Jewish Music through the Ages." *J of Synagogue Music* 1 (Feb. 1967): 3–25.

Goldfarb, I., and Samuel E. Goldfarb. *The Jewish Songster* (with music). N.Y.: 1919.

Heskes, Irene. "Jewish Music Literature." *JBA* 23 (1965): 34–41.

Idelsohn, Abraham Zvi. *Jewish Music in Its Historical Development*. N.Y.: Sacred Music Press and HUC–JIR, 1932 (reprinted 1968). 404 pp.

Kiell, Norman. *Phonograph Recordings of Jewish Interest*. Washington, D.C.: B'nai B'rith Hillel Foundation.

* Levy, Ezekiel. *Sacred Music and Festivals of Catholic, Jewish and Protestant Faiths*. New York U., 1955.

* Lorch, Steven Charles. *The Convergence of Hebrew Sacred Music and Western Culture as Exemplified Through Music: Some Educational Consequences*. Columbia U., 1977. 280 pp.

"Music." In *Enc Jud*, 12:552–715.

Rabinowitch, Israel. *Of Jewish Music, Ancient and Modern*. Translated from the Yiddish by A. M. Klein. Montreal: The Book Center, 1952. 321 pp.

Rinder, Reuben. *Music and Prayer, for Home, School and Synagogue*. N.Y.: UAHC, Sacred Music Press, 1959. 394 pp.

Rothstein, Arnold. "Synagogue Music in Our Day." *Jew Life* 18 (June 1951).

Rubin, Ruth. "Literature on Jewish Music." *JBA* (1947–48): 64–70.

———. *Voices of a People: The Story of Yiddish Folksongs*. Phila.: JPS, 1963, 1979. 558 pp.

Union of Orthodox Jewish Congregations of America, National Conference of Synagogue Youth. *NCSY Songster*. N.Y.: 1963?. 11 pp.

Union Songster: Songs and Prayers for Jewish Youth. N.Y.: CCAR, 1960. 438 pp.

Wahl, A. Z. (Music in Jewish Education). *Hadoar* (H.) 25 (June 17, 1946): 703–9.

Werner, Eric. "The Jewish Contribution to Music." In *Jews*, 1288–1321.

———, ed. *Reviews of Selected Recordings of Jewish Music*. N.Y.: National Jewish Music Council, 1953.

Yasser, Joseph. "The Musical Heritage of the Bible." *YA* 12 (1958/59): 157–75.

MUSIC IN THE SCHOOL

Altman, Shalom. "You Too, Can Teach a Song." *Jew Teach* 34 (Feb. 1966): 14–15.

Arian, Meri Lovenger. "Consider the Choir." *Compass* 1 (Spring 1978): 16.

Arian, Philip. "Structuring a Music Program for the School." *Syn Sch* 25 (Spring 1967): 26–29.

Brilliant, Nathan, and Libbie L. Braverman. "A Singing School Is a Happy School." In *Act*, 149–64.

Bryan, Marsha. "Choral Music: How to Organize a Jewish Choir." In *Cat 2*, 360–67.

Cook, Ray M. *The Complete Sing for Fun Book*. N.Y.: UAHC. Grades 1–6.

———. *The Tax Collector of Teplitz. A Three Act Operetta for Children*. N.Y.: UAHC, 1968.

Coopersmith, Harry. "The Choral Group in the School." *Jew Teach* 11 (Nov. 1942): 11–20.

———. "A Guide to Jewish Music in the Home." *Jew Teach* 10 (Nov. 1942).

———. "How to Teach a Song." *Jew Teach* 13 (1944–45): 1–6.

———. "Music in the Jewish School." *Jew Teach* 9 (June 1941): 1–7.

———. *The New Jewish Song Book*. N.Y.: Behrman, 1965. 192 pp.

———. *The Songs We Sing*. 2 vols. N.Y.: USCJE, 1950.

———. *Songs of Zion*. N.Y.: Behrman, 1942.

———. "The Teaching of Jewish Music." *Jew Ed* 2 (Jan. 1930): 25–28.

———. "They Sing Together." *Jew Ed* 23 (Feb. 1952): 59.

Eisenstein, Judith K. *Gateway to Jewish Song*. N.Y.: Behrman, 1939.

———. *History of Music: The Music of the Jewish People*. N.Y.: UAHC, 1973. 339 pp.

———. (Music in Jewish Education). In *Yesod* (H.), 148–53.

———. "A New Look at Music in Jewish Education." *Ped Rep* 22 (Mar. 1971): 7–8.

———. "שירי מועד„ (H.) (Festival Songs). N.Y.: Bloch, 1943. 64 pp.

Eisenstein, Judith K., and Ira Eisenstein. *The Seven Golden Buttons: A Cantata Based on a Hasidic Tale*. N.Y.: Jewish Reconstructionist Foundation.

Eisenstein, Judith K., and Frieda Prensky. *Songs of Childhood*. N.Y.: USCJE, 1935, 1955. 321 pp.

Frankel, Reuben. "Music in the Synagogue School Program." *Syn Sch* 20 (1962).

Goldfarb, Samuel E. "Music in the Jewish School." *Jewish Teacher* 2 (Apr. 1918): 65–70.

Goldstein, Rose B. *Songs to Share, Matnet Shir* (H.). N.Y.: USCJE, 1949.

Grossman, Reuben. "על שירי ילדים„ (On Children's Songs). *Sh Hah* (H.) 3 (1928): 239–42.

Heskes, Irene. "A Unit Outline Covering the Topic of Chasidic Music." *Jew Teach* 22 (Mar. 1954): 10–12.

Hofman, Shlomo. "חנוך דרך מוסיקה„ (Education Through Music). *Sh Hah* (H.) 23 (Fall/Winter 1963): 9–21, 85–98.

Idelsohn, Abraham Z. "הנעימה היהודית„ (The Jewish Melody). *Sh Hah* (H.) 4 (1929): 471–80.

———. *The Jewish Song Book for Synagogue, School and Home*. 3d ed. Cincinnati: Publication for Judaism, 1953. 548 pp.

———. "הזמרה בבית הספר העברי באמריקה„ (Music in the Hebrew School in America). *Sh Hah* (H.) 2 (1927): 23–32.

Jochsberger, Tziporah. "The Hebrew Arts School: Music Education for the Young." *Ped Rep* 36 (Jan. 1985): 10, 13.

———. "Teaching Children to Love the Arts," *Jew Music Educators Journal* 70 (Oct. 1983): 50–52.

Jospe, Erwin. *A Music Curriculum for the Jewish School*. N.Y.: UAHC.

———. "Toward a Music Program in the Jewish Religious School." *Jew Teach* 10 (Jan. 1942): 19–26.

Kane, Rhoda H. "Music in the Classroom." *Syn Sch* 16 (Dec. 1957): 27–28.

Kiell, Norman. "Phonograph Recordings as an Educational Tool in the Jewish Religious School." *Jew Ed* 14 (Jan./Mar. 1943): 151–54.

Klepper, Jeff. "Chai on Music—18 New Ideas for Jewish Music Education." In *JTH*, 1:151–64.

Koenig, Benjamin. "The Helen Laufer Ideas on Creative Music for Children." *Syn Sch* 22 (Spring 1965): 23–25.

Kohn, Harriet Korach. "The Euclid Avenue Temple Program—Hit Parade." *Jew Teach* 10 (June 1942): 28–29.

Krantzler, Harold. "The Jewish Choral Movement in the United States." Master's thesis, HUC–JIR, 1953. 139 pp.

Levy, Maria. "The Music of Tomorrow in the Religious School of Today." *Jew Teach* 28 (May 1960): 5–6.

Morton, Laurence. *Ruth* (an operetta). N.Y.: UAHC.

Neumann, Richard. "Quality Music in Jewish Schools." *Ped Rep* 32 (Winter 1981): 30 and 36 (Jan. 1985): 13–14.

Orbach, Harold. "The Teaching of Israel Through the Teaching of Jewish Music." *Jew Teach* 32 (Dec. 1963). Also in *Ped Rep* 15 (June 1964): 7–8.

Penn, Ascher. "געזאנג און דראמע ... אין אידישן שול-וועזן אין אמעריקע" (Song and Drama in the Jewish Schools of America). In *Penn* (Y.), 456–63.

Portnoy, Joseph L. "Music Art in the Classroom." *Jew Teach* 33 (Feb. 1965): 13–14.

———. *Music Curriculum for Jewish Religious Schools*. N.Y.: UAHC, c. 1967. 76 pp.

Preston, Shari Ann. "Utilizing Music to Teach the Concept of Kibbutz Galuyot to Fourth Graders in an Afternoon Hebrew School." Master's thesis, JTS Dept. of Education, 1989.

Regelson, Abraham. (Music Instruction). *Sh Hah* (H.) 1 (1940): 33–39.

Resnick, Hyman, and David Cedarbaum. "A Music Curriculum for the Jewish Holidays." *Jew Teach* 21 (May 1953): 11–13.

Rosewater, A. *Primary Songs and Games for Children in the Jewish Religious School*. Cincinnati: UAHC, 1938.

Shapiro, Roni. "A Practical Guide to Jewish Music Education for the Supplementary Religious School." Master's thesis, JTS Dept. of Jewish Education, 1989.

Sheinzon, I. D. "השירה במחלקות הנמוכות" (Music in the Elementary Classes). *Sh Hah* (H.) 10 (Mar. 1950): 73–78.

Silverstein, Philip. "On Teaching Torah and Haftorah Cantillation." *Syn Sch* 21 (1963).

Weissman, Jackie. "Musical Fun with Preschoolers." *AM* (Spring 1979).

Zimmer, Alex. "Teaching with Recordings." *Jew Teach* 23 (May 1955): 8–9.

GLEANINGS

Kaplan, Mordecai M.,

"Once Jewish life is capable of meeting the emotional, intellectual and social demands of human living, it will evoke functional creativity of the artist, and the secondary creativity of an audience conscious of art."

Judaism as a Civilization (1957), 487–88.

Gezari, Temima,

"When a child picks up a brush in a Hebrew school or messes around in clay, what he is doing is not frittering away precious time that might be spent on other things. He is proving that we were all born with more than two senses—the sense of sight and hearing—and that he can learn not only through reading of books and listening to the teacher, but also he can learn even more eloquently about Jewish life through his sense of taste, his sense of smell, and above all his sense of touch."

Jew Ed 23 (Fall 1952), 55.

Lapson, Dvorah,

"Jewish folk dance, both Israeli and European, plays an important part in any education dance program. Adolescents are particularly stimulated by the Israeli folk dances because of their vigorous and romantic character. Educators utilize this discovery for the creation of a firmer bond of confidence with the Jewish youth."

Jew Ed 23 (Fall 1952), 61.

Coopersmith, Harry,

"Music was a natural by-product of Jewish living. It was heard in the synagogue, at home, and in the street, at festivals and national lamentations, at weddings and at family gatherings. It was in the air, and its influence could not be escaped."

Quoted in *Act*, 149–50.

Kaplan, Mordecai M.,

"The arts by giving an emotionally stirring interpretation of the experiences shared by Jews, create a common intellectual and emotional content for Jewish life."

Questions Jews Ask (1956), 370.

Kayser, Stephen S.,

"When we speak of 'Jewish art' we mean the arts as they are applied to Judaism. This application, of course, is made principally in those areas where art is essen-

tial as a means to an end. Such a concept of Jewish art may be called functional, since it does not recognize anything Jewish in art unless it serves a purpose connected with Judaism as a way of life. The definition excludes creation by Jewish artists which are detached from Jewish objectives, but includes works which serve a Jewish purpose even though the makers were not Jewish, a situation quite common in western Europe before the Emancipation. Thus while there is no Jewish style, there is a Jewish art, the Jews expressing themselves in the art-forms of the surrounding world."
Jewish Ceremonial Art (1959), 9–10.

Heschel, Abraham J.,

"The only language that seems to be compatible with the wonder and mystery of being is the language of music,... a reaching out toward a realm that lies beyond the reach of verbal propositions.... Religious music is an attempt to convey that which is within reach but beyond our grasp."
The Insecurity of Freedom (1967), 245, 248.

Cohen, Joan Freeman, (on drama in the school)

"The 1970's brought a new interest in the development of alternative methods of education. Jewish educators began to realize that it was emotional impact of the school on its students that would be the distinguishing factor which would set Jewish education apart from general studies in the minds of pupils.... There is a scarcity of Jewish plays.... Our solution must be as follows:

1. Rewrite scripts, so that they are more relevant and personal to today's students....

2. We must pool the talented resources in the Jewish community and write Jewish plays with both content and pizzaz that will have the same appeal as the Hebraicized Broadway show which is the norm for so many of our youth.

It should be understood then, that we are referring to drama not as a subject title as in an elective chug at summer camp, but rather as a mode of teaching."
MJ 13 (Winter 1982), 8, 14.

5 | BAR/BAT MITZVAH

PRIOR TO 1950

Aronson, David. "What Jewish Equipment We Ought to Give the Bar Mitzvah or Confirmand." *RA* (1933–38): 324–29.

"The Bar Mitzvah Ceremony," *Syn Sch 7* (Feb. 1949).

Cohen, Samuel. "The Bar-Mitzvah and Democracy." *The Jewish School and Democracy* 2 (Apr. 1944): 91–92, 104.

Levitats, Isaac. "Communal Regulations of Bar Mitzvah." *JSS* 11 (Apr. 1949): 153–62.

Rivkind, Isaac. "לאות ולזכרון, תולדות בר מצוה". *(For a Sign and a Reminder—The History of Bar Mitzvah)* (H.). N.Y.: Shulsinger, 1942.

Scharfstein, Zevi. "הכנה לבר מצוה," (Preparation for Bar Mitzvah). *Sh Hah* (H.) 9 (Jan. 1949): 15–16.

Segal, Abraham. "Reconstructing Bar Mitzvah." *Recon* 10 (Jan. 26, 1945): 10–16.

"What to Do About Bar Mitzvah," *Syn Sch* 5 (Mar. 1947): 95–99.

SINCE 1950

Abrams, Sylvia F. "Charlie Brown's Bar Mitzvah." *Compass* 4 (Spring 1981): 12–13, 27.

Beckerman, Solomon. "Torah Reading for the Teenager." *Syn Sch* 19 (1961): 20.

Bender, Daniel. *Reading* Disabilities and Bar Mitzvah. A summary of behaviors associated with the reading disabled, including a set of lesson plans. Master's project, HUC–JIR, 1977.

Berger, Kenneth R. "Bar and Bat Mitzvah—A Creative Approach." *Recon* 42 (Sept. 1976): 29–31.

Bettan, Israel. "Bar Mitzvah Has No Place in Reform Jewish Practice." *CCAR J* (June 1954): 25.

Blitstein, Sheldon. "The Bar Mitzvah as an Experience in Family Growth." *J Jew Com Ser* (Fall 1982): 45–57.

Bloomstone-Korb, Deena. *Covenant: A Model for Responsibility and* Relationships. L.A.: HUC–JIR, Tartak Learning Center, 1986.

Blumental, Aaron. "Bar Mitzvah In Our Congregations." *Syn Sch* 12 (Sept. 1953): 11–18.

Borowitz, Eugene. *The Bar Mitzvah Book*. N.Y.: Praeger. Grades 6–9.

Central Conference of American Rabbis, *CCAR* 72 (1962). *Problems of Bar Mitzvah and Bas Mitzvah:*

> Martin, Bernard. "Bar Mitzvah and Reform Judaism." p. 158.
> Stern, Jack. "Bar Mitzvah and Reform Judaism." pp. 160–61.
> Stillpass, Leo J. "Survey of Present Practices." p. 157.

5 BAR/BAT MITZVAH

Cohen, Jack J. "Bar Mitzvah as a Stage in Jewish Education." *Ped Rep* (Sept. 1957): 5–6. See "Continuity in Jewish Education" in *JEDS*, 314–39.

Efron, Benjamin, and Alvan D. Rubin. "The Reality of Bar Mitzvah." *CCAR J* (Oct. 1960): 31–33.

———. *Coming of Age: Your Bar/Bat Mitzvah*. N.Y.: UAHC, 1977. Grades 6–8.

Eisenberg, Azriel. *The Bar Mitzvah Treasury*. N.Y.: Behrman, 1952. 316 pp. Grades 6–8.

Eisenberg, Azriel, and Leah A. Globe. *The Bat Mitzvah Treasury*. N.Y.: National Womens League of USA, 1965. 384 pp. Grades 6–8.

"Examinations for Candidates for Bar Mitzvah and Bat Mitzvah." *Syn Sch* 12 (Sept. 1953): 22–23.

Feuer, Leon I. "Second Thoughts about Bar-Bat Mitzvah," *RJ* (Winter 1980): 1–8.

Fox, Cherie Koller. "A New Look at Bat Mitzvah," in *The Jewish Woman: New Perspectives*, edited by Elizabeth Koltun, 31–42. N.Y.: Schocken Books, 1976.

Gaster, Theodor H. "What Does the Bar Mitzvah Signify?" *Commentary* (June 1951): 525–31.

Glasser, Benis. "One Family's Frustration: A Bat Mitzvah Mishap over 'regulations'." *Moment* 3 (Oct. 1978): 18–24.

Golinkin, Noah. "Enriching the Bar Mitzvah Ceremony." *Syn Sch* 12 (Sept. 1953): 19–21.

Greenberg, Sidney, and Abraham Rothberg. *The Bar Mitzvah Companion*. N.Y.: Behrman, 1959. 121 pp. Grades 6–9.

Greenfield, Howard. *Bar Mitzvah*. Holt, Rinehart, Winston, 1981.

Ingall, Carol K. *Bar/Bat Mitzvah* Program. Teacher's Guide. N.Y.: MRC of JTSA, 1984. 22 pp.

———. "On Becoming a Jewish Adult: Educating for Bar and Bat Mitzvah." *Con Jud* 3 (Spring 1976).

———. "Bar/Bat Mitzvah." *JPH* (1983), ed. Marcus and Zwerin, 421–26.

Isaac, Mel. "Bar Mitzvah and Bat Torah: A New Non-Focused Approach," *Ped Rep* 31 (Spring 1980): 25–26.

Katsh, Abraham I., ed. *Bar Mitzvah*. N.Y.: Shengold, 1955. 160 pp.

Levitats, Isaac. "בר-מצווה" (Bar Mitzvah) *DER* (Y.) 1 (1957): 482–90.

Lewisohn, Ludwig. "My Dear Boy," (A letter to a boy about to be called to the Torah). In *Bar Mitzvah*, edited by Katsh, 28–30.

Marcus, Audrey Friedman, et al. *Bar and Bat Mitzvah: A Family Education Unit*. Denver: ARE, 1977.

The Melton Research Center. *Together: Bar-Bat Mitzvah, A Child-Parent Kit*. N.Y.: MRC, 1984.

Millgram, Abraham E. *Your Son's Bar Mitzvah*. N.Y.: USCJE.

Ribicoff, P. "Bar Mitzvah at The Wall "*Moment* 3 (Dec. 1977): 31–37.

Rittner, Stephen. *All That You Want to Know about the Bar-Bat Mitzvah*. Milwaukee: Arbit Books.

Rosenberg, Stuart E. "The Right Age for Bar Mitzvah." *Jew Spec* 29 (Mar. 1964): 14–18. Also *Rel Ed* 60 (July/Aug. 1965): 298–99.

Roth, Cecil. "Bar Mitzvah—Its History and Its Association." In *Bar Mitzvah*, ed. Katsh, 15–22.

Routtenberg, Max J. "A Group Bat Mitzvah Service." *Syn Sch* 10 (Apr. 1952): 13–17.

Ruthen, Marlene Lobell. *My Bar/Bat Mitzvah*. N.Y.: UAHC, 1982.

Sachs, Moshe. "After Bar Mitzvah—What?" *Syn Sch* 10 (1951): 5.

Schoenberg, Elliot Salo. "The Bar/Bat Mitzvah: What Is the Rabbi's Role?" *Jew Ed* 55 (Fall 1987): 38–41.

Schwartz, E. "I don't gotta put on tefillin," *Jew Spec* (Sept. 1964): 23–25.

Segal, Abraham. *Your Daughter's Bat Mitzvah*. N.Y.: USCJE, 1954.

Siskin, Edgar E. "Bar Mitzvah American Style," *RJ* 28 (Winter 1981): 89–91.

Snyder, Herman E. "Is Bar-Bat Mitzvah Destroying Attendance at Synagogue Services?" *RJ* 27 (Winter 1980): 9–12.

Spiro, Jack D. "Bar Mitzvah Dropouts—A Juvenile Solution." *Jewish Teacher* 33 (Feb. 1965): 15–16

———. "The Educational Significance of the Bar Mitzvah Initiation." *Rel Ed* 72 (July–Aug. 1977): 389–99.

Swartz, Michael. "Bar and Bat Mitzvah Workshops." *Ped Rep* 35 (Jan. 1984): 26–27.

Union of American Hebrew Congregations. *Your Bar/Bat Mitzvah, Parashah and Haftarah with Commentary.* N.Y.: UAHC, 1983.

Wohlberg, Max. "Bar Mitzvah Instruction." *Syn Sch* 12 (Sept. 1953): 3–10.

Yedwab, Myra. "Temple Beth Am's Mitzvah Program." *Ped Rep* 31 (Spring 1980): 26–27.

GLEANINGS

Segal, Abraham,

"A few hundred years ago, the Bar Mitzvah ceremony was quite simple, without special preparations or fuss of any kind. It had, however, a valid social function, for it represented changes that took place in the lives of the boy and his parents. It thus symbolized problems and solutions to problems which had real meaning in the life of the people.

Today, pomp and circumstance have replaced the old simplicity and honesty, and showmanship has replaced achievement. Whatever may be true of his physical development, the thirteen-year-old of today is far from maturity in vocational preparation, in education, emotional experience. . . . Modern life is so complicated that practically nobody can grow to maturity in twelve or thirteen years. . . . We have retained the traditional number of years as a requirement for Bar Mitzvah, although at that age the boy is only halfway grown up, and we have retained, together with the traditional age requirement, also the traditional conventions and terminology, whereby we talk and think in terms of a maturity which does not exist. We have today, therefore, a ceremony, splendid in its outer shell but inwardly hollow and false."

"Reconstructing Bar Mitzvah" *Recon,* (Jan. 26, 1945), 10.

Gaster, Theodor H.,

"The existing ceremony of religious graduation does have a real function: our problem is created by the fact that it is not the function of the ceremony of Bar Mitzvah. Could we not, however, honestly recognize the present ceremony as a kind of initial matriculation, and add another, at a more mature age, which would have the value of full graduation, and which would really take over the function of the Bar Mitzvah institution? At the present moment, what happens is that the two stages are confused. As I have suggested, the lad of thirteen is, so to speak, being handed a cap and gown but denied any graduate standing. To put it differently, he has been given a certificate of citizenship without enjoying civil rights."

"What Does the Bar Mitzvah Signify?" *Commentary*, June 1951.

Commission on Jewish Education—CCAR and UAHC,

"If any ceremony connected with the education of the young is to be given precedence, there can be no question that it is the ceremony of Confirmation. Neither Bar Mitzvah nor Bas Mitzvah can be considered a substitute for Confirmation. . . . With regard to appropriate standards for Bar Mitzvah and Bas Mitzvah, the Commission believes that candidates for these ceremonies should be required as a minimum to have:

a. the ability to read fluently the major Hebrew prayers of the Sabbath service;

b. the ability to participate in the Torah service as a knowledgeable oleh latorah in accordance with the customs of the congregation;

c. an understanding of the Torah and Haftorah portions read the week of their Bar Mitzvah or Bas Mitzvah;

d. a mastery of selected Hebrew portions of the Torah;

e. attendance at Sabbath services regularly in the period preceding their Bar Mitzvah or Bas Mitzvah;

f. a commitment to continue their Jewish education through Confirmation."

Adopted by the Commission, June 21, 1960

5 BAR/BAT MITZVAH

A Former Bar Mitzvah Student (From an interview by Thomas Cottle. (Children of Divorce)

"Everybody knows . . . you don't become an adult just because you turn thirteen and memorize a lot of Hebrew words. I mean God doesn't make any magic when you have your Bar Mitzvah. You just do it because it is an old ceremony and because your parents, well, sort of order you to do it. But as I was doing all this work getting ready for my big day . . . I thought to myself . . . it may be a great joke this magic business of becoming an adult when you get Bar Mitzvahed or Batmitzvahed, but you get it through your thick skull that it's no magical joke at all. You're going to have to become an adult, Jewish joke or not. So the truth of it all that I became an adult quite a few months before I did it in the temple where it is supposed to be official."

Quoted by Norman L. Friedman, *Jew Ed* 52 (Summer 1984), 32.

6 THE BIBLE

GENERAL (SELECTED)

Adar, Zvi. *The Biblical Narrative*. Jerusalem: WZO, c. 1959. 280 pp.

Albright, William F. "The Biblical Period." *Jews*, 1:3–69.

———. "The Old Testament World." In *The Interpreter's Bible*, edited by G. A. Buttrick, 1:233–71. N.Y.: Abbington-Cokesbury, 1952.

Buttenweiser, M. *The Prophets of Israel*. N.Y.: Macmillan, 1934.

Chorowsky, Joshua. "The Influence of Biblical Ideas on the American Revolution and Constitution." *Ped Rep* 28 (Fall 1976).

Cronbach, Abraham. *The Bible and Our Social Outlook*. Cincinnati: UAHC, 1941. 383 pp.

Daiches, David. "The Influence of the Bible on English Literature." *Jews* 2:1452–71.

Durant, Will. "The People of the Book" and "The Literature and Philosophy of the Bible." In *Our Oriental Heritage*, 328–49. N.Y.: Simon and Schuster, 1954.

Goldman, Solomon. *The Book of Human Destiny*. 3 vols. 1st ed. (1) *The Book of Books: An Introduction*. N.Y.: JPS, 1948. (2) *In the Beginning*. N.Y.: Harper, 1949. (3) *From Slavery to Freedom*. N.Y.: Abelard-Schuman, 1958.

Gordis, Robert. "The Bible as a Cultural Monument." *Jews* 1:783–822.

Gordon, Cyrus H. "Genesis and Archaeological Discovery." *Jew Teach* 24 (Apr. 1961): 7–10.

Greenberg, Moshe. "The Heritage of Biblical Israel." *Understanding Exodus*. Melton Research Center and JTSA Series, vol. 2, part 1. N.Y.: Behrman, 1969.

Hertz, Joseph H., ed. *The Pentateuch and the Haftorahs*. London: Soncino, 1960. 1067 pp.

Heschel, Abraham J. *The Prophets*. Phila.: JPS, 1962. 518 pp.

Honor, Leo L. "The Role of Memory in Biblical History." In *Mordecai M. Kaplan Jubilee Volume*, ed. Moshe Davis. Also in *RTJH*, 71–90.

———. *Kings I: Commentary*. UAHC, 1955. 367 pp.

Kaufman, Yehezkel. "The Sources" and "Classical Prophecy." *The Religion of Israel*, trans. from Hebrew by Moshe Greenberg, 153–211, 343–446. Chicago: U. of Chicago Press, 1960. Abstracts from Kaufman in Leo Schwartz, ed., *Great Ages and Ideas of the Jewish People*, 1–92.

Leeman, S. "The New Torah Translation." *Jew Ed* 34 (Fall 1963): 51–62.

Licht, Jacob. *Story Telling in the Bible*. Jerusalem: The Magnes Press, The Hebrew University, 1978. 154 pp.

Margolis, M. J. *The Hebrew Scriptures in the Making*. Phila.: JPS, 1922.

Orlinsky, Harry W. *Understanding the Bible Through History and Archaeology*. N.Y.: Ktav, 1972. 292 pp.

Plaut, W. G. Gunther, Ed. *The Torah: A Modern Commentary.* N.Y.: UAHC, 1981. 1787 pp.

Weinstein, Jacob J. *The Place of Understanding: Comments on Portions of the Week and Holiday Cycle.* N.Y.: Bloch, 1959. 181 pp.

TEACHING THE BIBLE PRIOR TO 1950

Anspacher, Abraham S. "Archaeological Research In Bible Lands." A paper written principally with the needs of Sabbath School teachers in mind. *CCAR* 23 (1913): 362–82.

*Bemnion, Adam Samuel. *An Objective Determination of Materials for a Course of Study in Biblical Literature.* U. of California, 1924.

Chomsky, William. "The Problem of Bible Teaching in Our Hebrew Curriculum." *Jew Ed* 10 (June 1938): 85–90.

Downing, William L. "The Bible in Education, Considered Historically and Constructively." Master's thesis, Texas U., 1927.

Eisenberg, Israel (Azriel). "Planning a Lesson in Biblical Literature." *Jew Teach* 1 (Mar. 1933): 16–23.

———. "Teaching the Bible." *Jew Teach* 9 (Jan. 1941): 1–16.

Etan, Israel. "בינה במקרא.," (Understanding the Bible) *Sh Hah* (H.): vol. 1 (1925–26)—1:25–28, 2:25–30, 4:32–36; vol. 2 (1927)—3:38–42, 5:50–56; vol. 3 (1927) 2:111–18; vol. 4 (1928–29) 1:33–36, 5:247–51.

* Fineberg, Solomon Andhill. *Biblical Myth and Legend in Jewish Education: The Presentation of Biblical Myths and Legends in Books for Jewish Religious Schools.* Columbia U., 1932. 150 pp. Published by Behrman, 1932.

Frisch, Ephraim. "The Use of the Bible as a Textbook in the Religious Schools." *CCAR* 24 (1914): 343–45.

Gamoran, Emanuel. "Problems in the Teaching of Bible." *Jew Teach* 2 (Jan. 1933).

Gordon, Miriam. "Ethical Values in the Creation." *Jew Teach* 16 (June 1948): 1–8.

Gordon, Sh. L. "לשאלת למוד התנך בבית הספר." (Concerning the Question of Teaching the Bible in the School) *Sh Hah* (H.) 1 (1926): 28–38.

Hoffman, Meinrod L. "Educational Values of the Psalms." Master's thesis, Notre Dame U., 1930.

Kaplan, Louis L. "A New Approach to the Teaching of Humosh." *Jew Ed* 15 (Jan. 1944): 85–89.

Kaplan, Mordecai M. "הוראת התנ״ך בזמננו,, (Teaching of the Bible in Our Times). *Yesod* (H.), 48–75.

———. "A New Educational Approach to the Teaching of the Bible." *FAJ*, 447–68.

Kohn, Eugene. "How to Teach Biblical History." *Jew Teach* 21 (Apr. 1918): 4–8.

Kornfeld, Joseph S. "Our Biblical Histories." *CCAR* 19 (1909): 353–87.

Landesman, Alter Y. "Bible." *A Curriculum for Religious Schools.* (1922): 71–89.

Lucia, Sister. "Curriculum Possibilities of the Literature of the Old Testament" Master's thesis, U. of Cincinnati, 1929.

Melconian, Vartin. "The Pedagogy of the Pentateuch, with Special Reference to Moses as an Educational Leader." Master's thesis, New York U., 1927.

Rosenthal, Ira A., and Joel Zion. "Unit on the Prophets," *Jew Teach* 16 (Nov. 1947): 13–18.

* Roskies, Diana K. *Folklore and Myths as Resource Material in Early Education Curricula: A Case Study in Bible Education.* Harvard U., 1973.

Scharfstein, Zevi. "תנ״ך היסטוריה וספרי למוד.,, (Bible History and Textbooks) *Hadoar* (H.) 40 (1st of Elul 1925).

———. "על הוראת המקרא.,," (On Teaching the Bible) *Sh Hah* (H.) 4 (1929): 219–32.

———. "Traditional Versus Historical Approach in the Teaching of the Bible," trans. from the Hebrew by E. A. Nudelman and I. B. Rappoport. *Jew Ed* 2 (Jan. 1930): 4–15.

———. "המטרה הוראת התנ״ך.,, (The Goal in Teaching the Bible). In דרכי למוד התנ״ך. (*Methods of Teaching the Bible*) (H.), 11–33. N.Y.: JTI and JTSA, 1934.

Schechter, Solomon. "The Study of the Bible." In *Studies in Judaism*, 31–54. Phila.: JPS, 1908.

Schechtman, Aaron. "The Teaching of the Bible in the Three Year Congregational School." Master's thesis, Northwestern U., 1932.

Silverstone, Leslie. *Listening to the Voices of the Women in the Bible: A Ten Lesson Unit for High School Students*. L.A.: HUC–JIR, Tartak Learning Center, 1986.

Whiteman, Kalmen. "הוראת החומש" (Teaching the Pentateuch). *Sh Hah* (H.) 2 (1927): 31–38.

TEACHING THE BIBLE SINCE 1950

Ackerman, Walter I. "Bible Instruction in Conservative Congregational Schools." Part I, "Bible Instruction" *of NICD*.

Adar, Zvi. "הוראת התנ״ך בגולה" (Teaching the Bible in the Diaspora). *FPDE* (H.), 75–79.

Aphek, Edna, and Diane Romm. "The Bible and Independent Study." *Ped Rep* 30 (Spring 1979): 23–25.

Bamberger, Bernard J. "Concerning Prophetic Judaism." *Jew Teach* 31 (Apr. 1963): 5–7.

Bellin, H. "The Cognitive Basis for Development of Cognitive Concepts." In *NICD*, 22–30.

Blank, Sheldon. "What Do We Want Our Children to Know About the Bible?" *Jew Teach* 28 (Mar. 1960): 15–19.

Bogot, Howard. "Hi-Ways to the Bible: The Poetry of Children's Literature." *Ped Rep* 23 (Mar. 1972): 17.

Borowitz, Eugene B. "Theological Problems in Teaching the Bible." *Jew Teach* 29 (Apr. 1961): 10–15.

Brauner, Ronald A. "The Bible and the High School Student." *Syn Sch* 34 (Spring 1976): 36–45.

———. "Values in the Bible." *Ped Rep* 30 (Spring 1979): 2–5.

Brill, Sheraga F. "התרגילים לחומש—תועלתם וחסרונותיהם" (The Exercises for the Pentateuch—Their Advantage and Shortcomings). *Sh Hah* (H.) 26 (Fall 1966): 18–23.

Brown, Samuel Wolfe. "The Book of Genesis: An Affective and Cognitive Experience." Master's thesis, HUC–JIR, 1973.

Chomsky, William. "Melton Approach to Teaching the Bible." *Recon* 33 (1967): 22–25.

Cohen Jack J. "The Bible for Children." (Symposium—"The Use of the Bible in Religious Education") *Rel Ed* 52 (Jan.–Feb. 1957).

———. "The Bible for Children." *Ped Rep* 8 (May 1957).

———. "The Bible." In *JEDS*, 177–87.

Cohen, Judy R. "Noah's Ark." *Compass* 10 (Spring/Summer 1988): 8–9.

Cole, Bruce K. "Teaching the Bible Through Archaeology." *Ped Rep* 15 (Sept. 1963).

Colodner, Solomon. *Concepts and Values: On Weekly Torah Portions*. N.Y.: Shangold, 1969. 140 pp.

Divinsky, Oscar. "Teaching the Bible in English to Adolescents." *Syn Sch* 16 (Mar. 1958): 16–18.

Edelstein, Menachem M. "הכנה ללמוד החומש" (Preparation of Teaching the Pentateuch). *Sh Hah* (H.) 19 (May 1950): 165–71.

Fishman, Joshua A. "How Safe is Psychoanalysis?" (On "selecting" Biblical stories for children) *Jew Ed* 23 (Winter 1952): 45–48.

Fraenkel, Mira. "On The Teaching of the Book of Job." *Ped Rep* 30 (Spring 1979): 3.

Frost, Shimon. "Hidon, Ha-Tanakh (The Bible Quiz)—An Enrichment Program Opportunity." *Syn Sch* 21 (Feb. 1963).

Gamoran, Emanuel. "Teaching the Bible as Literature." *Jew Teach* 33 (Oct. 1964): 3–6.

Gertman, Stuart A. "Bible in the Primary School." *CCAR J* 22 (Spring 1975): 59–63.

Gevirtz, Stanley. "Humanism in the Bible." NATE 19th Annual Conference (1973), 16–22.

Ginsburg, Lenore. "We Study About Abraham and God." *Jew Teach* 26 (Jan. 1958): 11.

Goitein, Sh. D. "לימוד התנ״ך בחינוך היהודי בגולה" (Study of the Bible in Jewish Education in the Diaspora). *FPDE* (H.), 64–74.

Gold, Manuel. "Digging the Bible." *Ped Rep* 30 (Spring 1979): 6–8.

———. "Violence in the Bible: Guidelines for the Classroom." *Compass* 9 (Winter 1987): 6–7.

Greenberg, Moshe. "On Teaching the Bible in Religious Schools." *Jew Ed* 29 (Spring 1959): 45–53. Also in *MJET*, 79–88.

Greenberg, Shlomo. „הוראת החומש לתלמידים לפני גיל בר-מצוה" (Teaching the Pentateuch to Students before Bar Mitzvah Age). *Sh Hah* (H.) 25 (Fall 1965).

———. "Bible Study and the Conservative School." In *NICD*, 2–21.

Grossman, Barney. "Family Life and the Bible Stories." *Jew Teach* 22 (Nov. 1953): 4–7.

Halevi, Mordecai. „להוראת החומש למתחילים" (On Teaching the Pentateuch to Beginners). *Sh Hah* (H.) 10 (Sept. 1950): 249–54.

Hammer, Robert Alan. "Teaching the Bible Honestly." *Recon* (Feb. 25, 1962): 16–20. Also in *Ped Rep* 13 (May 1962).

Henkin, Anne D. "On Teaching the Humash." *Syn Sch* 22 (Summer 1964).

Herman, Menahem. "Trope Instruction." *Ped Rep* 34 (Jan. 1988): 33–34.

Hyman, Frieda Clark. "A Humash Siyum Project." *Syn Sch* 16 (Mar. 1958): 22–27.

Isseroff, Sampson. "Humash Workbooks." *Ped Rep* 30 (Spring 1979): 31–32.

Levin, Nancy Prager. "Strategies for Teaching Bible: A Three-Part Series of In-Service Workshops for Teachers." A presentation of three in-service workshops for teachers designed to enhance their professional growth and development in the techniques for teaching Bible. Master's project, HUC–JIR, 1980.

Lewittes, Mordecai H. "Hagigat B'Reishit." *Syn Sch* 12 (Feb. 1954): 21–23.

Matt, Hershel. "Miracle and B'rakhah: How Shall We Approach the Miracles of the Bible?" *Syn Sch* 22 (1964).

* Millburn, Ronald R. *Old Testament Scripture Learning Using Pictorial Mnemonic Associations*. Brigham Young U., 1980.

Nattiv, Rachel. "Bible Instruction in the State of Israel: Its Relevance for American Reform Jewish Education." Master's thesis, HUC–JIR, 1966.

Newman, Shirley. "Teaching the Bible in the Early Grades." *Ped Rep* 30 (Spring 1979): 9–12.

Pesselnick, Ruth. "Puppets as Visual Aids in Teaching Bible Stories." *Syn Sch* 16 (Mar. 1956): 22–23.

Pollak, George. "The Portion of the Week." *Ped Rep* 30 (Spring 1979): 17–18.

Radzik, Avraham. "The Bible and Creative Dramatics." *Ped Rep* 30 (Spring 1979): 33–34.

Ray, Natalie. "The Bible Through Media." *Ped Rep* 30 (Spring 1979): 15–16.

Revitch, Eugene. "How Dangerous Is the Apple?" (On psychological interpretations of Bible stories for children). *Jew Ed* 23 (Winter1952): 43–44.

Shifman, M. „ספרים ללמוד החומש באמריקה" (Texts for the Study of the Pentateuch in America). *Sh Hah* (H.) 14 (Apr. 1954): 180–90.

Silberman, Shoshana. "Seeds: A Thematic Approach to Biblical Study." *Compass* 1 (Winter 1977): 10–11.

Slesinger, Zalmen. "Observations on the Teaching of Bible." *Ped Rep* (Jan. 1958).

Spiro, Jack D. "The Bible—A Jewish Book." *Ped Rep* 19 (Dec. 1967): 13.

Spotts, Leon H. "Teaching Bible to Children of Eleven and Twelve." *Syn Sch* 16 (Mar. 1958): 8–15.

Weilerstein, Sadie Rose. "Teaching Bible to Children of Seven to Ten." *Syn Sch* 16 (Mar. 1958): 3–7.

Weintraub, Simkha. "Ah-Kay-Dah: A Midrash Making Experience." *MJ* 13 (Winter 1982): 5–6.

Werb, Sherry. "Towards an Approach to Bible Teaching in the Afternoon Elementary Hebrew School. Master's thesis, Brandeis U., 1970.

Wohl A. Z. „הוראת חומש למתחילים" (Teaching the Pentateuch to Beginners) *Sh Hah* (H.) 10 (Mar. 1950): 92–98.

Zeldner, Max. *Bible Teaching*. N.Y.: AAJE, 1960.

Zelenitz, Alan N. "The Bible in a Literature Class." *Ped Rep* 30 (Spring 1979): 13–15.

Zeligs, Dorothy F. "Psychological Factors in the Teaching of Bible Stories." *Jew Ed* 22 (Summer 1951): 24–28.

Zielenger, Ruth. "The Melton Approach to Teaching the Bible." *Ped Rep* 30 (Spring 1979): 26–27.

TEXTBOOKS AND GUIDES FOR TEACHERS PRIOR TO 1950

Alper, Michael. *The Bible Retold, with Notes, Maps, and Illustrations*. N.Y.: Behrman, ca. 1930, 336 pp.

Altman, Addie R. *Jewish Child's Bible Stories*. N.Y., 1926

———. *God's Agent, The Prophets and Other Biblical Tales*. 1926.

Bildersee, A. *Out of the House of Bondage*. Cincinnati: UAHC, 1925.

———. *The Story of Genesis*. N.Y.: UAHC, 1927.

Calisch, Edith L. *Bible Tales for the Very Young*. N.Y.: Behrman, 1930.

Cohen, Lenore. *Bible Tales for Very Young Children*. Cincinnati: UAHC, (vol. 1) 1934, 189 pp; (vol. 2) 1936, 231 pp.

Cohen, Mortimer J. *Pathways Through the Bible*. Phila.: JPS, 1946.

Comins, Harry L. *Teaching the Prophets*. Cincinnati: UAHC, 1936.

Cone, Molly. *Who Knows Ten? Children's Tales on the Ten Commandments*. N.Y.: UAHC, 1966. Grades 1–3.

Eisenberg, Azriel. *Into the Promised Land—A Teacher's Guide for the Period from Joshua to Solomon*. Cincinnati: UAHC, 1936.

———. *With Singer and Sage—A Teacher's Guide for the Teaching of the Writings*. N.Y.: UAHC, 1940.

Fox, Ethel. *Bible Primer for Tiny Tots*. N.Y.: Bloch, 1930. 102 pp.

Freehof, Solomon B. *Psalms*. N.Y.: UAHC, 1938.

Frishberg, I. Z. "ראשית למוד בחומש„ (*Beginning the Study of the* Pentateuch) (H.). 2 vols. N.Y.: Mashmer, 1923–24.

Gamoran, Emanuel. *Methods of Teaching the Bible*. N.Y.: UAHC, 1948. 44 pp.

Gamoran, Mamie. *The Voice of the Prophets*. Cincinnati: DSSE and UAHC, 1930. 240 pp.

———, Selector and Arranger. *With Singer and Sage*. Cincinnati: DSSE and UAHC, 1930. 369 pp.

Ish-Kishor, Sulamith. *The Children's Story of the Bible A Bible History for School and Home*. N.Y.: Educational Stationery House, 1930. 191 pp.

Kohn, Eugene. *A Manual for Teaching Biblical History*. N.Y.: USA, 1917. 220 pp.

Landman, I. *The Story of the Prophets*. Cincinnati, 1912.

Lehman, Eugene H. *The Jewish Teacher*. Series III, An aid for teaching the Bible. N.Y.: Bloch, 1915, 1923. 294 pp.

Magil, Joseph. *Linear School Bible*. N.Y.: Hebrew Pub. Co., 1905.

Polak, I. Ch. חומש לתלמידים (*The Pentateuch for Students—Genesis*) (H.). N.Y.: Hebrew Pub. Co., 1934.

Reizenstein, Jennie. *Biblical History for Jewish Religious Schools*. Baltimore: Warwick, York, 1925. 338 pp.

Scharfstein, Zevi. חומש למתחילים—בראשית (*Pentateuch for Beginners—Genesis*) (H.). N.Y.: Shiloh, 1933. 141 pp.

———. ספורי התורה צם ציורים (*Bible Tales with Illustrations* (H.). 3 vols. N.Y.: Shiloh, 1944.

———. עזר ללמוד החומש לתלמידים (*An Aid for the Study of the Pentateuch*) (H.). N.Y.: Shiloh, 1938. 48 pp.

Singer, Richard. *If the Prophets Were Alive Today*. N.Y.: Bookman, 1937.

Weingarten, J. *Torah Lemat'hilim* (H.). 2 vols. N.Y.

Whiteman, Kalmen. *Hadrakha B'horaat Hahumash (A Guide for Teaching the Pentateuch)* (H.). N.Y.: JEC, 1946.

Zaretski, Samuel. *In the Land of Kings and Prophets—A Teacher's Book*. N.Y.: UAHC, 1938.

Zeligs, Dorothy F. *The Story Bible: Together with Tales from the Midrash*. N.Y.: Behrman, 1949. 192 pp.

6 TEXTBOOKS, WORKBOOKS, AND GUIDES SINCE 1950

Efron, Benjamin. *The Message of the Torah*. N.Y.: Ktav, 1963. 152 pp.

Fischman, Joyce. *Bible Work and Play*. Illustrated by Heidi Steinberger. Rev. ed. 2 vols. N.Y.: UAHC, 1984. For the early grades.

Freehof, Lillian S. *The Bible Legend Book* and *The Second Bible Legend Book*. N.Y.: UAHC, 1952.

Freehof, Solomon B. *Prefact to Scripture*. N.Y.: UAHC, 1950.

Goodman, Hannah Grad. *The Story of Prophecy*, edited by E. B. Borowitz. N.Y.: Behrman.

Hollender, Betty Rosett. *Bible Stories for Little Children*. Rev. ed. 3 vols. N.Y.: UAHC, 1985. Grades 1–3.

Keeping Posted. *The Prophets*. Mini-Course, #840800, Leader Edition, #840802.

Levinger, Elma Ehrlich. *Wonder Tales of Bible Days: Legends Retold for Jewish Children*. Phila.: JPS, 1929. 348 pp.

Levitin, Miriam. *Workbook* (3 parts) for M. J. Cohen's *Pathways Through the Bible*. Phila.: JPS, 1956.

Liebert, Sarah L. *Stories from Hebrew Scriptures: A Collection of Biblical and Talmudic Tales*. N.Y.: Bloch, 1930. 68 pp.

Lewittes, Mordecai H., ed. *The Student Bible* (H.). 3 vols. N.Y.: Hebrew Pub. Co., c. 1950–62.

Loeb, Sorel Goldberg, and Barbara Binder Kadden. *Teaching Torah: A Treasury of Insights and Activities*. Denver: ARE, 1984.

Malofsky, Lyn. *Prophets and Prophecy—A Unit of Study*. A ten-lesson unit for the eighth grade. L.A: HUC–JIR, Tartak Learning Center, 1988.

Newman, Shirley. *A Child's Introduction to Torah*, edited by L. Newman. Workbooks by Stephen Kraft. Teacher's Guide by L. Newman with explanation of Melton Method. N.Y.: Behrman, ca. 1985. Primary Grades.

———. *A Child's Introduction to the Early Prophets*, edited by Louis Newman. Teacher's Guide by Shirley Newman. Workbooks by Anye Rosenberg. N.Y.: Behrman, 1972. Primary Grades.

———. *An Introduction to Kings*, edited by L. Newman. Workbook by Morris J. Sugarman. Teacher's Guide by Shirley Newman. N.Y.: Behrman. Primary Grades.

Orenstein, Walter, and Hertz Frankel. *Torah and Tradition: A Bible Textbook for Jewish Youth*. 2 vols. N.Y.: Hebrew Pub. Co., 1967.

Orleans, Ilo. *The First Rainbow*. N.Y.: UAHC, 1954. 72 pp. Primary Grades.

Sarna, Nahum M. *Understanding Genesis*. Teacher and Student Guide by Louis Newman et al. N.Y.: JPS. (For "Advanced" Students.)

———. *Exploring Exodus: The Heritage of Biblical Israel*. N.Y.: Schocken, 1986.

Schwartzman, Sylvan, and Jack Spiro. *The Living Bible: A Topical Approach to the Jewish Scriptures*. N.Y.: UAHC, 1962.

Silverman, Althea. *Behold My Messengers*. N.Y.: Bloch, 1955. 248 pp.

Simms, Laura et al. *Exploring Our Living Past*. Student Packet, Teacher's Guide, and Recording. N.Y.: Behrman. K through Primary Grades.

Zielenger, Ruth. *Bible*, edited by B. W. Holtz. 2d ed. Curriculum Supervisor, Seymour Fox. Level Dalet (4), *Genesis: A New Student Workbook* (3 booklets) Teacher's Edition. N.Y.: Melton Research Center and JTS, 1982. 215 pp.

———. *Genesis: A New Teacher's Guide*. Level Dalet. 2d ed. Edited by B. W. Holtz. Curriculum Supervisor, Seymour Fox. N.Y.: Melton Research Center and JTS, 1982. 473 pp.

———. *Bible*. Level He (5). Edited by B. W. Holtz. Curriculum Supervisor, Seymour Fox. *Exodus: A Teacher's Guide*. N.Y.: Melton Research Center and JTS, 1984. 367 pp. Experimental Edition.

GLEANINGS

Heine, Heinrich,

> "The Jews... trudged around with it [the Bible] all through the Middle Ages as with a portable fatherland." (1854)

Joseph L. Baron, *A Treasury of Jewish Quotations*, 27.

Schechter, Solomon,
"The Bible is our patent of Nobility" (1903)
Joseph L. Baron, *A Treasury of Jewish Quotations*, 27.

Rosenzweig, Franz,
"The Bible is a parable of a man's advance to the family, to the tribe, to a nation with a national ideal, to a nation with a universal ideal." (1906)
Joseph L. Baron, *A Treasury of Jewish Quotations*, 30.

Jacobs, Joseph,
"If it be true, as it obviously is, that the Bible is a creation of the Jews, it is also true, though not so obvious, that the Jews are the creation of the Bible."
Jewish Contribution to Civilization (1919), 63.

Zhitlovsky, Hayyim,
"The more critically and humanly we consider the Bible, the greater the merit of the people that produced it." (1922)
Baron, Joseph L., *Treasury of Jewish Quotations*, 30.

Gamoran, Emanuel,
"It seems to me that we can best understand the singular devotion with which the Bible has been held in Jewish life if we realize that while the many universalistic elements that enter into it have made it the book of the world, par excellence, yet in our history, it has become so keenly associated with our people, with our life, with our survival, that it is for us one of our chief survival, as well as humanistic values. In other words, we teach the Bible primarily not because it is a great book, not because it is a good book, but because it is our great book! Other people may teach it because it is good from a moral point of view. We, realizing both of these qualities, teach it because it is ours, because it has been associated with our life and with our people and with our history."
Jew Teach 2 (1933), and *Jew Ed* 34 (Winter 1964), 103.

Union of Orthodox Jewish Congregations
"In studying the Bible, children should be impressed with the idea that merely understanding it and remembering its contents are not enough, that the form itself is sacred and that verses should be memorized as far as possible." (1942)
A Model Program for the Talmud Torah, UOJC, 1942. Quoted in *Jew Ed* 15 (Jan. 1944), 105.

Zeligs, Dorothy F.,
"Certain biblical stories, namely those at the beginning of Genesis, the Creation stories and the ones immediately following, are not suitable for young children. It is preferable to teach them at a later age, about twelve or over. On the other hand, the stories beginning with Abraham and continuing through the life of Solomon, which might be termed the heroic period of early Jewish history, contain elements which make them particularly suited for children from the age of seven to ten or eleven."
Jew Ed 22 (Summer 1951), 24.

Revitch, Eugene,
"Strict adherence to any school of thought in raising a child only indicates insecurity on the part of the parent, and instead of helping the child it only strains the child-parent relationship. It is not so important what to tell a child, or what to do for him, as to how it is told and how it's done. A little child raised in a healthy atmosphere can be told the story of creation without harm, whereas a child raised in an unhealthy environment will not develop into an emotionally healthy human being whether he was or was not taught the story of the apple in paradise. The danger does not lie in the apple."
Jew Ed 23 (Winter 1952), 44.

Fishman, Joshua A.,
"How seriously . . . should we want our children to take the supernatural aspects of the Bible? The answer is—just as seriously as we ourselves take them. It would be a mistake for a parent or a teacher who does not himself believe in a literal interpretation of certain passages to teach these passages in such a manner as to lead the child to interpret them literally. It is not any discrepancy between faith and science that disillusions our children. It is the discrepancy between

the professed and the observed or practiced faith of those adults (parents, teachers and clergy) whom they set up as models. Dr. Mordecai M. Kaplan has stated that a major plague of Jewish education is that things are taught which neither the parent believes, nor the teacher believes, nor the child believes, but everybody keeps quiet about them."

Jew Ed 23 (Winter 1952), 45–46.

Goldman, Solomon,

"The Bible inspired authors unfolded their theme of themes in language as fluent and popular, as vivid and near to the comprehension of the senses as they did with all other ideas. They wrote history instead of theology or philosophy, and dramatized the destiny of all mankind in the career of a people, in a manner which across the centuries engages the uncultivated imagination of the common man as much as the subtle wit of the philosopher."

Samuel Caplan and Harold U. Ribalow, *The Great Jewish Books and Their Influence on History*, 22–23.

Kaplan, Mordecai M.,

"A radically different role ... was assumed by Torah during the greater part of the Second Commonwealth era. By that time it came to be identified with the written Pentateuch, or the Torah of Moses. As such, it was no longer the monopoly of the priests, but came to be gradually accessible to the people. Reading from it became an established practice throughout the land. It satisfied the spiritual craving to know what God would have His People do."

Questions Jews Ask, 380–81.

Albright, William F.,

"Aside from a few die-hards among older scholars, there is scarcely a single biblical historian who has not been impressed by the rapid accumulation of data supporting substantially the historicity of patriarchal tradition."

The Jews, 1:3.

Gordis, Robert,

"What is the significance of the Bible for the modern age? On the most obvious level, the Bible is literature. Within its covers repose some of the world's greatest masterpieces in poetry and prose.... But the importance of the Bible goes deeper. It is an indispensible element in the religious and moral education of the human race."

The Jews, 1:788.

Greenberg, Moshe,

"The object of teaching the Bible in a religious school is, I submit to make the student aware of the spiritual issues raised by the Bible and to delineate the manner in which these issues are answered or otherwise dealt with....

In order to carry out his duty the teacher is not required to assent personally to the answers given by the Bible, or to the manner in which it deals with the issues it raises. He may have a different viewpoint. This does not disqualify him from teaching. For the basic requirement of a Bible teacher is not faith, but understanding; not assent, but recognition of the profound issues of which the Bible treats."

Weinstein and Yizhar, eds. *Modern Jewish Educational Thought*, 79.

Zielenger, Ruth,
"Introduction To Teaching Bible"

"Two considerations underlie our approach to teaching Bible and must be mentioned at the outset:

A) Do not teach anything to your students that they will have to unlearn later, e.g., false information which will have to be discarded at some later date.

B) Do not "tell" or present your information if they can find this information by themselves when directed to the proper texts. Information which is "discovered" first hand by a student will be better understood and remembered than information presented by the teacher.

In our experience, the most effective way of learning Bible is through a careful analysis of a text, taught by means of a guided discussion or an 'inquiry.'"

Ruth Zielenger, *Genesis: A New Teacher's Guide*, 1.

Rothschild, Fritz A.,
"Truth and Metaphor in the Bible"

"If we believe that God's message is to be found in Scripture, we can expect that basic motifs, metaphors and paradigmatic tales contain guidance ("Torah") for all ages, and it becomes our duty to delve into their implications with reverence and seriousness.

On the same assumption, however, the timeless message can never be read through the spectacles of our great-grandparents. It becomes our duty and challenge to do what previous generations have done: to focus upon the sacred text the fullest light of knowledge at our disposal."

Ruth Zielenger, *Genesis: A New Teacher's Guide*, 451–52.

7 EARLY CHILDHOOD EDUCATION

PRIOR TO 1950

Chipkin, Israel S. "Pre-School Education." *RA* (1946): 167–69.

Cohen, Esther. "Jewish Education in the Primary Grades." *Jew Teach* 6 (Nov. 1937): 14–15.

Comins, Harry L. "Motivating a Holiday Curriculum for the Pre-Reading Grades." *Jew Ed* 3 (Apr.–June 1931): 77.

Folkman, Jerome D. "The Pre-School Mothers' Club." *Jew Teach* 14 (June 1946): 30–31.

Frank, Evelyn W. "Creative Work in the Primary Grades." *Jew Teach* 14 (June 1946): 26–29.

Gamoran, Emanuel. "Reaching the Pre-school Child." *Jew Teach* 4 (June 1936): 1–4.

Golub, Jacob S. "A Curriculum for the Primary Grades." *Jew Ed* 3 (Jan.–Mar. 1931): 49–55.

Hart, Elizabeth J., and Betty Furth Marx. "A Jewish Nursery School." *Jew Teach* 15 (Nov. 1946): 29–33.

Jacobs, Ella. *Methods of Teaching Primary Grades*. Course A (192 pp) and B (214 pp). Correspondence School for Religious School Teachers conducted by the Chautauqua Society. Phila., 1914.

Rips, Mrs. A. S. "The Enlarged Cradle Roll." *Jew Teach* 8 (Apr. 1940): 12–15.

Rosewater, Adeline R. "Songs and Games for the Primary Department." *Jew Teach* 4 (Apr. 1936): 24–30; 5 (Jan. 1937): 6–13; 6 (Nov. 1937): 6–13.

Rossel, Karen Trager. "The Development of Reform Religious School Materials for the Five-Year Old." Master's thesis, HUC–JIR, 1977.

Satlowe, Lewis, and Rose Skoble. "The Use of Supplementary Reading in Classroom Instruction." (Primary) *Jew Teach* 8 (Apr. 1940): 6–11.

Touroff, Nissan. "היסוד לבניין,, (The Foundation for the Edifice) On the Kindergarten. *Hadoar* (H.). 2:100, 26th of Shevat, 1922.

Whiteman, Kalman. "החנוך העברי לקטנים,, (Hebrew Education for Young Children). *Hadoar* (H.) 25 (Dec. 7, 1945): 105.

ARTICLES, MANUALS, AND BOOKS SINCE 1950

Abramovitz, Hayim. "Teaching Hebrew in the Kindergarten Through Nursery Rhymes." Master's thesis, Yeshiva U., 1954.

*———. *Hebrew Language Arts Instruction in Early Childhood*. Yeshiva U., 1965. 311 pp.

Averbach, Moshe. "תינוקות של בית רבן,, (Young School Children) (H. and E.) *Ped Rep* 31 (Spring 1980): 32–34.

Barnett, Sara. "An Early Childhood Activity Approach." COMPASS, 2 (Fall–Winter 1978): 18–19.

Behar, Rivka, and Faye Reichwald. "Jewish Values and Prayer in Early Childhood Education." *Ped Rep* 31 (Spring 1980): 7–8.

Bernstein, Bennie. "Bible and Music: A Sample Curriculum for Primary Grades." A sample curriculum for the primary grades utilizing music as a vehicle for the teaching of Biblical personalities and concepts; to be used as a supplement to an established text. Master's project, HUC–JIR, 1976.

———. "An Introduction to Bible Curriculum Using Music for Grades Kindergarten, First, and Second." An introduction to a primary curriculum which introduces Biblical personalities and concepts through music. Utilizes both established music and music composition. Master's project, HUC–JIR, 1975.

Biber, Barbara. "Nursery School as the Beginning of Education." *Ped Rep* 2 (Mar. 1952).

Bogot, Howard I. "The Rabbi and Early Childhood Education." *Ped Rep* 31 (Spring 1980): 2–3.

Brown, Sheldon S. "Hebrew Reading Readiness for the Pre-Hebrew School Teacher and for Parents of the Very Young." *Jew Teach* (Oct. 1963): 14–15.

Bubis, Gerald B. "Value Building in the Preschool Years." *Ped Rep* 24 (Fall 1972): 3.

Chankin, Beatrice. "Parents and Children Go To Nursery School." *Ped Rep* 30 (Fall 1978): 27.

Chanover, Hyman. "A Program of Weekday Hebrew Education for Sixes and Sevens." *Syn Sch*, 9 (Jan. 1951): 3–7.

———. "The Case for the Foundation School." *Syn Sch* 11 (Apr. 1953): 3–9.

———. "Some Administrative Problems in Organizing a Foundation School." *Syn Sch* 13 (Sept. 1954): 7–23.

———. "Worship for Children of Primary Age." *Syn Sch* 15 (Dec. 1956): 3–11.

———. "The Three-Fold Challenge of Early Childhood Education." *Syn Sch* 17 (June 1959): 19–26.

———. "Guidelines for the Primary Classroom." *Syn Sch* 18 (June 1960): 10–14.

Chernoff, Shulamith S. "Jewish Orientation in the Nursery School Program." *Jew Ed* 22 (Winter–Spring 1951): 40–43.

Chipkin, Israel S. "Jewish Education in Early Childhood." *Cong W* (Mar. 22, 1954): 6–8.

Cohen, Floreva. "Comment on Hebrew Language Instruction in the Kindergarten." *Jew Ed* 46 (Spring 1978): 52–53.

Cohen, Floreva, and Ruth Musnikow. "Trends in Jewish Early Childhood Education." *Jew Ed* 50 (Summer 1982): 29–31, 45.

Cohen, H. Hirsch. "A Systematic and Comparative Investigation of the Nursery School as a Method for Reform Jewish Instruction." Master's thesis, HUC–JIR, 1952.

Colton, Lawrence M. *Towards Primary Text on Life*. HUC–JIR, 1967.

Drasin, Mrs. Samuel. "Story Telling for Young Children." *Syn Sch* 17 (Dec. 1958).

Feinberg, Miriam. "Teaching Cooperation in the Jewish PreSchool." *Ped Rep* 35 (Mar. 1984): 12–16.

Feldman, Estelle, Ellen Rosen, and Ruth Wortman. "Creating a Nursery School." *Syn Sch* 17 (Dec. 1958).

Freidenreich, Fradle. "Idea Forum: Jewish Programming in the Pre-School." *Ped Rep* 24 (Fall 1972): 11.

Gelbart, Frances S. "An Experiment in Case Work Service in a Pre-School Program." *Jew Ed* 28, (Winter 1958): 42–48, 60.

Gertman, Stuart A. "Bible in the Primary School." *CCAR J* 22 (Spring 1975): 59–63.

Ginsberg, Marvell. "The Parent and Early Childhood Education." *Ped Rep* 31 (Spring 1980): 20–27.

———. "An Approach to Early Childhood Jewish Education." *Rel Ed* 68 (Mar.–Apr. 1973): 282–83.

———. "What Makes Early Childhood Education Jewish?" *AM* (Spring 1978).

———. "The Right of the Jewish Child to Be Jewish." *Rel Ed* 74 (May–June 1979): 287–94.

Green, Kathy. "Jewish Early Childhood Education," A new curricular "vision." *Melton Research Center Journal*, 12 (Spring 1981): 3, 20.

7 EARLY CHILDHOOD EDUCATION

* Gross, Morris B. *Exploration of the Differences in Pre-School Learning Readiness and Concomitant Differences in Certain Cultural Attitudes Between Two Subcultural Jewish Groups*. Columbia U., 1966. 149 pp.

Grunwald, Emily. "Teaching Three and Four-Year-Olds." *Ped Rep* 31 (Spring 1980): 11–12.

Harris, Hannah. "The Function of a Hebrew Kindergarten." *Ped Rep* 2 (Jan. 1951).

Havivi, Mrs. Moshe. "A Sabbath Unit for the First Grade." *Syn Sch* 10 (Sept. 1951): 10–15.

Institute for Jewish Life. *Why Didn't We Do This Before?* Changing the Jewish Pre-School. IJL, *Project Report* (Sept. 1975). 26 pp.

"Jewish Education: The Early Years." *Ped Rep* 24 (Fall 1972).

"The Jewish Foundation School: Some Questions and Answers." *Syn Sch* 10 (Apr. 1952): 25–27.

Kadden, Barbara Binder. *Jewish* Communities around the World. A series of learning packets for kindergarten through first grade focusing on the theme of Jewish families around the world. Master's project, HUC–JIR, 1979.

Karner, Alvin. "Passover." A unit of three lesson plans for use in the kindergarten and primary grades. *Jew Teach* 4 (Jan. 1936): 10–27.

Kassof, Marvin. "The Mekhinah Program." Orientation or Preparation Program (H.). *Ped Rep* 31 (Spring 1980): 18–19.

Katz, Betty. "Creating Materials for Early Childhood Classes." *Ped Rep* 31 (Spring 1980): 13–15.

Katzoff, Adina. "The Physical Aspect of the Nursery." *Syn Sch* 11 (Nov. 1952): 7–12.

———. "The Bilingual Program in the Jewish Nursery School." *Jew Ed* 24 (Spring 1953): 44–48, 57.

Krause, Sherri. "Tu'Bishvat and Purim." *AM* (Winter 1978).

Kupinsky, B. Z. "Bilingual Reading Instruction in the Kindergarten." *The Reading Teacher* 37 (Nov. 1983): 132–37.

Levine, Baruch A. "An Experimental High Holy Day Service for Children Five to Eight." *Syn Sch* 12 (Apr. 1954): 15–18.

Linzer, Lila. "Cooking as an Integrating Subject in Early Childhood Education." *Ped Rep* 31 (Spring 1980): 15–17.

Livingstone, Nancy. "Bilingual Class for Preschoolers." *Ped Rep* 34 (Jan. 1983): 9–10.

———. "Values in a Jewish Preschool." *Ped Rep* 34 (Oct. 1983): 15–17.

Moskowitz, Sarah. "Feer Kashes (Four Questions) about Jewish Nursery Education." *Jew Ed* 41 (Winter 1972–73): 19–25, 37.

Musnikow, Ruth A. "First Steps." *Ped Rep* 31 (Spring 1980): 8–10.

Newman, Mrs. Louis (Shirley S.). "Providing Meaningful Experiences in Hebrew for the Four and Five Year Olds." *Syn Sch* 14 (Nov. 1955), 7–8. Also in *RTHE*, pp. 56–58.

———. "The Religious Foundations of the Young Child." *Syn Sch* 17 (Dec. 1958): 10–13.

Nowak, Nancy Cohen. "Developing a Jewish Preschool." *JPH*, pp. 405–19.

Parelis, Mrs. Maurice. "A Chanukoh Unit for the Primary Department." *Jew Teach* 6 (Nov. 1937): 1–5.

* Pinkenson, Ruth S. *The Impact of the Jewish Day Care Experience on Parental Jewish Identity*. Temple U., 1987.

Pomerantz, Hyman. "Certification of Early Jewish Childhood Education." *Ped Rep* 31 (Spring 1980): 35.

Preiss, Madeline. "Creating a Living Environment." *Ped Rep* 24 (Fall 1972): 7.

Raphaels, Rose. "Programming for Festivals with the Nursery Group." *Ped Rep* 3 (Jan. 1952).

Ravid, Ruth. "The Effect of Jewish Early Childhood Education on Jewish Home Practices." *Jew Ed* (Fall 1985): 12–15.

Ray, Natalie. "Shabbat Is a Different Kind of Day." A slide and tape presentation intended for children from ages three to six. Master's project, HUC–JIR, 1978.

Ribner, R. "The Bible, the Young Child, and the Kindergarten." *Syn Sch* 26 (Summer 1968): 13–20.

Rotenberg, Rena. "A Survey History of Jewish Early Childhood Education." Master's thesis, Peggy Meyerhoff Pearlstone School of Graduate Study, Baltimore Hebrew College. 1977.

———. "Holidays in the Nursery School." *Ped Rep* 32 (Sept. 1981): 2–5.

Ruffman, Louis L. "Developing a Daily Primary Department." *Syn Sch* 17 (June 1959): 43–47.

Salinger, Rosemarie D. "Elements of the Nursery School Program." *Syn Sch* 17 (Dec. 1958).

Salvay, Betty. "'Daddy and Me' at Sinai Temple." *Ped Rep* 31 (Spring 1980): 23–24.

Schafler, Samuel. "The Status of Early Childhood Education in Congregational Schools Today." *Syn Sch* 18 (June 1960).

Schram, Peninnah. "Storytelling: Role and Technique." *JTH* 2:79–93.

Schwartzman, Louis. "Pre-School Education as a Jewish Educational Force." *Jew Ed* 22 (Winter–Spring 1951): 43–44, 58.

Sklar, Samuel. "A Congregation for Primary School Children." *Syn Sch* 22 (Mar. 1964).

Sussman, Eva W. "What Is Beth Ha Gan?" *Syn Sch* 24 (Fall 1965).

Tarasow, Morris. "Primary Department Course of Study." *SWJT* (1977): 21–23.

Zafran, Estelle. "Story Telling in Jewish Early Childhood Education." *Ped Rep* 31 (Spring 1980): 29–30.

Zusman, Mrs. Morris. "Teaching Prayer to Children Four to Seven." *Syn Sch* 15 (Dec. 1956): 13–20.

LITERATURE FOR THE VERY YOUNG (SELECTED)

Adler, David. *The House on the Roof: A Sukkot Story*, N.Y.: Bonim: 1976.

Bearman, Jane. *The Eight Nights: A Chanukah Counting Book*. N.Y.: UAHC, Blum Publishing Fund, ca. 1980. Grades 1–3.

———. *Fun on Sukkos*. N.Y.: UAHC, 1946.

———. *Happy Chanuko*. N.Y.: UAHC, 1943.

———. *Passover Party*. N.Y.: UAHC, 1946.

———. *Purim Parade*. N.Y.: UAHC, 1947.

———. *Shavuos Time*. N.Y.: UAHC, 1947.

Bin-Nun, Judy, with Nancy Cooper and Ruth Sternfeld. *Pesach: A Holiday Funtext*. Illustrated by Heidi Steinberger. N.Y.: UAHC, 1983. Grades 1–3.

Bin-Nun, Judy, and Franne Einhorn. *Rosh HaShanah: A Holiday Fun-text*. Illustrated by Heidi Steinberger. N.Y.: UAHC, ca. 1980. 32 pp. Grades 1–3.

Bogot, Howard I. *Yoni*. Illustrated by Heidi Steinberger. N.Y.: UAHC, 1984.

Bogot, Howard I., and Daniel B. Syme. *Books Are Treasures*. N.Y.: UAHC, 1982.

———. *I'm Growing*. N.Y.: UAHC, ca. 1986.

———. *My Body Is Something* Special. N.Y.: UAHC, ca. 1982.

———. *Prayer Is Reaching*. N.Y.: UAHC, 1983. Preschool.

Brichto, Mira. *God around Us: A Child's Garden of Prayer*. N.Y.: UAHC, 1958. Grades 1–3.

Calisch, Edith Landman. *Fairy Tales from Grandfather's Big Book: Jewish Legends of Old Retold for Young People*. N.Y.: Behrman, 1938. 130 pp.

Cedarbaum, Sophia N. *Chanuko: The Festival of Light*. N.Y.: UAHC.

———. *A First Book of Jewish Holidays*. 8 vols. N.Y.: UAHC, 1984. Grades 1–2.

———. *Passover: The Festival of Freedom*. N.Y.: UAHC.

———. *Purim: A Joyous Holiday*. N.Y.: UAHC.

———. *Sabbath: A Day of Delight*. N.Y.: UAHC.

Chanover, Hyman. *Home Start* (Holidays). N.Y.: Behrman, 1985.

Chanover, Hyman, and Alice Chanover. *Happy Hanukah Everybody*. N.Y.: USCJE, 1954. For the very young.

———. *Pesah Is Coming*. N.Y.: USA, 1954.

———. *Pesah Is Here*. N.Y.: USA, 1954.

Charles, Fred. *The Mystery of the Missing Challah*. N.Y.: Jonathan David, 1959. Grades K–3.

Cone, Molly. *Hear, O Israel: The Shema Story Books: First Say the Shema; about Learning; about Belonging; about God*. 4 vols. Teacher's Guide by D. B. Syme for complete series. N.Y.: UAHC, 1971, 1982. Grades 1–3.

Eichenbaum, Sharon, Alice Goldin, and Michael Korman. *The Jewish Holidays: Fall and Spring Holidays*. N.Y.: Behrman, ca. 1985. Grades 1–2.

Fishman, Joyce. *Holiday Work and Play: A Workbook*. N.Y.: UAHC, 1981. Grades 1–3.

———. *Let's Learn about Jewish Symbols*. N.Y.: UAHC, 1983. Preschool and Primary.

Friedman, Audrey, and Raymond A. Zwerin. *Our Synagogue. Set A—The Synagogue; Set B—The Holy Days; Set C—Shabbat and Jewish Ideals*. Teacher's Guide. N.Y.: Behrman, ca. 1985. Grades K–1.

Garvey, Robert. *Good Shabbos Everybody*. N.Y.: USCJE, 1951, 1956. For young children.

———. *Let's Learn about Jewish Holidays: Discover, Explore, Play*. Teacher's Guide. N.Y.: Ktav, 1956.

Grand, Tamar. *Kindergarten Kit for the Jewish Child*. N.Y.: UAHC, 1957.

Greenberg, Barbara, and Herbert Greenberg. *The Sabbath Kit*. Teacher's Manual for the Sabbath. N.Y.: UAHC and USA, ca. 1971. Grades 1–3.

Hirsh, Marilyn. *One Little Goat: A Passover Song*. N.Y.: Holiday, 1979.

Marcus, Audrey Friedman, and Raymond A. Zwerin. *But This Night Is Different: A Seder Experience*. N.Y.: UAHC, Blum Publication Fund, 1981. 44 pp. Grades 1–3.

Miller, Deborah Uchill. *My Siddur: A Prayer Readiness Book*. N.Y.: Behrman, ca. 1985. Grades K-2.

Post, Lillian. *Children's Megillah*. Cincinnati: UAHC, 1950.

Schlein, Miriam. *Our Holidays*. 8 vols. N.Y.: Behrman, ca. 1986. Grades K-2.

Siegel, Daniel, and Allan Sugarman. *And God Braided Eve's Hair*. N.Y.: Department of Youth Activities, USA, 1976. 123 pp.

Simon, Norma. *Festival Series of Picture Story Books*. 10 vols. N.Y.: USA, 1959–61.

Syme, Deborah Shayne. *The Jewish Home Detectives*. N.Y.: UAHC, ca. 1986.

Weilerstein, Sadie Rose. *The Adventures of K'tonton, a Little Jewish Tom Thumb*. N.Y.: National Women's League of the USA, 1935. 100 pp.

Zwerin, Raymond A., and Audrey Friedman Marcus. *Shabbat Can Be*. N.Y.: UAHC, Blum Publication Fund, ca. 1982. Grades 1–3.

GUIDES, CURRICULA, AND MANUALS PRIOR TO 1950

Harris, Hannah, Lillian Leiderman, and Annette Peikus. *Hebrew Kindergarten Manual*. N.Y.: Mizrachi National Education Committee, 1946. 111 pp.

Honor, Jennie J. *Kindergarten Manual for Jewish Religious Schools, Part I*. N.Y.: USA, 1927, USCJE, 1949. 64pp.

Jacobs, E. *The Methods of Teaching Primary Grades*. Phila.: The Jewish Chatauqua Society, 1914.

Klaperman, Libby L. *Jeremy and Judy Say the Sh'ma*. N.Y.: Behrman, and UOJCA, 1956.

Landman, Eva. *A Kindergarten Manual*. Cincinnati, 1918.

Pessin, Deborah, and Temima Gezari. *The Jewish Kindergarten*. N.Y.: UAHC, 1944. 329 pp.

Rosenzweig, Marion J., and Ephraim Rosenzweig. *Now We Begin: A Manual of Stories and Instructions for Home and School*. 6 pamphlets. Cincinnati: UAHC, 1936–37. First chapters in *Jew Teach* 4 (June 1936): 5–14.

GUIDES, CURRICULA, AND MANUALS SINCE 1950

Avner, Ailene, and Joel Wittstein. *Idea Exchange, 1980: The Year of the Senses*. Ideas for Jewish Preschool Activities. N.Y.: UAHC, 1980.

Bessler, Helen. *Bereshit: A Kindergarten Guide*. N.Y.: UAHC, 1969.

Chanover, Hyman. *Planning for Three to Eights in the Hebrew School: A Manual for Teachers and Administrators*. N.Y.: USCJE, 1954. 208 pp.

Chanover, Hyman, et al. *A Curriculum Guide for the Kindergarten.* N.Y.: USCJE, 1960. 130 pp.

Furfine, Sandy S., and Nancy Cohen Nowak. *The Jewish Pre-School Teachers Handbook.* Extensive bibliography on early childhood, pp. 107–32. Denver: ARE, 1981.

Gezari, Temima, and Dorothy Pessin. *The Jewish Kindergarten—A Manual.* Rev. Ed. N.Y.: UAHC, 1959.

Kohn, Rebekkah J. *Teaching Oral Hebrew to the Young Child.* N.Y.: AAJE, 1954.

Levy, Deborah, and Audrey Friedman Marcus. *The Learning Center Book of Jewish Holidays and Symbols.* Denver: ARE, ca. 1985.

Mirel, Joan, and Hilda Klein. *The Temple Nursery School—A Report and Analysis.* N.Y.: UAHC, 1959.

Union of American Hebrew Congregations, Central Conference of American Rabbis, and Commission on Jewish Education. *To See the World Through Jewish Eyes: Guide for the Pre-School Years.* N.Y.: National Curriculum Project of the UAHC, CCAR, and CJE, 1981. 82 pp.

GLEANINGS

United Synagogue Commission on Jewish Education,
"The Foundation School (Bet Ha-Yeled): Modern psychology recognized the crucial importance of early childhood experiences in molding adult character. For this reason, early developments of basic Jewish attitudes and habits profoundly affect the developments of a positive Jewish outlook in adulthood.

Hebrew language instruction on an oral-aural basis, and a Hebrew reading readiness program for the very young also offer the promise of more rapid acceleration in future achievement in the elementary Hebrew school. . . .

Congregations are urged to explore . . . the possibility of establishing Hebrew Foundation Schools to provide integrated, bi-cultural daily programs for children between three and eight."

Objectives and Standards for the Congregational School (1958), 16.

The Nursery School and Kindergarten (Gan): Where a Foundation School cannot be established, the congregation should organize a Gan, that is, a nursery school and kindergarten for children three to six. The Gan should meet daily for a minimum of two and a half hours."

Objectives and Standards for the Congregational School (1958), 17.

Central Conference of American Rabbis Conference, 1959,
"We applaud the increasing number of congregations which have established pre-school nursery schools, thereby reaching the children at an age when character influences are deeply felt, and bringing young parents in earlier contact with the synagogue. We urge that such nursery schools be integrated with the religious school and that a maximum of Jewish religious content be included in their programs.
CCAR (1959), 152.

Barnett, Sarah,
"Young children learn about the world through experiencing it. . . . A person blind from birth cannot understand the difference between red and blue, so a child cannot understand Shabbat without the experience of work and rest. Lighting candles is a hollow gesture if it is learned only from the pages of a book. It is not until all preparations for Shabbat have been experienced that a child can truly understand the special quality of the 7th day. . . . For those who do not have this home experience, it provides an introductory taste."
Compass (Fall/Winter 1978), 18.

Green, Kathy,
"In considering curriculum for any kind of new or extended program, it is imperative that we think carefully about our own underlying beliefs, assumptions, goals and objectives. It is no longer possible for Jewish nursery school teachers to limit themselves to dealing with customs and ceremonies as presented in the first grade Sunday school classrooms, especially if we are to be the child's principal educator for significant hours each day."
"Jewish Early Childhood Education," *MRCN* 12 (Spring 1981), 3.

8 | EXCEPTIONAL CHILDREN

SPECIAL EDUCATION

Aaron, Ruth S. "A Special Project for 'Slow Learners'." *Jew Teach* 24 (Jan. 1956): 10–11.

Abramowitz, Hayim. "The Interaction Concept and the Gifted Child." *Ped Rep* 31:1 (Fall 1979): 35–36.

———. "A Survey of Jewish Special Education Programs in the United States." The results of a survey conducted in 1976–77 involving Bureaus of Jewish Education and individuals involved in Jewish Special Education programs throughout the United States. Master's project, HUC–JIR, 1977.

Alper, Janice, and Vicki Reikes. "LD (Learning Disabilities) Programs: Where Are They?" *Compass* (Spring 1978): 19–20.

Amidon, Edmund, and Carl Hoffman. "Helping the Socially Isolated or Rejected Child." *Ped Rep* 15 (Mar. 1964).

Bemporad, Jack. "The Religious Program at Hawthorne Cedar Knolls School." *News and Views* (Sept./Oct. 1961).

* Biberfield, Marcee. *The Attitudes of Orthodox Jewish Mothers toward Their Mentally Retarded Children*. Yeshiva U., 1983.

Birner, Louis. "An Experimental Program for Retarded Children in a Part-Time Congregational Religious School." *American J of Mental Deficiency* 60 (July 1955): 95–97.

Bleich, J. David. "Torah Education for the Mentally Retarded." *J of Halacha and Contemporary Society* 4 (Fall 1982).

Bloom, David I., and David Cohen. "The Gifted Child in the Jewish School." *Syn Sch* 15 (1956).

Bogot, Howard I. "Special Education and the Arts: Judaism." *Rel Ed* 79 (Summer 1984): 456–61.

Brevis, Harry J. "The Story of Hebrew Braille." *AJA* 21 (Nov. 1969): 105–12.

Brown, Joni Bass. "Children with Special Needs," JPH, Eds., Marcus and Zwerin, (1983): 451–460.

———. "Special Needs Forum." *AM* Spring 1978, Fall 1978, Winter 1979, and Spring 1979.

Cohen, Henry. "A Very Special Confirmation." *Compass* (Fall 1981): 12, 18.

Eisenpreis, B. "UAHC Program for Learners with Special Needs." *RJ* 12 (Winter 1983/84): 27.

Fargell Harris C. "Jewish Special Education," *Had Mag* (Nov. 1985): 18–20.

Fleischmann, Rienne. Curriculum Guide to the Ezra-Kadima School. Downsview, Ont.: Beth Emeth Bais Yehudah Synagogue, 1976.

———. "Sources of Information in Jewish Special Education." *Ped Rep* 31 (Fall 1979): 17–18.

Freid, Jacob, and Richard Borgersen. "The Jewish Braille Library," *JBA* 1974–75, 37–43.

Frost, Shimon. "Meeting the Needs of Non-Language Students." *Syn Sch* 16 (Dec. 1957).

Geller, Bonnie S. "The Jewish Braille Institute," *For* (Aug 8, 1982): 9 (E section).

"General News and Notes: Special Education." *Ped Rep* 25 (Spring 1974): 20.

Gennert, Pamela. "A Hebrew Class for Special Needs." *Compass* 3 (Fall 1979): 20–21.

Gilbert, Arthur. "More Than a Penny," *Jew Ed* 24 (Spring 1954): 36–38, 61.

Goldhammer, Douglas. "Teaching Torah to Deaf Children." *Compass* 8:3 (Winter 1986): 9, 16.

Goldreich, G. "Operation Headstart—Jewish Style." *Had Mag* 52 (Sept. 1970): 12.

Goldstein, Martin. "The Evolution of an Intensive Educational Program." (A program for the gifted) *Syn Sch* 15 (Sept. 1956).

Gottlieb, Lynn. "The Jewish Deaf Community." In *Cat 2*, 151–66.

Green, Roberta M., and Elaine Heavenrich. *A Question in Search of an Answer: Understanding Learning Disability in Jewish Education*. N.Y.: UAHC, 1981. 262 pp.

Greenberg, Barbara, and Herbert A. Greenberg. "The North Bellmore Experience: A Proposed Community Model for Jewish Special Education." *Syn Sch* 31 (Summer 1973): 26–30.

———. *The Sabbath Kit*. N.Y.: USCJE. For preadolescents and adolescents.

———. "The Tikvah Program." (A Special Education Program at Camp Ramah) *Ped Rep* 31 (Fall 1979): 30–33.

Greenberg, Herbert A. "The Jewish Learning Disabled Child." *Con Jud* 28 (Spring 1974): 41–48.

———. "Tikvah is Special." *Your Child* 4 (Summer 1971): 14.

———. *Tikvah Program: Summer 1971. Phase II, Camp Ramah in Glen Spey, N.Y. Integration of Children with Learning and Emotional Difficulties—An Evaluation and Descriptive Analysis*.

Hammer, Reuven. "The Jewish School and the Special Child." *Con Jud* 36 (Summer 1983): 13–15.

———. *The Other Child in Jewish Education*. N.Y.: USCJE, 1970. 314 pp.

Haramati, Amnon. "הוראת תורה לכתת מחוננים בבית ספר תיכון" (Teaching Bible to a Class of Gifted Students in a Secondary School) (H. and E. summary) *Ped Rep* 31 (Fall 1979): 39–40.

Heilbraun, Judith. "Sweet Glow of Success." *Compass* 1 (Winter 1977): 8–9.

Heilbraun, Judith, and Dorothy Axelroth. "A Hebrew Learning Center for the Perceptually Disabled Child." *Ped Rep* 31 (Fall 1979): 7–9.

Henkin, Alan. "The Disabled in Our Midst," *Jud* 32 (Fall 1983): 452–62.

———. "Does God Understand Sign Language?" *Compass* 10 (Oct. 1987): 6–7.

Herman, Floyd L., Raymond Starr, and Janice Starr. "The Story of Matthew Starr's Bar Mitzvah." *Compass* 8 (Winter 1986): 5–6.

Jewish Braille Review 20th Anniversary Anthology, 1931–51.

"Jewish Education Brings Hope for Retarded Child." *Jew Digest* 17 (Nov. 1971): 55–58.

"Jewish Education and the Disabled." *Con Jud* 36 (Special Issue).

Jewish Society for the Deaf. *Community Center Chronicle*. N.Y.: Oct. 1955.

Kaiman, Arnold G. "The Bar Mitzvah of a 'Special Child,'" *Jew Teach* 32 (Dec. 1963): 15–16.

———. "Towards Making the 70's Special." *CCAR J* (Apr. 1970): 81–85.

* Kaminetzky, Edward. *Incorporating the Special Education Philosophy within American Jewish Education*. Columbia U., 1976. 237 pp.

———. *Sons of Omission: The Neglected Children*. A rationale for Jewish Special Education. N.Y.: Yeshiva U. Press, 1977. 135 pp.

Kelman, Joseph H. "Jewish Education and the Disabled." *Con Jud* 36 (Summer 1983): 5–12.

———. "The Kadima and Ezra Schools: Pioneers in Special Education." *Ped Rep* 31 (Fall 1979): 10–12.

———. "Special Education for All: Integrating the Handicapped Child into the Synagogue School." *Syn Sch* 23 (Spring 1965): 4–21.

Kelman, Naamith, and M. Levy. "The Jewish Blind." In *Cat* 2, 167–79.

Kohn, Sylvan H. "A 'Torah Workshop' for Handicapped Children." *Syn Sch* 16 (Dec. 1957): 21–23.

Landsberg, Z. ואס קינדער אידישע פאר סקול,, לערנען אין צוריקגעשטאנען זיינען" (School for Jewish Retarded Children). *Day* (Y.) Dec. 2, 1934.

Lawson, Martin S. "Toward a Program in Jewish Ethics for Primary-Intermediate Religious School Students with Reading Disabilities." Master's thesis, HUC–JIR, 1974.

Layman, Robert. "The Jewish Special Child." *Impact* 35 (Summer 1977): 33–40.

———. "The Parent and Special Education." *Ped Rep* 31 (Fall 1979): 21–22.

Lerer, Deborah. "Community-Wide Special Education," *Compass* (Summer 1980): 8–22.

Lerner, Jack. "The Brain Injured Child," *Syn Sch* 12 (Fall 1963): 10–11.

Leviant, D. "The Nir Group: Teaching a Special Child to Walk, Talk, Laugh and Love." *B'nai B'rith International Jewish Monthly* 99 (Dec. 1984): 37–38.

Levinson, B. M. "The Intellectually Gifted Child." *Yeshiva Education* 4 (1961): 3–20.

———. "The Mentally Defective Child." *Yeshiva Education* 3 (1959): 3–15.

Lichtman, William. "The Slow Learner: A Program to Meet His Needs." *Jew Teach* 32 (Oct. 1963): 7.

Lister, Louis. "Religious Education for the Emotionally Disturbed." *SWJT* 1 (Winter 1967–Spring 1968).

Lister, Rebecca. *Jewish Religious Education for the Retarded Child.* N.Y.: UAHC, c. 1959, 1970. 79 pp.

Mackmann, Beverly C. "Developing Services to the Mentally Retarded/Developmentally Disabled." *J Jew Com Ser* 61 (Winter 1984): 188–92.

Manual for Organizing Special Classes. N.Y.: USCJE.

Menachowski, M. קינדער צוריקגעשטאנענע,, ליטעראטור" יידישער דער אין (Retarded Children in Yiddish Literature). In *Almanac-Yiddish* (Y.), 293–306. 1961.

Milgram, Josephine. "An Experiment in Acceleration." *Syn Sch* 15 (1956).

Milgram, Rebecca. "The Role of the Parents in Raising the Gifted Child." In *Ed As* (1968), 45–50.

Nemzoff, Samuel A. "The Gifted Pupil." *Jew Teach* 32 (Feb. 1964): 16.

Oliansky, Carol. "The Hebrew School for the Deaf—A Special School for Special Children." (E.) *For* (Nov. 1981): B9, B13.

Olitzky, Kerry M. "Proceed with Caution: Mainstreaming in the Religious School." *Compass* 8 (Winter 1986): 8.

Olson, Sallie D. "All Your Children Shall Be Taught of the Lord." *Compass* 8 (Winter 1986): 3–4, 18.

Pallay, Eva. "The Talking Siddur." *Ped Rep* 33 (Dec. 1981): 26–27.

Passow, A. Harry. "Education of the Gifted and Talented: Some Basic Principles." *Ped Rep* 31 (Fall 1979): 5–7.

Penn, Ascher. וועלט דער אין שול בעסטע די,, שטימע-טויב פאר" (The Best School in the World for Deaf-Mutes). In *Penn* (Y.), 426–36.

———. "ליכט ברענגען,, (Bringing Light). (The New York Guild for the Jewish Blind whose members transcribe prayerbooks and other texts into Braille) In *Penn* (Y.), 413–25.

Pollak, George. "The Gifted Student in Our Schools." *Syn Sch* 23 (Spring 1965): 12.

Poisson, Joseph A. "Religious Education for Our 'Special Children'." *Compass* (Winter/Spring 1981/82): 11–20.

Rackman, Bennett M. "Jewish Special Education." *Ped Rep* 31 (Fall 1979): 2–4.

Rogow, Sally. "The Child with Learning Disabilities in the Synagogue School." *Syn Sch* (Summer 1974).

Rosenkranz, Samuel. "The Steps We Took With Tommy" *SMJT* 1 (Winter 1967–Spring 1968).

Rosenwasser, Rose K. "Serving the Shut-in." *Syn Sch* 18 (Dec. 1959): 21–22.

Schnaidman, Mordecai. "Judaic Studies Material for Handicapped Children." *Ped Rep* 31 (Fall 1979): 41.

Schwartz, Elliot S. *A Manual for Organizing Classes for Jewish Special Children* N.Y.: USCJE, 1975.

———. "A Very Special World." *Syn Sch* 31 (Summer 1973): 12–25.

Schwartz, Elliot S., and B. Zenofsky. "Special Education." *Ped Rep* 35 (Mar. 1984): 16–18.

Schwartz, Larry. "Educable Retarded Children." *SWJT* 1 (Winter 1967–Spring 1968).

Shapiro, B. M. "Religion and the Disabled Child: A Letter to My Son on His Bar Mitzvah." *The Exceptional Parent*. 13 (Apr. 1983).

Shapiro, E. "Special Education, Yeshiva Style." *Moment* 6 (May 1981): 50–53.

Shapiro, Helen. "Jewish Religious Education for Retarded Children." *Mental Retardation* 2 (Aug. 1964).

Shapiro, J. "Our Disadvantaged Jewish Children." *A Zion* 60 (Sept. 1969): 20–22.

Shuart, Adele Kronick. *Signs in Judaism: A Resource Book for the Jewish Deaf Community*. N.Y.: National Congress of Jewish Deaf, Bloch Publishing Co., 1986. 176 pp.

Shurin, Aaron B. „ווי אזוי אפגעשטאנענע קינדער קריגן א אידישע דערציאונג" (How Retarded Children Receive a Jewish Education). *For* (Y.) (July 24, 1962).

Siegel, Ernst. "Integrating Handicapped Children and Youth into Regular Religious Educational Programs." *Rel Ed* 62 (July–Aug. 1967): 355–59.

Siegel, Morton. "The Jewish View of Education for the Handicapped." *Ped Rep* 20 (Dec. 1968).

Silver, Daniel. "The Retarded Child and Religious Education." *Rel Ed* 52 (Sept–Oct. 1957): 361–64.

Simon, Sara. "Sh'ma V'Ezer (Hear and Help): A Community Model." *Ped Rep* 31 (Fall 1979): 12–14.

Slesinger, Zalmen. "Education for Creativity." *Ped Rep* 13 (1961). Gifted children.

Soifer, Maralyn. "A Special Shabbat." *Ped Rep* 36 (Jan. 1985): 34.

Spotts, Leon H. "Meeting the Jewish Educational Needs of the Exceptional Child." *Ped Rep* 31 (Fall 1979): 15–17.

Stadtler, Bea. "Religious Program Aids for Jewish Retarded." *Newsletter—Children Limited* 16 (1967). National Assoc. for Retarded Children, N.Y.

Stiskin, Herschel M. *A Curriculum Guide and Suggested Activities and Experiences for Teachers of Children with Retarded Mental Development in Jewish Religious Schools: The Holiday Cycle*. N.Y.: JEC Press.

———. "Curriculum Planning for the Special Religious Class." *Syn Sch* 22 (Fall 1963): 3–6.

———. *Religio-Ethnic Influences and Considerations in Curriculum Planning within the Maimonides Institute*. N.Y. JEC Press, Sept 8, 1965.

———. *A Survey of Jewish Religious Programs for the Handicapped*. N.Y.: AAJE, 1968.

Sulkes, Zena W. "An Expression of Our Commitment to Klal Yisrael, Mainstreaming in the Religious School." *Compass* 8 (Winter 1986): 8.

———. "The Gifted Student: A Potential Resource for Judaism's Future." *Compass* 9 (Spring/Summer 1987): 8–9.

———. "Providing for the Gifted Child." In *JPH*, 143–51.

Syden, Martin. "Religious Education for the Jewish Retarded Child." *American J of Mental Deficiency* 64: 689–94.

Tarasow, Morris. "Education for the Gifted Child." *Syn Sch* 16 (Dec. 1957 and Fall 1963).

Teller, Gerald. "Intensive Classes." *Ped Rep* 34 (Jan. 1988): 21–22. For gifted children.

Tendler, M. D. "Education of the Special Child: A Halachic Analysis." Annual Eastern Region Conference of National Commission on Torah Education, Dec. 22, 1974.

Vogelstein, Ilene. "Jewish Education and the Hearing Impaired." *Ped Rep* 31 (Fall 1979): 41.

Weisberg, Phyllis G. "Religious Education of the Jewish Retarded Child—What Next?" *Syn Sch* 22 (Fall 1963): 7–9.

Willner, Eric A. "A Program of Jewish Education in Blythedale." *News and Views* (Oct. 1961).

Witty, Y. "Educating the Bright." *Jew Spec* 29 (Feb. 1964): 17–18.

Worenklein, Abe. "Children with Learning Disabilities." *Compass* 1 (Fall 1977): 20–21.

* Zabell, Emil M. *A Study of Forty-Six Adult Deaf Who Are Known to the Jewish Society of the Deaf and Who Were Considered Rehabilitated by the Division of Vocational Rehabilitation.* Columbia U., 1955. 105 pp.

GLEANINGS

Kelman, Joseph,
"The fact that the Jewish community has not done enough for the disabled is not because rabbis, educators, professionals, and leaders of the social service agencies are insensitive to the needs of the disabled. The fact that they have not been integrated into the community has not been a deliberate omission. It is due to the attitudes and concepts that most people have had about the disabled. Their disabilities inhibit the community because of these attitudes and concepts. The experience of the last decade has clearly indicated that some exciting and innovative programs can take place so that Jewish life will be made accessible to the disabled."

Family Committee of the USCJE, *Your Child*, 18:1 (1982).

Kushner, Harold,
"For many years, I was bothered by the berakhah, we are supposed to recite on seeing a dwarf or deformed person, Barukh meshaaneh habriot, Praised are you, Oh Lord our God, ruler of the universe, who has created such variety among his creatures. The phrasing struck me as insensitive to the feelings of the deformed and handicapped people; whereas the handicapped want and need to be seen as people, not as freaks or walking ailments. (I hasten to add that my discomfort was strictly theoretical. For fourteen years, my wife and I were the parents of a physically handicapped child, and I don't recall any of our orthodox acquaintances reciting the berakha on meeting him.) It reminded me of St. Augustine's "argument from plenitude": Why are there misshapen people in the world? Because God in His grace realized how dull the world would be if we all looked the same and made it a more interesting place by populating it with dwarfs and cripples (a view I always found fatuous and condescending like the suggestion that God creates retarded children in order that we might learn compassion).

Recently, I have come to see the berakha differently. It no longer seems to say 'look how different the person is.' Rather, it says 'despite his different appearance, he too is fashioned in the image of God.' The berakha now strikes me as an implementation of Mishnah *Sanhedrin*, 4:5, 'A human being strikes many coins from the same mold, and they are all identical. But the Holy One, blessed be He, strikes us all from the mold of Adam, and each of us is unique.' It comes to affirm that all human beings, in their infinite variety, are flawed and incomplete, each in his way, but that all are bearers of the divine image. The one who recites the berakha on seeing a deformed person is, in effect, saying to himself 'were it not for the reminder of this berakha, I might respond to him with disgust or pity. But now I am reminded to see him bearing God's image.'"

Kol Bana'yikh—All Your Children (Spring/Summer 1984), 1

Liheyot (Becoming), CJE, UAHC, and CCAR
"The disabled did not choose to be disabled. We are 'dis'abled in that we cannot do what we would like to enable them. We must begin with accepting that a quality Jewish experience for some will not necessarily be the same quality Jewish experience as for others. Qualitatively, quantitatively, and subjectively our realities are different. That cannot be changed. Once we are sensitized to these realities we are free to choose from the breadth of options open to us to select those meaningful and communicable elements which a population or an individual can thrive upon. It may not be the 'usual' or anticipated so-called 'normal' reality—but no question about it, it is valid as

quality of life, quality of experience and as authentic quality Judaism."

"Sensory impairment is obvious but learning disability is 'hidden' or can be—unless someone spells it out to the religious school. As to learning style, there is no style suited to all. Each child is really unique—some may need multiple modality approaches and others may be confused or overstimulated by such stimuli and may require only modality in isolation. The Religious School does not need to discover or diagnose learning style but rather to receive input from other sources (parents, psychologists, schools). Another important notion is that modifications tailored to individual student needs may be incorporated into the regular classroom and often add additional enrichment for other students."

Liheyot (*The Connection*) (Fall 1982), Department of Education–UAHC, 1:1.

9 | GUIDANCE

IN THE SCHOOL

Arian, Philip. "Comment on Guidance in the Jewish School." *Jew Ed* 39 (Dec. 1969): 53–54.

Axelroth, Dorothy. "The Principal as Counselor in the Congregational School." *Ped Rep* 32 (Fall 1980): 10–11.

Baum, E. "Counseling in the Religious School." *Rel Ed* 61 (Mar.–Apr. 1966): 133–39.

Baxt, Roland, and David Preston. "Jewish Problems in Vocational Counseling." *JSSQ* (Mar. 1946): 274–79.

* Blass, Jerome Harold. *The Relationship of Psychological Values and Needs to Vocational Role Differences among Jewish Seminarians.* Fordham U., 1975. 166 pp.

B'nai B'rith Vocational Service. *Careers in Jewish Education, Community Organization Work, and Vocational Service in Jewish Agencies.* Washington D.C., 1961.

Brown, Sheldon S. *Guidance and Counseling for Jewish Schools.* N.Y.: Bloch, 1964. 88 pp.

* ———. *A Guidance Experiment in the Jewish Supplementary Weekday School.* Dropsie U., 1961. 850 pp.

———. "A Guidance Experiment in the Jewish Supplementary Weekday School." *Rel Ed* 57 (Sept.–Oct. 1962): 371.

———. "A Guidance Experiment in the Religious School." *Jew Ed* 33 (Fall 1962): 52–57.

———. "Guidance in the Jewish School." *Syn Sch* 16 (Dec. 1957): 17–23.

———. "What We Should Know About Our Pupils: Guidance in the Jewish School." *Syn Sch* 22 (Feb. 1964): 57–63.

Cohen, Samuel M. *Guiding Jewish Youth.* N.Y.: Young People's League, USA, 1939. 158 pp.

———. *Jewish Child Guidance and Leader's Guide and Student Manual.* National Federation of Jewish Men's Clubs, USA. 124 and 125 pp.

Duckat, Walter. "Extending Guidance Service to the Jewish Schools." *Jew Ed* 39 (July, 1969): 8–14. Also *J Jew Com Ser* 46 (Dec. 1969): 163–69.

———. "Guidance Program for Jewish Schools." *Jew Ed* 18 (Feb.–Mar. 1947): 21–23.

———. (All are in *Jew Life*.) "Careers for the Sabbath Observer." 20 (Sept. 1952); "New Careers for Jewish Women." 21 (Dec. 1953); "—in Social Work." 26 (Aug. 1959); "—in Commercial Art." 26 (Feb. 1959); "—with Mathematics." 27 (June 1960); "—in Business Administration." 27 (Apr. 1960); "—in Music." 27 (Dec. 1960).

* Goldman, Henry. *School Careers and Subsequent Careers: An Analytical and Comparative Study of the School Records and Subsequent Careers of Those Men Who Graduated from the Hebrew Technical Institute of New*

York from 1886 to 1907 Inclusive. N.Y.: N.Y.U., 1918. 304 pp.

Goodman, Nathaniel. "Consultative Casework Services to an Afternoon Hebrew School." *J Jew Com Ser* 45 (Win. 1968): 173–78.

* Grant, Arnold. *Perceptions of Yeshiva High School Students toward Career Education Needs*. Yeshiva U., June 1982.

Gross, Morris B. "Reaction to Walter Duckat's Paper on Guidance Service." *Jew Ed* 39 (July 1969): 15–16.

Jaskall, Ira L. "My Son the Computer Programmer: The Need for Career Education." (On the Bramson ORT Technical Institute) *Ped Rep* 32 (Fall 1980): 30–31.

Kaminetsky, Joseph. "Guidance in the Jewish School." *Jew Ed* 11 (Jan. 1940): 197–99.

Lang, Gerhard. "The Teacher As Counselor." *Ped Rep* 32 (Fall 1980): 12–13.

Levinger, Lee J. *Professional Opportunities for Jewish Youth*. Washington, D.C.: B'nai B'rith Vocational Service Bureau. 47 pp.

———. *Your Future Profession*. Cincinnati: B'nai B'rith.

Levinson, B. M. "The Vocational Interest of Yeshiva College Freshmen." *J of Genetical Psychology* 99 (1961): 235–44.

Lubinsky, Menachem. "Orthodox Vocational Guidance: Is There a Need?" *Jew Obs* (June 1976): 28–31.

The Pedagogic Reporter. 32 (Fall 1980). Special Issue on Guidance.

Reingold, Harold A. "A Guidance Program for Congregational Schools." *Ped Rep* 32 (Fall 1980): 6–9. See also "Update" 35 (Oct. 1984): 16–18.

Sobel, Louis, and Joseph Samler. *Group Methods in Vocational Guidance*. N.Y.: Furrow Press, 1938. 111 pp.

Swerdloff, S., and H. Rosen. *The College and Career Plans of Jewish High School Youth*. Washington D.C.: B'nai B'rith Vocational Service, 1964.

Wachstock, David. "Fostering Self-Esteem." *Ped Rep* 32 (Fall 1980): 14–16.

Zubin, Joseph. "Vocational Guidance and the American Jewish School." *Jew Ed* 4 (Oct.–Dec. 1932): 174–79.

———. *Choosing a Life Work*. Cincinnati: UAHC, 1937. 220 pp.

GLEANINGS

Duckat, Walter,
"Perhaps the supreme advantage of a well rounded adequately staffed guidance program is the sense of relevance that it conveys so compellingly to students. The guidance counselor may be the only person in the school who accepts the student as he is without admonishing him. This does not mean that he is unmindful of the grim realities of grades, college requirements, parent and teacher expectations, and the demands of peers. The counselor considers, with the student, those matters which concern the student most deeply, his attitudes and feelings about himself and others and his typical reactions to his daily life's demands. He also discusses with him his educational and vocational plans. He may help to clarify goals that may serve to release untapped capacities and interests."
"Guidance Services for Jewish Schools," *Jew Ed* 39 (July 1969), 13.

Arian, Philip (Comment on Duckat's remarks, *Jew Ed* 39 (1969))
"Generally, vocational workers, like other social workers, project as their overriding aim, the accomodation of the client to the surrounding society. Social workers may reject some of the values in this society, but their overriding goal is the enabling of the client to participate as a functioning member of this society. Many Jewish educators, on the other hand, totally reject the surrounding society and see their schools (especially Yeshiva day schools) as a vehicle for the structuring of a completely Jewish-oriented society. These schools invite the student to see his life orientation as one completely motivated by a total Jewish frame of reference. Anyone representing the larger society, who offers opportunities for the youngster to

'fit in' within this society's frame of reference is a threat."
Jew Ed 39 (Dec. 1969), 53.

Lewittes, Mordecai H., Editorial,
"Guidance refers to the services, such as testing and counseling, rendered to students to help them make decisions. Most day schools have done well in the area of college advising but not too well in the areas of career guidance and personal counseling. Many Jewish educators and boards of education feel that guidance is a frill that can be dispensed with . . .

Studies prove that guidance services have helped students to advance academically, emotionally and vocationally. We can no longer afford to neglect guidance services if we are truly interested in quality education . . ."
"Guidance Services," *Ped Rep* 32 (Fall 1980), 1.

Lang, Gerhard,
"We live in an era of specialization. For instance in medicine there exist more than two dozen specialties and within each specialty we find many sub-specialties . . .

In education, too, we have our specialists. We have guidance-counselors, school psychologists, school social workers and school nurses. . . . It is the classroom teacher, however, who is closest to the pupils and observes their day-by-day behavior. While teachers are not trained and licensed to practice psychotherapy, social work, medicine or dentistry they should be able to recognize symptoms which may be indicative of psychological and/or medical problem. If teachers report pupils to proper authorities, psychotherapy can be recommended before a neurosis or psychosis develops."
"The Teacher as Counselor." *Ped Rep* 32 (Fall 1980), 12.

Axelroth, Dorothy G.,
"It is true that in time one learns diplomatic reponses and an assortment of answers to a very wide variety of problems and situations. What qualifications does the educator need to do this? Courses in guidance and counseling are a prerequisite. In addition, understanding, empathy, objectivity and a large measure of old-fashioned horse sense are important. To couch it in more familiar terms, we need the wisdom of Solomon, the patience of Job, the devotion of Ruth, the compassion of Isaiah, and perhaps some of the cynicism of Koheleth. But lacking some of these qualities, as all do, we must rely ultimately on the essential requirement of honesty, to admit that we need help, coupled with the willingness to seek it and the knowledge of where to find it."
"The Principal as Counselor in the Congregational School." *Ped Rep* 32 (Fall 1980), 11.

10 HEBREW

HEBREW IN JEWISH LIFE (SELECTED)

Barish, Louis. "Is the Hebrew Language Indispensable to Judaism?" *Recon* 9 (1943).

Benderly, Samson. "Hebraism in America." *Jew Ed News* 1 (Jan. 1926).

Blumenfield, Samuel M. „הלשון העברית– יעודה הדתי והלאומי" (The Hebrew Language— Its Religious and National Mission). In *S Ed* (H.). A briefer version appears in *Wiseman* (H.), 205–9.

———. "The Story of Hebrew 'Past and Present'." *Jewish Heritage* 1 (1958). Also in Pilch, ed., *Thou Shalt Teach* (1973), 52–59.

Brody, Fannie M. "The Hebrew Periodical Press in America, 1871–1931." *PAJHS* 33 (1934): 127–70.

Chomsky, William. *Hebrew: The Eternal Language*. Phila.: JPS, 1957, 321 pp.

———. "The Hebrew Language Is Indispensable to Judaism." *Recon* 9 (1943).

———. „עברית כלשון הספר" (Hebrew as the Language of the Book). In *Ed Enc* (H.), 2:683–84.

Efros, Israel. *"The Hebrew Language." Day* (May 15, 1964).

Engelman, Uriah Z. "The Strength of Hebrew in America." *Menorah J* 16 (Mar. 1929): 230–40.

Gannes, Abraham P. *Hebrew Culture Foundation, 1955–1978*. N.Y.: HC Foundation, 1977. 18 pp.

Greenberg, Simon. „עברית כלשון התפילה והתורה" (Hebrew as the Language of Prayer and Torah). In *Ed Enc* (H.), 2:681–83.

Halkin, Abraham S. "Hebrew in Jewish Culture." In *Jan 1*, 122–33.

Halkin, Simon. *Modern Hebrew Literature: Trends and Values*. N.Y.: Schocken, 1950. 238 pp.

Hebrew Comes to Life. (Articles on Hebrew and its significance in Jewish life) N.Y.: Histadruth Ivrith of America. 43 pp.

* Kabakoff, Jacob. *The History of Hebrew Literature in America*. Jewish Theological Seminary, 1958.

Mikliszanski, Jacqes K. תולדות הספרות העברית באמריקה מראשיתה עד ימינו (The History of Hebrew Literature in America from the Beginning to the Present) (H.). N.Y.: Ogen and Histadruth Halvrith in America, 1966. 448 pp.

Mirsky, David. "Hebrew in the United States: 1900–1920." In *HYB* 5 (1963), 83–111.

Persky, Daniel. „חבואת הספרות העברית באמריקה" (The Harvest of Hebrew Literature in America). In *Sefer HaShanah* (H.) 10/11 (1949), 699–712.

Scharfstein, Zevi. „עברית כלשון חיה" (Hebrew as a Living Language). In *Ed Enc* (H.), 2:677–81.

Sheniak, Mazal. "„למה עברית?". (Why Hebrew?). Experimental Edition. Jerusalem: the University, the WZO, and MRC for Jewish Education in the Diaspora, 1955. 170 pp.

Spiegel, Shalom. *Hebrew Reborn*. N.Y.: Macmillan Co., 1930. 479 pp.

Spolsky, Bernard. "Teaching Hebrew in the Diaspora: Rationales and Goals." *Jew Ed* 54 (Fall 1986): 11–20.

Waxman, Meyer. "The Story of Hebrew." In *JMW* 2:377–409.

Zolotkoff, Leon. "Jewish Culture and the Printed Jewish Word." *Menorah J* 4 (Dec. 1920): 352.

METHODOLOGY AND TEACHING AIDS PRIOR TO 1950

Arzt, Morris. "The Method of Aggregation and the Method of Segregation in the Learning of Hebrew." *Jew Ed* 7 (Apr.–June 1935): 107–11.

———. "Methods of Learning Hebrew." *Jew Ed* 6 (Jan.–Mar. 1934): 30–36.

Benderly, Samson. "Hebrew Language and Literature in Jewish Religious Schools." *Jewish Comment* (Dec. 16, 1904).

Blumberg, Zevi. "„להוצאת עתון עברי בבית הספר" (On Publishing a Hebrew Newspaper in the School). *Sh Hah* (H.) 6 (Sept. 1946): 288–95.

Braverman, Libbie L. "Hebrew is a Popular Subject in Our School." *Jew Teach* 2 (June 1934): 10–14.

Chomsky, William. "Aims and Methods in Teaching Hebrew." *Jew Ed* 15 (May 1944): 148–51.

———. "The Hebrew Language in the Jewish Curriculum." *Recon* 8 (Mar. 20, 1942): 10–15, 20.

———. *How to Teach Hebrew in the Elementary Grades*. N.Y.: USCJE, 1946. 295 pp.

———. "The Place of Hebrew Grammar in the Hebrew School." *Jew Ed* 15 (Sept. 1943): 34–37.

———. "Training for Character Through the Study of Hebrew." *Syn Sch* 4 (Feb. 1946): 53–56.

Cohn-Schechter, A. "„השפה העברית והחנוך" (The Hebrew Language and Education). *Sh Hah* (H.) 3 (1928): 213–18, 286–91.

Deitchman, Emily. "A Device for Teaching Hebrew Reading." *Jewish Teacher* 1 (Jan. 1917): 120–24.

Edelstein, Menachem M. "„חנוך עברי לילד היהודי באמריקה" (Hebrew Education for the Jewish Child in America). *Hadoar* (H.) 26 (Oct. 17, 1947): 1239–40.

Efros, Israel. "„שעורים לדוגמא" (Model Lessons on Teaching Poetry). *Sh Hah* (H.) 6 (1926): 43–47.

Eisenberg, Azriel. "Celebrating Hebrew Month." *Syn Sch* 5 (Mar. 1947): 99–104.

———. "Objectives and Methods of Teaching Hebrew." *Jew Ed* 21 (Winter 1949): 57–63.

Eisenberg, Azriel, and Ida Mirel. "Teaching Hebrew by the Individual and Group Instruction Method." *Jew Ed* 14 (Jan.–Mar. 1943): 143–45. Also in *RTHE*, 105–8.

Elkin, Harry. "How to Make Hebrew Study Relevant." *Recon* (Apr. 6, 1945): 17–22.

Engelman, Uriah Z. *Hebrew Education in America*. N.Y.: Jewish Teacher's Seminary and People's U. Press, 1947. 60 pp.

Frishberg, I. Z. "„קריאת אותיות וקריאת מלים" (Reading of Letters and Reading of Words) *Sh Hah* (H.) 1 (Fall 1940): 20–32.

Gamoran, Emanuel. "A New Approach To The Teaching of Hebrew." *CCAR* 46 (1936): 304–17.

———. "On the Teaching of Hebrew." *Jew Teach* 14 (Jan. 1946): 17–20.

———. "Ten Reasons for Studying Hebrew." *Jew Teach* (1939).

Goldman, Sylvia G. "The Hebrew Department." *Jew Teach* 6 (Nov. 1937): 20–22.

Greenberg, Simon. *The First Year in the Hebrew School: A Teacher's Guide*. N.Y.: USCJE, 1946. 233 pp.

———. "Teaching Ideals Through the Hebrew Lesson." *Syn Sch* 3 (Jan. 1945): 38–41.

Grossman, Hanna. „על הוראת הלשון העברית למתחילים" (On Teaching the Hebrew Language to Beginners). (H.) *Jewish Teacher* 6 (Apr. 1924): 7–9.

Halevi, Mordecai. „ערכים בחנוך העברי" (Values in Hebrew Education). *Hadoar* (H.) 28 (Oct. 16, 1949): 1088–90.

Hanapolski, M. B. „השמוש במלון" (On the Use of a Dictionary). *Hadoar* (H.) 11 (16th of Heshvan 1935).

Hoffman, M. N. H. "The Measurement of Bilingual Background." Master's thesis, Columbia U. Teachers College, 1934. 76 pp.

Hurwich, Louis. "Word Frequency in Pre-Biblical Hebrew Textbooks." *Jew Ed* 7 (Jan. 1935): 40–43.

Kessler, Harry L. "Teaching Hebrew in Sunday School." *Jew Teach* 15 (June 1947): 20–25.

Kleiman, Blanche. "A Hebrew Club Paper as a Teacher's Technique." *Jew Teach* 8 (Apr. 1940): 1–5.

Kohn, Rebekah. "The Whole-Word Method of Teaching Hebrew." *Syn Sch* (Feb., Apr., and Sept. 1949).

Levinthal, L. „שנת עבודה על שדה החנוך העברי" (A Year Work in the Field of Hebrew Education). *Hadoar* (H.) 1 (June 6, 1922): 3.

Mehler, Judith. "Intensive Hebrew Course in Gilenu." *Jew Teach* 15 (Nov. 1946): 20–29.

Millgram, Abraham E. "Intensive Hebrew Training in the Small Congregational School." *Jew Ed* 11 (1939): 49–51.

The National Committee. "Plan of Transliteration from Hebrew into English for General Use." *Jew Ed* 8 (Apr.–June 1936): 89.

Nudelman, Edward A. "Three Years of Individual Instruction in the Teaching of Hebrew—An Evaluation." *Jew Ed* 1 (Oct. 1929): 154–64.

Pilch, Yehudah. „לשאלת העברית בבית הספר" (On the Question of Hebrew in the School). *Hadoar* (H.) 28 (Oct. 14, 1949): 1091–92.

———. "The Place of the Hebrew Language in the School." *Jew Ed* 19 (Spring 1948): 20–22.

Rappoport, Israel B. "The Elementary Jewish School of Tomorrow—Linguistic or Experimental." *Jew Ed* 5 (Apr.–June 1933): 89–95.

———. "New Type Devices in the Teaching of Hebrew." *Jew Ed* 2 (Oct. 1930): 146–56.

Rosen, Ben, and William Chomsky. "Improving the Teaching of Hebrew in Our Schools." *Jew Ed* 12 (Sept. 1940): 97–101, 113.

Rosenberg, Ariah. „פתיחה לפסיכולוגיה של למוד הלשון" (Introduction to the Psychology of Language Study). *Sh Hah* (H.) 9 (May 1949): 67–71.

Scharfstein, Zevi. „נסיונות בגדול ילדים דו-לשוניים באמריקה" (Experiments in Raising Bi-Lingual Children in America). *Hadoar* (H.) 18 (December 1938): 85–86, 120, 125, 135–36.

———. "Factors Making for Effective Language Teaching." *Jewish Teacher* 2 (June–Oct. 1918): 94–99.

———. „כמה מלים עבריות ידועות לילדי ישראל באמריקה?" (How Many Hebrew Words Do Jewish Children in America Know?). *Hinukh* 1 (Adar 1936): 66–70.

———. „כמה עברית יוכל בית הכנסת להקנות לתלמידים?" (How Much Hebrew Can the Synagogue Transmit to the Pupils). *Hadoar* (H.) 20 (Jan. 10, 1941): 177–78. Also in *Yesod* (H.), 88–96.

———. דרכי למוד לשוננו (Methods of Studying our Language) (H.). N.Y.: Shulsinger, 1940. 410 pp.

———. „דרכי למוד הכתיב" (Methods of Teaching Writing) *Sh Hah* (H.) (Special Issue, May-June 1939): 28–48.

———. „תפקיד הלשון העברית בחנוך" (The Role of the Hebrew Language in Education). In *Yesod* (H.), 31–47. Also in *ES* (H.), 9–26.

———. „הוראת הלשון העברית" (Teaching the Hebrew Language). (H.) N.Y.: JTI, 1922. 169 pp.

———. „למוד הלשון העברית" (Study of the Hebrew Language) *Hadoar* (H.) 3 (Aug. 22, 1924): 4–5.

———. „למה נלמד עברית?" (Why Should We Teach Hebrew?). In *ES* (H.), 27–34.

* Seidel, Julius. *The Affect of Bilingualism on the Measurement of Intelligence.* Fordham U., 1937.

Silverman, William B. "Code Fun in Hebrew." *Jew Teach* 18 (Nov. 1949): 5–9.

Simon, Ralph. "An Experiment in Intensified Hebrew Instruction." *Syn Sch* 7 (Apr. 1949): 8–10.

Sugarman, Lillian. "The Teaching of Liturgical Hebrew." *Jew Teach* 14 (Jan. 1946): 11–16.

Touroff, Nissan. "חנוך עברי וחנוך יהודי„ (Hebrew Education and Jewish Education). *Sh Hah* (H.) 1 (1926): 1–6.

———. "לתקנת החנוך העברי„ (Toward the Improvement of Hebrew Education). *Sh Hah* (H.) 1 (1926), 1–14; 2 (1926), 19–24, 16–22.

"Using the Hebrew Dictionary." *Syn Sch* 5 (Apr. 1947): 123–26.

Wallenrod, Reuben. "הוראת הדקדוק העברי„ (Teaching Hebrew Grammar). In *Yesod* (H.), 132–47.

Weiss, Fannie. "Hebrew Alphabet." *Jew Teach* 4 (Jan. 1936): 37–38.

Whiteman, Kalman. "ווי האלט עס מיט העברעאישער ערציהונג אין אמעריקע?„ (How Does Hebrew Education Fare in America?) *Day* (Y.) (Feb. 22, 1926).

———. "לאן?„ (Whither?). On the goals of Hebrew education. *Sh Hah* (H.) 1 (1926): 1–8, 15–21.

Zederbaum, A. D. "מספרים„ (Statistics on Hebrew Education in America). *Sh Hah* (H.) 4 (1929): 400–403.

METHODOLOGY AND TEACHING AIDS SINCE 1950

Abrams, Arthur I. "Toward a Course of Study in Hebrew for the Sixth Grade of the Religious School." Master's thesis, HUC–JIR, 1961.

Ackerman, Walter I. "Hebrew Language Instruction in the Conservative Congregation School." *Syn Sch* 23 (Summer 1965).

———. "Second Language Learning for the Child below Eight." *Syn Sch* 19 (1960).

* Adiv, Ellen. *An Analysis of Second Language Performance in two types of Immersion Programs.* McGill U., 1980.

Anisfeld, M. M., and W. E. Lambert. "Social and Psychological Variables in Learning Hebrew." *J of Abnormal and Social Psychology* 63 (1961): 524–29.

Aphek, Edna. "Teaching Hebrew Poetry." *Ped Rep* 4 (Jan. 1983): 20–23.

Aroestry, Ruth M. "Individualizing a Hebrew Program." *Syn Sch* 32 (Summer 1974): 22–24.

* Axelrod, Herman C. *Bilingualism Background and Its Relation to Certain Aspects of Character and Personality of Elementary School Children.* Yeshiva U., 1952.

Bargad, W. "Teaching Hebrew Through Creative Writing." *Con Jud* 27 (Summer 1973): 52–62.

Beckerman, Avi. "The Hebrew Language and Its Context." *Jew Ed* 55 (Spring 1987): 6–8.

Ben-Horin, Meir. (On Values and Language—or, The Hebrew Language and Jewish Education). *Hadoar* (H.) 54 (July 11, 1975).

Berkowitz, Alice J. "An Integrated Program of Hebrew and Religious Instruction." *Jew Teach* 32 (Oct. 1963): 12–13.

Bernstein, Eliezer Z. "החינוך העברי לאן?„ (Whither Hebrew Education?). *Hadoar* (H.) 52 (Sept. 7, 1973).

Blumberg, Harry. ספר הדקדוק והחבור (Hebrew Grammar and Composition) (H.) N.Y.: Hebrew Pub. Co., c. 1955. 410 pp.

Bortniker, Elijah. "שיטות למודה של שפה שניה„ (Methods for Teaching a Second Language). *Sh Hah* (H.) 16 (Spring 1956): 137–45.

Braverman, Libbie L. "Teaching Hebrew—A Joyous Experience." *Syn Sch* 11 (Feb. 1953): 27–28.

Bridger, David. "העברעאישע לערנביכער פאר די ערשטע צוויי יאר פון העברעאיש-לימוד אין דער אמעריקאנער העברעאישער עלעמענטאר שול„ (Hebrew Textbooks for the First Two Years in the American Hebrew Elementary Schools). In *DER* (Y.), 3:267–86.

Chasen, Simon. "Iconoscopy in Language Teaching." *Modern Language J* (Feb. 1955). Also in *RTHE*, 42–43.

Chomsky, William. "Aims and Techniques in Teaching Hebrew." *Jew Teach* 34 (Apr. 1966): 31–34.

———. "A Basic Problem in Hebrew Methodology." *Jew Ed* 29 (Winter 1959): 3–5.

———. "Principles of Teaching a Foreign Language to Young Children: Experiences in Hebrew." *Modern Language J* 39 (Feb. 1955).

———. "בעיות הוראתן של הלשון העברית ושל התרבות העברית באמריקה" (Problems of Teaching the Hebrew Language and Culture in America). *Hagut* (H.) 3 (1974): 379–88.

Cohen, Jack J. "Language." In *JEDS*, 171–76.

Cohen, Miles B. "The Melton Hebrew Language Program." *MRCN* 9 (Spring 1979): 3, 11.

Colbert, Scott E., and Pat Dinning. "A New Approach to Hebrew Instruction." *Compass* 4 (Spring 1981): 10–11.

Dori, Rivkah. "Hebrew From Within—A Confluent Approach." *AM* (Winter 1978).

Efron, Benjamin. *Suggested Hebrew Curriculum for Reform Jewish Schools*. Rev. ed. by Jack Horowitz. N.Y.: Ktav, 1970.

Ehrmann, Eliezer L. "Listening Comprehension: A Contribution to the Teaching of Hebrew." *Jew Ed* 32 (Winter 1972): 96–98.

Eisenberg, Azriel. "Audio-Visual Materials in the Teaching of Hebrew." In *RTHE*, 293–94.

Eisenberg, Azriel, and Seymour Warkow. "Continuity of Higher Hebrew Study and Jewish Home Environment." *Jew Ed* 26 (Spring 1956): 42–50.

Engel, David. "לימוד השפה העברית כחובה דתית" (Study of the Hebrew Language as a Religious Obligation). *Sh Hah* (H.) 39 (1980): 15–16.

Feinstein, Joseph. "A Curriculum for the Midweek Hebrew School." *Jew Teach* 33 (Oct. 1964): 23–25.

Frank, Beryl. "Art in a Hebrew Class." *Compass* (Mar.–Apr. 1971).

Frank, H. P. "A Study of the Impact of a Hebrew Program on Children and Their Parents." Master's thesis, Ohio State U., 1962.

Franzblau, Abraham N. "The New Hebrew Methodology Progress Report." *CCAR J* (Jan. 1954): 19–26.

———. "New Methods of Teaching Hebrew." *Jew Ed* 22 (Winter–Spring 1951): 15–28.

Frost, Shimon. "עברית-הגשר בין הארץ והגולה" (Hebrew—The Bridge Between Israel and the Diaspora). *Ped Rep* 34 (H. and E. summary) (Jan. 1983): 34–36.

Gamoran, Hillel. "Hebrew and the Reform Religious School." *Jew Teach* 26 (May 1958): 16–18.

Glasner, Samuel. "The Silent Reading Method." *Jew Ed* 33 (Summer 1963): 231–34.

Glasner, Samuel, and Samuel Grand. *Toward a Curriculum for Hebrew Instruction in Reform Jewish Religious Schools*. N.Y.: UAHC, CJE, and CCAR, 1964.

Glassman, Barbara. "The Creative Hebrew Teacher's Helper." In *JTH*, 2d ed., 53–68.

* Goelman, Elazar. *The Development of the Natural Method (Ivrit B'Ivrit) in the Teaching of Hebrew in Jewish Schools in Modern Times*. Dropsie College, 1953.

———. "Toward the Improvement of Teaching Hebrew." *Jew Ed* 25 (Fall 1954): 32–36, 79.

Goldman, Emanuel. "Goals for Hebrew Language Instruction." *Jew Ed* 49 (Summer 1981): 46.

Goldman, Robert. "A No-Nonsense Approach to Teaching Hebrew." *Compass* 4 (Fall–Winter 1980): 6–7, 21.

Gordon, Joel. "The Hebrew Program." In *JPH*, 301–10.

Gordon, Yosi. "Teaching Hebrew: Initial Considerations." In *JPH*, 109–14.

Grand, Samuel, and Moshe Genser. *Hebrew, the Audio-Lingual Way*. N.Y.: Ktav, 1963.

Grand, Samuel, and Tamar Grand. *Hebrew Through Stamps*. N.Y.: Tarbuth Foundation, 197?. 21 pp.

Halevi, Mordecai. "עברית בחינוך היהודי בגולה" (Hebrew in Jewish Education in the Diaspora). In *Ed Enc* (H.), 2:676–77.

Haramati, Shlomo. "Hebrew Language Education." *MRCN* 4 (Winter 1976): 1–6.

———. "דרכי הוראת העברית בתפוצות" (Methods of Teaching Hebrew in the Diaspora) (H.). Jerusalem: DEC and WZO, 1976. Introduction published in *Hadoar* (H.) 56 (Mar. 4, 1976).

Hoffman, Rae D. "The Need for a Remedial Reading Program." *Syn Sch* 15 (May 1957): 16–20.

Iram, Jacob. "להפסיק ללמד ספרות?" (Shall We Interrupt to Teach Literature? Aims and Methods in Teaching Hebrew Literature). *Hadoar* (H.) 52 (Dec. 8, 1972).

* Isseroff, Sampson A. *The Utilization of Hebrew Workbooks as Teaching Aids in Afternoon Hebrew Schools.* New York U., 1962. 220 pp.

Janowsky, Oscar. "Hebrew Education." *Day-Jewish Morning J* (May 16, 1956).

Kalband, Regina, and Rose Klaw. "Introducing the Study of Hebrew with a Filmstrip." *Jew Teach* 22 (May 1954): 13–14.

Kaminetsky, Alex. "The Use of Grouping in the Teaching of Hebrew." *Syn Sch* 12 (Feb. 1954): 3–8.

Klein, Joseph. "Hebrew in Reform Religious Education." *Jew Teach* 25 (Jan. 1957): 3–5.

Kohn, Rebekah J. "Selecting a First Year Hebrew Text." *Syn Sch* 9 (Apr. 1951): 13–16.

———. "The Use of the Workbook in Teaching Hebrew." *Syn Sch* 13 (Dec. 1954): 21–23.

Korman, Michael. "Criteria for Selecting Hebrew Language Textbooks." *Ped Rep* 34 (Jan. 1983): 27–28.

Lander, Harry, and Jordan Parr. *Effective Strategies for Hebrew Education.* HUC-JIR, Fall 1985.

Lazarus, Mrs. Louis. "Providing Meaningful Experiences in Hebrew for the Six and Seven Year Olds." *Syn Sch* 14 (Nov. 1955). Also in *RTHE*, 59–62.

Lear, Elmer N. "The Committee Method in the Classroom." *Jew Ed* 24 (Spring 1953): 41–46.

Levinson, Jay H. "Hebrew Language Instruction in the Synagogue School." *Syn Sch* 34 (Fall 1975): 33–34.

Levitats, Isaac. "העברעאיש (לערן-מעטאד)„ (Hebrew Methodology). In *DER* (Y.), 203–14.

Levy, Louis. "Teaching Hebrew to Beginners." *Jew Teach* 20 (Nov. 1951 and Jan. 1952): 16–30, 1–10.

Lister, Louis. "A Functional Hebrew Curriculum." *CCAR J* (June 1954): 43–45.

Lister, Rebecca. "The Lynnbrook Experiment with the One-Bond Method of Teaching Hebrew." *Jew Ed* 24 (Spring 1953): 47–54.

Marenof, Martha. "An Experiment in Teaching Values Through Hebrew." *Jew Teach* (Dec. 1963): 16–18.

———. "Teaching Hebrew for Meaning." *Jew Teach* 23 (Mar. 1955): 17–18.

Margoshes, Samuel. "צווייטע שפראך„ (Second Language). *Day* (Y.) (Nov. 4, 1961).

Mayo, Maxine. "Chazakah—A Summer Hebrew Correspondence Course." A three-month correspondence program, which stresses contact with the rabbi, educator, and synagogue. Master's project, HUC–JIR, 1976.

Medini, Mordecai. "רצון ויכולת בחנוך„ (Desire and Capability in Hebrew Education). *Hadoar* (H.) 30 (Apr. 13, 1951): 443–49.

Miller, Richard. "Hebraisms: A Conceptual Approach to Learning Hebrew." Master's thesis, HUC–JIR, 1976.

Mosenkis, Rebekkah Kohn. "מדריך לטירון„ (A Guide for the Beginner). *Ped Rep* 35 (Jan. 1984): 33–34.

Nadel, Max. "On Teaching a Hebrew Poem in Translation." *Ped Rep* 36 (Jan. 1985): 15–17.

Nahir, Moshe. "Teaching Hebrew as a Second Language: The State of the Art." *Modern Language J* 63 (1979): 423–29.

Nudelman, Edward A. "How Should Hebrew Be Taught?" *Ped Rep* (Jan. 1957): 9–12. Reprinted from *Teachers Bulletin*, vol. 19, no. 3 (Aug. 1956), Chicago, BJE.

* Parks, Miriam Ben-Hayne. *Teaching Hebrew to American Students.* Ann Arbor, Mich.: University Microfilms International, 1984. 262 pp.

Rabin, Chaim. "Reasonable Choice: Language of the Bible." *MRCN* 9 (Spring 1979): 3, 11.

Raphaeli, Ruth. "The Melton Hebrew Language Program." *Ped Rep* 34 (Jan. 1983): 12–14.

Reisman, Diana. "Providing Meaningful Experiences in Hebrew for the 12 to 15 Age Group." *Syn Sch* 14 (Nov. 1955): 12–14. Also in *RTHE*, 63–66.

Ribalow, Menachem. "The Role of Hebrew in Jewish Education." *Jew Ed* 22 (Summer 1951): 69–71. Also in *JJS*, 134–37.

Ribner, Israel. "Aural-Oral Is Not Enough." *Syn Sch* 26 (Fall 1967): 3–10.

Rieger, Eliezer. *Modern Hebrew: A Complete Program for Teaching Hebrew as a Modern Spoken Language.* N.Y.: Philosophical Library, 1953. 156 pp.

Robin, Robert. "Correlation of Hebrew and the Other Subjects in the Curriculum." *Syn Sch* 11 (Feb. 1953): 10–12.

Robin, Stanley. "Toward a Program in Liturgical and Biblical Hebrew for Primary Grades of the Reform Religious School." Master's thesis, HUC–JIR, 1962.

* Rosin, Avivah. *The Value of Contrastive Analysis A Priori in Predicting Interference in Learning the Syntax of a Foreign Language: A Study of Selected Grammatical Structures in Hebrew and in English*. New York U., 1977.

Rothman, Iris. "More Hebrew Need Not Be a Problem." *Jew Teach* 27 (Nov. 1958): 9–10.

Rubee, Lillie. "Transition from the Whole-Word Method to Phonetics—A Case Study." *Syn Sch* 11 (Apr. 1953): 22–24.

Sandberg, Jeanne Glazer. "A Proposed Hebrew School Curriculum for a Developing Community." (High School) Master's thesis, Brandeis U., 1970.

Schachter, Lifsa. "Memory and Meaning in the Teaching of Hebrew." *Ped Rep* 34 (Mar. 1983): 34–36.

Schafer, Molly A. "Success in Hebrew Language Study as a Function of Intelligence and Home Motivation." *Ed As* (1968): 7–25.

Schaffler, Israel. "Report on the Use of *Shalom Yeladim* in Teaching Hebrew." *Syn Sch* 11 (Nov. 1952): 10–13.

Schanzer, Sharon Stern, and Nathaniel A. Entin. "The Language Laboratory in the Congregational School." *Jew Ed* 39 (Jan. 1969): 49–53, 64.

Schremer, Oded. "The Teaching of Hebrew and the Jewish Curriculum." *Jew Ed* (Fall 1986): 21–27.

Shapiro, Max A. "Toward a Curriculum for Hebrew Comprehension." Master's thesis, HUC–JIR, 1955. 105 pp.

Shmueli, Ephraim. „הערכה מחדש של מטרות הוראת הלשון העברית ודדכי לימודה באמריקה" (A Reevaluation of the Goals of the Hebrew Language Instruction in America and Its Methodology). In *Scharfstein* (H.), 118–33.

Shohamy, Elana. "The State of the Art of the Hebrew Language Curriculum." *Jew Ed* 53 (Fall 1984): 23–30.

Shumsky, Abraham. "Approaches to Hebrew Instruction." *Con Jud* 24 (Summer 1970): 65–69.

Skolnick, Irving H. "Mastery Learning in a Jewish School Settting." *Jew Ed* 55 (Winter 1988): 9–11.

Sochen, Mordecai. "Hebrew Instruction—At What Age?" *Syn Sch* 14 (May 1956): 3–6.

Soviv, Aaron. „ערך השמיעה בלמוד הלשון" (The Value of the Aural Experience in the Study of Language). *Sh Hah* (H.) 24 (Summer 1964): 205–10.

———. "The Function of Hebrew in the Afternoon School." *Jew Ed* 43 (Fall 1973): 17–23.

Spicehandler, Ezra. "The Teaching of Hebrew and Applied Linguistics." *Jew Teach* 28 (May 1960): 12–15.

Spivack, Harold. "An Experimental Hebrew Curriculum in a Small Congregation." *Jew Teach* 29 (Dec. 1960): 10–11.

Steinberg, Samuel. "Hebrew in the Curriculum." *Ped Rep* 34 (Jan. 1983): 1–2.

* Turner, Pearl G. *The Tactile-Kinesthetic Technique in the Teaching of Hebrew*. Kent State U., 1968. 89 pp.

Weinstein, David, and Abraham Yanover. "Hebrew Through Pictures." *Syn Sch* 17 (Sept. 1958): 14–19, and *Ped Rep* 10 (Nov. 1958).

Willner, Eric. "Applying Principles of Readiness to the Teaching of Hebrew." Master's thesis, Yeshiva U., 1954.

Winter, Magda. "Experimental Biblical Language Program." *MRCN* (Apr. 1976): 3.

Wolf, Sylvia, and Francine Feierstein. "The Magic of Hebrew Calligraphy." *Compass* 3 (Summer 1980).

Yari, Hava. „שפור הנחלת הלשון בארצות הברית" (Improving Hebrew Language Instruction in the United States). *Sh Hah* (H.) 27 (Summer 1967): 219–21.

Yenish, Joseph. "Teaching Functional Hebrew." *Syn Sch* 19 (1960–61).

Zalesky, Jacob. "Teaching Hebrew in the Jewish Religious School." *Jew Teach* 22 (1953–54).

BASIC VOCABULARY LISTS PRIOR TO 1950

Chomsky, William. "A Basic Vocabulary in Hebrew for the First Three Years." *Jew Ed* 7 (Jan.–Mar. 1935): 44–47.

———. "Vocabulary Studies as a Basis for a Hebrew Methodology." *Jew Ed* 9 (Apr.–June 1937): 58–60, 112

Hurwich, Louis. "Word Frequency in Pre-Biblical Hebrew Textbooks." *Jew Ed* 7 (Jan.–Mar. 1935): 40–43.

Jabotinsky, Ze'ev (Vladimir). "תרי״ג מלים„ (613 words). *Sh Hah* (H.) 2 (1926): 23–27.

Lurie, Rose G. "A Selected Hebrew Vocabulary for the Classroom." *Jew Teach* 5 (Jan. 1937): 19–23.

Rappaport, David. "An Effective Reading Word List for the Elementary School." *Jew Ed* 21 (Winter 1949): 64–69.

Rieger, Eliezer L. "Selection of a Spelling Vocabulary in Hebrew." Master's thesis, Chicago U., 1931.

Scharfstein, Zevi. "מלות היסוד בלשוננו„ (Basic Hebrew Words). *Hinnuch* (H.) 2 (Nissan 1938): 139–49.

Segal, Abraham. "Functional Hebrew Vocabulary Curriculum." *Syn Sch* 5 (Oct. and Dec. 1946 and Feb. 1947): 3–6, 42–44, 84–87.

Mark, Yudl. "Some Comments and Suggestions on Hebrew Word Lists." *Jew Ed* 29 (Winter 1959): 51–52, 71.

Nahshon, Samuel. (List of 900 Easy Hebrew Words) (H.). In *RTHE*, 271–77. Also in *Sh Hah* (H.) 13 (Jan. 1953): 67–81.

Nudelman, Edward A. "Vocabulary Studies and the Teaching of Hebrew." *Jew Ed* 30 (Fall 1959): 62–66.

Rappaport, David. "A Basic Word List for the Elementary Hebrew School." *Jew Ed* 22 (Summer 1951): 52–56

Rieger, Eliezer L. "The Vocabulary." In *Modern Hebrew* (1953), 96–117. Also in *RTHE*, 223–64.

* Spotts, Leon H. "Foundations of Vocabulary Selections for the Teaching of Hebrew in America." *Jew Ed* 29 (Winter 1959): 6–15.

———. *Word Studies in Modern Hebrew Literature and Their Methodological Implications*. Dropsie U., 1959. 150 pp.

* ———. "רשימת מלים לספרות החדשה„ (A Word List for the New Hebrew Literature) (H.). In *RTHE*, 278–84.

* Weinstein, David. *A Comparative Study of the Adequacy of Selected Vocabulary Lists for Simplifying Hebrew Literature*. Harvard U., 1956. 168 pp.

———. "Vocabulary Studies: A Review and Revaluation." Comment by W. Chomsky and Response by Weinstein. *Jew Ed* 28: 13–25. Also in *RTHE*, 109–18.

BASIC VOCABULARY LISTS SINCE 1950

Benathan, Morris B. "Basic Vocabulary and Language Forms of the Siddur." *Jew Ed* 29 (Winter 1959): 16–46.

Bridger, David. "The Vocabulary Content of Hebrew Readers." *Ped Rep* 3 (Jan. 1952).

Brown, Sheldon S. "A Word Count of Basic Prayers." *Jew Ed* 29 (Winter 1959): 48–50.

Chomsky, William. "Some Guiding Principles in Textbook Analysis and Word List Construction." *Jew Ed* 25 (Fall 1954): 46–49, 73.

READING

Aaroni, Abraham. "The Teaching of Reading." *Jew Teach* 28 (May 1960): 10–12.

Abramson, Charlotte. "Teaching for Independent Reading in the Torah Curriculum." Master's thesis, Department of Jewish Education, JTS, 1989.

* Adini, Uziel. *Selected Hebrew Readings Studies in American and Israeli Hebrew High Schools: A Comparative Study of Values*. Dropsie U., 1969.

* Allouche, Edith K. *The Application of Miscue Analysis to the Oral Reading of Vocalized and Unvocalized Hebrew Texts*. Ohio State U., 1977. 104 pp.

Arzt, Morris. "How To Teach Reading." *Jew Ed* 8 (Apr.–June 1936): 83–88.

* Balgur, Raphael. *Problems of Teaching Hebrew (Reading Orientation) with Special Reference to Collateral Reading*. Dropsie U., 1964.

Berger, Philmore. "A Critical Evaluation of Current Methods of Teaching Hebrew Reading in the Reform Religious School." Master's thesis, HUC–JIR, 1953.

Birnbaum, David, and Bayle Koolak. "רשימת ספרים לקריאת עונג" (A List of Books for Reading for Pleasure) (H.). In *RTHE*, 286–90.

Borodkin, Thelma L., and Adina Ofek. "The Cloze Plus DTRA: A Technique for Teaching Metacognition in Modern Hebrew." *Jew Ed* 55 (Winter 1988): 30–37.

Bortniker, Elijah. "Supplemental Hebrew Reading." *Jew Ed* 30 (Winter 1960): 62–64.

Bridger, David. "A Review of Recent Hebrew Textbooks for the Primary Grades." *Jew Ed* 20 (Feb. 1949): 50–51.

Chomsky, William. "מקומם של ספרי קריאה בהוראות לשוננו" (The Place of Readers in the Instruction of Our Language). *Sh Hah* (H.) 2 (Oct. 1942): 259–67.

———. "The Problem of Reading in the Jewish School." *Jew Ed* 1 (Oct. 1929): 195–200.

———. "Reading Program in Hebrew." *Jew Ed* 8 (Oct.-Dec. 1936): 137–40.

———. "סיפורי" (Sippuri) (H.). 2 vols. Phila.: Gratz College, 1948. 47, 48 pp.

* Cooke, Bridget Litherland. *American Children's Perceptions of the Hebrew Alphabet*. Yeshiva U., 1979. 253 pp.

Copeland, Steven R. "The Oral Reading Experience in Jewish Learning." *Stu*, 193–211.

* ———. *Values and Experiences of Reading Aloud in Traditional Jewish Text Learning: A Study in the Coordination of Form and Meaning*. Harvard U., 1978. 196 pp.

Eisenberg, Azriel. "הקריאה המובנת כמטרה ראשית בהוראת העברית" (Reading Comprehension as a Primary Goal in Teaching Hebrew). *Sh Hah* (H.) 12 (June 1952): 143–49.

Engel, David. "Reading Hebrew." *Ped Rep* 34 (Jan. 1983): 30–31.

* Hammer, Robert A. *A Study of Hebrew Decoding Skills in Third and Fourth Grade English-Speaking Children*. Northwestern U., 1975. 208 pp.

Haramati, Shlomo. "בחינת מטרות הוראת הקריאה בחינוך היהודי בתפוצות" (Analysis of Objectives in the Teaching of Reading in Jewish Education in the Diaspora). In *Stu*, 7–39.

Hoffman, Rae D. "The Need for a Remedial Reading Program." *Syn Sch* 15 (May 1957): 16–20.

Karten, Esther. "Teaching Hebrew Reading: The Earlier the Better." *Compass* (Dec. 1976): 1–4.

King, Diane A. "Developing a Selected List of Co-Curricular Hebrew Reading." Readers evaluated. *Syn Sch* 27 (Spring 1969): 13–20.

Klarberg, Fred. "Beginning Reading and Hebrew." *Jew Ed* 51 (Winter 1983): 25–30.

Kramer, N. (Materials for Independent Reading). *Sh Hah* (H.) 3 (Mar. 1943): 83–88.

* Kupinsky, Bonnie Zwebner. *The Development of Visual Perception to Beginning Bilingual Reading Instruction in English and Hebrew*. Wayne State U., 1981. 180 pp.

Lenchner, Orna, and Rivka Dori. "Why Jonathan Can't Read (Hebrew)." *Compass* 6 (Summer 1983): 6–8, 19.

Lister, Rebecca. "Reading for Pleasure." *Jew Teach* 28 (May 1960): 8–9.

Margolis, Henry, and Chaim Ohel. "The Problem of Mechanical Reading." *Ped Rep* 34 (Jan. 1983): 32–33.

Millner, Achitob. *Does the Hebrew Program of Teaching Reading Need Revision?* N.Y.: 1957. 30 pp.

———. "Improving the Teaching of Reading." *Syn Sch* 14 (May 1956): 28–30.

* Nahshon, Samuel. *Readability Measurement of Hebrew Prose*. Columbia U., 1958. 156 pp.

———. "What Makes a Hebrew Book Readable?" *Jew Ed* 29 (Winter 1959): 53–63.

Nardi, Noah. "Language Difficulties and Reading Preferences." *Jew Ed* 14 (Apr.–June 1942): 30–35.

* Raphaeli, Ruth. *The Development of Materials for Teaching Reading Comprehension in Biblical Hebrew*. Columbia U. Teachers College, 1981. 280 pp.

Rappaport, David. "Reading—For What?" *Jew Ed* 21 (Summer 1950): 42–43.

* Saposnik, Tamar Lubin. *A Computer-Based Prototype for the Structure of a Hebrew Reading Program*. U. of Rochester, 1979. 144 pp.

Shpan, Shlomo. „הספרות העברית בחינוך היהודי בתפוצות" (Hebrew Literature in Jewish Education in the Diaspora) (H.). In *FPDE*, 109–17.

* Spector, Noya. *The Effect of Instruction in Reading, Writing, and Pronouncing Hebrew on Reading, Writing and Spelling English, among Children Who Are Slow Readers Studying Hebrew as a Foreign Language*. U. of Minnesota, 1980. 103 pp.

Stern, Jay B. "The Problem of 'Mechanical' Reading." *Syn Sch* 15 (May 1957): 21–25.

Tarnor, Pearl G. "Hebrew Reading for Pleasure." *Syn Sch* 15 (May 1957): 13–15.

"Teaching Hebrew Reading." *Syn Sch* 15 (May 1957): 13.

Weinstein, David, and Abraham Yanover. "Hebrew Through Pictures." *Syn Sch* 17 (Sept. 1958): 14–19, and *Ped Rep* 10 (Nov. 1958).

Zussman, Mrs. Morris. "Siddur Reading Remedial Chart." *Syn Sch* 15 (May 1957): 25–27.

Sud, Ira. "The Sephardic Pronunciation in the Hebrew School." *Syn Sch* 9 (Nov. 1950): 9–12.

ASSESSMENT PRIOR TO 1950

Braverman, Libbie L. "Hebrew in a Reform Temple School." *Jew Ed* (Jan.–Mar. 1933): 40–45.

Edidin, Ben. "Critique of the Hebrew Curriculum." *Jew Ed* 16 (Jan. 1945): 11–17.

Engelman, Uriah Z. "Problems of Hebrew Education in America." *Jewish Review* 2 (Jan. 1945): 231–56.

Essrig, Harry. "The Teaching of Hebrew in the Reform Religious School." *Jew Ed* 15 (1943): 28–33.

Konowitz, Israel. „מצב החנוך העברי באמריקה" (The Status of Hebrew Education in America). *Luach Ahi Ever* (1918). N.Y.: 3:39–62. Also in *Ha-Toren* (H.) 2 (Jan. 1915).

Nardi, Noah. "Studies in Attitudes Towards Hebrew Education." *J of Educational Research* 42 (1948): 37–46.

Pilch, Judah. „חובתנו בשעה זו" (Our Current Obligation). (On the need to intensify Hebrew education) *Sh Hah* (H.) 10 (1949): 3–5.

Reichert, Max. "The Instruction of Hebrew in Our Sunday Schools." *CCAR* 33 (1923): 281–85.

Rosen, Ben. "On 'The Strength of Hebrew in America'." *Menorah J* 16 (1928): 580.

PRONUNCIATION

Chomsky, William. "Problems of Pronunciation in Hebrew." In *Gratz College Anniversary Volume* (1971), 21–27.

Cohen, Carl. "The Pronunciation of Hebrew." *Con Jud* 7 (Apr. 1951).

Sheinzon, I. D. „נשפר את מבטאם הספרדי של תלמידינו" (Improving the Sephardic Pronunciation of Our Students). *Sh Hah* (H.) 11 (Dec. 1950): 28–34.

ASSESSMENT SINCE 1950

Axelroth, Dorothy. "Hebrew in the Reform Religious School." *Ped Rep* 31 (Jan. 1983): 8–9.

* Bridger, David. *The Consistency of Primary Hebrew Textbooks with the Curricula of the Hebrew Schools in the United States*. U. of Southern California, 1953. 323 pp.

———. "The Consistency of Primary Hebrew Textbooks with the Curricula of the Hebrew

Schools in the United States." *Jew Ed* 29 (Fall 1958): 50–55.

———. "Some Guiding Principles of Achievement of Hebrew Language Instruction on the Primary Level." *Jew Ed* 25 (Fall 1954): 37–45, 73.

Chomsky, William. "Another Look at the Problem of Teaching Hebrew in Our Schools." *Jew Ed* 33 (Fall 1962): 45–51, 57.

———. "Hebrew in America." *Jew Ed* 24 (Fall 1952): 47–54, 63.

———. „בעיות הוראתן של הלשון העברית ושל התרבות העברית באמריקה" (Problems of Teaching the Hebrew Language and Its Culture in America). *Hagut* (H.) 3 (1974): 379–88.

Engelman, Uriah Z. "The Congregation and Hebrew Education." *Jew Ed* 24 (Fall 1953): 39–46, 67.

Fishman, Joshua A. "Success and Failure in Language Education." *MRCN* 4 (Winter 1976): 1–6.

Friedman, Rivka. „נתיב חדש בחינוך העברי באמריקה" (A New Direction in Hebrew Education in America—Public High Schools and Colleges). *Bitzaron* (H.) (New series) 5–6 (Mar.–Apr. 1980): 34.

Frost, Shimon. "The Position of Hebrew in the Supplementary School." *Jew Ed* 45 (Winter 1977): 10–12, 38.

Gamoran, Hillel. "Hebrew and the Reform Religious School." *Jew Teach* 26 (May 1958): 15–16.

———. "The Study of Hebrew in Reform Congregations." *CCAR* 86 (1976): 70–91.

Gannes, Abraham P. "Hebrew Centered Curriculum vs. Value Centered Curriculum." *Impact* 35 (Summer 1977): 18–20.

Glasner, Samuel. "What Shall We Do About Hebrew?" *Jew Teach* 32 (Oct. 1963): 10–12.

Gopstein, Alizah. „על הוראת העברית באמריקה" (On the Teaching of Hebrew in America). *Hadoar* (H.) 58 (June 15, 1979).

Grand, Samuel. "The Implications of the Hebrew Survey for Temple Educators." *Jew Teach* (Apr. 1962): 23–27.

———. "The New Outlook for Hebrew in Reform Jewish Education." *Jew Ed* 34 (Winter 1964): 103–8.

———. *Report: Survey of Mid-Week Hebrew Instruction in Reform Religious Schools, 1960–61*. N.Y.: CJE of UAHC and CCAR, 1961–62. 39 pp.

———. "A Viable Hebrew Language Program for Our Schools." *Jew Teach* 32 (Apr. 1964): 10–13.

Halkin, Abraham S. "Hebrew During the Past Ten Years in Jewish Education." *Jew Ed* 21 (Spring 1950): 51–53.

Kaiman, Arnold. "Teaching Hebrew in a Small Congregation." *Jew Teach* 28 (Jan. 1960): 3–6.

Kapel, David E. "Parental and Student Reactions to an Alternative Summer Hebrew Program." *Jew Ed* 44 (Spring/Summer 1976): 43–50.

Klein, Joseph. "Hebrew in Reform Religious Education." *Jew Teach* 25 (Jan. 1957): 3–5.

Mark, Yudl. "Is There a One-Bond Method for Teaching Hebrew." *Jew Ed* 22 (Summer 1951): 31–36.

Nudelman, Edward A. "Notable Contribution to the Teaching of Hebrew." *Syn Sch* 19 (1960).

———. "The Teaching of Hebrew—Another Look Ten Years Later." *Jew Ed* 36 (Summer 1966): 133–42.

Rabinowitz, Zina. „שוחרי החנוך העברי" (Friends of Hebrew Education). *Hadoar* (H.) 35 (Mar. 9, 1956): 359.

Rosen, Harry J. "Hebrew in the Reform Religious School." *Jew Teach* 29 (Dec. 1960): 2.

Ruby, Hemdah. „שגיאות יסודיות בהוראת שפתנו" (Basic Errors in the Teaching of Our Language). *Sh Hah* (H.) 14 (Summer 1954): 248–52.

Scharfstein, Zevi. „עליות וירידות בחנוך העברי" (Ups and Downs of Hebrew Education). *Hadoar* (H.) 37 (11th of Tishri 1959).

Scheindler, Ronny. "The Computer as an Aid to Teaching the Hebrew Language in a Jewish School in the United States" (H.). Master's thesis, Department of Jewish Education, JTS.

Schiff, Alvin I. *Towards a Statement on the Significance of Hebrew*. N.Y.: DEC, Study and Teaching of Hebrew, Spring 1965.

Shereshevsky, Ezra. "Hebrew Alone Is Not Enough." *Jew Spec* 31 (Mar. 1966): 13.

Siegel, Morton. "Hebrew in the Afternoon Religious School." *Ped Rep* 34 (Jan. 1983): 2–4.

Slesinger, Zalmen. "The Place of Hebrew in the Curriculum of the Afternoon School—A Dilemma of Jewish Education." *Ped Rep* 21 (Sept. 1969).

Sochen, Mordecai. "Hebrew Instruction—At What Age?" *Syn Sch* 14 (May 1956): 3–6.

* ———. *The Teaching of Foreign Languages in the Period of 1940–1954*. JTS, 1955. 233 pp.

Spotts, Leon H. "Hebrew in the Context of the Philosophy of Conservative Judaism." *Syn Sch* 24 (Winter 1966): 4–14.

Wise, Aaron M. "The Place of Hebrew in Conservative Judaism: Its Philosophy, Problems, and Prospects." *Syn Sch* 23 (Summer 1965): 26–34.

Zeldner, Max. "Hebrew Is a Must in Jewish Education." *Jud* 26 (1977): 46–51.

TESTING AND EVALUATION

Bugatch, Simon, and Judah Pilch. *Tests in Advanced Hebrew*. (Grades 1–4 and 6–11) N.Y.: NCRI, AAJE, 1964.

Chomsky, William. "Experience with a Testing Program in Hebrew." *Jew Ed* 14 (Jan.–Mar. 1943): 134–37.

Eisenberg, Azriel, ed. "AAJE Tests"; "JEC Tests"; "Chomsky Tests." In *RTHE*, 152–221.

* Goodnick, Benjamin. *Measuring Aptitudes for Hebrew in the Jewish School*. Dropsie U., 1955. 105 pp.

* Grad, Edna. *Instruments for the Evaluation of Language Materials: An Example from Hebrew Textbooks*. U. of Texas, 1978. 208 pp.

Hebrew Language Achievement Tests: Lower, Intermediate and Upper Levels. N.Y.: AAJE.

* Hochberg, Hillel. *Hebrew Language Achievement in Accredited Orthodox Talmud Torahs*. Yeshiva U., 1966. 274 pp.

Maller, Julius B. "A Standardized Hebrew Prognosis Test." *Jew Ed* 3 (Oct.–Dec. 1931): 177–84.

Nardi, Noah. "Group Test for Siddur Reading." *Jew Ed* 18 (Nov. 1946): 49–51.

———. "Hebrew Achievement Tests." *Jew Ed* 15 (Sept. 1943): 21–27.

———. "A Test to Measure Aptitude in the Hebrew Language." *J of Educational Psychology* 38 (Mar. 1947): 167–76.

Nudelman, Edward A. "An Index for Testing Reading Facility." *Jew Ed* 1 (May 1929): 121–23.

* Plavin, Irving. *The Development and Preliminary Validation of an Auto-tutorial Program for Improving Skills in Recitation of Biblical Hebrew Texts*. Columbia U. Teachers College, 1976. 145 pp.

* Ravid, Ruth. *Development and Evaluation of an Achievement Test in the Hebrew Language*. Northwestern U., 1979.

Shluker, David. "At Last—Hebrew Achievement Test." *Ped Rep* 34 (Jan. 1983): 28–30.

* Shohamy, Elana Goldberg. *Investigation of the Concurrent Validity of the Oral Interview with Cloze Procedures for Measuring Proficiency in Hebrew as a Second Language*. U. of Minnesota, 1978. 337 pp.

Skolnick, Irving A. "Development of New Hebrew Language Tests." *Ped Rep* 30 (Winter 1979): 1–2.

Tarasow, Morris. "An Experiment in Standardizing a Hebrew Achievement Test for the Second Year." *Jew Ed* 26 (Spring 1956): 51–55.

HEBREW IN PUBLIC HIGH SCHOOLS

See also New York City in Chapter 37

Amirom, P. „הערות והצעות להוראת הלשון בב״ס העברי בארצה״ב" (Comments and Suggestions for the Instruction of Hebrew in Schools in the US). *Hadoar* (H.) 61 (Dec. 4, 1981).

Azrieli, Shlomo. "Hebrew in the Public High Schools and Colleges." *Jew Ed* 21 (Summer 1950): 5–7.

Blumberg, Harry. "Some Desiderated Materials in Hebrew Language Teaching in the Public High Schools." *Jew Ed* 12 (Jan. 1941): 166–70.

Haber, Leo. "Hebrew in Public High Schools and Colleges." *Ped Rep* 32 (Winter 1981): 13–15.

Katsh, Abraham I. "Hebrew in the High Schools." *Jew Fron* (Sept. 1953).

———. „הוראת העברית בבתי הספר האמריקאים" (Hebrew Instruction in American Schools). *Hadoar* (H.) 18 (Kislev 2, 1930).

Lapson, Judah. „עברית במערכת החינוך הצבורי בארצות הברית" (Hebrew in the U.S. Public School System). In *FPDE* (H.), 130–35.

Lewittes, Mordecai H. "Hebrew in the Public Schools." *Jew Ed* 48 (Winter 1980): 6–9.

Schechter, Jay. "Hebrew Studies in Public Schools." *Ped Rep* 33 (Mar. 1982): 14.

HEBREW TEXTBOOKS PRIOR TO 1950 (SELECTED)

Bachrach, Kalman. *HaSefer* (Part 1) (H.). 3 vols. N.Y.: Elat Pub. Co., 1941–47.

Feinberg, N. S. *HaYisod* (H.). N.Y.: Bloch, 1929. 60 pp.

Gamoran, Emanuel, and Abraham Friedland. *Gilenu: The Play Way to Hebrew* (H.). 2 vols. Cincinnati: DSSE of UAHC, 1933–45.

Golden, Hyman. *HaTzaad HaRishon*. 2 vols. N.Y.: Hebrew Pub. Co., 1929. 80 and 94 pp.

Greenberg, Simon. *HaRishon* (H.). 3 vols. N.Y.: USCJE of USA and Rabbinical Assembly, 1940–48, 1954. 40, 96, and 120 pp.

Grossman, Jacob D. *Reshit HaKriah* (H.). N.Y. 54 pp.

Klepper, Leah H. *Shalom U'Vrakha* (H.). N.Y.: Behrman, 1948. 79 pp.

Konowitz, Israel, et al. *Daat* (H.). First year. N.Y.: Hebrew Pub. Co., 1938. 128 pp.

Krinsky, M. *Reshit Daat* (H.). Rev. ed. N.Y.: Hebrew Pub. Co., 1938. 96 pp.

Marenoff, M., and L. Schultz. *HaIvri* (H.). 2 vols. Chicago: Teudah Pub. Co., 1939–41. 96 and 95 pp.

Polak, I. H. *Bet Sifrenu* (H.). N.Y.: Hebrew Pub. Co., 1939. 123 pp.

Rappoport, Israel B. *HaMitlamed* (H.). 2 vols. N.Y.: Hebrew Pub. Co., 1934–37. 32 and 88 pp.

Rubinstein, Simha, and Harry Kessler. *Elements of Hebrew* (H.). 2 vols. N.Y.: Bureau of Jewish Education, 1937, 1939.

Scharfstein, Zevi. *Amenu*. 2 vols. For third and fourth years. N.Y.: Shiloh 1938, 1941. 153 pp.

———. *Hayenu* (H.). 2 vols. N.Y.: Shiloh, 1938.

———. *Our People's Language* (H.). Reader for second year. N.Y.: c. 1927. 81 pp.

HEBREW TEXTBOOKS SINCE 1950

Adler, Lillian W. *Practice, Drill, and Review Book for Reading Hebrew* (H.). N.Y.: Behrman. Sephardi.

Band, Orah, and Bella Bergman. *Hebrew—A Language Course*. 3 vols. N.Y.: Behrman. For high school.

Blumberg, Harry, and Mordecai H. Lewittes. *Modern Hebrew: A Course in Reading, Grammar and Conversation*. 2 vols. N.Y.: Hebrew Pub. Co., 1952. For high school.

Castberg, C., and Lillian W. Adler. *Reading Hebrew*. Programmed instruction book, teacher's guide, practice drill, review book, filmstrip and cassette. N.Y.: Behrman.

Cohen, Miles B., and Ruth Raphaeli. *B'rinna Yiktzoru* (First Reader). Workbooks by Ruth Raphaeli; Curriculum Supervisor, Seymour Fox. N.Y.: MRC of JTSA, 1983.

———. *Alilot Uzial* (Third Reader). Curriculum Supervisor, Seymour Fox. 14 Workbooks (Units). N.Y.: MRC of JTSA, 1982, 1984.

Edelstein, Menahem M., E. Indelman, and Y. Weingarten. *Aleph with Workbook* (H.). Primer. Brooklyn, N.Y.: 1954.

Haramati, Shlomo. *Alfon Ivri: A Hebrew Primer*. Teacher's Guide developed by MRC. N.Y.: Behrman.

Kohn, Rebekah, and Nathaniel A. Entin. *Kra Na, Books I and II*. Workbook and illustrations. N.Y.: USCJE.

Mansoor, Menahem. *Contemporary Hebrew: An Introductory Course.* N.Y.: Behrman, c. 1976. 295 pp.

Persky, Elias, and Sol Scharfstein. *Bet Sefer—A.* Recordings. N.Y.: Ktav. 96 pp.

Raphaeli, Ruth, and Miles B. Cohen. *Agadat HaShamir.* Curriculum Supervisor, S. Fox. 14 Workbooks (Units) by Ruth Raphaeli. N.Y.: MRC of JTSA, 1984.

———. *Kol Rinna.* Curriculum Supervisor, S. Fox. Teachers Guide. 4 Workbooks (12 Units). N.Y.: MRC of the JTSA. Ages 8–10. Second Reader.

Scharfstein, Sol. *Hebrew Language Funbooks.* N.Y.: Ktav.

———. *Shaar Hakriah I and II.* Workbooks, cassettes, and flashcards. N.Y.: Ktav.

Schwartzman, Sylvan. *Rocket to Mars.* Cincinnati: Rocket Press, 1955.

Shumsky, Abraham, and Adina Shumsky. *Alef-Bet: A Hebrew Primer* and *The Alef-Bet Reading Practice Book.* Teachers Guide. N.Y.: UAHC. For beginners.

———. *Mah Tov.* 3 vols with teachers guides and workbooks. Illustrated by K. Plowitz, L. C. Wronker, and J. Maidoff. For intermediate grades. N.Y.: UAHC.

———. *Olam Gadol, Alef.* Teachers Guide. Illustrated by Leo Glueckselig. *Olam Gadol Bet—Reader.* Illustrated by M. Bloom, M. Garchik, C. M. Schulz, and S. Shimin. N.Y.: UAHC.

Silber, Theresa K. *Kadima Yeladim.* For second year. N.Y.: USCJE. 204 pp.

———. *Shalom Yeladim, Books I and II.* Teachers Guide, Workbooks. N.Y.: USCJE. 1951–76. 133 pp.

GLEANINGS

"W.A.," *The Quarterly Theological Magazine* II (1813), 92–95,

> Is Latin of more importance than Hebrew? I would ask, does it become us to employ months and years in learning a heathen tongue, and yet not to allot even a solitary day to the sacred Hebrew language.... Is it consistent with those precepts inculcated by the doctrines of Christianity, to elevate men above the Maker.... I would ask, can Horace, Juvenal, Virgil, Homer, and the whole catalogue of Pagan authors, produce one work or passage that can vie with many of the Old Testament in sublimity, beauty of imagery, purity of morality, and the importance and magnificence of the subject discussed."

Quoted by Wolfe and Whiteman, in *History of the Jews in Philadelphia* (1956), 309.

Edwards, B., Professor of Hebrew, Andover Theological Seminary (1838),

> I shall attempt ... to adduce some reasons why the study of the Hebrew language should be made a part of a liberal education....
> 1. An argument for the study of Hebrew may be derived from the fact that great eminence in the pursuit, on the part of a few individuals, cannot be expected in the absence of a general cultivation of the language....
> 2. My second argument for the more general study of the Hebrew is, that we may be better prepared to take all proper advantage of the immense stores of erudition on the general subject which have been collected in Germany....
> 3. The importance of the study of the Hebrew language may be argued from its effect in strengthening the faith of the student in the genuineness and divine authority of the Scriptures....
> 4. The influence of the study of the Hebrew Scriptures on the imagination and the taste....
> 5. Another important consideration is the bearing of the study of Hebrew upon the missionary enterprise."

Quoted in Blau and Baron, *The Jews of the United States, 1790–1840* (1963), 2:419–24.

Schechter, Solomon,
> "The Hebrew language is the great depository of all that is best in the soul-life of the Congregation Israel. Without it we will become severed from the great Tree which is life to those who cling to it."

Quoted by Zeldner, *Jud* (Winter 1977), 50–51.

Magnes, Judah L,.
"In every Jewish cultural revival the Hebrew language has played an important part, and today when the Jewish nation is again witness of the marvel of its own renaissance, when, like an old tree in springtime, it is shooting forth new cultural blossom, the Hebrew language is again fulfilling its mission as the natural vehicle through which young Judah expresses his fears and hopes."
Quoted in G. Plaut, *The Growth of Reform Judaism*, 320.

Spiegel, Shalom,
The revival of Hebrew and its transformation into a colloquial tongue with all the defects and virtues of a living language; the revival of Hebrew literature and its development within the last decades to a high intellectual and emotional level, and such progress in vocabulary as would have filled any civilized people with pride—these things have proven beyond a doubt the physiological genuineness of our rejuvenation as a people."
Hebrew Reborn (1930), 19–20.

Kaplan, Mordecai M.,
"Hebrew can no more be omitted from the child's training as a Jew than English from his training as an American."
JAC (1957), 483.

Gamoran, Emanuel,
"Suppose that music had to justify its existence in the eyes of people who are deaf, it would be highly unfortunate, would it not? Yet Hebrew is often asked to justify itself in the eyes of those who are, so to say, deaf to the sound of Hebrew. As sensible people we would contend that music must justify itself ultimately because of those who are not deaf and are able to appreciate the beauty of sound. So Hebrew must be justified in terms of those people who know it and appreciate it, and it is the function of the rabbi and teacher to convince the men and women in his congregation that there are some questions in Jewish life with reference to which the parents of our children are not in a position to pass judgement. On those questions they must abide by the advice of those who have studied, who know, and who love the Hebrew language and its literature."
CCAR Yearbook (1936), 306–7.

Mark, Yudl,
"There never was a time when the Yiddish school system did not include Hebrew. The question was only when to begin the study of Hebrew."
Jew Ed 17 (Feb. 1946), 43.

Halkin, Abraham S.,
"The truth is that the attitude to Hebrew in the western countries of Europe and America, in consonance with a general re-evaluation and reshuffling of general life, has been seriously affected because Hebrew has been made ancillary, a tool of religion—not to religion in the comprehensive sense, not as Jews understood and lived by until recently but strictly to religious service. In other words, Hebrew as related to religion has been interpreted to mean the ability to read prayers plus some inkling of their meaning.... 'Translation Judaism' may lead to a frightfully warped conception of both the religion and the civilization of the Jews."
Jew Ed 23 (Spring 1950), 51–52.

Ribalow, Menahem,
"There will be no integrated and wholesome Jews as long as our children are not brought up in Hebrew, the original language of Israel, as long as they are not taught to speak, read and write the language. Only through communication, through some communion with the Hebrew language, will they behold the full revelation of Judaism and become initiated into the mystery that preserved the Jewish people since the beginning of its history to this day of the renewal of Jewish sovereignty."
Jew Ed 22 (Summer 1951), 69.

United Synagogue Commission on Jewish Education,
"Hebrew is the historic language of the Jewish people, the language of the Bible, the Siddur, and Mahzor, the language of the renascent Jewish life in Eretz Israel.

It is the key to the vast spiritual treasures of Hebraic literature in all ages. Language study should constitute the principal area of instruction in the elementary division. At the junior high school the Bible and related content should be foremost. The materials should make active use of Hebrew to fortify language skills. At the same time, the content and ideals of the Torah must receive constant emphasis. With a Hebrew emphasis permeating both levels, students should derive living and meaningful experiences from their study of Hebrew."

Objectives and Standards of the Congregational School (1958), 10.

Ehrlich, Abraham J.,
"Any educator who says that he can teach these children (90–95% of the class) conversational Hebrew within the confines of an afternoon Hebrew School is fooling himself and misleading his congregation. What is worse, he is depriving his children of the only opportunity they have in Jewish Education. . . . I believe that the knowledge of Jewish values is more important than conversational Hebrew and that the teaching of Jewish ethics should take precedence over Hebrew writing or grammar."

Quoted by Walter I. Ackerman, *Syn Sch* 23 (Summer 1965), 18.

Resolution adopted by the Union of American Hebrew Congregations,
"Whereas, the aims of Reform Jewish education as articulated by our Commission on Jewish Education, include the preparation of the student to participate meaningfully in worship service and to derive religious and spiritual enrichment from our classic religious literature,

Therefore, be it recommended that, among the requirements for confirmation in any of the Reform religious schools there be included a reading knowledge of the Hebrew language, sufficient at least to read and comprehend the Hebrew portions of the Union Prayerbook and the Union Haggadah, as well as a minimum knowledge of Hebrew terminology dealing with religious life."

47th Biennial Assembly (1963), *Jew Ed* 34 (Winter 1964), 188.

Chomsky, William,
"In considering the problem of teaching Hebrew. . .we must bear in mind the distinction between techniques and methods. Techniques deal with the ways of doing things, with devices that make for economy, efficiency, and interest. In the case of methods, the emphasis is on aims and objectives: Why do these things? What goals do we want to attain? Once we determine the goals, we may look for effective techniques as aids in achieving these goals. We then have a method."

Jew Teach 34 (Apr. 1966), 31.

Haramati, Shlomo,
"Our vocabulary studies of the Bible and Siddur enable us to prepare materials which have the cumulative effect of giving the student the basic vocabulary of both of these texts. The entire Hebrew Bible contains only about 7500 different words—and there are 2000 basic roots. Our studies indicate that vocabulary of about 600 carefully chosen words enables a student to understand 80% of the narrative portions of the entire Bible—and over 90% of the central portions of the Siddur. Because our materials are based precisely on these 600 words, the transfer to the Biblical text itself should present no difficulty."

MRCN 4 (Winter 1976), 3.

Fishman, Joshua A.,
"We continue miraculously, generation after generation, to raise children who venerate, respect, and value the Hebrew language even as we have failed to give them speaking, reading, or even praying facility in the language."

MRCNA 4 (Winter 1976), 3.

Arzt, Raphael,
"A student whose consciousness is not enriched by Jewish memoirs must be convinced that the effort required to learn Hebrew will 'pay off'. Hebrew is not a self legitimating value. An educated Jew who does not know Hebrew is a cripple, but an uneducated Jew who perhaps knows 250–

1000 routine or even, Bible-related words is a Jewish non-entity. Hebrew as a strategic pillar to support educational efforts is ineffective. Only when we can solve the problem of deeper motivation can the strategy of teaching Hebrew come into meaningful focus."

Stu, 1:146.

Melton Hebrew Language Program,

"The Melton Hebrew Language Program is part of a curriculum for the afternoon Hebrew school which seeks to integrate the study of Bible, Siddur, holidays, Mitzvot, and Jewish thought, history, and community, in a graded, five-year program. . . .

The most important aspect of learning to understand a new language is learning the patterns of words and sentences which are most characteristic of that language. The meaning of individual words, though certainly important, is not as crucial in the long run. For even if the meaning of every word in a sentence is known, without a recognition of the sentence structure or pattern, that sentence remains nothing but a random list of words. It is the familiarity with the basic language patterns that turns those words into a meaningful thought."

Miles B. Cohen, *Preliminary Teachers Guide* (MRC of the JTSA, 1982), 1, 2.

11 | HISTORY

GENERAL HISTORY (SELECTED)

Baron, Salo W. *A Social and Religious History of the Jews*. 18 vols. Rev. ed. N.Y.: Columbia U. Press, 1952–83.

Ben-Sasson, H. H., ed. *A History of the Jewish People*. Cambridge: Harvard U. Press, 1976.

Dubnow, Simon. *World History of the Jews*. 11 vols. (G., H., Y., and E.). 1925–29.

Graetz, Heinrich. *History of the Jews*. 6 vols. Phila.: JPS, 1891–98.

Sachar, Howard M. *The Course of Modern Jewish History*. Rev. ed. N.Y.: Vintage Books, 1990.

PRIOR TO 1950

Baron, Salo W. "Emphases in Jewish History." *Jew Ed* 11 (Apr. 1939): 8–22, 39.

Calisch, Edward N. *Methods of Teaching Jewish History*. Senior Grade. Phila.: 1915. 264 pp.

Cohen, A. *Judaism in Jewish History*. N.Y.: Union of Orthodox Jewish Congregations of America, 1925. 22 pp.

Cohen, Morris R. "Philosophies of Jewish History." *JSS* 1 (1939): 39–72. Also in *RTJH*, 1–36.

Cowen, Ida G. "Project in American Jewish History." *Jew Teach* 12 (1944): 1–11.

Dreyfus, Miriam W. "A Jewish Current Events Project." *Jew Teach* 6 (June 1938): 16–21.

Eisenberg, Israel L. (Azriel). "Children's Reactions to Current Events and Keren Ami Letters." *Jew Teach* 5 (June 1937): 31–37; 6 (Jan. 1938), 19–24.

———. "Correlating Jewish Current Events." *Jew Teach* 4 (Apr. 1936): 1–7.

———. "Teaching Jewish Current Events." *Jew Teach* 2 (June 1934): 1–9.

Emil, N. Charles. "A Problem Course in World Jewry." *Jew Teach* 13 (Nov. 1944): 1–7.

Feinstein, Moses. "להוראת תולדות ישראל,, (On Teaching Jewish History). *Sh Hah* (H.) 1 (1925): 21–24; 1 (1926): 22–27; 2 (1926): 34–42; 2 (1927): 33–37, 47–49; 3 (1928); 4 (1928): 90–93.

Fineberg, Solomon A. *A Project in American Jewish History*. A manual for Jewish teachers. Cincinnati: DSSE and UAHC, 1921, 1931. 79 pp.

Fineschreiber, William. *Methods of Teaching Biblical History—The Prophets*. Phila.: Jewish Chautauqua Society, n.d.

Franzblau, Abraham N. *A Curriculum in History for Jewish Religious Schools—Elementary Grades*. Cincinnati: HUC, 1935. 103 pp.

Gamoran, Emanuel. "Concerning Workbooks." *Jew Teach* 3 (Nov. 1934): 21–22.

Golub, Jacob. "Goals in the Teaching of Jewish History." *Jew Ed* 15 (Jan. 1944): 90–95. Also in *RTJH*, 113–18.

———. "What Are Workbooks and Why?" *Jew Teach* 1 (Nov. 1932): 14–20; 3 (Nov. 1934): 11–14.

Green, Alan S. "Teaching Modern Jewish History through Fiction." *Jew Teach* 7 (Nov. 1939): 1–7.

———. *Teaching Modern Jewish History through Fiction.* N.Y.: UAHC, 1939. 96 pp.

Greenberg, Sidney J. "The Teaching of Jewish Current Events." *Jew Ed* (Oct.–Dec. 1935): 175–77.

Halkin, Abraham Sh. „תפקיד למוד ההיסטוריה בחנוך" (The Role of the Study of History in Education) *Yesod* (H.), 104–20.

Honor, Leo L. "Guiding Principles for Writing and Teaching Jewish History." *American Israelite* (Nov. 26, 1931). See also *Jew Ed* 42 (Fall 1957): 1, 55; *RTJH*, 91–96; and Honor, *Selected Writings*, 278–87.

———. "Methods of Teaching Jewish History." *Jew Ed* 28 (Fall 1957): 48–51, 55. See also Honor, *Selected Writings*, 257ff.

———. *Selected Writings.* Edited by Abraham P. Gannes. N.Y. Reconstructionist Press, 1965.

———. *Surveys of Jewish History.* Chicago: College of Jewish Studies, 1932.

———. "The Teaching of Jewish History." *The Jewish Teacher* 1 and 2 (1917–19). Also in Honor, *Selected Writings*, 257–77.

Kahn, Robert I. "A Problem Approach to the Teaching of Jewish History." *Jew Ed* 7 (Jan.–Mar. 1935): 51–54.

Kohn, Therese. "Home and Worship in Biblical Times." *Jew Teach* 11 (Nov. 1972), 1–10.

———. "Our Ancestors Build a Temple in Jerusalem." *Jew Teach* 13 (Nov. 1943): 10–16.

Kurzband, Toby. "Modern Motivations in Modern Jewish History." *Jew Teach* 13 (Jan. 1945): 16–23.

Leibman, Morris. *An Objective Determination of a Course of Study in Contemporary Jewish Life.* Master's thesis, Chicago U., 1931.

Lucks, Alvin S. "Teaching Jewish Personalities to Young Children." *CCAR* 44 (1934): 270–71.

Nadel, Max. "Contemporary Issues in the History of German Jewry." A unit in a course in modern Jewish history. *Jew Teach* 14 (Nov. 1945): 2–7.

———. "Democratic Organization of the Medieval Polish Jewish Community." *Jew Teach* 14 (Jan. 1946): 24–28.

———. "Jewish Immigration to America." *Jew Teach* 14 (Apr. 1946): 15–27.

———. "Unit in American Jewish History." *Jew Teach* 13 (Apr. 1945): 25–34.

Pollak, Jacob B. "Some Recent Textbooks and Materials for the Teaching of Jewish History." *Jew Teach* 1 (Jan. 1933): 16–21.

Pool, David de Sola. "Methods of Presenting Jewish History." *Bulletin of Young Judea* (Feb. 1916).

Rosenthal, Ira. "A Jewish-American Hall of Fame." *Jew Teach* 15 (June 1947).

Scharfstein, Zevi. „הערה על למוד ההיסטוריה בבית הספר הנמוך" (A Note on the Study of History in the Elementary School) *Sh Hah* (H.) 6 (1945): 56–59.

Schiff, Harold. "The Jew as an American Soldier." *Jew Teach* 13 (Jan. 1945): 7–15.

Schmidt, H. "A Broader Approach to Jewish History." 8 (Dec. 1949): 588–93.

Schneider, Louis. "Teaching Jewish Current Events." *Jew Teach* 4 (June 1936): 15–20.

Segal, Abraham. "A Jewish History Project." *Jew Ed* 5 (Jan.–Mar. 1933): 45–52.

———. "A Retrogressive Approach in Teaching Jewish History." *Jew Ed* (Jan.–Mar. 1934): 23–30.

Soloff, Mordecai I. "Jewish History in the Intermediate Grades." *Jew Teach* 2 (Apr. 1934): 1–8; 4 (Jan. 1936): 1–9.

———. "Problems in Supervised Study." *Jew Ed* 10 (Apr.–June 1938): 97–102. Also in *RTJH*, 133–40.

———. "Teaching of History in Intermediate Grades of the Sunday School." An experiment in supervised study. *Jew Ed* 1 (Oct. 1929): 200–203.

Starr, Joshua. "Some Current Issues in Teaching Jewish History." *Jew Ed* 4 (Apr.–June 1932): 104–9.

Steinberg, Milton. *A Guide to Jewish History*. 3 pamphlets. N.Y.: Education Department of Hadassah. 23 pp, 53 pp, and 54 pp.

Stolz, J. "Post Biblical Histories." A proposal for the study of post-biblical history. *CCAR* 20 (1910): 344–46.

Sussman, Samuel. "Current Events in Jewish Schools." *Jew Ed* 1 (May 1929): 109–14.

Tcherikover, E. M. "Jewish Historiography." *JPPP*, 1:223–32.

Tzipkin, Samuel. "על למוד ההיסטוריה שלנו„ (On the Study of Our History) *Hadoar* (H.) 11 (12th of Adar "A" 1932).

Wachsman, Celia. "An Introductory Lesson in Current Events." *Jew Teach* 1 (Apr. 1933): 24–29.

Waldstein, A. Sh. "למוד מדעי החברה בבתי- ספר„ (The Study of the Social Sciences in the Schools). *Sh Hah* (H.) 2 (1927): 11–22.

Weingarten, I. "שעור בהיסטוריה„ (A Lesson in History) *Sh Hah* (H.) 3 (Mar. 1943): 119–26.

Zeligs, Dorothy F. "The New History." *Jew Teach* 5 (1937): 32–36.

———. "The New Psychological Approach to the Teaching of History in Intermediate Grades." *Jew Ed* 4 (Jan.–Mar. 1932): 36–44.

———. "Why An Activity Program?" *Jew Ed* 15 (Jan. 1944): 96–104.

Zeligs, Dorothy F., and Jacob Golub. "A Symposium on the Workbook." *Jew Teach* 3 (Nov. 1934): 7–14.

SINCE 1950

Ackerman, Walter I. "Let Us Now Praise Famous Men and Our Fathers in Their Generations: History Books for Jewish School in America." *Dor l'Dor: Kvatzim L'Toldot Hachinuch Hayehudi* (H.) 2 (Sept. 1984): 82–116.

Bennett, Alan D. "In the Days of David and Solomon—Comments on a Class Unit." *Jew Teach* 25 (Nov. 1956): 11–12.

Bertisch, Felix P. "Ancient Israel in Relation to American History." *Jew Teach* 20 (Nov. 1951): 6–15.

Bogot, Howard. "A Walk Through History." *Jew Teach* 34 (Feb. 1966): 27–30.

Brandt, Dorey. "Literature Through the Looking Glass: A Means to Enhance an American Jewish History Unit." A supplement for use in the afternoon religious school program. Master's project, HUC–JIR, 1980.

Bronstein, Herbert. "A Project in American Jewish History." *Jew Teach* 22 (May 1954): 3–6.

Chomsky, William. "Varied Approaches in Teaching History." *Syn Sch* 13 (Sept. 1954): 10–16.

Cohen, Gerson D. "A Lesson on the Jews of Spain." *MRCN* 5 (Winter 1977): 1, 3, 4.

———. "Translating Jewish History into Curriculum. From Scholarship to Paideia—A Case Study." In *From the Scholar to the Classroom*, edited by Seymour Fox and Geraldine Rosenfield, 31–48. N.Y.: MRC for Jewish Education and JTSA, 1977.

Cohen, Jack J. "History." In *JEDS*, 188–96.

———. "The Tercentenary in the Jewish School." *Syn Sch* 13 (Sept. 1954): 3–4.

Ehrlich, Irvin S. "A Look at Jewish History Through Great Crises." *Jew Teach* 34 (Feb. 1966): 33–35.

Epstein, Seymour. "M'korot: Teaching Jewish History with Primary Sources." In *JTH*, 2:33–42.

Feldman, Egal. "Jewish History and American Jewish Education." *Jud* 21 (Fall 1972): 470–76.

Finkelstein, Milton. "Techniques in Teaching American Jewish History." *Jew Teach* 19 (May 1951): 20–25. 6th grade.

Friedman, Alfred. "Providing Meaningful Experiences in History for the Ten to Twelve Group." *Syn Sch* 14 (Nov. 1955): 17–18.

Gamoran, Emanuel. *The Teaching of Jewish History*. N.Y.: UAHC, 1958.

Garvine, H. "Jewish History and the Raising of Jewish Consciousness." *Recon* 41 (June 1975): 7–13.

Gittelson, Abraham J. "A Tour of Historical Places." *Ped Rep* 28 (Fall 1976): 19–20.

Grayzel, Solomon. "Jewish History as a Subject of Instruction in the Jewish School." *Jew Ed* 21 (Spring 1950): 40–45, 72.

Gribitz, Beverly. "Teaching the Crusades." *MRCN* 5 (Winter 1977): 4–5

Hyman, Frieda Clark. "Living History." *Syn Sch* 14 (Mar. 1955): 15–17. Also in *RTJH*, 175–78.

Ingall, Carol K. "Home Is Where the Start Is: Teaching Local Jewish History." *Ped Rep* 33 (Dec. 1981): 32–33.

Jacobs, Steven Bennet. "Toward a Source Book for the Religious School in Modern Jewish History, from the French Revolution to the Present." Master's thesis, HUC–JIR, 1967.

Kadden, Barbara Binder. "Data Bank: American Jewish History." A collection of primary sources such as diaries, newspapers, and pictures. Master's project, HUC–JIR, 1979.

Kaiman, Arnold G. "A Critical Evaluation of the Teaching of Chronological Jewish History in the Intermediate Grades of the Reform Religious School." Master's thesis, HUC–JIR, 1958. 487 pp.

Kamin, Benjamin A. "Toward a New Teaching Method for Jewish Teens: Dramatic Confrontations in History." Master's thesis, HUC–JIR, 1978.

Karbal, Albert, and Justin Lewis. "Teaching Teachers to Teach Jewish History." *Ped Rep* 29 (Winter 1978).

Katz, Dina. "Teaching History with a Focus on Values." Master's thesis, HUC–JIR, 1978.

Kravitz, Leonard S. "Some Reflections on the Teaching of Jewish History." *CCAR J* (Oct. 1962): 30–32.

———. "Toward a Contemporary Course of Study for the Reform Middle School." Master's thesis, HUC–JIR, 1974.

* Lakritz, William B. *The Aims and Methodology of Jewish History Textbooks in the Intermediate Grades of the Jewish School in America*. Dropsie U., 1968.

———. "Analyzing Jewish History Textbooks for the Intermediate Grades." *Ped Rep* 27 (Fall 1975): 25–26, 28–29.

Levitas, Irving. "The Use of Fiction in American Jewish History." *Jew Teach* 33 (Feb. 1965): 11–12.

Lewis, Adele. "The Drama of Modern Jewish History: Teaching History Through Modern Books." *Jew Teach* 29 (Feb. 1961): 9–10.

Lowe, William T. "Where Shall History Be Taught?" *Ped Rep* 16 (Mar. 1965).

Massar, Rita. "A New Approach to Teaching Jewish History in American Jewish Schools." Master's thesis, Brandeis U., 1971.

Meyer, Michael A. *Ideas of Jewish History*. N.Y.: Behrman, 1974. 360 pp.

Norov, Jacob. "‟כיצד מלמדים היסטוריה?„ (How Do We Teach History?). *Sh Hah* (H.) 29 (Spring 1969): 171–72.

Nudelman, Edward A. "The Tercentenary and the Jewish School." *Jew Ed* 25 (Fall 1954): 4–5.

Nussbaum, Aaron M. "The Jewish People." *Ped Rep* 31 (1979).

Olan, Levi A. "An Introduction to a Philosophy of History." *CCAR J* (Apr. 1954): 3–9. Also in *RTJH*, 63–70.

Ostrich, David E. "Different, but Still the Same: A Textbook Teaching Jewish History as a Developmental History." Master's thesis, HUC–JIR, 1982.

Paul, Simon M. ‟תקופת האבות לאור תגליות חדשות„ (The Ancient Period of Our Ancestors in Light of New Findings) (H.). *NICD*.

Peretz, Josephine and Class. "Original Conversations and Dialogues from Jewish History." *Jew Teach* 19 (Mar. 1951): 17–31.

Pessin, Deborah. "The Teaching of Jewish History." *Syn Sch* 13 (Sept. 1954): 5–9.

Plesur, Milton. "Correlation in the Teaching of Jewish History." *Syn Sch* 11 (Feb. 1953): 3–9.

Resnick, Martha. "Jewish History through Primary Texts: An Approach of Teaching the Golden Age of Spain to High School Teachers." Master's thesis, Department of Jewish Education JTS, 1989.

* Rosenzweig, Linda W. *Moral Dilemmas in Jewish History*. Carnegie-Mellon U., 1975.

Schaffzin, Linda K., and Stephen Schaffzin. "Teaching Jewish Current Events." *JPH*, 63–67.

Schwartz, E. "A Jewish View of History." *Jew Life* 36 (May–June 1969): 28–35.

11 HISTORY

Shudofsky, Adele A. "Individualizing Instruction in the Teaching of Jewish History in the Supplementary Religious School." Master's thesis, JTSA, 1989.

Siegel, Danny. "Talmudic Models: People." *Ped Rep* 2 (Fall 1980): 20–24.

Slesinger, Zalman. "Some Observations on the History Program of the Jewish School." *Ped Rep* 18 (Dec. 1966): 9–12.

Sokobin, Alan M. "Toward a Core Curriculum in American Jewish History for the Reform Religious School." Master's thesis, HUC–JIR, 1955.

Stroll, Milton. "American Jewish Heroes." *Jew Teach* 19 (May 1951): 12–19. Grade 8.

Tarnor, Pearl G. "The Newspaper Technique in Teaching Jewish History." *Syn Sch* 15 (Mar. 1957): 9–11.

Weingarten, I. "געשיכטע„ (History) (Methodology) *DER* (Y.), 2:241–62.

Whiman, David A. "Toward a Competency-Based Programmed Learning Course of Instruction in Jewish History: For the Intermediate Grades of the Reform Religious School." Master's thesis, HUC–JIR, 1979.

Zalesky, Mrs. Jacob. "Providing Meaningful Experiences in History for the Eight and Nine Year Olds." *Syn Sch* 14 (Sept. 1955): 15–16.

Zuckerman, Herbert. "An Activity Unit on the Prophets and Modern Palestine." *Jew Teach* 19 (Jan. 1951): 29–35.

SOCIAL STUDIES

Baylinson, David. "Toward the Development of the Primary Grade Curriculum in Jewish Social Studies." Master's thesis, HUC–JIR, 1956.

Efron, Benjamin. "The Times Themselves Call for Jewish Civics." *Ped Rep* 23 (June 1972): 3.

Ehrmann, Eliezer. "Teaching the Social Studies." *Jew Ed* 25 (Fall 1954): 50–54. Also in *RTJH*, 127–32.

———. "The Use of Audio-Visual Aids in the Jewish Social Studies." *Jew Ed* 26 (Fall 1955): 40–46.

Freidenreich, Fradle. "Expanding the Jewish Social Studies." In *JPH*, 29–48.

———. "Idea Forum: Creative Approaches to Teaching Social Studies." *Ped Rep* 23 (June 1972): 9.

Gannes, Abraham P. "Jewish Juvenile Periodicals as Aids in Teaching About Jewish Life." *Jew Ed* 30 (Winter 1960): 59–62.

Hessel, Carolyn S. "On Tour—An Israel Project for the Primary Grades." *Ped Rep* 29 (Winter 1978).

Lang, Gerhard. *The Teaching of Jewish Civics in Jewish Schools in the United States*. N.Y.: AAJE, 1970.

Lewittes, Mordecai H. "Trends in the Teaching of Social Studies." *Ped Rep* 29 (Winter 1978).

Moss, Penrod. "Launching the Social Study Unit on an Intermediate Grade Level." *Jew Teach* (Fall 1962).

Nadel, Max. "Jewish Social Studies Units in Public Schools." *Ped Rep* 29 (Winter 1978).

———. "The Struggle for Freedom." *Jew Teach* 21 (Jan. and March 1953): 6–8, 9–12.

Nudelman, Edward A. "Teaching the Jewish Social Studies." *Jew Teach* 8 (Jan. 1940): 1–9. See also *Jew Teach* 13 (Jan. 1945).

"The Place of Social Studies in the Jewish School." (Symposium) *Ped Rep* 29 (Winter 1978).

Powell, David R. "Toward a Textbook for the Intermediate Grades on Jewish Life in America." Master's thesis, HUC–JIR, 1961.

Roseman, Kenneth D. "Teaching History through Research." *Jew Teach* 34 (Feb. 1966): 17–18, 23.

Schwartz, Shuly Rubin. "A Lesson in Contemporary American Jewish History." *MRCN* 5 (Winter 1976): 2, 4.

Slesinger, Zalmen. "The Need for Jewish Social Studies Programs." *Ped Rep* 17 (Dec. 1965): 9–10, 29–30.

Soref, Irwin I. "Maps for Use in Teaching the Jewish Social Studies." *Ped Rep* 4 (Sept. 1952).

Spitzer, Frances. "Teaching Jewish Social Studies in the Elementary Grades." *Syn Sch* 15 (Mar. 1957): 3–8.

Waldstein, A. Sh. „למוד מדעי החברה בבתי הספר" (The Study of Social Science in Schools). *Sh Hah* (H.) 2 (1927): 11–12.

Wittstein, Joel. "Social Studies Curriculum—Wise Temple Religious School." *Ped Rep* 31 (Fall 1979): 24–25.

TEXTS, READERS, AND RESOURCES PRIOR TO 1950 (SELECTED)

Alofsin, Dorothy. *America's Triumph: Stories of America's Jewish Heroes*. Cincinnati: UAHC, 1949. 312 pp.

Bildersee, Adele. *Jewish Post-Biblical History through Great Personalities*. Cincinnati, 1918.

Comins, Harry L. *Activities in the Life of the Early Hebrews*. 2 vols. N.Y.: N.Y. Committee for School Extension, UAHC, 1931. 547 pp.

Edidin, Ben M. *Student's Workbook for* A History of the Jews in the United States *by L. Levinger*. Cincinnati: UAHC, 1942.

Goldberg, Israel, and Samson Benderly. *Outline of Jewish Knowledge*. N.Y.: BJE, 1929, 1931. 769 pp.

Golub, Jacob S. *The Golden Dawn (to 586 BCE)*. 1942, 56pp.

———. *In the Days of the First Temple*. 1931. 341 pp.

———. *In the Days of the Second Temple*. 1929. 191 pp; 1942–43, 341 pp.

———. *Israel in Canaan*. 1930. 356 pp.

———. *The Jewish Middle Ages, Part I*. Experimental ed. Cincinnati: DSSE, UAHC. 1937. 73 pp.

Goodman, Philip, ed. *Children's Books and Stories of American Jewish History*. N.Y.: JBC of America, 1954.

Grand, Samuel. *Program Resources for American Jewish History Week*. N.Y.: AJHS, 1962. 14 pp.

Ish-Kishor, Sulamith. *America's Promise*. N.Y.: Behrman, 1947. 209 pp.

Kalisher, Betty. *Watchmen of the Night: Stories about Eminent Jews*. Cincinnati: DSSE–UAHC, 1936. 205 pp.

Levinger, Elma C. *Great Jews since Bible Times for Young People*. N.Y.: Behrman, 1926. 195pp. Primary grades.

Levinger, Lee J. *A History of the Jews in the United States*. 20th ed. Cincinnati: UAHC, 1961. 616 pp.

Lurie, Rose G. *The Great March*. 2 vols. Cincinnati: UAHC, 1931, 1940.

Nudelman, Edward A. *Israel in Canaan*. Teacher's Guide. Cincinnati: DSSE and UAHC, 1935. 119 pp.

Pessin, Deborah. *Giants of the Earth: Jewish Heroes in America*. N.Y.: Behrman, 1940.

———. *Michael Turns the Globe*. Jews in various countries. Cincinnati: UAHC, 1946. 180 pp.

Roth, Cecil. *A Bird's Eye View of Jewish History*. Cincinnati: UAHC, 1935. 419 pp.

Scharfstein, Zevi. היסטוריה לילדים (History for Children) (H.). 3 Vols. N.Y.: Shiloh.

Schwartz, Jacob D. *Into the Promised Land*. Cincinnati: UAHC, 1927. 168 pp.

Soloff, Mordecai I. *How the Jewish People Grew Up*. 1936. 283 pp. Teacher's Book, 1939.

———. *When the Jewish People Was Young*. Cincinnati: DSSE and UAHC, 1934. 296 pp. Teacher's Book, 1939.

Tomrov, M., and Abraham Gold. תולדות ישראל לילדים (Jewish History for Children) (H.). 2 Vols. N.Y.: Hebrew Pub. Co.

Zeligs, Dorothy F. *A Child's History of the Hebrew People*. With pupil's activity book. N.Y.: Bloch, 1935, 1939. 149 pp.

———. *A Child's History of Jewish Life in the First Sixteen Centuries of the Common Era*. N.Y.: Bloch, 1937. 250 pp.

———. *A History of Jewish Life in Modern Times for Young People*. N.Y.: Bloch, 1938. 446 pp.

TEXTS, READERS, AND RESOURCES SINCE 1950 (SELECTED)

Ackerman, Walter I. *Out of Our People's Past* (Sources for teachers). N.Y.: USA, 1977. 718 pp.

11 HISTORY

Agus, Irving A. (History of the Jewish People) (H.). N.Y.: Jewish Agency and Department for Torah Education, 1957. 179 pp. Grades 7–8.

Axelroth, Dorothy G. *A Course Syllabus on Ancient Jewish History*. N.Y.: UAHC, Department of Continuing Education, 1971.

Brownstone, Nathan. *American Jewish Life in Story and Legend*. N.Y.: UAHC, 1954.

Butwin, Frances. *The Jews of America: History and Sources*. With student inquiry book by Frances Long. N.Y.: Behrman, 1973. 121 pp. Grades 6–7.

Charry, Elias, and Abraham Segal. *The Eternal People: The Story of Judaism and Jewish Thought through the Ages*. N.Y.: USCJE, 1967. 427 pp. Grades 7–12.

Chazan, Robert, and Marc Lee Raphael, eds. *Modern Jewish History: A Social Reader*. N.Y.: Schocken, 1974. 395 pp.

Eban, Abba. *My People: From the Beginning to the Threshold of Modern Times*. 2 vols. Adapted by David Bamburger. N.Y.: Behrman, 1968. Grades 6–7 and 7–8.

Eisenberg, Azriel. *Eyewitnesses to Jewish History: From 586 B.C.E. to 1967*. N.Y.: UAHC, 1973.

———, ed. *Eyewitnesses to American Jewish History Part 3:1881–1920*. Teacher's Guide by Eric Feldheim. N.Y.: UAHC, 1978. Grades 10–12.

———, ed. *Eyewitnesses to American Jewish History Part 4: 1915–1969*. N.Y.: UAHC, 1979. Grades 10–12.

Eisenberg, Azriel, and Hannah Grad Goodman. *Eyewitnesses to American Jewish History Part 2: 1800–1875*. Teacher's Guide by Eric Feldheim. N.Y.: UAHC, 1977. Grades 10–12.

Eisenberg, Azriel, Hannah Grad Goodman, and Alvin Kass, eds. *Eyewitnesses to American Jewish History Part 1: 1492–1793*. N.Y.: UAHC, 1976. Grades 10–12.

Gamoran, Mamie G. *The New Jewish History*. 7 vols. N.Y.: UAHC, 1953–56. Elementary grades.

Gay, Ruth. *Jews in America: A Short History*. N.Y.: Basic Books, 1965.

Grand, Samuel. *The Jews Settle in New Amsterdam*. N.Y.: UAHC, 1954. 28 pp.

Grayzel, Solomon. *A History of the Contemporary Jews*. Phila.: JPS, 1960.

Gumbiner, Joseph A. *Leaders of Our People: Jewish History through Personalities*. Teacher's guide by Rebecca Lister. 2 vols. N.Y.: UAHC, CJE, 1963, 1965.

Harlow, Jules. *Lessons from Our Living Past*. N.Y.: Behrman, 1972. Grades 4–6.

Hartstein, Jacob I., ed. *The Jews in American History: A Resource Book for Teachers of Social Studies and American History*. National Program Division of the ADL and the School of Education and Community Administration, Yeshiva U., 1955. 100 pp.

Hyman, Frieda Clark. *The Jewish Experience*. 2 vols. N.Y.: USCJE, 1972–74. 248, 448 pp. Junior high school.

Karp, Deborah. *Heroes of American Jewish History*. Workbook by L. and B. Efron. N.Y.: ADL and Ktav, 1972. 155 pp. Grades 5 and 6.

———. *Heroes of Jewish Thought*. N.Y.: Ktav, 1965.

———. *Heroes of Modern Jewish Thought*. N.Y.: Ktav, 1966. Grades 5–7.

Klaperman, Gilbert, and Libby Klaperman. *The Story of the Jewish People: Vol. I, From Creation to the Second Temple*. N.Y.: Behrman, ca. 1980. Grades 4–8.

———. *The Story of the Jewish People: Vol. II, From the Building of the Temple to the Ages of the Rabbis*. N.Y.: Behrman. Grades 4–8.

———. *The Story of the Jewish People: Vol. III, From the Golden Age in Spain to European Emancipation*. N.Y.: Behrman. Grades 4–8.

———. *The Story of the Jewish People: Vol. IV, From the Settlement in America through Israel Today*. N.Y.: Behrman. Grades 4–8.

Levinger, Elma E. *They Fought for Freedom*. N.Y.: UAHC, 1953. 264 pp.

Lewittes, Mordecai. *Heroes of Jewish History*. Vol. 1, Abraham to Moses; Vol. 2, Joshua to Jeremiah; Vol. 3, Daniel to Rambam. N.Y.: Hebrew Pub. Co., c. 1960. Grades 3–8.

———. *Highlights of Jewish History: Eight Centuries from the Middle Ages to the Crea-*

tion of Israel. N.Y.: Hebrew Pub. Co., 1972. Junior and senior high.

Lister, Rebecca, and Gerard P. Meyer. *Units of Instruction and Activity for the Tercentenary Year*. N.Y.: UAHC, 1954.

Loeb, Sorel Goldberg, and Barbara Binder Kaddan. *Jewish History, Moments and Methods: An Activity Source Book for Jewish Teachers*. Denver: ARE, 1980.

Lurie, Rose G. *American Jewish Heroes*. N.Y.: UAHC, 1960. 224 pp.

———. *A Guide to Taching of American Jewish Heroes and Transitional History*. N.Y.: UAHC, 1967. 71 pp.

Marcus, Audrey Friedman, M. Wolf, and Raymond A. Zwerin. *Jews in Spain*. Student manual and teacher's guide. Denver: ARE. Grades 7–12.

Meitzer, Milton. *World of Our Fathers: Jewish life in Eastern Europe prior to the Great Migration to America*. N.Y.:Farrar, Straus, and Giroux, 1974. Junior and senior high school.

———. *Taking Root: Jewish Immigrants in America*. N.Y.: Farrar, Straus, and Giroux, 1976. Grades 9–12.

Nadel, Max. *Teaching the Jewish Experience in America*. Units and Resources. N.Y.: AAJE and American Jewish Congress, 1975. 81 pp. Extensive bibliography.

Nudelman, Edward A., and Zalmen Slesinger. *The Jew in America: A Syllabus for Teachers*. 2 vols. Issued in observance of the American Jewish Tercentenary. N.Y.: AAJE, 1954. 127 pp and 169 pp.

Pessin, Deborah. *History of the Jews in America*. N.Y.: USCJE, 1957. 317 pp.

———. *The Jewish People*. 3 vols. With teacher's guides and pupil activity books. N.Y.: USCJE, 1951–53. Ages 10–13.

Porath, Jonathan. *Jews in Russia—The Last Four Centuries*. N.Y. USCJE, 1974. 224 pp. High school.

Rosen, Gladys. *Guidance to Jewish History in Social Studies Instructional Material*. N.Y.: AJC, 1971. 47 pp.

Rossel, Seymour. *Introduction to Jewish History: From Abraham to the Sages*. Activity book by Malkah Avarani. Teacher's guide by Lenore C. Picker. N.Y.: Behrman. Grades 4–5.

———. *Journey through Jewish History: The Age of Faith and the Age of Freedom*. Workbook and teacher's guide. N.Y.: Behrman, ca. 1981. Grades 5–6.

Ruderman, Jerome L. *Jews in American History: A Teacher's Guide*. N.Y.: ADL of B'nai B'rith, 1975.

Samuels, Ruth. *Jewish History Activity Funbook*. N.Y.: Ktav. Grades 2–4.

———. *Pathways through Jewish History*. With workbook. N.Y.: Ktav. Grades 7–9.

Sarna, Jonathan D., Benny Kraut, and Samuel K. Joseph. *Jews and the Founding of the Republic*. A resource volume. N.Y.: Markus Wiener, 1985. 145 pp.

Segal, Abraham. *Teacher's Guide to* The Jewish People, Book 1, *by D. Pessin*. N.Y.: USCJE, 1953. 179 pp.

Soloff, Mordecai Isaac. *The Covenant People*. 2 vols. Flushing, N.Y.: Jonathan David, 1975.

———. *How the Jewish People Lives Today*. Teacher's Guide. N.Y.: UAHC, 1952.

Stern, Shirley. *Exploring Our Jewish Heritage: A Course of Study for Intermediate Grades*. N.Y.: Ktav, n.d.

Sugar, Robert. *Focus Kit on the Golden Age of Spain*. N.Y.: UAHC, 1973.

———. *Journey of Fifteen Centuries: The Story of the Jews of Spain*. Teacher's edition. N.Y.: UAHC, ca. 1970. Grades 7 & up.

Weilerstein, Sadie Rose. *Jewish Heroes*. 2 vols. N.Y.: USCJE, 1953. Grades 3–4.

Weitz, Emil. *A Glimpse into Jewish History through Philately*. N.Y.: Israel Coin Distributors Corp., c. 1970. 128 pp.

Zeligs, Dorothy F. *Child's History of the Jewish People*. N.Y.: Bloch, 1951. 179 pp.

GLEANINGS

Dubnow, Simon S.,
"The first part of Jewish history, the Biblical part, is a source from which, for

HISTORY

many centuries, millions of human beings belonging to the most diverse denominations have derived instruction, solace, and inspiration.... But a time will come—perhaps it is not very far off—when the second half of Jewish history, record of the two thousand years of the Jewish people's life after the Biblical period, will be accorded the same treatment. The latter part of Jewish history is not yet known, and many, in the thrall of prejudice, do not want to know it. But ere long it will be known and appreciated. For the thinking portion of mankind, it will be a source of uplifting moral and philosophical teaching. The thousand years' martyrdom of the Jewish people, its unbroken pilgrimage, its tragic fate, its teachers of religion, its martyrs, philosophers, champions, this whole epic will in days to come sink deep into the memory of men. It will speak to the ear and the conscience of men, not merely to their curious mind. It will secure respect for the silvery hair of the Jewish people, a people of thinkers and sufferers. It will dispense consolation to the afflicted, and by its example of spiritual steadfastness and self-denial encourage martyrs in their devotion. It is our conviction that the time is approaching in which the second half of Jewish history will be to the noblest part of thinking humanity what its first half has been to believing humanity, a source of sublime moral truths." (1903)

Jewish History (1927), 182–84.

Peretz, I. L.,
"A people's memory is history; and as a man without a memory, so a people without a history cannot grow wiser, better."

Works (Y.), vol. 12; *ATJQ*, 180.

Honor, Leo L.,
"The purpose of the course in Jewish history shall be to instill in the child a love for his people and pride in its history. It should give him a clear and unbroken view of the development of the Jewish people from its beginnings until the present time."

Jewish Teacher (May 1917).

International Workers—Orden Schools,
"Through the study of history we do not strive to give the child an idealistic picture of the Jewish past. We do not seek to bring the child back to the 'fortunate past'. We wish to acquaint the child with the past of his people and from that past to extract all the positive moments and transmit them to the child as his historic heritage."

(Translation) Fifth Conference (1936) in *Almanac of IWO* (Y.) (1936), 85.

Golub, Jacob S.,
"We should avoid the so-called lachrymose conception of Jewish history. Some writers have written Jewish history as though it were a series of uninterrupted pogroms, disasters, massacres, and brutal killings. It is true that Jewish history has its fair proportion of these sad events, but our history is far from being a series of calamities. We have long periods of peaceful, happy living in the midst of other peoples."

Jew Ed 15 (Jan. 1944), 94–95.

Union of Orthodox Jewish Congregations,
"Jewish history must be taught in a manner which will make the child conscious of the immortality of his people, of Judaism as a message and a challenge and as God's voice in every age and climate."

A Model Program for the Talmud Torah (1942). Quoted in *Jew Ed* 15 (Jan. 1944), 105.

Grayzel, Solomon,
"To some extent the fault is that of our teaching staff. They know less about the teaching of history than they do about the teaching of Hebrew. I may be prejudiced, but I think that history is more difficult to teach than Hebrew; it certainly requires more information than the textbook provides, a vibrant attitude and a lively intelligence. The usual teacher is bound to the page. He does not master these little details with which to fill in the gaps in the story so as to make for interest and clarity. They are afraid of discussion. They do not know how to encourage the use of supplementary reading. In fact, they are often ignorant of the existence of such materials."

Jew Ed 21 (Spring 1950), 41.

Ehrmann, Eliezer L.,
"The content of Jewish history should be treated in large and significant units, i.e.,

organized around major ideas, through the study of which the pupils attain genuine understanding."
Jew Ed 25 (Fall 1954), 52.

Pessin, Deborah,
"Jewish history has been a creative history, a moving forward and development. To convey the essence of such a history, it must be taught creatively, so that the child feels himself a part of it, in harmony and in identification with his predecessors. But the feeling of identity cannot be imposed from above. It must be a development, through participation, within the child. The child must be not a recipient, but a participant. He must be a partner in the learning process."
Syn Sch (Sept. 1954). Also in *RTJH*, 145.

Neuman, Abraham A.,
"The texture of Jewish history is a unified composition. The thread of unity and continuity is the most colorful part of the design. Pull out this thread and you destroy the design. Break up Jewish history into fragments or disjointed parts and all we have are dead limbs torn from a living body. . . .The history of the Jews in America undoubtedly has special characteristics, but it is a part of world Jewish history and can be understood only in this relationship."
PAJHS 47 (Mar. 1958), 138.

United Synagogue Commission on Jewish Education,
"The Jewish past and present should be presented vividly and correctly to kindle the imagination and induce identification with Israel and its eternal hopes and ideals. The positive aspects of Jewish experience should be stressed; most important is the central role that religion has played in determining Jewish destiny. On all levels, but particularly on the higher ones, readings from literary masterpieces of each historic period should be integrated with Jewish History."
Objectives and Standards for the Congregational School (1958), 13.

Freehof, Solomon B. (On persecutions in Jewish history),
"All those bitter facts are not what we did; they are a description of what others did to us. The persecution should be part of German history, not of ours. What was done to us is not basically our history. Our history is how we responded; not that the Jews were driven out of the Rhineland City of Worms four times and the community destroyed, but that these scattered Jews from Worms crawled back and rebuilt it four times. That is (Jewish) history."
Quoted by Roland B. Gittelsohn in *Essays in Honor of Solomon B. Freehof*, edited by W. Jacob, F. C. Schwarts, and V. W. Kavalier (1964), 107.

Marcus, Jacob Rader (Address to AJHS, May 19, 1968)
"I would ask at this hour that we gird our loins and go out in quest of the new Jew of tomorrow, that individual who will somehow embody within himself the consensus of his people. Let us with our sophisticated techniques hold up the mirror to reality. Perspective is emancipation. To see where we are moving is an invitation to shape our course. Not to suffer history but to make history—this is the challenge that confronts the new historian. Knowledge, meticulous, painfully accurate, all-embracing knowledge, brings with it the power to create, to mould, to survive."
"The Quintessential American Jew." *AJHS* 68 (Sept. 1968), 22.

Schwartz, Shuly Rubin,
"The study of contemporary Jewish life is crucial for many reasons. . . . Our students' generation may be the last to have personal contact with those who experienced the trauma of immigration from Eastern Europe. Only they can tap the unknown wells of information which our older Jewish population possesses. Also, direct contact with those who survived the Nazi era may provide our students with some understanding of an otherwise incomprehensible tragedy. Events of Jewish history come alive when students see their effects on relatives and acquaintances.
MRCN 5 (Winter 1977), 2.

Yerushalmi, Yosef Hayim,
"The Hebrew Bible seems to have no hesitations in commanding memory. Its injunctions to remember are uncondi-

11
HISTORY

tional, and even when not commanded, remembrance is always pivotal. Altogether the verb zakhar (to remember) appears in its various declensions in the Bible no less than one hundred and sixty-nine times, usually with either Israel or God as the subject, for memory is incumbent upon both. The verb is complemented by its obverse—forgetting. As Israel is enjoined to remember, so is it adjured not to forget. . . . If Herodotus was the father of history, the fathers of meaning in history were the Jews. . . .

Only in Israel and nowhere else is the injunction to remember felt as a religious imperative to an entire people. . . .

'Remember the days of old, consider the years of ages past.'" (Deut. 32:7)'

Zakhor—Jewish History and Jewish Memory (1982), 5–9.

12 | THE HOLOCAUST

BACKGROUND MATERIALS (SELECTED)

Alk, Jeremy David. "Suffer Not the Children." An audio-visual program on American efforts to rescue German refugee children in 1939. Geared to high school students and adults. Master's project, HUC–JIR, 1979.

Baron, Salo W. "European Jewry before and after Hitler." *AJYB* 63 (1962): 3–53. Reprinted from *A Historian's Notebook*. 56 pp.

Bauer, Yehuda. *A History of the Holocaust*. N.Y.: Franklin-Watts, 1982. 398 pp.

* Bilik, Dorothy S. *The Immigrant Survivor: Post-Holocaust Consciousness in Recent Jewish American Fiction*. U. of Maryland, 1977. 295 pp.

Bogart, Leo. "The Response of Jews in America to the European Catastrophe." Master's thesis, U. of Chicago, 1948.

Boyle, Kay. *Breaking the Silence: Why a Mother Tells Her Son about the Nazi Era*. N.Y.: AJC, 1962. 39 pp.

Cain, Seymour. "The Questions and Answers after Auschwitz." *Jud* 20 (Summer 1971): 263–74.

Cohen, Arthur. *The Tremendum: A Theological Interpretation of the Holocaust*. N.Y.: Crossroads, 1981. 110 pp.

Cutter, William. "Literature and the Holocaust: A Review Essay." *Modern Judaism* 2 (May 1982): 213–20.

Dawidowicz, Lucy. *The War Against the Jews*. N.Y.: Holt, Rinehart-Winston, 1975. 460 pp.

Des Press, Terrence. "The Edge of Decency." *Moment* 1:43–48.

Dobroszycki, Lusjan, ed. *The Chronicles of the Lodz Ghetto, 1941–1944*. Trans. by Richard Lourie, Joachim Neugroschel, and others. New Haven and London: Yale U. Press, 1984. 551 pp.

Fackenheim, Emil L. *The Human Condition after Auschwitz* (The B. G. Rudolph Lectures in Judaic Studies). Syracuse: Syracuse U. Press, 1971. 17 pp.

Finger, Seymour. *American Jewry during the Holocaust*. N.Y.: American Jewish Commission on the Holocaust, 1984.

Friedlander, Albert H. *On the Holocaust: A Critique of the Treatment of the Holocaust in History Textbooks*. N.Y.: ADL of B'nai B'rith, 1972, 1973. 31 pp.

Friedlander, Saul. *When Memory Comes*. N.Y.: Farrar, Straus, and Giroux, 1979.

Friedman, Ph. ‏"דער גורל פון ייִדישן קינד און פון דער ייִדישער יוגנט אונטער נאצי-רעזשים"‎ (The Fate of Jewish Youth under the Nazi Regime) *YD* (Y.) (1949–50): 78–85, 109–12.

———. ‏"100 ביכער אין ייִדיש וועגן חורבן און גבורה"‎ (100 Yiddish Books on Destruction and Resistance During the Holocaust) (Y.). *JBA* (1950–51): 80–92. See also *JBA* (1958–59): 112–32.

Gladstone, Jacob, Israel Knox, and Samuel Margoshes, eds. *Anthology of Holocaust Literature*. Phila.: JPS, 1969. 412 pp.

Green, Gerald. *The Artists of Terezin*. Illustrations by the inmates of Terezin. N.Y.: Hawthorne, 1978. 191 pp.

Greenberg, Blu. "Talking about the Holocaust." *Had Mag* (Apr. 1985): 48–49.

Hellman, Peter. *Avenue of the Righteous*. Portraits of uncommon courage of Christians and the Jews they saved. N.Y.: Atheneum, 1980.

Hilberg, Raul. *The Destruction of the European Jews*. 3 vol. Holmes and Meier, 1985. 1300 pp.

Levin, Nora. *The Holocaust, 1933–1945*. N.Y.: Crowell, 1968. 768 pp.

* Lookstein, Haskel. *American Jewry's Public Response to the Holocaust, 1938–1944: An Examination Based upon Accounts in the Press and Periodical Literature*. Yeshiva U., 1979.

Michael, Robert. "America and the Holocaust." *Mid* 31 (Feb. 1985): 13–16.

Morse, Arthur D. *While Six Million Died: A Chronicle of American Apathy*. N.Y.: Random House, 1968. 420 pp.

Peck, Abraham J., ed. *Jews and Christians after the Holocaust*. Fortress, 1982. 128 pp.

Petuchowsky, Jacob J. "Dissenting Thoughts about the Holocaust." *RJ* 28 (Fall 1981): 1–9.

Pfeffercorn, Eli, and K. L. Ackerman. *Holocaust Memorial Observance: A Pilot Study*. N.Y.: Memorial Foundation of Jewish Culture, 1984. 26 pp.

Recess, Asher. "A Quarter Century of Books on the Warsaw Ghetto Battle." *JBA* (1968–69): 23–29.

Ringelbaum, Emmanuel. *Notes from the Warsaw Ghetto: The Journal of Emmanuel Ringelbaum*. Edited by Jacob Sloan. N.Y.: McGraw-Hill, 1958.

* **Rosenbloom, Noah H.** *The God-Ideas of Leading Hebrew Poets during the Period 1933–1948*. New York U., 1958.

Rosenfeld, H. "The Holocaust in American Popular Culture." *Mid* 29 (June/July 1983): 53–59.

Rubenstein, Richard L. *After Auschwitz: Radical Theology and Contemporary Judaism*. Indianapolis: Bobbs-Merrill, 1967. 207 pp.

* **Rugoff, Kathy.** *The Holocaust in American and British Poetry*. Florida State U., 1983. 318 pp.

Sachs, Nellie. *O the Chimneys: Selected Poems*. N.Y.: Farrar, Straus, Giroux, 1967. 387 pp.

Spiro, Jack. "Discussion Guide." Participants: Gideon Hausner, Bruno Bettelheim, Abraham J. Heschel, Elie Wiesel, and others. *Dimensions* 1 (Spring 1967).

Steckel, Charles W. "God and the Holocaust." *Jud* 20 (Summer 1971): 279–85.

Syrkin, Marie. *Blessed is the Match: The Story of Jewish Resistance*. Phila.: JPS, 1947. 361 pp.

Trachtenberg, Martin, and Minna Davis. "Breaking Silence: Serving the Children of the Holocaust Survivors." *J Jew Com Ser* 54 (Summer 1978).

Trunk, I. לאדזער געטא (The Ghetto of Lodz). A historical and sociological study. (Y.) N.Y.: Yivo, 1962. 528 pp.

———. "Religious, Educational and Cultural Problems in the Eastern European Ghetto under German Occupation." *YA* 14 (1969): 159–95.

"The Warsaw Ghetto Uprising." Special Issue. *Congress Bi-Weekly* 30 (Apr. 1, 1963).

Weinreich, Max. *Hitler's Professors*. N.Y.: Yivo, 1946. 291 pp.

Werner, Alfred. "Art of The Holocaust." *Dimensions* 4 (Fall 1969): 44–47.

Wiesel, Elie. *The Gates of the Forest*. N.Y.: Holt, Rinehart and Winston, 1966.

World Jewish Congress. *The Warsaw Ghetto Uprising and its Historical Significance*. N.Y.: 1968. 18 pp.

Wyman, David. *The Abandonment of the Jews: America and the Holocaust, 1941–1945*. N.Y.: Pantheon Books, 1984.

Wyschogrod, Michael. "Faith and the Holocaust: A Review Essay of Emil Fackenheim's *God's Presence in History*." *Jud* 20 (Summer 1971): 286–94.

The Zukunft. (Y.) Memorial Issue on the Holocaust (on the ghetto uprising). Apr. 1952 and Apr. 1963.

TEACHING AND COMMEMORATION

Addison, Robert. "The Use of Drama in Teaching the Holocaust." *Jew Ed* 33 (Mar. 1982): 20–21.

Akselrad, Sanford D. "Towards an Improved Holocaust Curriculum: Integrating Lawrence Kohlberg's Theory of Moral Development into the Teaching of the Holocaust." Master's thesis, HUC–JIR, 1984.

American Association for Jewish Education. "Holocaust Curriculum Project." *Ped Rep* 33 (Mar. 1952).

——. *The Holocaust: A Case Study of Genocide*. A guide teaching the Holocaust as a mini-course. N.Y.: National Curriculum Research Institute of the AAJE, 1974. 70 pp.

——. *Teaching and Commemorating the Holocaust*. Psychological guidelines—pedagogic strategies for teaching the Holocaust. N.Y.: National Curriculum Research Institute of the AAJE, 1975.

Anti-Defamation League. *Writings of the Nazi Holocaust: A Teacher's Study Guide*. 32 pp.

Arian, Philip. "Evoking the Holocaust for Our Children." *Syn Sch* 26 (Winter 1968): 26–33.

——. "Teaching the Holocaust" *Jew Ed* 41 (Fall 1972): 41–46, 51.

Bennett, Alan D. "Towards a Holocaust Curriculum." *Jew Ed* 43 (Spring 1974): 22–26.

Bloomberg, Jon. "Defining the Uniqueness of Holocaust Teaching in the Jewish School." *Jew Ed* 53 (Summer 1985): 21–23, 39.

Blumberg, Herman J. "Some Problems in Teaching the Holocaust." *Recon* 34 (Dec. 10, 1968): 13–20.

Bronznick, Norman. "A Theological View of the Holocaust." *Jew Ed* 42 (Summer 1973): 12–20, 28.

Carmon, A. "Teaching the Holocaust." *Jew Fron* (Apr. 1980): 11–13.

Charney, Israel W. "Teaching the Violence of the Holocaust." *Jew Ed* 38 (Mar. 1968): 15–24.

Coles, R. "The Holocaust and Today's Kids." *Learning* 12 (Nov. 1983): 42–46.

Egozi, Akivah. "הערות לבעית, 'הוראת השואה בבתי ספרנו'" (Notes on the Problems of "Teaching about the Holocaust in Our Schools.) *Sh Hah* (H.) 29 (Summer 1969): 224–28.

Epstein, Helen. *Children of the Holocaust*. N.Y.: Putnam and Sons, 1979.

Epstein, Kyla. *The Study of Values Through Holocaust Literature*. L.A.: HUC–JIR, Tartak Learning Center, 1984.

Franck, Isaac. "Teaching the Tragic Events of Jewish History." *Jew Ed* 34 (Spring 1964): 173.

Freeman, Elayne, ed. *Holocaust Literature for Young Readers*. Toronto: Canadian Jewish Congress.

Freidenreich, Fradle, and Leonard Rubin. *Holocaust Education in Informal Settings*. N.Y.: JWB, 1981.

Friedlander, Henry. "Toward a Methodology of Teaching the Holocaust." *Teachers College Record* 80 (Feb. 1979).

Friedman, S. S. "Teaching the Holocaust." *Jew Fron* 39 (July–Aug. 1972): 8–15.

Gershenzon, R., and W. Jacob. "On Teaching the Holocaust." *Rel Ed* 78 (Summer 1983): 441–46.

Glicksman, William. "Bias Against Whom?" *Jew Ed* 34 (Spring 1964): 181–86.

——. "Teaching the Shoah (Holocaust) in Jewish Schools." *Jew Ed* 36 (Summer 1966): 174–78.

Goldman, Solomon. "The Jewish Child during the Holocaust." *Jew Ed* 46 (Spring 1978): 40–51.

Hymovitz, Leon. "After the Holocaust: A Primer for Parents and Teachers." *Rel Ed* 72 (Sept.–Oct. 1977): 534–44.

Innovative Jewish Education. *Teaching the Holocaust: New Directions*. N.Y.: AAJE and AJC, 1973. 22 pp.

Israel, Eric. "Teaching the Holocaust: Yad Vashem's Education Department." *For* (English section) (Aug. 22, 1986): 23.

Jacob, Walter. "On Teaching the Holocaust." *RJ* (Winter 1984): 81–85.

Kates, Eileen, and Alisa Waldman-Lewin. "Adolescent Children of Holocaust Survivors. "*Jew*

Ed 49 (Summer 1981): 38–42. Also in *Ped Rep* 33 (Mar. 1982): 22–25.

Kaunfer, Neal. "An Inquiry Model as a Focus for Teaching the Holocaust." *Jew Ed* 44 (Spring–Summer 1976): 31–34.

Keeping Posted. *Art of the Holocaust.* Nos. 840590 and 840592.

———. *Aspects of the Holocaust.* Nos. 840440 and 840442.

———. *Children of the Holocaust.* Nos. 840710 and 840712.

———. *Nazi War Criminals.* Nos. 840770 and 840772.

———. *Righteous Gentiles.* Nos. 840640 and 840642.

———. *Survivors.* Nos. 841040 and 841042.

Korin, Uri. "A Community-Wide Holocaust Memorial." *Ped Rep* 33 (Mar. 1982): 25.

Lamm, Norman. "After the Holocaust." *Ped Rep* 33 (Mar. 1982): 3–4.

Lampert, S. "How Students Perceive the Holocaust." *Mid* 30 (Apr. 1984): 29–31. College level.

Leinwohl, Debi M. *The Defiant Palette.* A mediated instructional project bringing together 35 millimeter slides and an audio-tape narrative dealing with the theme of resistance to the Holocaust through art. Master's project, HUC–JIR, 1980.

Lerner, Israel. "Lessons from World Gathering of Holocaust Survivors." *Jew Ed* 49 (Fall 1981): 2–16.

Lewis, Judith S. "Integrating the Holocaust: A Graded Curriculum." *Ped Rep* 33 (Mar. 1982): 7–10.

Maller, Allan S. "The Shoah and Its Teachings." *CCAR J* (June 1969). See also *Rel Ed* 66 (Mar.–Apr. 1971): 149–51.

Matteoni, Louis. "Why Teach the Holocaust?" *Jew Ed* 49 (Summer 1982): 4–7.

Memorial Foundation for Jewish Culture. "The Basic Goals of the Holocaust Curriculum for Jewish Schools." Prepared by the Steering Committee of the Holocaust Curriculum for Jewish Schools.

Nadel, Max, and Shimon Frost. "Teaching the Holocaust in the Jewish School." *Jew Ed* 49 (Spring 1981): 30–33.

———. "A Holocaust Mini-Course." *Ped Rep* 33 (Mar. 1982): 15–17. High school age.

National Association of Temple Educators. שואה ותחיה (Holocaust and Rebirth). Dec. 1981 Aliyah Conference in Israel. Participants: Gerhardt Hausner, Yehudah Bauer, Sh. Bror, and others. Bibliography. N.Y.: UAHC, 1982. 130 pp.

The Pedagogic Reporter 25 (Winter 1974). Special issue. "Teaching and Commemorating the Holocaust."

> Bakst, Joshua S. "In the Day School," pp. 12–13.
> Frankel, Ephraim. "As a Vehicle to Strengthen Jewish Identity," pp. 11–12.
> Goelman, Elazar. "Highlights of a Survey—A Preliminary Report," pp. 3–4.
> Greenberg, Harold S. "In the Public Senior High School," pp. 18–20.
> Kaye, Gerard W. "In the Jewish Camp," pp. 16–18.
> Meisels, Stanley. "For Multi-Level Congregational Programming," pp. 6–10.
> Rosenthal, Norma. "In the Elementary Grades," pp. 4–6.
> Shapiro, Sara S., and Nathaniel Stampfer. "On a Communitywide Basis," pp. 15–16.
> Weinsberg, Edgar James. "As a Contemporary Teenage Concern," pp. 13–15.

Pilch, Judah, Sara Feinstein, and Zalmen F. Ury. "The 'Shoah' and the Jewish School." *Jew Ed* 34 (Spring 1964): 162–72.

Post, Albert. *The Holocaust: A Case Study of Genocide.* A teaching guide. N.Y.: Commission on Jewish Studies in Public Schools of the AAJE and Jewish Congregational Social Action Council of Southwest Nassau and the Rockaways, 1973. 67 pp.

Roskies, Diane. *Teaching the Holocaust to Children: A Review and Bibliography.* N.Y.: Ktav, 1975. 65 pp.

Rothschild, William Lee. "New Directions for Holocaust Studies." *Ped Rep* 33 (Mar. 1982): 10–12.

Sabar, Naama, and Sara Gurim. "The Effects of Teaching a Special Holocaust Curriculum." *Jew Ed* 48 (Fall 1980): 23, 27–39.

Sandler, Ron. "A Resource Unit for Teaching the Holocaust in the Jewish Religious Secondary School." Master's thesis, HUC–JIR, 1976.

Schechter, Jay. "Holocaust Studies in Public Schools." *Ped Rep* 33 (Mar. 1982): 14.

Schnaiderman, Sh. L. „אונטערערדישע שולען אין ווארשעווער געטא" (Underground Schools in the Warsaw Ghetto). *Day* (Y.) (Jan. 16, 1966).

Schulweiss, Harold M. "The Bias against Man." *Jew Ed* 34 (Fall 1963): 6–14.

Sherwin, Byron L. "Teaching about the Holocaust: Some Guidelines." *Ped Rep* 33 (Mar. 1982): 4–6.

Sherwin, Byron L., and Susan G. Ament. *Encountering the Holocaust*. N.Y.: Impact Press, 1979. 502 pp.

Silverberg, David. "Studying and Teaching the Holocaust." *Present Tense* 6 (Spring 1979): 43–47.

Slesinger, Zalmen. "The Film as a Resource in Teaching about the Holocaust—A Partial Bibliography." *Ped Rep* 23 (Dec. 1971): 33.

———. "Teaching about the Holocaust—Basic Questions for Consideration." *Ped Rep* 17 (June 1966).

Spicehandler, Arnold. "Teaching the Holocaust." *Mid* 26 (Apr. 1980): 37–39.

Spiegelman, Marvin J. "On the Holocaust and Jewish Education." *Jew Ed* 43 (Fall 1973): 36–37.

Stadtler, Bea. "Teaching the Holocaust to Children." In *Cat 2*, 216–32.

Suggested Background Materials on the Teaching of Martyrdom and Heroism: The Warsaw Ghetto Uprising. N.Y.: Jewish National Fund, Youth and Education Department.

Syrkin, Marie. "The Teaching of the Holocaust." *Mid* 30 (1984): 37–49; 31 (Feb. 1985): 47–49.

Toubin, Isaac. "How to Teach the Holocaust." *Con Jud* 18 (Summer 1964): 22–26.

United Federation of Teachers and Jewish Labor Committee. "The Holocaust: The Jewish Ordeal in Nazi-Occupied Europe, 1933–1945." N.Y.: Apr. 1974. High school.

Ury, Zalmen. „לבעית הוראת השואה" (On the Problems of Teaching the Holocaust). *Sh Hah* (H.) 25 (Summer 1965): 226–29.

Weinberg, E. "Teaching the Holocaust to Teenagers." A model lesson. *Syn Sch* 29 (Summer 1971): 45–58.

Weiss-Rosmarin, Trude. "Holocaust: How to Teach it to a New Generation." *RA* (1979): 79–83.

Zamichow, Abraham. "The Holocaust Curriculum in a Yeshivah." *Ped Rep* 33 (Mar. 1982): 13.

TEXTS AND LITERATURE FOR STUDENTS (SELECTED)

Altshuler, David A. *Hitler's War against the Jews: A Young Reader's Version of Lucy Dawidowicz's* The War against the Jews, 1943–1945. N.Y.: Behrman, 1978.

Eisenberg, Azriel, ed. *Witness to the Holocaust*. N.Y.: Pilgrim Press, 1981. Grades 10–12

Flinker, Moshe. *Young Moshe's Diary*. Edited by Saul Esh. (Diary of a young boy who died in Aushwitz.) N.Y.: JEC Press of BJE of N.Y., 1972. 126 pp. Grades 8 and up.

Frank, Anne. *The Diary of a Young Girl*. Garden City, N.Y.: Doubleday, 1952.

Friedlander, Albert H. *Out of the Whirlwind: A Reader of Holocaust Literature for High School Students*. Teacher's guide by Jack D. Spiro and discussion guide by Jack D. Spiro and Abraham Sheingold. N.Y.: UAHC, 1968. 540 pp. Grades 10 and up.

Gilbert, Martin. *The Final Journey*. N.Y.: Mayflower Books, 1979. Grades 9 and up.

———. *Holocaust: An Atlas*. N.Y.: Farrar, Strauss, and Giroux.

Hoffman, Judy. *Joseph and Me: A Holocaust Story and Text*. N.Y.: Ktav, n.d. Grades 4–5.

Koehn, Ilse. *Mischling, Second Degree: My Childhood in Nazi Germany*. N.Y.: Bantam, 1978. Grades 9–11.

Meltzer, Milton. *Never to Forget: The Jews of the Holocaust*. N.Y.: Harper and Row, 1976. Grades 7 and up.

Pilch, Judah, ed. *The Jewish Catastrophe in Europe*. Teacher's guide by Leon H. Spotts. N.Y.: AAJE, 1978. 230 pp.

Rabinowitz, Dorothy. *New Lives: Survivors of the Holocaust Living in America*. N.Y.: Alfred A. Knopf, 1976. Grades 10 and up.

Rossel, Seymour. *The Holocaust*. N.Y.: Franklin-Watts, 1981. 148 pp. Grades 9–11.

Stadtler, Bea. *The Holocaust: A History of Courage and Resistance*. Edited for schools by David Bial. Discussion guide by Nancy Karkawsky. N.Y.: Behrman, 1975. Grades 5–6.

Wertstein, Irving. *The Uprising of the Warsaw Ghetto*. N.Y.: Norton, 1968. Grades 7–10.

Zwerin, Raymond A., Audrey Friedman Marcus, and Len Kramish. *The Holocaust: A Study in Values*. Denver: ARE, n.d. Grades 7–12.

GLEANINGS

Moladowsky, Kadia,
>Choose another people, we are weary of dying...
>We have no more blood; can no longer be a
>sacrifice; our home is turned into desert; the earth too small for our graves; we have
>run out of lamentations; we cannot find a
>fitting song of sorrow in the old books ...

King David Remained Alone (Y.), translated by Yudl Mark. *JBA* 6 (1947), 57.

Pilch, Judah,
>"It has been pointed out time and again that our youth have little knowledge and less appreciation of the entire story of Jewish martyrdom, including the recent tragedy, the shoah. They do know and remember those events of the past which have become patterns of conduct in the home and in the synagogue.... The writer is convinced that if we fail to impress our children with the Jewish struggle for equality in the immediate past and with the shoah the marginality of their lives as Jews will become greater from year to year, and their descendants may have little or no concern for their people's future. We owe it, therefore, to ourselves and to history to keep the story of the shoah alive. Teaching it is not only a means for a better understanding of the history and destiny of the Jewish people, but it makes for a better appreciation of what makes a Jew a Jew."

Jew Ed 34 (Spring 1964), 163–64.

Wiesel, Elie,
>"During the war, some Jews attempted to escape and to survive for one reason only: to tell their story. Cynics were amazed and asked them: What for? The world does not deserve your sacrifice or your tale: it won't even believe you. But the cynics themselves were among those who tried, for the same reason, to preserve the tale. That very reason was, ironically, invoked by the Judenrat: let the few remain and transmit what happened to the many. Echad ba'ir ushnayim b'mishpacha—'Let one person bear witness for his whole town, and two for their entire family.' For deep down people lived and died in fear: perhaps the last Jew will disappear, and the tale will die with him. But then—so what? Let it not be told! Perhaps the 'post-Holocaust future' does not deserve its past! Why were we so concerned with mankind which chose to ignore our fate?
>Yet, we are concerned. We do try to put the experience into words. But can we? That is my question. Language is poor and inadequate. The moment it is told, the experience turns into betrayal. The Oral Tradition had to remain oral. The Kotzker Rebbe said: the Oral Torah that we know is not the real one; the true Torah she-b'al peh remained oral and secret.
>That is our problem, that is my fear: perhaps whatever we write and say about Jewish values and Jewish experience has no relationship to either."

"Jewish Values in the Post-Holocaust Future." *Jud* 16 (Summer 1967), 282–84.

Sherwin, Byron L.,
>"It is a basic pedagogic premise that one teaches not only a subject, but a class. The nature of the class determines how the subject may be taught. Therefore, the first question which the teacher of the Holocaust must ask him or herself is whether the students he or she is teaching have the intellectual, emotional, the-

ological and personal prerequisites necessary for handling a journey to the 'Holocaust Kingdom.' One cannot summarily jump into a study of the Holocaust. Study of the Holocaust is unlike any other subject. The student must be prepared in advance. Not so much the age of the student, but the educational and emotional status of the student would determine whether he or she should be taught about the Holocaust."

"Teaching About the Holocaust: Some Guidelines." *Ped Rep* 33 (Mar. 1982), 5.

Fackenheim, Emil

"The Jew is singled out for special contradictions. In America he enjoys a freedom and security unparalleled in history; yet he is but twenty years from the greatest and as yet uncomprehended Jewish catastrophe. His trust and joy in the modern secular world cannot but coexist with radical distrust and profound sorrow. Authentic Jewish religious witness in this age must both face up to Auschwitz and yet refuse a despair of this world which, wholly contrary to Judaism, would hand still another victory to the forces of radical evil. Insofar as he is commited to Jewish survival, the Jew has already taken a stand against these forces. But survival—for survival's sake—is an inadequate stand. The Jew can go beyond it only if he can reopen the quest of Jeremiah and Job, who for all their agony refused to despair either of God or the world."

Quoted by Rauch in *Religious Schooling in America*, edited by Carper and Hunt (1984), 153.

13 SCHOOL LIBRARY

THE LIBRARY

Abelson, Estelle. "The Library as Audio-Visual Center." *Jew Teach* 25 (Jan. 1957): 10–11.

———. "A New Library." *Jew Teach* 24 (Jan. 1956): 14–15.

Achtenberg, Minnie R. "A Sunday Morning Library Tea." *Syn Sch* 9 (Apr. 1951): 25–26.

Association of Jewish Libraries. Synagogue, School, and Center Division. *Standards for Jewish Libraries in Synagogues, Schools and Centers*. Rev. ed. N.Y.: Jewish Book Council of America, 1970.

Avner, Sylvia. "The Librarian and a Bar/Bat Mitzvah Program." *Ped Rep* 35 (Jan. 1984): 23–25.

Berman, Margot S. *How to Organize a Jewish Library: A Source Book Guide for Synagogue, School, and Center Libraries*. N.Y.: JBC, 1981–82. 77 pp.

Braverman, Libbie L., and Nathan Brilliant. "The Jewish School Library." *Jew Teach* 6 (June 1938): 1–11; 7 (Nov. 1938): 23–27.

———. "The Library—A Major Instrument for Education." In *Act*, 225–44.

Carsch, Judith, and Miriam Miller. *Creating a Collection: A Resource List for a Beginning Library*. N.Y.: Association of Jewish Libraries, 1982.

Cedarbaum, Sophia N. *A Manual for Jewish Community Center, School and Congregation Libraries*. N.Y.: JBC, 1962

Celnik, Max. *A Basic Book List for Synagogue and Religious School Libraries*. N.Y.: USA, 1960.

———. *The Synagogue Library—Organization and Administration*. N.Y.: USA, Library Service Bureau, 1968.

Chaikind, H. K. *Religious School Libraries in Temples of Reform Judaism: Factors for Success*. New Haven: Southern Connecticut State College, 1963.

Cohen, Frances L. "The Birth of a Synagogue Library." *Ped Rep* 23 (Sept. 1971): 25.

Cohen, Samuel. "School Library." In *Progressive Jewish School*, 170–71. 1932.

Dagani, E. "House of the Book." *Judaica Librarianship* 1 (Fall 1983): 32–33.

Ehrlich, Rae. "A Bilingual Library Program." *Ped Rep* 35 (Jan. 1984): 22–23.

Ehrmann, Eliezer. "A Library Project." *Jew Teach* 10 (June 1942): 15–27.

Eisen, Sylvia. "The Library as an Aid in Teaching Responsibility." *Ped Rep* 36 (Nov. 1985): 13–14.

Frank, Ruth S., and William Wollheim. *The Book of Jewish Books*. Annotated bibliography with introduction to each general area by a scholar in the field. San Francisco: Harper and Row, 1986.

Gamoran, Emanuel. "What Shall I Do for Jewish Book Week?" and "Suggested Books for Home and Religious School in Observance of Jewish Book Week." *Jew Teach* 2 (Apr. 1934): 23–28.

Gelfand, Sidney. "Organized Jewish Libraries." *Library Journals* (Jan. 1, 1962): 31–34.

Golinkin, Noah. "The Story of a Children's Library." *Syn Sch* 7 (Nov. 1948).

Golub, Jacob S. *Children's Library List*. Includes all the juvenile literature in English published up to 1948. N.Y.: JEC of N.Y., 1948.

———. *A Library List for Teachers in Jewish Schools*. N.Y.: JEC of NY.

Goodman, Philip. "Jewish Books in Jewish Schools." *Syn Sch* 10 (Sept. 1951): 16–22. Also in *Jewish Books in Jewish Schools*. N.Y.: JBA and NJWB, 1970.

Gup, Eva. "The Library Period." *Jew Teach* 8 (Apr. 1940): 16–18.

Halporn, Roberta. "The Temple Library." *Ped Rep* 22 (Sept. 1978): 20–22.

Heckelman, Tziporah. "The Role of the Library in the Jewish School." *Syn Sch* 21 (Feb. 1963).

Hyman, Ruth Salinger. "An Experiment with a School Library." *Syn Sch* 14 (Feb. 1956): 12–16.

Jewish Book Month Materials. N.Y.: JBC.

Kahn, Ruby. "A Rolling Library." *Jew Teach* (Dec. 1961).

Kallen, Horace. "The Library-Role in Jewish Life." *Day* (Aug. 23, 1961).

Karp, Hazel. *Jewish Children's Books: A Select Bibliography of 100 Books for a Beginning Library*. N.Y.: Association of Jewish Libraries, 1982.

Kurland, Mildred, and Mae Weine. *Subject Headings for a Judaica Library*. N.Y.: Association of Jewish Libraries, 1982.

———. *Weine Classification Scheme for Judaica Libraries*. 7th ed. 1982. Contains relative index to the *Weine Classification Scheme for Judaica Libraries*.

Landesman, Alter F. "A List of Books for a Small School Library." *A Curriculum for Jewish Religious Schools*. 1922, 272–76.

Leff, Barbara. "Creative Use of the Library." In *JTH*, 125–38.

———. "The Library/Media Center." In *JPH*, 247–65.

———. "What Is the Key to a Quality School Library." *Ped Rep* 35 (Jan. 1984): 19–21.

Leff, Barbara, and Anita Werner. "Audiovisual Equipment." In *JPH*, 227–45.

Leikind, Miriam. "Building a Temple Library." *Jew Teach* 5 (1937).

———. "The Library as an Aid in Religious Education." *Jew Teach* 9 (Jan. 1941): 12–15.

———. "Reading Interests of Children." *Jew Teach* 15 (Apr. 1947): 34–37.

———. "The Temple Library." In *Church and Synagogue Libraries*, edited by John F. Harvey, 73–80. Metuchen, N.J., and London: Scarecrow Press, 1980.

Leviton, Elsie. "The Temple Library—Fact or Fiction." *Jew Teach* 32 (Dec. 1963): 13–15.

Libby, Claire. "The Library Visits the Reader." *Syn Sch* 16 (May 1958): 26–27.

Linzer, Norman. *Around the World with Jewish Books*. N.Y.: JBC and NJWB, 1969, 1970.

Lubetski, Edith, and Meir Lubetski. *Building a Judaica Library Collection: A Resource Guide*. Littleton, Colo.: Libraries Unlimited, 1983.

Michelson, Mrs. Julius. "The Synagogue Library." *Syn Sch* 27 (June 1969): 4–8.

Neuman, Tillie, and Joel Zion. "A Jewish Book Month Project." *Jew Teach* 15 (June 1947): 26–36.

Packscher, Hazel G. "A Book House." *Jew Teach* 7 (Apr. 1939): 32.

———. "Chanuko—Book Club." *Jew Teach* 11 (Nov. 1942): 21–22.

———. "The Religious School Library." *Jew Teach* 3 (Apr. 1935): 30–32.

Raskin, Aliza. "The Class Library." *Syn Sch* 18 (Oct. 1959): 28–29.

Rosenwasser, Rose K. "The Organization of a Synagogue Library." *Syn Sch* 14 (Feb. 1956): 3–11.

Schwartz, M. G. "Conservative Synagogue Library: An Analysis and Evaluation." Master's thesis, Indiana U., 1962.

Segal, Judith. "On Jewish Libraries and Standards." *Syn Sch* 31 (Winter 1973): 15–26.

Slesinger, Zalmen. "The Library as an Integral Feature of the Jewish School." *Ped Rep* 10 (Mar. 1959).

Stone, Selma Weiss. "Build Your Own Library." *Jew Teach* 23 (May 1955): 6–7.

"The Story of a Children's Library." *Syn Sch* 7 (Nov. 1948).

Sugarman, Joan. "Building a Library in the Religious School.' *Jew Teach* 23 (Jan. 1955): 8–10.

Tuchman, Maurice S. "The Relationship of the Synagogue School and Its Library." In *Church and Synagogue Libraries*, edited by John F. Harvey, 59–72. Metuchen, N.J., and London: Scarecrow Press, 1980.

Weine, Mae. "The Association of Jewish Libraries." In *Church and Synagogue Libraries*, edited by John F. Harvey, 232–40. Metuchen, N.J., and London: Scarecrow Press, 1980.

———. *A Basic Periodical List for the Small Jewish Library*. Rev. ed. N.Y.: Association of Jewish Libraries, 1978.

———. "Libraries for the Jewish Layman." (Includes school library). In *JBA* (1966–67), 50–54.

———. "Survey of Synagogue Libraries in Philadelphia: The Synagogue Library as a Factor in Jewish Education." Master's thesis, Dropsie U., 1957.

"Why a Children's Library." *Syn Sch* 6 (1947).

GLEANINGS

Ibn Tibbon (1190),
 Make your books your companions; let your cases and shelves be your pleasure-grounds and orchards."
 Hebrew Ethical Wills, 63.

Landesman, Alter F., "The School Library,"
 "A school library will be necesary in order that the work suggested may be properly done.... The school library should contain a number of books which are to be used by the teacher, especially those books which are not to be found on the shelves of the public libraries, and in the libraries of other Jewish institutions in the city. The teacher must have tools with which to work....
 Children should have free access to the library at all out-of-school hours."
 A Curriculum for Jewish Religious Schools (1922), 17–19.

Nadich, Judah (on the Jewish Book Council of America)
 "Created in the dark days of the Holocaust when famous European Jewish scholars were annihilated and great Jewish libraries destroyed, the Jewish Book Council of America has steadfastly sought to aid in the creation of an American Jewish cultural renaissance. Sponsored by the National Jewish Welfare Board, the Council recognized that without the Jewish book, the Jewish group cannot survive. Our goals have been formulated as follows:
 To infuse in both young and old the traditional ardent zeal for Jewish knowledge through reading the Jewish classic as well as contemporary works.
 To encourage the establishment of Jewish book shelves as an integral part of the home environment.
 To help augment Jewish book collections in libraries of synagogues, schools, centers, and other institutions, and to stimulate their utilization....
 To make available books of Jewish interest for promoting reciprocal interfaith understanding and cooperation."
 Essays on Jewish Booklore, selected by Philip Goodman (1972), xiii.

Leff, Barbara,
 "The library improves the quality of Jewish education. The library provides a unique dimension to the learning process. The library promotes independent learning. The library has a lasting effect on Jewish children who are our Jewish future....
 In this information age, Jewish Schools have a responsibility with regard to library support. Somehow, they must provide adequate library personnel who can implement quality library programs and services."
 "What Is the Key to a Quality School Library?" *Ped Rep* 35 (Jan. 1984), 21.

14 | LIFE CYCLE OF A JEW

SYNAGOGUE AND PRAYER–GENERAL (SELECTED)

Asheri, Michael. *Living Jewish: The Lore and Law of the Practicing Jew*. N.Y.: Dodd, Mead and Co., 1983. 482 pp.

Baumgard, Herbert M. *Judaism and Prayer*. N.Y.: UAHC, 1964.

Bempord, Jack, ed. *The Theological Foundations of Prayer*. N.Y.: Commission on Worship, UAHC, 1967. 126 pp.

Bettan, Israel. "The Function of the Prayer Book." In *Reform Judaism*, edited by Joseph L. Blau, 285–301. 1973.

Cohon, Beryl D. *Introduction to Judaism: Customs and Ceremonies*. N.Y.: Bloch, 1942. 188 pp.

Cohen, Jack J. *The Religion of the Jewish Prayer Book*. N.Y.: Reconstructionist Foundation, 1948.

———. *Worship in the Modern Synagogue*. N.Y.: Jewish Reconstructionist Foundation.

A Course of Study on Jewish Prayer. N.Y.: Council of Jewish Women, 1923.

Donin, Hayim H. *To Be a Jew: A Guide to Jewish Observance in Contemporary Life*. N.Y.: Basic Books, 1972. 336 pp.

———. *To Pray as a Jew: A Guide to the Prayer Book and the Synagogue Service*. N.Y.: Basic Books, 1980.

Eisenberg, Azriel. *The Synagogue through the Ages*. N.Y.: Bloch, c. 1974. 206 pp.

Freehof, Solomon B. *The Small Sanctuary: Judaism in the Prayerbook*. Cincinnati: UAHC, 1942.

Goldstein, I. "The Concept of Jewish Prayer." Master's thesis, New York U., 1959.

Gordis, Robert. *The Ladder of Prayer: Prayer, Its Various Forms, the Conservative Approach*. N.Y.: NAAJS of USA, ca. 1957. 48 pp.

Green, Arthur, and Barry Holtz. *Your Word is Fire*. N.Y.: Paulist Press, 1977.

Greenberg, Simon. *The Jewish Prayer Book—Its Ideals and Values*. N.Y.: NAAJS and USA, 1957. 159 pp.

Gutman, Joseph, ed. *The Synagogue: Studies in Origin, Archaeology, and Architecture*. N.Y.: Ktav, c. 1975. 359 pp.

Heschel, Abraham J. "The Spirit of Prayer." *RA* (1953): 151–78.

Idelsohn, Abraham Z. *Jewish Liturgy and Its Development*. Cincinnati: Sacred Music Press, HUC, 1957.

Israel, Raymond. "A Reform Jew Looks to Prayer." *Jew Teach* 22 (Mar. 1953): 4–6.

Jacobson, Burt. "The Siddur Alienated Me from God." *Sh'ma* (Jan. 25, 1985): 44–45.

Jick, Leon A. *The Americanization of the Synagogue, 1820–1870*. Hanover, N.H.: U. Press of New England for Brandeis U. Press, 1976. 247 pp.

Kadushin, Max. *Worship and Ethics*. Evanston, Ill.: Northwestern U. Press, 1963–64.

Kohn, Eugene. "Prayer and the Modern Jew." *RA* (1953): 179–91.

Konvitz, Milton. "What Is Jewish Living?" *Jud* 1 (Jan. 1952): 11–18.

Kravitz, Leonard S. "Problems of Prayer." *CCAR J* 13 (Oct. 1965): 25.

* Lazowski, Philip. *The Role of Prayer in a Middle Sized American Jewish Community*. JTS, 1970.

Martin, Bernard. *Prayer in Judaism*. N.Y.: Basic Books, 1968.

Millgram, Abraham E. *Jewish Worship*. Phila.: JPS, 1971. 673 pp.

Neulander, Arthur H. *What Is in the Prayer Book?* N.Y.: JTSA.

Petuchowski, Jacob J. *Understanding Jewish Prayer*. N.Y.: Ktav, 1972.

Pool, David de Sola. "Judaism and the Synagogue." In *Jan* 1, 28–55.

"Prayer." *Response* 13 (Fall–Winter 1982). Focus on prayer.

Rackman, Emanuel. "The Study of Prayer." *Jew Life* 26 (Apr. 1959).

Riemer, Jack. *The First Words of Prayer*. N.Y.: Burning Bush Press, 1964.

Strassfield, Sharon, and Michael Strassfield. "The Geography of the Synagogue." In *Cat 2*, 264–95.

Weinberg, Dudley. *The Efficacy of Prayer*. N.Y.: Jewish Chautauqua Society and Commission on Interfaith Activities–UAHC, 1965. 20 pp.

SYNAGOGUE AND PRAYER IN THE CLASSROOM

Alper, Robert A. "A Common Prayerbook for Children." Master's thesis, HUC–JIR, 1972.

Angel, Marc D. "The Sephardic Approaches to Teaching Siddur." *Ped Rep* 33 (Dec. 1981): 19.

Arian, Philip, and Azriel Eisenberg. *The Story of the Prayer Book*. N.Y.: Prayer Book Press, 1969. 156 pp.

Arzt, Max. "Teaching Synagogue Schools." *Syn Sch* 7 (Nov. 1949).

Bamberger, David. *A Functional Teacher's Guide for When a Jew Prays*. N.Y.: Behrman, 1972.

Bennett, Mrs Leon. "Teaching Prayer to Children Eight to Ten." *Syn Sch* 15 (Dec. 1956): 21–22.

Birnbaum, Paltiel. "סדר התפילות והתנ״ך" (The Order of the Prayers and the Bible) (H. and E. summary) *Ped Rep* 33 (Dec. 1981): 35–36.

Bloom, Mrs. Joel. "Prayer: A Creative Approach." *Syn Sch* 28 (Winter 1970): 4–8.

Brown, Sheldon S. "A Word Count of Basic Prayers." *Jew Ed* 29 (Winter 1959): 48–50.

Cohen, Jack J. "Worship." In *JEDS*, 215–20.

Cohen, Samuel. "Worship." In *The Progressive Jewish School*, 66–97. 1932.

Cohn-Levine, Debra. *The Story of Jewish Liturgy: Jewish Values through Prayers*. 2 vols. A ten-lesson exploration of the Siddur for Bar/Bat Mitzvah students. L.A.: HUC–JIR, Tartak Learning Center, 1986.

Danzig, Jerry M. "Derech Ami: 'Az M'ken Lernen'." *Syn Sch* 29 (Summer 1971): 5–44.

Eisenberg, Azriel, ed. *Readings in the Teaching of Prayer and Siddur*. N.Y.: JEC Press, 1964.

Eisenberg, Yehuda. *A Curriculum in Tefillah*. N.Y.: 1976.

Feinstein, Jerome Tov. "An Experiment in Teaching Reading of Prayers." *Jew Ed* 22 (Summer 1951): 47–51.

Freehof, Solomon B. "Education for Worship." *Rel Ed* (July–Aug. 1946).

Gittelsohn, Roland B. "Educating for Worship in Our Religious Schools." *Jew Teach* 12 (Jan. 1942): 1–10.

Goldress, Leslie. "Alenu: A Teaching Unit on the Prayer." Master's thesis, JTSA–Teacher Institute, 1975.

Goldstein, Sheldon. "Outlines for the Study of the Siddur." Master's thesis, Yeshiva U., 1949.

Goodman, Robert. "Sequence in the Teaching of Siddur." *Ped Rep* 33 (Dec. 1981): 6–9.

Greenberg, Simon. "The Prayerbook in the Elementary Jewish School Curriculum." *Jew Ed* 10 (Jan.–Mar. 1938): 28–34.

Greenfield, Marcus. "Teaching Prayer to Eleven and Twelve Year Olds." *Syn Sch* (Dec. 1956): 23–26.

Harlow, Jules. "The Purposes of Prayer." *Ped Rep* 33 (Dec. 1981): 2–3.

Heilbraun, Regina. "Our Synagogue and Its Development." *Jew Teach* 13 (June 1945): 12–16.

Jacobson, Burt. "The Experiences of Worship." In *Teen*, 71–82.

———. *Teaching the Traditional Liturgy: An Experimental Edition for Teachers*. N.Y.: MRC–JTSA, 1980. 206 pp.

Kaplan, Mordecai M. "The Teaching of Prayer in Our Schools." *Con Jud* 10 (Summer 1956): 1–13.

Katzoff, Louis. "Objectives of Prayer Book Instruction." In *Issues*, 76–81.

Kelman, Stuart. "Prayer and Process." *Rel Ed* 75 (July–Aug. 1980): 462–73.

Kelman, Stuart, and Joel Lurie Grishaver. "Of Prayers and Progress: One Model for Teaching Jewish Prayer." In *JPH*, 115–32.

Kronish, Leon. "Educating Children and Young People for Public Worship." Master's thesis, HUC–JIR, 1942.

Lazar, Jeffrey B. "Toward a Program of Worship Experience of Primary Grade Pupils in the Religious School." Master's thesis, HUC–JIR, 1971.

Leibman, Moshe. "להוראת הסדור„ (On the Teaching of the Siddur) *Sh Hah* (H.) (May 1943): 147–58.

Lerner, Barry Dov. "Teaching Synagogue Skills." *Ped Rep* 33 (Dec. 1981): 20–21.

Maretz, Sylvia. "Project on the Temple." *Jew Teach* 8 (June 1940): 12–16.

Matt, H. J. "The Goals of Teaching Jewish Prayer." *Syn Sch* 31 (Summer 1973): 4–11.

Netter, Esther. "What Does a Praying Jew Look Like." *MJ* 14 (Spring 1982): 26.

Nudelman, Ludwig. "Conviction and Clarification." *Syn Sch* 15 (Dec. 1956): 27–29.

Panoff, Susan R. "Tefillot (prayers) in the First Grade." *Ped Rep* 33 (Dec. 1981): 9–12.

Peli, Pinchas. "Prayer, Prayer Books, and the Prayer" In *Cat 2*, 296–305.

"Prayer in the Melton Curriculum." *MRCN* 10 (Summer 1979): 1–4, 16, 20.

Richman, Milton. "The Art of Prayer." *Jew Teach* (Feb. 1964): 8–9.

Romm, J. Leonard. "On Teaching the Structure of Siddur." *Ped Rep* 33 (Dec. 1981): 23–25.

Roshal, Margit. *B'rakhot*. A ten-lesson curriculum for grades seven through ten. L.A.: HUC–JIR, Tartak Learning Center, 1986.

Schlager, Milton J. "A Course for the Intermediate Grades in the Understanding and Personal Relevance of the Traditional Jewish Prayers in the Reform Liturgy." Master's thesis, HUC–JIR, 1954. 150 pp.

Schmuckler, Miriam. "The Synagogue—An Integrated Course in Jewish History, Literature and Ceremonies." *Jew Teach* 13 (June 1945): 1–11; 14 (Nov. 1945): 8–14; 14 (Jan. 1946): 1–10; 14 (June 1946): 1–11.

Sherman, Robert. "Teaching Poetry as Prayer." *Ped Rep* 32 (Winter 1981): 17–19.

"The Siddur for Teaching Democracy: The Meaning of Worship." *The Jewish School and Democracy* 3 (Nov.–Dec. 1944): 19–20.

Sklar, Samuel. "A Congregation for Primary School Children." *Syn Sch* 22 (1964).

Slominsky, Henry. "Prayer." *Jew Teach* 33 (Feb. 1965): 3–7.

Steinberg, Theodore. "Concepts in the Siddur." *Ped Rep* 33 (Dec. 1981): 13–16.

"Symposium on Improving the Teaching of Prayer." *Syn Sch* 15 (Dec. 1956).

Thiemann, F., and Toby Kurzband. "A Course on the Synagogue." *Jew Teach* 12 (Apr. 1944): 26–31.

Tornberg, Robert. "A Guide for a Confluent Approach to the Teaching of the Siddur: The Amidah." Master's thesis, HUC–JIR, 1975.

* Wachs, Saul P. *An Application of Inquiry to Teaching Siddur*. Ohio State U., 1970.

———. "Discovering the Siddur: Overview of the Literature." *Syn Sch* 33 (1974): 4–31.

———. "Goals of Instruction in Siddur." *Ped Rep* 33 (Dec. 1981): 3–5.

———. "A Review of Materials for the Teaching of Prayer and the Siddur." *Syn Sch* 34 (Fall 1975): 4–32.

———. "Teaching the Siddur through Inquiry and Discovery." *Ed As*, 1972 (1973): 52–55.

Weissberg, Victor. "Worship in the Hebrew School." *Jew Teach* 28 (Oct. 1959): 15–16.

"Worship in the Classroom." *Syn Sch* 5 (Feb. 1947): 81–84; 5 (Apr. 1947): 115–17.

* Zuckerman, I. J. *Educational Values and Attitudes as Derived from the Siddur: The Jewish Prayer Book*. St. Louis U., 1967.

Zusman, Mrs. Morris. "Siddur Remedial Reading Chart." *Syn Sch* 15 (May 1957): 25–27.

Zyskind, Howard B. "Seeking to Overcome a Lost Art." *Jew Teach* 34 (Feb. 1966): 25–27.

THE JUNIOR CONGREGATION

Alper, Janice. "A Liturgy Curriculum for a Three Day a Week Religious School." For students in the second, third, and fourth years of a four-year Hebrew program. Master's project, HUC–JIR, 1978.

Brilliant, Nathan. "Children's Service" (criteria), *Jew Teach* 1 (Apr. 1933): 11–15.

Brilliant, Nathan, and Libbie L. Braverman. "Children's Services." In *Act*, 122–37.

"Ritual for Children's Service." CCAR Committee Report. *CCAR* 17 (1906): 181, 185, 192.

Chanover, Hyman. "The New Prayer Book for Junior Congregations: A Statement on Its Aims and Objectives in Behalf of the Authors." *Syn Sch* 18 (Dec. 1959): 13–20.

Colodner, Sol. "Stimulating Participation in the Junior Congregation." *Syn Sch* 10 (Sept. 1951): 6–9.

Davidson, Jerome E. "Creative Worship for Teen Agers in the Religious School." *Jew Teach* 23 (Mar. 1955): 8–10.

Davis, Moshe. "Towards a Modern Children's Service." *Jew Ed* 9 (Jan.–Mar. 1937): 26–33.

Einsider, Harold. "The Role of the Junior Congregation in Jewish Education." *Ped Rep* 32 (Winter 1981): 25–27.

Goldman, Yehudah. "בית הכנסת לילדים„ (The Junior Congregation). *Hinukh* (H.) 1 (Apr. 1935): 22–24.

Grossman, Jacob B. "The Junior Congregation." *RA* (1928): 149–53.

Lazaron, Morris S. "Religious Worship for Children." *Central Conference of American Rabbis Yearbook* 38 (1928): 344–60.

Millgram, Abraham E. "Meaningful Prayer for Our Children." *RA* (1959): 49–60.

Rosen, M. "A Second Look at the Junior Congregation." *Syn Sch* 26 (Spring 1968): 4–9.

Schwartz, Elliot. "The Junior Congregation Program." *Syn Sch* 10 (Sept. 1951): 3–5.

Sherman, Frank. "Children's Services." *Jew Teach* 2 (Nov. 1933): 13–17.

Spotts, Leon H. "Conducting a Successful Junior Congregation." *Syn Sch* 12 (Apr. 1954): 914.

Stampfer, Nathaniel I. "A Junior Congregation Program." *Syn Sch* 17 (Dec. 1958): 22–23.

Zussman, Evelyn. "Making the Torah Reading Meaningful at the Junior Congregation." *Syn Sch* 17 (1959).

———. "Telling Stories at the Junior Congregation" (with extensive bibliography). *Syn Sch* 11 (Apr. 1953): 16–21.

PRAYER BOOKS, GUIDES, AND TEXTBOOKS FOR SYNAGOGUE AND PRAYER

Abramson, Lillian S., and Lilian T. Leiderman. *Jeremy and Judy's Book of Blessings*. N.Y.: Behrman and UOJCA, 1957.

Bamberger, David. *A Functional Teacher's Guide for When a Jew Prays*. N.Y.: Behrman, 1972.

Birnbaum, Philip, ed. *Daily Prayer Book*. N.Y.: Hebrew Pub. Co., 1977.

Brown, Steven M. *Higher and Higher: Making Jewish Prayer Part of Us*. Teacher's guide. N.Y.: USA Department of Youth Activities, 1981. 196 pp.

Cedarbaum, David, and Libbie L. Braverman. *Teach Me to Pray*. N.Y.: Behrman, n.d.

Chanover, Hyman, and Evelyn Zusman. *A Book for Prayer for Junior Congregations: Sabbath and Festivals*. N.Y.: USCJE, 1959. 256 pp.

———. *My Book of Prayers*. 2 vols. N.Y.: USA, 1959.

Cheil, Arthur. *Pathways through the Torah*. Teacher's guide. 4 parts. N.Y.: Ktav, n.d.

De Koven, Ralph. *Mahzor Meforash*. N.Y.: Ktav.

———. *Siddur Meforash: A Prayer Book with Explanatory Notes*. N.Y.: Ktav, 1965. 595 pp.

Dorph, Gail Zaiman. *Prayer*. Edited by Barry W. Holtz. Curriculum Supervisor, Seymour Fox. The following are for teacher use only in conjunction with the holiday series written by Marcia Kaunfer. *Part One—The Torah Service, Shema U'Virkhoteha*. 145 pp. *Part Two—Geography of the Siddur, The Amidah*. 181 pp. *Part Three—Ashrei, Musaf, Minhah, Kaddish, Keva and Kavanna*. 55 pp. Melton Graded Curriculum Series. N.Y.: MRC–JTSA, 1984. For level gimmel (3) 10-year-olds.

Dorph, Gail Zaiman, and Victoria Koltun Kelman. *My Siddur Reader: Prayer Series*. Edited by B. W. Holtz. Curriculum Supervisor, Seymour Fox. N.Y.: MRC of JTS, 1981. 48 pp. Level bet (2).

Edelstein, Menachem M. *Seder Limud L'Tfilot*. N.Y.: Baronial Press, 1947. 102 pp.

Efron, Benjamin. *Pathways through the Prayerbook*. Teacher's guide. N.Y.: Ktav, 1962. 165 pp.

Ehrlich, Abraham. *Shiure Berachot* (H.). N.Y.: 1967.

Fields, Harvey J. *Bechol Levavcha: With All Your Heart*. 2 parts. N.Y.: UAHC, 1976. 171 pp. Grades 7–9.

Fishman, Priscilla. *Think and Thank*. Siddur program. Workbook. N.Y.: Behrman, 1982. 96 pp.

Freehof, Solomon B. *In the House of the Lord: Our Worship and Our Prayerbook*. N.Y.: UAHC, 1951. 162 pp.

Freeman, Grace, and Joan G. Sugarman. *Inside the Synagogue*. N.Y.: UAHC, 1971. Grades 3–4.

Grishaver, Joel Lurie. *Shema is for Real: A Book on Prayers and Other Tangents*. Teacher's guide. Chicago: Olin-Sang, Ruby, Union Institute, 1973. Grades 6–9.

Hertz, Joseph H. *The Authorized Daily Prayer Book*. N.Y.: Bloch, 1948. 1119 pp.

Kaplan, Aryeh. *Prayerbook Series*. National Conference of Synagogue Youth/Orthodox Union.

Kaplan, Mordecai M., and Eugene Kohn. *Sabbath Prayer Book*. N.Y.: Reconstructionist Press, 1977.

Levin, Meyer, and Toby K. Kurzband. *The Story of the Synagogue*. N.Y.: Behrman, 1957. 191 pp. Grades 5–6

Levinger, Elma Ehrlich. *With the Jewish Child in Home and Synagogue*. School ed. N.Y.: Bloch, 1930. 115 pp.

Mindel, Nissan. *My Prayer*. N.Y.: Merkas L'inyonei Chinuch, 1972.

———, ed. *Siddur Tehillat Hashem*. N.Y.: Merkas L'inyonei Chinuch, 1982.

Moskowitz, Nachama Skolnik. *A Bridge to Prayer: Volume 1—God, Prayer, and the Shema*. N.Y.: UAHC Press, 1988. 80 pp.

Persky, Elias, and Sol Scharfstein. *Reading and Prayer Primer—Kreah Ootfilah L'mathilim*. Teacher's guide, workbook, cassette, and flashcards. N.Y.: Ktav, 1965.

Pool, David De Sola. *The Traditional Prayer Book for Sabbath and Festivals*. N.Y.: Behrman. 897 pp.

Rossel, Karen Trager, and Patricia Goldstein Mason. *Hebrew through Prayer*. Teacher's guide; programmed text; practice, review, and game book; and flashcards. Level one. N.Y.: Behrman, n.d.

———. *Hebrew through Prayer: Baruch U'Mvorach*. Teacher's guide, practice book, and flashcards. N.Y.: Behrman, n.d.

Rossel, Seymour, Eugene B. Borowitz, and Hyman Chanover. *When a Jew Prays*. 2 vols.

Teacher's guide, student encounter book, and teacher's cassette. N.Y.: Behrman, 1973. 192 pp. Grades 4–5.

Schanin, Norman. *T'filah V'hag LaTalmid—Prayers and Holidays for the Student*. Designed by Ezekiel Schloss. Teacher's guide, workbook, and individualized instruction booklet. N.Y.: Ktav, 1960. 177 pp.

Scharfstein, Sol. *Shaar Hakriah*. Workbook, cassette, and flashcards. N.Y.: Ktav, n.d.

Scherman, Nosson. *The Complete Artscroll Siddur*. N.Y.: Mesorah Publications Ltd, 1987.

Shiloh Siddur. N.Y.: Shiloh Pub. Co.

Siegel, Seymour. *A Conceptual Teacher's Guide to When a Jew Prays*. N.Y.: Behrman, 1973.

Silberman, Morris. *Sabbath and Festival Prayer Book*. N.Y.: USA Book Service, n.d.

Singer, Howard. *With Mind and Heart—An Approach to Judaism for Young People*. N.Y.: USCJE, 1961. 312 pp.

Stern, Chaim, ed. *Shaarei Tefilah: Gates of Prayer* (The New Union Prayer Book). N.Y.: CCAR, 1975. 779 pp.

———, ed. *Shaarei Teshuvah: Gates of Repentance* (The New Union Prayer Book). 2 vols. N.Y.: CCAR, 1978.

Stern, Shirley. *Pathways through the Prayer Book*. Teacher's guide. N.Y.: Ktav.

Tochnit Gurim, Tefilot U'Brachot. N.Y.: Hanhala Artzit-B'nei Akiva of North America, 1954. 120 pp. Ages 11–13.

Union Hymnal: Songs and Prayers for Jewish Worship. N.Y.: CCAR, 1932. 588 pp.

Weisser, Michael. *My Synagogue*. N.Y.: Behrman, n.d. Grades 1–2.

HOLIDAYS, CEREMONIES, AND CUSTOMS

Applebaum, Morton. "The Observance of the Holy Days and Festivals." *CCAR* 68 (1958): 188–90.

Aronson, D. *The Jewish Way of Life*. N.Y.: USCJE–JTSA, 1946. 227 pp.

Balin, Harry. "A Purim Surprise." *Jew Teach* 11 (Jan. 1943): 31.

Barrington, Joanne. *The Sanctification of Jewish Time*. A ten-lesson unit that explores special aspects of holy times in Judaism. L.A.: HUC–JIR, Tartak Learning Center, 1988.

Bin-Nun, Judy, and Franne Einhorn. *Rosh Hashanah: A Holiday Funtext*. N.Y.: UAHC, c. 1978. 31 pp.

Blank, Irwin M. "The Teaching of Customs and Ceremonies to Eleven-Year-Olds." *Jew Teach* 14 (Jan. 1946): 21–24.

Bloch, Abraham P. *The Biblical and Historical Background of Jewish Customs and Ceremonies*. N.Y.: Ktav, 1980. 402 pp.

Bonder, Evelyn D. "Shadow Play for Passover Assembly." *Jew Teach* 9 (Apr. 1941): 1–12.

Borowitz, Eugene. "Mass Contests as a Chanuko Stimulant." *Jew Teach* 18 (Nov. 1949): 1–4.

Borowsky, Alice. "How a Bureau Can Help in Celebrating Yom-Tov." *Ped Rep* 32 (Sept. 1981): 5–7.

Braverman, Libbie L. "Chanuko and Our Neighbors." *Jew Teach* 11 (Apr. 1943): 13–17.

———. "A Purim Carnival." *Jew Ed* 7 (Jan.–Mar. 1935): 49–51.

Brilliant, Nathan, and Libbie L. Braverman. "Consecration and Confirmation." In *Act*, 200–224.

———. "Holiday Celebrations." In *Act*, 55–103.

* Bundt, Barbara A. K. *Leisure and Religion: A Contemporary Jewish Sabbath Paradigm*. U. of Minnesota, 1981.

Chomsky, Elsie S. "Experience with a Holiday Program as a Center of Interest in the Curriculum." *Jew Ed* 5 (Apr.–June 1933): 95–100.

Chorowsky, Joshua. "A Conceptual Graded Approach to the Teaching of Hanukkah." *Ped Rep* 32 (Sept. 1981): 10–11.

Cohen, Jack J. "Customs and Ceremonies." In *JEDS*, 202–14.

Cohen, Jeffrey. "A School Genizah Ceremony." *Ped Rep* 35 (Oct. 1984): 27–29.

Covich, Edith S. *The Jewish Child Every Day*. N.Y.: UAHC, 1947.

Department of Education and Culture, WZO, American Section. (Shavuot) (H.) (Rosh Hashanah and Yom Kippur) (H.) In *A Page for the Hebrew Teacher*. Prepared by Aviv Ekroni, Tamar Aryav, and Raphael Banai. May and Aug. 1983. 30 and 39 pp.

Dorph, Gail, and Vicky Kelman. "Fragment of a Shavuot Lesson" (First year religious school). *MRCN* 6 (Spring 1977): 3.

Dotan, Beth Seldin. *Ritual: How Ritual Re-enacts Covenant*. A ten-lesson unit. L.A.: HUC–JIR, Tartak Learning Center, 1988.

Dresner, Samuel H. *The Sabbath*. N.Y.: Burning Bush Press, 1970.

Edidin, Ben M. *Jewish Customs and Ceremonies*. N.Y.: Hebrew Pub. Co., 1941. 178 pp.

———. *Jewish Holidays and Festivals*. N.Y.: Hebrew Pub. Co., 1940.

———. *Projects about Religious Ideas and Customs*. Experimental ed. Cincinnati: UAHC and CJE, 1938. 54 pp.

———. "Teaching Holidays and Customs." *Jew Teach* 5: (Mar. 1937): 1–24; 5 (June 1937): 1–20.

Eisenstein, Ira. *The Sabbath*. Washington, D.C.: B'nai B'rith Organization, 1961. 27 pp.

Feuer, Leon I., Jerome Rosenblum, and William B. Levinson. "How to Have a Happy Hanukkah." *Jew Teach* (1935): 1–7.

* Fierman, Morton. *Selected Resource Units for the Holy Days and Festivals of Judaism in Seventh, Eighth, and Ninth Grades in American Reform Religious Schools*. Arizona State U., 1960. 231 pp.

Fischbach, Suzanne. "American Holidays and Jewish Festivals." *Jew Teach* 15 (Nov. 1946): 1–23.

Franzblau, Abraham N., and Alan S. Green. *A Curriculum in Jewish Ceremonials for Grades 4 through 12*. Cincinnati: HUC–JIR, ca. 1935.

Gamoran, Emanuel. "The Project Method in Teaching Customs and Ceremonies." *CCAR* 36 (1926): 322–52.

Gaster, Theodor H. *Festivals of the Jewish Year*. N.Y.: Sloan, 1953.

Gates, Edith B. "Succot: A Jewish Harvest Festival—A Multimedia Presentation." Master's thesis, California State U., Long Beach.

Glosser, Joanne Katz. "Ba-Or Chaim—In the Light of Life." A tenth-grade curriculum for moral growth and self-affirmation, structured to follow the course of Jewish holidays. Master's project, HUC–JIR, 1977.

Golden, Patti. "The Holiday Workshop Series: An Experimental Program." *Compass* (Fall/Winter 1978).

Golub, Jacob S. "Chanuko Projects." *Jew Teach* 12 (Nov. 1943): 17–26.

———. "Purim Projects." *Jew Teach* 12 (Jan. 1944): 11–20.

———. "Shevuos Projects." *Jew Teach* (Apr. 1944): 18–25.

Golub, Jacob S., and Noah Nardi. "A Study in Jewish Observance." *Recon* 11 (June 1945).

Goodman, Philip, ed. *The Passover Anthology*. Phila.: JPS, 1961. 498 pp.

———. *The Purim Anthology*. Phila.: JPS, 1947. 525 pp.

———. *The Rosh Hashanah Anthology*. Phila.: JPS, 1970. 378 pp.

———. *Shavuot Anthology*. Phila.: JPS, 1974.

———. *Sukkot/Simhat Torah Anthology*. Phila.: JPS, 1973. 475 pp.

———. *The Yom Kippur Anthology*. Phila.: JPS, 1971. 399 pp.

Gordis, Robert, and David M. Feldman. *Ritual in Jewish Life*. Washington, D.C.: B'nai B'rith Organization, 1960. 48 pp.

Green, Barry H. "Toward a Course of Study for the Third Grade in Relating Judaism to the American Holiday Cycle." Master's thesis, HUC–JIR, 1957.

Greenstone, Julius H. *Jewish Feasts and Fasts*. Phila.: JPS, 1945.

Hakimian, Leah. "Objectives, Instruction, Evaluation" (holidays). *Ped Rep* 32 (Sept. 1981): 8–9.

"Hamishah Asar—Tree Planting Ceremony." *Syn Sch* 4 (Jan. 1946): 46–47.

Heschel, Abraham J. *The Sabbath: Its Meaning for Modern Man*. N.Y.: Noonday Press, 1977.

Holtz, Barry W. "The Melton Graded Curriculum in Holidays/Mitzvot/Prayer." *MRCN* 10 (Summer 1979): 13.

Idelsohn, Abraham S. *Ceremonies for Judaism*. Cincinnati: UAHC, 1929.

Isserman, Ruth, and Albert E. Goldstein. "Tests for Holidays." *Jew Teach* 7 (June 1939): 8–21; 9 (Nov. 1940): 20–25; 9 (Jan. 1941): 23–28; 9 (Apr. 1941): 21–27; 9 (June 1941): 16–22.

Kabakoff, Jacob. "The Seder through the Ages." *Syn Sch* 4 (Apr. 1946): 91–96.

Kadison, Elaine F. "Fall Holidays." *Ped Rep* 34 (Sept. 1981).

Kaplan, Louis L. "Developments in Jewish Education on Jewish Life and Its Observances." *Jew Ed* 21 (Spring 1950): 46–50.

Kaunfer, Marcia. "Sample Outline of a Graded Holiday Curriculum for the Afternoon School." *MRCN* 6 (Spring 1977): 2, 5.

Kohler, Kaufmann. "The Origin and Function of Ceremonies in Judaism" (1907). In *Reform Judaism*, edited by Joseph L. Blau, 205–27. 1973.

Korenblit, Ari. "Shabbaton Educational Programs." *Ped Rep* 33 (Winter 1981): 24–25.

Langer, Hajnalka. "Ceremonial Object Work in the Jewish Schools." *Jewish Teacher* (May 1917).

Lasker, Arnold A. "Motivations for Attending High Holy Day Services." *J for the Scientific Study of Religion* 10 (Fall 1950): 241–48.

Laufman, Larry. "A Curriculum Evaluation of Teaching Pesach in the Religious School." Master's thesis, Brandeis U., 1971.

Lee, Barton. "Course in the Jewish Life Cycle for Grades 8–9." *Jew Teach* 34 (Feb. 1966): 30–32.

Lehrer, Leibush. "The Dynamic Role of Jewish Symbols in the Psychology of the Jewish Child in America." *YA* 6 (1951): 37–72. First published in *YB* (Y.) 28 (1946) and 29 (1947).

Lesser, Charles B. "Purim in Miniature." *Jew Teach* 6 (Jan. 1938): 9–18.

Lieb, David S. "Avodah L'Shabbat." *AM* (Fall 1971).

Lukinsky, Joseph. "Making the Seder a Personal Experience: A Workshop." *MJ* 15 (Winter 1983): 7, 24.

Maislin, Simeon J., ed. *Shaarei Mitzvah: A Guide to the Jewish Life Cycle*. N.Y.: CCAR, 1979. 176 pp.

Marcus, Jacob R. "The Life Cycle Ceremonies" (in early America). In *CAJ*, 2:984–99.

Miller, Deborah D. "Secret Sedarim." *Ped Rep* 32 (Sept. 1981): 14–15.

Millgram, Abraham E. *Sabbath—Day of Delight*. Phila.: JPS, 1952. 495 pp.

"Oneg Shabbat: Program and Games." *Syn Sch* 4 (Feb 1946): 55–60.

Packscher, Hazel G. "Chanuko in the Book Club." *Jew Teach* 11 (Nov. 1942): 21–22.

Pins, Arnulf M. "The Creative Use of the Haggadah for Specific Age Groups." *Jew Teach* (Mar. 1954): 2–4.

Plaut, W. Gunther. "The Sabbath in the Reform Movement" (1965). In *Reform Judaism*, edited by Joseph L. Blau, 229–54. 1973.

Podet, Allen H. "Secular Studies and Religious Uniqueness: A View of Hanukkah." *Rel Ed* 71 (Nov.–Dec. 1976): 596–602.

Pollak, George. "Rosh Hashanah and the Mahzor." *Ped Rep* 33 (Dec. 1981): 17–18.

Reichert, Irving F. "Shall We Teach Ceremonies in the Religious School." *CCAR* 33 (1923): 286–95.

Reimer, Joseph. "A Developmental Perspective on Teaching the Holidays." *MRCN* 6 (Spring 1977): 4, 5.

Rosewater, Adeline R. "The Megillah in Verse." *Jew Teach* 11 (Jan. 1943): 18–26.

Rosman, Steven M. "Holiday Programs for Teenagers." *Ped Rep* 32 (Sept. 1981): 18–19. For high school.

Rush, Barbara, and Eliezer Marcus. "Teaching the Holidays through Folk Tales." *Ped Rep* 32 (Sept. 1981): 20–22.

Schauss, Hayyim. *The Jewish Festivals*. Cincinnati: UAHC, 1938. 320 pp.

———. *The Lifetime of a Jew throughout the Ages of Jewish History*. N.Y.: UAHC, 1976. Grades 9 and up.

Schwartzman, Sylvan D. "Let's Have A Chanuko World's Fair." *Jew Teach* 9 (Nov. 1940): 1–13.

Sheinman, Hildy L. "Sukot: A New Approach to the Festival of Thanksgiving." *Compass* 6 (Fall 1982): 1, 22.

Shook, Mark L. "A Time to Remember, a Time to Forget: Holy Days and Festivals." *CCAR J* (Spring 1974): 21–26.

Silver, Sam, and Alvin Fine. "Chanuko Marches on." *Jew Teach* 8 (Nov. 1939): 8–17. School program.

Slonimsky, David T. "A Children's Seder Service." *Jew Teach* 11 (Apr. 1942): 18–30.

———. "A Sabbath Unit." *Jew Teach* 9: (Nov. 1940): 14–19.

Solis-Cohen, E., ed. *Hanukkah: The Feast of Lights*. Phila.: JPS, 1937. 400 pp.

Soloff, Mordecai I. "Objectives and Methods of Teaching Customs and Ceremonies." *Jew Teach* 5 (Jan. 1937): 1–10.

Solovy, Delores Kohl, and Betty Katz. "From Taxonomy to Purimspiel: Applying Thinking Skills to Holiday Study." *Ped Rep* 32 (Sept. 1981): 12–13.

Stein, Adele. "Teaching of Purim." *Jew Teach* 23 (Jan. 1955): 3–6.

Stern, Carolyn H., and J. Jacques Sone. "Purim Carnival." *Jew Teach* 2 (1933).

Thal, Linda. "Seder Table." *Compass* (Summer 1982): 3–6, 17.

Trepp, Leo. *The Complete Book of Jewish Observance*. N.Y.: Behrman, 1980.

Chanukah. 3d ed. N.Y.: UOJCA, National Conference of Synagogue Youth, n.d.

Vainstein, Jacob. *Cycle of the Year: Through the Ages of Jewish History*. Jerusalem: WZO Department of Torah Education and Culture in the Diaspora, 1953. 151 pp.

Vanek, Julie. *Exploring the Jewish Life Cycle through the Prism of Covenant*. A ten-lesson course for the fifth grade. L.A.: HUC–JIR, Tartak Learning Center, 1988.

Waskow, Arthur. *Seasons of Our Joy: A Handbook of Jewish Festivals*. N.Y.: Bantam, 1982. 272 pp.

Waxman, Robert. "Sukkot Retreat." *AM* (Spring 1978).

Williams, Dorothy S. "Older Children and the Jewish Life Cycle." *Jew Teach* 29 (Dec. 1960): 4–7.

Your Neighbor Celebrates: Jewish Holidays and Traditions in America. N.Y.: ADL, 1957.

Zussman, Evelyn. "A School Havdalah Service." *Syn Sch* 18 (1959).

TEXTS, GUIDES, AND BOOKS FOR HOLIDAYS, CEREMONIES, AND CUSTOMS

Abramson, Lillian S. *Jeremy and Judy's Hanukah*. N.Y.: Behrman for UOJCA, 1956.

Berman, Bonnie, and Laura Gladstein. *Holiday Game Pak*. Denver: ARE.

Bial, Morrison David. *The Hanukkah Story*. N.Y.: Behrman, 1952. 43 pp.

Bokser, Ben Zion. *A Young People's Mahzor*. N.Y.: USA, n.d.

Cedarbaum, Sophia N. *Rosh Ha-Shonoh, Yom Kippur, the High Holy days; Shovuos, the Birthday of the Torah; Sukos and Simchas Torah; Chanuko, the Festival of Lights; Passover, the Festival of Freedom; Purim, a Joyous Holiday; The Sabbath, a Day of Delight;* and *Tu Bi-Shvot, the New Year's Day for Trees*. N.Y.: UAHC, c. 1960–61.

Dorph, Gail Zaiman, and Victoria Koltun Kelman. *Holidays/Mitzvot/Prayer*. Edited by B. W. Holtz. Curriculum Supervisor, Seymour Fox.

> Level alef (1) units:
> Volume 1—*General Introduction*. Teacher's guide. 25 pp.
> Volume 2—*Talmud Torah, Rosh Hashanah/Yom Kippur, Sukkot, Simhat Torah, Prayer, Part One*. Teacher's guide. 185 pp.
> Volume 3—*Shabbat: Weekly Shabbat Ceremony*. Teacher's guide. 77 pp.
> Volume 4—*Hanukkah*. Teacher's guide. 67 pp.
> Volume 5—*Prayer, Part Two, Tu Bishvat, Purim, Pesah*. Teacher's guide. 159 pp.
> Volume 6—*Yom Ha'atzma'ut, Counting the Omer/Lag Ba'omer, Shavuot*. Teacher's guide. 123 pp.
> Level bet (2) units:
> Volume 1—*General Introduction, Talmud Torah, Rosh Hashanah/Yom Kippur, Sukkot/Simhat Torah, the Synagogue*. Teacher's guide. 185 pp.

Volume 2—*Birkat Hamazon, Family History, Tzedakah/Gemilut Hasadim, Hanukkah.* Experimental ed. 299 pp.
Volume 3—*Shema U'virkhoteha, Tu Bishvat, Lel Shabbat, Purim.* Teacher's guide. 266 pp.
Volume 4—*Pesah, Yom Ha'atzma'ut, Amidah.* Teacher's guide. 180 pp.
Volume 5—*Lag Ba'omer, Shavuot, Kashrut, Alenu.* Teacher's guide. 136 pp.

Edelman, Lily. *The Sukkah and the Big Wind.* N.Y.: USA, n.d.

Eisenberg, Azriel, and Jessie Robinson. *My Jewish Holidays.* N.Y.: USCJE, 1958. 208 pp.

Epstein, Morris. *All about Jewish Holidays and Customs.* Teacher's guide, workbook. N.Y.: Ktav, 1970. 142 pp.

Fass, David E. *The Shofar that Lost Its Voice.* N.Y.: UAHC, 1982. 48 pp. Grades 4–6.

Fine, Helen. *G'dee* and *G'dee's Book of Holiday Fun* (workbook). N.Y.: UAHC. Grades 4–6.

Freehof, Lillian S. *The Runaway Candle.* N.Y.: UAHC, 1950.

Gamoran, Mamie G. *Days and Ways—History of Jewish Holidays and Customs.* With pupil's activity book by Hannah G. Goodman (1950), 133 pp. N.Y.: UAHC, 1941. 205 pp. Grades 4–6.

———. *Fun Ways to Holidays.* N.Y.: UAHC. Grades 4–6.

———. *Hillel'S Calendar.* N.Y.: UAHC, 1960. Grades 1–3.

———. *Hillel's Happy Holiday.* Teacher's guide. N.Y.: 1939, 1944. 205 pp.

Garvey, Robert. *Good Shabbos, Everybody.* N.Y.: USCJE, c. 1951. 28 pp.

Gersh, Harry, Eugene B. Borowitz, and Hyman Chanover. *When a Jew Celebrates: The Jewish Life Cycle and the Jewish Year.* 2 vols. Teacher's guide, student encounter book, and teacher cassette. N.Y.: Behrman, n.d. Grades 5–6.

Goldin, Hyman. *Holiday Tales: Jewish Holidays and Their Legends.* N.Y.: Jordan Pub. Co., 1929. 259 pp.

Golub, Rose L. *Down Holiday Lane.* N.Y.: UAHC, 1947. 166 pp.

Goodman, Robert. *A Teacher's Guide to Jewish Holidays.* Denver: ARE, 1983. 224 pp.

Grand, Tamar. *Holiday Craft Kit for the Jewish Child.* N.Y.: UAHC. Grades 1–3.

Grishaver, Joel. *The Life-Cycle: A Workbook.* Denver: ARE, 1983. 49 pp. Grade 6.

Ingall, Carol K., and Marcia Kaunfer. Edited by B. W. Holtz. Curriculum Supervisor, S. Fox. *Holidays—Level 3: Yom Ha-'atzma'ut, Shavuot.* Teacher's guide. N.Y.: MRC of JTS, 1984. 135 pp.

Kaunfer, Marcia Lapidus. *Holidays.* Edited by B. W. Holtz. Curriculum Supervisor, S. Fox. N.Y.: MRC of JTSA, 1984.

>Level gimmel (3) units:
>Volume 2—*Hanukkah.* Teacher's guide. 27 pp.
>Volume 3—*Pesah.* Teacher's guide. 97 pp.
>Level dalet (4) student workbook and teacher edition (2 booklets):
>Volume 1—*Rosh Hashanah/Yom Kippur, Sukkot/Simhat Torah.* 1984.
>Volume 2—*Hanukkah.* 1984.
>Volume 3—*Tu Bishvat, Purim.* 1985.
>Volume 4 and 5—*Pesach, Part Two.* 1985.
>Volume 6—*Shavuot.* 1985.

Kieffer, Sam. *The Jewish Life Cycle: Rituals and Concepts.* Edited by Stephen Garfinkel. N.Y.: USA, Department of Youth Activities, 1984.

Kolatch, Mollie. *Sabbath Is Special.* N.Y.: Behrman for UOJCA, 1956.

Kozodoy, Ruth. *The Book of Jewish Holidays.* Teacher's guide, parent kit, work activities for children. N.Y.: Behrman. Grades 3–4

Kurzband, Toby K., and Meyer Levin. *The Story of the Jewish Way of Life.* N.Y.: Behrman, 1959. 192 pp.

Levine, Hadassah. *The Minor Festivals.* N.Y.: Women's Branch of the UOJCA, 1926. 20 pp.

Levinger, Elma E. *Jewish Festivals in the Religious School.* Cincinnati: UAHC, 1923.

———. *Passover Entertainments.* N.Y.: UAHC, 1924.

Levy, Deborah, and Audrey Friedman Marcus. *The Learning Center Book of Jewish Holidays and Symbols.* Denver: ARE, 1979.

Margolis, Isidor, and S. L. Markowitz. *Jewish Holidays and Festivals.* N.Y.: Citadel, n.d.

Markowitz, Samuel. *Living a Jewish Life in a Modern World.* On the place of holiday observances in the modern home. N.Y.: UAHC, 1942.

Maslin, Simeon J., ed. *Gates of Mitzvah: A Guide to the Jewish Life Cycle.* N.Y.: CCAR, 1979. 176 pp.

Mervis, Leonard. *We Celebrate the Jewish Holidays.* 6 pamphlets. N.Y.: UAHC, 1963–69.

Nanus, Susan. *Five in One: Holiday Plays for Jewish Children.* N.Y.: UAHC, ca. 1981. 45 pp. Grades 1–3.

Olitzky, Kerry M. *The Life Cycle Workbook.* Leader guide. Denver: ARE, 1983. 56 pp.

Orenstein, Walter, and Frankel Hertz. *Torah as Our Guide.* N.Y.: Hebrew Pub. Co., 1960.

Rembrandt, Elaine. *Heroes, Heroines and Holidays: Plays for Jewish Youth.* Denver: ARE, 1981.

Reznick, Anita. *Meet the Stickmans—A Trip through the Jewish Holiday Year.* 2 parts. N.Y.: Ktav, n.d.

Rosenberg, Amye. *My Calendar.* N.Y.: Behrman, n.d. Grades 1–3

Rush, Barbara, and Eliezer Marcus. *Seventy and One Tales for the Jewish Year: Folk Tales for Festivals.* 296 pp.

Sampter, Jessie E. *Around the Year in Rhymes,* N.p., n.d. Poetry on ceremonies.

Scharfstein, Sol. *Happy Holiday Pop-up.* N.Y.: Ktav. Kindergarten, n.d.

Scharfstein, Zevi. *Purim and Chanukah* (H.). Readers for children. N.Y.: Shiloh, 1925, 1928. 154 pp. and 25 pp.

Schwartzman, Sylvan D. *Once upon a Lifetime.* N.Y.: UAHC, 1958. 134 pp.

Shulman, M. *The Observance of Passover* (H.). N.Y.: Mizrachi, 1940.

Simon, Norma. *Every Friday Night.* N.Y.: USA. Ages 3–5.

———. *My Family Seder.* N.Y.: USA. Ages 3–5.

———. Festival Series of Picture Storybooks: *Rosh Hashanah; Yom Kippur; Our First Sukkah; Simhat Torah; Hanukah in My House; Happy Purim Night; The Purim Party.* N.Y.: USA, c. 1959–60. Ages 3–5.

———. *Tu Bishvat.* N.Y.: USA. Ages 3–5.

Soltes, Mordecai. *The Jewish Holidays: 250 Questions and Answers.* N.Y.: JWB, 1937.

Stadtler, Bea, and Shirley Simon. *Once upon a Jewish Holiday.* Workbook, flashcards. N.Y.: Ktav, 1965.

Sussman, A., and Abraham Segal. *Holy Days and Holidays.* N.Y.: Bloch, 1947.

Unterman, Isaac. *The Jewish Holidays.* 2 vols. N.Y.: Federal Press, 1950.

Weilerstein, Sadie Rose. *Molly and the Sabbath Queen.* N.Y.: Behrman, n.d.

———. *What the Moon Brought.* Phila.: JPS, 1942. 159 pp.

Weinstein, Deborah. *Chamishah Asar Bishvat.* N.Y.: Mizrachi, 1940.

Zeligs, Dorothy F. *The Story of Jewish Holidays and Customs.* N.Y.: Bloch, 1942.

———. *The Jewish Calendar.* Denver: ARE.

Zwerin, Raymond A., and Audrey Friedman Marcus. *A Purim Album.* N.Y.: UAHC, Blum Publication Fund. Grades 1–3.

GLEANINGS

Hirsch, Samson Raphael (1808–88),
"The catechism of the Jew consists of his calendar."
Judaism Eternal, edited and translated by L. Grunfeld (1956), 1:3.

Greenstone, Julius H.,
"The purpose of the work in this course, and indeed in all other courses of the religious school, should be to make the children feel that human life depends on God, and that the purpose of life is to serve God. And while they are made to feel their responsibility towards Him they should be made to realize that right conduct, based on Torah and tradition, is the most acceptable form of service that may be rendered to God."
The Jewish Religion (1920). Quoted in S. Cohen, *The Progessive Jewish School* (1922), 109.

Shapiro, Mannheim,
"The trend among American Jews seems

to be to retain those customs and practices which are annual rather than daily or weekly, which are festive and which involve family gatherings and relationships."

Quoted by B. Sherman in *Jan 2*, 48.

Horn, Ronnie M., "The Struggle to Celebrate,"
"In my family, we have noticed that what we did for holidays three years ago, is no longer appropriate for our children's level of interest and understanding. When many of the people around our seder table were very small we used to substitute a reading of Uri Schulevitz' *The Magician* for the Welcoming Elijah section of the UNION HAGGADAH."

Compass 1 (Winter 1977), 6.

Dorph, Gail Zaiman, and Victoria Koltun Kelman,
"This program addresses itself to a major problem in the current afternoon school: how can students develop a mature and intelligent understanding of the holiday cycle, the mitzvot of the tradition and Jewish prayer? Our answer is that a curriculum should be structured around Jewish thought—the value concepts and intellectual framework of our tradition. Thus, the Melton Graded Curriculum is not a "customs and ceremonies" approach to the tradition, but it explores the central ideas that underlie Jewish observances and traditional texts. On the other hand, the curriculum does not give up on basic skills for the sake of ideas."

Holiday/Mitzvoi/Prayer: Level Alef, Volume 1—General Introduction, 3.

Schechter, Solomon (1850–1915),
"When most Jewish children prayed, one text sufficed for all; now when few are given to prayer, we are blessed with a variety of prayer books."

Quoted in *Jew Ed* 15 (May 1944), 171.

Tochnit Gurim, Tefilot U'Brachot,
"To instill a sense of gratitude and indebtedness to our Creator (for the good as well for the seemingly bad) through the medium of Tefilot and Brachot and to develop a natural feeling of loyalty to Hakadosh baruch Hu.

To present an understanding of why we pray to G-d and how we should pray to G-d; how can we achieve sincere devotion during prayer." (Five more goals follow.)

Unit 1, page 7. N.Y.: Bnei Akiva of North America, 1954.

United Synagogue Commission on Jewish Education,
"*Prayer and Worship:* Pupils should be helped to develop strong emotional attachments to the prayer book, understanding of its main ideas, and, above all, deep trust in God which is the basis of all prayer."

Objectives and Standards for the Congregational School (1958), 12.

Richman, Milton,
"The decisive point for the religious school teacher is to recognize the potential dimensions of personal prayer and of group worship. Of all the things that have been said about prayer in the many religions, this much seems to be universal, that the person in the praying situation changes from his ordinariness. Whatever the meaning of the God to whom the prayer is directed, and whatever the meaning of the prayer, the person becomes something different, something extraordinary. In the Jewish tradition, the effective prayer is taken to be cooperative and reciprocal, which is to say that the prayer and God are being influenced. It is also a dictum of our tradition that the means of the prayer can be both formal and traditional, as well as informal and spontaneous."

Jew Teach 32 (Feb. 1964), 8.

15 | LITERATURE

See also Chapters 10 and 21.

JUVENILE LITERATURE PRIOR TO 1950

* Davidson, Israel. *Parody in Jewish Literature.* Columbia U., 1902.

Feuer, Leon I. *Jewish Literature since the Bible, Book One.* Cincinnati: UAHC, 1937. 206 pp.

———. "Post-Biblical Literature in the Curriculum of the Religious School." *Jew Teach* 2 (Nov. 1933): 18–25.

Feuer, Leon I., and Azriel Eisenberg. *Jewish Literature since the Bible, Book Two.* Cincinnati: UAHC, 1941.

Franzblau, Abraham A. *Stories from Hebrew and Yiddish Sources for Religious Schools.* Cincinnati: HUC, ca. 1935.

Gamoran, Emanuel. "A Selected List of Stories for Jewish Children." *Jew Teach* 3 (Nov. 1934): 15–19; 3 (Jan. 1935): 17–21.

Goelman, Eliezer. "Pupils' Reading Interests." *Jew Ed* 14 (Apr.–June 1942): 33–34.

Goodman, Abram V., and Mrs. A. V. Goodman. "Folklore in the Jewish Religious School." *Jew Teach* 4 (Nov. 1935): 8–14.

Lewittes, Mordecai, and Harry Blumberg. מספרות הדורות (Selected Readings from Hebrew Literature) (H.). N.Y.: Hebrew Pub. Co., 1942. 211 pp.

Lieberman, Morris. "The Use of Fiction in Jewish Education." Master's thesis, HUC–JIR, 1934.

Schaefer, Alice L. "Literature in the Junior High School." *Jew Teach* 6 (Nov. 1937): 17–20.

Scharfstein, Zevi. "יוצרי ספרות-הילדים שלנו„ (Creators of Our Children's Literature). Primarily Europe and Israel. In *Sefer Hashanah* (H.), 234–55. 1940.

Slouschz, Nahum. *The Renascence of Hebrew Literature, 1743–1885.* Phila.: JPS, 1909. 307 pp.

* Soviv, Aaron. *Attitudes towards Jewish Life and Education as Reflected in Yiddish and Hebrew Literature in America, 1870–1914.* Dropsie U., 1957.

Syrkin, Marie. "The Cultural Scene: Literary Expression." Covers first half of 20th century. In Jan 1, 92–121.

Stories from Jewish Literature: A Teacher's Manual. UAHC, 1914. 214 pp.

JUVENILE LITERATURE SINCE 1950

Abramowitz, Tammy Rubin. "Criteria for Selecting Jewish Literature for Use in the Kin-

15 LITERATURE

dergarten and First Grade of the Day School and One-Day School." Master's thesis, Department of Jewish Education, JTSA, 1989.

Amirom. P. „הערות להוראת הספרות העברית בבית הספר העברי באצרה"ב" (Notes on the Teaching of Literature in the Hebrew Schools of the U.SA). *Hadoar* (H.) 61 (Jan. 15, 1982).

Blatt, Gloria T. "The Jewish-American Experience: The View from Children's Fiction." *Top of the News* (Summer 1979): 391–97.

Bloore, John Stephen. "The Jew in American Literature, 1794–1930." Master's thesis, New York U., 1950.

"Children's Literature." In *Enc Jud*, 5:428–60.

Citron, Paul. "Using Fiction to Teach Ethics." *Compass* 10 (Spring/Summer 1988): 16–17.

Cohen, Jack J. "Useful Magazines for Teachers and Pupils." *Syn Sch* 5 (Dec. 1946): 39–41.

Colodner, Solomon. *Lessons in Jewish Literature: An Outline of Jewish Literature from its Early Beginnings to Modern Times*. N.Y.: Bloch, ca. 1963. 64 pp.

Daniels, Leona. "The 34th Man: How Well Is Jewish Minority Culture Represented in Children's Fiction?" *School Library J* (Feb. 1970): 38–43.

Davis, Enid. *A Comprehensive Guide to Children's Literature with a Jewish Theme*. N.Y.: Schocken, 1981. 177 pp.

Eisenberg, Azriel, ed. *The Golden Land: A Literary Portrait of American Jewry, 1654 to the Present*. N.Y.: Yoseloff, 1964. 518 pp.

———. *Modern Jewish Life in Literature*. N.Y.: USCJE, 1968.

Epstein, Morris. *"World Over* [children's magazine] Polls its Audience." *Jew Ed* 23 (Summer 1952): 40–44.

Fellus, Gail Teicher. "How to Teach with Fiction." *Compass* 10 (Spring/Summer 1988): 14–15.

Frischer, Rita Berman. "Seven Days of Signs and Wonders—A Marketful of Jewish Children's Literature." *MJ* 17 (Winter 1984): 5–6, 30.

Gannes, Abraham P. "Jewish Juvenile Periodicals as Aids in Teaching about Jewish Life." *Jew Ed* 30 (Winter 1960): 59–62.

Gertel, E. B. "Toward Jewish Standards of Literature." *Recon* 48 (Summer 1983): 7–14.

Goldreich, Gloria, ed. *A Treasury of Jewish Literature from Biblical Times to Today*. N.Y.: Holt, Rinehart and Winston, 1982. 256 pp. Grades 5 and up.

* Golub, Ellen. *Orality in Jewish Literature*. State U. of New York at Buffalo, 1978.

Golub, Jacob S. *Teaching*. N.Y.: JEC. 15 pp.

Grossman, Cheryl S., and Suzy Engman. *Jewish Literature for Children: A Teaching Guide*. Denver: ARE, 1985. 200 pp.

Grover, Judy. "Children's Books in Review." *MRCN* 11 (Fall 1980): 4.

Halkin, Simon. *Modern Hebrew Literature—Trends and Values*. N.Y.: Schocken, 1950. 238 pp.

Harap, Louis. *The Image of the Jew in American Literature from Early Republic to Mass Immigration*. Phila.: JPS, 1974. 586 pp.

* Hershinow, Sheldon Jay. *Jewish Writers and the Changing Novel in America*. U. of Hawaii, 1975.

Howe, Irving, ed. *Jewish-American Stories*. N.Y.: New American Library, 1977.

Hyman, Philip. *"Reading for a Broader Jewish Education." Syn Sch* 11 (Nov. 1952): 13–16.

Indelman, Elchanan. „ספרות-ילדים עברית באמריקה" (Children's Hebrew Literature in America). *Sh Hah* (H.) 36 (1976): 83–93.

Joseloff, Samuel H. *A Time to Seek: An Anthology of Contemporary Jewish American Poets*. Teacher's guide. N.Y.: UAHC, 1975. Grades 10–12.

Kahn, L. "New Faces in Modern Jewish Literature." *Recon* 48 (Summer 1983): 15–19.

Kapp, Lisa. "Books for Jewish Children." *Commentary* 8 (Dec. 1949): 547–53.

Kimmel, Eric A. "Confronting the Ovens: The Holocaust and Juvenile Fiction." *Horn Book Magazine* (Feb. 1977): 84–91.

———. "Jewish Identity in Juvenile Fiction: A Look at Three Recommended Books." *Horn Book Magazine* (Apr. 1973): 171–79.

* Kroloff, Theresa Klausner. *The Beginning of American Jewish Fiction*. Drew U., 1978.

Levin, Irene S. "A Content Analysis of Books for Children Suitable for Reform Jewish Education." Master's thesis, Palmer Graduate Library School, 1969. 98 pp.

* Lewis, Stuart Arthur. *Ghetto and Frontier: The Jewish Author in Search of America*. U. of Colorado at Boulder, 1975. 110 pp.

Lister, Louis. "Putting *World Over* to Work in Your Classroom." JEC *Bulletin* 83 (Oct. 1952). Also in *RTJH*, 203–6.

Lister, Rebecca, and Louis Lister. "*Keeping Posted*: Curriculum Enrichment for Teen-Agers." *Jew Teach* 33 (Oct. 1964): 17–22.

Lukinsky, Joseph. "Fairy Tales, Myths, and Jewish Education." *MJ* 13 (Winter 1982): 9.

Mikliszanski, J. K. "Hebrew Literature in the United States." In *JPPP*, 4:308–33.

Patai, Raphael. *On Jewish Folklore*. Detroit: Wayne State U. Press, 1983. 511 pp.

Patz, Naomi. "The Jewish Children's Periodical Study: Evaluation and Proposal." Master's thesis, HUC–JIR, 1979.

Patz, Naomi, and Philip Miller. "Jewish Religious Children's Literature in America: An Analytical Survey." *Phaedeus* 7 (Spring/Summer 1980).

Posner, Marcia. "Reading with Children." *Cong M* (Nov.–Dec. 1983): 12–17.

* ———. *A Search for Jewish Content in American Children's Fiction*. New York U., 1980.

Rauch, Eduardo. "Children's Books in Review." *MRCN* 11 (Fall 1980): 4, 8.

———. "Towards an Understanding of the Forgotten World of Myth: An Essay in Definition." *MJ* 13 (Winter 1982): 4, 18–19.

* Reiter-Zedek, Miriam. *The Impact of Children's Literature upon the Development of a Child's Personality*. JTS-Herzliah, 1968.

Rudavsky, David. "הספרות והחינוך," (Literature and Education). *Hadoar* (H.) 58 (Dec. 22, 1978).

Sadker, Myra Pollock, and David Miller Sadker. "Jewish Americans in Children's Books." In *Now upon a Time: A Contemporary View of Children's Literature*, 191–209. N.Y.: Harper and Row, 1977.

* Saperstein, Jeffrey. *A Craving for History: Immigrant Themes for Jewish-American Literature*. New Hampshire U., 1984.

Schram, Peninah. "Story-Telling: Creative Sharing, Listening, Teaching." *Ped Rep* 36 (Jan. 1985): 20–23.

———. "There is a Time to Tell Tales." *MJ* 13 (Winter 1982): 3, 19, 20, 24.

Schwartz, Howard. "On Jewish Fairy Tales." *MJ* 15 (Winter 1983): 32, 30, 31.

* Sherman, Bernard A. *The Fictive Jew: Jewish-American Novels, 1916–1964*. Northwestern U, 1966. 296 pp.

Silberschlag, Eisig. "Development and Decline of Hebrew Letters" (America). In *Jan 2*, 175–92.

Spotts, Leon H. "Magazines for Jewish Teenagers." *Jew Ed* 39 (Apr. 1969): 43–54, 59.

Waxman, Meyer. *A History of Jewish Literature*. 6 vols. N.Y.: Yoseloff, 1960. See especially "Hebrew Literature," 5:189–210.

PERIODICALS FOR CHILDREN AND YOUTH

(For Periodicals for JEWISH YOUTH Prior to 1900 see History of Jewish Education section)

Ben ha-Dor (H.). New York, 1927. Monthly.

Eden (H.). New York, 1924–26. Monthly.

Ha-Doar la No'ar (H.). New York, 1934–60. Biweekly.

The Jewish Child (Y.). New York Federation of Yeshivoth and Talmud Torahs, organ for national religious education. Monthly.

Jewish Current Events. Elmont, N.Y. Sixteen issues per year.

Jewish Youth. New York, 1967–?.

The Jewish Youth Magazine. New York, 1922–?

Keeping Posted. New York, 1955–present.

No'ar (H.). New York, 1930. Monthly.

Olam Hadash (H.). Jewish Agency, New York, 1961–?. Monthly.

Olomeinu—Our World. TU, New York, 1945–present.

Our Age (Dorenu). New York, 1959–?.

Shaharut (H.). New York, 1916–21. Monthly.

Shofar. Senior Publications, Ltd., Melville, N.Y., 1986–present.

World Over. New York, 1938–198?.

Young Judean. Hadassah Zionist Youth Commission, New York, 1912–present.

GLEANINGS

Grade, Chaim,
"As no Jewish writer before or after him, Sholem Aleichem succeeded in depicting children and childhood. Peretz was the portrait painter of the Jewish woman, Sholem Aleichem, of the Jewish child in his intimate relationship to the world around him. Sholem Aleichem links the child to the Jewish holidays and festivals as much through his interest in clothes, food and play, as through the spiritual aspect of these days. With poetic pathos he describes the holiday joy of the poor, their eternal optimism, their contentment with their lot, and their child-like dreams. Childhood figures of speech, songs, play, all come alive in his writings, and the children themselves glow with innocence and wholesomeness."

Jew Ed 30 (Fall 1959), 91.

Schwartz, Howard,
"Tales of magic and wonder can be found in every phase of Jewish literature, both sacred and secular. Among the post-biblical aggadot (legends) and the maasiot (tales) of Jewish folklore are to be found a number of stories which can easily be identified as traditional fairy tales. Some of these are the universal type of fairy tale set in an enchanted island and populated with a variety of human and supernatural beings, both good and evil, and are Jewish solely by virtue of their source. But many others, perhaps half of the existing body of Jewish fairy tales, have fused some specific aspects of Jewish life and tradition with the archetypal fairy tale framework. For the fairy tale version of the world as a stage on which good and evil struggle is fully compatible with the Jewish view of the essential condition of this world, where faith in God can defeat the evil impulse, known as the Yetzer Hara."

MJ 15 (Winter 1983), 32.

Davis, Enid,
"There is a broad spectrum of children's literature with Jewish themes covering such topics as history and biography, literature and the arts, Bible retelling and theology, folklore and fiction. This body of literature mirrors the richness, variety, and vicissitudes of Jewish life throughout the ages—the heroes and "schlemiels" (fools), innocents and monsters all express one or another aspect of this vast experience."

A Comprehensive Guide to Children's Literature with a Jewish Theme, 1.

16 MITZVOT/VALUES AND CONTEMPORARY ISSUES

PRIOR TO 1950 (SELECTED)

Baeck, Leo. "Faith in Man In Ourselves," "In One's Fellow Man," and "In Mankind." In *The Essence of Judaism*, 150–253. N.Y.: Schocken, 1948.

Birnbaum, Philip. *A Book of Jewish Concepts*. N.Y.: Hebrew Pub. Co., 1964. 717 pp.

Buber, Martin. "Education" and "The Education of Character." In *Between Man and Man*, translated by Ronald Gregor Smith. N.Y.: Macmillan, 1948.

"Character Building." Central Conference of American Rabbis Symposium. *CCAR* 25 (1915): 300–334.

> Buttenweiser, Moses. "Character Building and Ethics."
> Deinard, Samuel N. "Character Building and the Study of Hebrew."
> Freund, Charles J. "Character Building and the Home."
> Levi, Charles S. "Character Building and the Personality of the Teacher."
> Rappaport, Julius. "Character Building and Jewish History."
> Rypins, Isaac L. "Character Building and Social Apparatus of the Religious School."
> Wolfe, Horace J. "Character Building and Child Worship."

Chipkin, Israel. "Remedies for Causes of Prejudice through Religious Societies." *J of Educational Sociology* 16 (Feb. 1943): 385.

* Clinchy, Everett R. *Some Educational Aspects of Protestant, Catholic, Jewish Relationships in American Community Life*. Drew U., 1935. 681 pp.

Cohen, Irving B. "Some National Jewish Agencies and Social Action. 1939–1949." Master's thesis, HUC–JIR, 1953.

Cohon, S. S. "Religion and Ethics," and "Social Righteousness." In *Judaism: A Way of Life*, 99–111, 182–233. N.Y.: Schocken, 1962.

Cronbach, Abraham. "Judaism and Social Justice Historically Considered." *CCAR* 25 (1915): 414–22.

———. *The Social Outlook of Modern Judaism*. Cincinnati: UAHC and CCAR, ca. 1937, pamphlet.

Drachman, Bernard. "Jewish-Gentile Relations from the Jewish Viewpoint." In *Judaism in a Changing World*, edited by Leo Jung, 97–117. 1939.

* Eisenstein, Ira. *The Ethics of Tolerance Applied to Religious Groups in America*. Columbia U., 1941.

Finkelstein, Louis. "The Hebraic Doctrine of Human Equality." *Menorah J* 24 (1936): 16–29.

Foster, Solomon. "The Workingman and the Synagogue." *CCAR* 19 (1909): 432–94.

* Glazer, B. Benedict. *Christian-Jewish Relations in the United States with Particular Reference to Movement and Efforts for Goodwill and Better Understanding*. U. of Pittsburgh, 1938.

———. "A Re-Evaluation of the Good-Will Movement." Reprint. *CCAR* 57 (1947): 3–38.

Hirsch, Samson Raphael. "The Talmud and Its Teachings on Social Virtues, Civic Duties and Commercial Integrity" (1858). In *Judaism Eternal*, translated by I. Grunfield, 155–86. London: Soncino Press, 1956.

Kallen, Horace. "Prejudice—The American Way." *Jew Ed* 17 (Nov. 1945): 56–61.

Kaplan, Mordecai M. "Jewish Ethics" (1934). In *Judaism as a Civilization*, 460–78. N.Y.: Reconstructionist Press, 1957.

Kohn, Eugene. "The Synagogue and Social Problems." *RA* (1933–38): 78–85.

* Landes, Morris A. *Trends in American Jewish Thought with Respect to the Ritualistic Mitzvot and Maasiot*. U. of Pittsburgh, 1954.

Levine, Goldie S. "Our Religion and the Religion of Our Neighbors." *Jew Teach* 10 (Apr. 1942): 17–20.

Lewin, Kurt, Alfred Marrow, and Charles E. Hendry. *Accent on Action*. N.Y.: Commission on Community Interrelations of the American Jewish Congress.

* Mann, Louis L. *Social Ethics of the Talmud*. Yale U., 1920.

"Pronouncements of the Rabbinical Assembly of America on Social Justice." *RA* (1933–38): 156–64; (1941–44): 43–50.

Simon, Sidney. "The Jewish Community in the Springfield Plan." *Jew Ed* 17 (Nov. 1945): 29–30.

Steinberg, Milton, and Moshe Davis. "Contemporary Social Problems in the Light of Jewish Tradition." *Jew Ed* 13 (Jan. 1942): 194–98.

Weinstein, Jacob J. "Social Ideals and Ethics for the Jew of Our Time." *Recon* 11 (Feb. 23, 1945): 29–37.

Weintraub, Ruth G. *How Secure These Rights?: Anti-Semitism in the USA*. ADL Survey. Garden City, N.Y.: Doubleday, 1948. 215 pp.

SINCE 1950 (SELECTED)

Ackerman, Nathan W. *Prejudice, Mental Health and Family Life*. N.Y.: AJC Institute of Human Relations, 1961. 26 pp.

Adar, Zvi. *Humanistic Values in the Bible*. Translated from the Hebrew by Victor Tcherikover. N.Y.: Reconstructionist Press, 1967. 429 pp.

Agus, Jacob B. *The Vision and the Way: An Interpretation of Jewish Ethics*. N.Y.: Ungar, 1966. 365 pp.

Allport, Gordon W., and Bernard M. Kramer. "Roots of Prejudice." In *Jews in the Modern World*, edited by Jacob Fried, 1:253–78. N.Y.: Twayne, 1962.

Appel, Gerson. *A Philosophy of Mitzvot: The Religious-Ethical Concepts of Judaism, Their Roots in Biblical Law and the Oral Tradition*. N.Y.: Ktav, 1975. 288 pp.

Arzt, Max. *Justice and Mercy*. N.Y.: Burning Bush Press, 1963.

* Bannan, Rosemary Shamborsky. *Attitudes of Jewish High School Youth toward Catholics, Protestants and Jews*. Loyola U. of Chicago, 1964.

Bellin, L. E. "The Need to Revive Mussar." *Un Syn Rev* 28 (Spring/Summer 1976).

Belth, Nathan C. *A Promise to Keep: American Encounters with Anti-Semitism* (ADL). N.Y.: Times Books, 1979. 308 pp.

Bemporad, Jack. "Dimensions of Jewish Ethics." *A Jud* 15 (Fall 1965).

Ben-Horin, Meir. "The Teaching of Ethical Concepts and Conduct in Jewish Schools." *Rel Ed* 56 (Sept./Oct. 1961): 334–42.

Blumenfield, Samuel M., Judah Shapiro, Mannheim S. Shapiro, and H. Vogel. *New Realities and Changing Values*. Amer Jew Congress. 24 pp.

Bokser, Ben-Zion. "Problems in Bio-Medical Ethics: A Jewish Perspective." *Jud* 24 (1975): 134–43.

Borowitz, Eugene B. "Rethinking the Reform Jewish Theory of Social Action." *RJ* 27 (Fall 1980): 1–19.

Bread to the Hungry. This Is Our Home series, no. 14. N.Y.: AJC, 1956. 15 pp.

Brickner, Balfour. "God and Value in an Open Society." *Rel Ed* 69 (Mar.–Apr. 1974): 160–68.

Chai-Ways: Living Judaism Through Mitzvos. N.Y.: National Federation of Temple Youth, 1957. 96 pp.

Chazan, Barry. "Jewish Education and Moral Development." In *Moral Development, Moral Education and Kohlberg*, edited by B. Munsey, 298–325. Birmingham: Religious Education Press, 1980.

———. "Moral and Religious Education." In *LJE*, 77–94.

Children of One Father. N.Y.: AJC, 1966. 28 pp.

Chipkin, Israel S. "Judaism and Social Welfare." In *Jews* 2:1043–75.

Cohen, Henry. *Justice, Justice: A Jewish View of the Negro Revolt.* N.Y.: UAHC, 1968. 156 pp.

Cohen, Jack J. "The Arab-Israel Conflict: The Moral Dilemma." *Recon* 38 (Nov. 1972).

Cohn, Haim H. *Human Rights and Jewish Law.* N.Y.: Ktav, 1984.

"Conference on Jewish Values." *Congress Bi-Weekly* (Supplements to Jan. 16, 1961, June 26, 1961, and Apr. 2, 1962 issues).

* Cytron, Barry D. *A Rational and Proposed Curriculum for Jewish-Christian Dialogue.* Iowa State U., 1982. 298 pp.

Donin, Hayim Halevy. "Kindness: A Means to an End." In *To Be a Jew*, 41–60. N.Y.: Basic Books, 1972.

Dorff, Elliot K. "The Interaction of Jewish Law with Morality." *Jud* 26 (Fall 1977): 455–66.

Eckardt, A. Roy. "Recent Literature on Christian-Jewish Relations." *JBA* (1980–81): 47–61.

Edel, Abraham. "Some Current Trends in Ethical Theory." *CCAR J* (June 1968): 50–62.

Edelman, Lily, ed. *Face to Face.* Includes articles by Robert Gordis, Jay Kaufman, J. Lichtman, Reinhold Niebuhr, Ellis Rivkin, and others. Washington, D.C.: B'nai B'rith Adult Jewish Education and ADL, 1967. 122 pp.

Eisenstein, Ira. "Jewish Ethics." In *Creative Judaism*, 160–65. N.Y.: Jewish Reconstructionist Foundation, 1953.

Ende, George. "Teaching Jewish Values to High School Youth." *Ed As* (Mar. 1954).

Fenster, M. M. "Civil Rights and the Synagogue." *Syn Sch* 23 (Winter 1965): 2–6.

Finkelstein, Louis. "Human Equality in the Jewish Tradition." *Con Jud* (Fall 1955): 2–27.

———. "Prophetic Wisdom: Cure for the World's Ills." *Un Syn Rev* (18 Jan. 1966).

* Fisher, Eugene J. *A Content Analysis of the Treatment of Jews and Judaism in Current Roman Catholic Religious Text Books and Manuals on the Primary and Secondary Levels.* New York U., 1976. 383 pp.

Fox, Marvin, ed. *Modern Jewish Ethics: Theory and Practice.* Proceedings of the first conference of Institute for Judaism and Contemporary Thought. Columbus: Ohio State U., 1975. 262 pp.

Fox, Seymour. "The Values of Jewish Education." *RA* (1962).

Franck, Isaac. *The Concept of Freedom in Jewish Tradition.* Phila.: Gratz College, 1973. 16 pp.

* Frazin, Lester A. *The Relationship of Jewish Value Acceptance to Self-Esteem and Degree of Isolation among Reform Jewish Adolescents.* Northern Illinois U., 1971. 205 pp.

Freidenreich, Fradle Pomerantz. "The Unwritten Curriculum in the Jewish School." *Jew Ed* 52 (Spring 1984): 3–7.

Frimer, Norman E. *Judaism and Ethics.* Washington, D.C.: B'nai B'rith, 1959. 40 pp.

Frumkin, Norman. "The Jewish Passion for Social Justice: A Social Psychological Analysis." *Social Ethos* 2 (1957): 40–42.

Gendler, E. E. "To Violence No Sanction." *Jewish Heritage* 13 (Spring/Summer 1972).

Gittler, Joseph B., ed. *Understanding Minority Groups.* N.Y.: Wiley, 1956. 139 pp.

Glustron, S. "Confronting the New Morality." *Un Syn Rev* 22 (Summer 1969).

Golden, Harry, and Albert Vorspan. "Unease in Dixie." *Mid* 2 (Autumn 1956): 38–51.

Gordis, Robert. "A Basis for Morals: Ethics in a Technological Age." *Jud* 25 (Winter 1976): 20–43.

———. "The Ethical Dimension in Halakhah." *Con Jud* 26 (Spring 1972).

———. *Race and the Religious Tradition*. N.Y.: ADL, 1962.

Greeley, Andrew M. *Why Can't They Be Like Us?* N.Y.: AJC, Institute of Human Relations Press, 1969. 76 pp.

Green, Arthur. "How to be a Mentsh." In *Cat 3*, 390–94.

Greenberg, Irving. "Jewish Values and the Changing American Ethic." *Trad* 10 (Summer 1968): 42–74.

———. "The Open Society: Shaping Religion and Values." *Rel Ed* 68 (Sept/Oct. 1973): 558–61.

Greenberg, Simon. *The Ethical in the Jewish and American Tradition*. N.Y.: JTS, 1977. 327 pp.

* Gruesser, M. Jeanne. *Categorical Valuation of Jews among Catholic Parochial School Children*. Catholic U. of America, 1950. 227 pp.

Hartman, David. "Halakhah as a Ground for Creating a Shared Spiritual Language." *Trad* 16 (Summer 1976): 7–40.

Hirsch, Richard G. "The Relevance of Jewish Tradition for Contemporary Social Issues." *Jew Teach* 32 (Apr. 1964): 16–20.

———. *There Shall Be No Poor*. N.Y.: Commission on Social Action of Reform Judaism, UAHC, 1965. 134 pp.

"Interfaith at Fifty: An Evaluation of the Movement by Catholics, Protestants and Jews" (Symposium). *Jud* 27 (Summer 1978): 262–344.

Israel, Richard J. "Judaism as a Source of Social Values—Jewish Tradition and Political Action." In *Tradition and Contemporary Experience*, edited by Alfred Jospe, 189–204. 1970–71.

Jakobovitz, Immanuel. *Jewish Medical Ethics*. N.Y.: Bloch, 1975.

"Jewish Values and the Changing American Ethic" (Symposium). *Trad* 10 (Summer 1968): 42–74.

"Jewish Values in the Post-Holocaust Future" (Symposium). Participants: Emil L. Fackenheim, Richard H. Popkin, George Steiner, Elie Wiesel. *Jud* 16 (Summer 1967): 269–300.

Jung, Leo. *Human Relations in Jewish Law*. N.Y.: JEC Press, 1967.

Kallen, Horace. *Cultural Pluralism and the American Idea*. Phila.: U. of Pennsylvania Press, 1956.

Kaplan, Mordecai M. "A Philosophy of Jewish Ethics." In *Jews*, 2:1010–40.

Keeping Posted. *Bio-Ethics: Applying Moral Insights to Medicine and Science*. Mini-Course, no. 840490. Leader's edition, no. 840492.

Kellner, Menachem M., ed. *Contemporary Jewish Ethics*. N.Y.: Sanhedrin Press, 1978. 452 pp.

Klein, Edward E., and Roland B. Gittelsohn. "The Crisis of Civil Rights." In *Judaism and the Contemporary Crisis in Religion and Society*. Jewish Chautauqua Society, 1965.

Konvitz, Milton R., ed. "The Good Life." In *Judaism and Human Rights*, 216–24. N.Y.: Commission on Adult Jewish Education of B'nai B'rith and Norton, 1972.

———. *Judaism and the American Idea*. N.Y.: Schocken, 1980. 223 pp.

* Koolyk, Shirley. *A Comparison of the Underlying Philosophical Assumptions Concerning the Concept of Justice in Kohlberg's Theory of Moral Developments with those of Jewish Ethical Perspective from Halakhic Perspective*. Boston U. School of Education, 1978. 149 pp.

Krause, Allen S. "Rabbis and Negro Rights in the South: 1954–1967" (Reform rabbis only). Master's thesis, HUC–JIR, 1967. Summary in *Amer Jew Arc* 21 (Apr. 1969): 10–47. Also in *Jews in the South*, edited by Leonard Dinnerstein and Mary Dale Palsson, 360–85. Baton Rouge: Louisiana State U. Press, 1973.

Lamm, Norman, ed. *The Good Society: Jewish Ethics in Action*. N.Y.: Viking, 1974. 240 pp.

Lavender, Abraham D. "Jewish Values in the South." In *"Turn to the South": Essays on Southern Jewry*, edited by Nathan M. Kaganoff and Melvin I. Urofsky, 124–34. Charlottesville: University Press of Virginia for the American Jewish Historical Society, 1979.

Lederberg, J., W. Herberg, and P. G. Green. "Human Values in a Technological Society: Symposium." *Dimensions* 5 (Winter 1971).

Leigh, Ruth. *Man's Right to Life: The Issue of Capital Punishment*. N.Y.: Commission on Political Action of Reform Judaism. N.Y.: UAHC, 1959. 5 pp.

Lelyveld, Arthur J. "The Values We Stand for." *Congress Bi-Weekly* 35 (Mar. 25, 1968).

———. "Judaism as a Source of Social Values—Transient Isms and Abiding Values." In *Traditions and Contemporary Experience*, edited by Alfred Jospe, 176–88. 1970–71.

Lerner, Anne Lapidus. "Who Hast Not Made Me a Man: The Movement for Equal Rights for Women in American Jewry." *AJYB* 77 (1977):3–88.

Lerner, Israel D. "Maintaining Torah Values in a Changing Society." *Ped Rep* 24 (Fall 1972): 4.

Lichtenstein, Aharon. "Does Jewish Tradition Recognize an Ethic Independent of the Halakhah?" In *Contemporary Jewish Ethics*, edited by Menachem M. Kellner, 102–23. 1979.

Lieber, David. "The Religious Foundation of Ethics." *Un Syn Rev* 24 (Spring 1971).

Lipman, Eugene J., and Albert Vorspan. *A Tale of Ten Cities: Relations between Protestants, Catholics and Jews*. N.Y.: UAHC, 1962. 344 pp.

Lipset, Seymour M. "Intergroup Relations: The Changing Situation of American Jewry." In *JCA*, 312–38.

The Many Faces of Anti-Semitism. N.Y.: AJC, 1972. 40 pp.

Marx, Robert J. "The New Anti-Semitism and the Old." *RJ* 27 (Spring 1980): 1–11.

* Mervis, Leonard J. *The Social Justice Movement of the American Reform Rabbis, 1890–1940*. U. of Pittsburgh, 1952.

———. "The Social Justice Movement and the Reform Rabbi." *AJA* 7 (June 1955): 171–230.

Niebuhr, Reinhold. "The Relations of Christians and Jews in Western Civilization." *CCAR J* (Apr. 1958): 18–32.

Noar, Gertrude. *Information Is Not Enough*. N.Y.: ADL, 1958.

"Papers and Proceedings of a Conference on Negro-Jewish Relations in the United States." *JSS* 27 (June 1965): 3–66.

Passamaneck, Stephen. "Humanism in the Talmud." *NATE*, 19th Annual Conference (Dec. 1973): 16–22.

* Pearlstein, Mitchell B. *Selected Jewish Responses to Affirmative Action Admissions: Toward a Conceptual Understanding*. U. of Minnesota, 1980. 271 pp.

* Rinder, Irwin D. *Jewish Identification and the Race Relations Cycle*. U. of Chicago, Department of Sociology, 1953.

Rivkin, Sholom. "Jewish Concept of Social Responsibility." *Jew Life* (June–Aug. 1965): 12–20. Also appears as "The Application of Torah Ethics to Human Relations," in *The Jewish Concept of Social Responsibility*. N.Y.: UOJCA. 10 pp.

Roth, Norman, ed. *Justice, Justice, You Shall Pursue*. USA, 1968.

Schiff, Alvin I. "Developing an Approach to the Teaching of Religious Values." *Jew Ed* 36 (Spring/Summer 1966): 3–4.

Schulweiss, Harold M. "Some Principles of Jewish Ethics." *Jewish Heritage* 7 (Fall 1964).

Shaskolsky, Rinah Lipis. "The Prophets as Dissenters: Protest and Dissent in Jewish Tradition." *Jud* 19 (Winter 1970): 15–29.

* Shkedi, Asher. *Teacher Participation in Curriculum Development: A Case Study of Workshops for Teachers of "Jewish Values"* (H.). JTS, 1987.

Sidorsky, David, ed. *Essays on Human Rights: Contemporary Issues and Jewish Perspectives*. Phila.: JPS, 1979. 359 pp.

Siegel, Seymour. "Religion and Social Action." *RA* (1961): 143–63.

Silver, Daniel J., ed. *Judaism and Ethics*. N.Y.: Ktav, 1970. 338 pp.

Silverman, Charles, Arthur J. Lelyveld, and Bayard Rustin. "Negroes and Jews—3 Approaches." American Jewish Congress Convention, April 28, 1966.

Snitzer, Lee H., and Marci Dickman. "A Genesis of Ethics and Values: A Adaptation of the Cognitive-Developmental Approach to Moral Education for the Liberal Religious School, Using Biblical Texts to Illustrate Certain Ethics." Master's thesis, HUC–JIR, 1981.

* Steinberg, Paul M. *Selected Case Studies of Human Relations: Designed for a Human Relations Training Program for Rabbinic Students*. Columbia U., 1961.

Steiner, C. "Jewish Values in the Post-Holocaust Future: Symposium." *Jud* 16 (Summer 1967): 276–81.

"The Urban Crisis." *Syn Sch* 27 (Spring 1969): 27–29.

Ury, Zalman. *The Mussar Movement.* N.Y.: Yeshiva U. Press, 1970.

Vorspan, Albert. "Jewish Ethical Wills." *Dimensions* 3 (Winter 1968–69): 38–40.

Wax, James A. "The Attitude of the Jews in the South toward Integration." *CCAR J* (June 1959): 14–20.

Wiesel, Elie. "Jewish Values in the Post Holocaust Future" (Symposium). *Jud* 16 (Summer 1967): 281–84.

TRANSMITTING VALUES IN THE CLASSROOM PRIOR TO 1950

Assembly Programs on Social Justice. A series. N.Y.: UAHC.

Bergman, Shlomo. "How Can we Explain Anti-Semitism to the Child?" *Jew Teach* 10 (June 1942): 1–14.

Berman, Jeanne. "The Sunday School as an Agent in Combatting Anti-Semitism." *Jew Teach* 4 (Nov. 1935): 26–30.

"Brotherhood Week." *The Jewish School and Democracy* 3 (Feb. 1945): 56–61.

Cahnman, Werner. "Intercultural Education and Jewish Content." *Recon* (Apr. 29, 1948): 9–15.

Charry, Elias. "Jewish-Christian Interreligious School Activity." *RA* (1945): 79–83.

Cronbach, Abraham. *The Jewish Peace Book for Home and School*, edited by Emanuel Gamoran. Cincinnati: DSC, UAHC, 1932. 114 pp.

Dushkin. Alexander M. "Personal Values in Jewish Education." *JSSQ* 23 (1947): 285–90.

———. "Religion and Secularism in Character Training." In *Religious Education and the Public School*. N.Y.: AAJE, 1941.

"Education for Democratic Citizenship." *The Jewish School and Democracy* 3 (Apr. 1945): 83–85.

Feldman, Abraham J. "The Teaching of Jewish Ideals." *Jew Teach* 12 (Nov. 1943): 1–9.

Franzblau, Abraham N. "Jewish Religious Education: Desirable Character Objectives and Philosophy of Motivation." *Rel Ed* 25 (1930): 427–32.

Gamoran, Emanuel. "Jewish Curriculum and Character Education." *Rel Ed* 29 (1934): 135–40.

———. "Typical Jewish Values." In *Changing Conceptions in Jewish Education*, part II, 102–39. 1924.

———. "The World Neighborhood." *Rel Ed* 26 (Oct. 1931): 650–53.

Gittelsohn, Roland B. *A Project on Peace*. Cincinnati: CJE, 1937. 107 pp.

———. *Projects in Modern Ethics for Junior High Schools*. N.Y.: UAHC, 1937. 107 pp.

Greenstein, Harry. "New Reservoirs of Jewish Values." *Jew Ed* 11 (Jan. 1940): 186–87.

Heller, Bernard. "Ways to Better Understanding." *Jew Ed* 15 (Sept. 1943): 17–20.

———. *With Malice toward None: A Study of Commissions for Democratic Citizenship to Eliminate Bias in Textbooks*. N.Y.: Synagogue Council of America, ca. 1945.

Kadushin, Max. "The Teaching of Jewish Values." *Jew Ed* 19 (Summer 1948): 23–26.

Kahn, Alfred J. "Jewish Elements in the Development of the Child." *Jew Ed* 18 (Summer 1947): 12–17.

Kaplan, Harry. "Teaching Social Justice in the Jewish School." *Jew Teach* 2 (Apr. 1934): 22.

Kaplan, Mordecai M. "Character Training in Jewish Schools." *Jewish Teacher* 5 (Aug. 1923): 1–2.

Kohn, Eugene. "Character Training in the Jewish Religious School." *RA* (1930–32): 43–63. Also in *Jew Ed* 3 (Jan./Mar. 1931): 20–28.

———. "The Social Justice Ideal in Jewish Education." *RA* (1938): 117–38.

———. "The Values for Democratic Living in Jewish Education." *Jew Ed* 11 (Jan. 1940): 159–72.

Krass, Nathan. "A Review of Textbooks for Ethics." *CCAR* 19 (1909): 348–52.

Kronish, Leon. "Teaching History with a Focus on Values." Master's thesis, HUC–JIR, 1942. 132 pp.

Kurzband, Toby K., Selma Kramer, and Anna Lesser. "Brotherhood in a Festival Course of Study." *Jew Teach* 13 (Apr. 1945): 35–39.

Kushtai, Sh. "מוסר חוץ ומוסר—פנים בהוראה„ (Ethic—External and Internal Factors in Education). *Sh Hah* (H.) (1927): 57–63.

Landman, Isaac. "Survival Values in Jewish Religious Education." *Rel Ed* 34 (July/Sept. 1939): 135–42.

Lang, Leon S. "Social Ideals in the Curriculum of the Jewish School." *RA* (1930–32): 365–67.

Mahler, Yehudah. "מחקר באופי„ (Research in Character Education). *Sh Hah* (H.) 4 (1928): 1–9.

Maller, Julius B. "Character Education and the Jewish School." *Jew Ed* 1 (Jan. 1929): 14–24.

———. "Character Growth and Jewish Education." *Rel Ed* 25 (Sept. 1930): 627–30.

———. "Jewish Source Materials for Character Education." *Jew Ed* 7 (Jan./Mar. 1935): 47–48.

———. "Moral Instruction in the Jewish School." *Jew Ed* 4 (Apr./June 1932): 110–15.

Richman, Julia, and E. H. Lehman. *Methods of Teaching Jewish Ethics*. Phila.: Chautauqua Society, 1914. 274 pp.

Sachar, Abraham L. "Jewish Education and Moral Stamina." *Jew Ed* 14 (Sept./Dec. 1942): 77–84.

Zeligs, Rose. "Racial Attitudes of Jewish Children." *Jew Ed* 9 (Oct./Dec. 1937): 148–52.

———. "Racial Attitudes of Jewish and Non-Jewish Children in the Sixth Grade." Master's thesis, Cincinnati U., 1937.

TRANSMITTING VALUES IN THE CLASSROOM SINCE 1950

Abrams, Beverly. "The Mitzvah of Social Action." *Ped Rep* 34 (Oct. 1983): 22–23.

* Abrams, Solomon. *Principles of Human Relations in Curriculum Development*. U. of Pittsburgh, 1952.

Ackerman, Walter I. "Changing Race Relations Implications for the Jewish School." *Ped Rep* 17 (Sept. 1965). Also in *J Jew Com Ser* 41 (June 1965): 352–56.

———. "Ethics and the Jewish School." *Syn Sch* 17 (Sept. 1958).

* Adini, Uziel. *Selected Hebrew Readings Studied in American and Israeli Hebrew High Schools: A Comparative Study of Values*. Dropsie U., 1969.

———. "הנחלת ערכים במשנת החינוך היהודי„. (Teaching Values in Jewish Education). In Gratz College Anniversary Volume, 19–26. 1971. (H. section.)

Altshul, William. "Training for a Life of Mitzvot." *Ped Rep* 34 (Oct. 1983): 1–3.

Arian, Philip. "A Program for the Teaching of Jewish Concepts." *Jew Ed* 36: (Summer 1966): 162–66.

Aron, Isa, and David Ellinson. "The Dilemma of Jewish Education: To Learn and to Do." *Jud* (Spring 1984): 212–20.

Arzt, Raphael. "A Model of a Value-Frame for Jewish Education." *Ed As* (1967): 13–25.

Bacon, Brenda. "Sample Lessons for Twelve- and Thirteen-Year-Olds on the Problem of Evil." *MRCN* 8 (Winter 1978): 3–6.

Bahn, Charles, and Israel Mosenson. *A Mitzvah Pattern Program: A Recreational Program Based on Traditional Jewish Observances for Junior NCSY (Pre-Teens)*. Israel and N.Y.: UOJCA, Conference of Synagogue Youth, 197?. 16 pp.

Bamberger, Henry B. "An Interfaith Demonstration Seder Project." *Jew Teach* 34 (Dec. 1965).

* Baradon, Howard S. *Ethical Values of Jewish Adolescents and Implications for the Jewish Religious School Curriculum*. U. of Pittsburgh, 1964. 187 pp.

Barish, Shirley. *Six Kallot: Retreat for Jewish Settings*. Denver: ARE, 1979.

Baylor, Ruth M. "Development of Character through Bible Stories." *Jew Teach* 19 (Nov. 1950): 10–25.

Beilin, Harry. "The Cognitive Basis for Development of Moral Concepts." *Ed As* (1964): 22–40.

Bemporad, Jack. "The Ethics of 'An Eye for an Eye'." *Jew Teach* 33 (Feb. 1965): 8–10.

———. "Rabbinic Ethics." *Jew Teach* 34 (Dec. 1965): 4–7.

Ben Gurion, David. "ערכים בחינוך היהודי" (Values in Jewish Education) (H.). In *MJET*, 11–24.

Ben-Horin, Meir. "The Teaching of Ethical Concepts and Conduct in Jewish Schools." *Rel Ed* 56 (Sept./Oct. 1961): 334–41.

Bennett, James M. "Toward a Synthesis of Reform Jewish Education and Humanistic Education: A Curriculum for Personhood." Master's thesis, HUC–JIR, 1984.

Bernards, Solomon S. "Race Relations in the Jewish School Curriculum." *Rel Ed* 59 (Jan./Feb. 1964): 60–63.

Bernstein, Mashey M. "Films in a Class on Values and Ethics." *Ped Rep* 33 (Oct. 1982): 37–39.

Bleich, David J. "Sound Moral Principles." *Sh'ma* 14 (May 1984): 105–6.

Bogot, Howard I. "Mitzvah as Goal." *Ped Rep* 34 (Oct. 1983): 11–12.

Campeas, Hyman. "Course in Basic Jewish Concepts." *Jew Ed* 41 (Spring 1972): 12–14.

Canter, I. *Christmas in the Life of a Jewish Teenager*. N.Y.: B'nai B'rith Youth Organization and ADL, 1961. 19 pp.

Chazan, Baruch (Barry). "על החנוך המוסרי" (On Moral Education). *Sh Hah* (H.) 30 (1970): 48–51.

———. "Moral and Religious Education." In *LJE*, 77–94.

———. "Study and Moral Action in Contemporary Jewish Education." *J of Curriculum Studies* 12 (1980).

Churgin, Gershon A. "חינוך למוסר" (Moral Education). In *Scharfstein* (H.), 111–17.

Cohen, Burton I. "Some Considerations for Planners of Mitzvah Activities in the Jewish School." *Jew Ed* 47 (1979): 38–41.

Cohen Jack J. "Ethics." In *JEDS*, 221–33.

Cohen, Joel. "Pidyon Shevuyim" (Responsibility to Aid Jews who Are Deprived of Freedom). *Ped Rep* 36 (Nov. 1985): 20–21.

Cohen, Jonathan. "על המשמעות המוסרית של ההוראה: עיון בסיפור אגדה" (On the Moral Significance of Teaching: A Study of an Aggadic Story.) (H.). In *Stu*, 40–50.

Cohn, Edward L. "Towards the Development of Text on Comparative Religion for the Third Grade Child in the Reform Religious School." Master's thesis, HUC–JIR, 1961.

Davidson, Joan L. "Moral Education: A Coherent Approach for the Religious School." Master's thesis, HUC–JIR, 1982.

———. "A Religious School Model of Moral Education." *Ped Rep* 36 (Nov. 1985): 3–5.

Dorff, Elliott N. "A Renewed Understanding of Mission and Method in Jewish Education." *Rel Ed* 79 (Winter 1984): 78–87.

———. "Study Leads to Action." *Rel Ed* (Mar./Apr. 1980): 171–92.

Dresner, Samuel H. "Mitzvah: The Way of Man." In *NICD*, 7–35.

Duker, Abraham G. "Changing Values in American Jewish Life: A Challenge to Jewish Education." *Jew Ed* 40 (Winter 1970): 13–22.

Elkins, Dov Peretz. *Humanizing Jewish Life, Judaism and the Jewish Potential Movement*. N.Y.: Barnes, 1976.

———. "Value Strategies for Pesach." *AM* (Winter 1976).

Engel, David E. "Teaching Jewish Values to High School Youth." *Rel Ed* 65 (Jan./Feb. 1970).

Fox, Marvin. "Translating Jewish Thought into Curriculum: Moral Philosophy in Jewish Education." In *From the Scholar to the Classroom*, edited by Seymour Fox and Geraldine Rosenfield, 59–85. N.Y.: Melton Research Center for Jewish Education–Jewish Theological Seminary, 1977. Also in *MRCN* 8 (Winter 1978): 1–2, 6–8.

Friedman, Jerry. "Is There a Difference in Ethical Reasoning between Students in Jewish Schools and Public Schools." *Jew Ed* 55 (Fall 1987): 12–23.

* Friedman, Seymour I. *The Effect of Jewish Religious Education on the Moral Reasoning* *and Social Interest of Yeshiva High School Students.* Fordham U., 1983.

* Geller, Joshua. *A Study of Early Adolescent Attitudes toward Ethnic and Democratic Beliefs as Related to Attendance in the Public and Jewish Schools.* U. of Michigan, 1968. 252 pp. See also *J Jew Com Ser* 46 (Fall 1969): 93–100.

* Gentile, Michael. *Moral Adjustment throughout Adulthood among Four Jewish Religious Affiliations.* Fordham U., 1978. 120 pp.

* Gersten, Leon. *Cultural Presses and the Development of Moral Judgment.* Columbia U. Teacher's College, 1965.

Gertel, Eliot B. "The Talmud and Moral Instruction." *Syn Sch* 31 (Winter 1973): 16–25.

Gittelsohn, Roland B. "Teaching Ethics in the Religious School." *Jew Teach* 26 (May 1958): 3–7.

Glasser, Harry A. "Guides and Goals in Teaching Comparative Religion." *Jew Teach* 32 (Oct. 1963): 15–17.

Glosser, Joanne Katz. *Moral Development in Jewish Education: In Search of a Synthesis.* The theories of moral development proposed by Lawrence Kohlberg are examined in terms of their application to Jewish education. Master's project, HUC–JIR, 1977.

Goldstein, Martin. "Guidelines to the Teaching of Values in a Congregational School." *Syn Sch* 22 (1964): 36–42.

———. "A School's Experience with the 'Friendship through Adoption Project'." *Syn Sch* 17 (Mar. 1959).

Goldstein, Sidney I. "An Interfaith Project on the Primary Level." *Jew Teach* 19 (May 1956): 30–31.

Goodis, Sally. "Choosing Personal Ethics Based on the Ten Commandments." Master's thesis, HUC–JIR, 1975.

* Graber, Howard M. *Designing a Program for Teaching Jewish Ethics in the Senior High School: Rationale and Proposal.* U. of Pittsburgh, 1975. 359 pp.

Griffen, William L. "A Needed Dialogue: Schools and Values." *Ped Rep* 16 (1964).

Halpern, I. "Talmud Torah Students: Their Attitudes towards Jewish Values." Master's thesis, U. of Minnesota, 1962.

Heschel, Abraham J. "Idols in the Temples: On Religious Education and Race Relations." *Rel Ed* 58 (Mar.–Apr. 1963): 33–40.

———. "The Values of Jewish Education." *RA* 26 (1962): 83–100. Also in *MJET*, 24–37.

Hirsch, Richard G. "Who is a 'Good' Person?" *KP* (18 Apr. 1973).

Hofman, J. "Are We Teaching Our Values?" *Jew Life* 22 (16 Apr. 1955).

Hofmann, Justin. "The Case for Moral Education." *Rel Ed* 63 (May–June 1968): 207–14.

———. "Ends and Means in Moral Education." *Rel Ed* 63 (July/Aug. 1968).

———. "Religion, Ethics and Moral Education in Judaism." *Rel Ed* 77 (Jan./Feb. 1982): 57–68.

Honor, Leo. "Teaching Moral Standards and Ethical Conduct" (Committee report). *Syn Sch* 12 (Apr. 1954): 7–8.

Hopfinger, Jana. "Using Jewish Folktales to Teach Jewish Values." Master's thesis, Department of Jewish Education, JTS, 1989.

Humanistic Values in Jewish Education. NATE (Dec. 1973). 83 pp.

Israel, Sherry. "Experimental Methods." In *JPH*, 213–323.

Itkin, W., R. J. Marx, and S. S. Shapiro. "The Ethical Education of the Religious Child." *Rel Ed* 64 (July/Aug. 1969).

Jacobs, Steven. "What We Sometimes Forget." *Compass* 4 (Fall/Winter 1980): 3–4.

Johnson, S. Y. "Teaching Torah through Discussion—Based on Stages of Moral and Cognitive Development." Master's thesis, JTSA–Teacher Institute.

Joseph, Michael. "What Should We Teach Jewish Teens about Christianity?" *Compass* 9 (Fall 1986): 12, 21.

Joseph, Samuel K. "Caring, Judging, and Acting: How to Promote Jewish Values in the Religious School." *Compass* 9 (Winter 1987): 5–9.

* Karan, Val Elliot. *An Empirical Investigation of the Relationship between Exposure to For-*

mal *Jewish Education, Personal-Social Factors and Moral Judgments.* New York U., 1973. 152 pp.

Keeping Posted. Jews and Blacks (Micro-Course). No. 840700. Leader's edition, No. 840702.

———. *Justice, Mercy, Life, and Death.* Nos. 840290 and #840292.

———. *The Poor.* Nos. 841080 and 841082.

Kerzner, Jerome. "Guiding the Child's Spiritual Growth." *Ped Rep* 17 (Sept. 1965).

Kipper, Morris A. "Towards a Course of Study in Developing Jewish Spiritual Values in the Primary Grades of the Reform Religious School." Master's thesis, HUC–JIR, 1961.

* Kipust, P. J. *Moral Development and Self-Concept of Hasidic Adolescent Boys and Girls.* Dissertation Abstracts International, 3327A-28A. 44 pp.

Kling, Simcha. "The Value of Jewish Education." *RA* (1962): 101–5.

Korman, Michael. "Social Action and the Religious School." *Ped Rep* 32 (Winter 1981): 6–9.

Krumbein, Eliezer. "Educating for Understanding and Feeling in Judaism." *Syn Sch* 28 (1970): 4–24.

Kurzweil, Zvi E. "The Educational Philosophy of Mussar (Ethics)." *Jud* 8 (1959): 152–59.

Lear, Elmer. "An Experiment in Interfaith." *Jew Teach* 24 (Jan. 1956): 5–6.

Leibowitz, Yeshia. "חינוך למצוות„ (Education for Divine Precepts). In *MJET* (H.), 56–60.

Lerner, Israel D. "Maintaining Torah Values in a Changing Society." *Ped Rep* 24 (Fall 1972).

Levinson, B. M. "Traditional Jewish Cultural Values and Performance on the Wechsler Test." *J Educational Psychology* 50 (1959): 177–81.

———. "Yeshiva College Sub-Cultural Scale: An Experimental Attempt at Devising a Scale of the Internalization of Jewish Traditional Values." *J Genetic Psychology* 191 (1962): 375–99.

Levitats, Isaac. "On Teaching Mitzvot." In *NICD,* 45–61.

Lichtenstein, A. "Does Jewish Tradition Recognize an Ethic Independent of Halacha?" In *Modern Jewish Ethics,* edited by M. Fox. Columbus: Ohio State U. Press, 1975.

Lieber, David. "The Values of Jewish Education." *RA* (1962): 106–9.

Linzer, Norman. "Resolving Ethical Dilemmas in Jewish Education." *Jew Ed* 55 (Fall 1987): 7–11.

Lukinsky, Joseph. "Two Cheers for Value Confusion." *Rel Ed* 75 (Nov./Dec. 1980): 682–85.

Maier, J., and W. Spinrad. "Comparison of Religious Beliefs and Practices of Jewish, Catholic, and Protestant Students." *Phylong* 18 (1958): 355–60.

Mandelbaum, Bernard. "Two Principles of Character Education in the Aggadah." *Jud* 21 (Winter 1972): 84–92.

Mandelbaum, Naomi. "A Program for United Nations Day." *Jew Teach* 24 (Nov. 1955): 10–11.

Marcus, Audrey Friedman. "Another Look at Values Clarification." *Compass* (Oct. 1976).

———. "More Values Clarification." In *JTH* 2:105–20.

———. "Values Clarification." In *JTH,* 1:75–94.

———. "Value Sheets." In *JTH,* 1:95–112.

Marcus, Fred. "Values Clarification and Religious Education." Master's thesis, HUC–JIR, 1975.

Mark, Yudl. "Teaching Jewish Values through Stories." *Jew Ed* 24 (Fall 1953): 24–30, 64.

Matanky, Leonard A. "Outside The Classroom." *Ped Rep* 35 (Oct. 1984): 18–19.

Melamed, Israel. „החומש בתור ספר לימוד מצוות" (The Pentateuch as a Source for Teaching Mitzvot) (H.). *Ped Rep* 34 (Oct. 1984): 33–34.

* Menitoff, Michael N. *A Comparative Study of Moral Development in Jewish Religious School Settings.* UCLA, 1977. 286 pp.

Milgram, Roberta. "A Study of the Inquiry-Discovery Method in Teaching Moral Concepts." *Syn Sch* 28 (Spring 1979).

Morin, Cynthia, and Richard Morin. *Jewish Social Values.* N.Y.: UAHC, 1974.

Nadel, Max. "A Lesson Plan for Teaching Mitzvot." *Ped Rep* 35 (Oct. 1984): 23–24.

Nemzoff, Samuel. "A Faculty Institute on Human Relations." *Jew Teach* 25 (Mar. 1957): 12–15.

"New Approaches to Mitzvot" (Symposium). *AM* (Spring 1977):

> Jacoby, Emil. "The Thirteen Mitzvot Program."
> Radzik, Abraham. "The Mitzvah Motivational Point System."

Noar, Gertrude, ed. *Current Problems and Issues in Human Relations Education*. N.Y.: ADL, 1955. 70 pp.

Olitzky, Kerry M. "Teaching Mitzvot through Pirke Avot." *Ped Rep* 34 (Oct. 1983): 13–15.

Ornstein, Daniel. "Teaching Jewish Responses to Evil and Suffering to Adolescents and Young Adults: Theoretical and Practical Perspectives." Master's thesis, Department of Jewish Education, JTS, 1989.

Perlmutter, Philip. "The Teaching of Jewish-Christian Relations—A Demonstration Project." *Rel Ed* 62 (Nov./Dec. 1967): 477–78.

Pilch, Judah. "Civil Rights and Jewish Institutions." *Rel Ed* 59 (Jan./Feb. 1964): 86–88.

———, comp, and ed. *The Concept of Ahavot Haberiyoth in Jewish Literature* (Love of mankind). 7 units. N.Y.: NCRI and AAJE, 1967–68.

———. "הסרת המחיצה בין היהודי והאדם" (Judaism and Universal Values) (H.). *Ped Rep* 32 (Fall 1980): 35–36.

Polatnick, Samuel. "An Experiment in Teaching Ethical Ideals." *Jew Teach* 24 (Jan. 1956).

Portnoy, Joseph L. "An Experiment in Human Relations." *Jew Teach* 26 (May 1958): 16–18.

Press, Judith A. "The Dilemma: Key to Effective Moral Education." *Ped Rep* 36 (1985): 3–5.

Rackman, Emanuel. "Getting on Course Again: A Plea for Moral Education." *Jew Ed* 45 (Summer/Fall 1977): 6–12.

Riemer, Jack. "Teaching About Non-Jews in the Jewish School." *Syn Sch* 32 (Winter 1973–74): 22–31.

Reimer, Joseph. "The Moral Component of Religious Education." Master's thesis, Brandeis U., 1970.

Rosenfeld, David. "Judaism and Ecology as it is Transmitted in Informal Educational Settings." Master's thesis, Department of Jewish Education, JTS, 1989.

* Rosenkrantz, Samuel. *Religious Education for One World*. Washington U., 1950. 235 pp.

Rosenzweig, Linda W. "Toward Universal Justice: Some Implications of Lawrence Kohlberg's Research for Jewish Education." *Rel Ed* 72 (Nov./Dec. 1977): 606–15. See also *Jew Ed* 45 (1977).

Rossel, Seymour. "Developing Jewish Values Clarification." *Ped Rep* 27 (Fall 1975): 17.

———. "Lawrence Kohlberg and the Teaching of Jewish Ethics." *Jew Ed* 45 (Summer/Fall 1977): 20–23.

———. "On Teaching Jewish Ethics." *Response* 10 (1976).

Schafler, Samuel. "On Teaching Mitzvot Ma'asiyot." *Syn Sch* 18 (Oct. 1959): 19–22.

Schanin, Norman, et al. "Developing a Religious Personality: A Symposium." In *NICD*, 72–107.

* Schein, Jeffrey L. *"Genesis" and "In Their Footsteps": An Evaluation of Two Programs in Moral Education Designed for Jewish Schools*. Temple U., 1981.

———. "Lawrence Kohlberg's Theory of Moral Development: Some Implications for Jewish Schools." *AM* (Winter 1970).

———. "Moral Education in Jewish Schools." *Recon* 50 (Mar. 1985): 15–18.

———. "A Reconstructionist Approach to Teaching Mitzvot." *Ped Rep* 34 (Oct. 1981): 8–12.

Schiff, Alvin I. "The Challenge of American Jewish Values to Jewish Education" (Editorial). *Jew Ed* 40 (Winter 1970): 3–4.

———. "Developing an Approach to the Teaching of Religious Values." *Jew Ed* 36 (Spring/Summer 1966): 167–73.

———. "Programming Jewish Values for Jewish Adolescents in Jewish Community Centers." *J Jew Com Ser* 48 (Winter 1971): 174–81.

Schimmel, Solomon. "Ethical Dimensions of Traditional Jewish Education." In *Stu*, 91–111.

Schnaidman, Mordecai. "Values in Orthodox Yeshivot and Day Schools." *Ped Rep* 32 (Fall 1980): 16–19.

Schwartz, Earl. "Encouraging Moral Development." In *JPH*.

Segal, Abraham. "Valued Teachings Is Teaching Values." *Jew Teach* 34 (Oct. 1965): 12–19.

Segel, Kenneth I. "Ethical Values of Jewish Youth: The Implications for Our Schools." *CCAR J 23* (Winter 1976): 57–64.

Selig, Sidney, and Gerald Teller. "The Moral Development of Children in Three Different School Settings." *Rel Ed* 70 (July/Aug. 1975): 406–15.

Shevitz, Susan R. "Sexism in Jewish Education." *Response* 18 (Summer 1973): 107–13.

Shoham, Gilbert L. "On Jewish Morality vs. Kohlberg's Morality." *Jew Ed* 53 (Spring 1985): 33–35.

Siegel, Danny. "Talmudic Models—People." *Ped Rep* 32 (Fall 1980): 20–22.

Singer, Howard. *When Your Child Meets with Prejudice*. N.Y.: USCJE, 1956. 16 pp.

Singer, Richard E. "Thinking and Wondering—Children and Their Religion." *Ped Rep* 13 (May 1962).

Skolnick, Irving H. "Mitzvah Instruction in the High School—Halachah L'Maase." *Syn Sch* 34 (Fall 1975): 35–40.

———. "Where Do We Stand on Mitzvot?" *Syn Sch* 32 (Winter–Spring 1974): 5–15.

Slesinger, Zalmen, "Basic Considerations in Teaching Jewish Values." *Ped Rep* 18 (June 1967): 11–13.

———. "Social, Ethical Education—The Imperative of Our Time." *Ped Rep* 20 (Mar. 1969): 7–8.

Sodden, Jesse. "A Thematic Guide to Pirke Avos." *Jew Teach* 29 (Oct. 1960): 13–17.

"Some Mitzvah Projects." *Ped Rep* 34 (Oct. 1983): 24–26.

Sosovsky, Moshe Chaim. "Kohlberg's Moral Dilemmas and Jewish Moral Education." *Jew Ed* 48 (Winter 1980): 10–13.

Spiro, S. *Morality, Halacha and the Jewish Tradition*. N.Y.: Ktav, 1983.

Spitzer, Julie. *Mah La'asot: Making Decisions Jewishly*. A curriculum on Jewish values. LA: HUC–JIR, Tartak Learning Center, 1983.

Stein, Kenneth E. "Teaching the Three Pillars of Judaism." *Jew Teach* 29 (Dec. 1960): 7–8.

Steinbach, Alexander A. "Teaching the Jewish Values." *Jew Ed* 24 (Fall 1953): 20–23, 63.

Steinberg, Paul. "Teaching and Being." *Jew Teach* 28 (Mar. 1960).

* Stern, Leonard W. *A Study of the Perception of Reform Jewish Religious School Administrators Concerning the Value-Centered Approach to Reform Jewish Education*. St. John's U., 1974.

Teller, Gerald A. "Values and the Religious School Setting." *Syn Sch* 30 (Fall 1971): 27–46.

Ulman, Sh. B. "שנוי הערכין בחנוך היהודי" (Changing Values in Jewish Education). *Sh Hah* (H.) (Fall 1961): 11–25.

Ury, Zalman F. "Bridging the Gap Between Ethical Theory and Conduct." *Yeshiva Educator's Notebook* (Dec. 1979).

———. "Salanter Musar Guidance." *Jew Ed* 38 (Mar. 1968): 34–39.

"Values Clarification Ken or Lo" (Symposium). *AM* (Fall 1977):

> Cohen, David S. "The Use and Abuse of Values Clarification in the Jewish Classroom."
> Elkins, Dov Peretz. "Why I Love Values Clarification."
> Lieberman, Phyllis. "To Say Is Not Necessarily to Do: Teaching Ethics through Values."
> Rossel, Seymour. "Clarifying Jewish Values Clarification."
> Wolfson, Ron. "Values Clarification: A Goal-Setting Tool for Schools."

Vorspan, Albert. "The Racial Crisis and the Teacher." *Jew Teach* (Feb. 1964): 3–5.

Wachs, Saul P. "Affective Learning and the Teaching of Jewish Tradition." *Jew Ed* 43 (Spring 1974): 14–21.

* Weiss, Samuel Abraham. *Acceptance of Jews and Gentiles by Jewish Children*. New York U., 1957.

West, Jane Dora. *Unity within Diversity: Jewish Religious Pluralism in America*. A three-unit, nine-lesson curriculum for eighth and ninth grade students. LA: HUC–JIR, Tartak Learning Center, 1984.

Wittstein, Joel. "Toward a Program of Affective Pedagogy for the Development of Fundamental Jewish Values in the Intermediate Grades." Master's thesis, HUC–JIR, 1975.

KEREN AMI IN THE CLASSROOM

Edidin, Ben M. "The Keren Ami Project." *Jew Ed* 2 (June 1930): 68–77.

Eisenberg, Azriel, ed. *Tzedakah: A Way of Life*. N.Y.: Behrman, 1963. 127 pp.

Garfinkel, Marvin H. "Keren Ami as an Activity in the Jewish School." *Syn Sch* 14 (Sept. 1955): 3–6.

Goodis, Karen-Lipshutz. "Teaching Tzedakah." *Ped Rep* 36 (Nov. 1985): 8–9.

Kadden, Bruce. "A Tzedakah Project." *Ped Rep* 34 (Oct. 1983): 20–21.

Keeping Posted. *Tzedakah*. Mini Course. No. 840780. Leader's edition, no. 840782.

Kligfield, Bernard. "An Exciting School-Wide Keren Ami Activity." *Syn Sch* 14 (Sept. 1955): 19–24.

Landes, Sora. "An Inter-School Keren Ami Council." *Syn Sch* 14 (Sept. 1955): 7–18.

Lang, Gerhard. "Keren Ami Survey." AAJE *Information Bulletin* 32 (1969).

Marcus, Audrey F. "Teaching Tzedakah." *AM* (Spring 1978).

Ribner, Israel. "Teaching Jewish Values through Keren Ami." *Syn Sch* 14 (Sept. 1955): 25–27.

Shapiro, Mannheim. *Tzedakah—An Aspect of Jewish Uniqueness*. N.Y.: Council of Jewish Federations, 1966.

Shudofsky, Chanoch, and Morton Siegel, *Yad L'tikvah: A Tzedakah Syllabus*. N.Y.: USCJE, 1976.

Siegel, Danny. "13 Things Kids Don't Know about Tz'dakah." *Moment* 5 (May 1980).

———. "Tzedakah in a Brown Envelope." *Ped Rep* 33 (Dec. 1981): 28–30.

———. *Tzedakah: Righteous Actions*. Teacher's guide. N.Y.: CAJE, 1984. 16 pp.

Stein, Gisela. "A Ts'doko Project for the Young Child." *Jew Teach* 21 (April and May 1953): 7–9, 6–9.

Strauss, Ruby G. "Mitzvah Movies." *AM* (Spring 1977).

Summers, Barbara Fortgang. *Tzorchei Tzibbur: Community and Responsibility in the Jewish Tradition*. N.Y.: United Synagogue Youth. 250 pp.

Tarnor, Norman. "A High School Keren Ami Project." *Syn Sch* 19 (June 1961): 18–19.

Touber, Rosalyn. "Teaching Tzedakah, a School Project." *Syn Sch* 12 (Apr. 1954): 25.

Trainin, Isaac N. *Tzedakah and Jewish Education*. (Educational Council) N.Y.: CJF Philanthropies, 1964.

"Tzedakah." *The Jewish School and Democracy* 2 (Oct. 1943): 6–9.

Wieder, Leland E. "A Teaching Strategy of Jewish Identity through Tzedakah." In *Jewish Civics Workbook*, edited by Benjamin Efron and Hyman Chanover, 53–67. N.Y.: NCRI and AAJE, 1975.

Zwerin, Raymond A. *For One Another: Jewish Organizations that Help Us All*. N.Y.: UAHC, ca. 1980.

TEXTBOOKS AND TEACHER GUIDES

Axelrod, Herman. *In Their Footsteps*. 2 vols. (E. and H.). Teacher's guide. N.Y.: TU. 144 pp. High school students.

Baron, Leora. *What's the Way?* Introduction to Jewish law and ethics. Part 2, experimental ed. N.Y.: UAHC, 1980. 38 pp. Grade 7.

Bemporad, Jack, Abraham Segal, Jack Spiro, and R. Widom, eds. *Focus on Judaism, Science and Technology*. N.Y.: UAHC, 1970. 228 pp. High school students.

Borowitz, Eugene B. *How We Live*. N.Y.: UAHC, 1978. High school students.

———. *Understanding Judaism*. N.Y.: UAHC, 1979. 231 pp. Grades 8–11.

16 MITZVOT/VALUES AND CONTEMPORARY ISSUES

Brickner, Balfour, and Albert Vorspan. *Searching the Prophets for Values*. N.Y.: UAHC, 1981. 239 pp. High school students.

Bush, Lawrence. *Rooftop Secrets and Other Stories of Antisemitism*. Teacher's guide by Sherry Blumberg. N.Y.: UAHC, ca. 1987. 176 pp. Grades 7–9.

Cohen, Martin A., and Jack Zevin. *Survival*. N.Y.: UAHC, 1978.

Dorff, Elliott N. *Jewish Law and Modern Ideology*. Teacher's guide. N.Y.: USCJE, 1973. 263 pp.

Dresner, Samuel H., and Byron L. Sherwin. *Judaism, the Way of Sanctification*. N.Y.: USA, 1978. 355 pp.

Eisenberg, Azriel, and Abraham Segal. *Teaching Basic Jewish Values*. N.Y.: Behrman, 1954. 90 pp. Confirmation class.

Fine, Helen, *At Camp Kee Tov: Ethics for ages 9 to 12*. Teacher's guide and parent's manual by Edith Samuel. N.Y.: UAHC, 1963. 262 pp. Junior high school and high school.

Freehof, Lillian S. *The Right Way: Ethics for Youth*. N.Y.: UAHC, 1957. 233 pp. High school.

Jacobs, Louis. *Jewish Ethics, Philosophy, and Mysticism*. Teacher's guide by Ben Ezra Green. N.Y.: Behrman, 1969. 171 pp. High school.

Kipper, Lenore C., and Howard I. Bogot. *The Alef-Bet of Jewish Values: Code Words of Jewish Life*. N.Y.: UAHC, c. 1985. 43 pp.

Kripke, Dorothy K. *Let's Talk about Right and Wrong*. N.Y.: Behrman, 1955. 32 pp. Elementary school.

Levin, Meyer. *Beginnings in Jewish Philosophy*. Teacher's guide by W. J. Dannhauser. N.Y.: Behrman, 1971. 192 pp. High school.

Miller, Milton G., and Sylvan D. Schwartzman. *Our Religion and Our Neighbors*. N.Y.: UAHC, 1960, 1963. 297 pp. High school.

Neusner, Jacob. *Meet Our Sages*. N.Y.: Behrman. Grades 4–5.

———. *Mitzvah*. Chappaqua, N.Y.: Rossel Books, 1981. 110 pp. High school.

Persky, Elias, and Max Raiskin. *Mitzvot and Values* (H. and E.). N.Y.: Ktav, 1977. Elementary school.

Reisman, Bernard. *Jewish Experiential Book: The Quest for Jewish Identity*. N.Y.: Ktav, 1979. 449 pp. Grades 6–12.

Rosenberg, Amye. *Mitzvot*. N.Y.: Behrman. Grades 1–2.

———. *Tzedakah*. N.Y.: Behrman. Primary–grade 1.

Rosenberger, Mrs. Sh., Mrs. A. Halpert, and Mrs. Sh. Markowich. (Temporary Yiddish Reader No. 4) (Y.). Stories with a moral. Brooklyn, N.Y.: Beth Rachel of Satmar, 1974. 200 pp.

Rosenthal, Gilbert S. *Comparative Judaism*. Edited by S. Rossel (workbook) and W. B. Moshe Ben Aharon. Teacher's guide by Ellen Singer. N.Y.: Behrman. Grades 9–10.

Rossel, Seymour, et al. *Lessons from Our Living Past*, edited by Jules Harlow. Workbooks by M. Lipstein. Teacher's guide by Kelly Cherry. Parent's kit by Ruby Strauss. N.Y.: Behrman. Grades 3–4.

Rossel, Seymour, Hyman Chanover, and Chaim Stern. *When a Jew Seeks Wisdom: Sayings of the Fathers*. Teaching guides by Seymour Siegel. Functional guide by David A. Altshuler. Student encounter book by Laura Karp. Teacher's cassette by J. Margolis. N.Y.: Behrman, 1975. 255 pp.

Schwartz, Earl. *Moral Development: A Practical Guide for Jewish Teachers*. Denver: ARE, 1983. 188 pp.

Schwartzman, Louis, and Nathaniel Soroff. *Arakhim: Hebrew through Values*. Miami: BJE, 1968.

Segal, Abraham. *Comparative Judaism*. N.Y.: UAHC. Grades 5–6

Shumsky, Abraham, and Adaia Shumsky. *Mah Tov Series* (H.). N.Y.: UAHC:

1. *Asot Mishpat*—text, workbook, and teacher's guide.
2. *Ahavat Chesed*—text, workbook, and teacher's guide.
3. *Hatznea Lechet*—text, workbook, and teacher's guide.

Silverman, William B. *Rabbinic Wisdom and Jewish Values*. N.Y.: UAHC, 1971. 221 pp. High school.

———. *The Still Small Voice: The Story of Jewish Ethics*. N.Y.: Behrman, 1955, 1958. 218 pp. Grades 7–9.

Simms, Laura, et al. *Exploring Our Living Past*. Edited by Jules Harlow. Educational consultant, Seymour Rossel. Student and teacher package. N.Y.: Behrman. Grades 1–2.

Spiro, Saul. *Fundamentals of Judaism*. N.Y.: Ktav, 1969. 342 pp. High school.

Vorspan, Albert. *Giants of Justice*. N.Y.: UAHC, 1960. 260 pp.

———. *Jewish Values and Social Crisis: A Casework for Social Action*. N.Y.: UAHC, 1968. 306 pp. High school.

———. *To Do Justly: A Junior Casebook for Social Action*. N.Y.: UAHC, 1981. High school.

Vorspan, Albert, and Eugene J. Lipman. *Justice and Judaism*. N.Y.: UAHC, 1959. 272 pp. High school.

GLEANINGS

Midrash attributed to R. Tanhuma Bar Abba, 4th century C.E., "Justice, justice shalt thou pursue." Deut. 16:20,

"Why is the word justice written twice. To teach us that we must practice justice all times—whether it be for our profit or for our loss, and towards all men—towards Jews and non-Jews alike."

Tanhuma

Luzatto, Moses Hayyim (1707–46),

"Humility in thought means that a man should be wholly persuaded of his unworthiness to be the recipient of praise and glory. A man of this sort will surely find it impossible to consider himself superior to others. This attitude toward himself he will have not only because he is aware of his failings, but also because he realizes the insignificance of his attainments. . . . The possession of learning, for example makes dangerously for pride and self-esteem. . . . Yet there is no one so learned who does not make mistakes, or who is not in need of learning from his equals, and at times from his disciples."

The Faith of the Upright (1740), translated and edited by Mordecai M. Kaplan (1936, 1966), 386

A Rabbinic View,

"According to Jewish tradition two rabbis were debating the question: How do you know when the night ends and the day begins? The first rabbi said: "The night ends and a new day begins when you can tell the difference between a blue thread and a purple thread." The second rabbi said: "The night ends and a new day begins when you can see the face of your brother."

Quoted by William B. Silverman in *Rabbinic Wisdom and Jewish Values* (1971).

Noah, J. J.,

"A Hebrew would consider elementary education of but little avail were it not accompanied by a proper knowledge and appreciation of all the cardinal virtues, of morality, obedience to the laws, and particularly of obedience and reverence to parents. They seek to inculcate these essentials in the youthful mind, to the end that they may be conserved in manhood, and again taught to posterity."

"Hebrew Education" in the *Annual Report of the US. Commissioner of Education* (1870), 364.

Cohen, Samuel M.,

"The problem of living in a non-Jewish and often anti-Jewish environment is a peculiarly difficult one. It cannot be met by creating a sense of self-sufficiency and superiority. This would only lead to the destruction of the Jewish ideal of Human Brotherhood in which the value of every Citizen of the kingdom of God is unique and uncomparable. The best approach seems to be to live out in one's own life the Jewish ideal of peace and good will. The aspiration of being a brother to all mankind is accordingly emphasized as a part of Israel's mission or as a function of a Jewish national group. Without ignoring or belittling the actual injustice or wickedness in the world, the child is made to sense his membership in the human race by contact and cooperation with children of other races and creeds and by contact and cooperation with civic institutions and their officers."

The Progressive Jewish School (N.Y.: USA, 1932), 17–18.

Central Conference of American Rabbis (UAHC), 1937,
"In Judaism religion and morality blend into an indissoluble unity. . . . The love of God is incomplete without the love of one's fellow men. . . . Justice to all, irrespective of race, sect or class, is the inalienable right and the inescapable obligation to all."
Quoted by Blau in *The Characteristics of American Jews* (1965), 126.

Rabbinical Assembly of America,
"It is the duty of religion . . . to ally itself with those forces that make for social education and the fostering of a social conscience. . . . We who profess to dedicate ourselves to the advancement of the Jewish religion must bring it into the arena of social life as a force for reconstruction and rebirth."
Quoted by Blau in *The Characteristics of American Jews* (1965), 126.

Central Conference of American Rabbis (UAHC), 1943,
"1. We declare our concern for the rights of all racial groups within our country's boundaries who are denied the full privileges which are the birthright of every American."
CCAR (1943), 122.

Baeck, Leo,
"Man's duty toward man comes before the knowledge of God, and the knowledge of him is a process of seeking and inquiring rather than an act of possession."
The Essence of Judaism (1948), 14.

Menes, Abraham,
"The musar or "moralist" movement, initiated by Israel Salanter (1810–1883), became the moral force which helped Jewish youth in yeshivot to overcome the temptations of Haskalah. The great achievement of this movement was in revealing to the young student the rich moral content of Judaism, and thus strengthening his faith in himself and in the mission of the Torah. The spiritual life of the yeshivot took on a new richness and breadth of interest. . . . Whereas the Haskalah called the Jew—"know the world," the musar movement proclaimed—"know thyself.""
The Jewish People—Past and Present, 2:115.

Kadushin, Max,
"What the Jewish youth needs, and what he has a right to expect from his elders, is a pattern of values. He needs values that will give him inner security and poise, ideals of public and private conduct, concepts that interpret life and render it zestful. Only if Judaism can give him these values will it receive his full, deep-seated loyalty."
Jew Ed 19 (Summer 1948): 23.

A Charter of the Rights of the Jewish Child,
"An upbringing that will strenghten him in commitment to democracy as the way of life most in accord with Jewish teaching, with the welfare of America and with the dignity of humanity, and that will realize in him a deep sense of kinship with all mankind."
Jew Ed 22 (Summer 1951), 76.

Central Conference of American Rabbis (UAHC) on social justice (Teaching),
"1. Your Commission on Justice and Peace acknowledges with humility that its greatest failure to date has been in the area of implementing the social idealism of our people within our own congregations. With exceptions as notable as they are rare, we have limited ourselves to lofty pronouncements, but have not devised ways and means of teaching the practical application of these pronouncements to our people or of activating them in the search for a more decent society.

The practical work we do in our communities and even more the non-partisan political activity to which we can stimulate our congregants as an expression of their Jewish prophetic zeal will be both a manifest of our sincerity and a determinant of our effectiveness. We have always properly insisted that Judaism is a way of life. This must be as true in the areas represented by this Commission as with respect to ritual observance and to ethical conduct generally.

We would urge most strongly, therefore, that a major program in next year's Conference schedule should be devoted to the reporting in detail of successful committees on public affairs already in oper-

ation within our Congregations and specific practical proposals for the extension of such activity among the groups which the members of this Conference have the high privilege of serving."
CCAR (1951), 107.

Central Conference of American Rabbis (UAHC) on segregation,
"1. Righteousness is the pathway to peace. The historic decision of the Supreme Court outlawing segregation in our public schools is a forward step upon that path. The Court has now made known its program for implementing its unanimous decision. Mindful though we are of the many problems and passions involved, we call upon our colleagues to offer courageous leadership in helping to bring about the harmonious implementation of the Court's decision."
CCAR (1955), 65.

United Synagogue Commission on Jewish Education (USA),
"To provide opportunities for the child to develop spiritual and ethical sensitivity through curricular and co-curricular experiences which call for spiritual and ethical action."
Objectives and Standards for the Congregational School (1958).

Berkson, Isaac B.,
"The struggle for the preservation of Jewish life was never a struggle for mere survival. It was a struggle for the maintenance of a pattern of Jewish values as a basis for a way of life."
Jew Ed 30 (Fall 1959), 32.

Richman, Thelma,
"I doubt whether any other people had evolved so rich a repertoire of home "dramas" as the Jews. The Sabbath, the Seder, the Succah—all of these utilize the dramatic form, complete with script, stage-setting and cast of characters, to bring home to the child the meaning of values. And, the very fact that these were performed in the home served to institutionalize the family as other people have institutionalized a church or a flag. So that when the Jewish people began to remove this drama from the home-stage and place what little was left of it in the synagogue and in the school, they in effect, assimilated at the very core of their being. For in the Jewish home every table was an altar, every father the High Priest and every house a Temple. In other words, the household became the microcosm of the world and every family the microcosm of Mankind. It was there that the children learned what the world should be like, and what they should strive for in "remaking" it. It was there, in the relationship between its members, that the children learned what their relationship should be to their "brothers" outside. The lessons were hammered away day in and day out by precept and example."
In *Congress Bi-Weekly* Supplement (Jan 16, 1961).

Kurzweil, Zvi E.,
"The study of Mussar has given a powerful impetus to the re-evaluation of Judaism by placing emphasis on its ethical content; thus it helped to rescue Judaism from the shortcomings inherent in a formal legalistic interpretation of its teachings."
Modern Trends in Jewish Education (1964), 93.

National Community Relations Advisory Council,
"We recognize that discrimination and poverty are twin problems that must be combated simultaneously. If the principle of "Equality of Opportunity" is to have meaning, the opportunity must be provided, as well as the equity. . . . We once again pledge to do all in our power, in our individual capacities and as members of the Jewish community, to eradicate those twin evils from our society."
NCRAC, Plenary Session (June 1965), 87.

Hirsch, Richard G.,
"Judaism has something to contribute to America. The contribution is not in offering pat solutions to complex problems, but in projecting a system of values directing man to serve God by serving his fellow man. These values, an integral part of Jewish life through the ages, evolved under varying social, economic and political conditions. Judaism does not advocate any economic or political ideology,

but it is an advocate of a specific response to life's problems. It speaks to our day in the voice of the past, but in a language which is universal in time and place."

There Shall Be No Poor (1965), 9–10.

Heschel, Abraham J.,

"It is crucial to make Jewish youngsters and young adults aware that Jewish values are relevant to their daily life. . . . Our young people are bewildered, perplexed about the meaning of their existence, about the meaning of being human, about the meaning of being a Jew. There is a waiting for meaning, but meaning is kept a well-guarded secret. It is we who fail them. Instead of conveying the intellectual splendor of our heritage, we offer them infantile conceptions of Judaism, stereotypes, cliches."

Jew Ed 36 (Fall 1965), 16.

Schiff, Alvin I.,

"I have tried to develop some guide posts for the teaching of religious values. In order to teach for religious living, we must take into consideration the psychological factors which affect receptivity. We must be convinced that change is possible. Our teachers, rabbis and lay leaders must approach their work with increased optimism. Initially, the program must adapt to the level and needs of the students. Children must be conditioned to accept the responsibility of Judaism. Finally, instruction in religious values must stress activity, group experience, continuity of experience, relevance and multi-faceted influences."

Jew Ed 36 (Spring/Summer 1966), 173.

Vorspan, Albert,

"I believe that my generation has messed up America—and the world. I believe that the dreadful problems of our time—war, poverty, racial strife, hatred—are, despite everything, capable of solution. I believe that the ethical values of Judaism, as they were tested and refined through history, have something sharp and important to say about these problems and to the real world in our time. I believe that Jewish values can contribute to the social revolution of our age and I believe, very deeply, that the world has need of Jews who know, understand, and live by Jewish values. I believe that being Jewish is not merely an accident of birth but, rather, a high calling, a moral challenge, an eternal refusal to cop-out on the scene, and an ever new mandate to take the world in our hands, as co-partners with God, and beat it into better shape on the anvil of life. And I believe that America has the capacity to overcome any problem."

Jewish Values and Social Crisis: A Casebook for Social Action (1968), vii.

Geller, Joshua A.,

"The synagogue, as well as the school, will have to devise means to have youth see relevance in their education and in their prayers. Most important, it will be the task of the synagogue and the school to help youth become aware of the relationship that exists between Judaic religious values and democratic ideals and how they are both related to the contemporary scene, which require personal involvement and personal commitment."

Syn Sch 28 (Winter 1970), 13.

Ackerman, Walter I.,

"The quality of the life in the Jewish school is not significantly different than that of the public school. Although we do not have a detailed ethnography of the afternoon congregational school, anyone acquainted with that institution knows that it is, by and large governed by rules, practices and procedures which are remarkably like those which regulate life in our Jewish schools. That is a painful paradox: the Jewish religious school attempts to transmit a set of norms and values which are presented as unique and different but patterns its own behavior after a manner rooted in another tradition. If the Jewish religious school is to successfully fulfill its function of socialization for Jewish life, it must itself serve as an exemplar of Jewish living. Life in the school in all its varied aspects must be informed by principles drawn from the Jewish tradition. Neither the Melton Research Center nor the United Synagogue has addressed itself to this critically important factor in Jewish education. The programs they offer are necessary but not sufficient for the realization of the full po-

tential of the afternoon school."
Con Jud 32 (Fall 1970), 61–62.

National Jewish Community Relations Advisory Council, on Equal Rights Amendment,
"We reaffirm our recommendation that Jewish community relations agencies support ratification of the Equal Rights Amendment and also the extension of existing statutes against discrimination on grounds of religion or race to include prohibition of discrimination on grounds of sex. We recommend that Jewish community relations agencies vigorously recruit women in more than token numbers for both professional and voluntary positions in all aspects of Jewish communal activity, and at all policy and decision making levels."
Proceedings, 1974–75, 34.

Union of Orthodox Jewish Congregations of America, on Equal Rights Amendment,
"The Union of Orthodox Jewish Congregations of America oppose the enactment of the 27th Amendment even though it unequivocally champions equal rights for women. . . .
The UOJCA considers this legislation to be antithetical to the distinctiveness and sanctity which Jewish law, tradition and heritage have invested in the lives of men and women and in the creation of healthy family life. . . .
The concept embodied in the proposed constitutional amendment refuses recognition to the unique roles of partner in marriage and the merging of their distinct, but complementary existences, into a family unit, it confuses equality of status with identity of social roles."
Proceedings, 1974–75, 34.

National Jewish Community Relations Advisory Council, on affirmative action, preferential treatment, and quotas,
"We renew our recommendation that special provisions be made for compensatory education, training, retraining, apprenticeship, job counseling and placement, financial assistance and other forms of help for the deprived and disadvantaged, to enable them as speedily as possible to realize their potential capabilities for participation in the mainstream of American life. The sole criterion for such special services must be individual need; the services must not be limited or offered preferentially on the basis of race, color, national origin, religion or sex. . . .
The ADL of B'nai B'rith, the UOJCA, the JCRC of Minnesota, the JCRC of Omaha, of Palm Beach County, and of South Bend, Ind., dissent from the foregoing recommendation, deeming it to undercut the principle of equal opportunity for all Americans. . . .
The Jewish Labor Committee dissents from the foregoing recommendation for "special consideration," believing that it could be cited in justification of preferential treatment, which the JLC deems inconsistent with the principle of equal opportunity."
Proceedings, 1974–75, 35–36.

National Jewish Community Relations Advisory Council, on abortion,
"We believe that abortion in the early weeks of pregnancy is a matter for decision by individual women in accordance with their personal situations, and their religious, moral and ethical views, and should not be regulated by law. . . .We oppose proposals to amend the Constitution to invalidate the recent U.S. Supreme Court decision concerning abortion. . . ."
ADL abstained because "it believes that the foregoing section of the Joint Program Plan is too broad and fails to recognize the special role and capacity of non-sectarian and government agencies in dealing with this problem. . . ."
"The UOJCA dissent from this section. We believe that an unborn fetus has a right to life, and that society has the obligation to protect that life. It would therefore remain the responsibility of law to protect the child and society against abortion by convenience."
Proceedings, 1974–75, 42.

Rackman, Emanuel,
"In Judaism, in basic Judaism morality is stretched to the point that religion and morality are one."
Jew Ed 45 (Summer/Fall 1977), 6.

Fox, Marvin,
"No Jewish education can ignore the challenge of moral instruction. Neither can any serious Jewish education ignore

the challenges to Jewish morality posed by contemporary society. Even the youngest student can be helped to see the various ways in which Jewish thinkers have tried to come to terms with these problems. They can be shown that their own concerns were, in certain respects, shared by the greatest minds that Jewish learning produced. They will discover that Judaism does not expect blind and unthinking acceptance of its dogmas. They will see that inquiry, reflection, critical analysis are not only permitted but expected. In the process of study they will also come to realize that there are no easy answers to very complex questions. Finally, it will be evident that, having pushed rational reflection to its farthest limits, we are forced to take our stand with less than absolute certainty. It will be important for them to understand how much is at stake in such decision, to know what price we pay for the stance we take, what risks we run, what we sacrifice and what we gain."

From Scholar to the Classroom, edited by S. Fox and G. Rosenfield (1977), 81.

The Commission on Jewish Education—UAHC,

"The Commission on Jewish Education calls upon every synagogue to provide a program of Jewish education which will enable children, youth and adults to become: Jews who bear witness to the brit (the covenant between God and the Jewish people) by embracing Torah through the practice of mitzvot (commandments) as studied in Torah and the classic literature it has generated and interpreted in light of historic development and contemporary liberal thought."

Quoted by H. I. Bogot. "Mitzvah as Goal." *Ped Rep* 34 (Oct. 1983), 11.

17 TEXTBOOKS

1900 TO 1950

For texts prior to 1900, see history and Jewish education in the United States. After 1900 see also subject areas in curriculum section, day and Yiddish schools, and states and cities.

Comins, Harry L. "Recent Contributions to Jewish Education." (Review of new texts for teachers and students.) *CCAR* 43 (1933): 205–41.

Jung, Leo (chair of Textbook Committee of Synagogue Council of America). "Textbooks in Jewish Religious Schools." *Contemporary Jewish Record* 6 (1943): 79–84.

* Klein, Aaron. תולדות ספרי הלימוד לבתי הספר היהודים (History of Textbooks in Jewish Schools) (H.). N.Y.: JTSA, 1935.

Kohn, Eugene. "Books on Jewish Education." *JQR* 8 (1918): 201–22.

"Report of the Religious Education Committee: On Text-Book Commission and the Issue of Uniform Texts for Schools." *CCAR* 22 (1912): 176–201.

"Report of the Religious Education Committee: On Textbooks and Teacher Training." *CCAR* 21 (1911): 85–95.

"Report of the Text-Book Commission." *CCAR* 21 (1911): 94–95.

Werbe, Z. "ספרי לימוד חדשים„ (New Textbooks). *Sh Hah* (H.) 2 (1942): 108–13.

SINCE 1950

Greenberg, Cheryl. "Textbook Treatment of the Roles of Ritual and Women in Judaism." *JSS* 46 (Winter 1984): 73–82.

Grollman, Earl A., and Esor Ben-Sorek. "Textbooks and Ethnocentrism." *Jew Ed* 36 (Summer 1966): 179–80, 191.

* Klein, Aaron. *The Development of Textbooks for Jewish Schools in the United States*. N.Y.: JTSA, 1956. 210 pp.

———. „תולדות ספרי הלמוד לבתי הספר היהודים באמריקה" (History of Textbooks in American Jewish Schools). *Sh Hah* (H.) 17 (1956–57): 21–38, 72–81, 164–77.

Pollak, George and Gerhard Lang. *Inventory of Texts in Supplementary Jewish Schools*. JESNA Research and Information Bulletin no. 52 (September 1982). 47 pp.

Rose, Marvin. "The Treatment of Jesus in Jewish Textbooks." *Jew Ed* 40 (Summer 1970): 21–35.

* Shapiro, Max A. *An Historical Analysis and Evaluation of Jewish Religious Textbooks Published in the United States*. U. of Cincinnati, 1960. 262 pp.

* Shoop, Simon H. *A Study of Jewish Theological Concepts as Reflected in an Analysis of Textbooks of Jewish Religion, 1830–1956*. U. of Pittsburgh, 1956. 278 pp.

Strober, Gerald S. "Inter-Group Images in Textbooks." *Rel Ed* 68 (Mar.–Apr. 1973): 195–203.

Weinryb, B. D. "Intergroup Content in Jewish Religious Textbooks." *Rel Ed* 55 (Mar.–Apr. 1960): 109–16.

GLEANINGS

Rabbi Akibah (second century, CE),
"When thou teachest thy son teach in a well-corrected book."
Quoted by Nathan Morris, *The Jewish School* (1937), 241.

Leeser, Isaac,
"It has been my endeavor to make myself understood by children from eight to fourteen years old; yet I fear that I may have failed, oftener than I should do, of rendering subject-matter sufficiently clear. I trust, however, that teachers and parents will not put the book into the hands of children without giving at least a cursory explanation, which, it is confidently hoped, will be enough to assist the learner."
Preface to *Catechism for Younger Children* (Phila.: 1839), x–xi.

Benderly, Samson (1903),
"A definite progressive system of education will in course of time evolve its own text-books. Text-books, to be of any use, must be based upon the experience of able teachers. We must, therefore, first have the able teachers and the experience, and the text-books will follow as a natural result."
Quoted by Winter in *Jewish Education in a Pluralist Society* (1966), 54.

Schechter, Solomon,
After qualified teachers, "The second [need] is the almost utter lack of textbooks. Through some cause or other, we have as yet no Jewish history fit to place in the hands of a teacher or pupil. . . . We must have a whole series of primers and readers and text-books and histories extending at least over a course of eight years, commencing with the Hebrew alphabet and culminating somewhere in the later Hebrew literature."
Seminary Addresses and Other Papers (1907), 112.

Jung, Leo L., chair of Textbook Committee of the United Synagogue Council
"From Heinrich Cornill through Travers Herford, reverent and friendly to appreciate that prayers for divine wrath upon those 'who have devoured Jacob and laid waste his habitation' were psychological safety valves for a minority tortured by cruel and unconscionable wielders of temporal power. Yet, for the purpose of teaching the positive aspects of Jewish history rather than the glorious and heartrending account of its millennial martyrdom, we have favored for the textbooks of our school children the elimination, substitution or modification of such texts. . . . Another problem concerns the attitude of our textbooks toward the founder of Christianity. As a rule, Orthodox Jewish books contain no reference to him, yet our children should receive some authoritative information culled from our literature and free from any odium theologicum. One could quote without fear of objection from any side Rabbi Jacob Em-den's too little known *Iggereth Shalom*, recently published in English. Rabbi Em-den, zealot par excellence, in this epistle reveals true Jewish tolerance."
"Textbooks in Jewish Religious Schools." *Contemporary Jewish Record* 6 (Feb. 1943), 82 and 83.

Weinryb, Bernard D.,
"The curriculum materials of the Jewish school are, for the most part, centered on subject matter and its linguistic nature. The rest are mostly historical in character and deal very little with doctrine. The textbooks show a high rate of preoccupation with majority groups (more in terms of ethnic or political relations, less in terms of religion), and a smaller preoccupation with other minority groups and with intra-Jewish groups. Of negative imbalance, or prejudice, against non-Jewish groups—other religions or peoples, majority or minority—there is very little and this is exceeded at times by expressions of positive imbal-

ance-friendliness, anti-prejudice—found in Jewish curriculum materials. A somewhat higher negative imbalance is found in the category of intra-Jewish relations, mainly among textbooks originating from the more extreme groups. A similar pattern is discernible when using a qualitative analysis of self/other images."

"Intergroup Content in Jewish Religious Textbooks." *Rel Ed* (Mar.–Apr. 1960), 116. (Essay based in part on the results of the Dropsie College Intergroup Research Project, Bernard D. Weinryb, Director; Meir Ben-Horin, Consultant; Daniel Garnick, Researcher.)

Bennett, Alan D.
"The variety of textbooks used in the several grades of our schools is literally astounding. The 24 different texts reported in use by Kindergarten students is a paltry number compared, for example, with the 47 listed in 2nd grade, 61 in 3rd grade, 75 in 4th, and almost 70 in each of the remaining grades!"

Curriculum and Materials: Educational Research Survey No. 5 (N.Y.: NATE, CJE, UAHC, and CCAR, 1962), 25.

Grollman, Earl A., and Esor Ben-Sorek,
"An investigation of junior high and high school text-books reveal an ethnocentrism based not so much upon the heroics of the "good guy" but rather the decreasing of the Gestalt patterns of the surrounding culture—the totality of the historic event.

"Textbooks and Ethnocentrism." *Jew Ed* 36 (Spring/Summer 1966), 100.

Rose, Marvin,
"When writing about Jesus for adult readers in a Christian society, an author is faced with a tremendous task; when writing for children, who are far more easily impressed with the authority of the printed page, it is an awesome responsibility. The writer of a textbook for Jewish youth writes as an educator. Particularly, when writing about a subject like Jesus for Jewish children living in an open society, he cannot content himself with adapting the theory of his favorite historian. He has a responsibility not only to report the facts as he finds them, but to consider their implications in terms of the larger objective of helping each of his students to find his own Jewish identity. The authors of some of the more recent high school level textbooks included in the present study began to recognize and accept this responsibility, but the sad fact is that most of our children have not been motivated to continue their Jewish education long enough to ever see these books. What is needed, therefore, are textbooks on an elementary level that fully reflect this responsibilty."

"The Treatment of Jesus in Jewish Textbooks" *Jew Ed* 40 (Summer 1970), 35.

Study of textbooks and storybooks by the Religious Action Center, Washington, D.C. (1975),
"Most women are portrayed as housewives, while men are seen as doctors, judges, builders, etc. All temple activities are male-dominated, with rabbis, presidents, and members of the Boards of Trustees pictured as men. Men carry the Torah, read from the Torah, etc. Men play the more important roles while women, if they are portrayed as active in synagogue life at all, serve in the Sisterhood and are shown as part of the congregation at worship or opening the Ark, at best. Males are always shown as brighter and more active than females. In too many instances, the majority of main characters are men. Bible stories, history books and Hebrew books neglect the role of women, both historically and in story material."

Quoted by Susan Weidman Schneider in *Jewish and Female*, 167.

Gertman, Stuart A.
"As with curriculum, the use of textbooks in Reform religious schools is extremely diverse. . . .There are myriads of textbooks available and their usage depends in large measure on the educator's judgment about the quality and the place in the curriculum into which they fit. . . .

A little more than 50% of our religious schools use textbooks published by the Reform movement, although this varies slightly from grade to grade and changes when there is a strong textbook for a particular course by another publisher. Full-time educators tend to use non-Union textbooks more often than part-time educators (about three to two), and much more often than rabbi-educators (sometimes as much as three to one, but almost always twice as much). . . .

We also find that part-time educators tend to use no text more often than full-time educators. Smaller schools tend to use a text less frequently than large schools."

"And You Shall Teach Them Diligently": A Study of the Current State of Religious Education in the Reform Movement (N.Y.: NATE, in cooperation with the UAHC Department of Education, 1977), 38.

Pollak, George, and Gerhard Lang,
"The amount of time devoted to the three subjects: Hebrew, Prayer, and Customs, Ceremonies and Observances, the overlapping of the texts and their use in the teaching of any of the subjects, would seem to indicate that our supplementary schools are essentially "religious" schools and not oriented towards the teaching of Hebrew qua language as the name "Hebrew School" may imply."

Inventory of Texts in Supplementary Jewish Schools (JESNA Research and Information Bulletin no. 52, September 1982), 11.

Wachs, Saul,
"Teachers who must choose materials for Jewish studies are at a considerable disadvantage. There are fewer publishers, almost no writers who make a career of preparing materials, and little money for testing them. In short, from a commercial point of view, the size of the potential market for Jewish school materials does not warrant the publisher's investment of adequate sums of money. That is not to say that there are no good materials and no serious publishers in the field; valuable work has been and is being produced by national, local and Israeli insitutions, as well as by a few talented individuals and commercial houses. Nevertheless, there are great gaps between what there is and what is needed. Schools that teach prayer have few texts and workbooks designed for the purpose. Principals of American Jewish schools who need Hebrew language texts often feel forced to use texts from Israel which are indeed attractive, but which reflect an Israeli milieu remote from the world of students in this country and often include vocabulary increments beyond their grasp. There is little material for teaching the Bible beyond the fourth or fifth grades in day schools, so principals and teachers must choose texts written for Israelis and unabridged editions with or without medieval commentaries. In one case, the linguistic level is satisfactory but the explanatory notes do not necessarily reinforce the most important values in Bible Study, and in the other, students are asked to study ancient Hebrew with the help of a commentary written in medieval Hebrew."

The Jewish Teacher: Professional Status (1984), 21.

18 | THE HIGH SCHOOL

PRIOR TO 1950

Edidin, Benjamin M. "Teaching Holidays and Customs to High School Youth." *Jew Ed* 6 (Apr.–June 1934): 95–99.

Folkman, Jerome D. "Building the High School Department." *Jew Teach* 11 (Apr. 1943).

Fram, Leon. "Developing the High School Department." *Jew Teach* 11 (Apr. 1943): 1–7.

Franklin, Leo L. "Sabbath School Work for High-School Pupils." *CCAR* 21 (1911): 263–70.

Franzblau, Abraham. *Twenty Worship Services for the High School*. Cincinnati: HUC, ca. 1936.

Gittelsohn, Ronald B. "Aims and Objectives of the Jewish Religious High School." *Jew Ed* 8 (Apr.–June 1936): 79–82.

———. "Modern Jewish Problems." (A course proposed for the high school.) *Jew Teach* 3 (June 1935): 18–23.

———. "Teaching Religion to Children of High School Age." *Jew Ed* 9 (Apr.–June 1937): 74–77.

Greenstone, Julius H. *Methods: Teaching the Jewish Religion in Junior and Senior Grades*. (Correspondence School.) Phila.: Jewish Chautauqua Society, 1915. 349 pp.

Lang, Leon S. *A Curriculum for the High School Department of the Jewish Religious School*. N.Y.: USA, 1931. 77 pp.

———. "A Curriculum of a High School of a Jewish Religious School." Master's thesis, Columbia U. Teachers College, 1932.

Lazaron, Morris S. *Religious Service for Jewish Youth*. Baltimore: 1927. 275 pp. High school and Sunday school.

Levine, Abraham. "בית הספר העברי הגבוה,, (The Hebrew High School). *Hadoar* (H.) 4 (13th of Tevet, 1925).

Obasi, I. "הספרות העברית החדשה בבתי-הספר הגבוהים" (The New Hebrew Literature in the High Schools). In *Yesod* (H.), 92–103.

Pearlman, David W. "The Curriculum of a Congregational High School." *Jew Ed* 3 (Apr./June 1931): 98–110.

Pollak, Jacob B. "Jewish History Texts in the High School." *Jew Teach* 1 (Apr. 1933): 1–4.

Rudavsky, David. "Nature and Extent of Secondary Jewish Schooling in America." *Jew Ed* 12 (Apr. 1940): 25–32.

Wessel, Harvey E. "The Aim of a Curriculum for Jewish Religious High Schools." *CCAR* 33 (1923): 296–306.

SINCE 1950

Alk, Jeremy David. "Jews Who Are Black: A Study Guide." A study guide designed for high school students to broaden their understanding of what it means to be a Jew. Master's project, HUC–JIR, 1980.

Arian, Philip. "Temple Israel: A High School Challenges Its Congregation." *Syn Sch* 19 (June 1961): 8–13.

———. "Transforming the Jewish School." In *Teen*, 43–49. Also in *Jew Spec* 32 (Fall 1967).

Bauman, Morton. "Goals of the High School Department." In The High School Department, edited by Walter H. Plaut, 25–26. N.Y.: UAHC, 1962.

Berk, Aliza Wallin. "The Four Holy Cities in Israel." A slide-tape presentation on the historical development of the four holy cities of Israel—Hebron, Tiberias, Jerusalem, and Safed—as seen in art, poetry, and Midrash. Master's project, HUC–JIR, 1978. High school.

Berman, Myron. "Thy Son Shall Build the House—A Blueprint for the Religious Education of the Teenager." *Syn Sch* 23 (Winter 1965): 27–33.

Bissell, Sherry. "God: The Struggle and the Dialogue: Curricular Approach to the Teaching of God and a Curriculum for Junior High School." An analysis of the basic curricular approaches to the subject of God. Includes a curriculum for junior high students that utilizes varied methodologies and culminates in a weekend experience. Master's project, HUC–JIR, 1976.

* **Dinsky, Samuel.** *Secondary Jewish Education in the United States*. Dropsie U., 1962.

Dori, Rivka. "Confluent Education in Terms of the Language Teacher." An outline of an alternative approach to Hebrew language education via confluent education, structured around the confluence of the cognitive and effective processes. Includes lesson plans for College Hebrew I and evaluations of the lessons. Master's project, HUC–JIR, 1976.

———. *Programmed Instruction Unit: Piel*. Unit intended to be used along with an introductory high school/college Hebrew classroom sequence. Includes only regular verbs. Master's project, HUC–JIR, 1976.

Eisenberg, Azriel. "Bridging the Gap between Elementary School and the Jewish Teachers College." In *Jan* 2, 281–96.

———. "The Hebrew High School: Issues, Problems, and Opportunities." *Jew Ed* 37 (Winter 1967): 58–68.

———. "The Hebrew High School in the United States and Canada: The Present Picture." *Syn Sch* 27 (Fall 1968): 28–36.

———. "Index to Jewish Living." (Secondary education.) *Congress Weekly* (Oct. 27, 1958): 5–7.

———. "Problem Number One: The Hebrew High School." In *Wiseman*, 44–57.

———. ‏"החינוך התיכון בבית הספר העברי בתפוצות"‎ (Secondary Hebrew Education in the Diaspora). In *PDE* (H.), 100–106.

Eisenstein, Ira. "The Synagogue High School in the Metropolitan Community." *Syn Sch* 10 (Dec. 1961): 5.

Elazar, Daniel J. "Need: Hebrew High School." *Jew Spec* 29 (June 1964): 25–27.

Freidenreich, Fradle. "Idea Forum: Jewish Programming in the High School Years." *Ped Rep* 25 (Fall 1973): 11.

Frost, Shimon. "The Hebrew High School: For the Able and Willing." *Syn Sch* 23 (Winter 1965): 34–37.

Geffen, Peter A., and Lavey Derby. "The Synagogue High School." In *JPH*, 427–49.

Goldberg, Henry R. "Extension Education for the High School Student." *Syn Sch* 10 (Dec. 1951): 46.

Gordon, Susan. "Twentieth Century Jewish Women: A Teacher's Guide." A teacher's guide and anthology that examines feminist issues in secular and Jewish history and explores current attitudes in the Jewish community towards women in the Rabbinate and other areas of leadership. Master's, HUC–JIR, 1977. High school.

"High School Student Recruitment." *Ped Rep* 33 (May 1982): 14.

Jacobson, Burt, Mildred Brooks, and Michael Swirsky. "Towards the Value-Centered High School Community." *Ed As* (1970): 60–70.

Kerdeman, Deborah. "The Creation of an Institute: Melton and Reform Youth." *MJ* 18 (Summer 1984): 31, 32.

Kurzband, Toby K. *The Senior High School in Reform Jewish Religious Schools*. N.Y.: UAHC, 1970.

Levitsky, Louis M. "The High School Student and the Congregation." *Syn Sch* 10 (Dec. 1951): 26–30.

Lipman, Eugene J. "Greater Involvement of Youth." *Ped Rep* 23 (Mar. 1972): 15.

Luijken, Marianne. "A Guide to the Teaching of Joshua." An integrated approach for the teaching of Bible to junior high, high school, and adult students. Master's project, HUC–JIR, 1983.

Lukinsky, Joseph. "The Teenager and the Synagogue: Possibilities for Institutional Resolution." *Syn Sch* 21 (Fall 1962).

Margoshes, Samuel. "The Hebrew High School." *Day* (Nov. 15, 1961).

Millgram, Abraham E. "Hebrew High School: Education for All Our Children." *Con Jud* 15 (Winter 1961): 1–14. Also in a pamphlet, N.Y.: USCJE, 1961. 22 pp.

National Association of Temple Educators. "The High School—The Crucial Department of the Next Decade" (Panel discussion). *Jew Teach* 29 (Apr. 1961): 14–15, 20–21.

Nelson, Harry. "The Synagogue High School in the Social Community." *Syn Sch* 10 (Dec. 1951): 18.

Newman, L., and G. Watson. "Education for Jewish Teenagers." *RA* (1962).

Oberstein, Leonard. "Creating a Community High School." *Ped Rep* 29 (Spring 1978): 11.

Olitsky, Kerry M., and Gary P. Zola. "The High School Community Period." In *JPH*, 327–36.

Parzen, Herbert. "The Need for a System of Secondary Education." *Recon* (June 14, 1957): 18–23.

Penn, Ascher. „אידישע האי-סקול דערציאונג אין אמעריקע" (Jewish Secondary Education in America). *Penn* (Y.), 481–89.

Pilch, Judah. "Beyond the Elementary School." *Congress Weekly* (July 25, 1955): 7–8.

Plaut, Walter H., ed. *The High School Department*. N.Y.: UAHC, 1962.

Rose, Ruth W. "The Lore of Judaism: Concepts and Values Taught through Science Fiction and Fantasy." A series of units for junior and senior high school students that uses science fiction to teach Jewish lore, values, and culture. Master's project, HUC–JIR, 1977.

Rosenbloom, Milton. "Goals for the High School Department." In *The High School Department*, edited by Walter H. Plaut (N.Y.: UAHC, 1962).

Saltzman, Manuel. "The High School Student and the Community." *Syn Sch* 10 (Dec. 1951): 30–33.

Schindler, Alexander M. "Educating the Post-Confirmand." *Jew Teach* 32 (Apr. 1961): 25–27.

Schwartz, Elliot S. "Case Study of a High School Merger." *Jew Ed* 53 (Fall 1984): 34–36, 45.

———. "The Hebrew High School for All." *Syn Sch* 23 (Winter 1965): 38–42.

———. "The Intercongregational Hebrew High School." In *Teen* (1968), 88–92.

Shudofsky, Chanoch. "The Intercongregational High School." *Syn Sch* 34 (Spring 1976): 30–35.

Silver, Jeremy. "The Temple High School." *Jew Teach* 33 (Oct. 1964): 7–10.

Silverman, David Wolf. "Goals for the Conservative Hebrew High School in America." In *Teen* (1968), 11–13.

Spiro, Jack D. "Commission on Jewish Education, UAHC–CCAR." (Description of high school programs in the Reform movement.) *Ped Rep* 25 (Fall 1973): 15.

Tanenbaum, Roy. "A Want-to-Go High School." *Syn Sch* 30 (Summer 1972): 11–27.

United Synagogue Commission on Jewish Education. "The Afternoon High School Curriculum: A Statement of Goals." *Ped Rep* 23 (Sept. 1971): 28.

———. *Jewish High School Enrollment and Recruitment Manual*. N.Y.: USCJE, 1979. 52 pp.

CURRICULUM AND PEDAGOGY

Altman, Barry Martin. "A Bible Curriculum for the Junior High Department of a Religious School." Master's thesis, HUC–JIR, 1973.

Arian, Philip. "The Hebrew High As a World." *Syn Sch* 25 (Fall 1966): 11–16.

———. "The Hebrew High School as a Total Community." *Syn Sch* 27 (Fall 1968): 52–58. Also in *Ed As* (1968): 1–6.

Baron, Charlotte. "A Happy High School Program." *Jew Teach* 24 (Nov. 1955): 12–14.

Berlin, Donald B. "Toward a Course in Jewish Theology for the Reform Jewish Student." Master's thesis, HUC–JIR, 1965. 198 pp.

Brickner, Balfour. "A Curriculum of Some Jewish Theological Concepts of Interest to Reform Jewish High School Youth." Master's thesis, HUC–JIR, 1952.

Dinsky, Samuel H. "A Program for Secondary Jewish Education in the United States." *Jew Ed* 32 (Fall 1961): 8–18.

Ehrmann, Eliezer L. "Reflections on the Teaching of Jewish History in the High School." In *Teen*, 61–70

———. "Teaching Jewish Holidays in the High School." *Syn Sch* 26 (Fall 1967): 12–16.

Ende, George. "Formal Jewish Education for the High School." *Syn Sch* 10 (Dec. 1951): 42–45.

Ezring, Sheldon. "A Course in Jewish Literature and Cinema for High School." *SWJT* 9 (Fall/Winter 1976–77): 11–12.

———. "Toward an Experimental and Developmental Text Dealing with the Mitzvoth for Reform Jewish High School Youth." Master's thesis, HUC–JIR, 1974.

Fefferman, Michael. "Grades 9, 10 Curriculum." *SWJT* 9 (Spring/Summer 1977): 18–19.

Fox, Brian. "Toward a High School Program Dealing with Relevant Rabbinic Theology (The Living Rabbis)." Master's thesis, HUC–JIR, 1974.

Frank, Bernard S. "Toward Topical Approach to Jewish History for the Junior High School Department of the Reform Religious School." Master's thesis, HUC–JIR, 1960.

Gamoran, Emanuel, ed. *Units of Activity and Instruction for the Junior and Senior High School*. N.Y.: UAHC, 1956. 316 pp.

Goff, Ronald H. "Toward a Program of Experimental Holiday Worship for the Reform High School and Adults." Master's thesis, HUC–JIR, 1965.

Goldman, Mark N. "Toward a Course for the Reform Jewish High School on Personal Values through Rabbinic Literature." Master's thesis, HUC–JIR, 1967.

Goldstein, Martin. "Motivations and Attitudes of High School Students." *Syn Sch* 27 (Fall 1968): 70–80.

———. "The Motivation of High School Students." In *Teen*, 148–54.

Hailperin, Harriet. "A Sabbath Project for Teenagers." *Syn Sch* 10 (Sept. 1951): 23–24.

Hadoar (H.). "העברית בבית הספר הגבוה," (Hebrew in the High School). 27 (Oct. 15, 1948): 983–85.

Hershman, Morris M. "Toward a Curriculum in Bible for the Ninth and Tenth Grades." Master's thesis, HUC–JIR, 1957.

Isseroff, Sampson A. *National Commission on Torah Education Curriculum*. N.Y.: BJE, 1970. The 1970 high school curriculum developed by Isseroff is included with high school curricula developed after 1970 in the *Curriculum Guide for Afternoon Religious Schools*, edited by Eli Baum (1979), 179–204.

Kadosh, Mary Anne. "Curriculum for the Union Hebrew High School." Master's thesis, HUC–JIR, 1974.

Kantor, Nathan C. "Teaching Teenagers Hebrew Reading." *Jew Teach* 29 (Feb. 1961): 12–13.

Kaunfer, Neil. "Directions for Supplementary Hebrew High Schools in the Eighties." *Jew Ed* 48 (Winter 1980): 37–38, 48.

———. "A Radical Approach to Teaching the Biblical Narrative in the Hebrew High School." In *Teen*, 50–61.

Kraus, William H. "Thematic High School Textbook on Russian Jewry: During the Period of Mass Immigration to the United States." Master's thesis, HUC–JIR, 1980.

Lakritz, Isaac. "Create Drama! Create Involvement! Youth Education through Creative Drama." *J Jew Com Ser* (Fall 1982): 77–82.

Levi, Charles S. "Toward a Course of Study for the Young Reform Adolescent in the Great

Hymns of Jewish Liturgy." Master's thesis, HUC–JIR, 1977.

Lewis, Justin. "A Suggested Approach for Re-Structuring Social Studies Curriculum in Our High Schools." *Ha Manahel* (H.) (Spring 1975).

Lewittes, Mordecai H. "Values in the Jewish Secondary School." *Ped Rep* 29 (Spring 1978).

Malin, Penina C. "Creative and Meaningful Learning in the High School." *Impact* 35 (Winter 1976–77): 28–36.

Manual for a Comprehensive Jewish High School in Your Congregation. N.Y.: USCJE, 1973, 1974.

Mason, Patrice Goldstein. "Teaching of Jesus for Ninth Grade Reform Religious School Students." Master's thesis, HUC–JIR, 1977.

Matanky, Leonard A. "A Seminar with a Twist." *Ped Rep* 36 (Jan. 1985): 31–32.

Menitoff, Paul J. "Reform Judaism Viewed as a Polydoxy; Towards a Text for Teenagers." Master's thesis, HUC–JIR, 1970.

Miller, Milton G. "A Course of Study in Comparative Religions for the High School Department of the Reform Religious School." Master's thesis, HUC–JIR, 1953.

Morris, Herbert. "A Curriculum towards a High School Program of Teacher Training." Master's thesis, HUC–JIR, 1956.

Natkin, Fred A. "Art Is for Us: Toward a Curriculum for Teaching Jewish Art in the Senior High School Department of the Reform Religious School." Master's thesis, HUC–JIR, 1972.

Panoff, Mark J. "Our Inheritance from the Jewish Immigrant Community of 1880 to 1920: A Study in Current Jewish Values for the Reform High School Student." Master's thesis, HUC–JIR, 1973.

Pomerantz, Frederic S. "A Philosophy of Education for Ethics Instruction in the Junior High School Department of Reform Jewish Religious Schools." Master's thesis, HUC–JIR, 1968.

Preisand, Sally. "Toward a Course of Study for Reform High School Youth Dealing with the History and Changing Role of the Jewish Woman." Master's thesis, HUC–JIR, 1972.

Relkin, Stanley T. "Toward a Topical Course of Study for the High School Department of the Reform Religious School." Master's thesis, HUC–JIR, 1962.

Schanin, Norman. "Informal Education for Secondary Age Groups." *Jew Ed* 32 (Fall 1961): 20–26.

Shahar, Yonai. „נסוי בתאום בין המקצועות בביה״ס תיכון של אחה״צ" (Experiments in Coordinating the Curriculum of the Afternoon High School). *Sh Hah* (H.) 37 (Mar. 1978): 140–45.

Shevitz, Susan R. "Evaluation: A Tool for Program Development." (A case study in secondary education.) *Ped Rep* 36 (Sept. 1985): 10–13.

Smolar, Leivy. "The Na-aseh of Reform Jewish High School Education." *Jew Teach* 32 (Feb. 1964): 13–15.

* Sosevsky, Morris. *Incorporating Moral Education into the Jewish Secondary School Curriculum.* Yeshiva U., 1980. 62 pp.

Starr, Arthur F. "Preparing for College: A Guide for Jewish High School Seniors." Master's thesis, HUC–JIR, 1969.

Steinberg, Gerald D. "Toward a Curriculum in Jewish Values Based upon Jewish Literature for the High School Department of the Religious School." Master's thesis, HUC–JIR, 1965.

Teller, Gerald A. "A Creative Congregation High School Program." *Ped Rep* 29 (Spring 1978): 14.

To See the World through Jewish Eyes—The High School Years. Experimental ed. N.Y.: UAHC, 1984. 172 pp.

Selected Hebrew High School Curriculum Materials Kit. N.Y.: USCJE.

Wachs, Saul P., and Leon Waldman. "A Theory of Practice for the Conservative Congregational High School." In *Teen*, 33–43.

Warshal, Bruce. "A Study in the Separation of Church and State: Toward a Text for Reform High Schools and Relating Historical Jewish Values to the Problems of American Law." Master's thesis, HUC–JIR, 1969.

Warshaw, Ephraim. "New Dimensions in the Hebrew High School Curriculum." *Syn Sch* 27 (Summer 1969): 8–26.

Weiss, Dean Clifford. "A Selected Repertoire of Hebrew Sacred Music for Use in the Secondary School Choral Program." Master's thesis, California State U., Fullerton, 1974. 168 pp.

Wisnia, Eric B. "A Modified Contract/Open Classroom Approach to Teaching Mini-Courses in Judaica to Junior High School Students." Master's thesis, HUC–JIR, 1974.

Wolowelsky, Joel B. "Advanced Placement in the Jewish High School." *Ped Rep* 32 (Winter 1981): 15–16.

Zerin, Edward. "A High School Program for Living Judaism." *CCAR J* 10 (Jan. 1963): 23–26.

CONFIRMATION IN THE HIGH SCHOOL

Bennett, Alan D., ed. *Confirmation Practices*. Educational Research Survey, no. 2. N.Y.: UAHC, 1959.

———. "A Study Concerning the Optimum Age for Confirmation." *Jew Teach* 26 (Nov. 1957): 3–6.

Bissell, Sherry H. "God—The Struggle and the Dialogue: Curricular Approach to the Teaching of God and a Curriculum for Junior High School." Master's thesis, HUC–JIR, 1976.

Egelson, Louis I. "Confirmation Practices in One Hundred Jewish Religious Schools." *CCAR* 41 (1931): 366–99.

Essrig, Harry. "The Confirmation Class." *Jew Teach* 6 (Jan. 1938): 1–8.

———. "Confirmation in the Reform School." *Jew Ed* 12 (Jan. 1941): 178–82.

Fackenheim, Emil. "Apologia For a Confirmation Text." *Commentary* 32 (May 1961): 401–10. Also in *Judaism and the Jewish School*, edited by Pilch and Ben-Horin. N.Y.: Bloch, 1966. 281–94.

Feldman, Abraham. *Confirmation*. N.Y.: Bloch, 1948.

Feuer, Leon I., and B. Benedict Glazer. *The Jew and His Religion: A Guide for Confirmation and High School Classes*. N.Y.: Bloch, 1931. 158 pp.

Gittelsohn, Roland B. "Ideas of Religion as Reflected in the Confirmation Manuals and Catechisms Used by American Jews." Master's thesis, HUC–JIR, 1936.

Glasner, Samuel. "Learning Experiences for the Confirmation Class." In *The Confirmation Class*, edited by Walter H. Plaut, 23. N.Y.: UAHC, 1961.

Hennig, Helen Kohn. *Confirmation Workbook on the Religion of the Jews*. N.Y.: UAHC, 1943. 129 pp.

Klein, Debra L., and Karen A. Sobel. *The Holy Relationship: A 10th Grade Confirmation Class Curriculum*. L.A.: HÜC-JIR, Tartak Learning Center, 1982.

Lang, Leon S. "What Have We Done With Confirmation?" *RA* (1933–38): 288–307.

Levinger, Elma C, and Joseph Lee. *Folk and Faith: The Confirmand's Guide Book*. N.Y.: Bloch, 1942. 139 pp.

Lipman, Steve. *The Harvest Festivals: A Prism for Understanding Our Relationship to the Land of Israel*. A ten-lesson unit designed for use in a confirmation program. LA: HUC–JIR, Tartak Learning Center, 1988.

Mahrer, Lawrence M. "Toward a Course of Study on Prayer for the Confirmation Department of the Religious School." Master's thesis, HUC–JIR, 1959.

Nemzoff, Samuel L., compiler. *Confirmation Service Sampler*. N.Y.

Plaut, Walter H., ed. *The Confirmation Class*. N.Y.: UAHC, 1961.

Rosenthal, Frank, and Joseph Wagner. "Graduation Not Confirmation." *Syn Sch* 17 (1959).

Sager, Steven R. "The Jewish Identity of Confirmation: Problem and Proposal." *Rel Ed* 78 (Spring 1983): 201–9.

Scherer, Allan, and Toby Kurzband. "Jewish Ethics in Every-Day Life." (For confirmation class.) *Jew Teach* 23 (May 1955): 9–14.

Schwartzman, Sylvan D. *The Commitments of Confirmation*. Cincinnati: HUC, 1961.

* Shapero, Sanford M. *A Study of the Confirmation Process—Its Objectives and Its Contribution to the Religious Development of Students*. HUC–JIR, 1959. 254 pp.

Siegel, Berl. "Should We Confirm Those Who Know No Hebrew?" *Jew Teach* 29 (Dec. 1960): 9.

Spiro, Jack D. "A Curriculum for the Confirmation Department of the Religious School." Master's thesis, HUC–JIR, 1958.

Steinbach, Alexander A. "The Teaching of the God Idea to the Confirmands." *Jew Ed* 11 (Apr. 1939): 45–48.

Stern, Norton B. "A Unit on Jewish Theology, Ethics, and Comparative Religion for a 15–16 Year Confirmation Class." *Jew Teach* 24 (Jan. 1956): 12–13.

Weitz, Martin M. *A Tercentenary Manual for the Confirmation Class*. N.Y.: UAHC, 1954.

Wolfe, Arnold Jacob. *Challenge to Confirmands: An Introduction to Jewish Thinking*. N.Y.: Scribe, 1963. 161 pp.

ADOLESCENCE AND ITS IMPLICATIONS

Anisfeld, M., S. R. Manoz, and W. E. Lambert. "The Structure and Dynamics of the Ethnic Attitudes of Jewish Adolescents." *J of Abnormal Social Psychology* 66 (1963): 31–36.

Bauman, Morton A. "A Study of the Nature of and the Conflicts between the Jewish and Non-Jewish Environment of Adolescent Jewish Children." Master's thesis, HUC–JIR, 1937.

Berger, Helene. *The Teenager: A Major Target in Jewish Education*. General Assembly, Jewish Welfare Federations, Nov. 1978. 10 pp.

* Blank, Irwin. *A Guide for Teachers of Adolescents in Reform Jewish Religious Schools*. Columbia U., 1958. 193 pp.

Boroff, D. J. "The Structure and Dynamics of the Ethnic Attitudes of Jewish Adolescents." *Annals of the American Academy of Political and Social Science* 331 (1961): 79–80.

Brown, Fred. "The Nature and Needs of the Older Adolescent." In *The High School Department*, edited by Walter H. Plaut, 1–10. N.Y.: UAHC, 1962.

Cohen, Montague N. A. "Religious Influences of Childhood upon Adolescence." *CCAR* 17 (1908): 239–51.

Committee on Education, CCAR (Frederick C. Schwartz, chair). "Adolescent Education: Informal Structure in the Formal Setting," *CCAR*, 89 (1979): 23–29.

Davis, Maurice. "Accommodating Jewish Learning to the Adolescent Years." *Jew Teach* 32 (Feb. 1964): 10–13.

Davis, Moshe. "From Adolescence to Jewish Maturity." *Syn Sch* 10 (Dec. 1951): 4–7.

Dinerman, M. "Some Socio-Cultural Patterns of Jewish Teen-Agers." *JSSQ* 31 (1955): 353–58.

Dubin, C. "Democratic and Religious Attitudes of Jewish Adolescents." *Ped Rep* 20 (June 1969): 19–20.

Ephraim, Miriam R. "Meeting the Needs of Today's Jewish Teen Agers." *J Jew Com Ser* 36 (1959): 22–31.

Gerard, Bert S. *The Junior High School Youth Group*. N.Y.: UAHC.

Godshaw, Alfred T. "A Suggestion as to Reaching the Adolescent." *CCAR* 16 (1906): 251–61.

Goldstein, M. "Motivations and Attitudes of Hebrew High School Students." *Syn Sch* 27 (Fall 1968): 70–80.

Grad, Eli, ed. *The Teenager and Jewish Education*. Educators Assembly of the USA, 1967 Yearbook Committee.

Greenberg, Simon. "We and Our Teen Agers." *Syn Sch* 27 (Fall 1968). See also *Ped Rep* 20 (Mar. 1969): 18–23.

Hachen, David S. "An Experimental Problems Core Curriculum in Meeting the Life-Need of Jewish Adolescents in the First Year of the Religious High School." Master's thesis, HUC–JIR, 1952.

Harris, S. W. "The Expressed Interests of 200 Jewish Teenagers." *J Jew Com Ser* 32 (1956): 406–13.

Katzoff, Louis. "Jewish Youth and Their Values." In *Teen*, 138–45.

Lampner, Carl. "An Approach to Informal Jewish Education for Adolescents." In *Teen*, 160–67.

Landesman, Alter F. "The Adolescent: Some of His Interests and Conflicts." *RA* (1933–38): 308–21.

Lewis, Albert L. "The Jewish Teenager: A Rabbi's View." *Syn Sch* 21 (Feb. 1962): 2.

Lipnick, Bernard. "An Organic Peer Community—An Experiment in Jewish Teen-Age Education." *Jew Ed* 43 (Winter–Spring 1975): 38–41, 45.

Newman, Louis. "The Jewish Teenager." *Syn Sch* 21 (1962): 3.

Olitzky, Kerry M. "Spiritual Antidotes for Jewish Adolescents." *Compass* 9 (Fall 1986): 5, 20.

Peterson, J. L., and N. Zill. *American Jewish High School Students: A National Profile*. N.Y.: AJC, National Jewish Family Center. 32 pp.

Pollak, George. "Adolescent Attitudes." *Ped Rep* 29 (Spring 1978).

Rosen, Bernard Carl. *Adolescence and Religion: The Jewish Teenager in American Society*. Cambridge, Mass.: Schenkman, 1965. 218 pp.

Rosenbloom, J. R., and P. S. Dobinsky. "Student Attitudes in a Reform Jewish Religious School." *Rel Ed* 63 (July/Aug. 1968): 323–27.

Rudavsky, David. "Education for Adolescents." *Congress Weekly* (Mar. 22, 1954): 8–10.

Sanua, Victor D. "Empirical Studies on the Jewish Adolescent." In *The Jewish Adolescent*, edited by A. Pins and H. Sainer. N.Y.: JEC, 1965.

———. "The Jewish Adolescent." *Jew Ed* 38 (June 1968): 36–52.

———. "Jewish Education and Attitudes of Jewish Adolescents." In *Teen*, 112–37.

Schoenberg, Elliot S. "Conservative Judaism and Adolescence." *Rel Ed* 81 (Spring 1986): 251–56.

"Selected Papers Delivered at the Conference on the Needs of the Adolescent (Dec. 24–25, 1967)." *Syn Sch* 27 (Fall 1968). 89 pp.

Shapiro, Harvey. "Ha Lachma Anya and B'Chol Dor—Humility, Freedom, and Historical Transcendence: Teaching the Haggadah to High School Students." A guide to teach the Haggadah on an advanced level. Master's thesis, HUC–JIR, 1983.

Simon, E. "Suburbia, Its Effect on the American Jewish Teenager." *J of Educational Sociology* 36 (1962): 124–33.

Slesinger, Zalmen. "Programming for the Education of the Adolescent." *Ped Rep* 13 (1962).

Spiegler, S. "Teenagers, Jewish Tradition, and Modern Problems." *J Jew Com Ser* 46 (Winter 1969).

Spotts, Leon S. "The Student Council of Secondary Jewish Schools." In *Teen*, 95–99.

Teplitz, Saul I. "The Jewish Adolescent and Informal Education." *Syn Sch* 27 (Fall 1968): 41–45.

Tofield, Sanders A. "Adolescent Education in the Smaller Community." *Syn Sch* 10 (1951): 22.

USA. *Manual PEP II: Parent Education for Parents of Jewish Adolescents*. N.Y.: USCJE, 1976.

Wallace, Herrice P. "The Jewish Teenager in American Society from 1940–1965." Master's thesis, Tablet Theological Seminary.

Warshaw, Efraim. "Jewish High School Student Attitudes toward Education." *Jew Ed* 41 (Fall 1972): 25–32.

Wollman, Benjamin. "An Appraisal of Current Literature on the Jewish Adolescent." *JSS* 13 (Oct. 1951): 333–44.

———. "על היצירה הספרותית בגיל הנעורים„ (Literary Creativity in Adolescence). *Sh Hah* (H.) 9 (Oct. 1949): 163–75; 10 (Dec. 1949): 10–24.

EVALUATION

Braver, Joseph. "The Survey of United Synagogue High School—1973." *Syn Sch* 32 (Summer 1974): 4–7.

Carp, Joel M. "Social Group Work Impact upon the Jewish Identification of High School Age Youth: A Report on a Program Demonstration." *J Jew Com Ser* 43 (Winter 1966): 189.

Gillman, Neil. "The Hebrew High School and College." *Syn Sch* 26 (Fall 1967): 16–27.

Grad, Eli. "Factors Related to Continuity in Jewish Education." *Syn Sch* 23 (Fall 1964): 13.

Hochberg, Hillel, and Gerhard Lang. "The Jewish High School in 1972–73: Status and Trends." *AJYB* 75 (1974–75): 235–76.

Horowitz, David. "After High School—What?" *Jew Teach* 34 (Feb. 1966).

Hurvitz, Aharon. „מקומה של הלשון העברית בחינוכו של המתבגר" (Place of the Hebrew Language in the Education of the Adolescent) (H.). In *Teen*, 199–205.

"Jewish Education through the High School Years." *Syn Sch* 18 (Sept. 1959).

Krakower, Isidore E. "Maintaining Educational Standards for High School Students." *Syn Sch* 9 (Jan. 1951): 20–21.

Kuselewitz, David. "A Responsum—On Some Issues in Jewish Education." *Jew Ed* 43 (Spring 1974): 37–39. High school.

Lakritz, William B. "A Bird's-Eye View of Our High School Department." *Jew Teach* 15 (Apr. 1947): 1–21.

Lampner, Carl. "Youth Looks at Jewish Education." *Syn Sch* 25 (1966): 17.

* Levine, Ronald A. *Cultural Conflict, Personality Attributes, and Patterns of Achievement in a Jewish Secondary School*. California School of Professional Psychology, 1978. 220 pp.

Levitats, Isaac. „חינוך תיכוני, למה?" (Secondary Education—For What?). *Sh Hah* (H.) 28 (1968).

Lewis, Albert L. "Report on Preliminary Survey." *Syn Sch* 10 (Dec. 1951): 7–11. High school.

* Lilker, Martin. *Educational Policy and Decision-Making in the Jewish Secondary School*. Yeshiva U., 1977. 142 pp.

Lipman, Steve. "Curriculum Cutback: Survey Finds Few High Schools Offer Courses on Holocaust." *Jewish Week* (Aug. 23, 1985).

Pilch, Judah. *The Contemporary Jewish Scene for High School Students*. N.Y.: AAJE, 1963.

Pollak, George, and Gerhard Lang. *The Supplementary Jewish High School*. N.Y.: AAJE, 1980). 52 pp.

Ravid, Moshe. „הצעות לשיפורו של בית הספר העברי התיכון" (Proposals for the Improvement of Jewish Secondary Education). *Sh Hah* (H.) (Spring 1967): 78–85.

"Recent High School Texts on Jewish Religion." *Syn Sch* 19 (1961): 24.

Rudavsky, David. "Four Decades of the Hebrew High School." *Jew Ed* 24 (Fall 1953): 4–5.

———. "The Status of the Jewish Secondary School." *Jew Ed* 30 (Winter 1960): 64–65. See also *Rel Ed* 56 (Mar.–Apr. 1961).

Schindler, Pesach. "A 'Follow-Up' Survey of the United Synagogue High Schools: 1967." *Syn Sch* 27 (Fall 1968): 37–40.

———. "The Survey of the United Synagogue Hebrew High Schools: 1965–1966." *Syn Sch* 25 (Fall 1966): 4–10.

Siegel, Morton. "Effectiveness of the High School Curriculum." In *Teen*, 25–32.

Singer, Mrs. M. M. "Raising Standards for the High School." *Jew Teach* 24 (May 1956): 3–5.

Spotts, Leon S. "Structural Variations in the Jewish High School." *Syn Sch* 34 (Spring 1976): 20–29.

Tarnor, Norman. "Problems in the Hebrew High School Level: Student Caliber." *Jew Ed* 31 (Winter 1961): 34–37, 40.

Wachs, Saul P. "The Congregational Hebrew High School." *Syn Sch* (Fall 1968): 59–69.

Warshaw, Ephraim. "The Junior High School of Today and Tomorrow." In *Ed As* (1970), 71–78.

Winter, Nathan H. "A Shift in the Emphasis in the Structure of Jewish Education." (The junior high school.) *Syn Sch* 28 (Spring 1970): 12–16.

BOOKS, MINI COURSES, AND TEXTS (SELECTED)

(See also chapters 6, 11, 15, and 16)

Blumenthal, Aaron H. *If I Am Only for Myself: The Story of Hillel*. N.Y.: US Book Service. Grades 9–12.

Chazan, Robert L. *A Jewish History Syllabus*. Experimental ed. N.Y.: USCJE, ca. 1975. 65 pp. High school.

Cohen, Henry. *Why Judaism?* N.Y.: UAHC. Grades 8–11.

Eisenstein, Ira. *What We Mean by Religion.* N.Y.: Reconstructionist Press, 1958. 173 pp. High school.

Elkins, Marilyn. *Halakha and Jewish Values.* LA: HUC–JIR, 1986.

Fackenheim, Emil. *Paths to Jewish Belief.* N.Y.: Behrman, 1960. Teacher's guide. Grades 9–10.

Fox, Marcia. *Reform Judaism and Mitzvot.* L.A.: HUC–JIR, Tartak Learning Center, 1984.

Gittelsohn, Roland B. *Little Lower than the Angels.* N.Y.: UAHC, 1951, 1955. 334 pp.

———. *Modern Jewish Problems.* Cincinnati: UAHC, 1953. Teacher's guide by Harvey J. Fields (UAHC, ca. 1966). 123 pp.

Glustrom, Simon. *The Language of Judaism.* N.Y.: Jonathan David. Grades 9–11.

Grayzel, Solomon. *History of the Jews.* JPS. Grades 10–12.

Jacobs, Louis. *The Book of Jewish Belief.* Behrman. Grades 9–11.

Joseloff, Samuel H., ed. *An Anthology of Contemporary Jewish American Poets.* N.Y.: UAHC. Grades 10–12.

Karp, Abraham. *The Jewish Way of Life.* Englewood Cliffs, N.J.: Prentice-Hall, 1962. Grades 10–11.

Lutz, Barry. *The Mystic Perspective.* L.A: HUC–JIR, Tartak Learning Center, 1984.

Nadel, Max. *American Jewish Literature for High School Grades.* N.Y.: JEC Press, 1973.

Pilch, Judah. *Fate and Faith: The Contemporary Jewish Scene.* N.Y.: Bloch, 1963. 206 pp. High school.

Reich, Cindy. *Redemption—A Curriculum for High School Students.* L.A.: HUC–JIR, Tartak Learning Center.

Rosenthal, Gilbert S. *The Many Faces of Judaism: Orthodox, Conservative and Reform Ideologies.* N.Y.: Behrman, 1978. Junior and senior high schools.

Roth, Shana, and Sheri Ellowitz Silver. *A Course in Jewish Folk Art.* L.A.: HUC–JIR, Tartak Learning Center, 1982.

Sasso, Sandy Eisenberg, and Sue Levi Elwell. Jewish Women: *Preserving Life, Studying and Teaching, Seeking God, Building Community,* *Making Connections. KP* mini course. Student manual, 40 pp. Leader's manual, 53 pp.

Schwartzman, Sylvan D. *Reform Judaism Then and Now.* N.Y.: UAHC, 1971. Grades 10–12.

Serotta, Isaac. *Film and the Jewish Self.* L.A.: HUC–JIR, Tartak Learning Center, 1984.

Silverman, William B. *Judaism and Christianity: What We Believe.* N.Y.: Behrman. Grades 8–9.

Singer, Howard. *With Mind and Heart—An Approach to Judaism for Young People.* N.Y.: USCJE, 1961. 312 pp. Grades 8–12.

Trepp, Leo. *A History of the Jewish Experience: Eternal Faith, Eternal People.* N.Y.: Behrman. Grades 9–11.

GLEANINGS

Jewish Education Society of Chicago, September 15, 1876,

"Israelites of Chicago: What have you done for preserving our faith and transmitting the noble bequest of ages to posterity? . . . True, you have raised your children as Jews, but do you believe that they, after having attended the Sabbath school up to the time of their confirmation, will be able to expound and to defend Judaism before the world? Or do you know of any of them desirous of pursuing the study of Jewish lore and history, in order to know what Judaism is, and what it has accomplished in its wonderful march? And suppose there are such people, what opportunities have they of studying Hebrew and acquiring the knowledge indispensable for a thorough understanding of Judaism? Where are the schools from which you expect your future rabbis and teachers and the well-read laymen to come? The latter can certainly not be imported from the old country for the purpose of upholding our institutions.

We must have a Jewish high school in every large community, where especially gifted young people from their eleventh or twelfth year are to be advantageously taught in Hebrew literature and Jewish history, in addition to various branches of general high school the Hebrew forming an organic part of the entire school system; where, moreover, lessons in Jewish religion, history and literature are given twice or thrice during the week to such young people who are anxious to receive information about Judaism, while pursuing their mercantile or scientific course during the day."

Quoted by Louis Wirth in *The Ghetto* (1975), 176–77.

Wessel, Harvey A.,
"An identification of self with the eternal, wandering community of Israel—which is continually interrelating itself with non-Jewish communities and the Great Society—is the determining factor in the aim of a high school curriculum."
CCAR Yearbook 33 (1923), 306.

Essrig, Harry, on confirmation,
"The true religious expression of the child, in all its simplicity and naivete is more significant than an highly illuminating discourse on Israel's past memorized and spouted forth. There can be nothing finer nor more moving than the child's struggle for expression of his sentiments and emotions. The ceremony then ceases to be a parrot procession but becomes instead a sincere religious activity, long to be cherished in the memory of the participant."
Jew Teach 6 (Jan. 1938), 8.

Parzen, Herbert,
"Judaism is not a religion . . . that can be expressed or formalized in a creedal catechism. . . . It is the dynamic religious civilization of the Jewish people. . . . It has always required prolonged study to be understood. . . . Jewish educators are well aware that the elementary schools are not able to provide the Jewish community with a Jewish literate laity."
"The Need for a System of Secondary Jewish Education." *Recon* (June 14, 1957), 18.

Rudavsky, David,
"We may conclude that the movement for adolescent Jewish education beyond the elementary school has undergone an unprecedented numerical growth. In New York City, 7.4% of all Jewish students of high school age are exposed to some form of Jewish schooling; in the three adjacent counties, 11.3%; in the country as a whole 14%, or nearly twice the proportion in New York City. Outside the city, the ratio is even higher, around 18%. Though these figures still represent a small minority of our teen-agers, further quantitative expansion, though important, is not an immediate problem. We should be far more concerned with the absence of proper standards in our supplementary high schools and with the fact that such a large proportion of our youth—about 50%, receive only a minimal Jewish training in a One Day school."
Rel Ed (Mar./Apr. 1961).

USA Conference on the Needs of the Jewish Adolescent
"Whereas, Jewish Education on the secondary level constitutes an indispensible link in the chain of ongoing Jewish study, which has been an integral part of Jewish life throughout the ages, and inasmuch as the adolescent years provide a unique opportunity for the expansion of intellectual horizons and the development of deep-seated convictions and postures . . . Therefore, be it resolved that secondary Jewish Education should be the area of special and intensive concern in American Jewish Education and in the organized Jewish community at large."
Syn Sch 27 (Fall 1968), 81.

Hochberg, Hillel, and Gerhard Lang.
"The over-all enrollment prospects did not appear promising. . . . Of far greater and more immediate concern was the indication that the quality of schooling and exposure to instruction has been minimal for the large majority of pupils in the supplementary high school. Approximately 70 per cent of these youngsters attend school for two years or less, most of them about two hours per week. Even with the best teachers and the most intensive curriculum, it would be unreasonable to expect more than a modicum of achievement. . . . It was gratifying to find that a very large proportion of schools sponsored various types of informal educational programs."

"The Jewish High School in 1972–73." *AJYB* 75 (1974–75): 274–75.

AJC, *The Colloquium Papers,*
A. "The Colloquium recommends that it be a Jewish communal responsibility to make possible, in plural and diverse ways, educational opportunities and environments at a high school level of excellence for persons of high school age."
Jewish Education and Jewish Identity: Summary Report and Recommendations (N.Y.: AJC, 1976), 23.

Slesinger, Zalmen,
"Jewish education, particularly for high school-adult groups, must be largely contemporized in spirit and emphasis and concern itself with the entire spectrum of issues confronting the Jewish community."
Jud 28 (Spring 1979), 231–32.

Heimowitz, Joseph,
"The study indicates that there is a perceived school influence on the adult life style of the graduates of a yeshivah high school. It shows that a Yeshivah high school education is the most promising form of secondary education today in promoting Jewish awareness and commitment."
"Jewish Education Makes a Difference—A Study of the Graduates of a Yeshivah High School." *Jew Ed* 47 (1979), 33.

Kaunfer, Neil,
"As I see it, our basic decision regarding future directions for Hebrew high school is one of philosophy, which needs to be made in each school individually, between a more progressive and a more conservative model of education. This choice must be based upon consideration of the implications of each style not only for the present but based upon speculation of the evolving and changing needs of the future American Jewish community. But whichever direction chosen, there is need for curricular, methodological and administrative consistency with that philosophy. The current inconsistencies are sending off confusing messages to our youth."
"Directions for Supplementary Hebrew High Schools in the Eighties" *Jew Ed* 48 (Winter 1980), 38.

National Commission on Torah Education,
"The aim of the Hebrew High School Curriculum must be to attract students to the school, and then maintain the interest. Since student interests vary, the ideal secondary school curriculum:

1) Must be flexible and provide the widest choice of elective subjects.

2) Must be taught by inspiring, experienced, and sympathetic teachers who are aware of the special needs of the Jewish teenager.

3) Should contain many informal, social, and activity experiences that are so important to adolescents.

4) Must utilize the most modern media and instructional techniques that our students experience in their public high schools."
Curriculum Guide for Afternoon Religious Schools, edited by Eli Baum (1979), 179.

19 AMERICAN JEWRY AND THE LAND OF ISRAEL

PRIOR TO 1948 (SELECTED)

Adler, Cyrus. "American Jewry and Palestinian Jewry." In *Lectures and Selected Papers Addresses*. Phila.: 1933. 306–17.

Allen, Lewis I. "The Founding of the City of Ararat, on Grand Island by Mordecai M. Noah." In *Publications of the Buffalo Historical Society*, 305–28. 1979.

Avukah Annual: Fifth Anniversary Edition, 1925–1930. N.Y.: Avukah, American Student Zionist Federation, 1930. 135 pp.

Baron, Salo W., and Jeanette M. Baron. "Palestinian Messengers in America, 1849–1879." *JSS* 5 (Apr. 1943): 115–62.

Berger, Elmer. *The Jewish Dilemma*. N.Y.: Devin-Adair Co., 1945.

Berkowitz, Henry. "Why I Am Not a Zionist." *CCAR* 9 (1899): 167. Also in *BJR*, 371–73.

Brandeis, Louis D. *The Jewish Problem: How to Solve It*. (Address before the Eastern Council of the CCAR, June 1915.) N.Y.: ZOA, 1939. 15 pp.

Cohen, Naomi. "The Reaction of Reform Judaism in America to Political Zionism, 1897–1922." *Publications of the American Jewish Historical Society* 40 (June 1951): 361–94.

──────. "*The Maccabean*'s Message: A Study in American Zionism Until World War I." (Official American Zionist journal 1901–19?) *JSS* 18 (July 1956): 163–78.

Cohon, Samuel S. "Palestine in Jewish Theology." In *Hebrew Union College Jubilee Volume, 1875–1925*, 171–209. Cincinnati.

The Collegiate Zionist. N.Y.: Collegiate Zionist League, July 1910. 26 pp.

Doniger, A., ed. *A Zionist Primer*. N.Y.: Young Judea, 1917. 80 pp.

Eisenstein, Ira. "Reconstructionism and Zionism." *Recon* 8. See also *Zionism* (N.Y.: Jewish Reconstructionist Foundation, 1943), 23–30.

Epstein, Judith G. "Hadassah." In *PYB*, 1:384–88.

Feinstein, Marvin. *American Zionism 1884–1904*. N.Y.: Herzl Press, 1965. 320 pp.

* Fox, Maier B. *American Zionism in the 1920's*. George Washington U., 1979.

Fram, Leon. "Reform Judaism and Zionism—A Zionist Interpretation" (1920). In *Reform Judaism: Essays by HUC Alumni*, 174–95. Cincinnati: HUC Press, 1949.

Freehof, Solomon. "Reform Judaism and Zionism: A Clarification." *Menorah J* 32 (Spring 1944): 26.

Gellman, Leo. "Mizrachi Organization of America." In *PYB*, 1:405–6.

Glassman, Leo M. "Bnai Zion." In *PYB*, 1:389–91.

19 AMERICAN JEWRY AND THE LAND OF ISRAEL

Goldblatt, Charles Israel. "The Impact of the Balfour Declaration in America." *American Jewish History Quarterly* 57 (June 1968): 455–515.

Goldstein, Belle J. "Mizrachi Women's Organization of America." In *PYB*, 1:407–8.

Gottheil, Richard J. H. *Zionism*. Phila.: JPS, 1924. 258 pp.

* Grand, Samuel. *A History of Zionist Youth Organizations from Their Inception to 1940*. Columbia U., 1958.

Grinstein, Hyman B. "The Memoirs and Scrapbooks of Joseph Isaac Bluestone of New York City." (On Orthodox Jewry and Zionism in America.) *PAJHS* 35 (1939): 53–64.

———. "Orthodox Judaism and Early Zionism in America." In *EHZA*, 219–28.

Halpern, Ben. "The Americanization of Zionism, 1880–1930" *AJH* 69 (Sept. 1979): 15–33.

Hechalutz Organization of America. *Hechalutz, Builders and Fighters: Pioneering for Palestine*. N.Y.: HO of A, 1946.

Jastrow, Morris, Jr. "The Objections to a Jewish State." *Menorah J* 4 (June 1918): 130.

Eretz Israel. Jubilee volume, 30th anniversary of the Jewish National Fund (1901–30). N.Y.: Jewish National Fund for America, 1932. 300 pp.

Kabakoff, Jacob. "Beginnings of Hibbat Zion (Love of Zion) in America." In *Herzl Yearbook*, edited by Raphael Patai, 255–64. 1964–65.

Kaplan, Mordecai M. "The Land of Israel." In *Judaism as a Civilization*, 264–79. 1934, 1957.

Knee, Stuart E. "Jewish Non-Zionism in America and Palestine Commitment, 1917–1941." *JSS* 39 (Summer 1977): 209–26.

Kohler, Max J. "Some Early American Zionist Projects." *PAJHS* 8 (1900): 75–118.

* Kutcher, Carol B. *The Role of Hadassah in the American Zionist Movement, 1912–1922*. Brandeis U., 1975.

Levies, Caspar. "The Justification of Zionism." *CCAR* 9 (1899): 179. Also in *BJR*, 379–92.

Levin, Herschel. "The Other Side of the Coin." (On the pro-Zionist role of some Reform leaders prior to 1920.) In *Herzl Yearbook*, edited by Raphael Patai, 35–63. N.Y.: Herzl Press, 1963.

Levin, Meyer. *If I Forget Thee: A Picture Story of Modern Palestine*. N.Y.: Viking, 1947. 143 pp.

* Levine, Samuel H. *Changing Concepts of Palestine in American Literature to 1867*. New York U., 1953. 340 pp.

———. "Palestine in the Literature of the United States to 1867." In *EHZA*, 21–38.

Levitas, Irving. "Reform Judaism and Zionism, 1919–1922." *AJA* 14 (Apr. 1962): 5–19.

Lipsky, Louis. *Thirty Years of American Zionism*. N.Y.: 1927.

Melamed, Samuel M. *Forty Years of Zionism*. N.Y.: ZOA. 47 pp.

Meyer, Isidor S., ed. *Early History of Zionism in America*. N.Y.: AJHS and Theodor Herzl Foundation, 1958. 340 pp.

Noah, Mordecai Manuel. "Discourse on the Restorations of the Jews." In *Schappes*, 247–52. See also Isaac Goldberg, *Major Noah* (N.Y.: Knopf, 1937), 316.

Noble, Shlomo. "Pre-Herzlian Zionism in America as Reflected in the Yiddish Press." In *EHZA*, 39–54.

* Oder, Irwin. *The United States and the Palestine Mandate, 1920–1948: A Study of American Foreign Policy with Special Attention to the Influence of Jewish Groups*. Columbia U., 1956.

Parzen, Herbert. "The Federation of American Zionists (1897–1914)." In *EHZA*, 245–74.

Patai, Raphael, ed. *Herzl Yearbook: Studies in the History of Zionism in America, 1894–1919*. N.Y.: Herzl Press, 1963.

Plesur, Milton. "The American Press and Jewish Restoration During the Nineteenth Century." In *EHZA*, 55–76.

Pool, David De Sola. "Early Relations between Palestine and American Jewry." In *BAA*, 536–48.

Popper, William. "One Hundred Available Books in English on Palestine." *AJYB* 7 (1905–6): 153–62.

Richards, Bernard. "Zionism in the United States." In *The Zionist Movement*, edited by I. Cohen (N.Y: ZOA, 1946), 326–46.

Rischin, Moses. "The Early Attitude of the American Jewish Committee to Zionism." *PAJHS* 49 (Mar. 1960): 188–201.

Rothbard, Dvorah. "Pioneer Women's Organization." In *PYB*, 398–401.

Samuel, Maurice. *Harvest in the Desert*. Phila.: JPS, 1944. 316 pp.

Segal, Louis. "The Jewish National Worker's Alliance and Its Palestine Activities." In *PYB*, 402–4.

Seller, M. S. "Isaac Leeser's Views on the Restoration of a Jewish Palestine." *AJHQ* 58 (1968): 118–35.

Sherman, C. Bezalel. "The Beginnings of Labor Zionism in the United States." In *EHZA*, 275–88.

Shubow, Joseph Sh., ed. *The Brandeis Avukah Annual of 1932: A Collection of Essays in Contemporary Zionist Thought*. Boston: American Student Zionist Federation-Avukah, 1932. 808 pp.

Silver, Abba Hillel. "Israel." *CCAR* 45 (1935). See also *BJR*, 415–36.

Soltes, Avraham. "Palestine in the Poetry and Song of the Jewish Diaspora." Master's thesis, HUC–JIR, 1942.

Spiro, Saul. "Zionist Organization of America." In *PYB*, 374–83.

Spizman, L., ed. א פערטל יארהונדערט הסתדרות (A Quarter of a Century of Histadruth) (Y.). N.Y.: National Committee for Labor Palestine, 1946. 300 pp.

Steinberg, Milton. *The Creed of an American Zionist*. N.Y.: Committee on Unity for Palestine, 1945. 21 pp.

Sternstein, Joseph P. "Reform Judaism and Zionism 1895–1904." In *Herzl Yearbook*, edited by Raphael Patai, 11–31. N.Y.: Herzl Press, 1963.

Teller, Judd L. "Zionism, Israel, and American Jewry" (Historical). In *Jan 2*, 301–21.

Udin, Sophie A., ed. *PYB*.

Urofsky, Melvin J. *American Zionism from Herzl to the Holocaust*. N.Y.: Doubleday, 1975.

U.S. Congress. House. Committee on Foreign Affairs. *The Jewish National Home in Palestine: Hearings on H.R. 418 and H.R. 419*. 78th Cong. Washington, D.C.: Government Printing Office, 1944. 512 pp.

Weissman, Herman L. "American Zionist Youth." In *PYB*, 409–15.

Wertheim, David. "Poale Zion Organization in America." In *PYB*, 392–97.

Wice, David H. "Reform Judaism and Zionism—A Non-Zionist Interpretation" (1933). In *Reform Judaism: Essays by HUC Alumni*, 196–205. Cincinnati: HUC Press, 1949.

Zionism—Its Aspirations, Aims, and Accomplishments. N.Y.: ZOA, 1938. 14 pp.

SINCE 1948 (SELECTED)

An Approach to an American Judaism. N.Y.: American Council for Judaism, 1956.

Baron, Salo W. "The Dialogue between Israel and Diaspora." *Forum* 4 (1959): 236–44. Also in *JMW*, 617–31.

Berger, Elmer. *Judaism or Jewish Nationalism: The Alternative to Zionism*. N.Y.: Bookman-Twayne, 1957. 207 pp.

Blumenfield, Samuel M. "Israel and the Future of American Jewry." *Recon* 15 (1950). See also *TST*, 84–98.

Bokser, Ben Zion. "Israel and the American Synagogue." *The Torch* (July 1950). See also *RTJS*, 295–98.

* Breakstone, David. *The Dynamics of Israel in American Jewish Life: An Analysis of Educational Means as Cultural "Texts."* Jerusalem: Hebrew U., 1986.

Breslau, David. *Arise and Build: The Story of American Habonim*. N.Y.: Labor Zionist Youth, 1961. 207 pp.

Chertoff, Mordecai. *Zionism: A Basic Reader*. N.Y.: Herzl Press, 1975.

Cohen, Jack. "The Two-Way Stream: Israel and the Diaspora." *Recon* (Fall 1977).

Cohen, Naomi. *American Jews and the Zionist Idea*. N.Y.: Ktav, 1975. 172 pp.

"Conservative Judaism and Israel: A Symposium." *Con Jud* 11 (Spring 1957): 26–53.

Council of the Jewish Federation and Welfare Funds. "Travel, Study, and Work Opportunities for Jewish Youth in Israel." (Draft report) (May 1973). CP, 1925, 1974.

Dialogue in Israel, 1962–1989. Special annual issues on relationships between American Jewry and Israel. *Cong M.*

Dinur, Ben Zion. *Israel and the Diaspora.* Phila.: JPS, 1969. 206 pp.

Duker, Abraham G. "Some Aspects of Israel's Impact on Identification and Cultural Patterns." *JSS* 21 (1951): 25–45.

Dushkin, Alexander M. "Cultural Influences of Israel on American Jewry." *J of Educational Sociology* (Nov. 1948): 215–22.

———. "Implications of the New Developments in Palestine for Jewish Culture." *JSSQ* 26 (Sept. 1948).

„דער ערשטער מאי נומער לכבוד מדינת ישראל" (The First of May Issue in Honor of the State of Israel). *Zuk* (Y.) (May–June 1949): 259–318.

Freeman, Samuel D. "The Effects of the Establishment of the State of Israel upon Forum and Concert Programs." *JSS* 21 (Jan. 1959): 22–24.

Goldman, Nahum. "Israel and the Diaspora." *CCAR J* 19 (1972).

Grand, Samuel. *The Origins of the Hashomer Hatzair in America.* N.Y.: Hashomer Hatzair of North America, 1972. 36 pp.

"Hadoar (The Book of the Decade), Dedicated to 10 years of Israel's Independence, 1948–1958." *Hadoar* (H.) 38 (Oct. 17. 1958).

* Halperin, Samuel. *The Political World of American Zionism: Background of a Political Interest Group.* Washington U., 1956. (Detroit: Wayne State U. Press, 1961. 431 pp.)

Halpern, Ben. "The Impact of Israel on American Jewish Ideologies." *JSS* 21 (Jan. 1959): 62–81.

Hertzberg, Arthur, ed. *The Zionist Idea.* N.Y.: Herzl Press, 1963. 638 pp.

———. "Jewish Identification after the Six Day War." *JSS* 31 (1969): 267–71.

Hirsch, Richard G. "The Reform Movement's Zionism Radical Changes." *Forum* 1 (1977).

"The Influence of Zionism on the American Jewish Community: An Assessment by Israeli and American Historians" (Evyatar Friesel, Alton Gal, Melvin I. Urofsky, and Henry L. Feingold). *AJH* 75 (Dec. 1985): 129–83.

"Israel and the Diaspora: A Symposium." *Recon* 39 (Apr. 1973).

Kaplan, Mordecai M. *A New Zionism.* N.Y.: Herzl Press, 1959. 190 pp.

Karp, Abraham J. "Reactions to Zionism and to the State of Israel in the American Jewish Religious Community." *Jew J Soc* 8 (Dec. 1966): 150–74.

Klein, Debra Lynn. "North American Jews in Israel: Conflicts and Adjustments on Jewish Identity." An eight-session exploration of the dynamics of adjustment of Jewish identity when expressed in Israel. Master's project, HUC–JIR, 1982.

Laquer, Walter. *A History of Zionism.* Holt, Rinehart, and Winston, 1972. 640 pp.

Levine, Etan. "Confronting the Aliyah Option." *Con Jud* (July/Aug. 1981): 42–51.

———, ed. *Diaspora.* N.Y.: Jason Aronson-Scribner's, 1982. 350 pp.

Liebman, Charles S. "The Role of Israel in the Ideology of American Jewry." *Dispersion and Unity* 10 (Winter 1970): 19–26.

Margoshes, Samuel. "Zionism's Impact on Jewish Life." In *Two Generations in Perspective,* edited by H. Schneiderman, 146–61. 1957.

"Papers and Proceedings of the Joint Conference with the Theodor Herzl Institute on the Impact of Israel on the American Jewish Community." *JSS* 21 (Jan. 1959): 1–88.

Patai, Raphael, ed. *Encyclopedia of Zionism and Israel.* 2 vols. N.Y.: Herzl Press and McGraw-Hill, 1971.

Ribalow, Menachem, ed. „בשער הבית השלישי" (At the Gate of the Third Temple). In *Sefer Hashanah,* 13–27. N.Y.: Histadruth Ivrith, 1949.

* Rolnick, Don. *A Study of Attitudes toward Israel of American-Jewish Youth Participating in a Seminar Institute in Israel.* New York U., 1965. 332 pp.

Sachar, Howard M. *A History of Israel from the Rise of Zionism to Our Times.* N.Y.: Knopf, 1976. 883 pp.

"Salute to Israel." *Congress Weekly* 25 (May 12, 1958): 3–41.

Schindler, Alexander M. "Israel and the Diaspora—Our Responsibility." *CCAR* 84 (1974): 137–40.

* Schmidt, Sarah L. *Horace M. Kallen and the Americanization of Zionism*. U. of Maryland, 1973.

The Second Aliyah: An Anthology. N.Y.: Zionist Youth Council, 1955. 96 pp.

Selavan, Ida Cohen. "Attitudes of American Jews towards Palestine (Israel) from 1945–1950 as Reflected in the American Jewish Press." Master's thesis, Dropsie College, 1971.

Sherman, C. Bezalel. "Zionism or Pro-Israelism?" *Jew Fron* (Dec. 1959): 4.

Sklare, Marshall, and Benjamin B. Ringer. "A Study of Jewish Attitudes toward the State of Israel." In *JES*, 437–54.

Sloan, Jacob. "American Jewish Community and Israel." *AJYB* 55 (1954): 114–26.

Teller, Judd L. "America's Two Zionist Traditions." *Commentary* 20 (Oct. 1955): 343–52.

Urofsky, Melvin T. *We Are One: American Jewry and Israel*. Garden City, N.Y.: Anchor Press/Doubleday, 1978. 536 pp.

Whartman, Eliezer. "Attitudes of American Rabbis on Zionism and Israel." *JSS* 17 (Apr. 1955): 121–32.

* Zak, Ita. *Jewish Background, Self-Esteem, Jewish-American Identity and Attitudes toward Israel*. New York U., 1972.

ZION IN THE CLASSROOM BEFORE 1948

Alpert, Sumner. "Zionism on the Campus." *Jew Ed* 18 (Feb.–Mar. 1947): 40–43.

Bavli, Hillel. „מקומה של ארץ ישראל בחינוך העברי" (The Place of the Land of Israel in Jewish Education). In *Yesod*, 121–31.

Becker, Charles S. "On Trial: A Play about the White Paper Regarding Palestine." *Jew Teach* 12 (Apr. 1944): 1–17.

Chazan, Barry. "Palestine in American Jewish Education in the Pre-State Period." *JSS* 42 (Fall 1980): 229–48.

Dinin, Samuel. *Zionist Education in the United States*. N.Y.: ZOA, 1944.

Dushkin, Alexander M. "Palestine Talks to Teachers." *Jewish Teacher* 5 (1923).

———. "Sanity in the Teaching of Palestine." (Editorial.) *Jew Ed* 2 (June 1930): 65–67.

———. "Toward a Program of Zionist Education in America." In *Reorienting Zionist Education Today*. N.Y.: ZOA, 1940.

Edidin, Benjamin M. „למוד הציונות וארץ ישראל בבית הספר הגבוה" (Study of Zionism and the Land of Israel in the High School). *Sh Hah* (H.) 3 (Sept. 1943): 239–44.

———. "Teaching Palestine through Pupil Activity." *Jew Ed* 5 (Apr./June 1933): 103–8.

———. "Zionist Youth Camps." *Jew Ed* 17 (June 1946): 24–26.

Fineberg, Solomon A. "A Critical Evaluation of the Reform Religious School." (Calls for a greater emphasis on Palestine and includes discussion.) *CCAR* 39 (1929): 439–52.

Frishberg, Mrs. Leo. "March of Time." (Drama about Palestine, 1920.) *Jew Teach* 12 (Nov. 1943): 27–30.

Grand, Samuel. *Palestine and the Jewish School: A Comprehensive Manual*. N.Y.: American Zionist Youth Commission.

Honor, Leo. "A Zionist Program of Jewish Education in America." *Zionist Quarterly* (1939). Also in *Selected Writings of Leo Honor*, edited by Gannes. 1965.

Katzoff, Louis. "Objectives of Instruction on Palestine." In *Issues*, 89–95.

Nardi, Noah, ed. „ציונות וארץ ישראל בחינוך העברי באמריקה" (Zionism and the Land of Israel in Jewish Education in America). In *Jewish Education in the Diaspora* (H.) (proceedings of Foundation Conference of the World Union for Jewish Education in the Diaspora), edited by Rieger. Jerusalem: University Press, 1948.

Neumann, J. H. "The Study of the Geography of Palestine." *Jewish Teacher* 2 (June/Oct. 1918): 62–64, 80.

Palestine and the Jewish School. N.Y.: American Zionist Youth Commission, 1947.

Stright, H. L. "Teaching Values of the Legends and Myths of Israel." Master's thesis, Boston U., 1928–29.

Touroff, Nissan. „ארץ ישראל בתור גורם חנוכי" (Israel as an Educational Factor). *Sh Hah* (H.) 1 (1926): 16–25.

ISRAEL IN THE CLASSROOM SINCE 1948

Ackerman, Walter I. "Israel Today and the Jewish School." *Jew Ed* 56 (Spring 1988): 4.

———. "'The Land of Our Fathers' in the 'Land of the Free'—Textbooks on Israel in American Jewish Schools." *Jew Ed* 54 (Winter 1986): 4–14.

Adar, Zvi. „החינוך היהודי בישראל ובארצות הברית" (Jewish Education in Israel and the United States). (U.S. education on pages 161–269.) Tel Aviv: Gomeh, 1969. Available in English translation.

Ages, Arnold. "Zionist Ideologies." *Ped Rep* 30 (Winter 1979): 2–5. High school and adults.

Allon, Yigal. „תרומתה של ישראל לחינוך היהודי בגולה" (The Contribution of Israel to Jewish Education in the Diaspora). In *Proceedings of the Conference of Directors of Bureaus of Jewish Education in the United States and Canada, July 30–Aug. 15, 1971,* 119–26. Jerusalem.

———. "Education: The Key to Unity." *World Jewry* 13 (Jan./Feb. 1970): 12.

Ariav, Tamar. "Curriculum Change in the Teaching of Israel." *Ped Rep* 39 (Apr. 1988): 813.

Auerbach, Ephraim. "Response to Dr. Ernst Simon" (On the educational influence of Israel on American Jewry). In *JER,* 24–31.

Avital, Moshe. „החינוך היהודי בישראל ובתפוצות לאור מלחמת יום-הכיפורים" (Jewish Education in Israel and the Diaspora in Light of the Yom Kippur War). *Hadoar* (H.) 53 (June 14, 1974).

———. "Teaching Aliyah." *Ped Rep* 30 (Winter 1979): 14–15.

Axelroth, Dorothy. "Some Israeli Projects." *Ped Rep* 30 (Winter 1979): 28–29.

Azulary, Shimon. "The Teaching of Zionism and Israel through Biblical Sources." *Ped Rep* 30 (Winter 1979): 16–17.

Ben-Yehudah, Baruch. „מעמד בית ספר היהודי בתפוצות" (The Condition of Jewish Schools in the Diaspora) *In Honor of A. Tartakover* (Festschrift) (H.) (1970), 127–36.

———. „החינוך הציוני בבתי הספר בגולה" (Zionist Education in Schools in the Diaspora). In *PDE* (H.), 73–76.

Bennett, Alan D. "Israel and the Jewish School Today." *Jew Ed* 56 (Spring 1988): 6–8.

———. "The Teaching of Zionism in Reform Education." *Ped Rep* 30 (Winter 1979): 23–25.

———. "What Is My Responsibility to the State of Israel?" In *Jewish Community Resources,* AAJE, 1973, 93–94. Grades 6–9.

Berkson, Isaac B. „עם ישראל, הארץ והתפוצות" (The Jewish People: the land and the diaspora). *Sh Hah* (H.) 22 (Summer 1962): 217–25.

Bernstein, Louis. "Israel and the Jewish School Today." *Jew Ed* 56 (Spring 1988): 8–9.

Beth Arieh, David. „מדינת ישראל והחינוך בתפוצות כאלמנטים לאחדות האומה" (The Land of Israel and Education in the Diaspora as National Unifying Elements). In *PDE* (H.), 38–42.

Beyer, Arthur. "Unit Study Program—Modern Israel: An Effective Approach." *Compass* (Jan. 1971).

Blumenfield, Samuel M. "Department of Education and Culture of the Jewish Agency in America." *Jew Ed* 28 (Spring 1958): 64–73.

———. „חינוך ותרבות בתנועה הציונית" (Education and Culture in the Zionist Movement). In *S Ed* (H.), 119–29.

———. "Israel and American Jewry." *Syn Sch* 17 (1959): 48–52.

———. "Israel and Jewish Education in the Diaspora." *Jew Ed* 38 (Oct. 1968): 25–30.

———. „ישראל והחינוך היהודי בתפוצות" (Israel and Jewish Education in the Diaspora). *In Honor of A. Tartakover* (Festschrift) (H.) (1970), 169–74.

———. "Zionist Theory and Practice in Jewish Education." DEC, American Zionist Council, 1961. Also in *TST*, 28–35.

Bortniker, Elijah. "Nir" (Broken Ground). Published by the Teachers Council for the JNF. *Jew Ed* 21 (Spring 1950): 71–72.

Brickman, William W. "Comments on the Impact of Israel on American Jewish Education." *JSS* 21 (1959): 24.

Brickner, Balfour. "Israel, Judaism, Jewishness—and Our Youth." *CCAR J* (Apr. 1961): 39–44.

Bror, Chaim. „החינוך היהודי בין התפוצות והמדינה" (Jewish Education—A Bridge between the Diaspora and Israel). In *Scharfstein*, 134–37.

Chamiel, Haim. "Diaspora Education Today." *Mid* (May 1980): 36–39.

Charak, Gail. "Teaching Israel through Literature." Master's thesis, Brandeis U., 1972.

Chazan, Barry. "Israel in American Jewish Schools in the Mid-70's." *Jew Ed* 52 (Winter 1984–85): 9–12.

———. "Israel in American Jewish Schools Revisited." *Jew Ed* 47 (Summer 1979): 7–17.

———. "Israel and Jewish Education." In *LJE*, 95–121.

———. "The Role of Israel in Jewish Education." *Syn Sch* 24 (Winter 1966).

———. "Teaching Israel in the 70's." *CCAR J* 20 (Winter 1973): 60–70.

———. "Teaching Zionism in American Jewish Schools." *Ped Rep* 30 (Spring 1979): 28–30.

———. "Texts and Contexts: Israel in the Jewish Curriculum." *Con Jud* 25 (Winter 1971): 42–51.

———. "Towards a Theory of Israel in Jewish Education." *Dispersion and Unity* 13/14 (1971–72).

Chipkin, Israel. "Israel and American Jewish Education." *Day* (Feb. 18, 1949).

Chomsky, William. „החינוך באמריקה לאור מדינת ישראל" (Education in America—in Light of the State of Israel). *Hadoar* (H.) 37 (July 25, 1958): 650–51.

———. "Potentialities of Israel for American Jewish Education." 56 (Dec. 1965).

Cohen, Burton. "Israel and the Jewish School Today." *Jew Ed* 56 (Spring 1988): 9–11.

Cohen, Jack J. "Israel." In *JEDS*, 197–201.

———. "Israel and American Jewish Education—A View from Jerusalem." *Jew Ed* 42 (Spring 1973): 11–15.

Cohen, Steven M. *Attitudes of American Jews toward Israel and Israelis: The 1983 National Survey of American Jews and Jewish Communal Leaders*. N.Y.: AJC, 1983.

„ילקוט קטן" (A collection of materials and articles on teaching Israel in the afternoon schools) (H.). N.Y.: Jewish National Fund, Youth and Education Department, 1960. 64 pp.

"Commission on Teaching about Israel" (AAJE). *Jew Ed* (Nov. 1971).

Davis, Moshe. „החינוך כגשר בין ישראל לתפוצות" (Education as a Bridge between Israel and the Diaspora). *Gesher* (H.) (Fall 1984): 66–70.

———. "The Eretz Israel Dimension." *Con Jud* 29 (Fall 1969): 41–58.

Deutch, S. "An Approach to the Teaching of 'Israel' in Our Religious Schools." *Syn Sch* 13 (May 1954): 11–14.

Dinin, Samuel. "Israel in American Jewish Education." *Jew Ed* 42 (Spring 1973): 16–30, 33.

———. "The Role of Israel in Jewish Education." *Jew Ed* 38 (June 1968): 6–11.

Dinur, Ben Zion. „דעת העם ומקומו בחינוך היהודי בתפוצות" (View of Our People and Their Role in Jewish Education in the Diaspora.) (H.). In *FPDE*, 23–42.

Dushkin, Alexander M. "Analysis of Some Recent Developments of Jewish Education in the Diaspora." *Scripta Hierosolymitana* (1963): 56–74.

———. "The Development of a World Program for Jewish Education." *Jew Ed* 37 (1967): 169–73.

———. "Implications of the Jewish State for American Jewish Education" (Editorial). *Jew Ed* 19 (Spring 1948): 2–5.

———. "Israel and the Teaching of Jewish Identity." *Jew Ed* 42 (Spring 1973): 21–26.

———. "The Meaning of Israel for American Jewish Education." In *25th Anniversary Book of the Hebrew Teachers Federation*. L.A.: 1955.

Eisenberg, Azriel. "An Impressive Halutzic Achievement." *Syn Sch* (Summer 1972): 53–58.

———. "Israel's Impact on Jewish Education." *Jew Ed* 21 (Summer 1950): 4–5.

———. "Jewish Educational Exchange with Israel." *Jew Ed* 24 (Spring 1953): 5–6.

Elazar, Daniel J. "Israel and the Jewish School Today." *Jew Ed* 56 (Spring 1988): 11–12.

Elkin, Harry. "The Department of Education and Culture of the Jewish Agency." *Jew Ed* 34 (Fall 1963): 36–42, 50.

Engel, R. C., and J. M. Berman. "An Experimental Approach to Teaching Israel in Jewish Early Childhood." *Syn Sch* 32 (Spring 1974): 16–40.

Entin, Nathaniel A. "Recent Films and Filmstrips about Israel." *Ped Rep* 28 (1971).

Ettenberg, Sylvia C. "Opportunities for Learning about Israel for the High School Student." *Syn Sch* 27 (Fall 1968): 46–51.

Fein, Eve Melman. *In Relationship with Israel*. A ten-lesson course for high school students. L.A.: HUC–JIR, Tartak Learning Center, 1986.

Finkelstein, Hayim. „תרומה ישראל לחינוך היהודי בגולה" (The Contribution of Israel to Jewish Education in the Diaspora). *Hadoar* (H.) 50 (Aug. 6, 1971).

Fishman, Yehudah. "Zionist Education and the Youth Movements." *Ped Rep* 30 (Winter 1979.): 9–11.

Flam, Alan C. "Teaching Israel: Toward a Program for High School Youth Based upon Intensive Israel Experience." Master's thesis, HUC–JIR, 1978.

Fox, Seymour. "The Place of Israel in Our Religious Schools." *RA* (1968): 139–46.

———. *The Role of Israel in Jewish Education in the Diaspora*. Jerusalem: World Leadership Conference for Jewish Education, 1984. 8 pp.

Frank, Avraham. "Education towards Aliyah." *Ed As* (1968): 60–69.

Freidenreich, Fradle. "Idea Forum: Current Israel Programming." *Ped Rep* 24 (Winter 1973): 9–12.

Frost, Shimon. "The National Commission on the Teaching of Zionism and Israel." *Ped Rep* 30 (Winter 1979): 12–13.

Gamoran, Mamie. "Within Thy Gates—Teaching Israel." *Compass* 21 (1972–73).

Gannes, Abraham P. "Camping and Zionism/Israel." *Ped Rep* 39 (Apr. 1988): 35–37.

———. "The Centrality of Israel and the Decentrality of Jewish Education." *Forum* (Summer/Fall 1979): 41–59.

———. "Introduction" (to a symposium on teaching Israel). (Symposium participants: Hayim Abramowitz, Jacob Eckstein, Sara Feinstein, Cy L. Swartz, and Leon H. Spotts. *Ped Rep* 24 (Winter 1973).

———. "Israel's Role in American Jewish Education" (Editorial). *Jew Ed* 42 (Spring 1973): 6–10.

———. "Israel's Role in Diaspora Education." *Jew Ed* 52 (Winter 1984–85): 15–17, 28.

———. "National Council for Jewish Education: Annual Conference—Focus on Israel." *Jew Ed* 38 (Mar. 1968): 54.

———. *Report and Evaluation*. World Zionist Organization, Department of Education and Culture-American Section, 1968–78. 29 pp.

———, ed. הוראת ישראל (Teaching Israel). *Part II: An Annotated Guide to Textual Material*. (E. and H.) Jerusalem: Pedagogic Centre in Jerusalem for Jewish Education in the Diaspora, 1982. 121 pp. Comprehensive bibliography for teacher and student.

———. "When Should Your Child Visit Israel." *Your Child* 4 (Winter 1970): 10–13.

Gannes, Abraham P., and Moshe Avital. "High School Study in Israel." *Jew Ed* 42 (Spring 1973): 48–50.

Glatzer, Shoshana. "Developing a Curriculum for Teaching Israel." *Ped Rep* 39 (Apr. 1988): 13–16.

Goldberg, Hannah L. "The Educational Program of the Jewish Agency" (Interview with Hayim Greenberg). *Recon* (June 30, 1950): 8–13.

Goldman, Solomon. „הקרן המחנכת וקרן המחנך" (The Jewish National Fund and the Educator). *Ped Rep* 33:4 (Oct. 1982) (H.) 33–35.

———. "Jewish National Fund School Projects." *Ped Rep* (Apr. 1988): 30–32.

Golomb, Abraham. „על תכנית בית הספר בגולה" (On the Program of the School in the Diaspora). *Sh Hah* (H.) 14 (Fall 1954): 19–29.

Goodman, Robert. "An Israel Celebration." *Inkling* 5 (1977–78).

———. "Making Israel Come Alive." *Inkling* 4–5 (1977–78).

Greenberg, Hayim. "Jewish Culture and Education in the Diaspora" (Address at the Zionist Congress, 1951). *Jew Fron* (Mar. 1963): 18–25. Also in *YK* (Y.) (Jan. 27, 1950): 6–8, (Sept. 14, 1951): 2–4, (Nov. 16, 1951): 6–7, (Nov. 23, 1951): 9–11; *JJS*, 130–35; and *Hayim Greenberg Anthology*, edited by M. Syrkin (1968), 161–79.

Greenberg, Simon. *Israel and Zionism: A Conservative Approach*. N.Y.: USCJE. 28 pp.

———. "On the Relationship between Israel and the Diaspora." *Jew Ed* 21 (Spring 1950): 14–16.

———. "The Role of Israel in American Jewish Education." *Jew Ed* 42 (Spring 1973): 27–33.

Guttman, Nahum. "American Campers in Israel." *Jew Ed* 36 (Winter 1966): 108–11.

Hakimian, Leah. "Evaluation of Israel Summer Program." *Ped Rep* 30 (Winter 1979): 25–28.

Hammer, Zevulun. "A New Spirit in Israel-Diaspora Educational Relationships." *Jew Ed* 47 (Fall 1979): 4–5, 18.

Hartman, Emanuel. "The Day School, Israel, and Our Children." *Jew Parent* 27 (Jan. 1975).

Herman, Dorothy. *Touring Israel: An Experimental Approach to the Teaching of Israel*. Miami: CAJE, 1979.

Herman, Menahem. "A School Prepares for Israel's 40th Anniversary." *Ped Rep* 29 (Apr. 1988): 28–29.

Herman, Simon N. "American Jewish Students in Israel: A Social Psychological Study in Cross Cultural Education." *JSS* 24 (1962): 3–29.

———. "Education towards Zionism." *Forum* 5 (1962): 83–91.

Herson, Benjamin. "Providing Meaningful Experiences through Relating Ourselves to Israel." *Syn Sch* 14 (Nov. 1955): 23–24.

Hessel, Carolyn Starman. "The Kibbutz on Long Island." *AM* 7 (Fall 1976): 4–5.

———. "Teaching about Israel." *Ped Rep* 36 (Nov. 1955): 15–17.

Hirsch, Richard G. "Israel as a Resource for Jewish Education." *Jew Ed* 56 (Spring 1988): 35–38.

Horowitz, Jack. "Our Project of Friendship with the Children of Israel." *Jew Teach* 29 (Oct. 1960): 3–7. See also *Compass* 44 (Mar. 1977).

Horowitz, Stanley B., and Ben Hirsch. "Israel and the Jewish School Today." *Jew Ed* 56 (Spring 1988): 12–13.

„ידיעות למורים" (Information for Teachers) (H.). N.Y.: Council of Educators for the Jewish National Fund in the United States, 1949.

"Israel in the Classroom." *Syn Sch* 15 (Mar. 1957): 12–21.

Israel and the Jewish School in America, Objectives. N.Y.: AAJE Commission on Teaching about Israel in America, 1969.

"Israel and the Jewish School in America: A Statement of Objectives" (AAJE Commission on Teaching about Israel in America). *Jew Ed* 42 (Spring 1973): 69–70.

"Israel Study/Travel Programs for American Teen Agers" *Ped Rep* 26 (Fall 1974): 1–24.

Isseroff, Sampson A. „חידון התנ״ך הארצי" (The National Bible Contest) (H.). *Ped Rep* 39 (Apr. 1988): 41–42.

Jacoby, Emil. "Our Children Are Planting a Forest in Israel." *Syn Sch* 22 (Fall 1963).

"Jewry: Educating the Diaspora—Zionists Adopt New Priority." *Jew Obs* (July 9, 1971).

Joseph, Samuel K. "Israel as an Educational Laboratory." *Compass* 10 (Winter 1988): 13–15.

Kaufman, Jay. "The State of Israel—Means or End?" *Jew Teach* 33 (Apr. 1965).

Klein, Jenny Machlowitz. "Teaching Israel with Threads of Gold." *Ped Rep* 32 (Winter 1981): 11–12.

Kodesh, Shlomo. „חובת הציונים באמריקה לחינוך העברי" (The Obligation of American Zionists to Hebrew Education). *Hadoar* (H.) 51 (June 9, 1972).

19 AMERICAN JEWRY AND THE LAND OF ISRAEL

Kohn, Theresa. "Impact of the Jewish State on Jewish Education in America." *Recon* (Apr. 29, 1948): 17–23.

Kol, Moshe. „מהותה ותפקידיה של עליית הנוער" (Youth Aliyah: Its Task and Purposes). In *PDE* (H.), 67–72.

Kolodner, Milton A. "An Israeli Stamp Project." *Jew Teach* 22 (Mar. 1954): 12–14.

* Koolik, Murry W. *A Content Analysis of Educational Films about Israel*. New York U., 1971.

Korman, Michael. "Vision and Reality: A Message to Teachers and Parents." *Ped Rep* 39 (Apr. 1988): 25–27.

Kronish, Ronald. "Israel and the Religious School." *Jew Teach* 32 (Apr. 1964): 14–15.

———. "Israel as a Resource." In *JPH*, 293–300.

———. "Teaching Zionism." *Ped Rep* 39 (Apr. 1988): 4–7.

Krug, Mark M. "The Place of Israel in the Jewish School." *Syn Sch* 9 (Apr. 1951): 9–12.

Kuselewitz, David. "The Herzl Commemorative Year in the Jewish School." *Syn Sch* 13 (Dec. 1954): 3–7.

* ———. *Israel and American Jewry: A Curriculum Guide for Supplementary Jewish Schools*. Columbia U., 1958.

———. "Israel and Zionism in the Curriculum of Jewish Schools." *Jew Ed* 28 (Spring 1958): 74–83.

———. *Teaching Israel: A Guide for Curriculum Development*. N.Y.: Herzl Press, ca. 1964. 140 pp.

Langer, Michael. "Developing a Reform Zionist Leadership for Our Youth." *Compass* 37 (Jan. 1976).

———. *Reform Judaism and Zionism as Jewish Responses to the Modern Age*. N.Y.: Youth Division of the UAHC.

Lee, Sara S. "Defining Israel." *Compass* 10 (Winter 1988): 7, 25.

———. "Israel and the Jewish School Today." *Jew Ed* 56 (Spring 1988): 13–16.

Lehman, Emil. *Israel*. USCJE, United Synagogue of America, 1970.

Levine, Etan. "Israel, Aliyah, and Jewish Education." *Jew Ed* 48 (Winter 1980): 14–24.

Levine, Shlomo. "Israel and Jewish Education in America." *Jew Ed* 43:3, (Fall 1974): 46–47

Lewittes, Mordecai H. "Teaching Zionism" (Editorial). *Ped Rep* 30 (Winter 1979): 1.

Margolis, Henry. "Israel Programs—What's the Future?" *Jew Ed* 49 (Sum 1981): 47–48.

Margoshes, Samuel. "Practical Program for the ZOA—Educational and Aliyah." *Day* (Oct. 1, 1964).

Mehlman, Israel. „תכנית בסיסית לבתי הספר בתפוצות" (A Basic Program for Schools in the Diaspora). In *FPDE* (H.), 48–52.

Meir, Shlomo, and David Breakstone, eds. הוראת ישראל (Teaching Israel) (H. and E.). *Part 1: An Annotated Guide to Educational Media*. Jerusalem: Pedagogic Centre in Jerusalem for Jewish Education in the Diaspora, 1980. 101 pp. Extensive bibliography.

Melkman, Joseph. "Educational Policy in the Diaspora." *Forum* 4 (1959): 336–39.

Mendelsohn, Phyllis. "Yom Haatzmaut." *Compass* 17 (1970).

Miller, Israel. "Symposium: Teaching Zionism and Israel." *Jew Ed* 52 (Winter 1984–85): 4.

Mishaan, Marc. "Recommended Films and Filmstrips on Israel." *Ped Rep* 24 (Winter 1973): 27–28.

Nadel, Max. "Return to Israel." *Jew Teach* 10 (May 1952): 1–9. Grade 6.

———. "A Unit of Study on Israeli Literature." *Ped Rep* (Apr. 1988): 33–34.

Nahshon, Samuel. „מדינת ישראל ומקומה בחינוך העברי בארה״ב" (The State of Israel and Her Place in U.S. Jewish Education) *HaHinukh* (H.) 41 (Mar. 1969): 356–59.

Nardi, Noah, ed. „יסודות לחינוך העברי בתפוצות הגולה" (Fundamental Principles for Diaspora Education) (H.). Jerusalem: Department of Education and Culture of the Jewish Agency, 1958. 294 pp.

———. „ישראל וציונות בחינוך היהודי בתפוצות" (Israel and Zionism in Jewish Education in the Diaspora). In *FPDE* (H.), 101–8.

———, ed. בעיות החינוך העברי בתפוצות הגולה (Problems of Diaspora Education). In *Proceedings of the Second World Institute on*

Diaspora Education (H.). Jerusalem: DEC, 1961. 217 pp.

National Commission on Torah Education. "Suggested Hebrew School Assembly Program for Yom ha-Atzmaut." *Ped Rep* 22 (Mar. 1971): 23.

Neibert, Aimee. "Israel in Our School." *Compass* 21 (1972–73).

Neiman, David. "The UAHC Forest Project and the Religious School." *Jew Teach* 22 (May 1954): 10–12.

Novak, Bill. "Israel and Our Schools" (Editorial). *Dimensions* 5 (Summer 1971): 31–35.

Orbach, Harold. "The Teaching of Israel through the Teaching of Jewish Music." *Jew Teach* 32 (Dec. 1963). Also in *Ped Rep* 15 (June 1964): 7–8.

Penn, Ascher. „די צוויי קולטור אפטיילונגען פון דער אידישער אגענטור אין אמעריקע" (The Two Cultural Departments of the Jewish Agency in America). In *Penn* (Y.), 582–600.

Peri, Chaim. „חג העצמאות של מדינת ישראל בבית הספר היהודי-מטרות ודרכים" (Israel Independence Day in the Jewish School—Goals and Methods) (H.). *Ped Rep* 30 (Winter 1979): 32–33.

———. „על הוראת ישראל בתפוצות בשנת השלושים למדינה" (On Teaching Israel in the Diaspora on Israel's 30th Anniversary). *Hadoar* (H.) 57 (June 9, 1978).

Perla, Shoshana, Sam E. Bloch, and Abraham P. Gannes, comps. and eds. יום העצמאות (Israel Independence Day). Program materials. N.Y.: DEC–American Section. 336 pp.

Pilch, Judah. "Education for Halutziut." *Jew Ed* 32 (Winter 1962): 79–84.

———. „החינוך לציונות בארה״ב" (Education for Zionism in the U.S.). *Hadoar* (H.) 55 (Aug. 6, 1976).

Pilchik, Ely. "Teaching Israel Today." *Jew Teach* 18 (Mar. 1950): 26–27.

Pollak, George. "Israel in American Jewish Schools in the 1980's." *Jew Ed* 52 (Winter 1984–85): 12–14.

———. *A Survey on Israel/Zionism in American Jewish Schools*. N.Y.: JESNA and WZO, 1984.

Program and Activities. Jerusalem: Hebrew U., Centre for Jewish Education in the Diaspora, 1970. 12 pp.

Rackman, Emanuel. "Israel: Three Principles of Faith." *Jew Ed* 42 (Spring 1973): 34–40.

Raphael, Jacob. "Israel in the Classroom." *Jew Teach* 18 (Mar. 1950): 15–25.

Reinhold, H. "The Development of Youth Aliyah." *Jew Ed* 28 (Spring 1958): 58–63.

Reisman, Bernard, and Barry Chazan. "Israel as Jewish Education: An Analysis of the Short-Term Study Program in Israel." *Forum* 30/31 (Spring/Summer 1978).

Resnick, David. "Israel and the North American Jewish Educational Community." *Jew Ed* 56 (Spring 1988): 39–43.

Rich, S. Esther. "Collecting Israel Stamps." *Syn Sch* 13 (May 1955): 22–23.

Ronen, D. "A Study of the Effect of a Summer in Israel on American Jewish Youth." *In the Dispersion* 5/6 (Summer 1966): 211–80.

Rosenak, Michael. "On the Teaching of Israel in Jewish Schools." *Jew Ed* 42 (Winter 1972–73): 9–18.

Rosenberg, Samuel. "An Israel Activity Program for Nine and Ten Year Olds." *Syn Sch* 15 (Mar. 1957): 17–19.

Rudavsky, David. "Israel and American Education." *Jew Ed* 26 (Fall 1955): 3–4.

Rudin, Jacob. "The Place of Israel in the Curriculum of Our Religious Schools" *Jew Teach* 26 (Mar. 1958): 7–9, 12.

Sachar, Howard M. "The Diaspora and Israel: A New Dimension of Support." *Jew Ed* 45 (Winter 1977): 32–38.

Sachs, Moshe. "Teaching Mature Zionism." *Syn Sch* 9 (Spring 1951): 3–8.

Samlan, Arnold D. "Zionist Youth Groups." *Ped Rep* 39 (Apr. 1988): 38–40.

Schachter, Lifsa. "The Role of Israel, Hebrew Language and School Structure." *Jew Ed* 51 (Spring 1983): 45–48.

Schaktman, Peter B. "Israeli Arabs: The Missing Piece of Israel Education." *Compass* 10 (Winter 1988): 10, 29.

Schanin, Norman. "The Centrality of the Jewish People in Israeli and Diaspora Jewish Schools." *Jew Ed* 47 (Spring 1979): 6–13, 48.

Scharfstein, Zevi. „תקומת ישראל ותקומת החינוך העברי" (Revival of Israel and the Revival of Jewish Education). *Hadoar* (H.) 27 (12th of Tishri, 1949).

———. „השפעה של תקומת מדינת ישראל על החינוך העברי באמריקה" (Influence of the Revival of the State of Israel on Jewish Education in America). *Hadoar* (H.) 28 (Oct. 14, 1949): 1087–88.

Schenker, Avraham. "Zionist Camping in America." *Jew Ed* 36 (Winter 1966): 103–7.

Schiff, Alvin I. "Israel-Diaspora Relationships—How Can They Be Mutually Beneficial?" *Jew Ed* 49 (Fall 1981): 4–8.

———. "Israel in American Jewish Schools." *Jew Ed* 38 (Oct. 1968): 6–24.

———. "Israel in American Jewish Schools in the 1960's." *Jew Ed* 52 (Winter 1984–85): 59.

———. "Israel and the Jewish School Today." *Jew Ed* 56 (Spring 1988): 16–18.

Segal, Abraham. "Israel in Your Classroom." *Compass* 21 (1972–73).

———. "Teaching Israel." In *Teaching in the Religious School*, edited by Meyers. 1967.

Segal, Benjamin J. "'Israel' vs. 'Zionist' Education—The Summer Trip Model." *Jew Ed* 55 (Fall 1987): 30–36.

Shapira, Rina. *Attitudes toward Israel among American Jewish Adolescents*. N.Y.: Center for Urban Education.

Shapiro, Ezra. "Aspects of the WZO Role in Diaspora Jewish Education." In *Intrater*, 33–34.

Shapiro, Miriam Klein. "Israel and the Jewish School Today." *Jew Ed* 56 (Spring 1988): 18–20.

Shubow, Joseph Sh. "Jewish Education and Zionism." *American Zionist* (Sept./Oct. 1965): 20–21; (Nov. 1965): 20–22.

Siegel, Gertrude. "Return to Palestine—Then and Now." *Jew Teach* 19 (May 1951): 26–29.

Siegel, Morton. "United Synagogue Commission on Jewish Education: How Israel Is Taught." *Ped Rep* 24 (Winter 1973): 21.

Silberschlag, Eisig. "Hebrew Literature: Architect of the State of Israel." *Jew Teach* 29 (Apr. 1961).

Simon, Ernst. "The Educational Influence of Israel on American Jewry." In *JER*, 8–18.

Skirball, Haim. "Israel and the Jewish School Today." *Jew Ed* 56 (Spring 1988): 20–21.

Slesinger, Zalmen. "The Filmstrip as a Resource in Teaching about Israel." *Ped Rep* 22 (Mar. 1971): 39.

———. "Israel's Potential Role in the Education of the American Jew." *Ped Rep* 22 (June 1971): 13.

———. "The Place of Israel in the Curriculum of the Jewish School." *Ped Rep* 16 (June 1965): 13–15.

———. "Six Days in June—Some Implications for Jewish Education." *Ped Rep* 19 (Mar. 1968).

Soref, Irwin. "The Challenge of Israel." (Commentary by Sara Feinstein.) *Jew Ed* 39 (Dec. 1969): 48–52.

Soshuk, Levi, and Azriel Eisenberg, eds. *Momentous Century: Personal and Eyewitness Accounts of the Rise of the Jewish Homeland and State, 1875–1978*. Cranbury, N.J.: Cornwall Books, 1984. 421 pp.

Spiegel, Elliot D. "Israel and the Jewish School Today." *Jew Ed* 56 (Spring 1988): 21–22.

Spiro, Jack D. "Commission on Jewish Education, UAHC–CCAR." (Description of UAHC materials for Israel's 25th Anniversary.) *Ped Rep* 24 (Winter 1973): 18.

Spotts, Leon H. "Instructional Materials about and from Israel." *Jew Ed* 56 (Spring 1973): 62–68.

———. "Israel and the Jewish School Today." *Jew Ed* 56 (Spring 1988): 22–24.

Stein, Gizela. "The Teaching of Israel in the Religious School—An Exploration of New Activities and Methods." *Jew Teach* 20 (Jan. 1952): 11–26.

Steinberg, Paul. "Israel in American Reform Jewish Education." *Jew Ed* 42 (Spring 1973): 41–43.

Stern, Heidi. "Teaching Zionist Thinkers to the Adolescent." Master's thesis, HUC–JIR, 1978.

Straus, Livia. "The History and Present Reality of Israel as an Educational Imperative." *Jew Ed* 56 (1988) 31–34.

A Survey on Israel/Zionism in American Jewish Schools. (Report of the National Commission on the Teaching of Zionism and Israel, George Pollak, director, Gerhard Lang, consultant.) N.Y.: JESNA and World Zionist Organization of America, 1984. 51 pp.

"Teaching Israel in Our Schools." *JESNA Research and Information Bulletin* 58 (Aug. 1984).

"Teach Us What We Want to Know about Israel." *Compass* 21 (1972–73).

Telsner, David. "Ten Years of Zionist Torah Education in America." (Program of American Zionist Council.) *Jew Ed* 33 (Fall 1962): 42–44.

Tishkoff, Larry. *If I Forget Thee, O Jerusalem: The Centrality of Jerusalem in Jewish Life.* L.A.: HUC–JIR, Tartak Learning Center, 1984.

Tropper, Daniel. "Israel and the Jewish School Today." *Jew Ed* 56 (Spring 1988): 24–25.

Tulin, David P. "Myths and Facts about Israel and Zionism." *Ped Rep* 30 (Winter 1979): 6–9.

Yom Ha-atzmaut Observance Kit (for youth, religious school and congregational groups). N.Y.: UAHC, CJE, 1972. Includes:

    (1) Bennett, Alan D. "A Teaching Prospectus for Yom Ha-atzmaut."
    (2) Bronstein, Herbert. "A Worship Service for the Sabbath and Yom Ha-atzmaut."
    (3) "How to Organize an Israel Expo, Based on the Experience of Congregation B'nai Jeshurun, Short Hills, N.J."
    (4) "Rejoice in Zion: A Service for Israel Independence Day."
    (5) Weisberg, Stephen E. "A Worship Serice for the Sabbath and Yom Ha-atzmaut."

Warschauer, Heinz. "Israel Program for Primary Grades." *Compass* 21 (1972–73).

Weiss, Carole. "The Role of Teaching Israel in American Jewish Education." Master's thesis, Brandeis U., 1968.

Wolfson, Ronald G. "A Description and Analysis of an Innovative Living Experience in Israel." In *Stu*, 2:65–81.

———. "An Innovative Living Experience in Israel" *Jew Ed* 44 (Spring/Summer 1976): 68–80.

Wollman, Benjamin. "מקומה של ארץ ישראל בחינוך העברי באמריקה" (The Place of Israel in Jewish Education in America). *Sh Hah* (H.) 11 (1951): 84–93, 120–24.

Woocher, Jonathan S. "Israel and the Jewish School Today." *Jew Ed* 56 (Spring 1988): 25–27.

Yeger, Dvorah. "Israel Working toward the Future." *Jew Ed* 56 (Spring 1988): 28–30.

Zlotowitz, Bernard. "Israel in the Temple." *Compass* 2 (1972–73).

TEXTS AND FICTION PRIOR TO 1948 (SELECTED)

Braverman, Libbie. *Children of the Emek.* N.Y.: Furrow Press, 1937. 120 pp. Grades 2–5.

Edidin, Benjamin M. *Rebuilding Palestine.* N.Y.: Behrman, 1939. 264 pp.

Eisenberg, Azriel. *Into the Promised Land.* Cincinnati: UAHC, 1936.

Ish Kishor, Judith. *Adventure in Palestine.* 241 pp.

King, Marian. *Amnon, A Lad of Palestine.* N.Y.: Houghton Mifflin, 1931. 96 pp.

Rubinstein, Simha. *We Are Traveling to the Land of Israel* (H.). N.Y.: 1941.

Sampter, Jessie E. *The Emek: Poems on the New Palestine.* N.Y.: Bloch, 1927. 87 pp.

Scharfstein, Zevi. *Our Land* (H.). N.Y.: Shiloh, 1939.

Schwarz, J. D. *Into the Promised Land.* Cincinnati: UAHC, 1927.

Zeligs, Dorothy F. *The Story of Modern Palestine for Young People.* N.Y.: Bloch, 1944. 339 pp.

ELEMENTARY TEXTBOOKS AND WORKBOOKS SINCE 1948 (SELECTED)

Fine, Helen. *Behold the Land: A Social Studies Text.* Illustrated by R. Zamoski. N.Y.: UAHC,

**19
AMERICAN
JEWRY AND
THE LAND
OF ISRAEL**

1968, 1977. Rev. ed., 263 pp. Teacher's guide, 1971, 489 pp. Grades 5–6.

Frankel, Max, and Judy Hoffman. *I Live in Israel*. Text and activity book. N.Y.: Behrman, 1979. 127 pp. Grades 3–5.

Grand, Tamar, and Samuel Grand. *The Children of Israel*. Illustrated by A. Frankel. N.Y.: UAHC, 1973. 55 pp. Activity book, teacher's guide, 1974, 68 pp. Grades 1–3.

———. *Israel Fun Book*. Activity Book. N.Y.: WZO, 1978. Grades 4–6.

Jaffe, Bernadette. *Builders of the State of Israel*. Cleveland: Jaffe Publications. Grades 4–6.

Sasek, M. *This Is Israel*. N.Y.: Macmillan, 1962. Grades 1–3.

Scharfstein, Sol. *Israel Activity Kit*. N.Y.: Ktav. Kindergarten through grade 3.

Segal, Sheila. *Joshua's Dream*. Illustrated by Jana Peiss. N.Y.: UAHC, c. 1985. Ages 6–8.

Weilerstein, Sadie Rose. *K'Tonton in Israel*. N.Y.: National Women's League of USA, 1964. 93 pp.

Zeligs, Dorothy F. *The Story of Modern Israel*. Rev. ed. N.Y.: Bloch, 1961. 437 pp. Grades 5–6.

Hirschfield, Burt. *A State is Born*. N.Y.: Messner, 1967.

Kagan, Joan, comp. *Beyond Six Days*. N.Y.: UAHC, 1971. 104 pp. Teacher's guide, 1974, 17 pp.

Keeping Posted. *The Palestinians*. Nos. 840920 and 840922.

———. *Zionism*. No. 840450. Leader's edition no. 840452.

Kubie, Nora Benjamin, and Marc R. Silverman. *The Jews of Israel: History and Sources*. N.Y.: Behrman, 1975. 132 pp.

Lehman, Emil. *Israel: Idea and Reality*. N.Y.: USCJE, 1962, 1965, 1967. 244 pp.

Roos, Roberta M. "Haaretz—The Land: A Student Manual for Use in a Program to Teach Quasi-Philosophical Issues Relating to Zionism in the Upper Grades." Master's thesis, HUC–JIR, 1979.

Rossel, Seymour. *Israel: Covenant People, Covenant Land*. N.Y.: UAHC, 1985. 256 pp. Teacher's guide by Russell Herman.

Rothenberg, Joshua. (A Trip to Israel) (Y.). N.Y.: National Committee of LZOA, 1964. 93 pp.

SECONDARY TEXTBOOKS, GUIDES, AND WORKBOOKS

Breakstone, David, and Cindy Jochnowitz. *The Israel Experience Book*. N.Y.: Bloch, 1977. 249 pp.

Eisenberg, Azriel, and Leah Ain-Globe, eds. *Home at Last*. N.Y. Bloch, 1977. 181 pp.

Eisenberg, Azriel, and Dov Peretz Elkins. *Treasures from the Dust*. Illustrated by Michael Hopkins. (Jewish history and archaeology.) N.Y.: Abelard-Schuman, ca. 1972. 149 pp.

Elon, Amos. *Understanding Israel*. N.Y.: Behrman, 1976. 246 pp. Student workbook and teacher's guide by M. J. Sugarman. 362 pp.

Essrig, Harry, and Abraham Segal. *Israel Today*. Rev. ed. N.Y.: UAHC, 1977, 1986. 365 pp. Student workbook and teacher's guide, 61 pp.

CURRICULA, UNITS, MINI COURSES, AND MATERIALS FOR STUDENTS AND TEACHERS

Avital, Moshe, and Chaim Peri. *Israel Lamed*. N.Y.: WZO–DEC, 1977–79. Five bulletins on Israel. High school.

Bennet, Daniel. *Yisrael: A Curriculum*. N.Y.: UAHC, 1976. Elementary.

Breakstone, David. *The Israel Connection: Issues in Israeli-Diaspora Relations*. Jerusalem: Hebrew U., Samuel Mendel Melton Centre for Jewish Education in the Diaspora, 1984. 123 pp.

Brickner, Balfour. *Helping Our Children Identify with Israel*. N.Y.: UAHC, 1969. High school.

Cohen, Jack. *Israel, Zionism and the American Jew*. Washington, D.C.: B'nai B'rith Youth Organization, 1970. 62 pp.

Feinstein, Sara, and Hyman Chanover, eds.

Viewpoints: Major Issues Facing the State of Israel.

    Bruckerman, Yigal. *Aliyah.*

    Bruckerman, Yigal, and Marcia Kaunfer. *Coming of Age in Israel.*

    Feder, Chaim, and Sara Feinstein. *Swords into Plowshares: Ethics of War and Peace.*

    Seldin, Ruth. *The Arab Minority.*

    ———. *Israel: Your Neighbor and You.*

    ———. *Jewish State and the Jewish Religion.*

    ———. *A New Society.*

    ———. *The Roots of the Jewish-Arab Conflict.*

    ———. *Why a Jewish State.*

    Singer, Herman. *Israel on the World Scene.*

Goodman, Robert. *Zionism and Israel.* N.Y.: National Commission on the Teaching of Zionism and Israel. Study guide for students by Max Nadel. 1978. 190 pp. High school.

Herman, Dorothy C. *Touring Israel: An Experimental Approach to the Teaching of Israel.* Miami: CAJE and JNF of Greater Miami, 1979. 93 pp.

Israel and Zionism: An Anthology of Classroom Activities. Wilmette, Ill.: Delores Kohl Educational Foundation, 1980.

Keeping Posted. *Digging into Our Past.* Nos. 840050 and 840052.

———. *Fighters of Israel.* Nos. 840610 and 840612.

———. *Jerusalem: Why Are Nations in an Uproar?* Nos. 840120 and 840122.

———. *The Kibbutz . . . Past, Present and Future.* Nos. 840170 and 840172.

———. *The Palestinians.* Nos. 840920 and 840922.

———. *The Palestinians, the Refugees and the PLO.* Nos. 840360 and 840362.

———. *Speaking out for Israel.* Nos. 840390 and 840392.

———. *Theodore Herzl and the Zionist Dream.* Nos. 840860 and 840862.

———. *Zionism: What It Is and Is Not.* Nos. 840450 and 840452.

Korman, Michael. *Zionism and Israel: The Student Activity Book.* N.Y.: USCJE and NCTZI, 1979. 163 pp. High school.

Kuselewitz, David. *Teaching Israel.* N.Y.: Herzl Press, 1965. 140 pp.

Pilch, Judah. *The Concept of Eretz Israel in Jewish Literature.* N.Y.: AAJE, 1967. 37 pp.

Rosenak, Michael. *Israel: "Eretz Israel" Land of Promise.* N.Y.: UOJCA, Youth Division (NCSY), 1968. 108 pp. High School.

Siegel, Morton. *A Syllabus on Israel—Part I: Roots.* Experimental ed. N.Y.: USA, CJE, 1976. 51 pp.

Soshuk, Levi. *A Course on the Jewish State.* N.Y.: UAHC, 1971. 65 pp.

———. *Ten Lesson Plans on Israel.* WZO-DEC, 1973. 40 pp.

GLEANINGS

Union of Orthodox Jewish Congregations of America (1942),

    "Eretz Yisrael, Zion and Jerusalem are brought to the fore of the curriculum. They are means of binding us to our past; they express the hope of the future. Pictures of the holy places and of the new life and progress in the rebuilding of the Land, together with excerpts from the old and new literature stressing the duty of every Jew to participate in the rebuilding of Eretz Yisrael and expressing the hope of the redemption of Zion should be brought to the attention of the pupils."

Leo Jung and Joseph Kaminetsky, *A Model Program of the Talmud Torah*, 30–31. Quoted by Chazan, *JSS* 43 (Summer/Fall 1980), 231.

First World Conference for Hebrew Education in Diaspora, held at the Hebrew University in Jerusalem, July 29–Aug. 6, 1947, resolution,

    1. "Jewish education in the Diaspora should be Hebraic and Zionist in the spirit of the Torah and the classic tradition of Israel."

Jew Ed 19 (Fall 1947), 55.

Greenberg, Hayyim,

"The fundamental objective of Jewish education in the Diaspora is thus, not Zionism, in the specific or programmatic sense of the word but Jewishness. Zionism should be the natural product of an organic education in Jewishness, the culmination not the point of departure. Without such education, Zionism may be a doctrine, a convincing theory, a program, a plan, an undertaking of desperate urgency, an appeal to sentiment, a noble humanitarian enterprise, but not a profound creative experience. Hebrew is naturally a very, very important element in this sort of education, but I should prefer to use the word, Hebraism rather than 'Hebrew'. I use the word, Hebraism, here not in the polemical sense which in our time signifies an extreme language preference, a purely linguistic shibboleth, but in the same way that I should use the term, for example, as Hellenism. Hellenism is more than the Greek language. . . . It is a current in the infinite ocean of mankind's searchings, of humanity's passionate will to find security within itself, an anchorage in the cosmos of its striving toward truth, beauty and harmony. Judaism, too, is such a mighty current."

Address at the World Zionist Congress in Jerusalem, August 1951. See "Jewish Culture and Jewish Education in the Diaspora" in Greenberg's *The Inner Eye*, 1:83. Also in *Judaism and the Jewish School* (1966), 131–35.

Workmen's Circle (Arbeiter Ring),

"The epic of the State of Israel, too, has an important place in the curriculum of the Peretz School. The view, however, is stressed, that the vast majority of our people is destined to live among nations of the world; also, that Jews led a creative life throughout the centuries prior to the State of Israel." (Curriculum–1952).

Quoted by Krug in *Jew Ed* 25 (Fall 1954), 68–69.

The AAJE Commission on Teaching about Israel in America,

A Statement of Objectives:
1. To familiarize Jewish students with the basic similarities between the democratic ideals of the United States and Israel.
2. To relate them to the Jews of Israel in firm bonds of kinship.
3. To tie Jewish students more closely to the Jewish people throughout the world.
4. To help them to consider favorably the various opportunities of Aliyah to Israel.
5. To teach modern Hebrew as the living language of the Jewish people.

(Adopted by the Governing Council of the AAJE, May 18, 1969.) *Jew Ed* 42 (Spring 1973): 69.

Hertzberg, Arthur, on the response of young and old to the 1967 Six Day War:

"At least a third of all the ten thousand (youths) who ultimately came to volunteer had had a substantial Jewish education and a continuing Jewish concern. In their answers to the political questions, another third showed that they had spent their young adult years worrying about race and Vietnam, and that they now lacked any organizational Jewish ties. Yet even this group had had some Jewish education in childhood or even into the teens. . . . There is some reason for thinking that American Jewish education, despite all its inadequacies, has played a significant role in implanting an often hidden loyalty in many younger people."

Commentary 44 (Aug. 1967), 71–73.

Dushkin, Alexander M.,

"I went to Palestine then [1919] not to settle, but to learn what I thought would be of importance upon my returning to do educational work in America. In 1917, I wrote: "To indulge in prophecy, it appears that the time is not far distant when no serious Jewish professional worker will consider his training complete before visiting the Land of the Fathers, there to drink deep of the reawakened fountain of Jewish life and to bring back from there inspiration and redoubled zeal for his work in this country. Indeed, I went there myself as the first such professional 'student': My goal was American Jewish education as I envisaged it."

Living Bridges: Memoirs of Alexander M. Dushkin (1975), 25.

JESNA and WZO–American Section, "The essential constituents of the Zionist program are the unity of the Jewish people, with its common history and destiny; the centrality of Israel in Jewish national life; the ingathering of the Jewish people in its historic homeland; the realization in the State of Israel of the prophetic vision of social justice and peace; the preservation of the Jewish people through the fostering of Jewish education; and the protection of Jewish rights everywhere."
A Survey on Israel/Zionism in American Jewish Schools (Dec. 1984), 49.

20 | DAY SCHOOL

HISTORY

See also chapters 21 and 29.

Brickman, William W. „יחסו של בית-הספר היהודי היומי אל בית-הספר הציבורי האמריקני בפרספקטיבה היסטורית" (The Attitude of the Jewish Day School to American Public Education in Historical Perspective). *Hagut* (H.) 3 (1974): 343–53.

Dushkin, Alexander M. "Concerning the Jewish Parochial School Thirty Years Ago." *Jew Ed* 20 (Nov. 1948): 15, 32.

Feuerstein, Samuel L. "Torah Umesorah—A Quarter of a Century." In *HDS*, 71–77.

Goldberg, Martin. "A History of Jewish Education, 1840–1860." Master's thesis. HUC–JIR, 1953.

Grinstein, Hyman B. "An Early Parochial School." *Jew Ed* 13 (Apr. 1941): 23.

* Hallowicz, George. *Jewish Day School in the United States*. U. of California at Berkeley, 1959.

Hurwitz, Solomon. "The Jewish Parochial School." *Jewish Teacher* 1 (May 1917): 211–15.

Kaminetsky, Joseph. "The Mystique of the Day School Movement." *Jew Ed* 50 (Fall 1982): 38–41.

* Kramer, Daniel J. *The History and Impact of Torah Umesorah and Hebrew Day Schools in America*. Yeshiva U., 1976. 277 pp.

Schiff, Alvin I. "In Early America," "The Pioneer Yeshivot," and "Emergence of the Modern American Yeshivah." In *The Jewish Day School in America*, 20–47. 1966.

Syme, Daniel. "Reform Judaism and Day School: The Great Historical Dilemma." *Rel Ed* 78 (Spring 1983): 153–81.

Torah Umesorah. *National Society for the Establishment of Jewish All-Day Schools*. History, objectives, and activities. 1948.

TYPES

Ackerman, Walter I. "The Day School in the Conservative Movement." *Con Jud* 15 (Winter 1961): 46–51.

Bokser, Ben Zion. "Solomon Schechter Day School Education and the Conservative Movement." *Ped Rep* 19 (June 1968): 22–25.

———. "The Solomon Schechter Day Schools." *Un Syn Rev* (Mar. 1957): 11.

Diskind, Zalman. "Views on Jewish Religious Education by American Orthodox-Jewish Leaders." *Rel Ed* 63 (Jan./Feb. 1968): 63–67.

Dushkin, Alexander M. "The Range of Educational Philosophies in Jewish Day Schools." *Jew Ed* 16 (May 1945): 6–8.

Gordis, Robert. "The Conservative School." *RA* (1962).

Greenberg, Simon. "The Conservative Movement and the Jewish Day School." *Syn Sch* 24 (Fall 1965): 4–14.

Klein, Isaac. "The Jewish All Day School." *RA* (1946): 159–66.

Lesser, Sim. "An Experimental Reform Day School." *Ped Rep* 23 (Mar. 1972).

Malzberg, Amy S. *The Jewish Day School in the United States*. N.Y.: AJC, 1970. 10 pp.

Shurin, Aaron Ben Zion. „חנוכת הבית פון שולמית, די ערשטע און עלטסטע מיידל שול אין אמעריקע" (Dedication of Shulamit—First and Oldest School for Girls in America). (Founded in 1929.) *For* (Y.) (May 6, 1983).

Singer, David. "Voices of Orthodoxy." *Commentary* 58 (July 1974): 54–60.

———. "The Yeshiva World." *Commentary* 62 (Oct. 1976): 70–73.

GOALS

Frankel, Edwin R. "Is A Statement of Ideology Enough?" *Jew Ed* 55 (Winter 1988): 28–29, 37.

Frost, Shimon. "Goals and Objectives For the Solomon Schechter Schools." *Ed As* (1970): 47–57.

Goldberg, Henry. "The Jewish All-Day School." *RA* (1962): 46–57.

Greenberg, Simon. "The Philosophy of the Conservative Day School." *Syn Sch* 16 (Sept. 1957): 3–13.

Holtz, Avraham. "Rationale and Purpose of Solomon Schechter Day Schools." (Solomon Schechter Day School Association, Resource Library.) N.Y.: USA Department of Education, 1966.

Hutner, Yitzchak. "A Shiur in Hilchos Chinuch: A Discourse on the Laws of Education." *Jew Parent* 11 (Dec. 1959) (Y., Mar. 1967). Also in *HDS*, 3–12.

Kaminetsky, Joseph. "In Quest of Tradition for Jewish Education." *Trad* 8 (Winter 1966): 112–16.

Kaminetzky, Yaacov. "Aims in Jewish Education." *Jew Parent* 5 (Apr. 1954). Also in *HDS*, 13–17.

Klughaupt, Sol. "The Goals of a Yeshiva Day School." *Ped Rep* 37 (Feb. 1986).

* Leary, Carolyn Frances. *Perceived Goals and Characteristics of Jewish Day Schools and Catholic Parochial Schools*. Fordham U., 1978. 200 pp.

Siegel, Morton. "The Goal of the Schechter Day School." *Ped Rep* 37 (Feb. 1986): 7–8.

———. "What Kind of a Child Do We Want to Produce in the Solomon Schechter Day Schools?" *Syn Sch* 25 (Spring 1967): 13–21.

Taback, Ben Zion. „מה היא ישיבה קטנה רצויה?" (What Are Criteria [Yeshiva] for the Young?). *Sh Hah* (H.) 14 (Apr. 1954): 172–74. See also *Sh Hah* 24 (Fall 1964): 26–28.

United Synagogue CJE (Jack J. Cohen, Chair). "A Charter for Day Schools." *Syn Sch* 19 (June 1961): 3–4.

———. "In Our School System." *Ped Rep* 19 (Dec. 1967): 23–26.

Whiteman, Kalman. „הישיבות הקטנות" (The Yeshivot for the Young). *Hadoar* (H.) 22 (10 Kislev 1943).

THE DEBATE

Belsky, Meir. "The Day Schools in the United States: Another View." *Jew Obs* 12 (Jan. 1977): 5–7.

Bickel, Shlomo. „דעמאקראטיע און טאג-שולן" (Democracy and Day Schools). *YK* (Y.) (June 20, 1952): 3–4.

———. „אידישע טאג-שולן" (Jewish Day Schools). *Day* (Y.) (Aug. 31, 1962).

Blau, Joseph L. "The Jewish Day School." *Recon* (Nov. 14, 1958): 29–32.

Bleiberg, James S. "The Debate over Day School Education in Reform Judaism: A Historical Study." Master's thesis, HUC–JIR, 1982.

20 DAY SCHOOL

CCAR Commission on Jewish Education. "Fulltime Reform Jewish Education." *CCAR* 79 (1969): 90–96.

Cohen, Jack J. "American Education and the Jewish Day School." *Syn Sch* 16 (Sept. 1957): 29–35. Revised in *JEDS*, 300–313.

"Conservative Day Schools" (editorial). *Un Syn Rev* 19 (Apr. 1966).

Diamond, Joseph. "The Case for Jewish Day Schools." *National Jewish Monthly* 64: 190, 192, 203, 221, 242–44.

Dinin, Samuel. "All-Day Jewish School." *Recon* (Oct. 5, 1945): 11–20.

Eisenberg, Azriel. "Let's Take a Long, Hard Look at Jewish Education." *National Jewish Monthly* (Mar. 1965): 24, 61–63.

Fox, Marvin. "The Case for the Day School." *Jew Parent* (Sept. 1953). Also in *Judaism and the Jewish School*, edited by Pilch and Ben-Horin. N.Y.: Bloch, 1966. 207–13.

Fried, Jacob. "Public School or Jewish Day School." *Congress Weekly* (May 25, 1953): 11–12.

Gamoran, Emanuel. "Liberal Judaism and the Day School." *Jew Teach* (Mar. 1951.) Also in *Gamoran*, 65–71.

Glasner, Samuel. "The Day School and Reform Jewish Education: The Case for a Reform Jewish Day School." *Jew Teach* 26 (Apr. 1963): 15–18. See also *Dimensions* 3 (Summer 1969): 36–39.

Goldberg, Ben Zion. "שאג-שולן" (Day Schools) (Y.). *Day* (Oct. 10, 13, 1964).

Goldberg, Henry R. "Now Is the Time." *Syn Sch* 23 (Fall 1964): 29–32.

Goldburg, Norman M. "Why Indeed Jewish Day Schools?" *Congress Weekly* (Jan. 25, 1946): 7–8.

Golomb, Abraham. "Development of Jewish Children in All-Day Schools." *Jew Ed* 16 (Jan. 1945): 40–44.

Gordis, Robert. "The Conservative Day School." *RA* (1963): 58–66.

Grossman, Mordecai. "Parochial Schools for Jewish Children—An Adverse View." *Jew Ed* 16 (May 1945): 20–25.

Hachen, David S. (Chair of the UAHC Ad Hoc Committee on Day Schools). "Day Schools." (May 1968). 3-page report.

Jakobovits, Immanuel. "The Potential of Day School Education." *Jew Parent* (Dec. 1960).

"A Joint Call: The Day School Movement." *Syn Sch* 24 (Spring 1966).

Kallen, Horace M. "Why Jewish Day Schools?" *Jew Spec* 37 (Dec. 1972): 6–7.

Karff, Samuel E. "Are Day Schools Right for Reform?" *RJ* (Summer 1982).

Kaufman, Jay. "Day Schools: Not Whether but How." *CCAR J* (Oct. 1963): 3–9.

Klein, Isaac, "The Jewish All Day School." *RA* (1946): 159–66.

Lookstein, Joseph H. "בית ספר יהודי כל-יומי" (The Jewish All-Day School). *Sh Hah* (H.) 6 (Oct. 1946): 3–9.

LZOA. "The Jewish Day School." *Jew Fron* (Aug. 1963): 28–30.

Maller, Allen S. "Day School and Reform Judaism." *Jew Spec* (Dec. 1964): 18–21.

Margoshes, Samuel. "The Jewish Day School." *Day* (May 5, 6, 1965).

National Council for Jewish Education. "Resolution on All-Day Schools" (Feb. 21, 1962). *Jew Ed* 32 (Winter 1962): 123.

Pilch, Judah. "Day Schools Versus Supplementary Jewish Education." In *Wiseman*, 58–63.

Revel, Bernard. "The Day School and the Yeshiva in Jewish Education." Proceedings of the NCJSS (1926), 293–303.

Rosenkrantz, Samuel. "The Day School and Reform Jewish Education: The Case Against a Reform Jewish Day School." *Jew Teach* 31 (Apr. 1963): 19–21.

Rosenstock, E. D. "The Case For/Against a Reform Jewish Day School." *Dimensions* 3 (Summer 1969): 36–39.

Rubin, Philip. "Why Jewish Day Schools." *Congress Weekly* (Sept. 8, 1958): 12–14.

Schiff, Alvin I. "From Sunday School to Day School." *Jew Ed* 50 (Summer 1982): 6–13.

Schwartzman, Louis. "Day School—Public School." *RA* (1962): 71–75.

Schwartzman, Sylvan D. "Who Wants Reform Jewish Day Schools?" *CCAR J* (Apr. 1964).

Segal, Jacob. "The Jewish Day School." *RA* (1962): 71–75.

Skydell, A. "A Home for the Wandering." *Jew Life* 14 (Feb. 1947).

Spiro, Joseph. "Why the Jewish Day School? A Trainee Speaks out." *Jew Parent* 17 (June 1966): 12–13.

"Statement on Day Schools" (LZOA). *Jew Ed* 34 (Summer 1964): 277–78.

United Synagogue, CJE. "Resolution on Day School Education." *Syn Sch* 16 (Sept. 1957): 28.

Weiss-Rosmarin, Trude. "In Defense of Jewish Day Schools." *Congress Weekly* (May 26, 1952): 5–7.

Zeldin, Michael. "Full-Time Jewish Education in the Reform Movement." A proposal for a secondary level institute of full-time education through the perspective of the history and development of Reform Jewish education. Master's project, HUC–JIR, 1975.

GROWTH AND DEVELOPMENT

‏„ארום 70 טויזענט אידישע קינדער לערנען אין ישיבות און טאג-שול"‎ (About 70,000 Jewish Children are now attending Yeshivot and Day Schools). *Day* (Y.) (Sept. 13, 1962).

Axelrod, Herman C. "Trends in the Newer Day Schools." *Jew Ed* 24 (Spring 1954): 39–44, 64.

Basic Questions People Ask about the Hebrew Day Schools. N.Y.: TU, 198?.

Berman, Jeremiah J. "The Return to the Jewish Day School." *Con Jud* 8 (Jan. 1951): 1–13.

Bernstein, Mendel. "Around the Day School Circuit: Jewish Day Schools in the South." *Jew Parent* 16 (Jan. 1965): 25.

Brickman, William W. "The American Jewish Day School Movement." (Review article.) *Trad* 9 (Spring/Summer): 176–93.

Derby, Josiah. "The Jewish Day School." *RA* (1962): 76–78.

Engelman, Uriah Z. *All-Day Schools in the United States, 1948–1949.* N.Y.: AAJE, 1949. 40 pp.

———. *Jewish All Day Schools in the United States.* Bulletin no. 22. N.Y.: AAJE Department of Research, 1953. 62 pp.

———. ‏„בתי ספר כל יומיים"‎ (Jewish Day Schools). *Sh Hah* (H.) 9 (Aug. 1949): 115–22.

* Fried, Irving. *Trends and Issues in Hebrew Day School Education.* Ohio State U., 1973. 228 pp.

F.R.S. "ORT Enters the United States Day School Movement." *ORT Reporter* (Fall 1981).

Goldenberg, Bernard. "Have You 'Sold' Your School Lately?" *Jew Parent* 17 (Mar. 1961).

Halpern, Harry. "The Jewish All-Day School." *RA* (1962): 42–45.

Horowitz, David. "The Jewish Day School." *RA* (1962): 67–70.

Jewish Agency, Department of Education and Culture. *The Hebrew Day School.* N.Y.: Jewish Agency, 1950.

"Jewish Day School" (report on LZOA conference). *Jew Fron* 30 (Aug. 1963): 28–30.

"Jewish Day School Statistics: United States and Canada." *School and Society* 89 (1961): 219.

Joint Advisory Committee of the Synagogue Council of America. *The Jewish Day School: A Policy Statement of the Synagogue Council of America* (circular letter). July 22, 1971.

Kaminetsky, Joseph. "The Hebrew Day School Movement." *School and Society* 82 (Oct. 1955): 105–7.

———. "I Have Seen the Jewish Day School." *Jew Spec* (May 1947): 21–22.

———. "Interpreting the Day School to the Community." *Jew Parent* 17 (Jan. 1966).

———. "Jewish Day School." *Day* (July 1, 1962).

Kaminetsky, Joseph, ed., and Murray I. Friedman, comp. *Hebrew Day School Education: An Overview.* N.Y.: TU, National Society for Hebrew Day Schools, 1970. 311 pp.

Lewis, Schnayer. "Hebrew Day School Enrollment for the 70's." *Jew Parent* 21 (Apr. 1970): 20–21.

Machlis, Leon. "More Dynamic Community Relations for Our Yeshivos." *Jew Parent* (June 1960): 10.

Margoshes, Samuel. "The Jewish Day School." *Day* (Jan. 16, 1961; June 23, 1962; June 2, 3, 1968; June 2, 1972).

Mark, Yudl. „דער פראבלעמען-קנויל-ישיבה און טאג שול" (The Problem-Cluster—Yeshiva and Day School). *Zuk* (Y.) (Dec. 1949): 564–68.

Nardi, Noah. "The Growth of Jewish Day Schools in America." *Jew Ed* 20 (Nov. 1948): 23–32.

———. "Jewish Day Schools in America." *Congress Weekly* (Jan. 3, 1947): 11–13.

———. "A Survey of Jewish Day Schools in America." *Jew Ed* 16 (Sept. 1944).

Pelcovitz, Ralph. "The Day School and the Emerging Jewish Community." *Jew Parent* (Mar. 1961): 10.

Penn, Ascher. „אידישקייט אין אמעריקע" *Judaism in America* (Y.). N.Y.: Judaism in America Library, 1958.

    Ch. 25—"Torah Umesorah," 297–306.
    Ch. 26—"Mizrachi National Education Committee," 307–12.
    Ch. 27—"Conservative Jews," 313–24.
    Ch. 28—"Reform Movement," 325–35.
    Ch. 30—"Folk Schools of LZOA," 349–63.
    Ch. 41—"Jewish Day School for Girls—The Beth Jacob Schools," 473–80.
    Ch. 56—"Lubavitcher Rabbi," (Chabad Headquarters in New York), 635–47.

Rosenberg, Stuart C. "The Purpose of the North American Day School Conference of the Conservative Movement." *Syn Sch* 24 (Spring 1966).

Saphire, Shelley R. "The Talmudical Academy of Yeshiva University." *Jew Ed* 20 (Nov. 1948): 40–42.

Schiff, Alvin I. "Jewish Day Schools in America, 1962–1977." *Ped Rep* 29 (Fall 1977). Extensive bibliography.

Shereshevsky, Ezra. "The Jewish Day School." *Syn Sch* 17 (Spring 1959). See also *Sh Hah* (H.) 21 (Spring 1961): 162.

Shulman, Avi. "Your Day School and Public Relations." *Jew Parent* 18 (June 1967): 31–32.

Siegel, Morton. "The Conservative Day School: The Solomon Schechter Day School Association." *Ped Rep* 29 (Fall 1977).

———. "The Day School: The 'Life School'." *Un Syn Rev* 29 (Apr. 1977): 12–13.

Singer, David. "The Growth of the Day School Movement." *Commentary* (Aug. 1973): 53–57.

Skaist, Solomon N. „בתי הספר הכל-יומיים" (The Day Schools). *Sh Hah* (H.) 26 (Summer 1966): 251–52.

Spero, Robert. "The Day School Changes Communities." *Jew Parent* (Mar. 1961): 8.

Syme, Daniel B. "The Reform Day School: Its History and Future Prospects." *Ped Rep* 29 (Fall 1977).

Taschman, Dershon. "Yeshiva High School for Girls?" *Jew Parent* 26 (Mar. 1969): 16–17.

Torah Umesorah. *Statistical Summary*. Dec. 1970.

Toubin, Isaac. "Some Vital Statistics on the Jewish Day School." *Reg* (1965): 12–24.

Unger, Menasha. „תלמידים אין די 50,000 אמעריקאנער ישיבות" (50,000 pupils in American Yeshivot). *Day* (Y.) (May 27, 1963).

Zeldin, Michael. "Building a Reform Day School." *Compass* 9 (Spring/Summer 1987): 5, 22.

CURRICULUM AND PEDAGOGY

Ackerman, Walter I. "Developing the Program of Jewish Studies on the Day School." *Syn Sch* 16 (Sept. 1957): 14–21.

———. "The Pre-School and the Early Years of the Day School." *Syn Sch* 17 (1959).

Adiv, Ellen. "Jewish Day Schools as Multi-Lingual Models of Education." *Jew Ed* 53 (Fall 1984): 10–14.

Agus, Abraham. *Hatzaah L'tokhnit Limudim L'Yeshivot* (A Proposal for a Course of Study in the Yeshivot) (H.). N.Y.: Council for Torah Education of Mizrachi, 1953.

Axelrod, Herman C. "Guidance in the Jewish Day School." *The Principal* 6 (Apr. 1961).

———. "Learning Another Language." *Jew Parent* 1 (Fall 1949). Also in *HDS*, 215–18.

———. *Tokhnit Limudim* (A Course of Study) (H.). 1952.

Barash, Y. "Tomorrow's Technology—Afraid to Use it Today?" *Jew Obs* 16 (Mar. 1983): 16–19.

Barthold, Judith Bin-Nun. "Employing Creative Techniques and Materials in the Teaching of Judaic and General Studies." *Syn Sch* 28 (Winter 1970): 14–24.

* Berdugo, Yehuda. *The Design, Implementation and Evaluation of a Theme-Centered Interaction Program for Adolescents in a Jewish Day School*. U. of Pittsburgh, 1978. 197 pp.

Berger, Herschel. "Co-Curricular Programs Bridge the Gap." *Jew Parent* 23 (June 1972): 12–13.

* Bernstein, David I. "A Study of the Teaching of Jewish History in Modern Orthodox Yeshivah High Schools." *Jew Ed* 54 (Winter 1986): 27–38.

———. *Two Approaches to the Teaching of Jewish History in Orthodox Yeshiva High Schools*. New York U., 1986.

Bin-Nun, Judith. "The Emanuel Day School Judaic/Hebrew Curricular Framework Scope and Sequence Chart." A comprehensive guide in chart form of the Judaic and Hebrew curriculum of a synagogue day school, early childhood through third grade, with an integrated programmatic thrust. Master's project, HUC–JIR, 1976.

———. "The Emanuel Day School Slide Show—Rationale, Process, Script and Slide/Cassette Production." The process and outline of how to create a promotional media presentation for a day school. Master's project, HUC–JIR, 1976.

———. "Toward a Singular Jewish Experience—The Emanuel Approach." A handbook for the establishment of a liberal Jewish Day School. Master's project, HUC–JIR, 1975.

Boxerman, Nahoma. "Jewish 'Headstart'." *Jew Parent* 17 (June 1966).

Brandt, Doray. "Reading Miscues Inventory and Its Possible Uses with Hebrew Instruction in a Hebrew Day School." An application of the Reading Miscues Inventory to Jewish day schools as a means of providing educators with information about student strengths and weaknesses in reading Hebrew and English. Master's project, HUC–JIR, 1979.

Braverman, Jay. "The Jewish Day School from a Trilingual Perspective." *Jew Ed* 51 (Spring 1983): 20–24.

Breslavner, S. N. "Yeshiva Education: Reclaiming the Secular Departments." *Jew Obs* 8 (Jan. 1973): 13–19.

* Burack, Solomon. *Ancillary Jewish Education Material Paralleling Grades 7–9 Science Course*. Yeshiva U., 1967. 266 pp.

Charner, M., and F. S. Morris. "Curricular Enrichment at Yeshiva Dov Revel." *Yeshiva Education* 3 (Fall 1959).

Chwat, Sheldon, and Charles Baskett. "New School Responds to Needs of Modern Yeshiva Day Schools." *Jew Parent* 27 (Apr. 1975): 10–15.

Cohen, Alfred. "The Need for Individualized Instruction." *Jew Parent* 23 (Jan. 1972): 14–15.

Cohen, Yehuda. "Creative Jewish Day School Education." *Jew Parent* 21 (Oct. 1969): 10–11, 22.

Colandra, Alexander. "The Day School and the Modern Curriculum." *Jew Parent* 18 (June 1967): 22–24.

Day Schools in the United States and Canada (Directory of Yeshiva all-day schools). N.Y.: TU, 1954, 1956, 1957.

Deitcher, Howard. "Teaching the Rites of Passage in Orthodox Yeshiva Education." *Jew Ed* 54 (Winter 1986): 39–42.

Diner, Loisan. "An Art Program in a Jewish Day School." *Ped Rep* 36 (Jan. 1985): 1–3.

Dolgin, S. A. "The Personal Equation." *Jew Life* 20 (Feb. 1953).

Dolins, Joseph Lehman, Walter Martin Greene, and Gail Porter Lissek. "A Cooperative Program between a Jewish Day School and Jewish Family Center." *Jew Ed* 49 (Winter 1981): 14–22.

Dorph, Gail Zaiman, Victoria Koltun Kelman, and Barry W. Holtz. "The Melton Curriculum in the Conservative Day School: A Report on a Pilot Project." *MJ* 16 (Spring/Summer 1983): 13–14.

Edelstein, Rosalind. "Casework Services for the Hebrew Day School." *J Jew Com Ser* 45 (Winter 1968): 179–84.

Egozi, Akivah. "A Day School Curriculum from the Teacher's Point of View." *Ped Rep* 29 (Spring 1978): 19–20.

———. "הכנה צורך הוראה„ (Guidelines for Lesson Planning). *Sh Hah* (H.) 37 (Dec. 1977.): 86–92.

———. "Hebrew in a Day School." *Ped Rep* (Jan. 1983): 5–7.

Eliach, David. "The Centrality of Israel in the Day School Curriculum." In *Compendium: The Jewish Educational Scene*, edited by R. S. Hirt. 1972.

Elkin, Joshua, and Risa Rosenbaum Krohn. "Building an In-House Teacher Resource Center: A Case Study." *MJ* 21 (Winter 1987): 14, 22.

Elkind, Alan, and Nachman Sorkin. "Mentoring—An Enrichment Program for Day Schools." *Ped Rep* 34 (Mar. 1984): 33–34.

Feinstein, Moshe. *Bastion of Faith: A Collection of Expositions on Bible and Jewish Holidays as Heard from Rabbi Moshe Feinstein*. Compiled and edited by Abraham Fisheles. N.Y.: 1973. 256 pp.

Friedlander, Dov. "Counseling and Guidance Services." *Jew Parent* 17 (Mar. 1966).

Friedman, Murray J. "An Essential History of American Jewry." *Jew Parent* 22 (Mar./Apr. 1971): 7–10.

———. "A Genetic Approach to Jewish History." *Jew Parent* (Jan. 1972).

Gans, Manfred, ed. *Yeshiva Children Write Poetry: From the Heart We Sing*. (Published under the auspices of TU, the National Conference of Yeshiva Principals, and the American Jewish Museum of Art and Culture.) N.Y.: Hebrew Pub. Co., ca. 1976. 145 pp.

Garfinkel, Helen. "Establishing a Learning Environment." *Jew Parent* 22 (Jan. 1971).

* Gittelson, Abraham J. *The Application and Adaptation of the "Teaching Improvement Process" in an Elementary Jewish Day School*. U. of Miami, 1985.

———. "Approaches to Curriculum Design." In *IL*, 53–73.

Gold, Milton J. "New Developments in Educational Techniques." *Syn Sch* 24 (Spring 1966).

Goodside, Samuel. "Religious and Secular Subjects in the Day School." *Jew Ed* 24 (Fall 1953): 55–58.

Greenberg, M. "Teaching Values in the Modern Day School" *Jew Parent* 15 (1963): 8–9.

Greenfield, M. "The Rebbe-Talmid Relationship." *Jew Obs* (June 1979): 8–11.

Gross, Maurice B. "Psychological Services for Yeshivoth." *Jew Ed* 30 (Spring 1960): 22–32.

———. "Reporting Meaningful Test Results in the General Studies Program." *Jew Parent* 16 (Mar. 1965): 12–13.

Gruenberg, Sandra S. "Roots and Thanksgiving" (Social studies). *Ped Rep* 34 (Sept. 1981).

Hebrew Curriculum for the Day School. N.Y.: TU.

Hecht, Abraham B. "Reaching Out to the Adolescent." *Jew Parent* 23 (Mar. 1972): 12–14.

———. "To Teach and to Guide." *Jew Parent* 15 (June 1964). Also in *HDS*, 151–57.

Hoffnet, N. "The Ideological Gap." *Jew Life* 21 (Apr. 1954).

Horowitz, David A. "Developing a General Studies Program." *Syn Sch* 16 (1957): 35–39.

Implementation of a Diagnostic and Remedial Program at a Hebrew Day School. N.Y.: TU.

Kaminetsky, Joseph. "A Program for the Day School Movement in the 70's and Beyond." *Trad* 16 (Summer 1976): 120–26.

Kapel, Marilyn B., and David E. Kapel. "Hebrew, English Reading Achievement in a Jewish Day School." *Jew Ed* 40 (Winter 1970): 23–32.

Karlin, Meyer. "Teaching Love for Eretz Yisroel in Our Yeshivos." *Jew Parent* 8 (Dec. 1956). Also in *HDS*, 200–204.

Kessler, Harry. "The Sager Solomon Schechter School." *Ped Rep* 23 (Mar. 1972): 3–4.

Kohn, Rebekah J. *Hebrew in the First and Second Grades of the Foundation School and Day School*. N.Y.: USCJE, 1960. 95 pp.

Krantzler, Gershon. "Incentives to Jewish Learning." *Jew Parent* 8 (Mar. 1957). Also in *HDS*, 191–99.

———. "Preparing Students for Yeshiva High School." *Jew Parent* 9 (Dec. 1957): 301–11.

———. "Vital Functions of Jewish Children's Literature." *Jew Parent* 23 (Oct. 1971): 7–8.

Kranzler, Moses N. "Elementary Guidance: A New Horizon in Yeshiva Education." *Jew Parent* 17 (June 1966): 8–19.

* ———. *Guidance in Selected Elementary Jewish Day Schools: An Attempt to Develop a More Effective Guidance Program in a Growing Movement*. Columbia U., 1967. 277 pp.

Krauss, Simcha. "Techniques of Torah Education for the 70's." *Jew Parent* 23 (Oct. 1971): 9–10.

* Kreinan, Fannie. *A Music Syllabus for Jewish All-Day Schools*. New York U., 1956. 512 pp.

Kutzin, Margaret, and Irving Fried. "Health Services in the Day School." *Jew Parent* 14 (June 1963): 26–27.

Latham, Luisa. "A Hebrew Language Curriculum for the First Grade Level of the Day School." A primary Hebrew curriculum integrating Jewish values and concepts with the teaching of language skills. Master's project, HUC–JIR, 1977.

Lerner, Benjamin. "The Psychologist's Role in Day Schools." *Jew Parent* 14 (Oct. 1962): 8–9.

Levi, Linda. "The Teaching of Israel to Adolescents in an Orthodox Day School." Master's thesis, Brandeis U., 1972.

Levinson, Boris M. "Emotional Disorders of Infancy and Childhood and Their Relation to the Day School." *Yeshiva Education* 5 (Winter 1964).

Lewis, Justin. "Structure, Readiness and Intuition: Applying These New Vital Concepts to the Day School Program." *Jew Parent* 17 (June 1966): 10–11.

———. "A Suggested Approach for Re-Structuring Social Studies Curriculum in Our High Schools." *Ha Manahel* (H.) (Spring 1975).

Lewittes, Mordecai H. "Guidance in the Senior High School." *Ped Rep* 32 (Fall 1980): 4–6. Review of N. Shudofsky's dissertation (below).

Lobman, Frances Weingarten. "In Favor of Immersion Programs in Day Schools." *Ped Rep* 43 (Jan. 1983): 14–16.

Lookstein, Joseph H. *Course of Instruction in Judaic Studies, Upper Level of Ramaz*. N.Y.: 1979.

Mermelstein, Jacob. "Children's Aggressiveness." *Jew Parent* 17 (June 1966).

———. "The Child's Need to Explore." *Jew Parent* 17 (Oct. 1965).

* Messinger, Howard. *A Dinim Curriculum: Content and Methodology*. Yeshiva U., 1981.

Mindel, Nissan. "Textbooks and Literature for Hebrew Day Schools." *Jew Parent* 19 (Mar. 1968): 13–15. Also in *HDS*, 242–50.

Mir, Donia. "Mishnah in Grade 2?" *Jew Parent* 20 (Mar. 1968): 20–21.

Nardi, Noah. ‏"הסברים להצעת תכנית לימודים היומיים לבתה"ס שהוגשה לכינוס"‏ (Comments on the "Proposed Curriculum for the Hebrew Day Schools"). In *PDE* (H.), 81–84.

———, ed. *A Proposed Curriculum for All-Day Schools in the Diaspora* (H.). Jerusalem: DEC for the Diaspora, WZO, 1958. 60 pp.

Nudelman, Edward A. "An Approach to the Teaching of Hebrew Reading in a Day School." *Ped Rep* 2 (Nov. 1950).

Nulman, Louis. "Programmed Instruction: Its Potential for Torah." *Jew Obs* 6 (Apr. 1970): 8–10, 23.

Paskind, Judy. "Reform Jewish Day Schools." Report prepared for the UAHC–CCAR Commission on Jewish Education, May 1974.

* Peretz, David J. H. *Source Material for Sex Education in the Jewish Day School*. Yeshiva U., 1975. 237 pp.

Pick, Manfred. "How to Develop An Effective Tefillah Program." *Jew Parent* 23 (Jan. 1972): 11–13.

Program of Study for the Hebrew Day School. N.Y.: Yeshiva Etz Chaim, 1975.

Raphael, Ruth. "Hebrew and Bible in the Day School: An Alternative Approach." *MJ* 16 (Spring/Summer 1983): 13–14, 23.

Rephun, Sholom. *Grouping for Instruction*. N.Y.: TU, 1969.

———. "Grouping for Instruction with Special Reference to Co-education." *Jew Parent* 20 (June 1969).

Rischall, Joseph. "Innovations in Education." *Jew Parent* 26:1 (Oct. 1973): 27–30

Rokeach, M. "The Kollel: American Phase." *Jew Life* 30 (May/June 1963): 13–21.

Rosenblum, Paul C. "Educational Innovation and the Day Schools." *Jew Parent* 18 (Oct. 1966): 4–5.

Salczer, David. "Why Should Hebrew Language Instruction in the All-Day Schools Begin in the Kindergarten?" *Jew Ed* 45 (Summer 1977): 40–43; (Fall 1977): 12.

Schlussel, J. L. "A Teaching Method for the Automation Era." *Jew Life* 29 (Aug. 1962).

Sherman, Robert. "Creative Writing in the Judaic Studies Classroom." *Ped Rep* 36 (1985): 27–29.

Shuchatowitz, Joseph L. "Educational TV in the Day School." *Jew Parent* 15 (June 1964): 20–21.

Shudofsky, Chanuch. *Curriculum Compendium for Solomon Schechter Day Schools*. N.Y.: USCJE. 274 pp. See also *Ped Rep* 29 (Spring 1978).

* Shudofsky, Noam. *The Nature and Role of Guidance in the Jewish All-Day Senior High School*. Yeshiva U., 1977. 210 pp.

Shulamit School for Girls. *Suggested Currirulum Enrichment for the Hebrew Day School*. N.Y.: 1975.

Shulman, Avi. *How to Teach, Enjoy and Survive Primary Grades*. TU.

Silver, A. M. "May Women Be Taught Bible, Mishnah, and Talmud?" *Trad* (Summer 1978): 74–83.

* Sivan, Tamar. *Kindergarten Perceptual and Language Factors as Predictors of Third Grade Hebrew and English Reading Comprehension among Jewish Day School Students*. JTSA, 1984. 180 pp.

Soffer, Abraham. "Daily Prayer in a Day School Can Succeed." *Ped Rep* 33 (Dec. 1981): 22–23.

Solovy, D. K. "Potential and Reality: Can Computers Help Meet the Goals of the Day School?" *Ped Rep* 35 (Jan. 1984): 10–12.

Steinberg, Barbara. "Bilingual Education: What Is It and Why Do We Need It?" *Ped Rep* 36 (Jan. 1985): 32–33.

Swift, Isaac L. "Meeting the Pressures of Adolescence." *Jew Parent* 11 (Apr. 1965). Also in *HDS*, 134–40.

Teaching Procedures for the Day School (Digest of lecture delivered at Torah Umesorah summer session on Yeshiva education). N.Y.: TU, 1951.

Teitelbaum, Eli. "The Overhead Projector in the Hebrew Department." *Jew Parent* 20 (June 1969): 36.

Tendler, Moses D. "Science in the Day School." *Jew Parent* 9 (Mar. 1958). Also in *HDS*, 229–33.

Tokayer, Shmuel. "Mental Health and the Day School." *Jew Parent* 22 (June 1971): 13–14.

Ury, Zalman F. "Interpreting the Holocaust to Our Children." *Jew Parent* 18 (Jan. 1967). Also in *HDS*, 205–14.

———. "Problems of Adjustment of All-Day School Pupils and Their Guidance Problems." *Jew Ed* 37 (Oct. 1967): 188–98.

———. "Understanding the Shoah." *Jew Parent* 27 (Jan. 1975): 20–21.

Weiss, Benjamin. "On Teaching Talmud in the Day Schools." *Gesher* (H.) 2 (1964): 22–26.

Weitzman, Laura. "Guidance in the Day School." *Ped Rep* 32 (Fall 1980): 2–4.

Willner, Eric. "Problems of Adjustment of All-Day School Pupils and Their Guidance Implication." *Jew Ed* 37 (Oct. 1967): 188–98.

Young, Moshe L. "Why Torah Should Not Be Taught in Ivrit." *Jew Parent* 25:2 (Apr. 1973): 6–8

Zamichow, Abraham. "The Hebrew Curriculum in a Yeshivah." *Ped Rep* 33 (Mar. 1982).

PROGRAMS FOR EXCEPTIONAL CHILDREN

Brickman, S. "Day School Special Education within the Mainstream." *Ped Rep* 33 (May 1982): 21–22.

David, G. "Needs of the Special Child—A Broken Promise: Free and Appropriate Special Education for Disabled Jewish Children." *Jew Obs* 17 (Oct. 1983): 7–9.

Egozi, Akivah. "Programs for Exceptional Children." *Jew Parent* 10 (Sept. 1958). Also in *HDS*, 276–80.

Friedman, R. "Students with Special Needs." *Ped Rep* 33 (May 1982): 21–22.

Kahn, Blanche. "Educating the Physically Handicapped: New Potential for the Day School Movement." *Jew Parent* 17 (Jan. 1966): 10–13.

Kahn, Max. "The Hebrew Academy for Special Children." *Jew Parent* 22 (Mar./Apr. 1971): 32–34.

Levi, Miriam. "On Children with Learning Disabilities." *Jew Parent* 21 (Jan. 1970): 23–25.

Muschel, Nahum. "Aiding the Slow Learner." *Jew Parent* 10 (Sept. 1958). Also in *HDS*, 281–87.

"Special Education: Day High School Program for Learning Disabled." *Ped Rep* 33 (May 1982): 16–17.

Ribowsky, H. "Needs of the Special Child—R=1: A Dangerous Equation." *Jew Obs* 17 (Oct. 1983): 4–6.

Seidman, Aaron B. "Teaching Hebrew to the Deaf." *Jew Parent* 23 (Jan. 1972): 16–18.

Shapiro, E. "Special Education, Yeshiva Style." (May 1981): 50–53.

Stiskin, Herschel M. "Curriculum Planning for the Special Religious School." *Syn Sch* 22 (1964): 17–19.

———. "Maimonides Institute—The School and the Movement." *Yeshiva Education* 5 (Winter 1964).

———. "The Slow Learner and the Yeshiva." *Jew Parent* 17 (Oct. 1965): 8–9.

INTEGRATION OF CURRICULUM

Abrams, Solomon. "Report on Session on Integrative Learning." In *IL*, 72–75.

Axelrod, Herman C. "Integration in the Day School." *Jew Parent* (Feb. 1953): 10–11, 15.

Ben-Haim, Meir. "Dual Curriculum: Open Forum." *Jew Spec* 36 (Apr. 1971): 26–27.

Bieler, Jack. "Integration of Judaic and General Studies in the Modern Orthodox Day School." *Jew Ed* 54 (Winter 1986): 15–26.

Bokser, Ben Zion. "Integrating the Jewish and General Studies Program." *Syn Sch* 16 (Sept. 1957): 39–42.

Braverman, Jay. "Integration in the Jewish Day School—In Practice." In *IL*, 36–39.

Brickman, Benjamin. "Integration and Interrelationships." *Jew Ed* 46 (Winter 1978): 29–31.

Brown, Stephen Ira, and Joseph Lukinsky. "Integration of Religious Studies and Mathematics in the Day School." *Jew Ed* 47 (Fall 1979): 28–35.

Charney, Baruch. „אינטגרציה בלמודים בישיבות" (Integration of Curriculum in the Yeshivot). *Sh Hah* (H.) 12 (Mar. 1952): 67–72.

Davis, Perry. "Integration: External Concerns." *Jew Ed* 46 (Winter 1978): 28.

Diamond, Joseph. "Towards an Integrated Jewish Community School." In *Wiseman*, 32–43.

Elias, Joseph. "The Hebrew and General Studies Departments." *Jew Parent* 14 (Spring 1961). Also in *HDS*, 219–28.

———. "Torah and Secular Studies: The Two Sides of the Coin." *Jew Obs* 4 (Apr. 1967).

Finell, David. "Integration of General and Judaic Studies in Jewish Day Schools—An Overview." Master's project, HUC–JIR, 1979.

Freidenreich, Fradle, and Abraham J. Gittelson. *Interdisciplinary Integration in the Jewish Day School: The Process of a Pilot Project*. A report on an experimental three-year project of the AAJE and the CAJE of Miami. Edited by Malvina W. Liebman. Miami: 1979. 143 pp.

———. "Subject Integration: A Process Model." *Jew Ed* 46 (Winter 1978): 32–36.

Frost, Shimon. "Integrated Learning—Between Theory and Practice." *Jew Ed* 46 (Winter 1978): 19–21.

———. "Integrating the Judaic and General Studies Curriculum." *Syn Sch* 24 (Mar. 1966): 29–34.

Goodside, Samuel. "Integration is Not an Educational Slogan." *Jew Ed* 46 (Winter 1978): 18–19.

———. "Integration of Jewish and Social Studies in the Jewish Day School." *Jew Ed* 23 (Summer 1952): 29–32, 36.

———. "Religious and Secular Studies in the Day School." *Jew Ed* 24 (Fall 1953): 55–58.

Greenberg, Menachem. "The Yeshiva World's Outlook on Torah and Secular Studies." *Jew Obs* (Dec. 1969): 11–14.

Greenberg, Simon. "Limitations of Integration." *Jew Ed* 46 (Winter 1978): 21–22.

Halzel, Michael. "Report on Integrative Learning Session." In *IL*, 80–81.

Hoenig, Sidney. "The Social Studies Program in Yeshiva Education." *Yeshiva Education* 5 (Winter 1964).

Holtz, Barry W. "Towards an Integrated Curriculum for the Jewish School." *Rel Ed* 75 (Sept./Oct. 1980): 546–57.

"Integrating Studies in Day Schools." *Ped Rep* 26 (Spring 1975): 25.

Kurtz, Shoshana. "Integration in the Jewish Day School—In Practice." In *IL*, 40–43.

Latham, Luisa. "An Integrated Social Studies Framework for the Day School." Summary of the process of developing a social studies curriculum. Master's project, HUC–JIR, 1977.

* Lieberman, Sidney. *Integrating the World History Curriculum with Jewish Historical Developments for the Yeshiva High School*. Yeshiva U., 1959.

Lookstein, Joseph. "True Integration." *Jew Ed* 46 (Winter 1978): 37–38.

Lukinsky, Joseph. "Integrating Jewish and General Studies in the Day School: Philosophy and Scope." In *IL*, 1–35.

Mars, Alvin. "A Day School Dilemma: Two Curricula." *Impact* 35 (Winter 1976–77): 17–27.

Nadel, Max, ed. *Integrative Learning: The Search for Unity in Jewish Day School Programs:*

    Braverman, Jay, Shoshana Kurtz, and Ruth Rittenband, "Integration in the Jewish Day School," 36–46.

    "The Holocaust: Causes and Responses" (Rabbinics—Abraham Soffer, Social Studies—Lee Lipskin, English Literature—Phyllis L. Berk, Hebrew Literature (H.)—Igal Mishiah), 135–55.

    Nussbaum, Aaron M., "Integration of Studies: Some Procedures and Proposals," 121–24.

    Rosenblatt, Howard B., "An Integrated Non-Karaitic Approach to Teaching Torah," 125–29.

    Sheinkopf, David J., and Geraldine T. Vayer, "The Psalms as a Source of Poetry," 109–19.

Nussbaum, Aaron, M. "The Integrated Curriculum in the Conservative School." *Ed As* (1970): 53–58.

———. "Integration of Studies in Our Day School." *Iggeret* (H.) 3 (May 1968): 4–8; 4:1 (Nov. 1969).

Peri, Chaim. "Integration: The Overlooked Aspects." *Jew Ed* 46 (Winter 1978): 42–43.

Ritterband, Ruth. "Reaction to Joseph Lukinsky's 'Integrating Jewish and General Studies in the Day School'." In *IL*, 44–46.

Schnaidman, Mordecai. "Integration in Centrist Jewish Day Schools." *Jew Ed* 47 (Fall 1979): 11–18.

———. "Integration in the Jewish Elementary All-Day School in America." Master's thesis, Yeshiva U., 1958.

Siegel, Morton. "Clearing the Air on Definitions of Integration." *Jew Ed* 46 (Winter 1978): 22–33.

Silberberg, Yaffa. "Coordination of the Jewish and General Studies Curriculum for the School Year 1968–69." *Iggeret* (H.) 4 (Nov. 1969): 4–6.

Skaist, Solomon W. "Definitions of Integration Can Be Misleading." *Jew Ed* 46 (Winter 1978): 23–25.

Skolnick, Irving. "Integration of Formal and Informal Education." *Syn Sch* 22 (Winter 1964): 43–47.

Solomon, Bennett I. "A Critical Review of the Term 'Integration' in the Literature on the Jewish Day School in America." *Jew Ed* 46 (Winter 1978): 24–28.

* ———. *Curricular Integration in the Jewish All-Day School in the United States*. Harvard U., 1979. 174 pp.

———. "Curricular Integration in the Jewish All-Day School in the United States." *Rel Ed*

77 (July/Aug. 1982): 445–46. Abstract of Solomon's dissertation above.

———. "Theory into Practice: Creating Integrated Experiences within the Jewish Day School." *Ped Rep* 34 (Mar. 1985): 9–13. See also *Stu*, 150–74.

Teutch, Betsy Plotkin. "The Integration of Secular and Judaic Tracks in a Reform Day School: Curricular Units Designed for Fourth Grade Social Studies." Master's thesis, HUC–JIR, 1979.

Ury, Zalman F. "Integration Does Not Mean 'Melting Pot'." *Jew Ed* 46 (Winter 1978): 25.

Wolf, Michael. "Report on Integration Project in Miami." In *IL*, 77–80.

Zalenitz, Alan N. "Correlating General and Judaic Subjects in High School." *Ped Rep* 29 (Spring 1978).

Zeldin, Michael. "Mixing General and Jewish Studies in the Reform Jewish Day School." *Compass* 4 (1981): 3–4, 18.

ORGANIZATION AND ADMINISTRATION

* Berger, Felix. *Yeshivah High School Principals in America*. Yeshiva U., 1970. 267 pp.

Charish, Sharon. "Classroom Climate: Guidelines for the Effective Teacher." *Ped Rep* 35 (Oct. 1984): 5–6.

The Dean's Administrative Manual. 2 Parts. N.Y.: TU. 180 pp.

Egozi, Akiva. "The New Teacher in the Out-of-Town Day School." *Jew Parent* 15 (June 1964): 10–12.

* Flatto, Zehava. *Role Congruency and Job Satisfaction of Principals in Jewish Day Schools*. Yeshiva U., 1978. 151 pp.

Frost, Shimon. "Staffing a Day School." *Ped Rep* 29 (Fall 1977).

Glickman, Leah. "Teaching in a Hebrew Day School is Unique." *Jew Parent* 21 (June 1970): 14–15.

Greenfield, Yeshayahu. „סדר עדיפויות בעבודת מנהל בית-הספר הכל יומי" (A Principal's Priorities in the Day School) (H.) *Ped Rep* 34 (Mar. 1983): 28–30.

Himmelstein, Samuel A. "Day School Teachers' Satisfactions and Dissatisfactions." *Jew Ed* 44 (Spring/Summer 1976): 51–56.

Jordan, Cecille Blank. "In-Service Education: An Innovative Approach." *Ped Rep* 33 (Oct. 1982): 17–19.

* ———. *Perceptions of Role Conflict Problems Reported by Heads of Selected Private Schools: The Solomon Schechter Day School in North America*. U. of Houston, 1983. 153 pp.

———. "Written Job Descriptions, Role Conflict and Day School Heads." *Jew Ed* (Fall 1975): 16–18.

Kaminetsky, Joseph. "Establishing a Jewish Day School." *Jew Ed* 20 (Nov. 1948): 33–39.

———. "Personnel, Finances and Polarization." *Jew Ed* 51 (Spring 1983): 27–29, 48.

Kobrin, Lawrence A. "A Layman Views the Organization and Structure of a Day School." *Jew Ed* 51 (Winter 1983): 31–34, 45.

Lakritz, William B. "Planning a New Day School." *Syn Sch* 16 (Sept. 1957): 22–28.

* Lebovitz, George. *Satisfaction and Dissatisfaction among Judaic Studies Teachers in Midwestern Jewish Day Schools*. U. of Cincinnati, 1981.

* Levi, Jossef. *Formulation and Validation of an Instrument for Interview in Judaic Studies Teachers for Jewish Day Schools*. Catholic U. of America, 1983.

Levinson, B. M. "The Intelligence of Applicants for Admission to Jewish Day School." *JSS* 19 (1957): 129–40.

Mars, Alvin. "A Staff Development Model for the Jewish Day School: Peer Coaching and Teaching Skills." *Jew Ed* 52 (Winter 1984–85): 18–21, 28.

Mermelstein, Jacob. "To Be a Teacher." *Jew Parent* 27 (Jan. 1975): 24–25, 34.

Millgram, Abraham E. "The Day School Teacher." *Syn Sch* 16 (Sept. 1957): 43–47.

Outline of Administrative Responsibilities in a Hebrew Day School. N.Y.: TU.

Pollak, George, and Gerhard Lang. "Teacher Stress in Day Schools—Does It Exist?" *Jew Ed* 52 (Summer 1984): 34–39.

Proceedings, First National Summer Workshop for Principals, Aug. 18–20, 1953. N.Y.: TU.

Rosenberg, Stanley, and Victor B. Geller. "Planning the New Day School." *Jew Parent* 20 (June 1969): 30–32.

Rosenthal, Stephen. "Directors of Non-Orthodox Jewish Day Schools: Who Are They?" *Jew Ed* (Winter 1988): 25–27.

* Schachter, Lifsa B. *Professional Growth of Teachers: A Case Study in Staff Development in a Jewish Day School*. JTSA, 1986.

Schindler, Pesach. "Organizing and Developing a New Day School." *Syn Sch* 24 (Spring 1966): 6–13.

Schwarcz, Ernest. "What Do Tests Test?" *Jew Parent* 22 (Oct. 1970): 16–17.

Shulman, Avi. "The Principals' Workshop: An Experiment in Self-Analysis." *Jew Parent* 22 (Oct. 1970): 26–27.

Shulman, S. N. "I Teach at a Yeshivah." *Jew Life* 17 (Feb. 1950).

Skaist, Solomon N. "The Education of Day School Teachers." In *Jan 2*, 167–74.

Spotts, Leon H. "Organizing the Jewish Day School." *Ped Rep* 29 (Fall 1977).

Teitelbaum, Simcha. "A Principal Looks at the Day School." *Jew Parent* 14 (Summer 1963).

PROFESSIONAL ORGANIZATIONS

Agudath Israel of America—Children's, Girls', and Young Men's Divisions.
"Educates Orthodox Jewish children in Torah; encourages sense of communal responsibility." *Darkenu*; Leaders Guides "Sponsors regular weekly programs on the local level and unites girls from throughout the Torah world with extensive regional and national activities." *Newsletter*; "Educates youth to see Torah as a source of guidance for all issues facing Jews as individuals and as a people. Inculcates a spirit of activism through projects in religious, Torah-educational, and community-welfare fields." *Zeirie Forum, Am Hatorah, Daf Chizuk*, Yom Tov Publications, *Torah Lodaas Ohr Hakollel*.
(*AJYB*, 1988), 442.

Merkos L'inyonei Chinuch (Central Organization for Jewish Education) (educational arm of the Lubavitcher movement).
"Seeks to promote Jewish education among Jews regardless of their background, in the spirit of the Torah-true Judaism; to establish contact with alienated Jewish youth; to stimulate concern and active interest in Jewish Education on all levels; and to promote religious observance as a daily experience among all Jews." *Schmuessen mit Kinder un Yugent, Sihot la Noar, Talks and Tales*.
(*AJYB*, 1988), 449.

Mesivta Yeshiva Rabbi Chaim Berlin Rabbinical Academy.
"Maintains fully accredited elementary and high schools; collegiate and postgraduate school for advanced Jewish studies, both in America and Israel."
(*AJYB*, 1988), 449.

Torah Umesorah–National Society for Hebrew Day Schools.
"Establishes Hebrew day schools throughout the United States and Canada, and services them in all areas, including placement and curriculum guidance, conducts teacher-training institutes on campuses of major yeshivas and seminars and workshops for in-service training of teachers." *Olomeinu—Our World, Vision*.
(*AJYB*, 1988), 452.

UOJCA.
"Serves as the national central body of Orthodox synagogues; sponsors National Conference of Synagogue Youth, Our Way Program for the Jewish deaf, Yachad program for developmentally disabled youth." *Our Way Magazine, Yachad Magazine, Jewish Action Magazine*.
(*AJYB*, 1988), 454.

PARENTS AND THE JEWISH DAY SCHOOL

Adams, Louise L., J. Frankel, and N. Newbauer. "Parental Attitudes toward the Jewish Day School." *Jew Ed* 42 (Winter 1972–73): 26–30.

* Bachelis, Faith G. *Regional Origin, Personality, and Mothers' Attitudes of Jewish Day School Students.* Yeshiva U., 1966. 266 pp.

Benov, Ethel. "The Parent's Role in Motivating Religious Training." *Jew Parent* 17 (Oct. 1965).

Dembicer, P. "Our Children Go to Day School." *National Jewish Monthly* 81 (Feb. 1967): 6–7.

Feitman, Yaakov. "Helping the Parent to Be a Parent: New Role for the Yeshiva Day School." *Ped Rep* 30 (Fall 1978).

Feuer, Avraham C. "Give and Take: Torah Insights into Parent-Child Relationships." *Jew Parent* 22 (Mar./Apr. 1971): 14–16.

Fried, Irving. "Family Education—A Critical Issue in the Hebrew Day School." *Jew Parent* 17 (June 1974): 8–10.

———. "Hebrew Day School Program Diluted by Pressures of Non-Orthodox Parents." *Young Israel Viewpoint* (Oct. 1975).

Handel, Yitzchak. "Aspects of Parenting: A Torah View." *Jew Ed* 52 (Summer 1984): 40–44.

Hirsch, B. "What Shall I Tell My Teacher?" *Jew Life* 14 (Feb. 1948).

Isaac, F. "The Jewish Home Versus College Temptations." *Jew Life* 16 (Oct. 1948).

Israel, Richard J. "Reflections on a Solomon Schechter Day School Education." *MJ* 20 (Spring 1986): 9–10.

Kaminetsky, Joseph. "Parents Too Grow through the Day School." *Orthodox Jewish Life* 19 (Mar./Apr. 1952): 25–28.

———. "Ways to Religious Growth in the Home." *Jew Parent* 1 (Fall 1949). Also in *HDS*, 122–25.

Kapel, David E. "Parental Views of a Jewish Day School." *Jew Ed* 41 (Spring 1972): 28–38.

* Kelman, Stuart L. *Motivations and Goals: Why Parents Send Their Children to Non-Orthodox Jewish Day Schools.* U. of Southern California, 1978.

———. "Parent Motivations for Enrolling a Child in a Non-Orthodox Jewish Day School." *Jew Ed* 47 (Spring 1979): 44–48.

———. "Why Parents Send Their Children to Non-Orthodox Jewish Day Schools: A Study of Motivations and Goals." In *Stu*, 289–98.

Kleinhaus, Rosalie. "A Parents Council's Contribution to a Jewish Day School." *Jew Ed* 56 (Summer 1988): 29–31.

Krupnick, Lillian. "The Parent's View of the Day School." *Jew Parent* 14 (Apr. 1963).

Lamm, Norman. "Taking the Reins Back: How to Restore Effective Parental Responsibility in the Upbringing of Children." *Jew Parent* 18 (Apr. 1967).

Lichtblau, Amy P. "The Parent between Child and Day School." *Jew Parent* 26 (Jan. 1974): 20–21.

Mermelstein, Jacob. "On Psychological Issues: The School and the Home Intervening Therapeutically." *Jew Parent* 23 (June 1972): 24–25.

———. "The Overinvolved Parent: Anxiety and How It Is Learned." *Jew Parent* 26 (June 1974): 28–29.

Miller, Paul A. "The Home, the Synagogue and the School." *Jew Parent* 22 (Mar.–Apr. 1971): 21.

Neusner, Jacob. "The Non-Orthodox Parent in the Orthodox Day School." *Jew Parent* 26 (Mar. 1974): 15.

* Nulman, Louis. *The Parent and the Jewish Day School.* Scranton, Pa.: Parent Study Press, 1956. 119 pp.

———. "Parents' Reaction to the Hebrew Day School." *Ped Rep* 7 (Mar. 1956).

———. *The Reaction of Parents to a Jewish All-Day School.* U. of Pittsburgh, 1955. 146 pp.

Panich, Avigdor. "Explaining the Hebrew Curriculum to Our Parents." *Jew Parent* 15 (Jan. 1964): 10–11.

Parnes, Hannah. "Preparing Children for Family Living." *Jew Parent* 22 (Oct. 1970): 10–11.

Ribalow, Harold U. "My Child Goes to a Jewish Parochial School." *Commentary* (Jan. 1954): 64–67.

Rosenfeld, Israel. "The Parent's Role in the Gamarah Program." *Jew Parent* 18 (Oct. 1966): 9–10.

Schwartz, Elkhanan. "Education for Parents." *Jew Parent* 17 (Jan. 1966).

Singer, Howard. *Why Should I Send My Child to a Day School.* N.Y.: Isaiah Day School, 1966.

Sokol, Moshe Z. "The Psychology of Guilt and the Orthodox Jew." *Jew Parent* (Jan. 1973). Also in *BJC*, 313–18.

Steinberg, Arthur. "Progress Reporting through Home Visitation." *Jew Parent* (June 1966).

Suskowitz, Meir. "Tips to Parents." *Jew Parent* 17 (1965–66).

Twerski, Michael. "The Day School and the Broken Home." *Jew Parent* 26 (June 1974): 15–17.

* Twersky, David. *Attitudes as Indicators of Social Groups: A Case Study of the Parents of Hebrew Day School Students.* Rutgers U., 1965. 104 pp.

Weiss, Samuel A. "Emotional Security in Jewish Children." *Jew Parent* (Dec. 1957).

Willner, Eric A. "A Comparative Study of Home Backgrounds: Factors of All-Day and Afternoon Hebrew School Students." *Jew Ed* 40 (Mar. 1970): 130–35.

ASSESSMENT

Alkin, Abraham. "Needed Now—Unity of Purpose in the Day School Movement." *Jew Parent* 9 (Mar. 1958).

Appel, Gerson. "Are We Educating for Orthodoxy?" *Jew Parent* (Feb. 1955).

Belsky, Meir. "The Day School as an Instrument of Change." *Jew Parent* 26 (Oct. 1973): 14–16.

Belsky, Yisrael. "What Can a Yeshiva Bocher Do?" *Jew Obs* 9 (June 1973): 12–16.

Berman, Jack. "The Making of Hebrew Day School Students." *Jew Parent* 22 (Oct. 1970): 33.

Berman, Saul J. "The Jewish Day School." *Trad* 13 (Summer 1972): 96–99.

Bernstein, Dorothy. "Pre school: Preparation for the Future." *Jew Parent* 25 (June 1973): 16–17.

Bin-Nun, Judith. "The 'Kesher' Response: A Modest Proposal in Support of Reform Day School Education." *Compass* (Dec. 1975): 1–3.

Blau, Yoseph. "Day School—Seven Days a Week." *Jew Parent* 17 (Mar. 1966): 10–11, 29.

Brafman, Aaron. "The Mesivta High School: Time for a Reassessment." *Jew Obs* 6 (Oct. 1970): 8–10.

Brafman, M. "The Yeshivah Problem—A New Approach." *Jew Life* 26 (Dec. 1958).

Breslavener, S. N. "Torah Education's Neglected Frontier: The Yeshiva's English Department." *Jew Obs* 8 (Dec. 1972): 8–12.

Breuer, Jacob. "An Urgent Inner-Yeshiva Project." *Jew Parent* 22 (Jan. 1971): 22–23.

Brickman, William W. "The Day School." (Symposium—Jewish Education in a Secular Society, 45–48.) N.Y.: Synagogue Council of America, Institute for Jewish Policy Planning and Research, 1971.

———. "The Jewish Day School—Backbone of Jewish Education." *Day* (July 22, 1964).

———. "The Jewish Day School's Contribution to American Public Education." *Jew Life* 38 (May/June 1971): 10–21.

———. "The National Report on Jewish Education and the Yeshiva Movement." *Parents Association Bulletin* (May 1960): 2.

———. "Status and Needs of American Jewish Education: The Day School." *Jew Parent* 23 (Oct. 1971): 4–6, 30.

Bridger, David. "Discussion on A. I. Schiff's Paper on Jewish Day School." *Jew Ed* 37 (Winter 1967): 83–86.

Bulman, Nachman. "The Day School Changes People." *Jew Parent* (Mar. 1961): 4.

Cohen, David. "Counteracting Spurious Ideologies." *Jew Parent* 22 (Oct. 1970): 6–7.

Cohen, David Sanford. "American Reform Judaism and the Jewish Day School." Master's thesis, Hebrew University of Jerusalem, 1974.

Cohen, Jack J. "The Jewish Day School." *Recon* (Dec. 26, 1958): 27–28.

Cohen, Michael. "The Anglo-Jewish Day School at the Crossroads." *Jew Ed* 54 (Winter 1986): 43–45.

Cohen, Yehuda. "Creative Day School Education: Myth or Reality?" *Jew Parent* 27 (Oct. 197?): 10–11.

Derby, Josiah. "The Jewish Day School." *RA PROC* (1962): 76–78.

Diamond, Stanley C. "A Look at the Contemporary Jewish Teen-Ager." *Jew Parent* 26 (Jan. 1974): 9–11, 32.

Domb, Cyril. "Oasis in the Desert." *Jew Parent* 20 (Mar. 1969).

Dushkin, Alexander M. "The Role of the Day School in American Jewish Education." *Jew Ed* 20 (Nov. 1948): 5–15.

Egozi, Akivah. "החינוך בישיבות ותרומתו„ (Education in the Yeshiva and Its Contribution). *Sh Hah* (H.) 26 (Fall 1966): 80–85.

Eisemann, Meir. "Helping Our Graduates Continue Their Jewish Education." *Jew Parent* 18 (Apr. 1967): 12–13.

———. "Public Relations for Our Schools." *Jew Parent* 14 (Apr. 1963): 8–9, 29.

Eliach, David. "The Jewish Day School." *Trad* 13 (Summer 1972): 99–105.

Fasman, Oscar Z. "Trends in the American Yeshiva Today." *Trad* (Fall 1967): 48–60.

Feder, Shirley Sloan. "Who Needs the Jewish Day School." *National Jewish Monthly* 85 (Oct. 1970).

Feldman, Emanuel. "Trends in the American Yeshivot: A Rejoinder." *Trad* 9 (Spring 1968): 54–64.

Fendel, Meyer. "Reaching and Teaching More Students." *Jew Ed* 51 (Spring 1983): 41–42.

Feuerman, Chaim. "Critical Challenges Facing the Jewish Day School in the Coming Decade." *Jew Ed* 51 (Summer 1983): 20–22.

* Finkelstein, Eleanor. *A Study of Female Role Definitions in a Yeshiva High School*. New York U., 1980. 274 pp.

Fox, Marvin. "Day Schools and American Jewish Patterns." *Jew Parent* 5 (Sept. 1953). Also in *HDS*, 78–85.

Friedman, Hillel. "Why Chaim Can't Read." *Jew Parent* 26 (Mar. 1974): 14–15.

Frost, Shimon. "Crucial Challenges to the Non-Orthodox School." *Jew Ed* 51 (Spring 1983): 25–26, 37.

———. "Day Schools: A Practitioner's View." (The needs of the Solomon Schechter day schools.) *Con Jud* 33 (Spring 1980): 74–79.

Gelman, Reuben. "The Challenge of the Cheder: A Report on an Old-New Approach to Teaching." *Jew Obs* 5 (May 1968): 15–18.

Gifter, Mordecai. "The Function of Torah Chinuch in Our Generation." *Jew Parent* 15 (June 1960). Also in *HDS*, 18–24.

* Gladstein, Sally S. *Teachers'Mainstreaming inside Priorities in Jewish Elementary Day Schools*. Yeshiva U., 1986.

Goldenberg, Bernard. "Reclaiming the Wasteland." *Jew Parent* 25 (Jan. 1973): 18–19.

Gordis, Robert. *The Day School and the Public School: A Strategy for Jewish Survival Today*. N.Y.: A J Congress.

Greenberg, Simon. "The Religious Policy of the Solomon Schechter Day School." *Syn Sch* 24 (Spring 1966): 11–28.

Grob, Paul. "Self Concept, Sex, Intelligence and Achievement of Jewish Day School Students." *Jew Ed* 41 (Fall 1972): 19–24.

Gross, Alexander. "Who Is Running Our Yeshivas?" *Jew Life* (Fall 1979).

Gross, Maurice. "Reporting Meaningful Test Results in the General Studies Program." *Jew Parent* 16 (Mar. 1968): 12–13.

Heimowitz, Joseph. "Commitment through Learning: How Best to Maintain the Day School's Integrity of Principle." *Jew Parent* 15 (Jan. 1964): 6–7.

———. "Jewish Education Makes a Difference—A Study of the Graduates of a Yeshivah High School." *Jew Ed* 47 (Summer 1979): 28–34.

Himmelfarb, Milton. "Reflections on the Jewish Day School." *Commentary* (July 1960): 29–36.

Hirsch, B. "Dilemmas on the Education Front." *Jew Life* 16 (Apr. 1949).

Hollander, B., and J. Hollander. "Proposal for a Pluralistic Day School." *Recon* 36 (Mar. 27, 1970): 23–25.

Inbar, Efraim. "The Hebrew Day Schools—The Orthodox Communal Challenge." *J of Ethnic Studies* 7 (Spring 1979): 13–29.

Jacobson, Isaac W. "Our Children in Contemporary Society." *Jew Parent* (Feb. 1960).

Jakobovitz, Immanuel. "Jewish Day Schools—Comparison and Challenge." *Jew Parent* 14 (Apr. 1963): 4–5, 24.

———. "The Strength of the Yeshiva Movement." *Jew Parent* (Feb. 1961). Also in *HDS*, 86–91.

"Jewish Education in the Spotlight" (editorial). *Jew Life* 18 (Feb. 1951).

Kaminetsky, Joseph. "The Day School—Action and Reaction." *Jew Life* 20 (Sept. 1952).

———. "The Day School—Crises and Mystique." *Jew Parent* 22 (June 1971): 17–18.

———. "The Jewish Day School." *Trad* 13 (Summer 1972): 106–11.

———. "Orthodox Unity and the Day Schools." *Jew Life* 18 (Sept. 1950).

———. "The Present Challenges to Torah Umesorah." *Jew Parent* 22 (Jan. 1971): 7–9.

———. "Preserving the Integrity of the Day School." *Jew Parent* 15 (June 1964): 6–7, 14.

———. "The Program and Effectiveness of the All-Day School." *Jew Ed* 27 (Winter 1957): 39–49.

Kelman, Stuart, and William Cutter. "The Next Step in the Day School Movement." *Sh'ma* 11 (Oct. 2, 1981): 141–42.

Klein, Stephen. "Jewish Education: How High Should We Aim." *Jew Parent* 27 (Jan. 1975): 22–23.

Kohn, Eugene. "The Zionist Interest in the Jewish Day School." *Jew Ed* 20 (Nov. 1948): 16–22.

Koppman, L. "Bachurei Chemed: An Experiment That Worked." *Jew Life* 17 (Dec. 1949).

Kramer, Daniel J. *The Day School and Torah Umesorah: The Seeding of Traditional Judaism in America*. N.Y.: Yeshiva U. Press, 1984. 211 pp.

* Lazar, Meyer. *Religious Academic Achievement of Boys and Girls of Hebraic Jewish Orthodox Day Schools as Related to Selected Variables*. St. John's U., 1969. 208 pp.

Leiman, Shnayer Z. "The Campus Problem and Jewish Education." *Jew Life* (Mar./Apr. 1968): 22–28.

Lesser, Sim. "Thoughts after One Year's Operation of an Experimental Reform Day School." *Ped Rep* 23 (Mar. 1972): 13–14.

Levinson, B. M. "Problems of Yeshiva Boys." *Yeshiva Education* 1 (Winter 1958): 2–13.

Lookstein, Haskel. "The Jewish Day School." *Trad* 13 (Summer 1972): 112–15.

Lorch, Steven C. "Needed: Quality Curriculum Materials." *Jew Ed* 51 (Spring 1983): 34–37.

Lukinsky, Joseph. "The Jewish Day School Confronts Modernity." *Jew Ed* 51 (Summer 1983): 23–24, 26. Also in *Jew Digest* 39 (Jan. 1984): 20–22.

Lustig, Shane. "What is behind the Success of the Yeshivah and the Failure of Modern Education." *Jew Obs* 6 (July 1970): 9–11.

Marcus, Charles. "Discipline in the Day School." *Jew Parent* 19 (June 1968): 32–33.

Marguleas, Anton. "Proposal for a Pluralistic Day School." *Recon* 36 (May 29, 1970): 27–28.

Martin, Alon. "Maimonides School: A Description of and a Curricular Evaluation of an Orthodox Day School." Master's thesis, Brandeis U., 1971.

Matzner-Bekerman, Shoshana. *The Jewish Child: Halakhic Perspectives*. N.Y.: Ktav, 1984. 314 pp.

Mirsky, Samuel. „לדמותו של חנוך הישיבות הקטנות" (On the Image of the Day Schools). *Hadoar* (H.) 36 (Oct. 6, 1957): 733–35; (Oct. 20, 1957): 758–60.

Neumann, Fannie R. "A Modern Jewish Day School in Quest of a Synthesis." *Jew Ed* 4 (Jan.–Mar. 1932): 25–26.

Newman, A. "The Lesson of the Churbon." *Jew Life* 26 (Aug. 1959).

Newman, L. "The Akiba Hebrew Academy." *Con Jud* 15 (Winter 1961): 15–27.

Noble, Shlomo. "The Yeshiva Today: The Significance of this National Institution throughout History and in our Days." *Jew Obs* 6 (Apr. 1970): 8–10, 23.

* Nussbaum, Aaron M. *A Study of the Degree of Dogmatism Expressed by Junior High School Students in the Jewish Day School*. JTSA, 1973.

Oberstein, Elchonon. "The Day Schools: A Postscript—The Way Things Really Are." *Jew Obs* 12 (Jan. 1977): 7–8.

Ohana, Samuel. "Where is the Day School Headed?" *Jew Parent* 23 (June 1972): 10–11.

Opender, Barry T. "The Jewish Day School: Problems and Issues." Master's thesis, JTSA–Teachers Institute, 1975.

* Orlow, Eva D. K. *Factors Affecting Reading Achievement in Hebrew and in English of Third Grade Day School Students*. Temple U., 1977. 141 pp.

"Perils of Day School Success" (editorial). *Jew Life* 33 (May/June 1966).

Perr, Yechiel. "The Yeshiva World and Orthodoxy: Self Protection . . . or Encounter." *Jew Obs* 6 (Jan. 1970): 22–23.

* Pollak, George. "The Day School in Light of Research." *Ped Rep* 29 (Fall 1977).

———. *The Graduates of the Jewish Day School: A Follow-up Study*. Case Western Reserve U., 1961.

———. "The Jewish Day School Graduate." *Jew Spec* (Feb. 1962): 11–14.

Rauch, Eduardo. "The Jewish Day School in America." In *Religious Schooling in America*, edited by J. C. Carper and T. C. Hunt, 130–65. Birmingham, Ala.: Religious Education Press, 1984.

* Ravin, Noach. *The Effects of Individual and Job Characteristics on Job Satisfaction of Supplementary and Hebrew Day Schools' Hebrew Teachers*. American U., 1981.

———. "The Effects of Individual and Job Characteristics on Job Satisfaction of Supplementary and Hebrew Day Schools' Hebrew Teachers." *Jew Ed* 50 (Spring 1982): 28–35.

Riskin, Steven. "The Jewish Day School." *Trad* 13 (Summer 1972): 115–18.

Rosen, Morton. "Solomon Schechter Day School for All: At What Age?" *Syn Sch* 28 (1970): 4–11.

Rosenblum, William. "Does the General Studies Department Need Overhauling?" *Jew Parent* 15 (Sept. 1963): 14–15.

* Rosenthal, Stephen M. *An Analysis of Factors Affecting the Mobility of Private Non-Orthodox Jewish Day School Directors*. U. of San Francisco, 1987.

Rothkoff, Aaron. "Why A Yeshiva High School?" *Jew Parent* 20 (Jan. 1969): 18–19.

Rothman, Eugene. "Whither the Hebrew Day School?" *Mid* 17 (June–July, 1971): 19–30.

Routtenberg, Max. "A Joint Call: The Day School Movement." *Syn Sch* 24 (Spring 1966): 5–6.

Schachter, Lifsa B. "Three Ways to Evaluate a Day School." *Jew Digest* 30 (Sept. 1984): 35–39.

Schefler, Sh. "בתי ספר יומיים על שם שכטר„ (The Schechter Day Schools). *Sh Hah* (H.) 22 (Fall 1961): 32–34.

Schiff, Alvin I. "An Appreciation of the Jewish Day School in America." *Jew Ed* 37 (Winter 1967): 69–83.

* ———. *A Critical Evaluation of the Policies and Practices of Administration and Supervision of Teacher Personnel in Selected Jewish Elementary Day-Schools*. Yeshiva U., 1959.

———. "Day School Education Today." *Jew Digest* 29 (Sept. 1983): 36–43.

———. "The Jewish Day School." *Trad* 13 (Summer 1972): 118–24.

———. "The Jewish Day School and the Jewish Community." *Jew Ed* 33 (Fall 1962).

———. "The Jewish Day School—The Next Half Century." *Jud* 36 (Spring 1987): 220–25.

———. "On the Status of All-Day Jewish Education." *Jew Ed* 51 (Spring 1983): 2–7.

Schindler, Pesach. "The Solomon Schechter Day School Movement: Post Infancy Challenges." *Ed As* (1970): 39–46.

Schlossberg, David. "The Day School Graduate: Are We Neglecting Him?" *Jew Parent* (Oct. 1964): 20–21.

Schnaidman, Mordecai M. "The Orthodox Day School: An Overview of the Day and High School." *Ped Rep* 29 (Fall 1977).

Schwarcz, Ernest. "Yeshiva Education is Human-Centered: Some Thoughts Regarding the Essential Spirit of Yeshiva Education." *Jew Parent* 13 (Dec. 1961).

Schwartz, Elkhanan. "How Our Children Will Live and Learn in the Future." *Jew Parent* 18 (Jan. 1967): 8–10.

———. "The Problem of Fulfillment: The Quandry Our Yeshiva Graduates Face." *Jew Parent* 18 (Oct. 1966): 6–7.

———. "Yeshiva Graduates as Yeshiva Leaders." *Jew Parent* 16 (Jan. 1965): 6–9.

Segal, Samuel M. "Evaluation of the Jewish Day School." *Jew Ed* 25 (Winter 1955): 46–62.

Shulman, Avi. "On Continuing Yeshiva Education." *Jew Parent* 22 (Mar.–Apr. 1971): 22.

Shurin, Aaron Ben Zion. „די אמעריקאנער ישיבות און דאס פראבלעם פון תנ״ך לערנען" (American Yeshivot and the Problem of Learning Bible). *For* (Y.) (Nov. 23, 1984).

———. „40 יאריקער יוביליי פון תורה ומסורה" (Fortieth Anniversary of Torah Umesorah). *For* (Y.) (Jan. 13, 1984).

———. „באטראכטונגען פון ישיבה לערער און פירער" (Thoughts on Day School Teachers and Lay Leaders). *For* (Y.) (July 1986).

Siegel, Morton. "Some Sobering Concerns." *Jew Ed* 51 (Spring 1983): 30.

Silver, David L. "The Enrollment Plateau: Have We Lost Our Early 'Spark'?" *Jew Parent* 17 (Mar. 1966): 18, 20.

Skydell, A. "A Home for the Wandering." *Jew Life* 14 (Feb. 1947).

Slesinger, Zalmen. "Surveying the Day Schools." *Ped Rep* (Sept. 1966).

Soloveichik, Aaron. "Standards for Achievement on the Day School." *Jew Parent* 16 (June 1965): 4–5, 24.

Syme, Daniel B. "Reform Day Schools: Explosive Growth Ahead?" *RJ* 5 (Mar. 1977): 1, 7, 12.

Taback, Ben Zion. „מה היא ישיבה קטנה רצויה?" (What Constitutes a Good Day School?). *Sh Hah* (H.) 14 (Apr. 1954): 172–74; 24 (Fall 1963): 26–28.

Teitelbaum, Simcha. "Meeting the Challenge Head-On: Finishing Yeshiva High School Education in Israel." *Jew Parent* 23 (Oct. 1971): 11–12.

Teitz, Pinchas M. "Communicating Effectively to the Community." *Jew Parent* 19 (June 1968). Also in *HDS*, 158–63.

———. "Evaluating Our Goals and Outcomes." *Jew Parent* 10 (June 1958): 47–52. Also in *HDS*, 47–52.

Turk, Samuel D. "Something Wrong With Yeshiva Day Schools." *Day* (Mar 9, 1959).

Ury, Zalman F. "Shall the Day School Be Open to All?" *Jew Life* 25 (Aug. 1958).

———. "The Yeshiva-Kollel System." *Jew Ed* 51 (Spring 1983): 17–19.

Wadler, N. H. "What Happens to the Day School Graduate?" *Jew Life* 20 (Aug. 1953).

Wilchesky, Nachman. "The Human Condition, the Jewish Community and the Jewish Day School." *Jew Ed* 51 (Spring 1983): 8–10.

Wohlgemuth, Isaiah. "Continuing Yeshiva Education into Adolescence." *Jew Parent* (June 1960): 4.

Wolpin, Nissan. "The American Hebrew Day School Comes of Age: A Report and Analysis." *Jew Obs* (Oct. 1976): 3–10.

———. "Where is the Day School Headed?" *Jew Parent* 23 (June 1972): 10–11.

Zeldin, Michael. "Beyond the Day School Debate." *RJ* (Spring 1986): 10–11.

Ziprin, Nathan. "The Jewish Day Schools." *Day* (Nov. 15, 1961).

Zuroff, Abraham N. "The Jewish Day School." *Trad* 13 (Summer 1972): 124–30.

VALUES AND IDENTITY

Aboff, Samuel E. "New Approaches to Emotional Health and Moral Guidance." *Jew Parent* (June 1962). Also in *BJC*, 277–83.

Altusky, Zev W. "What Our Children Read Molds Them." *Jew Parent* 11 (Oct. 1959).

Axelrod, Herman C., S. Silverman, and L. Neuman. *A Comprehensive Program of Middos—Character, Education.* N.Y.: TU, 1969.

———. "The Teaching of Middos in Jewish Schools." *Ped Rep* 21 (Mar. 1970). Also in *BJC*.

Bekritsky, Morris. "Introduction to Jewish Ethics." *Jew Parent* (Mar. and June 1969). Also in *BJC*, 203–12.

Brickman, William W. "Ethical Values, Education and the Moral Crisis." *Jew Parent* (Mar. 1971). Also in *BJC*, 118–21.

Bulman, Nachman. "Reason, Emotion and Habit in the Training of a Torah Personality" (Annual Fryer Memorial Lecture). *Jew Parent* 23 (Mar. 1982): 5–7, 34. Also in *BJC*, 28–37.

Cohen, David. "The Relevancy of Torah to the Social and Ethical Issues of Our Time." *Jew Parent* 26 (Jan. 1974): 4, 6, 32. Also in *BJC*, 47–54.

Dove, Y. "Kindliness." *Jew Parent* (Mar. 1956). Also in *BJC*, 259–64.

Elias, Joseph. "The Teaching of Middos." *Jew Parent* (Jan. 1965). Also in *BJC*, 77–85.

Elkin, Joshua. "Bar/Bat Mitzvah as a Unique Dimension within a Day School." *Ped Rep* 31 (Spring 1981): 27–28.

Finkel, Nisson Z. "Kindness as an Expression of Faith." Translated by Joseph Kaminetsky from *Or Hatzofun* for *Jew Parent* (Jan. 1968). Also in *BJC*, 186–90.

Fox, Marvin. "Character Training in the Face of Environmental Pressures." *Jew Parent* 16 (Oct. 1964). Also in *BJC*, 92–98.

Friedman, Murray J. "Solving Ethical Problems." In *BJC*, 61–70.

———. "The Sources of Jewish Ethics." In *BJC*, xi–xix.

* Fuchs, Jay Levi. *Relationship of Jewish Day School Education to Student Self-Concepts and Jewish Identity*. UCLA, 1978. 193 pp.

Gifter, Mordecai. "Ahavas Chesed." *Jew Parent* (Dec. 1950). Also in BJC, 219–29.

———. "The Philosophy and Structure of the Middos Program." *Jew Parent* 18 (June 1967). Also in *BJC*, 3–10.

Glick, Seymour. "To Put Mitzvah Back into Bar Mitzvah." *Jew Parent* 21 (Jan. 1970): 25–26.

Glicksberg, Avraham A. "Respect—A Basic Educational Principle in the Shulchan Aruch." *Jew Parent* (Jan. 1971). Also in *BJC*, 230–35.

* Golovensky, David I. *Ingroup and Outgroup Attitudes of Young People in a Jewish Day School Compared with an Equivalent Sample of Pupils in Public (Mixed) Schools*. New York U., 1954. 321 pp.

Greenberg, M. "Teaching Values in the Modern Day School." *Jew Parent* 15 (1963): 8–9.

Halberstam, Chaim. "The Identity Crisis of the Non-Observant Child in the Hebrew Day School." *Jew Parents* (Apr. 1973): 10–11, 34.

Helmreich, William B. *Wake up, Wake up, to Do the Work of the Creator*. N.Y.: Harper and Row, 1976.

Horovitz. Moshe. "Creative Approaches to Keeping Our Teenagers." *Jew Parent* 17 (Mar. 1966).

Hurwitz, Joseph Zatzal. "To Turn the Many to Righteousness." Translated by Shraga Silverstein and adapted by Joseph Kaminetzky. *Jew Parent* (Mar. 1971). Also in *BJC*, 180–85.

Kagan, I. M. *Ahavath Chesed: Kindness as Required by God*. Translated by Leonard Oschry. Jerusalem and N.Y.: Philip Feldheim, 1967.

———. "A Behavioral Analysis of Teaching Ethics." *Jew Parent*. Also in *BJC*, 284–90.

Kahn, Paul. "Psychological Facts in Yeshiva Education." *Jew Parent* 17 (Jan. 1966): 14–15.

Kaminetsky, Joseph. "Aids to Character Formation." *Jew Parent*. Also in *BJC*, 99–104.

———. "The Day School and the Identity Crisis." *Jew Parent* 26 (Oct.1973): 8–11.

Kaminetsky, Joseph, and Murray I. Friedman, eds. *Building Jewish Ethical Character*. N.Y.: TU, 1975. 318 pp.

Lasson, Morris. "Alienation among Yeshiva Youth." *Jew Obs* 6 (July 1970): 12–15.

Leibowitz, A. H. "Chochmas Hamussar" (The Wisdom of Morality). In *BJC*, 55–60.

Levine, Aaron. "The Ideal Day School Child." *Jew Parent* 15 (Jan. 1964): 14–15.

Mayefsky, Isaac. "Curing Our Ambivalence." *Jew Parent* 20 (Jan. 1969): 28–29.

Mykoff, David. "Experiment at Camp Dora Goldberg" (camp program on ethics). *Jew Parent* (Apr. 1970). Also in *BJC*, 149–55.

Nulman, Louis. "The Launching of the Middos Curriculum." *Jew Parent* (Jan. 1969). Also in *BJC*, 127–33.

———. "A Personal Code of Ethics." *Jew Parent* (July 1957). Also in *BJC*, 105–12.

Schnaidman, Mordecai. "Values in Orthodox Yeshivot and Day Schools." *Ped Rep* 32 (Fall 1980): 16–19.

Schwartz, Elkanan. "The Pursuit of Personal Perfection." *Jew Parent* (June 1969). Also in *BJC*, 246–51.

———. "The Three Dimensions of Piety." *Jew Parent* (Jan. 1975). Also in *BJC*, 252–58.

Schwartz, Gedalia. "Crisis in Education—Aspects of Morality." *Jew Parent* 22 (Oct. 1970): 8–10.

Silverman, Shraga. "Rationale of Middos Character Instruction." In *BJC*, 142–48.

* Silverman, Simon G. *The Psychological Adjustment of All-Day Yeshiva Students*. Yeshiva U., 1954. 195 pp.

Soloveitchik, Aaron. "The Fire of Sinai." In *BJC*, 11–18.

———. "Law and Morality in Modern Society." In *BJC*, 19–27.

Sondhelm, Uri. "Why Not Wednesday?: A Study of Yeshiva Students' Attitude toward Authority—Both in the General Scene and in Religious Life." *Jew Obs* 11 (Sept. 1975): 9–12.

Swift, Isaacs L. "Torah Values for Every Day Living." *Jew Parent* 8 (Sept. 1956). Also in *HDS*, 33–46.

Torah Umesorah. "Program Objectives of the Middos Program." In *BJC*, 125–26.

Twerski, Abraham. "Mental Health in the Yeshiva." *Jew Parent* 22 (Oct. 1970): 4–6.

Ury, Zalman. "Beyond Behaviorism." *Jew Parent* (Mar. 1972). Also in *BJC*, 291–95.

———. "Bridging the Gap Between Ethical Theory and Conduct." In *BJC*, 38–40.

———. *A Program for Teaching Jewish Values, Laws and Customs*. N.Y.: TU, 1967.

Wachs, Saul P. "Teaching Mitzvot in the Conservative Day School." *Ped Rep* 34 (Oct. 1983): 3–7.

Weinberg, Jacob S. "Mitzvos as 'Springboards' for Ethical Behavior." *Jew Parent* (Jan. 1963). Also in *BJC*, 73–76.

Weisfogel, Alex. "Achieving Social Refinement." *Jew Parent* (Apr. 1960). Also in *BJC*, 270–74.

* Willner, Eric. *The Adjustment of Jewish All-Day School Pupils Compared to That of Public School Pupils Attending Afternoon Hebrew Schools: As Determined by the Mooney Problem Check List of "Problems Related to Religion" and an Adaptation of the Maslow S-I, Inventory*. New York U., 1963. 287 pp.

Winter, Herman. "Derech Eretz (Respect) in Yeshivos." *Jew Parent* (Mar. 1955). Also in *BJC*, 265–69.

Yaget, Moshe. "Kibbud Ov (Honor or Esteem for Father)—An Analysis." *Jew Parent* (Apr. and June 1973). Also in *BJC*, 236–45.

FINANCIAL SUPPORT

Brickman, William W. "The Educational Scene—A Moral Issue, the 'Constitutionality' Problem, Freedom for Religious Education." *Jew Parent* 16 (Mar. 1965): 22–23.

———. "Federal Support for Hebrew Day Schools." *Jew Parent* (June 1961): 8.

———. "The Need for Public Support for Jewish Day Schools." *Jew Parent* 15 (Mar. 1964): 37–39.

Budoff, Lippman. "The Government's Aids in a Day School's Dream." *Jew Parent* 17 (June 1966): 18–19.

Deinard, Amos. *Jewish Education: All Day Schools—A Federation Responsibility*. N.Y.: CP, 1961.

Dick, Judah. "The Tuition Squeeze on Yeshiva Parents." *Jew Obs* 51 (Mar. 1968): 3–5.

Dinin, Samuel. "The Jewish All-Day Schools: Federal or Federation Aid?" (editorial). *Jew Ed* 32 (Spring 1962): 133–34.

Dushkin, Alexander M. "Notes on the Relations of Governments to Jewish Day Schools." In *Lown*, 70–76.

Elliott, Roberta. "Tuition Trauma'—Cost Squeeze is Hitting Parents in Day Schools." *Jew Week* (Aug. 23, 1985).

Engelman, U. Z., and Isaac Toubin. *Study on Financing Jewish Day Schools and Related Factors—Summary*. (Prepared for the 31st General Assembly of CJFWF.) CJFWF, Nov. 1962. 22 pp.

Feldman, Irving. *Funding Day School Education*. GA, Nov. 1979.

Federation Support of Day Schools: Background Information. N.Y.: CJF, April 1972.

Federation Support of Day Schools. N.Y.: CJF, November 1976. 15 pp.

Goldenberg, Bernard. "Educational Needs of the Seventies: Testimony Before General Sub-

Committee on Education." *Jew Parent* 21 (Jan. 1970): 20–22.

Guidelines for Federation Assistance to Day Schools. CJFWF, Mar. 1972. 5 pp.

Hartstein, Jacob J. "Jewish Community Parochial Elementary Schools." *Jew Ed* 9 (Oct.–Dec. 1937): 136–42.

Isaacs, Benjamin. "Why Not a United Yeshiva Appeal." *Jew Parent* (Feb. 1961): 10.

"אידישער חנוך אין פאדערגרונט" (Jewish Education in the Foreground) (editorial). *Day* (Y.) (Nov. 24, 1961).

Missri, M. A. "Federation and the Day Schools: A Parent's View." *Jew Life* 38 (Mar./Apr. 1971): 21–28.

National Policy Statement on Communal Support for Jewish Education and Communal Support for Jewish Day Schools. AAJE, 1972.

Pollak, George. *Budget and Financing in Jewish Day Schools.* AAJE *Bulletin* 41 (Mar. 1979). 39 pp.

Pollak, George, and Gerhardt Lang. *Budget and Financing in Jewish Day Schools 1979–80–81.* AAJE *Bulletin* 48 (May 1981).

Raab, Menachem. "Make Jewish Day School Education Free." *Jew Ed* 51 (Spring 1983): 38–40.

———. "Tuition Assistance for the Jewish Day School." *Jew Ed* 47 (Winter 1979): 17–19.

Schrayer, Robert M. *Funding Day School Education.* GA, Nov. 1979.

Sherer, Moshe. "דאס שטיף קינד פון אידישע בודזשעטן" (The Step-Child of Jewish Budgets). *Dos Yiddishe Vort* (Y.) (Aug. 1965): 2–3, 23.

Stewart, Eliyahu. "Federation Support for the Day School." *Jew Parent* 21 (June 1970): 16–17.

Stone, Irving. *Jewish Education: All Day Schools—A Federation Responsibility.* CP, 1961.

———. "Our Case at Federation." *Jew Parent* (Sept. 1961).

Summary and Interpretation of the Study on Financing Jewish Day Schools and Related Factors. N.Y.: AAJE, 1962.

Summer, Morton J. "Cost Effectiveness and Day School Financing." *Jew Parent* 19 (Mar. 1968): 31.

Toubin, Isaac. *The Relationship of the Jewish Welfare Federation to the Jewish Day School.* N.Y.: AAJE, 1961.

"Tuition Compilation Survey." Solomon Schechter Day Schools. N.Y.: United Synagogue, CJE, 1979.

* Well, Harvey A. *Finances and the Jewish Day-School: An Analysis of the Relationship of Teacher, Instructional, and Per-Pupil Costs to Scholastic Achievements.* Loyola U. of Chicago, 1975. 158 pp.

Wolpin, Nisson. "Moment of Truth for Torah Education: For the Federation." *Jew Obs* 9 (May 1973): 14–18.

PERIODICALS FOR CHILDREN AND YOUTH

Olomeinu—Our World. TU, New York, 1945–present. Monthly.

Shmuesen Mit Kinder Un Yugent (Y.) (Conversations with Children and Youth). Merkos L'Inyonei Chinuch, Inc., New York, 1942–present. Monthly.

TEXTS AND GUIDES

(See also texts in curriculum section)

Atkin, Abraham. *Chelkeinu* (H.). Hebrew language text and workbook. N.Y.: TU. 200 pp. Intermediate and senior grades.

———. *Darkenu Aleph and Bais in One Volume* (H.). Two-part workbook on observance of holidays. N.Y.: TU. Intermediate grades.

———. *Darkenu Daled* (H.). Workbook on Shabbos. N.Y.: TU. Grades 7–12.

———. *Darkenu Gimel* (H.). Complete workbook on daily laws and customs. N.Y.: TU. Grades 4 and up.

Blumenthal, Y. C., comp. *Hamishkan V'keilov* (The Tabernacle and Its Utensils) (H.). N.Y.: TU.

Dessler, N. W. *Tokhnit Halimudim—Curriculum for the All Day School*. N.Y.: TU, 1958.

Directory of Yeshiva High Schools for Boys and for Girls. N.Y.: TU, 1986. 147 pp.

Epstein, Ita. *Ba'Sha'ar Yehadus and Middos* (Basic Concepts of Judaism Ethical Values). Workbook. N.Y.: TU. Intermediate grades.

Friedman, L. *The Jewish Year* (Y.). Textbook for religious girls' schools—customs, values, history, etc. Brooklyn, N.Y.: Beth Rachel of Satmar, 1961. 252 pp.

Galupkin, Esther. *Kindergarten Curriculum for the Day School*. N.Y.: TU.

Gross, Sukey. *How and What to Teach a Pre-School and Kindergarten*. Curriculum guide. N.Y.: TU, ca. 1981. 118 pp.

Guide for Women Teachers (Y.). Brooklyn, N.Y.: Beth Rachel of Satmar, 1976. 104 pp.

Isaacs, Jacob. *Our People—History of the Jews*. Brooklyn, N.Y.: Merkos L'Inyonei Chinuch, 1946. 167 pp.

Lifshitz, I. I. *Our Book—a text for Yiddish* (Y.). Brooklyn, N.Y.: Merkos L'Inyonei Chinuch, 1946, 1961. 64 pp.

Lomner, Nathan Perek. *Hamafkid*. Talmud for beginners. N.Y.: TU.

Mindel, Nissan. *Complete Story of Passover*. 8th ed. Brooklyn, N.Y.: Merkos L'Inyonei Chinuch, 1960. 77 pp.

———. *Complete Story of Shovuoth*. Brooklyn, N.Y.: Merkos L'Inyonei Chinuch, ca. 1972. 86 pp.

My Aleph Beth (Y.). Brooklyn, N.Y.: Beth Rachel of Satmar, 1973. 30 pp.

Rabinowitz, C. D. *Divrei Y'mei Yisroel* (H.). History text "from the Year 1 until the present." N.Y.: TU. Upper grades.

Rivkin, Mrs. Nacha. *Reishis Chochmah* (H.). Workbook. N.Y.: TU, c. 1960. 64 pp.

Rosenberger, Mrs. B. Sh., Mrs. Sh. Markowitz, and Mrs. E. Halpert. *Temporary Yiddish Reader 4* (Y.). On values. Brooklyn: Beth Rachel of Satmar, 1974. 200 pp.

Rosenfeld, Israel. *Gemorah L'mas'chilim—Talmud for Beginners* (H.). Workbook and teacher's guide. N.Y.: TU.

———. *Targilon for Sefer Bamidbar: A Workbook* (H.). 2 vols. N.Y.: TU.

Shulman, Avi. *A Guide to the Bais Hamikdosh*. N.Y.: TU.

Sippurim. Collection of stories for the use of youth leaders, translated from modern Hebrew literature. N.Y.: B'nei Akiva of America, ca. 1960.

Stories (with illustrations and guide for female teachers) (Y.). Brooklyn, N.Y.: Beth Rachel of Satmar, 1976. 114 pp.

Stories with a Moral (Y.). Brooklyn, N.Y.: Beth Rachel of Satmar, 1975–77.

The Study of Zionism and Israel in the Yeshiva Day School: A Teacher's Curriculum Guide. N.Y.: National Commission on the Teaching of Zion and Israel, WZO–America, and AAJE, 1980. 87 pp.

A Teacher's Guide and Syllabus for the Teaching of the Weekly Haftorah (H.). N.Y.: TU.

A Teacher's Guide for the Teaching of Prayer (H.). N.Y.: TU

A Teacher's Guide for the Teaching of Tanach (H.). N.Y.: TU.

Ury, Zalman. *The Story of Rabbi Yisroel Salanter* (ethics). N.Y.: TU, 1976. 98 pp.

Yavne, National Religious Jewish Students Association. *College Guide for Jewish High School Students*. N.Y.: Youth Division of UOJCA, ca. 1968. 11 pp.

Sefer Ha-Zikaron (Y.). Brooklyn, N.Y.: Yeshiva and Mesivta Arugath Habosem of Williamsburg, 1985. 127 pp.

GLEANINGS

Bush, Isidor (St. Louis, 1855),
    "After mature reflection and due consideration of all its bearings, I am utterly opposed to all sectional or sectarian schools, nor would I change my opinion if our means are as ample as they are deficient. . . . I have . . . given my views of the most feasible plan by which a good religious instruction might be given to our children without retarding their progress in other

knowledge, and by which the boon might be extended to a much larger number...."

Another objection raised against the public schools is, that it might be demanded of our children to read the Bible in some Christian version, or even the books called gospels, &c. But this is as futile an argument as the rest; for in most of the States this question has been fully dicussed against the admission of any Bible or religious instruction whatsoever."

Quoted in Gartner, *JEUS*, 68–69, 71.

Felsenthal, Bernard (Chicago, 1865),
"We would be entirely against specifically Jewish schools, if the body of Jewish knowledge which we consider desireable for our children could easily be acquired in Sabbath schools. But there is too large an amount of subject matter to master."

Quoted in Gartner, *JEUS*, 83–84.

Benderly, Samson (1926),
"We who are interested in this American system of Jewish Education are fully convinced that the only hope for Jewish education in this country lies in schools supplementary to the Public School. It may be quite possible and would probably be worth while to have a number of Jewish Day Schools in which both secular and Jewish subjects can be taught. And if they will only be conducted along lines that will reckon with modern educational theory and pedagogic principle we should welcome them."

Quoted in Nathan Winter, *Jewish Education in a Pluralist Society* (1966), 49.

Revel, Bernard,
"The Jewish day school brings about a closer unification of the forces of education. It will, by its simultaneous human and religious appeal, quicken the moral consciousness and widen the spiritual and moral horizon of the Jewish child."

"The Day School and the Yeshiva in Jewish Education." NCJSS Proceedings (1926), 296.

Dinin, Samuel, on Jewish parochial schools,
"The secular subjects are taught, presumably, as in the public schools, full sway being given to the teacher to teach what and how he pleases. The Jewish subjects, however, are taught as gospel truth, and the methods of science are proscribed.... It makes for the worst kind of dualism, and for serious maladjustments. Parochial schools, being religious, are open to the same criticism as the congregational schools. Being dogmatic, they are anti-scientific and anti-"experimental." Being doctrinaire, they are no respecters of the child as he is, or of the world he lives in. Consequently they are undemocratic and unsocial, and should be condemned as such."

Judaism in a Changing Civilization (1933), 192.

Grossman, Mordecai,
"As a matter of far-reaching policy, Jewish individuals and Jewish communities should discourage the establishment of parochial schools."

Jew Ed 16 (May 1945), 25.

Honor, Leo L.,
"A remarkable and even striking change in Jewish educational attitudes is indicated by the recent growth of Jewish all-day schools.... Total enrollments for all-day schools in 1946–47 was 14,835, (6.3% of total enrollments in all Jewish schools)."

In *JPPP*: 2:169–70.

Reichert, Victor E.,
"I see the Jewish All-Day as a phenomenon that must be interpreted in the context of the eclipse of humanistic liberalism and withdrawal in the shell of separatism. This may make for intensity, but not for real illumination. The inculcation of intense and narrow Jewish loyalty, purchased at the price of voluntary withdrawal and segregated sectarian study, comes too high. Like many private systems of education that withdraw children from the public schools in their most pliable and most impressionable years when they should be experiencing the free association, the friendship and the fight of the democratic way of life—and not merely learning to speak the phrase—the scar of a certain snobbish, warped and narrow mental outlook is fairly sure to result."

Jew Teach 19 (Jan. 1951), 7.

Fox, Marvin (1953),
"The Hebrew Day School movement has come of age. Even its sharpest critics and bitterest opponents can no longer dismiss it contemptuously as of no consequence. Those who in their prejudiced blindness conceived of the Day Schools as the passing effects of an extremist fanaticism must now admit that their vision was myopic. For it is unquestionably a matter of public record that the Day School has established itself as one of the stable and growing elements in the pattern of Jewish education in America. . . .

The Hebrew Day School must be candidly explicit in announcing that it is committed to a particular set of values which are embodied in Jewish religion and rooted in the whole of established tradition."
Hebrew Day School Education (1970), 78, 80–81.

USCJE—National Conference on Day School Education (April 30–May 1, 1957),
"We further call upon the USCJE to expand forthwith its program of educational services to provide for the establishment and operation of a Committee on Day School Education whose purposes it will be:
A. To stimulate, guide and direct the development of day schools in our Movement.
B. To gather and disseminate to these, and to prospective schools, materials and information pertinent to the organization, administration, and the curriculum of such units.
C. To stimulate and foster creative thought, research and activity which will enable these institutions to attain their fullest potential and to make their maximum contribution to the spiritual and cultural enrichment of their charges and through them to the American Jewish Community."
Syn Sch 16 (Sept. 1957), 28.

Fourth NCJE Conference (June 1959),
"Whereas the Jewish Day School has increased rapidly during the past decade, indicating that they have met a deeply felt need of groups within the Jewish community for intensive Jewish education. . . .

Therefore Be It Resolved that as a partial solution for the need for more intensive Jewish education for some children, communities be advised to accept among the schools which they support or service the Jewish Day Schools that meet objective standards of school management and public requirements for general education."
Jew Ed 30 (Fall 1959), 95.

NCJE Adopts Resolution on All-Day School,
"The National Council for Jewish Education notes with deep satisfaction the significant growth of the all-day school and its emergence as a major form of Jewish education in numerical strength and wide-spread appeal manifesting, as it does, the increasing commitment of a substantial segment of American Jewry to Jewish education in a greater degree of depth than that which the predominant supplementary school can offer."
Jew Ed 32 (Winter 1962), 123.

LZOA Statement on Day Schools,
"We regard the Jewish Day School as being potentially best for the Jewish child in that it provides him with a maximal opportunity to become imbued with Jewish learning through study and close association with the treasures of Jewish culture in their original, thus making for his personal enrichment and laying the foundation for those Jewish commitments and habits of Jewish study so basic to sound growth into knowledgeable Jewish adulthood."
Jew Ed 34 (Summer 1964), 277.

Birnbaum, Herbert A.,
"There is no significant relationship between the religious attitudes, observances, and beliefs of Jewish pupils and the type of school (Day school, Hebrew school, Sunday school) the affiliation of the school (Orthodox, Conservative, Reform) they attend. However, the Day school pupils seem to have a greater degree of "self-acceptance" as Jews than Hebrew school pupils."
A Study of Religious Attitudes, Beliefs, and Observances of Jewish Pupils with Varying Religious Educational Experiences (U. of Maryland, 1963). Quoted in *Jew Ed* 35 (Summer 1965), 241.

Berkson, Isaac B. (1964),
"We need the intensive Orthodox Jewish Day Schools—the yeshivot—with their religious and educational intensity. We need them realizing full well that many of them do make accommodations. They need not make accommodations. We need their strong conviction and commitment. They are going to persist and they should persist."
Quoted by Alvin I. Schiff in *Jew Ed* 37 (1967), 75.

Frost, Shimon,
"Need I tell you that our day schools are anything but unitary in their program? The typical day school is bi-departmental. The school day is dichotomized. The administrative apparatus is frequently run by two principals, and there are two faculties. The educational climate permeating one part of the program is far removed from whatever transpires in the other. Not only do the two faculties operate in different universes of discourse, they, at times, are not, literally, on speaking terms."
"Integrating the Judaic and General Studies Curriculum." *Syn Sch* 24 (Spring 1966). Quoted by Bennett I. Solomon in *Stu*, 2:150.

Schiff, Alvin I.,
"The Jewish Day School has demonstrated convincingly that it is one of the best ways of combatting the corrosive effects of assimilation. It has become a most effective instrument for transmitting the Jewish heritage to Jewish youth, and consequently a sure method of insuring American Jewry's creative continuity and abilty to enrich American life."
Jew Ed 37 (Winter 1967).

Bridger, David,
"I cannot agree that the day school is communal simply because it receives a communal subsidy. The determining factor is not what the community does for the school but what the school does for the community. A communal school is, to my understanding, one which serves as an educational institution for those who support it, for all parents and their children who are part of the community.
The curriculum of the day school is . . . not balanced. It is mainly based on the study of Humash and Talmud, and other subject matter is either incidental or auxiliary in nature. . . . I can see only two basic textbooks in the day school, and those were authored two thousand years ago. . . . The children of the day school live in two worlds which do not touch each other, not only from the standpoint of content and language, but also from the standpoint of the tempo, the teaching-learning process, and the materials and methods of instruction. In the English department, the child is exposed to a variety of colorful learning materials; to well graded, attractive, and well-organized textbooks. This is not the case in the Hebrew department. The child in the English department proceeds from the easy to the difficult, from the near to the distant, from the concrete to the abstract. . . . There is full recognition of "individual differences." The process and experience is quite often reversed in the Hebrew department."
Jew Ed 37 (Winter 1967): 84–86.

Kaminetsky, Joseph, and Murray J. Friedman,
"The permissive nature of American society, the separation of church and state which resulted in the dissolution of congregational discipline, and other related factors made it necessary for a different type of school organization to be designed in order to conduct a program of intensive Jewish education. Thus arose a school structure in which the administration of religious and secular studies took place under one roof. In addition, the function of the school was not only to transmit Torah knowledge but also to revive the observance of mitzvos which the home neglected and to foster sympathy for the school's objectives."
HDS, 189.

Sklare, Marshall (1971),
"Despite the wide differences among day schools, sophisticated observers claim that all of them suffer from a similar defect: the two-track approach. The result of such compartmentalization is that the secular curriculum never receives the benefit of cross-fertilization by Jewish culture and vice versa. To its detriment

Jewish culture is doomed to exist in splendid isolation from the general culture. Furthermore, the student may be taught one thing in the secular curriculum and its precise opposite in the Jewish curriculum. Sensitive educators concede the danger of curricular separatism and the consequent desirability of integrating secular and Jewish studies, but little progress has been made."

Quoted by Eduardo Rauch in *Religious Schooling in America*, edited by J. C. Carper and T. C. Hunt (1984), 145.

Berman, Saul J.,
"While the traditional yeshivot may continue to attract predominantly students who are sufficiently sheltered from the outside world as to maintain their basic similarity to the students of the past generation, even they, and certainly the more open Day Schools, are attracting in increasing numbers, students whose life styles are being shaped by the new cultural patterns in American society. If the Day School continues to teach in the old, even previously successful, fashions, they wiil fail to accomplish their goals with the new students."
Trad 13 (Summer 1972), 96.

Eliach, David,
"We educate our students in two separate directions—philosophically and psychologically. On the one hand we guide our students in the belief that Torah is a way of life which encompasses every way of life. On the other hand, we expose them in the humanities department to a secular way of life influenced by the sciences, history and world literature, with an entirely different approach to life. . . . It is clear that we need a complete change in thinking to save our future generations. . . . To establish a national central committee for Yeshiva education where Gedolim and great educators will work out together a new approach to our education which will be relevant and meaningful."
Trad 13 (Summer 1972), 100, 104.

Rubin, Israel,
"In summary, Satmarer [Hasidim] want their schools to serve primarily as a bastion against undesireable acculturation, as a training ground for Torah knowledge in the case of the boys, and, in the case of girls, as a place to gather knowledge they will need as adult women."
An *Island in the City* (1972), 140. Quoted by B. Steinberg in *Jew J Soc* 21 (June 1979), 53.

Schiff, Alvin I.,
"If I were on the fence in the past regarding government aid to Jewish day schools. I now stand squarely for it. If I had hesitation about its de jure legality, I am convinced about the soundness of its de facto reality. If I had concerns about the negative effects of breaching the wall of separation between church and state, these have completely dissipated. The 'wall' has been breached without any ill effects on the political and national security of the United States. Indeed, other kinds of breaching and breaking should concern us much more. If I questioned the absolute need to help sustain Jewish day schools and help the Jewish community maintain quality all-day education, the sky-rocketing costs of schooling have disabused me concerning any doubts of this need. If there ever was a time for gaining the full support of government funding for Jewish day schools it is now."
Jew Ed 42 (Summer 1973), 11–12.

Sklare, Marshall,
"Until the nineteen-forties parochial education constituted a heretical idea. Obedience to the American system of public education was a religious commandment. By the post-World War II era there had emerged a group of first, second, and third generation Jews who felt safe enough as Americans to reject public education. Unlike their predecessors they did not require the common school in order to validate their American identity."
Quoted by Eduardo Rauch in *Religious Schooling in America*, edited by J. C. Carper and T. C. Hunt (1984), 155.

Slesinger, Zalmen,
"The dramatic growth of the day school during the past four decades should not delude us as evidence of the superiority of its program. The sharp increase in day school registration is largely the result of unwelcome conditions within the public school rather than the outcome of a spurt

of Jewish consciousness, or a surge of interest in intensive traditional Jewish education or a growing realization that day school education is the response par excellence to the educational needs of our times."

Jew Fron (Aug./Sept. 1975), 37.

Elazar, Daniel J.,
"The biggest development in Jewish education in recent years is the spread of day schools. While enrollment in other forms of Jewish education stabilized by 1962 and then began to decline the enrollment of the day schools continued to rise, although it now seems to have leveled off. By 1971 nearly seventy thousand students were registered in Jewish day schools, in contrast with forty-three thousand in 1969 and four thousand (all in New York City) in 1935. In 1972 day school students constituted slightly over 14 percent of all pupils in Jewish schools of any kind."

Community and Polity (1976), 290.

Berkovitz, Eliezer (1976),
"There is at least one serious shortcoming in our educational philosophy. In our day schools and Yeshiva high schools, the curriculum is divided into Limudei Kodesh and Limudei Hol, sacred studies, the teaching of Jewish subjects on the one hand, and secular studies of a general nature on the other. . . . The two areas of knowledge cannot be kept apart in the mind and soul of the student. If one may paraphrase the words of Maimonides from the Introduction to his *Guide for the Perplexed*, by this kind of educational process one either does violence to one's intellect by one's faith, or one violates one's faith by one's intellect."

Quoted by Eduardo Rauch in *Religious Schooling in America*, edited by J. C. Carper and T. C. Hunt (1984), 145–46.

Schiff, Alvin I.,
"As the Jewish day school movement has developed, the schools more and more reflect the diversity of the Jewish community. There are as many kinds of Jewish-all-day programs as there are ideological shadings and spectrums of American Jewry. They include Hasidic, sectarian Orthodox yeshivot and mesivot; centrist Orthodox yeshivot and day schools; communal-traditional institutions; Conservative, Reform and general secular schools."

Jew Ed 51 (Spring 1983), 2.

Frost, Shimon,
"These five challenges—professional leadership, academic excellence, the Hebraic/Judaic program, day high school or reasonable facsimiles thereof for smaller communities, and the need for a social/cultural/religious milieu—will have to be addressed and met if the non-Orthodox day school is to flourish as a vigorous force for creative Jewish survival."

Jew Ed 51 (Spring 1983), 37.

21 YIDDISH SECULAR SCHOOLS

BACKGROUND MATERIALS (SELECTED)

Many of the periodicals listed are from Ephim H. Jeshurin's Bibliography on Yiddish Schools, Part 2 of his *One Hundred Years of Modern Yiddish Literature* (Y.) (1965).

Abramowicz, Dina. *Yiddish Literature in English Translations: Books Published*. N.Y.: Yivo, 1967. 35 pp.

Algemeine Encyclopedia—General Encyclopedia, Yiddish Section. "ייִדישע שולן אין די פאראייניקטע שטאטן און קאנאדא" (Jewish Schools in the United States and Canada). In *Yidn*, 407–20. 1942.

אלמאנאך פון די ייִדישע קינדער שולן (Almanac on Yiddish Schools). N.Y.: International Workers Orden, 1941. 100 pp.

לעקסיקאן פון דער נייער ייִדישער ליטעראטור (Biographical Dictionary of Modern Yiddish Literature) (Y.). 8 vols. N.Y.: World Jewish Congress, 1956–82.

Boraisha, Menachem. *The Story of Yiddish*. N.Y.: 1946. 23 pp. Also in *JMW*, 2:356–76.

Doroshkin, Milton. *Yiddish in America: Social and Cultural Foundations*. Rutherford, N.J.: Fairleigh Dickinson U. Press, 1969. 281 pp.

Fishman, Joshua. *Never Say Die*. N.Y.: Hague Moulton Publishers, 1981. 763 pp.

———. "Yiddish in America." *Jewish Heritage* (Fall 1962): 5–12.

* Garfinkle, Harry. *Ideological Elements in the Development of the American Yiddish School Movement*. Columbia U., 1953. 345 pp.

Goldberg, I. *Jewish Secular Education: Its Values and Meanings*. N.Y.: Kinderbuch, 1961.

Goldsmith, Emanuel S. *Architects of Yiddishism at the Beginning of the Twentieth Century: A Study in Cultural History*. Cranbury, N.J.: Fairleigh Dickinson U. Press, 1976. 309 pp.

Howe, Irving. *World of Our Fathers*. N.Y.: Harcourt, Brace, Jovanovich, 1976. 714 pp.

Hyman, Sh. "דער לימוד פון ייִדיש אין אמעריקאנער אוניווערסיטעטן" (The Study of Yiddish in American Universities). *Zuk* (Y.) (May/June 1974): 196–97.

Landis, J. C. "The Relevance of Yiddish." *Jewish Heritage* 12 (Fall 1969): 14–19.

Lehrer, Leibush. די מאדערנע אידישע שול (The Modern Yiddish School) (Y.). N.Y.: Meisl Pub., 1927. 190 pp.

Niger, Shmuel. "וועלטלעכע ייִדישע שול" (Secular Yiddish School). In *DER* (Y.), 3:381–400.

———. אין קאמף פאר א נייער דערציאונג (Struggling for a New Education) (Y.). N.Y.: Education Department of the WC, 1940. 226 pp.

———. "Yiddish Culture." In *JPPP*, 4:264–307.

Poll, Samuel. "The Role of Yiddish in America." *YA* 13 (1965): 125–52.

Pomerantz, I. Chaim, and Shloime Bercovich, eds. *Shul-Pinkes* (Y.). Materials on schools in Chicago and studies on Yiddish education in general. Chicago: SAFI, 1948. 674 pp.

Samuel, Maurice. *In Praise of Yiddish*. N.Y.: Cowles. 283 pp.

Zhitlowsky, Chaim. „דער ערשטער פערטל יארהונדערט פון אונדזערע שול" (The First Quarter-Century of Our Schools). In *S Alm*, 9–14.

HISTORY OF YIDDISH SECULAR SCHOOLS

Bass, Hyman. „פון קאסמאפאליטיזם ביזן אויפקום פון נאציאנאלע אידייען" (From Cosmopolitanism until the Rise of National Ideas). *Zuk* (Y.) 59 (Dec. 1954): 453–58.

Berg, Jacob. „אביסל זכרונות" (Some Memories). On the history of the Sholem Aleichem Schools. In *Jubilee Volume—40 Years* (Y.), 63–65. N.Y.: SAFI, May 1964.

Bialostotzky, B. J. „דער 50 יאריגער יובילעאום פון אידישע קינדער-שולן אין אמעריקע" (The 50th Jubilee of Yiddish Secular Schools). *For* (Y.) (June 10, 1961).

Chaikin, J. „די באציאונג פון יידישע צייטונגען אין אמעריקע צו דער באוועגונג פאר יידישע שולן" (The Attitude of the Yiddish Press to the Yiddish School Movement). In *Yiddish Pages in America* (Y.), 352–65. 1946.

Chanin, Nathan. „50 יאר יידיש-וועלטלעכע שולן אין אמעריקע" (50 Years of Yiddish Secular Schools in America). *Zuk* (Y.) (Sept. 1961): 310–12.

„די בר מצוה פון די שלום עליכם שולן" (The Bar Mitzvah of the Sholem Aleichem Schools). *Day* (Y.) (Dec. 30, 1926).

Doroshkin, I. „ווי אלט זיינען אונדזערע שולן?" (How Old Are Our Schools?). *Pro D* (Y.) (Feb. 1937): 16–17.

Elbe, Leon. „דער ארבייטער רינג און די אידיש ראדיקאלע שולן" (The WC and the Yiddish Radical Schools). *Zuk* (July 1916): 632–44.

Entin, Joel. „די נייע אידישע דערציאונג" (The New Jewish Education—Beginning of Jewish Folk Schools). In *Jewish National Workers Alliance, 1910–1946* (Y.), 145–97.

———. „25 יאר נייע אידישע דערציאונג" Years of New Jewish Education). *Jewish Worker's Voice* (Y.) (June 1937): 17–19.

Gladstone (Glatstein), Jacob. „40 יאר שלום עליכם אינסטיטוט" (40 Years of the Sholem Aleichem Folk Institute). In *Jubilee Book* (Y.), 23–24. N.Y.: 1954.

Glantz, A. „די נאציאנאל-ראדיקאלע שוהלען" (The National-Radical Schools). *Zuk* (Y.) (July 1914): 709–12.

Glantz-Leyelis, A. „זכרונות וועגן דער יידישער שול-באוועגונג אין אמעריקע" (Memoirs of the Yiddish School Movement in America). In *Shu P*, 200–212.

———. „44 יאר שלום עליכם שולעס" (44 Years—Sholem Aleichem Schools). *Day-Journal* (Y.) (May 15, 1957).

Gold, I. „70סטער יובילייי פון די ארבעטער-רינג שולן" (70th Jubilee of the Workmen's Circle Schools). *For* (Y.) (Dec. 2, 1988).

Goldberg, Ben Zion. „דרייסיק יאר וועלטלעכע שולן" (30 Years of Secular Schools). *Day* (Y.) (Dec. 11, 1943).

Goodman, Saul L., ed. *The Faith of Secular Jews*. N.Y.: Ktav, 1976. 301 pp.

———, ed. *Our First Fifty Years* (E. and Y). N.Y.: SAFI, 1972. 187 pp.

Hertz, J. B. „יידישע וועלטלעכע שולן" (Yiddish Secular Schools). In *Fifty Years of the Workmen's Circle in American Jewish Life* (Y.), 197–209.

Hurwitz, Maximilian. "The Schools." In *The Workmen's Circle: Its Ideals, Organization and Institutions*, 166–77. N.Y.: 1936.

דער פעוציק-יאריקער יובילעאום פון די יידישע פאלק שולן (Jubilee Volume in Honor of 40 Years) (Y.). N.Y.: SAFI, 1954.

יובל-בוך לכבוד 50 יאר שלום עליכם פאלק-שולן (Jubilee Volume in Honor of 50 Years) (Y.). N.Y.: SAFI, 1963. 100 pp.

Knox, Israel. "The Arbeiter Ring [WC] at Sixty." *Recon* 26 (Nov. 18, 1960).

Lehrer, Leepe. „דער שלום עליכם פאלקס אינסטיטוט" (Sholem Aleichem Folk Institute). In *S Alm* (Y.), 134–47.

21 YIDDISH SECULAR SCHOOLS

Lehrer, Leibush. „דער אנהייב פון דער יידיש-וועלטלעכער שול" (Beginning of the Yiddish Secular School). In *The Modern Yiddish School*, 24–32. N.Y.: Meisl Pub., 1927.

———. „די יידישע פארגאנגענהייט און די יידישע שול" (Jewish Past and the Jewish School). In *From Generation to Generation* (Y.), 41–50. 1959.

Levine, Jacob. „35 יאר ארבעטער רינג שול" (35 Years of WC Schools). *CE* (Y.) (Jan. 1954).

Mark, Yudel. „אן איבערבליק איבער דער געשיכטע פון יידישער דערציאונג אין אמעריקע" (An Overview on the History of Jewish Education in America). *Zuk* 59 (Dec. 1954): 491–94.

———. „30 יאר יידישע שול אין אמעריקע" (30 Years of Yiddish Schools in America, 1918–1948). *Jewish Review* 5 (1947) (Y. section): 1–41. See also *Zuk* (Mar. 1946): 152–61.

———. „צוויי דורות פון אונדזער שול" (Two Generations of Our School). *CE* (Y.) 33 (Feb. 1963): 4–5.

———. „בתי הספר האידיים בארצות הברית ובקנדה" (Yiddish Schools in the United States and Canada). In *JB* (H.), 195–205.

———. "Towards a History of the Sholem Aleichem Folk Institute." In *OFFY*, 17–32.

Milbauer, I. „אין אנהייב" (In the Beginning). In *Jubilee Volume—40 Years* (Y.), 66–67. N.Y.: SAFI, May 1964.

Mlotek, Joseph. „די בריק צווישן דורות" (The Bridge between Generations). 35 years of WC in America. *Der Veker* (Y.) (Oct. 1, 1952): 9–10.

———. „50 יאר י. ל. פרץ שולן פון ארבעטער רינג" (50 Years I. L. Peretz Schools of the Workmen's Circle). *For* (Y.) (Jan. 28, 1968).

Niger, Shmuel. „היסטארישער הינטערגרונט" (Historical Background). In *SNE* (Y.), 23–40.

———. „וואָרצלען אין דער אַלטער היים" (Roots in the Old Home). In *SNE* (Y.), 1–22.

Noveck, H., ed. „שול אלמאנאך" (School Almanac) (Y.). Phila.: WC, 1935. 416 pp. Articles on ideologies and histories of various Yiddish school systems.

Penn, Ascher. "The First Quarter Century." On the history of SAFI. In *OFFY*, 3–16.

Sandler, P. „פופצן יאר פראגרעסיווע יידיש-שול-וועזן אין אמעריקע" (15 Years of Progressive Yiddish Schools in America). *Yiddish Culture* (Y.) (Jan. 1942): 39–45.

Shapiro, Solomon. „דער אנהייב פון די פאלקשולן" (The Beginning of the Folk Schools). *YD* (Y.) (Spring 1962): 27–33.

———. „דער פופציק-יאריקער יובילעאום פון די יידישע פאלק שולן" (50 th Jubilee of the Yiddish Folk Schools). *YD* (Y.) 10 (Dec. 1962): 76–83.

Silver, L. „יידישע דערציאונג אין אמעריקע" (Yiddish Education in America). Historical account. *CE* (Y.) 11 (Mar. 1941): 113–14; (Nov. 1941): 15–17; and (Dec. 1941): 15–16.

Simon, Solomon. "Fifty Years of the Sholem Aleichem Folk Institute." In *OFFY*, 109–16.

———. „40 יאר אידיש-וועלטלעכע שולען" (40 Years Yiddish Secular Schools). *Morning Journal* (Y.) (Jan. 8, 1953).

Talmach, Regina Entin. "A Child Goes to the First Folkschule." *For* (E. section) (Feb. 25, 1983): 23–24.

Tsivion (B. Hoffman). „די ערשטע ארבעטער רינג שול" (The First WC School in Our Times). *Der Friend* (Y.) (Jan. 1939).

Yefroikin, Zalman. "The Yiddish Secular School in the United States." In *JPPP*, 2:144–50.

———. „די יידיש-וועלטלעכע שול אין ליכט פון דרײַ הונדערט יאר יידיש לעבן" (Yiddish Secular Schools in Light of 300 Years of Jewish Life in America). *CE* (Y.) (Nov. 1953): 4–6.

RATIONALE

Entin, Joel. אידישע דערציאונג (Jewish Education) (Y.). Edited by Solomon Shapiro. N.Y.: Farlag Gingold—JNWA–LZOA, 1960. 378 pp.

———. „די אידישע פאלק שול" (The Jewish Folk School). Ideals and program. *YK* (Y.) (Aug. 4, 1950): 5–8.

———. „די אידישע פאלק שול, איר תוך איר נשמה" (The Yiddish Folk School—Its Substance and Soul). *Day* (Y.) (Jan. 4, 1936).

———. „די אידישע פאלק שול" (Yiddish Folk Schools). In *S Alm* (Y.), 119–33.

Gingold, Pinchos. „די יידישע פאלקשולן" (The Yiddish Folk Schools). In *Gingold* (Y.), 31–44.

Glicksman, William. "One Man's Opinion Concerning the Place of the Yiddish Secular School in America Today." *Jew Ed* 39 (July 1969): 17–22.

Golomb, Abraham. „די אידיש-וועלטלעכע שול" (The Yiddish Secular School). In *S Alm* (Y.), 15–26.

Goodman, Saul L. „דער וועלט באנעם פון דער יידישער שול" (The World Outlook [Weltanschaung] of the Yiddish School). *CE* 30 (Jan. 1960): 14–17.

Hadoar. „אידיש בבית הספר הצבורי" (Yiddish in the Public Schools) (H.) (editorial). 37 (Apr. 11, 1958): 425–26.

Kantor, M. „וועלטלעכקייט אין אונדזערע שולן" (Secularism in Our Schools). *YD* (Y.) (Aug. 1950): 108–10.

Knox, Israel. "Yiddish and the Peretz Schools of the WC." *For* (E.) (May 14, 1958).

Lazarson, I. „סאציאלע דערציאונג אין אונדזערע שולן" (Social Values in Our Schools). *CE* (Y.) 11 (Apr. 1941): 13–15.

Lehrer, Leibush. „דערציאונג און באוועגונג" (Education and Ideology). *CE* (Y.) 11 (Nov. 1941): 6–8.

———. „דער צוועק פון דער שול" (The Purpose of the School). In *The Modern Yiddish School* (Y.), 152–62. N.Y.: Meisl Pub., 1927.

———. „זוכנדיק א וועג" (Searching a Direction). *zuk* (Y.) (Sept. 1953): 355–59.

Leivick, H. „לאמיר בויען די אידישע שול" (Let Us Build the Yiddish School). *For* (Y.) (Nov. 20, 1949).

Levine, Jacob. „די אידישע ארבעטער רינג שול איר ציל און פראגראם. ווי אזוי אזא שול צו עפענען און אנצופירן" (The Jewish Workmen's Circle School—Goal and Program: How to Open and Administer this Type of School). N.Y.: Education Committee of the WC, 1920. 64 pp.

Margoshes, Samuel. "The Sholem Aleichem Schools in Defense of Yiddish." *Day* (June 17, 1963).

Mark, Yudel. „וועגן הייטנצייטיקער אידעאלאגיע פאר דער יידישער שול" (Concerning a Contemporary Ideology for the Yiddish School). *BYD* (Y.) (June/Sept. 1951): 1–12.

———. „דערציאונג פאר צווי קולטורן" (Education for Two Cultures). *BYD* (Y.) (Apr./June 1953): 17–25.

———. „פארמולירונג פון דעם הויפטציל פאר יידישער דערציאונג" (Formulating the Primary Goal for Jewish Education). In *Wiseman* (Y.), 245–60.

———. „די שליחות פון דער יידישער שול" און „אויפן שוועל פון פערטן יארהונדערט פון יידיש לעבן אין אמעריקע" ("The Mission of the Yiddish School" and "On the Threshold of the Fourth Century of American Jewish Life") (Y.). N.Y.: Kaminsky, 1954.

———. „די נאציאנאלע בארעכטיקונג פאר דער יידישער שול" (The National Justification for the Yiddish School) (Y.). *BYD* 1 (Spring 1962): 1–12.

———. "Secular Jewishness: The Basis of the Sholem Aleichem School." In *OFFY*, 85–96.

———. „אונדזער יידישע וועלטלעכקייט" (Our Yiddish Secularism). *CE* (Y.) 28 (Jan. 1958): 3–5.

Niger, Shmuel. „איז גענוג פאר אונדז די פאבליק סקול?" (Is the Public School Enough for Us?). *Day* (Y.) (Sept. 17, 25, 1926).

———. „א צונג פאר שטומע" (A Tongue for the Mute). *CE* (Y.) 11 (Oct. 1941): 3–4.

Pat, Emanuel. „70 יאר פון נאציאנאלער וועלטלעכער יידישקייט" (Seventy Years of National Secular Jewishness). *CE* (Y.) 37 (Feb. 1967): 5–7.

Shapiro, Yehudah. „די אנדערשקייט פון די יידישע פאלק שולן" (The Difference in the Yiddish Folk Schools). *YD* (Y.) (Dec. 1962): 20–23.

Sholem Aleichem Folk Institute. *Principles of the Sholem Aleichem Folk Institute, Adopted in 1927 and in 1953.* In *OFFY*, 135–37, 138–39.

———. *Why Yiddish for Our Children?*. N.Y.: SAFI, 1956.

Wiseman, Shlomo. „אונזער וועג" (Our Path). *Jewish Worker* (Y.) (official biweekly of the LZOA) (Nov. 3, 1926): 8–9.

21 YIDDISH SECULAR SCHOOLS

YD (Y.) LZ)A — Farband. די פראגראם פון די יידישע פאלקשולן. (The Program of the Yiddish Folk Schools). *YD* 8 (Aug. 1950).

Yefroikin, Zalman. „דער אידייאישער וועג פון די ארבעטער רינג שול" (The Ideological Path of the Workmen's Circle Schools) In *S Alm* (Y.), 91–101.

———. „די פאזיטיווע ראלע פון די ארבעטער רינג שול". (The Positive Role of the Workmen's Circle School). *CE* 11 (May 1941): 15–20.

———. „די יידישע שול אין אמעריקאנער לעבן" (The Yiddish School in American Life). *CE* (Y.) (May 1946): 14–19.

Zaltsman, D. די שול פאר אייער קינד. (The School for Your Child) (Y.). N.Y.: International Workers' Orden, 1935. 40 pp.

CURRICULUM—GENERAL

Bass, Hyman. „די פראגראם פון א יידישער שול," (The Program of a Yiddish School). *BYD* (Y.) (June/Sept. 1951): 87–93.

Bridger, David. „אן אינטעגרירטער קוריקולום פאר דער יידישער שול" (An Integrated Curriculum for the Yiddish School). *BYD* (Y.) (June/Sept. 1949): 24–32.

Gingold, Pinchos. „דער אינהאלט פון אונדזער פאלק-שול וועזן" (The Content of Our Folk Schools—1952). In *Gingold* (Y.), 68–75.

Golomb, Abraham. „אלגעמיינע יסודות פון איינהייטלעכער יידישער דערציאונג" (General Principles for a Coordinated Jewish Education). In *Between Eras* (Y.), 210–17. 1967.

Jewish Folk Schools of America. „די פראגראם פון די פאלק שולן" (Program of the Jewish Folk Schools of America). *YD* (Y.) (June 1946): 99–106.

Labor Zionist-Farband. (Report on 1950 Education Conference). *YD* (Y.) (Aug. 1950). 120 pp. Various articles.

Mark, Yudel. „די יסודות פאר א פראגראם פון דער יידישער שול" (Principles for a Program of the Yiddish School). *Zuk* (Y.) (Oct. 1946): 686–90.

Niger, Shmuel. "פראגראם„ (Program). Historical review of the WC curriculum, 1917–1840. In *SNE* (Y.), 107–39.

* Parker, Sandra. *Inquiry into the Yiddish Secular Schools in the United States: A Curriculum Perspective*. Harvard U., 1973. 275 pp.

Sholem Aleichem Folk Institute. „קוריקולום פון א 5-טאגיקער שלום עליכם שול" (Curriculum of a 5-Day-a-Week School). In *OFFY* (Y.), 120–31.

———. "The Curriculum of a One-Day Sholem Aleichem School." In *OFFY* (E. and Y.), 141–57.

Shtern, I. „די לימודים אין דער יידישער שול" (The Course of Study of the Yiddish School). In *Shu P* (Y.), 385–417.

Wiseman, Shlomo. „אמעריקע אין אונדזער יידישער דערציאונג-וועגן אן אינטעגרירטער יידישער דערציאונג" (America in Our Jewish Education: On Integrated Education). *Jewish Review* (Y. section) (Dec. 1943): 129–46.

Workmen's Circle. *The Curriculum of the I. L. Peretz School of the WC* (Y.). N.Y.: WC Education Committee, 1952.

פראגראם פון די ארבעטער רינג שולן (Program of the Workmen's Circle Schools) (Y.). Adopted at 6th Conference. WC Education Department, 1927.

LANGUAGE

Bass, Hyman. „גרינגע און שווערע ווערטער אין יידיש" (Easy and Difficult Words in Yiddish). *BYD* (Y.), (Nov. 1949): 66–68, 77.

———. שפראך און דערציאונג (Language and Education) (Y.). Teacher's guide for teaching Yiddish. N.Y.: Educational Department of the WC, 1950. 400 pp.

———. „צו דער מעטאדיק פון ליינען און שרייבן" (On the Methodology of Reading and Writing). *BYD* (Y.) (Nov. 1949): 52–60.

———. „אפטסטע ווערטער אין יידיש" (Most Frequent Words in Yiddish). In *DER* (Y.), 1:373–79.

———. „דער וויזועלער ליין-מעטאד אין די פאראייניקטע שטאטן" (The Visual Reading

Method in the United States). *BYD* (Y.) 1 (June/Sept. 1950): 64–75.

Bloom, Sh. Z. „הבעיה הלשונית באפע״ל (פארבאנד)" (The Problem of Language in the Farband Schools) (LZOA). *Hadoar* (H.) 39 (Jan. 1, 1960).

Bridger, David. „לערן-כללים און זייער אנװענדונג ביים שפראך-למוד" (Learning Principles and Their Application in Language Teaching). *BYD* (Y.) 1 (June/Sept.1950): 36–42.

———. „דער װאקאבולאר מוז קאנטראלירט װערן" (The Vocabulary Must Be Controlled). In *Shu P* (Y.), 462–67.

Fishman, Joshua A. „צװײ שפראכיקײט אין א ײדישער שול" (Bilingualism in a Yiddish School—Yiddish and Hebrew). *BYD* (Y.) (June/Sept. 1951): 32–42.

———. "Degree of Bilingualism in a Yiddish School and Leisure Time Activities." *J of Social Psychology* 36 (1952): 155–65.

———. "Language Maintenance and Language Shift: The American Immigrant Case within a General Theoretical Perspective." *Sociology* 16 (1965): 19–39.

Goichberg, I. „פראבלעמען און מעטאדן פון דעם ײדיש לימוד" (Problems and Methods in the Study of Yiddish). In *Shu P* (Y.), 468–75.

* Hodes, Phyllis. *A Psycholinguistic Study of Reading Miscues of Yiddish-English Bilingual Children*. Wayne State U., 1976. 254 pp.

Levine, Jacob. „װעגן די גרונט פראבלעמען ביים לערנען ײדיש" (Concerning the Basic Problems in Teaching Yiddish). In *Shu P* (Y.), 476–85.

Mark, Yudel. „נאך באמערקונגען צו די פראבלעמען פון ײדיש לימוד" (Further Observations on the Problems in Teaching Yiddish). In *Shu P* (Y.), 495–502.

———. „גראמאטיק פאר דער ײדישער כלל-שפראך" (A Grammar of Standard Yiddish) (Y.). Congress for Jewish Culture, 1978. 394 pp.

———. „אַרײנפיר צו די מעטאדישע פראבלעמען פון ײדיש לימוד" (Introduction to the Problems of Method in the Teaching of Yiddish). In *Shu P* (Y.), 457–61.

———. „װעגן מאטיװירונגען פאר ײדיש" (On Motivations for Yiddish). In *Golomb* (Y.), 615–28.

———. „די ראלע פון העברעאישן עלעמענט אין ײדיש" (The Role of Hebrew in Yiddish). *YD* (Y.) 1 (Mar. 1937): 46–50; (Aug./Nov. 1937): 39–47.

Shapiro, Isaac. „פארגרײזונגען אין ײדישער אױסשפראך" (Errors in Yiddish Expression). *YD* (Y.) 1 (Nov. 1936): 34–38.

———. „אױסשפראך און אױסלײג פון װערטער מיט װײכע קלאנגען" (Expressions and Spelling of Words with Soft Sounds). *YD* 1 (Nov. 1937): 22–24.

———. „װעגן שפראכאיבונגען באם לערנען ײדיש" (On Language Exercises in the Teaching of Yiddish). In *Shu P* (Y.), 486–94.

———. „דער לימוד פון אידישן אױסלײג" (The Subject of Yiddish Spelling). *YD* (Y.) 1 (Mar. 1937) 34–40.

Shichman, V. „דער לימוד ײדיש אין קלאס ב" (The Teaching of Yiddish in the Second Grade). *YD* (Y.) (Aug. 1950): 96–101.

Shtern, I. „װעגן לימוד פון ײדיש אין דער פאלקשול" (On the Teaching of Yiddish in the Folk School). *YD* (Y.) (June 1946): 15–27.

Steinbaum, Israel. „אונטערשײדן אין לערנען שרײבן און לײענען אידישע און העברעאישע װערטער" (Differences in Teaching the Reading of Yiddish and Hebrew Words) (Y.). Report on a study. *Our School* 4 (Mar. 1934): 21–25.

———. „א נייער שטורעם ארום דער פראגע װי צו לערנען לײנען" (A New Storm on the Question of Teaching Reading). *CE* 29 (Jan. 1959): 11–13.

———. „דער לימוד פון פרעמד-שפראכן אין די פאראײניקטע שטאטן" (The Study of Foreign Languages in the United States). *BYD* 1 (June/Sept. 1950): 43–54.

Steinbaum, Israel, David Bridger, and Yudel Mark. „דער װאקאבולאר פאר אנהייבער קלאס אין דער אמעריקאנער ײדישער שול" (The Vocabulary for the Beginning Grade in the American Yiddish School) (Y.). N.Y.: Yivo, Psychology-Education Section, 1944. 32 pp.

Weinreich, Uriel. *College Yiddish: An Introduction to the Yiddish Language and to Jewish Life and Culture*. N.Y.: Yivo, 1949. 397 pp.

Yefroikin, Zalman. „דער ציל פון אידיש לימוד" (The Goal for the Study of Yiddish). *Our School* (Y.) 6 (Nov. 1936): 4–6.

LITERATURE

Bass, Hyman. „הונדערט יאר יידישע ליטעראטור און פופציק יאר יידישע שול" (One Hundred Years of Yiddish Literature and Fifty Years Yiddish Schools). *CE* (Y.) 36 (May 1965): 12–15.

———. „די פרץ טראדיציע און די יידישע שול" (The Peretz Tradition and the Yiddish School). The literary impact on the founding of the Yiddish school. *BYD* (Y.) (Apr./July 1953): 1–8.

———. „דיכטונג" (Poetry). In *DER* (Y.), 2:394–400.

Bialostotzky, B. J. „וועגן קינדער ליטעראטור" (On Children's Literature). *CE* 26 (Dec. 1956): 1–2.

Entin, Joel. „ליטעראטור אין דער פאלקשול" (Literature in the Folkschool). *YD* 6 (Mar. 1939): 11–14.

Gingold, Pinchos. „צו דער פסיכאלאגיע פון קינדער ליטעראטור" (On the Psychology of Children's Literature). In *Gingold* (Y.), 104–11.

Golomb, Abraham. „ליטעראטור און דערציאונג" (Literature and Education). *CE* 28 (Feb. 1958): 5–7.

———. „אונדזער ליטעראטור און אונדזער קיום" (Our Literature and Our Survival). *BYD* (Y.) (Apr./July 1953): 42–50.

Grant, Ch. „פאסיקע טעג פאר ביכער מתנות צו קינדער" (Suitable Days for Books as Gifts for Children). *JBA* (Y. section) (1942): 78–82.

Katz, M. „אונדזער שול און אונדזער קינדער-ליטעראטור" (Our School and Our Children's Literature). *Pro D* (Y.) 3 (Apr. 1937): 4–5.

Kazdan, Ch. Sh. „ווי אזוי צו לערנען פאעזיע אין שול" (How to Teach Poetry in School). *BYD* (Y.) (June/Sept. 1950): 25–35.

———. „שלום עליכם, דאס קינד און די יידישע שול" (Sholem Aleichem, the Child, and the Jewish School). *Zuk* (Y.) 64 (May/June 1959): 253–57.

———. „דער לימוד פון ליטעראטור" (The Subject of Literature). *BYD* (Y.) (Nov. 1949): 10–31.

———. „פינף און דרייסיק יאר יידישע קינדער ליטעראטור" Thirty-five Years of Children's Literature) (1911–46). In *Shu P* (Y.), 355–79.

Lehrer, Leepe. „די ביכער פון פארלאג, מתנות" (The Books of Farlag Matones). (Yiddish publishing house of the Sholem Aleichem Folk Institute—primarily books for children). *JBA* 4 (1946): 126–29.

Leivick, H. „ליטעראטור פאר קינדער און ליטעראטור פאר דערוואקסענע" (Literature for Children and Literature for Adults). *BYD* (Y.) (Nov. 1949): 17–18.

Mark, Yudel. „יידישע קינדער און יוגנט-ליטעראטור אין אמעריקע" (Yiddish Literature in America for Children and Youth). *JBA* (Y.) (1944–45): 136–41.

Menachowsky, M. „צוריקגעשטאנענע קינדער אין דער יידישער ליטעראטור" (Retarded Children in Yiddish Literature). In *Almanac Yiddish* (Y.). N.Y.: Congress for Jewish Culture, 1961.

Mlotek, Joseph. „דער אידישער שרייבער און די אידישע שול" (The Jewish Author and the Jewish School). *The Mirror* (Y.) (1949): 6.

———. „יידישע קינדער ליטעראטור אין די פאראייניקטע שטאטן" (Yiddish Literature for Children in the United States). In *Algemeine Encyclopedia* (Y.), "Yidn" section, 5:220–25. N.Y.: Central Yiddish Culture Organization (CYCO). 1950.

———. „די יידישע שול און די יידישע ליטעראטור" (The Yiddish School and Yiddish Literature." *CE* 34 (Oct. 1964): 1–5.

Niger, Shmuel. „וועגן אידישער קינדער ליטעראטור" (Concerning Yiddish Literature for Children). In *S Alm* (Y.), 188–95.

Novak, H. „אברהם רייזען און די אידישע שול" (Abraham Raizin and the Yiddish School). *Zuk* (Y.) (Nov. 1948): 781–82.

Pat, Jacob. „י. ל. פרץ און די יידישע שול" (I. L. Peretz and the Yiddish School). *BYD* (Y.) (June/Sept. 1950): 92–96.

Rabinowitz, I. „דער לימוד פון ליטעראטור" (The Study of Literature). *YD* (Y.) (June 1946): 31–37.

Rojanski, Samuel, ed. דאס קינד אין דער יידישער פאעזיע און פראזע ביי 95 שרייבער (The Child in Yiddish Poetry and Prose—95 Authors) (Y.). Buenos Aires: Yivo, 1971. 316 pp.

Simon, Solomon. „קינדער ליטעראטור אדער ליטעראטור פאר קינדער" (Children's Literature or Literature for Children). *BYD* (Y.) (June/Sept. 1949): 33–39.

Zaltzman, R. „ביכער פאר אייך און אייערע קינדער" (Books for You and Your Children). *Pro D* (Y.) 3 (May 1937): 19–21.

Zilberberg, Israel. „אברהם רייזען און די יידישע שול" (Abraham Raizin and the Yiddish School). *Zuk* (Y.) (Nov. 1948): 784–86.

———. „דער לימוד פון ליטעראטור אין דער יידישער שול" (The Subject of Yiddish Literature in the Yiddish School). *BYD* (Nov. 1949): 32–35.

———. „די יידישע ליטעראטור און די יידישע שול" (Yiddish Literature and the Jewish School). *CE* (Y.) 17 (May 1947): 5–7.

Zipper, J. „וועגן ליטעראטור אין דער עלעמענטאר שול" (Concerning Literature in the Elementary School). In *Shu P* (Y.), 427–32.

BIBLE

Dunsky, Shimshon. "חומש פראגראם" (The Pentateuch Program). *YD* (Y.) 1 (Mar. 1937): 18–26.

Pedagogic Bulletin (Y.). „פראבלעמען ביים לערנען תנך" (Problems in Teaching the Pentateuch). 184 (May 1962): 9–12.

Rabinowitch, I. „וועגן דעם לימוד חומש" (On the Study of Pentateuch). *YD* (Y.) 9 (May 1954): 82–88.

Schauss, H., ed. מעשיות פון בראשית (Tales from Genesis) (Y.). N.Y.: CYCO, 1945. 328 pp.

Schechter, Joseph. „צוליב וואס לערנען מיר תנ״ך און אגדה?" (Why Do We Teach the Bible and Aggadah?). *YK* (Y.) (Apr. 1950): 24–28.

Schwartz, I. I., ed. משה רבינו (Moses—Our Teacher) (Y.). Folk tales and legends about Moses. N.Y.: CYCO, 1953. 344 pp.

Schwartzman, M. „דער לימוד פון נביאים ראשונים" (The Study of the Early Prophets). *YD* (Y.) (June 1946): 38–42.

Shtern, I. „דער תנ״ך לימוד אין אונדזערע שולן" (The Study of Bible in Our Schools). *BYD* (Y.) (June/Sept. 1950): 51–59.

Simon, Solomon, comp. and translator. יהושע און שופטים (Joshua and Judges) (Y.). N.Y.: Farlag Matones, 1952. 112 pp.

———. „פארוואס נביאים ראשונים פאר דער יוגנט?" (Why the Early Prophets for Our Youth?). *CE* (Y.) 29 (Dec. 1959): 11–13.

Yehoash. חומש פאר קינדער (Pentateuch for Children) (Y.). Arranged by Solomon Simon. 1938, 1940. 214 pp.

HEBREW

Barkan, H. „העברעאיש אין דער עלעמענטאר שול" (Hebrew in the Elementary School). *CE* (Y.) (Mar. 1946): 6–7.

Dunsky, Shimon. "אשכנזיש אדער ספרדיש?" (Ashkenazic or Sephardic?). Pronunciation. *BYD* (Y.) (Nov. 1949): 92–96.

———. „דער מעטאד פון העברעאיש לערנען" (Methodology in the Teaching of Hebrew). *YD* (Y.) 1 (Nov. 1936): 26–33.

Goldoftas, M. „שפראכן אין אונדזערע פאלקשולן" (Languages in Our Schools). *YD* (Y.) 10 (Dec. 1962): 51–59.

Golomb, Abraham. „וועגן דער העברעאיש-לימוד אין שול און וועגן דער הברה" (On the Study of Hebrew—and On Its Pronunciation). *BYD* (Y.) (June/Sept. 1950): 55–63.

Goobkin, I. „וועגן דער הברה אין העברעאיש-לימוד" (On the Pronunciation of Hebrew). *YD* (Y.) (Nov. 1949): 86–89.

Levine, Jacob. „וועלכע הברה באנוצן ביים לערנען העברעאיש אין די יידישע שול" (Which Pronunciation to Use in Teaching Hebrew in the Yiddish School). *BYD* (Nov. 1949): 88–91.

Mark, Yudel. „די ווירקונג פון העברעאיש אויפן יידישן סינטאקסיס" (The Effect of Hebrew upon Yiddish Syntax). *YD* 2 (June 1938): 34–41.

Meyerowitz, Abraham. „דער לימוד פון העברעאיש" (The Study of Hebrew). *YD* (Y.) 6 (Mar. 1939): 25–26; (June 1946): 28–30.

Zilberberg, Israel. "אױף װעלכער הברה דאַרף מען לערנען העברעאיש אין אונדזערע שולן?" (Which Pronunciation Should We Use to Teach Hebrew in Our Schools?). *BYD* (Y.) (June/Sept. 1949): 100–103.

HISTORY

Bass, Hyman. "געשיכטע און נאַציאָנאַלע דערציִונג" (History and National Education). In *DER* (Y.), 2:231–40.

———. "ייִדישע געשיכטע און נאַציאָנאַלע דערציִונג" (Jewish History and National Education). *BYD* (Y.) (June/Sept. 1949): 3–10.

Bressler, G. "די פּראָבלעמען פֿון געשיכטע לימוד אין אונדזערע שולן" (The Problems of Teaching Jewish History in Our Schools). *Our School* (Y.) 7 (Apr. 1937): 11–13.

Bridger, David. "דער לימוד פֿון דער ייִדישער געשיכטע אין דער פֿאָלקשול" (The Teaching of Jewish History in the Folk School). *YD* (Y.) (Aug. 1950): 418–26.

Dunsky, Shimon. "דער לימוד געשיכטע אין אונדזערע שול" (The Study of History in Our Schools). In *Shu P* (Y.), 418–26.

Gingold, Pinchos. "װעגן דעם לימוד פֿון ייִדישער געשיכטע" (On the Study of Jewish History). *YD* (Y.) (June 1946): 43–46.

Glicksman, William. "דער לימוד פֿון ייִדישער געשיכטע" (The Study of Jewish History). *CE* (Nov. 1963): 6–8.

Goldberg, A. "געשיכטע אין אונדזערע שולן" (History in Our Schools). *Pro D* (Y.) 3 (Feb. 1937): 8–10.

Katz, M. "דער לימוד ייִדישע געשיכטע קלאַפּט אין אונדזערע טירן" (The Subject of History Knocks at Our Doors). *Pro D* (Y.) (July/Aug. 1937): 6–8.

Lehrer, Leibush. "ייִדישע געשיכטע פֿאַר ייִדישע קינדער" (Jewish History for Jewish Children). *YK* (Y.) (June 1960): 7–9.

Lifshitz, I. "דער זין פֿון געשיכטע לימוד אין די פֿאָלקשולן" (The Rationale for Jewish History in the Folk School). *YD* (Y.) (Aug. 1950): 77–84.

Menes, Abraham. "װעגן לימוד פֿון ייִדישער געשיכטע" (On the Study of Jewish History). *CE* (Y.) 11 (Feb. and Apr. 1941): 7–8, 15–17.

Pedagogic Bulletin (Y.) "לאָמיר ברענגען אין אַרדענונג דעם לימוד געשיכטע" (Let Us Bring Order to the Subject of History). 76 (Apr. 1949). 24 pp.

Shapiro, Isaac. "װעגן עטלאַכע הילפֿסמיטלען צום לימוד פֿון געשיכטע" (Teaching Aides in the Subject of History). *YD* (Y.) 2 (June 1938): 18–22.

Snyder, Wolf. "געשיכטע פֿון די איִדן אין אַמעריקע אלס לימוד פֿאַר אונדזערע שול" (The History of the Jews in America as a Subject for Our Schools). *YD* (Y.) (Mar. 1939): 14–17.

Weingarten, I. "אַריינפֿיר צו דער מעטאָדיק פֿון ייִדי שער געשיכטע אין דער עלעמענטאַר שול" (Introduction to the Methodology of Jewish History in the Elementary School). *BYD* (Y.) (June/Sept. 1949): 11–19.

———. "(געשיכטע) (מעטאָדיק)" (Methodology—History). In *DER* (Y.), 2:241–62.

———. "מעטאָדיק פֿון ייִדישער געשיכטע" (Methodology of Jewish History). *BYD* (Y.) (June/Sept. 1950): 1–12.

PEDAGOGY AND RELATED PROGRAMS

Badanes, Ida. "די נויטיגע דיסציפּלין פֿאַר קינדער" (Discipline Necessary for Children). *Day* (Y.) (Aug. 21, 1926).

Bernstein, I. "אונדזער לערן-פּראָגראַם אין דער איצטיקער צײַט" (Our Program at the Present Time). *CE* (Y.) 6 (May 1966): 17–20.

Bets, Johanna. "פֿאַרװאָס קינדערגאַרטנס?" (Why Kindergartens?). *Our School* (Y.) 6 (May 1936): 15–17.

Bridger, Hyman. "דראַמאַטישע אויפֿפֿירונגען" (Dramatic Performances). In *DER* (Y.), 3:168–74.

———. "היים אַרבעט" (Homework). *BYD* (Y.) 4 (June/Sept. 1951): 190–94.

———. "לערנען און געדענקען" (Learning and Retention). *BYD* (Y.) 4 (June/Sept. 1951): 25–31.

Chaikes, E. „ארץ ישראל אין אונדזערע שולן" (Israel in Our Schools). *YD* (Y.) 7 (June 1946): 66–68.

Chanin, Nathan. „די ראלע פון שול פארוואלטער אין דער ארבעטער רינג שול" (The Role of School Committee Members in the WC School). *Our School* (Y.) 5 (Nov. 1935): 19–12.

Gelbart, Michael. לאמיר קינדער זינגען לידער (Children—Let Us Sing). N.Y.: WC Central School Board, 1955.

——— . לידער (Songs) (Y.). N.Y.: WC Education Committee, 1941–42.

——— . „לאמיר זינגען א ליד צו דער יידישער שול" (Let Us Sing a Song to the Yiddish School). *For* (Y.) (June 14, 1958).

Goldberg, G. „די אינטעליגענץ פון יידישע און אנדערע קינדער" (The Intelligence of Jewish Children and Other Children). *CE* (Y.) 11 (Dec. 1941): 17–19.

Goodman, Saul L. „וואס איז דער ענדציל פון יידישער דערציאונג?" (What Is the Goal of Jewish Education?). *CE* (Y.) 30 (Oct. 1960): 5–8.

Grabla-Valetsky, Tzirl. מאל און דערצייל (Draw and Tell) (Y.). WC Education Committee, 1963. 46 pp.

Indelman, A. *Happy Holiday Children* (Y.). Illustrated by I. Goitein, A. Lobel. Songs for children. N.Y.: JEC, 1958.

Jakabov, B. „וואס טוט מען מיט די געראטענע קינדער?" (What Shall We Do with Our Talented Students?). *Morning Freiheit* (Y.) (Mar. 3, 1947).

Kaplan, Rivkah. „אונדזער קינדער גארטן" (Our Kindergarten). *Morning Freiheit* (Y.) (Oct. 26, 1926).

Kazdan, Ch. Sh. „דער לימוד פון שרייבן און זיין ראלע אין דער אמאליקער דערציאונג ביי יידן" (The Subject of Writing and Its Role in Early Jewish Education). *CE* (Y.) (Dec. 1946): 13–15.

Lehrer, Leibush. „צווייי שפדאכיקייט און אינטעליגענץ" (Bilingualism and Intelligence). *YD* (Y.) 1 (Mar. 1937): 8–14.

——— . „דיסציפלין" (Discipline). Address before WC school conference. *School Bulletin* (Y.) (Nov. 1926).

——— . „באמערקונגען וועגן דער פילאזאפיע פון טראדיציאנאלן חינוך ביי יידן" (Observations on the Philosophy of Traditional Education among Jews). In *Wiseman* (Y.), 229–44.

——— . פסיכאלאגיע און דערציאונג (Psychology and Education) (Y.). N.Y.: Farlag Matones, 1937. 488 pp.

Levine, Jacob. „וועלטלעכע און רעליגיעזע יידישקייט" (Secular and Religious Jewishness). *CE* (Y.) 28 (Feb. 1958): 7–9.

Menachowsky, M. „וועגן שול-דיסציפלין" (About School Discipline). *Our School* (Y.) (Oct. 1933): 19–23; (Dec. 1933): 20–25.

Mlotek, Eleanor Gordon. *A List of 55 Recommended Yiddish Records: Index of 500 Recorded Songs.* N.Y.: WC Educational Department, 1964. 38 pp.

——— . מיר טראגן א געזאנג (We Carry a Song) (Y.). N.Y.: WC Education Committee, 1972. 201 pp.

Mlotek, Joseph. „פראבלעמען פון אום ארום ערשטן קלאס" (Problems Concerning the First Grade). *CE* (Y.) (Mar./Apr. 1957).

Niger, Shmuel. „פארשול-בילדונג" (Pre-School Education). In *SNE* (Y.), 140–42.

——— . „שולביכער, פעדאגאגישע זשורנאלן קינדער ליטעראטור" (Schoolbooks, Pedagogic Journals, and Children's Literature). In *SNE* (Y.), 184–91.

Otrovsky, B. „דער קינדער קלוב ביי דער ארבעטער רינג שול" (The Children's Club in the WC School). *The Friend* (Y.) (Jan. 1929): 17–18.

Shapiro, I. „וועגן פארבעסערן דעם לימוד פון יידיש און העברעאיש" (On Improving the Study of Yiddish and Hebrew). *YD* (Y.) 7 (1946).

Shapiro, Solomon. „אויסער קלאס און אויסער שול טעטיקייטן" (Activities outside the Classroom and the School). *YD* (Y.) (June 1946): 47–57.

——— . „אמעריקע און ישראל אין אונזער דערציאונג" (America and Israel in Our Education). *YD* (Y.) 9 (May 1954): 51–64.

Snyder, Wolf. „צו דער פראגע וועגן קלאס פירונג" (On the Question of Classroom Management). *YD* (Y.) 1 (Nov. 1936): 11–17.

Steinbaum, Israel. „פראבלעמען ארום דעם לימוד פון א צווייטער שפראך" (Problems in

Teaching a Second Language). *CE* (H.) 31 (Oct. 1961): 7–10; 31 (Nov. 1961): 8–10.

Tarant, Devorah. "פאר-שול דערציאונג„ (Pre-School Education). *Pro D* (Y.) (Dec. 1936, Jan. 1937).

Weisbard, M. "דער לימוד געזאנג אין אונזער שול„ (Singing in Our School). *Our School* (Y.) 4 (Dec. 1934): 21–23.

Wiseman, Shloime. "וועגן לייענען„ (On Reading). *YD* (Y.) 9 (May 1954): 77–81.

Yamen, Ben, ed. לידער פאר שול און היים (Songs for School and Home) (Y.). N.Y.: Workers-Orden, Bronx Teachers Council, 1944.

THE DAY SCHOOL

(See also chapter 20)

Berkowitz, A. L. "טאג שולן„ (Day Schools). *YD* (Y.) (June 1946): 93–98.

Brusilov. Nathan. "רעיונות וועגן יידישן שול-וועזן„ (Thoughts on Jewish Schools in America). On the Kineret Day School. *ZuK* (Y.) (Dec. 1959): 515–17.

Goodman, Saul L. "יידישע טאג שולן אין אמעריקע„ (Jewish Day Schools in America). In *Uniqueness of American Jewry* (Y.), 398–405. Tel Aviv: I. L. Peretz, 1980.

Kazdan, Ch. Sh. "די יידישע שול פאר נייע אויפגאבעס„ (The Yiddish School Faces New Challenges). *CE* (Y.) 17 (Oct. 1947): 3–5.

Kersht, I. M. "די טאגשול כנרת צו איר דריטן לערן-יאר„ (The Day School Kineret in its Third School Year). *For* (Y.) (Oct. 28, 1949).

Lehrer, Leibush. "די היים שול„ (The Home School). Yiddish Day School for Children Who Live away from Home. *Freie Arbeiter Shtimme* (Y.) (Apr. 3, 1926): 6.

Novak, H. "יידישע טאג שולן„ (Yiddish Day Schools). *Zuk* (Y.) (Mar. 1946): 185–88.

Saks, Honan. "The Kineret Day School." *Jew Fron* 31 (Sept. 1964): 55–57.

Spizman, L. "פראגרעסיווע טאג שולן„ (Progressive Day Schools). On Kineret. *Day* (Y.) (July 2, 1947).

Weingarten, I. "טאגשולן און נאכמיטאג שולן„ (Day Schools and Afternoon Schools). *YD* (Y.) (May 1954): 65–72.

———. "אונזער ערשטע טאג שול„ (Our First Day School). *YK* (Y.) 31 (Jan. 27. 1950): 8.

———. "שאלות ותשובות וועגן כנרת„ (Questions and Answers about Kineret). *YK* (Y.) (May, 1952).

Winer, Gershon. "אונזער אידיש שול-וועזן—בלויז איין ברירה„ (Our Jewish Schools—Only One Option). *YK* (Y.) (Oct. 9, 1970).

SECONDARY EDUCATION

Chanin, Nathan. "40 יאר ארבעטער רינג מיטלשול„ (Forty Years of WC Secondary Schools). *CE* (Y.) (Sept. 1961): 4–5.

Entin, Joel. "דערגרייכונגען פון יידיש אין פאלקשול און מיטלשול„ (Achievements in Yiddish in Elementary and Secondary Schools). *YD* (Y.) (May 1954): 46–51.

———. "יידישע עטנאלאגיע און לעבנס שטייגער„ (Jewish Ethnology and Manner of Living). Proposed secondary school program. *YD* (Y.) 8 (Aug. 1950): 15–68.

Farber, Sh. "וואס די מיטל-שול גיט דער יידישער יוגנט„ (What the High School Gives to Jewish Youth). *Morning Freiheit* (Y.) (July 13, 1946).

Goobkin, I. "פראבלעמען פון דער מיטלשול„ (Problems in the Secondary School). *YD* (Y.) (Aug. 1950): 89–92.

———. "מיטלשול דערציאונג און די יוגנט„ (Secondary School and Youth). *YD* (Y.) 9 (May 1954): 72–77.

Kahn, S. "די אינטערעסן פון די מיטלשול תלמידים„ (Interests of Secondary Students—Findings of a Survey). *CE* (Y.) 17 (Apr. 1947): 4–5.

Lazarson, I. "דארף מען לערנען העברעאיש אין אונזערע מיטלשולן?„ (Should We Teach Hebrew in Our High Schools?). *Our School* (Y.) 7 (Apr. 1937): 49–52.

Levine, Jacob. "די ארבעטער רינג מיטלשול„ (The WC Secondary School). *CE* (Y.) (May 1957): 6–7.

Niger, Shmuel. "די מיטלשולן" (The Secondary Schools of the WC). In *SNE* (Y.), 143–53.

———. "אידישע ליטעראטור און די מיטלשול" (Yiddish Literature and the High School). *YD* (Y.) 1 (Mar. 1937): 15–17.

Vladovsky, M. "דארף מען טאקע לערנען העברעאיש אין אונזערע מיטלשולן?" (Should We Teach Hebrew in Our High Schools?). *Our School* (Y.) (Apr. 1937): 52–54.

Wohl, Joseph. "די שלום עליכם מיטל-שול" (The Sholem Aleichem Secondary School). In *Year Book of the SAFI* (Y.), 51–52. 1928.

Yefroikin, Zalman. "וואס די מיטל שול האט אונדז געגעבן" (What the High School Has Given Us). *CE* (Y.) 31 (Dec. 1961).

TRADITION

Barkan, H. "קדושה אין אונדזער שול ארבעט" (Sacredness in Our School Activities). *CE* (Y.) (Feb. 1947): 6–8.

Bass, Hyman. "דער נייער טראדיציאנאליזם אין די מאדערנע דערציאונג" (The New Traditionalism and Modern Education). In *Wiseman* (Y.), 262–70.

Biederman, I. M. "אמונה און טראדיציע אין אונזער שול ווען" (Faith and Tradition in Our Schools). *YD* (Y.) (May 1954): 89–96.

Dunsky, Shimon. "וועגן דעם לימוד פון רעליגיע אין אונדזער שול" (On the Study of Religion in Our School). *YD* (Y.) (June 1946): 76–79.

Feldman, Esther. "א יום טוב פראגראם פאר אונדזער שול" (A Holiday Program for Our Schools). *CE* (Y.) 26 (Mar. 1956): 4–6.

Golomb, Abraham. "די נאציאנאלע יסודות פון דער טראדיציאנאלער דערציאונג ביי יידן" (The National Foundations of Traditional Education among Jews) (Y.). 1944. 33 pp.

———. "פאזיטיוויסטישע און נאציאנאל-עטישע צילן אין דערציאונג" (Positivistic and National-Ethical Goals in Education). *BYD* (Y.) (June/Sept. 1954): 16–22.

Goodman, Saul L., ed. הגדה של פסח (Passover Haggadah) (Y., H., E.). SAFI, 1962. 64 pp.

Lehrer, Leibush. "רעליגיע און טראדיציע" (Religion and Tradition). *YK* (Y.) 44 (1963): 54–58.

Maltz, Sh. "יום טובים אין אונדזער שול" (Holidays in Our School). *CE* (Y.) 28 (May 1958): 31–34.

Mark, Yudel. "דער נייער טראדיציאנאליזם און די מאדערנע יידישע דערציאונג" (The New Traditionalism and the Modern Yiddish Education) (Y.). 1964.

Mlotek, Chane, and Malke Gottlieb. יום-טובדיקע טעג (Festival Days) (Y.). N.Y.: Jewish Education Press, 1972. 122 pp.

Olitzky, M. גוט יום טוב קינדער (Happy Holiday Children). With English translation by M. Rosenfield. N.Y.: WC Education Committee, 1981. 32 pp.

Rabinowitz, Zina. דער ליבער יום טוב (The Dear Holiday) (Y.). N.Y.: Farlag Matones, 1958. 196 pp.

Schauss, H. דאס יום טוב בוך (The Holiday Book) (Y.). N.Y.: Published by the author, 1933. 274 pp.

School Center for Yiddish Culture. ראש-השנה און יום-כפור בוך סוכות און שמחת-תורה בוך—פורים איז א שפיל אזא (Rosh Hashanah and Yom Kippur Book, Sukkot and Simhat Torah, and Purim) (Y.). N.Y.: School Center for Yiddish Culture, 1967, 1968.

Simon, Solomon. "אינטעגראלע יידישקייט אבער אן גאט" (Integral Jewishness—But without God). *YK* (Y.) (Feb. 22, 1963): 9–12.

Steinbaum, Israel. א יום טוב-בוך (A Holiday Book) (Y.). N.Y.: 1925. 320 pp.

Weiner, Lazar. כארען זינגען (Choirs Sing). 2 vols. N.Y.: WC Education Press, 1941.

Wiseman, Shlomo. "די יידישע יום טובים און די יידישע דערציאונג" (Jewish Holidays and Jewish Education). In *Shu P* (Y.), 216–59.

———. טראדיציע און לעבנסשטייגער (Tradition and Way of Life). *YD* (Y.) (1946): 3–14.

Workmen's Circle Education Committee. פסח, פורים, חנוכה, רות (Passover, Purim, Chanuko, and Ruth) (Y.). 4 pamphlets.

———. א נייע הגדה של פסח (A New Haggadah for Passover) (H. and Y). Compiled by I. I. Schwartz, H. Noveck, Jacob Levine, and Michael Gelbart. N.Y., 1941 (17 pp), 1960 (32 pp).

Zaltz, F. „טראדיציע אין אונדזערע פאלק-שולן" (Tradition and Our Folk Schools). *YD* (Y.) (Aug. 1950): 101–7.

Zipper, I. „יום-טובים פייערונגען" (Holiday Celebrations). *YD* (Y.) (June 1946): 58–62.

CHANGE

Bass, Hyman. „א נייע פראגראם פאר אונדזער שול" (A New Program for Our School). *CE* (Y.) 17 (Mar. 1947): 7–11.

———. „דיפראגראמאטישע ענדערונגען אין דער ארבעטער רינג שול" (The Programmatic Changes in the WC School). In *S Alm* (Y.), 67–70.

Chanin, Nathan. „מיט וואס האבן זיך אונדזערע שול געענדערט?" (How Have Our Schools Changed?). *CE* (Y.) 17 (Dec. 1947): 11–12.

Entin, Joel. „אונדזער אידישע דערציאונג" (Our Jewish Education). Changes in the Program of the Folk Schools. *YD* (Y.) (May 1954): 3–29.

Gingold, Pinchos. „ווי זאלן מיר זיך באציען צום בר מצוה יום טוב?" (How Should We Relate to the Bar Mitzvah Program?) (1939). In *Gingold* (Y.), 90–103. Also in *YD* 6 (Mar. 1939): 20–22.

Mark, Yudel. „וועגן א הייצטצייטיקער פראגראם פאר די עלעמענטאר שול" (About a Contemporary Program for the Elementary School). *CE* 31 (Feb. 1961): 1–3.

———. "Changes in the Yiddish Schools." *Jew Ed* 19 (Fall 1947): 31–38.

———. „עס טאר ניט בלייבן ווי געווען" (It Must Not Remain the Way It Was). *CE* (Y.) 11 (Apr. 1941): 8–10.

Pomerantz, I. Chaim. „צום תיקון פון אונדזער שול ארבעט" (Toward the Improvement of Our School Work). Includes findings of survey by author and recommendations for change. In *Shu P* (Y.), 95–118.

Rubinstein, I. Chaim. „צי דארף פארקומען א שינוי הערכין פון אונדזער שול פראגראם?" (Is There a Need for Change in the Values of Our School Program?). *YD* (Y.) (Dec. 10, 1962): 85–92.

Steinbaum, Israel. „עקספערימענטן אין דערציאונג" (Experiments in Education). *CE* 30 (Nov. 1960): 13–14.

Yefroikin, Zalman. „דארפן געמאכט ווערן ענדערונגען אין אונדזער שול-פראגראם?" (Should Changes Be Made in Our School Program?). *CE* (Y.) 11 (Jan. 1941): 3–8.

TEXTBOOKS

Bridger, David. „ווי אזוי אפצוקלייבן און אפשאצן לערנביכער" (How to Select and Evaluate Textbooks). *BYD* (Y.) (Apr./July 1953): 51–56.

———. „אנהייבער ביכער אין דער מאדערנער יידישער שול" (Primers in the Modern Yiddish School). In *DER* (Y.), 1:332–50.

———. „אן אויספארשונג וועגן וואקאבולאר פון די יידישע אנפאנגערס" (A Survey on Vocabulary in Yiddish Primers). *BYD* (Y.) 22 (Sept./Oct. 1943): 84–103.

Mark, Yudel. „די לערנביכער פאר דער יידישער שול אין אמעריקע" (The Textbooks of the Yiddish School in America). Historical evaluation of textbooks in the Yiddish Secular Schools. In *Shu P* (Y.), 260–334.

Niger, Shmuel. „שולביכער" (Textbooks). In *SNE* (Y.), 184–91.

THE TEACHER

Altman, M. „לערער און סביבה" (Teacher and Environment). *YD* (Y.) (June 1946): 80–85.

Bass, Hyman. „די סאציאלע ווארצלען פון דעם יידישן לערער" (The Social Roots of the Yiddish Teacher). In *Shu P* (Y.), 130–50.

Blaushtein, M. „א לערער רעדט זיך אראפ פון הארצן" (A Teacher Gets Things off His Chest) (Y.). Mexico: 1959. 689 pp.

Gingold, Pinchos. „די ראלע פון דעם לערער אין דער מאדערנער דערציאונג" (The Role of the Teacher in Modern Education). In *Gingold* (Y.), 85–89.

Gladstone, Jacob. „דער מאנגל אין אידישע לערער" (The Shortage of Yiddish Teachers). *Day-MJ* (Y.) (Mar. 22, 1957).

Goldstein, M. „די ראלע פון לערער אין די שלום עליכם שולן" (The Role of the Teacher in the SAFI). In *OFFY*, 110–13.

Golomb, Abraham. „מיט די אויגן פון א יידישן לערער" (With the Eyes of a Jewish Teacher). Autobiographical. In *Toward the Depths of Jewish Thought* (Y.), 283–87. Tel Aviv: J. L. Peretz, 1974.

Kaufman, Kopl Leib. „מיינע ערשטע טעג אין דער יידישער שול" (My First Days in the Yiddish School). *CE* (Y.) (May 1957): 58.

Knox, Israel. „די לאגע פון אמעריקאנער און אידישע לערער" (The Condition of the American and Jewish Teacher). *Day* (Y.) (Nov. 2, 1951).

Lazarson, I. „דער יידישער לערער און די ארבעטער רינג שול באוועגונג" (The Yiddish Teacher and the WC School Movement). *CE* (Y.) (Oct. 1963): 13–14.

Lehrer, Leibush. „די פסיכאלאגיע פון דער לערער פערזענלעכקייט" (The Psychology of the Teacher Personality). *YB* (Y.) 4 (Sept. 1932): 97–119.

———. „לערער און שולן אין פארשיידענע קולטורעלע און פסיכאלאגישע סיטואציעס" (Teachers and Schools in Various Cultural and Psychological Situations). *YB* (Y.) 9 (Jan./Mar. 1936): 76–106.

———. „דער יידישער לערער" (The Yiddish Teacher). *BYD* (Y.) (June/Sept. 1951): 12–15.

Litvak, A. „אונזער לערער" (Our Teacher). WC School Bulletin (Y.) 18 (1926).

Mendelsohn, Sh. „דער לערער" (The Teacher). *CE* (Y.) (Nov. 1946): 12–15.

Mlotek, Joseph. „זארג פארן יידישן לערער" (Concern for the Teacher). *CE* (Y.) 37 (Jan. 1967): 3–4.

———. „ווענן באציאונגען צווישן לערער" (Relationships among Teachers). *BYD* (Y.) (Nov. 1949): 90–103.

Olgin, Moshe. „די שול און דער לערער" (The School and the Teacher). *Home and Education* (Y.) (Jan. 1940): 7–8.

Pedagogic Bulletin (Y.). „גוטס און שלעכטס אין דער לערערישער פראקטיק" (Strengths and Weaknesses in Teacher Practice). (Dec. 1954): 17–20; (Apr. 1956): 15–17.

Pomerantz, I. Chaim. „יידישע לערעריי—די ניט דערצאלטע מלאכה" (Jewish Teaching—The Underpaid Profession). *CE* (Y.) (Dec. 1947): 12–14.

Rabinowitch, I. „דער לערער און זיין פלאנירן" (The Teacher and His Planning). *YD* (Y.) (June 1946): 86–89.

Ronch, I. A. „אונזער לערער און זיין ארבעט" (Our Teacher and His Work). *Jewish Workers School Bulletin* of WC Schools (Y.) (Nov. 12, 1926).

Unger, M. „דער נייער טיפ לערער אין די אידישע וועלטליכע שולען" (The New Type of Teacher in the Yiddish Secular Schools). *Day* (Y.) (Dec. 25, 1946).

HIGHER EDUCATION AND TEACHER TRAINING

Baker, Shimon. „45 יאריקער יוביליי פון אידישן לערער סעמינאר" (45th Anniversaey of the Yiddish Teachers Seminary). *Canadian Eagle* (Y.) (Mar. 25, 1963).

Bleter far Yiddisher Dertsiung. „דער יידישער פאלקסאוניווערזיטעט און לערער סעמינאר אין ניו יארק" (The Jewish Teachers Seminary and Folk University in New York). *BYD* (Y.) 1 (Nov. 1949): 108–10.

The Day. „פערציק נייע אידישע לערער" (Forty New Yiddish Teachers). On the commencement of the Jewish Teachers Seminary of the WC. *Day* (Y.) (June 27, 1926).

Gingold, Pinchos. „צו דער געשיכטע פון יידישן לערער סעמינאר" (On the History of the Jewish Teachers Seminary). *Jewish Review* (Y. section) 1 (1943): 122–26.

———. „דאס פראבלעם פון העכערער יידישער בילדונג" (The Problem of Higher Jewish Education). *Jewish Worker's Voice* (Y.) (June 1937): 26–27.

———. „דער אידישער לערער סעמינאר" (The Yiddish Teachers Seminary). In *S Alm* (Y.), 204–12.

Izban, Sh. „דער אידישער לערער סעמינאר—יאר אלט" (The Jewish Teachers Seminary—

21 YIDDISH SECULAR SCHOOLS

32 Years Old). *Morning Journal* (Y.) (Mar. 6, 1950).

Jewish Teachers Seminary and People's University. *In Honor of the 30th Anniversary of the Seminary Charter* (Y.). N.Y.: Jewish Teachers Seminary and People's University, ca. 1948.

Kirk, F. „די לערער קורסן פון די ארדן שול" (The Teacher Courses of the Orden Schools). *Pro D* 3 (Oct. 1937): 7–8.

Knox, Israel. „א געוווינס פאר אידישער דערציאונג" (A Gain for Jewish Education). On the new Horace Kallen School. *For* (Y.) (July 18, 1976).

Marmor, Kalman. „צען יאר אידישער ארבעטער יוניווערזיטעט" (Ten Years of the Jewish Workers University). *Pro D* (Y.) 3 (June 1937): 16–17.

Niger, Shmuel. „העכערע קורסן ..." (Teacher Training and the Higher Courses in Jewish Culture of the WC). In *SNE*, 153–60.

Penn, Ascher. „אידישער לערער סעמינאר און פאלקס אוניווערזיטעט" (Jewish Teachers Seminary and Folk University). On training of teachers and general Judaic studies. In *Penn* (Y.), 505–17.

Steinbaum, Israel. „די געשיכטע פון יידישן לערער סעמינאר און פאלקס אוניווערזיטעט" (The History of the Jewish Teachers Seminary and Folk University in New York, 1928–1968) (Y.). Jerusalem: 1979. 184 pp.

Weinryb, D. „בית המדרש היהודי למורים" (The Yiddish Teacher Seminary). In *JB* (H.), 272–75.

Winer, Gershon. "The Education of Yiddish Teachers." In *Jan 3*, 175–83.

HOME AND EDUCATION

Davidson, B. „די מאמע—איר גרויסער ווירקונג אויף דער דערציאונג פון קינד" (The Mother and Her Great Influence on the Education of the Child). *Our School* (Y.) (Jan. 1935): 5–7.

Entin, Joel. „די שול און היים" (The School and Home). *YD* (Y.) 1 (Aug. 1937): 15–21.

Feldman, Esther. „די ווירקונג פון אונדזער שול אויף דער היים" (The Influence of Our School

on the Home). *CE* (Y.) 28 (May 1958): 34–35.

Fell-Yellin, Sarah. „די הויפט פאקטארן אין קינדער דערציאונג שול, גאס און היים" (The Chief Factors in Children's Education—School, Street, and Home). *Freiheit* (Y.) (May 23, 1926).

Golomb, Abraham. „עלטערן און קינדער ביי יידן אין אמעריקע" (Parents and Children among Jews in America). *BYD* (Y.) (June/Sept. 1949): 40–48.

Goodman, Saul. „די נייע עלטערנשאפט אין דער יידיש-וועלטלעכער שול" (The New Parenthood in the Yiddish Secular Schools). *BYD* (Y.) (Apr./July 1953): 38–42.

Katz, Moshe. „א געשפרעך מיט טאטעס און מאמעס—וועגן קינדער שולן" (A Conversation with Fathers and Mothers about Schools for Children). *Pro D* (Y.) (Sept. 1936): 4–5.

Levine, Jacob. „די יידישע שול און די עלטערן" (The Jewish School and the Parents). *CE* (Y.) 26 (Nov. 1956): 9–10.

Mark, Yudel. „וועגן געווינען די עלטערן" (On Winning over the Parents). *CE* (Y.) 36 (Mar. 1966): 3–4.

Meckler, D. L. „אידישע דערציאונג פאנגט זיך אן מיט די עלטערן" (Jewish Education Begins with the Parents). *Day-MJ* (Y.) (Aug. 19, 1969).

Meisl, Nachman. „די יידישע שול איז און דארף זיין מער ווי בלויז א שול" (The Yiddish School Is and Must Be Much More than a School). *Home and Culture* (Y.) (Nov. 1940): 8–9.

Menes, Abraham. „אידישע דערציאונג און די אידישע פאמיליע" (Jewish Education and the Jewish Family). *For* (Y.) (July 24, 1966).

Mlotek, Joseph. „די נייע יידישע היים און אונדזער שול" (The New Jewish Home and the School). *CE* (May 1954).

———. „די עלטערן וואס שיקן זייערע קינדער אין די ארבעטער רינג שולן" (The Parents Who Send Their Children to the WC School). *CE* (Y.) (May 1963): 12–18.

Mokdoni, A. „די שותפות צווישן דער יידישער שול און היים" (The Partnership between the Jewish School and Home). *Morning Journal* (Y.) (Nov. 23, 1949).

Novadaska, Rose. „די היים אונזער ערשטע שול" (The Home, Our First School). *Our School* (Y.) (Apr. 1934).

Ronch, I. A. „וואס אונזערע עלטערן טוען יא און טוען ניט פאר זייערע קינדער" (What Parents Do and Do Not Do for Their Children). *Morning Freiheit* (Y.) (Oct. 24, 1926).

Sigalowski, M. „ווי ארגאניזירט מען מוטער קלובן" (How to Organize Mother Clubs). *CE* (Y.) (May 1947): 17.

Yefroikin, Zalman. „די שול און די עלטערנשאפט" (The School and the Parents). *CE* (Y.) (Mar. 1962) 1–3.

ON CONSOLIDATING YIDDISH SCHOOLS

Bickel, Shlomo. „פאראייניגונג אדער פארווירקלעכער אידעאל?" (Consolidation or Realized Ideal?). *Day* (Y.) (May 19, 1944).

———. „אידישע שול מוזען זיך פאראייניקן". (Yiddish Schools Must Unite). *Day* (Y.) (Mar. 25, 1942).

Drachler, Israel. „די לאגע פון די אידישע וועלטלעכע שולן און די פראגע פון פאראייניגונג" (The Condition of the Yiddish Secular Schools and the Issue of Consolidation). *Zuk* (Y.) (Nov. 1930): 794–97.

Lehrer, Leibush. „אידישע שולן—צעטיילט אדער פאראייניגט?" (Yiddish Schools—Divided or United?). *Zuk* (Y.) (June 1930): 401–4.

Niger, Shmuel. „קאנען אלע אידן האבן איין שול פאר זייערע קינדער?" (Can All Jews Have One Type of School for Their Children). *Day* (Y.) (Feb. 6, 1926).

Schwartzman, M. „פאראייניקונג אדער ליקווידאציע" (Consolidation or Liquidation). *YD* (Y.) (Aug. 1950): 92–95.

CAMPS

B-N, T. „דער ארבעטער רינג קעמפ—א דערציאונגס-אינסטיטוציע פאר קליין און גרויס" (The WC Camp—An Educational Institution for Children and Adults). *CE* (Y.) 26 (Feb. 1956): 32–33.

Buchover, E. „קעמפ ניי בוי בעריק—דער אפרוה פאר אידישע קינדער" (Camp New Boiberik—Rest Area for Jewish Children). *Morning Journal* (Y.) (Aug. 26, 1926).

Gingold, Pinchos. „קינדערוועלט אלס דערציאונגס-אינסטיטוציע" (Kinderwelt as Educational Institution). *Farband Shtimme* (Y.) (LZOA) (Oct. 1941).

Kohn, Fannie. „דער צוועק פון קעמפס און קלובן פאר ארבייטער" (The Purpose of Camps and Clubs for Workers' Children). *Gerechtigkeit* (Y.) (Justice) (Published by International Ladies Garment Workers) (1926).

Lehrer, Leibush. *Camp Boiberik: The Growth of an Idea*. N.Y.: 1959. 44 pp.

———. „די אידישע וועלטלעכע קעמפס" (The Yiddish Secular Camps). In *S Alm* (Y.), 196–98.

Sholem Aleichem Folk Institute. קעמפ בויבעריק (Camp Boiberik). SAFI, 1928.

Silver, L. „די יידישע דערציאונג אין קעמפ קינדער-רינג" (Jewish Education in Camp Kinder-Ring, WC). *CE* (Y.) 17 (May 1947): 14–16.

Skooler, Chaim. „קינדערלאנד—די זומער היים פון די ארדן-שולן" (Kinderland—The Summer Home of the Orden Schools). *Home and Education* (Y.) (May 1939): 15.

ASSESSMENT PRIOR TO 1950

Almazov, Sh. „די קינדער האבן ליב די אידישע ראדיקאלע שול" (The Children Like the Yiddish Radical School). *Morning Freiheit* (Y.) (Oct. 27, 1926).

Bass, Hyman. „אן איבערבליק איבער די פראבלעמען פון יידישע דערציאונג" (An Overview of the Problems in Yiddish Education). *CE* (Y.) 11 (May 1941): 3–10.

Ben-Mayer, M. Sh. „חנוך אידי באמריקה" (Yiddish Education in America). *Sh Hah* (H.) 2 (June 1942): 184–89.

Bercovich, Shloime. „די סתירות צווישן טעאריע און פראקטיק אין אונדזער יידישער שול" (The Discrepancies between Theory and Pratice in Our Schools). In *Shu P* (Y.), 170–99.

21 YIDDISH SECULAR SCHOOLS

Bercovici, Konrad. ‏"סאָציאַליסטישע קינדער שול"‎ (Socialist School for Children). *The Friend* (Y.) (Oct. 1911): 529–34.

Bergman, A. ‏"אונדזער יוגנט"‎ (Our Youth). *Home and Education* (Y.) (Feb. 1940): 15–16.

Bialostotzky, B. J. ‏"וואָס די יוגנט זאָגט"‎ (What Youth Is Saying). *CE* (Y.) (Dec. 1945).

Botwinik, B. ‏"די יוגנט אַרום אַרבעטער רינג"‎ (The Youth around the Workmen's Circle). *The Friend* (Mar./Apr. 1931): 6–8.

Bridger, David. ‏"די ייִדישע דערציאונג מוז איופגעריכט ווערן"‎ (Yiddish Education Must Be Restored). *YK* (Y.) (Dec. 20, 1946): 4–6.

Chanin, Nathan. ‏"דער קריטיקער פון אונדזערע שול"‎ (The Critic of Our Schools). *CE* (Y.) 11 (Apr. 1941): 2–4.

———. ‏"די זשאַנדאַרן פון דער תורה"‎ (The Gendarmes of the Torah). Response to a critic of a WC textbook. *CE* (Y.) 11 (Feb. 1941): 3–5.

Chinsky, Bloome. ‏"מיינונגען פון תלמידים וועגן דער אַמעריקאַנער ייִדישער שול"‎ (Views of Students on the American Yiddish School). In *Shu P* (Y.), 521–31.

Engelman, Uriah Z. ‏"לעתידותיה של השפה האידית באמריקה"‎ (On the Future of the Yiddish Language in America). *Sh Hah* (H.) 4 (1928): 63–72.

Entin, Joel. ‏"די טעותן פון דער נאציאנאל-ראדיקאלער שול באוועגונג"‎ (The Errors of the National-Radical School Movement). *The Jewish Worker* (Y.) (Official Organ of the LZOA) (1926): 16–17.

———. ‏"די ייִדישע פאלקשול"‎ (The Jewish Folkschool). *YD* (Y.) (Nov. 1936): 3–10.

———. ‏"די ייִדיש-וועלטלעכע סאָציאַליסטישע שול"‎ (The Yiddish-Secular Socialist School). *CE* (Y.) (Apr. 1944): 9–11.

Fishman, Joshua A. ‏"די שול יוגנט—אירע שטריכן און האפענונגען"‎ (The School Youth—Its Characteristics and Hopes). In *Shu P* (Y.), 503–15.

Gingold, Pinchos. ‏"ייִדישע דערציאונג אין דעם איצטיקן מאמענט און די באוועגונג פון די ייִדישע פאלקשולן"‎ (Jewish Education at the Present Moment and the Movement of the Yiddish Folkschools). *BYD* (Y.) 4 (June-Sept. 1951): 83–86.

———. ‏"די ראָלע פון אידיש-נאציאנאלן אַרבעטער פארבאנד אין דעם אידיש-קולטור לעבן אין אמעריקע"‎ (The JNWA in the Jewish Cultural Life of America). In ‏"אידישער נאציאנאלער אַרבעטער פארבאנד 1910-1946"‎ (Jewish National Workers Alliance, 1910–1946) (Y.), 339–86. LZOA.

———. ‏"די אידישע יוגנט און די אידישע קולטור"‎ (Jewish Youth and Jewish Culture). In *Gingold*, 124–29.

———. ‏"די ייִדישע פאלקשולן—זייער צושטייער און זייערע פראבלעמען"‎ (The Yiddish Folk Schools—Their Contribution and Their Problems). *Zuk* (Y.) (Mar. 1946): 195–97.

Gladstone, Jacob. ‏"גאנצע ייִדישע דערציאונג"‎ (Whole Jewish Education). *CE* (Y.) 26 (Nov. 1956): 5–6.

Goldberg, A. ‏"די אָרדן-שולן"‎ (The Orden Schools). In *Almanac* (Y.) 10th Anniversary of Orden School—Assessment of Curriculum, 67–192. N.Y.: 1940.

———. ‏"די אידיש-וועלטלעכע שולן"‎ (The Yiddish Secular School). *Pro D* (Y.) 3 (Sept. 1937): 3–5, 16.

Goldberg, Ben Zion. ‏"אונזערע אומפארטייאישע שולען"‎ (Our Non-Partisan Schools). On the Sholem Aleichem Schools. *Day* (Y.) (Dec. 26, 1926).

Goldstein, Sh. ‏"ווי האלט עס מיט אונזער שול באוועגונג?"‎ (How Does Our School Movement Fare?). *Pro D* (Y.) (May 1935): 11–13.

Golomb, Abraham. ‏"דער וועג פון דער ייִדישער דערציאונג אין אמעריקע"‎ (The Path of Jewish Education in America). *Zuk* (Y.) (Mar. 1946): 175–77.

———. ‏"קיום און דערציאונג"‎ (Survival and Education). *Zuk* (Y.) 53 (Sept. 1948): 518–21.

Goodman, Saul. ‏"די שלום עליכם שולן"‎ (The Sholem Aleichem Schools). *BYD* (Nov. 1949): 104–6.

Gordon, Abba. ‏"די וועלטליכע שולען אין אמעריקע"‎ (The Yiddish Secular School in America). *Zuk* (Y.) (Nov./Dec. 1937): 653–56.

Grossfield, A. ‏"די אַרבעטער רינג שול—אַ טאלמוד טורע אף אידיש"‎ (The WC School—A Talmud Torah in Yiddish). *Pro D* (Y.) (May 1935): 11–13.

Hurwitz, Sh. ‏"די אידישע וועלטליכע שול אין אמעריקע—וואס זי איז און וואס זי דארף זיין"‎

(The Yiddish Secular School in America: What It Is and What It Should Be). *Zuk* (Y.) (Jan. 1928): 40–44.

Hyamson, D. „ייִדיש װעלטלעכע שול דארפן זיין ייִדיש און װעלטלעכער" (Yiddish Secular School Must Be Yiddish and Secular). *CE* (Y.) 11 (1941): 15–16.

Katz, Moshe. "דערציאונג און קלאסן-קאמף„ (Education and Class Struggle). *Pro D* (Y.) 3 (May 1937): 3–4, 18.

———. „די אידישע װעלטלעכע שול אין אמעריקע" (The Yiddish Secular School in America). *Pro D* (Y.) 3 (Jan. 1933): 11–12, 33.

Lehrer, Leibush. „אונזער װעלטלאכע שול אין די פאראייניגטע שטאטן" (Our Secular School in the United States). *New Life* (Y.) 1 (1923): 54–59, 38–44.

———. "די שלום עליכם פאלק-שולן„ (The Sholem Aleichem Folk Schools). *Zuk* (Y.) (Nov. 1943): 682–86.

———. "Trends in Yiddish Education." *Congress Weekly* 13 (Oct. 25, 1946).

———. "The Yiddish Secular School." *Jew Ed* 4 (Apr./June 1932): 103–4.

Leivick, H. „לאמיר בויען די אידישע שול" (Let Us Build the Jewish School). *For* (Y.) (Nov. 1920).

Levine, Jacob. "די װעלטלעכע ייִדישע שול„ (The Secular Yiddish School). *Zuk* (Y.) (Mar. 1946): 189–93.

Lieberman, Herman (Chaim). „אין קאמען פאר אידישער דערציאונג" (The Struggle for Jewish Education) (Y.). A critique of the Yiddish secular school. N.Y.: Pardes Pub. House, 1941. 116 pp.

Mark, Yudel. "דאס קינד איז ניט דער ציל„ (The Child is Not the Goal). *CE* (Y.) 11 (Nov. 1941): 13–15.

———. „ייִדישקייט און װעלטלעכקייט אין און ארום אונדזערע שולן" (Jewishness and Secularism in and about Our Schools). In *Shu P* (Y.), 9–68.

———. „דער אלװעלטלעכער קולטור קאנגרעס און די ייִדישע שול" (The Worldwide Cultural Congress and the Yiddish School). *Zuk* (Y.) (Sept. 1948): 513–17.

Mendelsohn, Sh. „די אויפגאבעס פון אונדזער שול אין דער איצטיקער צייט" (The Tasks of Our

School at the Present Time). *CE* (Y.) (May 1946): 9–13.

———. "מיר מוזן אפהיטן די ייִדישע שול„ (We Must Preserve the Yiddish School). *CE* (Y.) 11 (Oct. 1941): 5.

Milstein, M. „צום איצטיקן מאב פון אונדזערע שולן" (On the Present Condition of Our Schools). *CE* (Y.) 17 (Dec. 1947): 14–15.

Niger, Shmuel. „װאס האט די מאדערנע שול אויפגעטאן" (What Has the Modern School Accomplished?). *Shoolblat* (Y.) (Sept. 1937): 3.

Noveck, H. „ייִדיש װעלטלעכע שולן העלפן פארשפרייטן ייִדישע ביכער" (Yiddish Secular Schools Help to Spread Yiddish Books). *JBA* (Y. section) (1942): 62–69.

Pinski, David. „אונדזערע װעלטלעכע שולן" (Our Secular Schools). *Zuk* (Y.) 51 (Mar. 1946): 139.

Pomerantz, I. Chaim. „שולטוער דארף מען לערנען" (School Board Members Must Be Educated). *CE* (Oct. 1947): 7–8.

Pomerantz, N. „די הויפט אויפגאבע פון דער אידישער שול" (The Major Task of the Yiddish School). *Our School* (Y.) 4 (Mar. 1939): 16–20.

Raizin, Abraham. „די אידיש-װעלטלעכע שול אין אמעריקע" (The Yiddish Secular School in America). *For* (Y.) (Nov. 20, 1949).

Rivkin, B. „די אידישע שול 'אידיזירט' און אמעריקאניזירט" (The Yiddish School, "Yiddicized" and Americanized). *Zuk* (Y.) 43 (Nov. 1938): 642–48.

Rotenberg, I. "די פועלי ציון װעגן אידישן חינוך„ (The Poale Zion [LZOA] on Jewish Education). *YK* (Y.) (July 26, 1963).

Simon, Solomon. „די שלום עליכם שולן און זייערע פראבלעמען" (The Sholem Aleichem Schools and Their Problems). *Zuk* (Y.) (Mar. 1946): 197–99.

Steinbaum, Israel. „אידישע שולן—װאס האבן זיי אויפגעטאן?" (What Have the Yiddish Schools Accomplished?). *Zuk* (Y.) (Mar. 1946): 191–94.

"דאס אידיש לימוד„ (The Study of Yiddish) (Symposium). Participants: R. Kaplan, Yudel Mark, B. Siegel, Israel Steinbaum, and Zalman Yefroikin. *Our School* 7 (Feb. 1937): 1–21.

Unger, M. „װאס איז געװארן פון די קינדער װאס האבן זין געלערנט אין די װעלטליכע

"איידיש שולען?" (What Became of the Children Who Learned in the Yiddish Secular Schools?). *Day* (Y.) (Feb. 19, 1939).

Weisbard, M. "דער איצטיקער מצב פון אונדזער שול" (The Present Condition of Our School). *CE* (Y.) (Apr. 1947): 13–15.

Whiteman, Kalman. "היש עתיד לחנוך האידישאי?" (Is There a Future for Yiddish Education?). *Hadoar* (H.) 18 (4th of Nissan, 1939).

Workmen's Circle "אין קאמף פאר אונדזער שול" (The Struggle for Our School) (Y.). N.Y.: WC-Teacher Organization, April 1931. 33 pp.

די יוגנט רעדט (Youth Speaks) (Y.). N.Y.: Central Committee, WC Schools, 1934. 64 pp.

Yefroiken, Zalman. "ארום אונדזער שול" (Around Our School). Critique of pedagogic practices. *CE* (Y.) 17 (Mar. 1947): 4–5.

——. "איידישע דערציאונג אין די וועלטלעכע שולן אין אמעריקע" (Jewish Education in the Yiddish Secular Schools in America). Survey of Several Decades of School Work. *Zuk* (Y.) 44 (May 1939): 283–85.

——. "אונדזערע אידעאלאגישע פראבלעמען" (Our Ideological Problems). *CE* (Y.) (Jan. 1946): 7–15.

——. "די פערספעקטיוון פון דער יידיש וועלטלעכער שול אין אמעריקע" (Perspectives on the Yiddish Secular School in America). *Zuk* (Y.) (Mar. 1946): 181–84.

——. "די ארבעטער רינג שול אין ליכט פון אונזער צייט" (The WC School in the Light of Our Time). *Der Vecker* (Y.) (Nov. 24, 1934): 7–8.

Zaltsman, R. "1926–1936." Report on 10 years of education of the Orden Schools). *Pro D* (Y.) 3 (Jan. 1937): 3–5.

"16 יאר שולן, 16 יאר ארדן" (16 Years of Orden Schools). *Freiheit* (Y.) (Apr. 4, 1946).

"וועגן יידיש וועלטלעכע שולן אין די פאראייניגטע שטאטן" (On Yiddish Secular Schools in the United States). In *World Yiddish Culture Congress* (Y.), 226–32. Paris: 1937.

ASSESSMENT SINCE 1950

Auerbach, Ephraim. "איידישע דערציאונג" (Jewish Education). *Day* (Y.) (July 11, 1958).

——. "איידיש-וועלטלעכע דערציאונג" (Yiddish Secular Education). *Day* (Y.) (Aug. 14, 1961).

Bass, Hyman. "די יידישע דערציאונג אויפן שיידוועג" (Jewish Education at the Crossroads). *World of Yiddish* (Y.) 9. 20 pp. Also in *Zuk* (Y.) (Nov. 1976): 353–58.

——. "יידישע דערציאונג אין אונדזער תקופה" (Jewish Education in Our Era). *Zuk* (Y.) (Feb./Mar. 1953): 156–61.

——. "אונדזער דור מוז אנטשיידן" (Our Generation Must Decide). *BYD* (Y.) (Spring 1962): 12–19.

——. "וועגן אונדזער עיקרדיקסטער פראבלעם—יידישע דערציאונג" (Our Most Pressing Problem—Jewish Education). *Zuk* (Y.) (July/Aug. 1965): 273–78.

——. "דאס ארט פון דער יידישער שול אין אמעריקאנער יידיש לעבן" (The Place of the Yiddish School in American Jewish Life). *CE* (Y.) (Oct. 1952): 11–17.

——. "פראבלעמען פון יידישן חינוך ביים הײַנטיקן טאג" (Problems of Jewish Education in Our Day) (Y.). N.Y.: World Jewish Congress, 1957.

——. "דער וועג צו אונדזער יוגנט" (The Road to Our Youth). *Zuk* (July/Aug. 1961): 253–59.

——. "Some Problems of Jewish Education: The Yiddish Progressive Standpoint." In *JJS*, 188–91.

——. "טענדענצן אין יידישער דערציאונג" (Tendencies in Jewish Education). *CE* (Y.) (Oct. 1954): 8–11.

——. "The Yiddish Schools." *Jew Ed* 21 (Spring 1950): 56–57.

Bickel, Shlomo. "אידישע דערציאונג" (Jewish Education). *Day* (Y.) (May 14, 1965).

——. "שלום עליכם שולען" (Sholem Aleichem Schools). *Day* (Y.) (Nov. 29, 1963).

Chanin, Nathan. "א דור פון גרויסן אידעאליזם" (A Generation of Great Idealism). *Zuk* (Apr. 1958): 172–76.

——. "א פראגרעסיווע יידישע דערציאונג אין די פאראייניגטע שטאטן" (A Progressive Jewish Education in the United States). *Zuk* (Y.) (Sept. 1961): 330–32.

Dawidowicz, Lucy. "The Relevance of an Education in the Sholem Aleichem Schools." In *OFFY*, 117–23.

Dawidowitch, Sh. „די יידישע קינדער שולן פֿון דעם אינטערנאַציאָנאַלן אַרבעטער אָרדן" (The Jewish Children's Schools of the International Workers Orden). *Day* (Y.) (Jan. 14, 1951).

Entin, Joel. „דערגרייכונגען פֿון אידיש אין פֿאָלקשול און מיטלשול" (Achievements of Yiddish in Elementary Folkschool and High School). *YD* (Y.) (May 1954) 46–51.

———. „אונדזער יידישע דערציאונג" (Our Jewish Education). *YD* (Y.) 9 (May 1954): 3–28.

Feder, Sarah. „די פּיאָנערן פֿרויען און די אידישע פֿאָלקשולן" (The Pioneer Women [LZOA] and the Yiddish Folkschools). *YD* (Y.) 9 (May 1951): 36–41.

———. „ציוניזם און דערציאונג" (Zionism and Education). *YD* (Y.) 10 (Dec. 1962): 5–11.

Field, Ben. „דער כאַראַקטער און אינהאַלט פֿון די אָרדן-שול" (The Character and Content of the Jewish Orden Schools). *Morning Freiheit* (Y.) (Sept. 26, 1950).

Gingold, Pinchos. „יידישע דערציאונג אין דער הײַנטיקער תּקופֿה" (Jewish Education in the Present Era). *YK* (Y.) (Jan. 27, 1950): 27–28.

———. „אונדזער שול-וועזן אינעם איצטיקן מאָמענט" (Our Schools at This Momemt). *YD* (Y.) (Aug. 1950): 3–8.

Glazman, Sh. „דער חשבון הנפֿש פֿון די פּראָגרעסיווע וועלטלעכע אידישע קינדער שול" (An Introspective View of the Progressive Yiddish Schools). *Morning Freiheit* (Y.) (June 13, 1962).

Golomb, Abraham. „דערציאונג צו אינטעגראַלער אידישקייט" (Education toward Integral Jewishness). *YK* (Y.) (Sept. 10, 1954): 7–8.

———. „פֿאַלשע דערציאונג" (False Education). *YK* (Y.) (Nov. 18, 1965): 6–7.

———. „אויף אייגענע וועגן" (On Our Paths). *Zuk* (Y.) (Oct. 1960): 383–86.

Goodman, Saul. „דאָס פּנים פֿון יידישן חינוך אין אַמעריקע" (The Features of Jewish Education in America). *Zuk* (Y.) (Sept. 1960): 313–60.

———. "The Future of the Yiddish Secular School in America." *Recon* (May 29, 1964): 7–13. Also in *Zuk* (Y.) (Dec. 1962): 484–88.

———. „די שלום עליכם שול—די עוואָלוציע פֿון דער יידיש-וועלטלעכער שול אין אַמעריקע" (The Sholem Aleichem School—The Evolution of the Yiddish Secular School in America). *BYD* 4 (June-Sept. 1951): 79–82.

———. "Whither the Yiddish School?" *Congress Biweekly* (Mar. 13, 1961): 7–9.

Greenberg, Hayim. „אונדזער דערציאונג און קולטור אַרבעט אין חוץ לארץ" (Our Education and Culture in the Diaspora). *YK* (Y.) (Jan. 27, 1950): 6–8. See also *YK* (Sept. 14, 1951): 2–4; (Nov. 16, 1951): 6–7, 9; and (Nov. 23, 1951): 9–11.

Isaacman, Daniel. „ווי יידיש וועלן אונדזערע קינדער זײַן?" (How Jewish Will Our Children Be?). *YD* (Y.) 10 (Dec. 1962): 12–19.

Kantor, M. „וועלטלעכקייט און אונדזערע שולן" (Secularism and Our Schools). *YD* (Y.) (Aug. 1950): 108–10.

Kazdan, Ch. Sh. „דורות קייטלען זיך" (Links between Generations). *BYD* (Y.) (Spring 1962): 20–27.

Knox, Israel. „אידיש און אידישע דערציאונג" (Yiddish and Yiddish Education). *For* (Y.) (June 5, 1977).

Kolodner, S. „יידישער קיום און יידישע דערציאונג" (Jewish Survival and Jewish Education). *Zuk* (Y.) (July/Aug. 1977): 231–33.

Lazarson, M. „עטיק און די מאָדערנע יידישע שול" (Ethics and the Modern Jewish School). *YD* (Y.) 7 (May 1940): 11–12.

Lehrer, Leibush. „די יידישקייט פֿון צווייטן דור וועלטלעכע" (The Jewishness of the Second Generation of Secular Jews). *YB* (Y.) 42, 1948 (1962): 167–80. See also *YA* 13 (1962): 79–94.

Levine, Jacob. „די יידישע דערציאונג אין אונדזער שול" (Jewish Education in Our School). *CE* (Y.) 26 (Mar. 1956) 1–3.

Maltz, Saul. „דער אַרבעטער רינג און די אַרבעטער רינג שול" (The WC and the WC School). *CE* (Y.) 36 (Mar. 1961): 10–11.

Mark, Yudel. „פֿערציק יאָר און וואָס ווײַטער?" (40 Years and What Is Ahead?). *CE* (Y.) (Dec. 1961): 11–12.

———. "Fragments of a Summation." (Autobiographical credo.) *Jew Ed* 39 (Apr. 1969): 5–12.

Millstein, M. „הײַנטיקע פּראָבלעמען און אונדזערע שולן" (Current Problems and Our Schools). *CE* (Y.) 30 (Nov. 1960): 9–10.

Millstone, Mark. "Trends in American Yiddish Education." *Jew Spec* (Oct. 1953): 25–27.

Mlotek, Joseph. „האבן מיר טאקע פארלארן אונדזער יוגנט?" (Have We Really Lost Our Youth?). *CE* (Y.) (Jan. 1950): 11–12.

———. „טרײ דעם גײסט פון די פיאנערן" (In Keeping with the Spirit of Its Pioneers). On the 35th jubilee of the WC schools. *Der Freind* (Y.) (Sept./Oct. 1953): 4–5.

———. "Jewish Education." *The Call* (Sept. 1962): 4–5.

———. „אונדזערע געוועזענע תלמידים" (Our Former Students). Summary of a survey. *CE* (Y.) 29 (May 1958): 5–10. See also *For* (Y.) (June 14, 1958).

———. „וואס ווייסן אונדזערע קינדער און אייניקלאך פון אונדזער נעכטן" (What Do Our Children and Grandchildren Know about Our Yesterday?). *Day-Journal* (Y.) (Sept. 7, 1959).

———. „די יוגנט פון ארבעטער רינג" (The Youth of the Workmen's Circle). *CE* (Y.) (Mar. 1952): 7–8.

Niger, Shmuel. „לאמיר זיך באראטן" (Let Us Confer). *Day* (Y.) (Sept. 10, 1955).

Noskowitz, I. „דערגרייכונגען פון אונדזערע שולן" (Achievements of Our Schools). *CE* (Y.) (Mar. 1959): 3–4, 10.

———. „דער מצב פון די ייִדיש וועלטלעכע שולן" (The Condition of the Yiddish Secular Schools). *Pio Woman* (Y.) (Oct./Nov. 1967): 3–4, 7.

———. „דערציאונג פאר דערוואקסענע" (Education for Adults). *CE* (Y.) 31 (Feb. 1961): 2–5.

Olitsky, M. „קינדער וואס גייען אוועק פון שול" (Children Who Leave School). *CE* (Y.) 26 (Oct. 1956): 13–14.

Orlant, A. Sh. „ארבעים שנות חנוך יהודי חילוני" (Forty Years of Jewish Secular Education). *Hadoar* (H.) 37 (June 20, 1958): 597–98.

Parker, Sandra. "An Educational Assessment of the Yiddish Secular School Movement in the United States." In *Never Say Die*, 496–511. N.Y.: Hague Moulton Publishers, 1981.

Penn, Ascher. „די פראגרעסיווע אידישע שולן (געוועזענע ארדן-שולן) דערנענטערן זיך אויך צו טראדיציאנאלער אידישקייט" (Progressive Yiddish Schools [former Orden Schools] Come Closer to Jewish Tradition). In *Penn* (Y.), 389–400.

———. „די פאלק שול און פולע טאג שול פון דער ציוניסטישער ארבעטער באוועגונג אין אמעריקע און קאנאדא" (A Review of the LZOA-Farband Secular Schools and the Beginning of Their First Day School in the US and Canada). In *Penn* (Y.), 349–63.

———. „די שלום עליכם שולן—דער וועג פון עקסטרעם אידישער וועלטלעכער קולטור צוריק צו טראדיציע און ... בית מדרש" (The SAFI Schools Return to Tradition). In *Penn* (Y.), 376–89.

———. „די שולן פון ארבעטער רינג פארענענטערן זיך אלץ מער צו די אלטע אידישע קוואלן" (The WC Schools Draw Closer to Early Jewish Sources). In *Penn* (Y.), 364–75.

Rudman, S. „דערציונג אדער כאאס?" (Education or Chaos?). *Zuk* (Y.) (June 1955): 196–201.

Shapiro, Solomon. „אמעריקע און ישראל אין אונדזער דערציאונג" (America and Israel in Our Education). *YD* (Y.) 9 (May 1954): 51–64.

Shefner, B. „פרומע עצות פאר וועלטלעכע אידן" (Pious Advice for Secular Jews). The condition of the Yiddish secular school. *For* (Y.) (Oct. 22, 1960).

Sherman, Bezalel C. „וועלטלעכע שולן—אמאל און הײנט" (Secular Schools—Past and Present). *YK* (Y.) (Aug. 13, 1954): 7–8, 13.

Shulman, A. „צוויי שפראכיקייט אין אמעריקע און די מעגלעכקייט פאר ייִדיש" (Bilingualism in America and the Potential for Yiddish). *CE* (Y.) 37 (Jan. 1967): 1–3.

Simon, Solomon. „דער גורל פון אונדזערע אידישע שולן" (The Fate of Our Yiddish Schools). *Freie Arbeiter Shtimme* (Y.) (May 18, 1956). Also in pamphlet of the same title published by SAFI, ca. 1956. 32 pp.

Singer, Sh. D. „דער לימוד פון ייִדיש לעבן איבער דער וועלט הײנט צו טאג" (The Study of Jewish Life in the World Today). *CE* (Y.) 31 (Mar. 1961): 7–11.

Spizman, L. „ליכט און שאטן אין אידישן חינוך" (Light and Shadow in Jewish Education). *Day-Morning Journal* (Y.) (Nov. 3, 1956).

———. „די ארבעט פאר דער אידישער שול" (The Work in Behalf of the Yiddish School). In *History of the Labor Zionist Movement in*

North America (Y.), 1: 261–73. N.Y.: Yiddisher Kemfer, 1951.

———. „אידישע דערציאונג אמאל און היינט" (Yiddish Education—Past and Present). *YD* (Y.) (May 1954): 41–46.

WC I. L. Peretz Schools. „ארבעטער רינג י. ל. פרץ שולן" Articles in honor of 50th anniversary of WC schools by: Joseph Mlotek, P. Geleibter, Zalmen Yefroiken, Nathan Chanin, A. Lessin, M. Chait, and Tsivion. *For* (Y.) (Jan. 28, 1968).

Wineshenker, I. „וואס עס פעלט אין אונדזער חינוך" (What Is Lacking in Our Education). In *Golomb* (Y.), 557–60.

World Congress for Yiddish Culture. „פארשלאגן און רעקאמענדאציעס" (Proposals and Recommendations on Yiddish Education) (Y.), 235–37. Tel Aviv, 1977.

Yefroikin, Zalman. „דאס ארט פון אונדזער שול אין היינטיקן אידישן לעבן" (The Place of Our School in Today's Jewish Life). *CE* (Y.) 26 (Nov. 1956): 1–4.

———. „די יידישע וועלטלעכע שול" (The Yiddish Secular School). *CE* (Y.) 36 (Feb.1966): 9, 20.

Zipper, I. „אידישע דערציאונג אין ליכט פון מדינת ישראל" (Jewish Education in Light of the State of Israel). *YD* (Y.) (Aug. 1950). Also in *Golomb* (Y.), 567–74.

ORGANIZATIONS SPONSORING YIDDISH EDUCATION

Labor Zionist Alliance (formerly Farband Labor Zionist Order; now uniting membership and branches of Poale Zion-Labor Zionist Organization of America and American Habonim Association): "Seeks to enhance Jewish life, culture, and education in the United States and Canada." Publishes *Jew Fron* and *YK* (Y.). (AJYB, 1989)

Sholem Aleichem Folk Institute: "Aims to imbue children with Jewish values through teaching Yiddish language and literature, Hebrew and the Bible, Jewish history, the significance of Jewish holidays, folk and choral singing, and facts about Jewish life in America and Israel." Publishes *Kinder Journal* (Y.) (AJYB, 1989)

WC: "Provides fraternal benefits and activities, Jewish educational programs, secularist Yiddish schools for children, community activities, both in Jewish life and on the American scene, cooperation with labor movement." Publishes *The Call, Kinder Zeitung* (Y.), and *Kultur un Lebn* (Y.). (AJYB, 1989)

BOOKS FOR CHILDREN AND YOUTH (SELECTED) (TITLES TRANSLATED)

Auerbach, Ephraim. *Moses* (Y.). Farlag Yiddish, 1918.

———. *Three Giants* (Y.). N.Y.: Kinder Ring, WC Education Committee, 1932. 64 pp.

Barkan, H. *Once There Was* (Y.). Legends and stories. Edited by Y. Mark. 3d ed. 1948, 1957. 48 pp.

Elbe, Leon. *Yingele Ringele* (Y.). N.Y.: Farlag Matones, SAFI, 1929, 1932. 200 pp.

Fogelman, L. *Our Ring* (Y.). A history of the WC. N.Y.: Kinder Ring Education Committee, 1931. 32 pp.

Goichberg, I. *Good Morning* (Y.). N.Y.: Farlag Matones, SAFI, 1928. 60 pp.

Gold, H. *A Lass with a "Tzepl" [Pigtail] Tastes an Apple* (Y.). N.Y.: M. Shklarsy, 1941. 48 pp.

Gross, Naphtali. *Eugene V. Debs* (Y.). N.Y.: Kinder Ring, WC Education Committee, 1938. 64 pp.

———. *Legends* (Y.). N.Y.: Kinder Ring, WC Education Committee, 1935. 144 pp.

Kaminsky, I. *A Story about Three Small Goats* (Y.). N.Y.: Kinder Ring, WC, 1927. 32 pp.

———. *A Tiny Chick Strolls to Brownsville* (Y.). N.Y.: Kinder Ring, WC, 1937. 100 pp.

Kozlowski, Ida Glazer. *A Trip to the Moon* (Y.). N.Y.: 1940.

Leib, Mani. *Wonder Follows Wonder* (Y.). N.Y.: Kinder Ring, WC, 1930. 160 pp.

Levitan, Ruth, ed. *Listen to a Tale! Listen to a Tale!* (Y.). N.Y.: 1982. 94 pp.

Mark, Yudel. *All Mothers Are Pretty* (Y.). N.Y.: Kinder Ring, WC, 1941. 480 pp.

Menes, G., ed. *Elijah the Prophet* (Y.). N.Y.: CYCO, 1955. 343 pp.

Opatoshu, Joseph, ed. *Tales about the Ba'al Shem Tov* (Y.). N.Y.: CYCO, 1957. 306 pp.

Osherowitz, H. *Moses Montefiore*. N.Y.: Farlag Kinder Ring, WC, 1951. 48 pp.

Radin, H. *Alef Avremel* (Y.). N.Y.: Farlag Matones, 1946.

Raizin, Abraham. *50 Songs and Poems* (Y.). Illustrations in color by 9 artists. N.Y.: Farlag Matones, SAFI, 1926.

Segal, Berl. *Moses Mendelsohn* (Y.). N.Y.: Kinder Ring, WC, 1941. 46 pp.

Segal, J. J. *Poems for Jewish Children* (Y.). N.Y.: WC Education Department, 1961. 111 pp.

Shifris, Moshe. *Lenin Shows the Way*. Young International Orden, 1933. 16 pp.

———. *Mother Week and Her Seven Days* (Y.). N.Y.: Yungvarg, 1941. 78 pp.

Sholem Aleichem. *Motl, the Cantor's Son* (Y.). Abridged by I. Zilberberg. N.Y.: Farlag Matones, SAFI, 1946. 237 pp.

Simon, Solomon. *The Clever Tailor* (Y.). N.Y.: Farlag Matones, SAFI, 1933. 127 pp.

———. *Foolish Shmerl* (Y.). N.Y.: Farlag Matones, SAFI, 1931. 104 pp.

———. *The Heroes of Chelem*. N.Y.: Farlag Matones, 1942.

Steinberg, Yehudah. *Stories* (Y.). Edited by S. Shapiro. N.Y.: Folkschools of the JNWA, 1926. 146 pp.

Tashrak. *All the Legends of the Talmud* (Y.). 3 vols. N.Y.: Hebrew Pub. Co., 1922.

———. *Tales for Children* (Y.). N.Y. Hebrew Pub. Co., 1928. 222 pp.

Weinstein, B. *Sketches from the Life of American Jewish Workers*. Rewritten by N. Gross. N.Y.: Kinder Ring, WC, 1935. 139 pp.

PERIODICALS FOR YOUTH (SELECTED)

Kinder Journal (Y.). SAFI, 1920–8? Monthly.

Kinderland (Y.). WC, 1921–23. Monthly.

Kinderwelt—Olam haYalodim (Y. and H.). JNWA, ca. 1915–2?

Kinder Zeitung (Y.). WC, 1934–8? Monthly.

Unzer Zeitung (Y.). JNWA, 1948–? Monthly.

Dos Yiddishe Kind. (Y.). JNWA–LZOA, 1934–? Monthly.

Yiddisher Kinder Journal (Y.). JNWA, 1914–16.

Yungvarg (Youth) (Y.). Orden, 1937–4?

PERIODICALS FOR EDUCATORS AND PARENTS (SELECTED)

Bieter far Yiddisher Dertsiung (Y.). Congress for Jewish Culture, New York, 1949–5?. Monthly.

Bulletin (Y.). SAFI, New York, 1941–6?. Published 7–8 times per year.

Culture and Education (formerly *Our School*) (Y.). WC, New York, 1938–84.

Home and Education (Y.). Orden, New York, 1935–45. Bimonthly.

Our School (Y.). WC, New York, 1931–37. Monthly.

Pedagogic Bulletin (Y.). Commission of Yiddish Schools and JEC of New York, New York, 1941–66.

Proletarian Education (Y.). Orden, New York, 1935–? Monthly.

Quarterly Pedagogic School Journal, LZOA–JNWA, 1936–40.

School Bulletin (Y.). WC, New York, 1924–?

School and Home (Y.). WC Teachers Organization, New York, 1927–?

School and Teacher (Y.). JNWA–LZOA, New York, 1927–? Quarterly.

Shoolblat (Y.). WC, New York, 1937–46.

Yiddishe Dertsiung (Y.). LZOA, New York, 1932–5?

TEXTBOOKS, READERS, WORKBOOKS, AND TEACHER GUIDES (SELECTED)

Barkan, H. *Our People* (Y.). Vol. 1. N.Y.: WC Education Department.

Bass, Hyman. *Jews in Ancient Times* (Y.). Workbook and reader from Babylonia until after the uprising of Bar Kohba. N.Y.: WC, 1933.

———. *Program for Jewish History* (Y.) Manual for teaching Jewish history. N.Y.: WC Education Department, 1952. 164 pp.

———. *Workbook for Jewish History—Wanderings in the Desert—Until the Babylonian Exile* (Y.). N.Y.: WC, 1931. 96 pp.

Bass, Hyman, and Zalman Yefroikin. *My Language Book* (Y.) and *My Language Book—Read!*. 3d ed. N.Y.: WC Education Committee, 1946, 1948.

Bergman, A., and A. Goldberger, eds. *Our Book* (Y.). Chrestomathy for high school. N.Y.: Committee for Progressive Jewish Education, 1937, 1952. 208 pp.

Bridger, David. *The Primer* (Y.). 4th ed. N.Y.: Farlag Matones, 1981. 155 pp.

Dubnow, Shimon. *Jewish History for School and Home* (Y.). Edited by M. Sklarsky. N.Y.: Central Committee of the Jewish Folk Schools (LZOA/JNWA), 1941, 1954.

Elbe, Leon. *The Yiddish Language* (Y.). For the National Radical School. N.Y.: M. Gurevitch, 1914. 138 pp.

Entin, Joel. *From the People's Mouth* (Y.). Collection of stories and folk tales for the school and home. N.Y.: 1914. 201 pp.

———, ed. and comp. *Yiddish Poets* (Y.). 2 vols. Handbook of Yiddish poetry. N.Y.: Folk School Organization, JNWA and LZOA, 1927.

Entin, Joel, and Leon Elbe. *From Jewish Sources* (Y.). Textbook—anthology. N.Y.: M.N. Maisel, 1916. 306 pp.

Feldman, Moshe. *My Yiddish Book* (Y.). N.Y.: Farlag Fraternal Folks Orden, 1946. 192 pp.

Goodelman, Israel. *Jewish History* (Y.). 3 vols. (Notebooks.) N.Y.: Farlag Matones, 1945–65.

Grant, Hyman. *First Steps* (Y.). Primer. N.Y.: Hebrew Pub. Co., 1934. 134 pp.

Kaminsky, I. *In the Home and in the School* (Y.). Primer and workbook. N.Y.: WC. 128 pp.

———. *My Alef-Bet* (Y.). N.Y.: 1927. 50 pp.

Levine, Jacob. *Jewish History for Children from Abraham to Ezra*. N.Y.: Farlag Yiddish, Hebrew Pub. Co., 1946. 189 pp.

———. *Primer* (Y.). 8th ed. N.Y.: Hebrew Pub. Co., 1921, 1929. 116 pp.

Levitz, J. *Yiddish: Listen and Speak Method* (Y.). Experimental project. N.Y.: WC Education Committee, 1972. 63 pp.

Liebert, Sarah. *Word and Picture* (Y.). N.Y.: Farlag Matones, SAFI, 1933. 78 pp.

Maladowsky, Kadya. *On the Paths of Zion* (Y.). N.Y.: Jewish Folk Schools–LZOA, 1957. 364 pp.

Mark, Yudel. *History-Workbook* (Y.). N.Y.: WC Education Committee, 1967. 32 and 33 pp.

———. *Yiddish for School and Home* (Y.). Experimental ed. plus workbook. N.Y.: Committee for Yiddish in Public High Schools, 1941, 1961.

Mlotek, Joseph. *Jewish Children* (Y.). Workbook. N.Y.: WC Education Committee, 1959, 1961, 1971. 128 pp.

Mlotek, Joseph, and Matis Olitzky. *Jewish Children* (Y.). N.Y.: WC Education Committee, 1975. 120 pp.

Noskowitz, I. *My People* (Y.). History textbook for elementary school. 2 vols. N.Y.: WC Education Committee, 1962, 1967. 167 pp. and 195 pp.

Olitzky, M., and Joseph Mlotek. *Jewish Children* (Y.). N.Y.: WC Education Department, 1975. 120 pp.

Ostrowsky, B., and Sh. Hurwitz. *Yiddish for Beginners* (Y.). N.Y.: Farlag Folk School, 1926. 89 pp.

Rotenberg, Joshua. *A Trip to Israel* (Y.). Textbook for the study of Israel. N.Y.: Pinchos Gingold Farlag—JNWA and LZOA, 1964. 93 pp.

Rudai, Pinchos. *Workbook for the Jewish Child, Part 1* (Y.). N.Y.: Hebrew Pub. Co., 1941. 74 pp.

Schauss, Hayyim. *Jewish History for School and Adults* (Y.). N.Y.: WC Education Committee, 1927. 159 pp.

Shapiro, Isaac. *My Book: Primer and second year*. 2 vols. N.Y.: Central Committee for the Yiddish Folk Schools in the United States and Canada, Farband–LZOA, 1961.

Shapiro, Solomon. *Primer for School and Home* (Y.). N.Y.: Central Committee of Farband and LZOA, 1944, 1946. 64 pp.

Shapiro, Solomon, and I. Goobkin. *The New Word* (Y.). Anthology. N.Y.: Pinchos Gingold Farlag-Farband–LZOA, 1954.

Shifris. Moshe. *My Yiddish Book—Two* (Y.). 3d ed. N.Y.: Committee for Progressive Jewish Education, 1953, 1961. 63 pp.

Silver, L. *Jew in America—Episodes and Portraits* (Y.). N.Y.: WC Education Committee, 1955.

Snyder, Wolf. *Syllabus for Jewish History for the Jewish Folkschools* (Y.). N.Y.: Central Committee of JNWA and LZOA, 1941. 116 pp.

Steinbaum, Israel. *Methods for the First Year Yiddish* (Y.). For teachers. N.Y.: Farlag "Education," 1924. 127 pp.

———. *My Reader* (Y.). 2d ed. N.Y.: Farlag "Education," 1926.

———. *Our People* (Y.). Reader for older students. N.Y.: Farlag "Education," ca. 1932. 41 pp.

Tarant, Dvorah. *My Reader* (Y.). N.Y.: Committee for Yiddish in the High School. 94 pp.

Wiseman, Shlomo. *The Word* (Y.). 2 vols. Anthology. N.Y.: Yiddish Folk Schools of JNWA–LZOA, 1931.

Yefroikin, Zalman. *Peretz Anthology* (Y.). On Peretz's 100th birthday. N.Y.: WC Department of Education, 1952. 264 pp.

———. *The Yiddish Word* (Y.). Reader. N.Y.: WC Education Committee, 1947, 1968. 320 pp.

Yefroikin, Zalman, and Hyman Bass. *The Living Word* (Y.). 3 vols. Reader. N.Y.: WC Education Committee, 1958–59. 3rd and 4th grades.

———. *Our Word* (Y.). Literary chrestomathy for 3rd and 4th grades. N.Y.: Meisel, WC, 1933. 408 pp.

Yefroikin, Zalman, and H. Sh. Kazdan. *At the Source* (Y.). Literary anthology. N.Y.: WC Education Committee, 1948. 110 pp. High school.

Yefroikin, Zalman, and Yudel Mark. *Jewish Children*. Reader. N.Y.: WC Education Committee, 1956. Revised 1962. 167 pp. 2nd grade.

Zilberberg, Israel, and Yudel Mark. *Anthology of Yiddish Literature for Youth* (Y.). 2d ed. 1974. 366 pp.

Zumoff, Nachum. *Learning Yiddish* (Y.). Workbook. N.Y.: WC Education Committee, 1956. 37 pp. Preschool.

GLEANINGS

Entin, Joel, on early Yiddish secular schools, 1909,

"The Jew who is neither religious nor nationalistic—what is he to do? It is for these Jews that the Folk Schools have a program. There is a certain something that binds these Jews to the Jewish past, makes them interested in the Jewish present, and they will even listen of a brighter future. These parents do not wish their children to be different than they are themselves. Very few of these parents would like their children to be other than Jews."

Quoted by B. Segal, *Jew Ed* 32 (Winter 1963), 11.

Sholem Aleichem Folk Institute—"Principles" (1927),

"4. This, as yet incomplete, Jewish secular school must offer such a program and possess such a character that would express and fortify the aforementioned basis of Jewish secular life. This means that its chief requisite must be the subjects and activities that bear on Jewish secular life and its creativeness, as for example, Yiddish, Yiddish literature, Yiddish folklore, and Jewish history. Religious beliefs and customs must be considered from the cultural, historic standpoint. Hebrew and Hebrew literature should be studied in the upper grades (this means in high school) as a part of the total Jewish cultural treasure."

In Goodman, ed., *Our First Fifty Years* (E. and Y.) (N.Y: SAFI, 1972), 136.

Mark, Yudel,
"The Yiddish school regards itself as a young branch on the old trunk of Jewish education."
Jew Ed 17 (Feb. 1946), 43.

Yefroikin, Zalman,
"In the schools of the Jewish National Workers Alliance special attention was devoted to the study of Hebrew. In the schools of the Workmen's Circle and in the Sholem Aleichem Schools emphasis was placed on 'education and achievements relating to Jewish secular life and activity; Yiddish literature, Jewish folk creativity, Jewish history'; and further on the need 'to acquaint our children with the treasures of Jewish culture and literature, new and old, in order to assure the continuity of Jewish cultural life.'"
"Yiddish Schools," in *JPPP*, 2:125.

Pomerantz, I. Chaim, on Sholem Aleichem Schools (excerpts from his survey on Yiddish schools),
"The basic principles of the Yiddish school are still sound. . . .

Without Hebrew we cannot build our school system. We begin with Yiddish—since even today, after the Hitler slaughters, it is still the living language of the East-European Jew. . . . Since Yiddish could be a debatable issue with some parents we must concentrate on its significance in [Jewish life]. . . .

A school of a group or . . . of a party is actually not a school from an educational point of view. . . . We have in mind only a school that is dedicated to the well-being of the Jewish people. . . .

We need not change our principles . . . but examine the changes that have taken place in American life during the past thirty-five years and implement the necessary changes. . . .

Today's leaders of our school belong to one generation and the parents of the children to another . . . and a bridge is lacking between school, lay-leadership and parents. . . .We must strengthen our dialogue with the parents of our students . . . and prospective parents as well. . . . Our parents today are more educated than in previous decades—and have much to offer to the enrichment of the school. . . . We must remake ourselves to be worthy of the challenge to save our schools from the current crisis. . . .

We must reeducate ourselves—both educators and lay leaders. To renew our school-work we must begin with ourselves."
"Towards the Improvement of Our School Work." In *Shu P* (Y.), 90, 91, 92, 93, 96, 98. Translated from the Yiddish.

Chanin, Nathan, on WC (1950),
"The school must become what the home is no longer—in order that it might give the children the Jewish way of life and the Jewish holidays. The school must arm the Jewish child in America with Jewish values."
Quoted by Krug, *Jew Ed* 25 (Fall 1954), 69.

WC (1952),
"It is the aim of the Arbeiter Ring Schools [WC schools] to familiarize its pupils with Jewish life, history, folklore, literature and the story of the Bible. In addition, it seeks to develop in the children a feeling for the creatuve social ideas of the times. The school sees an affinity between the moral values in Jewish history and the ideals of democracy and freedom as conceived in the United States. Its purpose is to nurture in the young an appreciation of the positive elements in both American and Jewish life."
Quoted by Krug, *Jew Ed* 25 (Fall 1954), 68.

Bass, Hyman (1952),
"The Yiddish school must remember that only the vital life of a people which possesses all the needed elements of traditions, statutes and continuity, can be educationally effective and can educate a generation. It must also recognize the national poetic value of the people's creativity, the Chumash, the Midrash, the ancient literary treasures, and to create in the child the receptivity to accept this heritage and be influenced by it."
Introduction to *Manual for the Teachers of Jewish History* (N.Y: WC Education Department, 1952). Quoted by Krug, *Jew Ed* 25 (Fall 1954), 69.

21 YIDDISH SECULAR SCHOOLS

SAFI,

"We teach Yiddish—the language and literature, Hebrew and the Bible, Jewish History—from the earliest to the present. The Jewish Way of Life,—Jewish holidays and their significance, Jewish Life in America and Israel, Folk Songs and Choral Singing, Extra-Curricular Activities—Children Celebrate Bar Mitzvah and Jewish holidays."

Reproduction of a circular from the 1950s in *OFFY*, 140.

Lehrer, Leibush (1962)

(reflections on Camp Boiberik, founded in 1922 by the Sholem Aleichem Folk Institute of New York, which conducted Yiddish secular schools in New York and other cities). Lehrer was camp director for many years.

"When a school organization establishes a camp it has a right to expect the latter to be an extension of the work of the school.... In the early years, we were all victims of this mistaken illusion.... We found that a camp has potentials which a school cannot possibly fulfill. The object of a school is to see that its pupils acquire as much knowledge as possible, whereas the primary object of a camp is to teach children the value of cooperation, good moral habits and, in Jewish matters, to stress the Jewish way of life, forms of natural Jewish expression, a readiness to experience in concrete ways the symbolic expressions of Jewishness derived from our great heritage....

Any effort to introduce into Boiberik, among the children and guests as well, the slightest hint of traditional content had to be undertaken in gradual stages, with teaspoon doses....

The systematic drawing closer to tradition remained localized, a permanent concern in Boiberik. Here the objectives have remained as they were as they first blossomed forth. Only in one task, and a very vital one, it is not possible to report any progress: the furtherance of Yiddish as the normal medium for the children's camp....

It is easier to state ideas than to discover proper methods for their implementation. Our aim is to provide sound camping experience and to imbue our campers with the educational and moral values of wholesome fun, recreation and cooperative living. On the other hand, since we are dealing with Jewish children, effective expression should be given to the campers' consciousness of Jewish belonging and to the feeling of loyalty to the interests of Jewish people."

"The Objectives of Camp Boiberik—In the Light of its History." In Goodman, ed., *Our First Fifty Years* (E. and Y.) (N.Y: SAFI, 1972), 61–62, 64, 68, 71.

Mlotek, Joseph, on 50 years of the WC,

"During the fifty years, tens of thousands of children were educated, who today are active young men and women participating in Jewish communal life, plus the thousands of adults who were educated in our adult programs. The Workmen's Circle was also the cultural home, where thousands quenched their thirst for cultural growth. In the cities where there were Workmen's Circle Schools, these schools were transformed into cultural centers, where Yiddish authors appeared, where a Jewish library was established, where there were hundreds of lectures, forums, concerts, and drives for important communal purposes. Around the Workmen's Circle Schools gathered creative Jewish groups, dramatic circles and choirs who brought the sparkling Yiddish word and song to the Jewish masses....

The Workmen's Circle did not fulfill all of its hopes during these past fifty years. Many stronger forces in American society prevented that around the school there flourish a full Jewish life. Often the Yiddish School remained an isolated Yiddish island surrounded by a sea of self-denial and conformity."

"With a Deep Belief in the Future." *For* (Y.) (Jan. 28. 1968). Translated from the Yiddish.

Mark, Yudel,

"I tell myself (it does not help) that the Yiddish schools has done so much. It gave meaning to the lives of the poor working people, who supported the schools, it provided self-esteem for the immigrants of two generations; it was an important factor in the great historical process, the rise of the common man; that it brought elements of Jewishness into empty homes; it gave children at least a part of that precious treasure called Yiddish; it planted in the hearts of its pupils, the noblest passion, the passion of justice; it combined the Jewish experience of the children with happy experiences; it educated a considerable number of people who are active in every area of Jewish communal life in this country.

All this is true, but my heart aches because of the grinding poverty of our schools, which is almost shameful; because they remained afternoon schools with fewer and fewer hours of instruction and because there is not understanding of the importance of converting to Day schools; because there are no young reserves to replace the teachers; because they failed to educate the parents; because achievement in Yiddish is going down; because the process of fortifying the children with Jewishness is such a slow one."

Jew Ed 39 (Apr. 1969), 11.

SAFI,

"As Jews who identify themselves with the Jewish people we must imbue our children with a feeling of kinship with Jews throughout the world, with everything that it implies.

1. Active participation in Jewish life.

2. Readiness to help Jews in other lands and a deep interest in the future of Israel.

3. To preserve and perpetuate those elements of the Jewish tradition which are in harmony with Jewish life in America.

"Basic Principles of Education in the SAFI School." In *OFFY*, 138.

Dawidowicz, Lucy S.,

"In the Sholem Aleichem School I first encountered history. There we learned Jewish history, we learned a sense of history, and we learned the role that history played in shaping our national ethos and our national fate."

In Goodman, ed., *Our First Fifty Years* (E. and Y.) (N.Y.: SAFI, 1972), 119.

Katzman, Jacob,

"The keystone of the Labor Zionist cultural and educational enterprise was the Folkshul—the People's School [Jewish Folk Schools]. Alongside their devotion to Eretz Israel, was the singular devotion the Folkshul aroused in my parents and many of their chaverim. Into it they poured their love, their unstinting effort and their readiness for sacrifices in time and money."

In *Commitment: The Labor Zionist Life-style in America*. (Personal memoir, 1975), 115.

22 | HIGHER EDUCATION

(See also Higher Education and Teacher Training in Chapter 21)

TEACHER TRAINING PRIOR TO 1925

Berkowitz, Henry. "Correspondence School for Jewish Teachers." *CCAR* 21 (1911): 235–40.

Gamoran, Emanuel. *Teacher Training for Jewish Schools*. Cincinnati: DSSE, 1924. 89 pp.

Grossman, Louis. *The Aims of Teaching in Jewish Schools: A Handbook for Teachers*. Cincinnati: 1919.

———. *A Course of Work for Teachers in Jewish Schools*. Cincinnati: Teachers' Institute of the HUC, 1919. 61 pp.

———. "The Teachers' Institute of the Hebrew Union College." *CCAR* 24 (1914): 325–28.

Kordimon, Sh. „שעורי-קיץ למורים" (Summer Courses for Teachers). *Hadoar* 3 (1st of Av, 1924).

Waxman, Meyer. *Mizrachi Teachers' Institute: Statutes, General Statement and Program of Studies*. N.Y.: 1918.

TEACHER TRAINING 1925–1950

Abrams, N. B. Nir: *Annual Publication of the Teachers Institute of Rabbi Elchanan Theological Seminary*. N.Y.: 1925.

Blumenfeld, Samuel M. „המורה, הכשרתו ובעיותיו" (The Teacher, His Training and His Problems). *Sh Hah* (H.) 6 (Sept. 1946): 274–79. Also in *S Ed* (H.), 274–79.

Churgin, Pinchos. "The Teachers Institute in the Present and the Future." N.Y.: Teachers Institute of Yeshiva College, 1944.

Dinburg, Ben Zion. „הכשרת מורים לבתה"ס העבריים בגולה ודרכיה" (Training of Teachers for Jewish Schools in the Diaspora). In *JED* (H.), 56–63.

Dinin, Samuel. "Twenty-Five Years of Teacher Training." *Jew Ed* 7 (Jan.–Mar. 1935): 25–33. On the Teachers Institute of JTSA.

Essrig, Harry. "The Training of Educators for Reform Schools—A Proposal." *Jew Ed* 10 (Apr.–June 1938): 77–81.

Feinstein, Moses. „בית הספר הגבוה ובית מדרש למורים, הרצליה" (Herzliah—the High School and Teachers' College). *Sh Hah* (H.) 2 (1942): 138–49. See also *Sh Hah* 7 (Oct. 1947): 196–205. Also in pamphlet (H. and E.) (1942), 15 pp.

———. „הכשרת המורים בגולה" (Teacher Training in the Diaspora). In *JED* (H.), 37–46.

Franzblau, Abraham. *An Introduction to Jewish Religious Education: A Syllabus—Education I*. Cincinnati: HUC, 1937. 78 pp.

Gamoran, Emanuel. *Introductory Course in Education: A Syllabus*. Cincinnati: UAHC, 1926. 98 pp.

———. *Train Your Teachers.* Cincinnati: DSSE, UAHC, 1928. 11 pp.

Greenstone, Julius H. "גרץ קוליג׳" (Gratz College). *In JB* (H.), 276–79.

Halel's, Shlomo. "בית הספר הגבוה ובית המדרש למורים, הרצליה" (Herzliah—the High School and Teachers' College). In *JB* (H.), 262–67.

Hartstein, Jacob. "בית מדרש למורים של ישיבת רבנו יצחק אלחנן" (Teachers College of the Rabbi Elchanan Theological Seminary). In *JB* (H.), 259–62.

Hoenig, Simcha. "בית מדרש למורות בניו יורק" (Hebrew Teachers' College for Women). In *JB* (H.), 268–71.

Honor, Leo L. "Comparative Study of Hebrew Teacher Training Schools in the United States." *Jew Ed* 7 (June 1935): 71–90.

Honor, Leo L., and Azriel Eisenberg. "Educating Personnel for the Profession of Jewish Education." *Jew Ed* 19 (Fall 1947): 19–22. Committee report.

Horowitz, A. L. "בתי-מדרש למורים בארצות הברית" (Teacher Colleges in the U.S.). *Sh Hah* (H.) 10 (Sept. 1950): 179–223.

Kaplan, Mordecai M. "The Teachers Institute and Its Affiliated Departments." In *The Jewish Theological Seminary*, edited by C. Adler, 121–43. 1939.

Kimmel, Meyer. "תולדות ישיבת ר׳ חיים ברלין" (The History of Yeshiva Rabbi Chaim Berlin). *Sh Hah* (H.) 9 (Jan. 1949): 51–54.

Levenson, Jacob. "On The Twenty-Fifth Anniversary of the Teachers Institute." N.Y.: Teachers Institute of Yeshiva College, 1944.

Maller, Julius. *Educational Psychology: A Syllabus.* Cincinnati: DSSE, UAHC, 1928. 112 pp.

Margoshes, Samuel. "The Herzliah." *Day* (Mar. 19, 1944).

NIR: An Annual of the Student Organization of the Isaac Elchanan Yeshiva. Twentieth anniversary jubilee issue. Essays on the history and organization of the college. N.Y.: 1938. 138 pp.

Pollak, Jacob B. *Classroom Organization and Management: A Syllabus for Jewish Teachers.* Cincinnati: DSSE, UAHC, 1927?. 99 pp.

Pollock, Shimon. "הכשרת מורים" (Training of Teachers). In *JED* (H.), 47–52.

Rabbinical Assembly, The. "The Training of Teaching and Leadership Personnel—A Report." (1941–44): 348–60.

Shulman, Moses L. "The Yeshiva Etz Hayim Hebrew Institute of Boro Park [N.Y.]." *Jew Ed* 20 (Fall 1948): 47–48.

Waxman, Meyer. "Some Recollections on the First Period of the Teachers Institute." N.Y.: Teachers Institute of Yeshiva College, 1944.

Yihiel, B. "בית המדרש למורים, מיסודו של בית המדרש לרבנים בניו יורק וסניפיו" (History of the Teachers of the Rabbinical College in New York and Its Branches). In *JB* (H.), 249–58.

TEACHER TRAINING SINCE 1950

Ackerman, Walter I. "A Profile of the Hebrew Teachers College." In *Jan 3*, 41–69.

Alter, Robert. "Teaching Jewish Teachers." *Commentary* 46 (July 1968): 60–65.

Benathan, Morris B. "Teacher Education—Realities and Needs." *Jew Ed* 31 (Spring 1961): 2–12, 45.

Blumenfield, Samuel M. "The Education of the Jewish Teacher: Some Reflections." *Jew Ed* 40 (Spring 1970): 46–49.

———. "לבעיות הכשרתו של המורה היהודי באמריקה" (On the Problems of Training the Jewish Teacher in America). *Hadoar* (H.) 50 (Oct. 22, 1971).

Cagan, Jack. "The Institutional Training of Teachers for Religious Schools of Reform Congregations." Master's thesis, HUC–JIR, 1959.

Chomsky, William. "A Review of *The Education of American Jewish Teachers.*" *JSS* 31 (Jan. 1969): 41–48.

Cutter, William. "Rationale for Graduate Professional Training in Jewish Education at Hebrew Union College in California." *Jew Ed* 43 (Fall 1974): 7–10, 20.

———. "Thoughts on Jewish Professional Training." *J Jew Com Ser* 52 (Summer 1976): 331–37.

22 HIGHER EDUCATION

Dinin, Samuel. "The Curricula of the Hebrew Teachers College." In *Jan 3*, 61–81.

———. "A Program of Teacher Education to Meet the Needs of Jewish Education Today." *Jew Ed* 27 (Spring 1957): 23–28.

Dushkin, Alexander M. *Analysis of Opinions and Proposals Regarding Supply and Training of Jewish Teachers in the Diaspora*. Research survey submitted to World Council on Jewish Education. Geneva, Switzerland: 1964.

———. *Comparative Study of Jewish Teacher Training Schools in the Diaspora*. Jerusalem: Institute of Contemporary Jewry, Hebrew University, 1970. 150 pp.

———. "Israel and the Training of Jewish Teachers for the Diaspora." In *Jan 3*, 208–25.

———. (Jewish Education in the Diaspora—The Problems of Teachers and Teaching) (H.). Jerusalem: Institute of Contemporary Jewry, Hebrew U., 1968. 94 pp.

———. "The Supply and Training of Jewish Educational Personnel." *Ed As* (1966): 13–25.

———. "Supply and Training of Teachers for the Jewish Schools in the Diaspora." *Jew Ed* 35 (Fall 1964): 22–36.

Ehrlich, Irvin Sigo. "Toward a Teacher Training Program through Audio-Visual Techniques for a Reform Religious School." Master's thesis, HUC–JIR, 1970.

Ettenberg, Sylvia C. "The Changing Image of the Combined Program." (Jewish and general education for Jewish teachers.) In *Jan 3*, 123–28.

Fox, Seymour. "Planning For Teacher Education: An Interim Report." In *Jan 3*, 297–302.

Goelman, Elazar. "Training of Jewish Teachers for Supplementary Educational Functions." In *Jan 3*, 198–204.

Goldberg, Henry R. "Program of Jewish Teacher Education." *Jew Ed* 25 (Fall 1951): 21–31, 79.

Goldin, I. E. "Some Attitudes of Jews toward Higher Education." Master's thesis, U. of Chicago, 1950.

Goldin, Judah. "Japhet in Shem's Tent." On a combined program of Jewish and General Education for Jewish Teachers. In *Jan 3*, 111–21.

Greenberg, Simon. "The Role of Higher Learning: An Evaluation of the Jewish Teachers Seminary." In *Foundations of a Faith*. N.Y.: Burning Bush Press, ca. 1967. 340 pp.

Grinstein, Hyman B. "The History of the Teachers Institute at Yeshiva University" (H.). In *Samuel Belkin Memorial Volume*. N.Y.

———. "The Orthodox, Conservative, and Nationalistic Teacher-Training Schools." In *Jan 3*, 303–9.

Honor, Leo L. "Educating Teaching Personnel for Jewish Schools, 1897–1918." *Huc Annual* 23 (1950–51): 617–47.

Hurwich, Louis. "Hebrew Teachers' Colleges in the United States." *Jew Ed* 22 (Winter–Spring 1951): 73–96.

———. "Origin and Development of Jewish Teacher-Training Schools in the United States: A Brief Historical Survey." In *Jan 3*, 3–10.

———. *A Survey of Hebrew Teachers Training Schools*. N. Y: AAJE, 1950.

Janowsky, Oscar I., ed. "The Education of American Jewish Teachers." In *The Education of American Jewish Teachers*, 317–46. Boston: Beacon, 1967.

Jew Ed. "New Models in Preparing Personnel for Jewish Education." Responses by Alan D. Bennett, Sheldon Chwat, and Irving Skolnick. 43 (Fall 1974): 27–32.

Jick, Leon A. "Can Minimal Jewish Education Be Made Viable?" In *Jan 3*, 311–15.

Kaunfer, Neil. "Retraining Jewish Teachers." *Response* 30/31 (Summer/Fall 1976): 193–99.

Levine, Etan B. "Educating Jewish Educators." *Jew Spec* 33 (Dec. 1968): 17–20.

Levow, Mordecai. "An Inquiry-Skills Teacher Education Program—Report on an NCRI Project." *Ped Rep* 23 (Dec. 1971): 3–6.

Lukinsky, Joseph. "The Education Program at the Jewish Theological Seminary—Basic Distinctive Assumptions." *Jew Ed* 43 (Fall 1974): 11–13, 39.

Margolis, Isidor. "Hebrew Teacher Training Schools in the United States in the First Half of the Twentieth Century." *Jew Ed* 31 (Spring 1961): 13–21, 53.

* ———. *A History of Teacher-Training for Teachers in Jewish Schools in the United*

States in the First Half of the Twentieth Century. New York U., 1960. Published as *Jewish Teacher Training Schools in the United States*. N.Y.: National Council for Torah Education of Mizrachi-Hapoel, Hamizrachi, 1964. 349 pp.

National Board of License. *Criteria for the Evaluation of Hebrew Teachers Colleges*. N.Y.: AAJE, 1955.

National Committee of Teacher Education and Welfare. *Current Needs in Hebrew Teacher Education*. N. Y: AAJE, 1958. 14 pp.

Rabinowitz, J. "The Yeshiva University Teacher Training Program." *Ped Rep* 33 (Oct. 1982): 2–4.

Rauch, Eduardo, and Barry W. Holtz. "Jewish Teacher Education: New Answers to Tough Old Problems." *MJ* 18 (Summer 1984): 4–5, 21. See also *J Jew Com Ser* 61 (Fall 1984).

Resnick, Martha. "Jewish History through Primary Texts: An Approach to Teaching Golden Age of Spain to High School Teachers." Master's thesis, Department of Jewish Education, JTS, 1989.

Rosenmond, A. „בית המדרש למורות—ישיבה אוניברסיטה" (College for Women Teachers—Yeshiva U.). *Sh Hah* (H.) 21 (Winter 1961): 90–95.

* Rosenthal, Lester H. *Professional Laboratory Experiences for Secondary School Teachers in a Fifth Year Internship Program: An Exploratory Study of the Teaching Fellowship Program at Yeshiva University with Recommendations*. Columbia U., 1964. 364 pp.

Saltzman, Elly. "Teacher Training." *Jew Teach* 23 (Jan. 1955): 11–12.

* Schachter, Lifsa. *An Overview of the Literature on General and Jewish Teacher Education in the United States*. JTSA, 1983.

———. "The Practicum: Teacher Education as Initiation." *Ped Rep* 33 (Oct. 1982): 16–17.

Schiff, Alvin I. "New Concepts in Teacher Education." *Jew Ed* 38 (Jan. 1968): 10–18.

———. "Overview of Programs for the Preparation of Jewish Educational Personnel." *Jew Ed* 43 (Fall 1974): 5–6, 32.

———. "The Students of the Hebrew Teachers Colleges: Profile and Career Choice." In *Jan 3*, 83–110.

Schoolman, Albert P. "Lay Leadership and Finances of Hebrew Teachers Colleges." In *Jan 3*, 129–52.

Schwartzman, Sylvan D. "Planning for Teacher Growth." *Jew Teach* 34 (Apr. 1966): 16–17.

———. *Syllabus: Religious School Teaching*. Rev. ed. Cincinnati: HUC, 1956. 190 pp.

Scult, Mel. "Mordecai Kaplan, the Teachers Institute, and the Foundation of Jewish Education in America." *Amer Jew Arc* 38 (Apr. 1986): 57–84.

Segal, Abraham. "The Education of Non-Hebrew Teachers." In *Jan 3*, 155–65.

Silberschlag, Eisig. "Accreditation of Hebrew Teachers' Colleges." In *Jan 3*, 27–40.

———. „חינוך על-יסודי בתפוצות" (Higher Education in the Diaspora). In *MJET* (H.), 69–74.

Wachs, Saul P. "The Philip W. Lown Graduate Center for Contemporary Jewish Studies." *Jew Ed* 43 (Fall 1974): 14–20.

Winter, Nathan. "Recruitment and Training of Personnel for Jewish Education Agencies." *Jew Ed* 43 (Winter–Spring 1975): 26–32.

JEWISH INSTITUTIONS OF HIGHER LEARNING PRIOR TO 1950 (INCLUDING JUDAIC STUDIES IN GENERAL COLLEGES AND UNIVERSITIES)

Adler, Cyrus, ed. *The Jewish Theological Seminary of America, Semi-Centennial Volume*. N.Y.: JTSA, 1939. 194 pp.

American Jewish Yearbook. "American Colleges in Which Hebrew Is Taught." In *AJYB* 19 (1917–18): 406.

Benderly, Samson. "The Hebrew Union College—Fifty Years and After." *Jew Ed News* (Nov. 1925).

Berger, Isaiah. „ליובלה של ישיבת ר' יצחק אלחנן" (On the Jubilee of Rabbi Isaac Elchanan Yeshiva) (1896). *Hadoar* (H.) 16 (16th of Tammuz, 1937).

22 HIGHER EDUCATION

Blumenfield, Samuel M. *Higher Jewish Education and the Emerging Pattern of American Jewry*. N.Y.: Jewish Institute of Religion, 1941. 11 pp.

Davis, Moshe. „ראשית החנוך העברי הגבוה באמריקה" (Beginnings of Jewish Higher Education in America). In *Yesod* (H.), 197–210.

Dinin, Samuel. "Higher Jewish Education." *Jew Ed* 10 (Jan.–Mar. 1938): 11–19.

Feinberg, Charles K. "Jewish Studies in American Universities." *Menorah J* 2 (Dec. 1916): 319–21.

* Fierstein, Robert. *From Foundation to Reorganization: The Jewish Theological Seminary of America, 1886–1902*. JTSA, 1986.

Finkelstein, Louis. "The Seminary as a Center of Jewish Learning." In *The Jewish Theological Seminary of America, Semi-Centennial Volume*, edited by Cyrus Adler, 163–77. N.Y.: JTSA, 1939.

Grayzel, Solomon. "Gratz College, Fifty Years of Educational Service." *Jewish Exponent* (Dec. 7, 1945).

———. "Jewish Expectations in Higher Education." *Jew Ed* 10 (Jan.–Mar. 1938): 20–24.

Hall, G. Stanley. "A Suggestion for a Jewish University." *Menorah J* 3 (Apr. 1917): 98–101.

Hartstein, Jacob J. "Yeshiva Education in America." In *Israel of Tomorrow*, edited by Jung, 446–77. 1946.

———. "The Yeshiva Looks Back over Fifty Years." *Jew Ed* 9 (Apr.–June 1937): 53–57.

———. "Yeshiva University." *AJYB* 48 (1946–47): 73–84.

Hurwitz, Henry. "The Idea of a Menorah College for Jewish Cultural and Social Science." *Menorah J* 34 (1946): 1–28.

Karpf, Maurice J. "A Proposal for the Establishment of an Educational Fund for Maintaining Jewish Institutions of Higher Jewish Learning in the United States." *Jew Ed* 10 (Apr.–June 1938): 65–69, 76.

Katsh, Abraham I. "Jewish Student Activities in American Universities, with Special Reference to New York University Jewish Culture Foundation." *Jew Ed* 18 (Feb./Mar. 1947): 30–34.

———. *Hebrew in American Higher Education*. N.Y.: 1941. 182 pp.

———. „מקומה של השפה עברית במכללות של ארצות הברית בעבר ובהווה" (The Place of the Hebrew Language in American Colleges in the Past and Present). In *JB* (H.), 89–98.

———. "The Status of Hebrew in American Colleges and Universities." *Jew Ed* 13 (Sept. 1941): 108–9, 142.

———. "The Study of Hebrew Culture in American Universities." *Jew Ed* 18 (Nov. 1946): 32–42.

Kiev, I. Edward, and John J. Tepfer. "Jewish Institute of Religion." *AJYB* 49 (1947–48): 91–100.

* King, Diana A. *A History of Gratz College, 1893–1928*. Dropsie U., 1979.

Kohler, Kaufmann. "The Hebrew Union College of Yesterday and a Great Desideratum in Its Curriculum Today." In *Hebrew Union College Jubilee Volume, 1875–1925*, 71–78. Cincinnati: 1925.

Lookstein, Joseph H. "The Modern American Yeshiva." *Jew Ed* 16 (May 1946): 12–16.

Malachi, Eliezer R. „יובל בית המדרש" (Jubilee of the Jewish Theological Seminary). *Hadoar* (H.) 16 (10th of Shevat, 1937).

Marshall, Louis. "The Jewish Theological Seminary." In *Louis Marshall: Selected Papers and Addresses*, edited by C. Reznikoff, 859–94. 1937.

Mendes, Henry P. "The Beginning of the Seminary." In *The Jewish Theological Seminary of America, Semi-Centennial Volume*, edited by Cyrus Adler, 35–45. N.Y.: JTSA, 1939.

Newman, Louis I. *A Jewish University in America?* ("With a symposium of opinions.") N.Y.: Bloch, 1923. 94 pp.

Philipson, David, ed. "The History of the Hebrew Union College." In *Hebrew Union College Jubilee Volume, 1875–1925*, 1–70. Cincinnati: 1925.

Reeder, Joseph. „בית מדרש לחכמת ישראל" (Judaica—Higher Education). *Hadoar* (H.) 13 (19th of Shevat, 1934).

Revel, Bernard. "The Message and Meaning of Yeshiva." In *Historical Souvenir Journal*. N.Y.: Yeshiva College Building Fund, 1926.

Rosenau, William. "Semitic Studies in American Colleges." *CCAR* (1896): 99–113.

Rosenblatt, Samuel. "American Jewish Scholarship and the Jewish Theological Seminary." *RA* (1938): 372–87.

Rubenstein, Frank J. *The Early Years, 1908–1919: Dropsie College for Hebrew and Cognate Learning.* Phila.: Dropsie U., 1977. 48 pp.

Sachar, Abraham L. *A Host at Last.* (History of Brandeis U.) Boston: Little Brown and Co., 1976. 308 pp.

JEWISH INSTITUTIONS OF HIGHER LEARNING SINCE 1950

AJHQ "Contemporary Jewish Civilization on the American Campus: Research and Teaching." 63 (June 1974):
  Elazar, Daniel J. "The Place of Jewish Political Studies on the Campus," 334–39.
  Faur, Jose. "Introducing the Materials of Sephardic Culture to Contemporary Jewish Studies," 240–49.
  Fox, Marvin. "Philosophy and Contemporary Jewish Studies," 350–55.
  Neusner, Jacob. "Departments of Religious Studies and Contemporary Jewish Studies," 356–60.
  Sklare, Marshall. "Problems in the Teaching of Contemporary Jewish Studies," 361–68.
    Discussants: Joshua A. Fishman (369–73), George L. Moore (373–75), Laurence J. Silberstein (375–78), and Moshe Davis (379–81).

Askowith, Dora. "The Role of Women in the Field of Higher Jewish Education." *Jud* 5 (1956): 169–72.

Band, Arnold J. "Jewish Literature in the University." *Jud* 11 (1962): 319–33. Also in *MJET*, 64–78.

———. "Jewish Studies in American Liberal-Arts Colleges and Universities." *AJYB* 67 (1966): 3–30. Also in *Jan 3*, 255–64.

Ben-Horin, Meir. "Some Implications for Jewish Educational Institutions of Jewish Studies in American Institutions." In *Jan 3*, 265–78.

Bernstein, S. "Touro College." *Jew Life* 38 (May/June 1971): 8–9.

Bomzer, Herbert W. *The Kollel in America.* (Schools for advanced Talmudic study.) N.Y.: Shengold, 1985. 182 pp.

Brickman, William W. "Judaism—Higher Education." (Historical review and analysis.) In *The International Encyclopedia of Higher Education*, edited by Asa S. Knowles, 8:3537–39. San Francisco: Jossey/Bass, 1977.

Brickner, Barnett R. "The Hebrew Union College at 75." *Jew Ed* 21 (Summer 1950): 7–8.

Chanover, Hyman. "Horizons for the Communal Hebrew Colleges." *Jew Ed* (Fall 1973): 5–10.

Cohen, Jack J. "Higher Jewish Education." In *JEDS*, 263–78.

Cohen, Samuel S. "The History of the Hebrew Union College." *PAJHS* 40 (Sept. 1950): 17–55.

Con Jud "A Symposium on Jewish Studies in the University." 27 (Winter 1972): 3–34.

David, L. "Jewish Higher Education: Its Value Today." *Jew Life* 29 (Dec. 1961).

Davis, Moshe. *Jewish Studies in Universities: Alternate Approaches in Different Parts of the World.* Jerusalem: Institute of Contemporary Jewry, Hebrew U., 1974. 19 pp.

* Dekel, Aviva L. *The Idea of a Jewish University.* Vanderbilt U., 1984.

Feldman, Emanuel. "Trends in American Yeshivot." *Trad* 9 (Spring 1968): 56–64.

* Fine, Irene. *Developing a Jewish Studies Program for Women: A Springboard to History.* Union for Experimenting Colleges and Universities, 1980.

Finkelstein, Louis. "The Seminary and the Future of Jewish Scholarship." *RA* (1951): 220–24.

* Fish, Sidney M. *History of Gratz College* (H.). Phila.: Dropsie U.

Goelman, Elazar. "New Directions for Hebrew Colleges in the United States." *Intrater*, 35–38.

Goldberg, Hillel. "From Berkeley to Jerusalem." *Mid* 28 (June/July 1982): 41–43.

Greenberg, Irving. "Jewish Survival and the College Campus." *Jud* 17 (Summer 1968): 259–81.

Hartman, Geoffrey. "Judaic Studies as the Third Pillar." *Cong M* (May/June 1987): 7–9.

Helmreich, William B. "Old Wine in New Bottles: Advanced Yeshivot in the United States." *AJH* 69 (Dec. 1979): 234–56.

———. *The World of the Yeshiva*. N.Y.: Free Press, 1982. 412 pp.

Hoffmann, Justin. "The Case for Jewish Studies on the Campus." *Jew Ed* 46 (Summer 1978): 27–35.

Hollender, C. T. "The Telsher Yeshiva." *Jew Parent* 18 (Mar. 1957): 12–13, 25.

* Honan, Bernard W. *A Model for Examination of the Feasibility of Developing a Consortium of Judaic Studies in the Southeastern United States*. U. of Alabama, 1976. 240 pp.

* Huttler, Rubin. *An Exploratory Study of Development of Judaic Studies in American Higher Education with Special Emphasis on Three Contemporary Programs*. U. of Southern California, 1979.

Jick, Leon A., ed. *The Teaching of Judaica in American Universities: The Proceedings of a Colloquium*. N.Y.: Association for Jewish Studies-Ktav, 1970 (all page numbers refer to first page of article):

    Band, Arnold J. "Modern Hebrew Literature," 73.
    Blau, Joseph. "A Proposal for a Professional Association," 89.
    Branscomb, Harvie. "A Note on Establishing Chairs of Jewish Studies," 95.
    Cohen, Gerson D. "An Embarrassment of Riches: Reflections on the Condition of American Jewish Scholarship," 135.
    Greenberg, Irving. "Scholarship and Continuity: Dilemma and Dialectic," 115.
    Hallo, William. "Biblical Studies in Jewish Perspectives," 43.
    Jick, Leon A. "Introduction," 3, and "Tasks for a Community of Concern," 83.
    Levine, Baruch A. "On the Teaching of Talmud in the American University," 49.
    Neusner, Jacob. "Graduate Education in Judaica: Problems and Prospects," 19.
    Sandmel, Samuel. "Scholar or Apologist?," 105.
    Sarna, Nahum. "The Bible and Jewish Studies," 35.
    Silberman, Lou H. "The University and Jewish Studies," 9.
    Sklare, Marshall. "The Problem of Contemporary Jewish Studies," 57.

Jospe, Alfred, ed. *Judaism on the Campus: Essays on Jewish Education in the University Community*. Washington, D.C.: B'nai B'rith Hillel Foundation, 1964.

Kaminetsky, Joseph. "Our Higher Yeshivos." *Jew Parent* 23 (Jan. 1972).

Kaplan, Louis L. "Judaic Studies on Campus: New Horizons." *Jewish Heritage* 12 (Fall 1969): 39–44.

Kaplan, Mordecai M. "Towards a University of Judaism." *Recon* (Oct. 7, 1955): 27–29.

Katsh, Abraham I. "Growth of Modern Hebrew in American Colleges and Universities." *Jew Ed* 21 (Summer 1952): 11–15.

———. "Hebraic Studies in American Higher Education: An Evaluation of Current Trends." *JSS* 21 (1959): 15–21.

———. "Hebrew in American Higher Education." *Congress Weekly* 22 (Mar. 22, 1954): 13–15.

———. *Hebrew Language, Literature and Culture in American Colleges and Universities*. N.Y.: Payne Educational Foundation, 1950.

Katz, I. E. "Some Attitudes of Jews toward Higher Education." Master's thesis, U. of Chicago, 1950.

* Klaperman, Gilbert. *The Beginning of Yeshiva University: The First Jewish University in America*. Yeshiva U., 1955. 240 pp.

———. *The Story of Yeshiva University*. N.Y.: Macmillan, 1969.

———. "Yeshiva University: Seventy Years in Retrospect." *PAJHS* 54 (Sept. 1964): 5–50; (Dec. 1964) 198–201.

Kresel, G. "עם שנת המאה להיברו יוניון קולג׳„ (The Hebrew Union College—100 Years). *Hadoar* (H.) 54 (Mar. 9, 1975).

Lapson, Judah. *Hebrew in Colleges and Universities: A Guide to Courses Offered in the United States*. N.Y.: Hebrew Culture Council, 1958.

Levin, Leo. "Can A College Education Supplement the Yeshiva Program?" *Jew Parent* (Oct. 1959).

* Lewitter, Sidney R. *A School for Scholars: The Beth Medrash Govoha, the Rabbi Aaron Kottler Jewish Institute of Higher Learning in Lakewood, N.J. A Study of the Development and Theory of One Aspect of Jewish Education in America.* Rutgers U., 1981.

Lipset, Seymour, and E. C. Ladd, Jr. "Jewish Academics in the United States: Their Achievements, Culture, and Politics." *AJYB* 72 (1971): 89–128.

* Loren, Morris J. *Hebrew Higher Educational Institutions in the United States.* Wayne State U., 1976. 199 pp.

Mansoor, Menahem. "Jewish Studies in the University." *Jew Spec* (Summer 1974).

Meyer, Michael M. "A Centennial History, Part One." In *At One Hundred Years* (HUC–JIR), 32–47. HUC–JIR, 1976.

Moore, Deborah Dash. "Yeshiva College: Orthodox Hedge." In *A Home in America*, 177–99. 1981.

Neuman, Abraham. "The Dropsie College for Hebrew and Cognate Learning: Basic Principles and Objectives." In *The Seventy-Fifth Anniversary Volume of the* Jewish Quarterly Review, 18–46. Phila.: 1967.

Neusner, Jacob. "Jewish Studies in American Universities." *Congress Weekly* (Oct. 1962): 7–9.

———. "Modes of Jewish Studies in the University." In *The Academic Study of Judaism: Essays and Reflections.* 2 vols. N.Y.: Ktav, 1975, 1977.

———. "The Promise of Jewish Studies in the University." In *MJET*, 60–63.

———. "The Selling of Jewish Studies." *Moment* 3 (Mar. 1978): 61–62.

Panzer, Mitchell E. "Gratz College—A Community's Involvement in Jewish Education." In *Gratz College Anniversary Volume, 1895–1970*, edited by I. D. Passow and S. T. Lachs, 1–19. Phila.: Gratz College.

Penn, Ascher. „העברעאיש אין אמעריקאנער קאלעדזעס" (Hebrew in American Colleges) (Y.). In *Penn*, 529–38.

Perr, Yechiel. "The Yeshiva World and Orthodoxy: Self Protection . . . or Encounter." *Jew Obs* (1970): 22–23.

Rackman, Emanuel. "From Synagogue toward Yeshiva: Institutionalized Cult or Congregations of the Learned?" *Commentary* 21 (Apr. 1956): 352–56. Also in *JJS*, 219–36.

———. "Yeshiva University—the Challenge of Higher Jewish Education." *Gesher* (E.) 2 (1964).

Rudavsky, David. „הוראת המקצועות העבריים באוניברסיטאות ובקולג׳יס האמריקאיים" (Hebraic Studies in American Colleges and Universities). *Hadoar* (H.) 50 (Sept. 17, 1971).

———. "The National Association of Professors of Hebrew." *Jew Ed* 23 (Winter 1952): 5.

———. "A Note on the Teaching of Hebrew in American Colleges and Universities." *Jew J Soc* 14 (June 1972): 85–92.

———. „מעמד העברית ולמודי היהדות במכללות ובאוניברסיטאות באמריקה" (The Status of Hebrew and Jewish Studies in American Colleges and Universities). *Sh Hah* (H.) 34 (1974): 169–75. See also *Bitzaron* (H.) (Elul 1972): 349–55.

Schaffler, Lawrence D. "Preliminary Report on Federation Involvement with Jewish Studies in Colleges and Universities." CP, July 1973. 3 pp.

Sherwin, Byron L. "Teaching Judaism at College and University." *RA* (1975): 213–19.

Silver, Daniel Jeremy. "The American University and Jewish Learning." *Jud* 25 (1976): 281–89.

———. "Higher Jewish Learning." In *Movements and Issues in American Judaism Since 1945*, edited by Bernard Martin. Westport, Conn.: Greenwood, 1978. 207–16.

Silverberg, David. "Jewish Studies on the American Campus." *Present Tense* 5 (Summer 1978): 52–56.

Singer, David. "A Profile of the Jewish Academic: Some Recent Studies." *Mid* 19 (June/July 1973): 57–64.

Sofer, B. "Restoring the Missing Rung." *Israel Scene* 4 (Aug. 1983): 9–11.

Syme, Daniel B. "The College Connection." *Compass* 2 (Fall–Winter 1978): 10.

22
HIGHER EDUCATION

Wechsler, H. S., and P. Ritterband. "Jewish Learning in American Universities: The Literature of a Field." *Modern Judaism* 3 (Oct. 1983): 253–89.

Zeidman, Hillel. „ישיבה אוניברסיטה ופעלה ביהודית אמריקה" (Yeshiva University and Its Activities in American Jewish Life." *Hadoar* (H.) 50 (Apr. 23, 1971).

GLEANINGS

Leeser, Isaac, on the proposed Maimonides College (1867),
"Some may object to the movement, that is not pledged to either reform or orthodoxy. These hateful words are always at hand when anything is to be done from the election of a secretary to a society, to printing a book or establishing a college. The illiberal always ask: To what party does he or it belong? For our part, strange as it may sound, we belong to no party. We commenced life with certain convictions and have not swerved from them. We know only Judaism: and if you call it 'orthodox,' you do so—not we."
Quoted in *The Jewish Theological Seminary of America, Semi-Centennial Volume*, edited by Cyrus Adler (N.Y: JTSA, 1939), 4.

Charter of the Rabbi Isaac Elchanan Theological Seminary (later Yeshiva University) (1897)
"The particular objects for which the corporation is to be formed are to promote the study of the Talmud and to assist in educating and preparing students of the Hebrew faith for the Hebrew Orthodox Ministry."
AJHQ 54 (Sept. 1964), 49.

American Hebrew Congregations decide to establish a college,
"The Congregations do unite themselves into a Hebrew Congregational Union with the object to preserve and advance the union of Israel; to take proper care of the promulgation of Judaism; to establish and support a scholastic institute and library appertaining thereto, for the education of rabbis, preachers and teachers of religion."
Hebrew Union College Jubilee Volume 1875–1925 (Cincinnati: 1925), 9–10.

Charter of the Jewish Theological Seminary (1886),
"The purpose of this Association being the preservation in America of the knowledge and practice of historical Judaism . . . proposes . . . the following specific objects:
1. The establishment and maintenance of a Jewish Theological Seminary for the training of Rabbis and teachers.
2. The attainments of such cognate purposes as may upon occasion be deemed to be appropriate."
The Jewish Theological Seminary of America, Semi-Centennial Volume, edited by Cyrus Adler (N.Y: JTSA, 1939), 6–7.

Revel, Bernard, Yeshiva University (1925),
"The Yeshiva proposes to establish a College of Liberal Arts and Sciences . . . with the double purpose of educating both liberally and Jewishly a number of young men who have been already imbued with the spirit and the sanctity of Judaism and its teachings so that these men may not be lost to us."
Quoted by Gilbert Klaperman, *AJHQ* 54 (Sept 1964), 40.

Leiser, Jacob,
The Rabbi Isaac Elchanan Theological Seminary [later Yeshiva University], organized in 1896, . . . is a Russian Yeshiva transplanted to the East Side of New York. It is an ultra orthodox, and wholly out of sympathy with American democracy, as one might infer, from the provisions of its foundation, namely: legalized Judaism. Naturally its faculty regards Reform Judaism as the next to apostasy, since American Judaism abrogated rabbinism. The antediluvian seminary has been liberally endowed, but has no future here." *A Jud* (1925), 163.

Placard Distributed in Orthodox Synagogues, 1932,
"We Jews of New York discovered that in the Yeshiva Rabbi Isaac Elchanan . . . there is a nest of atheism and Apikursus

[denial of God]. Therefore we do warn and announce, that you should not send your children or the children of your acquaintances into the Yeshiva until you will find out what is going on in the Yeshiva, who is responsible for the terrible situation, and how it is to be remedied."

Quoted by William B. Helmreich in *The World of the Yeshiva* (N.Y: Free Press, 1982), 22–23.

Kotler, Reb. Aharon, on the Beth Medrash Govoha in Lakewood, N.J. (ca. 1943),

"I don't want you to misunderstand me; I don't want to mislead you. There is a need for rosh yeshivas [heads of Yeshivot] in this country and elsewhere and Lakewood will produce them. There is a need for effective teachers and for the right kind of rabbis and Lakewood will produce these too. There is a need for baalei-batim-talmidei chachomim [lay scholars] and Lakewood will send them forth. However, the raison d'etre of Lakewood is 'limud ha Torah lishmo,' to learn Torah for its own value. It is with this understanding, and for this purpose, that I am asking for your support."

Quoted by William B. Helmreich in *The World of the Yeshiva* (N.Y: Free Press, 1982), 43.

Band, Arnold, defining Judaic studies,

"We would . . . consider Judaic studies as the discipline which deals with the historical experiences, in the intellectual, religious, and social spheres of the Jewish people in all centuries and countries."

AJYB 66 (1967), 5.

Cohen, Gerson D.,

"In the community at large, in recent years, there has been evident an increasing interest in placing and supporting Jewish studies on the university campus, not so much as vehicles of knowledge and research for their own sake, as of stimuli and aids to Jewish identity and pride on the campus. I do not believe that there can be any objection to these motives, provided they remain confined to board rooms and do not in any way interfere with scholarly detachment essential to our work; which is to say, provided they do not in any way pressure the faculty man to serve as a quasi-chaplain or advocate of any form of affiliation or for that matter of disaffiliation. From our point of view, the mere presence of Jewish studies on the campus, provided they are a fair representation of the totality of Jewish life and are treated as an academic discipline, are by their presence an affirmation of the corporate identity of the Jews."

In Leon A. Jick, ed., *The Teaching of Judaica in American Universities: The Proceedings of a Colloquium* (N.Y.: Association for Jewish Studies-Ktav, 1970), 147–48.

Silver, Daniel Jeremy,

"The field of Jewish Studies has made, and continues to make, significant contributions to the critical understanding of the Jewish experience, but it is not Jewish learning in the traditional, value-laden talmud torah sense. Jewish Studies refines a perception of Torah which binds the dimension of time and the study of mankind into the received tradition. Its results present a stimulating challenge to the faith and faithful. It is the responsibility of the seminary to blend the new insights with the old. Whether such a Torah can inspire and bind men to it remains an open question, one which, in the final analysis, the field of Jewish Studies is not compelled to answer."

In Bernard Martin, ed., *Movements and Issues in American Judaism Since 1945* Westport, Conn.: Greenwood, 1978, 216.

Lamm, Norman, on Yeshiva University (1981),

"We are committed to secular studies, including all the risks that this implies, not only because of vocational or social reasons, but because we consider it is the will of God that there would be a world in which Torah would be effective; that all wisdom issues ultimately from the Creator and therefore it is the Almighty who legitimizes all knowledge."

Quoted by Gurock, *Amer Jew Arc* 35 (Nov. 1983), 159.

Rauch, Eduardo, and Barry W. Holtz,

"Jewish teachers need to be offered new forms of in-service education which, beyond enrichment experiences in pedagogy and Jewish texts, will permit them to become more spiritually aware and more religiously sensitive. Only then will teachers be able to transcend the general poverty of their present roles in Jewish life, and become in some ways leaders toward change in the Jewish community as a whole. We live during a time in which hunger for wonders and a strong attraction toward a spiritual path among the present generation of young adults offer strong opportunities for innovative forms of teacher education. Presently university education focuses almost exclusively on the rationally intellectual. By expanding education in the spiritual, artistic and religious realms, a Jewish teacher retreat as proposed below by the Melton Research Center could expand the learning and growth experiences of teachers well beyond their present opportunities."

MJ 18 (Summer 1984), 4.

THE PROFESSION

PART II | THE PROFESSION

CONTENTS

23 | ADMINISTRATION 245

    School Organization, Supervision, and Practices 245
    Pedagogic Issues 247
    The Principal 247
    In-Service Training 250
    The Profession of Jewish Education 251
    Professional Organizations 252
    Educational Journals (Selected) 253
    The Teacher Shortage 253
    Teacher Aides 254
    Standards and Codes for the Profession 255
    Evaluation 256
    Enrollment prior to 1950 257
    Enrollment since 1950 258
    Retention and Dropouts in Jewish Education 258
    Small Schools 259
    Gleanings 259

24 | THE TEACHER 263

    Prior to 1950 263
    Since 1950 263
    The Profession prior to 1950 264
    The Profession since 1950 265
    Israelis Teaching in American Jewish Schools 266
    Gleanings 267

25 | THE RABBI AND JEWISH EDUCATION 270

    General (Selected) 270
    Role in Jewish Education 271
    Gleanings 272

26 | CONFERENCES IN JEWISH EDUCATION, 1890–1988 274

27 | MEN AND WOMEN WHO INFLUENCED JEWISH EDUCATION 287

23 ADMINISTRATION

SCHOOL ORGANIZATION, SUPERVISION, AND PRACTICES

(See also Chapters 20, 21)

AAJE. *Women in Jewish Schools: Better Personnel Practices.* N.Y.: 1979.

Adelman, Philip J., and Hannah B. Adelman. "Time Management." In *JPH*, 91–100.

Bayar, Steven. "Religious School Mergers: A Congregational Rabbi's Perspective." *Jew Ed* 55 (Winter 1988): 20–24.

Bennet, Alan D. "Supervising the Classroom." *NATE News* (June 1959).

Bloom, David I. "Toward a Solution of Our Problems." *Ed As* (1970): 88–94.

Dubb, Allie A. "Jewish Schools in the Diaspora: A Statistical Description." *Stu* vol. 3, ed. Aviad, 246–61.

* Epstein, David H. *A Model for Educational Supervision Drawn from Classical Jewish Sources.* Georgia State U., 1978. 200 pp.

Feinstein, Sara, Ellen Rosen, and Ruth Wortman. "Portrait of a Supervisor." *Syn Sch* 16 (1958).

Franzblau, Abraham. *Organization, Supervision and Administration of the Jewish Religious School: Syllabus for Education.* Cincinnati: Department of Jewish Religious Education, 1935. 53 pp.

Gannes, Abraham P. "The Executive's Job." *Jew Ed* 18 (Summer 1947): 45–48.

———. "Supervision in Agencies with Limited Personnel." *Jew Ed* 21 (Spring 1950): 30–31.

Glasner, Samuel. "Memorandum on Supervision." *Jew Teach* 26 (May 1958): 10–12.

Glickman, Carl D. "The Developmental Approach to Supervision." *Ped Rep* 34 (Mar. 1984): 19–20.

* Goldman, Emanuel. *An Inquiry into the Philosophy of Time and Its Meaning to the Study of Judaism.* Boston U. School of Education, 1978. 114 pp.

Golub, Jacob S. "Supervision for the Creative Teacher." *Jew Ed* 21 (Spring 1950): 26–29.

Gottlieb, Albert S. "Religious School Architecture and Equipment." *CCAR* 26 (1916): 83, 247.

Grad, Eli. "Supervision for What?" *Syn Sch* 20 (1961).

Kohn, Eugene. "A New System for Classifying Children in the Jewish Schools." *Jew Ed* 4 (Oct.–Dec. 1932): 163, 173.

Konowitz, Israel. „תולדות המחלקות בבתי התלמוד תורה" (On the Development of Grouping in the Talmud Torah). *Sh Hah* (H.) 1 (1941): 32–40.

Krug, Mark M. "The Executive in Jewish Education and the Lay Board." *Jew Ed* 22 (Summer 1951): 44–46, 84.

23
ADMINISTRATION

Landman, Isaac. "School Organization." *CCAR* 20 (1911): 330–43.

Lang, Gerhard, Maureen Carroll, and Leslie Liebman. "Women in Jewish Schools." *Jew Ed* 46 (Autumn 1978): 30–36, 41.

Leibson, Howard. "Crossing the Threshold: Some Guidelines for Classroom Observation." *Compass* 4 (Summer 1981): 8–9, 19.

Levitats, Isaac. „די ארגאניזאציע און די אנפירונג פון די יידישע שולן אין אמעריקע" (The Organization and Administration of Jewish Schools in America). *YB* (Y.) 40 (1956): 120–56. See also *YA* 11 (1956–57): 82–104.

Linick, Samuel. "The Teacher's View on Supervision and the Supervisor." *Jew Ed* 21 (Spring 1950): 31–33.

Marcus, Audrey Friedman. "Resource Guide for Jewish Educators." In *JTH*, 1:189–204.

Margoshes, Samuel. „רעדע צו דערציער" (A Talk to Educators). *Day* (Y.) (June 12, 1953).

Millgram, Abraham E. "Can the American City and County School Boards Provide a Pattern for the Congregational School Board?" *Syn Sch* 11 (Nov. 1952): 3–6.

Nadel, Max. "What Can We Learn from General Education?" *Ped Rep* 35 (Mar. 1984): 1–3.

National Committee on Leadership Development of CJF and JESNA. *Major Issues in Jewish Education: A Leadership Development Training Program Manual*. Developed and co-ordinated by Jack H. Mayer, Fradle Freidenreich, and Theodor Comet. 2d ed. April 1984.

Polish, David. "A Radical Departure." Plan for a second Congregational Board devoted to education. *Compass* 2 (Spring 1979): 5–6.

Pollak, George. "The Carnegie Report and Jewish Education." *Ped Rep* 35 (Mar. 1984): 3–7.

Pollak, Jacob B. *Classroom Organization and Management: A Syllabus for Normal Schools and Classes*. Cincinnati: Department of Synagogues and Schools of the UAHC, 1927. 99 pp.

Rappoport, Israel B. "Is Supervision Essential in a Program of Jewish Education?" *Jew Ed* 6 (Apr.–June 1934): 87–94.

Reynolds, Ronald Lewis. "Goals and Effectiveness in Jewish Education: An Organizational Perspective." In *Stu* 3, 91–115.

* ———. *Organizational Goals and Effectiveness: The Function of Goal Ambiguity in Jewish Congregational Afternoon Schools*. UCLA, 1982.

Rosen, Ben. "Coordination Between Week-Day and Sunday Schools." *Jew Ed* 1 (Jan. 1929): 44–46.

Ruffman, Louis L. "Supervision Program." *Jew Ed* 21 (Spring 1958): 7–8.

Schachter, Stanley J. "An Experiment That Failed." Consolidation of schools in a large city. *Syn Sch* 26 (Summer 1968): 21–25.

Schiff, Alvin I. "School Management and Organization." *Jew Ed* 37 (Winter 1967): 69–83.

Schreiber, Max and Nathan Stern. "The Classroom," "The Cleaning of the School Plant," and "Planning the Jewish School Building." In *Library on Jewish School Buildings*, edited by David Rudavsky. N.Y.: JEC, 1948.

Schwartz, Elliot S. "Supervision in the Jewish School." *Syn Sch* 30 (Summer 1972): 48–52.

Schwartzman, Sylvan D. *Syllabus: Religious School Administration for College Students*. Cincinnati: HUC, 1956. 142 pp.

Shluker, David. "Creative Supervision." *Ped Rep* 34 (Mar. 1983): 21–24.

Slesinger, Zalmen. "Resource Material for the Jewish Teacher and Administrator." In *Reg*, 28–40 (1959) and 64–90 (1965). N.Y.: AAJE.

* Small, Sarah L. *Attitudes of Professionals and Lay Leaders of Congregations in a Major Metropolitan Jewish Community, Chicago, toward the Employment of Women as Administrators of Congregational Schools*. U. of Missouri, Kansas City, 1983. See also Small's article in *Jew Ed* 52 (Spring 1984): 23–28.

Sokolow, Judy. "Middle Management Positions in Our School." *Jew Ed* 49 (Fall 1981): 36–39.

Sorin, Morris. "Accountabilty in the Open Classroom and Jewish Education." *Jew Ed* 43 (Fall 1974): 33–35.

Soviv, Aaron. „תפקיד הפקוח בבית-הספר העברי באמריקה" (The Role of Supervision in the American Jewish School). *Sh Hah* (H.) 26 (Summer 1966): 243–46.

Steinbach, Alexander A. "Raising Standards of Achievement in Religious Schools." *Jew Teach* 24 (Mar. 1956): 3–6.

Stern, Jay B. "Accountabilty and Jewish Education." *Ed As* (1972): 63–71.

———. "Some Supervisory Techniques for the Hebrew School." *Syn Sch* 16 (1958): 15–18.

Targan, Judith. "Jewish Education." In *Cat 2*, 176–209.

Weinstein, Marvin. "Supervision in the Experience of a Young Teacher." *Syn Sch* 20 (1962).

PEDAGOGIC ISSUES

Ackerman, Walter I. "Discipline in the Jewish School." *Syn Sch* 16 (Dec. 1957): 9–12.

Ben-Shoham, Hannah. "Creating Environments for Learning." *AM* Fall 1978.

Brilliant, Nathan, and Libbie L. Braverman. "Recognition of Achievement: Honors and Awards." *Jew Teach* 11 (June 1943): 13–16.

Cohen, Jack J. "Useful Magazines for Teachers and Pupils." *Syn Sch* 5 (Dec. 1946): 39–41.

Daum, Annette. "Sexism in Jewish Religious Education." *Jew Fron* 50 (Oct. 1983): 12–16.

Dembo, Myron. "An Evaluation of Confluent Education: Theory and Practice in the Jewish Setting." Master's thesis, UCLA, 1975.

Drachler, Norman. "The Problem Years in the Religious School." *Jew Teach* 26 (Jan. 1958): 3–6.

Frost, Shimon. "Is Jewish Education a Discipline?" *Ped Rep* 36 (Sept. 1985): 27.

Gewirtz, Max. "To Promote or Not to Promote." *Jew Teach* 23 (Mar. 1955): 7.

Glasser, Harry A. "Behavior Problems in the Religious School." *Jew Teach* 23 (Nov. 1954): 8–10.

Grand, Samuel. "The Problem Years in the Religious School" *Jew Teach* 26 (Jan. 1958): 3–6.

Grishaver, Joel Lurie, and Joyce Seglin. "Designs for Jewish Learning Spaces." In *JTH*, 2:1–9.

Isseroff, Sampson A. "How the Consultant Can Help the Teacher." *Ped Rep* 33 (Oct. 1982): 23–24.

Katz, Sally Klein. "Problems and Issues from a School Person's Perspective." *Jew Ed* (Summer 1983): 3–5.

Levin, Nancy Prager. "A Training Model for Cross-Age Teaching in the School Setting." Program based on research in secular education of cross-age teaching (tutoring and teaching of younger students by older students, who serve as models). Master's project, HUC–JIR, 1981.

Lister, Louis. "Towards Solving the Problem of the Problem Grades." *Jew Teach* 26 (Nov. 1957): 6–10.

Merel, Sheldon F. "Now Is the Time to Discuss Report Cards." *Jew Teach* 29 (Oct. 1960): 7–8.

Milgram, Roberta M. "Discipline in the Religious School." *Syn Sch* 23 (Fall 1964).

Schimmel, Solomon. "Corporal Punishment of School Children: The Teacher's Tort Liability in Jewish Law." *Jew Ed* 45 (Fall/Winter 1976): 32–41.

Schneider, Susan Weidman. "Battling Sexism in Jewish Schools." *Lilith* 10 (Winter 1982/83): 18–22.

Schwartz, Elliott. "Team Teaching: Applications and Implications in Jewish Education." *Syn Sch* 21 (Feb. 1963): 3–10.

Schweitzer, Ira H. "Discipline: The Classroom Teacher as Social Group Worker." *Ped Rep* 35 (Oct. 1984): 14–15.

Shiloni, Nathan Ariah. "המשמעת בבתי הלמוד„ (Discipline in the Schools). *Sh Hah* (H.) 3 (May 1943): 170–75.

Silberman, Melvin. "Discipline." In *JPH*, 7–11.

Syn Sch. "Disciplinary Control." 25 (Fall 1967): 79–81.

Weinstein, Joshua. "Competency Based Education in Jewish Education." *Ed As* (1972): 41–51.

Weinstein, Joshua, and W. Robert Houston. "Competency Based Education." *Jew Ed* 43 (Fall 1974): 21–26.

THE PRINCIPAL

Ackerman, Walter I. "The Educational Director and Curriculum Development." *Syn Sch* 22 (Fall 1964).

23
ADMINISTRATION

American Association for Jewish Education. *Better Personnel Practices*. N.Y.: AAJE, 1963, 1979, 1980.

Axelroth, Dorothy. "The Principal as Counselor in the Congregational School." *Ped Rep* 32 (Fall 1980): 10–11.

Baum, Eli. "The Role of the Administrator in Religious Education." *Rel Ed* 60 (Sept.–Oct. 1965): 370–74.

Behrman, Nicolas L. "Know before Whom You Stand: A Matter of Principal." *Compass* 2 (Fall/Winter 1978): 17.

Bennet, Alan D. "Budget and Priorities." In *JPH*. 49–67.

———. "The Roles of the Reform Jewish Educator." *Jew Teach* 33 (Dec. 1964): 7–12.

Bloom, D. I. "The Status of the Jewish School Principal: A Limited Study." *Jew Ed* 39 (Apr. 1969): 55–59.

Braver, Joseph L. "The Education Director as an Educational Leader: Innovation and Change in the Religious School—Theory, Method, and Approach." *Ed As* (1970): 98–108.

Braverman, Jay. "The Challenge to the Jewish Educational Leader." *Ped Rep* 34 (Mar. 1983): 1–2.

Campeas, Hyman J. "A Principal Looks at Home-School Cooperation." *Ped Rep* 30 (Fall 1978): 15–17.

Chein, Isidor. "The Faculty Educational Model." *Ped Rep* 12 (Jan. 1961).

Colodner, Sol. "How Do I Rate? A Self Evaluation Scale for Principals." *Syn Sch* 20 (Fall 1961).

Davis, Stuart E. "Towards the Orientation of the New Teacher for the Reform Religious School." Master's thesis, HUC–JIR, 1962.

Egozi, Akivah. „המנהל ותפקידו בהדרכת המורה הצעיר" (The Principal and his Role in the Guidance of the Young Teacher). *Sh Hah* (H.) 20 (Fall 1960): 29–31.

Eisenberg, Israel L. (Azriel). "The Principal's Job—An Activity Analysis." *Jew Ed* 3 (Oct.–Dec. 1931): 164–72.

———. „חשיבות המנהל ותפקידו" (The Significance of the Principal and His Role). *Sh Hah* (H.) 12 (Mar. 1952): 78–89.

* Elbaz, Nissim Maxim. *A Study of Job Satisfaction and Dissatisfaction of Administrators of Jewish Schools*. U. of Cincinnati, 1979. 225 pp.

Ende, George. "The Faculty Meeting as an Instrument of School Administration." *Syn Sch* 9 (Nov. 1950): 3–9.

Feldheim, Eric. "Administration and Supervision." *NATE* (24th annual conference, Dec. 1978): 30–34.

Franzblau, Abraham N. "The Contribution of Psychiatry to the Principal's Task." *Jew Teach* 23 (May 1955): 2–6.

Gittelsohn, Roland B. "Teachers' Meetings: Outlines for Discussion." *Jew Teach* 8 (June 1940): 17–24.

———. "The 'What' and 'Why' of Teachers' Meetings." *Jew Teach* 6 (Apr. 1938): 1–15.

Glasman, Naftali. „מנהל בית הספר כמנהיג וכסוכן שינויים" (The Principal as Leader and Agent of Change). *Sh Hah* (H.) 38 (Mar. 1979): 165–69; (June 1979): 199–205; 39 (Sept. 1979): 52–56.

Gross, Victor. "Stress." In *JPH*, 101–16.

Gruber, Ruth. "Public Relations Planning." In *JPH*, 69–75.

Himelstein, Schmuel. "'Back to School' for School Principals." *Jew Ed* 47 (Spring 1979): 33–34.

Joseph, Samuel K. "The Crisis of Change: A Guide to Change Management." *Compass* 9 (Spring/Summer 1987): 6–7.

———. *Day-to-Day Administration of the Religious School*. Cincinnati: HUC–JIR, 1984. 188 pp.

———. "The TI Guide." (Informing parents about school activities.) *Compass* (Fall 1977).

Klein, Betty Dolgin. "A Teacher Center in Your School." In *JPH*, 267–75.

Konowitz, Israel. "How to Organize a Hebrew School." *Jewish Teacher* 2 (Apr. 1918): 21–25; 2 (Jan. 1919): 100–103.

Kostman, Samuel. "The Principal and Classroom Supervision." *Ped Rep* 34 (Mar. 1983): 17–20.

Kramish, Leonard. "The Total Temple Educator." *Compass* 4 (Fall/Winter 1980): 9, 20.

Krug, Mark M. "The Jewish Principal and the School Committee." *Jew Ed* 23 (Summer 1952): 25–28.

Kurzband, Toby. *A Manual of Religious School Administration*. N.Y.: UAHC, 1959. 445 pp.

Lee, Sara S. "The Principal as Leader." In *JPH*, 519–20.

M. H. L. "The Effective Principal." *Ped Rep* 34 (Mar. 1983): 7–9.

Libman, Melvin L. "The Recruitment of Personnel for Informal Education." *Ed As* (1966): 78–80.

Marcus, Audrey Friedman, and Raymond A. Zwerin. *The Jewish Principal's Handbook*. Denver: ARE, 1983. 525 pp.

Moskowitz, Nechama Skolnik, and Charlene Neeley. "The Physical Environment." In *JPH*, 3–6.

Nardi, Noah. „היסודות הפסיכולוגיים בתכנית הלמודים של אגדת המנהלים" (The Psychological Principles in the Curriculum of the Principals' Association). *Sh Hah* (H.) (Mar. 1944): 126–32.

Oliker, Lilyan G. "A New Teacher Comes to School." *Compass* 3 (Summer 1980): 10–11, 21.

Perlman, Milton. "The Function of the Principal in Directing Behavior Attitudes." *Syn Sch* 10 (Apr. 1952): 3–8.

Pins, Arnulf M. "Helping Teachers through a Program of Supervision." *Jew Teach* 23 (Nov. 1954): 3–8.

Podolsky, Judy. "Managing the School." In *JPH*, 23–47.

Pollak, George. "School Climate and Administration." *Ped Rep* 35 (Oct. 1984): 6–8.

———. "Staff Relations." *Syn Sch* 31 (Winter 1973): 27–31.

Ranson, Marius. "A Completely Departmentalized Religious School." *CCAR* 45 (1935): 432–41.

Rauchwanger, Diane. "Orientation Innovation." (For parents.) *Compass* 2 (Summer 1979): 10–11.

Resnick, David. "School Models and the Role of the Principal." In *JPH*, 513–18.

Ruffman, Louis L., and Henry Goldberg. "The Job of the Principal." *Ped Rep* 4 (Nov. 1952): 3–5.

Schanin, Norman. "Developing a Favorable Climate for Jewish Education in the Congregation." *Syn Sch* 19 (Mar. 1961): 34, 36.

Scheirer, Elinor, and David Resnick. "Creating Better Designs for Teaching." *AM* 9 (Fall 1978): 4–6.

Schiff, Alvin I. "Focus on the Jewish School Principal" (editorial). *Jew Ed* 48 (Winter 1980): 2–5.

———. "Jewish School Principalship at the Crossroads." *Ped Rep* 24 (Mar. 1983): 3–7.

* Schneider, Paul David. *The Training of the Jewish Principal*. Columbia U.–Teachers College, 1980. 150 pp.

Segal, Abraham. "Encouraging Teacher Creativity." *Jew Teach* 34 (Apr. 1966).

———. "Expanding the One-Shot Teachers' Conference." *Compass* 4 (Autumn 1970).

Selig, Sidney. "Our Souls Are Not Raisins Either." *Ed As* (1972): 72–75.

Shapiro, Miriam Klein. "Eliminating Sexism from Jewish Education." *Jew Ed* 48 (Spring 1980): 42–44.

* Silberman, Rosalind M. R. *Teacher Expectations of Jewish Afternoon School Principals: Role Responsibilities, Relationships, and Decision-Making*. Temple U., 1983.

Silberman, Shoshana. "Jewish Teachers' Expectations of Their Principals." *Jew Ed* 52 (Spring 1984): 19–22.

Silverman, Hillel. "Relationship with Staff and Laymen." *RA* (1972).

Slesinger, Zalmen. "The Role of the Principal—A Job of Multiple Responsibilities." *Ped Rep* 13 (Nov. 1961): 10–12, 31.

Spotts, Leon H. "The Congregational Educator: His Problems and Prospects." *Syn Sch* 21 (Fall 1963).

———. "A New Design for the Role of the Educational Director in the Conservative Congregation." *Syn Sch* 20 (Fall 1961).

Steinberg, Barbara Summers. "How Principals Can Help Teachers." *Ped Rep* 33 (Oct. 1982): 20–22.

Stern, Jay. *Know Your School.* N.Y.: JEC Press, 1961.

Steven, Reuben. "Staff Professional Growth and Evaluation." *NATE* (24th Annual Conference, Dec. 1978): 42–45.

Tarasow, Morris. "The Principal as Supervisor." *Syn Sch* 16 (May 1958): 3–7.

Tornberg, Robert E. "Recruiting, Hiring, and Firing." In *JPH*, 119–33.

———. "The Teachers' Handbook." In *JPH*, 135–58.

Toubin, Isaac. *Preliminary Report on Administrators Training Program.* N.Y.: AAJE, 1972.

Troy, Dov. "Team Teaching: A Personal Experience." *Syn Sch* 21 (Feb. 1963): 11–20.

Wolk, Asher. „מחנכים רעדן זיך אראפ פון הארצן" (Educators 'Get Things off Their Chests'). *Day* (Y.) (June 21, 1965).

Zuckerman, Herbert. "Efficient Administration in the Religious School." *Jew Teach* 26 (Jan. 1958): 6–8.

IN-SERVICE TRAINING

Blumenfield, Samuel M. "In-Service Jewish Teacher Education." In *Jan 3*, 185–95.

Council of Jewish Federations and Welfare Funds. *Federation Planning for Jewish Education.* Recommended Priority Programs Proposed by Special Subcommittee: 1. Training Principals, Adminstrators and Counsultants; 2. In-Service Summer Institute for Teachers in the Midwest. October 11, 1968. 5 pp.

Gamoran, Emanuel. "The Training of the Jewish Teacher." *The Hebrew Standard* (Nov. 24, 1922).

———. *Train Your Teachers.* Cincinnati: DSSE, 1928.

Gold, Manuel. "Teaching the Teacher." *Ped Rep* 23 (Dec. 1971): 15.

Goldstein, Mark. "How We Conduct a Teacher-in-Service Training Program." *Syn Sch* 19 (Mar. 1961): 37–41.

Gorr, A. "Simulations for the Training of Jewish Educators." *Syn Sch* 32 (Winter 1973–74): 32–41.

Jordan, C. "In-Service Education: An Innovative Approach." *Ped Rep* 33 (Oct. 1982): 17–19.

Joseph, Samuel K. "Teaching and Learning." (Teacher training program.) *Compass* 6 (Fall 1982): 7–8, 16–17.

Katz, Dina. "The WATE Teacher Training Program." *Ped Rep* 33 (Oct. 1982): 14–15.

Korman, M. "Teacher-in-Service: Synagogue Based." *Syn Sch* 31 (Winter 1973): 4–14.

Lee, Sara S. "In-Service Education: A Priority for All Seasons." *Ped Rep* 34 (Mar. 1983): 21–23.

Leibman, Morris. "Supervision through in Service Training, Conferences and Demonstration Teaching." *Jew Ed* 21 (Spring 1950): 23–25.

Levow, Mordecai. "An Inquiry Skills Teacher Education Program." Report on an NCRI Project. *Ped Rep* 23 (Dec. 1971): 3.

Levy, Phyllis S. "Teachers' Centers: Application for in-Service Education in Jewish Education." *Jew Ed* 45 (Winter 1977): 20–31.

Marcus, Audrey Friedman. "Teacher Training." In *JPH*, 159–74.

Pomerantz, Hyman. "FIJEL [Fellowships in Jewish Educational Leadership]—A Training Program." *Ped Rep* 34 (Mar. 1983): 26–27.

Rauch, Eduardo. "Crystalizing the Beginnings of a Dream—A Working Paper: Towards Imagining a Teacher Retreat." *MJ* 20 (Spring 1986): 5, 29.

Selig, Sidney. "An Experimental Teacher Training Program." *Ed As* (1966): 36–39.

Shapiro, Sara S. "The Training of Master Teachers." *Ped Rep* 34 (Mar. 1983): 30–32.

Soref, Irwin. "Films to Use in a Teacher-Training Program." *Jew Ed* 23 (Summer 1952): 37–39.

United Synagogue Commission on Jewish Education. "Professional Growth Programs." *Ped Rep* 22 (June 1971): 23.

THE PROFESSION OF JEWISH EDUCATION

Bayar, Steven. "The Professional Must Learn How to Cope." *Ped Rep* 35 (Oct. 1984): 25–26.

Bennett, Alan D. "The Reform Jewish Educator—Then and Now." *RJ* 16 (Spring 1988): 13.

Bortniker, Elijah. „כתבי-עת לחינוך יהודי בארצות הברית" (Periodicals for Jewish Education in the United States). *HaHinukh* (H.) 28 (1956): 227–29.

Chipkin, Israel S. "Fate of the Jewish Education Profession in America." *Jew Ed* 24 (Spring 1953): 10–12.

———. "Improving the Status of the Hebrew Teacher." *Jew Ed* 16 (Sept. 1944): 3–5.

Clark, Matthew. "The Leadership of the CJE." *Ped Rep* 34 (Mar. 1983): 25–26.

———. "Professionalism in Jewish Education." *Jew Ed* 50 (Spring 1980): 37–40.

Conference of Jewish Educator Organizations. *Advocacy Plan for Enhancing the Jewish Educator Profession*. COJEO, 1986.

Coun, Ronald. "The Role of the Jewish Educational Professional in the Jewish Communal Setting." *Jew Ed* 55 (Summer 1987): 3–5, 17.

Dinin, Samuel, and I. L. Eisenberg. "Professional Prospects in Jewish Education." *Jew Ed* 5 (Jan./Mar. 1933): 52–56.

———. "Strengthening the Profession of Jewish Education." *Jew Ed* 35 (Fall 1964): 4–13.

Diskind, Zalman. "A Profile of Seventy-Five NCJE Members." *Jew Ed* 34 (Fall 1963): 43–50.

Drachler, Norman. "The Role of the Professional Educator." *CCAR* 68 (1959): 156–58.

Dushkin, Alexander M. "The Profession of Jewish Education." *Menorah J* 3 (Apr. 1917): 90–97; (June 1917): 174–81.

———. "The Role of the Professional Worker in Jewish Education." *Jew Ed* 5 (Jan./Mar. 1933): 3–13.

Dushkin, Alexander M., and Leo L. Honor. "Aims and Activities of Jewish Educational Organizations in America." *Jew Ed* 5 (Oct.–Dec. 1933): 136–46.

Edelstein, Menachem M. "The Status of the Jewish Education Profession." *Jew Ed* 24 (Spring 1953): 23–38.

Eisenberg, Azriel. "The National Council for Jewish Education Faces the Future." *Jew Ed* 32 (Fall 1961): 43–44.

Frankel, Max. "The State of NATE." *Jew Teach* 34 (Apr. 1966): 9–12.

Freidenreich, Fradle, and Miriam Klotz. *To Build a Profession: Careers in Jewish Education—Project Round up*. JESNA, June 1986.

Goldman, Israel M. "New Directions for the Profession of Jewish Education." *Jew Ed* 14 (Sept/Dec. 1942): 106–9.

Goldman, Solomon. "Is a Jewish Educator a Professional?" *Ed As* (1970): 95–97.

Grand, Samuel. "Role of NATE in Creating a Profession in Jewish Education." *Jew Teach* 25 (May 1957): 8–9.

———. "Ten Years of NATE." *Jew Teach* 33 (Dec. 1964): 3–6.

Handler, Zevi. „יסוד אגודת המנהלים" (The Founding of the Principals' Association). *Sh Hah* (H.) 23 (Autumn 1963): 38–46.

Honor, Leo L. "Twenty-Five Years of NCJE." *Jew Ed* 22 (Summer 1951): 2–5.

"Inter-Organizational Plenary Session, May 1, 1974." Resolutions adopted: 1. Interlocking Structure of Jewish Educational Professionals; 2. Federation and Jewish Education; 3. Israel; 4. Think-Tank in Jewish Education; 5. Pedagogic Supervision. *Jew Ed* 43 (Fall 1974): 62–63.

National Board of License for Teachers and Principals in American and Canadian Jewish Schools: Requirements and Procedures. Rev. ed. N.Y.: JESNA, 1982. 15 pp.

Jewish Teacher, The. "The First Decade" (special issue on NATE). *Jew Teach* 33 (Dec. 1964).

Justman, Joseph. "Educational Leadership in the Coming Years." *Syn Sch* 20 (1961).

Kelman, Stuart. "Preparation for a Profession." *NATE* (24th Annual Conference, Dec. 1978): 17–24.

Kessler, Aharon. "The Jewish Teaching Profession." *Reg* (1951): 51–58.

23
ADMINISTRATION

Pilch, Judah. "Fifty Years of Jewish Educational Professional Leadership." *Jew Ed* 44 (Spring/Summer 1976): 19–24.

Pollak, George. "A Vision of the Jewish Educator." *Jew Ed* 48 (Summer 1980): 39–43.

———. *Who's Who in Jewish Education: A Profile of the Jewish Educator*. N.Y.: AAJE and WZO, 1980. 105 pp.

Reimer, Joseph, ed. *To Build a Profession: Careers in Jewish Education*. Hornstein Program in Jewish Communal Service, Brandeis U., May 1987.

Ribner, Israel. "The Jewish Educator—The Status of the Educator." *Ed As* (1970): 81–87.

Rosenbaum, Jonathan. "The Community Teacher Concept: A Different Approach to Professionalizing Jewish Pedagogues." *Jew Ed* 52 (Summer 1983): 27–31.

Schiff, Alvin I. "The Crisis in the Jewish Education Profession." *Rel Ed* 67 (Sept./Oct. 1972): 342–44.

Schwartz, Elliot S. "Council for Jewish Education Challenges." *Jew Ed* 51 (Winter 1983): 43–45.

Slesinger, Zalmen. "Jewish Education: A Crisis in Orientation and Educational Leadership." *Jew Fron* (Aug.–Sept. 1975): 34–42.

* Sparks, Jack L. *Jewish Educators' Perceptions of Professional Role, Problems and Issues: An Exploratory Study*. Boston U., 1985.

Woocher, Jonathan. *Building Educational Leadership: The Current Challenge*. N.Y.: JESNA, 1986.

PROFESSIONAL ORGANIZATIONS

(See also Chapters 20, 21)

Coalition for Alternatives in Jewish Education, founded 1976. Includes Jewish educators from various ideological sectors. Sponsors Bikurim, Crisis Curriculum, Mekasher, CAJE.

Council for Jewish Education, founded 1982 (formerly the National Council for Jewish Education). Publications: *Jewish Education* and *Sheviley Hahinuch* (H.).

Jewish Education Service of North America (JESNA) (formerly AAJE, founded 1939). "Coordinates, promotes, and services Jewish education in federated communities of North America.... Maintains a National Educational Resource Center.... Sponsors the National Board of License... and provides placement of upper-level bureau and communal school personnel and educators." Publications: *Pedagogic Reporter, Jewish Education Directory*. See *AJYB* (1989).

Jewish Theological Seminary of America, Melton Research Center, founded 1960. Develops new curricula and materials for Jewish education and conducts training sessions for Jewish educators. Publications: *Melton Journal*.

Union of American Hebrew Congregations and Central Conference of American Rabbis: Commission on Jewish Education. "Develops curricula and teachers manuals; conducts pilot projects and offers educational guidance ... to member congregations." Publications: *Compass* (formerly *The Jewish Teacher*). See *AJYB* (1989).

Union of American Hebrew Congregations, National Association of Temple Educators, founded 1955. "Represents the temple educator.... Reform Judaism, fosters the full-time profession of the temple educator; encourages growth and development of Jewish religious education." Publications: *NATE News, Proceedings of NATE Annual Conference*. See *AJYB* (1989).

United Synagogue of America, Commission on Jewish Education. "Promotes higher educational standards in Conservative congregational schools and Solomon Schechter Schools and publishes material for the advancement of their educational program." Publications: *Briefs, Impact* (formerly *The Synagogue School*), *In Your Hands*, and *Your Child*. See *AJYB* (1989).

United Synagogues of America, Jewish Educators Assembly. "Promotes, extends, and strengthens the program of Jewish education on all levels in the community in consonance with the philosophy of the Conservative movement." Publications: *Jewish Educators Assembly Yearbook, Newsletter, Tamtzit*. See *AJYB* (1989).

EDUCATIONAL JOURNALS (SELECTED)

Alternatives in Religious Education. ARE, Denver, 1970–78.

CAJE Jewish Education News, CAJE, 1976–1991.

Compass (formerly *The Jewish Teacher*). UAHC Department of Education and School of Education of HUC–JIR, New York, 1933–1991). Three times per year.

HaHinukh (H.). NCJE, New York, 1935–38. Quarterly.

Impact (formerly *The Jewish School and Democracy* and *Synagogue Scholar*). USA–CJE, 1943–present.

The Inkling (newsletter for teachers). ARE, Denver.

The Jewish Audio-Visual Review. AAJE, New York, 1951–60.

Jewish Education. CJE, New York, 1929–present.

Jewish Parent. TU, 1948–77.

Kol Bana'Yikh (All Your Children). Special Education Committee of the USCJE, 1986–present. Quarterly.

The Lehiyot Connection (Lihiyot program for special needs learners). UAHC, 1987–1991.

The Melton Journal (formerly *Melton Research Center Newsletter*). New York, 1982–present.

Pedagogic Reporter. JESNA, New York, 1949–1991.

Sheviley Hahinuch (H.). CJE, New York, 1925–39 and 1940–1991.

Shoah. National Jewish Resource Center, New York.

Tekumah (H.). Jewish National Fund, New York, 1935–?

THE TEACHER SHORTAGE

AAJE. The Personnel Problem in Jewish Education. N.Y., 1955.

AAJE. *Some Practical Proposals for Increasing the Supply of Qualified Educational Personnel.* CJFWF, Mar. 1958. 11 pp.

Aron, Isa. "From Where Will the Next Generation of Jewish Teachers Come?" *Compass* 10 (Spring/Summer 1988): 5, 24, 26.

Aron, Isa, and Adrianne Bank. *Dealing with the Shortage of Supplementary School Teachers: An Exploratory Study.* N.Y.: JESNA, 1987.

Chanover, Hyman. "The Manpower Crisis in Jewish Education." *Jew Ed* 27 (Spring 1957): 11–17.

Chipkin, Israel S. "Problem Number One in Jewish Education" (shortage of personnel). *Jew Ed* 26 (Summer 1955): 2.

Clark, Matthew. "Teacher Recruitment and Retention." *Jew Ed* 49 (Spring 1981): 26–29.

Congress Weekly. "The Manpower Crisis in Jewish Education" (special issue). (Oct. 29, 1956).

Danzig, Yehuda. "On the Use of Public School Personnel in Jewish Education." *Ed As* (1966): 51–54.

Davis, Moshe. "The Crisis in Jewish Education—Teacher Shortage, Teacher Training." *Day* (Apr. 13, 1949).

Deutch, Samuel. "A Word of Caution." (On the utilization of public school personnel.) *Ed As* (1966): 58–60.

Gattman, Eric. "Utilizing Para-Professionals." *NATE* (19th Annual Conference, Dec. 1973): 58–59.

Gross, Ted. "Lay People as Specialized Instructors." *Ed As* (1966): 65–67.

Hollander, Arthur S. "Developing Sources for Personnel Recruitment." *Ed As* (1966): 26–31.

Hurwich, Louis. "The All Day Hebrew Teachers College as a Remedy for Teacher Shortage." *Jew Ed* 27 (Spring 1957): 29–30.

JESNA. "Alternative Solutions to the Shortage of Supplementary School Teachers." *Trends* 12 (Fall 1986).

Jewish Educators Assembly. *Recruitment and Training of Educational Personnel.* Jewish Educators Assembly, CJE–USA, 1970.

Kaplan, Louis L. "The Problem of the Shortage of Teachers in Jewish Schools." *Jew Ed* 35 (Fall 1964): 14–21.

Katzoff, Louis. "Teacher Selection and Recruitment—Problems in General and Jewish Education." *Jew Ed* 24 (Spring 1954): 29–34, 61.

Levinthal, L. "Challenge and Opportunity." *Congress Weekly* (Oct. 29, 1956): 5–7.

Liebman, Melvin S. "The Recruitment of Personnel for Informal Education." *Ed As* (1966): 78–80.

Lown, Philip W. "A Clear and Present Danger" (personnel shortage). *Jew Ed* 27 (Spring 1957): 6–7.

Margolis, Henry. "Personnel Crisis in Jewish Education." *Jew Ed* 43 (Winter/Spring 1975): 55–56.

Millgram, Abraham E. "The Jewish Educator: His Woes and Joys" (recruitment of personnel). *Congress Weekly* (Mar. 31, 1958): 10–11.

Nudelman, Edward A., and Zalmen Slesinger. "The Personnel Problem in Jewish Education." *Jew Ed* 26 (Summer 1955): 6–13.

Ped Rep. "Personnel Crisis in Jewish Education." (Dec. 1963): 9–12.

Pilch, Judah. "Teacher Shortage: Problem and Solution." *Congress Weekly* (Oct. 29, 1956): 2–5.

Pollak, George. "Jewish School Problem." *Jew Ed* 49 (Summer 1981): 43–45.

Preil, Joseph J. "The Personnel Crisis and Population Erosion." *Jew Ed* 51 (Spring 1983): 31–33.

Reisman, Bernard. "Recruitment of Professionals." *Jew Ed* 51 (Summer 1983): 5–9.

Rosenberg, Benjamin B. "The Crucial Gap in Qualified Teachers." In *What Can the Federation Do to Strengthen Jewish Education?* CJF-WF, Nov. 1966.

Rubin, Ph. "A Confusing Picture." *Congress Weekly* (Oct. 29, 1956): 9–12.

Schiff, Alvin I. "The Man Power Crisis in Jewish Education: Real Problem and Realistic Solutions." *Jew Ed* 38 (June 1968): 12–23.

———. "A Response to the Manpower Problem." *Jew Ed* 40 (Mar. 1970): 36–41.

———. "Some Modest Proposals for Improvement of Hebrew Teacher Recruitment and Training Programs." In *Report of Proceedings of the World Presidium Conference*, World Council of Jewish Education, (Dec. 6, 1965): 16–35.

Schoolman, Albert P. "Crisis in Jewish Education" (editorial on teacher shortage). *Jew Ed* 27 (Spring 1957): 3–5.

Segal, Bernard. ". . . Pivotal and Indispensible" (personnel). *Syn Sch* 25 (Winter 1968): 13–15.

Shevitz, Susan Rosenblum. "Communal Responses to the Teacher Shortage in the North American Supplementary School." In *Stu* 3, 25–61.

Shoham, Joseph. "A Teacher Views Recruitment." *Ed As* (1966): 46–48.

Siegel, Morton. "On Placement and Personnel." *Syn Sch* 26 (Winter 1968): 16–25.

Silberschlag, Eisig. "Critical Shortage in Teacher Personnel." *Jew Ed* 32 (Fall 1961): 40–43.

Slesinger, Zalmen. "The Personnel Crisis in Jewish Education." *Ped Rep* 15 (Dec. 1963): 9–12, 28.

Stern, Jay B. "Losing One's Faculties in Jewish Education." *Con Jud* 24 (Summer 1970): 58–64.

———. "Taking the Teacher Recruitment Bull by the Horns." *Ed As* (1966): 33–35.

Ury, Zalman Halevi. „לבעית המחסור המורים באמריקה" (On the Problem of Teacher Shortage in America). *Sh Hah* (H.) 33 (1973): 201–5.

Wahlberg, Jeffrey A. "Problem Solving: The Congregational School-By-Products of the Teacher Shortage." *Con Jud* 26 (Winter 1972): 57–59.

Wasserman, Joy Beth. "Training Avocational Teachers for the Congregational School." A critical presentation of the current realities of recruiting staff for the Jewish supplementary school. Master's project, HUC–JIR, 1987.

Whiteman, Kalman. „המחסור במורים עברים" (The Shortage of Hebrew Teachers). *Hadoar* (H.) 249 (Oct. 5, 1945): 101.

TEACHER AIDES

Beizer, Ruth. "A Project for the Training of Teacher Helpers." *Ed As* (1966): 42–46.

Gattman, Eric. "Creatively Using Teacher's Aides in Our Classrooms." *AM* (Spring 1975): 14–15.

Grad, Eli. "Toward a Program of Total Judaism" (cadet training). *Syn Sch* 19 (Oct. 1960): 20–29.

Hirt, Robert S. "Recruiting Young People for Avodat Hakodesh." *Jew Ed* 53 (Summer 1985): 36–39.

Kaplan, Louis L. "An Untapped Reservoir of Potential Teachers" (utilization of Hebrew high school alumni). *Ed As* (1966): 60–61.

Karbal, Harold. "Student Teaching in the Religious School." *Ped Rep* 22 (Sept. 1970).

Katz, Sally Klein, and Karen Trager Rossel. "Co-op Teacher Training." *Compass* 2 (Winter 1979): 14–15.

Kling, S. "Problem Solving: The Congregational School—Non-Professionals in the Classroom." *Con Jud* 26 (Winter 1972): 55–57.

Korin, Uri. "Teacher Training for High School Students—The Cadet Program." *Jew Ed* 49 (Winter 1981): 44–46.

Kurzband, Toby, and Paul Warner. "A Student-Teaching Program for Post Confirmands." *Jew Teach* 21 (Mar. 1953): 2–6.

Levin, Nancy Prager. "Training Aides, Assistants, and Tutors." In *JPH*, 183–200.

Marcus, Fred. "A Teacher and Teacher Assistant Training Session." *AM* (Spring 1975): 16–19.

Meyers, Larry. "Students as Teachers." *The Living Light* 29 111–17.

Rosoff, Barbara. "The Teacher Aide Program in the Religious School." (Extensive bibliography.) *Syn Sch* 32 (Summer 1974): 10–21.

Schlaffman, Helene. "Working with Teen Aides." In *JTH*, 2:121–28.

Schwartz, Elliot S. "The Teacher-Aide Program." *Syn Sch* 25 (1966).

Silver, Menachem. "Student Tutors as a Potential Source of Personnel." *Ed As* (1966): 40–41.

Spotts, Leon H. "Recruitment and Training of Cadet Teachers." *Ed As* (1966): 61–65.

Tonger, Judith. "Para-Professionals—Our Madrichim." *AM* (Spring 1975): 12–14.

STANDARDS AND CODES FOR THE PROFESSION

AAJE. *National Board of License—Requirements and Procedures*. Rev. ed. N.Y., 1977. 12 pp.

Chanover, Hyman. *Guide to a Code of Practice for Teachers and Schools*. Better Personnel Practices, No.1. N.Y.: AAJE, Mar. 1963.

* ———. *A History of the National Board of License for Teachers and Supervisory Personnel in American Jewish Schools: The Struggle to Improve the Quality of Instruction in Jewish Schools in the United States*. New York U., 1971. 449 pp.

———. "The National Board of License—Its Function, Composition and Affiliates." *Reg* (1965): 25–41.

Golub, Jacob S. (Chair, National Council for Jewish Education). "A Code of Practice for Executives in Jewish Education" (committee report). *Jew Ed* 2 (Oct. 1930): 144–45. See also *Jew Ed* (Sept. 1944): 43–47.

Honor, Leo. "Proposal to Establish a National Board of License" (editorial). *Jew Ed* 11 (Jan. 1940): 157–58.

Horowitz, C. Morris. "The National Board of License and the Accredited Board of Certification." *Reg* (1959): 17–25.

JESNA. *National Board of License for Teachers and Principals in American and Canadian Jewish Schools: Requirements and Procedures*. N.Y., 1982. 15 pp.

NATE. *Guide of Ethical and Personnel Practices of the National Association of Temple Educators*. Rev. ed. N.Y.: NATE–UAHC, December 1978.

———. A Guide to Personnel Practices of the National Association of Temple Educators. Approved by NATE and the Joint Commissions on Jewish Education of the UAHC and CCAR, 1962–63. 11 pp.

Pilch, Judah. "The National Board of License and the Training of the Jewish Teacher." *Jew Ed* 22 (Winter/Spring 1951): 2–3.

Pomerantz, Hyman. "Certification in Jewish Education." *Ped Rep* 31 (Spring 1980).

———. "The National Board of License." *Jew Ed* 46 (Autumn 1978): 40–44.

Ruffman, Louis L. "Code for Executives." *Jew Ed* 24 (Spring 1953): 4–5.

EVALUATION

(See also Chapters 10, 20, 21, and 42)

Alexander, Chanan. "Evaluating Jewish Educational Programs." *MJ* 12 (Spring 1981): 7, 16.

* Alexander, Henry A. *The Qualitative Turn in Evaluation: An Ecumenical Analysis.* (Jewish Education.) Stanford U., 1985.

Bank, Adrianne. "Evaluation: Is It Good for Jewish Education?" *Ped Rep* 36 (Sept. 1985): 1–6. See also Bank's article on evaluation in *Stu* 3, 116–33.

Brav, Stanley T. "Attitudes toward Jewish Education: A Sample of Reform Jewish Opinion." *Jew Ed* 24 (Spring 1954): 35, 60.

Brody, H. (Definition of a Good Teacher). *Sh Hah* (H.) (Spring 1970).

Bugatch, Simon. *Guide to Interpretation and Use of Test Scores.* (For use by Jewish schools in the United States). N.Y.: NCRI, 1967. 12 pp.

Burnstein, Steven. "An Exploratory Study of the Relationship between Teacher Qualifications and Degree of Personal Feelings of Success in the Afternoon Hebrew School." Master's thesis, Department of Jewish Education, JTS, 1989.

Cedarbaum, David I. *Guide for School Evaluation for Religious Schools of Reform Congregations.* N.Y.: UAHC, 1964.

Chipkin, Israel S. "Proposals for the Study of Evaluation and Reconstruction of the Jewish Educational System in America." *Jew Ed* 16 (Jan. 1945): 34–36.

Cohen, Burton, and Joseph Lukinsky. "The Evaluator as Change Agent: A Practical Approach in a Limited Time Frame." *Jew Ed* 49 (Spring 1981): 4–9.

* Corseri, Richard Alan. *The Development and Testing of Group Instructional Modules for the Teaching of Judaica.* College of Boca Raton (Florida), 1977.

Eisenberg, Azriel. (Criteria for Measuring Quality in Jewish Education). *Sh Hah* (H.) 24 (Winter 1964): 72–74.

Fineberg, Solomon A. "A Critical Evaluation of the Reform Religious School." *CCAR* (1929): 439–52.

Fishman, Joshua A. "Educational Evaluation in the Context of Minority Group Dynamics." *Jew Ed* 29 (Fall 1958): 17–24.

———. "Evaluation of Results in Current American Education." *Jew Ed* 24 (Spring 1954): 22–28.

Freidenreich, Fradle. "The Evaluation Process: Two-Way Interaction." *Ped Rep* 23 (Sept. 1971): 7.

Freidenreich, Fradle, and Jay B. Stern. "Responses to 'Accountabilty in the Open Classroom and Jewish Education.'" *Jew Ed* 43 (Fall 1974): 36–39.

Friedman, Norman L. "Reform Jewish Sunday School Primary Grade Department: An Ethnography." *Jew Ed* 55 (Spring 1987): 18–26.

Goodnick, Bernard. "The Evaluation of Attitudes and the Jewish School." *Jew Ed* 30 (Fall 1959): 34–48, 59.

Gordon, Susan. "Underground vs. Open Evaluation." *Compass* 8 (Spring 1985): 9, 15.

Gutman, Jacob. "An Objective Test in General Knowledge of Judaism." Master's thesis, U. of Minnesota, 1930.

Hakimian, Leah. "Objectives, Instruction, Evaluation." *Ped Rep* 32 (Sept. 1981): 8–10.

———. "Teacher Evaluation." *Ped Rep* 33 (Oct. 1982): 33–34.

* Hartman, Eliyahu E. *A Follow-Up Study of Graduates of Selected Hebrew Elementary Educational Institutions.* Memphis State U., 1976. 183 pp.

* Henkin, Hillel. *Evaluation of Jewish Education in the United States with Special Emphasis on Testing, 1910–1965.* Dropsie U., 1965.

Hillelsohn, Michael J. "Evaluation of a Congregational School's Principal." *Jew Ed* 49 (Spring 1981): 10–15.

Isserman, Ruth, and Albert F. Goldstein. "Tests for the Holidays." *Jew Teach* 9 (Jan. 1941): 23–28.

Joseph, Samuel K. "Teacher Effectiveness." *Ped Rep* 33 (Oct. 1982): 31–32.

Karten, Esther. "Teacher Evaluation." *Compass* 1 (Winter 1977): 14.

Latham, L. "Telling Tales out of School: Student Evaluation." In *JTH*, 2:129–140.

Leibman, Morris. "An Evaluation of the Afternoon Hebrew School." *Jew Ed* 37 (Winter 1957): 29–38.

Levy, Phyllis S. "Evaluation Strategies for Student Success." *Compass* 3 (1979): 4–6.

Makovsky, Nancy. "Evaluation." *Ped Rep* (Winter 1979).

Maller, Julius B. *Attitudes of Jewish Students*. N.Y.: UAHC, 1931.

———. "Testing Achievement in Jewish Schools." *Jew Ed* 2 (Oct. 1930): 154–65.

———. *Testing the Knowledge of Jewish History*. Cincinnati: DSSE, 1932. 252 pp.

———. "Tests in History." *Jew Ed* 2 (June 1930): 96–103.

Maller, Julius B., and Jacob B. Pollack. *Jewish History Achievement Test*. 8 parts. Cincinnati: UAHC, ca. 1930.

Musella, Donald. "Improving Teachers' Evaluation." *Ped Rep* 22 (Sept. 1970): 3–6.

Poisson, Joseph A. "The Role of Evaluation in the Hebrew School System." *Syn Sch* 20 (1961).

* Press, Judith Ann. *An Ethnographic and Phenomenological Study of Students' Perceptions about Hebrew School*. U. of Connecticut, 1982. See also *Jew Ed* 53 (Fall 1984): 15–24.

Reuben, Steven. "Staff Professional Growth and Evaluation." *NATE* (24th annual conference, Dec. 1978): 42–45.

Reynolds, Ronald L. "Program Evaluation." In *JPH*, 385–402.

Ruffman, Louis L. "Criteria for Evaluating a Weekday Hebrew School." *Jew Ed* 29 (Fall 1958): 25–31. See also *Ped Rep* 10 (Mar. 1959).

———. "Curriculum Development and Pupil Achievement." *Jew Ed* 31 (Fall 1960): 25–35.

Schwartzman, Louis. "The Good Jewish School: An Evaluation." *Jew Ed* 30 (Winter 1960): 56–59.

Shapiro, Jonathan Z. "The Accountability Movement: Prospects and Proposals in Jewish Education." *Ped Rep* 35 (Mar. 1984): 24–26.

Shluker, David. "Evaluation Is Jewish." *Ped Rep* 36 (Sept. 1985): 7–9.

Slesinger, Zalmen. "Evaluation, the Key to Progress in Jewish Education." *Ped Rep* (Jan. 1962).

———. "Guidelines for Judging the Quality of a School." *Ped Rep* (Mar. 1963).

Steinberg, Harriet P. "The Evaluation Study: A Vehicle for Improving Administration." *Syn Sch* 24 (Winter 1966).

Vanek, Zdenek. "Testing in American Jewish Education." Master's thesis, Teachers Institute, Columbia U., 1952. See summary by Vanek in *Jew Ed* 25 (Winter 1954–55): 36–45.

Weinsbank, Annette B., and Lee S. Shulman. "What Is Taught and What Is Learned: Evaluating a Religious School Program." *Rel Ed* 68 (Nov.–Dec. 1973): 737–48.

Wolfson, Ronald. "Evaluating and Choosing Learning Materials." In *JPH*, 153–59.

ENROLLMENT PRIOR TO 1950

Berkson, Isaac, and Ben Rosen. "Social and Economic Change Reflected in Jewish School Enrollment." In *Jewish Education in the United States*, 174–75. (Selected from Berkson's and Rosen's 1936 *Jewish Education Survey of Cleveland*, Part I.)

Engelman, Uriah Z. "Enrollment in Jewish Schools—Spring 1947." *Jew Ed* 19 (Summer 1948): 31–40.

Synagogue School, The. "Statistics for the Jewish School." *Syn Sch* 5 (Jan. 1947): 59–61.

The Story of Jewish Education in the United States in 1927 in Figures. N.Y.: BJE, Department of Information.

23
ADMINISTRATION

Zederbaum, A. D. "מספרים„ (Data on Jewish Education in the United States in ten large cities: Baltimore, Boston, Chicago, Cincinnati, Cleveland, Newark, New York, Philadelphia, Pittsburgh, and St. Louis). Based on 1927 study. *Sh Hah* (H.) 4 (1929): 400–403.

ENROLLMENT SINCE 1950

AAJE. *Jewish School Census. Information Bulletin* No. 44. Prepared by George Pollak and Gerhard Lang. N.Y., Aug. 1979.

———. *National Census of Jewish Schools. Information Bulletin* No. 28. Prepared by Gerhard Lang. N.Y., 1967.

———. *Trends in Jewish Enrollment.* Prepared by Murray Rockowitz and Gerhard Lang. N.Y., 1976.

Bobrowsky, Ida. "Conducting an Enrollment Campaign." *Ped Rep* 23 (Sept. 1971): 34.

Chipkin, Israel S. "Enrollment in Jewish Schools." *Day* (Jan. 1954).

Della Pergola, Sergio. "Toward a System of Statistical Indicators on Jewish Education in the Diaspora: First Data on Hours of Total and Judaic Instruction in Jewish Schools, 1981/82–1982/83." In *Stu* vol. 3, ed. Aviad, 226–45.

Dubb, Allie A., and Sergio Della Pergola. *First Census of Jewish Schools in the Diaspora, 1981–82, 1982–83: United States of America.* N.Y.: JESNA, 1986. 102 pp.

Eisenberg, Azriel. "The AAJE's 1967 National Census of Jewish Schools." *Jew Ed* 38 (June 1968): 3–5.

———. *World Census of Jewish Education.* N.Y.: World Council on Jewish Education, 1968.

Engelman, Uriah Z. "Jewish Education in Facts and Figures." *Reg* (1951): 27–57; (1959): 56.

———. "Jewish School Enrollment." *AJYB* 56 (1955): 247–51.

Himmelfarb, Harold S., and Sergio Delia Pergola. *Enrollment in Jewish Schools in the Diaspora, Late 1970s.* Jerusalem: Institute of Contemporary Jewry, Hebrew U.

Horowitz, C. Morris. "Estimated Jewish Population and School Enrollment in the United States." *Ped Rep* 4 (Jan. 1953).

———. "Jewish Education in Facts and Figures." *Reg* (1965): 9–24.

Lestchinsky, Jacob. "וויפל אידישע קינדער לערנען איצט אין די אידישע שולען" (How Many Jewish Children Attend Jewish Schools Now?). *For* (Y.) (Oct. 6, 1956).

Malin, Harry "Increasing the Enrollment of Girls." *Syn Sch* 13 (Dec. 1954): 8–9.

Pat, Jacob. "איבער א פערטל מיליאן אידישע קינדער אין אמעריקע באזוכן שולען פאר אידישער ער ציאונג" (Over a Quarter Million Jewish Children in America Attend Jewish Schools). *For* (Y.) (June 10, 1950).

Pickett, Winston. "Census Study on Jewish Education Reveals Surprises." *Northern California Jewish Bulletin* (May 16, 1986): 12.

Schiff, Alvin I. "Student Enrollment and Educational Funding." *Jew Ed* 51 (Summer 1983): 12–17.

Zeitlin, Aaron. "וויפל קינדער אין אמעריקע קריגן אידישע דערציאונג?" (How Many Children in America Receive a Jewish Education?). *Day* (Y.) (Mar. 21, 1956).

RETENTION AND DROPOUTS IN JEWISH EDUCATION

Eisenberg, Azriel. "A Study of 4473 Pupils Who Left High School in 1932–33." *Jew Ed* 7 (Apr.–June 1935): 91–97.

Eisenberg, Azriel, and Seymour Fromer. "Why They Continued: A Study of 553 students in Hebrew High Schools and Colleges." *Jew Ed* 23 (Winter 1952): 49–53, 68.

Grad, Eli. "Factors Related to Continuity in Jewish Education." *Syn Sch* 23 (Sept. 1964): 13.

Klein, Aaron. "Retention of Students in the Elementary Hebrew School." *Syn Sch* 10 (Dec. 1951): 38–41.

Leibman, Morris. "Registration and Elimination in Hebrew Schools." *Jew Ed* 14 (Jan–Mar. 1943): 138–42, 182.

* Selig, Sidney. *Profiling Withdrawals from a Jewish Supplementary School*. Wayne State U., 1972. 276 pp.

Slesinger, Zalmen. "Increasing the Retention Power of the Jewish School." *Ped Rep* 16 (Mar. 1965): 13–16, 31.

Spiro, Jack D. "Bar-Mitzvah Dropouts—A Juvenile Solution." *Jew Teach* 33 (Feb. 1965).

SMALL SCHOOLS

Albert, Burton. *Jewish Education in the Small Community: Partnership between Synagogue and Federation*. CP, GA, 1974. 4 pp.

Eisenberg, Azriel. "Jewish Education in the Small Community." *Un Syn Rev* 27 (Winter 1975): 12–13.

Folkman, Jerome D. "Some Problems in Smaller Religious Schools." *Jew Teach* 15 (Apr. 1947): 29–33.

Frankel, Ephraim. "The School in the Intermediate Size Community." *Jew Ed* 51 (Spring 1983): 11–16.

Ginsburgh, Sylvan J. "Three Years in Rural Jewish Education." *Jew Ed* 18 (Summer 1947): 27–31.

Goldstein, Fabian. "A One Man Faculty." *Syn Sch* 31 (Summer 1973): 31–34.

Gordon, Susan. "Curriculum for the Small, One-Day-a-Week Jewish School." A total curriculum for ages 5–12. Master's project, HUC–JIR, 1976.

———. "The Small Congregation." In *JPH*, 363–81.

Hefterman, A. "החנוך העברי בערי השדה" (Jewish Education in Suburbia). *Sh Hah* (H.) 3 (Sept. 1943): 234–238.

Hollander, Arthur S., and Moses B. Sachs. "Program of Studies for Schools in Smaller Congregations." *Syn Sch* 23 (Fall 1964): 19–23.

Kaplan, Deborah B. "A Joint School Adventure: A Consolidated School for Small Communities." *Compass* 4 (Spring 1981).

Lipson, Norman S. "Rearing and Educating Children in the Small Community—or, Ana-tevka American Style." *SWJT* 7 (Spring 1975): 7–8.

Lister, Rebecca, and Louis Lister. *The Smaller Religious School*. UAHC.

Moskowitz, Nachama Skolnick. "The Teacher in the Small School." *Ped Rep* 33 (Oct. 1982): 24–26.

Page, Fred G. "The Small Synagogue School." *Syn Sch* 26 (Spring 1968): 17–31.

Shostuk, Robert. *Small-Town Jewry Tell Their Story: A Survey of B'nai B'rith Membership in Small Communities in the United States and Canada*. Washington, D.C.: B'nai B'rith Vocational Bureau Service, 1953.

Wachs, Saul P. "Supervision in a Small School." *Syn Sch* 20 (1961).

GLEANINGS

Krug, Mark M.,
"The success or failure of the principal or educational director depends primarily upon the degree in which he will succeed in establishing an effective and mutually respectful relationship with his school board, the faculty, the rabbi, the pupils and the parents. . . . First and foremost it is imperative for a principal to gain the respect and support of a well knit and influential faculty. At the same time we must recognize that in some congregations the position of the principal and his re-engagement will depend upon his development of a satisfactory relationship with the chairman of the board."
"The Principal and the School Committee." *Jew Ed* 23 (Summer 1952), 26.

Ruffman, Louis L., and Henry R. Goldberg,
"The principal is in key position to determine the character, direction, emphasis and effectiveness of the school. He is effective to the extent that, by virtue of his personality, training and relationship he

maintains with all elements involved in the conduct of the school, he gives constant evidence that he is actually exercising his role of leadership. He cannot function only as an administrative technician. He is constantly faced with the responsibility of judging values and determining policy. . . . He must continue to think in terms of the philosophy and aims of Jewish education and keep abreast of all significant developments in the field, if his leadership is to be effective in developing a dynamic program for his school and a high level of achievement from his staff. He must have a definite philosophy of Jewish education which he transmits and interprets to his teachers, parents, and lay leaders. Above all, he must be imbued with a sense of dedicated leadership."

"The Job of the Principal." *Ped Rep* 4 (Nov. 1952), 3.

Franzblau, Abraham N.,
"The capacity of the teacher to identify with the principal is another very important element. That is the essence of drama. The good play is the one with which you can identify. It lifts you out of yourself and you get something out of it. It may influence your life, your thinking.

As a principal, you've got to bear that fact in mind. You cannot be isolated from your teachers. You cannot be a voice speaking to them out of a box. You've got to be a real individual with whom they can identify, a sound, acceptable authority figure. They also have to identify with the goals of the institution, to transmit them effectively to the children. These unconscious things are very influential in the kind of situation we deal with in our schools.

In psychologically sound supervision we build up the teacher's ego, not tear it down; we stimulate the teacher's drive to want to advance, to want to achieve. We recognize that what we put into the teacher is of minimal value in comparison with what we bring out of her. We increase to the greatest extent by pointing up a direction here and there, and allowing the teacher to grow. If we could just unlock a small portion of what the teacher already has inside of herself, we could make supervisory work more effective.

One reason why we often have difficulties with our 7th, 8th and 9th graders (everybody knows those are the tough years) is because we continue to treat them like children. We assume that religious school is a continuum, whereas there is a very sharp dichotomy, at this point.

There are many who look with anguish at the declining enrollment figures of the high school years. What is happening is not a rejection of what we have to offer but a momentary shift in interest. Our children begin to be interested in different things, girls in boys, and boys in girls. The whole realm of sex and family life opens up before them, a realm which is very important for us and in which Judaism has a great stake. When we recognize this, we have very exciting religious high school programs. We can almost set up a test of how effective a religious school high school department is by the number of 'shidduchim' which come out of it.

Instead of making the children feel guilty when they say 'I'm not interested in the textbook anymore, we ought to make their desire for togetherness the springboard for our youth activities. The study comes second, but it comes along. In places where this is done, a well-rounded program of youth work and education has proven successful."

"The Contribution of Psychiatry to the Principal's Task." *Jew Teach* 23 (May 1955), 3, 4, 5.

Dushkin, Alexander M., and Uriah Z. Engelman,
"Possessing Jewish school principal's licenses (from any source whatever): One-day school principals 12.9%, Weekday Afternoon schools 12.3%, Day schools less than 1%. It would seem therefore that the majority of Jewish school principals do not have Jewish teaching licenses and only a small proportion have special training for their tasks as principals. We point the finger to this phase of the Jewish educational problem in the belief that it is crucial to the future improvement of

Jewish teaching. The programs for training Jewish teachers have been inadequate enough but practically nothing has been done thus far by the American Jewish community to train school principals and supervisors. At present there are very few 'sources' for licensing Jewish principals. It is one of the tasks which the National Board of License must undertake in cooperation with its local accredited boards. A large plan of proper compensations, fellowships and other inducements needs to be developed as part of a national effort to procure trained school principals and supervisors...

"Evidently, Jewish educators are right in insisting that our problem is no longer that of getting our children in Jewish school, but rather of having them stay in the school long enough to make that education valuable...

"Enrollment is proportionately higher in the smaller communities than in the larger, in the less populous than in the more populous, in towns than in big cities."

Jewish Education in the United States (1959), 126, 226, 228.

NATE,
"Whereas the 88th Annual Convention of the Central Conference of American Rabbis adopted a resolution on congregational professionals....
We call upon the professional organizations of Cantors, Educators and Administrators to maintain their efforts to achieve a higher degree of professionalism in within their own range. We call upon the Central Conference of American Rabbis to be in the forefront of the effort to assure that those who occupy such positions in our congregations are individuals who meet the professional standards."

NATE (23rd annual conference, Dec. 1977), 64.

Syme, Daniel,
"The Total Temple Educator must be a literate Jew and a trained educational specialist. Accordingly, I believe that those of us who have not already done so must obtain at least a Masters Degree in Jewish Studies and at least a Masters Degree in education, specializing in curriculum, teacher training, and methodology. Three summers spent at the HUC–JIR schools of Education, Gratz College, Spertus College, or local universities will help to begin that lifelong process of professional development. Next, the Total Temple Educator will have to know and administer programs of informal education. Experience at our UAHC camps, work with chavurot, familiarity with station learning, values clarification, confluent education, role-play, simulation, and other similar techniques will, therefore, be essential. Third, the Total Temple Educator will be required to administer programs for adults, parents and families. Libraries of materials from the UAHC and elsewhere should be accumulated now, course outlines prepared, booklets of activities compiled. We must become human computer retrieval systems in anticipation of the demands soon to be made of us."

"Shaping Our Destinies—the New Temple Educator." *NATE* (24th annual conference, Dec. 1978), 10–11.

Rosen, Gladys,
"The Jewish Woman's educational wagon is still hitched to a patriarchal star. Most study materials ascribe social roles and character traits according to sex in such a way as to reserve to men the most highly prized characteristics such as intelligence, initiative and emotional strength while women have been defined in socio-biological terms with their functions largely limited to the home and family life."

"Teaching about the Role of Women." *Ped Rep* 32 (Fall 1980), 27.

National Board of License–JESNA,
"Cognizant of the fact that the principal of the Jewish school cannot hope to gain the community's recognition and respect for himself and his profession unless he demonstrates his qualifications and all-around preparedness for his tasks, the National Board of License in February 1962, decided to award deserving school administrators with a special license. Its program for certification of principals came in response to the rapidly expanding role of the Jewish school administrator and

the need to enforce professional standards in this vital area of Jewish education.

To implement its decision, the National Board appointed a standing Committee for Principals' Certification. In addition to carrying responsibility for procedures and standards, the Committee is charged with administering qualifying examinations, interviewing applicants, and coordinating the four affiliated local licensing boards—in New York, Philadelphia, Chicago, and Los Angeles—whose principals' certification program antedated its own."

National Board of License: Requirements and Procedures (Rev. ed. N.Y.: JESNA, 1982), 12.

Joseph, Samuel K.,
"There are four major weaknesses in teacher evaluation as it is presently practiced by Jewish schools:

1. Teacher evaluation has a low priority in our Jewish schools.
2. Teacher evaluation is filled with discord. There is suspicion and uncomfortableness.
3. Evaluation is generally done to teachers. The teacher is the passive object in the process.
4. Teacher evaluation is often used to make judgments whether the teacher is 'good' or 'bad.' It does not tell a teacher how he/she can improve."

"Teacher Effectiveness." *Ped Rep* 33 (Oct. 1982), 31.

Schiff, Alvin I.,
"Many principals gravitate toward the administrative dimensions of their positions because they feel more comfortable with them. It is to be hoped that once they gain more competence and self-confidence in their roles as educational supervisors, they will spend the necessary time—indeed, the largest segment of their daily schedule—working in those areas of principalship that ultimately lead to better teaching and more learning."

Ped Rep 24 (Mar. 1983).

Bennett, Alan D.,
"Reform education has been transformed . . . by NATE's profound preoccupation with professional standards. When first efforts to provide correspondence and regional study through HUC–JIR did not succeed, NATE devised its own professional development programs, utilizing educational colleagues and rabbis and linking membership requirements to professional growth. School certification standards were enunciated, standards which still serve NATE's accreditation teams. Curriculum award projects (Gamoran, Kaminker and Chapman Awards) continue to motivate educators to experiment towards educational excellence. The Fellow in Religious Education (FRE) title, administered through the Commission, encouraged many NATE members to reach ever higher levels of competence and excellence.

Yet, as forward looking and as demanding as the FRE was, it did not fully satisfy the quest for recognized excellence. That need is now met through the Reform Jewish Educator (RJE) program, which rewards the very highest of standards and recognizes that the educator is competent in all aspects of synagogue education, not only in the religious school."

"The Reform Jewish Educator—Then and Now." *RJ* 16 (Spring 1988), 13.

24 THE TEACHER

PRIOR TO 1950

(See also chapters 20, 21, 22, 23)

Chipkin, Israel S. "The Jewish Teacher and the Jewish Community." *Recon* 2 (Oct. 12, 1936): 11.

Finkelstein, Louis. "Our Teachers." *RA* (1934): 158–78.

Gamoran, Emanuel. "המורה העברי באמריקה" (The Hebrew Teacher in America). *Sh Hah* (H.) 3 (1928): 279–85.

Glick, M. "למצב המורה העברי באמריקה" (On the Status of the Hebrew Teacher in America). *Sh Hah* (H.) 2 (1927): 41–44.

Golub, Jacob S. "An Experiment with a Full-Time Sunday School Teacher." *Jew Ed* 18 (Summer 1947): 22–26.

Isorov, A. "גורל המורה" (The Fate of the Teacher). In *JB* (H.), 458–62.

Jew Ed. "The Jewish Teacher and Economic Realism" (editorial). 8 (Apr./June 1936): 61–62, 88.

The Jewish School and Democracy. "The Jewish Teacher and the Peace." 4 (Nov. 1945): 3–5.

Kushtai, Sh. "על המורה" (On the Teacher). *Sh Hah* (H.) 2 (1926): 28–33.

Levinson-Lavi, M. "נחפשה דרכנו" (Let Us Seek Our Direction). On the teacher's role. *Hadoar* (H.) 12 (Nov. 4, 1932).

Simon, Abram. "The Task of the Jewish Religious School Teacher." *Jew Teach* 1 (Nov. 1932): 5–6.

Singer, A. *The Jewish Educator.* Jamaica, N.Y.: printed by the author, 1922. 84 pp.

Touroff, Nissan. "השתתפות המורה העברי בחיים הציבוריים" (Participation of the Hebrew Teacher in Communal Life). *Sh Hah* (H.) 5 (1931): 6–12.

Zeligs, Dorothy. "The Teacher Looks at His Job." *Jew Ed* 19 (Summer 1948): 26–30.

SINCE 1950

AAJE. *Our Teachers* (newsletter of the National Committee on Teacher Education and Welfare). N.Y.

———. *There's a Career for You in Jewish Education.* Compiled by Hyman Chanover. N.Y.

Adler, Morris. "Eulogy For A 'Moreh Vatik'." *Jew Ed* 34 (Winter 1964): 118–19.

Adri, Battya. "יחסי המורים והתלמידים באמריקה" (Relationships between Teachers and Students in America). *Hadoar* (H.) 50 (Mar. 5, 1971).

Azrieli, Shlomo. "Oh, Jewish Teacher, What Is Required of Thee?" (editorial). *Jew Ed* 24 (Fall 1953): 2–3.

Baumgard, Herbert M. "The Teacher as Role Model." *Compass* 4 (Spring 1981): 24.

Brickman, William W. "Teachers for Today and Tomorrow." *RA* (Spring 1961): 22–36.

Cahn, Steven M. "Ten Commandments for Teachers." *Recon* 44 (June 1978): 11.

Chanover, Hyman. "The Central Role of the Teacher." *Congress Biweekly* 26 (May 25, 1959): 7–10.

———. "Will These Be Tomorrow's Teachers?" *Jew Ed* 31 (Spring 1961): 22–36.

Chanover, Hyman, and Zalmen Slesinger. "What Price the Jewish Teacher?" *Congress Weekly* (Oct. 29, 1956): 12–14.

Chomsky, William. "עשר מדות טובות במורה" (Ten Good Qualities of the Teacher). *Sh Hah* (H.) 11 (1951): 186–91.

Cohen, Beryl D. "The Jewish Teacher." *Jew Spec* 27 (Dec. 1962).

Cohen, Jack J. "The Future of the Hebrew Teacher." *Jew Ed* 27 (Spring 1957): 18–22.

Dubin, Bernard. "The Role of the Jewish Educator in the Planning Process." *Jew Ed* 47 (Winter 1979): 4–7.

Hadoar. "בעית המורה ובעית החנוך העברי" (The Problem of the Teacher and of Jewish Education). (H.) 40 (June 16, 1961): 533–34.

Honor, Leo L. "The Teacher's Calling." *Congress Weekly* 23 (Oct. 29, 1956): 7–9.

Jew Ed. "The Jewish School Teacher—Today and Tomorrow." Articles by 24 participants. 55 (Spring 1987): 4–62.

Klutznick, Philip M. "The Role of the Teacher in Giving Meaning to Our Cultural Heritage." *Jew Ed* 27 (Spring 1957): 37.

Levitsky, J. "Jewish Education and the Jewish Teacher." *A Zion* 57 (Oct. 1966): 23–25.

Millgram, Abraham E. "The Jewish Educator: His Woes and Joys." *Congress Biweekly* 23 (Oct. 29, 1956): 7–9.

Pilch, Judah. "Jewish Teachers for Tomorrow." *Jew Ed* 27 (Spring 1957): 38–40.

Pollak, George. "A Vision of the Jewish Educator." *Jew Ed* 48 (Summer 1980): 39–43.

Ravid, Zvulun. "הפסיכולוגיה של המורה" (The Psychology of the Teacher). *Sh Hah* (H.) 30 (1970): 156–64.

Savan, Isaac. "המורה כמנהיג חנוכי" (The Teacher as Educational Leader). *Sh Hah* (H.) 37 (1978).

Scharfstein, Zevi. "אורח חיים למורה: עיונים בנפש הילד ובדרכי הלמוד" (A Guide for the Teacher—Studies about the Nature of the Child and Methodology) (H.). N.Y.: JEC, 1959. 156 pp.

———. "אשיחה עם המורים" (Talks with Teachers) (H.). Israel: Organization of Teachers in Israel, 1962. 180 pp.

———. "הרהורים על הגורל המורה" (Thoughts on the Fate of the Teacher). *Sh Hah* (H.) 11 (Sept. 1951): 183–85.

Schiff, Alvin I. "The Jewish School Teacher—Today and Tomorrow." *Jew Ed* 55 (Spring 1987): 4–7.

———. *Salute to the Teachers.* N.Y.: JEC, 1959.

Wolk, A. "מחנכים ריידן זיך אראפ פון הארצן" (Educators Express Their Inner Feelings). *Day* (Y.) (June 21, 1965).

THE PROFESSION PRIOR TO 1950

Blumenfield, Samuel M. "The Elementary Jewish Teacher in Jewish Tradition—His Economic Status and Social Position." *Jew Ed* 17 (Feb. 1946): 24–30.

Chipkin, Israel S. "המורה העברי בארצות הברית ומשכורתו" (The Hebrew Teacher in the United States and His Salary). *Hadoar* 9 (Oct. 3, 1930): 756–57; (Oct. 17, 1930) 774–75.

Dushkin, Alexander M. "Qualifications of the Ideal Jewish Teacher." *Jew Teach* 1 (Jan. 1916): 51–61.

———. "דרגות משכורת למורים עברים" (Salary Levels for Hebrew Teachers). *Sh Hah* (H.) 3 (1937): 150–52.

Edelstein, Menahem M. "מעמד המורה העברי באמריקה" (Status of the Jewish Teacher in America). In *JB* (H.), 221–45.

Eisenberg, Azriel, Leo L. Honor, David Todes, Shimon Pollock, and Uriah Z. Engelman. "A Report: The Professionalization of the Jewish Teacher." *Jew Ed* 19 (Fall 1947): 14–24.

Friedland, A. H. "The Profession of the Hebrew Teacher." *Jew Ed* 6 (Jan./Mar. 1934): 6–13.

Gamoran, Emanuel. "The Growth of the Jewish Teacher." *Jew Teach* (Nov. 1932): 7–13.

Nudelman, William A. "The Social Philosophy of the Jewish Teacher." *Jew Ed* 5 (Oct.–Dec. 1933): 156–60.

Schoolman, Albert P. "The Jewish Teacher and the Profession of Jewish Education." *Jew Ed* 3 (Oct.–Dec. 1931): 152–55, 184.

———. "Jewish Teachers Unionize" (editorial). *Jew Ed* 11 (Apr. 1939): 4–5.

Twersky, Yochanan. "המורה וחניכו„ (The Educator and His Student) (psychological study). *Sh Hah* (H.) 3 (1927): 5–8.

Whiteman, Kalman. "מדבור למעשה„ (From Theory to Practice) (teacher's role). *Hadoar* (H.) 1 (Dec. 15, 1921): 2.

THE PROFESSION SINCE 1950

AAJE. *Better Personnel Practices*. N.Y., 1963, 1971, 1980.

———. *Our Teachers* (newsletter of the National Committee on Teacher Education and Welfare). N.Y.

———. *Salaries of Teachers in Jewish Schools*. George Pollak and Gerhard Lang, comps. N.Y., 1980. 25 pp.

———. *Salary Scales for Full-Time Teaching, 1975–1976*. N.Y., April 1977. 20 pp.

Ackerman, Walter I. "Of Jewish Schools, Teachers and Other Things Too." In *Jewish Education and Jewish Identity: An Update*. N.Y.: AJC, 1982.

Agris, Aryeh. "Teacher Unionization as a Positive Force in Jewish Education." *Ped Rep* 33 (Apr. 1982): 6–8.

Chanover, Hyman. "What Price the Jewish Teacher?" *Congress Weekly* (Oct. 29, 1956): 12–14.

———. *There's a Career for You in Jewish Education*. N.Y.: AAJE.

Chazan, Barry. "Perspectives on the Jewish Teaching Profession." *Jew Ed* 40 (Mar. 1970): 24–29.

Dinin, Samuel. "The Future of the Jewish Teaching Profession" (editorial). *Jew Ed* 35 (Fall 1964): 3.

* Edelstein, Menachem M. *The Status of the Professional Jewish Teacher in the Schools of America with Special Reference to New York City*. Dropsie U., 1951. 225 pp.

———. "History of the Development of a Jewish Teaching Profession in America." *Jew Ed* 23 (Winter 1952): 36–42, 62; (Summer 1952): 45–53, 68; (Fall 1952): 34–48; 25 (Fall 1954): 55–66.

Frankel, Max. "Our Teacher Incentive Program." *Ped Rep* 36 (Jan. 1985): 30–31.

Gamoran, Emanuel, and Mamie Gamoran. *Talks to Jewish Teachers*. N.Y.: 1967. 175 pp.

Glass, Charlotte. "Teachers Do Have a Role in Curriculum Development." *Ped Rep* 32 (Fall 1980).

Glatzer, Shoshana. "The Teachers' Center—Food for the Teacher's Soul." *Ped Rep* 33 (Oct. 1982): 27–29.

Grishaver, Joel Lurie. "You Too Can Own Your Own Plastic Inflatable Teachers'." *AM* (Winter 1978): 6–7.

Hershon, Jerome L. "How Can Teachers Train Students in Self-Discipline?" *Ped Rep* 35 (Oct. 1984): 10–12.

Hochberg, Hillel, and Gerhard Lang. "Salary Scales for Full-Time Teaching in Jewish Schools Outside New York City, 1969–1970." *Ped Rep* 23 (Sept. 1971): 3.

Honor, Leo L. "הוראת עברית בתור פרופסיה„ (Hebrew Teaching as a Profession). *Sh Hah* (H.) 11 (Sept. 1951): 162–72.

Joseph, Samuel K. *How to Be a Jewish Teacher: An Invitation to Make a Difference*. L.A.: Torah Aura Productions, 1987.

Katz, Betsy Dolgin. "The Jewish Teacher Center." *Compass* 1 (Summer 1978): 5–7.

Klein, Aaron. "על חובת המורה להשתלם„ (The Teacher's Obligation for Self Improvement). *Sh Hah* (H.) 27 (Fall 1967): 59–63.

Kodesh, Shlomo. "החינוך היהודי בארצה"ב בעיני מחנך ישראלי„ (Jewish Education in the

United States as Viewed by an Israeli Educator). *Hadoar* (H.) 51 (June 1972).

Lamm, Norman. "The Jewish Educator and Jewish Education: Four Myths." *Jew Ed* 45 (Spring 1977): 29–32.

Levitats, Isaac. "מעמד המורה העברי באמריקה" (The Status of the Hebrew Teacher in America). *Sh Hah* (H.) 13 (Summer 1953): 240–43.

* Lukinsky, Joseph Sender. *Teaching Responsibility: A Case Study in Curriculum Development*. Harvard U., 1967–68.

Marcus, Audrey Friedman, ed. *The Jewish Teacher's Handbook*. 2 vols. Denver: ARE, 1980, 1981.

Morris, Elaine. "The Melton Approach: Accent on the Teacher." *Un Syn Rev* (Winter 1979).

Pollack, Shimon. "המורה העברי ומעמדו באה״ב" (The Hebrew Teacher and His Status in the United States). In *PDE* (H.), 107–13.

Pollak, George. "Teaching Conditions in Jewish Schools." *Ped Rep* 33 (Oct. 1982): 8–10.

Rabinowitz, Zina. "המורה העברי בארצות הברית" (The Hebrew Teacher in the United States). *Hadoar* (H.) 31 (Oct. 31, 1952): 838–45.

Rose, Ruth W. "The Life Cycle Pinah Limud." Brief discussion of the development and construction of a life cycle learning center (teacher resource center). Master's project, HUC-JIR, 1977.

Rosenberg, Chaim. "המורה, האגודה והצבור" (The Teacher, the Union and the Community). *Hadoar* (H.) 34 (Feb. 25, 1955): 319.

Rosoff, Barbara. "Improving the Teacher-Student Relationship." *Ped Rep* 37 (Feb. 1986): 9–12.

Rossel, Seymour. *Managing the Jewish Classroom: How to Transform Yourself into a Master Teacher*. L.A.: Torah Aura Productions, 1987.

Rubinstein, Simha. "דיוקונו של מורה" (Profile of a Teacher). *Hadoar* (H.) 34 (Sept. 30, 1955): 783, 791.

Rubinsztejn, Zionna. "Using an Outdated Textbook as the Basis for Sub-Group Teaching and Learning Centers." Master's thesis, Department of Jewish Education, JTS, 1989.

Schatz, Shirley. "Teacher Retreats." In *JPH*, 175–82.

Schiff, Alvin I. "Focus on the Teacher" (editorial essay). *Jew Ed* 40 (Winter 1970): 9–12.

———. "Looking towards the 21st Century: Who Needs Hebrew Teachers in Our Supplementary Schools" (editorial essay). *Jew Ed* 51 (Winter 1983): 3–7.

———. "On the Making of the Jewish Teaching Profession." *Jew Ed* (Fall 1985): 2–5.

Schoem, David. "Inside the Classroom: Reflections of a Troubled People." *Jew Ed* 48 (Spring 1980): 35–41.

Schwartzman, Sylvan D. "Planning for Teacher Growth." *Jew Teach* 34 (Apr. 1966): 16–17.

Schweitzer, Ira H. "Discipline: The Classroom Teacher as Social Group Worker." *Ped Rep* 35 (Oct. 1984): 14–15.

Shane, Paul. "An Exploration of the Content and Structure of Hebrew School Teachers' Conceptions of Their Own Teaching." Master's thesis, Brandeis U., 1971.

Shloush, Rita. "Using Teaching Centers to Teach Judaic Studies." *Ped Rep* 32 (Winter 1981).

Stern, Jay. "The Jewish School Teacher—Today and Tomorrow." *Jew Ed* 55 (Winter 1988): 38–40.

Stern, Kenneth E. "Emotional Conditioning." *Jew Teach* 32 (Oct. 1963): 3–5.

Teller, Gerald A. "Teacher Burn-Out." *Ped Rep* 33 (Oct. 1982): 10–11.

Wachs, Saul. *The Jewish Teacher: Professional Status*. N.Y.: AJC, 1984. 36 pp.

ISRAELIS TEACHING IN AMERICAN JEWISH SCHOOLS

Chanover, Hyman. "Israelis Teaching in American Jewish Schools: Findings of an Exploratory Survey." In *Jan 3*, 227–51.

Dushkin, Alexander M. "Israel and the Training of Jewish Teachers for the Diaspora." In *Jan 3*, 208–25.

Feldman, Lisa, Ari Lloyd Fridkus, and Bonnie Slavitt-Moore. "Israelis Teaching in American Jewish Schools: A Comparative Study." *Jew Ed* 53 (Summer 1985): 24–26.

Glickman, Jacob. „בשולי בעיותיו של השליחות הישראלית" (On the Problems of the Israeli Teacher Exchange) (H.). *Ed As* (1966): 120.

Goelman, Elazar. "The Vanguard Role of the Israeli Teacher." *Jew Ed* 25 (Summer 1954): 42–49, 64.

Grad, Eli. "The Israeli Teacher in Our Classroom" *Ed As* (1966): 68–77.

Israeli, Eytan. *Al Ha'mifgash Shel Morim Sh'lihim Mi'Yisrael im Ha'hinuch HaYehudi Ha'Amerikani* (On the Meeting of Exchange Teachers from Israel with American Jewish Educators) (H.). N.Y.: Council on the Teaching of Hebrew, 1970.

———. "On Israeli Teachers in American Jewish Education." *Hadoar* (H.) 51 (Feb. 1972).

———. *Morim Sh'lihim Mi'Yisrael Hoveh V'Sikuyim* (Israeli Exchange Teachers: Present and Prospects) (H.). N.Y.: DEC, WZO, 1972.

Kessler, Aharon. "Israeli Teachers in American Jewish Schools." *Jew Ed* 42 (Spring 1973): 55–61.

Kochvi, I. B. „מורים ישראלים וילדי אמריקה" (Israeli Teachers and American Children). *Sh Hah* (H.) 12 (June 1952): 166–67.

Kodesh, Shlomo. „הפגישה הגורלית בחדר הכיתה" (A Fateful Meeting in the Classroom—An Israeli Teacher's Experience in an American Classroom) (H.). *Ed As* (1966): 120–36.

* Levine, Allan Marshall. *Influence of Different Cultural Backgrounds on Teacher-Pupil Interaction and Teacher Attitudes of Israeli and American Teachers in Jewish Education*. U. of Southern California, 1978.

Pomerantz, Hyman. "The Exchange Visitors Program" (teachers from Israel). *Ped Rep* 33 (Oct. 1982): 12–13.

Shneider, Sh. „המורה הישראלי והוראת היסטוריה וספרות באמריקה" (The Israeli Teacher and the Instruction of History and Literature in America). *Hadoar* (H.) 51 (June 30, 1972).

———. „על מידת נחיצותם של מורים מישראל" (On the Need of Teachers from Israel). *Hadoar* (H.) 51 (July 7, 1972).

———. „לבעית המורים-השליחים מישראל" (On the Problems of Exchange Teachers from Israel). *Hadoar* (H.) 51 (June 2, 1971).

* Weinbaum, Joseph. *Educational Problems Arising from Cultural Differences between Israeli Teachers and Jewish American Students*. Northwestern U., 1977. 193 pp.

GLEANINGS

Benderly, Samson (1903),
"A definite progressive system of education will in course of time evolve its own text-books. Text-books, to be of any use, must be based upon the experience of able teachers. We must, therefore, first have the able teachers and the experience, and the text-books will follow as a natural result."
Quoted by Nathan Winter in his *Jewish Education in a Pluralist Society* (1966), 54.

Greenstone, Julius (1914),
"It is essential that teaching in the Jewish religious schools becomes an honorable profession, commanding the respect and the appreciation of the community expressed in adequate remuneration. The salaries of the Jewish religious school teachers should be proportionally higher than those of the secular teacher, because the qualifications demanded of the former are higher."
Quoted by Israel Chipkin, *AJYB* 38 (1936–37), 107–8.

A. Eisenberg, L. L. Honor, S. Pollock, D. Todes, and U. Z. Engelman, report on the professionalization of the Jewish teacher, Recommendation, 3.
"While every effort should be made to improve the economic status of the teacher and to give consideration to his material welfare, it is important at the same time from the standpoint of those who are in the profession and those who are being encouraged to enter the profession, that Hebrew teaching be presented as an ideal. Unless teachers have faith in the value of the work which they are doing, unless

they recognize that this work is fundamental to the building of future American life, their work will be of little value. In other words, Jewish education must be accepted as a Profession, not from the standpoint of a career but from the standpoint of a calling or an ideal."
Jew Ed 19 (Fall 1947), 23.

Heschel, Abraham Joshua,
"We do not celebrate kings and heroes—we celebrate teachers—Moses and Rabbi Akiba. The teacher is the central pillar of Jewish living, past, present, and future. ... Judaism is teacher centered. And, according to its tradition, God Himself teaches. This implies, however, that the teacher has a very great responsibility. ...

"The teacher is not an automatic fountain from which intellectual beverages may be obtained. He is either a witness or a stranger. To guide a pupil into the promised land, he must have been there himself. When asking himself: Do I stand for what I teach? Do I believe what I say? He must be able to answer in the affirmative.

"What we need more than anything else is not textbooks but text people. It is the personality of the teacher which is the text that the pupils read; the text they will never forget. The modern teacher while not wearing a snowy beard, is a link in the chain of a tradition. He is the intermediary between the past and the present as well. Yet he is also the creator of the future of our people. He must teach the pupils to evaluate the past in order to clarify their future."
Jew Ed 24 (Fall 1953), 9, 19. See also *The Insecurity of Freedom* (1965), 223–41.

Silver, Abba Hillel (1955),
"The profession of teacher is a noble one. The profession of the teaching of religion is the noblest. Teaching is vital for the survival of any civilization. It is the sine qua non—the indispensable condition for our survival as a Jewish community. ... This is the major highway leading to the solution of nearly all of our problems—more time, more teachers and better teachers."
Quotable Quotes (AAJE), 3.

Honor, Leo L.,
"We have made a great deal of progress in Jewish education during the past forty-odd years. Beautiful and adequate school buildings are now a common sight. Fine textbooks are being written. The curriculum has been enriched through music, artcraft, and visual aids. Moreover, our conception of curriculum has been enlarged. We are in great danger, however, of losing all we have gained if we permit the disappearance of the full-time professional teacher who gives all of his time and energy to Jewish education.

"The teacher must be concerned with the future of Jewish life in America. He must be convinced that only through his efforts and those of his colleagues in his and kindred professions, together with the influence and inspiration which will emanate from Israel, can we help build the kind of Jewish life which will make it a dynamo of future creativity."
Congress Weekly 23 (Oct. 29, 1956), 8.

Cohen, Jack J.,
"Spiritual leadership has no necessary connection with a man's office. But every office must become for its holder a sanctuary within which he strives for spiritual perfection. The Hebrew teacher is no less subject to this demand than anyone else, and the Jewish community can as little afford to ignore his contribution to Judaism than it can ignore that of the rabbi."
Quotable Quotes (AAJE), 4.

Millgram, Abraham E.,
"The businessman may regard with pride his financial success, the physician his medical achievements. But he who has labored patiently in the field of Jewish education can look with satisfaction at personalities he has influenced, changed and, in a sense, created."
Quotable Quotes, 4. Also in *Congress Weekly* (Mar. 31, 1958).

Schiff, Alvin I.,
"Jewish teaching is now beginning to assume the status of a profession. Despite many set-backs the emergence and growth of new educational institutions have aided the teaching profession. Various landmarks highlight the development

of the Hebrew teaching profession in New York City. These are: the Hebrew Teachers Union, founded in 1923; the Board of License, established in 1923; the Board of Review, organized in 1929; the Jewish Education Association Code of Practice issued in 1933, and reformulated by the Board of Review in 1944; the Group Insurance Plan, initiated in 1934; the Jewish Teachers Retirement Association founded in 1946; and the SAAD plan, initiated in 1947. All told, the Hebrew teacher has come a long way. A challenge, however, still remains for teachers to help their own cause."

A Salute to the Hebrew Teacher (N.Y.: JEC Press, 1960), 6.

Dinin, Samuel,

"We must recognize . . . that a strictly professional or even unionist approach, important as it is to the solution of some of the problems posed before this conference, cannot contribute much to the solution of all of the problems raised. The status of the profession of Jewish Education rests ultimately on the quality of Jewish life lived in America, on the level of aspirations of the parents of our children, on the values and commitments by which American Jews live, on the understanding of our lay leaders, and on the direction and control of the institutions and agencies which serve the Jewish community. Hence, even more than the public school teacher, the professional Jewish teacher must be totally involved in the life of the community, if he is to effect any appreciable change in the profession of Jewish education."

"Strengthening the Profession of Jewish Education." *Jew Ed* 35 (Fall 1964), 6.

Kaunfer, Neil,

"Jewish education is an unrewarding profession financially and in terms of status. It is also part-time work. The result of all this is that only the very dedicated or the very incompetent would choose to enter the field."

In *Cat 2*, p. 208.

25 THE RABBI AND JEWISH EDUCATION

GENERAL (SELECTED)

Bamberger, Bernard J. "The American Rabbi—His Changing Role." *Jud* 3 1954): 488–497.

Baron, Salo W. "The Image of the Rabbi, Formerly and Today." *RA* 24 (1960): 84–92. Also in his *Steeled by Adversity*, 147–57.

Ben-Horin, Meir. "Toward a New Generation of American Rabbis." *Recon* (Sept. 19, 1969): 7–14.

Bernstein, Philip. "The Role and Functions of the America Rabbi." *CCAR* 79 (1966): 226.

Con Jud. "The Congregational Rabbi and the Conservative Synagogue" (symposium). 29 (Winter 1975).

Eckstein, Simon L. "The Rabbi in a Changing Community." *Jew Life* 19 (Nov. 1951).

Elazar, Daniel J., and Rela Geffer Monson. "The Evolving Roles of American Rabbis." *Modern Judaism* 21 (Feb. 1982): 73–89.

* Engel, Gerald. *Sons of the Prophets: The Training Needs and Functions of the American Rabbi*. Columbia U., 1954.

Feldman, Abraham J. *The American Reform Rabbi: A Profile of a Profession*. N.Y.: Bloch, 1965. 242 pp.

Friedman, Leslie. "Role-Related Stress: A Report on a Nationwide Study of Conservative and Reform Rabbis." *RJ* 32 (Winter 1985): 53–63.

Goldin, Judah. "Interdenominational Activities of American Rabbis." *Contemporary Jewish Record* 4 (Aug. 1941): 349–56.

———. "The Thinking of the Rabbis." *Jud* 6 (1956): 3–12.

Gottschalk, Alfred. *Your Future as a Rabbi*. N.Y.: Rosen, 1987. 127 pp.

Greenberg, Simon. "The Rabbinate and the Jewish Community Structure." *Con Jud* 23 (Spring 1969): 52–59.

* Greenwald, Eli B. *Rabbinic Education in the United States, 1867–1939*. Dropsie U., 1975.

Gurock, Jeffrey S. "Resisters and Accommodators: Varieties of Orthodox Rabbis in America, 1886–1983." *Amer Jew Arc* 35 (Nov. 1983): 100–187. Also in *The American Rabbinate*, edited by Jacob Rader Marcus and Abraham J. Peck, 10–97. Hoboken, N.J.: Ktav, 1985.

Hertzberg, Arthur. "The Changing American Rabbinate." *Mid* 12 (Jan. 1966): 16–29.

Hoenig, Martin A., and Stuart H. Gilbreath. "The Counseling and Pastoral Role of the Rabbis in the American Jewish Community." *JSS* 31 (Jan. 1969): 20–24.

Kaplan, Mordecai M. "The Rabbinic Training of Our Day." *Jew Ed* 5 (Apr./June 1933): 67–78.

Karp, Abraham J. "The Conservative Rabbi—'Dissatisfied But Not Unhappy'." *Amer Jew Arc* 35 (Nov. 1983): 188–262. Also in *The American Rabbinate*, edited by Jacob Rader Marcus and Abraham J. Peck, 98–172. Hoboken, N.J.: Ktav, 1985.

Katz, Robert. *The Role of the Rabbi: Selected Readings.* Rev. ed. Cincinnati: HUC-JIR, 1974.

Lenn, Theodore I., et al. *Rabbi and Synagogue in Reform Judaism.* N.Y.: CCAR. 412 pp.

Lieberman, Morris. "The Role and Function of the Modern Rabbi." *CCAR* 79 (1969): 211–24.

Mantinband, Anna K. "Vignettes from the Life of a Rabbi Confronting Racism in Mississippi, 1952–1963." *RJ* 27 (Summer 1980): 83–98.

Marcus, Jacob Rader, and Abraham J. Peck, eds. *The American Rabbinate: Century of Continuity and Change, 1883–1983.* Hoboken, N.J.: Ktav, 1985. 261 pp.

* Mirsky, Norman. *The Making of a Reform Rabbi.* Brandeis U., 1971.

Orkand, Robert. "The Rabbi in the Small City." RJ (Winter 1981): 66–75.

Plaut, W. Gunther. "New Directions for the Rabbi." *CCAR J* (Oct. 1971): 24–27.

Polish, David. "The Changing and the Constant in the Reform Rabbinate." *Amer Jew Arc* 35 (Nov. 1983): 263–41. Also in *The American Rabbinate*, edited by Jacob Rader Marcus and Abraham J. Peck, 173–251. Hoboken, N.J.: Ktav, 1985.

Polner, Murray. "Master and Teacher: An Historical Review of the American Rabbinate." In *Rabbi: The American Experience*, 1–30. N.Y.: Holt, Rinehart and Winston, 1977.

Rosenberg, Stuart. "The Changing Role of the Rabbi." Master's thesis, Columbia U., 1948.

Rubenstein, Richard L. "The Rabbi and Social Conflict." *Rel Ed* 59 (Jan.–Feb. 1964): 100–106.

Sarna, Jonathan D. "Introduction" (analysis of the history of the rabbinate in America). *Amer Jew Arc* 35 (Nov. 1983): 91–99. Also in *The American Rabbinate*, edited by Jacob Rader Marcus and Abraham J. Peck, 1–9. Hoboken, N.J.: Ktav, 1985.

Shankman, Jacob K. "The Changing Role of the Rabbi." In *Retrospect and Prospect, 1889–1964*, 230–50. CCAR, 1965.

Sklare, Marshall. "On the Conservative Rabbi." In his *Conservative Judaism*, 164–74. 1955.

Tobin, Herbert, Elliot Skiddell, and Sidney H. Schwartz. "Three Perspectives on the Rabbi's Role" (community-school-synagogue). *Recon* 46 (Aug. 1980): 15–20.

Weinberger, Bernard. "Confessions of an Orthodox Rabbi or a Talk of These Three Bridges." *Jew Life* 4 (Winter 1975): 15–27.

Weiss-Rosmarin, Trude. "The New American Rabbi." *Jew Spec* 31 (Fall 1966): 3–7.

* Zeitlin, Joseph. "Rabbi's Views on Some Issues Concerning Education" (public education). In *Disciples of the Wise: The Religious and Social Opinions of American Rabbis*, 131–38. Teachers College, Columbia U., 1961.

ROLE IN JEWISH EDUCATION

* Adams, Theodore L. *The USA Rabbi: His Contribution to Jewish Education, 1810–1930.* Followed by an empirical survey, 1930–60. Yeshiva U., 1962.

Angel, Marc D. "Learning from/with/about the Rabbi." *Ped Rep* 32 (Winter 1981): 23–24.

Aronson, David. "The Place of the Pulpit in Adult Education." *The Torch* (Winter 1951–52). See also *RTJS*, 258–64.

Cohn, Hillel. "Making an Impact on Your Synagogue School." *Raayonot* 4 (Spring 1984): 12–14.

Dushkin, Alexander M. "The Educational Training of Rabbis" (editorial). *Jew Ed* 5 (Oct.–Dec. 1933): 134–35, 155.

———. "The Profession of Jewish Education and Its Relation to the Rabbinate." *CCAR* 41 (1931): 400–431.

Ettenberg, Sylvia. "The Rabbi: A Force in a Program for Recruiting Teachers." *RA* (1956): 223–28.

Goldstein, David A. "The Role of the Rabbi as an Educational Statesman." *RA* (1955): 214–16.

Golub, Jacob S. "Towards a Better Understanding Between Rabbis and Educators" (editorial). *Jew Ed* 10 (Oct./Dec. 1938): 132–33.

Greenberg, Shlomo. "הרב האמריקני כמחנך" (The American Rabbi as Educator). In *Yesod* (H.), 183–91.

Karp, Abraham J. "Rabbis as Educational Statesmen." *RA* (1953): 217.

Korman, Michael. "The Rabbi-Educational Director Relationship." *Jew Ed* 49 (Winter 1981): 34–43. See also *Con Jud* 36 (Winter 1982–83): 58–68.

Kronish, Ronald. "The Rabbi as Educator." *RJ* (Spring 1978): 55–60.

Levitsky, Louis M. "The Rabbi is a Teacher of Judaism." *CCAR J* (June 1957): 23–26.

Millgram, Abraham E. "Rabbis as Educational Statesmen." *RA* (1955): 204–13.

"הרב המודרני באמריקה וחנוך הדור" (The Modern Rabbi and Contemporary Education). Participants: H. Greenberg, Sh. Bernstein, Sh. Shulman, M. Halevi, E. Lisitzky, M. Waxman, and Sh. B. Maximon. *Sh Hah* (H.) 3 (1927): 79–104.

Narot, Joseph R. "First Teachers in Last Resorts." *CCAR J* (Winter 1978): 45–51.

RA. The Rabbi in Jewish Education. (1946):
    Chipkin, Israel S., 167–69.
    Davis, Moshe, 180–84.
    Greenberg, Simon, 172–76.
    Katzoff, Louis, 176–79.
    Klein, Isaac, 159–66.
    Millgram, Abraham E., 169–72.

———. *The Role of the Rabbinate in Elementary and Secondary Education.* RA (1962):
    Eisenberg, Azriel, 20–24.
    Greenberg, Simon, 1–19. (Also in *MJET*, 25–34.)
    Weinstein, David, and Michael Yizhar, 45–59.

Rosenberg, Stuart E. "The Rabbi as a Teacher." *Rel Ed* 56 (May–June 1961): 168–72.

Sandberg, Ruth. "How a Rabbi Creates a School." *Raayonot* 4 (Spring 1984): 5–11.

Schein, Jeff. "Adult Learning Styles and the Congregational Rabbi." *Raayonot* 4 (Spring 1984): 16–18.

———. "Rabbi as Teacher: The Process of Formulating Educational Goals for Jewish Leadership." *Jew Ed* 56 (Summer 1988): 15–17.

Scherman, N. "The Rabbi and the Rosh Yeshiva: A Look at Their Respective Roles in American Jewish Life." *Jew Obs* (June 1964): 14–16.

Schwartzman, Sylvan D. "Thirty Years of Rabbinic Theses in Education." *RJ* 28 (Winter 1981): 76–78.

———. "Training the Rabbi for His Role in the Educational Program of the Temple." *Jew Teach* 25 (May 1957): 12.

Singer, Aaron. "The Rabbi as Educator of Youth." *RA Proc.* (1965): 101–13.

Zerin, Edward. "The Rabbi as Counselor." *RJ* 32 (Winter 1985): 21–29.

GLEANINGS

Kaplan, Mordecai M. (1940),
"It will not be possible for the rabbi, whose official duties bind him to the synagogue, to be able to keep up with the growing needs of Jewish life. . . . The principle of division of labor would have to be applied to the function of the rabbi. Some rabbis would serve congregations, others would specialize in educational work, and still others in the various types of communal endeavor. . . . It will be necessary for men with a rabbinic training and outlook to serve in administrative capacities in every phase of Jewish activity. When Jewish institutions come to prefer as administrators those who have had an extensive Jewish training, the entire trend of Jewish life will be transformed from one of decline to one of ascent."
Quoted in *AJA* 35 (Nov. 1983), 221.

Adler, Morris (1940),
"As our teacher, the late Professor Davidson, once pointed out, whereas in our day of specialization every profession contracted the area of its intensive study and operation, the office of the rabbi, has on the contrary, assumed new and multiple duties. . . . He is, or is expected to be, at once scholar, teacher, priest, pastor, preacher, administrator, communal leader, social worker, and ambassador of good-will. To him come many and diverse appeals for assistance."
Quoted in *AJA* 35 (Nov. 1983), 220–21.

Levi, S. Gershon (1949),
"A direct, personal relationship to the school of his synagogue is the duty, rather than an option, of every rabbi. . . . He should observe classroom teaching . . . [and] make a practice of having pupils visit his study for short chats."
Quoted in *AJA* 35 (Nov. 1983), 225.

Engelman, Uriah Z.,
"Unfortunately, the American Rabbi unoriented either to the power and prestige inherent in his position, or to the problems that faced Israel, fell under the spell of the same conditions which molded the lives of his parishioners. Hence, he was extremely cautious about offering effectual guidance to the laymen in shaping the course of Jewish education in the land."
Hebrew Education in America, 38–39. 1947.

Bamberger, Bernard J.,
"The American rabbi is a novel and unique phenomenon in Jewish experience. His office is related to the earlier forms of leadership by a tie of historic continuity; yet the modern rabbinate presents so radical a change both in function and temper as to constitute a virtually new profession. . . . This statement applies to orthodox, conservative, and reform rabbis alike."
Jud 3 (Fall 1954), 488.

Greenberg, Simon,
"As the Jewish community in America becomes increasingly acculturated and the State of Israel becomes more stabilized, the eternally cardinal concern of Jewish life, 'to study and to teach the Torah,' resumes its place of centrality with renewed vividness and cogency. To that central task the rabbi in America has heretofore not given his chief energies. We feel the time has come for him to do so, and if he does, it will constitute a radical change in his own life, a change which is bound to have radical and beneficial effects upon the life of the entire Jewish community."
MJET, 58–59.

Korman, Michael,
"Unless the role of the professional educational director in the congregational school is clearly defined and he is provided the necessary status that goes along with educational responsibility, the quality of Jewish education in the congregational school will continue to deteriorate, including the respective roles and status of laity, educators and rabbis in the overall congregational setting, as well as in the school."
"The Rabbi-Education Director Relationship." *Jew Ed* 49 (Winter 1981), 34–43.

26 | CONFERENCES IN JEWISH EDUCATION, 1890–1988

CONFERENCES IN JEWISH EDUCATION, 1890–1988

If not reported directly from proceedings, conferences are listed by the date reported in a journal or newspaper.

1890
CCAR 1 (1890): "Sabbath School," 27–28, 31–32.

1891
CCAR 2 (1891): 14.

1892
CCAR 3 (1892): "Call for preparation of textbooks for Sabbath School," 45–46.

1894
CCAR 5 (1894): Catechism, Hebrew instruction, manual of instruction, and plan of instruction, 26, 35, 44, 77, 89, 90, 95, 97.

1896
CCAR 6 (1896): Committee on Plans of Instruction, "Plans of Instruction in the Jewish Sabbath School—A Manual," 25, 30–40.

1897
CCAR 7 (1897): "Catechism Literature and Manual," xlvi, lv.

NCJW, *Proceedings* (Nov. 15–19, 1896) (Phila.: JPS, 1897): "Our Religious Schools, What Can the Council Do for Them?," 356–63.

1898
CCAR 8 (1898): 56.

1901
CCAR 11 (1901): "Catechism," 77, 90.

1902
CCAR 12 (1902): "Resolutions," 35, 70, 72, 173, 187–201.

1904
CCAR 14 (1904): "Bible History," 149.

1905
CCAR 15 (1905): "Religious School Committee to Be Appointed," 162.

1906
CCAR 16 (1906): "Ritual for Children's Service," and "Committee for Religious School Day Established," 181, 185, 192.

1907
CCAR 17 (1907): "Report of Committee on Religious Schools: Bible History, Propaganda, Uniformity of Curriculum," 43, 124–138.

1908
CCAR 18 (1908): "Report of the Committee on Religious Schools: Exhibit and Library List," 57, 58, 81–85, 139.

1909
CCAR 19 (1909): "Report of the Committee on Religious Schools: Review of Books, List of Suggested Pictures, and Exhibit," 33, 108–19.

1910
CCAR 20 (1910): "Committee Report on Textbooks," 87–90.

1911
CCAR 21 (1911): "Report of the Religious Education Committee," 89–94, and "Report of the Text-Book Commission," 94–95. See also pp. 113 and 136.

1912
CCAR 22 (1912): "Report of the Religious Education Committee," "The Issue of Uniform Textbooks," 176–201.

1913
CCAR 23 (1913): "Report of the Committee on Religious Education," 161–64.

1914
CCAR 24 (1914): "Report of the Committee on Religious Education," 66–68. Also "Symposium on Recent Progress in Religious Education," 312–38.

1915
CCAR 25 (1915): "Symposium on Character Building," 300–334. See also pp. 69, 128, and 148.

1916
CCAR 26 (1916): Symposium on "How Can the Personal Side of Religion Be Cultivated in the Jewish Child?" 224–46. See also pp. 82, 83.

1917
CCAR 27 (1917): 125.

1919
CCAR 29 (1919): 67.

1920
CCAR 30 (1920): "Aims of Religious Education," 125, 361–76.

1921
CCAR 31 (1921): 66, 68, 75.

1922
CCAR 32 (1922): "Proposal for a National Federation of Religious Schools," 55–62.

1923
CCAR 33 (1923): "Report of Commission on Jewish Education, UAHC," 307–13. Also "The Curriculum of the Jewish Religious School—Elementary and High School Departments," 314–43, 75.

1924
NCJSS *Proceedings* (1924): "Jewish Education," 248–88.

1925
CCAR 35 (1925): 156.

Farband Schools–LZOA. „א באריכט וועגן די שולן וואס ווערן אויסגעהאלטן פונם אידיש נאציאנאלן ארבעטער פארבאנד איבער גאנץ אמעריקע" (Report on Farband Folk Schools in America). *Jewish Workers Voice* (Y.) 2 (Aug. 1925).

1926
CCAR 36 (1926): 96, 332.

NCJSS *Proceedings* (1926): "Jewish Education," 272–312.

1927
CCAR 37 (1927): 114.

NCJSS *Proceedings* (1927): "The Development of a Community Program in Jewish Education," and "The Bureau of Jewish Social Research," 210–49.

RA Proceedings (27th Annual Conference, 1927): "The Place of Religion in Jewish Education."

WC. „פראגראם פון די ארבעטער רינג שולן" (Program of the WC) (Adopted at the Sixth Conference) (Y.). N.Y.: WC Education Department, 1927. 95 pp.

1928
CCAR 38 (1928): 114.

National Association of Hebrew Teachers and Principals of America. „הועידה לשם יסוד..." (Founding Conference) (Pittsburgh, Oct. 13–15, 1927). *Sh Hah* (H.) 3 (1928): 327–37; 4 (1929): 556.

1929
CCAR 39 (1929): 101–2.

Dushkin, Alexander M. "Third Annual Conference of the National Council for Jewish Education." *Jew Ed* 1 (Jan. 1929): 6–13.

Edidin, Ben M. "Fourth Annual Conference of NCJE" (summary of proceedings). *Jew Ed* 1 (Oct. 1929): 191–94.

Naman, P. „דין וחשבון מהועידה השניה של ההסתדרות מורים ומנהלים בארצות הברית" (Report on the Second Conference of the Teachers' and Principals' Association in the United States). *Sh Hah* (H.) 4 (1929): 599–611.

1930

CCAR 40 (1930): 112, 115.

Dinin, Samuel. "Proceedings of the Fifth Annual Conference of the NCJE." *Jew Ed* 2 (Oct. 1930): 137–43.

Jew Ed. "Program for the 5th Annual Conference of the NCJE." *Jew Ed* 2 (June 1938): 104.

1931

CCAR 41 (1931): 132, 168.

Lapson, Judah, recorder. "Proceedings of the Sixth Annual Conference of the NCJE." *Jew Ed* 3 (Oct.–Dec. 1931): 185–91.

Jew Ed. "Program for 6th Annual Conference of NCJE." *Jew Ed* 3 (Apr. 1931): 126.

1932

CCAR 42 (1932): "Report of the Committee on Religious Education," 107–24, 128. Includes a list of all previous conference papers on religious education.

Eisenberg, Israel L. (Azriel). "Proceedings of the Seventh Annual Conference of the NCJE." *Jew Ed* 4 (Oct.–Dec. 1932): 180–89.

1933

CCAR 43 (1933): 24, 63, 169.

Eisenberg, Israel L. (Azriel), recorder. "Proceedings of the Eighth Annual Conference of the NCJE." *Jew Ed* 5 (Oct.–Dec. 1933): 168–74.

1934

CCAR 44 (1934): "Report of the Commission on Jewish Education," 55–64.

Dinin, Samuel. "Proceedings of the Ninth Annual Conference of the NCJE." *Jew Ed* 6 (Oct.–Dec. 1934): 167–71.

1935

CCAR 45 (1935): 93, 100.

Eisenberg, Azriel L., recorder. "Proceedings of the Tenth Annual Conference of the NCJE." *Jew Ed* 7 (Oct.–Dec. 1935): 170–74.

Jew Ed. "Preliminary Program for the 10th Annual Conference of the NCJE." 7 (Apr. 1935): 128.

1936

CCAR 46 (1936): "Report of Committee on Religious Work in Universities," and "Report of Committee on Religious Education," 107–13, 114–15.

Eisenberg, Azriel I. "Proceedings of the 11th Annual Conference of the NCJE." *Jew Ed* 8 (Oct.–Dec. 1936): 147–54.

1937

CCAR 47 (1937): 126.

Dinin, Samuel. "Proceedings of the 12th Annual Conference of the NCJE." *Jew Ed* 9 (Apr.–June 1937): 87–94.

Goldberg, A. "דער צוזאמענפאר פון די ארבעטער שולן" (The Conference of the Workers' Schools). *Pro D* (Y.) 3 (June 1937): 4–6, 17.

International Workers Orden. "באשלוסן וועגן פראגראם" (Decisions on Curriculum). *Pro D* (Y.) 3 (Feb. and Mar. 1937): 17, 18.

WC. "קאנפערענץ פארהאנדלונגען" (Conference Proceedings) (Apr. 1937). *Our School* (Y.) 7 (May 1937).

World Yiddish Culture Congress, Paris (Sept. 20, 1937): "רעזאלוציע" (Resolution on Education and Discussion) (Y.), 286–92, and 336–37.

1938

Brilliant, Nathan, recorder. "Proceedings of the 13th Annual Conference of the NCJE." *Jew Ed* 10 (Apr.–June 1938): 103–10.

CCAR 48 (1938): 105, 116.

1939

CCAR 49 (1939): CJE, Report on Jewish Education, 35, 86–95, 201.

RA (1939): "Education Committee," 165.

1940

CCAR 50 (1940): 135, 146.

Edidin, Ben M. "ועידת המועצה הארצית" (The Conference of the NCJE). *Sh Hah* (H.) 1 (1940): 89–90.

———. "Proceedings of NCJE" (June 14–18, 1939). *Jew Ed* 11 (Jan. 1940): 240–44.

———. "Proceedings, NCJE" (May 22–26, 1940). *Jew Ed* 12 (Sept. 1940): 123–28.

RA (1940): "Committee on Adult Jewish Education," 36–38, "Education Committee," 38–41.

1941

Lapson, Judah, recorder. "Proceedings of the Sixteenth Annual Conference of the NCJE." *Jew Ed* 13 (Sept. 1941): 137–40, 217–23.

"דער צוועלפטער צוזאמענפאר פון די ארבעטער רינג שול" (The 12th Conference of the WC Schools) (Apr. 25–27, 1941): *CE* (Y.) (May 1941): 2–25, 32.

1942

Halevi, Mordecai. "מועצת המחנכים העברים—תש"ב" (Council of Hebrew Educators—1942). *Bitzaron* (H.) 7 (Oct. 1942): 59–67.

Levinson, I. "כנוס חנוכי במערב התיכון" (Educational Conference in the Midwest). *Sh Hah* (H.) 2 (1942): 153–57.

Mizrachi, Sh. "ועידת המורים עברים במערב התיכון" (Conference of Hebrew Teachers in the Midwest). *Sh Hah* (H.) 2 (1942): 233–35.

1943

Lapson, Judah, recorder. "Proceedings of the 17th Annual Conference of the NCJE." *Jew Ed* 14 (Jan.–Mar. 1943): 183–91.

Rinegrad, N. "ועידת המחנכים עברים במערב התיכון" (Midwest Conference of Hebrew Educators). *Sh Hah* (H.) 3 (1943): 62–63.

Wertheim, David H. "רשימות להועידה השנתית של אגודת המורים" (Summary of the Annual Teachers Conference). *Bitzaron* (H.) (Apr. 1943): 62–64.

1944

Baron, A. "הכנוס הפדגוגי של המנהלים" (Pedagogic Conference of Administrators). *Sh Hah* (H.) 4 (1944): 74–77.

CCAR 54 (1944): "Report of CJE," 113–21, and "Report on Religious Work in Universities," 129–32.

1945

Jewish Education. "Proceedings of the 19th Annual Conference of the NCJE." *Jew Ed* 17 (Nov. 1945): 57–62.
USCJE: *RA* (1945), 11–12.

Wertheim, David. "ועידה הסתדרות המורים הארצית בדיטרויט" (National Teachers Conference in Detroit). *Sh Hah* (H.) 5 (1945): 277–84.

1946

Chanin, Nathan. "באריכט פון בילדונגס קאמיטעט צום 14טן שול צוזאמענפאר אין באסטאן" (Report of the WC Education Committee at the 14th Conference in Boston). *CE* (Y.) 16 (May 1946): 19–23. Resolutions, 23–27.

Labor Zionist-Farband Folk Schools. "ספעציעלער נומער לכבוד דעם דרייצנטן צוזאמענפאר פון די יידישע פאלקשולן" (Special issue on the 13th Annual Conference of the Yiddish Folk Schools, June 1945). *YD* (Y.) (June 1946): 108. "רעזאלוציעס" (Resolutions), 69–75.

Rudavsky, David. "Proceedings of the 20th Annual Conference of the NCJE." *Jew Ed* 18 (Nov. 1946): 61–68.

USCJE, *RA* (1946): 317–19.

1947

Dushkin, Alexander M. "World Union for Jewish Education." (editorial on World Conference in Jerusalem, July 29–Aug. 6, 1947). *Jew Ed* 19 (Fall 1947): 2–5.

Edidin, Ben M. "ועידת עולמית לחנוך העברי" (World Conference on Hebrew Education). *Sh Hah* (H.) 7 (1947): 95.

NCJE. "Resolutions Adopted at 21st Annual Conference." *Jew Ed* 19 (Fall 1947): 57–58.

RA, Second Annual Rabbinical Conference on Jewish Education, in Cooperation with USCJE and the Teachers Institute of JTS. *The Structure of Jewish Education in Conservative Judaism* (Dec. 22–23, 1947). 176 pp. (E. and H.). Report of USCJE (1947), 87–93.

Jew Ed. "Resolutions of the First World Conference for Hebrew Education in the Diaspora" (Jerusalem). *Jew Ed* 19 (Fall 1947): 55–57.

Scharfstein, Zevi. "אחרי הכנוס" (After the Conference). *Sh Hah* (H.) 7 (1947): 179–81.

Torcyk, D., and Z. Schwartz. "הועידה השנתית של ההסתדרות המורים" (Annual Conference of the Teachers Organization). *Sh Hah* (H.) 7 (1947): 244–50.

1948

Edelstein, Menachem M. "כינוס הועד הפועל הגדול באטלאנטיק סיטי" (Conference of the Large Executive Board in Atlantic City). *Sh Hah* (H.) 8 (1948): 195–98.

Mark, Yudl. "דער אלוועלטלאכער קולטור קאנגרעס און די יידישע שול" (World Cultural Congress and the Yiddish School). *Zuk* (Y.) 53 (Sept. 1948): 513–17.

RA (1948): 49–52.

World Conference on Jewish Education in the Diaspora (Jerusalem, July–Aug. 1947). "החנוך"

"העברי בתפוצות הגולה" (Jewish Education in the Diaspora). Addresses and Resolutions by the Diaspora Delegates. World Union for Jewish Education in the Diaspora. "החלטות הכינוס של מורי התפוצות" (Resolutions Adopted by Conference on Goals of Jewish Education in the Diaspora and a Minimum Program for Supplementary Afternoon Schools in the Diaspora). In *JED* (H.), 207–10.

1949

Adler, I. N. "חוברת הכינוס הארצי הראשון למען החינוך השלם. מטעם ועד החינוך היהודי של המזרחי בא״הב" (The First National Conference on Day School Education by the Orthodox Council of Mizrachi in the United States) (H.). 1949. 62 pp.

Alper, M. "Proceedings of the Joint Conference [NCJE and AAJE] on Jewish Education in Atlantic City, N.J., May 26–31, 1949." *Jew Ed* 21 (Winter 1949): 71–81.

Edelstein, Menachem M. "הועידה השנתית של הסתדרות המורים העברים" (Annual Conference of the Hebrew Teachers Organization, Dec. 1948). *Sh Hah* (H.) 9 (1949): 55–64.

Kuselewitz, David. "ועידת אגודי החנוך העברי" (Conference of Hebrew Education Association). *Sh Hah* (H.) 9 (1949): 197–202.

NCJE. "Resolutions Adopted at 1949 Conference of NCJE." *Jew Ed* 21 (Winter 1949): 83–84.

———. "Resolutions Adopted by the 1949 Conference of the AAJE." *Jew Ed* 21 (Winter 1949): 85.

———. "Resolutions of Annual Conference." *Jew Ed* 20 (Feb. 1949): 63–64.

Sheviley Hahinuch. "כנוס השנתית של הסתדרות המורים העברים" (Annual Conference of the Hebrew Teachers Organization). *Sh Hah* (H.) 9 (1949): 149–54.

USCJE, *RA* (49th Annual Convention), 72–82.

1950

AAJE. "The Call to a National Conference on Jewish Education" (October 1950). *Jew Ed* 21 (Summer 1950): 2.

Chipkin, Israel S. "The 1950 American Conference on Jewish Education." *Jew Ed* 21 (Summer 1950): 3–4.

CCAR, CJE 60 (1950): "Report of CJE," 123–30, "Report of the Committee on Religious Education," 131–35.

LZOA. "דעקלאראציע און רעזאלוציעס פון דער דערציאונגס קאנפערענץ" (Declaration and Resolutions of the Educational Conference). *YK* (Y.) (Sept. 1950): 12–13. *YD* (Y.) (May 1954): 102–5.

LZOA–Jewish National Workers Alliance-Farband and Pioneer Women. "לערער קאנפערענץ פון די יידישע פאלקשולן אין אמעריקע און קאנאדא" (Teacher Conference of the Labor-Zionist Movement of the US and Canada, Aug. 7–9, 1950). *YD* (Y.) (Aug. 1950): 115.

NCJE, Mid-Year Conference. *Jew Ed* 21 (Summer 1950): 69.

USCJE, *RA* (1950): 55–56.

1951

Auerbach, Ephraim. "קולטור ירידה אדער שאפערישער קיום" (Cultural Decline or Creative Survival—at First National Conference on Jewish Education). *YK* (Y.) (Jan. 26, 1951): 4–6.

Ben-Israel, M. "הכנוס הרביעי של המחנכים במערב התיכון" (Fourth Conference of Educators in the Midwest). *Sh Hah* (H.) 11 (Mar. 1951): 105–7.

Bleter far Yiddisher Dertsiung. "די ערשטע לאנד קאנפערענץ פאר יידישער דערציאונג אין די פאראייניקטע שטאטן" (Addresses and Resolutions of the First National United States Conference on Jewish Education). *BYD* (Y.) 4 (June/Sept. 1951): 64–93.

Bortniker, Elijah. "דינאמיקה בחיינו" (Dynamics in Our Lives) (on the First National Education Conference). *Sh Hah* (H.) 11 (Mar. 1951): 79–83.

CCAR 61 (1951): "CJE," 149; Committee on Adult Education, 159; Committee on Religious Education, 33, 156.

Chipkin, Israel S. "The First National Conference Concerning Jewish Education in the USA and Its Aftermath." *Jew Ed* 22 (Summer 1951): 10–12.

Ed As. "Resolutions Adopted at the Founders Session of the Educators Assembly." *Syn Sch* 10 (Dec. 1951): 55–56.

First National Conference on Jewish Education. "A Charter of the Rights of the Jewish Child." *Jew Ed* 23 (Summer 1951): 77.

———. Excerpts from papers: Michael A. Stavitsky, Samuel J. Borowsky, Samuel L. Blumenfield, Ephraim Auerbach, Eisig Silberschlag, Bernard Semel, Philip S. Bernstein, Ira Eisenstein, Sh. Niger, Menachem Ribalow, David W. Petagorsky, and Harry Starr. *Jew Ed* 22 (Summer 1951): 57–72. "Resolutions," 73–75.

Goodman, Saul. —„די שלום עליכם שולן— עוואלוציע פון דער יידיש-וועלטלעכער שול אין אמעריקע" (The Sholem Aleichem Schools—the Evolution of the Yiddish-Secular School in America). (Presented at First National Conference on Jewish Education.) *BYD* (Y.) (June/Sept. 1951): 79–82.

NCJE, "Resolutions of the 1950 NCJE Conference." *Jew Ed* 22 (Spring 1951): 114–15.

USCJE. *RA* (1951): 62–63

RA. "Program of the Fourth Rabbinical Assembly Conference on Jewish Education" (Feb. 13, 1951). *Syn Sch* 10 (Dec. 1951): 59–62.

Sherman, Bezalel C. „ארום דער קאנפערענץ פאר אידישער דערציאונג" (On the Conference for Jewish Education). *YK* (Y.) (Jan. 5, 1951).

Spizman, L. „דערציאונג—נאך דער קאנפערענץ" (Education after the Conference). *YK* (Y.) (Jan. 26, 1951): 2–3.

Yefroiken, Zalmen. „די י.ל. פרץ שולן פון ארבעטער רינג" (The I. L. Peretz Schools of the WC—at First National Conference on Jewish Education.) *BYD* (Y.) (June–Sept. 1951): 76–78.

Zuto, A. „ועידת החנוך של הרבנים המשמרים" (Education Conference of the Conservative Rabbis). *Sh Hah* (H.) 11 (Mar. 1951): 108–10.

1952

Avironi, Israel. „הכנוס החמישי של המחנכים העברים במערב התיכון" (The Fifth Conference of Hebrew Educators in the Midwest). *Sh Hah* (H.) 12 (Mar. 1952): 120–24.

CCAR 62 (1952): "CJE," 259–67, "Committee on Religious Education," 43, 268.

Goodman, Philip. "Proceedings of the 25th Anniversary Conference of the NCJE" (digest). *Jew Ed* 23, (Fall 1952): 63–64.

First National Conference on Jewish Education (1950). Panel discussions, *Jew Ed* 23 (Winter 1952).

Ruffman, Louis L., recorder. "Personality Growth of the Jewish Child." Participants: Isidor Chein, Mrs. Morris Marshall Cohn, Samuel Dinin, Edward A. Nudelman, Eugene Revitch, Albert P. Schoolman, and Zalmen Slesinger.

Krug, Mark M., recorder. "Cultural Expressions of Jewish Life." Participants: Mrs. Rebecca Brickner, Azriel Eisenberg, Stanley Rabinowitz, Miriam Ephraim, Mark M. Krug, Amram Pero, and Herman A. Bachrack.

Kohanski, A. S., recorder. "Content of the Jewish School." Participants: Hyman B. Bass, Barnett R. Brickner, Abraham N. Franzblau, Jacob J. Hartstein, Louis E. Levinthal, Herman M. Pekarsky, and Zevi Scharfstein.

Kallen, Horace M. "The National Conference for Jewish Education and Democratic Living." *Jew Ed* 23 (Winter 1952): 54–55, 68.

NCJE. "Resolutions of 1951 Conference." *Jew Ed* 23 (Winter 1952): 65 and 68

USA. "Resolutions on Jewish Education." Adopted May 14–18, 1952. *Syn Sch* 11 (Sept. 1952): 29.

1953

CCAR Proc 63 (1953): "CJE," 111, Committee on Religious Education, 150, Committee on Adult Education, 336, New Goals in Religious Education, 431.

Glatstein, Zevi. „הועידה הארצית של הסתדרות המורים העברים באמריקה" (The National Conference of the Organization of Hebrew Teachers in America). *Sh Hah* (H.) 13 (1953): 263–67.

USCJE, *RA* (1953): 36–38.

1954

Bass, Hyman B. „די דערציאונגס קאנפערענץ פון קולטור קאנגרעס" (The Educational Conference of the Congress for Jewish Culture). *Zuk* (Y.) (Jan. 1954): 7–11.

Bortniker, Elijah. "Summary of the 27th Annual Conference of the NCJE." *Jew Ed* 24 (Spring 1954): 56–57.

CCAR 64 (1954): Committee on Adult Education, 33, CJE, 48–52, Committee on Religious Education, 120–22.

Chipkin, Israel S. "A National Conference on the Shortage of Jewish Educational Personnel" (editorial). *Jew Ed* 25 (Feb. 1954): 2–3.

———. "The Second National Conference on Jewish Education." *Jew Ed* 24 (Spring 1954): 2–4.

Day. „ארבעטער רינג צוזאמענפאר דיסקוטירט וואס פאר א דערציאונג צו געבן די אמעריקאנער געבוירענע קינדער" (WC Conference Discusses the Type of Education to Offer American-Born Children). (Y.) (May 17, 1954).

RA Proc (1954): 41–49.

USCJE, RA. *Six Approaches to Adult Education in Conservative Synagogues*. 1954.

1955

Bortniker, Elijah. "Summary of the 28th Conference of the NCJE." *Jew Ed* 25 (Winter 1955): 65–69.

CCAR 65 (1955): Committee on Adult Education, 37, CJE, 57, Committee on Religious Education, 82, Symposium on adult religious education, 121.

Grand, Samuel, comp. "Conference of Principals of Reform Schools—Eastern Seaboard" (Dec. 26–28, 1954). *Jew Teach* 23 (Mar. 1955): 11–16.

USCJE, RA (1955): 27–30.

1956

CCAR 66 (1956): Adult Education Committee, 37, CJE, 61, resolution for experts to evaluate work of CCAR in education, 135, Committee on Religious Education, 102, Special Commission on Education, 24.

Dinsky, Samuel H. "Summary of the 29th Conference of the NCJE." *Jew Ed* 26:3 (Spring 1956): 56–59

Lerman, H. K. „כנסת המחנכים על יד בתי הכנסת המאוחדים" (Educators Assembly of the United Synagogue). *Sh Hah* (H.) (Fall 1956): 57–58.

NATE. "Raising Standards of Educational Achievement and Religious Commitment in Our Schools" (founding conference, Dec. 26–29, 1955). *Jew Teach* 24 (May 1956): 7–16.

USA—National Biennial Convention, Nov. 13–17, 1955. "Resolutions." *Syn Sch* 14 (Feb. 1956): 24.

1957

AAJE. *Proceedings of the First Meeting of the National Commission on Teacher Education*. N.Y.: AAJE, 1957. 51 pp. Mimeo.

AAJE. National Conference on Manpower Crisis in Jewish Education, Nov. 1956. "Summary of Proceedings." *Jew Ed* 27 (Spring 1957): 41–62.

CCAR 67 (1957): Committee on Adult Education, 33, CJE, 53, Committee on Religious Education, 80, "The Pulpit as an Educational Medium—the Total Program of Education in the Synagogue," 117, 118.

Department of Education and Culture of the Jewish Agency in Cooperation with the AAJE, May 10–12, 1957. *Jewish Education in Response to the Challenge of Our Times* (Rockaway Park, N.Y.). *Proceedings of the Institute on Jewish Education*. N.Y.: Dec. 1957. 99 pp. Mimeo.

Elkin, Harry. "Summary of the 30th Conference of the NCJE." *Jew Ed* 27 (Winter 1956–57): 57–62.

NATE, Dec. 23–26, 1956. "Goals and Realities in Religious Education for Reform Judaism." *Jew Teach* 25 (May 1957) 13–18.

RA. "Resolution on Jewish Education Adopted at the Annual Assembly of the Rabbinical Assembly of America, May 1957." *Syn Sch* 16 (Dec. 1957): 29.

Third National Conference on Jewish Education (Teacher Shortage). "Resolutions." *Jew Ed* 27 (Spring 1957): 63–65.

Wohl, I. Z. „הועידה השנתית של המועצה הארצית למען החנוך היהודי" (The Annual Conference of the NCJE). *Sh Hah* (H.) 17 (Winter 1957): 117–28.

1958

CCAR 68 (1958): Committee on Adult Education, 22, 37; Committee on Religious Education, 24, 117–18; CJE, 73–78; Commission Director's Report, 79–83.

DEC. „יסודות לחינוך העברי בתפוצות הגולה" (Fundamental Principles for Diaspora Education). *Proceedings of the Institute on Diaspora Education* (H.) Aug. 14–18, 1955. Jerusalem: DEC, 1958. 205 pp.

Educators Assembly, Sixth Annual Assembly Convention, Mar. 17–21, 1958. *Syn Sch* 16 (1958).

NATE, Dec. 25–28, 1957. "NATE Takes a Stand On Basic Issues in Reform Jewish Education." *Jew Teach* 26 (1958): 2–19.

TU. *Program of the First PTA Conference. Jew Parent* 10 (June 1958).

USA Convention, Nov. 17–21, 1957. "Resolutions on Jewish Education." *Syn Sch* 16 (Mar. 1958): 28–29.

1959

AAJE. "Proceedings of the Fourth National Conference of Jewish Education, Jan. 3–5, 1959." *Jew Ed* 30 (Fall 1959): 75–95.

CCAR 69 (1959): Committee on Adult Education, 24, 39; CJE, 75; Committee on Religious Education, 24, 116.

Dinsky, Samuel H. "Proceedings of the 32nd Annual Conference of the NCJE." May 1–4, 1958. *Jew Ed* 29 (Winter 1959): 72–78.

Jew Ed. "Proceedings of the Fourth National Conference on Jewish Education." 30 (Fall 1959).

Jewish Education News. Third National Jewish Education Conference, Feb. 1959. 8 pp.

NATE, Dec. 1958. "The Emerging Patterns of Reform Jewish Education." *Jew Teach* 27 (Mar. 1959): 17–30.

World Jewish Congress. "Fourth Plenary Assembly." Symposium on International Cooperation in Jewish Education. Stockholm, Aug. 6, 1959.

1960

CCAR 70 (1960): Committee on Adult Education, 21 and 31; Committee on Religious Education, 21, 93; CJE, 59; Refining the Goals of Reform Jewish Education, 159; Goals in Primary Education, 160; Goals in Hebrew Instruction, 160.

LZOA—Farband. „ראציע און רעזאלוציע דעקלא" (Declaration and Resolution). *YK* (Y.) (Nov. 18, 1960): 78.

NATE. "New Insights from Jewish Scholarship for the Temple Educator, Dec. 1959." *Jew Teach* 28 (Mar. 1960): 2–19.

Soviv, Aaron. "Proceedings of the 33rd Annual Convention of the NCJE." *Jew Ed* 30 (Winter 1960): 50–55.

———. "Proceedings of the 34th Annual Conference of the NCJE." *Jew Ed* 31 (Fall 1960): 53–57.

1961

CCAR 71 (1961): Committee on Adult Education, 35, 36; CJE 59; Committee on Religious Education, 123.

Nardi, Noah, ed. „בעיות החינוך העברי בתפוצות הגולה" (Problems of Diaspora Education) (H.). *Proceedings of the Second World Institute on Diaspora Education, Aug. 1958.* Jerusalem: DEC, 1961. 217 pp.

NATE, Dec. 25–28, 1960. "Challenge of the Sixties in Jewish Education." *Jew Teach* 29 (Apr. 1961): 2–28.

Soviv, Aaron. "Summary of the Proceedings of the 35th Annual Conference of the NCJE, May 25–28, 1961." *Jew Ed* 32 (Fall 1961): 45–49.

1962

World Conference on Jewish Education, Jerusalem, Aug. 12–17, 1962.

Auerbach, Ephraim. „די חינוך קאנפערענץ" (The Education Conference–Jerusalem) (Y.). (Aug. 16, 1962).

„וועלט קאנפערענץ פאר יידישער דערציאונג" (World Conference in Behalf of Jewish Education). *BYD* (Spring 1962): 39–42.

„אידישע קאנפערענץ אין ירושלים פאדערט אויף אידן געבן גרעסטע שטיצע צו טאג-שולן" (Jewish Education Conference in Jerusalem Calls for Highest Support to Jewish Day Schools). *Day* (Aug. 16, 1962).

Hyamson, B. „די וועלט קאנפערענץ פאר אידישער דערציאונג" (The World Conference for Jewish Education). (Y.) Aug. 3, 1962.

Ivri, I. „וועלט קאנפערענץ פאר אידישער דערציאונג" (World Conference for Jewish Education). *Day* (Y.) (Jan. 1, 1962).

Janowsky, Oscar I. "The World Conference on Jewish Education." *Recon* 28 (Oct. 5, 1962): 22–26.

"The World Conference of Jewish Organizations called the Conference." *Jew Ed* 32 (Winter 1962): 123.

Margoshes, Samuel. "World Conference of Jewish Education." *Day* (Feb. 14, 1962, Aug. 16, 1962).

Pat, Jacob. „אויפן דערציאונגס-

26 CONFERENCES IN JEWISH EDUCATION, 1890–1988

"צוזאממענפאר אין ירושלים" (At the Education Conference in Jerusalem). *Zuk* (Y.) (Oct. 1962): 357–60.

Pilch, Judah. "World Assembly on Jewish Education." *Congress Biweekly* (Mar. 1962): 7–8, 13.

Rubenstein, L. "די וועלט קאנפערענץ אין ירושלים פאר אידישן חינוך" (The World Conference of Jewish Education in Jerusalem). *YK* (Y.) (Oct. 26, 1962): 10–12.

Tartakover, Arieh. "The World Conference on Jewish Education." *Day* (Sept. 2, 1962).

"הועידה העולמית לחנוך היהודי: סקירה וסכומים" (World Conference on Jewish Education: Review and Summaries) (H.). Jerusalem: Aug. 12–17, 1962.

CCAR 72 (1962): Committee on Adult Education, 41; CJE, 42, 61; Committee on Religious Education, 116.

NATE. *Relating Learning to Jewish Living—Current Issues in Jewish Education*. Dec. 1962.

NCJE. "Resolutions on All Day Schoool" (February 2, 1962). *Jew Ed* 32 (Winter 1962): 123.

Unger, M. "די וועלט קאנפערענץ פון קאנסערוואטיווע אידן" (World Conference of Conservative Jews, Jerusalem). *Day* (Y.) (April 29, May 27, 1962).

WC Conference. "ארבעטער רינג שול צוזאממענפאר הערט בארירט אז פיל הי-געבוירענע עלטערן ווילן אז זייערע קינדער זאלן לערנען אידיש..." (Report at WC Conference States That Many American-born Parents Want Their Children to Learn the Yiddish Language). *Day-Jewish Journal* (Y.) (April 29, 1962).

———. "ארבעטער רינג שולן ראנגלען זיך מיט פראבלעם פון עלטערן וואס ציען זיך אריבער אין די סאבורבס" (WC Conference Struggles with Problem of Families Moving to Suburbs). *Day–Jewish Journal* (Y.) (Apr. 29, 1962).

———. "ארבעטער רינג שולן ווערן מער אידיש-נאציאנאל ווערט באטאנט ביים שול קאנפערענץ" (WC Schools' Growing Emphasis on Jewish Nationalism is Stressed at Conference). *Day–Jewish Journal* (Y.) (Apr. 30, 1962).

YD "Report on Our School Conference at Unzer Camp, July 1961" (LZOA–JNWA, Pioneer Women). (Y.) (Dec. 1962): 95–100.

1963

Avidor, M. "לאחר ועידת החנוך" (After the Conference on Education [Jerusalem]). *Sh Hah* (H.) (Winter 1963): 102–6.

Borowsky, Samuel J. "Proceedings of the 36th Annual Conference" (NCJE). *Jew Ed* 33 (Winter 1963): 121–26.

CCAR 73 (1963): Adult Education Committee, 33–34, CJE, 54, Committee on Religious Education, 84.

Glatstein, Zevi. "הועידה הארצית של ההסתדרות המורים והמנהלים" (National Conference of Teachers' and Principals' Association). *Sh Hah* (H.) 23 (1963): 185–88.

Goldmann, Nahum. "Jewish Education and the Future" (on 1962 World Conference in Jerusalem). *Jew Ed* 33 (Winter 1963): 72–80.

Jew Ed. "Resolutions Adopted at the 36th Annual Conference of the NCJE." 33 (Spring 1963): 186–88.

NATE. "Proceedings of the 8th Annual Convention of NATE (Dec. 1962)." *Jew Teach* 31 (Apr. 1963): 2–25.

Pilch, Judah. "The World Conference on Jewish Education: A Summary and an Evaluation." *Jew Ed* 33 (Winter 1963): 81–88.

RA Proc (May 27–28, 1963).

Recon. "Reconstructionism and Jewish Education." Annual Conference of Federation of Reconstructionist Congregations and Fellowships, May 2–5, 1963 (Part I). 29 (Oct. 18, 1963).

Rotenberg, I. "פועלי ציון וועגן אידישן חינוך" (Labor Zionists on Jewish Education) (review of recent resolutions). *YK* (Y.) (July 26, 1963).

Syn Sch. "Proceedings of the 1963 Convention of the Educators Assembly." 22 (Winter 1964): 3–72.

1964

CCAR 74 (1964): Committee on Adult Education, 41, 67.

Isaacman, Daniel. "Summary of Proceedings of the 37th Annual Conference of the NCJE." *Jew Ed* 34 (June 1963): 209–12.

NATE, Dec. 1963. "Reform Jewish Education for the Family." *Jew Teach* 32 (Apr. 1964): 2–28.

NATE, 10th Anniversary Convention, Dec. 1964. Phoenix.

Resnik, Reuben. "World Conference on Jewish Education." *Day* (Sept. 30, 1964).

1965

World Conference of Yiddish Schools, New York City, May 1965

„אידישע שולן אין דער וועלט א פעסטונג קעגן אסימילאציע—הערט די קאנפערענץ" (Education Conference States That Yiddish Schools Represent a Fortress against Assimilation). *Day* (Y.) (May 8, 1965).

„צוזאמענפאר פאר שולן פאדערט מער פאנדן פאר אידישער דערציאונג" (Gathering Calls for More Funds in Behalf of Yiddish Education). *Day* (Y.) (May 9, 1965).

Glanz, Aaron. „וועלט צונויפקום פאר אידישע שול" (World Gathering in Behalf of Yiddish Schools). *Day* (Y.) (Apr. 28, 1965).

„וועלט קאנפערענץ פאר אידישע שולן פייערלעך דערעפנט" (Impressive Opening of World Conference of Yiddish Schools). *Day* (Y.) (May 7, 1965).

Margoshes, Samuel. "World Conference on Jewish Education." (Secular Yiddish Schools). *Day* (May 6, 1965).

Mark, Yudl. „א וועלט צוזאמענפאר פון דער יידישער שול" (A World Conference of the Yiddish School). *Zuk* (Y.) (Mar. 1965): 100–103.

„וועלט קאנפערענץ פון אידישע שולן עפנט זיך אין רוזוועלט האטעל" (World Conference of Yiddish Schools Opens at the Roosevelt Hotel). *Day* (Y.) (May 6, 1965).

„אידיש שולן צוזאמענפאר רופט פארשטארקן אידישע דערציאונג" (Yiddish Schools Conference Calls for the Strengthening of Yiddish Education). *Day* (Y.) (May 10, 1965).

Zilberberg, Israel. „וועלט צוזאמענפאר פאר אידישער דערציאונג" (World Conference for Yiddish Education). *Day* (Y.) (Apr. 23, 1965).

———. „דער וועלט צוזאמענפאר פאר יידישער דערציאונג" (The World Conference for Yiddish Schools). *CE* (Y.) 35 (Mar. 1965): 1–3.

AAJE. *Proceedings, National Conference on Adult Jewish Education* (Feb. 28, 1965) (New York).

CCAR Proc 75 (1965): Committee on Adult Education, 35, 93; Committee on Religious Education, 96.

Margolis, Henry. "Proceedings of the 39th Annual Conference of the NCJE (May 1965)." *Jew Ed* 36 (Fall 1965): 58–61.

S.A. „הועידה הל״ח של המועצה למען החנוך העברי" (The 38th Conference of the NCJE). *Sh Hah* (H.) 25 (Fall 1965): 53–54.

1966

CCAR 76 (1966): CJE, 46, Committee on Religious Education, 48.

Fifth National Conference on Jewish Education, Proceedings (personnel shortage). N.Y.: AAJE, Mar. 17–20, 1966

LZOA. "Problems of Jewish Education Discussed at 35th Labor Zionist Convention." *Israel Digest* 9 (June 12, 1966).

NATE, *Affirmations of Faith in an Age of Doubt.* Dec. 1966.

———, Dec 1965. "The American Jew: Retrospect and Prospect." *Jew Teach* 34 (Apr. 1966): 3–42.

RA (1966): Resolutions, Recruitment and Training of Educational Personnel, 107–10.

Reznik, Reuben. „הועידה הל״ט של המועצה למען החנוך" (The 39th Conference of the NCJE). *Sh Hah* (H.) 26 (Fall 1966): 54–56.

Yefroiken, Zalmen. (We Continue to Build). 21st Conference of WC Schools. *CE* (Y.) (Apr./May 1966): 1–10.

1967

Dinin, Samuel. "The Jerusalem Conference (July 1966)" (editorial). *Jew Ed* 37 (Winter 1967): 3–5.

Ed As 14th Annual Convention, Mar. 1966: 1966 Yearbook, *The Recruitment and Training of Educational Personnel*, edited by Eli Grad. N.Y.: Educator's Assembly, 1967.

NATE. *Thou Hast Sanctified Us by Thy Commandments.* Dec. 1967

Pilch, Judah. „כנסת מחנכי אמריקה במדינת ישראל" (Assembly of American Educators in Israel). *Sh Hah* (H.) 27 (Winter 1967): 116–17.

Spotts, Leon. "Proceedings of the 40th Anniversary Conference of the NCJE" (in Jerusalem). *Jew Ed* 37 (Winter 1967): 24–43. Part 2 in *Jew Ed* 37 (Spring 1967): 122–24. Also in *Sh Hah* (H.) 27 (1967): 121–28.

1968

CCAR 78 (1968): CJE, Director's Report, 79, 81; Committee on Religious Education, 109.

Ed As, Mar. 1967. *The Teen Ager and Jewish Education*, edited by Eli Grad. N.Y.: Ed As–USA, 1968. 205 pp. See also "Resolutions of the 1967 Assembly" and "The Needs of the Jewish Adolescent," *Syn Sch* 27 (Fall 1968): 81–89.

Gannes, Abraham P. "NCJE Annual Conference—Focus on Israel." *Jew Ed* 38 (Mar. 1968): 23.

NATE. *A Time for Learning.* Dec. 1968.

Spotts, Leon H. "Proceedings of the 42nd Annual Conference of the NCJE." *Jew Ed* 38 (Oct. 1968): 41–50. Resolutions, 51–52.

Syn Sch. "Selected Papers Delivered at the Conference on the Needs of the Adolescent, Dec. 24–25, 1967." 27 (Fall 1968). 89 pp.

1969

CCAR 79 (1969): CJE–Day School, 90, Committee on Religious Education, 117.

Ed As–USA, Mar. 1968. *The Parent and Jewish Education*, edited by Jay B. Stern. N.Y.: Ed As–USA, 1969. 90 pp.

Jew Ed. "NCJE Annual Conference, May–June 1969." 39 (Dec. 1969): 23–58.

NATE, Dec. 1969. *For Our Time: A Philosophy of Jewish Education.* N.Y.: NATE. 70 pp.

Schiff, Alvin I. "Challenge in Jewish Education—43rd Annual Conference Program" (editorial). *Jew Ed* 39 (Dec. 1969): 3. See also p. 23.

1970

Ed As–USA, Mar 1970. *Jewish Education in the 70's: Challenge and Promise*, edited by Abraham J. Gittelson. N.Y.: USA, 1970. 138 pp.

Goelman, Elazar. "The 6th National Conference on Jewish Education." *Jew Ed* 40 (Summer 1970): 6.

Isaacman, Daniel. "Proceedings: 44th Annual Conference of the NCJE." *Jew Ed* 40 (Winter 1970): 49–61.

Mosenkis, Matthew. "The 44th Annual Conference of the NCJE." (May 1970): *Jew Ed* 40 (Mar. 1970): 3.

Rabbi Isaac Elchanan Theological Seminary. *Proceedings of the Conference on Torah Education.* Convention in Commemoration of the 25th Anniversary of the Community Service Division, Jan. 25, 1970.

Shurin, Zvi H. "The 19th Annual Summer Seminar" (TU). *Jew Parent* 22 (Oct. 1970): 21–30.

1971

CCAR. "Concern for Improving Jewish Education." Discussed at Conference, March 1971.

RA 70th Annual Convention. May 9, 1971.

TU, Convention, 400 day schools in the United States and Canada. Feb. 12, 1971. (Data for 1971 from *AJYB* 72 (1971), 251. Compiled by Geraldine Rosenfield.)

1972

NATE, Dec. 1972. *Chai—Toward a Richer Life.* N.Y.: NATE, 1972. 148 pp.

WZO and AAJE. *Proceedings of the Conference of Directors of Bureaus of Jewish Education in the United States* (H.). July 30–Aug. 15, 1971. Jerusalem: WZO and AAJE, 1972. 222 pp.

1973

NATE, Dec. 1973. *Humanistic Values in Jewish Education.* N.Y.: NATE, 1973. 82 pp.

National Commission on Torah Education "to consider effectiveness of Orthodox educational institutions." *AJYB* 74 (1973), 227. Compiled by Geraldine Rosenfield.

RCA, Conference on Education, Dec. 19–20, 1973. *AJYB* 74 (1973): 228. Compiled by Geraldine Rosenfield.

TU, Conference Crisis in Staff Recruitment, May 3–7, 1973. *AJYB* 74 (1973): 228. Compiled by Geraldine Rosenfield.

1974

Inter-Organizational Plenary Session, May 1, 1974. "Resolutions Adopted by IOPS." *Jew Ed* 43 (Fall 1974): 62–63. (NCJE, Educators Assembly, Educators Council of America and NATE.)

Mosenkis, Matthew. „ועידת הליכוד של המחנכים היהודים באמריקה" (United Conference of Jewish Educators in America) (Aug. 16, 1974). *Hadoar* (H.) 53 (28th of Ab 1974).

NATE. *Meeting the Realities of Reform Education*. Dec. 1974.

UOJCA, 76th Anniversary Biennial Convention, Nov. 27–Dec. 1, 1974.

1975

NATE, Dec. 1975. *Exploring Israel for Jewish Education in America* (conference in Israel). N.Y.: NATE. 116 pp.

1976

NATE, Dec. 1976. *Goals and Realities: A Challenge for Now*. N.Y.: NATE. 197 pp.

North American Jewish Student (network): National Conference on Jewish Education at Brown University, Providence, R.I., Aug. 1976. (Became CAJE in 1977.)

1977

CAJE, Second National Conference, in Rochester, N.Y., Aug. 1977.

NATE, Dec. 1977. *Diversity in Jewish Education: Choices and Challenges*. N.Y.: NATE, 1978. 69 pp.

NCJE, Jubilee Conference. "Retrospect and Prospect." In N.Y., Feb. 1976. See also "Zionism and the Jewish People in Jewish Education" (Aug. 1976 in Jerusalem). *Jew Ed* 45 (Spring 1977): 8–40.

World Conference for Yiddish and Jewish Culture. „באריכט פון דער וועלט-קאנפערענץ פאר ייִדיש און ייִדישער קולטער" (Proceedings) (Y.). Jerusalem, Aug. 23–26 1976. "Recommendations on Yiddish Education," 235–37. Tel Aviv: World Bureau for Yiddish and Jewish Culture, 1977. 247 pp.

1978

Ackerman, Walter. "Irvine and Jerusalem" (CAJE). *Moment* 3 (Oct. 1978): 14–17.

CAJE, Third Annual Conference. "A Celebration of Jewish Teaching." Aug. 1978, Irvine, California.

NATE, Dec. 1978. *Shaping Our Destiny: The New Temple Educator*. N.Y.: NATE. 81 pp.

1979

CAJE, 4th Conference, Aug. 1979. At Rutgers U.

Moroz, Sh. "דרכים ודרך בחנוך„ (Paths and a Path—in Education). *Hadoar* (H.) (Nov. 23, 1979).

NATE, Dec. 1979. Silver Jubilee Volume, 1954–1979. *Change and Jewish Education*. N.Y.: NATE. 88 pp.

Rossel, Seymour. "The Educational Imperative." Report on the 4th Annual Conference on Alternatives in Jewish Education." *Response* 38 (Winter 1979–80): 47–54.

1980

NATE, Aliyah Conference in Israel. „שואה ותחיה" (Holocaust and Rebirth) N.Y.: NATE (Dec. 18–28, 1980). 130 pp.

NCJE. "Selected Papers and Presentations from the Annual Conference of the NCJE" (Mar. 1980). *Jew Ed* 48 (Summer 1980): 38–50.

1981

CAJE, 6th Conference, Aug. 1981, at Oberlin College. See *Forward* (English section) (Sept. 27, 1981): 16.

NATE. *Spiritual and Professional Concerns for the 80's*. Denver, Dec. 25–29, 1981. 124 pp.

Rosenblatt, Gary. "A Celebration of Jewish Teaching" (CAJE). *Had Mag* (Dec. 1981): 13–15, 39–40.

1982

NATE. *The Ecology of Values*. N.Y., Dec. 1982.

Pilch, Judah. "World Assemblies in Jewish Education" (review of world conferences on Jewish education). *Jew Ed* 50 (Fall 1983): 48–49.

1983

CAJE. 8th Conference, San Antonio, Texas, Aug. 1983.

Bell, Roselyn. "And in This CAJE—1200 Teachers." Account of the 8th Conference with some background on CAJE. *Moment* 9 (Dec. 1983): 45–50.

NATE—Choices and Challenges: Visions and Hope. Costa Mesa, California, Dec. 1983.

1984

CAJE, 9th Conference. Stanford U., Aug. 1984.

Kamin, Ira. "New Alternatives to Alef, Bet, Gimel..." *California Bulletin* (Aug. 17, 1984): 2, 5.

NATE, 30th Anniversary, 1955–1984. "After Bar/Bat Mitzvah, What?" Clearwater, Florida, Dec. 1984. 28 pp.

Schiff, Alvin I. "World Jewish Leadership and Jewish Education." *Jew Ed* 52 (Summer 1984): 2–6.

Smolar, Boris. „צוזאמענפאר פאר אידישע דערציער" (Conference for Jewish Educators) (CAJE). *For* (Y.) (Aug. 24, 1984): 12, 22.

———. "Jewish Education Gets a Big Dose of Judaism from CAJE." *For* (Y.) (Aug. 31, 1984): 14.

World Leadership Conference for Jewish Education. Jerusalem, June 18–20, 1984.

1985

Schiff, Alvin I. "Erev CAJE 10" (editorial comments). 53 (Summer 1985): 2–3.

1987

Adler, Andrew B. "Annual Conference of CAJE." *For* (English section) (Sept. 11, 1987).

1988

Carroll, Andrew Silow, and Leon Cohen. "CAJE Marks 'Bar Mitzvah' with Conclave in Israel." *For* (English section) (July 27, 1988): 16.

Gluck, Peggy Isaak. "Educators use Israel as Living Classroom at CAJE Meeting." *Northern California Bulletin* San Francisco (Aug. 19, 1988): 6.

UAHC Department for Religious Education and NATE. *Liheyot—(Becoming)*. "Chesed, Chinuch, Kedushah: Jewish Values for Jews with Special Needs." Phoenix, Arizona, Oct. 28–30, 1988.

27 | MEN AND WOMEN WHO INFLUENCED JEWISH EDUCATION

MEN AND WOMEN WHO INFLUENCED JEWISH EDUCATION

Abrams, Israel A., ?–1971

Abrams, Sol. "Israel A. Abrams—In Memoriam." *Jew Ed* 41 (Spring 1972): 4.

Halevi, Mordecai. "ישראל אברמס" (Israel Abrams). In *AJE* (H.) 13–16.

Liebman, Moshe. "יובלו של ישראל אברמס" (On the Jubilee in Honor of Israel Abrams). *Sh Hah* (H.) 21 (Spring 1961): 174–77.

Ahad Ha-Am, 1856–1927

Blumenfield, Samuel M. "Ahad Ha-Am: His Present Significance—On the 100th Anniversary of His Birth." *Jew Fron* (Nov. 1964): 15–23.

———. "אחד העם—מחנך הדור" (Ahad Ha-Am—Teacher of the Generation). In *SEd* (H.), 163–72.

Friedlander, Israel. "Ahad Ha-Am." In *Past and Present*, 275–98. 1961.

Gottschalk, Alfred. "Redefining Ahad Ha-Am: Israel and the Diaspora as Coexisting Centers of Jewish Life." *Amer Jew Arc* 40 (Apr. 1988): 25–39.

* Gringardas, Nordchajus. *Asher Ginzberg (Ahad Ha-Am): The Exponent of Spiritual Zionism*. U. of Pittsburgh, 1934.

Kahn, Eugene. "The Wisdom of Ahad Ha-Am." *Recon* (June 27, 1956): 16–21.

Maximon, Sh. B. "המורה" (The Teacher). On the 70th birthday of Ahad Ha-Am. *Sh Hah* (H.) 2 (1927): 1–3.

Noveck, Simon. "Ahad Ha-Am." In *GJT*, 11–44.

Pilch, Judah. "Ahad Ha-Am: His Ideology and His Legacy." *Jew Fron* (May 1977): 17–20.

Simon, Leon. "Ahad Ha-am." *AJYB* 30 (1928–29): 87–99.

* Taback, Samuel. *Ahad Ha-Am's Influence on Jewish Educational Thinking in America*. Dropsie College, 1966.

Weiss-Rosmarin, Trude. "Ahad Ha-Am—Prophet of Jewish Survival." (A century after his birth.) *Congress Weekly* (Dec. 17, 1956).

Alper, Michael, 1902–55

"Alper, Michael." *AJYB* 57 (1956): 605.

Altaian, Shalom, 1911–1986

"Altman, Shalom." *AJYB* 88 (1988): 500–501.

Arian, Shraga (Philip), 1919–72

Gittelson, Abraham. "Shraga Arian—In Memoriam." *Jew Ed* 41 (Fall 1972): 8–9.

Picker, Chaim, ed. *He Kindled a Light: A Philosophy of Jewish Education. From the Speeches and Writings of Shraga Arian*. N.Y.: USCJE, 1976. 142 pp.

27 MEN AND WOMEN WHO INFLUENCED JEWISH EDUCATION

Bardin, Shlomo H., 1898–1976

"Bardin, Shlomo." *AJYB* 78 (1979): 538.

Powell, B. "Shlomo Bardin as Educator." *Jew Spec* 43 (Spring 1978): 36–38.

Bass, Hyman B., 1904–86

"Bass, Hyman B." *AJYB* 85 (1985): 412–13.

"Bass, Hyman B." In *Enc Jud* 4, 413.

"חיים בעז," (H. B. Bass). In *Biographical Dictionary of Modern Yiddish Literature* (Y.), 355–56.

Bavli, Hillel, 1893–1961

"Bavli, Hillel." In *Enc Jud* 4, 348–49.

Dinin, Samuel. "Hillel Bavli—In Memoriam." *Jew Ed* 32 (Winter 1962): 69.

Halevi, Abraham Zvi. "יהלל בבלי המבקת והמחנך" (Hillel Bavli—the Critic and Educator). *Sh Hah* (H.) 23 (Winter 1963): 82–84.

Belkin, Samuel, 1911–76

Hartstein, Jacob I. "About Two Unsung Heroes." *Jew Ed* 50 (Fall 1982): 28–31.

The Inauguration of Rabbi Samuel Belkin. Yeshiva U., 1945.

Leaf, Hayim. "Dr. Samuel Belkin—Scholar, Educator and Community Leader" (H.). In *Samuel Belkin Memorial Volume*, ix–xx. N.Y.: 1981.

Schiff, Alvin I. "Samuel Belkin—in Memoriam." *Jew Ed* 44 (Spring/Summer 1976): 17.

Stitskin, Leon. "Dr. Samuel Belkin as Scholar and Educator." In *Studies in Judaica in Honor of Dr. Samuel Belkin as Scholar and Educator*, 3–18. N.Y.: 1974.

Benathan, Morris, ?–1967

Eisenberg, Azriel. "Morris Benathan—In Memoriam." *Jew Ed* 38 (Jan. 1968): 8.

Gopstein, Alizah. "לזכרו של מ. בן נתן ז"ל" (M. Benathan—In Memoriam." *Sh Hah* 27 (Fall 1966): 63.

Benderly, Samson, 1876–1944

Alper, Michael. "Dr. Benderly as a Teacher of Liberal Rabbis." *American Hebrew* 86 (Mar. 14, 1910). See also *Jew Ed* 20 (1949).

Honor, Leo L. "שלשה שהשפיעו" (Three Who Were Influential). In *JB* (H.), 343–51.

"Samson Benderly Memorial Issue." *Jew Ed* 20 (Summer 1949). Includes articles by Alexander M. Dushkin, Mordecai M. Kaplan, Israel S. Chipkin, Samuel Dinin, Abraham P. Gannes, and others.

Scharfstein, Zevi. "שמשון בנדרלי" (Samson Benderly). In *GJE* (H.), 179–207.

———. "שמשון בנדרלי" (Samson Benderly—Ten Years after His Death). *Sh Hah* (H.) 14 (April 1954): 67–80, 131–46.

* Winter, Nathan H. "An Early Educational Blueprint for the Jewish School." In *Jewish Education in a Pluralist Society: Samson Benderly and Jewish Education in the United States*, 239–52. N.Y.: New York U. Press, 1966).

———. *The Role of Samson Benderly in Jewish Education in the United States*. New York U., 1963. 344 pp.

Ben-Horin, Meir, 1918–88

"Ben-Horin, Meir." In *Enc Jud* 4, 520.

Braver, Haim. "Education versus Religion." *Sh Hah* (H.) 46 (Winter 1988): 83–85.

Eisenstein, Ira. "In Memory: Dr. Meir Ben-Horin." *Recon* 54 (Oct/Nov. 1988): 8.

Ravid, Zvulun. "פרופסור מאיר בן-חורין" (Professor Meir Ben-Horin). *Sh Hah* (H.) 46 (Winter 1988): 79–82.

Berdichevsky, Zalman, ?–1971

D.I.B. *"Zalman Berdichevsky—In Memoriam." Jew Ed* 41 (Spring 1972): 6.

Berkson, Isaac B., 1891–1974

Ben-Horin, Meier. "על הגותו הקהילתית והחינוכית של יצחק בר ברקסון" (On Berkson's Communal and Educational Philosophy). *Sh Hah* (H.) 44 (Spring 1985): 177–81.

———. "Isaac Baer Berkson—In Memoriam." *Jew Ed* 43 (Winter/Spring 1975): 6–7.

"Berkson, Isaac B." *AJYB* 77 (1977): 592.

Dinin, Samuel. "Isaac B. Berkson" (editorial). *Jew Ed* 32 (Spring 1962): 134.

Goelman, Elazar. "Three American Educators in Israel." *Jew Ed* 47 (Winter 1979): 20–25.

Halevi, Mordecai. "יצחק ברקסון וספרו האחרון" (Isaac Berkson and His Last Book). In *AJE* (H.), 49–59.

Merowitz, Morton. "Some Aspects of the Educational Thought of Isaac B. Berkson." *Rel Ed* 64 (July/Aug. 1969): 286–91.

Pilch, Judah. "ד"ר יצחק ב. ברקסון ז"ל המחנך הפילוסוף" (In Memory of Dr. Berkson, the Educator and Philosopher). *Hadoar* (H.) 54 (Apr. 25, 1975).

* Skirball, Henry F. *Isaac Baer Berkson and Jewish Education*. Columbia U., 1977. 339 pp.

Berkson, Mrs. Isaac B. (Libbie Suchoff), ?–1970

Dushkin, Alexander M. "Mrs. Isaac B. Berkson (Libbie Suchoff)—In Memoriam." *Jew Ed* 40 (Winter 1970): 8.

Berlin, Meyer, 1880–1949

"Bar-Ilan, Meir." In *Enc Jud* 4, 224–25.

"Berlin, Meyer (Meir Bar-Ilan)." *AJYB* 51 (1950): 519.

Berlin, Naphtati Levi Judah, 1817–93

Jung, Leo. "Naphtali Zevi Judah Berlin." In *Men of Spirit*, 285–99. 1964.

Scharfstein, Zevi. "ר' נפתלי צבי יהודה ברלין (הנצי"ב)" (N. L. J. Berlin, Ha-Neziv). In *GJE* (H.), 57–67.

Blumenfield, Samuel M., 1901–72

"Blumenfield, Samuel M." *AJYB* 74 (1973): 554.

Bortniker, Elijah. "Samuel M., Blumenfield—In Memoriam." *Jew Ed* 41 (Fall 1972): 6–7.

Feigin, Samuel I. "ד"ר שמואל בלומנפילד" (Dr. Samuel Blumenfield). *Sh Hah* (H.) 5 (Sept. 1945): 242–48.

Gannes, Abraham P. "Dr. Blumenfield and the Department of Education and Culture." In *Thou Shalt Teach*, edited by Judah Pilch, xiii–xix.

Ravid, Zvulun. "ד"ר שמואל בלומנפילד" (Dr. S. Blumenfield). *Sh Hah* (H.) 5 (Sept. 1945): 49–50.

Borowsky, Samuel I., 1895–1965

Blumenfield, Samuel M. "ליובלו של שמואל י. בורובסקי" (On the Jubilee of Samuel I. Borowsky). *Sh Hah* (H.) 25 (Summer 1965): 208–9.

"Borowsky, Samuel I." *AJYB* 68 (1967): 524.

Davis, Moshe. "דברים על יד קברו של שמואל יהודה בורובסקי ז"ל" (Samuel Yehudah Borowsky—In Memoriam). *Sh Hah* (H.) 26 (Summer 1966): 278.

Diamond, Joseph. "על מות שמואל י. בורובסקי" (Samuel Yehudah Borowsky—In Memoriam). *Sh Hah* (H.) 26 (Summer 1966): 274–75.

Dushkin, Alexander M. "דברי הספד" (Samuel Y. Borowsky—In Memoriam). *Sh Hah* (H.) 26 (Summer 1966): 277.

Kodesh, Shlomo. "דברי הספד על שמואל יהודה בורובסקי ז"ל" (Samuel I. Borowsky—In Memoriam). *Sh Hah* (H.) 26 (Summer 1966): 277–78.

Bragin, Joseph, ?–1932

Benderly, Samson. "Tribute to Joseph Bragin." *Jew Ed* 5 (Jan./Mar. 1933): 20–21.

Kaplan, Mordecai M. "Tribute to Joseph Bragin." *Jew Ed* 5 (Jan./Mar. 1933): 18–20.

Brickman, William W., 1913–86

"Brickman, William W." *AJYB* 88 (1988): 501.

Brickner, Barnett R., 1892–1958

"Barnett Brickner—In Memoriam." *J Jew Com Ser* (Fall 1958): 3.

"Brickner, Barnett R." *AJYB* 60 (1959): 354–55.

"Brickner, Barnett Robert." In *Enc Jud* 4, 1369–70.

Gamoran, Emanuel. "Barnett R. Brickner in Memoriam." *Jew Ed* 29 (Winter 1959): 2, 15.

Brilliant, Nathan, 1894–1983

Braverman, Libbie. "Nathan Brilliant—In Memoriam." *Jew Ed* 51 (Winter 1983): 2.

Levitin, Bernard. (Nathan Brilliant—In Memoriam). *Sh Hah* (H.) 43 (Winter 1983–84): 75.

Buber, Martin, 1878–1965

Ben-Yosef, I. A. "Buber's Dialogue Principle in Education." *Jew Ed* (Fall 1985): 19–22.

Bick, A. "מארטין בובער און זיין דערציאונגס-טעאריע" (Buber and His Theory of Education). *CE* (Y.) 11 (Nov. 1941): 17–18.

Birnbaum, Ruth. "The Man of Dialogue and the Man of Halakhah." *Jud* 26 (Winter 1977): 52–62.

27 MEN AND WOMEN WHO INFLUENCED JEWISH EDUCATION

Churgin, Gershon. „מהגיונותיו של בובר על החינוך" (Buber's Reflections on Education). *Sh Hah* (H.) 26 (Winter 1966): 131–36. See also *Hadoar* (H.) 56 (Dec. 10, 1976).

Cohen, A. "The Question of Values and Value Education in the Philosophy of Martin Buber." *Teachers College Record* 80 (May 1974).

Cohen, Adir. *The Educational Philosophy of Martin Buber*. Rutherford, N.J.: Fairleigh Dickinson U. Press, 1983. 274 pp.

Etscovitz, L. "Religious Education as Sacred and Profane: An Interpretation of Martin Buber." *Rel Ed* (July/Aug. 1969): 279–86.

* Falk, Randall M. *The Philosophy of Martin Buber on Christian-Jewish Relations and Its Relevance for the Contemporary American Community*. Vanderbilt U. Divinity School, 1969. 136 pp.

Friedman, Maurice. "Martin Buber." In *GJT*, 183–209.

———. "Martin Buber and Religious Education." *Rel Ed* 54 (Jan./Feb. 1959): 5–17.

Iram, Yaakov. „משנתו החינוכית של מרטיו בובר—עיון מחדש" (Martin Buber's Educational Philosophy Reconsidered). *Sh Hah* (H.) 39 (Sept. 1979): 29–33; (Dec. 1979): 97–102.

Kiner, Edward D. "Martin Buber's Concept of 'Living Truth' and Jewish Education." *CCAR J* (Apr. 1969): 73–76.

Kurzweil, Zvi. "Buber on Education." *Jud* (Winter 1962): 44–55.

"Martin Buber on His Centennial—A Tribute and An Evaluation" (various authors). *Jud* 37 (Spring 1975): 135–213.

Rachlis, A. "Martin Buber's Dialogical Principles in Religious Education." *Recon* 40 (June 1974): 18–25.

Chajes, Hirsch (Zevi) Perez, 1876–1923

Baron, Shalom. „הרב צ. פ. חיות בתור חוקר ומורה" (Rabbi H. P. Chajes—As Researcher and Teacher). *Sh Hah* (H.) 4 (1928): 37–45.

Federbush, S., ed. "Rabbi Chajes." In Hokhmat Yisrael be-Eiropah) (The Wisdom of Israel in Europe) (H.), 1:241–53. 1958.

Chanin, Nathan, 1886–1965

"Chanin, Nathan." *AJYB* 67 (1966): 533.

„נחום כאניו" (Nathan Chanin). In *Biographical Dictionary of Modern Yiddish Literature* (Y.), 372–76.

Yefroiken, Zalman. (N. Chanin—Leader in Education and Culture). In כאניו .נ (N. Chanin) (Y.), 142–72. N.Y.: N. Chanin Jubilee Committee, 1946.

Charna, Shalom Yonah, 1878–1932

Abramovitz, Hirsch. „שלשה מחנכים עברים מפרסמים" (Three Famous Hebrew Educators). *Sh Hah* (H.) 14 (Winter 1954): 88–98.

"Charna, Shalom Yonah." In *Enc Jud* 5, 360–61.

Scharfstein, Zevi. „אהרן כהנשטם וד"ר יונה טשרני" (Aharon Kahnshtam and Dr. Yonah Charna). In *GJE* (H.), 115–35.

Chipkin, Israel S., 1891–1955

Berkson, Isaac B. "Israel S. Chipkin—Servant of the Jewish Renaissance." *Jew Ed* 27 (Fall 1956): 7–9, 28.

"Chipkin, Israel S." *AJYB* 58 (1957): 475–76.

"Dedicated to the Memory of Israel S. Chipkin." *Jew Ed* 27 (Fall 1956).

Elkin, Harry. "Writings of Israel S. Chipkin." *Jew Ed* 27 (Fall 1956): 61–63.

Engelman, Uriah Z. "Dr. Chipkin as Pioneer in Jewish Research." *Jew Ed* 27 (Fall 1956): 35–37.

Gamoran, Emanuel. „ד"ר עזריאל שלמה טשיפקין ע"ה" (Dr. Israel S. Chipkin—In Memoriam). *Sh Hah* (H.) 16 (Winter 1956): 73–75.

Halevi, Mordecai. „ישראל טשיפקיו—ז"ל" (Israel Chipkin—In Memoriam). In *AIE* (H.), 117–25.

Honor, Leo L. "In Memoriam." *Jew Ed* 27 (Fall 1956): 5–6.

Kaplan, Mordecai M. "Israel Chipkin." *Jew Ed* 27 (Fall 1956): 5–6.

Pilch, Judah. "Dr. Israel S. Chipkin—In Memoriam." In *Reg* (1959), v–i.

Chomsky, Elsie, ?–1972

Goelman, Elazar. "Elsie Chomsky—In Memoriam." *Jew Ed* 42 (Winter 1972–73): 7.

Chomsky, William, 1896–1977

"Chomsky, William." *AJYB* 79 (1979): 368.

"Dedicated to the Memory of Dr. William Chomsky." *Sh Hah* (H.) 37 (June 1978): 196–210. Includes tributes by: Uziel Adini, T. Baker,

Abraham P. Gannes, Elazar Goelman, Abraham Martan, and Zvulun Ravid.

Eisenberg, Azriel. "ד"ר חומסקי ליובלו הששים" (Dr. Chomsky on His 60th Birthday). *Sh Hah* (H.) 17 (Summer 1957): 196–200.

Gannes, Abraham P. "כתבי הד"ר זאב חומסקי" (Writings of Dr. William Chomsky). *Sh Hah* (H) 18 (Fall 1958): 54–55.

Glenn, Menahem. "ד"ר זאב חומסקי" (Dr. William Chomsky). *Sh Hah* (H.) (Winter 1956): 104–8.

Goelman, Elazar. "William Chomsky, in Memoriam." *Jew Ed* 43 (Summer/Fall 1977): 5.

Ravid, Zvulun. "לד"ר זאב חומסקי ליובלו" (To Dr. Chomsky on His Jubilee). *Sh Hah* (H.) 25 (Fall 1965): 3–6.

Churgin, Gershon A., 1903–78

"Churgin, Gershon A." *AJYB* 80 (1980): 363.

Churgin, Pinchos, 1894–1957

Benathan, Morris. "Dr. Pinchos Churgin." *Jew Ed* 28 (Winter 1957–58): 2–3.

"Churgin, Pinchos M." *AJYB* 60 (1959): 354.

Hoenig, Sidney B. "Pinchos Churgin." *JBA* 16 (1958): 105–7.

Lander, Dov Ber. "ד"ר פנחס חורגין ז"ל" (Dr. Pinchos Churgin—In Memoriam). *Sh Hah* (H.) 18 (Spring 1958): 162–64.

Leaf, Hayim. "על המעוט והמרובה בחינוך העברי" (Minimum and Maximum in Jewish Education). *Sh Hah* (H.) 46 (Winter 1988): 86–92.

Ravid, Zvulun. "Churgin's Vision upon Contemporary Jewish Educational Development." *Sh Hah* (H.) 46 (Winter 1988): 93–99.

Reznik, Reuben. "ד"ר פנחס חורגין המורה" (Dr. Pinchos Churgin, the Teacher). *Sh Hah* (H.) 28 (Winter 1968): 123–24.

Smolar, Levi. "פנחס חורגין ותרגום יונתן על הנביאים" (Pinchos Churgin and Targum Jonathan on the Prophets). *Sh Hah* (H.) 43 (Fall 1983): 23–30.

Citron, Samuel J., 1908–79

Avital, Moshe. (Dr. Samuel J. Citron—In Memoriam). *Sh Hah* (H.) 39 (Sept. 1979): 25–28.

Gannes, Abraham P. "Samuel Citron—In Memoriam." *Jew Ed* 47 (Summer 1979): 5–6.

Mosenkis, Matthew. "ד"ר שמואל י. צטרון ז"ל" (Dr. Samuel J. Citron—In Memoriam). *Sh Hah* (H.) 38 (June 1979): 196.

Colodner, Solomon, 1908–86

"Colodner, Solomon." *AJYB* 88 (1988): 502.

Davis, Moshe, 1916–

"Davis, Moshe." In *Enc Jud* 5, 1369–70.

Dushkin, Alexander. "Dr. Moshe Davis, Ph. D., Hebrew University." *Jew Ed* 18 (Feb. 1947): 2, 43.

Wigoder, Geoffrey, ed. *Contemporary Jewry: Studies in Honor of Moshe Davis* (H. and E.) (on Davis's 70th birthday). Jerusalem: Institute of Contemporary Jewry/Hebrew U., 1984. 441 pp.

Dewey, John, 1859–1952

Ben-Horin, Meir. "John Dewey and Jewish Education." *Recon* (Oct. 30, 1959): 15–19. See also *Ped Rep* 11 (Jan. 1960) and *Rel Ed* 55 (May/June 1960): 201–2.

Berkson, Isaac B. "Some Dewey Ideas and Their Implications for Jewish Education." *Jewish Institute Quarterly* 3 (Jan. 1927): 13–21; (Mar. 1927): 22–32; (May 1927): 19–22. See also *Sh Hah* (H.) 3 (Nissan 1927): 23–32; 3 (Tishre 1928): 203–12.

Blumenfield, Samuel M. "משנת דיואי והחנוך העברי" (John Dewey and His Contribution to Jewish Education). In *S Ed* (H.), 173–83. See also *Sh Hah* (H.) 20 (Winter 1960).

———. "John Dewey and Jewish Education." *Rel Ed* 67 (May/June 1972): 163–69.

———. "ג"ון דיואי ותרומתו לחינוך היהודי" (The Teachings of John Dewey and Jewish Education). *Sefer Ha shanah* (H.) 5 (1940): 291–300.

Dinin, Samuel. "The Influence of John Dewey on Some Pioneer Jewish Educators." *Jew Ed* 48 (Spring 1980): 6–11, 18.

* Kronish, Ronald. *The Influence of John Dewey on Jewish Education in America*. Harvard U. Graduate School of Education, 1979.

———. "The Influence of John Dewey on Jewish Education: Preliminary Findings." *Con Jud* (Winter 1976): 44–57.

———. "John Dewey and Jewish Education Today." *Jew Ed* 48 (Fall 1980): 24–26; 51 (Winter 1983): 35–37.

Scharfstein, Zevi. "דיואי כמורה„ (John Dewey as a Teacher). *Sh Hah* (H.) (Fall 1960): 76–77.

Dinin, Samuel, 1902–

"Dinin, Samuel." In *Enc Jud* 6, 57.

Dinsky, Samuel H., ?–1970

Toubin, Isaac. "Samuel H. Dinsky—In Memoriam." *Jew Ed* 40 (Winter 1979): 7–8.

Dushkin, Alexander M., 1890–1976.

Davis, Moshe. "שלש הקאריירית של אלכסנדר דושקין„ (Three Careers of Alexander M. Dushkin). *Hadoar* (H.) 59 (Sept. 5, 1966).

Eisenstein, Ira. "Alexander M. Dushkin at Seventy-Five." *Recon* 31 (Jan. 7, 1966).

Gannes, Abraham P. "Alexander M. Dushkin—In Memoriam." *Jew Ed* 44 (Spring/Summer 1976): 14–15.

———. "בונה גשרים„ (A Builder of Bridges). *Sh Hah* (H.) (Winter 1986): 69–73.

———, ed. "Introduction." In *Alexander M. Dushkin, Jewish Education: Selected Writings*, 9–21. Jerusalem: Hebrew U. School of Education and Ministry of Education and Culture, Magnes Press, Hebrew U., 1980. Annotated bibliography, 163–80.

Goldstein, Israel. "On Professor Dushkin." *Day* (July 25, 1965).

* Iram, Yaacov. *Half a Century of Jewish Education in the United States as reflected in A. M. Dushkin's Thought and Work*. Dropsie U., 1972.

———. הלכה ומעשה בחינוך היהודי (Theory and Practice in Jewish Education) (H.). A. M. Dushkin's thought and work in the United States and Israel. Tel Aviv: 1977. 294 pp.

"A. M. Dushkin: His Contributions in America and Israel" (special issue). *Jew Ed* 41 (Summer/Fall 1971): 43–125. Includes editorial by Abraham P. Gannes ("Our Debt to Alexander M. Dushkin) and articles by Zevi Adar, Isaac B. Berkson, Samuel M. Blumenfield, Moshe Davis, Tamar De Sola Pool, Yohanan Ginat, Israel Goldstein, Avraham Harman, Mordecai M. Kaplan, Moshe Kol, Edward A. Nudelman, Judah Pilch, Zvulun Ravid, Chanoch Rinott, Nathan Rotenstreich, Louis Ruffman, Alvin I. Schiff, Albert P. Schoolman, and Ernst Simon. Bibliography, 37–40.

Levitats, Isaac I. "חלוץ התחייה באמריקה ובישראל„ (A Pioneer of the Rebirth in America and Israel). *Hadoar* (H.) 54 (May 30, 1975).

Dushkin, Julia Aronson, ?–1975

Gamoran, Mamie. "Julia Aronson Dushkin—In Memoriam." *Jew Ed* 44 (Spring/Summer 1976): 16.

Edelstein, Menachem M., 1892–1954

Azrieli, Shlomo (Israel Chipkin). "Menahem M. Edelstein—In Memoriam." *Jew Ed* 25 (Fall 1954): 9–10.

"Edelstein, Menachem M." *AJYB* 57 (1956): 605.

Halevi, Mordecai. "לדמותו של ד"ר מנחם אדלשטיין ז"ל„ (On the Personality of Dr. M. Edelstein—In Memoriam). *Sh Hah* (H.) 16 (Fall 1956): 3–8. Also in *AJE*, 17–28.

Pilch, Judah, "Kalman Whiteman and Menachem Edelstein." *Jew Ed* 40 (Spring 1971): 19.

Tabak, Ben-Zion. "מנחם ע. אדלשטיין ז"ל„ (Menachem Edelstein—In Memoriam). *Sh Hah* (H.) 16 (Fall 1956): 14–15.

Edidin, Ben M., 1899–1948

Dushkin, Alexander M. "Ben M. Edidin—In Memoriam." *Jew Ed* 20 (Fall 1948): 2–3.

Halevi, Mordecai. "Benjamin Edidin—In Memoriam" (H.). In *AJE*, 126–29.

Efros, Israel, 1891–1981

"Efros, Israel Isaac." In *Enc Jud* 6, 468–69.

Goelman, Elazar. "Israel Efros—In Memoriam." *Jew Ed* 49 (Spring 1981): 3.

Eisenberg, Azriel, 1903–85

"ספרי עזריאל אייזנברג„ (The Books of Azriel Eisenberg). *Sh Hah* (H.) 21 (Winter 1965): 137–38.

Chomsky, William. "ד"ר עזריאל אייזנברג—איש ההלכה למעשה„ (Dr. Azriel Eisenberg—From Theory to Practice). *Sh Hah* (H.) 25 (Winter 1965): 68–69.

Gannes, Abraham P. "Azriel Eisenberg at Seventy-Five." *Jew Ed* 46:3 (Autumn 1978): 5–9.

———. "עזריאל אייזנברג ע״ה" (Azriel Eisenberg—The Man and the Educator). *Sh Hah* (H.) 45 (Winter 1985): 85–88.

Halevi, Mordecai. "עזריאל אייזנברג וספריו" (Azriel Eisenberg and His Writings). In *AJE* (H.), 29–38.

Millgram, Abraham E. "Azriel Eisenberg—In Memoriam." *Jew Ed* 53 (Winter 1985): 4–6.

Mosenkis, Matthew. "עזריאל אייזנברג ז״ל" (Azriel Eisenberg—Eulogy). *Sh Hah* (H.) 45 (Winter 1985): 89–90.

Ravid, Zvulun. "פרס שז״ר לעזריאל אייזנברג" (The Shazar Award to Azriel Eisenberg) (editorial). *Sh Hah* (H.) 38 (Oct. 1978): 7–8; (1979): 134.

Elijah Ben Solomon Zalman, "Gaon of Vilna," 1720–97

Charna, Sh. I. "הגאון מווילנה על עניני חנוך" (The Gaon of Vilna on Education." *Sh Hah* (H.) 4 (1929): 189–97.

———. (The Gaon of Vilna—His Methodology in Education). In *DER* (Y.), 3:310–38.

Ginzberg, Louis. "The Gaon, Rabbi Elijah of Wilna." In *Students, Scholars and Saints*, 125–44. 1928.

Greenstone, Julius H. "The Books of Elijah Gaon." *JBA* 6 (1947/48): 76–83.

Schechter, Solomon. "Rabbi Elijah Wilna, Gaon." In *Studies in Judaism*, 73–98. N.Y.: JPS, 1896.

Waxman, Meyer. "The Gaon of Vilna." *Jew Life* (Oct. 1948): 17–24.

———. "Vilna Gaon." In *GJP*, 317–27.

Elkin, Harry, ?–1964

Pilch, Judah. "Harry Elkin—In Memoriam." *Jew Ed* 34 (Summer 1964): 221–221.

Engelman, Uriah Z., ?–1972

Segal, Leon. "Uriah Engelman—In Memoriam." *Jew Ed* 41 (Fall 1972): 7.

Entin, Joel, 1874–1959

"Entin, Joel." In *Enc Jud* 6, 801.

Gladstone, Jacob. "יואל ענטין" (Joel Entin). *Day* (Y.) (Oct. 1, 1961).

Jeshurin, Ephim H. *Bibliography of Joel Entin* (Y.). N.Y.: 1960. 16 pp.

Lehrer, Leibush. "יואל ענטין" (Joel Entin). *YK* (Y.) (Jan. 31, 1965).

Mendelson, I. "יואל ענטין דער מענטש פון תורה און מעשים" (Joel Entin, the Man of Torah and Deeds). *CE* 29 (May 1959): 1–17.

Shoob, E. "יואל ענטין" (Joel Entin). *For* (Y.) (May 17, 1964).

Shulman, Elias. "יואל ענטין" (Joel Entin). In *Bibliographical Dictionary of Modern Yiddish Literature* (Y.), 3–8.

Epstein, Izhac, 1863–1943

"Epstein, Izhac." In *Enc Jud* 6, 826–27.

Scharfstein, Zevi. "יצחק אפשטיין" (Izhac Epstein). In *GJE* (H.), 143–62.

Feigin, Samuel I., 1893–1950

Blumenfield, Samuel M. "ד״ר שמואל י. פייגין ז״ל" (Dr. Samuel I. Feigin—In Memoriam.") *Sh Hah* (H.) 10 (1951): 53–54.

"Feigin, Samuel I." *AJYB* 52 (1951): 501.

"Feigin, Samuel I." In *Enc Jud* 6, 1207.

Golub, Jacob S. "We Mourn Our Losses." *Jew Ed* 21 (Summer 1950): 10.

Halkin, A. Sh. "שמואל י. פייגין איש המדע" (Samuel Feigin—The Scientist). *Sh Hah* (H.) 10 (Summer 1950): 150–53.

Feinstein, Moses, 1895–1986

"Feinstein, Moses." *AJYB* 66 (1988): 503.

"Feinstein, Moses." In *Enc Jud* 6, 1213.

Helmreich, William D. *The World of the Yeshiva: An Intimate Portrait of Orthodox Jewry*. N.Y.: Free Press, 1982. See index p. 407 regarding Feinstein.

Felsenthal, Bernhard, 1822–1908

Felsenthal, Emma. *Bernhard Felsenthal, Teacher in Israel*. N.Y.: Oxford U. Press, 1924. 362 pp.

* Ludlow, Victor L. Bernhard Felsenthal: Quest for Zion. Brandeis U., 1984.

Soviv, Aaron. "Bernhard Felsenthal, a Great American Jewish Educator." *Jew Ed* 25 (Summer 1954): 35–41, 64.

Stolz, Joseph. "Bernhard Felsenthal." *CCAR* (1909): 161–67. See also *AJHS* 17 (1909): 218–22.

Feuerstein, Samuel C., 1893?–1983

"Feuerstein, Samuel C." *AJYB* 85 (1985): 414–15.

Franzblau, Abraham N., 1901–82

"Franzblau, Abraham." *AJYB* 84 (1984): 332.

"Franzblau, Abraham N." In *Enc Jud* 7, 110.

Freehof, Solomon B., 1892–

Jacob, Walter, Frederick C. Schwartz, and Vigdor W. Kavaler, eds. *Essays in Honor of Solomon B. Freehof*. Pittsburgh: Rodef Shalom Congregation, 1964. 331 pp. Essays include:
- Bamberger, Bernard J., "Solomon Freehof in the Central Conference of American Rabbis," 97–104.
- Gittelsohn, Roland B., "Dr. Freehof, Teacher of His Time," 105–11.
- Pilchik, Ely, "Our Mentor, Solomon B. Freehof," 112–17.

Friedland, Abraham H., 1891–1939

Blumenfield, Samuel M. "מחנך אסתיטיקן" (Educator—Aesthete). In *Friedland* (H.), 52–54.

———. "Friedland, the Educator." *Recon* (Sept. 29, 1931). See also *S Ed* (H.), 208–10.

Braverman, Libbie. "Profile of a Pedagogical Giant." *Jew Ed* 50 (Fall 1982): 3–5.

Feinstein, M. "המחנך" (The Pedagogue). In *Friedland* (H.), 43–47. See also *Sh Hah* (H.) 1 (1940): 66–68.

Gamoran, Emanuel. "Abraham H. Friedland." *AJYB* 42 (1940–41): 145–152.

———. "ח. א. פרידלנד—המחנך העברי" (A. Friedland, the Hebrew Educator). *Hadoar* (H.) 18 (10th of Elul 1939).

———. "כתר התורה שלו" (His Prime Teachings). In *Friedland* (H.), 38–42.

Golub, Jacob S. "Abraham H. Friedland." *Jew Ed* 11 (Jan. 1940): 182–85.

Haramati, Shlomo. "ח"א פרידלנד בסיפורים יפים שלו" (A. Friedland in His *Beautiful Stories*). *Hadoar* (H.) (Oct. 18, 1974).

Isaacs, Bernard. "ח. א. פרידלנד—איש האשכולות" (A. Friedland, a Man of Parts). In *Sefer B. Isaacs* (H.), 88–90.

Orlan, Hayim. "עם זכרו של ח. א. פרידלנד" (The Memory of H. A. Friedland—Twenty Years after His Death). *Sh Hah* (H.) 21 (Winter 1961): 114–15.

Persky, Daniel. "לזכר פרידלנד" (In Memory of H. A. Friedland). In *Friedland* (H.), 15–30.

Ribalow, Menahem. "בחייו ובמותו" (In Life and In Death). In *Friedland* (H.), 10–14.

Scharfstein, Zevi. "ח. א. פרידלנד" (H. A. Friedland). In *GJE* (H.), 251–65.

Friedlander, Israel, 1876–1920

Cohen, Boaz. *Israel Friedlander: A Bibliography of His Writings with an Appreciation*. N.Y.: Moinester Publishing Co., 1936.

Honor, Leo L. "שלשה שהשפיעו" (Three Who Were Influential). In *JB* (H.), 343–51.

Kohn, Jacob, "Israel Friedlander: A Biographical Sketch." *AJYB* 23 (1921–22): 65–79.

Magnes, Judah L. "The Work of Israel Friedlander: Friedlander the Student." *Menorah J* 6 (Dec. 1920): 351–54.

Marx, Alexander. "Israel Friedlander, Zionist and Scholar." *Maccabean* 34 (Aug. 1920): 33–35.

———. "The Work of Israel Friedlander: Friedlander the Scholar." *Menorah J* 6 (Dec. 1920): 344–50. Also in his *Essays in Jewish Biography*, 280–89. 1947.

Parzen, Herbert. "Israel Friedlander—A Teacher of Cultural Judaism." In *Architects of Conservative Judaism*, 155–88. N.Y.: Jonathan David, 1964.

Schussheim, Morris. "Recollections of Israel Friedlander." *RA* (1945).

Shargel, Baila Round. *Practical Dreamer, Israel Friedlander and the Shaping of American Judaism*. N.Y.: JTSA, 1985. 223 pp.

Frisch, Daniel, 1897–1950

"Frisch, Daniel." In *Enc Jud* 7, 197.

Golub, Jacob S. "We Mourn Our Losses." *Jew Ed* 21 (Summer 1950): 9–10.

Frishberg, Israel Z., 1876–1955

"Frishberg, Israel Z." *AJYB* 58 (1957): 476.

Halevi, Mordecai. "י. ז. פרישברג ז"ל" (I. Z. Frishberg—In Memoriam) (H.). In *AJE*, 148–50.

Gamoran, Emanuel, 1895–1962

Berkson, Isaac B. "A Personal Memorial—Emanuel Gamoran." *Jew Ed* 34 (Winter 1964): 6–7.

Dinin, Samuel. "Emanuel Gamoran—In Memoriam." *Jew Ed* 33 (Winter 1963): 70–71.

"Gamoran, Emanuel." *AJYB* 65 (1964): 432.

Gamoran, Hillel. "Father and Teacher." In *Gamoran*, 6–9.

Gittelsohn, Roland B. "Not Afraid of Change." In *Gamoran*, 18–21. Also in *Jew Ed* 34 (Winter 1964): 80–83.

Golub, Jacob. "ד״ר עמנואל גמראן לשנתו החמישים" (Dr. Emanuel Gamoran on His 50th Birthday). *Sh Hah* (H.) 6 (1946): 154–56.

Grand, Samuel, and Mamie G. Gamoran, eds. *Emanuel Gamoran, His Life and His Work*. N.Y.: Emanuel Gamoran Memorial Fund, 1979. See especially bibliography, pp. 160–64.

Halevi, Mordecai. "עמנואל גמראן ז״ל" (E. Gamoran—In Memoriam). In *AJE* (H.), 60–62.

Kaufman, Jay. "Eulogy—Dr. Emanuel Gamoran." In *AJE*, 16–17.

Olitzky, Kerry M. "The Gamoran Revolution: Its Incipient Stages." *Jew Ed* 52 (Winter 1984–85): 29–34.

Schoolman, Albert P. "Emanuel Gamoran—His Life and Work." *Jew Ed* 34 (Winter 1964): 69–79. See also *Sh Hah* (H.) 23 (Winter 1963–64): 79–81.

* Wechman, Robert J. *Emanuel Gamoran: Pioneer in Jewish Religious Education*. Syracuse U., 1970.

Gelbart, Frances Spitzer, ?–1969

Mosenkis, Matthew. "Frances Spitzer Gelbart—In Memoriam." *Jew Ed* 39 (Dec. 1969): 6.

Gelbart, Gershon, ?

Gamoran, Emanuel. "Dr. Gershon Gelbart—In Memoriam." *Jew Ed* 29 (Winter 1959): 15.

Gingold, Pinchas M., 1892–1953

Brown, Meyer. "דער מאמין" (The Believer) (Y.). In *Gingold*, 325–28.

Edelstein, Menachem. "פנחס גינגאלד—דער איד" (Pinchas Gingold, the Jew). In *Gingold*, 282–89.

Eisenberg, Azriel. "מענטשן פון צוויי וועלטן" (People of Two Worlds). In *Gingold*, 290–94.

Even-Shmuel (Kaufman), Judah. "דרכים און מידות" (Paths and Values) (H.). In *Gingold*, 270–77.

Golub, Jacob S. "We Mourn Our Losses." *Jew Ed* 24 (Spring 1954): 11–.

Goobkin, I. "דער דערציער און חבר" (The Educator and Friend). In *Gingold*, 295–298.

Maladowsky, K., M. Mashewitzky, and L. Rubinstein, eds. פנחס גינגאלד בוך (Pinchas Gingold Book) (Y. and H.). N.Y.: Pinchas Gingold Publishing Foundation of the National Committee of the Jewish Folk Schools, 1955. 328 pp. Includes articles on and by Gingold.

Mokdoni, A. "פנחס גינגאלד" (P. Gingold). *Day* (Y.) (Dec. 16, 1953).

Pat, Jacob. "ווי אזוי איך האב געזען פנחס גינגאלד" (How I Saw P. Gingold) (Y.). In *Gingold*, 304–6.

Schichman, Z. "פנחס גינגולד ע״ה" (P. Gingold in Memoriam). *Sh Hah* (H.) 14 (Winter 1954): 114–15.

Schneierson, Fishel. "דאס פארבארגענע אין מענטשן" (The Hidden or Concealed in People) (Y.). In *Gingold*, 278–81.

Shapiro, Sh. "פנחס גינגאלד" (P. Gingold). *YK* (Y.) (Nov. 6, 1953).

Simon, Solomon. "א שמועס" (A Conversation) (Y.). In *Gingold*, 299–303.

Ginzberg, Louis, 1873–1953

Finkelstein, Louis. "Louis Ginzberg." *AJYB* 56 (1955): 573–79.

"Ginzberg, Louis." In *Enc Jud* 7, 584–85.

Golub, Jacob S. "We Mourn Our Losses." *Jew Ed* 24 (Spring 1953): 10.

Marx, Alexander, ed. "ספר היובל לכבוד לוי גינצבורג" (Louis Ginzberg Jubilee Volume) (2 vols.—H. and E.). 1945, 1946.

Glenn, Menahem G., 1900–1978

"Glenn, Menahem G." *AJYB* 80 (1980): 365.

Goelman, Elazar, 1913–

Adini, Uziel. "לד״ר אלאזר גואלמן, בחג יובלו השבעים" (To Dr. Elazar Goelman at 70). *Sh Hah* (H.) 43 (Summer 1984): 209–10.

Goldberg, Henry R., 1904–66

"Goldberg, Henry R." *AJYB* 68 (1967): 526.

Goldman, Solomon, 1893–1953.

Blumenfield, Samuel M. "Rabbi Goldman, the Educator." *Jew Ed* 10 (Oct. 1938): 131–32.

"Goldman, Solomon." *AJYB* 55 (1955): 456.

"Goldman, Solomon." In *Enc Jud* 7, 722.

Golomb, Abraham, 1888–1982

Shtarkman, Moshe, ed. „אברהם גאלאמב— זיין לעבן און שאפן" (Abraham Golomb—Life and Work). In *Golomb* (Y.), pp. 3–30.

Alifaz, Abner. „גאלאמב דער מחנך און שריפטסטעלער" (Golomb the Educator and Author). In *Golomb* (Y.), 31–33.

Barakin-Melamdavitch, Feigl. „זכרונות פון לעבן אין יידישן לערער סעמינאר" (Memories of the [Vilna] Teachers' Seminary). In *Golomb* (Y.), 253–61.

Elishav, Mordecai. „אברהם גולומב בארץ ישראל" (Golomb in Israel). In *Golomb* (Y.), 35–38.

"Golomb, Abraham." In *Enc Jud* 7, 763.

Leftwich, I. "Abraham Golomb's Influence on the Jewish Community." *B'nei Yiddish* (Y.) 32 (Nisan/Iyar 1974): 5–10.

Liptzin, Sol. „דריי שטעלונגען צו יידיש נאך דער ערשטער וועלט מלחמה" (Three Stands on Yiddish after World War I). In *Golomb* (Y.), 93–100.

Mann, Mendl. „א. גאלאמב דער פעדאגאג" (Golomb the Pedagogue). In *Golomb* (Y.), 101–4.

Mark, Yudl. „אברהם גאלאמבן צו זיינע 80 יאר" (To A. Golomb on His 80th Birthday). In *Golomb* (Y.), 105–7.

———. „לערער במשך א האלבן יארהונדערט" (A Teacher for a Half Century). *CE* (Y.) 30 (Jan. 1960): 1–3.

Menachowski, M. „א. גאלאמב—דער לערער פון לערערס" (Golomb—The Teacher of Teachers). In *Golomb* (Y.), 109–14.

Rapchinski, B. „צום אכציג-יאריקן יובל פון א. גאלאמב" (On the 80th Birthday of Golomb). In *Golomb* (Y.), 189–97.

Rapoport, I. „צוריק צו גאלאמבן!" (Back to Golomb). In *Golomb* (Y.), 187–88.

Ron, Lazer. „די אינסטיטוציע—גאלאמב" (The Institution—Golomb). In *Golomb* (Y.), 181–86.

Shlavin, Benjamin. „צו מיין לערער און רבי ר' אברהם גאלאמב" (To my Teacher and Mentor—A. Golomb). In *Golomb* (Y.), 209–11.

Zuckerman, Baruch. „אברהם גאלאמב און זיין וועלט-באנעם" (Golomb and His View of the World). In *Golomb* (Y.), 129–37.

Golub, Jacob, ?–1959?

Azrieli, Shlomo (Israel Chipkin). "To Dr. Jacob Golub." *Jew Ed* 24 (Spring 1952–53): 8–9, 54.

Cohen, Jack J. "Jacob S. Golub—In Memoriam." *Jew Ed* 29 (Spring 1959): 2.

Gordon, Aharon David, 1856–1922

Cohen, Jack J., and Simon Noveck. "Aaron David Gordon." In *GJT*, 45–71.

Halevi, Menachem. *A. D. Gordon and His Philosophy*. N.Y.: Hechalutz Organization of America, 1947. 32 pp.

Kurzweil, Zvi E. "The Educational Philosophy of A. D. Gordon." *Jew Ed* 32 (Spring 1961): 37–45. See also *MTJE*, 95–114.

Rose, Herbert H. *The Life and Thought of A. D. Gordon*. N.Y.: Bloch, 1964. 151 pp.

———. "The Relevancy of A. D. Gordon's View of Man." *Jud* 10 (1961): 40–48.

Rotenstreich, Nathan. "A. D. Gordon." In *Jewish Philosophy in Modern Times*, 239–52. 1968.

Gordon, George J., 1874–1943

Ben-Tsemach, Sh. „ד"ר גרשון יעקב גורדון ז"ל" (Dr. Gershon Jacob Gordon—In Memoriam). *Sh Hah* (H.) 5 (1945): 86–95. (See also Minneapolis, Minnesota.)

Gordon, Louis, ?–1969

Galin, Meyer. "Louis Gordon—In Memoriam." *Jew Ed* 39 (July 1969): 7.

Gordon, Samuel, ?–1967

Margolis, Isidor. "Samuel Gordon—In Memoriam." *Jew Ed* 38 (Jan. 1968): 9.

Gratz, Rebecca, 1781–1869

Marcus, Jacob R. "Rebecca Gratz—The Idol of Her Generation." *Mem*, 1:272–80. See also index of his *The American Jewish Woman: A*

Documentary History and *The American Jewish Woman, 1654–1980*.

Morais, Sabato. *Address Delivered before . . . the Hebrew Sunday School, Philadelphia, on the Life and Character of Rebecca Gratz*. Phila.: Collins, 1869. 15 pp.

Osterweis, R. *Rebecca Gratz: A Study in Charm*. N.Y.: G. P. Putnam's Sons, 1935. 244 pp.

Philipson, David, ed. *Letters of Rebecca Gratz*. Phila.: JPS, 1929. 454 pp.

* Rosenbloom, Joseph R. "Rebecca Gratz and the Jewish Sunday School Movement in Philadelphia." *PAJHS* 48 (1958): 71–77.

———. *And She Had Compassion: The Life and Times of Rebecca Gratz*. HUC–JIR, 1957.

———. "Some Conclusions about Rebecca Gratz." In *Ess*, 171–86.

Greenberg, Hayim, 1889–1953

Bickel, Shlomo. "חיים גרינבערג,, (Hayim Greenberg). In *Writers of My Generation* (Y.), 256–66. 1958.

Blumenheld, Samuel M. "חיים גרינברג,, המחנך הציוני" (Hayim Greenberg—The Zionist Educator). In *S Ed* (H.), 203–7.

Gladstone, Jacob. "חיים גרינבערג,, (Hayim Greenberg). *Day* (Y.) (May 8, 1966).

Goldman, Nahum. "Hayim Greenberg—Artist and Moralist." *Jew Fron* (May 15, 1953): 7–9.

Halpern, Ben. "Greenberg in His Generation." *Jew Fron* 30 (Mar. 1963): 5–7.

Kaplan, Mordecai M. "Hayim Greenberg: Realist, Humanist, Idealist." *Jew Fron* (Mar. 1957): 5–7.

Lehrer, Leibush. "חיים גרינבערג,, (Hayim Greenberg). *YK* (Y.) (Apr. 19, 1963).

Shazar, Zalman. "חיים גרינבערג,, (Hayim Greenberg). *Day* (Y.) (June 12, 1966).

Shulman, Charles E. "Hayim Greenberg: An Enduring Force." *Congress Weekly* (Mar. 18, 1963).

Syrkin, Marie. "Hayim Greenberg." In *Hayim Greenberg Anthology*, 7–19. Detroit: Wayne State U. Press, 1968.

Greenberg, Irving, 1933–

"Greenberg, Irving." In *Enc Jud* 7, 904.

Greenberg, Simon, 1901–

"Greenberg, Simon." In *Enc Jud* 7, 906.

Greenstone, Julius H., 1873–1955

Chomsky, William. "Dr. Julius H. Greenstone—In Memoriam." *Jew Ed* 26 (Summer 1955): 4–5.

"Greenstone, Julius H." *AJYB* 57 (1956): 606.

"Greenstone, Julius H." In *Enc Jud* 7, 911–12.

Grinstein, Hyman B., 1899–1982

"Grinstein, Hyman B." *AJYB* 84 (1984): 334.

Halevi, Mordecai 1890–1978

Chomsky, William. "מרדכי הלוי איש הדעים,, (Mordecai Halevi—A Man of Knowledge). *Sh Hah* (H.) 26 (Fall 1966): 5–7.

Gannes, Abraham P. "על מרדכי הלוי שהגיע לגבורות" (On Mordecai Halevi at Eighty). In *AJE* (H.), 7–12.

———. "מרדכי הלוי ז״ל,, (Mordecai Halevi—In Memoriam). *Sh Hah* (H.) 38 (Oct. 1978): 61–62.

Hayim of Volozhin, 1749–1821

Charna, Sh. I. "רבי חיים מולוזין בתור פדגוג,, (Rabbi Hayim of Volozin as Pedagogue). *Sh Hah* (H.) 4 (1929): 309–17.

Scharfstein, Zevi. "ר' חיים מוולוזין,, (Rabbi Hayim of Volozin). In *GJE* (H.), 50–57.

Wurtzburger, Walter S. "Rabbi Hayim of Volozin." In *GOH*, 189–206.

Heilpern, Jehiel, 1880–1943

Scharfstein, Zevi. "יחיאל היילפרין,, (Jehiel Heilpern). In *GJE* (H.), 244–50.

Heschel, Abraham Joshua, 1907–72

Borowitz, Eugene B. "Abraham Joshua Heschel, Model." *Sh 'ma* (Jan. 19, 1973).

Breslauer, S. D. "Abraham Joshua Heschel and Religious Education." *Rel Ed* 72 (Oct. 1977): 484–90.

Dresner, Samuel H. "The Contribution of Abraham Joshua Heschel." *Jud* 32 (Winter 1983): 57–69.

Fierman, Morton. "The Educational Philosophy of A. J. Heschel." *Rel Ed* (July/Aug. 1960): 272–79.

27 MEN AND WOMEN WHO INFLUENCED JEWISH EDUCATION

Goldberg, Hillel. "Abraham Joshua Heschel and His Times." *Mid* 28 (Apr. 1982): 26–42.

Lookstein, Joseph H. "The Neo-Hasidism of Abraham J. Heschel." *Jud* 5 (1956): 248–55.

Parzen, Herbert. "Abraham Joshua Heschel—A New Teacher and Personality." *The Torch* (Spring 1958). Also in *RTJS*, 79–86.

Rothschild, Fritz. "Abraham Joshua Heschel, 1907–1972: Theologian and Scholar." *AJYB* 74 (1973): 533–44.

Spiro, Jack D. "Rabbi Abraham Heschel: An Appreciation." *Rel Ed* 68 (Mar./Apr. 1973): 218–25.

Tanenzapf, Sol. "Abraham Heschel and His Critics." *Jud* 23 (Summer 1974): 276–86.

Hirsch, Samson Raphael, 1808–88

Breuer, Isaac. "Samson Raphael Hirsch." In *Jewish Leaders*, edited by Leo Jung. 1953.

Breuer, Mordecai. "Samson Raphael Hirsch." In *GOH*, 265–99.

Elias, Marcus. "The Educational Work of Rabbi S. R. Hirsch: Jewish Schools in Western Europe." In *Ateret Zwi, in Honor of Joseph Breuer*. 1962.

Grunfeld, I. "Samson Raphael Hirsch—The Man and His Mission." In *Judaism Eternal: Selected Essays from the Writings of Samson Raphael Hirsch*, xiii–xlvii. 2 vols. 1956.

* Gundersheimer, Ernest M. *Samson Raphael Hirsch as an Educator*. Dropsie College, 1957. 176 pp.

Guttman, Julius. "S. R. Hirsch." In *Philosophies of Judaism*, translated by David W. Silverman, 313–21. 1964.

Heller, Max. "S. R. Hirsch." *CCAR* 18 (1908): 179–216.

Jelenko, Edward W. "Samsom Raphael Hirsch." In *GJP*, 69–96.

Kurzweil, Zvi E. "Samson Raphael Hirsch: Educationist and Thinker." In *MTJE*, 46–70. See also *Trad 2* (Spring 1960): 286–303.

Rosenbloom, Noah H. "Religious and Secular Co-Equality in S. R. Hirsch's Educational Theory." *JSS* 24 (Oct. 1962): 223–47.

———. *Tradition in an Age of Reform: The Religious Philosophy of Samson Raphael Hirsch*. Phila.: JPS, 1976. 480 pp.

Rotenstreich, Nathan. "S. R. Hirsch." In *Jewish Philosophy in Modern Times*, 121–36. 1969.

"Samson Raphael Hirsch." In *Enc Jud* 8, 508–15.

Schwarzschild, Steven. "Samson Raphael Hirsch—The Man and His Thought." *Con Jud* 13 (Winter 1959).

Stein, Regina. "Samson Raphael Hirsch: Orthodox Reformer." Master's thesis, JTSA-Teachers Institute, 1973.

Hoenig, Sidney B., 1907–79

Schiff, Alvin I. "Sidney B. Hoenig—In Memoriam." *Jew Ed* 48 (Spring 1980): 5.

"Sidney B. Hoenig." *AJYB* 81 (1981) 367.

Honor, Leo L, 1894–1956

Berkson, Isaac B. "In Memoriam—Leo L. Honor." *Jew Ed* 27 (Winter 1956–57): 4–5.

Chomsky, William. "אליעזר האיש—הונור הדגול" (Leo Honor—A Man of Distinction). *Sh Hah* (H.) 17 (Winter 1957): 67–69.

Elkin, Harry. "ד״ר א. ל. הונור ז״ל" (Dr. L. L. Honor—In Memoriam). *Sh Hah* (H.) 24 (Spring 1964): 167–70.

Gannes, Abraham P., ed. "Introductory Essay on Honor." In *Selected Writings of Leo L. Honor*. N.Y.: Reconstructionist Press, 1965. 329 pp.

———. "לזכר ד״ר אליעזר ל. הונור" (Leo L. Honor—The Man and Educator). *Sh Hah* (H.) 45 (Spring/Summer 1986): 219–22.

Halevi, Mordecai. "אליעזר ל. הונור ז״ל" (Leo L. Honor—In Memoriam). In *AJE* (H.) 63–82.

"Honor, Leo L." *AJYB* 59 (1959): 474.

Jew Ed (dedicated to the memory of Leo L. Honor) 28 (Fall 1957): 3–68.

    Dinin, Samuel M., "Leo L. Honor and Teacher Education," 29–33.

    Futorian, Naomi, "Eulogy—L. L. Honor," 11–12.

    Gamoran, Emanuel, "Scholar and Pedagogue," 24–28.

    Gannes, Abraham P., "Selections from the Writings of Leo L. Honor," 36–65.

    Gannes, Abraham P., and Ruth Honor Robbins, "Bibliography of Writings of L. L. Honor," 66–68.

    Grayzel, Solomon, "Eulogy—L. L.

Honor," 8–11.

Kaplan, Mordecai M., "Eulogy—L. L. Honor," 5–8.

Neuman, Abraham A. "Eulogy—L. L. Honor," 4.

Pilch, Judah, "Dr. Leo L. Honor—The Teacher," 34–36.

Ruffman, Louis L., "Dedication on a Yahrzeit," 3.

Schoolman, Albert P., "Leo Lazarus Honor," 14–23.

Pilch, Judah. "Leo L. Honor." *Rel Ed* 52 (Jan./Feb. 1957): 49.

Scharfstein, Zevi. "אליעזר הונור ע״ה„ (Eliezer Honor—In Memoriam." *Sh Hah* (H.) 17 (Winter 1957): 70–71.

Hurwich, Louis, 1886–1967

Ackerman, Walter I. "Louis Hurwich—In Memoriam." *Jew Ed* 38 (Jan. 1968): 6–7.

Halevi, Mordecai. "אריה ליב הורוויץ ז״ל„ (Louis Hurwich—In Memoriam). In *AJE* (H.), 83–87.

"Hurwich, Louis." In *Enc Jud* 8, 1117.

Pilch, Judah. "Louis Hurwich." *Jew Ed* 40 (Spring 1971): 15–16.

Ravid, Zvulun. "ד״ר א. ל. הורוויץ—מורה למורים„ (Dr. A. L. Hurwich, Teacher of Teachers). *Sh Hah* (H.) 8 (Winter 1968): 122.

Intrater, Aaron, 1913–78

Bennet, Alan D., ed. Commitment: *A Tribute to Aaron Intrater by his Colleagues in Jewish Education*. Cleveland: 1977. 46 pp.

Margolis, Henry. "Aaron Intrater—In Memoriam." *Jew Ed* 46 (Autumn 1978): 4.

Isaacman, Daniel, 1924–82

Adini, Uziel. "ד״ר דניאל איזקמן דברים לזכרו„ (Dr. Daniel Isaacman—In Memoriam." *Sh Hah* (H.) 41 (Summer 1982): 211–12.

Lakritz, William B. "Daniel Isaacman—In Memoriam." *Jew Ed* 50 (Spring 1982): 3–4.

Isaacs, Bernard, 1882–1975

Nobel, Morris, ed. ".ספר ב. אייזעקס„ (Sefer B. Isaacs) (H., E., and Y). N.Y.: 1977. 284 pp. Articles include:

Kabakoff, Jacob. "על מבחר סיפורים„ (On Mivhar Sippurim [Hebrew stories]) (H.), 148–49.

Nobel, Morris, "עיונים בספורי אייזקס„ (Reflections on Hebrew Stories by Isaacs) (H.), 135–47.

Ravid, Zvulun, "יצירתו הספרותית של ב. אייזקס„ (B. Isaacs—His Literary Contribution) (H.), 102–34.

Shmueli, Ephraim. "דוב אייזיקס„ (Bernard Isaacs) (H.), 99–101.

Weine, Max. "Bernard Isaacs: A Memoir," 81–100.

Ravid, Zvulun. "אייזקס—אחרון הראשונים„ (Isaacs—The Last of the Pioneers). *Sh Hah* (H.) 36 (1976): 130–37, (1976/77): 195–200; 37 (1977): 103–12; 38 (1978): 106–17, (1979): 176–185, 238–44.

Israel Meir Ha-Kohen ("Hafez Hayim"), 1838–1933

"Israel Meir Ha-Kohen." In *Enc Jud* 9, 1068–70.

Scharfstein, Zevi. "ר׳ ישראל מאיר הכהן—החפץ חיים„ (Rabbi Israel Meir Ha-Kohen—The "Hafez Hayim"). In *GJE* (H.), 89–114.

Yoshor, M. M. "Saint and Sage." In *Jewish Leaders*, edited by Leo Jung, 459–73. 1953.

Judah Loew Ben Bezalel ("MaHaRal" of Prague), c. 1525–1609

"Judah Loew Ben Bezalel." In *Enc Jud* 10, 374–379.

Kleinberger, Alex Fritz. "The Didactics of Rabbi Loew of Prag." *Scripta Hierosolymitana* (1963): 32–55.

———. *The Pedagogic Thought of the MaHaRAL of Prague* (H.). Jerusalem: Magnes Press, 1962. 195 pp.

Scharfstein, Zevi. "המהר״ל מפראג„ (The MaHaRal of Prague). In *GJE* (H.), 9–24.

Kadushin, Max, 1895–1980

"Kadushin, Max." *AJYB* 81 (1982): 368.

"Kadushin, Max." In *Enc Jud* 10, 668–669.

* Steinberg, Theodore. *Max Kadushin, Scholar of Rabbinic Judaism: A Study of His Life, Work and Theory of Vocational Thought*. New York., 1980.

———. "Max Kadushin's Contribution to the Study of Jewish Thought and Its Implications for Jewish Education." *Jew Ed* 48 (Winter 1980): 21–27.

Kahnstam, Aharon, 1859–1921

Berger, Mira. „המוסדות להכשרת מורים עברים בוילנה ובגרודנה" (Institutions for Training Hebrew Teachers in Vilna and Grodno). In „החנוך והתרבות העברית באירופה". (Hebrew Education and Culture in Europe between the Two World Wars) (H.), edited by Zevi Scharfstein, 391–431. N.Y.: Ogen, Histadruth Ivrith of America, 1957.

Golomb, Abraham. "א. קאנשטאם," (Aharon Kahnstam). *School and Life* (Y.). Kiev, 1920.

Newman, I. M. "אהרון כהנשטם וד"ר טשרנא" (Aharon Kahnstam—In Memoriam). *Sh Hah* (H.) 1 (1925): 141–42.

Scharfstein, Zevi. "אהרון כהנשטם וד"ר שלום יונה טשרנא" (Aharon Kahshtam and Yonah Charna). In *GJE* (H.), 115–30.

Kallen, Horace M., 1882–1974

Education and the Creative Life: In Honor of Horace M. Kallen. Addresses by Phillip W. Lown, Buel Gallagher, and Milton R. Konvitz. Response by Kallen. N.Y.: AAJE, 1957. 31 pp.

Hook, Sidney, and Milton Konvitz, eds. *Freedom and Experience: Essays Presented to H. M. Kallen.* N.Y.: Cooper Square Publishers, 1947, 1974. 343 pp.

* Kaplan, Louis. *Judaism and Jewish Education in Horace M. Kallen's Philosophy of Cultural Pluralism.* Dropsie U., 1971.

Konvitz, Milton R. "Horace Meyer Kallen—Philosopher of the Hebraic-American Idea." *AJYB* 75 (1974–75): 55–80. See also an undated pamphlet written by Konvitz and published by the AAJE that contains a bibliography of Kallen's writings on Jewish education.

Kronish, Ronald. "John Dewey and Horace Kallen on Cultural Pluralism: Their Impact on Jewish Education." *JSS* 44 (Spring 1952): 135–45.

Ratner, Sidney, ed. *Vision and Action: Essays in Honor of H. M. Kallen on His 70th Birthday.* New Brunswick, N.J.: Rutgers U. Press, 1953. 277 pp.

Ruffman, Louis L. "Salute to Horace Kallen." *Jew Ed* 28 (Winter 1958): 5–6.

Schmidt, Sarah L. "Horace M. Kallen: An American Jewish Philosopher." *Jud* 25 (Spring 1976): 217–29.

Waldridge, Earle E. "Horace Meyer Kallen: A Bibliography." In *Freedom and Experience*, edited by Sidney Hook and Milton Konvitz, 334–45. N.Y.: Cooper Square Publishers, 1947, 1974.

Kaminetsky, Joseph, 1911–

"Kaminetsky, Joseph." In *Enc Jud* 10, 729.

Kaminker, Samuel, ?–1964

Soref, Irwin I. "Samuel Kaminker—In Memoriam." *Jew Ed* 34 (Summer 1964): 222.

Kaplan, Mordecai M., 1881–1983

Ackerman, Walter I. "On the Making of Jews." *Jud* 30 (Winter 1981): 87–95.

* Alper, Michael. *Reconstructionism and Jewish Education: Implications of Reconstructionism for Jewish Education in the United States.* Columbia U., 1954. 449 pp.

Ben-Horin, Meir. "The Influence of Mordecai M. Kaplan." *Recon* 49 (Apr.–May 1984): 8–9.

———. „פרופיסור מרדכי מנחם קפלן ז"ל" (Professor Kaplan—In Memoriam). *Sh Hah* (H.) 43 (Winter 1983–84): 86–89.

———. „עיונים במשנתו של מרדכי מ. קפלן" (Reflections on the Educational Philosophy of Kaplan). *Sh Hah* (H.) 36 (1976): 74–77, (1976–77): 160–67.

Blumenfield, Samuel M. „מרדכי קפלן—אחד העם של יהדות אמריקה" (Mordecai Kaplan, Ahad Ha-Am of American Judaism). In *S Ed* (H.), 232–39.

Chipkin, Israel S. "Dr. Mordecai M. Kaplan and Jewish Education." In *M. M. Kaplan, An Evaluation*, edited by I. Eisenstein, and E. Kohn, 85–118. 1952.

Cohen, Gerson D. "Bibliography of the Writings of Professor M. M. Kaplan." In „ספר היובל לכבוד מ. מ. קפלן" (Jubilee Volume in Honor of M. M. Kaplan), edited by Moshe Davis (H. and E.), 9–33. N.Y.: JTSA, 1953.

Dushkin, Alexander M. „השפעתו של ד"ר קפלן כיהודי וכמחנך" (Dr. Kaplan's Influence as a Jew and an Educator) (H.) 50:30 June 11, 1971.

Eisenstein, Ira. "Mordecai M. Kaplan." In *GJT*, 253–79.

Liebman, Charles S. "Reconstructionism in American Jewish Life." *AJYB* 71 (1970): 3–99.

Kami, Leon J., ?–1953

Golub, Jacob S. "We Mourn Our Losses." *Jew Ed* 24 (Spring 1954): 10–11.

Kaufman, Yehezkel, 1889–1963

Blumenfeld, Samuel M. „משנתו החינוכית של יחזקאל קויפמן" (The Educational Philosophy of Yehezkel Kaufman). In *S Ed* (H.), 225–31.

"Kaufman, Yehezkel." In *Enc Jud* 16, 1349–51.

Lieber, David. "Yehezkel Kaufman's Contributions to Biblical Scholarship." *Jew Ed* 34 (Summer 1964): 254–61.

Kohler, Kaufmann, 1843–1926

Cohon, Samuel M. "Kaufmann Kohler." In *GJT*, 227–52.

"Kohler, Kaufmann." *AJYB* 28 (1926–27): 235–60.

"Kohler, Kaufmann." In *Enc Jud* 10, 1142–43.

Kohut, Rebecca B., 1864–1951

"Kohut, Rebecca." In *Enc Jud* 10, 1150–51.

"Kohut, Rebecca B." *AJYB* 54 (1953): 539.

Konowitz, Israel, ?–1959

Gamoran, Emanuel. "Dr. Israel Konowitz—In Memoriam." *Jew Ed* 29 (Winter 1959): 2.

Joseph, Samuel K. "Israel Konowitz: Jewish Education in America at the Beginning of the Twentieth Century." *Jew Ed* 51 (Fall 1983): 315.

Woll, A. Z. "ד"ר ישראל קנוביץ ז"ל" (Dr. Israel Konowitz—In Memoriam). *Sh Hah* (H.) 19 (Spring 1959): 67–69.

Kook (Kuk), Abraham Isaac, 1865–1933

Agus, Jacob B. "Abraham Isaac Kuk." In *GJT*, 73–96.

Bokser, Ben-Zion. "Jewish Universalism: An Aspect of the Thought of Harav Kook." *Jud* 8 (1959): 214–19.

———. "The Religious Philosophy of Rabbi Kook." *Jud* 19 (1970): 396–405.

Epstein, I. "Abraham Yitzhak Hacohen Kook." In *GOH*, 483–509.

———. *Abraham Yitzhak Hacohen Kook: His Life and Times*. 1951.

Kurzweil, Zvi E. "Rabbi Kook—His Influence on Jewish Education." In *MTJE*, 244–57.

Rotenstreich, Nathan. "Harmony and Return." In *Jewish Philosophy in Modern Times*, 219–38. 1963.

Yaron, Zvi. *The Philosophy of Rabbi Kook* (H.). WZO, Torah and Culture Department, 1974. 383 pp.

Korczak, Janusz, 1878–1942

Bettelheim, Bruno. "Janusz Korczak: Champion of the Children." *RJ* 14 (Spring 1986): 8–9, 38.

Buckley, J. J. "Janusz Korczak Bibliography." 11 (Winter 1975–76): 85–92.

Cohen, Adir. „יאנוש קורצ'אק המחנך" (Janusz Korczak the Educator) (H.). Tel Aviv: 1974. 232 pp.

Frost, Shimon. "Janusz Korczak: His Life and Work." *Jew Ed* 33 (Winter 1963): 89–96.

Korzcak, Janusz. "Memory." Translated by Adele Milch. *Moment* 6 (Sept. 1981): 25–29.

Kurzweil, Zvi E. "Janusz Korczak." In *MTJE*, 171–97.

———. "Korczak's Educational Writings and the Image of the Child." *Jew Ed* 38 (Jan. 1968): 19–28.

Scharfstein, Zevi. „יאנוש קורצ'אק" (Janusz Korczak). In *GJE* (H.), 266–92.

Turkow, Y. „דער הייליקער קינדער-דערציער" (Janusz Korczak—The Saintly Child-Educator). *Almanac Yiddish* (Y.), 73–90. 1961.

Ungerfeld, M. „יאנוש קורצ'אק המחנך" (Janusz Korczak the Educator). *Hadoar* (H.) 54 (Nov. 1, 1975).

Wohlman, L. „ד"ר יאנוש קארטשאק—זיין לעבן און שאפן" (Janusz Korczak—His Life and Work). *BYD* (Y.) (Apr./July 1953): 12–16.

Kotier, Aaron, 1891–1962

"Aaron Kotler." In *Enc Jud* 10, 1221–22.

Egozi, Akivah. „לדמות דיוקנו של הגאון ר' אהרן קוטלר ז"ל" (On the Personality of the Gaon Rabbi Aaron Kotier of Blessed Memory). *Sh Hah* (H.) 23 (Spring 1963): 138–43.

Helmreich, William B. "Rabbi Ahron Kotier." In *The World of the Yeshiva: An Intimate Portrait of Orthodox Jewry*, 40–45. N.Y.: Free Press, 1982.

Kagan, Shaul. "From Kletzk to Lakewood." *The Torah World: A Treasury of Biographical Sketches*, edited by Nisson Wolpin, 184–205. 1962.

———. "Reb Aharon Kotler: Ten Years after His Passing." *Jew Obs* (May 1973).

"Kotler, Aaron" *AJYB* 65 (1964): 434.

Penn, Ascher. "...דער בית מדרש גבוה„ (The Beth Medrash Gavoha). In *Penn* (Y.), 683–91.

Kraft, Louis, 1891–

Edidin, Ben N. "Louis Kraft." *Jew Ed* 19 (Fall 1947): 2, 38.

"Kraft, Louis." *Enc Jud* 10, 1235–1236

Kuselewitz, David, ?–1978

Goelman, Elazar. "David Kuselewitz—In Memoriam." *Jew Ed* 46 (Spring 1978): 5.

Lang, Leon S., 1898–1956

"Lang, Leon S." *AJYB* 58 (1957): 477.

Lapson, Dvorah, 1907–

"Lapson, Dvorah." In *Enc Jud* 5, 1272.

Lapson, Judah, 1901–85

Avital, Moshe. (50 Years on Behalf of Hebrew in Public Education). *Sh Hah* (H.) 39 (June 1980): 197–205.

Eisenberg, Azriel. "ד"ר יהודה לפסון ותרומתו רבת החשבת לחנוך העברי„ (Dr. Judah Lapson and His Major Contribution to Hebrew Education). *Hadoar* (H.) 59 (Aug. 8, 1980).

"Judah Lapson." *AJYB* 87 (1987): 441.

Leeser, Isaac, 1806–68

Davis, Moshe. "ר' יצחק ליסר—מראשוני הבונים של יהדות אמריקה„ (Rabbi Isaac Leeser—Among the Early Builders of American Judaism). *Hadoar* (H.) (Dec. 13 and 20, 1940).

Englander, Henry. "Isaac Leeser, 1806–1868." *CCAR* 28 (1918): 213–52.

* Feierstein, Milton. *Isaac Leeser (1806–1868): Founder of Jewish Education in the United States*. State U. of New York at Buffalo, 1971. 198 pp.

Korn, Bertram W. "Isaac Leeser—Centennial Reflections." *AJA* 19 (Nov. 1967): 127–41.

Marcus, Jacob R. "Isaac Leeser—American Jewish Missionary." *Mem* 2 (1955): 58–87.

* Seller, Maxine Schwartz. *Isaac Leeser, Architect of the American Jewish Community*. U. of Pennsylvania, 1965.

Sulzberger, Mayer. "No Better Jew, No Purer Man." *Occ* 25 (1868): 593–601. See also *AJA* (Nov. 1969): 140–48.

Sussman, Lance J. "Isaac Leeser and the Protestantization of American Judaism." *AJA* 38 (Apr. 1986): 1–21.

Todes, David U. "The Life and Character of Isaac Leeser, the Educator." *Jew Ed* 26 (Fall 1955): 30–39, 56.

Wolf, Simon. Address on the Life and Service of Isaac Leeser. Under the auspices of Elijah Lodge 50, I.O.B.B. Washington, D.C.: Philip and Solomon, 1868. 13 pp.

Lehrer, Leibush, 1887–1964

Goodman, Saul L. "In Memoriam—Leibush Lehrer." *Jew Ed* 35 (Spring 1965): 132–34.

"Lehrer, Leibush." *AJYB* 66 (1965): 578.

"Lehrer, Leibush." In *Enc Jud* 10, 1585.

"לייבוש לערער„ (Leibush Lehrer). In *Biographical Dictionary of Modern Yiddish Literature* (Y.), 5:235–39.

Sherman, Bezalel. "לייבוש לעהרער'ס ירושה„ (The Heritage of Leibush Lehrer). *Zuk* (Y.) (Dec. 1964): 485–89.

Yearbook Dedicated to the Memory of Leibush Lehrer (Y. and E.). N.Y.: SAFI, 1965. 85 pp. Includes articles by Sh. Bikel, Charles Sherman, I. Goichberg, A. Zeitlin, and others.

Zilberberg, I. "לייבוש לעהרער„ (Leibush Lehrer). *YK* (Y.) (Oct. 16, 1964): 9–11.

Leibman, Morris, 1897–1969?

Dinin, Samuel. "Morris Leibman—In Memoriam." *Jew Ed* 40 (Winter 1970): 5–6.

Leibovutz, Harry H., ?–1954

Golub, Jacob S. "We Mourn Our Losses." *Jew Ed* 2A (Spring 1954): 11, 64.

Leibowitz, Shmaya, ?–1979

Gannes, Abraham P. "Shmaya Leibowitz—In Memoriam." *Jew Ed* 47 (Spring 1979): 5.

Levine, Yaacov, 1884–1958

"Jacob Levine." *AJYB* 61 (1060): 418.

Lehrer, Leibush. "יעקב לעווין„ (Jacob Levine). In *Biographical Dictionary of Modern Yiddish Literature* (Y.), 5:510–14.

Lehrer, Leibush. "יעקב לעווין„ (Jacob Levine). *YK* (Y.) (Mar. 8, 1963).

Mark, Yudl. "יעקב לעווין ע״ה„ (Jacob Levine—In Memoriam). *JBA* 17 (1959–60): 43–48 (Y. section).

Shefner, B. "יעקב לעווין„ (Jacob Levine). *For* (Y.) (Jan. 17, 1959).

Levinsohn, Isaac Baer, 1788–1860

Glenn, Menahem G. "Isaac Baer Levinsohn." *JBA* (1959): 59–64.

Greenberg, Louis S. *Isaac Baer Levinsohn*. N.Y.: Bloch, 1930. 80 pp.

"Isaac Baer Levinsohn." In *Enc Jud* 11, 116–19.

Raab, David. "The Religious and Educational Teaching of Isaac Baer Levinsohn." Master's thesis, HUC-JIR, 1945.

Raisin, J. S. "Isaac Baer Levinsohn." In *Haskalah Movement in Russia*, 204–13. 1913.

Lewin, Kurt Z., 1890–1947

Amitzer, N. "קורט לוין„ (Kurt Lewin). *Sh Hah* (H.) (1947): 96–97.

Dushkin, Alexander M. "Kurt Lewin." *Jew Ed* 18 (Feb.–Mar. 1947): 2–3.

"Kurt Zadek Lewin." In *Enc Jud* 11, 172–73.

Lehrer, Leibush. "די פסיכאָלאָגישע טעאָריעס פון קורט לעווין„ (The Psychological Theories of Kurt Lewin). *BYD* (Y.) 1 (June-Sept. 1950): 12–24.

Marrow, Alfred J. *The Practical Theorist: The Life and Work of Kurt Lewin*. 1969.

Nardi, Noah. "Kurt Lewin—The Man and the Psychologist." *Recon* 14 (1948): 17–20.

Rothman, J. *Minority Group Identification and Intergroup Relations: An Examination of Kurt Lewin's Theory of Jewish Group Identity*. N.Y.: Research Institute for Group Work in Jewish Agencies, 1967. 263 pp.

* Seligman, Ralph. *A Test of the Lewinian Hypothesis on Self-Hatred among the Jews*. New York U., 1966. 562 pp.

Lilienthal, Max, 1815–82

Hershfield, Nathan. "Max Lilienthal's Contribution to American Judaism." *CCAR J* (Oct. 1959): 28–31.

"Lilienthal, Max." In *Enc Jud* 11, 243–45.

Merowitz, Morton J. "Max Lilienthal, Jewish Educator in Nineteenth Century America." *YA* 15 (1974): 46–65.

Philipson, David. "Max Lilienthal." *CCAR* 25 (1915): 191–220.

———. "Max Lilienthal." In *Centenary Papers and Others*, 149–90. 1919.

———. *Max Lilienthal, His Life and Writings*. 1915.

Lisitzky, Ephraim E., 1885–1962

Blumenheld, Samuel M. "אפרים ליסיצקי—המשורר המחנך„ (Ephraim Lisitzky—The Poet, the Educator). In *S Ed* (H.), 217–24.

Karp, Abraham. "Ephraim E. Lisitzky—The Poet." In *Golden Door to America*, 240–51. 1976.

"Lisitzky, Ephraim E." *AJYB* 64 (1963): 495.

Ravid, Zvulun. "Lisitzky: A Pioneer in Hebrew Instruction in America." *Sh Hah* (H.) (Summer 1972): 226–34.

Shpall, Leo. "אפרים ליסיצקי ז״ל„ (Ephraim Lisitzky—In Memoriam). *Sh Hah* (H.) 23 (Winter 1963): 75–76. See also *Jew Ed* 33 (Fall 1962): 5–6.

Silberschlag, Eisig. "אפרים ליסיצקי: המשורר המחנך„ (Ephraim Lisitzky—The Poet-Educator). *JBA* (H.) (1963–64): 66–71. Hebrew section.

Lookstein, Joseph H., 1902–79

"Joseph H. Lookstein." *AJYB* 81 (1981): 371.

"Lookstein, Joseph Hyman." In *Enc Jud* 11, 487–88.

Schiff, Alvin I. "Joseph Hyman Lookstein—In Memoriam." *Jew Ed* 47 (Fall 1979): 2.

Lown, Philip W., 1890–1976

Janowsky, Oscar I., and Jacob S. Lown. "Philip W. Lown: A Biographical Sketch." In *Lown*, 1–3.

"Lown, Philip W." *AJYB* 78 (1978): 543–44.

"Lown, Philip W." In *Enc Jud* 11, 535.

Magnes, Judah L, 1877–1948

Bentwich, Norman. *For Zion's Sake: A Biography of Judah L. Magnes*. Phila.: JPS, 1954. 329 pp.

Dushkin, Alexander M. "Our Educational Debt to Judah L. Magnes." *Jew Ed* 20 (Spring 1949): 2–3, 7.

Finkelstein, Louis. "Magnes, Son of the Hebrew Prophets." *Jew Ed* 20 (Spring 1949): 10.

Goren, Arthur A. "Introduction." *Dissenter in Zion: From the Writings of Judah L. Magnes*, 3–57. Cambridge: Harvard U. Press, 1982.

———. "Judah L. Magnes." In *New York Jews and the Quest for Community, 1908–1922*.

Judah L. Magnes. Berkeley: Judah L. Magnes Memorial Museum, 1977. 56 pp.

Lehman, Herbert H. "Magnes, the Champion of Justice." *Jew Ed* 20 (Spring 1949).

"Magnes, Judah Leon." *AJYB* 51 (1950): 522–23.

Marshall, James. "Judah L. Magnes." *AJYB* 51 (1950): 512–15.

Roth, L. "Judah L. Magnes and the Hebrew University." *Jew Ed* 20 (Spring 1949): 4–7.

Maimonides, Moses ("Rambam"), 1135–1204

Blumenfield, Samuel M. „למשנתו החינוכית של הרמב״ם" (On the Educational Teachings of the Rambam). In *S Ed* (H.), 143–62.

———. "Towards a Study of Maimonides the Educator." *HUC Annual* 23 (Part 2) (1950–51): 555–91.

Bokser, Ben Zion. "Maimonides' Response to the Challenge of His Time." *Jud* (1952): 366–71.

* Elefant, William L. *The Educational Ideas and Related Philosophical Concepts in the Writings of Maimonides*. U. of Denver, 1972. 166 pp.

———. „ה׳אני מאמין׳ של הרמבם" (The Principles of Faith by Maimonides). *Sh Hah* (H.) 40 (Summer 1981): 238–45.

Gamoran, Emanuel. "What Can We Do to Celebrate the Maimonides Octocentennial?" *Jew Teach* 3 (Apr. 1935): 1–4.

Garfinkel, Joseph I. "Educational Principles of Maimonides." *Jewish Teacher* 2 (Apr. 1918): 34–41.

Marx, Alexander. "Maimonides." In *Essays in Jewish Biography*, 87–111. 1947.

Mihaly, Eugene. "Moses Maimonides, Author and Teacher for the Ages." *CCAR J* (Oct. 1955): 19–27.

Minkin, Jacob S. "Education." In *The World of Moses Maimonides*, 284–91. N.Y.: Thomas Yoseloff, 1957.

Rawidowicz, Shimon. „רבנו משה בן מימון" (Our Teacher Moses Ben Maimon). *Zuk* (Y.) (May–June 1955): 203–10.

Twersky, Yochanan. "Introduction." In *A Maimonides Reader*, 1–29. Phila.: JPS and Behrman, 1972.

———. „הרמב״ם והשקפותיו על החנוך" (Maimonides and His Conception of Education). *Sh Hah* (H.) 4 (June 1944): 257–344.

———. „אפלטון, אריסטו, והרמב״ם" (Plato, Aristotle and the Rambam—Three Directions in Education). *Sh Hah* (H.) 4 (Dec. 1944): 3–22, 2 (1944): 83–112.

Weinstein, Joshua. „הרמב״ם—המורה לדורות" (The Rambam—The Teacher for Generations). *Sh Hah* (H.) 34 (1974): 17–22, 81–89, 152–59.

Yellin, David, and Israel Abrahams. *Maimonides*. Phila.: JPS, 1908. 239 pp.

Malachi, Eliezer R., 1895–1980

Ravid, Zvulun. „א. ה. מלאכי" (Eliezer R. Malachi—In Memoriam). *Sh Hah* (H.) 39 (June 1980): 219–22.

Margolis, Isidor, 1904–69

Dinsky, Samuel H. "Isidor Margolis—In Memoriam." *Jew Ed* 39 (Dec. 1969): 5–6.

"Margolis, Isidor." *AJYB* 71 (1970): 606.

Margoshes, Samuel, 1887–1968

"Margoshes, Samuel." *AJYB* 70 (1969): 523.

Mark, Yudel, 1897–1975

Fishman, Joshua. "Yudel Mark." *JBA* 34 (1976–77): 94–97.

Pilch, Judah. "Philip W. Lown and Jewish Education." In *Lown*, 26–29.

———, ed. *Philip W. Lown: A Jubilee Volume*. N.Y.: Bloch, 1967. 137 pp.

Goodman, Saul. "יודל מארק—פראקטיקער און טעארעטיקער פון דער יידיש-וועלטלעכער שול אין אמעריקע" (Yudel Mark—Practitioner and Theoretician of the Yiddish Secular School in America). In *Uniqueness of American Jewry* (Y.), 300–304.

"Mark, Yudel." In *Enc Jud* 11, 998–999.

Meitlis, J. "יודל מארק—דערציִער און פארשער" (Yudel Mark—Educator and Researcher). *Zuk* (Y.) (Dec. 1975): 81 (Dec. 1979): 381–84.

"יודל מארק" (Yudel Mark). In *Biographical Dictionary of Modern Yiddish Literature* (Y.), 5:510–14.

Marshall, Louis, 1856–1929

Adler, Cyrus. "Louis Marshall: A Biographical Sketch." *AJYB* 32 (1931): 21–55.

Benderly, Samson. "Louis Marshall and Jewish Education." *Jew Ed* 1 (Oct. 1929): 144–47.

Dawidowicz, Lucy S. "Louis Marshall's Yiddish Newspaper, *The Jewish World*: A Study in Contrasts." *JSS* 25 (1963): 102–32.

Dushkin, Alexander M., "Louis Marshall" (editorial). *Jew Ed* 1 (Oct. 1929): 141–42.

Reznikoff, Charles. "The Jewish Theological Seminary of America" and "Jewish Education." In *Louis Marshall, Champion of Liberty: Selected Papers and Addresses*, 2:859–913. Phila.: JPS, 1957.

Rosenstock, Morton. *Louis Marshall, Defender of Jewish Rights*. Detroit: Wayne State U. Press, 1965. 334 pp.

Marx, Alexander, 1878–1953

Alexander Marx Jubilee Volume (H. and E.). 2 vols. 1950.

Golub, Jacob S. "We Mourn Our Losses." *Jew Ed* 24 (Spring 1954): 10.

Halkin, Abraham S. "Alexander Marx." *AJYB* 56 (1955): 580–88.

"Marx, Alexander." In *Enc Jud* 11, 1070–71.

Melton, Samuel Mendel, 1900–

"Melton, Samuel Mendel." In *Enc Jud*, 1295.

"Sam Melton: Nurturing the Jewish Education Enterprise with Love." *MJ* 2, 22.

Mendelsohn, Moses, 1729–86

Agus, Jacob B. "The Age of Reason." In *Evolution of Jewish Thought*, 371–95. 1959.

Altmann, Alexander. *Moses Mendelssohn: A Biographical Study*. Phila.: JPS, 1973. 900 pp.

———. "The Philosophical Roots of Mendelssohn's Plea for Emancipation." *JSS* 26 (1974): 191–202.

Jospe, Alfred. "Moses Mendelssohn." In *GJP*, 11–42.

Rawidowicz, Simon. "Mendelssohn, the German and Jewish Philosopher." In *Studies in Jewish Thought*, edited by Nahum N. Glatzer, 327–49. Phila.: JPS, 1974.

Rosen, Leah. "Moses Mendelssohn as Educator." Master's thesis, City College of New York, 1933. 55 pp.

Rotenstreich, Nathan. "The Rule of Ethics." In *Jewish Philosophy in Modern Times*, 6–29. 1968.

Mendes, Henry Periera, 1852–1937

Pool, David de Sola. "Henry Periera Mendes." *AJYB* 40 (1938–39): 41–60.

Mendlowitz, Shraga Feivel, 1886–1948

"Mendlowitz, Shraga Feivel." In *Enc Jud* 11, 1346.

Gross, Alexander, and Joseph Kaminetsky. "S. F. Mendlowitz." In *Men of Spirit*, edited by Leo Jung, 553–72. 1964.

* Parsons, Sanford Bernard. *The Role of Feivel Mendlowitz in the Founding and Development of Hebrew Day Schools in the United States*. New York U., 1983.

Seidman, Hillel. *Shraga Feivl Mendlowitz* (H.). N.Y.: Shengold, 1976.

Miller, Linda R., 1878–1936

"Linda R. Miller." *AJYB* 39 (1937): 594.

Davidson, Israel, ed. *Essays and Studies in Memory of Linda R. Miller*. N.Y.: JTSA, 1938.

Millgram, Abraham E., ?-

Eisenberg, Azriel. "פתיחה, לכבוד ד"ר אברהם עזור מילגרם" (A Start—A Tribute to Dr. A. E. Millgram). *Sh Hah* (H.) 22 (Fall 1962): 3.

Mirsky, Samuel K., 1878–1967

Appel, Gershon, ed. *Samuel K. Mirsky Memorial Volume: Studies in Jewish Law, Philosophy, and Literature* (E. and H.). N.Y.: Yeshiva U. and Ktav, 1971. 601 pp.

Bernstein, Simon, and Gershon A. Churgin. ספר יובל לכבוד שמואל קלמן מירסקי (Samuel K. Mirsky Jubilee Volume) (H.). N.Y.: Jubilee Committee, 1958. 558 pp.

Brickman, William B. "Samuel K. Mirsky's Contribution to Jewish Educational Historiography." In *Samuel K. Mirsky Memorial Volume*, edited by Gershon Appel, 271–81. N.Y.: Yeshiva U. and Ktav, 1971.

Preshl, T. "כתבי פרופ. שמואל ק. מירסקי„ (The Writings of Professor Samuel K. Mirsky—Bibliography) (H.). In *Samuel K. Mirsky Jubilee Volume*, 538–58. N.Y.: Jubilee Committee, 1958.

Ravid, Zvulun. "S. K. Mirsky—In Memoriam." *JBA* 26 (1968): 64–67.

Morris, Nathan, 1890–1970

Eisenberg, Azriel. "Nathan Morris—In Memoriam." *Jew Ed* 41 (Spring 1972): 5–6.

"Morris, Nathan." In *Enc Jud* 12, 351

Naaraani, Israel G., 1915–79

"Naamani, Israel G." *AJYB* 81 (1981): 372.

Ravid, Zvulun. "ישראל נעמני„ (Israel Naamani). *Sh Hah* (H.) 38 (Oct. 1978): 11–12.

Rudavsky, David. "Israel Naamani—In Memoriam." *Jew Ed* 47 (Summer 1979): 4.

Nardi, Noah, 1902–

Goelman, Elazar. "Three American Educators in Israel." *Jew Ed* 47 (Winter 1979): 20–25.

Newman, Louis, ?–

Shapiro, Alexander M., and Burton I. Cohen. *Studies in Jewish Education and Judaica in Honor of Louis Newman*. N.Y.

Cohen, Burton I. "Louis Newman, Wisconsin: Innovations and Their Effect Upon the Ramah Camping Movement. In *Studies in Jewish Education and Judaica in Honor of Louis Newman*, edited by Alexander M. Shapiro and Burton I. Cohen, 23–38.

Noble, Moshe, 1910–83

Ravid, Zvulun. (Moshe Noble—In Memoriam." *Sh Hah* (H.) 43 (Spring 1984): 142.

Nudelman, Edward A., ?–1985

Ehrmann, Eliezer. "Edward A. Nudelman—In Memoriam." *Jew Ed* 53 (Summer 1985): 4.

Perkal, Ezra, ?–1982

Schafler, Samuel. "Ezra Perkal—In Memoriam." *Jew Ed* 50 (Summer 1982): 4.

Perl, Joseph, 1773–1839

Friedman, Philip. "יוסף פערל ווי א בילדונגס-טוער און זיין שול אין טארנאפאל" (Joseph Perl as Educator and His School in Tarnopol). *YB* (Y.) 31/32 (1948): 131–92.

Scharfstein, Zevi. "יוסף פרל„ (Joseph Perl). In *History of Jewish Education* (H.), 1:151–57.

Weinlez, I. "יוסף פערל׳ס לעבן און שאפן„ (Joseph Perl's Life and Work). In *Joseph Perl's Yiddish Writings* (Y.), vii–lxx. Vilna: Yivo, 1937.

Persky, Daniel, 1887–1962

Arfa, Milton. "דניאל פרסקי בדורותיו„ (Daniel Persky in His Generation) (*H.*).*JBA* 19 (1961): 98–106.

Glenn, Menahem. "דניאל פרסקי—המורה והמחנך" (Daniel Persky—Teacher and Educator). *Sh Hah* (H.) 18 (Fall 1948): 44–47.

Indelman, Elchanan. "דניאל פרסקי ז״ל—עבד לעברי„ (Daniel Persky—In Memoriam: "Toiler in Behalf of Hebrew"). *Sh Hah* (H.) 37 (June 1978): 210–15.

McDonald,———. "On Daniel Persky." *The New Yorker* (Nov. 26, 1959): 57–105.

"Persky, Daniel." *AJYB* 64 (1963): 495.

Ravid, Zvulun. "דניאל פרסקי ע״ה„ (Daniel Persky—In Memoriam). *Sh Hah* (H.) 22 (Summer 1962): 255.

Pilch, Judah, 1902–1986

Ben-Horin, Meir. (Judah Pilch—The Man and Educator). *Sh Hah* (H.) 45 (Winter 1985): 9, 98.

Bortniker, Elijah. "ליהודה פילטש בגבורותיו„ (Tribute to Judah Pilch on His 80th Birthday). *Sh Hah* (H.) 42 (Summer 1983): 213–15.

Gannes, Abraham P. "Judah Pilch—In Memoriam." *Jew Ed* 54 (Fall 1986): 2–4.

Goelman, Elazar. "יהודה פילטש בראי ה, ילקוט׳ שלו" (Judah Pilch in the Reflection of His "Yalkut"). *Sh Hah* (H.) 45 (Spring/Summer 1986): 223–24.

Mosenkis, Matthew. "תואר כבוד ליהודה פילטש„ (A Tribute to Judah Pilch). *Sh Hah* (H.) 38 (Mar. 1979): 133–34.

"Pilch, Judah." *AJYB* 88 (1988): 505–6.

Pitlick, Samuel, ?–1975

Chomsky, William. "Samuel Pitlick—In Memoriam." *Jew Ed* 45 (Fall/Winter 1976): 42.

Pollock, Shimon, ?–1976

Eisenberg, Azriel. "Shimon Pollock—In Memoriam." *Jew Ed* 45 (Fall/Winter 1976): 42.

Rapoport, Solomon Judah Loeb, 1790–1867

Barzilay, Isaac. *Solomon Judah Rapoport and His Contemporaries*. Ramat Can: Massada, 1969. 214 pp.

* Pitlick, Samuel. *Solomon Judah Loeb Rapoport, His Life and Works*. Dropsie U., 1937.

"S. J. L. Rapoport." In *Enc Jud* 13, 1555–56.

Rashi (Solomon ben Isaac), 1040–1105

Agus, I. A. "Rashi and His School." In *The Dark Ages*, edited by C. Roth, 210–48. 1966.

Aptowitzer, Avigdor. „רבן של ישראל" (Rashi the Teacher of Israel) (H.). *Bitzaron* 2 (Aug./Sept. 1940): 324–32.

* Blumenfield, Samuel M. *Master of Troyes: A Study of Rashi the Educator*. N.Y.: Behrman, 1946. 208 pp.

———. "Rashi." In *The Great Jewish Books*, edited by Samuel Caplan, and Harold Ribalow, 113–30. 1952.

———. *Rashi—Master of Troyes*. HUC-JIR, 1944.

Federbush, Simon, ed. „רשי—רבן של ישראל" (Rashi—Teacher of Israel) (H.). In *Rashi, His Teachings and Personality* (on the 850th anniversary of his death), 31–43. N.Y.: Culture Department of the World Jewish Congress and the Torah Department of the Jewish Agency, 1958.

Glenn, Menahem G. "On Rashi's Life and Teaching." In *Rashi, His Teachings and Personality*, edited by Simon Federbush, 131–42. N.Y.: Culture Department of the World Jewish Congress and the Torah Department of the Jewish Agency, 1958.

Hailperin, H. *Rashi and His World*. 1957.

Liber, Maurice. *Rashi*. Translated by Adele Szold. N.Y.: JPS, 1906. 278 pp.

Marx, Alexander. "Rashi." In *Essays in Jewish Biography*, 61–86. 1947.

* Shereshevsky, Ezra. *Rashi as Teacher, Interpreter of Text, and Builder of Character*. Dropsie U., 1957. 180 pp.

Waxman, Meyer. "Rashi as Commentator of the Bible." In *Rashi, His Teachings and Personality*, edited by Simon Federbush, 9–47. N.Y.: Culture Department of the World Jewish Congress and the Torah Department of the Jewish Agency, 1958.

———. „רש״י כמחנך" (Rashi as an Educator). In Generations and Their Educators (H.), 61–69. N.Y.: JEC Press, 1959.

Zeitlin, Solomon. "Rashi." *AJYB* 41 (1939): 111–40.

Reines, Isaac Jacob, 1839–1915

Fishman, L. J., ed. "Reines." In *Sefer Ha-Mizrachi* (H.), 93–101. 1946.

Newman, Aryeh. "Rabbi Jacob Reines—Torah Statesman and Educational Trailblazer." *Jew Life* (Jan./Feb. 1966): 20–25.

"Reines, Isaac Jacob." In *Enc Jud* 14, 58–59.

Revel, Bernard, 1885–1940

Churgin, Pinkhos. "Rabbi Dr. Revel and His Creation." In *Eidenu: Memorial Publication in Honor of Rabbi Dr. Bernard Revel* (H.), edited by A. Poupko, 14–17. N.Y.: Rabbi Isaac Elhanan Theological Seminary, 1942. See also *JEUS*, 153–56.

Hoenig, Sidney B. *Rabbinics and Research: The Scholarship of Dr. Bernard Revel*. 1968.

Jung, Leo. "Bernard Revel." *AJYB* 43 (1941/42): 415–24.

Rothkoff, Aaron. *Bernard Revel: Builder of American Jewish Orthodoxy*. Phila.: JPS, 1972. 378 pp.

Ribalow, Menahem, 1895–1953

Halevi, Mordecai. „מנחם ריבולוב" (Menahem Ribalow—In Memoriam). In *AJE* (H.), 158–62.

Pilch, Judah. "Menahem Ribalow—In Memoriam." *Jew Ed* 24 (Fall 1953): 7–8.

"Ribalow, Menahem." In *Enc Jud*, 149–150.

Rieger, Eliezer, 1896–1954

Dushkin, Alexander M. „אליעזר ריגר" (Eliezer Rieger—In Memoriam." *Sh Hah* (H.) 15

(Spring 1955): 151–55. See also *Jew Ed* 25 (Fall 1954): 7–8.

* Mars, Alvin. *A Pioneer of Jewish Education, Eliezer Rieger, 1896–1954*. Dropsie U., 1970.

Rosen, Ben, ?–1944

"Ben Rosen—In Memoriam." *Jew Ed* 16 (Jan. 1945): 2–3.

Edidin, Ben. "בן רוזן ע״ה„ (Ben Rosen in Memoriam.) *Sh Hah* (H.) 5 (1945): 126–27.

Rosenzweig, Franz, 1886–1929

Glatzer, Nahum N. "פראנץ ראזנצווייג„ (Franz Rosenzweig). *YB* (Y.) (Jan./Feb. 1945): 33–69. Also in *GJT*, 159–82.

———. "החנוך היוצר המאמין והמדע של פראנץ רוזנצווייג" (Rosenzweig's Creative Religious Educational Credo). In *Sefer Ha Shanah* (H.), 405–16. 1946.

Kurzweil, Zvi E. "Franz Rosenzweig as an Educationist." In *MTJE*, 198–219.

Levinas, Emanuel. "Franz Rosenzweig." *Mid* 29 (Nov. 1983) 33–40.

Simon, Ernst. "Franz Rosenzweig and Jewish Education." *Con Jud* 18 (Winter 1964): 10–24.

Trepp, Leo. "Franz Rosenzweig." *Liberal Judaism* (May 1948): 45–

Ruffman, Louis L, 1904–82

Bortniker, Elijah. "Louis L. Ruffman—In Memoriam." *Jew Ed* 50 (Winter 1982): 48.

Pilch, Judah. "אריה ל. רופמן„ (Louis L. Ruffman—In Memoriam). *Sh Hah* 42 (Winter 1982–83): 213–15.

Salanter, Israel Lipkin, 1810–1883

* Etkes, Emanuel. *Rabbi Israel Salanter and the Origins of the Musar Movement* (H.). Jerusalem: Hebrew U., 1975.

Ginzberg, Louis. "Rabbi Israel Salanter." In *Students, Scholars, and Saints*, 145–94. 1928.

Glenn, Menahem G. *Israel Salanter, Religious Thinker*. N.Y.: Bloch, 1953.

* ———. *Rabbi Israel Lipkin Salanter—Man of Musar: His Work, Influence and Disciples*. Dropsie U., 1945.

Kurzweil, Zvi E. "Rabbi Israel Salanter and the Musar Movement." In *MTJE*, 71–94.

Scharfstein, Zevi. "ר׳ ישראל סלנטר„ (Rabbi Israel Salanter). In *GJE* (H.), 68–88.

* Ury, Zalman F. *The Ethic of Israel Salanter, and Moral Education in Jewish Schools*. UCLA, 1966. 196 pp.

———. "The Legacy of Rabbi Israel Salanter." *Jew Parent* (Mar. 1968). Also in *BJC*, 159–67.

———. "Salanter Musar Guidance." *Jew Ed* 38 (Mar. 1968): 34–39.

Scharfstein, Zevi, 1884–1972

Ben-Ezra, Akivah. "הביבליוגרפיה של צבי שרפשטיין„ (The Bibliography of Z. Scharfstein). In *Scharfstein*, 25–67.

Ben-Horin, Meir. "Zevi Scharfstein: 1888–1972." *JBA* (1983/84): 112–21.

Gannes, Abraham P. "ברכת המועצה למען החנוך לפרופ׳ צבי שרפשטיין" (Greetings to Professor Scharfstein on Behalf of the National Council for Jewish Education). *Sh Hah* (H.) 29 (Spring 1969): 131.

Malachi, Eliezer R. "כתבי צבי שרפשטיין„ (The Writings of Zvi Scharfstein). *Sh Hah* (H.) 4 (1944): 192–206; 15 (Fall/Winter 1955): 23–28.

Pilch, Judah. "צבי שרפשטיין בכתביו„ (Scharfstein in His Writings). *JBA* 21 (1963–64): 132–36.

Ravid, Zvulun, ed. "ספר שרפשטיין„ (Zevi Scharfstein Jubilee Volume) (H.). Tel Aviv: Scharfstein Jubilee Committee and Hebrew Teachers Union in Israel, 1970. 421 pp.

———. (Zevi Scharfstein and the Periodical Literature in Hebrew Education). *Bitzaron* (H.) 50 (1964): 118–26.

Sh Hah (dedicated to Zevi Scharfstein) (H.) 4 (June 1944): 166–256.

Zeitlin, Aaron. "יום טוב פון העברעאישען חינוך" (A Celebration of Hebrew Education). In honor of Zevi Scharfstein's 70th birthday. *Day* (Y.) (July 1, 1954).

Schechter, Solomon, 1849–1915

Adler, Cyrus. "Solomon Schechter." *AJYB* 18 (1916–17): 25–67.

Bentwich, Norman. "Solomon Schechter." In *GJP*, 35–161.

Marx, Alexander. "Solomon Schechter." In *Essays in Jewish Biography*, 229–50. 1947.

Parzen, Herbert. "Solomon Schechter, the Seminary, and the United Synagogue." In *Architects of Conservative Judaism*, 26–78. 1964.

"Schechter, Solomon." In *Enc Jud* 14, 948–950.

Schenirer, Sarah, 1880–1939

Grunfeld-Rosenbaum, Judith. "Sara Schenirer." In *The Jewish Woman*, edited by Leo Jung. 1934.

Kurzweil, Zvi E. "Sarah Schenirer." In *MTJE*, 266–74.

Prager, Moshe. *Sarah Schenirer: Em be-Israel* (Mother in Israel) (H.). Jerusalem: Merkaz Beth Jacob.

Scharfstein, Zevi. "שרה שנירר„ (Sarah Schenirer). In *GJE* (H.), 226–43.

Shurin, Aaron Ben-Zion. "די נייטארן וואס האט געשאפן רעליגיעזע שולן פאר מיידלעך„ (The Seamstress Who Created Religious Schools for Girls). *For* (Y.) (Mar. 15, 1985): 12, 28.

Schneerson, Isaac Joseph, 1880–1950

"Schneerson, Isaac." *AJYB* 52 (1951): 504.

"Schneerson, Isaac." In *Enc Jud* 14, 1431–39.

Schneerson, Menachem M., 1902–

"Schneerson, Menachem M." In *Enc Jud* 14, 1431–39.

Penn, Ascher. "דער ליובאוויטשער רבי„ (The Lubavitch Rabbi) (Y.). In *Penn*, chapters 56, 57.

Schoolman, Albert P., 1894–1980

"Schoolman, Albertx P." *AJYB* 82 (1982): 372–73.

Dushkin, Alexander M. "A. P. Schoolman, the Story of a Blessed Life." *Jew Ed* 36 (Winter 1966): 71–76.

Gannes, Abraham P. "Albert P. Schoolman" (editorial). *Jew Ed* 36 (Winter 1966): 67.

Pilch, Judah. "Albert P. Schoolman—In Memoriam." *Jew Ed* 48 (Summer 1980): 4.

———. "A. P. Schoolman—On the Occasion of His 70th Birthday." *Jew Ed* 36 (Winter 1966): 68–69. See also *S/? Hah* (H.) 25 (Spring 1965): 147–48.

Segal, Abraham, 1910–77

"Segal, Abraham." *AJYB* 79 (1979): 373.

Semel, Bernard, 1878–1959

Dushkin, Alexander. "Bernard Semel—Maggid and Parnass, [preacher and communal leader] of Jewish Education." *Jew Ed* 20 (Spring 1949): 16.

Penn, Ascher. "בערנארד זעמעל: קא-עקזיסטענץ פון די פארשיידענע אידישע גרופן אין אמעריקע איז נויטיק„ (Semel Spokesman for Coexistence among the Various Jewish Groups in America). In *Penn* (Y.), 134–40.

Pilch, Judah. "Bernard Semel" (editorial). *Jew Ed* 26 (Spring 1956): 3.

Rudavsky, David. "Bernard Semel: A Leader in Israel." *Jew Ed* 26 (Spring 1956): 5–9.

"Semel, Bernard." *AJYB* 61 (1960): 418.

Shapira, Meir, 1887–1934

Frenkel, L. "Meir Shapira." In *Men of Distinction*, 2:31–39. 1967.

"Meir Shapira." In *Enc Jud* 14, 1299–1300.

Nadler, Meir, ed. "ספר היובל ... מאיר שאפירא„ (Jubilee Volume in Honor of Meir Shapira, Renowned Educational Scholar and Founder of "Yeshivot Hakhmei Lublin."). Lodz, Poland: Mesorah, 1930.

Shapiro, Solomon, 1889–1973

"Shapiro, Solomon." *AJYB* (1974–75): 657.

Shevach, Benjamin, ?–1978?

Ackerman, Walter I. "Benjamin Shevach—In Memoriam." *Jew Ed* 46 (Winter 1978): 47–48.

Slesinger, Zalmen, 1906–85

Ben-Horin, Meir. "הצנע לכת וחינוך„ (The Man of Modesty and Thought). *Sh Hah* (H.) 45 (Spring/Summer 1986): 211–18.

Soloveitchik, Joseph B.. 1903–

Birnbaum, Ruth. "The Man of Dialogue and the Man of Halakhah." *Jud* 26 (Winter 1977): 52–62.

"Soloveitchik, Joseph Dov." In *Enc Jud* 15, 132–33.

Lichtenstein, Aharon. "R. Joseph Soloveitchik." In *GJT*, 281–97.

Soltes, Mordecai, 1893–1957

Gamoran, Emanuel. "Mordecai Soltes—In Memoriam." *Jew Ed* 29 (Winter 1959): 2.

"Mordecai Soltes—In Memoriam." *J Jew Com Ser* (Fall 1958): 3.

"Soltes, Mordecai." *AJYB* 59 (1958): 477.

Szold, Henrietta, 1860–1945

Dushkin, Alexander M. "Henrietta Szold—Teacher." *Jew Ed* 16 (May 1945): 2–3.

Fineman, I. *Woman of Valor: The Life of Henrietta Szold*. 1961.

Glenn, Menahem. *Henrietta Szold—Mother in Israel* (H.). N.Y.: JEC, "Ledor," 1964. 39 pp.

"Szold, Henrietta." In *Enc Jud* 15, 665–668

Tchernowitz, Chaim (Rav Zair), 1871–1949

* Hoffseyer, Benjamin. *Rabbi Chaim Tchernowitz: "Rav Tzair" and the Yeshiva of Odessa* (H.). Yeshiva U., 1967. 201 pp.

"Rav Tzair Memorial Issue." *Bitzaron* (H.) (Apr. 1949).

"Rav Zair Jubilee Issue." *Bitzaron* (H.) (Apr. 1948).

"Tchernowitz, Chaim." *AJYB* 51 (1950): 524.

"Tchernowitz, Chaim." In *Enc Jud* 15, 883–884.

Teitelbaum, Joel, 1888–

"Joel Teitelbaum of Satmar." In *Enc Jud* 15, 909.

Penn, Ascher. „דער סאטמארער רבי און די גרויסע חסידישע קהילה, וואס ער האט אויפגעבויט אין ווילאמסבורג, ברוקלין" (The Rabbi of Satmar and the Large Jewish Community He Has Developed in Williamsburg, Brooklyn). In *Penn* (Y.), 513–22.

Toubin, Isaac, 1915–86

"Toubin, Isaac." *AJYB* 88 (1988): 509.

"In Tribute to Isaac Toubin" (memorial meeting by JESNA, May 29, 1986). *Ped Rep* 37:3 (Oct. 1986): 1–2. Includes tributes by Philip Bernstein, Fradle Freidenreich, and Nathan Winter.

Touroff, Nisson, 1877–1953

Abramovitz, Hirsch. „שלשה מחנכים עברים מפרסים" (Three Famous Jewish Educators). *Sh Hah* (H.) 14 (Winter 1947): 88–98.

Bavli, Hillel. „ניסן טורוב" (Nisson Touroff). *Sh Hah* (H.) 1 (1940): 68–69.

Ben-Ezra, Akivah. „הביבליוגרפיה של הד"ר טורוב" (The Bibliography of Dr. Touroff). *Sh Hah* (H.) 8 (1947): 46–53; 14 (1954): 98–110.

„בטאון" (*Bitaon*) (dedicated to Touroff) (H.) 3/4 (1937).

Blumenheld, Samuel M. „ניסן טורוב—העברי ללא תנאי" (Nisson Touroff—The Unconditional Jew). *In S Ed* (H.), 211–13.

Edelstein, Menachem. „למודה המורים—לד"ר ניסן טורוב ליובלי השבעים" (To the Teacher of Teachers—To Dr. Nissan Touroff on His 70th Birthday). *Sh Hah* (H.) 8 (1947–48): 83–85.

Hurwich, Louis. "Dr. Nissan Touroff" (editorial). *Jew Ed* 9 (Oct./Dec. 1937): 117–18.

Malachi, Eliezer R. „הביבליוגרפיה של ניסן טורוב" (The Bibliography of Dr. Nissan Touroff). In *Sefer Touroff* (H.), edited by I. Silberschlag and Y. Twersky, 64–82. Boston: Hebrew Teachers College, 1938.

Pitlick, Sh. „ד"ר ניסן טורוב" (Dr. N. Touroff). *Bitaon* (H.) 3 (1937): 5–10.

Scharfstein, Zevi. „ד"ר ניסן טורוב—המחנך הלאומי" (Dr. Nisson Touroff—The Nationalist Educator). In *GJE* (H.), 208–25. See also *Sh Hah* (H.) 14 (1947/48): 67–80.

Sh Hah (H.) (May 1948) (dedicated to Touroff).

Silberschlag, I., and Twersky, Y., eds. „ספר טורוב." (Sefer Touroff) (H.). Boston: Hebrew Teachers College, 1938. 114 pp.

"Touroff, Nisson." *AJYB* 55 (1954): 460.

Tuchman, Hyman, ?–1972

Lerner, Israel. "Hyman Tuchman—In Memoriam." *Jew Ed* 41 (Spring 1972): 5

Ullman, Solomon Baruch, ?–1972

Brown, Alexander, "Solomon Baruch Ullman—In Memoriam." *Jew Ed* 42 (Winter 1972–73): 6.

Veret, Paul, ?–1970

Gamoran, Emanuel, "Paul Veret—In Memoriam." *Jew Ed* 41 (Spring 1972): 4–5.

Walkomitz, Simha Hayyim, 1871–1918

Scharfstein, Zevi. „שמחה חיים ולקומיץ" (Simha H. Walkomitz). In *GJE* (H.), 136–42.

"Walkomitz, Simha Hayyim." In *Enc Jud* 16, 253.

Waxman, Meyer, 1887–1969

Mishkin, Laonard C. "Meyer Waxman: An Appreciation and Bibliography." *JBA* 13 (1955): 39.

Rosenthal, Judah, ed. *Meyer Waxman—Jubilee on the Occasion of his 75th Birthday* (E. and H.). 1967.

Rothblat, Ch. M. „ד"ר מאיר וקסמן—הסופר העברי" (Dr. Meyer Waxman—The Hebrew Author). In *Pakim Ktanim* (H.), 7–32. 1956.

Weinstein, Joshua, ?–1985

Goldman, Emanuel. „לזכרו של יהושע וינשטין" (Joshua Weinstein—In Memoriam." *Sh Hah* (H.) 45 (Autumn 1985): 31–32.

Ravid, Zvulun. „לזכרו של יהושע וינשטין" (Joshua Weinstein—In Memoriam." *Sh Hah* (H.) 45 (Autumn 1985): 18–30.

Wessely (Weisl), Naphtali Herz, 1725–1805

Kurzweil, Zvi E. "N. H. Weisel." In *MTJE*, 13–40.

Scharfstein, Zevi. „נפתלי הירץ וויזל" (Naphtali Herz Weisl). In *GJE* (H.), 29–49.

"Wessely, Naphtali Herz." In *Enc Jud* 16, 461–63.

Whiteman, Kaiman, c. 1882–1946

Churgin, Pinkhos. „קלמן וויטמאן, איש הרוח ואיש המעשה" (Kalman Whiteman, Intellectual and Man of Action). *Sh Hah* (H.) 7 (1947): 48–50.

Dushkin, Alexander M. "Kaiman Whiteman—In Memoriam." *Jew Ed* 18 (Nov. 1946): 2.

Edelstein, Menachem. „ר' קלמן וויטמן ע"ה" (Kaiman Whiteman—In Memoriam). *Sh Hah* (H.) 7 (1947): 83–85.

Frishberg, I. Z. „הסופר והפדגוג" (The Author and Pedagogue). *Hadoar* (H.) 18 (1939).

Halevi, Mordecai. „קלמן וויטמאן" (Kaiman Whiteman). *Sh Hah* (H.) (1939): 93–94. Also in *AJE* (H.), 91–94.

Wise, Isaac Mayer, 1819–1900

Akselrad, Sidney. "Studies in the Development of Conservative and Reform Judaism in the United States: A Comparison of the Views of Isaac Leeser and Isaac Meyer Wise, with Respect to the Messiah and Mission of Israel." Master's thesis, HUC-JIR, 1942.

Heller, James G. *Isaac Mayer Wise*. 1965.

Knox, Israel. "Isaac Mayer Wise." In *GJP*, 103–25.

* Temkin, Sefton David. *Isaac Mayer Wise, 1819–1900*. 2 vols. HUC-JIR, 1964.

"Wise, Isaac Mayer." In *Enc Jud* 16, 563–565.

Wise, Stephen S., 1874–1949

Bernstein, Philip S. "Stephen S. Wise." *AJYB* 51 (1950): 515–18.

"Wise, Stephen S." *AJYB* 51 (1950): 525–26.

"Wise, Stephen S." In *Enc Jud* 16, 566–568.

Wiseman, Shloime, 1899–

Dunsky, Shimshon, ed. „שלמה וויסמאן בוך" (Shloime Wiseman Book) (Y., H., and E.). Montreal: Jewish Peoples Schools, 1961. 464 pp. Articles include:

    Bickel, Shlomo. „א דערמאנונג און א בוך—א סאלוט צו שלמה וויסמאן" (A Reminder and a Book—A Salute to Wiseman) (Y.), 320–23.

    Korn, Rachel. „א פאר ווערטער צו שלמה וויסמאנ'ס יום טוב" (Some Remarks on Wiseman's Jubilee) (Y.), 316–18.

    Reich, Nathan, „זכרונות און אפשאצוונגען" (Memories and Evaluations) (Y.), 323–330.

    Segal, Louis, „א פיאנער פון נאציאנאלער יידישער דערציאונג" (A Pioneer of National Jewish Education) (Y.), 337–41.

    Zaltz, F. „ש. וויסמאן דער מענטש פון מעשים" (Wiseman—The Man of Deeds), 333–37.

(Shloime Wiseman). In *Biographical Dictionary of Modern Yiddish Literature* (Y.), 3:414–15.

Wohl, Harry, ?–1982

Cohen, Nathaniel. "Harry Woll—In Memoriam." *Jew Ed* 50 (Summer 1982): 4.

Isaacs, David L. „ואהל בן השבעים" (A Tribute to Wohl on His 70th Birthday). *Sh Hah* (H.) 29 (Spring 1969): 184–85.

Yefroikin, Zalman, 1895–1966

Culture and Education (Y.) (dedicated to Yefroikin and Tanhum Bernstein). Dec. 1967. 39 pp.

27 MEN AND WOMEN WHO INFLUENCED JEWISH EDUCATION

Shmulevitch, I. "זלמן יעפרויקין," (Zalman Yefroikin). *For* (Y.) (Feb. 25, 1959).

Simon, Solomon. "זלמן יעפרויקין," (Zalman Yefroikin). *CE* (Y.) (Mar. 1959).

"Yefroikin, Zalmen." *AJYB* 68 (1967): 535.

"יעפרויקיו, זלמן," (Zalman Yefroikin). In *Biographical Dictionary of Modern Yiddish Literature* (Y.), 4:281–82.

Yellin, David, 1864–1941

"David Yellin." In *Enc Jud* 16, 736–38.

Dinur, Ben Zion. *Benei Dori* (My Contemporaries) (H.), 86–99. 1963.

Malachi, Eliezer R. "דוד ילין," (David Yellin). *Hadoar* (H.) 12, 19 (1941).

Scharfstein, Zevi. "דוד ילין," (David Yellin). In *GJE* (H.), 163–78.

Zalesky, Noses, 1905–70

Furer, Max M. "Moses Zalesky—In Memoriam." *Jew Ed* 40 (Winter 1970): 6–7.

Halevi, Mordecai. "משה זלסקי ז"ל," (Moses Zaleski—In Memoriam). In *AJE* (H.), 95–101.

Zhitlowsky, Chaim, 1865–1943

Bickel, Shlomo. "חיים זשיטלאווסקי," (Chaim Zhitlowsky). In *Writers of My Generation* (Y.), 195–202. 1958.

Epstein, Melech. "Chaim Zhitlowsky." In *Profiles of Eleven*, 295–322. 1965.

Goldsmith, Emanuel S. "Chaim Zhitlowsky." In *Architects of Yiddish*, 161–81. 1976.

———. "Zhitlowsky and American Jewry." *Jew Fron* (Nov. 1975): 14–17.

Knox, Israel. "Zhitlowsky's Philosophy of Jewish Life." *Contemporary Jewish Record* 6 (1945): 172–82.

Lehrer, Leibush. "ד"ר חיים זשיטלאווסקי," (Dr. Chaim Zhitlowsky). In *Jubilee Volume—Dr. Chaim Zhitlowsky on His 70th Birthday* (Y.), edited by David Pinski, 23–24. 1935.

Mahler, Raphael. "די אידישע ירושה פון חיים זשיטלאווסקי" (The Jewish Legacy of Zhitlowsky). In *Historians and Spiritual Guides* (Y.), 111–51. 1967.

Niger, Sh. "דה. היים זשיטלאווסקי און אונדזער שול" (Dr. Zhitlowsky and Our School). *Our School* (Y.) (1936).

Noveck, H. "דה. היים זשיטלאווסקי און זיין באדייט פאר דער יידישער שול" (Dr. Zhitlowsky and His Significance for the Yiddish School Movement). In *Shu P* (Y.), 151–69.

COMMUNITY AND JEWISH EDUCATION

PART III | COMMUNITY AND JEWISH EDUCATION

CONTENTS

28 | HISTORICAL BACKGROUND OF JEWISH EDUCATION   317

Ancient Period (Selected)   317
The Middle Ages (Selected)   320
The Heder (Primarily Modern Period)   321
Modern Period (Selected)   322
Education in Modern Israel prior to 1948 (Selected)   326
Education in Modern Israel since 1948 (Selected)   327
Gleanings   332

29 | HISTORY OF JEWISH EDUCATION IN THE UNITED STATES   335

History   335
Jewish Education in the United Sates prior to 1900   337
History of American Jewry (Selected)   347
Institutions and Organizations (Selected)   348
Jewish Religious, Organizational, and Cultural life (Selected)   348
Gleanings   350

30 | THE AMERICAN JEWISH COMMUNITY   353

General (Selected)   353
The Community and Jewish Education prior to 1950   354
Tlx Community and Jewish Education since 1950   355
The Synagogue and Jewish Education   359
Lay Leadership and Jewish Education   360
Financial Support for Jewish Education prior to 1950   362
Financial Support for Jewish Education since 1950   363
The Rationale for Central Agencies of Jewish Education   364
Assessing Central Educational Agencies and New Needs   365
Women and Jewish Education in the United States   366
Women and the Rabbinate in the Community   367
The Jewish Center and Other Communal Agencies Related to Jewish Education   367
The Jewish Community in the Jewish Curriculum prior to 1950   368
The Jewish Community in the Jewish Curriculum since 1950   369
Changing Jewish Communities—Implications for Jewish Education (Selected)   370
Gleanings   371

PART III   COMMUNITY AND JEWISH EDUCATION

31 | THE HOME AND JEWISH EDUCATION   379

School Relationships prior to 1950   379
School Relationships since 1950   380
The Jewish Family (Selected)   385
Gleanings   388

32 | ADULT EDUCATION   390

General (Selected)   390
In the Community   393
Methodology and Evaluation   395
Gleanings   397

33 | THE WOMAN'S ROLE AND JEWISH EDUCATION   398

European Background (Selected)   398
In the United States prior to 1900   399
In the United States 1900–1950   399
In the United States since 1950   400
Gleanings   403

34 | SEPHARDIM AND JEWISH EDUCATION   405

General (Selected)   405
Education   407
Periodicals (Selected)   408
Gleanings   408

35 | YOUTH AND JEWISH EDUCATION   409

Prior to 1950   409
Since 1950   410
Gleanings   415

36 | CAMP   417

Camping Programs and Jewish Education   417
Gleanings   420

37 | LOCAL SOURCES FOR JEWISH EDUCATION   422

Alabama   422
Alaska   423
Arizona   423
Arkansas   424
California   424
Colorado   432
Connecticut   433
Delaware   435
District of Columbia   435
Florida   436
Georgia   438
Hawaii   440
Idaho   440

PART III COMMUNITY AND JEWISH EDUCATION

Illinois 440
Indiana 447
Iowa 448
Kansas 449
Kentucky 449
Louisiana 449
Maine 451
Maryland 451
Massachusetts 454
Michigan 458
Minnesota 463
Mississippi 464
Missouri 464
Montana 466
Nebraska 467
Nevada 467
New Hampshire 467
New Jersey 467
New Mexico 471
New York 471
New York City 475
North Carolina 493
North Dakota 494
Ohio 494
Oklahoma 499
Oregon 499
Pennsylvania 500
Rhode Island 507
South Carolina 509
South Dakota 509
Tennessee 510
Texas 510
Utah 512
Vermont 512
Virginia 512
Washington 514
West Virginia 515
Wisconsin 515
Wyoming 516

28 | HISTORICAL BACKGROUND OF JEWISH EDUCATION

ANCIENT PERIOD (SELECTED)

* Amir, Abraham. *The Tanna, Amora, Sidra, and Kallah in the Years 200–300 C.E.* (H.). Yeshiva U., 1972. 335 pp.

Arzt, Max. "The Teacher in Talmud and Midrash." In *Kaplan*, 35–48.

Atkins, W. A. "Educational Philosophies and Practices in the Old Testament." *Rel Ed* 45 (Sept./Oct. 1976): 500–508.

Averbach, Moshe. „התפתחות החנוך העברי" (The Development of Jewish Education). *Sh Hah* (H.) 26 (Winter 1966): 90–94, (Spring 1966): 157–58; 27 (Winter 1967): 103–9, (Summer 1967): 242–46.

———. "The Development of the Jewish Elementary and Secondary School System during the Talmudic Age." *Stu*, vol. 3, 290–301.

———. "Educational Institutions and Problems during the Talmudic Age." *HUC Annual* 37 (1966): 107–20.

———. „המורה העברי בתקופת התלמוד" (The Hebrew Teacher during the Talmudic Era). *Sh Hah* (H.) 31 (1971): 6–15, 140–44; 32 (1972): 5–13.

———. „החינוך היהודי בתקופת המשנה והתלמוד" (Jewish Education during the Eras of the Mishnah and the Talmud). Jerusalem: Rubin Mass Ltd. and the Hebrew College of Baltimore, 1982. 344 pp.

———. „היחסים בין הרב והתלמיד בתקופת התלמוד" (Teacher-Student Relationships during the Talmudic Era). *Sh Hah* (H.) 33 (1973): 6–12, 17–18; 34 (1974): 5–10, 69–75, 207–13; 35 (1975): 7–77; 37 (1977–78): 41–49, 121–27, 187–92, 244–93; 38 (251–55).

———. „תינוקות של בית רבן" (Young School Children). (H., and E. summary). *Ped Rep* 31 (Spring 1980): 32–34.

Baumel, Morris. "Philo Judaeus, His Educational Significance." Master's thesis, New York U., 1932.

Berger, Julius. *Elementary Education in the Talmud, the Fountainhead of Many Modern Pedagogical Ideas*. Montreal: Eagle, 1929.

* Berlin, Lewis L. *Health Teaching and Practices Derived from the Hebrew Bible*. New York U., 1952. 386 pp.

* Beyer, Jimmie Lee. *The Educational Concept of Parent-Child Relationship Based on Major Jewish and Christian Philosophies to the Second Century A.D.* New Orleans Baptist Theological Seminary, 1971.

Blumenfield, Samuel M. "Thou Shalt Teach." In *Great Jewish Ideas*, edited by Abraham Ezra Millgram, 133–46. Washington, D.C.: B'nai B'rith Department of Adult Jewish Education, 1964.

Brickman, William W. „אלט-יידישע דערציאונג אין אמעריקאנער פעדאגאגישע לערנביכער" (Ancient Jewish Education in American Pedagogic Textbooks). *YB* (Y.) 31–32 (1948): 389–400.

28
HISTORICAL BACKGROUND OF JEWISH EDUCATION

* Carlson, E. Leslie. *The Pedagogy of the Old Testament in the Light of Hebrew Terminology*. Southwestern Baptist U., 1936.

* Carpenter, James Walter. *The Jewish Educational System in Palestine during the Time of Jesus*. American U., 1958. 276 pp.

Charna, Y. לתולדות החינוך בישראל (On the History of Education in Israel) (H.). Parts 1 and 2, Biblical and Talmudic periods. Jerusalem: 1939.

Chertoff, Sheraga. "למוד התלמוד בחנוך העם" (The Study of the Talmud in the Education of the Nation). In *Yesod* (H.), 76–91.

Cornill, Carl. "The Education of Children in Ancient Israel." In *The Culture of Ancient Israel*, 68–100. Chicago: Open Court, 1914.

Cubberley, Ellwood P. "Hebrew Education." In *Syllabus of Lectures of the Study of Education*, 19–23. N.Y.: Macmillan, 1904.

Demsky, A. "Education in the Biblical Period." In *Enc Jud*, 6:382–98.

* Drazin, Nathan. "דידאקטישע פרינציפן" (Didactic Principles in Accordance with the Talmud) In *DER* (Y.), 2:358–68.

———. *History of Jewish Education from 515 B.C.E. to 220 C.E.* Johns Hopkins U., 1937. Also published by Johns Hopkins U. Press, 1940. 161 pp.

Duggan, Stephen. "Jewish Education." In *A Student's Textbook in History of Education*, 7–14. N.Y.: Appleton-Century, 1927.

* Ebner, Eliezer. *Elementary Jewish Education in Palestine during Tannaitic Times*. Dropsie U., 1949. 80 pp. Published as *Elementary Education in Ancient Israel*. N.Y.: Bloch, 1956. 128 pp.

Eby, Frederick, and C. F. Arrowood. "Theocratic Education Among the Hebrews." In *The History and Philosophy of Education, Ancient and Medieval*, 108–59. N.Y.: Prentice-Hall, 1942.

Ed Enc "התקופה העתיקה—החינוך היהודי" (Ancient Jewish Education). 4:136–84. Jerusalem, 1964.

Ed Enc "אנציקלופדיה חינוכית" (H.) Jerusalem: The Ministry of Education and Culture and the Bialik Institute, 1961–1969. 5 volumes. Includes Jewish Education in the United States and other lands. Extensive bibliographies in the language of the original publication.

Franklin, Leo. "Education among the Jews in Biblical and Talmudic Times." Master's thesis, HUC, 1892.

* Fried, Haya Rachel Greenberg. *Education in the Bible, the Talmud, and the Prayer Book*. Ann Arbor: U. of Michigan Microfilms International. 237 pp.

* Gafni, Y. *The Babylonian Yeshiva: Internal Structure and Social Function among the Jewish Community in the Period of the Amoraim*. Harvard U., 1977.

Gands, Solomon. "The Robeh or the Official Memorizer of the Palestinian Schools." *American Academy of Jewish Research Proceedings* 7 (1935–36): 5–12.

Gollancz, Herman. *Pedagogics of the Talmud and That of Modern Times: A Comparative Study*. London: Oxford U. Press, 1924.

Hefterman, A. "החנוך בספרות התלמודית" (Education in Talmudic Literature). *Sh Hah* (H.) 5 (May 1945): 147–56.

Hirsch, Samson Raphael. "The Talmud and Its Teachings on Social Virtues, Civic Duties, and Commercial Integrity." In *Judaism Eternal*, translated by I. Grunfield, 2:155–86.

Hoffmann, Justin. "The Ends of Jewish Education in Classical Judaism." *Jew Ed* (Winter 1962): 72–78.

———. "The Pre-Eminence of Education in Classical Judaism." *Jew Ed* 36 (Spring/Summer 1966): 155–61, 191.

———. "The Student in Classical Judaism." *Jew Ed* 38 (Jan. 1968): 50–58.

———. "The Teacher in Classical Judaism." *Rel Ed* 62 (July–Aug. 1967): 335–43.

———. "The Teaching-Learning Process in Classical Judaism." *Rel Ed* 65 (May–June 1970): 225–44.

Honor, Leo. "The Role of Memory in Biblical History." In *Kaplan*. Also in *RTJH*, 71–90.

* James, Muriel Marshall. *The Development of Hebrew Adult Education as Related to National Crisis from 1800 B.C. to 220 A.D.* U. of California-Berkeley, 1964. 295 pp.

Kane, W. "Education of the Hebrews." In *A History of Education*, 20–29. Chicago: Loyola U. Press, 1930.

* Kretzman, Paul E. *Education among the Jews from the Earliest Times to the End of the Talmudic Period.* U. of Minnesota, 1916.

Lauterbach, Jacob Z. "The Names of the Rabbinical Schools and Assemblies in Babylon." In *HUC Jubilee Volume*, 211–22. Cincinnati: 1925.

Lehrman, Irving. "Early Sources for Jewish Education: Talmud Torah as Found in the Pesikta De-Rab Kahana." Master's thesis, JIR, 1942.

Leipziger, Emil William. "Talmudic Education." Master's thesis, HUC, 1900.

* Leipziger, Henry M. *The Education of the Jews.* Educational Monograph no. 6, 187–221. N.Y.: Columbia U. College for the Training of Teachers, 1890.

* Maller, Julius B. *A Psychological Study of Talmudic Folklore with Comparison between Babli and Yerushalmi.* JTS, 1927.

Marinoff, Shlomo. "לתולדות החנוך בימי משה" (On the History of Education in the Days of Moses). *Sh Hah* (H.) 11 (Dec. 1950): 3–8.

Marsh, Leon. "The Philosophy and Practice of Hebrew Education from the Post-Exilic Era through the Tannaitic Period." Master's thesis, Southwest Baptist Theological Seminary, 1959. 303 pp.

* Maynard, John A. *A Survey of Hebrew Education.* New York U., 1919. 88 pp.

Melconian, Vartin. "The Pedagogy of the Pentateuch with Special Reference to Moses as an Educational Leader." Master's thesis, New York U., 1927.

Mirsky, Samuel K. "ראשיתו של בית-הספר העברי" (The Beginnings of the Jewish School). In *Sefer Hadoar: 35 Years of* Hadoar (H.), 64–67. 1957.

———. "לראשיתה הישיבה ומהותה" (The Origin of the Yeshiva and Its Intrinsic Nature.). *Horeb* (H.) 5 (1939): 133–42.

———. "Types of Lectures in the Babylonian Academies." In *Baron*, 375–402.

Moore, George Foot. "The Idea of Torah in Judaism." *Menorah J* 8 (1921).

———. "The Schools." In *Judaism*, 1:308–22. 3 vols. Cambridge: Harvard U. Press, 1946.

Moriel, Yehuda. "Education in the Talmud." In *Enc Jud*, 6:398–403.

Morris, Nathan. *The Jewish School.* N.Y.: JEC, 1964. 277 pp.

———. "זכרון, זיין ארט אין אלטן יידישן חנוך" (Memory: Its Place in Ancient Jewish Education). In *DER* (Y.), 3:480–87.

———. "הלכה ומעשה" (Theory and Practice) (Y.). In *DER*, 3:195–202.

Moses, Isidor R. "Post-Exile Hebrew Education." Master's thesis, New York U., 1918.

Orner, G. "לדמותו של המורה בתקופת התלמוד" (The Image of the Teacher during the Era of the Talmud). *Hadoar* (H.) 57 (Aug. 25, 1978).

Pearce, C. S. "The Education of Hebrew Youth from the Earliest Times to the Maccabean Period." Master's thesis, Cincinnati U., 1930.

* Polzin, Robert M. *An Analysis of the Language of the Chronicler and of the Priestly Document: Toward an Historical Typology of Biblical Hebrew Prose.* Harvard U., 1971.

* Pratt, Charles Lynn. *The Moral Teachings of the Jews at the Time of Christ.* Harvard U., 1916.

* Resnikoff, Moses B. *Social Aspects of Jewish Elementary Education in the First Centuries of the Christian Era.* Columbia U., 1966. 170 pp.

Rosenberg, Meyer J. "The Historical Development of Hebrew Education from Ancient Times to 135 A.D." Master's thesis, New York U., 1926. Published by the author in 1927, 135 pp.

Rosman, Steven M. "Classical Jewish Pedagogy: Its Prescription and Practice." *Jew Ed* 53 (Summer 1985): 27–35.

———. "A Study of a Child's Formal Introduction to Education in Poland and Germany: From the End of the Sixteenth to the End of the Seventeenth Centuries." Master's thesis, HUC–JIR, 1983.

* Roth, Alvin S. *Rabbinic Foundations of Jewish Education as Reflected in Talmudic Literature 10 C.E. to 499 C.E.* Northwestern U., 1957. 175 pp.

Sacks, Maxwell L. "Fundamental Issues in Buddhist and Jewish Education." Master's thesis, New York U., 1925.

Sandmel, Samuel. "Philo and His Pupils: An Imaginary Dialogue." *Jud* 4 (1955): 47–57.

* Sawdayee, Maurice M. *The Impact of Western European Education on the Jewish Millet of Baghdad, 1860–1950*. New York U., 1976. 328 pp.

Scharfstein, Zevi. "החנוך הישן,", (Ancient Education). *History of Jewish Education* (H.) 1 (1946): 1–31.

Shapiro, Israel. "השוואת הפדגוגיה המודרנית אל הפדגוגיה התלמודית" (A Comparison of Modern Pedagogy to the Talmudic Pedagogy). *Sh Hah* (H.) 3 (1927): 33–39, 126–31.

* Shapiro, Joseph. *Education among the Early Hebrews with Special Emphasis on the Talmudic Period*. U. of Pittsburgh, 1938. 248 pp.

Shifman, Pinchos. "הילד באגדה,", (The Child in the Aggadah). *Sh Hah* (H.) 4 (1929): 435–40.

* Shunk, William R. *The Educational Contribution of the Hebrew Prophets*. U. of Texas, 1961. 268 pp.

Simon, Abram. *The Principle of Jewish Education in the Past*. Washington, D.C.: 1909. 36 pp.

Simon, Joseph. *L'education et L'instruction des enfants, Chez les Anciens Juifs* (History of the Education and Instruction of Children among the Ancient Jews) (French). 2d ed. Paris: Librairie Sandoz and Fischbacher, 1870. 63 pp.

Sonne, I. "The Schools of Shammai and Hillel Seen from within." In *Louis Ginzberg Jubilee Volume*, edited by Saul Lieberman et al., 245–91. 1945

Spiers, B. *The School System of the Talmud*. London: E. Stoick, 1898. 111 pp.

Swift, Fletcher Harper. *Education in Ancient Israel to 70 A.D.* Chicago: Open Court, 1919. 134 pp.

Ulich, Robert. "The Judaic Tradition." In *Three Thousand Years of Educational Wisdom* (contains excerpts from the Bible, Baba Bathra, and Jewish educators), 643–48. Cambridge: Harvard U. Press, 1954. See also "The Judaic Tradition" in Ulich's *A History of Religious Education*, 3–20. New York U. Press, 1968.

Waldman, Elliot D. "The Significance of Learning as Reflected in Talmudic Literature: With Special Consideration of the Halachic Aspects." Master's thesis, HUC–JIR, 1959.

* Waldman, Mark. *Ideal View of Pre-Exile Education as Introductory to the Talmud, the Medieval and the Modern Era*. New York U., 1910.

Webb, Arnold Henry. "Hebrew Education." Master's thesis, U. of Kentucky, 1945. 65 pp.

Winters, Alton. "Elementary Education as Reflected in the Talmud." Master's thesis, HUC–JIR, 1947.

Wortman, David A. "An Introduction to Akkadian: A First Semester Text for English Speaking Students." Master's thesis, HUC–JIR, 1973. (On an early language with some influence on Hebrew.)

Yerushalmi, Yosef Hayim. *Zakhor: Jewish History and Jewish Memory*. U. of Washington Press and JPS, 1982. 144 pp.

THE MIDDLE AGES (SELECTED)

Abrahams, Israel. *Hebrew Ethical Wills* (H. and E.). Phila.: JPS, 1926, 1976. 384 pp. (Various wills stress the importance of education.)

———. "The Medieval Schools" and "The Scope of Education." In *Jew Life in the Middle Ages*, 340–72. Phila.: JPS, 1896.

Assaf, Simha. מקורות לתולדות החנוך בישראל (Sources on the History of Jewish Education) (H.) (from the Middle Ages to Haskalah). 4 vols. Tel Aviv: Davir, 1925–42.

Baron, Salo W. "Education and Public Enlightenment." In *The Jewish Community, 1300–1776*, 2:169–207. 3 vols. Phila.: JPS, 1942.

Blumenfield, Samuel M. "Education in the Age of Rashi." In *Rashi: His Teachings and Personality*, edited by Federbush, 90–106. 1958.

———. "Education in France in the Age of Rashi—Christian and Jewish Educational Practices" and "Jewish Education in the Days of Rashi." In *Master of Troys: A Study of Rashi the Educator*, 9–19, 23–71. N.Y.: Behrman, 1946.

Bortniker, Elijah. "Education in the Middle Ages." In *Enc Jud*, 6:403–14.

Finkelstein, Louis. *Jewish Self-Government in the Middle Ages*. N.Y.: Feldheim, 1964.

Furie, William B. "Adult Education in the Medieval Period." *Jew Ed* 14 (Apr./June 1942): 23–27.

Gantzfried, Solomon. "The Study of the Torah." In *Code of Jewish Law*, translated by H. E. Golden, 87–89. N.Y.: Hebrew Pub. Co., 1961. See also "Honor Due to the Teacher, the Scholar, the Aged, and the Priest," 4–6, and "The Training of Children," 47–49.

Goitein, S. D. "Education." In *A Mediterranean Society: The Jewish Communities of the Arab World as Portrayed in the Documents of the Cairo Geniza*, 2:171–211, 555–565. Berkeley: U. of California Press, 1971.

———. "Side Lights on Jewish Education from the Cairo Geniza." In *Gratz Anniversary Volumes*, 83–110. 1971.

* Gordon, Macy Aaron. *Collegial Relationships among Ashkenazi Jewish Scholars, 1100–1300*. Yeshiva U., 1977. 258 pp.

Greenberg, Simon. "Jewish Educational Institutions" (biblical period to modern times). In *JEWS*, 2:1254–87.

Gudemann, Moritz. Das Judische Unterrichtswesen Wahrend der Spanisch-Arabischen Periode (Jewish Education during the Spanish-Arabic Period) (German). Vienna: 1873.

———. "דערציאונג אין מיטל-עלטער" (Education during the Middle Ages—German Jews). In *DER* (Y.), 2:93–108.

———. Geschichte des Erziehungswesens un der Kultur Abend-Laendischen Wahrend des Mittelalters (The History of Instruction and Education and Culture of Western Countries during the Middle Ages) (German). 3 vols. Vienna: 1880–88. Translated into Hebrew by A. Sh. Friedberg. "ספר התורה והחיים" 3 vols. Warsaw: 1890. Also translated into Yiddish by Nahum Shtiff. "אידישע קולטור געשיכטע אין מיטלאלטער" Berlin: 1922. 250 pp. Recently reprinted by World Jewish Congress.

———. Quellenschriften zur Geschichte des Unterrichts und Erziehung bei der Deutschen Juden (Sources on the History of Instruction and Education Among the German Jews—from the Early Period until the Mendelssohn Era) (German). Berlin: A. Homan, 1891. 324 pp.

Jacobson, David. "Education in Rashi's Time." *Jew Ed* 12 (Sept. 1940): 79–87.

Marcus, Jacob R. "Jewish Education" (documents). In *The Jew in the Medieval World*, 373–80. 1961.

Mikliszanski, I. K. "חיי המורה" (The Life of the Teacher) (H.). In *Rashi*, edited by Federbush, 13–30. 1958

Morris, Nathan. תולדות החינוך של עם ישראל (The History of Jewish Education from the Ancient Period to the 18th Century) (H.). 2 vols. Tel Aviv: 1960.

Neumann, Abraham A. "Schools, Curricula, and Educational Ideas." In *The Jews in Spain*, 2:64–96. Phila.: JPS, 1944.

Reines, Chaim Wolf. "תמיכה פאר תורה-לערנערס" (Public Support for Study in Ancient and Medieval Periods). *YB* (Y.) 29 (1946): 291–336. See also *YA* (E.) 7 (1952): 84–109.

THE HEDER
(PRIMARILY MODERN PERIOD)

Abram, L., Abraham Knikhon, and I. K. Kaplan. "דער משפט איבערן חדר" (The Trial over the Heder—Vitebsk, Belorussia) (Y.). 1922.

Ahyloni (Sh. Niger). "די חדר פראגע" (On the Heder Question). *The Jewish World* (Y.) 3 (Mar. 1923): 108–22.

Birnbaum, I. "דער אלף-בית מעטאד אין חדר" (The Aleph Bet Method in the Heder). In *DER* (Y.), 1:3–7.

Carlebach, Joseph. Der Chederprocess in Stadttheater zu Witebsk, USSR, ein Kulturgeschichtlecher Dokument (The Heder Trial at the Theatre of Vitebsk—A Historic Document) (German). Berlin: 1924. (On a court trial initiated to close the Heder because of its "harmful effects.")

Cohn, S. "דער גורל פונעם חדר אין סאוועט-רוסלאד" (The Fate of the Heder in Soviet Russia). *CE* (Y.) (Oct. 1944): 15–17.

Gamoran, Emanuel. "Elementary Education—The Heder" and "The Method in the Heder." In *CCJE*, 59–89, 90–124.

Ginzberg, Louis. "The Jewish Primary School" (1907). In *Students, Scholars, and Saints*, 1–34. Phila.: JPS, 1928. See also *JJS*, 20–31.

Kazdan, Ch. Sh. „דער חדר אין צאַרישן רוסלאַנד" (The Heder in Czarist Russia). *CE* (Y.) (Mar. 1946): 13–16; (May 1946): 33–37; (Oct. 1946): 18–20.

———. „דער חדר אין שפיגל פון דער ליטעראטור" (The Heder as Reflected in Literature). In *A History of Jewish Education—From the Heder, "Shkoles" [government schools] to "Tzisho" [modern Yiddish schools in Poland]* (Y.), 139–68. 1956.

———. „חדר מתוקן—זיין ראל, געשיכטע און פראגראם" (The Improved Heder, Its Role, History, and Program). *BYD* (Y.) (Apr./July 1953): 57–67.

Lehrer, Leibush. „חדר און חינוך" (Heder and Education). *YK* (Y.) (Sept. 1959): 33–37.

Lifshitz, A. M. „החדר" (The Heder). *HaTekufah* (H.) (1920): 294–352. (Seminal study of the Heder.) *DER* (Y.) has an extensive summary of the above. 3:507–28.

Maimon, Solomon. *1754–1800, An Autobiography* (Available in English, Hebrew and Yiddish translations. Maimon, a philosopher, recalls negative memories of his Heder days. His memoirs were introduced at the Vitebsk Trial in 1921.)

Noble, Shlomo. „חומש טייטש" (Pentateuch Translation) (Y.). (Traditional methodology with Yiddish translation.) N.Y.: Yivo. 87 pp.

* Pilch, Judah. *The Heder Metukan* (The Improved Heder). Dropsie U., 1952.

Roskies, Diana K. "Alphabet Instruction in the East European Heder." *YA* 17 (1978): 21–53.

———. *Heder: Primary Education among East European Jews—A Selected and Annotated Bibliography of Published Sources*. N.Y.: Yivo. 14 pp.

———. „דער חדר פראיעקט ביי דער פסיכאלאגיש-פעדאגאגישער סעקציע פון ייוואָ" (The 'Kheyder Project' of the Psychological-Pedagogic Department). *YB* (Y.) 46 (1980): 269–80.

Scharfstein, Zevi. החדר בחיי עמנו (The Heder in the Life of Our People) (H.). N.Y.: Shiloh, 1943. 301 pp.

Shtern, Yekhiel. „באַשרייבונגען פון א חדר אין טישעוויץ..." (Descriptions of a Heder in Tyszowce, Poland). In *Studies in Psychology and Education, Yivo* (Y.), 1:327–54. Vilna: Yivo, 1933.

———. „חדר און בית המדרש" (Heder and House of Study). *YB* (Y.) 31–32 (1948): 37–130. Also published (Y.) N.Y.: YIVO, 1950. 128 pp.

Stampfer, Shaul. "Heder Study, Knowledge of Torah, and the Maintenance of Social Stratification in Traditional East European Jewish Society." In *Stu*, vol. 3, 271–89.

Zborowski, M., and E. Herzog. "From the Kheyder to the Grave" and "Sealed on Mount Sinai." In *Life Is with People*, 58–104, 105–23. 1952.

MODERN PERIOD (SELECTED)

Abramowitch, Stanley. "Jewish Education in Europe" (WWII and postwar). In *Enc Jud*, 6:433–47.

* Atkin, Abraham. *Beth Jacob Movement in Poland*. Yeshiva U., 1959. (Schools for girls.)

* Avital, Moshe. *The Yeshiva and Traditional Education in the Literature of the Hebrew Enlightenment Period* (H.). Yeshiva U., 1977. 332 pp.

Baron, Salo W. „דערציאונג" (Traditional Education). In *DER* (Y.), 3:108–37.

Berger, Myra. „העברעאישע פאלקס-שולן אין פוילן" (Hebrew Folk Schools in Poland). In *DER*, 3:214–39.

———. „העברעאישע פעדאגאגישע לערן-אנסטאלטן אין פוילן" (Hebrew Pedagogic Teacher Institutes in Poland). In *DER* (Y.), 3:239–67.

———. „געשיכטע אין די יידיש-וועלטלעכע שולן אין פוילן" (History of Yiddish Secular Schools in Poland). In *DER* (Y.), 2:263–84.

Borowitz, Eugene B. "Judaic Roots of Modern Education." In *Heritage of American Education*, edited by Richard E. Gross, 67–102.

Bortniker, Elijah. "Jewish Education, 16th-18th Centuries." In *Enc Jud*, 6:414–20.

———. "Jewish Education, The Modern Period, 1800–1939." In *Enc Jud* 6, 420–30.

* Colodner, Samuel. *Jewish Education in Nazi Germany*. Dropsie U., 1954. Published N.Y.: JEC Press. 139 pp.

Cooperstein, L. „האבקותו הפוליטית והמשפטית של החינוך העברי באירופה המזרחית" (The Political and Legal Struggle for Jewish Education in Eastern Europe). *Sh Hah* (H.) 8 (Aug. 1948): 98–107; 9 (Jan. 1949): 8–14, (Oct. 1949): 176–83.

Dinburg, Ben Zion. „ישראל בגולה" (Israel in the Diaspora) (H.). (Language spoken, writing, and educational methods.) 2:347–60.

Drazin, Nathan. „דערציאונגס פילאזאפיע" (Educational Philosophy of Traditional Jewish Education). In *DER* (Y.), 72–93.

Dubnow, Simon. "The Instruction of the Young." In *History of the Jews in Russia and Poland*, translated into English by I. Friedlander, 1:114–38. 3 vols. Phila.: JPS, 1916–20.

* Eisenstein, Miriam. *Jewish Schools in Poland, 1919–1939: Their Philosophy and Development*. Columbia U., 1950. Published by King's Crown Press, Columbia U., 1950. 112 pp.

Fishman, I. *The History of Jewish Education in Central Europe* (from the end of the 18th century). London: E. Goldstone, 1944. 176 pp.

* Friedman, Armin. *Major Aspects of Yeshiva Education in Hungary, 1848–1948*. Yeshiva U., 1971.

* Furie, William. *A History of Jewish Education in Poland before 1765*. Boston U. School of Education, 1939. 215 pp.

* Glicksberg, Abraham A. *Educational Principles and Practices in the Shulchan Aruch*. New York U., 1962.

Glueckl von Hamil. *Memoirs* (1645–1724) (Y.). (Translated into Hebrew and English). Buenos Aires: Yivo, 1967 (first published 1896). 363 pp.

Goitein, Sh. D. „לימוד התנ״ך בחינוך היהודי בגולה" (The Study of the Bible in Jewish Education in the Diaspora) (H.). In *FPDE* (H.), 64–74.

* Goldman, Solomon. *Education among Jewish Displaced Persons: The Sheerat Hapletah [Survivors] in Germany, 1945–1950*. Dropsie U., 1975.

Golomb, Abraham. „תקופות און דערציאונג" (Eras and Education). In *Eternal Paths of the Eternal People* (Y.), 155–228. 1964.

———. „טראדיציאנעלע דערציאונג" (Traditional Education). In "Yidn," *General Enc* (Y.), 3:368–77. See also *JPPP* (E.), 2:102–7.

Grade, Chaim. *The Yeshiva*. 2 vols (A novel with insights on the European Yeshiva).

Grossman, Louis. "Pedagogics." In *The Jewish Encyclopedia*, edited by I. Singer, 9:550–77. New York, 1906.

Gruenwald, Uri. "Education and Culture of the German Jews under Nazi Rule." *Jewish Review* 5 (1948): 56–83.

Halevy, Zvi. *Jewish Schools under Czarism and Communism*. N.Y.: Springer, 1970. 298 pp.

Hirsch, Samson Raphael. "Education" and "Educational Talks." In *JUET*, 1:155–220, 223–51.

Hurwitz, Marc. *Soviet Educational Policy and the Jews*. Washington, D.C.: National Center for Jewish Policy Studies, 1971. 19 pp.

Hurwitz, Sh. „די אידישע שול אין סאוועט-רוסלאנד" (The Jewish School in Soviet Russia). *Zuk* (Y.) (May 1928): 278–81.

Kahane, Sh. Z. „על החינוך הדתי בפולין" (On Religious Education in Poland). *Areshet* (H.) (1943): 117–30.

Kahn, Robert I. "Jewish Academic Goals in Germanic Lands during the 17th and 18th Centuries." Master's thesis, HUC–JIR, 1935.

Kaitz, Abraham. „הישיבות הגדולות של ואלוז׳ין ומיר" (The Yeshivot of Volozhin and Mir). *Hadoar* (H.) 60 (Dec. 19, 1980).

Kastelianski, N. „דאס אידישע שול-וועזן אין ראטן פארבאנד" (The Jewish School System in the Soviet Union). *S Alm* (Y.), 252–71.

Kazdan, Chaim S. „די געשיכטע פון יידישן שולוועזן אין אומאפהענגיק פויליז" (The History of Yiddish Schools in Independent Poland) (Y.). Mexico, 1947. 571 pp.

———. "The Yiddish Secular School Movement between the World Wars. In *JPPP*, 2:131–43.

28 HISTORICAL BACKGROUND OF JEWISH EDUCATION

Klarberg, Manfred. "Teachers from Afar—Itinerant Teachers in European and Western Jewish Communities." *Jew Ed* 47 (Winter 1979): 33–38.

Kohler, Kaufmann, and Morritz Gudemann. "Education." In *The Jewish Encyclopedia*, edited by I. Singer, 5:42–48. N.Y.: 1906.

* Kranzler, David H. *The History of the Jewish Refugee Community of Shangai, 1938–1945.* Yeshiva U., 1971. 520 pp.

Lestschinsky, Jacob. „די רדיפות אויף אידישע קהילות, ציוניזם, העברייאיש און החלוץ" (Attacks on Organized Jewish Communities, Zionism and Hebrew in Soviet Russia). In *Soviet Jewry* (Y.), 323–43. N.Y.: Poale-Zion-Zeire Zion, 1941.

Levitats, Isaac. „השכלה" (Haskalah—Educational Ideals of the Haskalah Movement). In *DER* (Y.), 3:286–92.

———. „חברות פאר דערציאונג און לערנען אין מזרח אייראפע" (Societies for Education and Study in Eastern Europe). In *DER* (Y.), 3:497–507.

* Levitz, Jacob. *The Jewish Community in Mexico: Its Life and Education.* Dropsie U., 1954. 241 pp.

* Lipset, Harry. *Jewish Schools in the Soviet Union, 1917–1941: An Aspect of Soviet Minorities Policy.* Columbia U., 1965. 372 pp.

Maller, Julius B. "The Role of Education in Jewish History." In *Jews*, 2:1239–53.

* Mannenberg, Eliezer. *The Evolution of Jewish Educational Practices in the Canzak (Eyalet) of Jerusalem under Ottoman Rule: An Historical and Philosophical Analysis of the Relationships between the Social and Philosophical Changes of the Local Jewish Communities, the Western Consulates, the Evolution of Jewish Educational Practices, and Their Effect on the Emergence of the Hebrew Educational System.* U. of Connecticut, 1976. 397 pp.

* Margoshes, Samuel. *The Curriculum of the Jewish School in Germany from the Middle of the Seventeenth to the Middle of the Nineteenth Century.* JTS, 1917.

Mehlman, Israel. החינוך היהודי בתפוצות הגולה בימינו (Jewish Education in the Diaspora in Our Times) (H.). Tel Aviv: 1969. 97 pp.

Mendelsohn, Ezra. The *Jews of East Central Europe between the Two World Wars.* (See "schools" in index for Jewish education in various countries.) Bloomington: Indiana U. Press, 1983.

Menes, Abraham. "Patterns of Jewish Scholarship in Eastern Europe." In *Jews*, 1:376–424.

———. „דער איצטיקער שטאנד פון דער טראדיציאנעלער דערציאונג" The Present Status of Traditional Education). In "Yidn," *General Enc* (Y.), 3:378–82. 1942.

———. "The Yeshivot in Eastern Europe." In *JPPP*, 2:108–18.

Mirsky, Samuel, ed. מוסדות תורה באירופה בבנינם ובחורבנם (Jewish Institutions of Higher Learning in Europe, Their Development and Destruction) (H.). N.Y.: Ogen (publishing house of Histadrut Ivrit of America), 1958. 730 pp.

Montenette, Marcia. "Jewish Life in the Middle East—A Teacher's Resource Unit and Curriculum Guide." Master's thesis, HUC–JIR, 1975.

* Moskowitz, Aron. *The History of Jewish Education in Hungary.* Dropsie U., 1960. Published as *Jewish Education in Hungary, 1848–1948.* N.Y.: Bloch for Dropsie College, 1964. 357 pp.

Noble, Shlomo. "The Yeshiva Teacher: The Significance of this National Institution throughout History and in Our Days." *Jew Obs* 6 (Apr. 1970): 8–10, 23.

Ormian, Hayim. המחשבה החינוכית של יהדות פולניה לאור הספרות הפדגוגית והפסכולוגית (The Educational Thought of Polish Jewry in Light of the Pedagogical and Psychological Literature) (H.). Tel Aviv: 1939.

Ozer, Charles. "Jewish Education in the Transition from Ghetto to Emancipation." *Historia Judaica* 9 (Apr. 1947): 75–94; 10 (Oct. 1947): 137–58.

Petuchowsky, Jakob J. "Manuals and Catechisms of the Jewish Religion in the Early Period of Emancipation." In *Studies in Nineteenth-Century Jewish Intellectual History*, edited by Alexander Altmann, 47–64. Cambridge: Harvard U. Press, 1964. (Includes several texts that were translated and used in American Jewish schools in the 19th century.)

Plaut, W. Gunther. "Jewish Education." Views of David Einhorn, Abraham Geiger, Michael Creizenach, Levi Herzfeld, and a resolution of the Leipzig Synod on Jewish Education. In *The Rise of Reform Judaism*, 48–52. N.Y.: World Union for Progressive Judaism. 1963.

Plontovski, Noah. לתולדות מוסדות החנוך של "תרבות" בפולן (Towards a History of Educational Institutions of "Tarbut" in Poland) (H.). Jerusalem: 1946. 46 pp.

* Rohn, Aryeh. *Jewish Education in Vienna between the Two World Wars*. Dropsie U., 1966.

Rosenzweig, Franz. *On Jewish Learning*. Edited by N. N. Glatzer. N.Y.: Schocken, 1955. 128 pp.

Scharfstein, Zevi. "תולדות החנוך בישראל בדורות האחרונים" (The History of Jewish Education in Modern Times (H.). 4 Vols. The first three volumes deal primarily with Europe, the fourth with Israel, 1945–1964. New York and Jerusalem: Ogen and Rubin Mass.

———. "מה נתנה החסידות לחנוך?" (What Has Hasidism Given to Education?) (H.). In *ES*, 209–16.

Schiff, Alvin I. "Jewish Teacher Personnel Practices in European Countries 16th–18th Centuries." *Jew Ed* 26 (Winter 1958): 26–37.

Schulman, Elias. *A History of Jewish Education in the Soviet Union*. N.Y.: Ktav and P.W. Lown Graduate Center, 1971. 184 pp.

Segel, Alexander. "Jewish Education in the Period following Mendelssohn." Master's thesis, HUC, 1918.

Shatzky, Jacob. "מקורים צו דער געשיכטע פון יידישן חינוך" (Sources for Jewish Educational History). Critical review of major works on Jewish Educational History. *YB* (Y.) 22 (Nov./Dec. 1943): 215–25. See also Yivo's *Psychology and Education*, 1:375–77.

———. יידישע בילדונגס-פאליטיק אין פוילן *Jewish Educational Policies in Poland, 1806–1866* (Y.). N.Y.: Yivo, 1943. 272 pp.

Soviv, Aaron. "חסידות וחנוך" (Hasidism and Education). *Sh Hah* (H.) 21 (1961): 198–211.

Spizman, L. "דאס העברעאישע שול וועזן" (The Hebrew School Movement—Europe). In *General Enc* (Y.), 3:425–48. See also *JPPP* (E.), 2:119–30.

* Stern, Nathan. *The Jewish Historico-Critical School of the Nineteenth Century*. Columbia U., 1901. 82 pp.

Strassburger, B. *Geschichte der Erziehung und des Unterrichts bei den Israeliten* (History of Jewish Education and Instruction) (German). Breslau: Jacobson, 1885. 310 pp. (Extensive bibliography in chronological sequence.)

Szajkowski, Zosa. *Jewish Education in France, 1789–1939*. N.Y.: Conference on Jewish Social Studies, 1980. 66 pp.

Tartakover, Arieh. "עם ישראל בהווה בחינוך היהודים" (Contemporary Jewry in Jewish Education). In *FPDE* (H.), 186–89.

———. "Das Mittelschulwesen in Polen" (Secondary Jewish Education in Poland). *Der Jude* (G.) (1926): 76–89.

Trachtenberg, Joshua. "Jewish Education in Eastern Europe at the Beginning of the 17th Century." *Jew Ed* 11 (Sept. 1939): 121–37.

* Velder, Eli. *Teaching the Bible in the Jewish Schools of Europe in the Fifteenth and Sixteenth Centuries*. Johns Hopkins U., 1953.

Weinryb, Bernard D. *Jewish Vocational Education: History and Appraisal of Training in Europe*. N.Y.: Jewish Teachers Seminary Press, 1948.

* Weiss, Ernest Yehudah. *The Impact of Enlightenment upon the Educational Writings of the Hebrew Maskilim in Germany*. Dropsie U., 1970.

Weiss, Isaac. דור דור ודורשיו (A History of the Founders and Builders of Jewish Tradition) (H.). Germany: 1924. (Vols. 4 and 5 include the development of traditional education. Written between 1871 and 1891.)

Wessely, Naphtali. "State of Education among the Jews in the Eighteenth Century." *New Era* 3 (1873): 186–89.

Yodfat, Aryeh. "Jewish Religious Education in the USSR." *Jew Ed* 42 (Winter 1972–73): 31–33, 37.

———. "The Soviet Struggle to Destroy Jewish Religious Education in the Early Years of the Regime, 1917–1927." *Jew Ed* 40 (Winter 1970): 33–41.

28 EDUCATION IN MODERN ISRAEL PRIOR TO 1948 (SELECTED)

Ahad Ha-Am. "הגימנסיה העברית ביפו" (The High School in Jaffa—1912) (H.). In The Complete Writings of Ahad Ha-Am, 415–20. 1947.

Ashkenazi, T. "חנוך ותרבות בארץ ישראל" (Education and Culture in the Land of Israel). Sh Hah 7 (1947): 27–38.

* Bardin, Shlomo. *Pioneer Youth in Palestine*. Columbia U., 1932.

Bentwich, Norman. "Jewish Schools in Palestine." *Jewish Review* 2 (Sept 9, 1911): 258–72.

Ben-Yehuda, Baruch. "לתולדות החינוך בארץ ישראל עד קום המדינה" (On the History of Education in the Land of Israel until the Establishment of the State). In *Education in Israel* (H.), edited by Haim J. Ormian, 3–33. Jerusalem: Department of Education and Culture, 1973.

Berkson, Isaac B. "A Centralized System of Jewish Education in Palestine." *Jew Ed* 21 (Jan 1930): 29–41.

——. "The Hebrew School System in Palestine and Decentralization." *Jew Ed* 6 (Oct./Dec. 1934): 151–61.

——. "Jewish Education in Palestine." *Annals of the American Academy of Political and Social Science* 164 (Nov. 1932): 139–54.

Chipkin, Israel S. "The Educational System in Palestine." *Jew Ed* 16 (Jan 1945): 37.

Dushkin, Alexander M. "The Department of Education at the Hebrew University." *Bulletin* (Hebrew University) 4 (Jan. 1938): 21–27.

——. "The Education Department at the Hebrew University in Jerusalem." *Jew Ed* 8 (Oct./Dec. 1936): 101–9.

——. "The Hebrew University." *Jewish Teacher* 2 (1918).

——. "How Much Do Our Children Receive? A Preliminary Study in the Problem of Elimination and Retardation of Pupils in the Hebrew School System of Palestine." In *Magnes Anniversary Volume* (H.), 105–21. 1938.

——. "Second Annual Report of the Education Department at the Hebrew University, Jerusalem." *Jew Ed* 9 (Apr./June 1937): 113–16.

Frankel, A. H. "The Hebrew University and the Regulation of Secondary Education." *Jew Ed* 18 (Fall/Winter 1947): 18–19.

Gamoran, Emanuel. "לשאלת החנוך בארץ ישראל" (Questions Concerning Education in Israel). *Hadoar* (H.) (Apr. 4, 25, 1930).

Goldberg, Ben Zion. "די שולן פון יידישן ישוב אין ארץ ישראל" (The Jewish Schools in Israel). *YB* (Y.) 20 (Nov.–Dec. 1942): 199–222.

Goldberg, Nathan. "Jewish School Systems in Palestine." *YA* (1946): 134–55. First published in *YB* (Y.) 20 (1942).

Itzkowitz, Benjamin. "Education and the Labor Movement in Palestine." Master's thesis, City College of N.Y., 1933.

Kahn, Juliette B. "The Hebrew University Program." *Jew Ed* 6 (Jan.–Mar. 1934): 20–22.

Klausner, J. "The Hebrew University in Jerusalem." *AJYB* 39 (1937–38): 179–92.

* Kokhba, Moshe. *Interest Patterns in Composition of Fifth Grade Pupils in American and Palestinian Schools*. Columbia U., 1936. 56 pp.

Konowitz, Israel. "למודי הקדש בבתי הספר שבארץ ישראל" (Religious Education in the Israeli Schools). *Sh Hah* (H.) 4 (1929): 252–59.

L. L. "The Hebrew University Experiment in Secondary Education." *Jew Ed* 17 (Nov. 1945): 34–35.

Menuhin, Moshe. "Elementary Education in Palestine." *Jewish Teacher* 2 (June–Oct. 1918): 70–77.

Mossinsohn, Ben Zion. "A Hebrew University in Jerusalem." *Menorah J* 6 (Dec. 1918).

Mumford, Lewis. "The Hebrew University." *Menorah J* 8 (1922): 33–36.

Napaha, Shraga. "The Philosophy of the European Double and the American Single Educational Ladders and Its Bearing to the Zionist Educational System in Palestine." Master's thesis, Yale U., 1931. 77 pp.

* Nardi, Noah. "In Defense of Palestinian Education" (editorial). *Jew Ed* 18 (Nov. 1946): 4–5.

——. "Industrial Education in Palestine." *Jew Ed* 16 (Jan. 1945): 29–33.

———. "Labor Education in Palestine." *Jew Ed* 9 (Oct./Dec. 1937) 132–35..

———. *Zionism and Education in Palestine*. Columbia U., 1935. Published by the ZOA, 1945. 255 pp.

Pheley, Gordon E. "The Development of Education in Palestine under the British Mandate." Master's thesis, U. of Southern California, 1937.

Rieger, Eliezer. "Education and a Free Society in Palestine." *Jew Ed* 12 (Jan 1941): 146–53.

———. החנוך העברי בארץ ישראל (Jewish Education in Israel) (H.). 2 parts. Israel: Davir, 1940. 303 pp. and 328 pp.

Roth, H. I., ed. *On Jewish Secondary Education in Israel* (H.). Jerusalem: Mass, 1939. 274 pp.

Sampter, Jessie E. "On the Mount of Olives—The Hebrew University." *Menorah J* 8 (Feb. 1922): 36–40.

Scharfstein, Zevi. החנוך בארץ ישראל (Education in Israel) (H.). N.Y.: Ogen (publishing house of Histadrut Ivrit of America), 1928. 191 pp.

———. "Education in Palestine—Modern Times." In *JPPP*, 2:189–200.

———. "מעמד המלמד בישראל" (The Status of the Teacher in Israel). *Sefer Hashanah* (H.) 6 (1947): 180–204.

Schatz, Boris. "The Bezalel School of Jewish Arts and Crafts." *The Maccabbean* (Nov. 1906).

Shvadron, Benjamin. "החנוך בארץ ישראל ובעיותיו" (Education in Israel and Its Problems). *Sefer Hashanah* (H.) 8–9 (1946): 601–16.

Simon, Ernst. "Department of Education of the Hebrew University." *Jew Ed* 17 (June 1946): 49–51.

———. "The Future Teachers of Palestine." *Jew Ed* 15 (Sept. 1943): 10–13.

Spiegel, Shalom. "חנוך וחברה בארץ־ישראל" (Education and Society in Israel). *Sh Hah* 1 (1925–26): 6–13, 16–21.

Wolman, Benjamin. "מבעיות החנוך בקבוצות ובקבוצים בארץ ישראל" (On the Problems of Education in Collective Settlements). *Sh Hah* (H.) 2 (1942): 83–96, 175–183.

Yaari, Abraham. "ספרי־חנוך וספרי ילדים שנדפסו בארץ ישראל בשנת תר׳ן־תרפ׳ח" (Our Children's Books: Textbooks Published in Israel, 1890–1928) (H.). In *Jubilee Book of the Teachers Federation*, 338–69. Jerusalem: 1929.

EDUCATION IN MODERN ISRAEL SINCE 1948 (SELECTED)

Ackerman, Walter I. "Education in Israel." *Jew Ed* 29 (Spring 1959): 54–59.

———. "Education in Israel, 1959—Second Annual Survey of Pedagogic Literature in Israel." *Jew Ed* 30 (Spring 1960): 39–44.

———. "Education in Israel—1960." *Jew Ed* 31 (Spring 1961) 54–59.

———. "Education in Israel—Fourth Annual Survey of Pedagogic Literature." *Jew Ed* 32 (Spring 1962): 173–79.

———. "Education in Israel (Fifth Annual Survey) *Jew Ed* 33 (Summer 1963): 219–25.

———. "Education in Israel—Sixth Annual Survey." *Jew Ed* 34 (Summer 1964): 238–43.

———. "Education in Israel—Seventh Annual Survey." *Jew Ed* 35 (Summer 1965): 231–37.

———. "Education in Israel—1965: Eighth Annual Review of Periodical Literature." *Jew Ed* 37 (Winter 1967): 15–23.

Adar, Zvi. החינוך היהודי בישראל ובארצות הברית (Jewish Education in Israel and in the United States) (H.). Tel Aviv: Gomeh, 1969. 277 pp.

———. "The Teaching of the Bible in Israel and the Problems of Religious Education." *Scripta Hierosolymitana* (1963): 77–104.

* Al-Agha, Reyad Fahmi. *Arab-Jewish Public Education in Israel from 1948–1967, and Implications for Palestinian Arab Minority Education*. U. of Kansas, 1978.

* Alkalay, Judith. *Health Education Teaching Program in Israel*. New York U., 1961.

* Al-Sa'ad, Farouk F. *The Impact of Zionism on Israeli Education: A Study of Israeli Jewish Secondary Education and Its Multiple Trends*. Indiana State U., 1977.

* Ariam, Sima. *The Effect of Subliminal Symbiotic Stimuli in Hebrew on Academic Performance of Israeli High School Students.* New York U., 1970.

Arrane, Z. „תכנית 'התודעה היהודית' במערכת החינוך הישראלית" ("Jewish Consciousness" in Israeli Education). In *MJET*, 31–35.

Avidor, M. "Ten Years of Education in Israel." *Jew Ed* 28 (Spring 1958): 3–8, 42.

Avigal, Moshe. „תכנית הלימודים בביה״ס בישראל" (The Educational Program in Israel's Schools). In *FPDE* (H.), 59–63.

Azrieli, Yehuda, ed. (80 החינוך הדתי בגבורותיו Years of National Religious Education) (H.). Jerusalem: Central Committee for Religious Education, Ministry of Education and Culture, WZO-DEC, 1986. 410 pp.

Ben-Horin, Meier. "Israel's Educational Frontiers." *School and Society* (Aug. 18, 1956): 58–62.

Ben-Jacob, J. "Israel's State Education." *Congress Weekly* (Dec. 20, 1954).

Ben-Vered, Tamar, and A. Ekrony. "The Ulpan Method." *Ped Rep* 34 (Jan. 1983): 10–11.

Ben-Yehuda, Baruch. „מפעל החינוך במדינת ישראל" (The Educational Enterprise in Israel). *Sh Hah* (H.) 10 (May 1950): 115–24.

Benor, J. "Ten Years of Arab Education." *Jew Ed* 28 (Spring 1958): 35–42.

Bentwich, Joseph S. *Education in Israel.* Phila.: JPS, 1965. 204 pp.

Bergman, Robert. "A Study of the Educational Principles and System of Hakibbutz Ha'artzi-Hashomer Hatza'ir and Their Implications for Jewish Education in the United States." Master's thesis, HUC–JIR, 1955.

Blackstone, T. "Education and the Underprivileged in Israel." *J of Jewish Social Services* 13 (Dec. 1971): 173–87.

* Bortniker, Elijah. *The Multiple Trends in Israel's Jewish Elementary School System: Investigation into the Origin, Development and Present Status of Israel's School System and its Political Subdivisions Known as "Trends".* New York U. School of Education, 1954. 385 pp.

Brademus, John, Chairman. *Education in Israel: Report of the Select Subcommittee on Education, House of Representatives, 91st Congress, Jan. 1970.* Washington, D.C: Government Printing Office, 1970. 227 pp.

* Brawer, Chaim Isaac. *Suggestions for Improving the Israeli Urban High School.* Columbia U., 1954. 130 pp.

Brickman. William W. "Religion in the Israeli Public Schools." *Trad* 2 (Spring 1960): 237–61.

Carlebach, Shmuel. *Our Path in Education* (H.). Bnai Brak: 1964. 150 pp.

Chertoff, Esther. "Origin and Development of the Modern School in Israel." Master's thesis, City College of N.Y., 1956.

Cohn, J. "Yeshivath B'nei Akiva" (Israel). *Jew Life* 15 (June 1948).

Dror-Elboim, Rachel. „תמורות במערך העוצמה וכוח ההחלטה בחינוך בישראל" (Changes in the Israeli System of Education and Power for Decision Making in Israel). *Sh Hah* (H.) 46 (Spring/Summer 1988): 156–65.

———. "Educational Research in Israel." *Scripta Hierosolymitana* 13 (1963): 156–86.

———. *Problems of Educational Administration in Israel* (reprinted from *Public Administration in Israel and Abroad*). Jerusalem: 1961.

* ———. *The Relation of Teacher Salary Levels to the Selection of Elementary School Teaching as a Vocation.* Harvard U., 1954.

———. *The Status and Conditions of Secondary School Teachers.* Jerusalem: 1961.

Dushkin, Alexander M. "Higher Education in Israel." *Jew Ed* 28 (Spring 1958): 42–51.

———. "Israel in Unesco." *Jew Ed* 22 (Winter Spring 1951): 100–102.

———. "The State Education Law in Israel." *Jew Ed* 25 (Fall 1954): 11–20.

Eban, Abba. „די דערציאונג אין מדינת ישראל פאראייניקט דאס גאנצע פאלק" (Education in Israel Unites the Jewish People). *Day-MJ* (Y.) (Apr. 20, 1961).

———. "Educating a Nation." *Congress Biweekly* (Apr. 17, 1961): 4–16.

———. "Education in a New Society." *The Atlantic* (Nov. 1961): 88–91.

———. "Perspectives of Jewish Education in Israel and in the Diaspora." *Jew Ed* 33 (Spring 1963). Also in *MJET*, 11–23.

Ed Enc (H.). "חנוך משלים," (Extra-Curricular [Supplementary] Education. In *Educational Encyclopedia* (H.), 3:610–30.

Ezrachi, Elan. "Informal Jewish Education in Israel." *MJ* 16 (Spring/Summer 1983): 7–8, 23.

Finstenberg, Rochelle. "Israel's Ulpan System: One-Stop Education." *Had Mag* (Jan. 1984): 5–6, 31.

Firer, Ruth. "Israeli Education under Begin and Hammer." *Jew Fron* 50 (May 1983): 18–20.

Fox, Seymour. "Education: Problems and Challenges." In *Israel—A Pictorial Celebration of Israel's 25th Birthday*, 140–43. 1963.

* Frank, Ivan Cecil. *The Degree to Which an Educational Youth Encampment Program, the Youth Aliyah Remedial Program in Kibbutz, Influences the Attitudes toward Social Integration of Socially Maladjusted Eastern Jewish Youth of Multi-Problem Families from Urban Slums*. U. of Pittsburgh, 1981.

Freudenberg, I. G. "Adult Education in Israel." *Jew Ed* 28 (Spring 1958): 52–57.

Gamoran, Emanuel. "Education in Israel." *Hadassah Newsletter* (Oct. 1954). See also *Gamoran*, 121–25.

Gannes, Abraham P. "The David Yellin College at Seventy." *Jew Ed* 52 (Summer 1984): 45–48.

* Ginsburgh, Sylvan J. *An Historical Study of Adult Hebrew Language Instruction in Palestine from 1917 to 1948 and of Its Continuation in Israel's Ulpanim, 1948–1960*. Dropsie U., 1964.

Glassman, Naftaly. "The Structural Reform in Israeli Education." *Jew Ed* 39 (Apr. 1969): 25–32.

Goldgraber, Elizabeth. "Reading Instruction in Israel." *Jew Ed* 45 (Fall 1980): 16–23.

Goldschmidt, J. "Integration in Israel and the Future of Religious Jewry." *Jew Life* 27 (June 1960).

———. "Jewish Identification in Israel." *Jew Life* 25 (Apr. 1958).

———. "Religious State Education in Israel." *Jew Life* 24 (Aug. 1957).

Golomb, Abraham. "Hebrew Education in Israel and Outside of Israel." *Zuk* (Y.) (Jan. 1966).

Greenspon, Bennett H. "The Presentation of Reform Judaism in the Israeli Educational System." Master's thesis, HUC–JIR, 1977.

* Haklai, Michael. *Mizrachi Education in Israel*. Yeshiva U., 1954.

Halevi-Levin, I. "Education, Constitution and Kulturkampf." *Jew Life* 17 (Summer 1950).

———. "Education and Politics." *Jew Life* 18 (Apr. 1951).

———. "State Education Gets Under Way." *Jew Life* 21 (1954).

———. "Is Israel's Cultural Cold War Becoming Hotter?" *Jew Life* 26 (Dec. 1958).

* Halper, Jeffrey Lewis. *Ethnicity and Education: The Schooling of Afro-Asian Jewish Children in a Jerusalem Locality*. U. of Wisconsin, 1978. 408 pp.

Hauslich, A. "Facing the Education Crisis" (Israel). *Jew Fron* (Summer 1963): 8–12.

Hebrew University, John Dewey School of Education. *The National Council of Jewish Women Center for Research in Education of the Disadvantaged*. Jerusalem: Department of Information and Public Affairs of the Hebrew University, 1971.

Herzog, Chaim. "Israel and the Jewish Heritage." *Jew Ed* 46 (Summer 1978): 4–8.

Hornstein, Shmuel. "A Program toward Meeting the Spiritual Needs of the Israeli High School Student." Master's thesis, HUC–JIR, 1962.

Horowitz, Bethanie. "The Two Israels: A Problem for Jewish Education." *MJ* 16 (Spring/Summer 1983): 10–11.

* Hurvitz, Liane. *The Influence of Child Rearing Environments in Israel on First, Second and Third Grade Children's Level of Resistance to Temptation and Stages of Moral Judgment*. U. of Southern California, 1979.

Jew Ed. "The Israel Compulsory Education Act, 1949." 21 (Summer 1950): 62–65.

Jew Ed. Israel Office of Information. "The Israel School System Today." 23 (Fall 1952): 65–66, 71.

Kaminetsky, Joseph. "Education in Israel and America: A Comparative Study." *Jew Parent* 24 (Oct. 197?): 4–6, 34.

Kaniel, Shoshana. *The Social Background of Students and Their Prospect of Success at School*. Israel: Ministry of Education and Culture-Israel National Commission for Unesco, Jan. 1971. 48 pp.

Kessler, A. A. "Financing Jewish Education: Yeshivot and Universities in Israel." *Jew Ed* 53 (Fall 1984): 39–42.

Kleinberger, A. F. "Legislation and Politics of Education," "The Schools," and "Some Major Problems." In *Society, Schools and Progress in Israel*, 116–50, 151–227, 275–330. 1969.

* Kneller, Herbert Samuel. *Israeli Youth Education Today and Tomorrow: An Administrative Plan for the Introduction of an Experience-Centered Curriculum into Israeli Education*. Columbia U. Teachers College, 1953. 85 pp.

Kol, Moshe. "Israeli Education for Tradition." *Recon* (Apr. 7, 1961): 5–8.

Kronish, Ronald. "Educating for Jewish-Zionist Identity in Israel." *MJ* 16 (Spring/Summer 1983): 7, 12.

Kurzweil, Zvi H. "How Jewish Are Israeli General Schools?" In *MTJE*, 275–303.

———. "Israel's Educational Scene." *Jew Life* 25 (June 1958).

———. "Some Aspects of Kibbutz Education." In *MTJE*, 146–70.

Kutner, Joel. "מועדי ישראל בישראל„ (Holidays in Israel) (H.). *Ped Rep* 32 (Sept. 1981): 34–36.

Lateef, Nasir Abed. "Analysis of Institutions in Ein Yabroud Village, Palestine." Master's thesis, Tennessee U., 1949.

Levenberg, A. *Welding a Nation: Education in Israel*. Tel Aviv: Ihud Olami. 48 pp.

* Levin, Nehemia. *The Attitudes of Jewish Administrators of Russian, Polish and Israeli Descent in Institutions of Higher Education in Israel toward Students of Ashkenazic and Sephardic or Oriental Background*. U. of Connecticut, 1977. 132 pp.

M. A. "פראבלעמען פון דערציאונג און יוגנט„ (Problems of Education and Youth). Report on a conference in Israel. *YK* (Y.) (Jan. 4, 1963): 4–5.

Meyouhas, J., ed. 35 Years of Supplementary Education (H.). Jerusalem: Ministry of Education and Culture, Youth Department, 1970.

Minkovich, A., ed. *Success and Failure in Israeli Elementary Education: An Evaluation Study with Special Emphasis on Disadvantaged Students*. N.Y.: Transaction Books, 1982. 539 pp.

Nardi, Noah. "First Decade of the Israeli School System." *Jew Ed* 28 (Spring 1958): 9–28.

Nardi, Noah, Moshe Avigal, and Naftali Githon. ספר החינוך והתרבות (A Book on Education and Culture) (H.). N.Y.: DEC, 1952. 350 pp.

Newman, A. "A New Curriculum for the Sabra." *Jew Life* 26 (Feb. 1959).

Nir, Amos. "Suggested Program for Pupil Personnel Services in the Elementary Schools in Israel." Master's thesis, U. of Maryland, 1952.

* Norman, Jean Schiffer. *Working Together for Better Schools in Israel: A Report of a Type C Project*. Columbia U. Teachers College, 1954. 178 pp.

Ormian, Haim J., ed. החינוך בישראל (Education in Israel) (H.). Jerusalem: Department of Education and Culture, 1973.

Ped Rep. "Education in Israel—A Survey." 8 (Jan. and May 1957).

* Portowicz, David J. *Values and School Achievement among Middle Class and Disadvantaged Sephardic Youths in Israel*. Brandeis U., 1981.

Rabin, A. I., and Bertha Hazan, eds. *Collective Education in the Kibbutz: from Infancy to Maturity*. N.Y.: Springer, 1973. 184 pp.

Rabinowitz, Dorothy. "Israeli Universities in a Time of Siege." *Change* (Feb. 1972): 42–47.

* Rauch, Max. *Higher Education in Israel*. U. of Southern California, 1971. 291 pp.

Reed, Judith, ed. *Impressions of Education in Israel: A Report of the Educational Staff Seminar Study Mission* (Feb 13–29, 1976).

Washington, D.C.: Institute for Educational Leadership, 1976. 123 pp.

Rimon, Pinchas. "A Profile of the Kfar Blum America-Israel Secondary School Program." *Ped Rep* 39 (Apr. 1988): 17–20.

* Ronen, Chanan. *A Study of Mainstreaming Educable Mentally Retarded Children in Israel*. U. of Wisconsin, 1980.

Rotenstreich, Nathan. סוגיות בחינוך (Issues in Education) (H.). Jerusalem: Hebrew U. School of Education, 1964. 177 pp.

Rothman, R. C. "Education and Participation in the Israeli Defense Forces." *JSS* 34 (1972): 155–72.

Samuels, Robert. "Education and the Progressive Movement in Israel." *NATE Proceedings* (Dec. 1975): 43–50.

Scharfstein, Zevi. תולדות החינוך בארץ ישראל (The History of Jewish Education in the Land of Israel) (H.). Jerusalem: R. Mass, 1965. 276 pp.

Schiff, Gary S. "The Socialization of Values in Israel's Educational System." *Jew Ed* 44 (Spring/Summer 1976): 57–67.

* Schmida, Mirjam. *Assumptions Underlying Major Developments in the System of Universal, Free, Public Secondary Education in the United States and the High School System of the Municipality of Tel Aviv with Certain Implications for the Future*. Columbia U., 1964.

———. "Extra Curricular Activities in the Israeli High School." *Jew Ed* 49 (Summer 1981): 18–27.

———. "Informal Education in Israel: The Case of the Community Center." *Jew Ed* 51 (Winter 1983): 19–24, 37.

Schweid, E. הכרת העם היהודי בחינוך בישראל (Recognition of the Jewish People in Israeli Education) (H.). Jerusalem: Hebrew U., 1974. 46 pp.

* Shapiro, Zipora. *A Comparative Study of Methods Teaching Arithmetic in the First Grade in Louisville Public Schools and in the Religious Schools, Haifa, Israel*. U. of Louisville, 1957.

* Sheier, Ira Jay. *Academic Problems of United States Students at Hebrew University*. Indiana U., 1973. 104 pp.

Sheintuch, I. "ייִדיש-לימוד אין ישראלישער מיטל-שול-דערציאונג" (The Study of Yiddish in Israeli Secondary Education). *Die Goldene Keyt* (Y.) 91 (1976): 51–60.

Shraga, Sh. Z. "נייע דערציאונגס-פראבלעמען אין דער אידישער מדינה" (New Educational Problems in Israel). *Day* (Y.) (Dec. 9, 1959).

* Shumsky, Abraham. *An Analysis of the Ethnic Group Problem in Israel with Implications for the Role of the School*. Columbia U., 1955. Published as *The Clash of Cultures in Israel*. N.Y.: Columbia U. Teachers' College, Bureau of Publications, 1955. See in particular "The Ethnic Problem and the School," 91–124, and "The Role of the School," 125–56.

* Smilansky, Moshe. *Analysis of the Problems Involved in Initiating an Action Research Program in Israel*. Ohio State U., 1954.

Snarey, John R. "The Kibbutz as Moral Educator." *For* (E. section) (Nov. 1, 1984): 13–14.

Sneh, Shlomo. "וואס מיינט די רעווזיע אין אונזער דערציאונג?" (What is the Meaning of the Revision in Our Education? [Israel]). *YK* (Y.) (Nov. 8, 1957): 7–9.

* Tadmor, Shlomo. *Adult Education in Israel—Problems and Principles for Future Development*. Columbia U., 1958.

Tropper, Daniel. "The Bar Mitzvah Program in Israel." *Jew Ed* 50 (Spring 1982): 5–9.

Tsamriyon, Tsemach. "דברים הטעונים תיקון" (Items That Need Improvement in Israeli Education." *Sh Hah* (H.) 46 (Spring/Summer 1988): 166–71.

Tsanin, M. "די יוגענט אין ישראל זוכט נייע וועגן" (The Education of Children in Israel). *For* (Y.) (May 24, 1953).

———. "די ערציהונג פון קינדער אין ישראל" (Youth in Israel Seeks New Paths). *For* (Y.) (Feb. 26, 1951).

Tseitman, Chanan. "אינטעגראציע פון עולים קינדער אין דער ישראל׳דיקער שול" (The Integration of Newly Arrived Children in the Israeli Schools). *YK* (Y.) (Nov 3, 1972): 3–4.

Urial, Akivah. "הוראת העברית לעולים חדשים" (Teaching Hebrew to New Immigrants). *Sh Hah* (H.) 12 (Dec. 1951): 30–35.

Walters, Joel. "The Anglos Are Coming, the Anglos Are Coming: English Language Instruction in Israeli Schools." *Jew Ed* 50 (Spring 1982): 16–21.

Weisman, Deborah. "Education in the Israeli Army: Towards an Enlightened Pluralism." *MJ* 16 (Spring/Summer 1983): 11–12.

* Winer, Gershon. *Philosophical Foundations for Education in Israel*. U. of Michigan, 1959.

Wolman, Benjamin. (Aspirations of Jewish Education in Israel). *BYD* (Y.) (June–Sept. 1949): 86–91.

———. „די אינטערעסן, שטרעבונגען, און אידעאלן פון דער יידישער יוגנט אין ארץ ישראל" (Interests, Aspirations and Ideals of Jewish Youth in Israel). *YB* (Y.) 31–32 (1948): 267–92.

———. "המדינה והחינוך בארץ ישראל„ (The State and Education in Israel). *Talpiot* (H.) 5 (Teveth 1952): 619–36.

Zisenwine, David. "Jewish Curriculum in Israeli Schools." *Jew Ed* 49 (Winter 1981): 30–33, 43.

———. "Professional Issues in Israeli Education, 1981–82." *Jew Ed* 39 (Fall 1981): 9–11.

Zisenwine, David, and Ruth Kopinski. "Parshat Ha-Shavua—An Innovation in the Israel Secular School." *Jew Ed* 51 (Summer 1983): 32–36.

GLEANINGS

A Talmudic discussion on study and action, first century C.E.,

"R. Tarfon and the Elders were once reclining ... when this question was raised before them. Is study greater, or practice? R. Tarfon answered, saying: Practice is greater. R. Akiba answered, saying: Study is greater, for it leads to practice. Then they all answered and said: Study is greater for it leads to action."

Kiddushin (Hebrew-English edition of the Babylonian Talmud). Soncino Press, 1966, 40b.

The Talmud on Class Size, 3rd-4th centuries C.E.,

"Raba further said: The number of pupils to be assigned to each teacher is twenty-five. If there are fifty, we appoint two teachers. If there are forty, we appoint an assistant at the expense of the town."

Baba Bathra (Hebrew-English edition of the Babylonian Talmud). Soncino Press, 1976, 21a.

Maimonides (1135–1204),

"Every man in Israel is obliged to devote himself to study, be he rich or poor, of good health or afflicted by diseases, a youngster or a doddering elder; even if he be a beggar or living on charity or a father burdened with a family, he ought to set aside time for study by day and night. . . . Among the greatest scholars of Israel there were wood-pickers and water carriers, even blind men, and they nevertheless studied the Torah by day and night. . . . Up to what age is one obliged to study the Torah? Unto the day of death."

Quoted by Salo W. Baron in *The Jewish Community, 1300–1776* (3 vols. Phila.: JPS, 1942), 2:169.

Synod of Castilian Jews at Valladolid (1432), on class size,

"Every community of fifteen families shall maintain a proper teacher for the children of primary school age who shall instruct them in Scripture. They shall also allow him a reasonable salary according to his needs. The fathers of the children shall pay the teacher each according to their means, and if the amount paid by the fathers is insufficient for the maintenance of the teacher, the community (Jewish) shall be obliged to pay the remainder necessary for his livelihood.

Whereas according to the Talmudic law no teacher is permitted to teach more than twenty-five pupils, unless he have an assistant, therefore we ordain that no teacher shall teach Scriptures to more than twenty-five children, but that if he have an assistant he may teach forty in accordance with the law of the Talmud. A community having fifty children shall be obliged to maintain two teachers; the same law to be applied to any number above forty."

Quoted in Louis Finkelstein, *Jewish Self-Government in the Middle Ages* (N.Y.: Feldheim, 1964), 353–55.

Eliakim, Isaac C., of Posen, in his *Lev Tov* **(1620),**

"Everyone should rear his child in Torah and mitzvot and good deeds while still in his youth, teaching him according to his intellectual capacity, his age, and that he is able to accept. Prior to his beginning to talk, get him used to kissing books, thus training him to treat them with respect. When the child begins to speak teach him . . . the first verse of the Shema. As he grows older, teach him Torah. Then hire a teacher to teach him Torah."

Quoted by Steven M. Rosman, *Jew Ed* 53 (Summer 1985), 30.

Hannover, Nathan Note, (d. 1683),

"Nowhere in all the dispersions of Israel was the study of the Torah so widespread as in the kingdom of Poland. For there every community maintained a yeshivah, and all were generous in their support of the academy's head . . . to enable him to occupy himself solely with the study of Torah."

Yeven Metsulah (Deep Mire) (H.). Venice, 1653. Quoted by Abraham Menes in *JPPP*, 2:110.

The Lithuanian Council on Advanced Study (1661),

"Every community and settlement having a rabbi of its own shall maintain an academy for advanced and younger pupils and give them on Sabbaths as well as weekdays, a decent livelihood as non-paying guest of the respective family. Some householders shall extend such hospitality for a continuous period of two, three or four weeks, each group by rotation, in accordance with its means, and with the proper order to be instituted by their communal leaders in consultation with their rabbi. . . . For every ten taxpayers households entered in the communal register there shall be allotted one advanced and two younger students."

Quoted by Salo W. Baron in *The Jewish Community, 1300–1776* (3 vols. Phila.: JPS, 1942), 2:189.

Maimon, Solomon (1754–1800), on the Heder,

"The school is commonly a small, smoky hut and the children are scattered, some on benches, some on the bare earth. The master in a dirty blouse, sitting on the table, holds between his knees a book on which he grinds tobacco with snuff, with a huge pestle like the club of Hercules, while at the same time he wields his authority. The assistants give lessons, each to his corner, and rule those under their charge quite as despotically as the master himself. Of the breakfast, lunch and other food sent to the school for the children, these gentlemen keep the larger share for themselves. Sometimes, the poor youngsters get nothing at all; and yet they dare not make any complaint on the subject, if they will not expose themselves to the vengeance of these tyrants. Here the children are imprisoned from morning to night and have not an hour for themselves, except on Friday and a half holiday at the new moon."

Quoted by Salo W. Baron in *The Jewish Community, 1300–1776* (3 vols. Phila.: JPS, 1942), 1:199.

Hirsch, Samson Raphael (1854),

"We require schools, in which equal attention shall be paid to the old sacred inheritance of the community of Jacob, Biblical and Rabbinical knowledge, and all that is true, noble and good in European culture, and both shall be cultivated hand in hand from the Aleph Beth and ABC through all stages of knowledge and progress. In this way the minds of boys and girls will be trained from the first in such a way that when they grow up they will be able to conduct themselves as truly educated Jews and truly educated men and citizens."

JUET, 156.

Maller, Julius B.,

"Among the basic concepts that appear to have been accepted in Jewish lore, the following may be noted: (1) An abiding faith in the efficacy of education, that human character is modifiable and improvable. (2) Learning and doing must be integrated; knowledge of ethics must be expressed in proper conduct. (3) Education is a continual process, to be carried on literally from the cradle to the grave. (4) Environment is an important factor in the educative process. (5) Education, to be most effective, must start with the very young. (6) Individual differences among pupils must be recognized; tests reveal differences in knowledge and convictions. (7) The process of education must be gradual from the known to the unknown, from the simple to the complex, and from the immediate to the remote. (8) Responsibility for education rests with the parents and community. (9) Training for work is regarded as both essential and honorable. (10) The teaching of history illustrates the continuity and meaning of Jewish experiences.

Jewish teaching emphasized above all else that study is essential and worth while and must be brought to the people for guidance in everyday affairs. The emphasis was definitely on the pragmatic aspects of education. The Greek concepts of contemplation or dialogue as forms of diversion and enjoyment were uncommon in Jewish lore."

"The Role of Education in Jewish History." In *Jews*, 2:1235.

The Heder in the Soviet Union (1920),

"To all Education Departments, sections, instructors, about liquidating Hadorim and Yeshivot:

The Jewish Education Department, taking into consideration the resolution of the all-Russian conference of Jewish educational workers and the reports that are being received from the various cities, has decided to start a militant campaign against the hadorim and yeshivot.

The struggle must begin at once, even while we have no opportunity as yet to take all the children into the Soviet schools....

The mere fact of destroying the hadorim, the Jewish Education Department considers to be a positive factor of creating and building. The children must be liberated from the terrible prison, from the full spiritual demoralization and from physical deterioration. The local education sections must consider the work of liquidating the hadorim for their number one aim."

Quoted by Elias Schulman in *A History of Jewish Education in the Soviet Union* (N.Y.: Ktav and P.W. Lown Graduate Center, 1971), 59.

Louis Ginzberg on the European Heder,

"The school is the most original institution created by post-biblical Judaism—a magnificent institution, a veritable fortress unshaken by the storms of the ages. To borrow a simile from the Midrash, the school was the heart that kept watch while the other organs slept.... The Heder! In the face of the misunderstanding with which friend and foe alike have treated it, it is difficult to speak calmly of this, one of the greatest institutions of post-biblical Judaism.... The Jewish religion is not a religious arithmetic. It does not permit the idea to usurp the place of the spirit. From the first the Jew has felt that reality is not abstract but individual. Religion to be a vital influence must be lived, not taught, and this condition was fulfilled in the Heder."

In *Students, Scholars, and Saints* (1928), 5, 16, 27.

Franz Rosenzweig (1886–1929), on the Eastern European Heder,

"In its actual effect the Heder is closer to the ideal of an educational institution than the Western European school. The latter produces fragmentary people, totally lacking orientation, but from the Heder there springs the constant renewal of a whole people."

Quoted by Kurzweil in *Modern Trends in Jewish Education* (1964), 202.

29 | HISTORY OF JEWISH EDUCATION IN THE UNITED STATES

(See also chapters 20, 21, and 37)

HISTORY

Bass, Hyman B. "בתי-ספר כנסתיים" (Congregational Schools). In *DER* (Y.), 1:490–98.

———. "זונטאג שולן אין די פאראייניקטע שטאטן" (Sunday Schools in the U.S.—Reform Movement). In *DER* (Y.), 3:463–80.

Ben-Horin, Meir. "From the Turn of the Century to the Late Thirties" (19th and 20th Centuries). In *AJHE*, 51–118.

Benderly, Samson. "Fifty Years of Jewish Education in America." *NCJSS Proceedings* (1926): 303–12.

Ben Levi, Joshua. "הנסיונות שהמורה העברי באמריקה עומד בהם" (The Trials of a Hebrew Teacher in America). *Sh Hah* (H.) 6 (Mar. 1946): 149–53.

* Blackman, Murray. *The History of Jewish Education in the United States from 1654 to 1881.* HUC–JIR, 1946.

Blumenfeld, Samuel M. "Historical Developments of Jewish Education in America, 1917–1949." *Jew Ed* 21 (Winter 1949): 44–51.

Chipkin, Israel S. "A Decade of Progress in Jewish Education." *Jew Ed* 21 (Winter 1949): 9–18, 51.

———. "Jewish Education in the United States at the Midcentury." In *Reg* (1951), 7–26. See also *Rel Ed* 48 (Sept.–Oct. 1953): 327–50.

———. "Twenty-Five Years of Jewish Education in the United States." *AJYB* 38 (1936): 27–116.

Chomsky, William. "Beginnings of Jewish Education in America." *Gratz College Annual of Jewish Studies* 5 (1976).

———. "Hebrew Grammar and Textbook Writing in Early Nineteenth Century America." In *Ess*, 123–45.

Cohen, Morris R. "Jewish Education." In *Recollections of a Wondering Jew* (1950), 23–30.

Colodner, Solomon. "Half a Century in Jewish Education." *Jew Ed* 51 (Fall 1983): 37–39.

Dushkin, Alexander M. "Antaeus—Autobiographical Reflections." *Amer Jew Arc* 21 (Nov. 1969): 113–39.

———. "הערכת ששים וחמש שנים של החנוך באה"ב" (Assessment of 65 Years of Jewish Education in the United States). *Sh Hah* (H.) 35 (1975): 140–51.

———. "מנסיונו של מחנך עברי" (Experiences of a Hebrew Educator). *Sh Hah* (H.) 21 (Spring 1961): 131–41.

———. "Fifty Years of American Jewish Education Retrospect and Prospects." *Jew Ed* 37 (Winter 1967): 44–57.

29 HISTORY OF JEWISH EDUCATION IN THE UNITED STATES

———. "Forty Years in Jewish Education in America." *Rel Ed* (Sept.–Oct. 1944).

———. *Living Bridges: Memoirs of an Educator*. Jerusalem: Keter, 1975. 310 pp.

Eisenstein, Ira. "Fifty Years in Jewish Education." *Jew Ed* 50 (Fall 1982): 8–11.

* Fierman, Floyd S. *Efforts toward Reform in American Jewish Education prior to 1881*. U. of Pittsburgh, 1950. 243 pp.

———. *Sources of Jewish Education in America prior to 1881*. El Paso, 1960. 243 pp.

Fox, J. S. "Sixty Year Effort: From Sunday Classes to Day Schools." *Jew Obs* 15 (Nov. 25, 1966): 13–14.

Freehof, Solomon. "Thirty Years of Reform Jewish Education." In *30th Anniversary, UAHC–CJE*, 5–11. 1953.

Friedman, Lee M. "Judah Monis, First Instructor in Hebrew at Harvard University." *PAJHS* 22 (1914): 1–24. See also *PAJHS* 37 (1947): 121–34.

Fromer, Seymour. "The First Survey of Jewish Education" (United States). *Congress Weekly* (May 25, 1959).

———. "In the Colonial Period." In *AJHE*, 1–24.

Gamoran, Emanuel. "The Commission on Jewish Education: Thirtieth Anniversary." *Jew Teach* 21 (Nov. 1952): 1–4.

———. "Seventy-Five Years of Liberal Education." *Liberal Judaism* (Nov.–Dec. 1948).

———. "Two Decades of Jewish Education." *Liberal Judaism* (June–July 1947).

Gartner, Lloyd P., ed. "Jewish Education in the United States." In *JCA*, 221–48.

———. *Jewish Education in the United States: A Documentary History* (18th–20th century). N.Y.: Teachers College, 1969. 224 pp.

Goelman, Elazar. "Gleanings." *Jew Ed* 50 (Fall 1982): 20–22.

Goldberg, Martin. "A History of Jewish Education, 1840–1860." Master's thesis, HUC–JIR, 1953.

Grand, Samuel. "Years of Challenge." *Jew Ed* 50 (Fall 1982): 23–26.

Greenberg, Simon. "Some Reminiscences." *Jew Ed* 50 (Fall 1982): 27–28.

Greenstone, Julius H. „ראשית החנוך העברי באמריקה" (The Beginnings of Jewish Education in America). *Sh Hah* (H.) 3 (1927): 17–22.

———. "Jewish Education in the United States." *AJYB* 16 (1914): 90–127.

Grinstein, Hyman B. "In the Course of the Nineteenth Century." In *AJHE*, 25–50.

Hertzberg, Arthur. "Seventy Years of Jewish Education." *Jud* 1 (Oct. 1952): 361–65.

Honor, Leo L. "Jewish Education in the United States." In *JPPP*, 2:151–11.

———. "Jewish Elementary Education in the United States." *PAJHS* 52 (Sept. 1952): 1–42.

Hurwitz, Louis. זכרונות מתנך עברי (Memoirs of a Jewish Educator) (H.). 3 vols. Boston: BJE, 1960.

Jaffe, Philip. "Serving Reform Jewish Education." *Jew Ed* 50 (Fall 1982): 31–34.

Jewish Chautauqua Society. *History of the Jewish Chautauqua Society* (educational correspondence society). N.Y.: 1953.

Kaplan, Louis L. "How I Became a Jewish Teacher." *Jew Ed* 50 (Fall 1982): 41–43.

Katzoff, Louis. "Rise of the Conservative Congregational School in America." In *Issues*, 15–21.

———. "Unpredictabilities: Reflections on the Past" *Jew Ed* 50 (Fall 1982): 43–44.

Konowitz, Israel. „בראשית החנוך העברי באמריקה" (Jewish Education in America—Early Years of 20th century). In *JB* (H.), 114–41.

Korn, Bertram W. "The First American Jewish Theological Seminary Maimonides College, 1867–1873." In *Eventful Years*, 151–95. 1954.

Landesman, Alter F. *Forty Years of Service in a Congested Metropolitan Neighborhood*. N.Y.: Hebrew Educational Society, 1939.

Malachi, Eliezer R. „מקורות לתולדות החינוך העברי באמריקה" (Sources on the History of Jewish Education in the United States). *Sh Hah* (H.) 38 (Mar. 1979): 156–61, (June 1979): 217–22; 39 (Mar. 1980): 57–60, (June 1980): 111–14.

Marcus, Jacob R. "Jewish Education." In *The Colonial American Jew, 1492–1976*, 2:1056–68. 1970.

Margoshes, Samuel. "Fifty Years of Bureaus of Jewish Education." *Day* (Y.) (Mar. 11, 1961).

Nemzoff, Samuel L. "Zichronot." *Jew Ed* 50 (Fall 1982): 45–48.

Olitzky, Kerry M. "Sunday Schools: The Beginning." *Jew Ed* (Fall 1985): 6–11.

* Orentlicher, Edward. *The Talmud Torah in America: Its Structure, Philosophy, and Decline, 1860–1960*. Dropsie U., 1961.

Ormian, Haim J. "תנועה חינוכית יהודית בארצות-הברית" (The Jewish Education Movement in the United States). In *Ed Enc* (H.), 1:975–82. Jerusalem, 1961.

Persky, Daniel. "Fifty Years of Teaching Hebrew in America." *Hadoar* (H.) (Jan. 5, 1951).

Pilch, Judah, ed. "From the Early Forties to the Mid-Sixties" (20th Century). In *A History of Jewish Education in the United States*, 119–76. N.Y.: National Curriculum Research Institute of the AAJE, 1969.

———. "Jewish Education in the United States of America." In *Enc Jud*, 6:437–46.

Pollak, Jacob B. "Forty Years of the Reform Religious School: Its Achievements and Its Failures." *CCAR* 39 (1929): 402–38.

Pool, David de Sola. "The Earliest Jewish Prayer Book Printed in America." *Jewish Tribune* (Sept. 5, 1928).

———. "The Earliest Religious School in America." *Jewish Teacher* (1917): 161–67.

* Rauch, Eduardo. *Jewish Education in the United States, 1840–1920*. Harvard U., 1978. 517 pp.

———. "Some Aspects of the Education of Jews in the United States from 1840–1920." In *Stu*, 21–51.

Resnik, Reuben. "Four Decades in the Profession of Jewish Education." *Jew Ed* (Fall 1983): 40–42.

Rudavsky, David. "After Fifty Years: Spotlight on Five Central Agencies for Jewish Education." *Jew Ed* 44 (Summer 1975): 6–8.

———. "Four Decades of the Hebrew High School." *Jew Ed* 24 (Fall 1953): 4–5.

Schafler, Samuel. "Observations on the History of Jewish Education in the United States." *Jew Ed* 49 (Fall 1981): 17–20.

Scharfstein, Zevi. "חמשים שנות חנוך יהודי באמריקה" (Fifty Years of Jewish Education in America). In *JB* (H.), 155–83.

———. "לתולדות החינוך היהודי בארצות הברית" (On the History of Jewish Education in America). In *Sefer HaShanah* (H.), 7:538–55. N.Y.: Histadrut Ivrit, 1944.

———. "בארצות הברית" (History of Jewish Education in the United States). In *History of Jewish Education in Modern Times* (H.), 2:155–366.

———. "החינוך היהודי—בארצות-הברית" (Jewish Education in the United States). In *Ed Enc* (H.), 4:593–600. Jerusalem: 1961.

Seybolt, R. F. "Hebrew in the Schools of Colonial America." *PAJHS* 32 (1931): 113–14.

Silberschlag, Eisig. "Reminiscence as Education." *Jew Ed* 50 (Fall 1982): 54–59.

Sochen, Mordecai. "From City to City." *Jew Ed* 50 (Fall 1982): 60–64.

* Stern, Jay B. *History of the United Synagogue Commission on Jewish Education, 1945–1960*. JTS, 1963–64.

Touroff, Nissan. "פרקי חיים" (Memoirs of an American and Israeli Educator). *Sh Hah* (H.) 8 (May 1948): 6–32.

* Yapko, Benjamin L. *Jewish Elementary Education in the United States: Colonial Period to 1900*. American U., 1958. 197 pp.

Yashuv, Shlomo Shulsinger-Shear. "Memoirs of a Hebrew Educator." *Jew Ed* 50 (Fall 1982): 50–54.

Yefroikin, Zalman. "יידישע דערציאונג אין די פאראייניקטע שטאטן" (Jewish Education in the United States). In *General Encyclopedia in Yiddish* (Y.), 5:166–219. 1957.

JEWISH EDUCATION IN THE UNITED STATES PRIOR TO 1900

Most of the descriptions for the items prior to 1850 are from W. S. Rosenbuch's *An American Jewish Bibliography*, vol. 30 (American Jewish Historical Society, 1926). Many items from 1851 to 1875 were found in Allan E. Levine's

29 HISTORY OF JEWISH EDUCATION IN THE UNITED STATES

An American Jewish Bibliography (Amer Jew Arc (1959).).

(Selected list in chronological order)

1640
Bay Psalm Book. Cambridge: Stephen Daye, 1640. 148 pp. "Faithfully translated into English." First book published in the English settlements in America. Hebrew letters precede each of the 22 stanzas in Psalm 119, in keeping with traditional practice.

1719
Josephus, Flavius. *Wars of the Jews.* 2 vols. Boston: S. Kneeland, 1719. (First of many editions printed during the 18th and 19th centuries.)

1735
Monis, A. Judah. דקדוק לשון עברית (A Grammar of the Hebrew Language). Boston: Jonas Green, 1735. 96 pp. (See Lee M. Friedman, *Early American Jews.* Cambridge: Harvard Univ. Press, 1934. 34.) Monis taught Hebrew at Harvard from 1722 to 1762. His grammar was one of several published in America during the 18th and 19th centuries.

1760
"Shearith Israel [Portuguese and Spanish] Congregation Employs a Schoolmaster." *PAJHS* 21 (1913):85 and 27 (1920):17. Also in *JEUS,* 41–42.

1761
Evening Service of Roshashanah and Kippur or the Beginning of the Year and the Day of Atonement [sic]. N.Y.: W. Weyman. 1761. 53 pp.

1763
Sewell, Stephen. *An Hebrew Grammar.* Boston: R. and S. Draper for the Honorable and Reverend the President and Fellows of Harvard College, 1763. 84 pp.

1766
Pinto, Isaac. *Prayers for Shabbath, Rosh-Hashanah, and Kippur, or the Sabbath, the Beginning of the Year, and the Day of Atonement; with the Amidah, and Musaph of the Moadim, or Solemn Seasons, According to the Order of the Spanish and Portuguese Jews* [sic]. N.Y.: John Holt, 1766. 190 pp.

1773
Karigal, Haim Isaac. *The Salvation of Israel: A Sermon preached at the Synagogue in Newport, R.I., May 26, 1773—Being the Anniversary of giving the Law at Mount Sinai—By the Venerable Hocham (The Learned Rabbi) . . . of the City of Hebron, near Jerusalem in the Holy Land.* Newport, R.I.: S. Southwick, 1773. 20 pp.

1789
Seixes, Gershon. *Religious Discourse: Delivered in the Synagogue in This City on Thursday the 26th of November, 1789, Agreeable to the Proclamation of the President of the United States of America, to be Observed as a Day of Public Thanksgiving and Prayer.* N.Y.: A. Mclean, 1789. 10 pp.

1797
Levi, David. *Defence of the Old Testament: A Series of Letters to Thomas Paine.* New York: W. A. Davis, 1797.

1802
Pike, Samuel. *A Compendious Hebrew Lexicon.* Cambridge: Printed for the University, 1802. 187 pp.

1804
"The Purposes of Jewish Education." *PAJHS* 27 (1920): 82–83. See also *JEUS,* 43–44.

1806
Lopez, Moses. *A Lunar Calendar, 1806: A Lunar Calendar of the Festivals and Other Days in the Year, Observed by the Israelites . . . begins September 24th, 1805, and Will End in the Same Month, in the Year 1859.* Newport, R.I.: Printed at the office of the *Newport Mercury,* 1806. (First Jewish calendar printed in America.)

1808
"Aims of the Polonies Talmud Torah" (1808). In *Schappes,* 113–17.

1812
Adams, Hannah. *History of the Jews from the Destruction of Jerusalem to the Nineteenth Century.* 2 vols. Boston: John Eliot, 1812.

1815
Biblia Hebraica. תורה נביאים וכתובים Prospectus of a Hebrew Bible from the Edition of Evarardo Van Der Hoogt. New York: Fanshaw and Clayton, 1815. 112 pp. (First attempt in America to publish the Bible in Hebrew.)

Carvalho, E. N. מפתח לשון עברית (Key to the Hebrew Tongue). Phila.: Wm. Fry, 1815. 32 pp.

1817
Cohen, S. I. *Elements of the Jewish Faith.* Richmond: Wm. W. Gray, 1817. 56 pp.

1823
The Jew (1823–25). First Jewish periodical in America (not published regularly).

1826
The Form of Daily Prayers According to the Custom of the Spanish and Portuguese Jews . . . Translated into English from the Hebrew by Solomon H, Jackson, the Hebrew Text carefully Revised and Corrected by E. S. Lazarus, First Edition. N.Y.: S. H. Jackson, 1826.

1827
Stuart, Moses. *Dissertation. On the Importance and Best Method of Studying The Original Languages of the Bible. By Jhan and Other Translations and Notes by Stuart.* Andover: Flagg and Gould, 1827. 96 pp.

1828
Solis, Jacob S. *Calendar of the Festivals and Lunar Months of Every Year Observed by Israelites.* New Orleans: F. Delaup, Printer of the Congregation, 1828.

1829
Constitution and Bye-Laws of the "United Hebrew Beneficent Society of Philadelphia." חברה גמילות חסדים וחנוך נערים Instituted, June 16, 1822, Incorporated, 1829. Phila.: Garden and Thompson, 1829. (A society to aid the poor as well as educate poor youth.)

Lowth, Robert. *Lectures on the Sacred Poetry of the Hebrews. Trans, by G. Gregory. A New Edition with Notes by Calvin E. Stowe.* Andover: Flagg and Gould, 1829 461 pp.

1830
Dwyer, Alexander. *A Discourse on the Structure of Poetry of the Hebrews.* Utica: Hastings and Tracy, 1830.

Leeser, Isaac. *Instruction in the Mosaic Religion.* Translated from the German of J. Johlson. Phila.: A. Waldie, 1830. 139 pp.

Peixotto, Daniel M. *Anniversary Discourse Pronounced to the Society for the Education of Orphan Children and the Relief of Indigent Persons of the Jewish Persuasion.* N.Y.: J. Seymor, 1830. (Proposed a school based on Pestolozzian principles.)

The Sabbath Service and Miscellaneous Prayers, Adopted by the Reformed Society of Israelites. Founded in Charleston, South Carolina, Nov. 21, 1825. Compiled by Isaac Harby, Abraham Moise and David Nunes Carvahlo. Charleston: J. S. Burges, 1830. 68 pp.

1831
Milman, Henry Hart. *The History of the Jews.* 3 vols. N.Y.: J. and J. Harper, 1831.

1833
Leeser, Isaac. "The Duty of Instruction" (Sept. 18, 1833). In *Discourses—Argumentative and Devotional on the Jewish Religion*, 2:1–13. 1837.

1834
Leeser, Isaac. "Religious Education" (June 2, 1834). In *Discourses—Argumentative and Devotional on the Jewish Religion*, 117–31. 1834

Seixas, James. *Manual of Hebrew Grammar, 2nd Edition, Enlarged and Improved.* Andover: Gould and Newman, 1834. 119 pp.

1835
Frey, J. S. C. F. *The Hebrew Student's Pocket Companion. 1. All the Hebrew roots translated. 2. Most important words in English, with their Corresponding Hebrew words.* 2d ed. N.Y.: Moore and Payne, 1835. 143 pp.

Leeser, Isaac. *To the Jewish Inhabitants of Philadelphia.* Phila.: 1835. 24 pp. Proposal to establish a school "where the children might acquire a correct knowledge of the Hebrew together with a thorough English education."

———. "Religious Education" (June 2, 1835) (stresses need to educate girls). In *Discourses—Argumentative and Devotional on the Jewish Religion*, 2:117–31 1837. Jacob R. Marcus quotes this section in *The American Jewish Woman A Documentary History*, 129–32. 1982.

1837
Noah, Mordecai M. *Discourse on the Evidence of the American Indians Being the Descendants of the Lost Tribes of Israel.* N.Y.: Mercantile Library Association, 1838. See also *JDH*, 2:419–24.

1838
Leeser, Isaac. *The Hebrew Reader: Hebrew and English Designed as an Easy Guide to the He-*

29 HISTORY OF JEWISH EDUCATION IN THE UNITED STATES

brew Tongue for Jewish Children and Self-Instruction. Phila.: Haswell, Barrington and Haswell, 1838. 40 pp.

Nordheimer, Isaac. *A Critical Grammar of the Hebrew Language, 1838–1841*. 2 vols. N.Y.: Wiley and Putnam. [Introduction, pp. iii–xv, contains discussion of early-19th-century philological studies on Hebrew.) Excerpts in *JDH*, 2:429–36.

1839

Leeser, Isaac. *Catechism for Younger Children*. (Dedicated to Rebecca Gratz.) Phila.: A. Waldie, 1839. 168 pp. Excerpts of the introduction in *JDH*, 2:451–54 and *JEUS*, 50–53.

1840

Leeser, Isaac, and Moses N. Nathan. *Second Annual Examination of the Sunday School for Religious Instruction of Israelites in Philadelphia. Held at the Synagogue Mikveh Israel, March 29, 1840*. Phila.: Printed by Order of the Congregation, 1840. 28 pp.

1841

Leeser, Isaac. "Religious Education." 3 sermons. In *Discourses—Argumentative and Devotional on the Jewish Religion*, 188–233. 1841.

Loeb, Henri. דרך האמונה (The Road to Faith). Translated from the German by Moses N. Nathan. Kingston, Jamaica: J. R. de Cordova, 1941. 63 pp. (For Jewish elementary schools.)

Solomon, Louis. *The Mosaic System in Its Fundamental Principles*. Phila.: E. G. Dorsey, 1841. 215 pp.

1843

"Founding of Talmud Torah and Hebrew Institute, Jan. 1843 in New York City." *Occ* 3:24–25.

Leeser, Isaac. "Jewish Children under Gentile Teachers." *Occ* 1 (Dec. 1843): 408–14.

———. "Sunday School . . . Philadelphia." *Occ* 1 (Apr. 1843): 38–46. See also "Fifth Anniversary of the Hebrew Sunday School." *Occ* 1 (May 1843): 61–64.

Noah, Mordecai M. "Hebrew College." *Occ* 1 (Aug. 1843): 301–7. See *AJA* 12 (Oct. 1960): 143–49.

"Public Religious Education" (editorial). *Occ* 1 (Nov. 1843): 361–64.

"Report of the Committee of the Society for the Education of Poor Children and Relief of Indigent Persons of the Jewish Persuasion. New York, Jan. 30, 1843." In *Schappes*, 217–22.

1844

Cohen, M. *A Catechism of Religious and Moral Instruction*. Translated from the French. Phila.: 1844. 36 pp.

Isaacs, Samuel M. "Religious Education." *Occ* 1 (Jan. 1844): 469–73.

Noah, Mordecai M. *Discourse of the Restoration of the Jews (Oct. 28 and Dec. 2, 1844)*. N.Y.: Harper and Bros., 1845. 56 pp. See also *Schappes*, 241–52.

"On Education" and "Objects and Means of Religious Education." *Occ* 2 (July 1844): 175–85, 185–95.

1845

"An American Jewess." *The Teachers' and Parents' Assistant, "Conveying to uninformed minds the first ideas of God and His Attributes"*. Phila.: C. Sherman, 1845. 36 pp. "Attributed to Rebecca Gratz—the celebrated Rebecca in Sir Walter Scott's Ivanhoe" (Rosenbach).

"Efforts to Open Religious Schools in Baltimore, New Orleans, and Montreal." *Occ* 3 (1845): 211.

"Establishment in 1845 of a School for Religious Instruction in Augusta, Georgia." *Occ* 3 (1845): 211.

Goldsmith, Harry. *Catechism for Hebrew Children*. N.Y.: S. H. Jackson, 1845. 20 pp.

"Jacob J. M. Falkenan's Evaluation of Societies Organized for the Promotion of Religious Education in 1845." *Occ* 3 (1845): 233.

Leeser, Isaac. "The Talmud Torah School of New York." *Occ* 3 (Apr. 1845): 21–29.

Lyon, George. "Freedom of Religion" (urged building of colleges by Jews). *Occ* 3 (1845): 468–69.

Lyons, L. L. *Rules and Regulations for the Government of a School for Gratuitous Instruction in the Hebrew Language and Forms of Prayer, According to the Custom and Mode of the Portuguese Jews*. N.Y.: Shearith Israel, 1845.

Phillips, Jonas B. *Address at Talmud Torah Institute of New York, Jan. 26, 1845*. Occ 3 (1845): 26–37.

"Public Education" (editorial). *Occ* 3 (Oct. 1845): 313–18.

1846

Bernal, A. I. H. "On Religious Education." *Occ* 4 (Aug. 1846): 250–51.

Leeser, Isaac. *The Forms of Prayers According to the Customs of the Spanish and Portuguese Jews*. 2d ed. 6 vols. Phila.: C. Sherman, 1846.

———. "A Plea for Education" (editorial). *Occ* 4 (May 1846): 61–67. See also 4 (June 1846): 109–14.

———. "Societies for the Religious Instruction of Jewish Youth." *Occ* 4 (July 1846): 187–97. (On reformers in Jewish education.)

Leven, L. T. "Hebrew Sunday School." *Occ* 4 (Apr. 5, 1846): 151–52.

Lilienthal, Max L. "On the Needs of Religious Education." *Occ* 3 (1846): 591–92.

1847

Gutheim, J. K. "Religious Education." *Occ* 4 (June 1847): 178–84.

Hart, H. *Jewish Creed, Arranged for the Sunday School of Charleston, for Teaching of Jewish Doctrine*. Phila.: C. Sherman, 1847. 17 pp.

Hurwitz, Hyman. *Hebrew Tales. Selected and Translated from the Ancient Hebrew Sages, to Which is Prefixed an Essay on the Uninspired Literature of the Jews*. N.Y.: Spalding and Shepard, 1847. 171 pp.

Leeser, Isaac. "Demand For Education" (editorial). *Occ* 5 (Apr. 1847): 1–9.

———. "A Visit to a New York All Day School." *Occ* 5 (Nov. 1847): 412–15.

Pray, Lewis G. "Jewish Education." In *The History of Sunday Schools*, 13–18. Boston: Wm. Crosby and H. P. Nichols, 1847.

"Religious Education, Beth El Congregation, Albany, N.Y. 1842." *Occ* 4 (1847): 600.

"Report on Jewish Education at Charleston, South Carolina." *Occ* 5 (Aug. 1847): 260–65.

1848

D'Israel, L. S. *Talmudic Maxims*. Translated from the Hebrew together with other sayings compiled from various authors. Boston: J. French, 1848. 198 pp.

1849

Asmonean. New York, 1849–58. Weekly.

Israel's Herald. Published for three months. First Jewish weekly in America (New York).

1850

Haggadah. סדר הגדה של פסח. מתורגם מלשון הקודש ללשון ענגליש (Seder for the Two First Nights of the Passover). With English translation. N.Y.: J. M. Jackson. 80 pp.

Herxheimer, S. יסודי התורה. (Catechism of the Faith and Moral Obligations for the Use of Schools and Private Families). Translated by Dr. Felsenthal and Mr. David Barnard as Revised by the Rev. Dr. Merzbacher Under the Patronage of the Congregation. N.Y.: Henry Franks, 1850. 96 pp.

Schwarz, Joseph. *Descriptive Geography and Brief Historical Sketch of Palestine*. Translated by Isaac Leeser. Phila.: A. Hart, 1850. 519 pp.

1851

Henry, H. A. ספר החנוך לילדי בני ישראל. (A Class Book for Jewish Youth of Both Sexes). Cincinnati: C. Cropper and Son, 1851. 133 pp.

"The Value of Jewish Day Schools." *Asmonean* (May 2, 1851). Also *JEUS*, 63–67.

1852

Raphall, Morris Jacov. *Devotional Exercise for the Use of the Daughters of Israel*. Compiled and translated with emendation from the German of Letteris, Miro and Stern; and edited by M. J. Raphall. N.Y.: L. Joachimssen, 1852. 139 pp.

1853

"Talmud Yelodim School, Cincinnati, Ohio." *Occ* 11 (Apr. 1853): 49–62.

1854

"Judah Touro's Will" (Jan. 6, 1854). (Includes many educational institutions throughout the U.S.). In *Schappes*, 333–41. Also in Leon Huhner's *Life of Judah Touro*, 129–39, and *Occ* 11 (1854): 592.

Kalisch, Isidor. "On the Value of the Study of the Talmud." *Occ* 11 (Feb. 1854): 552–56.

Leeser, Isaac. "Education" (1854). In *Discourses—Argumentative and Devotional on the Jewish Religion*, 252–57. 1867. (On the public schools and the need for Jewish education.)

———, ed. *Select Sentences: Designed as a Moral Guidebook for Young Israelites*. Phila.: L. Johnson Co., 1854. 200 pp.

Lilienthal, Max. "Do We Educate Our Children in Our Religion?" *Asmonean* (Aug. 11, 1854): 132.

Peixotto, Simha C. *Elementary Introduction to the Scriptures, for the Use of Hebrew Children*. 3d ed. Phila.: 1854, 175 pp.

Wise, Isaac M. *History of the Israelitisch Nation*. Albany: J. Munsell, 1854. 560 pp.

1855

Bush, Isidore. "The Task of the Jews in the United States." *Occ* 13 (May 1855): 85–89. See also *JEUS* 68–75 and *Amer Jew Arc* 18 (Nov. 1966): 155–59. (Opposed Jewish day schools.)

Leeser, Isaac. "A Plea for Religious Education" (Nov. 12, 1855). In *Discourses—Argumentative and Devotional on the Jewish Religion*, 117–59. 1867–68.

Lilienthal, Max. "The Aims of Our Schools." *Israelite* (later *American Israelite* 2 (Sept. 14, 1855).

1856

Leeser, Isaac. *The Twenty-Four Books of the Holy Scriptures*. Phila.: C. Sherman, 1856. 1243 pp.

Mayer, Isaac. *Systematical and Practical Hebrew Grammar. . . with a Chrestomathy Containing an Epitome of History from the Creation of the World to the Destruction of the Second Temple*. Cincinnati: Office of *The Israelite* and *Deborah*, 1856. 107 pp.

Raphall, Morris. "Education among the Hebrews" (ancient). *American Journal of Education* (Mar. 1856): 243–46.

1857

Aguilar, Grace. *Home Influence*. Boston: Hickling, Swan and Brewer, 1857. 386 pp.

Carvalho, Solomon Nunes. *incidents of Travel and Adventures in the Far West*. 1857. Reprinted by JPS in 1954.

Jacobs, Solomon. "Religious Education." *Occ* (1857): 246.

Kalisch, Isidor. *A Guide for Rational Inquiry into the Biblical Writings*. Cincinnati: Bloch, 1857. 193 pp.

Kalisch, Isidor, W. Rothenheim, and I. M. Wise. מנהג אמעריקא. תפלות בני ישורון (American Mode—Prayers B'nai Jeshurun). Cincinnati: Bloch, 1857. 142 pp.

"What Is Needed." (Editorial for the establishment of a "Jewish College of America.") *Jewish Messenger* (July 17, 1857).

1858

Einhorn, David, ed. עלת תמיד (Perpetual Offering Sabbath and Festival Prayers) (for Reform Congregations). Baltimore: C. W. Schneidereith, 1858. 492 pp.

1859

Hebrew Leader (E. and G.). New York, 1859–1974. Weekly.

Henry, Abraham A. *A Synopsis of Jewish History from the Return of the Jews of the Babylonian Captivity, to the Days of Herod the Great; Giving an Account of the Sects of Those Days; the Introduction of Prayer amomg the Jews; the Ureem and Thumeem, the Mishna or Oral Law, the Gemara-Completion, Usually Styled the Talmud*. San Francisco: Towne and Bacon, 1859. 187 pp.

Sherith Israel (congregation). *Elementary Instruction in the Hebrew Faith for the Jewish Youth of Congregation Sherith Israel*. San Francisco: Towne and Bacon, 1859. 187 pp.

186?

Dessor, Julius Heinreich. *First Elements of the Hebrew Grammar*. Cincinnati: Bloch, 186?. 18 pp.

1860

Adler, Samuel. *Leitfaden fur den Isrealitschen Religionsunterricht* (A Guide for the Instruction of the Jewish Religion) (G.). N.Y.: Thalmessinger, Cahn and Benedicks, 1860. 59 pp.

Emanu-El (congregation). *Order of Prayers for Hebrew School. Temporarily Compiled for the Devotion of the School on Solemn Holidays and Succoth, of the Year 5621*. San Francisco: 1860. 114 pp.

1861

Harris, Sarah. *Thoughts Suggested by Bible Texts*. Edited by Isaac Leeser. Phila.: Hebrew Sunday-School Society, 1861. 138 pp.

Wise, Isaac Mayer. *The Essence of Judaism*. Cincinnati: Bloch, 1861. 65 pp.

1862

Benjamin, I. I. "The Rearing of a Jewish Daughter." In *Three Years in America, 1859–1862*, 1:85–87. 2 vols. Phila.: JPS, 1956. (First published in Hanover, Germany, 1862.) See also *JEUS*, 76–79.

1863

Fischer, Wilhelm. זמירות ישראל (Hymns Set to Music) (E. and G.). Phila.: L. N. Rosenthal, 1863. 160 pp.

Hecht, Emanuel. *Biblical History for Israelitisch School . . . Revised and Corrected by S. Adler*. Translated from the German by M. Mayer. N.Y.: Thalmessinger and Cahn, 1863. 144 pp.

1864

Aguilar, Grace. *The Spirit of Judaism*, edited by Isaac Leeser. 3d ed. Phila.: 1864. 263 pp.

Henry, Abraham H. *Discourse on the Book of Genesis*. San Francisco: H. H. Bancroft, 5624 (1864). 246 pp.

Szold, Benjamin. *Abodath Israel* (Service of Israel). Baltimore: 1864.

1865

De Solla, J. Mendes. כל דברי התורה (A Vocabulary of the Pentateuch . . . with English Translation) (H.). Phila.: Published by the author, 1865. 152 pp.

1866

Congregation Emanu-El. *Duties and Powers of the Board of School Directors, Together with the School Rules, Regulations and Routine of Instruction. Adopted November 11, 1866, 5627*. San Francisco: Office of the Hebrew, 1866. 14 pp.

Einhorn, David. נר תמיד (Eternal Light) (H.). (Teachings of Judaism for school and home). Phila.: Stein and Jones, 1866. 112 pp.

Felsenthal, Bernard. *Judisches Schulwesen in America* (Jewish Education in America) (G.). Chicago: 1866.

מחזור. *Festival Prayers* (Polish rite with English translation) (H.). 3d ed. N.Y.: L. H. Frank, 1866.

1867

Lazarus, Emma. *Poems and Translations*. N.Y.: Hurd and Houghton, 1867. 297 pp.

Pyke, C, and E. Pyke. *Scripture History*. N.Y.: L. H. Frank, 1867. 84 pp.

Szold, Benjamin. אורים ותומים (Outlines of the System of Judaism). Baltimore: W. Palmyer, 1867. 32 pp.

1868

Appeals to the Israelite of the United States for the founding of a college, and by-laws of the American Hebrew College of the City of New York. N.Y.: M. Thalmessinger, 1868. 23 pp.

Aufrecht, L. ללמוד בני יהודה (The American Hebrew Primer) (H.). Cincinnati: Bloch. 23 pp.

Cahen, G. M. *The Little Bible or, The Instruction or Religion and Morals for Young and Old*. Cleveland: Nevint's Steam Press, 1868. 295 pp.

Deutsch, Solomon. *A New Practical Hebrew Grammar*. N.Y.: Leypoldt and Holt, 1868. 268 pp.

Eppstein, E. *Confirmand's Guide to the Mosaic Religion*. Detroit: F. A. Schorer and Bros., 1868.

Felsenthal, Bernhard. *A Practical Grammar of the Hebrew Language*. N.Y.: L. H. Frank, 1868. 99 pp.

למודי הקריאה *The Hebrew Reader*. An easy method for the instruction of Jewish children. Compiled by R. Lasker. N.Y.: L. H. Frank, 1868. 24 pp.

Jewish Times. New York, 1868–80. Weekly.

Meyers, M. H., and I. H. Meyers. *Twelve Hundred Questions on the Bible*. Phila.: Stein and Jones, 1868. 237 pp.

Neida, Fanny (Schnied). *Hours of Devotion: A Book of Prayers and Meditations for the Use of the Daughters of Israel*. Translated from the German. N.Y.: L. H. Frank, 1868, 1872. 185 pp.

Wise, Isaac M. *Hymns, Psalms and Prayers* (E. and G.). Cincinnati: Bloch, 1868.

1869

Israel, A. B. *Key to Israel's Outline Maps and Geographical Teaching*. St. Louis: Published by the author, 1869. 191 pp.

1870

Die Iddishe Tseitung (Y.). New York, 1870–72? First Yiddish weekly (although not published regularly). English title was *The New York Hebrew Times*.

29
HISTORY OF JEWISH EDUCATION IN THE UNITED STATES

Ha-Tsofeh (H.). New York, 1870–76. First Hebrew weekly.

Lilienthal, Max. "Is the Bible Fit to be Used as a School Book?" *Jewish Times* 1 (1869–70): 5.

Noah, J. J. "Hebrew Education, A Brief Report on Jewish Education in Ancient Times, Europe and the United States." Followed by statements of Dr. Sonneschein for St. Louis, B. Felsenthal for Chicago, I. M. Wise for Cincinnati, G. Jacobson for Philadelphia, and reports for Baltimore and Washington, D.C. In *Annual Report of the U.S. Commissioner of Education*, 359–70. Washington, D.C: 1870. The Wise report is also in *JEUS*, 85–86.

Sonneschein, Solomon H. *The Influence of the B'nai B'rith upon the Education of Our Children* (original in German). St. Louis: 1870. 8 pp.

Wise, Isaac Mayer. *Minhag America: The Daily Prayers for American Israelites* (H.). Cincinnati: Bloch, 1870. 138 pp.

1871

Cohen, Samuel. *A Catechism . . . for children of the Hebrew Faith. . . Published for the Sunday School of the Congregation B'nai Jeshurun*. N.Y.: L. H. Frank, 1871. 30 pp.

De Solla, J. Mendes. *A Catechism of the Jewish Religion*. San Francisco: Bacon and Co., 1871. 56 pp.

Frank, L. H. לשון הקדש אונד אידיש דייטש, למודי התורה, אדער אונטערריכט אים לעזן דעם בעארבייטעט ... פיר דיא איזרעליטישו שולען (Reading Instruction, or, Teaching the Reading of the Holy Language and Judeo-Yiddish in the Israelitisch schools) (Y. and H.). N.Y.: L. H. Frank, 1871. 21 pp.

Sherith Israel Congregation, San Francisco. *Rules and Regulations for the Government of the Hebrew School. Adopted January, 1871, 1896.* 12 pp. and 14 pp.

1872

Wise, Isaac Mayer. *Judaism, Its Doctrines and Duties*. Cincinnati: Office of *The Israelite*, 1872. 83 pp.

1873

Hecht, Simon. *First Lessons in Hebrew*. Cincinnati: Bloch, 1873. 44 pp.

Mannheimer, Sigmund. *The Leveler of the Path: Hebrew Reader and Translator*. From A. Kohn. N.Y.: Published by the author, 1873. 88 pp.

Szold, Benjamin. ראשית דעת (Catechism designed for the religious instruction of Israelitisch Children). Baltimore: Machsam and Seimers, 1873. 76 pp.

Wessely, Naphtali. "State of Education among the Jews in the Enlightened Century." *New Era* 3 (May 1873): 186–89.

1874

Mayer, Isaac. מעין הישועה (Source of Salvation). Brooklyn, N.Y.: Hebrew Pub. Co., 1874. 106 pp.

1875

Choynski, I. N. *Antiquarian Spelling Book* (for teaching Hebrew). San Francisco: 1875?.

Jewish Messenger, New York, 1875–190?. Weekly (later merged with *American Hebrew*).

Kaiser, Alois. שירי חנוך (Confirmation Hymns with English and German Words). Baltimore: 1875. 19 pp.

———. *Tunes for the Israelitisch School*. Written with B. Szold. Baltimore: 1875.

Piexotto, Simha C. *Elementary Introduction to the Scriptures for Use of Hebrew Children*. 13th ed. Phila.: T. K. Collins, 1875. 175 pp.

Polano, Hymen. חנך לנער (The Hebrew Speller). For Jewish children and self-instruction according to the German and Portuguese mode of pronunciation. N.Y.: L. H. Frank, 1875.

Szold, B. *Gebete fuer Kinder fuer Haus un Schule* (Children's Prayers for Home and School) (G.). Written by B. Szold and revised by M. Jastrow. Phila.: 1875. 20 pp.

Temple Emanu-El, N.Y. *The Temple Emanu-El Hymn Book*. Words selected by A. J. Davis. N.Y.: W. A. Pond and Co., 1875.

1876

Jewish Education Society of Chicago. "A Letter to the 'Israelites of Chicago'." (Call for an all-day Jewish high school in Chicago.) Sept. 15, 1876. In Louis Wirth, *The Ghetto*, 171. 1975.

1879

American Hebrew. New York, 1879–194?. Weekly (merged with *Jewish Messenger* and later became *American Hebrew Jewish Tribune*).

HISTORY OF JEWISH EDUCATION IN THE UNITED STATES

Beth Israel (congregation). *Catechism for the Congregation "Beth Israel" of San Francisco, California.* San Francisco: M. Weiss, 1879.

Meyers, E. M. *The Jews: Their Customs and Ceremonies with a Full Account of All Their Religious Observances from the Cradle to the Grave.* N.Y.: Worthington, 1879. 112 pp.

1880

Ben Ra-Shalom, Avrael. *Hebrew First Reader: A Progressive Method of Learning to Read Hebrew Correctly, and to Accentuate Accurately, with an Appendix of Prayers for Children's Sabbath Services.* San Francisco: M. Weiss, 1880. 40 pp.

Board of Delegates of American Israelites and the Union of American Hebrew Congregations. *Statistics of the Jews of the United States.* Phila.: UAHC, 1880. 59 pp. Excerpt in *Jew Ed* (Apr–June 1934): 110. Includes survey of Jewish education by state and city.

Felsenthal, Baruch Arieh. למען ילמדו (So That They Shall Be Taught) (H.). Chicago: 1880. 47 pp.

1881

Moses, Isaac S. *The Pentateuch.* Milwaukee: 1881. Children's edition that "omits embarrassing passages."

1885

Iddishes Tageblatt (Y.). New York, 1885–1928. Daily (merged with *Jewish Morning Journal*).

Kohler, Kaufmann. "Concerted Action for Sabbath School Reform" (conference papers). *American Hebrew* (1885): 1–23.

1886

Eisenstein, J. D. "Correspondence with Parents in Europe on the Education of his Son" (1881–86). *AJHQ* 52 (Mar. 1963): 241–43. See also *JEUS*, 102–3.

1887

Kohler, Kaufmann. *Manual of Religious Instruction.* N.Y.: 1887.

Mendes, Frederick de Sola. *The Child's First Bible, for Synagogue and Home.* N.Y.: 1887. Hymns, songs, and religious memoranda for Jewish congregations.

Messing, Aron. *Catechism for Instruction to the Mosaic Religion for the Hebrew Free School of San Francisco.* 2d ed. San Francisco: M. Weiss, 1887. 46 pp.

Weinberger, Moses. היהודים והיהדות בניו יורק (Jews and Judaism in New York) (H.). N.Y.: 1887. Translated from the Hebrew by Jonathan D. Sarna as *People Walk on Their Heads.* N.Y.: Holmes Meier, 1981. 137 pp. For Weinberger's educational views see "Education" in Sarna's translation, 51–56. See also excerpt in *JEUS*, 104–7.

1888

Krauskopf, Joseph. "Fifty Years of Judaism in America." *American Jews' Annual* 4 (1888): 65–95.

Sulzberger, Mayer. *Address on the 50th Anniversary of the Hebrew School of Philadelphia.* Phila.: 1888.

1889

Schindler, Solomon. *Israelites in Boston: A Tale Describing the Development of Judaism in Boston.* Boston: 1899.

Vidaver, Falk. *Israel's Religion.* San Francisco: M. Weiss, 1889. 48 pp. Catechism containing the essential teachings of Judaism written and composed for the instruction of the Hebrew School of the Sherith Israel Congregation of San Francisco, by their Rabbi, Rev. Dr. Falk Vidaver.

1890

Drachman, Bernard. "Jewish Educational Needs and Methods." *The Menorah* (official organ of B'nai B'rith) 8 (Jan. 1890).

Lucas, Alice. "Jewish Religious Education." *JQR* 2 (1890): 270–90.

Philipson, David, "Confirmation in the Synagogue." *CCAR* 1 (1891): 43–58.

Schreiber, Emanuel. "How to Teach Biblical History in Our Sabbath Schools." *CCAR* 1 (1891): 59–61.

1891

Bamberger, Gabriel. "Methods of Instruction in the Sabbath Schools." *Reform Advocate* 2 (Nov. 7, 1891): 190–92, (Nov. 21, 1891): 230–32.

1892

American Jewish Historical Society. "Organized at New York, June 7, 1892. Papers Presented at the First Scientific Meeting, Held at Philadelphia, December 15, 1892." Publication 1, 1893.

Daniels, Abraham G. *History of the Jews in Boston and New England.* 1892.

Ha-Ivri (H.). New York, 1892–98, 1901–2. Weekly.

Messing, Aaron. שפת עבר (A Hebrew Primer) (H.). Chicago: Rubowitch, 1892. 31 pp.

Die Zukunft (Y.). די צוקונפט (literary journal). New York, 1892–present. Monthly.

1893

Central Conference of American Rabbis. "Call for Preparation of Textbooks for Sabbath School." *CCAR* 3 (1892–93): 45–46.

Felsenthal, Julia I. "The Influence of the Jewish Religion in the Home." In *Papers of the Jewish Women's Congress* (1893), 122–32. Phila.: JPS, 1894.

Louis, Minnie D., and Rebecca Kohut. "Mission—Work among the Unenlightened Jews." In *Papers of the Jewish Women's Congress* (1893), 170–86, 187–95.

1894

Calisch, Edward., 4 *Child's Bible.* 2 vols. Richmond: 1894.

Harris, R., and L. M. Simmons. "Jewish Religious Education" *JQR* 6 (1894): 74–81.

Hecht, Sigmund. "A Sabbath School Union." *Reform Advocate* 2 (Nov. 21, 1891); 6 (Jan. 20, 1894).

Morais, Henry Samuel. "Religious Education" and "Educational and Industrial" (on the Hebrew Education Society). In *The Jews of Philadelphia*, 146–53, 154–61. Phila.: 1894.

Moses, Isaac S. *Hebrew Reader* (prayers and psalms). Chicago: Bloch, 1894. 48 pp.

1894–95

Imber, Naphtali Herz. "Education and the Talmud." In *Report of the U.S. Commissioner of Education*, 2:1795–1820. Washington, D.C.: U.S. Government Printing Office, 1894–95.

———. "The Letters of Rabbi Akibah, or the Jewish Primer as It Was Used in the Public Schools Two Thousand Years Ago." In *Report of the U.S. Commissioner of Education*, 1:709–19. Washington, D.C.: U.S. Government Printing Office, 1894–95. (Both Imber articles were described by Eisig Silberschlag as "irresponsible ventures into the arcana of post-biblical literature." See *Jan 2*, 181.)

1895

American Jewess. New York, 1895–99. Monthly (later quarterly). Edited by Rosa Sonnenschein. ("The Only Publication in the World Devoted to the Interests of Jewish Women.")

Cohen, Isabel E., comp. *Reading and Recitations for Jewish Homes and Schools.* Phila.: JPS, 1895.

Deutsch, Emanuel. *The Talmud.* Phila.: 1895. 107 pp.

Grossman, Louis. *Report of the Superintendent, Sabbath School of Temple Beth El, Sept. 29, 1895.* Detroit: Franklin Press, 1895.

Hecht, S. *Post Biblical History of the Jews.* Milwaukee: 1895.

Karpeles, Gustav. *Jewish Literature.* Phila.: JPS, 1895. 404 pp.

Kohut, George A. "Early Jewish Literature in America." *PAJHS* 3 (1895): 103–47.

1896

Central Conference of American Rabbis. "Plan of Religious Instruction in the Sabbath School." *CCAR Yearbook.* 6 (1896): 30–42.

Schechter, Solomon. "The Child in Jewish Literature." In *Studies in Judaism*, 282–312. Phila.: JPS, 1896.

1897

The Forward (Y. and E.). פארווערטס New York, 1897–present. Daily (later weekly).

Joseph, Morris. "Jewish Religious Education." *JQR* 9 (1897): 631–38.

Mordecai, Rosa. "Memoir of Rebecca Gratz and the Hebrew Sunday School of Philadelphia." *The Hebrew Watchword and Instructor* (1897) (serially). Excerpts in *PAJHS* 42 (1953): 397–406; J. R. Marcus, *Memoirs*, 1:281–88 (1955–56); and *JEUS*, 54–60.

Szold, Henrietta. "Knowledge versus Spirituality in the Curriculum of the Jewish Religious School." *The Menorah* 23 (Sept. and Oct. 1897).

1898

Moskowitz, Henry. "A Study of the East Side Chedar." University Settlement of New York. U. Settlement Associate Studies, 1898.

1899

American Jewish Year Book. Philadelphia, 1899–1990. Vol. 1 (1899), 299 pp.

פרייע ארבעטער שטימע *(Freie Arbeiter Shtimme)* (Y.). New York, 1899–1977. Weekly, later biweekly.

פריינד *(Friend)* (Y.). New York, 1899–194?. Weekly.

Levi, A. R. ראשית למודים (A Beginner's Text for the "Children of Abraham") (H.). Chicago: 1899. 31 pp.

Weiner, Leo. *The History of Yiddish Literature in the 19th Century.* N.Y.: Charles Scribner's Sons, 1899. 400 pp.

1900

Richman, Julia. "The Jewish Sunday School Movement in the United States." *JQR* 12 (1900): 563–601.

HISTORY OF AMERICAN JEWRY (SELECTED)

Blau, Joseph L., and Salo W. Baron. *The Jews of the United States: A Documentary History, 1790–1840.* 3 vols. Phila.: JPS, 1962.

Dawidowicz, Lucy S. "A Century of Jewish History, 1881–1981: The View from America." *AJYB* 82 (1982): 3–98.

Eidlin, Harold. "The English Weekly Press as Communicator for American Jewry." Master's thesis, American U., 1964.

Elazar, Daniel J., and Stephen K. Goldstein. "The Legal Status of the American Jewish Community." *AJYB* 73 (1972): 3–94.

Feingold, Henry L. *A Midrash on American Jewish History.* Albany: State U. of New York Press, 1982. 241 pp.

———. *Zion in America: The Jewish Experience from Colonial Times to the Present.* N.Y.: Hippocrene Books, 1974.

* Goodman, Abram V. *American Overture: Jewish Rights in Colonial Times.* U. of Texas, 1949.

Handlin, Oscar. *Adventure in Freedom.* N.Y.: McGraw, 1954. 282 pp.

Handlin, Oscar, and Mary F. Handlin. "Acquisition of Political and Social Rights by the Jews in the United States." *AJYB* 56 (1955): 43–98.

Herscher, Uri D. *Jewish Agricalatural Utopias in America, 1880–1910.* Detroit: Wayne State University Press, 1981.

Kabakoff, Jacob. "Hebrew Sources of American Jewish History." In *A Bicentennial Festschrift for Jacob Rader Marcus,* edited by Korn, 219–34. 1976.

Karp, Abraham J. *Haven and Home: A History of the Jews in America.* N.Y.: Schocken, 1985. 401 pp.

Katz, Nancy H. "Jewish Agricultural Colonies in the United States." Master's thesis, Southern Methodist U., 1964.

Konvitz, Milton R. *Judaism and the American Idea.* N.Y.: Schocken, 1980. 223 pp.

Korn, Bertram W. *American Jewry and the Civil War.* Phila.: JPS, 1951. 331 pp.

Learsi, Rufus. *The Jew in America.* N.Y.: World, 1954. 382 pp.

Lebeson, Anita L. *Jewish Pioneers in America, 1492–1848.* N.Y.: Behrman, 1938. 371 pp.

Mandel, Irving Aaron. "The Attitude of the American Jewish Community toward East-European Immigration." Master's thesis, HUC–JIR, 1947.

Marcus, Jacob R. *The Colonial American Jew.* 3 vols. Detroit: Wayne State U. Press, 1970.

———. *Early American Jewry.* 2 vols. Phila.: JPS.

Meyer, Isidore S. "Hebrew at Harvard—1636–1760." *PAJHS* 35 (1939): 145–70.

Pool, David de Sola. "Hebraic Learning among the Puritans of New England Prior to 1700." *PAJHS* 20 (1911): 31–83.

Raphael, Marc Lee. *Jews and Judaism in the United States—A Documentary History.* N.Y.: Behrman, 1983. 348 pp.

Sarna, Jonathan D., ed. *The American Jewish Experience: A Reader.* N.Y.: Holmes and Meier, 1986. 303 pp.

Schappes, Morris U. *A Documentary History of the Jews in the United States.* N.Y.: Citadel Press, 1950. 762 pp.

Shipton, Clifford K. "The Hebraic Background of Puritanism." *PAJHS* 47 (Mar. 1958): 140–53.

* Tarshish, Allan. *The Rise of American Judaism: A History of American Jewish Life from 1848 to 1881.* HUC–JIR, 1940.

INSTITUTIONS AND ORGANIZATIONS (SELECTED)

Bloom, Bernard H. "'Die Zukunft,' 1892–1905: A Study of the Early Jewish Socialist Movement of the United States of America." Master's thesis, HUC–JIR, 1957.

Cohen, Naomi. *Not Free to Desist: A History of the American Jewish Committee, 1907–1966.* Phila.: JPS, 1972. 652 pp.

Elazar, Daniel J. *Community and Polity: The Organizational Dynamics of American Jewry.* Phila.: JPS, 1976. 421 pp.

* Elwell, Ellen S. H. *The Founding and Early Problems of the National Council of Jewish Women: Study and Practice as Jewish Women's Religious Expression.* Indiana U., 1982.

Epstein, Melech. *Jewish Labor in the USA: An Industrial, Political and Cultural History of the Jewish Labor Movement, 1914–1952.* 2 vols. N.Y.: Trade Union Sponsoring Committee, 1952.

* Fromer, Morris. *The American Jewish Congress: A History, 1914–1950.* 2 vols. Ohio State U., 1978.

Graziani, Bernice. *Where There's a Woman: 75 Years of History as Lived by the National Council of Jewish Women.* N.Y.: McCall, 1967. 128 pp.

Grusd, Edward E. *B'nai B'rith: The Story of a Covenant.* N.Y.: Appleton-Century, 1966. 315 pp.

Herberg, Will. "Jewish Labor Movement in the United States." *AJYB* 53 (1952): 3–74.

Hurwich, Maximilian. *The Workmen's Circle: Its History, Ideals, Organization, and Institutions.* N.Y.: WC, 1936. 246 pp.

Lurie, Harry L. *A Heritage Affirmed: The Jewish Federation Movement in America.* Phila.: JPS, 1961. 481 pp.

* Miller, Donald H. *A History of Hadassah, 1912–1935.* New York U., 1969.

Morris, Robert, and Michael Freund, eds. *Trends and Issues in Jewish Social Welfare in the United States, 1889–1952.* Phila.: JPS, 1966. 642 pp.

National Federation of Temple Sisterhoods. *Through the Years—Jewish Women in American History: A Filmstrip.* N.Y., 1954.

National Jewish Community Relations Advisory Council. Reports of plenary sessions (annually since 1943).

National Women's League of the USA. *A History of the National Women's League, 1918–1968.* N.Y., 1967. 107 pp.

Rabinowitz, Benjamin. *The Young Men's Hebrew Associations, 1854–1913.* JHS 37 (1947).

Shapiro, Judah S. *The Friendly Society: The History of the Workmen's Circle.* N.Y.: Media Judaica, 1970.

———. "National Foundation for Jewish Culture." *Jew Ed* 31 (Fall 1960): 46–50.

Welt, Mildred G. "The National Council of Jewish Women." *AJYB* 46 (1944–45): 55–72.

JEWISH RELIGIOUS, ORGANIZATIONAL, AND CULTURAL LIFE (SELECTED)

Angoff, Charles. "Three Hundred Years of Jewish-American Culture." *Recon* 19 (Nov. 6, 1953).

Bernheimer, Charles S. "Summary of Jewish Organizations in the United States" (includes Jewish education). *AJYB* 2 (1900–1901): 496–506.

Bernstein, Saul. *The Renaissance of the Torah Jew: The History of Orthodox Judaism in the 20th Century.* Hoboken, N.J.: Ktav, 1985. 412 pp.

Berlin, Charles. "Library Resources for Jewish Studies in the United States." *AJYB* 75 (1974–75): 3–54.

Blau, Joseph L. *Judaism in America: From Curiosity to Third Faith*. Chicago: U. of Chicago Press, 1978.

———. "Spiritual Life of American Jews, 1654–1954." *AJYB* 56 (1955): 99–170.

Brown, Michael Gary. "All, All Alone: The Hebrew Press in America from 1914–1924." *AJHQ* 59 (1969–70): 139–75.

Chorowsky, Joshua. "The Influence of Biblical Ideas on the American Revolution and the United States Constitution." *Ped Rep* 28 (Fall 1976): 2–7.

Davis, Moshe. *The Emergence of Conservative Judaism: The Historical School in 19th Century America*. Phila.: JPS, 1963.

———. "Jewish Religious Life and Institutions in America: A Historical Study." In *Jews*, 1:488–587.

Doroshkin, Milton. *Yiddish in America: Social and Cultural Foundations*. Rutherford, N.J.: Fairleigh Dickinson U. Press, 1969. 281 pp.

Gladstone, J., Sh. Niger, and H. Rogoff, eds. (75 Years of the Yiddish Press in America, 1870–1945) (Y.). N.Y.: I. L. Peretz Writers Association, 1945. 197 pp.

Goldberg, Ben Zion. "Centennial of the Yiddish Press in America." *Un Syn Rev* (Fall 1970): 4–5.

Kabakoff, Jacob. "Hebrew Culture and Creativity in America." In *Jewish Life in America*, edited by T. Friedman and R. Gordis. 1965.

———. *Seekers and Stalwarts: Essays and Studies on American Hebrew Literature and Culture*. Jerusalem: Mass, 1978.

Karff, Samuel E., ed. *Hebrew Union College-Jewish Institute of Religion, at One Hundred Years*. Cincinnati: Hebrew Union College Press, 1976. 501 pp.

Karp, Abraham J. "A Century of Conservative Judaism in the United States." *AJYB* 86:3–61.

———. "Education, Religion, and Culture." In *The Jewish Experience in America* (selections from the Publications of the American Jewish Historical Society). 5 vols. N.Y.: Ktav, 1969.

———. *A History of the United Synagogue of America, 1913–1963*. N.Y.: USA, 1964.

Levin, Shalom Dober. *History of Chabad in the United States of America, 1900–1950*. Brooklyn, N.Y.: Kehot Publication Society, 1988. 400 pp.

Liebman, Charles S. *The Ambivalent American Jew: Politics, Religion and Family Life in American Jewish Life*. Phila.: JPS, 1973.

———. "Orthodoxy in American Jewish Life." *AJYB* (1965): 21–97.

———. "Reconstructionism in American Jewish Life." *AJYB* (1970): 3–99.

Malachi, Eliezer R. „יובל המאה לעתונות האידיש באמריקה" (The 100th Anniversary of the Yiddish Press in America). *Bitzaron* (H.) (Nissan 1970): 146–53.

Raphael, Marc Lee. *Profiles in American Judaism: The Reform, Conservative, Orthodox, and Reconstructionist Traditions in Historical Perspective*. San Francisco: Harper and Row, 1984. 238 pp.

Rudavsky, David. *Modern Jewish Religious Movements*. N.Y.: Behrman, 1972.

Sarna, Jonathan D. *The JPS and the Americanization of Jewish Culture, 1888–1988: A Centennial of the Jewish Publication Society*. Phila.: JPS, 1989. 430 pp.

Schmeltzer, Menahem H. "Jewish Scholarship in the United States: Selections from the Literature, 1965–1967." *AJYB* 69 (1968): 344–67; 71 (1970): 308–29.

* Schwarts, Sidney Howard. *Law and Legitimacy: An Intellectual History of Conservative Judaism*. Temple U., 1982. 442 pp.

Shtarkman, Moshe. „דער אנהייב פון דער יידישער ליטעראטור אין אמעריקע" (The Beginning of Yiddish Literature in America, 1870–1886) (Y.). *JBA* (1943–44): 89–95.

———. „ווען העברעאיש און יידיש זיינען געקומען קיין אמעריקע" (When Hebrew and Yiddish Came to America). In *Collected Works* (Y.), 1:25–48. Tel Aviv: Or Press, 1979.

Smolar, Boris. "A Century of the Yiddish Press." *Jew Digest* (Oct. 1970): 8–10.

29 HISTORY OF JEWISH EDUCATION IN THE UNITED STATES

Temkin, Sefton D. "A Century of Reform Judaism in America." *AJYB* 74 (1973): 3–75.

GLEANINGS

The Shearith Israel Congregation of New York (1737),

"David Mendes Machado, was elected to act as hazan or reader to this our K. K. de Seherit Yiserael. The said Mr. Machado promising and obliges himself to keep a publick school in due form for teaching Hebrew language, either the whole morning or afternoon as he shall think proper and any poor that shall be thought unable to pay for their children's learning they shall be taught gratis."

Quoted by A. Dushkin, JE NYC, *Jewish Education on New York City*. N.Y.: The Bureau of Jewish Education, 1918. 449. From the minutes of the Shearith Israel Congregation, Jan. 30, 1737.

Congregation in Newport, Rhode Island, asks assistance from New York congregation (Mar. 21, 1759),

"When we reflect on how much it is our Duty, to Instruct Children, in the Path of Vertuous Religion: and how unhappy the portions must be, of those Children, and their Parents, who are thro neccesity, educated in a place where they must remain almost Totally uninstructed . . . we now supplicate assistance."

Signed by Jacob Rods Rivere et al. Reprinted in *PAJHS* 27 (1920): 178.

Letter from Congregation Shearith Israel, New York to Mr. Benjamin Pereira (Jamaica) (Dec. 16, 1760),

"After our compliments to you and your family we . . . should apply to you . . . that you will be good enough to Engage a Suitable Master Capable to Teach our Children ye Hebrew Language. . . . He will not Suit unless he understands Hebrew and English at Least. . . . A Single: modest: Sober: person will be most agreeable."

PAJHS 27 (1920): 17.

The Board of Trustees of Congregation Shearith Israel issues a call for a meeting on April 21, 1804, to assess "the present State of the School of Polonies Talmud Torah,"

"In order to make your children truly Virtuous, You must rear them in the strict principles of our Holy religion, and this cannot be efficiently done without they understand what they are saying. . . . Education, generally speaking, is the first thing which ought to be pursued in life, in order to constitute us rational."

PAJHS 27 (1920): 81–82.

Aims of the Polonies Talmud Torah, opened in 1808,

"To instill in the youthful mind a love of learning, a veneration for religion and morality, and an attainment of useful instruction; whilst all visionary and impractical schemes should be rejected on the one hand, just as salutary maxims ought to be adopted on the other."

Quoted by Pool, *An Old Faith in the New World*, 217.

An Act, To Incorporate a Society of Israelites in New Orleans, March, 25, 1828,

Sec. 8. And be it further enacted, That, no Israelite child shall be excluded either from the schools, from the temple or from the burial ground, on account of the religion of the mother."

New Orleans First Congregation, 1828. Quoted in *Schappes*, 181.

Leeser, Isaac (1830),

"In an age, when science of every kind is pursued with avidity, no astonishment can be manifested at the attempt of an Israelite to give his brethren a clear knowledge of the religion which they have inherited from their ancestors."

Instruction in the Mosaic Religion (1830), v.

Peixotto, Dr. D.L.M., proposes a modern Jewish school before the Society for the Education of Poor Children and the Relief of Indigent Persons of the Jewish Persuasion (1830),

"1. The first [proposal] is the formation of a school on principles similar to those of Pestalozzi. . . . I would direct that one of the first objects to be taught the pupil should be a knowledge of the Hebrew language."

Quoted in *JDH*, 2:437.

Preamble of the Hebrew Education Society of Philadelphia (1848),

"Penetrated with the conviction of the necessity of a thorough religious education of all Israelites, and in view of the absence of proper school ... we the subscribers have associated ourselves of raising funds, and to effect therewith the establishment of such schools."

Fifty Years' Work of the Hebrew Education Society of Philadelphia, 1848–1899, 9.

Abrams, A. A., of Milwaukee, on parental attitude to Jewish education (1880),

"Even the activity of the best teacher cannot be fruitful if he has to fight the indifference of the home. It is a strange fact that parents who take great care to see to it that their children attend public school regularly and punctually keep the very same children at home for nonsensical reasons, since it is the Sabbath School that they are missing."

Quoted in *JEUS*, 98–101.

Benderly, Samson (1903),

"Shall we withdraw our children from the public schools and establish schools of our own as the Catholics are doing? In such schools the Jewish spirit would predominate. The purely Jewish studies would find their proper place in the curriculum and our children's health would not be endangered. This plan, even if practical otherwise, should be banished from our minds. In spite of the fact that isolation in the midst of a Christian environment greatly contributed to our preservation in the past, we have paid dearly for this isolation. What we want in this country is not Jews who can successfully keep up their Jewishness in a few large ghettos, but men and women who have grown up in freedom and assert themselves wherever they are. A parochial system of education among the Jews would be fatal to such hopes."

Quoted by Nathan H. Winter, *Jewish Education in a Pluralist Society* (1966), 48.

Benderly, Samson, on the Heder (1909),

"I must... say that the 40, 000 boys who attend the Chedarim are worse off than the 90, 000 boys who attend no school."
Jew Ed 20 (Summer 1949), 83.

The American Hebrew, March 4, 1910, on New York City,

"We have several times had to call attention to the lamentable state of religious instruction among the Jews of the city. Only a very small proportion are receiving any kind of religious instruction, and in many cases the instruction received is of very little value. If as is usually asserted, the Jewish population of New York has reached one million, there are at least two hundred thousand Jewish children of school age. Allowing for all corrections of insufficient calculations, and for those children receiving instruction at home, it is certain that a very large number of Jewish children of New York are growing up without receiving the slightest instruction in Hebrew and Bible or in the tenets of their religion."

Quoted by Nathan H. Winter, *Jewish Education in a Pluralist Society* (1966), 24.

Benderly, Samson, on the New York BJE (1910),

"Never before in Jewish history has so large a Jewish community as we form in this country had both the opportunity and the responsibility of proving that the essentials of Judaism, so far from being in contradiction to the cardinal elements of modern civilization, are complementary to them, the two sides being mutually indispensable to each other."

Quoted by Israel Friedlander in *Report of the U.S. Commissioner of Education* (1913), 379–80. Also in *Jew Ed* 20 (1949), 110.

Friedlander, Israel, on the New York Jewish BJE,

"The first systematic attempt to deal with the problem of Jewish education in America on its various phases is of recent origin."

Report of the U.S. Commissioner of Education (1913), 365.

Friedlander, Israel (1914),

"We in America are on the eve of such a magnificent outburst, for we have been gradually and unobservedly accumulating the immense stores of energy of Eu-

ropean Jewry, and they are now seeking an outlet. Woe to us if we allow the next spurting forth to go to waste; if we fail to catch the precious liquid of Jewish productivity and to preserve it for the future."
Past and Present, 264–65.

Kallen, Horace (1915),
"The immigrant group is still a national group, modified, sometimes improved, by environmental influences, but otherwise a solitary spiritual unit, which is seeking to find its way out on its own social level. . . . Americanization has not repressed nationality. Americanization has liberated nationality."

Quoted by Eduardo L. Rauch in *Religious Schooling in America*, edited by Carper and Hunt (1984), 140.

Blumenfield, Samuel M. (1948)
"In America, for the first time in the history of the Jewish diaspora, society and government, instead of seeking to disparage the Jewish cultural and religious heritage or to convert its followers to another creed, are favoring the Jewish group to remain loyal to its faith and traditions."
Jew Ed 21 (Winter 1949): 48.

Rackman, Emanuel,
"To prevent the institutionalized synagogue from turning Judaism into a temple cult and the rabbi into a public relations man, orthodoxy today is transferring its prime emphasis from the synagogue to the school—preferably the yeshiva. The shift of emphasis is in part a kind of holding operation, aimed at recreating an elite of scholars who will preserve Judaism through a period of agnosticism and non-observance. But the more immediate hope of the program is to train a substantial body of people literate enough in Torah to demonstrate by their way of life that a fully traditional Judaism can stand up to the intellectual and emotional challenges of our day."
Commentary (April 1956), 356.

Hertzberg, Arthur,
"Each of the colonial communities tries to regulate the religious behavior of its individual members. One vital ingredient had changed, however. In Europe governmental power usually enforced at least some of the decrees of the Jewish elders, because the Jewish community existed as a legal entity. In America this was not true."
In *Jan 2*, 152.

Pilch, Judah,
"Judaism in America has been taking a new turn from the thirties on, when the chapter of adjustment to conditions of life and culture in America ended. With the passing of the Yiddish language as a folk possession; with the break-up of typical Jewish neighborhoods; with the replacement of the leaders of European origin by American born; with the development of suburbanism, the process of acculturation became an accomplished fact. Ideas were expressed that religion, now as ever, was the beginning and the end, our very life and the length of our days. The nationalist-secular approach was being questioned, together with its emphasis on the study of the Hebrew language. The institutionalized religion of suburbia began to hold sway in the new neighborhoods."
In *JJS*, 107.

Sklare, Marshall,
"The favor that the public school system found in the eyes of the immigrant is a highly significant index of his secularization and desire to accommodate to America. And the public school in turn served to speed the process of integrating both parent as well as child into American culture. Given the attitudes of those who came to America during the period of mass migration, together with the challenges and opportunities of American life (and particularly the way such challenges and opportunities were interpreted by the immigrant), the traditional orientation toward Jewish learning was abandoned and a new orientation to secular studies came into being. It is possible to contend that the shift was so extreme that values actually became transposed: secular education assumed the place that Jewish education had occupied, while Jewish education was shifted to the position formerly assigned to secular education."
Quoted by Eduardo L. Rauch in *Religious Schooling in America*, edited by Carper and Hunt (1984), 137.

30 THE AMERICAN JEWISH COMMUNITY

(See also chapter 20)

GENERAL (SELECTED)

Bellen, L. E. "Jewish Decision Making." *Un Syn Rev* 30 (Summer 1977): 8–9.

Berkson, Isaac B. "The 'Community' Theory." In *Theories of Americanization*, 97–118. 1920.

Brickner, Balfour. "The Challenge of Community Pressures." *Jew Ed* 39 (Dec. 1969): 33–42.

Chanover, Hyman. "Observations on Lay-Involvement in Decision-Making." *Jew Spec* 43 (Fall 1974): 53–55.

Duker, Abraham G. "The Problem of Coordination and Unity." In *Jan 2*, 323–38.

———. "Structure of the Jewish Community." In *Jan 1*, 134–60.

———. *Workshop in Jewish Community Affairs: Three Syllabuses*. N.Y.: American Jewish Congress, 1952. 10 pp., 25 pp., and 27 pp.

Dushkin, Alexander M. "The Place of Jewish Education in Jewish Social Service." *NCJSS Proceedings* (June 1924): 267–79. Reprinted in *Trends and Issues in Jewish Social Welfare in the United States, 1889–1952*, edited by Robert Morris and Michael Freund, 220–25. Phila.: JPS, 1966.

Elazar, Daniel J. "Building Citizenship in the Emerging Jewish Community." CP, General Assembly–CJF, 1972. 16 pp.

———. *Community and Polity: The Organizational Dynamics of American Jewry*. Phila.: JPS, 1976. 421 pp.

———. "Decision-Making in the Jewish Community." In *FJCA* 4, 271–316.

———. "The Institutional Life of American Jewry." *Mid* (June–July 1971): 31–50.

———. "The Organic Jewish Community." *Recon* (Oct. 16, 30, 1964.

Fried, Jacob, ed. *Judaism and the Community*. South Brunswick, N.J.: Yoseloff, 1968.

Goldberg, S. P. *The American Jewish Community: Its Structure, Role, and Organizations*. N.Y.: Women's American ORT Community Service Publications, 1964.

Grayzel, Solomon. "Jewish Community Organization." Master's thesis, Columbia U., 1920.

Hertzberg, Arthur. "Community and Nation: Basis for Jewish Commitment." *Jew Ed* 45 (Fall/Winter 1976): 17–24.

Huberman, S. "Burning Bridges: Towards Realistic Links between Research and Planning in Jewish Communal Life." *J Jew Com Ser* 57 (Fall 1980): 37–43.

Janowsky, Oscar I. "The Image of the American Jewish Community." In *Jan 2*, 385–99.

Kaplan, Mordecai M. "The Organization of American Jewry." *Jew Ed* 7 (Oct.–Dec. 1935): 131–54.

Karpf, Maurice J. *Jewish Community Organization in the United States*. N.Y.: Bloch, 1938. 250 pp.

Koenig, S. "Socio-Economic Structure of an American Jewish Community." In *Jews in a Gentile World*, edited by Graeber. 1942.

Kohs, Samuel C. "Jewish Community Organization—As It Might Have Been." *Recon* 11 (Feb. 23, 1945): 47–54.

———. "The Jewish Community." In *Jews*, 2:1267–1324.

Levy, Charles S. "Jewish Communal Services: Health, Welfare, Recreational and Social." In *Jan 2*, 253–76.

Linfield, Harry S. "The Communal Organization of the Jews in the United States, 1927." *AJYB* 31 (1929–30): 126–52.

———. *Statistics of Jews and Jewish Organizations: Historical Review of Ten Censuses*. N.Y.: AJC, 1939. 64 pp.

MacIver, R. M. *Report on the Jewish Community Relations Agencies*. N.Y.: National Community Relations Advisory Council, 1951. 281 pp.

Maslow, Will. *The Structure and Functioning of the American Jewish Community*. N.Y.: American Jewish Congress, 1974.

National Commission on Communal Services. *Report of the Commission on the Structure, Function and Priorities of the Organized Jewish Community*. N.Y., June 1974.

National Jewish Community Relations Advisory Council. *Reports*. N.Y., annually since 1943.

Raphael, Marc Lee. *Understanding American Jewish Philanthropy*. N.Y.: Ktav, 1979.

Richards, Bernard G. *Organizing American Jewry*. N.Y.: Office of Information, American Jewish Congress, 1947.

Shapiro, Mannheim S. "The American Jewish Community." In *Currents and Trends in Contemporary Jewish Thought*, edited by Benjamin Efron, 156–75. N.Y.: Ktav, 1965.

———. "An Appraisal of the Current Needs of the American Jewish Community." *J Jew Com Ser* 40 (1963): 36–47.

Sherman, Bezalel C. "Jewish Communal Organizations in the United States." In *JPPP*, 2:217–30.

———. "Uniqueness of the American Jewish Community." In *The Jew within American Society: A Study in Ethnic Individuality*, 117–36. Detroit: Wayne State University Press, 1961.

Sklare, Marshall, ed. *The Jewish Community in America*. N.Y.: Behrman, 1974. 383 pp.

Soviv, Aaron. "Community and Education in America." *JSS* 31 (Jan. 1969): 65.

Steg, A. "Jewish National Identity: Jewish Community and Its Environments." WZO 53 (Fall 1984): 12–14.

THE COMMUNITY AND JEWISH EDUCATION PRIOR TO 1950

Baron, Salo W. "Communal Responsibility for Jewish Education." *Jew Ed* 19 (Spring 1948): 7–13, 40. See also *JJS*, 7–13, 40, and Baron's *Steeled by Adversity*, 518–31.

———. "Education and Public Enlightenment" (historical analysis). In his *The Jewish Community*, 2:169–207. 3 vols. Phila.: JPS, 1942. See also "A Historical Critique of the Jewish Community." *Jew Ed* 8 (Jan.–Mar. 1936): 2–8.

Benderly, Samson. "Jewish Education—A Communal Responsibility." *Jewish Education News* (Oct. 1925).

Blumenfield, Samuel M. "A Study of the Correlation between Elementary Jewish Education and Interest in Jewish Life and Problems." *Jew Ed* 9 (Oct.–Dec. 1937): 143–47.

Cahn, L. M. "Why Federation of Charities Are Interested in Jewish Education" (1924). *NUJSS Proceedings* (1925): 264–67.

Chomsky, William. "The School and Community in Jewish Education." *Recon* (Mar. 3, 1944): 15–19.

Davis, Moshe. "Leadership Training Fellowship." *RA* (1946), 180–84. N.Y.: JTS, 1947.

Dinin, Samuel. "A Community System of Jewish Schools." *Recon* (Jan. 9, 1948): 9–15.

———. „התאחדויות מוסדות הצדקה שאלת הקהלה והחנוך" (The Federation—Questions on the Community and Education). *Hinukh* (H.) (Spring 1935): 4–7.

Dushkin, Alexander M. "The Community Principle in Jewish Education." *Jew Ed* 17 (Feb. 1946): 17–23.

———. "The Development of a Community Program in Jewish Education." *NCJSS Proceedings* (1927): 211–27.

———. "Essentials of a Community Program for Jewish Children." *Jew Ed* 6 (Oct.–Dec. 1934): 130–36.

———. „החנוך העברי והקהלה היהודית" (Hebrew Education and the Jewish Community). *Hadoar* (H.) 21 (Dec. 12, 1941): 83–84.

———. „יידישע דערציאונג—א געמיינשאפט־לעכע אויפגאבע" (Jewish Education—A Communal Responsibility). *Shulblatt* (Y.) (June 1946): 9–10.

Egelson, Louis I. "The Part of Laymen in the Promotion of Judaism." *CCAR* 38 (1928): 521–60.

Hartstein, Jacob I. "Jewish Community Parochial Elementary Schools." *Jew Ed* 9 (Oct.–Dec. 1937): 136–42.

Honor, Leo L. "Community Program for Jewish Education and Recreation: From the Point of View of the Jewish Educator." *NCJSW Proceedings*, 1937.

———. „תפקיד הקהלה בחנוך היהודי" (The Role of the Community in Jewish Education). *Sh Hah* (H.) 3 (Dec. 1942): 39–43.

Hyman, H. Joseph. "A Community Program for Jewish Education." *Jew Ed* 10 (Jan.–Mar. 1938): 25–27.

Jew Ed. "The Federation as the Vital Community Agency." Report of the Committee on Finances and Governmental Welfare Policies of the NCJFWF. 6 (Jan.–Mar. 1934): 14–19, 36.

JSSQ. "Jewish Community Organization from Standpoint of Federation, Jewish Education and the Jewish Center" (symposium). Participants: George Rabinoff, Emanuel Gamoran, and Louis Kraft. 11 (Sept. 1934): 72–75.

Kallen, Horace M. "Jewish Education and the Future of the American Jewish Community." *Jew Ed* 16 (Sept. 1944): 6–11.

Kohn, Eugene. "Foundations of a Cultural Program for the Jewish Community." *Jew Ed* 8 (Jan.–Mar. 1936): 12–28.

Magnes, Judah L. "Jewish Education and the Jewish Community, 1914–1915." *Jew Ed* (Winter 1949): 12–17

Margoshes, Samuel. "Public Opinion and Jewish Education." *Jew Ed* (Jan. 1929): 47–51. See also *Sh Hah* (H.) 4 (1929): 260–63.

Mizberg, I. D. "A Problem in Jewish Education." *Recon* (Dec. 8, 1939): 8–13.

Monsky, Henry. "Jewish Education Is a Community Responsibility." *Jew Ed* 10 (Oct.–Dec. 1938): 139–43.

Rappoport, Israel S. "Priorities in the Jewish Community." *Contemporary Jewish Record* 6 (Aug. 1943): 352–65.

Rosen, Ben. "Jewish Education—What Program Should the Jewish Community Support?" *Jew Ed* 9 (Jan.–Mar. 1937): 5–11.

———. "Programs of Communal Agencies for Jewish Education." *Jew Ed* 13 (Jan. 1942): 170–75.

Schoolman, Albert. "Jewish Education and the Jewish Community." *JSSQ* (1932): 39–43.

THE COMMUNITY AND JEWISH EDUCATION SINCE 1950

Abeles, Herbert R. "The Role of the Community in Meeting the Manpower Crisis in Jewish Education." *Jew Ed* 27 (Spring 1957): 31–34.

Ackerman, Walter I. "New Models of Jewish Education: Formal and Informal. What Learning Is Most Worth?" General Assembly, CJF, Nov. 1986. Also in *Jew Ed* 54 (Summer 1986): 3–7.

AJC. *Organization and Control of Jewish Education.* 1959.

Alper, Michael. "Current Unifying and Communal Tendencies in Jewish Education" (editorial). *Jew Ed* 23 (Winter 1952): 3–4.

Avrunin, William. "Jewish Education towards Relevance and Quality." (Remarks: Mannheim S. Shapiro, Elijah Bortniker, Marvin Fox, and

William B. Goldfarb. CJFWF, Dec. 1965. CP. 26 pp.

Azrieli, Shlomo. "The Child and the Jewish Community." *Jew Ed* 23 (Summer 1952): 2–3.

Baron, Salo W. "Transmitting and Enriching the Heritage of Judaism." (Assembly Paper, Nov. 1970) CP, 1972.

Bayme, Steven, and Adrianne Bank. "Urge Greater Jewish Education Accountability." *For* (E. section) (Apr. 10, 1987): 26, 32.

Bennett, Alan D. "The Community Stake in the Personnel Crisis." *Jew Ed* 55 (Fall 1987): 3–6. (Presented at a meeting of Bureau Executives and Federation Planners, GA *Quarterly*. New York, Sept. 13, 1987.)

Bennett, Daniel W. "A Community Day School Network." *Ped Rep* 34 (Jan. 1988): 13–16.

Berkson, Isaac B. "The Community Idea for Jewish Education." In *JER*, 59–67.

Bernstein, Elliot M. *Implications for Communities—Guidelines for Federation's Role in Planning and Financing Jewish Education.* CP, 1969. 7 pp.

Bernstein, Philip. "Jewish Education." In *To Dwell in Unity*, 107–23. 1983.

Brody, Arthur. *Workshop on Planning and Financing Jewish Education—Advance Report for Community Discussion.* Council of Federations, Nov. 1978.

Chanover, Hyman. "Community Planning for Commitment." In *Intrater*, 20–23.

Chipkin, Israel S. "Community Coordination of Jewish Schools." *Day* (Dec. 30, 1953).

Chomsky, William. "Communal Responsibility for Jewish Education." *Recon* (June 29, 1951): 24–27.

———. "Mutual Responsibilities of the School and Community in Jewish Education." *Jew Ed* 38 (Mar. 1968): 25–32.

CJFWF. *Breakdown of Allocations to Jewish Education by Classification.* 1973–74.

CJFWF. *Community Responsibility for Jewish Education.* Advance Report for Community Discussion. Nov. 13–16, 1958. 4 pp.

CJFWF. *Community Responsibility and Planning for Jewish Education—Discussion Outline.* CJFWF Advance Report for Community Discussion at 22nd General Assembly, Cleveland, Nov. 20–22, 1953. 2 pp.

CJFWF. *The Community School 1974: Status, Problems, and Potentials.* Mar. 1974. 7 pp.

CJFWF. *Federation Involvement in Upgrading Jewish Education.* Assembly Papers: Charles Froug and Donald Tranin. Nov. 1970. 7 pp.

CJFWF. *Federation's Role in Jewish Education.* Discussion Outline and Background, Nov. 1962. 6 pp.

CJFWF. *How Federations Are Planning and Acting to Improve Jewish Education.* Report for 32nd General Assembly, Oct. 1963. 3 pp.

CJFWF. *Is Jewish Education a Community Responsibility?* Symposium: Western States Regional Assembly, Phoenix, Jan. 11, 1958. 13 pp.

CJFWF. *Jewish Education: Current Problems and the Role of the Federation.* Advance Report for Discussion at the Two Workshops, Detroit, Nov. 10–13, 1960. 3 pp.

CJFWF. *Major Issues: The Organized Jewish Communities' Jewish Education.* Symposium, Georgia, Nov. 1963. Panel: Azriel Eisenberg, Isaac Toubin, and Louis L. Kaplan.

CJFWF. *National-Local Cooperation in Federation Planning for Jewish Education.* Panel: Mandell L. Berman, Sol Drachler, Abraham P. Gannes, Alvin I. Schiff, Morton Siegel, and Jack D. Spiro. CJFWF Dec. 1967. 9 pp.

CJFWF. *Resolution on Jewish Education Adopted by the 34th General Assembly.* Nov. 11–14. 1965.

Cohen, Jack J. "The Partners in Jewish Education." In *JEDS*, 117–63.

Cohen-Keiner, Andrea. "School As Community." *Ped Rep* 34 (Jan. 1988): 29–30.

Curtis, Jerome M. "Current Problems and the Role of the Federation." In *Jewish Education: Rethinking the Federation's Role.* CJFWF, Dec. 1960.

Diamond, Joseph. "Community Responsibility for Jewish Education." *Jew Ed* 31 (1960).

———. "For an Integrated Community School System." *J Jew Com Ser* 39 (Spring 1963): 313–19.

Dinin, Samuel. "Jewish Education, Jewish Culture and the Jewish Community" (editorial). *Jew Ed* 33 (Winter 1963): 67–69.

Dinsky, Samuel. *A Community Approach to Jewish Education*. CJF Assembly Papers (37), 1968.

Ducoff, Bernard. *New Programs in Jewish Education*. CJFWF, July 1971. 3 pp.

Duker, Abraham G. "The Community and Education." *Congress Weekly* (Jan. 8, 1951): 14–17.

Dushkin, Alexander M. "Changing Conceptions of Community Responsibility in Jewish Education." *Jew Ed* 26 (Spring 1956): 136–46.

———. "The Patterns of Community Thinking in Jewish Education." *Jew Ed* 35 (Spring 1965): 136–47.

Eisenstein, Ira. "A Community School for Teenagers." *Jew Ed* 33 (Spring 1963): 144–57. See also *MJET*, 38–44.

Elazar, Albert. "Community Organization in the Field of Jewish Education." *J Jew Com Ser* (Fall 1958): 93.

Elkin, Harry. "Comments on 'Community Responsibility for Jewish Education'." *Jew Ed* 31 (Fall 1960): 44–45.

Engelman, Uriah Z. "Community Responsibility for Jewish Education." In *AJHE*, 177–200.

Feinstein, Sara. "Jewish Education—A Federation Perspective." *J Jew Com Ser* 54 (Spring 1978): 247–57.

Freeman, Julian. "The Role of the Community in Jewish Education." *Jew Ed* 22 (Summer 1951): 13–18.

Froug, Charles. "Federation Involvement in Upgrading Jewish Education" (assembly paper) (Nov. 1970). CP, 1972.

Gannes, Abraham P. "Community Responsibility for Jewish Education in the United States." In *Intrater*, 24–27.

———. "I Believe in the Community Idea." *Jew Ed* 50 (Fall 1982): 16–20.

———. "Needs in Jewish Education as Reflected in Recent Community Studies." *Jew Ed* 44 (Summer 1975): 42–49, 59.

———. "Reflections on the Community Idea in Jewish Education." *Jew Ed* 40 (Spring 1971): 26–35.

Garvett, Morris. "Community Responsibility for Jewish Education." CJFWF, 1954.

Goldstein, Israel. "Jewish Education—A Community Responsibility." *Day* (Feb. 3, 1966).

Goodman, Nathaniel. "Consultative Casework Service in an Afternoon Hebrew School." *J Jew Com Ser* (Dec. 1968): 170.

Gordon, Samuel. "The School, the Synagogue and the Community." *Syn Sch* 8 (Feb. 1950): 7–12.

Greenberg, Simon. "Jewish Education and Jewish Welfare Funds." *Un Syn Rev* 20 (Jan. 1968): 10. See also *Syn Sch* 26 (Winter 1968): 4–12.

Gurin, Arnold. *Community Planning: Jewish Education, Recreation, and Cultural Services*. N.Y.: CP, May 1957. 8 pp.

Heller, Robert I. "Jewish Education—Community Planning and Financing." In *Jewish Education: Rethinking the Federation's Role*. CJFWF, Dec. 1960.

Horn, Susan. "Communal Funding as a Qualitative Educational Tool." *Jew Ed* 55 (Spring 1987): 27–35, 41.

*———. *Communal Responsibility for Jewish Education: Concept and Application*. New York U., 1987.

Janowsky, Oscar. "Community Responsibility for Jewish Education." CJFWF, 1954.

———. "Jewish Education and the Community." *Congress Biweekly* (June 26, 1961): 35–37.

Jew Ed. "The Jewish Community School" (symposium). Participants: Meir Ben-Horin, Elijah Bortniker, Albert Elazar, William B. Lakritz, Joseph Diamond, Matthew Mosenkis, Edward A. Nudelman, Louis Schwartzman, and Harry L. Woll. 35 (Winter 1965): 67–95.

Jew Ed. "Jewish Education at the General Assembly of the Council of Jewish Federations." 54 (Summer 1986). Jewish education drop-in center sponsored by JESNA and the Conference of Jewish Educator Organizations. CJF and JESNA jointly issued mimeographed proceedings, compiled by Fradle Freidenreich. Articles include:

    Berkey, Jane, and Jack Meyers, "The Communal Role in Jewish Education in Communities without Central Agencies for Jewish Education," 23–26.

    Chanover, Hyman C, "The Communal Role on Jewish Education: The Bureau

Community Perspective," 8–10.

Frost, Shimon, "Developing an Approach to Jewish Federations and the CJF," 38–40.

Hyman, Robert S, "The Communal Role in Jewish Education: Federation Planning in a Small Community," 19–22.

Israel, Richard J., "The Context of Informal Education," 27–30.

Lauer, Chaim, "Future Models for Jewish Education," 15–18.

Schiff, Alvin I., "Jewish Education Arrives at the GA," 2.

Schiff, Gary, "Funding by Federations and Non-Federation Sources for Jewish Education," 31–37.

Spotts, Leon H., "A New Mission for Bureaus and Boards of Jewish Education," 11–14.

Joseph, Samuel K. "Pluralism in the Community." *Ped Rep* 34 (Jan. 1988): 31–32.

Kahn, Edward M. "Jewish Education—Current Problems and the Role of the Federation." In *Jewish Education: Rethinking the Federation's Role*. CJFWF, Dec. 1960.

Kaplan, Louis L. "Community Responsibility for Jewish Education." CJFWF, 1954.

———. "Jewish Education and the Community" *Jew Ed* 36 (Fall 1965): 5–16. Also *J Jew Com Ser* 42 (Summer 1966): 303–12.

Kelman, W. "On Funding Jewish Education." *Un Syn Rev* 23 (Spring 1970): 8–9.

Kobernick, Gerald. "Federations and Jewish Education" (San Diego General Assembly). *Jew Ed* 53 (Spring 1985): 2–5.

Kohanski, Alexander S. "Community Endeavor in Jewish Education." In *Lown*, 5–25.

Kosberg, J. Livingston. "Education and Culture." (Assembly Paper, Nov. 1971). CP, 1972

Levine, Eric. "The Concept of K'lal Yisrael." *Ped Rep* 34 (Jan. 1988): 5–9.

Levy, Beverly. "A Jewish Community's Compromise." *Compass* 10 (Spring/Summer 1988): 7, 25.

Mark, Yudel. „אידישע דערציאונג און אידישע געזעלשאפטלעכקייט" (Jewish Education and Jewish Community). *YK* (Y.) (Jan. 27, 1950): 9–12.

———. „די קהילה און די יידישע שול" (The Community and the Yiddish School). *CE* 32 (May 1962): 23–25.

Neusner, Jacob. "Jewish Education and Jewish Culture and the Jewish Welfare Fund." *Syn Sch* (Winter 1967): 6–56.

Olshansky, Bernard. "The Community Organization Component in Jewish Education." *J Jew Com Ser* (Mar. 1968): 271.

Pearlman, Ezekiel. "Jewish Education and the Community." *J Jew Com Ser* (June 1966): 313.

Perlmutter, Elsie, and Etta Soloshin. "How Social Work Helped Our School." *J Jew Com Ser* (Winter 1956): 193. See also *Jew Ed* 28 (Winter 1959): 38–41.

Pins, Arnulf M. "Professional Personnel in the Social Services of the Jewish Community." *AJYB* 64 (1963): 203–35.

Pollak, George. "AAJE's Role in Ironing out Community Problems in Jewish Education." *Ped Rep* 27 (Fall 1975): 32.

Rand, Baruch. "Jewish Education under Communal Auspices." *Jew Ed* 50 (Summer 1982): 18–23.

Recon. "Reinstating Jewish Education" (editorial). 16 (Jan. 26, 1951): 1–3.

Roseman, Saul. "Education and Culture." (Assembly Paper, Nov. 1971). CP, 1972.

Scharfstein, Zevi. „חינוך עברי—חובת הכלל" (Hebrew Education—Responsibility of the Community). *Hadoar* (H.) 39 (Nov. 30, 1959): 34.

———. „העם, הקהילה והחינוך" (The People, the Community and Education). *Hadoar* (H.) 42 (Sept. 6, 1963): 688–89.

Schiff, Alvin I. "Advocating for Jewish Education—A Heart-to-Heart Talk with Federation Leadership" (editorial). *Jew Ed* 55 (Winter 1988): 2–3.

———. "Communal Planning and Jewish Education." *Jew Ed* 44 (Spring/Summer 1976): 3–13.

———. "Funding Jewish Education—Whose Responsibility?" *Jew Ed* 42 (Summer 1973): 6–12.

Schulweis, Harold M. "The Public and Private Agenda in Jewish Education." *Ped Rep* 30 (Fall 1978).

Schwartzman, Louis. "Community Organization Component in Jewish Education." *J Jew Com Ser* 44 (Sept. 1968): 280–83.

Seligson, Isaac. "Community Organization in the Field of Jewish Education." *J Jew Com Ser* (Fall 1958): 87.

Shapiro, Max A. "The Religious School Cannot Stand Alone." *Jew Teach* 21 (May 1953): 14–15.

Silver, Abba Hillel. "Community Responsibility." *Day* (June 5, 1959).

Slesinger, Zalmen. "The Critical Lag in Community Commitment to Jewish Education." *Ped Rep* 17 (Mar. 1966).

———. "For a *U.J.A.* of Jewish Education: A Plan for Financing Jewish Education." *Jew Digest* 8 (June 1963): 1–7.

———. "Toward a Community Perspective of Jewish Education and the Jewish School." *Jew Fron* (Jan. 1977): 23–26.

———. "Toward a Contemporary and Community-Wide Perspective of Jewish Education and the Jewish School." *Jew Fron* 42 (Aug.–Sept. 1976): 20–25.

Smolar, Boris. „געמיינדע זארגען וועגן אידישער קולטור אין אמעריקע" (Communal Concerns about Jewish Culture in America). *For* (Y.) (Oct. 10, 1976).

Solender, Stephen D. "The Federation Role in Jewish Education." *Jew Ed* 51 (Summer 1983): 17–19.

Solender, Stephen D., Harry Barron, and Isaac Toubin. "National Programs for Jewish Commitment, Knowledge and Culture." *J Jew Com Ser* (June 1967).

Teller, Gerald A. "Community and Jewish Education." *Jew Ed* 53 (Spring 1985): 42–44.

Toubin, Isaac. "The Council of Jewish Federations Committee on Jewish Education—An Appraisal." *Jew Ed* 37 (Spring 1967): 99–103.

Tranin, Donald. "Federation Involvement in Upgrading Jewish Education." (Assembly Paper, Nov. 1970). CP, 1972.

Vincent, Sidney Z. "Post Elementary Education." In *What Can Federation Do to Strengthen Jewish Education?*. Nov. 1966.

———. "Priorities and Planning for Jewish Education." *J Jew Com Ser* 48 (Fall 1971): 49–53.

Woocher, Jonathan S. "Education and Community: Toward a Program of Jewish Civic Education." *Ped Rep* 34 (Jan. 1988): 1–4.

Yapko, Benjamin L. "Jewish Social Service Agencies and the Jewish School." *J Jew Com Ser* (Dec. 1968): 165.

Zeltzer, George M. "National Planning for Jewish Education and Culture" (General Assembly, 1975). N.Y.: CP. 6 pp.

Zibbell, Charles. "Federations and Jewish Education." *Jew Ed* 38 (Oct. 1968): 31–35.

———. "Federations and Jewish Education." *J Jew Com Ser* 50 (Fall 1973): 50–57.

Zibbell, Charles, et al. *The Community Stake in Jewish Education* (General Assembly, 1972). N.Y.: CP. 16 pp.

THE SYNAGOGUE AND JEWISH EDUCATION

Arzt, Max. "Some Problems of the Congregational School." *RA* (1928): 143–47.

Berkson, Isaac B. "Communal and Congregational Schools." *Recon* 3 (June 11, 1937): 7–11.

Berkson, Isaac B., and Ben Rosen. "Is There Intrinsic Opposition between Congregational and Communal Schools?" *Jew Ed* 22 (Apr. 1940): 8–13.

Brickner, Barnett R. "Communal Responsibility of the Synagogue to Jewish Education." *Jew Ed* 3 (Oct.–Dec. 1931): 142–51.

CJF, AAJE. *Guidelines for Federation Support of Congregational Education*. Revised draft. April 1975.

Dashevsky, Arieh. „דאס פנים פון יידישן חנוך" (The Face of Jewish Education) (on the congregational school). *YK* (Y.) (Mar. 30, 1962): 5–8.

Ducoff, Bernard. "Synagogue Center and Bureau: Confrontation and Direction." *Con Jud* 16 (Winter/Spring 1962): 1–12.

Dushkin, Alexander M. "Congregation and Commmunity in Jewish Education." *Jew Ed* 1 (May 1929): 73–81.

Engelman, Uriah Z. "Unpopular Issues in Jewish Education." *Recon* 25 (Jan. 25, 1963): 6–10.

Essrig, Harry. "The Congregation as an Educational Enterprise." *CCAR J* (Jan. 1954): 32–37.

Feldman, Abraham J. "The Role of the Synagogue in the American Community." *RA* (1957): 190–98.

Gamoran, Emanuel. "The Communal Responsibility of the Synagogue to Jewish Education." *Jew Ed* 3 (Oct.–Dec. 1931): 135–41.

Greenberg, Simon. "The Conservative Movement and the Community." *Syn Sch* 23 (Summer 1965): 14–16.

Greenstone, Julius H. *The Congregational School in a System of Jewish Education.* N.Y.: 1937.

JESNA. *Suggested Guidelines on Communal Support for Congregational Schools, 1983.* N.Y.: April 13, 1983.

Katzoff, Adina. "Interaction of School and Sisterhood." *Syn Sch* 17 (Sept. 1958).

Katzoff, Louis. "The Conservative School and the Jewish Community." In *Issues*, 96–106.

Krug, Mark M. "The Bureau of Jewish Education and the Congregational Schools." *Jew Ed* 21 (Winter 1949): 52–56.

Lehman, Emil. "Synagogue Leadership and the Congregational Schools." *Jew Ed* 26 (Fall 1955): 24–29, 56.

Lieber, David. "The Conservative Congregational School." *Con Jud* 46 (Spring 1978): 13–21.

Millgram, Abraham E. *Handbook for the Congregational School Board Member.* N.Y.: USCJE, 1953. 107 pp.

———. "Next Steps for the Congregational School." *Syn Sch* 16 (Dec. 1957): 3–8.

Pilch, Judah. "The Role of the Synagogue School." *Syn Sch* 18 (1960).

Schiff, Alvin I. "The Synagogue and the Jewish Supplementary School." *Jew Ed* 46 (Spring 1978): 13–21.

Schindler, Alexander M. "Bureau-Congregational Relationship." *Jew Teach* 33 (Feb. 1965): 2, 31–32.

Schwartz, Elliot S. "Bureau-Synagogue Relationships through Funding." *Jew Ed* 49 (Spring 1981): 19–22.

Siegel, Morton, and Pesach Schindler. *Manual for Congregational School Board Members.* N.Y.: USCJE, 1973. 160 pp.

Spiro, Jack D. "Congregational Lifestyles and Their Educational Offspring." *NATE Proceedings* (1972): 37–46.

UAHC. "Commission on Jewish Education Promotes Communal Cooperation in New Policy Statement" *Compass* (Mar. 1969): 1–3.

Wachs, Saul P. "The Congregational School: Crisis of Identity." *Impact* 35 (Winter 1966–67).

Weisband, Howard. "A Study of Federation-Synagogue Relations as Related to Inter-Organizational Analysis." Master's thesis, HUC–JIR, 1975.

Zibbell, Charles. "Federations, Synagogues, and Jewish Education in the '70'S" *Jew Ed* 43 (Fall 1974): 40–45.

LAY LEADERSHIP AND JEWISH EDUCATION

Abrams, William. "A Challenge and an Opportunity." *Ped Rep* 34 (Mar. 1983): 14.

Barkan, Irving. "The Parent-Teacher Council Plan of Organization." *Syn Sch* 11 (Sept. 1952): 13–15.

Bernstein, Philip. "The American Association for Jewish Education, Jewish Education, and the Community." *Jew Ed* 29 (Spring 1959): 27–34.

Borowitz, Eugene B. " 'Tzimtzum': A Mystic Model for Contemporary Leadership." *Rel Ed* 69 (Nov.–Dec. 1974): 687–700.

Botwinick, Chaim Y. "Human Resource Planning for Jewish Education: A Challenge to Jewish Leadership." *Jew Ed* 54 (Fall 1986): 42–45.

———. "Lay Leadership and Accountability." *Ped Rep* 36 (Sept. 1985): 23–25.

Charry, Elias. "The Class Mother's Group Organization." *Syn Sch* 11 (Sept. 1952): 15–18.

Chipkin, Israel S. "The American Association for Jewish Education" (editorial). *Jew Ed* 13 (Jan. 1942): 146.

———. *Planning for American Jewish Education*. N.Y.: AAJE, 1946.

Cohen, Burton I. "Leadership Development Programs in the Conservative Movement—A Response." *MJ* 16 (Spring/Summer 1983): 20–21.

Duker, Abraham G. "Historical and Sociological Factors in Jewish Communal Leadership." *JSS* 17 (1955): 183–92.

Eisenberg, Azriel. "An Experience with a Parent Association and an Adult Group." *Jew Ed* 3 (Apr.–June 1931): 91–95.

Eisner, Mark. "An American Association for Jewish Education." *Jew Ed* 11 (Sept. 1939): 90, 104.

Elazar, Daniel J. *The Role of Voluntary Leadership in Jewish Education*. Jerusalem: World Leadership Conference for Jewish Education, 1984. 13 pp.

Elfenbaum, Esther. "The Role of the Community in Nursery Education." *Ped Rep* 31 (Spring 1980).

Engelman, Uriah Z. "A Study of Parent-Teacher Groups." *Jew Ed* 21 (Summer 1950): 43–47.

Finkelstein, Hayim. (American Association for Jewish Education). *Sh Hah* (H.) 31 (Spring 1971): 152–62.

Fishman, Joshua A. *The Attitude of Jewish Community Leaders toward Current American Jewish Education*. Phila.: U. of Pennsylvania, Albert M. Greenfield Center for Human Relations, 1959.

Frost, Shimon. "JESNA: The Catalyst for Lay Leadership in Jewish Education." *Ped Rep* 34 (Mar. 1983): 10.

Goldberg, Henry. "A Year-Round Program for the PTA." *Syn Sch* 11 (Sept. 1952): 3–9.

Goldman, Sylvia. "Is Your PTA a Success?" *Jew Teach* 20 (May 1952): 19–22. Also in *Ped Rep* 4 (Nov. 1952).

———. "PTA Is Everyone's Business." *Jew Teach* 22 (Mar. 1954): 6–7.

Grad, Eli. "Lay Leadership of Education as Viewed by the Professional." *Syn Sch* 18 (Sept. 1959).

Hartstein, Jacob I. "Preparation for Jewish Leadership in Yeshiva University." *Jew Ed* 21 (Spring 1950): 61–63.

Institute for Jewish Life. *Fellowships in Jewish Educational Leadership*. 1973. 8 pp.

Jew Ed. "Perceptions of Bureau Executives Concerning the Future Role of the American Association for Jewish Education." Participants: Alan Bennett, Hyman Chanover, Gene Greenzweig, Daniel Isaacman, Samuel Schafler, Irwin Witty, and AAJE staff. 47 (Summer 1979): 22–27.

Joint Committee, NJWB and AAJE, *Recommendations on Jewish Education for Youth*. Jan. 1951.

Joseph, Aaron. "Lay Leaders with Vision: Termed Key to Better Jewish Education." *Jewish Week* (Aug. 23, 1985).

Kallen, Horace M. "American Association for Jewish Education and Jewish Education." *Jew Ed* 29 (Spring 1959): 21–26.

Kurzband, Toby, and Howard Levinson. "The PTA—A Necessary Part of the Religious School." *Jew Teach* 18 (Jan. 1950): 1–5.

* Levitats, Isaac. *Jewish Boards of Education in America*. Syracuse U., 1953. 323 pp.

———. "Jewish School Boards in America." *Jew Ed* 25 (Summer 1954): 28–34, 57.

———. "Jewish School Boards—A Comparative Study." *J Jew Com Ser* (Winter 1957): 205.

Lister, Louis, and Rebecca Lister. *The Religious School Board: A Manual*. N.Y.: UAHC. c. 1978. 109 pp.

Lown, P. W. "A Significant Anniversary" (AAJE–20 years). *Jew Ed* 29 (Spring 1959): 7–8.

Meyer, H. Jack., Fradle Freidenreich, and Theodor Comet. *Major Issues in Jewish Education: A Leadership Development Training Program Manual*. 2d ed. N.Y.: CJF National Committee on Leadership Development and JESNA Department of Pedagogic Services, 1984.

Miller, Norman. "Changing Patterns of Leadership in the Jewish Community." *JSS* 17 (July 1955): 179–82.

Musher, Ruth Weiss. "Volunteer Leadership." *Ped Rep* 34 (Mar. 1983): 12–13.

Nemzoff, Samuel A. "Look, Listen, Learn—A PTA Program." *Jew Teach* 28 (Jan. 1960): 14–15.

Penn, Ascher. „די אמעריקאנער אסאסיאציע פאר אידישער דערציאונג און איר טעטיקייט איבערן גאנצן לאנד" (The AAJE and Its Activities throughout the Land). In *Penn* (Y.), 222–38.

Pilch, Judah. "The Development of the AAJE and Its Program." *Jew Ed* 29 (Spring 1959): 9–20.

———. „תולדותיה של החברה האמריקנית למען החנוך העברי באמריקה" (History of the American Association for Jewish Education). *Sh Hah* (H.) 26 (Summer 1966): 205–17.

———. "Lay Participation in Jewish Education." *Jew Ed* 27 (Fall 1956): 43–46.

Rosen, Ben. "American Association for Jewish Education." *Jew Ed* 15 (Jan. 1944): 64–69.

Saretsky, Augusta. "An Effective Educational Instrument—the PTA." Address given at NCJE Conference, May 1954.

———. "Growth through Parent Education." *Jew Ed* 33 (Oct. 1964): 11–16.

———. "Parent-Teacher Association—A Force in Jewish Education." *Jew Teach* 18 (May 1950): 7–12.

Schiff, Alvin I. "A National Jewish Education Agency: Communal Perspectives" (study of the AAJE). *Jew Ed* 46 (Fall 1978): 19–25.

Schlussel, Mark E. "Jewish Education in Transition—A Layman's View." *Jew Ed* 50 (Spring 1982): 22–27, 36.

Schwartz, Elkhanan. "Yeshiva Graduates as Yeshiva Leaders." *Jew Parent* 16 (Jan. 1965): 6–9

Seman, Philip. "American Association for Jewish Education." In *Southwest Jewry*, edited by J. L. Malamut, 3:41–42. 1957.

Shabatay, Y. "Involving Laymen in the Decision Making Process." *Jew Ed* 43 (Fall 1974): 48–55.

Shoulson, Bruce D. "The Role of the Layman." *Ped Rep* 34 (Mar. 1983): 11–12.

Silverman, Hillel. "Relationship with Staff and Laymen." *RA* (1972).

Slesinger, Zalmen. "Jewish Education: A Crisis in Orientation and Educational Leadership." *Jew Fron* 42 (Aug.–Sept. 1975): 34–35, 37, 39, 41–42.

———. "Lay Involvement in Jewish Education." *Ped Rep* 22 (Dec. 1970): 9–12.

Stein, Louise S. "The Role of the School Board." *Ped Rep* 36 (Sept. 1985): 21–23.

Well, Harvey A. "The Challenge to Lay Leadership." *Jew Ed* 51 (Spring 1983): 43–44, 48.

Wolf, Edwin, II. "Leadership in the American Jewish Community." In *Jan 3*, 363–71.

Wolf, Larry M. "Observations on Lay-Professional Relationships." *Ped Rep* 34 (Mar. 1983): 15–16.

Woocher, Jonathan, and Daniel Elazar. *Jewish Community and Leadership: Issues and Historical Perspectives*. N.Y.: CP, 1983.

FINANCIAL SUPPORT FOR JEWISH EDUCATION PRIOR TO 1950

AAJE. *Budgeting and Financing of Central Agencies for Jewish Education, Parts I and II*. N.Y., 1949.

AAJE. *Community Allocations for Jewish Education*. N.Y., 20 pp.

AAJE, *Community Responsibility for Jewish Education*. N.Y., 1940, 1945. 25 pp.

AAJE. *Financing and Budgeting of Central Agencies of Jewish Education*. N.Y., 45 pp.

Assembly of the Jewish Theological Seminary. "Open Letter to Federations and Congregations" (regarding communal financial support for Jewish education). *Jew Ed* 4 (Oct.–Dec. 1932): 129–30.

Benderly, Samson. "Can a System of Jewish Education Be Self-Supporting?" *Jewish Teacher* 1 (Dec. 1917): 204–10.

Cedarbaum, David I. "Extent and Cost of Jewish Education in the United States." *Jew Ed* 1 (Jan. 1929): 52–55.

Chipkin, Israel S., and Ben Rosen. "Probable Trends in Costs and Income of Jewish Schools." *Jew Ed* 5 (Apr.–June 1933): 115–26.

Dushkin, Alexander M. "The Jewish Charities and Jewish Education." *Jew Ed* 3 (Jan.–Mar. 1931): 10–19.

Engelman, Uriah Z. "Federation Subvention for Jewish Education." *Jew Ed* 20 (Feb. 1949): 44–47.

Gamoran, Emanuel. "Jewish Education and the Economic Depression." 31st Annual Convention of the RA. *RA* (1930–32): 204–10.

Ginzberg, Sh. "מה לעשות?" (What Is To Be Done?). On the economic crisis and Jewish Education. *Hadoar* (H.) 11 (7th of Iyyar, 13th of Sivan, and 25th of Tammuz 1932).

Golub, Jacob S. "The Responsibility of Federation to Jewish Education." *Jew Ed* 4 (Jan.–Mar. 1932): 18–25.

Rosen, Ben. "The Effect of the Economic Depression upon Jewish Educational Institutions." *Jew Ed* 3 (Jan.–Mar. 1931): 4–9.

———. *Existing Practice in Community Support for Jewish Education*. N.Y.: AAJE.

———. "The Relationship of Federation of Charities to Jewish Education." *Jew Ed* 4 (Apr.–June 1932): 71–75, 80.

———. "Supplementary Statement on the Effect of Economic Depression upon the Communities' Educational Institutions and Suggestions for Dealing with the Situation." *Jew Ed* 3 (Oct.–Dec. 1931): 156–63.

Scharfstein, Zevi. "על המשבר" (On the Crisis-Impact of Depression on Jewish Education). *Hadoar* (H.) 11 (12th of Adar A' 1932). See also *Hadoar* (April 16, 30, 1943).

Schoolman, Albert. "Education and Philanthropy." *Jew Ed* 4 (Oct.–Dec. 1932): 131–38.

———. "School, Community Center and Federation." *Jew Ed* 5 (Oct.–Dec. 1933): 147–51, 155.

Silver, Abba Hillel. "The Relation of the Depression to Cultural and Spiritual Values of American Jewry." *Jew Ed* 4 (Oct.–Dec. 1932): 148–49.

FINANCIAL SUPPORT FOR JEWISH EDUCATION SINCE 1950

Alper, M. "Jewish Education and Jewish Communal Budgets." *Jew Ed* 21 (Spring 1950): 2.

AAJE. *Federation Allocations for Jewish Education, 1936–1951*. Prepared by Engelman, Uriah Z., and C. Morris Horowitz. N.Y., AAJE, 1952.

———. *Economic Status of Jewish Educational Personnel*. N.Y., 1956.

———. *Why a Pension Program for Teachers and Administrators?* N.Y., 1957.

———. *Budgeting and Financing of Central Agencies for Jewish Education*. Prepared by Chanover, Hyman, and Leon Spotts. N.Y., 1968. 35 pp.

———. *Long Term Trends in Federation and Chest Allocations for Local Jewish Agencies and Federation Allocations for Jewish Education*. Information Bulletin no. 26. N.Y., 1962. 45 pp.

———. *Budgeting and Financing of Central Agencies*. Information Bulletin no. 27. Prepared by Engelman, Uriah Z. N.Y., 1963.

———. *Communal Financing of Local Jewish Education—Three Decades, 1936–1966*. Prepared by Chanover, Hyman, and C. Morris Horowitz. N.Y., 1966.

———. *National Policy Statement on Communal Support for Jewish Education*. N.Y., June 1968.

———. *A Study on Tuition Fees and Related Matters*. N.Y., 1968.

———. *Community Grants to Local Jewish Schools*. Information Bulletin no. 31. N.Y., 1969. 80 pp.

———. Hochberg, Hillel, and Gerhard Lang. *Tuition Fee Scales and Policies in Jewish Schools*. N.Y., 1972.

———. *Budget and Financing of Central Agencies for Jewish Education*. N.Y., 1978.

———. *Tuition Fee Scales and Policies in Jewish Schools, 1978–1979*. Information Bulletin no. 43. N.Y., June 1979. 34 pp.

Chanover, H. "Translating the Economic Needs of the Jewish Education Profession into Reality." *Jew Ed* 32 (Fall 1961): 34–39.

———. *Patterns of Financing Jewish Education*. (37th GA, Nov. 13–19, 1968.) CJFWF, CP, 1968. 23 pp.

Council of Jewish Federations, American Association for Jewish Education, *Recommendations Made by the Large City Budgeting Conference on the Basis of a Program and Budget, Council Reports-Budgeting*. N.Y.: CJFWF, CP, May 1951. 9 pp. See also *Jew Ed* 22 (Summer 1951): 78.

———. *Federation Financing of Jewish Education as Related to Total Federation Campaign: Results and Allocations, 1955–1962* (statistical data). N.Y.: CP, May 1964.

———. *Federation Allocations to Jewish Education, 1964–1974*. N.Y.: CJFWF, Dec. 3, 1975.

———. *Federation Allocations to Jewish Education, 1966–1976: A Ten Year Analysis of Federation Support to the Field of Jewish Education*. N.Y.: CJF, Nov. 1977. 48 pp.

———. *Federation Allocations to Jewish Education, 1978*. N.Y.: CJF.

———. *Federation Allocations to Jewish Education*. N.Y.: CJF, Dec. 1982.

Donin, Hayim. "On Funding for Jewish Values and Commitments." *Jew Parent* 22 (Jan. 1971): 13–14.

Federman, Allan, comp. *Federation Allocations to Jewish Education, 1973–1977*. N.Y.: CJF, Nov. 1978. 27 pp.

———. *Federation Allocations to Jewish Education, 1974–1978*. N.Y.: CJF, Dec. 1979. 35 pp.

JESNA. *Allocations to Jewish Education*. Dec. 1982.

———. *Budgeting and Financing in Jewish Supplementary Schools*. N.Y.: JESNA, June 1983. 60 pp.

Large City Budgeting Conference. "Resolutions by Large City Budgeting Conference." *Jew Ed* 22 (Summer 1951): 77.

Margolis, Henry M. "The Economics of Jewish Education." *Jew Ed* 45 (Winter 1977): 16–19, 38.

Pilch, Judah. "Discussions on Jewish Education" (finance, personnel, etc.). *Jew Fron* (Apr. 1975): 19–26.

Pollak, George. "On Subsidies to Congregational Schools." *Jew Ed* 49 (Spring 1981): 16–18.

Rosenbaum, Jonathan. "Allocation Formulae: A New Solution." *Jew Ed* 52 (Spring 1984): 16–18, 22.

Schiff, Alvin I. "Responding to Budgetary Challenges" (editorial). *Jew Ed* 43 (Fall 1981): 1–2.

———. "Student Recruitment and Educational Funding." *Jew Ed* 51 (Summer 1983): 12–17.

* Skoff, Benson. *Tax Funds for Jewish Education: Presentation and Analysis of Various Jewish Views, 1947–1974*. Washington U., 1975. 389 pp.

Slesinger, Zalmen. "Financing Jewish Education—A Proposal." *Recon* 289 (Jan. 25, 1963): 10–15.

Smolar, Boris. „אידישע דערציאונג אין אמעריקע קאסט 250 מיליאן דאלאר א יאר" (Jewish Education Costs $250 Million a Year). *For* (Y.) (Nov. 2, 1975).

Spiegler, S. "Jewish School Costs." *J Jew Com Ser* 59 (Spring 1983).

Spotts, Leon H. "Funding Jewish Education in the Mid-Seventies." In *Intrater*, 28–32.

THE RATIONALE FOR CENTRAL AGENCIES OF JEWISH EDUCATION

AAJE. *Central Agencies of Jewish Education*. Prepared by Hyman Chanover. N.Y.: 1966.

———. *Central Organization of Jewish Education—A Statement of Purpose, Aims and Functions*. N.Y.: AAJE, May 27, 1967. 5 pp. mimeo.

———. *Central Agencies for Jewish Education Functions and Services*. Pollak, George.

Information Bulletin no. 47. N.Y.: AAJE, 1981. 51 pp.

Chanover, Hyman. "Central Organization of Jewish Education—A Concept and Mechanism." *Jew Ed* 35 (Summer 1965): 217–30.

Dinin, Samuel. "Central Agencies for Jewish Education." *Jew Ed* (Winter 1960): 3–16.

———. "The Role of the Central Agency in the Improvement of Jewish Education." *Jew Ed* (Summer 1975): 28–35.

Dinsky, Samuel H. *Functions of a Central Agency for Jewish Education*. N.Y.: AAJE, June 1969. 3 pp.

* Gannes, Abraham P. *Central Community Agency for Jewish Education*. Dropsie University, 1954. 300 pp. See also "The Forces Which Led to the Establishment of the Central Educational Agency," 1–28, chapters 7 and 8, and the appendix.

Honor, Leo L. "Aims and Objectives of the Bureau of Jewish Education." In *Proceedings of the Conference of Jewish Education and Center Work*. N.Y.: AAJE and NJWB, 1946.

———. "The Function of a Community Agency for Jewish Education." *Reg* (1951): 58–63.

———. "Functions of the Central Agency in a Community Program of Jewish Education." *Reform Advocate* (Apr. 16, 1937).

———. "תפקידה של לשכת החנוך בתכנית הקהילה" (The Role of the Bureau of Education in the Community). In *Yesod* (H.), 165–82.

JESNA, *Governance of Central Agencies for Jewish Education*. Research Information Bulletin no. 56. N.Y., Jan. 1984.

Levitats, Isaac. "ביוראען פאר יידישער דערציאונג" (Bureaus for Jewish Education). *YB* (Y.) 26 (Sept.–Oct. 1945): 20–36. See also *DER* (Y.), 1:456–63.

Rosen, Ben. "Efforts and Tendencies in Four Types of Communal Organization: Bureaus of Jewish Education." *NCJSS Proceedings*. 1923.

Winter, Nathan H. "An Early Educational Blueprint for the Jewish School." (Samson Benderly's Concept for a Central Jewish Educational Agency.) In *Jewish Education in a Pluralist Society*, 47–57. 1966.

ASSESSING CENTRAL EDUCATIONAL AGENCIES AND NEW NEEDS

AAJE, *Bureau and Congregational School Relationships*. N.Y., 1950. Also in *CA*, 231–33.

Arian, Philip. "Structuring a New Bureau for the '70's." *Jew Ed* 42 (Winter 1972–73): 34–37.

AAJE and USCJE. *Report of Findings on the Relationships between Central Agencies of Jewish Education and Parochial (All Day) Schools in America*. Prepared by David Rudavsky. N.Y.: AAJE Department of Research, Information and Publications, 1945.

Ben-Horin, Meir. "Ebbtide in Jewish Education." *Jew Fron* (July 1985): 18–20, 25–26.

Bennett, Alan D. "Central Agency Responsibility to the Community." *Jew Ed* 53 (Summer 1985): 6–8.

Bortniker, Elijah. "The Community Office of Jewish Education in the Mid Sixties." *Jew Ed* 35 (Spring 1965): 166–75. Includes reactions from Walter I. Ackerman, Samuel M. Blumenfield, Abraham P. Gannes, Alexander Schindler, Isaac Toubin, and Charles Zibbell, pp. 176–95.

Chanover, Hyman. "Seventy-Five Years Later: Issues Confronting Central Agencies for Jewish Education." *J Jew Com Ser* 63 (Fall 1986).

Gannes, Abraham P. "Boards of Bureaus of Jewish Education." *Jew Ed* 26 (Summer 1955): 32–39.

———. "לשכת החנוך בהתפתחותה" (The Development of the Bureau of Jewish Education). *Sh Hah* (H.) 17 (Fall 1957): 3–9.

———. "Jewish Communal Education at Fifty." *Recon* (Jan. 13, 1961): 7–12.

———. "ששים שנה של אחריות קהילתית לחינוך היהודי" (Sixty Years of Communal Responsibility for Jewish Education). In *Scharfstein* (H.), 146–52.

Horowitz, A. L. "יחס גומלין בין לשכות החנוך ובין בתי-הספר" (Mutual Relationships between Offices of Education and Schools). *Sh Hah* (H.) 11 (Mar. 1951): 67–78.

Jew Ed. "Key Challenges the Local Agencies for Jewish Education Should Address in the

Coming Decade." 44 (Summer 1975): 50–59. Participants: Hyman Chanover, Jack D. Spiro, Louis Schwartzman, Emanuel Rackman, Eli Grad, Edward T. Sandrow, Isaac Toubin, and Sidney Z. Vincent.

Laver, H. C. "Perspectives in Jewish Education." *J Jew Com Ser* 61 (Winter 1984): 144–47.

Lipnick, Bernard. "An Organic Peer Community in Jewish Teen-Age Education." *Jew Ed* 43 (Winter/Spring 1975): 38–41, 45.

Mann, David. "Informal Jewish Education and the Bureau." *Jew Ed* 48 (Fall 1980): 9–15.

National Council for Jewish Education. "The Role of the Central Agency for Jewish Education" (symposium). Participants: Meir Ben-Horin, Elijah Bortniker, Joseph Diamond, Albert Elazar, William B. Lakritz, Matthew Mosenkis, Edward A. Nudelman, Louis Schwartzman, and Harry A. Woll. *Jew Ed* 35 (Spring 1965): 67–95.

Pearlman, Ezekiel. "The Jewish Educator in the Jewish Communal Planning Process." *Jew Ed W* (Fall 1979): 44–48.

Ped Rep. "Increasing the Effectiveness of Our Public Relations Program." 15 (Sept. 1963): 9–10.

Pollak, George. "The Changing Central Agencies for Jewish Education." *Jew Ed* 44 (Summer 1975): 36–41.

Rand, Baruch. "The Central Agency for Jewish Education: Responsibility to the Learner." *Jew Ed* 53 (Summer 1985): 9–16.

———. "The Challenge of a Communal Educational System in Small and Middle Size Communities." *Jew Ed* 47 (Summer 1979): 35–37, 41.

———. "Dynamics of Communal Cooperation" (includes adult education). *Jew Ed* 48 (Fall 1980): 4–8, 48.

Rudavsky, David. "After Fifty Years: Spotlight on Five Central Agencies for Jewish Education." *Jew Ed* 44 (Summer 1975): 6–8.

Samber, Moshe. "Bureau Sets Tone for Raising the Status of Family Education." *Ped Rep* 30 (Fall 1978).

Schafler, Samuel. "The Central Agency for Jewish Education: Educating for Family Responsibility." *Jew Ed* 53 (Summer 1985): 17–20.

Scharfstein, Zevi. "השפעה מרכזית בחינוך" (Communal Influence Upon Education). *Hadoar* (H.) 40 (25th of Sivan 1961).

———. "פזור וריכוז בבית הספר העברי באמריקה" (Decentralization and Centralization in the Jewish Schools in America). In *ES* (H.), 110–14.

Schwartz, Elliot. "The Central Agency and Educational Responsibility to the Learner, Family and Community." *Jew Ed* 53 (Summer 1985): 5.

Shapiro, Jack. "Bureau Personnel as Agents for Change." *Jew Ed* 48 (Summer 1980): 47–49.

Skolnick, Irving H. "Upgrading School and Bureau Effectiveness through Service Agreements." *Jew Ed* 47 (Fall 1979): 22–27, 35.

Spotts, Leon H. "Fiscal Efficiency of Central Agencies for Jewish Education." *Jew Ed* 49 (Winter 1981): 23–29.

———. "Funding Relationships between Bureaus and Federation." *Jew Ed* 47 (Spring 1979): 14–22.

WOMEN AND JEWISH EDUCATION IN THE UNITED STATES

(*See also chapters 23 and 33*)

Daum, Annette. "Sexism in Jewish Religious Education." *Jew Fron* 50 (Oct. 1983): 12–16.

Klein, Aaron. "Now There Are Girls in Our Religious School." *Syn Sch* 13 (Dec. 1954): 10–14.

Levitats, Isaac. "Girls in Our Weekly Schools." *Syn Sch* 17 (Sept. 1958): 10–13.

Malin, Harry. "Increasing the Enrollment of Girls." *Syn Sch* 13 (Dec. 1954): 8–9.

Rosen, Gladys. "Teaching about the Role of Women." *Ped Rep* 32 (Fall 1980): 27–30.

Schneider, Susan Weidman. "Battling Sexism in Jewish Schools." *Lilith* 10 (Winter 1982–83): 18–22.

———. "Women and Jewish Education." *Women's American ORT Reporter* (Sept.–Oct. 1979): 13–14.

Shapiro, Miriam Klein. "Eliminating Sexism from Jewish Education." *Jew Ed* 48 (Spring 1980): 42–44.

Shevitz, Susan R. "Sexism in Jewish Education." *Response* 18 (Summer 1973): 107–13.

Stein, Jacob. "Jewish Education for Our Daughters—A Layman's View." *Syn Sch* 14 (May 1956): 7–12.

Tzemnon, Tsemach. "האשה בחנוך ובהוראה„ (The Woman in Education and in Instruction). *Sh Hah* (H.) 35 (1975): 30–37.

WOMEN AND THE RABBINATE IN THE COMMUNITY

Aronson, L. J. "Women in the Minyan And in the Rabbinate." *Jew Spec* 49 (Winter 1984): 56–57.

Cohen, Elaine Shizgal. "Women Rabbinical Students Reflect on Their Calling." *MJ* 22 (Fall 1987): 6–9.

Cohen, Gerson D. "On the Ordination of Women." *Con Jud* 32 (Summer 1979): 56–62.

Fox, Karen L. "Whither Women Rabbis?" *Rel Ed* 76 (July–Aug. 1981).

Freidman, Reena Sigman. "The Politics of Women's Ordination." *Lilith* 6 (1979): 9–15.

———. "Women in the Rabbinate: A Moment of Real Change." *Jew Fron* 49 (Jan. 1982): 12–16.

Gordis, Robert. "The Ordination of Women." *Mid* 26 (Aug.–Sept. 1980): 25–32. See also *Mid* 27 (Apr. 1981): 60–64.

———. "The Ordination of Women—A History of the Question." *Jud* 33 (Winter 1984): 6–12. (Entire issue is on women as rabbis.)

Greenberg, Simon. *The Ordination of Women as Rabbis: Studies and Responsa*. New York: JTSA, 1988. 223 pp.

Lerner, Anne Lapidus. "In God's Image Was Humanity Created." *Jud* 33 (Winter 1984): 34–38.

Perlmutter, Fishel A. "The Case for Women Rabbis." *Jud* 33 (Winter 1984): 50–53.

Rackman, Emanuel. "Suggestions for Alternatives." *Jud* 33 (Winter 1984): 66–69.

Sasso, Sandy Eisenberg. "Women in the Rabbinate: A Personal Reflection." *Recon* (Mar. 1984): 18–20.

Seidler-Feller, Chaim. "Female Rabbis: Male Fears." *Jud* 33 (Winter 1984): 13–20.

Zola, Garry P. "JTS, HUC and Women Rabbis." *RJ* 31 (Fall 1984): 39–45.

THE JEWISH CENTER AND OTHER COMMUNAL AGENCIES RELATED TO JEWISH EDUCATION

AAJE and NJWB. *Conference on Jewish Education and Center Work*. N.Y., ca. 1947.

Abrams, Percy. "The Role of the 'Y' in Formal and Informal Jewish Education." *J Jew Com Ser* 43 (Summer 1967).

* Banchefsky, Howard S. *An Analysis of the Differential In-Service Training Needs of New Bachelor Degree Workers in the Jewish Center Field*. Ohio State U., 1976. 168 pp.

Berger, Graenum. *The Jewish Community Center: A Fourth Force in America*. N.Y.: JEC Press, 1966. 344 pp.

Bubis, Gerald. "Today's Role of the Jewish Community Center in Jewish Education." *J Jew Com Ser* 49 (Fall 1972): 48–57.

Dinin, Samuel. "What Is a Jewish Community Center School?" *Jew Ed* 23 (Summer 1952): 9–10, 36.

Divinsky, Oscar, Ben M. Edidin, Julian Greifer, and Mordecai Soltes. "The Jewish School in the Community Center." *Jew Ed* 11 (Apr. 1939): 29–39.

Dubin, David. "Jewish Education in the Jewish Community Center." *J Jew Com Ser* 61 (Fall 1984): 64–69.

Elwell, Sue Levi. "The Jewish Community Center as a Primary Vehicle for Jewish Education in Contemporary America." Master's thesis, Brandeis U., 1972.

Freeman, Samuel D. "Adult Jewish Education in the Jewish Community Center." *Jew Ed* 25 (Summer 1954): 22–27, 59.

* ———. *The Adult Program of the Jewish Community Center in the United States*. Columbia U., 1953. 191 pp.

———. "The Adult Program of the Jewish Community Center in the United States." *Jew J Soc* 5 (1963): 187–97.

Gannes, Abraham P. "Bureaus of Jewish Education and Group Work Agencies." *JSSQ* 26 (1950): 439.

Grand, Samuel. "The Study of Cultural Factors in Jewish Social Service." *Jew Ed* 20 (Feb. 1949): 24–28.

Greifer, Julian E. "Realities in Jewish School and Jewish Center Cooperation." *Jew Ed* 23 (Summer 1952): 15–20, 24.

Jacobs, Herman. "Adult Education in the Jewish Center." *Jew Ed* 5 (Oct./Dec. 1933): 161–67.

Janowsky, Oscar I. *The JWB Survey: A Study of the Jewish Center*. N.Y.: Dial Press, 1948. 490 pp.

Jew Ed. "Common Objectives and Areas of Cooperation in the Field of Jewish Education and Jewish Center Work" (joint statement by Jewish educators and center workers, Nov. 1946). 18 (Summer 1947): 10–12.

JWB. *Maximizing Jewish Educational Effectiveness of Jewish Community Centers*. N.Y., 1984.

Kraft, Louis. *A Century of the Jewish Center Movement*. N.Y.: JWB, 1966. 315 pp.

———. "Community Centers." In *The Golden Heritage: A History from 1917 to 1967*, 342–45. N.Y.: ca. 1969.

Linzer, Norman. "Jewish Education for Jewish Agencies." *Jew Ed* 49 (Winter 1981): 9–13.

Livingstone, Nancy. "How Is the Pre-School Doing in the Jewish Community Center?" *J Jew Com Ser* 55 (Autumn 1978): 90–97.

———. "What Is a Pre-School Doing in a Jewish Community Center?" *J Jew Com Ser* 54 (1977): 39–42.

Picheny, Elias, and Ben M. Edidin. "Developing an Integrated Center Program." *Jew Ed* 15 (May 1944): 155–63.

Ribner, I. "The Jewish School and the Case Work Agency." *Jew Ed* 23 (Summer 1952): 21–24.

* Robbins, Edward. *An Approach to Planning and Development of Adult Education Programs in Jewish Community Centers*. St. Louis U., 1976.

Setleis, Lloyd. "An Inquiry into the Jewish Character of the Jewish Communal Agency: A Challenge to the Jewish Educator." *Jew Ed* 49 (Summer 1981): 32–37.

Soltes, Mordecai. "Integrating the Work of the Jewish Elementary School with the Center Program." *Jewish Center* (Dec. 1940).

———. "The Role of the Jewish Center in Jewish Education." *Jew Ed* 9 (Oct.–Dec. 1937): 128–31; 10 (Jan.–Mar. 1938): 1–10.

Tropp, E. "Testing Teenage Attitudes and Interests: The Place of the Center in the Life of the Teenager." *J Jew Com Ser* 37 (1961): 292–300.

Yapko, B. L. "Jewish Social Work Service Agencies and the Jewish School." *J Jew Com Ser* 45 (Winter 1968): 165–72.

THE JEWISH COMMUNITY IN THE JEWISH CURRICULUM PRIOR TO 1950

Alofsin, Dorothy. *The Stream of Jewish Life*. Cincinnati: UAHC, 1943. 360 pp.

Berkson, Isaac B. "The Community School Center" (policy and plan of the Central Jewish Institute). *Jewish Teacher* (May 1917): 224–34.

Blumenfield, Samuel M. "A Community Program for Jewish Youth Work." *CCAR* 44 (1934): 273–76. See also *Jew Ed* 7 (Jan.–Mar. 1935): 20–25.

Conovitz, Michael. *Dorothy and David Explore Jewish Life*. Cincinnati: UAHC, 1938. 206 pp.

Dushkin, Alexander M. "Community in Jewish Education." *Jew Fron* 10 (May 1943): 13–16.

———. "The New Community Program in Jewish Education." *JSSQ* 16 (Mar. 1940).

Edidin, Ben M. "Aims of Teaching Jewish Community Life." *Jew Ed* 7 (Apr.–June 1935): 101–6.

———. "School and Community." In *Jewish Community Life in America*, 37–52. N.Y.: Hebrew Pub. Co., 1947.

* ———. *Teaching Jewish Community Life.* U. of Buffalo, 1934. 342 pp.

Eisenberg, Azriel. "A Project in Teaching the Jewish Community." *Jew Teach* 8 (Nov. 1939): 1–7, (Jan. 1940): 26–33, (Apr. 1940): 19–27, (June 1940): 25–38.

Kurzband, Toby K. *Source Book for the Study of the Jewish Community: Part I, Jewish Welfare Organizations* and *Teacher's Manual for an Activity Course in the Jewish Community.* N.Y.: UAHC, 1931. 82 and 37 pp.

Levitats, Isaac. "Education in Community Living." *Recon* (Nov. 15, 1946): 9–13.

———. "An Experiment in Communal Education." *Jew Ed* 16 (Sept. 1944): 35–38.

Rosenthal, Ira. "Our Neighborhood." *Jew Teach* 14 (June 1946): 18–25.

Sellinger, Benjamin. "An Approach to a Course in Jewish Community Organization." *Jew Teach* 14 (Apr. 1946): 1–14.

Weitz, Martin M. *Jewish Demography: A Proposal for the Study of the Jewish Community.* Cincinnati: CJF-UAHC, 1935. 63 pp.

———. *Jewish Life in Our Community* (workbook). Cincinnati: UAHC–CJE, 1935. 63 pp.

———. "Possibilities of Contemporary Jewish Community' as Content for the Religious School." *Jew Ed* 8 (Oct.–Dec. 1936): 127–36.

THE JEWISH COMMUNITY IN THE JEWISH CURRICULUM SINCE 1950

AAJE. *The Jew in America: Selected Aspects of His History and Community Life.* 2 vols. N.Y., 1954.

———. *The Teaching of Jewish Civics in Jewish Schools in the United States.* Information Bulletin no. 33. N.Y., 1970.

———. *Exploring Your Jewish Community: An Adventure in Jewish Identity.* N.Y., 1972. See also *Ped Rep* 23 (Dec. 1971): 10.

———. *Meet Your Jewish Community.* Benjamin Efron, ed. N.Y.: AAJE Commission on Jewish Civics, a division of the NCRI, 1973.

———. *Multi Media Resources of the Jewish Community.* A selected, annotated and graded listing of materials for teaching Jewish civics. Benjamin Efron and Lionel Koppman. N.Y.: Commission on Jewish Civics, a division of the NCRI, Spring 1973. 98 pp.

———. *Jewish Civics: A Guide for Teaching Citizenship in the Jewish Community.* N.Y.: NCRI, 1975. 110 pp.

American Jewish Tercentenary Committee. *The Community Manual, 1654–1954.* N.Y., 1954. 77 pp.

Bennett, Alan D. "Demonstrating Concern for Other American Jews." In *Jewish Civics*, 89–93. Grades 6–9.

Berkson, Isaac B. "The Community Theory and the Jewish School Curriculum." *Jew Ed* 30 (Fall 1959): 24–33.

Bogot, Howard I. "Jewish Education in the Group Work Setting." *J Jew Com Ser* 50 (Summer 1974): 327–31.

Colodner, Sol. "The Jewish Community—A Project for Study and Activity." *Syn Sch* 17 (Mar. 1959): 15–18.

Efron, Benjamin, ed. *Currents and Trends in Contemporary Jewish Thought.* N.Y.: Ktav, 1965. 311 pp. High school and adults.

———. "Programs and Projects Involving Personal Contact with the Jewish Community in Action." *Ped Rep* 23 (Sept. 1971): 11.

Feldman, Sadie. "Our Jewish Community." *Jew Teach* 29 (Feb. 1961): 7–8.

Finnel, David B. "The Fairfax: A Jewish Community and You." A slide-tape presentation for ages twelve to fifteen designed to increase awareness of what constitutes one's own community and of how that community is changing. Master's project, HUC–JIR, 1980.

Isser, Stanley. "The Jewish Community in the Jewish School Curriculum." *Ed As* (1970): 29–36.

Kahan, Linda S. "Generations: A Unit on the Elderly." In *Jewish Civics*, 83–88. Grades 8–10.

Kohanski, Alexander S. "Education in Communal Living." *Recon* (Nov. 15, 1946): 9–13.

Kronish, Ronald. "The Community in the Classroom." *AM* (Spring 1976).

Lear, Elmer. "Providing Meaningful Experiences through Developing Identification with the American Jewish Community." *Syn Sch* 14 (Nov. 1955): 19–22.

Lipnick, Bernard. "The Class as a Community" (alternatives to conventional education). *Moment* 4 (June 1979): 58–61.

Lister, Rebecca, and Azriel Eisenberg. *Federation and Tzedakah in the Religious School*. N.Y.: CJFWF, May 1966.

Marenof, Martha. "Teaching Community Responsibility." *Jew Teach* 24 (Mar. 1956): 13–14.

Monson, Rela Geffen. "The Jewish Political Tradition—A Resource for Jewish Education in America." *Ped Rep* 34 (Jan. 1988): 10–12.

Nadel, Max. "The Jewish Community—Its Concerns and Organizations." In *Teaching the Jewish Experience in America*, 31–40. N.Y.: AAJE, 1975.

Pollak, George, and Benjamin Efron. "Current Trends in Jewish Communal Education." *Ped Rep* 27 (Spring 1976): 2–3, 5–9; 31 (Winter 1980): 19.

Schickler, Rolf W. "A Unit Curriculum in Jewish History for the Eighth Grade: Related to Community Experiences." Master's thesis, HUC–JIR, 1955.

Schindler, Alexander M. "Jewish Scholarship and the Jewish Community—A Reform Perspective." In *From the Scholar to the Classroom*, edited by Fox and Rosenfield, 86–97. 1977.

Slesinger, Zalmen. "Orienting Our Children into the Contemporary Jewish Scene." *Ped Rep* 15 (Mar. 1964): 9–13.

Teitz, Pinchos. "Communicating Effectively to the Community." *Jew Parent* 19 (June 1968). See also *HDS*, 158–63.

Warshaw, E. "The School as Community." *Syn Sch* 30 (Summer 1972): 28–47.

Wolfson, Ronald G. "Creating Community in the Classroom." In *JTH*, 2:11–22.

Zwerin, Raymond A. *For One Another: Jewish Organizations that Help Us All*. N.Y.: UAHC-AAJE, 1975. 192 pp. Grades 10–12.

———. "Toward a Course in the Functions of the Jewish Community for the Religious School." Master's thesis, HUC–JIR, 1964.

CHANGING JEWISH COMMUNITIES– IMPLICATIONS FOR JEWISH EDUCATION (SELECTED)

(See also chapter 44)

AJC. *Trends: Reports on Jewish Communal Developments*. N.Y.: Library of Jewish Information of the AJC, June 1959. 33 pp.

Blumenfeld, Samuel M. "American Jewry—Reflections on Social, Communal, and Spiritual Trends." In *Baron*, 99–117.

Elazar, Daniel. "The Jewish Community—Changing Patterns." GA, 1976.

Engelman, Uriah Z. "Medurbia." *Contemporary Jewish Record* 4 (Aug. 1941): 339–48, (Oct. 1941): 511–21.

Fishman, Joshua A. "Moving to the Suburbs: Its Possible Impact on the Role of the Jewish Minority in American Jewish Life." *Phylon* 24 (1963): 146–53.

Franck, Isaac. "The Changing American Jewish Community." In *AJ*, 18–45.

Gamoran, Emanuel. "Jewish Education in a Changing Jewish Community." *Jew Teach* 23 (Fall 1952): 9–16. Also in *Jew Ed* 34 (Winter 1964): 87–95.

Gans, Herbert J. "The Origin and Growth of a Jewish Community in the Suburbs." In *JES*, 205–48.

Goldfarb, William B. *Jewish Education and a Changing Society* (33rd GA, Nov. 1964). N.Y.: CP, Dec. 1964.

Handlin, Oscar. "Changing Patterns in Group Life in America." *J Jew Com Ser* (1983).

Intrater, Aaron. "Emerging Changes in Planning for Jewish Education." *Jew Ed* 34 (Fall 1963): 23–28.

Krug, Mark M. "Changes in the American Jewish Community and Its Impact on Jewish Education." *Jewish Cultural Affairs* 3 (1956): 1–3.

Rose, O. L. "Small Town Jews and Their Neighbors." *Jew J Soc* 3 (1961): 174–91.

Rudin, Marcia R. "The New Religious Cults and the Jewish Community." *Rel Ed* 73 (May–June 1978): 350–59.

Schottland, Charles I. "The Changing American Community: Its Significance for the American Jewish Community." *Jew Teach* 29 (Apr. 1961): 15–19.

Simon, E. "Suburbia, Its Effects on the American Jewish Teenager." *J of Educational Sociology* 36 (1962): 124–33.

Solender, Sanford. *The Changing Situation in the Jewish Community and Implications for Federation* (July 9, 1978). N.Y.: CP. 12 pp.

Teller, Gerald. "Impact of Culture on Structure of Jewish School." *Jew Ed* 48 (Summer 1980): 44–47.

Zibbell, Charles. "Emerging Changes in Planning for Jewish Education." *Jew Ed* 34 (Fall 1963): 15–22.

———. *New Directions in Federation Planning for Jewish Education*. CJF Planning Institute, Dec. 29, 1969. 5 pp.

GLEANINGS

Magnes, Judah L., on New York City (1909),

"Thousands of dollars and boundless energy and affection are expended each year in the education of the Jewish child, but it may be said that we have no Jewish educational system. Some schools are good, some are not. What the community might do is to help such a movement as is now beginning to develop, that of forming a Board of Jewish Education, and of employing a Superintendent of Instruction. . . . It would help to correct many abuses practiced by unlicensed and incompetent private schools and teachers. It would also show the necessity for additional schools for thousands of Jewish children who are now willing to go to Jewish school but find no schools to receive them."

Quoted by Nathan H. Winter, *Jewish Education in a Pluralist Society* (1966), 61.

Magnes, Judah L. (1915),

"The theory of the Kehillah has been that the community must be aroused so as to make provision for a system of various kinds of Jewish education for the more than one hundred and fifty thousand Jewish children who are without it."

Jew Ed 20 (Feb. 1949), 17. (See "Kehillah" in New York City.)

Marshall, Louis (1923),

"For some years past, I have repeatedly expressed the opinion that the time is rapidly approaching when it will become imperative for the Jews of the United States to tax themselves annually ten million dollars as a minimum for the purpose [of Jewish education]. Further reflection has convinced me that the estimate is moderate. We must establish and support religious schools in such number as to accommodate every Jewish child whose parents desire that it shall be given a thorough training in the principles, literature, history, and traditions of our people. We must supply them with suitable textbooks, properly equip them, train an abundance of competent and enthusiastic teachers, and make them in every way attractive."

1923 Conference of the UAHC. Quoted by W. Gunther Plaut in *The Growth of Reform Judaism* (1963), 319.

Selekman, Ben M., chair, *Extracts from a Report of the Committee on Finances and Governmental Welfare Policies of the National Federation of Jewish Federations and Welfare Funds*. Prepared for discussion at the General Assembly meeting on Jan. 6–7, 1934. On education and culture,

"When we pass to these functions, we confront a segment of the community program which, though receiving a limited share of Federation funds, cannot be transferred to governmental or non-Jewish auspices. Moreover, the sharpened thrust of Anti-Semitism, that dark feature of our present situation, makes more than ever imperative the strengthening of inner resources among our people. Unless our Jewish youth is brought up to understand deeply the historical experience of their people and the values of their cultural heritage in relation to the modern world, they lack an intelligent basis for a satisfying and rational adjustment to the general, and unfortunately antagonistic, environment in which they must live. To refuse one's Jewishness is not to escape its penalties in a period of intense nationalism and confused racial prejudices; it is merely to forfeit its recompenses of spiritual dignity and armor."

Jew Ed 6 (Jan.–/Mar. 1934), 17.

Dushkin, Alexander M.,
"Our faith in the community principle in Jewish education is based on both ideological and practical grounds. Ideologically we are influenced by our pedagogic training, by our evaluation of the changing Jewish scene and by our democratic environment. Pedagogically we have been trained to think of good education as a social process which takes best when schools are conceived as communities of children."

Jew Ed 17 (1946), 18–19.

Mark, Yudl,
"We can have a true community only when we do not merely tolerate one another but when we recognize our relatedness one to the other."

Jew Ed 17 (Feb 1946), 41.

Kaplan, Mordecai M.,
"The principal aim to be kept in mind in the Jewish education of the American-Jewish child, from the standpoint of his maximum self-fulfillment as an American and as a Jew, is, accordingly, to render the Jewish heritage relevant to his moral and spiritual needs, and to qualify him, when he matures to establish the kind of Jewish communal environment that will provide opportunities for the satisfaction of these needs."

In his *The Future of the American Jew* (1948), 446.

Arzt, Max,
"The Synagogue Center, being at the core a religious institution, fits perfectly into the pattern of American life. Its religious services, its religious classes and even its recreational and social activities, are the outgrowth of the desire to strengthen the loyalty to an historic faith. The faith that is Judaism embraces the totality of life and hallows even its 'secular' aspects."

Quoted in *Issues*, 100.

Katzoff, Louis,
"Today the real problem is the interrelation of the congregational school and the coordinating communal educational agency: the Bureau of Jewish Education. As long as the Bureau attempted the incorporation of the existing schools within its orbit of control, the congregation resisted its influence, lest it lead to an encroachment upon their jurisdiction. At present Dushkin's indication of the healthy process of integration and diversification is best manifested in the emerging synthesis of the two contending trends, as seen in the developing relationship of the congregational school and the Bureau."

In *Issues*, 106.

Ginzberg, Eli,
"Since most welfare funds and federations from the start were assiduous in avoiding entanglements in ideological conflicts, they concentrated on "uncharged" areas such as the support of the needy, health, and social services. For a long time, they have been reluctant to assume responsibility for the partial or complete support of Jewish education. However, a marked trend in this direction is now discernible. . . . It is likely that some of the difficulties that have confronted Jewish education in the United States during the past decades will slowly be resolved as communities reassess the danger of remaining aloof from the support of cultural objectives."

"Agenda for America." In *Jews*, 40.

Honor, Leo L.,
"We must recognize that a unified Jewish community must provide for differences, that in encouraging differences we are not helping to break up unity but rather

to maintain unity on a higher plane."

In *Selected Writings of Leo L. Honor,* edited by Gannes, 10.

Honor, Leo L., "The Function of a Community Agency for Jewish Education."

1. A community agency for Jewish education must serve all elements of the community who maintain a positive attitude towards Judaism and Jewish life.

2. This implies helping each element maintain its educational program on the highest plane possible. It does not necessarily imply trying to find a common denominator.

3. Unity is essential; uniformity is not desirable. Many false programs arise from the false identification of the two concepts. History is replete with instances where the dominant element tried to create a unified society through enforced uniformity. One of the glories of Jewish history is the Jewish people's fight for the right to be different and for the concept of Unity in Diversity....

Influencing without controlling is possible even if extremely difficult. The community agency should make available to all constituent schools the services of trained experts whom rabbis, principals, teachers, and lay-leaders can consult freely in regard to all phases of the Jewish educational process."

Reg (1951), 59, 61.

Berkson, Isaac,

"The idea of community responsibility for Jewish education was not, in the first instance, a principle of efficient organization. It was, at a deeper level, the expression of a positive philosophy of Jewish life, of a vision one might say, a vision of building in this land a great Jewish community which would share the responsibilities of mutual aid with Jews all over the world, would play its due part in recreating the Jewish homeland in the Land of Israel, would carry forward the agelong culture and spiritual heritage of the Jewish people."

Jew Ed 24 (Fall 1953), 35.

Klutznick, Philip,

"In many ways, one of the step-children of our community has been Jewish education, both formal and informal. We seem to have found extraordinary resources for many causes, but much too little for this purpose."

Quoted by Philip L. Seman in *Southwest Jewry,* edited by J. L. Malamut (1957), 3:42.

Commission on Jewish Education, USA, "Participation in Jewish Community Life,"

"The curriculum should provide the students with experiences in Jewish community life and responsibilities. These experiences should be provided in the next curricular area, 'The Jewish People.' Courses leading to understanding in all its manifestation should precede the Bar Mitzvah, graduation, and Confirmation ceremonies."

Objectives and Standards for the Congregational School (USCJE, 1958), 12–13.

Commission for the Study of Jewish Education in the United States (1959),

"Communities should establish community loan funds for building repair and construction, which if wisely and generously applied would help to meet minimal housing requirements and aid in planning and erecting buildings in new neighborhoods. A social-planning committee should concern itself with projecting plans for school buildings with a view to the movement of the population....

For the convenience of the children and for the better management of the schools, communities should organize common transportation systems, such as developed in Detroit and elsewhere."

A. M. Dushkin and Uriah Z. Engelman, *Report,* 233–34, 236.

Adler, Morris,

"A communal school system may,... remain quite as parochial and restricted in program as any congregational school with which it is generally placed in contrast. Deficit financing by the so-called community does not of itself fashion a communal outlook or motivation.... Our organized life, local and national, is still, despite the appearance of unity, a thing of shreds and fragments, of autonomies jealously held and sovereignties determinedly defended. The leadership is still one dominated by paternalism, in whose selection the community at large plays no part. The rhetorical pronouncements and sonorous statements made on public occasions abound in democratic phraseology, but the facts are sadly otherwise. There is no evidence of comprehensive thinking or a vital rationale on the part of those who assumed the dignity and responsibility of leadership.

Under such conditions, to act or speak as if the long-desired community were here, reflects a misreading of the present scene, and betrays the future of the idea which alone spells hope for organized American Jewish life. If we are to have a community, we must realize that 'community' is yet a myth. It is ours to make it a reality."

Recon 26 (Mar. 1960), 16, 18.

Slesinger, Zalmen,
"To remedy the existing state of affairs and to secure fully the financial means for the currently unmet needs of the community, our present methods of financing will have to be radically revised. What is urgently needed is to abandon gradually the widespread practice of relying on local resources and develop instead a community-wide policy for the financial support of Jewish education. We must seriously consider the advisability of pooling the financial resources for the American Jewish community as a whole."

Recon (Jan. 25, 1963), 13.

Intrater, Aaron,
"The recent recommendations, on the part of experienced observers, regarding the need of a return to the communal school system warn us that we must not abandon those communal schools which by virtue of their satisfactory results have proved a boon to their communities. But the realities of congregational life, confront us with the recognition that, with a present enrollment of approximately 90% of our children, the congregational schools will remain reality. We must, therefore, direct our concentrated attention to the strengthening of congregational school programs, the intensification of supervision, and the attainment of accreditation standards."

"Emerging Changes in Jewish Education." *Jew Ed* 34 (Fall 1963), 27.

Zibbell, Charles,
"Although we gain little in pointing out the limited scope of community responsibility in our early tradition, it is a healthy balance against an emotional approach which cries out for 'community responsibility' as the panacea for all ills of Jewish education. No responsible leader questions that there is some responsibility for Jewish education, and all agree that the community does not have the total responsibility. When we are able to define clearly the specific of that responsibility it will be an important first step towards our objectives. Moreover, it may be necessary to concede that this definition may encompass wide differences of community responsibility, one community from another, and one period of time from another. What may have been appropriate in the decade of the 40's, may be out-moded in the 50's, and suicidal in the 60's. What may be good for Detroit may be impractical for Los Angeles."

"Emerging Changes in Planning for Jewish Education." *Jew Ed* 34 (Fall 1963), 19.

Soboloff, Simon,
"One of the less happy consequences of the so-called religious boom is the divisiveness and denominationalism which are beginning to characterize the American Jewish community. We are becoming more and more denomination minded and the bridges of communication between Jewish groups are being broken down. We who insist that the meaning of America is diversity with unity must demonstrate that we can implement this idea within the life of the American Jewish community. It is not uniformity that we desire. We want the richness of creative difference and variety, but we must have the communication between the groups and the cross-fertilization which results from the meeting together of people of different views and different ideas."

Quoted by Rudavsky in *Yivo Annual* 13 (1965), 123.

Janowsky, Oscar I.,
"If community funds are applied to in-

crease the salaries of licensed teachers, and to enable schools to achieve accreditation and affiliation with the central agency, and if schools are held accountable for the proper use of funds, a powerful instrument will be forged for the betterment of Jewish education."

In *Jan 2*, 172.

Engelman, Uriah Zvi,

"Can the congregation be entrusted with the sponsorship of Jewish education? The answer is 'No.' Congregations have not in the past, and will probably not succeed in the future in developing an effective school system.... The congregation's failure was not due to its lack of appreciation of the importance of Jewish education.... The cause of the failure was found in the limitation inherent in the congregational structure and its institutional objective."

"Unpopular Issues in Jewish Education." *Recon* 28. Quoted in *Jew Ed* 35 (Spring 1965), 164.

Schindler, Alexander M., UAHC–CJE,

"There is much that we can do to deepen the devotion of our children to the larger community, to extend their reach of heart and mind to encompass all of Israel....

We can begin by teaching Judaism in our schools, teaching it, moreover, not as some kind of denominational possession, but as a shared possession to which variant interpretations have a vital relation. And when we speak of our differences as they really are, we can approach them, examine them—teacher and student both—in an atmosphere of respectful inquiry.

We can bring our children into contact with one another crossing denominational barriers for communal programs of education and for united activity arising to advance our common cause. Surely more than ideas are involved in our problem. People are involved. The sense of communion is sustained by encounter."

Remarks before the Rabbinical Assembly (Conservative) 66th Annual Convention, May 18, 1966.

Neusner, Jacob,

"I believe that all schools have a right to community support, and that all Jewish educational ventures and youth programs have a right to turn to the community for assistance. Here we can admit no discrimination; we should help whoever comes to ask our help to study the Torah, whether he be Orthodox, or Reform, or Conservative, or Reconstructionist, or secularist, or Zionist, or Yiddishist, or what have you. We must ask only that he maintain high standards of Jewish educational achievement and present a serious and appropriate program to meet these standards.... The greater part of the blame for the current situation belongs, therefore, to us, to the synagogues and their lay and rabbinical leadership, for these people could make of the allocations of Federation an instrument for the cultivation of the richest and best treasures of the Jewish spirit, instead of an instrument, as at present, for the starvation and destruction of the very institutions which, properly developed, might ensure its present and future prosperity. If synagogue leaders would apply to community affairs the very values which they profess in the synagogue, which they create and support, I have no doubt whatever that things would be very different. But they seem to regard the synagogue as a spiritual ghetto, which is intended to affect nothing outside of its walls, and the Torah as a kind of mumbo-jumbo, to be read in a formalistic way, as a Tibetan lama spins his prayer wheel, and then forgotten."

Syn Sch 25 (Winter 1967): 17, 37.

AAJE,

"The major objective of the activities of the organized Jewish community is the meaningful preservation of Jewish life, through maintaining the allegiance and esprit de corps of its young people.

Jewish education is regarded as the essential instrument through which the community hopes to achieve this objective. Whether Jewish education is provided under denominational auspices, or by communally sponsored schools, its potential can best be achieved through overall community planning. The quality of education, its intensity and duration, the number of young people whom it can effectively reach, is in large measure determined by the imaginative use of communal resources, particularly in the financing institutions and programs calculated to improve the educational establishment and attract and retain an ever increasing number of students.

Communal responsibility for the financing of Jewish education implies a commitment that no child be left to the caprice of a good or bad school, a good or bad teacher, interested or indifferent parents; but that the resources of the community in personnel, skills, facilities and funds, shall be made equally and fully available to all. It is with this objective in mind that the AAJE proposed this National Policy Statement to Jewish Federations, and Welfare Funds, Bureaus of Jewish Education, congregational bodies and individual schools, as a rationale and formula, to guide communal bodies in the financing of their Jewish educational systems."

"Preface" to *National Statement on Communal Support for Jewish Education*. 1968, 1971.

CCAR, CJE,
"Let us frankly proclaim that inadequate, incomplete, undistinguished Jewish education is a form of slow suicide for American Jewry, and a drastic change must be instituted in our approach to the problem throughout the country before it is too late. Recognizing the shortage of educators, as well as of facilities, in all segments of American Jewry, the UAHC–CCAR Commission on Jewish education submits that the old patterns of educational separation no longer serve the highest interests of the American Jewish community, the urgent educational needs of every man, woman, and child affiliated with Reform Judaism. While striving to increase the resources at our command, let us see that those we have are wisely utilized in a common effort for the common good.

A. When a congregation—particularly a small one—cannot offer such a [quality education] program, this commission recommends that wherever geographically possible, congregations shall cooperate in forming an intercongregational school or department, or a community school in partnership with other congregations, regardless of ideological affiliation.

B. The commission further recommends that all Reform congregational schools cooperate with one another and the local central agency for Jewish education, to upgrade the quality of Jewish education for every member of the Jewish community."

CJE Promotes Communal Cooperation in New Policy Statement. *Compass* 3 (Winter 1969), 1–3.

Vorspan, Max, and Lloyd P. Gartner,
"The congregations did poorly what no one else did at all."
History of the Jews of Los Angeles (1970), 170.

Gannes, Abraham P.,
"The main function of the central agency was to foster the development and expression of Jewish education for all age groups, leaving it to each element to expand its programs in the light of its particular ideology, to help each element raise the standards of its educational work. The central agency should in no way attempt to interfere with or influence the ideological orientation of any school but should rather implement its educational program in accordance with its own orientation through setting standards for housing of schools, the qualification of teachers and methods employed in the instructional program."
Jew Ed 40 (Spring 1971), 29–30.

Schafler, Samuel,
"I do not share the prevailing mood of pessimism bordering on despair on the possibilities of achievement, including Hebrew language achievement, within the framework of a congregational school. Congregational schools can continue to be useful vehicles for Jewish education, provided we do not burden the congregational schools with unrealistic expectations. And here I am not referring to curricular expectations."
Jew Ed 56 (Fall 1978), 17–18.

Elazar, Daniel J.,
"As two separate worlds emerged within Jewish life, the leading Jewish educators failed to learn the ways of getting on in the world of communal leadership. Whether it was because of their low opinion of the communal leaders or simply their different language and style (and style here is of the utmost importance): there was simply no real communication between the two elements.

In sum, two things are needed to recruit voluntary leadership of the highest caliber to become involved in Jewish education. One is a structural change as to where Jewish education is located within the Jewish community structure. Jewish education must become a community function, one that is intimately linked to the framing institutions of the community and to the strongest among them. . . .

Jewish education can only be the concern of voluntary leaders who believe that Jewish study, learning and teaching are important for all Jews, not just for children, that Jewish education is not a matter of minimal socialization or acquisition of 'synagogue skills' however important both are, but is a major function of being Jewish. . . .

"The new interest of the voluntary leadership is a reflection of their own perceptions of the change that is taking place among their constituencies, namely the rise in the perceived importance of Jewish education as a major responsibility of the Jewish community that behooves the voluntary leadership to become involved in that for which they will be held accountable in any case."

Voluntary Leadership in Jewish Education (Jerusalem: World Leadership Conference for Jewish Education, June 1984), 6, 9–10, 13.

Schiff, Alvin I.,
"The annual expenditures of the Jewish community in North America for the Jewish community exceeds a half billion dollars. At an average per pupil cost of $2500, the Jewish community expends about $250,000,000 for Jewish day schools. At an annual cost of $700, it expends $161,000,000, for supplementary Jewish education. Together this amounts to $411,000,000 per year. To this figure we must add the expenditures for informal Jewish education, teacher pre-service and in-service programs, central agency for Jewish education activities, adult and family education, higher education, and Jewish education camping. All these probably amount to $100,000,000 per year. In sum, over $500,000,000 is being expended in North America each year for Jewish educational activities."

Jew Ed 51 (Summer 1983), 15.

JESNA,
"The principles underlying the two AAJE policy statements [1967, 1971—See AAJE above] are as valid today as they were at the time of issuance. . . . By 1982, school enrollments were down to 55% of the 1968 figures. . . . In spite of economic pressures, many congregations and their schools have made continuing efforts to maintain and improve educational standards; to attract qualified staff; to involve parents in the educational process; to reach out to the unaffiliated; and to reorder their priorities with a view of giving the educational budget a higher proportion of the congregational income. Nonetheless, cost of maintaining the level of instruction and quality of education have far outstripped congregational income and are undermining the efforts of congregational schools to provide the best education to their students. . . . As of 1982, only a relatively small number of congregational schools received a cash subsidy. . . . Since more than half of all the students now receiving a Jewish education do so in a synagogue-related school, it is recommended that greater considerations be given to communal support for students in congregational schools, provided the recipient institutions meet the conditions specified."

Suggested Guidelines on Communal Support for Congregational Schools (N.Y.: JESNA, 1983).

Ben-Horin, Meir,
"In general, the 'central agencies' nationwide have never, as far as I know, been seriously and critically examined. It is as

if they are exempt from accountability and public scrutiny for their activities. But in view of the state of Jewish education in North America, such a searching inquiry, by an authority other than the agencies themselves, needs to be undertaken in the interests of truth, economy and recovery. American Jewry is entitled to know how 'central' these bodies really are and to what end, and how competent their staffs really are, in what measure they are to be held responsible for what is wrong in Jewish education—and to what extent they deserve credit for its attainments. More must be known by the public about Jewish educational thinking and doing than can be learned from the generalizations of critics, and from the often self-serving pronouncements of office holders and 'professionals' in a profession not yet really ranking as such."

Jew Fron (June–July 1985), 20.

Cardin, Shoshana,

"The 1985 General Assembly . . . marked the coming of age of Jewish education on the agenda of Jewish Federations and their leadership in North America. The primacy of quality Jewish education on Federation agendas was reflected in the scheduling of 17 designated sessions and six "Lunch and Learn" experiences. Jewish education was all-pervasive and ever-present throughout the breadth, depth and scope of this Assembly, beginning with JESNA and COJEO's innovative Jewish Education Drop-in Center, through the specific sessions, seminars and discussions directly dealing with Jewish education. Other sessions while not specifically related to Jewish education, surely had a strong component regarding this critical, vital and far-reaching enterprise of Jewish life. Our sages understood this well by enunciating early in the Talmudic exposition of Jewish priorities that talmud torah k'negged kulam. Education Torah, from the earliest inception of our people, was the foundation upon which almost everything in Jewish life was developed—family, community, leadership, and religious behavior. The Council of Jewish Federations and the Federation movement have a commitment to this principle. We are devoted to transmitting this fundamental understanding for we know that our future depends upon a sound foundation of quality Jewish education. This commitment will assure our creative continuity."

Quoted by A. I. Schiff, *Jew Ed* 54 (Summer 1985), 3.

31 THE HOME AND JEWISH EDUCATION

SCHOOL RELATIONSHIPS PRIOR TO 1950

(See also chapters 20 and 21)

Bausel, R. Barker. "Teaching Your Child." *Rocky Mountain News* (Feb. 18, 1941).

Block, Asher. "Education and Religion in the Home." *Recon* (Nov 2, 1945): 13–18.

Brilliant, Nathan, and Libbie L. Braverman. "Relating the Parent to the School." *Jew Teach* 8 (Nov. 1939 and Jan. 1940): 18–27 and 15–26.

Cohen, Samuel M. "Jewish Parental Education." *RA* (1933–38): 144–55.

———. "The School and the Home." In *The Progressive Jewish School*, 158–63. 1932.

Coopersmith, Ethel, and Harry Coopersmith. "Jewish Music in the Home." *Jew Teach* 10 (Nov. 1941): 20–25.

Eisenberg, Azriel. "Dear Parents" (monthly letter on school topics). *Syn Sch* 5 (May 1947): 133–35.

Folkman, Jerome D. "The Pre-School Mothers' Club." *Jew Teach* 14 (June 1946): 30–31.

Gamoran, Emanuel. "Moral and Religious Training in the Jewish Home." *Rel Ed* 25 (Dec. 1930): 915–19.

Goldblath, Maurice. "You, Too, Can Have a Chanuko Party in Your Home." *Jew Teach* 10 (Nov. 1941): 6–13.

Golub, Rose. "Parent-Teacher Cooperation." *Jew Teach* 10 (Jan. 1942): 27–29.

———. "Sabbath in the Home." *Jew Teach* 10 (Apr. 1942): 1–12.

Gordon, Albert I. *How to Celebrate Passover at Home*. N.Y.: USA, 1947.

Grand, Samuel. "An Experiment in Parent Cooperation in a Congregational School." *Jew Teach* 10 (Apr. 1942): 21–23.

Greenberg, B. D., and A. O. Silverman. *The Jewish Home Beautiful*. N.Y.: Women's League of the USA, 1941.

Greenfield, William P. "How Can Religion Make the Home and Family Life More Effective." *RA* (1940): 190–96.

Halevi, Mordecai. "יחס ההורים לחנוך העברי" (Relationship of the Parents to Jewish Education). *Sh Hah* (H.) 1 (Fall 1940).

Indelman, Ruchla L. "Parents and Children of Jewish Families." Master's thesis, Columbia U., 1939.

Jewish School and Democracy "The Jewish Home and Family" (May 1943): 33–37.

Kohn, Therese. "A Movie Project" (home worship). *Jew Teach* 11 (Jan. 1943): 9–17.

Kramer, N. "ביקורים בבתי ההורים" (Visits in Parents' Homes). *Sh Hah* (H.) 2 (Tishri 1942): 40–44.

Kurzband, Toby K., and Temima Gezari. "Artcraft in the Home." *Jew Teach* 9 (Jan. 1941): 8–11.

31 THE HOME AND JEWISH EDUCATION

Lehrer, Leibush. „די אמעריקאנער יידישע "היים" (The American Jewish Home). In *Shu P* (Y.), 69–84. Also in his *Dor Tzu Dor* (Y.), 89–104.

Levine, A. "יחס האבות אל חנוך הבנות„ (The Relationship of the Fathers to the Education of the Daughters). *Sh Hah* (H.) 2 (Spring 1926): 32–40.

Levinthal, L. L. "The Role of the Parent and Layman in Jewish Education." *Jew Ed* (Jan.–Mar. 1933): 14–17, 56.

Levitan, Sar. "Parent Opinion in Formulation of a School Curriculum." *Jew Ed* 13 (Jan. 1942): 180–86.

Markowitz, Samuel H., and Mrs. David K. Studner. "Introducing Home Observances through the Religious School." *Jew Teach* 6 (Apr. 1938): 16–26.

Nardi, Noah. "Studies in Jewish Home Environment." *Jew Ed* 17 (Feb. 1946): 44–49.

Shapiro, D. S. "Jewish Education through the Home." *Jew Life* 15 (Apr. 1948).

Touroff, Nissan. "„הורים ומורים" (Parents and Teachers). *Hadoar* (H.) 2 (12th of Shevat 1922).

Votheek, K. "Have You Read?" *Jew Life* 14 (Feb. 1947).

Yehudah, R. "„בית הספר ובית האב" (Home and School). *Sh Hah* (H.) 6 (Summer 1946): 311–13.

SCHOOL RELATIONSHIPS SINCE 1950

Ackerman, Walter I. "„בית הספר וההורים" (The School and the Parents). *Sh Hah* (H.) 23 (Fall 1963): 33–37.

Aft, Martha. "Parental Partnership." *Compass* 2 (Winter 1979): 9–10.

———. "Parent Involvement." In *JPH*, 79–85.

Andrews, Violet, and Joseph Andrews. "Jewish Education: A Parent View." *Syn Sch* 19 (Fall 1960).

Artzt, Edya. "Are Parents Accountable?" *Ped Rep* 36 (Sept. 1985): 25–26.

———. "Parental Involvement: How the Parent Should Relate to the Adolescent." *Ped Rep* 29 (Spring 1978).

———. "Parent and Child Learn Together." *Ed As* (1970): 9–10.

Ashkenazi, Ellen. "Today's Jewish Family: To Learn or Not to Learn." *Jewish Exponent* (Sept. 2, 1977).

Axelroth, Dorothy. "Shabbat Workshop: An Experiment in Parent-Child Education." *AM* (Fall 1977).

Barwell, B. "Home and School: The Great Divide." *Jew Obs* 24 (Nov. 21, 1975): 18.

Baum, Emanuel. "School-Parent Communication." *Syn Sch* 21 (June 1963): 19.

Bial, Morrison David. *Liberal Judaism at Home: The Practices of Modern Reform Judaism*. N.Y.: UAHC, 1971.

———. *Your Jewish Child*. N.Y.: UAHC, 1978. 96 pp.

Bissel, Sherry, and Ann Eisenberg. "Primary Family School." *AM* (Spring 1979).

Blaser, Elissa. "Lost Jewish Memory." *Compass* 2 (Fall/Winter 1978): 15–16.

Blumberg, Sherry Bissel. "Family Education." In *JPH*, 461–72.

Bogot, Howard I. "Parent Participation in Jewish Education." *Compass* (Sept. 1971).

Braver, Joseph. *Parent Education Program Packet—"PEP"*. Syllabi for grades 1–5. N.Y.: USCJE, 1973.

Bregman, Alan. "Single Parent Family Weekend." *UAHC Program Perspective* (Jan. 1979).

———. "Our Sabbath Institute" (for parents). *Syn Sch* 9 (Sept. 1950): 7–11.

Brilliant, Nathan, and Libbie L. Braverman. "The Parent in the Jewish School." In *ACT*, 3–35.

Brown, Leonard N. "Involving Parents in Religious School Classes." *Compass* (Nov.–Jan. 1971–72).

Campeas, Hyman. "Course in Basic Jewish Concepts" (for parents). *Jew Ed* 41 (Spring 1972): 12–14.

Chanover, Hyman, and Zalmen Slesinger. *The Jewish School, Your Child and You*. N.Y.: AAJE. 24 pp.

Charry, Elias. "The Class Mother's Group Organization." *Syn Sch* 11 (Sept. 1952): 15–18.

Chipman, Fannie. "Parents . . . Are They Expendable?" *Jew Ed* 41 (Spring 1972): 7–12.

Cohen, Lauren Marshal, and Cynthia Thai Mascatel. "Religious School: A Family Experiment." *Compass* 3 (Fall 1979): 12–13.

Cohn, Hillel. "Toward a Program of Training in Jewish Background for Parents and Teachers of the Reform Religious School." Master's thesis, HUC–JIR, 1963.

Cole, Melanie Joy. *Jewish Light: Signs and Symbols—A Curriculum for First Grade Students and Their Parents*. Designed as a family education model. L.A.: HUC–JIR, Tartak Learning Center, 1986.

Comer, Gerald. "Home and School: The Interaction between Jewish Education and Family Background." *Jew Ed* 43 (Fall (1973): 29–35.

Compass "Five Steps for Setting up a Jewish Parenting Center." 9 (Spring/Summer 1987): 11.

Cutter, William. "Rupture, Repair and Memory: Poetics and Family Value." *MJ* 20 (Spring 1986).

Dreyfus, A. Stanley. *Parents and Children*. N.Y.: UAHC, Department of Adult Jewish Education, Nov. 1963. 25 pp.

Efron, Ben. "Home and School Cooperation." *Jew Teach* 25 (Mar. 1957): 9–10.

———. "The Thoughts Some Parents Have." *Jew Teach* 26 (May 1958): 12–14.

Eisenberg, Azriel. *Talks with Parents*. N.Y.: USCJE, 1954. 40 pp.

———. „וואס אידישע עלטערן דארפן טאן פאר דער אידישער דערציאונג פון זייערע קינדער" (What Jewish Parents Should Do for the Jewish Education of Their Children). *Day* (Y.) (Feb. 13, 1951).

Eisenberg, Rubin L. "Shabbat Can Be a Family Education Day." *Compass* (Fall 1981): 9, 17.

Elkins, Dov P. "The Family Center: A New Model for Jewish Education." *Un Syn Rev* 28 (Spring/Summer 1976): 18–19.

———. "Jewish Family Education." *Ped Rep* 30 (Fall 1978): 7–10.

———. "Tzedakah as a Given." *Had Mag* (Mar. 1985): 42–43.

Feinberg, Miriam. "Learning Together: A Program for Parents and Children." *Ped Rep* 32 (Winter 1981): 31–32.

Feinstein, Joseph H. "Between Jewish Parent and Child." *AM* 5 (Winter 1975).

———. "A Pilot Parent Education Project and After." *Jew Ed* 41 (Spring 1972): 15–16.

Feintech, Vivian. *Developing a Congregational Jewish Parenting Center*. N.Y.: UAHC, 1984. 29 pp.

———. "UAHC Establishes Parenting Centers." *RJ* (Winter 1984–85): 9.

Fishman, Hertzel. "Raising Your Children Jewishly." *Ped Rep* 37 (Feb. 1986): 1–3.

Fishman, Joshua A. *The Attitudes of American Jewish Parents towards the Education of Their Children*. Phila.: U. of Pennsylvania, Greenfield Center. 86 pp.

———. "Home-School Relations as Reciprocal Influences in a Majority Context." *Syn Sch* 18 (Spring 1959).

Freeman, Mrs. Edward M. "How Can Sisterhood Aid Religious School Program." *Jew Teach* 18 (May 1950): 1–6.

Freidenreich, Fradle. "Parent Education in the Jewish School." *Ped Rep* 23 (Mar. 1972): 9.

Glustrom, Simon. *When Your Child Asks: A Handbook for Jewish Parents*. N.Y.: Bloch, 1956. 164 pp.

Golden, Patti. "The Holiday Workshop Series: An Experimental Program." *Compass* 2 (Fall/Winter 1978): 12–14.

Goldenberg, Rose L. *The Crossroads: A Play for Jewish Living*. Institute for Jewish Life, 1975. 46 pp.

* Goldmeier, Harold. *An Evaluation of the Parent Education Program of the USA at Three Sites in the New England Area*. Harvard U., 1975.

Goldstein, Martin. "Introducing Mitzvot Maassiot into the Home." *Syn Sch* 21 (Mar. 1963).

Gordis, Robert. "The Broken Vase or Our Jewish Grandparents and Our Jewish Children" (GA). CP, 1976. 16 pp.

Gordon, Miriam. "Jewish Home and Family: Today and in Bible Times." *Jew Teach* 18 (Mar. 1950): 6–14.

Grad, Eli. "Developing a Favorable Home Climate for Jewish Education." *Syn Sch* (Mar. 1961): 30–33.

Green, A. S. "Needed: Jewish Home Life for Children." *Jew Life* 24 (Apr. 1957).

Green, Alan S. *Return to Prayer: Home and Student Devotions for Sabbath, Every Day and Special Occasions*. N.Y.: UAHC, c. 1971. 83 pp.

Greenberg, Blu. *How to Run a Traditional Jewish Home*. N.Y.: Simon and Schuster, 1983.

Griffel, Rhina. "Shabbat Sharing." *Compass* (Aug. 1975).

Grishaver, Joel. "Family Kallah: A Program Guide." *AM* (Spring 1974).

Grollman, Earl A. "Talking about Death." *Had Mag* (Aug.–Sept. 1988): 36–37.

Gross, Barbara, Rinna Khodosh, and Dan Rosoff. "Tot Shabbat at Temple Sholom" (program for children and parents). *Compass* 9 (Spring/Summer 1987): 13–14.

Grossman, Herman E. "Parents Involvement in School Problems." *Syn Sch* 13 (Dec. 1954): 15–17.

Hakimian, Leah. *Parents Participate*. St. Louis: Central Agency for Jewish Education.

———. "School Evaluation by Parents." *Ped Rep* 30 (Fall 1978).

Handel, Yitzhak. "Aspects of Parenting—A Torah View." *Jew Ed* 52 (Summer 1984): 40–44.

Heschel, Abraham. "Duty of Parents." *Day* (July 13, 1966).

Hillman, Andy. "Chazak V'Amatz: The Chazak Program of Family Education." *AM* (Winter 1977).

Himmelfarb, Harold S. "The Interaction Effects of Parents and Schooling: Comparing the Impact of Jewish and Catholic Schools." *Sociological Quarterly* 18 (Autumn 1977): 464–77.

Hirt-Manheimer, Aron, and Judith Hirt-Manheimer. "Terrific Tots" (program for children and parents). *Compass* 9 (Spring/Summer 1987): 11–12.

Holin, Elliot. "Torah La-Mishpacha" (Torah for the Family). *Compass* 1 (Spring 1978): 17–18.

Home Start Evaluation. N.Y.: AAJE, June 1981.

Horowitz. I. "Education Begins at Home." *Jew Life* 19 (May 1952).

Institute for Jewish Life. *A Guide to Jewish Family Life Education Programming*. 48 pp.

Irlen, Barbara. "Helping Families Plan Family Education." *AM* (Fall 1975).

Jacobs, N. L. "The Changing Family: Its Implications for Early Childhood Centers." *J Jew Com Ser* 54 (Fall 1979): 43–49.

JESNA. *Home Start Programs* (packets of materials for parents). N.Y.

JTSA. *Havruta: Home-Study Program Catalogue*. A Torah L'Shma Program.

Karp, Abraham J. "What Shall Parents Tell Their Children about God?" *Syn Sch* 9 (Sept. 1950): 11–15.

Karp, B. I. "Training for the 'Jewish' in Jewish Family Life Education." *J Jew Com Ser* 61 (Fall 1984): 70–78.

Karp, Renee. "The Mini School: A Family Program." *Compass* 4 (Fall/Winter 1980): 8, 20.

Kastle, Harold D. "Seminar for Jewish Parents." *Syn Sch* 18 (Sept. 1959): 23–24.

Katz, David A. "Jewish Family Theatre." A new educational tool seeking to integrate theater and family education. Master's project, HUC–JIR, 1980.

Kay, J. "Family Education: P.A.C.E." *Compass* 3 (Winter/Spring 1980).

Keeping Posted. *The Jewish Family: Continuity and Change*. Nos. 840620 and 840622.

———. *Peace in the Home* (parents and youth, drug abuse, problems). Nos. 840040 and 840042. UAHC, N.Y.

———. *Problems of Jewish Family Life* (abortion, divorce, proselytizing, etc.). Nos. 849389 and 840382.

Kimel, Meyer. "הבית ובית הספר„ (The Home and the School). *Sh Hah* (H.) 11 (June 1951): 130–37.

Kiner, Edward D. "Focus on Family Education." *AM* (Winter 1976).

———. "Total Family Education." *CCAR J* 22 (Winter 1975).

Kitov, A. E. *The Jew and His Home.* Translated and with an introduction by Nathan Bulman. N.Y.: Shengold, 1963. 233 pp.

Klausner, Bertram. "Family Worship Services for Jewish and American Holidays." *Jew Teach* 32 (May 1954): 6–9.

Knoff, H. M., and C. R. Smith. "The Relationship of Student Attitude toward Religious Education and Parent Involvement" (program at a Jewish supplementary school). *Jew Ed* 48 (Spring 1980): 27–34, 41.

Koblenz, Maxine L. "Involving the Parent." *Ped Rep* 30 (Fall 1978): 23–24.

Kohn, J. "Modern Problems of Jewish Parents." *Recon* 45 (Jan. 1980): 18–21.

Kozberg, Cary. "A Family-Value Sukkot Experience." *Compass* (Summer 1975).

Krantzler, Harold I. *The Family in the Congregation and in the Community.* N.Y.: UAHC, Department of Adult Education, Nov. 16, 1963. 25 pp.

Kripke, Mrs. Myer S. "The Jewish Mother: Portrait or Caricature." *Your Child* 4 (Winter 1970): 14–18.

Kurtz, V. "Family Life Education in an Urban Synagogue." *Rel Ed* 77 (May–June 1982): 321–25.

Kurzband, Toby. *Parents Are Partners in Jewish Education.* N.Y.: UAHC, 1970.

Landau, Diane Fishman. "Family Chai: A Family Education Program Integrating Family Systems Theory with Jewish Values." A program focusing on nine Jewish values that affect family relations, based on family systems theory. Master's project, HUC–JIR, 1983.

Landes, Sora. "An Experiment in Parent Education." *Syn Sch* 13 (May 1955): 3–8. See also *Syn Sch* 23 (Winter 1965): 22–26.

Lasker, Arnold A. "Identifying and Changing Parental Attitude." *RA* (1977): 73–75.

———. "Parents as Partners: Report of a Research Project." *Impact* 35 (Winter 1976–77): 4–16.

———. "What Parents Want from the Jewish Education of Their Children." *J Jew Com Ser* 52 (Summer 1976): 393–403.

Lichtig, Judith. "The Hearts of Parents and Children." *Compass* 9 (Fall 1986): 6–7, 19.

Linzer, Norman. "The Future of the Jewish Family: Personal and Communal Responsibility." *Jew Ed* 52 (Spring 1984): 10–15.

Lippman, Froma. "Four Questions for Parents of Jewish Teens." *Compass* 9 (Fall 1986): 8, 17.

Lipschutz, Karen S. "A Family Shabbat Experience." *AM* (Fall 1976).

Livingstone, Nancy. "Our Children's Jewishness: Sharing Goals with Parents." *Ped Rep* 33 (Dec. 1981): 34.

Louis, Roberta L. "Parents' Attitudes and the Supplementary Jewish School." A study that documents and examines parental attitudes concerning supplemental Jewish schooling. Master's project, HUC–JIR, 1981.

Marcus, Audrey Friedman. "Involving Parents." In *JTH*, 2:141–47.

Meckler, D. L. „אידישע דערציאונג פאנגט זיך אן מיט די עלטערן" (Jewish Education Begins with the Parents). *Day* (Y.) (Aug. 19, 1962).

Melamed, Joseph. "Toward a Course in Adult Education in the Jewish Family." Master's thesis, HUC–JIR, 1966.

Melton Research Center. *Together: A Child-Parent Kit.* Created by Vicky Kelman, Joel Grishaver, and Jane Golub.
> *Issue One: Happy New Year*, 31 pp.
> *Issue Two: Gifts*, 28 pp.
> *Issue Three: The Magic Land*, 52 pp.
> *Issue Four: Hanukkah*, 24 pp.
> *Issue Five: Hide and Seek: A Game about God.* For children, 12 pp., for parents, 12 pp. Game board and audio tape.
> *Issue Six: Trees*, 35 pp.
> *Issue Seven: Purim*, 38 pp.
> *Issue Eight: Passover*, 40 pp.
> *Issue Nine: Israel and Torah*, 28 pp.

Menes, Abraham. „אידישע ערציהונג און די אידישע פאמיליע" (Jewish Education and the Jewish Family). *For* (Y.) (July 24, 1966).

Milch, Robert. "The Home as a Hebrew School." *Moment* 4 (June 1979): 51–57.

Millgram, Abraham E. "New Trends in Parent Education." *Syn Sch* 9 (Sept. 1950): 16–21.

Narot, Joseph B. "Reform Judaism—Its Challenge to the Family and the Religious School." *Jew Teach* 32 (Apr. 1964): 6–9.

National Federation of Temple Sisterhoods, UAHC. *Parents Are Teachers Too: A Home-*

Based Jewish Education Program. N.Y. See also *Ped Rep* 35 (June 1984): 20–21.

Oblath, Sunny Romer, and George Rubin. "A Course in Jewish Values for the Family." Eleven-session course dealing with Jewish values, written in the form of a facilitator's guide, for adolescents and their parents. Master's project, HUC–JIR, 1976.

Olitzky, Kerry M. "Across the Generations: A Family Shabbat Experience." *Compass* (Winter/Spring 1981–82): 3–4, 18.

Ped Rep. "Family Kallah." 24 (Fall 1972): 21.

Ped Rep. "In the Conservative Movement: Family Kallot." 25 (Fall 1973): 20.

Ped Rep. "In the Conservative Movement: Parent Education." 25 (Spring 1974): 17.

Ped Rep. "Winning the Jewish Home: A New Frontier in Jewish Education." 28 (Spring 1977).

Pilch, Judah. "Words that Preserve" (The Jewish Home). *Congress Weekly* (Nov. 11, 1957).

Pins, Arnulf. "What Teachers Can Do with Parents." *Jew Teach* 29 (Oct. 1960): 9–13.

Raik, Jerome. "Maximizing Parent Participation." *Sh'ma* (Sept. 1978): 146–49.

Rauch, Eduardo. "Families of Our Time." *MRCN* 11 (Fall 1980): 6, 16.

Ray, Natalie. "Kehilla: A Home Study Program for Isolated Families (in small towns or otherwise out of reach of Jewish resources)." Master's project, HUC–JIR, 1977.

Reneh, H. "Victim is the Child." *Congress Biweekly* 34 (Jan. 9 1967): 4–5.

Rosenthal, Ira. "Marriage and the Family" (high school unit). *Jew Teach* 18 (Jan. 1950): 6–11.

Rosman, Steven M. "Making Jewish Homes Jewish Schools: The Babayit Program." *Compass* 9 (Spring/Summer 1987): 15.

———. "What Do You Say When Your Child Asks about God?" *Compass* 9 (Fall 1986): 9, 17.

Saretsky, Augusta. "Bringing up Jewish Parents." *Adult Jewish Education* (Winter 1955): 19–20.

Schafler, Samuel. "Teaching Conservative Judaism and the Jewish Family." *Con Jud* 33 (Fall 1979): 73–78.

Scharfstein, Zevi. „די ראלע פון דער פאמיליע און דער אידישער דערציאונג" (The Role of the Family in Jewish Education). In *Yiddish Schools in Mexico* (Y.), 65–76. Mexico, 1950.

Scheindling, Lawrence. "School and Family." *Ped Rep* 37 (Feb. 1986): 3–6.

Schlosser, Sonya. "The Educator and the Parent." *Ed As* (1970): 111–18.

Schwartzman, Sylvan D. "Parent Education." *CCAR J* 19 (Autumn 1972): 43–72.

Shabatay, Y. "Involving Parents in the Decision Making Process." *Jew Ed* 43 (Fall 1974): 48–55.

Shereshevsky, Esra. "The Problem of Home School Relationship." *Jew Ed* 25 (Winter 1955): 33–35.

Siegel, Max. "Psychological Factors in Parent-School Relationships." *Ed As* (1968): 51–58.

Siegel, Morton. "Parental Options." *Syn Sch* 29 (Fall 1970): 37–39.

———. "The United Synagogue Family Education Program." *Ped Rep* 30 (Fall 1978): 11–12.

Silver, Cheri Ellowitz. "An Evaluation of Parent Involvement: Resources Designed for a Jewish Community Center Day Camp." A presentation of the philosophy that family and home learning are essential to the development of committed Jewish individuals. Master's project, HUC–JIR, 1982.

Sklare, Marshall. "The New American Jewish Parent and Jewish Education." *Ed As* (1968): 77–83.

Slesinger, Zalmen. "Our Silent Partners—the Teacher, the Parent and the Child." *Ped Rep* 19 (June 1968): 5–8.

Slonimsky, David. "Reporting to the Parent." *Ped Rep* 30 (Fall 1978).

Smolar, Boris. „א אידישע דערציאונג פאר עלטערן אין אמעריקע" (Jewish Education for Parents in America). *For* (Y.) (Oct. 5, 1980).

Spiro, Jack D. "Family Life and Jewish Education." *Dimensions* (Summer 1971): 38–41.

Starr, Earl S. "Toward a Program of Adult Education for Parents of Children in the Elementary Grades." Master's thesis, HUC–JIR, 1957.

Steinhorn, Sharon. "Tri-Generation Family Kallah." *AM* (Winter 1978).

Stern, Chaim, ed. "שערי הבית" (Gates of the House: The New Union Home Prayerbook). N.Y.: CCAR, 1977. 296 pp.

Stern, Jay B., ed. *The Parent and Jewish Education, 1968.* N.Y.: Ed As, 1969. 90 pp.

Strassfield, Sharon, and Kathy Green. *The Jewish Family Book.* N.Y.: 1981. 453 pp.

Syme, Daniel B. *The Jewish Home: A Guide for Jewish Living.* UAHC, 1988. 128 pp.

———. *The Jewish Home Series.* N.Y.: UAHC, 1982–85.
1. *Shabbat.*
2. *Pesach.*
3. *Chanukah and Purim.*
4. *Rosh Hashanah and Yom Kippur.*
5. *Tu Bishevat, Lag Ba'omer, Shavuot, and Tisha Be'av.*
6. *Sukot and the Value of Hoshana Rabbah, Shemini Atzeret, and Simchat Torah.*
7. *Berit Milah, Berit Chayim, and Names.*
8. *Pidyon Haben, Bar-Bat Mitzvah, Confirmation.*
9. *The Jewish Wedding* (part one).
10. *The Jewish Wedding* (part two).
11. *The Jewish Divorce.*

———. "Promoting Family Education." *Compass* (Mar. 1974).

Syn Sch. "Parent Education: A Program, Manual-Syllabus, Bibliography." 29 (Fall 1970): 14–63.

Szonyi, David M. "Jewish Family Education." *Had Mag* 66 (Oct. 1984): 46–47.

Toubin, Isaac. "Family Education: A New Frontier." *Ped Rep* 28 (Spring 1977).

UAHC, *Do It Yourself Shabbat.* N.Y., 1982.

USCJE. *So You Are Having a Family Kallah.* N.Y., 1975.

USCJE. "Syllabus: A Program for Parents Correlating with the Child's Course of Study" *Syn Sch* 29 (Fall 1970): 22–63.

Vernon, Lisa. "The Jewish Family: A New Approach to Bar/Bat Mitzvah." A family Bar/Bat Mitzvah program with both parallel and joint activities for students and family. Master's project, HUC–JIR, 1977.

Waldenberg, Shelley Michael. "The Family School of Temple Isaiah." *Compass* 1 (Fall 1977): 5–7.

Wall, Susan. "Hearing Parents Speak: A New Opportunity for Jewish Educators." *MJ* 20 (Spring 1986): 32, 30.

Weine, Max. "An Experiment in Parent Education." *Syn Sch* 9 (Sept. 1950): 3–6.

Weiss, Gabriele. "Parents Go to School." *Ped Rep* 32 (Winter 1981): 33–34.

Willner, Eric. "Home Background Factors of Students in Jewish Schools." *Jew Ed* 40 (Mar. 1970): 30–35.

Wittstein, Ailene, and Joel Wittstein. "The Parent Manual." In *JPH*, 87–89.

Wolf, Michael. "Perspectives on Jewish Family Education." *Ped Rep* 35 (Jan. 1984): 28–31.

Your Child and You (pamphlet series for Jewish parents). N.Y.: USCJE, 1954–58.
    Brevis, Anna Bear, *Jewish Education Begins at Home.*
    Karp, Abraham J., *When Your Child Asks about God.*
    Lewin, Kurt, *Bringing up the Jewish Child.*
    Millgram, Abraham, *Your Son's Bar Mitzvah.*
    Revitch, Eugene, *The Mental Hygiene Value of Jewish Education.*
    Segal, Abraham, *Your Daughter's Bat Mitzvah.*

Zaiman, Joel H. "An Approach to Jewish Parent Education." *Jew Ed* 41 (Spring 1972): 17–22.

———. "Parent Education." *Ped Rep* 22 (Mar. 1971): 17–21.

———. "Parent Education: Its Rationale." *Syn Sch* 29 (Fall, 1970): 5–13.

———. "Problem Solving: Jewish Parent Education." *Con Jud* 26 (Summer 1972): 69–71.

Ziprin, Nathan. "Call to Jewish Parents." *Day* (Sept. 4, 1960).

Zlotowitz, Bernard. "Three Generations Can Learn and Do Together." *Jew Ed* 41 (Spring 1972): 23–27.

THE JEWISH FAMILY (SELECTED)

* Abramowitz, Naomi Ruth. *The Investigation of Family Size Decisions in the Context of*

Marital Interaction: An Analysis of the Responses of Fifteen Jewish Couples Interviewed Conjointly about Their Decision to Terminate Child Bearing. Columbia U., 1972. 187 pp.

AJC. "Consultation on the Jewish Family: Its Role in Jewish Identity." *Summary Proceedings, May 1977*. N.Y.: Jewish Communal Affairs Department, 1977.

AJC. *National Family Center Newsletter*. N.Y.: AJC Jewish Communal Affairs Department, Mar. 1980.

AJC. *Summary Report* (AJC National Committee on Jewish Family Life). N.Y.: AJC, Jewish Communal Affairs Department, Aug. 1979.

AJC. *Sustaining the Jewish Family: A Task Force Report on Jewish Family Life*. N.Y.: AJC, Communal Affairs Department.

Alper, Janice, ed. *Learning Together: A Sourcebook on Jewish Family Education*. Denver: ARE, 1987.

Balswick, Jack. "Are American Jewish Families Closely Knit?" JSS 28 (July 1966): 159–67.

Bardis, P. D. "Familism among Jews in Suburbia." *Social Science* 36 (1961): 190–96.

Benson, Paulette, and Joanne Altschuler. *The Jewish Family, Past, Present and Future*. Student manual. Denver: ARE, 1979. Grade 7–adult.

Berman, Myron. "The New Morality and the Jewish Family." *Recon* 33 (Nov. 1967): 16–22.

Blau, Zina Smith. "The Strategy of the Jewish Mother." In *JAS*, 167–87.

Boroff, D. "The Over-Protective Jewish Mother." *Congress Weekly* 24 (Nov. 4, 1957): 6–8.

Brav, Stanley R. *The Jewish Family*. Vicksburg: 1940.

———. *Jewish Family Solidarity: Myth or Fact*. Nogales Press, 1940. 130 pp.

Bressler, M. "Selected Family Patterns in W. I. Thomas's Unfinished Study of the Bintel Brief [of the New York *Daily Forward*]." *American Sociological Review* 20 (1955): 33–39.

Bubis, Gerald, ed. *The Changing Jewish Family*. GA, 1976. 10 pp.

———. *The Contemporary Jewish Family*. Reprinted from *JWB Yearbook*, 1977. N.Y.: JWB.

———. *Serving the Jewish Family*. N.Y.: Ktav. 367 pp.

Cardozo, Arlene Rossen. *Jewish Family Celebrations: Shabbat, Festivals and the Traditional Ceremonies*. N.Y.: St. Martin's Press, 1982.

Christopherson, V. A., and J. Walters. "Responses of Protestants, Catholics, and Jews Concerning Marriage and Family Life." *Sociology and Social Research* 43 (1958): 16–22.

* Cohen, Jessica Lynn. *A Comparison of Norms and Behaviors of Child-Rearing in Jewish and Italian Mothers*. Syracuse U., 1977.

Cohen, Steven Martin. "The American Jewish Family Today." *AJYB* 82 (1982): 136–54.

Cohen, Steven Martin, and Paula E. Hyman, eds. *The Jewish Family: Myths and Reality*. N.Y.: Holmes and Meier, 1986. 242 pp.

Dimensions. "The Jewish Family in a Changing Society" (symposium). 4 (Fall 1969): 14–23. Participants: S. Hofstein, Mannheim S. Shapiro, and L. A. Berman.

Epstein, David, and Suzanne Stutman. *Torah with Love: A Guide for Strengthening Jewish Values within the Family*. N.Y.: Prentice-Hall, 1986.

Fishman, Joshua A. "The American Jewish Family." *The Jewish Family* 2 (1959).

Franzblau, Abraham. "A New Look at the Psycho-Dynamics of Jewish Family Living." *J Jew Com Ser* 35 (1955): 55–71.

Gittleman, Sol. *From Shtetl to Suburbia: The Family in Jewish Literary Imagination*. Boston: Beacon Press, 1978.

Glustrom, S. *The Jewish Teenager and the Family*. Washington, D.C.: B'nai B'rith. 60 pp.

* Goldberg, Stella. *A Study of Family Life Patterns as Expressed in Practices of Members in the Three Movements of Judaism*. Columbia U., 1957.

Grayzel, Solomon. *Jewish Books for Your Home*. N.Y.: JBA and NJWB, 1950. 16 pp.

* Harper, Sheila Zarb. *A Comparison of the Academic Achievement of Jewish and Non-Jewish ChiLdren After Parental Separation*. U.S. International U., 1982.

Hartman, David. *Memory and Values—A Traditional Response to the Crisis of the Modern Family*. Jerusalem: Posner, 1978.

Hofstein, Saul. "The Critical Role of the Family in a Changing Society." *Dimensions* 4 (Fall 1969).

Josephy, Marcia R. "The Social Structure of a Jewish Family Organization." Master's thesis, Columbia U., 1967.

Jung, M. "Changing Patterns in Jewish Family Life." In *CPA*, 51–66.

Kagan, Henry E. "The Jewish Family." *CCAR J* (Oct. 1954): 10–16.

———. "Sex in the Family." *Rel Ed* 57 (Nov–Dec. 1962): 419–35.

Keeping Posted. *The Jewish Family: Continuity and Change*. Nos. 840620 and 840622 (leader edition).

* Kohn, Jacob. *Modern Problems of Jewish Parents*. Yale U., 1932. Published under the same title by the Women's League of the USA, 1932. 130 pp.

Landes, Ruth, and Mark Zborowski. "Hypothesis Concerning the Eastern Jewish Family." *Psychiatry* 13 (Nov. 1950): 447–64.

Lang, Judith. "The Changing Jewish Family and the Crisis of Values: The Role and Impact of the Professional in Jewish Communal Services." *J Jew Com Ser* 56 (Summer 1980).

Lang, Leon S. "Jewish Values in Family Relationships." *Con Jud* 1 (June 1945): 9–18.

* Levin, Kay L. *Attitudes toward Education among Jewish Parents in an Enclaved and Non-Enclaved Jewish Community*. U. of Arizona, 1975. 150 pp.

Linzer, Norman. *The Jewish Family*. N.Y.: Human Sciences Press, 1984. 217 pp.

Lobel, Eve. "Family Camp: A Format for Jewish Education which Responds to the Needs of the Contemporary Jewish Family." Master's thesis, JTS Department of Jewish Education, 1989.

Mallay, Ruth. "What American Jewish Families Think the Future Holds for Their Children." Master's thesis, Vassar U., 1940.

———. "What Seventy Jewish Families Think the Future Holds for Their Children." *Jew Ed* 12 (Apr. 1940): 21–24.

Mailer, A. S. "The Jewish Family Today." *Recon* 46 (Jan. 1981).

Mayer, Egon. *Children of Intermarriage: A Study in Patterns of Identification and Family Life*. N.Y.: AJC, 1983.

———. "Myths of the Jewish Family." *RJ* (Mar. 1978): 6, 12.

Reisman, Bernard. *The Emerging Jewish Family: A Program for the Jewish Family Service Agency*. Institute for Jewish Life, CP, Oct. 1974. 55 pp.

———. "The Jewish Family and Jewish Communal Service: A Crisis of Values." *J Jew Com Ser* 56 (Fall 1979).

Rose, Nathan H. "A New Approach for the New Family." *Ped Rep* 34 (Jan. 1988): 23–25.

Rosen, Gladys. "The Jewish Family: An Endangered Species." *J Jew Com Ser* 55 (June 1979).

Rosenman, Yehudah. "Research on the Jewish Family and Jewish Education." *J Jew Com Ser* 60 (Spring 1984): 185–92.

Rossel, Seymour. *Family*. N.Y.: F. Watts, 1980.

Sanua, Victor D. "The Contemporary Jewish Family: A Review of the Social Science Literature." *J Jew Com Ser* 50 (Summer 1974): 297–312.

Schulweiss, Harold. "The Jewish Family: Religious Perspective." *CCAR* 93 (1983): 25–29.

Strodtbeck, Fred L. "Family Interaction, Values, and Achievement." In *JES*, 147–65.

Verbit, Mervin F. "The Jewish Family in America Today and Tomorrow: Family Life and Jewish Communal Policy: Some Proposals." GA, Nov. 1979. 17 pp.

Waxman, Chaim J. *The Jewish Father: Past and Present*. N.Y.: AJC, National Jewish Family Center, 1984. 20 pp.

———. *Single Parent Families: A Challenge to the Jewish Community*. N.Y.: AJC, 1980.

Weiss-Rosmarin, Trude. "The Family and Jewish Survival." *Jew Spec* 13 (May 1968): 7–11.

Wessel, Bessie Bloom. "Ethnic Family Patterns: The American Jewish Family." *American Journal of Sociology* 53 (May 1948): 439–42.

Wirth, Louis. "Cultural Conflicts in the Immigrant Family." Master's thesis, U. of Chicago, 1925.

Wolfenstein, M. "Two Types of Jewish Mothers." In *JES*, 520–34.

31 GLEANINGS

Hirsch, Samson Raphael (1854) (Germany),
"More than any other institution the school has to rely upon the confidence of the public, and it needs this confidence not only for the creation and maintenance of its internal requirements, but also for the performance of its essential function. Even for the fixing and defining of the curriculum the agreement of the parents is necessary."
Judaism Eternal, 1: 158–59. 1956.

Kaplan, Mordecai M.,
"If Jewish education is to prove its worth in this country, the scope of the Jewish teacher must be enlarged to include the home of the child."
Judaism as a Civilization, 496. 1957.

Engelman, Uriah Z.,
"In this contest between the liberating and assimilative forces in American life, Jewish parents, by virtue of the kind of Jewish home they establish for the young to be nurtured in will be, as they are now, the decisive factor."
Jew Ed 21 (Summer 1950): 47.

Rosenberg, Stuart E.,
"If our homes give the children the feeling of security, if they confer status upon them, if they teach respect for others, if they give meaning to dependability, if they radiate warmth and hope, if they provide opportunity for shared experiences, if they teach the thrill of new adventure, if, above all, they are loving and beloved, then we have found God. We need not worry about the need to paint for our little ones a verbal picture of God. God will be experienced through actions that speak louder than words."
"Should We Teach Tots about God."
Recon (May 2, 1952), 26.

Saretsky, Augusta,
"We must point out that until now the place of the parent has had a narrow academic interpretation. There has been a tendency until recently to relegate parents to the background, and not give them their rightful place. But a new point of view has been emerging, which is to invite the parent as a partner in planning and participating in the work of the Hebrew School. Rabbis and educators must understand the needs of parents and work with them. Jewish parents must be helped to possess the Jewish heritage before they can link themselves into the continuing chain of generations."
Adult Jewish Education (Winter 1955), 20.

Dinin, Samuel,
"A curriculum reflects what is lived and believed and thought by the community. Only if it is enriched by, as it enriches, Jewish life in the home and the community, will it have real meaning."
AJYB 63 (1962), 220.

Aft, Martha,
"Since we share a responsibility for transmitting our heritage with the home, we in the schools must seek new avenues for truly involving our parents in their children's religious education. Parents refuse to be invited 'to serve food' as their contribution to the school. The involvement must be central to our program, not a peripheral addition. This will truly strengthen both our school programs and the fabric of the besieged American Jewish family."
Compass 2 (Winter 1979), 9–10.

Cohen, Gerson D. (1979),
"Let us make one statement so that you will understand where I stand. A major word of heresy on my part. Ladies and gentlemen, the Jewish family never sustained the Jew. That is a myth that is being perpetrated by people who are dissatisfied with the synagogue and find themselves failures. The family, as a unit in a strongly organized community, had very little to do except to generate, feed, and clothe kids. The community educated them. Where? In the street, in the market place, in the synagogue, in the house of study, in the assembly hall. The family today is being asked to do things which it can't possibly do. It is being asked to replace community, to provide leisure, love, respect, satisfaction, fulfillment. But that's impossible, we cannot do these things in isolation. We can do them only

as a community."
MRCN (Fall 1980), 6.

Rauch, Eduardo,
"It is possible to speculate that what worries us so much today is not the apparent demise of the family as we have come to know it, but rather the loss of a framework within which some basic social functions were performed in an orderly fashion; functions such as child-rearing, inculcation of values, intimacy, sexuality and others. We must be able to continue to evolve societal models able to perform the functions which, while fulfilling our halakhic obligations, will respond to the ever-changing need imposed by the social-historical context. In brief, values insofar as they reflect Torah and human nature, do not change, but their forms of expression do, and do so dramatically. When we are unable to distinguish between value and its transitory expression, we are most likely to become paralyzed."
MRCN (Fall 1980), 6.

Reisman, Bernard,
"Recent research in education clearly calls for an educator-family partnership. The problem, however, is bringing about the two-way street. The situation in Jewish education is more accurately represented by a one-way street: educators moving in one direction working with children, but without a reciprocal flow from parents. And Jewish communal leaders looking on, like traffic cops, interested in being helpful, but uncertain of whether or how to intercede."
Jew Ed 53 (Spring 1985), 17.

32 | ADULT EDUCATION

GENERAL (SELECTED)

Abrams, William. "A Challenge and an Opportunity." *Ped Rep* 34 (Mar. 1983): 14.

Agus, Jacob B. *Study-Guide for the Evolution of Jewish Thought* (Beth El Congregation, Baltimore). N.Y.: Abelard Schuman. 37 pp.

Arffa, Elaine, and Gerald Arffa. "What's Happening in Adult Education?" (survey of temple programs). *Compass* 10 (Spring/Summer 1988): 10–12.

Aron, Isa, et al. "Alternative Jewish Education: The Havurah Model." *Response* 30–31 (Fall 1976): 185–92.

Aronson, David. *The Jewish Way of Life*. N.Y.: NAAJS of the USA, ca. 1946. 191 pp.

Atzmon, Ezri. „חינוך יהודי למבוגרים בארצות-הברית" (Jewish Education for Adults in the United States). *Hagut* (H.) (1974): 364–77.

AvRutick, A. N. "The Eggheads Came to Learn." *Jew Life* 26 (Oct. 1958).

Ballonof, Martin. "Retreat to Progress: Adult Education Comes of Age." *Con Jud* (Summer 1975): 79–89.

Beckerman, Marvin. "Adult Jewish Education: Present and Future Directions." *Rel Ed* (Jan.-Feb. 1973).

Ben-Horin, Meier. "Re-Schooling American Jewry." *J Jew Com Ser* (Spring 1976): 278.

Blinder, Robert. "Towards a Program of Adult Jewish Education for Parents of Pupils in Religious School." Master's thesis, HUC–JIR, 1957.

Blumenfield, Samuel M. "The Scope and Content of Adult Jewish Education as a Function of a Jewish College." *Jew Ed* 9 (Apr–June 1937): 78–86.

———. "Some Aspects of Adult Jewish Education." *Jew Ed* 10 (Oct.–Dec. 1938): 148–56. Also in *RA* (1933–38): 448–60.

Bregman, Alan, and Betsy Katz. "Encountering God in Your Life" (developing adult Jewish spirituality). *Compass* 10 (Fall 1987): 11–12.

Brodsky, Edith. "Combatting Jewish Illiteracy." *Congress Weekly* (Sept. 12, 1955): 10–13.

———. "Laboratory of Jewish Learning." *Congress Weekly* (Dec. 22, 1958): 5–7.

———. "The Search for Jewish Knowledge." *Congress Weekly* (Jan. 16, 23, 1956): 10–13, 7–10.

Buber, Martin. „מטרותיו של חינוך מבוגרים" (The Aims of Adult Education). *Ed Enc* (H.), 1:502–11. Jerusalem.

* Campbell, Kenneth James. *Determination of Participation in Jewish Adult Education*. U. of Maryland, 1978.

Cedarbaum, David I. "Adult Education and the Democratic Way." *Rel Ed* 37 (1942): 51–54.

———. "The Extent of Adult Education." *Jew Teach* 7 (Jan. 1939): 23–24.

Chipkin, Israel S. "The Israel Friedlander Classes—An Experiment in Jewish Education for Youth and Adults." *RA* (1930–32): 167–88.

Chomsky, William. "התנועה לחנוך מבוגרים" (Adult Education Movement). *Sh Hah* (H.) 24 (Fall 1963): 10–14.

Cohen, Jack J. "Continuity in Jewish Education." In *JEDS*, 314–42.

Cohen, Samuel I. "Adult Jewish Education." *Chicago Jewish Forum* 24 (Fall 1965): 2–9. See also *Rel Ed* 60 (Sept.–Oct. 1965): 381–88.

———. "Adult Jewish Education." *AJYB* 66 (1965): 277–90.

Danzig, Jerry M. "Derech Ami: 'Az M'Ken Lernen'." *Syn Sch* 29 (Summer 1971): 5–44.

Diamond, L. A. "Brotherhood's Stake in Adult Education." *A Jud* 16 (Winter 1966–67): 51.

Dinin, Samuel. "What Is Adult Jewish Education?" *Adult Jew Ed* (Winter 1955): 6–7.

Dushkin, Alexander M. "The Child and the Adult in Jewish Education." *Jew Ed* 13 (Jan. 1942): 165–69.

Edelman, Lily. "B'nai B'rith and Adult Education." *Recon* 30: 15–20.

* Elkin, Harry. *Adult Jewish Education in the United States.* Dropsie U., 1954. 206 pp.

———. "Jewish Education for Adults." *Jew Ed* 25 (Summer 1954): 9–21, 54.

Enelow, Hyman G. *Adult Education in Judaism.* Cincinnati: DSSE, UAHC, 1927. 18 pp.

———. "On Adult Education." *CCAR* 37 (1927): 264–70.

* Epstein, Jerome Michael. *The Contributions of Selected Traditional Jewish Literature to Understanding the Androgogy of and Practice of Adult Education.* Temple U., 1980. 157 pp. Digest in *Rel Ed* 77 (June–July 1982): 441.

Essrig, Harry. *The American Jew Takes Inventory—A Bold New Project in Adult Education.* Grand Rapids, Mich.: Temple Emanuel, 1950.

Essrog, Chaim I. *Adult Jewish Education Materials* (available at UAHC). N.Y.: UAHC, Department of Adult Jewish Education, 1965. 17 pp.

———. "The Primacy of Adult Jewish Education." *Jew Teach* 32:4 Apr. 1964.

Essrog, Chaim I., and Meir Ydit. *God's World and Man's World: A Study Guide for Adults.* N.Y.: UAHC, Department of Adult Jewish Education, 1963. 38 pp.

Feinberg, Paul. "Bat Kol—A Heavenly Echo in Search of a Studying Elite." *Compass* 3 (Fall 1979): 14, 22.

Feinstein, Morley. "Learning Packet on Judaism and Older People." Four-part learning packet that provides the learner the opportunity to both understand and act upon a complex social issue. Master's project, HUC–JIR, 1980.

* Feinstein, Sara. *A Content Analysis of the First National Conference on Adult Jewish Education.* Columbia U., 1967. 352 pp.

Feldman, Leon A. *Aspects of American Jewish Life: Proceedings of the Jewish Orientation and Training Session.* 2d ed. N.Y.: JEC Department of Adult Education, 1961. 80 pp.

———. "Some Selected Goals and Methods in Adult Jewish Education." *J Jew Com Ser* 33 (Summer 1957): 353.

———. "Wanted: The Facts on Adult Education." *Congress Weekly* (Mar. 22, 1954): 15–17.

* Feldman, Patricia Shirley. *Identification of Some Religious and Cultural Perceptions of Select Population of Aging Jewish Persons with Implications for Jewish Educational Programming.* U. of Pittsburgh, 1978. 233 pp.

Fisher, Gershon. "Toward the Creation of a Course of Study for the Convert to Reform Judaism." Master's thesis, HUC–JIR, 1964.

Fram, Leon. "The Trend Toward Adult Education." *Jew Ed* 6 (Jan. 1934): 5.

Frankel, P., and M. Golant. "A Family Education Program for Soviet Jewish Seniors." *J Jew Com Ser* 58 (Spring 1982): 223–30.

Freeman, S. D. "The Adult Program of the Jewish Community in the United States." *Jew J Soc* 5 (1963): 187–97.

Friedman, Theodore. "A Four Year Adult Jewish Education Curriculum." *RA* (1960): 43–48.

32 ADULT EDUCATION

Gamoran, Emanuel. "Toward a Program of Adult Education." *Jew Teach* 10 (Jan. 1943): 1–8.

———. "What Is Adult Jewish Education?" *Adult Jew Ed* (Winter 1952): 4.

Glasner, Samuel. "Three Principles in Adult Jewish Education." *Ped Rep* 20 (Mar. 1969).

Goldman, Israel M. "Adult Jewish Education in Terms of Contemporary Needs." *Jew Ed* 15 (Jan. 1944): 75–78, 84.

———. "Jewish Educational Content (for) Adult Group." *RA* (1941–44): 190–99.

———. *Lifelong Learning among Jews: Adult Education in Judaism from Biblical Times to the Twentieth Century.* N.Y.: Ktav, 1975. 364 pp.

———. "Objectives in Adult Jewish Education." *Jew Ed* 10 (Oct.–Dec. 1938): 167–75. See also *RA* (1939): 434–47.

Goodman, Philip. *Adult Jewish Courses in the Jewish Community Center.* N.Y.: JWB

Green, Alan Singer. "An Application of Modern Educational Theory to the Problem of Orienting and Integrating Adults in Modern Jewish Life: A Project in the Motivation of Adult Activity." Master's thesis, HUC–JIR, 1934.

———. "A Functional Approach to Adult Jewish Education." *Jew Ed* (Jan.–Mar. 1936): 43–45.

———. *A Project in Adult Participation in Present-Day Jewish Life.* Syllabus for adult congregational group. Cincinnati: Department of Jewish Religious Education–HUC, 1935. 88 pp.

Greenberg, Simon. "Lifetime Education as Conceived and Practiced in the Jewish Tradition." *Rel Ed* (May–June 1973): 339–47.

Halkin, Abraham, S. "החנוך לבוגרים„ (Adult Education). *Hinukh* (H.) 1 (Heshvan 1936): 52–56.

———. "Intensive Jewish Education: A Proposed Program." *Adult Jew Ed* (Spring 1957).

Heilman, Samuel C. *The People of the Book.* Chicago: U. of Chicago Press, 1983.

Honor, Leo L. "Adult Jewish Education." In *Adult Jewish Education*, Series 2. N.Y.: NAAJS, Proceedings of National Conference on Adult Education, Nov. 10, 1942.

———. "Moral and Spiritual Values in Adult Education from a Jewish Standpoint." *Jew Ed* 24 (Fall 1953): 31–34, 58.

———. "What Is Adult Jewish Education?" *Adult Jew Ed* (Winter 1955): 5.

Horn, Ronnie M. "Gates of Identity: An Adult Study Course Based on Gates of Repentance." Master's thesis, HUC–JIR, 1962.

Imber, Rebecca, and Jack J. Cohen, eds. *The Creative Audience.* N.Y.: The Reconstructionist Press, 1954. 152 pp.

Ingall, Carol K. "On Becoming a Jewish Adult." *Con Jud* 30 (Spring 1976): 63–71.

Israeli, Eitan. "חינוך המבוגרים היהודי באה"ב ובישראל„ (Adult Jewish Education in the United States and Israel). *Hadoar* (H.) 53 (Nov. 1973).

Kallen, Horace M. "Towards a Philosophy of Adult Education." In *Lown*, 45–61.

Kamrat, Mordecai. "הוראת עברית למבוגרים„ (Teaching Hebrew to Adults). In *FPDE* (H.) 118–122

Kaplan, Mordecai M. "What the American Woman Can Do for Adult Jewish Education." *Jew Ed* 4 (Oct./Dec. 1932): 139–47.

Kelson, Benjamin. "The Philosophy of Adult Education." *Jew Teach* 7 (Jan. 1939): 13–22.

Klein, Aaron. "חנוך לבוגרים—נסיון שהצליח„ (Education for Adults—An Experiment that Succeeded). *Sh Hah* (H.) 35 (1975): 198–204.

Landman, Isaac. "Adult Education—A Function of the Jewish School." *Jew Ed* 5 (Apr.–June 1933): 79–87.

Lang, Leon. "Adult Education." *RA* (1940): 36–37.

Lear, Elmer N. "Jewish Culture in the Summer Time." *Recon* (Feb. 24, 1956): 19–25.

Locke, Shawn. "A Study of Adult Learning in Havurot." Focuses on the learning component of synagogue Havurot and the adult learners who participate in Havurah education. Master's project, HUC–JIR, 1985.

Marcus, Audrey Friedman, and Kerry M. Olitzky. "Teaching and Reaching Adults and the Elderly." In JTH, 149–59.

Markowitz, Samuel H. "What Is Adult Jewish Education." *Jew Ed* 6:2 (Apr.–June 1934): 72–75.

Matz, Marcia S. "The Holiday Workshop Series: A Longitudinal Study of Impact." The history, format, goals, and teacher training of this series are reviewed as a model for adult education. Master's project, HUC–JIR, 1981.

NAAJS. *Adult Jewish Education in Time of War*. N.Y., 1943. 92 pp.

NAAJS. *Objectives, Standards, and Program for Adult Jewish Education in the Congregation*. N.Y., 1961.

Nadich, Judah. "Adult Education." *RA* (1976): 127–38.

National Council on Adult Jewish Education. *Guide to Select Adult Jewish Educational Materials*. N.Y.: AAJE, 1969.

Neulander, Arthur H. *The Sabbath Prayers*. N.Y.: NAAJS and JTSA.

Neusner, Jacob. "The Kinds of Adult Education." *Adult Jew Ed* (Spring/Summer 1962).

NJWB. *Learning for Jewish Living*. Jewish Center Lecture Bureau, NJWB.

Noveck, Simon. "New Trends in Adult Jewish Education." *RA* (1954): 201–11.

———, ed. *Suggested Courses for Adult Jewish Studies*. N.Y.: NAAJS–USA, 1954. 193 pp.

———. "Toward a Curriculum for Adult Jewish Education." *CCAR J* (June 1957): 27–30.

Noveck, Simon, and Lily Edelman. "Adult Jewish Education in 1954–1955." *Adult Jew Ed* 2 (Summer 1955): 3–4.

———. *The Enduring Heritage: An Anthology of Readings for Adult Study*. Washington, D.C.: B'nai B'rith Department of Adult Education, 1960. 154 pp.

———. *The Laymen's Institute—An Adventure in Jewish Living*. N.Y.: NAAJS–USA, 1954. 34 pp.

Pollak, George, and Israel D. Lerner. *The Aged in Jewish Tradition*. N.Y.: Council for Jewish Education, Apr. 1982.

RA. "Committee on Adult Jewish Education." (1940): 36–38.

Ravid, Zvulun. "חנוך מבוגרים" (Adult Education). *Sh Hah* (H.) 25 (Fall 1965): 57–58.

Recon. "Long Range and Immediate Tasks in Adult Jewish Education." 31 (Mar. 19, 1965).

Recon. "Needed: A Major Assault on Jewish Ignorance" (editorial). 32 (Feb. 17, 1967).

Ribner, Sol. "The Effects of Intensive Jewish Education on Adult Jewish *Life-Styles*." *Jew Ed* 46 (Spring 1978): 6–12.

Rosenthal, Henry W. "The Essentials of Jewish Knowledge for the American Jew." *Jew Ed* 15 (Sept. 1943): 14–16.

Rothstein, D. G. "Developing a Voluntary Neighborhood Intergenerational Program." *J Jew Com Ser* 60 (Fall 1982): 48–52.

Segal, Abraham. "Continuing or Adult—What's in a Name." *Ped Rep* 22 (June 1971): 18.

Sherwood, John M. "Toward an Introduction to Judaism for Adult Jews and Proselytes." Master's thesis, HUC–JIR, 1967.

Singer, Jacob. "Adult Education." *CCAR* 38 (1928): 361–85.

———. "Outline for Adult Education in Judaism." Includes bibliography by topic. *CCAR* 40 (1930): 428–64.

Slesinger, Zalmen. "Adult Jewish Education and the 'Dilemma of Freedom'." *Ped Rep* 16 (Dec. 1964): 13–16.

———. "Adult Jewish Education: A Four Dimensional Approach." *Ped Rep* 11 (Nov. 1959).

———. *Guide to Select Adult Jewish Educational Materials*. AAJE National Council on Adult Jewish Education, 1970.

Smolar, Boris. "אידישע דערציאונג פאר עלטערן אין אמעריקע" (Jewish Education for Parents in America). *For* (Y.) (Oct. 5, 1980).

Weiss, S. R. "New Vistas for Adult Jewish Education." *Jew Life* 15 (Oct. 1947).

Weiss-Rosmarin, Trude. "Observations on Adult Jewish Education." *Jew Spec* (May 1957): 3–8.

White, Martha. "Adult Education." In *JPH*, 473.

Wolf, A. "Adult Education in the American Synagogue." *Jud* 10 (Fall 1961).

IN THE COMMUNITY

AAJE. *The Adult Jewish Education Activities of the American Jewish Community: Highlights and Insights*. N.Y., 1964.

32 ADULT EDUCATION

Adult Jew Ed. "Adult Jewish Education—For the Few or the Masses?" Participants: Paul C. Behrman, Israel M. Goldman, and Samuel M. Burstein. (Winter 1957–58): 4–11.

Appel, George. *A Guide to an Adult Education Program in the Synagogue.* N.Y.: UOJCA.

Blumenfeld, Samuel M. "Adult Jewish Education in the Jewish Community." *Rel Ed* (Oct./Dec. 1939).

Braun, Barbara. "Havurah as a New Dimension in Congregational Life." In *Serving the Jewish Family*. N.Y.: Ktav, 1977.

Bubis, Gerald B., Henry W. Wasserman, and Alan Lerit. *Synagogue Havurot: A Comparative Study*. Lanham, Md.: U. Press of America, 1983.

Cohen, Beryl D. "The Teaching Synagogue." *Jew Teach* 7 (Apr. 1939): 1–16.

* Cohen, Samuel J. *History of Adult Jewish Education in Four National Jewish Organizations*. Yeshiva U., 1967. 426 pp.

———. "New Directions in Adult Jewish Education." *Jew Ed* 38 (Mar. 1968): 5–14.

Davis, David. *Adult Jewish Education Programs in Reform Congregations, 1959–1963*. N.Y.: UAHC, 1962. 24 pp.

Edelman, Lily. "B'nai B'rith and Adult Jewish Education." *Recon* (May 1, 1964): 15–20.

Edidin, Ben M. "A Community Program of Extension Education." *Jew Ed* 1 (Oct. 1929): 173.

———. "Institutes of Jewish Studies." *Jew Ed* 7 (Jan.–Mar. 1935): 34–39.

Eichhorn, Jonathan. *Outline of Twenty-Six Adult Education Courses in Reform Congregations, 1958–1959*. N.Y.: UAHC, 1959.

Einstein, Stephen J., and Lydia Kukoff. *Introduction to Judaism: A Course Outline*. N.Y.: UAHC, 1983.

Fishman, Priscilla. *Adult's Guide to Genesis*. 2 vols. N.Y.: U.S. Book Service–MRC, 1972.

Fram, Leon. "Adult Education in the Reform Temple." *Jew Teach* 9 (Apr. 1941): 13–17.

Garfiel, Evelyn. *The Service of the Heart: A Guide to the Jewish Prayer Book*. Study guide by Seymour Siegel. N.Y.: USA and NAAJS, 1958.

Goldman, Israel M. "National Academy for Adult Jewish Studies." *RA* (1941–44): 129–36.

Goldsmith, Bernard. *Adult Jewish Education Courses and Lectures Given in Reform Congregations, 1959–1960*. N.Y.: UAHC, 1960.

Goodman, Philip. *Adult Jewish Courses in the Jewish Community Center*. N.Y.: NJWB, 1949.

Greenberg, Simon. *The Conservative Movement in Judaism: An Introduction (Study Guide)*. N.Y.: NAAJS–USA. 16 pp.

Grossman-Sherman, Hannah. "נסיונותי בהוראת הלשון העברית לבוגרים מתחילים" (Experiences in Teaching Hebrew to Adult Beginners). *Sh Hah* (H.) 5 (Sept. 1945): 249–53.

Gumbiner, Abigail. "Chavurah." In *JPH*, 493–510.

Hachen, David. "Testing a New Method of Teaching Hebrew to Adults." *Jew Teach* 28 (Jan. 1966): 11–12.

Herman, Dorothy C. *From Generation to Generation: An Experimental Approach to the Teaching of the Elderly in Our Community*. Miami: Central Agency for Jewish Education, 1985.

Hoenig, Sidney B. *A Guide to Jewish History*. N.Y.: Department of Adult Education, Yeshiva U., 1960.

Horn, David. "The Struggle to Celebrate." *Compass* 1 (Winter 1977): 5–7.

* Jaffe, Reuven Ralph Martin. *The Berkeley Lehrhaus Judaica—An Alternative Model of Adult Jewish Education: A Case Study of Adult Jewish Education*. U. of Southern Cal., 1983.

Kamrat, Mordecai. "הוראת עברית למבוגרים" (Teaching Hebrew to Adults). In *FPDE* (H.), 118–22.

Kline, David. *Selected Adult Jewish Education Programs Offered in Reform Congregations, 1960–61*. N.Y.: UAHC, 1961.

Krantzler, Harold. *Your Congregation's Adult Education Committee: A Manual*. N.Y.: UAHC, 1978. 69 pp.

Kuselewitz, David. "Presenting Israel to American Jews." *Adult Jew Ed* (Winter 1955): 10–12.

Landau, S. "Jewish Music in Adult Jewish Education." *Adult Jew Ed* (Winter 1957–58): 15–18.

Lang, Leon S. "Adult Education through the Synagogue." *RA* (1939): 48–62.

Langh, Philip A. "Adult Education and the Synagogue." *RA* (1933–38): 139–43.

Mark, Yudel. *Invitation to Yiddish* (for adults). Includes two records. N.Y.: Commission on Jewish Affairs, American Jewish Congress, 1962. 128 pp.

Mintz, Charles D. "Toward an Adult Study Course in Great Jewish Literature." Master's thesis, HUC–JIR, 1956. 221 pp.

NAAJS. *Objectives, Standards and Programs for Jewish Adult Education in the Congregation.* N.Y., 1965.

Neusner, Jacob. "Defining the Havurah." In *Contemporary Judaic Fellowship in Theory and in Practice*, 67–73. N.Y.: Ktav, 1972.

Noble, Shlomo. "How Shall We Approach the Bible?" *Adult Jew Ed* (Spring 1957).

Noveck, Simon. *Adult Jewish Education in the Modern Synagogue.* N.Y.: NAAJS, 1959. 64 pp.

* Poupko, Bernard A. *Forms of Jewish Adult Religious Education in America: A Study of the History, Curriculum and Objectives of Jewish Adult Religious Programs Conducted by the Synagogue, Temple and Jewish Religious Organizations.* U. of Pittsburgh, 1953. 323 pp.

RA. *Six Approaches to Adult Education in Conservative Synagogues.* N.Y., 1954. 22 pp.

Reisman, Bernard. *The Chavurah.* N.Y.: UAHC, 1977.

———. "Professional Leadership for the Havurah." *RJ* (Winter 1977): 51–63.

* Rose, Isaac B. *A Clientele Analysis of Participants and Non-Participants in Synagogue Adult Jewish Education.* Columbia U., 1974. 143 pp.

Routtenberg, Max J. "Adult Education as a Congregational Function." *Adult Jew Ed* (Fall 1960–61).

Schafler, Samuel. "Congregation's Role in Adult Jewish Education." *Adult Jew Ed* (Spring/Summer 1964): 3–5.

Schwartz, Dannel I. "A Sunday School That's Not Just for Kids." *AM* (Winter 1979).

* Shangold, Benjamin. *Community Organizations and Adult Education.* Teachers College, Columbia U., 1957.

Siegel, Morton K. *Handbook for the Adult Education Committee Member.* N.Y.: Adult Education Committee of the USCJE, 1981.

———. "United Synagogue of America on Adult Jewish Education." *Ped Rep* 21 (June 1970): 22–23.

Stein, Jonathan. "In Defense of the Congregational Havurah." *RJ* (Summer 1983): 43–49.

Sundheim, Frank. "Towards a Course of Study for Reform Jewish Adults Dealing with Contemporary Religious Problems." Master's thesis, HUC–JIR, 1958. 200 pp.

SCA. *That Thy Days May Be Long in the Good Land: A Guide to Aging Programs for Synagogues.* Washington, D.C., 1975.

UAHC Department of Adult Education. *Basic Courses in Adult Jewish Studies:*
1. Blank, Irwin M., *How Judaism Grew.*
2. Hachen, David, *Making the Modern Jewish Home.*
3. Miller, Milton G., *Comparative Religion.*
4. Rose, Emanuel, *Understanding the State of Israel.*
5. Brickman, Jay R., *Basic Jewish Beliefs.*
6. Blackman, Murray, *Reform Judaism.*

———. *Union Havurah* (source materials for students and teachers). N.Y.: UAHC, 1977–78. 94 pp.

———. *Aging and Retirement.* N.Y., 1974.

———. *Death, Dying and Bereavement: A Jewish View.* Prepared by Gary H. Huber. N.Y.: UAHC Department of Adult Jewish Studies, 1980. 11 pp.

———. *Introducing the Book of Numbers.* N.Y., 1980.

Warshal, Bruce S. "The Language of Survival: Adult Education and Congregational Programs." *CCAR J* (Summer 1977): 49–58.

Zola, Gary P., and Kerry M. Olitzky. *My People Jacob, Thy Tents Have Grown Old: A Manual for Planning Weekend Kallot for Older People.* N.Y.: UAHC, 1981.

METHODOLOGY AND EVALUATION

Besdin, Abraham. *Life-Long Jewish Education: A Case History of an Adult Education Program.* N.Y.: Yeshiva U. Department of Adult

32 ADULT EDUCATION

Education, Community Service Division, 1957.

Chefitz, Mitchel. "How To Succeed in Adult Education without Really Trying." *Compass* 3 (Summer 1980): 12–13, 22.

Cohen, Israel M. "Adult Jewish Education—1975." *Rel Ed* 72 (Jan.–Feb. 1977): 44–60.

———. "Influencing Participation in Adult Jewish Education Programs." *Jew Ed* 39 (Apr. 1969): 33–42.

———. *Report on the Conditions and Present Status of Adult Jewish Education in the United States*. N.Y.: AAJE, Oct. 29, 1964.

Duker, Abraham G. *An Investigation of the Status and Problems of Jewish Adult Education in the United States*. N.Y.: American Jewish Congress, 1951.

Edelman, Lily. "Are We Asking the Right Questions?" *Information Bulletin on Adult Jewish Education* 1 (Mar. 1966).

Elkin, Harry. "Adult Jewish Education Developments in the United States during the Nineteenth and Twentieth Centuries." *Jew Ed* 26 (Summer 1955): 40–54.

———. "Evaluation and Measurement in Adult Education." *Jew Ed* 31 (Winter 1961): 38–40.

Elkin, Harry, and Shlomo Haramati. „בעיות ומגמות בארצות-הברית" Adult Education—Problems and Trends in the United States). *Ed Enc* (H.), 1:545–47. Jerusalem: 1961.

Essrig, Harry. *The CCAR Adult Education Survey, 1957–1958*. N.Y.: CCAR and UAHC, 1958.

———. "A New Look at Adult Education." *CCARJ* (June 1957): 7–11.

Feldman, Leon A. "The Student's Role in Adult Jewish Education." *Recon* 20 (Feb. 4, 1955).

Hirt-Mannheimer, Aron. "The Jewish Periodical and Adult Education." An investigation of the role that periodicals play in adult Jewish education, tracing the historical development of the Jewish press (English and Yiddish) in the United States as well as the adult Jewish education movement. Master's project, HUC–JIR, 1976.

* Israeli, Eitan. *Comparative Analysis of Program Development Processes in Synagogue Adult Jewish Education*. Columbia U., 1974. 146 pp.

Janowsky, Oscar I. "Adult Education—Analysis of a Survey." *Jew Ed* 36 (Fall 1965): 17–23.

* Kaplan, Felisa Berman. *Programmed Instruction: Teaching the Basic Skills of Hebrew to Post High School Students*. Syracuse U., 1973. 166 pp.

Kaplan, Mordecai M. "How to Vitalize Adult Jewish Study." In *FAJ*, 469–79.

Kieval, Herman. "A New Technique for Teaching the Weekly Sedrah from the Pulpit." *RA* (1960): 246–51.

Klein, Jenny Machlowitz. "Yom-Tov Workshops." *Ped Rep* 34 (Sept. 1981): 22–23.

Matz, Marcia S. "Impact of an Adult Education Program." *Jew Ed* 53 (Spring 1985): 36–41.

NFTB. *Findings of NFTB'S Survey of Laymen's Attitudes*. N.Y.: NFTB, UAHC, 1953.

NFTB. *A Kit to Stimulate Jewish Adult Education*. N.Y.: NFTB, UAHC, 1958.

Noveck, Simon. "Adult Jewish Education Reconsidered." *RA* (1981): 183–90.

Pilch, Yehudah. „גישתו של ד"ר קפלן לחינוך המבוגרים" (Dr. Kaplan's Approach to Adult Jewish Education). *Hadoar* (H.) 50 (June 11, 1971).

Reisman, Bernard, et al. *Experiential Learning in Jewish Groups*. Waltham, Mass.: Brandeis U., 1975.

Roberts, Daniel A. "Group Dynamics as a Media for Adult Religious Education." Master's thesis, HUC–JIR, 1969.

Schaalman, H. E. "Scholar-in-Residence—A New Approach to Adult Education." *Amer Jud* 13 (Spring 1964): 26.

USA. *National Survey III: Target Adult Jewish Education*. N.Y., Fall 1950.

Wiener, Marvin S. "Workshop Report: Objectives and Standards for Adult Jewish Education." *Rel Ed* 72 (Mar.–Apr. 1977): 233–35.

Zahn, Jane C. "Differences between Adults and Youth Affecting Learning." *Adult Jew Ed* (Spring/Summer 1969).

Zlatin, Edward. "University Accreditation of the Synagogue Adult Education Program." *Rel Ed* 74 (July–Aug. 1979): 396–401.

GLEANINGS

Ginzberg, Louis,
"In the olden time the opinion prevailed that the fathers were to be educated first and then the children, not in the reverse order."
In *Students, Scholars and Saints*, 87. 1928.

Baron, Salo W.,
"In their endeavor to stimulate adult education, many rabbis advised fathers to take teachers for their children rather than tutor them personally and thus infringe on the time set aside for their own study. 'Although one is obliged to teach Torah to his son,' says Ibn al-Nakawa, "self-instruction precedes that due to a son."
In *The Jewish Community*, 2:174. 1942.

Elkin, Harry,
"Jewish courses for adults reflect chiefly the goal of transmitting the Jewish heritage. Thus, the emphasis is toward Bible, Jewish History, and Hebrew. Limited attention is given to contemporary Jewish life and history, or to the needs of the modern Jew living in a democratic society."
Jew Ed 25 (Summer 1954), 15.

Gamoran, Emanuel,
"In days of adversity it is natural for people to ask themselves, 'Wherefore do we continue our unique way of life?' Here, it would seem, lies the answer to the question of what adult education is, or rather what it should be. It could answer the needs of adult Jews in a modern world in which the great Jewish ideals are continuously challenged."
Adult Jew Ed (Winter 1955), 4.

Dinin, Samuel,
"I should like to see as the outcome of the adult education process a literate Jew at home in the languages, the literature and culture of the Jewish people; a Jew who identifies himself with his people and participates in the organized life of the Jewish community ... a Jew who understands his intimate relationships to Israel, America and the world; a Jew who makes the ethical and moral teachings of Judaism the pattern of his behavior and conduct in his daily life; a Jew who lends his support to the perpetuation to all that is worthy in Jewish life and gives aid and comfort to all human causes that make for the perpetuation of freedom, justice and peace."
Adult Jew Ed (Winter 1955), 6.

Cohen, Jack J.,
"We must change the psychology of adult Jewish education. . . . We must supplement our 'big attractions' with seminar and text courses which will respect and challenge the intellectual capacity of many congregants."
In *JEDS*, 317.

Cohen, Samuel J.,
"The sore spot of contemporary adult Jewish education is in evaluation. The study [1964 AAJE study, *The Adult Jewish Education Activities of the American Jewish Community: Highlights and Insights*] revealed that attempts of evaluation were largely sporadic, fragmentary, and superficial, with most efforts based upon attendance records. Few programs involved professional Jewish education personnel in those efforts, and only token evaluation was made of curricula, methodology, personnel, instructional materials, and participants' reactions."
AJYB 66 (1965): 288–89.

Mann, David,
"If, in fact Jewish survival and Jewish education are synonymous, as we all believe they are, and if the vast majority of our people are not enrolled in formal Jewish educational institutions, it is incumbent upon us to reach out and to educate through all channels available to us. While informal Jewish education cannot be viewed as a substitute for formal educational programs, it must be seen as one vehicle for reaching those who are not likely to engage in Jewish learning through self-motivation."
"Informal Jewish Education and the Bureau." *Jew Ed* 48 (Fall 1980), 15.

33 | THE WOMAN'S ROLE AND JEWISH EDUCATION

(See also chapters 17, 23, 29, 30, 45)

EUROPEAN BACKGROUND (SELECTED)

Adler, Ruth. *Women of the Shtell through the Eyes of Y. L. Peretz.* Fairleigh Dickinson U. Press, 1980. 144 pp.

Aptchik, T., and D. Notik. "The 'Yehudiah,' a School for Girls in Wilno, 1917." *Jewish Teacher* 1 (1917).

* Atkin, Abraham. *Beth Jacob Movement in Poland* (schools for girls). Yeshiva U., 1959.

Brayer, Menahem. *The Jewish Woman in Rabbinic Literature.* 2 vols. Hoboken, N.J.: Ktav, 1986.

Keyserling, Meyer. *Jewish Women in History, Literature and Art* (G.). Leipzig: 1879. 375 pp.

Kohler, Kaufmann. "Women's Influence on Judaism." *Menorah* 29 (1914–15): 134–52.

Kurzweil, Zvi F. "Sarah Schenirer" (educator who founded the Beth Jacob Schools for girls in Poland). In *MTJE*, 266–74.

Niger, Sh. „די יודישע ליטעראטור און די לעזערין" (Yiddish Literature and the Female Reader). *Der Pinkes* (Y.) (1913): 84–138.

Noble, Shlomo. "The Jewish Woman in Medieval Martyrology." In *Studies in Jewish Bibliography, History, and Literature in Honor of I. Edward Kiev*, edited by Charles Berlin. N.Y.: Ktav, 1971. 347–66.

Reines, Ch. Z. „למוד הנשים בדורות הקודמים" (Education of Women in Prior Generations). *Sh Hah* (H.) 35 (1975): 172–76.

Roth, Cecil. "Outstanding Jewish Women in Western Europe." In *The Jewish Woman*, edited by Leo Jung. 1934.

Scharfstein, Zevi. „שרה שנירר" (Sarah Schenirer). In *GJE* (H.), 226–43.

Schechter, Solomon. "Memoirs of a Jewess of the Seventeenth Century" (on the *Memoirs* of Gluckel of Hameln. Translated from the Yiddish by Marvin Lowenthal. N.Y.: Schocken, 1977.) In Schechter's *Studies in Judaica*, 126–47. 1908.

Schenirer, Sarah. „וואס דארף זיין מיט דער יודישער טאכטער?" (What Are the Needs of the Jewish Daughter?). *Beth Jacob J* (Y.) (1930): 11 pp.

———. „מה תפקידה של בת-ישראל?" (What Is the Role of a Jewish Daughter?) (H., Y., G.). Jerusalem: 1934. 6 pp.

———. „צו וואס דארף מען בית-יעקב שולען?" (Why Are Beth Jacob Schools Necessary?) (Y.). Warsaw: Menrah, 1933. 31 pp. Also published in Jerusalem (H.) in 1933.

Shatzky, Jacob. „די עלטסטע שול פאר יודישע מיידלעך אין ווארשע" (The Oldest School for Girls in Warsaw). In his *Jewish Educational Policies in Poland from 1808 to 1866* (Y.), 210–22. N.Y.: Yivo, 1943.

Shemen, N. "די יידישע פרוי אין חינוך„" (The Jewish Woman in Education). In *Golomb* (Y.), 797–807.

Shurin, Aaron Ben-Zion. "די ניטאַרן וואָס האָט געשאַפֿן רעליגיעזע שולן פֿאַר מיידלעך„" (The Seamstress Who Created Religious Schools for Girls). *For* (Y.) (Mar. 15, 1985): 12, 28.

Suchoff, Libbie. "The Educational and Social Status of the Jewish Woman of the Past." Master's thesis, Columbia U.

Taube, Herman. "The Woman as Matriarch of Yiddish Literature" (on Glueckel of Hameln, 1645–1724). *For* (June 5, 1987): (E. section) 18, 35.

Weiss-Rosmarin, Trude. *Jewish Women through the Ages*. N.Y.: Jewish Book Club, 1940.

Wengeroff, Pauline (1833–1916). "Memoirs of a Grandmother" (education in transition from Orthodox to Haskalah to general learning). In *The Golden Tradition*, edited by Lucy Dawidowicz, 160–68. 1967.

IN THE UNITED STATES PRIOR TO 1900

Benjamin, I. I. "The Rearing of a Jewish Daughter." In his *Three Years in America, 1859–1862*, 1:85–87. Phila.: JPS, 1956. Also *JEUS*, 76–79, and in *The American Jewish Woman: A Documentary History*, edited by Jacob R. Marcus, 225–28. N.Y.: Ktav and AJA, 1981.

Block, C. "Our Religious Schools, What Can the National Council of Jewish Women Do for Them?" In *Papers of the Jewish Women's Congress, 1893*, 356–63.

Golomb, Deborah Grand. "The 1893 Congress of Jewish Women: Evolution or Revolution in American Jewish Women's History?" *AJH* 70 (Sept. 1960): 52–67.

Porter, Jack Nussan. "Rosa Sonnenschein and *The American Jewess*: First Independent English Language Jewish Women's Journal in the United States" (1895–99). *AJH* 68 (1978–79): 57–63. See also *AJA* 32 (1980): 125–31.

Rose, Ernestine. "On an Anti-Semitic Editorial in a Boston Newspaper." In *Ernestine Rose and the Battle for Human Rights*, by Yuri Suhl, 220–22. 1959. (Editorial was in Boston *Investigator*, October 28, 1863.)

Rosenbloom, Joseph R. "Rebecca Gratz and the Jewish Sunday School Movement in Philadelphia." *PAJHS* 48 (Dec. 1958): 71–77.

Szold, Henrietta. "What Has Judaism Done for Women?" In *The World's Parliament of Religion*, edited by J. H. Barrow, 1052–56. 1893.

Zirndorf, Henry. *Some Jewish Women*. Phila.: 1892. 280 pp.

IN THE UNITED STATES 1900–1950

Benderly, Samson. "The Problems of Educating the Jewish Girls." *American Hebrew* 88 (Jan. 6, 1911).

Berkson, Isaac B. "A System for Jewish Education for Girls." *Jew Teach* 1 (Jan. 1917): 95–112.

Comay, Joseph, and Israel Drachler. "יידישע פֿרויען לייענקרייזן אין דעטרויט„" (Women's Yiddish Reading Circles in Detroit) (Y.). Aims and activities of 26 women's reading circles. Detroit: Colonial Printing Co., May 1939. 28 pp.

Hapgood, Hutchins. "The Old and New Woman." In *The Spirit of the Ghetto*, 71–89. N.Y.: 1902.

The Hebrew Standard, April 5, 1907. Jewish Women's issue, with achievements and biographies of Jewish women in America and elsewhere.

Hirschowitz, Abraham E. *Religious Duties of the Daughters of Israel*. 3d ed. N.Y.: 1902. 77 pp.

Huhner, Leon. *The Jewish Woman in America*. Council of Jewish Women, New York section, Nov. 21, 1916.

Kaplan, Mordecai M. "The Status of the Jewish Woman in Jewish Law." In *FAJ*, 402–12.

Kohut, Rebecca. "Jewish Women's Organizations." *AJYB* 33 (1931/32): 165–201.

Korman, Ezra. "יידישע דיכטערינס„ (Anthology of Yiddish Poetry by Women Poets) (Y.). Chicago: 1928. 374 pp.

Levine, A. "יחס האבות אל חנוך הבנות„ (Relationship of the Fathers to the Education of Daughters). *Sh Hah* (H.) 2 (Spring 1926): 32–40.

Levinger, Emma Ehrlich. *Great Jewish Women.* N.Y.: Behrman, c. 1940.

* Lewis, Theodor N. *Women under Rabbinic Judaism.* HUC–JIR, 1933.

Pratt, Norma Fain. "Culture and Radical Politics: Yiddish Women Writers, 1890–1940." *AJH* 70 (Sept. 1980): 68–90.

Sinkoff, Nancy B. "Educating for Proper Jewish Womanhood: A Case Study in Domesticity and Vocational Training, 1897–1926." *AJH* 77 (June 1988): 572–99.

IN THE UNITED STATES SINCE 1950

AJC. *The Role of Women in Jewish Religious Life: A Decade of Change, 1972–1982* (proceedings and papers). N.Y.: AJC, Jewish Communal Affairs Department, 1982. 29 pp.

Baum, Charlotte, Paula Hyman, and Sonya Michel. *The Jewish Women in America.* N.Y.: Dial, 1976.

Berkowitz, Gila. "'Lifting the Yoke': Is There Hope for Ending Jewish Legal Discrimination against Women?" *Lilith* 16 (Spring 1987): 25–26.

Berman, Saul. "The Status of Women in Halachic Judaism." *Trad* 14 (Fall 1973): 5–28.

Biale, Rachel. *Women and Jewish Law.* N.Y.: Schocken, 1984.

Blumenthal, Aaron H. "An Aliyah for Women." *RA* 55 (1955): 168–81.

Braude, A. "The Jewish Woman's Encounter with American Culture." In *Women and Religion in America*, edited by R. R. Reuther and R. S. Keller, 1:150–92. San Francisco: Harper and Row, 1981.

Charry, Dana. "Women and Change in Jewish Law." *Con Jud* 29 (Spring 1975): 29–35.

Cohen, Elaine Shizgal. "Women Rabbinical Students Reflect on Their Calling." *MJ* 22 (Fall 1987): 6–9.

Cohen, Steven M., Susan Dessel, and Michael Pelavin. "The Changing (?) Role of Women in Jewish Communal Affairs: A Look into the UJA." In *The Jewish Woman: New Perspectives*, edited by Elizabeth Koltun. N.Y.: Schocken, 1976.

Cohn-Sherbok, D. "Women and Intellect." *Jew Spec* 48 (Fall 1983): 24–25.

Dresner, Ruth Rapp. "The Work of Bertha Pappenheim." *Jud* 30 (Spring 1981): 204–11.

Duckat, Walter. "New Careers for Jewish Women." *Jew Life* 21 (Dec. 1953).

Eisenberg, Dov. *A Guide for the Jewish Woman and Girl: A Detailed Manual of Jewish Laws, Customs and Practices, as They Apply to or Are Observed by Women and Girls.* Brooklyn: Moriah, 1978. 158 pp.

Elazar, Daniel J., and Rela Geffen Monson. "Women in the Synagogue Today." *Mid* 27 (Apr. 1981): 25–30.

Elwell, Ellen Sue Levi, and Edward R. Levenson. *The Jewish Women's Study Guide.* Fresh Meadows, N.Y.: Bantam, 1979.

Ezrat Nashim. "Jewish Women Call for a Change." (In March 1972 Ezrat Nashim, a women's organization, appeared before the RA and presented this document. See *The American Jewish Woman—A Documentary History*, by Jacob R. Marcus, 894–96. N.Y.: Ktav and AJA, 1981. 1047 pp.

* Fastenau, Maureen K. *Maternal Government: The Social Settlement House and the Politicization of Women's Sphere, 1889–1920.* Duke U., 1982. 281 pp.

Feinstein, Sara. "Opening Opportunities for Women in Jewish Communal Service." *J Jew Com Ser* 52 (Winter 1975).

Feldman, David M. "Women's Role and Jewish Law." *Con Jud* 26 (Summer 1972): 29–39.

* Fisch, Linda Y. *Patterns of Religious and Feminist Socialization among Jewish College Women.* Columbia U., 1983.

Fishman, Leora. "Jewish Women: The Struggle for Liberation." *Jew Fron* (Aug.–Sept. 1984): 11–19.

Fishman, Leora, and Aviva Zuckoff. "A Guide to Jewish Women's Activities." In *Cat 1*, 252–60.

Friedman, Reena Seegman. "Jewish Women: The Struggle for Liberation." *Jew Fron* (Aug.–Sept. 1984): 11.

Gertel, Elliot B. "Women and Change in Jewish Law." *Con Jud* 29 (Spring 1975): 50–52.

Gittelsohn, Roland B. "Women's Lib and Judaism." *Mid* 17 (Oct. 1971): 51–58.

Graubert, David. "Women and Change in Jewish Law." *Con Jud* 29 (Fall 1974): 17–18.

Green, Arthur E. "Women and Change in Jewish Law." *Con Jud* 29 (Spring 1975): 36–43.

Green, Kathy. "Many Hyphens: Reflections of an American-Jewish Feminist." *MJ* 22 (Fall 1987): 12, 23.

Greenberg, Blu. "Recent Literature on Jewish Women." *JBA* 35 (1977–78): 97–107.

———. *On Women and Judaism: A View from Tradition*. Phila.: JPS, 1981. 178 pp.

Gross, Rita M. "Steps toward Feminine Imagery of Deity in Jewish Theology." *Jud* 30 (Spring 1981): 183–93.

Hauptman, Judith. "Women and Change in Jewish Law." *Con Jud* 29 (Fall 1974): 20–21.

———. "Women's Liberation in the Talmudic Period." *Con Jud* 26 (Summer 1972): 22–28.

Heschel, Susannah, ed. *On Being a Jewish Feminist: A Reader*. N.Y.: Schocken, 1983.

* Hochman, Judith Whitman. *An Exploratory Investigation into the Nature of the Adult Years in the Life Cycle of a Selected Group of Jewish Women*. Temple U., 1984.

Hoenig, Sidney B. *Jewish Family Life: The Duty of the Woman*. 12th ed. N.Y.: Spero Foundation, 1974. 93 pp.

Hollander, Vicki Lee. "And Sarah Laughed: Towards an Educational Guide for the Study of the Jewish Woman." Master's thesis, HUC–JIR, 1979.

Horowitz, Cyma, ed. *The Jewish Woman in the Community*. N.Y.: AJC, Dec. 1976.

Hyman, Paula. "The Other Half: Women in Jewish Tradition." *Response* (Summer 1973): 14–21.

Jewish Media Service. "The Jewish Woman" (film). Brandeis U., Winter 1977.

Jud. "The Emerging Personality of Women" (several articles). 30 (Spring 1981): 183–224.

* Kaplovitz, Abbey P. *Mother Images in American Jewish Fiction*. U. of Denver, 1985.

Katz, F. "The Attitude of Jews toward the Education of Girls." Master's thesis, U. of Chicago, 1950.

Keeping Posted. *The New Jewish Woman*. Nos. 840740 and 840742 (leader's edition). High school and adults.

Klein, Aaron. "Now There Are Girls in Our Religious School." *Syn Sch* 13 (Dec. 1954): 10–14.

Koltun, Elizabeth, ed. *The Jewish Woman: New Perspectives*. N.Y.: Schocken, 1976.

Kuzmack, Linda Gorden, and George Solomon. *Working and Mothering: A Study of 97 Jewish Career Women with Three or More Children*. N.Y.: AJC, 1981.

Lebeson, Anita Libman. *Recall to Life: The Jewish Woman in America*. South Brunswick, N.J.: Yoseloff, 1970.

Lerner, Anne Lapidus. "In God's Image Was Humanity Created." *Jud* 33 (Winter 1984): 34–38.

———. "Who Hast Not Made Me a Man": The Movement for Equal Rights for Women in American Jewry." *AJYB* 77 (1977): 3–38.

Levin, Marlin. *Balm in Gilead: The Story of Hadassah*. N.Y.: Schocken, 1973. 274 pp.

Levitats, Isaac. "Girls in Our Weekly Schools." *Syn Sch* 17 (Sept. 1958): 10–13.

Lilith: The Jewish Woman's Magazine. Great Neck, N.Y., 1971–present. Quarterly.

Linn, Louis. "Women and Change in Jewish Law." *Con Jud* 29 (Fall 1974): 5–17.

Lubavitch Educational Foundation for Jewish Marriage Enrichment. *One Modern Jewish Woman: A Unique Perspective*. Brooklyn, N.Y., ca. 1984. 179 pp.

Maisl, N. "The Jewish Woman: The Martyr, Fighter, and Portrayer of the Holocaust and Resistance." *Yiddish Culture* (Y.) (Feb. 1972): 11–20, 20–28.

Malev, Milton. "Women and Change in Jewish Law." *Con Jud* 29 (Fall 1974): 18–20.

Marcus, Jacob R. *The American Jewish Woman, 1654–1980*. N.Y.: Ktav and American Jewish Archives, 1981. 231 pp.

———. *The American Jewish Woman: A Documentary History*. N.Y.: Ktav and AJA, 1981. 1047 pp.

Mathews, Carole, and Sandra Rubenstein. "Lesbian Jews: Recalling a Dual Identity." Master's thesis, U. of Southern California, 1980.

Meiselman, Moshe. *Jewish Woman in Jewish Law*. N.Y.: Ktav/Yeshiva U. Press, 1978. 218 pp.

Miller, Yisroel. *In Search of the Jewish Woman*. Feldheim, 1984.

MJ 23 (Spring 1990). Focus on women.
    Aschkenasy, Nehama, "Women Reacting to Oppression," 1.
    Avgar, Amy, "The Changing Status of Women," 13, 30.
    Lefkovitz, Lori, "When Lilith Becomes a Heroine," 5–7.
    Rauch, Eduardo, "Reaching for the Elusive Feminine," 13, 30.

Ostow, Mortimer. "Women and Change in Jewish Law." *Con Jud* 29 (Fall 1974): 5–12, 22–24. See also "Women and Change in Jewish Law: Responses to the Fall 1974 Symposium." *Con Jud* 29 (Spring 1975): 46–50.

Ozick, Cynthia. "Torah as Feminism, Feminism as Torah." *Cong M* (Sept.–Oct. 1984): 7–10.

Pfeifer, Paula. "Portrait of a Reformer: Esther Loeb Kohn." Master's thesis, Northwestern Illinois U., 1974.

Plaskow, Judith. "Halakha as a Feminist Issue." *MJ* 22 (Fall 1987): 3–5, 25.

Priesand, Sally. *Judaism and the New Women*. N.Y.: Behrman.

Reifman, Toby Fishbein. "Women and Change in Jewish Law." *Con Jud* 29 (Spring 1975): 48–50.

Rosen, Gladys. "The Impact of the Women's Movement on the Jewish Family." *Jud* 28 (Spring 1979): 160–68.

Schneider, Susan Weidman. *Jewish and Female: Choices and Changes in Our Lives Today*. N.Y.: Simon and Schuster, 1984. 640 pp.

Shoub, M. "State of the Field—Jewish Women's History: Development of a Critical Methodology." *Con Jud* 35 (Winter 1982): 33–46.

Siegel, Seymour. "Women and Change in Jewish Law." *Con Jud* 29 (Fall 1974): 13–15, 24.

Sigal, Philip. "Women in a Prayer Quorum." *Jud* 23 (Spring 1974): 174–82.

Silver, A. M. "May Women Be Taught Bible, Mishnah and Talmud?" *Trad* (Summer 1978): 74–83.

Snitow, Virginia, and Jacqueline Levine. "Role of Jewish Women." *Congress Biweekly* (June 18, 1971).

Sochen, June (guest editor). "American Jewish Women." *AJH* 70 (Sept. 1980): 5–118.

———, ed. *Consecrate Every Day: The Lives of American Jewish Women, 1880–1980*. Albany: SUNY Press, 1981.

Soloveitchik, Aaron. "The Jewish View of the Higher Nature of Women." *Jewish Horizon* (Nov.–Dec. 1969).

Stein, Jacob. "Jewish Education for Our Daughters—A Layman's View." *Syn Sch* 14 (May 1956): 7–12.

Switkin, Linda R. "Women and Change in Jewish Law: Responses to the Fall 1974 Symposium." *Con Jud* 29 (Spring 1975): 43–45.

Tofield, Aaron. "Women's Place in the Rite of the Synagogue." *RA* 55 (1955).

Tolidano, J. M. „על חנוך בנות ישראל" (On the Education of Jewish Women). *Sh Hah* (H.) 24 (Fall 1963): 29–35.

Tropper, S. "Some Unorthodox Reflections of Feminism and Torah." *Jew Obs* 17 (Summer 1984): 21–26.

Tzemnon, Tsemach. "The Woman in Education and in Instruction." *Sh Hah* (H.) 35 (1975): 30–37.

Umansky, Ellen. "Women in Judaism: From the Reform Movement to Contemporary Jewish Feminism." In *Women of Spirit: Female Leadership in the Jewish and Christian Tradition*. N.Y.: 1979.

* Vignola, Susan L. *The American Jewish Woman's Socialization Process*. Catholic U. of America, 1979.

Weiss-Rosmarin, Trade. "Women in the Jewish Community." *Jew Spec* (Feb. 1972).

Weissman, Debbie. "Women's Studies: Sources of Religious Renewal." *MJ* 22 (Fall 1987): 13, 25.

* Willensky, Marjory Koch. *The Effects of a Career Workshop on Aspects of Career Exploratory Behavior, Locus of Control, and Self-Concept of Jewish Married Women.* Boston U., 1979. 171 pp.

Winer, Toby, and Sophie B. Engel. *The Status of Women in Jewish Communal Service: A Report at the 79th Annual Meeting of the National Conference of Jewish Communal Service, June 5, 1977.*

Yudkin, Marjorie S. "The Shalom Ideal." *Jud* 33 (Winter 1984): 85–90.

Zelizer, Gerald L. "Women and Change in Jewish Law." *Con Jud* 29 (Spring 1975): 47–48.

Zuckoff, Aviva Cantor. "The Oppression of the Jewish Woman." *Ort Reporter* (Sept.–Oct. 1972).

GLEANINGS

Leeser, Isaac (1846),
"It may not, perhaps, not be improper to remark here, that there appears to be an indifference, or rather a total carelessness, in regard to the religious education of females, even among persons who are otherwise religiously inclined. Why such a state of things should exist, we cannot even conjecture. Is a woman a less responsible being than a man? Is it not the mother from whom the child receives his first ideas, thoughts, and impressions. Parents beware! How you trifle with the felicity of your daughters."
Occ 4 (May 1846), 99.

The Asmonean, May 2, 1851, praising Philadelphia's day schools,
"There are at present two schools in this city for boys, and one for girls, each of which possesses capabilities of the highest order, deserving the patronage and support of our co-religionists."
In *JEUS,* 64.

Jewish Women's Congress, 1893,
"Resolved, That we, Jewish women, sincerely believing that a closer fellowship will be encouraged, a closer unity of thought and sympathy and purpose, and a nobler accomplishment will result from a widespread organization, do therefore band ourselves together in a union of workers to further the best and highest interests of Judaism and humanity, and do call ourselves the 'National Council of Jewish Women'."
Papers of the Jewish Women's Congress, 1893, 264–65.

Berkson, Isaac B.,
"It is obvious that... the new conditions of our life in America must bring about a changed conception as to the educational needs of the Jewish Woman."
Jewish Teacher 1 (Jan. 1917): 95.

Kaplan, Mordecai M.,
"Though the traditional status of the Jewish woman compares favorably with that of the woman in other civilizations in the past, it is today a stumbling block. It stands in the way of contributing her best to her people. It prevents her from enhancing her life as much as it could. There is no way of reconciling that status with her welfare and highest interests in our day. It is high time for the Jewish women throughout the world to inaugurate a movement that will aim to remove the religious, civic and judicial disabilities which traditional Jewish law imposes upon them and that will win for them the status of equality."
FAJ, 412.

Greenberg, Blu,
"Throughout the centuries, Judaism generated revolutionary ethical teachings. Why will it not now incorporate the lessons of feminism? Equality, in various spheres long has been fundamental to Judaism; indeed, biblical teachings enjoin equality before law, equal ownership of property, equality of all men. Logically, therefore, should not feminist goals be embraced by Judaism today as a means of achieving equality for men and women in the eyes of God and the community?"
On Women and Judaism: A View from Tradition (Phila.: JPS, 1981), 3–4.

33 THE WOMAN'S ROLE AND JEWISH EDUCATION

Schneider, Susan Weidman,

"While many argue that Jewish women have traditionally occupied an honorable position within the home and family, there is little doubt that they were relegated to second-class status in the central arenas of public prayer and sacred study throughout much of Jewish history. The potential danger inherent in this situation, as the German Maskilim clearly recognized, was that the Jewish woman who had achieved recognition and a measure of equality in secular society would no longer be content with limitations imposed on them as Jews, and would therefore seek to abandon their Jewish heritage. The efforts of the Maskilim to improve Jewish education for women constituted a vigorous response to that challenge, one that is still very much with us today."

Jewish and Female: Choices and Changes in Our Lives Today (N.Y.: Simon and Schuster, 1984), 161.

34 SEPHARDIM AND JEWISH EDUCATION

(Data from Sephardic periodicals was provided by Joseph M. Papo. *See also* chapters 29, 37)

GENERAL (SELECTED)

American Sephardi Federation. *First National Convention Report, Feb. 25–26, 1973.*

Angel, Marc D. *La America.* (See index, p. 219, "Talmudei Torah" for Jewish education.) Phila.: JPS, 1982.

———. "Ruminations on Sephardic Identity." *Mid* (Mar. 1972): 64–67.

———. "Sephardic Culture in America." *Jew Life* 38 (Mar.–Apr. 1971): 7–11.

———. "Sephardim in America." *Present Tense* 4 (Autumn 1976): 12–14.

———. "The Sephardim of the United States: An Exploratory Study" (contains data on education). *AJYB* 74 (1973): 77–138.

———, ed. *Studies in Sephardic Culture.* N.Y.: David N. Barocas Memorial Volume, 1980.

Ashton, Eliyahu. *The Jews of Moslem Spain.* Phila.: JPS, 1974.

Baer, Yitzhak. *A History of the Jews in Christian Spain.* 2 vols. Phila.: JPS, 1961, 1971.

Barnett, Richard, ed. *The Sephardic Heritage.* N.Y.: 1970.

Benardete, Mair Jose. *Hispanic Culture and Character of the Sephardic Jews.* 2d ed. N.Y.: Sepher-Hermon Press for the Foundation for the Advancement of Sephardic Studies and Culture and Sephardic House at Congregation Shearith Israel, 1982.

Birmingham, Stephen. *The Grandees: America's Sephardic Elite.* N.Y.: Harper and Row, 1971. 368 pp.

Birnbaum, Ruth. "The Uniqueness of the Early Sephardic Community in America." *Jud* 25 (Winter 1976): 44–53.

Campeas, Hyman. "A Bird's-Eye View of the Magen David Congregation." *The American Sephardi* (Dec. 1966): 9.

Cardozo, D. A. J. "The Sephardim." *Jew Life* 18 (Nov. 1950).

Cong M. "How an Ashkenazi American Jewry Relates to a Sephardi Israel: The 21st Annual America-Israel Dialogue, Jerusalem, July 1985. Sponsored by the AJC" (special issue). 53 (Mar.–Apr. 1986).

* Dobrinsky, Herbert C. *Selected Laws and Customs of Sephardic Jewry.* Yeshiva U., 1980. 859 pp.

Elazar, Daniel J. *Sephardic Jewry in a New World Role* (GA, Nov. 1982). CP, 19 pp.

———. "Sephardim and Ashkenazim: The Classic and Romantic Traditions in Jewish Civilization." *Jud* 33 (Spring 1984): 146–59.

Faur, Jose. "Early Zionist Ideals among Sephardim in the Nineteenth Century." *Jud* 25 (Winter 1976): 54–64.

———. "Introducing the Materials of Sephardic Culture to Contemporary Jewish Studies." *AJHQ* (June 1974): 340–49.

———. *Sephardic Life and Culture* (GA, Nov. 1980). CP, 23 pp.

———. "The Sephardim: Yesterday, Today and Tomorrow." *The Sephardic World* 1 (1972): 5–6.

Fidanque, E. Alvin. "Early Sephardic Settlers in North America and the Caribbean." *RJ* 25 (Fall 1978): 77–82.

For. "Sephardi Jewish Identity Examined at International Congress." (Feb. 8, 1985): (E. section) 12.

Jochnowitz, George. "Ladino." *Mid* 27 (Feb. 1981): 29–32.

Joseph, A. B. *Aleppo Chronicles.* N.Y.: Thayer-Jacoby, 1988.

* Katz, Israel Joseph. *Judeo-Spanish Traditional Ballads from Jerusalem.* UCLA, 1967.

Lavender, Bernard. "The Sephardic Revival in the United States: A Case Study of Ethnic Revival in a Minority within a Minority." *J of Ethnic Studies* 3 (Fall 1975): 21–31.

Lazar, Moshe. *The Sephardic Tradition: Ladino and Spanish Literature.* B'nai B'rith, Jewish Heritage Classic.

Levenberg, M. "The Role of Sephardim in Jewish Life." *For* (Mar. 25, 1988): (E. section) 7, 35.

Levy, Louis N., comp. *Four Reviews of Stephen Birmingham's Book*, The Grandees. N.Y.: The Foundation for the Advancement of Sephardic Studies and Culture, June 1971. 37 pp.

Luria, Max Aaron. "The Language and Traditions of the Spanish Jews." Master's thesis, Columbia U., 1918.

Marcus, Jacob R. *The Colonial American Jew, 1492–1976.* 3 vols. Detroit: Wayne State U. Press, 1970. See index in vol. 3, entries for "Minhag," "Portuguese and Spanish Jews," and "Sephardim" for extensive data on Sephardim in colonial America.

———. *The Sephardic Period: U.S. Jewry, 1776–1985.* Detroit: Wayne State U. Press, 1990. 805 pp.

Matza, Diane. "Sephardic Jews in America: Why They Don't Write More." *AJA* 39 (Nov. 1987): 115–26.

———. "Sephardic Jews Transmitting Culture across Three Generations." *AJH* 79 (Spring 1990): 336–54.

Papo, Joseph M. "The Sephardic Community of America." *Recon* 12 (1946): 12–18.

———. "The Sephardic Press in the United States." *Sephardi Heritage* (Winter 1982): 37–39; (Winter 1983): 26–29

———. "The Sephardim—Jewry's Stepchildren." *Chicago Jewish Forum* (Fall 1949).

———. *Sephardim in Twentieth Century America: In Search of Unity.* San Jose and Berkeley, Calif.: Pele Yoetz Books and Judah L. Magnes Memorial Museum, 1987. 450 pp.

Polner, Murray. "Sephardim in America." In *The Rabbi*, 200–207. 1977.

Pool, David de Sola. "The Immigration of the Levantine Jews into the United States." *Jewish Charities* (June 1914).

———. "The Levantine Jews in the United States." *AJYB* 15 (1913–14): 207–20.

Raphael, Chaim. *The Road from Babylon: The Story of the Sephardic and Oriental Jews.* N.Y.: Harper-Row, 1985. 320 pp.

Roth, Cecil. *History of the Marranos.* N.Y.: 1966.

———. "On Sephardic Jewry." *Dispersion* (Spring 1966): 40–51.

The Sephardi. "United Sephardim of Brooklyn Report Progress." (Sept. 1954).

Shirazi, Helen. "The Communal Pluralism of Sephardi Jewry in the United States." *Le Judaism Sephardi* (F.) (Jan. 1966): 23–25, 32.

Staub, Sholom. "The Yemenite Jewish Dance: An Anthropological Perspective." Master's thesis, Wesleyan U., 1978.

Yerushalmi, Yoseph H. *From Spanish Court to Italian Ghetto—Isaac Cardoso: A Study in Seventeenth Century Marranism and Jewish Apologetics.* N.Y.: Columbia U. Press, 1971. 524 pp.

———. "A Review Essay on Sephardic Studies" (on the first symposium of Sephardic studies, held in Madrid in 1964). *AJHQ* 62 (Dec. 1972): 180–89.

EDUCATION

Alcalay, Isaac. "Widen Religious Education for Our Sephardi Children." *The Sephardi* (Dec. 1949).

Angel, Marc D. "Sephardic Approaches to Teaching Siddur." *Ped Rep* 33 (Dec. 1981): 19.

Baum, Eli, ed. "Sephardic Jewry." In *Curriculum Guide for Afternoon Religious Schools*. N.Y.: National Commission on Torah Education, 1979, 129–31.

Cohen, Edward M. "Toward a Program for Sephardi Youth." *The Sephardi* (Dec. 1950).

Community Sephardic Bulletin. New York, Nov. 1928, Mar. 1929, May 1929, Mar. 1930.

Delouya, Achiah. "A Curriculum of Sephardic Jewish History for Yeshivah and Day Schools in the United States." Yeshiva U., 1979.

Erdberger, A. "On Jewish Education." "טאגעבלאט„ (*Tageblatt*) (Y.) (Feb. 27, 1927).

Frank, Ben G., Tina Levitan, Mitchell Serels, and Raymond Harari. *Reawakening of American Sephardim*. KP Nos. 840330 and 840322 (leader's edition).

Hacohen, Devora, and Menahem Hacohen. *One People* (textbook). N.Y., 1969.

Hochstein, Joshua. "The Place of Sephardim on Present-Day Jewish Cultural Agenda." *Le Judaisme Sephardi* (F.) (Aug. 1964).

La America (Judeo-Spanish [Ladino] Hebrew letters). References to Jewish education: Dec. 9, 1910; May 26, 1911; Jan. 5, Feb. 9, Aug. 9, Sept. 6, 20, Oct. 11, 18, Nov. 29, 1912; May 16, Dec. 26, 1913; Aug. 28, Sept. 4, 1914; May 28, July 30, Oct. 15, 1915; Apr. 14, Aug. 25, Nov. 10, 1916; Jan. 19, Feb. 2, 9, Apr. 20, Oct. 12, 25, Nov. 9, 23, Dec. 28, 1917; Oct. 18, Nov. 8, Dec. 6, 1918; Apr. 11, Dec. 12, 19, 1919; Jan. 16, Aug. 20, 1920; Apr. 20, Dec. 2, 1921; Nov. 17, 1924; Apr. 17, May 15, July 10, 1925.

La Bos del Pueblo (Judeo-Spanish [Ladino] Hebrew letters). References to Jewish education: Mar. 17, 1916; Jan. 5, 19, Apr. 20, June 1, 1917; Feb. 8, 15, May 24, 1918; Mar. 21, 1919.

La Epoca de New York (Judeo-Spanish [Ladino] Hebrew letters, also English in later years): Dec. 5, 19, 1919.

La Luz (Judeo-Spanish [Ladino] Hebrew letters): Dec. 18, 1921; May 2, July 30, 1922.

La Vara (Judeo-Spanish [Ladino] Hebrew letters, also English in later years): Sept. 8, 1922; Feb. 16, Oct. 19, Nov. 23, 1923; July 4, 11, 1924; July 19, 1925; Oct. 18, 1926; Jan. 7, Mar. 11, Dec. 23, 1927; Nov. 20, Dec. 18, 1942; Nov. 15, 1945.

Levy, Albert J. "Education is the Best Weapon." *La Bos del Pueblo* (Judeo-Spanish [Ladino] Hebrew letters) (Nov. 8, 1918).

Mishkin, Madelyn. *Sephardic Jewry: A Curriculum for the Seventh Grade*. L.A.: HUC–JIR, Rhea Hirsch School of Education, 1984.

Papo, Joseph M. "Jewish Education Report." *The Sephardi* (Sept. 1946).

Ped Rep. "Teaching about Sephardic Culture" (special issue). 37 (Jan. 1987):
    Angel, Marc D., "An Approach to Teaching about Sephardic Oriental Jews," 1–2.
    "Films about Sephardic and Oriental Jews" (from *Medium*, Summer 1985), 13–15.
    Glicksman, David, "Sephardic Oriental Jewish Studies for the High School," 6–8.
    Haddad, Heskel M., "Sephardic Communities around the Mediteranean and in the Middle East," 8–10.
    Hessel, Carolyn Starman, "Some Books about the Sephardic/Oriental Heritage" (annotated), 16–17.
    Lebow, Karen, "The Sephardic Family Heritage Project," 3–5.
    Serels, M. Mitchell, "Materials for Teaching about Sephardic Jewry," 11–12.
    Shamah, Lind, "The Spirit of Aleppo" (an exhibit), 18–19.

Sassoon, Solomon David. *The Spiritual Heritage of the Sephardim* (F.). Paris: *Le Judaisme Sephardi*, Oct. 1957.

Sephardi World. March, May 1976; Apr. 1979.

Sugar, Robert. *Journey of Fifteen Centuries: The Story of the Jews of Spain* (textbook). N.Y.: UAHC. Grades 7–9.

Ventura, Moise. "View of Our Educational Activities." *The Sephardi* (Sept. 1952).

PERIODICALS (SELECTED)

(See also chapter 37)

El Progresso—La Bos del Pueblo—La Epoca de New York. 1915–21.

La Vara (The Staff). New York, 1922–48. Weekly.

Le Judaisme Sephardi (F.). Paris, 1932–40, 1950, 1953–56.

The Sephardi. Central Sephardic Jewish Community of America, New York, 1943, 1945–59.

The Sephardic Bulletin. 1937–39.

The Sephardic Home News, 1950–88.

The Sephardi World. World Sephardi Federation and World Zionist Organization, 1973–79, 1984.

GLEANINGS

Faur, Jose,
"The Sephardic response to the demands of the pluralistic society may be of interest to the American Jew. Rather than assimilate or live in a spiritual ghetto, the Sephardi succeeded in capturing the cultural stimuli of his society and used the key symbols of the non-Jewish world to express the values and ideologies of the Jewish people. He thus created something that was part and parcel of the general intellectual and cultural climate of his society and at the same time uniquely and distinctly Jewish."

"Introducing the Materials of Sephardic Culture to Contemporary Jewish Studies." *AJHQ* 63 (June 1974), 342.

Angel, Marc D.,
"The assimilation of American Sephardim of Judeo-Spanish background unto American society has been pervasive. Whether from the standpoint of religious observance or cultural behavior or language of communication, there is a chasm that separates third- and fourth-generation American-born Sephardim from their immigrant forbears. Aside from the Americanization process, Sephardim have also been significantly influenced by their far more numerous Askenazic coreligionists. Almost all of the Jewish day schools and yeshivot in the United States are run by Askenazim, and these schools exert little effort to make Spanish youngsters understand anything about their own specific heritage. Askenazic foods and Yiddish phrases have found their way into the life of Sephardim."

La America (Phila.: JPS, 1982), 178.

Papo, Joseph M.,
"The Syrian Sephardim have been the one segment of the Sephardi community to have maintained religious education as an integral part of their communal life. Thus, the Magen David Yeshiva, which, in 1943, had provided both secular and religious education to some 90 children, had expanded to a student body of some 700, mostly children of Aleppoan ancestry. Families stemming from Damascus have founded their own elementary school, in 1960, teaching more than 1,000 boys and girls, separately, as ordained by strict Orthodox tradition. For students of high school age, the acclaimed Sephardic Institute provides a well-rounded secular and Jewish education for both sexes, while the recently established post-high school Yeshiva Mikdash Melech, leans strongly towards rabbinical training. In addition, the various Syrian congregations conduct their own afternoon Hebrew schools."

Sephardim in Twentieth Century America: In Search of Unity (San Jose and Berkeley, Calif.: Pele Yoetz Books and Judah L. Magnes Memorial Museum, 1987), 197.

35 YOUTH AND JEWISH EDUCATION

PRIOR TO 1950

Blumenfeld, Samuel M. "A Common Program for Jewish Youth Work." *CCAR* 44 (1934): 273–76. See also *Jew Ed* 7 (Jan.–Mar. 1935): 20–25.

———. "Jewish Youth and Tomorrow." *Recon* (May 29, 1940).

———. "בעיות הנוער לאור ימינו" (Problems of Youth in Light of Our Times). *Hadoar* (H.) 20 (4th of Sivan 1941).

Boraisha, Menachem. "The Voice of Youth." *Congress Weekly* (Feb. 28, 1947): 11–14.

Chipkin, Israel S." The I.F.C.—An Experiment in Youth and Adult Jewish Education." *RA* (1930): 1–2.

Cohen, Samuel M. *Guiding Jewish Youth.* N.Y.: Young People's League of USA, 1939. 187 pp.

Cohon, Beryl David. *Introduction to Judaism: A Book for Jewish Youth.* N.Y.: Bloch, 1942. 188 pp.

Doniger, S., comp. *Course of Study and Syllabus for Young Judea Circles.* N.Y.: Young Judea, 1914. 46 pp.

Dushkin, Alexander M. "Achad Ha-Am's Message to the Jewish Youth of America." *The Jewish Youth Magazine* (Feb. 1927): 5–6.

Essrig, Harry. "Cultural Program of Hillel Foundation." *Jew Ed* (Feb.–Mar. 1947): 35–39.

* Ginsburgh, Stanley. *Organized Jewish Youth Groups in America.* U. of Massachusetts, 1940.

Goldberg, Ben Zion. "װאס די יוגנט טראכט" (Thoughts of Youth). *Day* (Y.) (Dec. 18, 1942).

Goldberg, Nathan. "א בינטל פאקטן װעגן דער ייִדישער יוגנט אין אמעריקע" (Some Facts about Jewish Youth in America). *YB* (Y.) 17 (Jan.–Feb. 1941): 28–42.

———. "Religious and Social Attitudes of Jewish Youth in the United States." *Jew Rev* (Y.) 1 (Dec. 1943): 135–68.

* Golub, Jacob S. *Jewish Youth and Tradition.* New York U., 1928.

Gordon, Albert I. "Frustration and Aggression among Jewish University Students." *JSS* 5 (Jan. 1943): 27–42.

Greenberg, Meyer. "The Jewish Student at Yale: His Attitude Toward Judaism." *YA* 1 (1946): 217–40.

Jewish Center "Jewish Attitudes of Jewish College Youth" (symposium). (Sept. 1945).

Katsh, Abraham. "Jewish Student Activities in American Universities with Special Reference to New York University-Jewish Culture Foundation." *Jew Ed* 18 (Feb.–Mar. 1947): 3–34.

Knox, Israel. "װעגן דער ייִדישער יוגנט אין אמעריקע" (On Jewish Youth in America) (Y.). N.Y.: WC National Executive Committee, 1962. 32 pp.

Lehrer, Leibush. "שטימונגען ביי אונדזער יוגנט" (Moods among Our Youth). *YA* 2 (Y.) (1939): 133–146.

35 YOUTH AND JEWISH EDUCATION

Lennard, Henry L. "Jewish Youth Appraising Jews and Jewishness." *YA* 2, 3 (1948): 262–81. (Originally published in *YB* (Y.) 29 (1947).

Maller, Julius B. "The Personality of Jewish College Students." *Jew Ed* 3 (Apr–June 1939): 11–19.

Nathan, Marvin. "The Attitude of the Jewish College Student towards Judaism." *Jew Ed* 4 (Jan.–Mar. 1932): 48–53.

———. *Attitudes of the Jewish Student in Colleges and Universities toward His Religion.* N.Y.: Bloch, 1932. 264 pp.

* ———. *The Attitudes of the Jewish Student in the Colleges and Universities toward His Religion: A Social Study of Religious Changes.* U. of Pennsylvania, 1932. 264 pp.

Perilman, Nathan A. "Where Are Our Youth?" In *Reform Judaism: Essays by Hebrew Union College Alumni*, 163–73. Cincinnati: HUC Press, 1949.

Rudavsky, David, David Bonder, Leslie L. Flaxman, and Ben M. Edidin. "Aspects of Jewish Youth Education." *Jew Ed* 11 (Jan. 1940): 218–27.

Schwartz, Lawrence W. "Study of Jewish Youth Education." Master's thesis, HUC–JIR, 1928.

Teller, I. L. „די דערוואכונג פון דער אידישער יוגנט" (The Awakening of Jewish Youth). *Morning Journal* (Y.) (Feb. 2, 1947).

Zhitlowsky, Chaim. „וואס גיבען מיר אונזער יוגנט?" (What Are We Giving to Our Youth). *Day* (Y.) (Sept. 17, 1932).

———. *The Future of Our Youth in This Country and Assimilation* (address—May 4, 1935). Translated by H. H. Weinberg. Pittsburgh Yiddish Culture Society. 15 pp.

SINCE 1950

Adelsberg, David. „טראגעדיע פון היינטיגער יוגנט" (Tragedy of Today's Youth). *Morning Journal* (Y.) (Mar. 11, 1951).

Adler, Morris. "American Jewish Youth—A Profile." *Jewish Heritage* (Summer 1966): 14–18.

AJC. *What We Know about Young American Jews.* N.Y.: 1970. 20 pp.

Alperson, M. "The Many Faces of American Jewry: Jewish Student Press." *Present Tense* 11 (Autumn 1983): 30–33.

Arzt, Raphael. "The Qualities of a Good Youth Leader." *Ed As* (1966): 80–84.

B'nai B'rith Hillel Foundation. *Jewish Life on Campus, 1981–82: A Directory of B'nai B'rith Hillel Foundations and other Jewish Campus Organizations.* Washington, D.C.: 1982. 64 pp. Also 1985, 96 pp.

Boroff, David. "Jewish Teen Age Culture." *The Annals* (Nov. 1961).

Borowitz, Eugene. "Making Sense out of God." *Jewish Connection* 5 (Winter 1985).

Breslau, David. *Arise and Build: The Story of American Habonim.* N.Y.: Ichud-Labor Zionist Youth, 1961. 260 pp.

Budick, Isadore. "Jewish College Youth." *Jew Ed* 26 (Fall 1955): 52–56.

Cahnman, Werner J. "The Cultural Consciousness of Jewish Youth." *JSS* 14 (July 1952): 195–208.

Chomsky, William. "The Youth Rebellion and Jewish Education." *Recon* 36 (Mar. 6, 1970): 16–21. See also *Ped Rep* 21 (June 1970): 7–10.

CJFWF. *Guidelines for the Development of Youth and Faculty Programs in Small City Federations.* N.Y., 1972. CP, 34 pp.

CJFWF. *Youth Looks at the Jewish Community.* N.Y.: October 1965. CP, 71 pp.

* Cohen, Joseph L. *Group Membership and a Belief System: A Study of the Relationship between Membership in a National Jewish Religious Youth Organization (United Synagogue Youth) and the Religious Attitudes of Its Membership.* New York U., 1970. 118pp

Cohen, Steven Martin. "Radical Jewish Youth and This America." *Sh'ma* (Apr. 27, 1973): 103–4.

Davidson, Jerome K. "Jewish Youth Today." *CCAR* 76 (1966): 198–203.

———. "The Religious Attitudes of Reform Jewish Youth." Master's thesis, HUC–JIR, 1958. Summary in *Jew Teach* 27 (Mar. 1959): 3–16.

Davis, Maurice. "How Effective Is Our Temple Youth Program?" *CCAR J* (Apr. 1961): 50–52.

* Dayan, S. I. *A Comparative Study of the Personality Structure of Male and Female Freshmen of Traditional Background*. Yeshiva U., 1958.

De Nola, D. "The Jewish Student Press—Pulsebeat of the Movement." *JBA* (1974–75): 33–36.

Dimensions. "Jewish Youth and the Sexual Revolution" (symposium). 3 (Winter 1968–69).

Drew, David E. "Jewish Student Today: Radical or Conservative?" *Transaction* (Oct. 1971): 46–48.

Einhorn, David. „רעליגיעזע זוכענישן ביי דער אידישער יוגנט" (Religious Quests among Jewish Youth). *For* (Y.) (Dec. 20, 1959).

———. „די פארבלאנדזשענע אידישע יוגנט אין אמעריקע" (The Straying Jewish Youth in America). *For* (Y.) (Mar. 4, 1950).

Eisendrath, Maurice N. „יוגנט אין רעפארם-רייען שטרעבט צו א טיפערן אידישן לעבן" (Youth in the Reform Movement Strive toward a Deeper Jewish Life). In *Penn* (Y.), 104–10.

Ellman, Eugene B. "Jewish Identity among American Jewish Youth." *Dispersion and Unity* 15/16 (1972): 133–44.

Engel, G., et al. "An Investigation of Anti-Semitic Feeling in Two Groups of College Students—Jewish and Non-Jewish." *J of Social Psychology* 48 (1958): 75–82.

Ephraim, Miriam R. "Implications of the JWB Young Adult Study." In *The Crisis in Values of the Young Adult in Our Society*. N.Y.: 92nd Street YM–YWHA, May 13, 1964.

———, chair. "Informal Jewish Education of Jewish Youth and Adults in America" (committee report). *Jew Ed* 27 (Fall 1956): 47–56.

Etzioni, A. "Campus Ferment: Search for New Values." *Had Mag* 50 (May 1969).

Feingold, Henry L. "Youth in Politics: Promises, Promises." *Congress Biweekly* (Dec. 8, 1972): 5.

Feldman, L. A. "The Personality of the Jewish College Student: A Portrait." *Jew Spec* (Dec. 1955): 11–17.

Feldman, Sara. "A New Jewish Voice on Campus." *Dimensions* (Winter 1970): 4–11.

Fishman, Shikl (Joshua). „איז דא א וועג צו דערנענטערן די יידישע סטודירנדיקע יוגנט אין אמעריקע צו יידישקייט?" (Is There a Way to Draw College Youth in America Nearer to Jewishness?) *Zuk* (Y.) (July–Aug. 1967): 273–77.

Fishman, Yehuda. "Zionist Education and the Youth Movements." *Ped Rep* 30 (Winter 1979).

* Freedman, Joseph L. *A Life-Coping Skills Approach to Guiding College-Bound Jewish Students*. Columbia U. Teachers College, 1980. 224 pp.

Fried, Jacob. "American Jewish Youth: Two Generations." In *JMW*, 171–92.

Friedman, Theodore. *Letters to College Students*. N.Y.: Jonathan-David, 1965. 223 pp.

Fromer, Seymour, and I. Rabinowitz. "Jewish Attitudes of Jewish College Youth." *Jewish Center* 23 (Sept. 1954).

Furman, Phyllis. "The Kesher Connection." *MJ* 18 (Summer 1984): 18.

* Garte, Sumner H. *The Relationship between Ethnic Identification and Academic Achievement in Jewish College Students*. Loyola U. of Chicago, 1973. 163 pp.

Gittelsohn, Ronald B. *The Extra Dimension: A Jewish View of Marriage*. N.Y.: UAHC, 1983.

———. "How to Survive Today's Youth: A Review Essay." *Dimensions* 1 (Winter 1967): 45–46.

———. *My Beloved is Mine: Judaism and Marriage*. N.Y.: UAHC, 1969. 320pp

Gladstone, Jacob. „אידישע יוגנט וואוהין?" (Jewish Youth—Whither?). *Day* (Y.) (Dec. 28, 1958).

Glicksberg, Charles I. "College Youth and the Future of Judaism?" *Jud* 4 (Winter 1955): 42–46.

———. "Our College Youth." *Congress Weekly* (May 18, 1953).

———. "The Questing of Jewish College Youth." *Congress Weekly* (June 10, 1955): 9–11.

Goodman, Isaac M. "A Correlation Study of Jewish Education and Hashkafah (mental view) among College-Age Jewish Students." In *Stu.*

*———. *Jewish Education and Religious Attitudes: A Correlation Study of College-Age Jewish Students.* Yeshiva U., 1978.

Goodman, Saul L. „געפעכטע טענות פון אונדזער יוגנט" (Justified Claims of Our Youth). In *Uniqueness of American Judaism* (Y.). Tel Aviv: I.L. Peretz, 357–62. 1980.

———. „זוכונגען פון דער אמעריקאנער יידישער יוגנט" (Quests of American Jewish Youth). In *Uniqueness of American Judaism* (Y.). Tel Aviv: I.L. Peretz, 367–87. 1980.

Gordon, Theodore H. "Ma'ayan—Torah Lish'mah for Youth." *CCAR J* (Winter 1978): 53–57.

Gorodetzer, Philip. "A Study of the Home Environment, Background and Attitudes of Jewish College Students." Master's thesis, U. of Houston, 1962.

Graubart, Judah L. "Jewish Youth and the Establishment." *Jew Fron* (Oct. 1971): 11–16.

Greenberg, Irving. "Jewish Survival and the College Campus." *Jud* 17 (Summer 1968): 281–95.

Greenberg, Meyer. "Social Characteristics of the Jewish Students at the University of Maryland." *JSS* 23 (Jan. 1961): 21–37.

Greenberg, M. "Kashruth and College." *Jew Spec* 29 (1964): 14–15.

Himmelfarb, Milton. "The Jewish College Student and the Intellectual Community." *Jud* 17 (1968): 3–9.

Hirt-Manheimer, Aron. "A Critical History of Reform Youth Magazines." A study of the evolution of four instructional youth magazines from 1907 to the present. Master's project, HUC–JIR, 1975.

Hoffmann, Justin. "Toward an Understanding of the Jewish College Student." *Rel Ed* 60 (Nov.–Dec. 1965): 443–50.

Horowitz, David. "After High School What?" *Jew Teach* 34 (Feb. 1966): 35–36.

Hurvitz, Mark. "The Depoliticization of Jewish Youth." *Sh'ma* (Apr. 27, 1973): 101–3.

Hurvitz, Nathan. "Understanding the Self-Hate of Jewish Young Adults." *Recon* (Nov. 14, 1952): 18–24.

Israel, Richard J. "From Protest to Brown Rice: Some Options for Jewish Students in a Post Drug Culture." *Jew Fron* (Jan. 1973): 7–10.

Jospe, Alfred. "Jewish College Students in the United States." *AJYB* 65 (1964): 131–45.

Kadushin, Max. "A New Approach to the Education of Jewish Youth" (interview by Howard J. Goldberg). *Recon* (May 24, 1950): 18–23.

Kahn, Benjamin M. "Jewish Youth in a Changing World." *The Jewish Community* 19 (Mar. 1964).

Kaplan, Harry. *Jewish Youth and the Jewish Community—Concerned or Indifferent?* CP, Dec. 1964. 9 pp.

Krasner, Norman. "Feedback: The Extent to Which Jewish Youth Groups Supply Professional Personnel for Jewish Life." *Ed As* (1960): 88–90.

Kronish, Ronald. "Communications: Reform College Students." *RJ* 30 (Fall 1983): 65–66.

Kruger, Laurie. "The Needs of Jewish Students on a 'Third World' Campus." Master's thesis, HUC–JIR, 1977.

Lamm, Norman. *The Sabbath: A Model for a Theory of Leisure for High School, College and Adults.* N.Y.: BJE, 1969. 34 pp.

* Lampner, Carl. *An Approach to Religious Youth Work.* Columbia U., 1965. 242 pp.

Lander, Adele. "Judaism for Friendly Skeptics." A guideline for Hillel staff members who teach a course in basic Judaism. Master's project, HUC–JIR, 1980.

———. "Listening to the Jewish College Student." Includes 65 articles on the Jewish college student from 1967 to 1977. Master's project, HUC–JIR, 1979.

Lavender, A. D. "Jewish Identity on the College Campus: An Experiment in Identity Maintenance." *Jew Ed* 46 (Spring 1978): 33–39.

Leeson, Jerrold I. "Informal Education: Its Thrust, Challenge and Its Emerging Professional Leader." *Ed As* (1973): 76–85.

Lehrer, Leibush. "Jewish Belongingness of Jewish Youth." *YA* 9 (1954): 137–65. Also in *YB* (Y.) 38 (1954): 78–105.

Leiman, Shnayer. *The Campus Problem and Jewish Education.* N.Y.: UOJCA. 8 pp.

Levine, Hillel. *Reaching the New College Generation*. CJF, Board Institute, 1982.

Levinson, B. M. "The Problem of Jewish Religious Youth." In *The Psychodynamics of American Jewish Life: An Anthology*, edited by Norman Kiell. 1967.

——. "The Problems of Yeshiva and Stern College Freshmen." *Yeshiva Education* 2 (Fall 1958): 13–25, 45.

Levy, Henry W. "Jewish Youth in Revolt." *Pio Woman* (Sept.–Oct. 1969): 3–5.

Levy, R. N. "Is College a Jewish Dead End or New Beginning?" *RJ* 12 (Winter 1983–84): 18–19.

Liebman, Charles. "Jewish Youth." In *The Ambivalent American Jew: Politics, Religion, and Family in American Jewish Life*, 122–34. Phila.: JPS, 1973.

Lookstein, Joseph H. "The Youth as Citizen." *Rel Ed 56* (Jan.–Feb. 1961): 17–19.

* Mailbaum, Matthew. *The New Student and Youth Movement, 1965–1972: A Perspective View on Some Social and Political Developments in American Jews as a Religio-National Group*. Claremont College, 1980.

Margoshes, Samuel. *"The Jewish Youth: Why Is It Not Jewish? Failures of the Jewish School and the Jewish Home." Day* (Jan. 12, 1966).

Menes, Abraham. „ווי האלט עס מיט דער אידישער יוגנט אין אמעריקע?" (How Do We Fare in Regard to Jewish Youth in America?). *For* (Y.) (Mar. 25, 1951).

Meyer, Eric M. "The Jewish Student Today: Patterns and Prospects." *Jew Ed* 38 (June 1968): 30–35.

Monson, Rela Geffen. *Jewish Campus Life: A Survey of Student Attitudes toward Marriage and Family*. N.Y.: AJC, 1984. 43 pp.

Novak, Bill. *"Genesis 2:* A Voice of the New Jewish Consciousness." *National Jewish Monthly* (July–Aug. 1974): 18–27.

Novak, Bill, and Robert Goldman. "The Rise of the Jewish Student Press." *Con Jud* (Winter 1971): 5–19.

Olitzky, Kerry M., and Elyce Azriel. *Critical Issues Facing North American Jewish Youth: A Resource Guide*. N.Y.: UAHC, 1982. 28 pp.

Ostow, Mortimer. "Jewish Youth in Dissent: A Psychoanalytic Portrait." In *FJCA*, 213–38.

Popkin, Zelda. "The 'Drop-Outs'." *Jew Fron* (Sept. 1966): 16–21.

Porter, Jacob Nusan, Boris Rockovsky, and Anita Bach Agrillo. "The Jewish Student: A Comparative Analysis of Religious and Secular Attitudes." *YA* 15 (1974): 297–338.

Potok, Chaim. "L.T.F. [Leaders Training Fellowship—for youth]: A New Image." *The Torch* (Spring 1965). Also in *RTJS*, 220–25.

Rabinowitz, Dorothy. "Are Jewish Students Different?" *Change* (Summer 1971): 47–50.

Radke, Marion. *The Meaning of Minority Group Membership to Jewish College Students*. N.Y.: 1951.

Raphael, Ahi Shimshun. „סטודענטן דעמאנסטראציעס און פאראנטווארטליכע אידישע פאליטיק" (Student Demonstrations and Responsible Jewish Politics). *Dos Vort* (Y.) (Apr.–May 1966): 25–27.

Rosenthal, Frank. "Youth and the Dialogue: A New Look." *Syn Sch* 22 (Fall 1963).

Roskin, Laurie. "Young Judea's Educational Program." *Ped Rep* 32 (Winter 1981): 9–11.

Rothstein, Ann, ed. *A Guide to Jewish Student Groups*. N.Y.: North American Jewish Students' Network, 1971. 80 pp.

Rutchik, Allen. "An Aggravating Challenge." *Syn Sch* 27 (Summer 1969): 4–7.

Saks, Robert J. "Jews, Judaism, and the New Left." *Con Jud* (Summer 1967).

Sanua, Victor D. "A Comparative Study of the Religious Attitudes and Practices of Different Groups of Jewish Students." *Jew Ed* 39 (July 1969): 27–36.

Saperstein, Marc E. "Jewish Youth Today." *CCAR* 76 (1967): 192–97.

Schanin, Norman. "Forty Years of Young Judea." *Jew Ed* 21 (Summer 1950): 37–41, 43.

* ——. *Young Judea: A Survey of a National Jewish Youth Movement in 1951–52*. New York U., 1959.

* Schlessinger, June Hirsch. *A Comparison of Documented Concerns of American Jewry with the Concerns Expressed in Accessible Jewish Fiction about Jewish Life Published in 1930 to 1935 and 1970 to 1975 and Suggested*

for Young Adult Readers. U. of Connecticut, 1979. 185 pp.

Schwartz, Howard. *Jewish College Youth Speak Their Minds*. N.Y.: AJC, 1969. 36 pp.

Schwartz, Lita Linzer. "Cults and the Vulnerability of Jewish Youth." *Jew Ed* 46 (Summer 1978): 23–26, 42.

* Segal, Jack. *Premarital Sexual Activities and Religious Practices of Jewish Female College Students Attending South Central United States Universities*. U. of Houston, 1973. 465 pp.

Segel, Kenneth I. "Ethical Values of Jewish Youth: The Implications for Our Youth." *CCAR J.*, (Winter 1976): 57–64.

Seltzer, S. "Assessing the Jewish Attitudes of Reform College Students." *RJ* 30 (1983): 67–77.

Shabatay, Yehuda. "United Synagogue Youth Reaches Maturity." In *Teen*, 170–78.

Sherwin, Byron L. "Reaching Out to the Collegian." *RA* (1975): 139–44.

Sh Hah (H.). "סמפוזיון על הנוער היהודי באמריקה" (Symposium on Jewish Youth in America). Participants: Sh. Belkin, Jacob Neusner, Morton Siegel, and I. Rabinowitz. 30 (1970).

Shosteck, Robert. *The Jewish College Student: Report of the Third Decennial Census of Jewish College Students in the United States and Canada*. Washington, D.C.: B'nai B'rith Vocational Service, 1955. 61 pp.

* Silverman, S. S. *Relationship of Personality Factors and Religious Background among College Students*. Yeshiva U., 1951.

* Slade, Irving L. *An Introductory Survey of Jewish Student Organizations in American Higher Education*. Columbia U., 1966. 175 pp.

Sleeper, James A. "Activists and a New Judaism." *Con Jud* 23 (Summer 1967): 25–32.

Spotts, Leon H. "The Challenge of Jewish Youth." *Jew Ed* 39 (Dec. 1969): 43–47.

Stavsky, David. *The Attitudes of a Jewish College Student toward His Religion as Reflected in Two Reference Groups*. Columbus, Ohio: Samuel Mendel Melton Foundation, 1966. 69 pp.

Stern, Jack, Jr. "Jewish Youth Today." *CCAR* 76 (1966): 204–7.

Stolper, Pinchas, ed. *Tested Teen Age Activities: A Guide to Programming*. N.Y.: UOJCA, National Conference of Synagogue Youth, 1964. 140 pp.

———, ed. *Text and Source Book for National Conference of Synagogue Youth* (E. and H.). N.Y.: UOJCA, National Conference of Synagogue Youth, 1961. 48 pp.

Summers, Barbara F. *Community Responsibility in the Jewish Tradition: A Study and Action Program*. USA Department of Youth Activities, 1978. 250 pp.

Swerdloff, S., and H. Rosen. *The College and Career Plans of Jewish High School Youth*. Washington, D.C.: B'nai B'rith Vocational Service, 1964.

Teitelbaum, Samuel. "The Jewish College Student." *Chicago Jewish Forum* (Spring 1953).

* ———. *Patterns of Adjustment among Jewish Students in Midwestern Universities*. Northwestern U., 1953.

Troupp, Leonard B. "Informal Education and the Reform Movement." *Ped Rep* 29 (Spring 1978).

UAHC. *Quest: Four Workshops on Important Issues Confronting Jewish Youth*. N.Y.

United Synagogue Youth. "Resolution on Youth and Jewish Education." *Syn Sch* 14 (May 1956): 16–18.

UOJCA. *Yamim Noraim*. N.Y.: National Conference of Synagogue Youth, 1961. 47 pp.

* Verbit, Mervin. *Referents for Religion among Jewish College Students*. Columbia U., 1968.

Wachs, Saul F. *Quality Control of Jewish Life* (GA, 1973). CP, 1974. 13 pp.

Wunsch, Lee R. "Meeting the Challenge of Contemporary Jewish Youth." *Ped Rep* 33 (Mar. 1982): 32–34.

Yavneh: A Guide to Jewish Life on the College Campus. N.Y.: Yavneh, 1975. 92 pp.

Zeitlin, Aaron. "וואוהין גייט די יוגנט?" (Whither Jewish Youth). *Day* (Y.) (May 21, 1958).

* Zerin, Edward. *Selected Theological and Educational Factors in the Personality Development of Jewish Youth*. U. of Southern California, 1953. 66 pp.

Zigmond, Maurice L. "Some Observations on the Jewish College Student." *CCAR* 76 (1966): 179–81.

GLEANINGS

American Jewish Archives,
"A survey was made by the American Council on Education in 1938 on the activities and attitudes of the youth of America. In this volume called *Youth Tell Their Story* a chapter is devoted to the religious attitudes of youth, and it was amazing to discover the strong attachment of Christian youth to the church in contrast to our Jewish youth. Whereas 85% of the Catholic youth and 65% of the Protestant youth attend their church service at least once a month, only 15% of Jewish youth come to the synagogue that often."

Quoted in AJA 35 (Nov. 1983): 222.

Kadushin, Max,
"What our youth need is a pattern of values that will give them inner security and wholesome satisfaction. Our youth need ideals that can be employed in public and in private conduct. They need concepts that interpret life and render it worthwhile. These values are all found in Judaism and it is our job to identify, interpret and apply these values to everyday living. Only in this way will Judaism command the loyalty and devotion of Jewish youth."

"A New Approach to the Education of Jewish Youth: An Interview with Max Kadushin." *Recon* (Mar. 24, 1950), 18–19.

Lelyveld, Arthur J.,
"Let us . . . selectively train the most promising of them [youth] to be maladjusted to their environment of mass-produced dreams of acquisition, to lead them to a moving concern with life's vertical dimension, the covenant ideal, the commitment to values larger than self and beyond price. Let us provoke them in a healthy and meaningful rebellion that they may dream once more the dreams which are the precious right of youth and that they make demands upon the synagogue in the name of the God who makes demands upon them and upon each and everyone of us."

"What Youth Demands of the Congregation They Will Inherit" (45th GA, Nov. 16, 1959), 11.

Greenberg, Irving,
"The Jewish community has been depending on a nominal Jewishness combined with neighborhood and social concentration to carry it through. College is destroying this possibility socially and culturally. Only a major upgrading in informed Jewish commitment and deepening of Jewish knowledge can save the day. It has been said that the British Empire was lost and won on the playing fields of Eton. The crown of Judaism and Jewishness will be won or lost on the campus of America."

Jud 17 (Summer 1968), 281.

CCAR,
"The Central Conference of American Rabbis urges its members to recognize the high priority that needs to be given to programs and activities for the young people of our movement. We recommend to our colleagues that the youth activities of the congregations deserve renewed and continued rabbinic interest on both the high school and college level. We, therefore, recommend that since regional activities represent the focal point of need, a rotating system be established which involves each of our colleagues in at least one regional conclave or related activity in the course of a year, and that calendars of youth regions be set after consultation with rabbis to provide for most effective rabbinic involvement."

Resolution adopted 1969, 147.

Soloveitchik, Joseph B.,
"Young people are more complicated religiously, more dynamic in their religious search. Moreover, they are infected with a degree of "chutzpah." They want a service which is more spontaneous and volatile, more fervent than fixed, more flexible than rigid. They are interested more in a house of study than a house of prayer.

35 YOUTH AND JEWISH EDUCATION

They are alienated from scrupulous, formalized and tightly organized worship."

Quoted by Ruth Birnbaum (*Jud* 26 [Winter 1977], 62) from Joseph B. Soloveitchik's *Shirei Harav: A Conspectus of the Public Lectures of Rabbi Joseph B. Soloveitchik*. 1974.

36 CAMP

CAMPING PROGRAMS AND JEWISH EDUCATION

(See also chapters 20 and 21.)

AAJE. "Camping as an In-School Experience." *Ped Rep* 26 (Spring 1975).

Ackerman, Walter I. "Camp and School: Year-Round Education." *Jew Ed* 36 (Winter 1966): 93–96, 120.

Alexander, Chanan. "Ometz: A New Conception of Leadership Development for the Conservative Movement" (Camp Ramah). *MJ* 15 (Winter 1983): 4, 25.

Arian, Philip. "Camp Ramah in the Congregational School." *Syn Sch* 22 (1964).

———. "The Camp Setting: Alternative to Never-Never Land." *Syn Sch* 23 (1965).

Arzt, Raphael. "The Camp as Setting for Jewish Education." Colloquim for Jewish Education. Sponsored by the Philip W. Lown Graduate Center for Contemporary Studies, Brandeis U., and the American Jewish Committee. Feb. 1971. 17 pp.

Aviad, Janet. "Subculture or Counterculture: Camp Ramah." In *Stu* 3, 197–225.

Bardin, Shlomo. "The Camp Brandeis Institute." *Jew Ed* 17 (June 1946): 26–27.

———. "The History of Brandeis Camp Institute." In *Southwest Jewry*, edited by S. L. Malamut, 3:197–200. 1957.

* Bekerman, Zvi. *The Social Construction of Jewishness: An Anthropological Interactional Study of a Camp [Ramah] System.* JTSA, 1986.

Bender, Daniel. "All Israel Are Brothers One to Another: A Unit Covering World Jewish Communities." A three-week camp unit on World Jewish Communities, with special emphasis on exotic communities. Master's project, HUC–JIR, 1977.

Benderly, Samson. "Possible Significance of the Summer Camp." *Opinion* (Apr. 11, 1932).

Berkson, Isaac B. "Thirty Years of Cejwin Camps." *Jew Ed* 21 (Winter 1949): 7–8.

Bernstein, Louis. "מסד" (Camp Massad). *Ped Rep* 32 (Winter 1981): (H. section) 35–36.

Blumenfield, Samuel M. "Summer Camp Institute Sharon." *Jew Ed* 22 (Summer 1951): 37–40.

Breslau, David, ed. *The Story of 25 Years of Habonim Camping.* N.Y.: Chai Commission of LZOA Movement, 1957. 198 pp.

Breuer, Stephen E. "Camping as an In-School Experience—Questions for Consideration." *Ped Rep* 26 (Spring 1975): 5.

Brodkin, Arthur. "Potentialities of Jewish Education in Camps under Jewish Community Center and JWF Auspices" (Federation planning for Jewish education). N.Y.: CJFWF, 1970. CP, 9 pp.

36 CAMP

Chazan, Barry. "Summer Reflections: A Look at Mahaneh Givah." *Syn Sch* 26 (Spring 1968): 10–16.

Cohen, Burton T. "Learning Hebrew at Ramah." *Ped Rep* 34 (Jan. 1983): 17–20.

———. "The Ramah Experience in Utilizing the Education Capabilities of Israelis." *CAJE Jewish Education News* (Winter/Spring 1988): 39.

Dickman, Marci. *M'soret and Me: A Curriculum for Special Needs Children on Jewish Symbols and Rituals Used in Camp*. L.A.: HUC–JIR, Rhea Hirsch School of Education, 1982.

Dover, Amy. "Planning Staff Training Programs in Jewish Resident Camping: Questions to Ask." Master's thesis, HUC–JIR, 1983.

Ephraim, Miriam R. "A Look at Jewish Communal Camping." *Jew Ed* 36 (Winter 1966): 97–102.

* Farago, Uri. *The Influence of a Jewish Summer Camp's Social Climate on the Camper's Identity*. Brandeis U., 1972.

Feinberg, Paul R. "Chalutzim in Oconomowoc." *Ped Rep* 33 (Mar. 1982): 34–35.

Fox, Frank. "Day Camp Hebrew Program for 8–10." *Syn Sch* 17 (Mar. 1959): 12–15.

———. "A Synagogue Summer Day Camp for Young Children." *Syn Sch* 15 (May 1957): 8–12.

Freidenreich, Fradle. "Camping as an In-School Experience—Introduction." *Ped Rep* 26 (Spring 1975): 1–3.

Gannes, Abraham P. "Camp—A Children's Jewish Community." *Jew Ed* 36 (Winter 1966): 87–92.

———. "Camps Solve a Problem—Through Jewish Living." *Nat Jew M* (Feb. 1969).

Gannes, Abraham P., and Levi Soshuk. "The Kvutzah and Camp Achvah." *Jew Ed* 20 (Summer 1949): 61–69.

Gillman, Neil G. "Ten Years of Ramah: Achievement and Challenge." *Syn Sch* 15 (May 1957): 3–7.

Gittelson, Abraham J. "Summer Enrichment Program." *Syn Sch* 27 (Spring 1969): 21–25.

Golub, Jacob S. "An Educational Program for Jewish Camps." *Jewish Teacher* 6 (June 1924): 1–2.

Goodman, Philip. "The Jewish Home Camp." *Jew Ed* 17 (June 1946): 30–35.

* Hamburger, Lewis D. *A Study of the Failures and Dilemmas of Part-Time Jewish Education and Implications of Elements from Talmudic Schools and Educational Camping*. U. of Maryland, 1971.

Isaacman, Daniel. "Jewish Education in Camping." *AJYB* 67 (1966): 245–52.

* ———. *Jewish Summer Camps in the United States and Canada, 1900–1969*. Dropsie U., 1970.

———. *Summer Camping and Jewish Education: Federation Planning for Jewish Education*. CJFWF, Mar. 21, 1968. 9 pp.

Jabotinski, Vladimir. „זומער קעמפס און לשון קודש" (Summer Camps and Hebrew). *Morning Journal* (Y.) (July 26, 1926).

JWB. *Directory of Summer Camps, under the Direction of Jewish Communal Organizations*. N.Y., 1937.

Kaye, George W. "A Post-High School Program" (camping). *Ped Rep* 26 (Spring 1975): 19–22.

Kilstein, Sandra. "Jewish Leadership Camping: A Model Jewish Counselor Training Project." *Jew Ed* 49 (Fall 1981): 23–26.

Klein, Aaron. "Camp Ramah—The Growth of an Idea." *Syn Sch* 11 (Feb. 1953): 19–24.

Klotz, Ronald. "Toward a Survey of the Union of American Hebrew Congregations' Camp Educational Program." Master's thesis, HUC–JIR, 1977.

Kornblum, Sholem. „בית-הספר ומחנה-קיץ— הפרדה או שתוף-פעולה?" (The School and the Camp—Separation or Partnership?). *Hadoar* (H.) 53 (27th of Nissan 1974).

Leiman, Sandra. "Creating an Ideal Camp for Jewish Children." *Compass* 8 (Winter 1986): 17.

Leinow, Benjamin J. "Toward a Year-Round Temple Camping Program." Master's thesis, HUC–JIR, 1966.

Lerner, Stephen C. "Camp Ramah and Its Critics." *Con Jud* 25 (Summer 1971): 1–28.

Levine, Gene N. "An Adventure in Curing Alienation." *Jew Ed* 41 (Fall 1972): 10–18.

Levow, Mordecai. "Various School Programs in Our Community" (school continuity in the camping program). *Ped Rep* 26 (Spring 1971): 7, 9–11.

Libenson, Michael A. "A Tool for Summer Continuity." *Ped Rep* 26 (Spring 1975): 15, 18–19.

* Luckens, Reuben. *Jewish Educational Camping in the United States*. Jewish Teachers Seminary-Herzliah, 1967–68.

Lurie, Rose G. "Summer Work in the Jewish School—Integrating the Recreation Program with the Curriculum." *Jew Ed* 5 (Apr.–June 1933): 100–108.

Marcus, George. "Jewish Camping and the Personnel Problem." *Ed As* (1966): 84–87.

Monson, Rela Geffen. "Education through Experience: Teaching the Jewish Political Tradition in the Summer Camp Setting." *Jew Ed* 49 (Fall 1981): 27–32.

NJWB. *Directory of Jewish Resident Summer Camps*. N.Y., 1973–74.

Novak, William. "Notes on Summer Camps: Some Reflections on the Ramah Dream." *Response* (Winter 1971–72).

Ped Rep. "The Use of Camping in the Jewish Schools." 23 (Dec. 1971): 8.

Reich, Zvi. "The Camp as an Unexcelled Educational Program." *Ped Rep* 22 (June 1971): 26.

Resnikoff, M. Bernard. "Ramah—A Thinking Child's Camp." *The Torch* (Spring 1959). Also *RTJS*, 214–19.

Schenker, Avraham. "Zionist Camping in America." *Jew Ed* 36 (Winter 1966): 103–7.

Schoolman, Albert P. "Jewish Educational Camping—Its Potentialities and Realities." *Jew Ed* 36 (Winter 1966): 77–86.

———. "The Jewish Educational Summer Camp: A Survey of Its Development and Implications." *Jew Ed* 17 (June 1946): 6–15.

———. "The Jewish Summer Camp." In *Jewish Schools in America*, 50–59. N.Y.: AAJE.

Schwartz, Shuley Rubin. "Ramah—The Early Years, 1947–1952." Master's thesis, JTSA, 1971.

———. "Ramah Philosophy and the Newman Revolution." In *Studies in Jewish Education and Judaica in Honor of Louis Newman*. Alexander M. Shapiro and Burton I. Cohen. N.Y. 1985.

Shapiro, Harvey. "Utilizing Judaic Resources for Camp Counselor Training." Outline of a counselor-training program for Jewish summer camps that promotes interaction between counselors, Jewish texts, and campers. Master's project, HUC–JIR, 1980.

Shreiber, Ben Zion. "The Summer Camp and Education for Jewish Living." *Recon* (Oct. 6, 29, 1950): 16–20, 25–29.

Shulsinger, Shlomo. "Hebrew Camping—Five Years of Massad." *Jew Ed* 17 (June 1946): 16–23.

* Sierad, Jack. *The Enhancement of Ethnic Identity: The Brandeis-Bardin Experiment*. UCLA, 1982.

———. "Hebrew Camping—The Creating of a Hebrew World." *Jew Ed* (Winter 1967): 6–14.

Skolnik, Nachama. "The Camp Connection." *Compass* 12 (Summer 1979): 7, 20.

———. "Outreach and the Jewish Residential Camp." On reinforcing the religious and educational qualities of the Jewish residential camp. Master's project, HUC–JIR, 1976.

Slesinger, Zalmen. "Summer Camping—The New Dimension in Jewish Education." *Ped Rep* 28 (Mar. 1967).

Smolar, Boris. ‏,,90 טויזנט קינדער אין 200 אידישע זומער קעמפס‏" (Ninety Thousand Children in 200 Jewish Summer Camps). *For* (Y.) (July 29, 1983).

Soshuk, Levi. "The Ramah Camp." *Syn Sch* 18 (1960).

Strauss, Herschel Ira. "Toward the Development of an Informal Camp Program for the Young Adolescent in Understanding Reform Judaism, Emphasizing Values Clarification." Master's thesis, HUC–JIR, 1975.

Swerling, Norman P. "Teaching Jewish Values in a Summer Camp." *Ped Rep* 36 (Nov. 1985): 22–24.

Syn Sch. "Camp Ramah in the Congregational School." 22 (Summer 1964): 3–17.

Teller, Gerald. "A Cooperative Effort between Formal and Informal Education Agencies." *Jew Ed* 49 (Fall 1981): 21–22.

Ward, Nahum. "A Judaic Curriculum for High School Age People in a Camp Setting." An experientially oriented curriculum that explores some of the major historical forces that have shaped modern Jewish life. Master's thesis, HUC–JIR, 1977.

———. "An Investigation of Social Interaction Values Using Rabbinic Sources." An experiential curriculum for children and adolescents in a camp setting that deals with three categories of values: relations between people, understanding human nature, and community. Master's project, HUC–JIR, 1977.

Werber, Bracha. "Eretz Yisrael through the Ages: A Curricular Model for Informal Education at Camp Ramah." Master's thesis, JTS Department of Jewish Education, 1989.

Zeldin, Michael. "Shabbat Manual for Reform Camps." For counselors and programmers to help create more of a balance between the emotional and intellectual aspects of the camp Shabbat experience. Master's project, HUC–JIR, 1976.

———. "Shabbat-Program Sourcebook for Reform Jewish Summer Camps." *SWJT* 9 (Spring/Summer 1977): 14–15.

GLEANINGS

Lehrer, Leibush, reflections (1962) on Camp Boiberik, founded in 1922 by the Sholem Aleichem Folk Institute of New York, which conducted Yiddish secular schools in New York and other cities. Lehrer was camp director for many years.

"When a school organization establishes a camp it has a right to expect the latter to be an extension of the work of the school.... In the early years, we were all victims of this mistaken illusion.... We found that a camp has potentials which a school cannot possibly fulfill. The object of a school is to see that its pupils acquire as much knowledge as possible, whereas the primary object of a camp is to teach children the value of cooperation, good moral habits and, in Jewish matters, to stress the Jewish way of life, forms of natural Jewish expression, a readiness to experience in concrete ways the symbolic expressions of Jewishness derived from our great heritage....

Any effort to introduce into Boiberik, among the children and guests as well, the slightest hint of traditional content had to be undertaken in gradual stages, with teaspoon doses....

The systematic drawing closer to tradition remained localized, a permanent concern in Boiberik. Here the objectives have remained as they were as they first blossomed forth. Only in one task, and a very vital one, it is not possible to report any progress: the furtherance of Yiddish as the normal medium for the children's camp....

It is easier to state ideas than to discover proper methods for their implementation. Our aim is to provide sound camping experience and to imbue our campers with the educational and moral values of wholesome fun, recreation and cooperative living. On the other hand, since we are dealing with Jewish children, effective expression should be given to the campers' consciousness of Jewish belonging and to the feeling of loyalty to the interests of Jewish people."

"The Objectives of Camp Boiberik—In the Light of its History." In *Our First Fifty Years: The Sholem Aleichem Folk Institute*, edited by Goodman (1972), 61–62, 64, 68, 71.

Isaacman, Daniel,

"What can be done in Jewish camping is dramatically demonstrated in Cejwin, Ramah, Massad, and some of the Zionist camps, where the leadership and staff are committed. These camps fill the void between June and September, when whatever a child may have learned during the formal Hebrew-school year is usually unlearned. What is even more important, these camps fill an emotional void. A Tish'ah be-Av program in a Habonim camp like Galil, or taking part in a play at Cejwin, can be an experience that no amount of formal study duplicates. The tranquility and repose of the Sabbath in

Ramah create an atmosphere and spirit which the camper may carry with him for the entire year, and the Havdalah near the lake demonstrates the concept of 'distinguishing between Sabbath and week days.'"

"Jewish Education in Camping." *AJYB* 67 (1966), 252.

Lerner, Stephen C.,
"Ramah has succeeded over the years because, with intelligence and sensitivity, it has introduced youngsters to intensive and unadulterated Jewish living. In its hothouse atmosphere, it could implement those ideals which rabbis, at best, would laud. Youngsters lived all the slogans which seemed so empty in Hebrew school back home. Ramah appropriated the most enduring aims of Conservative Judaism—the importance of Jewish study in Hebrew, regular prayer, significant . . . observance of Shabbat and Kashrut, concern for one's fellowman, identification for Israel—and made them work."

"Ramah and Its Critics." *Con Jud* 25 (Summer 1971). Quoted by Sheldon A. Dorph in *Stu*, 91.

37 | LOCAL SOURCES FOR JEWISH EDUCATION

For data prior to 1900 see Chapter 29. American Jewish Year Books list current periodicals for each state.

ALABAMA

"Alabama." In *Enc Jud*, 2:505–7.

"Alabama." In *Post*, 3–12.

Fishman, Joshua A. "Southern City." *Mid 7* (Summer 1961): 39–56. Also in *JIS*, 307–33.

Lowi, Theodore. "Southern Jews: The Two Communities." *Jew J Soc* 6 (July 1964). Also in *JIS*, 265–82.

Birmingham

Elovitz, Mark H. *A Century of Jewish Life in Dixie: The Birmingham Experience*. U. of Alabama Press, 1974. 258 pp.

Newfield, Morris. "The History of the Jews of Birmingham." *The Reform Advocate* (Nov. 4, 1911): 5–32.

Temple Emanu-El. *A Century of Reverence, 1882–1982*. Birmingham, 1983. 129 pp.

Mobile

Eichold, Samuel. *Without Malice: The 100th Anniversary of the Comic Cowboys, 1884–1984*. Mobile: R. E. Publications, 1985?. 177 pp.

Korn, Bertram W. *Congregation Shaarai Shomayim, Mobile, Alabama: Centenary Celebration, 1844–1944*. Mobile: 1944.

———. *The Jews of Mobile, Alabama, 1763–1841*. Cincinnati: HUC Press, 1970.

———. "The Jews of Mobile, Alabama, prior to the Organization of the First Congregation." *HUC Annual* (1969–70): 469–502.

Moses, Alfred G. "A History of the Jews of Mobile." *PAJHS* 12 (1904): 113–25.

The Jewish Ledger (New Orleans). "Mobile's Old Synagogue." June 21, 1907.

Mobile: Education

Dinsky, Samuel. *Report to the Jewish Welfare Fund on Improving Education*. N.Y.: AAJE, 1969.

Montgomery

Hanan, Rubin Morris. *The History of Ahayen Congregation, 1906–1962* (Sephardic). Montgomery: 1962. 34 pp.

Messing, A. J. "'Old Mordecai'—The Founder of the City of Montgomery." *PAJHS* 13 (1905): 71–81.

Moses, Alfred G. "A History of the Jews of Montgomery." *PAJHS* 13 (1905): 83–88.

Sheffield

Jewish Monitor. 1948–present. Weekly.

ALASKA

"Alaska." In *Enc Jud*, 2:513–14.

Bloom, Jessie S. "The Jews of Alaska." *AJA* 15 (Nov. 1963): 97–116.

Glantz, Rudolph. *The Jews in American Alaska 1857–1880*. N.Y.: 1953. 46 pp.

Postal, Bernard. "Alaska—Jewish Population and its History." *AJYB* 61 (1960): 165–69.

Ripinsky, Sol. "An Alaskan Report, 1909." *WSJH* 11 (Oct. 1978): 56–59.

Shirpser, Sol. "An Alaskan Memoir." *WSJH* 10 (Oct. 1977): 16–24.

Anchorage

Jewish Community of Anchorage. *Jewish Life in Alaska: Fulfilling an Alaskan Dream*. Catalog of an exhibition. Anchorage, 1987. 5 pp.

ARIZONA

"Arizona." In *Enc Jud*, 3:449–50.

"Arizona." In *Post*, 12–18.

AJA. "An Arizona Pioneer—Memoirs of Sam Aaron." 10 (Oct. 1958): 95–120.

———. "Trail Blazers of the Trans-Mississippi West." 8 (Oct. 1956): 94–98.

Fierman, Floyd S. "Peddlers and Merchants on the Southwest Frontier, 1850–1900." (Also New Mexico.) *Password* 8 (Summer 1963): 43–55.

———. *Roots and Boots: From Crypto-Jew in New Spain to Community Leader in the American Southwest*. Hoboken, N.J.: Ktav. 241 pp.

Glantz, Rudolph. "Notes on the Early Jews of Arizona." *WSJH* 5 (July 1973): 243–55.

Goldberg, Isaac. "Reminiscences of an Arizona Pioneer." *WSJH* 2 (Apr. 1970): 172–81.

* Lamb, Blaine P. *Jewish Pioneers in Arizona*. Arizona State U., 1982.

Lamont, Marian S. "Many Jews Helped the Pioneers Settle Arizona." *Nat Jew M* (Sept. 1951): 71–76.

Rochlin, Harriet, and Fred Rochlin. "Pioneer Jews: Humdingers in the Far West." *Arizona Highway* 61 (Sept. 1985): 51–102.

Stocker, Joseph. *Jewish Roots in Arizona*. Phoenix: JCC, 1954. 36 pp.

Wilson, Don W. "Pioneer Jews in California and Arizona, 1849–1875." *J of the West* 6 (Apr. 1967): 226–36.

Wollenberg, Charles M. "Recollections of Arizona, 1876–1891." *WSJH* 15 (Oct. 1982): 31–39.

Isaacson

Stern, Norton B., and William S. Kramer. "Who Was Isaacson, Arizona, Named for?" *WSJH* 19 (Jan. 1987): 121–24.

Phoenix

Greater Phoenix Jewish News. 1947–present. Biweekly.

Jewish Federation of Greater Phoenix. *The Greater Phoenix Jewish Population Study, 1983–84* (plus Report No. 2–9). Phoenix, 1983–84. 33 pp.

Lamb, Blaine. "Jews in Early Phoenix, 1870–1920." *J of Arizona History* 18 (Autumn 1977): 299–318.

Temple Beth Israel. *Yovel, Dedication Souvenir, 1950: Temple Beth Israel, 1920–1970*. Phoenix, 1970. 295 pp.

Phoenix: Education

JESNA. *Needs Assessment of the City's Centralized Education Services*. N.Y., 1983–84.

Tombstone

Stern, Norton B. "The Tombstone, Arizona, Jewish Saga." *WSJH* 19 (Apr. 1987): 217–30.

Tucson

Arizona Post. 1946–present. Fortnightly.

Hertzberg, Nat. "Cornerstone Laying of the First Synagogue in Arizona—1910." *WSJH* 19 (Apr. 1987): 255–56.

Temple Emanu-El . . . Commemorative Book in Recognition of the Sixtieth Anniversary of . . . Founding as the First Synagogue on the

ARKANSAS

"Arkansas." In *Enc Jud*, 3:458–59.

"Arkansas." In *Post*, 19–27.

Kohut, George A. "Arkansas." *PAJHS* 6 (1897): 158.

Le Master, Carolyn Gray. "The Jews of Arkansas." *Arkansas Times* 10 (Dec. 1983): 42–43, 82–90.

Shain, Samson A. "The Story of Arkansas Jewry, 1836–1953." Unpublished (American Jewish Archives).

AJA. "Trailblazers . . ." 8 (Oct. 1956): 67–71.

Little Rock

Sanders, Ira E., and Elijah E. Palnick. *The Centennial History of Congregation B'nai Israel*. Little Rock: B'nai Israel, 1966.

CALIFORNIA

"California." In *Post*, 27–65.

Carvalho, Solomon Nunes. *Incidents of Travel and Adventure in the Far West*. 1857. Reprint. Phila.: JPS, 1954. 325 pp. (Carvalho was Fremont's official artist for his expedition to the Pacific.)

Cogan, Sarah G., comp. *Pioneer Jews of the California Mother Lode, 1849–1880*. Includes annotated bibliography. Berkeley: Western Jewish History Center, Judah L. Magnes Memorial Museum, 1968. 54 pp.

Friedland, I. (Data on the History of the Jewish Community in California). *Cheshbon* (Y.) (Oct. 1955): 11–23.

Glanz, Rudolph. *The Jews of California from the Discovery of Gold until 1880*. N.Y.: Privately printed, 1960. 188 pp.

Territory of Arizona, Mar. 20, 1910. Tucson, 1970. 92 pp.

Goldmann, Jack B. "A History of Pioneer Jews in California, 1849–1870." Master's thesis, U. of California, 1940.

Iser, Alexander, comp. *The California Hebrew and English Almanac for the Year 5612, corresponding with the years, 1851–1852*. S.F.: Albion Job Press, 1851. 30 pp.

Kramer, William M. *The Western Journal of Isaac Mayer Wise, 1877*. Berkeley: Western Jewish Historical Center, 1974. 85 pp.

Levinson, Robert E. *The Jews in the California Gold Rush*. N.Y.: Ktav, 1978. 232 pp.

———. *A Preliminary Report on Pioneer Jewish Cemeteries of the California Mother Lode*. Oakland: Commission for the Preservation of Pioneer Jewish Cemeteries and Landmarks, 1964. 7 pp.

Los Angeles Yiddish Writers Society of YKUF. "קאליפארניער שריפטן„ (Writings on California, 1854–1954) (Y.). Jubilee ed. L.A.: Yiddish Writers Society, 1955. 240 pp.

Malamut, J. L. (Materials on the History of Jews in California). *Cheshbon* (Y.) (Oct. 1955): 24–31.

———. "The Yiddish Press in California." *Zunland* (Y.) (Sept. 1925): 92–101.

Meyer, Martin A. *Western Jewry: An Account of the Achievements of Jews and Judaism in California*. S.F.: Emanu-El, June 1916. 245 pp.

Naamani, Israel. "Giants in the West." *Ogen* (H.) (1968). 117 pp.

Newmark, Harris. *Sixty Years in Southern California, 1853–1913*. Edited by Maurice H. Newmark and Marco R. Newmark. 3d ed. Boston and N.Y.: Houghton Mifflin, 1930.

* Portnoy, Joseph. *An Analysis of Reform Youth Participation in Jewish Activities in the Northern California Council Region*. New York U., 1980.

Rafael, Ruth Kelson. *Western Jewish History Center: Guide to Archival and Oral History Collection*. Berkeley: Western Jewish History Center, J. L. Magnes Historical Museum, 1987. 207 pp.

Rischin, Moses, ed. *The Jews of the West: The Metropolitan Years*. Berkeley: AJHS and Western Jewish History Center, J. L. Magnes Memorial Museum, 1979. 159 pp.

Stern, Norton B. *California Jewish History: A Descriptive Bibliography, Selected and Annotated by N. B. Stern.* Glendale, Calif.: A. H. Clarke Co., 1967. 175 pp.

Stern, Norton B., and William M. Kramer. "Anti-Semitism and the Jewish Image in the Early Years." *WSJH* 6 (Jan. 1974): 129–40. Also in *The American West and the Religious Experience*, edited by William M. Kramer, 105–16. Western American Study Series. L.A.: 1975.

———. "The Historical Recovery of the Pioneer Sephardic Jews of California." *WSJH* 8 (Oct. 1975): 3–25.

———. "Sephardic Leadership in Early California Jewish Life." *WSJH* 17 (Apr. 1975): 227–30.

Wechsler, Harold S. "Community and Academy: Jewish Learning at the University of California." *WSJH* 18 (Jan. 1986): 131–42.

Wilson, Don W. "Pioneer Jews in California and Arizona, 1849–1875." *J of the West* 6 (Apr. 1967): 226–36.

Berkeley

* Jaffe, Reuven Ralph Martin. *The Berkeley Lehrhaus Judaica: An Alternative Model of Adult Jewish Education—A Case Study.* U. of Southern California, 1983.

The Jewish Radical. Student publication, 1969–75.

Butte County

Levinson, Rosaline. "Jewish Communities of Butte County, Rise and Development in the 19th Century." *Butte County Historical Society Diggin's* 29 (Fall/Winter 1985): 51–100.

———. "Jewish Communities of Butte County, Part II: the 20th Century, Chico, Decline and Resurgence." *Butte County Historical Society Diggin's* 30 (Fall/Winter 1986): 51–112.

Contra Costa

Tornheim, William. "Pioneer Jews of Contra Costa." *WSJH* 16 (Oct. 1983): 3–23.

Jackson, Amador County

Sharfman, I. Harold. *Nothing Left to Commemorate: The Story of the Pioneer Jews of Jackson, Amador County, California.* Glendale, Calif.: A. H. Clark, 1969. 181 pp.

Long Beach, Lakewood, and Los Alamitos

Hartmann, Sidney A. *History of the Long Beach Jewish Community.* Long Beach, Calif.: JCC, 1957. 64 pp.

Massarik, Fred A. *A Study of the Jewish Population of Long Beach, Lakewood, and Los Alamitos, 1962.* Long Beach: Jewish Community Federation, 1962. 72 pp.

Long Beach: Education

Spiro, Saul S. *Survey of Educational Needs and Community Attitudes.* N.Y.: AAJE, 1972.

Los Angeles

Barryte, Marcia Aron. "Dance among the Sephardic Jews from Rhodes Living in Los Angeles." Master's thesis, UCLA, 1984.

———. "Dance Events of Sephardic Jews from Rhodes: A Comparative Study." *J of Dance Ethnology* 8 (1984): 8–15.

Bibliograph, A. ״דאס יידישע בוך אין לאס אנדזעלאס״ (The Yiddish Book in Los Angeles 1916–1945). (51 Yiddish books published in Los Angeles.) *Oifn Shvel* (Y.) 32 (Apr.–May 1946).

* Bin-Nun, David. *Religious and Other Cultural Factors in Racial Control Affecting the Assimilation of Jews in Los Angeles.* U. of Southern California, 1953.

* Biskar, Herbert Morris. *A History of the Jewish Centers Association of Los Angeles with Special Reference to Jewish Identity.* U. of Southern California, 1972. 156 pp.

* Chammou, Eliezer. *Migration and Adjustment: The Case of the Sephardic Jews in Los Angeles.* UCLA, 1976.

Cogan, Sara G., comp. *The Jews of Los Angeles, 1849–1945: An Annotated Bibliography.* Berkeley: Western Jewish History Center, J. L. Magnes Memorial Museum, 1980. 237 pp.

* Cohen, Benjamin L. *Constancy and Change in the Jewish Family Agency of Los Angeles, 1854–1970.* U. of Southern California, 1972. 163 pp.

Davka. "Los Angeles Jewry." (Y.) Several articles on early Jewish life. 4 (Oct. 1973). 36 pp.

* Gelfand, Mitchell. *Chutzpah in El Dorado: Social Mobility of Jews in Los Angeles, 1900–1920*. Carnegie-Mellon, 1982.

———. "Jewish Economic and Residential Mobility in Early Los Angeles." *WSJH* 11 (July 1979): 332–47.

———. "Progress and Prosperity: Jewish Social Mobility in Los Angeles in the Booming Eighties." *AJH* 68 (July 1979): 408–32.

Hassan, Aron. "The Sephardic Jews of Rhodes in Los Angeles." *WSJH* 6 (July 1974): 241–54.

Huberman, Steven. *Demographic Highlights of the Los Angeles Jewish Community*. L.A: Jewish Federation Council of Greater Los Angeles, 1983.

Jewish Federation Council of Greater Los Angeles. *Jewish Los Angeles Planning for the Future: A Report on the Regional Needs Survey*. L.A., 1983. 132 pp.

Klein, Adaire. *A Guide to Los Angeles Orthodox Community*. Beverly Hills, Calif.: Beth Jacob Congregation, 1978. 27 pp.

Kohs, Samuel C. "The Jewish Community of Los Angeles." *Jewish Review* 2 (July–Oct. 1944): 87–126.

Kramer, William M., and Reva Clar. "Rabbi Edgar F. Magnin and the Modernization of Los Angeles Jewry." *WSJH* 19 (Apr. 1987): 233–51, (July 1987): 346–62.

Lipman, Eugene J., and Albert Vorspan. "Los Angeles—Explosive Metropolis." In *Ten*, 78–110. 1962.

Los Angeles, City of Los Angeles Cultural Affairs Department Folk Arts Program. *Treasures of Fairfax: A Salute to Jewish Cultural Traditions*. L.A., 1988. 8 pp.

Malamut, J. L., ed. "History of the Jewish Centers in Los Angeles." In *Southwest Jewry*, 3:134–35.

* McAllister, Joy T. *A Study of Delinquent Jewish Youth in Los Angeles*. U. of California, 1968. 200 pp.

Meltz, Jacob J., ed. *Associated Organizations of Los Angeles: Mount Sinai Year Book*. Los Angeles: 1946. 432 pp. Contains information on L.A. Jewry and Jewish institutions and includes Samuel Reichler's "The History of Jewish Religious Life in Los Angeles" (pp. 11–72).

Naumoff, I. Sh. "די יידישע פרעסע אין לאס אנגעלעס" (The Yiddish Press in Los Angeles). *Cheshbon* (Y.) (1946): 44–50. See also *Cheshbon* (Oct. 1955): 32–37.

Nussbaum, Max. "History of Zionism in Los Angeles." In *SWJ*, 3:56–58.

Owen, Tom. "The First Synagogue in Los Angeles." *WSJH* 5 (Oct. 1968): 9–11.

Philips, Bruce A. "Los Angeles Jewry: A Demographic Portrait." *AJYB* 86 (1986): 126–95.

Recon. "Los Angeles Issue." A self-study of America's fastest growing Jewish community. 18 (Nov. 28, 1952): 8–32.

Reisner, Neil, ed. *Jewish Los Angeles: A Guide*. L.A.: Jewish Federation Council of Greater L.A., 1978. 114 pp.

Sandberg, Neil C. *Jewish Life in Los Angeles: A Window to Tomorrow*. Lanham, Md.: U. Press of America, 1986. 211 pp.

Sass, Stephen J., ed. *Los Angeles—A Guide: Everything Jewish Under the Sun*. L.A.: Jewish Federation Council of Greater L.A., 1982. 184 pp.

Soref, Irwin. "The Jewish Community of Los Angeles in Retrospect." *Recon* 18 (1952): 812.

Spiegel, M. "Jewish Alcoholism Growing Problem for Community." *Los Angeles Jewish Community Bulletin* (Dec. 1, 1978).

Stern, Norton B., ed. *Bicentennial Digest: A Perspective of Pioneer Los Angeles Jewry* (collection of articles from the *WSJH*). L.A.: Jewish Federation Council of Greater L.A., 1976. 96 pp.

———, comp. *The Birth of Modern Los Angeles Jewry*. L.A.: L. L. Morrison, 1973.

———. "Jews in the 1870 Census of Los Angeles." *WSJH* 9 (Oct. 1976): 71–86.

———, ed. *The Jews of Los Angeles: Urban Pioneers*. L.A.: Southern California Jewish Historical Society, 1981.

Stern, Norton B., and William Kramer, eds. *Leo Newmark—California Family Newmark—An Intimate History*. Santa Monica, Calif.: N. B. Stern Publisher, 1970. 110 pp.

* Stern, Stephen. *The Sephardic Jewish Community of Los Angeles: A Study in Folklore and Ethnic Identity*. Indiana U. 1977.

Turner, Justin G. "The First Decade of Los Angeles Jewry, 1850–1860." *AJHQ* 54 (Dec. 1964): 123–64.

———. "Los Angeles Jewry: A Saga of Command Growth, 1854–1954." In *Los Angeles Jewish Tercentenary, 1654–1954*, 7–13. L.A.: JCC, 1954.

Varon, Isaac M. "The Sephardic Community of Los Angeles." *Les Cahiers Sefardis* (F.) (Sept. 30, 1947).

* Vorspan, Max. *History of the Jews in Los Angeles, 1850–1900*. U. of Judaism, 1961. 350 pp.

Vorspan, Max, and Lloyd P. Gartner. *History of the Jews of Los Angeles*. Phila.: JPS, 1970. 362 pp.

Los Angeles: Education

Bardin, Shlomo. "The History of Brandeis Camp Institute." In *SWJ*, 197–200.

Bridger, David. בוקר טוב (Good Morning) (primer) (H.). 1954.

———. הספר הראשון למתחילים (HaSefer HaRishon LaMathilim) (H.). Van Nuys: Delta, 1950, 1961.

———. „דער יידישער חינוך אין לאס אנגעלעס" (Jewish Education in Los Angeles). *Cheshbon* (Y.) (Sept. 1957): 60–63.

———. "The Los Angeles Yiddish High School." In *SWJ*, 159–60.

———. הוראת ספר בראשית (Teaching the Book of Genesis) (H.). L.A.: 1962. 60 pp.

———. הספר השלישי למתחילים (The Third Book for Beginners) (H.). L.A: 1960. 76 pp.

Dorph, Isaac. „מערכת החינוך היהודי" (The System of Jewish Education in Los Angeles). *Hadoar* (H.) (July 18, 1975). This issue of *Hadoar* is primarily on Los Angeles.

Egozi, Akiva. "The Development of the Day School in Los Angeles." *Jew Ed* 33 (Spring 1963): 158.

Eichenbaum, Rose. "A Comparative Study of the Liturgical Practices and Accompanying Dance and Ritualized Movement Behavior of the Ashkenazic and Sephardic Jews Living in Los Angeles." Master's thesis, UCLA, 1980.

Eisenberg, Yehuda. *A Dinim Curriculum from Kindergarten to Grade 12* (H.). L.A: Jewish Community Enrichment Press, 1979. 76 pp.

Engelman, Uriah Z. *The Study of Jewish Education in Greater Los Angeles, 1956*. N.Y.: Commission for the Study of Jewish Education in the United States, 1958. 216 pp.

———. "Survey of Surveys." *Jew Ed* 19 (Spring 1948): 31–37.

Goldblum, Chaim. *Legenden un Meiselach* (Legends and Stories) (Y.). L.A.: L.A. Culture Club, 1935. 233 pp.

Greenberg, Sydney J., David Engel, and John F. Rothman. "Havurat Noar of Los Angeles." *Ped Rep* 25 (Fall 1973): 8.

Gurov, Jacob. „בית מדרש למורים בלוס אנג'לס" (The College for Teachers in Los Angeles). *Sh Hah* (H.) (Fall 1967): 55–56.

———, ed. (25th Anniversary Jubilee Book) (H.). L.A.: Hebrew Teachers Federation of Los Angeles and Vicinity, 1955. 56 pp.

Hadoar. „המכללות למדעי היהדות" (The Universities for Judaica in L.A.). (H.) 54 (July 18, 1975).

Kaminker, H. „ארבעטער רינג שול" (Workmen's Circle School). *Marev* (Y.). (Feb. 1925): 60–61.

Katzir, Isoschar. „החנוך העברי בלוס אנג'לס" (Jewish Education in Los Angeles). *Sh Hah* (H.) 31 (1971): 47–53.

Kohs, Samuel K., and Louis Blumenthal. "Jewish Education." In *Survey of the Recreational and Cultural Needs of the Jewish Community of Los Angeles conducted by the National Jewish Welfare Federation*, part 17. 1942. 42 pp.

Maimoodes, I. „אידישע דערציאונג אין לאס אנדזעלאס" (Jewish Education in L.A.). In *YKUF* (Y.), 91–96.

Malamut, J. L., ed. "The Los Angeles Hebrew Junior High School." In *SWJ*, 3:43.

Miller, Sh. „וואס אונזערע היגע שולן דערציילן" (What Our Local Schools Report). *Marev* (Y.) (Feb. 1925): 59–60.

Radin, Hayim. „די לאס אנדזשעלעס יידישע מיטל-שולביי דער ארבעט" (The L.A. Yiddish High School). *Freie Arbeiter Shtimme* (Y.) (Mar. 5, 1948): 5–6.

———. „די יידישע וועלטלעכע שולן אין לאס אנדזשעלעס" (The Yiddish Secular School in L.A.). *Oifn Shvel* (Y.) (Jan. 1946): 18–20.

37 LOCAL SOURCES FOR JEWISH EDUCATION

CALIFORNIA

Soref, Irwin. *Chapters in the History of Jewish Education in Los Angeles*. Chicago: College of Jewish Studies, 1950. 133 pp. See also his article in *Cheshbon* (Y.) (Oct. 1955): 38–45.

———. "History of Jewish Education in Los Angeles." Master's thesis, U. of Chicago, 1949.

Ury, Zalmen F. "The Development of the Day School in Los Angeles." *Jew Ed* 33 (Spring 1963): 158–61.

Weiss, Samuel. (Die Ortodoksishe Yeshivot in Los Angeles) (The Orthodox Yeshivot in Los Angeles) (Y.). *For* (Y.) (July 5, 1973): 3.

Zuckerman, Ben. „מכוח דעם מצב פון יידישן חינוך אין לאס אנגעלעס" (On the State of Jewish Education in Los Angeles). *Cheshbon* (Y.) 3 (Oct. 1955): 53–56.

Los Angeles: Bureau of Jewish Education

Bank, Adrianne. "Evaluation and Accountability in Jewish Education: The Case of the Los Angeles BJE Review." *Jew Ed* 53 (Spring 1985): 20–32.

Bauman, Morton A. *Children's Worship Services for Rosh Hashanah and Yom Kippur*. L.A.: BJE, 1959. 59 pp.

Ben-Zvi, Hava, comp. *The Holocaust—Dramatic Material for Classroom Use*. L.A.: Jewish Community Library, 1976.

———. *Israel at 30: A Selective Bibliography of Books, Films, and Drama*. L.A.: Jewish Community Library, 1978.

———, comp. and ed. *A Source Book for Teaching the History of Los Angeles Jewry*. L.A.: Jewish Community Library–BJE, Jewish Federation of Greater L.A.

———. "Teaching Jewish History: Selected Materials." L.A.: Jewish Community Library, 1980.

Ben-Zvi, Hava, and Sandra R. Bernstein. *Los Angeles Jewry—A Salute!* L.A.: Jewish Community Library. 153 pp.

Bridger, David. *Curriculum for Hebrew and Yiddish Schools*. Jewish Community Council–BJE, 1947. 66 pp.

———. מדריך ללמוד הלשון (Guide for the Study of Hebrew) (H.). L.A.: BJE, 1952. 60 pp.

———. *How to Teach Hebrew (Phonetics)*. L.A.: BJE, 1952–53. 53 pp.

———. *Syllabus for the Teaching of Jewish History*. L.A.: BJE, 1955.

BJE. *Catalog of Audio-Visual Materials*. L.A., 1968. 132 pp.

———. *Curriculum for Hebrew and Yiddish Schools*. L.A., 1947. 66 pp.

———. *Curriculum of the Jewish Secular Schools*. L.A., 1962.

———. *Hebrew Secondary Schools*. L.A., June 1974. 5 pp.

Chochem, Corrine. *Jewish Holiday Dances and Songs*. L.A.: BJE.

Dinin, Samuel. "Bureau of Jewish Education." In *SWJ*, 3:41–42.

———. *A Five-Year Plan for Jewish Education in Los Angeles*. Jewish Education Pamphlet No. 2. L.A.: BJE, Nov. 1950. Also in *Jew Ed* 22 (Winter/Spring 1951): 59–62 and in *California Jewish Life* (Y.) (Jan. 15, 1951): 8, 11.

———. "Los Angeles—Three A.D." *Jew Ed* 19 (Spring 1948): 37–42.

Dinin, Samuel, and M. E. Fischman. "Jewish Center Schools and the Bureau of Jewish Education of Los Angeles." *Jew Ed* 23 (Summer 1952): 11–14.

Dorph, Sheldon. *Hebrew Program for the High School*. L.A.: BJE, 1973.

Dushkin, Alexander M. *Survey of Jewish Education in Los Angeles, 1944*. L.A.: BJE, 1944. 102 pp.

Egozi, Akiva. *Report on Bureau-Affiliated Day Schools*. L.A.: BJE, 1960.

Goldman, Maurice. *New Songs for the Jewish School*. L.A.: BJE.

Jacoby, Emil. *A Study of School Continuation and Dropout Following Bar Mitzvah*. L.A.: Institute for Jewish Social Research, U. of Judaism, BJE, 1969.

Jewish Education, celebrating the 50th anniversary of the Bureau of Jewish Education of Greater L.A. 56 (Winter 1988). Articles include:

Alexander, H. A., Gail Dorph, and Ronald Wolfson, "Opening Their Eyes: Being a Teacher in Jewish Schools—A Preliminary Report on the Qualitative Dimension of the L.A. Teachers Study," 29–33.

Aron, Isa, "The Relationship between Research and Practice in Jewish Education: Can We Close the Gap?" 34–40, 53.

Ben-Zvi, Hava, "Heartbeat: The Central Role of the Library," 51–53.

Dinin, Samuel, "Jewish Education and the Jewish Community," 21–28.

Elfenbaum, Esther, "Early Childhood Programming: Growing to Meet the Challenges of the 1990s," 49–50.

Fein, Eve M., "Education as Dialogue: An Approach to Staff Development," 54–58.

Graf, Gil, "Community-Based Models of Post-Bar/Bat Mitzvah Jewish Education: The L.A. Experience," 41–44.

Jacoby, Emil, "The Los Angeles Bureau of Jewish Education Responding to Changing Needs," 3–12, 20.

Schiff, Alvin I., "Marking a Jewish Communal Jubilee," 2.

Soref, Irwin I., "The Los Angeles Bureau of Jewish Education in Retrospect, 1937–1975," 13–20.

Ury, Zalman E., "Yeshiva Education in Los Angeles," 45–48.

Leibman, Morris. *The Teaching of Prayers in the Jewish School.* L.A.: BJE, 1949–50. 50 pp.

Los Angeles Bureau of Jewish Education, "Rules and Regulations Governing Subsidies to Schools." In *CA*, 226–30.

Soref, Irwin. *Handbook for the Jewish Parent-Teacher Group.* L.A.: BJE, 1955. 80 pp.

Ury, Zalmen F. *Suggested Outline for Teaching of Jewish History in the Day School.* L.A.: BJE, 1965.

Wyenn, Than R. *Parallel Dramatics* (for teaching of Bible). L.A.: BJE, 1957. 78 pp.

Los Angeles: Press and Periodicals (Selected)

B'nai B'rith Messenger. 1897–present. Weekly.

Heritage-Southwest Jewish Press. 1914–present. Weekly.

Jewish Journal. 1986–present. Weekly.

California Jewish Bulletin and Directory: The Only Jewish Magazine in Los Angeles Printed in English. 1933–?

California Jewish Voice. 1922–47 (Y.) and 1947–73 (E.). Weekly.

Der Yiddisher Biznessman (The Jewish Businessman) (Y. and E.). 1925–28. Weekly.

Die Yiddishe Presse (The Jewish Press) (Y. and E.). 1934–36. Weekly.

Folks Zeitung (People's Newspaper) (Y. and E.). 1936–37. Weekly.

Jewish Community Press. 1934–38. Weekly.

Jewish Times—Die Zeit (Y. and E.). 1918–192?

Marev (Y.). Feb. 1925 (only known issue) (61 pp.). Articles, poetry, and book reviews. Quarterly.

Pasific (Y.). 1929 (4 known issues). Literary quarterly.

The Scribe (E. and Y.). 1931–34.

The Messenger. (E. and Ladino). 1933–34? Monthly.

Zunland (Sun Land) (Y.). 1925 (6 issues published). Literary journal. Monthly.

Nevada City

Janicot, Michel. "The Jewish Cemetery of Nevada City." *WSJH* 21 (Oct. 1988): 58–66.

Oakland

Fohrman, Nadine, and Sara Ginsberg, eds. *A Jewish Guide to the Bay Area.* Oakland: Hillel Academy of the East Bay, 1978. 190 pp.

Kramer, William M. "History of Oakland Jewry." *WSJH* 10 (Jan. 1978) 99–125, (Apr. 1978): 238–59, (July 1978): 353–73; 11 (Oct. 1978): 69–86, (Jan. 1979): 173–86, (Apr. 1979): 265–78, (July 1979): 364–76.

Massarik, Fred. *A Report on the Jewish Population of Alameda and Contra Costa Counties.* Oakland: 1970.

Oakland Jewish Welfare Federation Files. "Historical Summary of Jewish Activities in Oakland for the Past 50 Years." 1926. Unpublished.

Rosenbaum, Fred. *Free to Choose: Oakland, California.* Berkeley: Judah Magnes Memorial Museum, 1976. 164 pp.

37 LOCAL SOURCES FOR JEWISH EDUCATION

CALIFORNIA

Oakland: Jewish Education

Zatkin, Joseph. *The Oakland Experience in Synagogue-Federation Cooperation in Jewish Education*. June 1974. 4 pp.

Oakland Press

East Bay Echo. 1930–?

The Jewish Bulletin of the East Bay. 1967–85. Weekly.

The Jewish Observer of the East Bay. 1968–82. Fortnightly.

The Menorah. 1928–29.

Tikkun. 1986–present.

Petaluma

Gottfried, Z. „דער אידישער ישוב אין פּעטאלומא" (The Jewish Community of Petaluma). In *YKUF* (Y.), 96–103.

Kann, Kenneth. "Reconstructing the History of a Community." *International J of Oral History* 2 (Feb. 1981): 4–12.

Sacramento

Altman, Hal. "The Pioneer Jewish Community of Sacramento." *The Far Westerner* 2 (Apr. 1961): 11–18.

Gaines, Marlene S. "The Early Sacramento Jewish Community." *WSJH* 3 (Jan. 1971) 65–85.

San Bernardino

Glanz, Rudolph. "Early Meeting of Jew and Mormon." In *Jew and Mormon*, 156–83.

The Pinkos (Jewish Chronicle). Commemorating 75 years of Jewish activities in San Bernadino and Riverside counties. San Bernadino: Diamond Jubilee Committee, 1935.

Stern, Norton B., and William M. Kramer. "The San Bernardino Hebrew and English Academy, 1868–1872" (Jewish all-day school). *WSJH* 8 (Jan. 1976): 102–17.

San Diego

Heritage—Southwest Jewish Press. 1914–present. Weekly.

Schwartz, Henry. "The First Temple Beth Israel: San Diego." *WSJH* 11 (Jan. 1979): 153–61.

San Francisco

Benjamin, I. I. *Three Years in America, 1859–1862*, 1:119–293. Phila.: JPS, 1956.

Blumenthal, Louis H. *Three Generations of Service to the Community, 1877–1954: The Story of the San Francisco Jewish Community Center and YM–YWHA*. San Francisco JCC 77th Anniversary Committee, 1954. 44 pp.

Cogan, Sara G., comp. *The Jews of San Francisco and the Greater Bay Area, 1849–1919: An Annotated Bibliography*. Berkeley: Western Jewish History Center, J. L. Magnes Memorial Museum 1973. 127 pp.

Daggett, Emerson. "History of Foreign Journalism in San Francisco." WPA Project 1000S (Mar. 15, 1939). In *History of Journalism in San Francisco*, 36–39.

* Dalin, David G. *Public Affairs and the Jewish Community: The Changing Political World of San Francisco*. Brandeis U., 1978.

Danziger, Gustav Adolf. "The Jew in San Francisco in the Last Half Century." *Overland Monthly* (Apr. 1895): 381–410.

Decker, Peter R. "Jewish Merchants in San Francisco: Social Mobility on the Urban Frontier." *AJH* 68 (June 1979): 396–407.

Kahn, Edgar. "The Saga of the First Fifty Years of Congregation Emanu-El." *WSJH* 3 (Apr. 1971): 129–47.

Kohut, Rebekah. *My Portion: An Autobiography*. N.Y.: Th. Seltzer, 1925. See pp. 35–86. (Rebekah, daughter of Rabbi Bettelheim, came to San Francisco in 1875 as a young girl.)

Massarik, Fred. *The Jewish Population of San Francisco, Marin County and the Peninsula, 1973: Basic Findings*. S.F.: 1974.

———. *A Report on the Jewish Population of San Francisco, Marin County, and the Peninsula, 1959*. S.F.: JWF, Marin County and the Peninsula, 1959. 154 pp.

Moment, Samuel. "A Study of San Francisco Jewry, 1938." In *Pop*, 160–82.

Narell, Irena. *Our City: The Jews of San Francisco*. San Diego: Howell-North Books, 1981. 424 pp.

Raab, Earl. "There's No City Like San Francisco—Profile of a Community." *Commentary* 10 (Oct. 1950): 369–78.

Rafael, Ruth Kelson. "The YMHA and the YWHA in San Francisco." *WSJH* 19 (Apr. 1987): 208–16.

Rosenbaum, Fred. *Architects of Reform: The Rabbis of Temple Emanu-El, San Francisco, 1850–1980*. (Analysis of ideologies of the rabbis and their influence.) Berkeley: Western Jewish History Center, J. L. Magnes Memorial Museum, 1980. 241 pp.

Temko, Allan. "Temple Emanu-El of San Francisco—A Glory of the West." *Commentary* 26 (Aug. 1958): 107–18.

Voorsanger, Jacob. *The Chronicles of Emanu-El, Being an Account of the Rise and Progress of the Congregation Emanu-El Which Was Founded in July 1850—and Will Celebrate its Fiftieth Anniversary, Dec. 23, 1900*. S.F.: 1900. 169 pp.

———. "A Few Chapters from the History of the Jews of the Pacific Coast from 1849–1860." *American Jews' Annual* (1889): 51–66.

Wiener, C. L. "A Merger of Synagogues in San Francisco." *Jew J Soc* (Dec. 1972): 167–96.

Zarchin, Michael M. *Glimpses of Jewish Life in San Francisco*. Berkeley: Judah L. Magnes Memorial Museum, 1964. 264 pp.

San Francisco: Education

* Gates, Gunther G. *A Study of Achievement of German-Jewish Refugee Students in American Public High Schools of the San Francisco Bay Area*. U. of California–Berkeley, 1955. 105 pp.

Honor, Leo L. *Survey of Jewish Education in San Francisco*. S.F.: Federation of Jewish Charities, 1938.

Kohanski, Alexander S. *Annual Report: 1949*. S.F.: Jewish Education Society, 1949.

———. *Curriculum for Jewish Religious Schools*. S.F.: Jewish Education Society, 1950. 128 pp.

———. "Jewish Education in San Francisco." *Jew Ed* (Summer 1952): 54–57.

Menuhin, Moshe. "Jewish Education Situation in San Francisco." *WSJH* 21 (Jan. 1989): 99–102. Reprinted from *Jewish Education News* (Mar. 1926).

Ruffman, Louis L. *Study of Jewish Education in San Francisco*. N.Y.: AAJE and Study Committee of the JWF for San Francisco, Marin County and the Peninsula. 1967.

Tollier, A. „על החנוך בסאן-פראנציסקו, קאליפורניה" (On Jewish Education in San Francisco). *Sh Hah* (H.) 2 (1927): 71–74.

Voorsanger, Jacob. "The Emanu-El Religious School." In *The Chronicles of Emanu-El, Being an Account of the Rise and Progress of the Congregation Emanu-El Which Was Founded in July 1850—and Will Celebrate its Fiftieth Anniversary, Dec. 23, 1900*, 132–37. S.F.: 1900.

———. *Services for Children*. Prepared and collected for the use of religious schools. Music composed by Cantor E. J. Stark. S.F.: Congregation Emanu-El, Standing Committee on Religious Education, 1908. 69 pp.

San Francisco: Bureau of Jewish Education

BJE. *By-Laws of the BJE of San Francisco, Marin County and the Peninsula*. S.F.: 1976.

———. "Ideas and Resources for Teaching about Israel." *Bay Area Teachers' Newsletter* 4 (1987–88): 24 pp.

———. "Study of Jewish Education in the San Francisco Area: A Report." 1979. Unpublished.

Ducoff, Bernard. *Report on San Francisco Experience in the Area of Federation-Bureau Relationship to Congregational Schools*. June 1974. 2 pp.

* Emanuel, Itzhak. *The Bureau of Jewish Education of San Francisco, Marin County and the Peninsula, in the State of California: The Effectiveness of Implementation of Goals, 1977–1982*. U. of San Francisco, 1983. 253 pp.

Greenberg, Sydney J. "The Jewish School and the Jewish Welfare Federation." S.F.: BJE of San Francisco, Marin County and the Peninsula, 1980?.

Kellman, Beth. *Affiliated School Statistics*. S.F.: BJE, 1982.

Schiftan, Harriet Kaplowitz. *Children of Inter-faith Families—Implications for the Classroom*. S.F.: BJE.

37
LOCAL SOURCES FOR JEWISH EDUCATION

COLORADO

San Francisco: Periodicals

The Gleaner. 1857–68. Weekly.

The Hebrew (E. and G.). 1863–87. Weekly.

Hebrew Observer (E. and G.). 1856–188?. Weekly.

Jewish Journal. 1928–31?. Semi-monthly.

Jewish Messenger of the Pacific (E. and G.). 1860–61.

Jewish Progress. 1875–96. Weekly.

Jewish Star. 1956–present. Bimonthly.

Jewish Times. 1880?–88?. Weekly.

Jewish Times and Observer. 1888?–1924. Weekly.

Jewish Tribune. 1933–47.

Jewish Voice (Y.). 1912–17.

Northern California Jewish Bulletin (formerly *San Francisco Jewish Bulletin*). 1946–present. Weekly.

The Progress. 1877–96. Weekly.

Emanu-El. Temple Emanu-El, 1895–1945. (Merged with the *Oakland Menorah* in 1930, the *Jewish Journal* in 1931, and the *Jewish Community Bulletin* in 1946.) Weekly.

Voice of Israel. 1870–74?. Biweekly with German supplement.

San Jose

Kinsey, Stephen D. "The Development of the Jewish Community of San Jose, California, 1850–1900." *WSJH* 7 (Oct. 1974): 70–87, (Jan. 1975): 163–82, (Apr. 1975): 264–73.

———. "They Called It Home: The Development of the Jewish Community of San Jose, California, 1850–1900." Master's thesis, California State U.-San Jose, 1973.

Temple Emanu-El. *Centennial Anniversary, 1861–1961.* San Jose: 1962. 24 pp.

Santa Ana

Stern, Norton B. "Santa Ana, California: Its First Jews and Jewish Congregations." *WSJH* 14 (Apr. 1942): 248–56.

Santa Cruz

Fogelson, George. "The Jews of Santa Cruz: The First Eighty Years, 1854–1934." *WSJH* 14 (Jan. 1982): 99–115.

Santa Monica

Jewish Spectator. 1935–1989?. Edited by Trude Weiss-Rosmarin. (In New York prior to 1978.) Quarterly.

Stern, Norton B. *Jews in Early Santa Monica: A Centennial Review.* (From the *WSJH*, July 1975.) Santa Monica: Western Area Council, Jewish Federation Council of Greater L.A., 1975. 24 pp.

Western States Jewish Historical Quarterly. 1968 to present. Edited by Norton B. Stern.

Stockton

Clare, Rosa. "Early Stockton Jewry and its Cantor-Rabbi Herman Davidson." *WSJH* 5 (1972–73): 166–87.

COLORADO

AJA. "Trailblazers . . ." 8 (Oct. 1956): 86–92.

Breck, Allen D. *A Centennial History of the Jews of Colorado, 1859–1959.* Denver: U. of Denver, Hirschfield Press, 1960. 360 pp.

"Colorado." In *Post*, 66–79.

Kauvar, C. E. Hillel. "The Colorado Jewish Community, 1859–1953." Unpublished (American Jewish Archives).

Sandler, P. דער פון געשיכטע דראמאטישע די„ קאלאראדא" אין געמיינדע יידישער (The Dramatic History of the Jewish Community in Colorado). *CE* (Y.) 28 (Jan. 1958): 13–15. (Review of Ida Uchill's *Pioneers, Peddlers and Tsadikim.*)

Uchill, Ida L. *Pioneers, Peddlers and Tsadikim: Jewish life in Colorado.* Denver: Sage Books, 1957. 327 pp.

Colorado: Education

Abrams, Jeanne, and Norma Schier Hitch. *Colorado Jewish History: A Guide for Teachers.*

Denver: Rocky Mountain Jewish Historical Society, 1983. 37 pp.

Colorado Springs

Meyers, Myron T. *The Early History of B'nai Israel Synagogue*. 1951.

The Cotopaxi Colony

Herscher, Uri D. "Cotopaxi, Colorado." In *Jewish Agricultural Utopias in America, 1880–1910*, 55–62. Detroit: Wayne State U. Press, 1981.

Roberts, Dorothy. "The Jewish Colony of Cotopaxi" (settled by Russian Jews in 1882). *Colorado Magazine* 18 (July 1941): 124–31.

Satt, Flora Jane. "The Cotopaxi Colony." Master's thesis, U. of Colorado, 1958.

Denver

Abrams, Jeanne E. *Historic Jewish Denver*. Denver: Rocky Mountain Jewish Historical Society, 1982. 26 pp.

Allied Jewish Federation of Denver. *The Denver Jewish Population Study, 1981*. Denver: 1982. 79 pp.

Beth HaMedrash HaGadol. *Historic Manual, 1879–1929*. Denver: 1929.

Breck, Allen D. "Education, Culture, and Society." In *A Centennial History of the Jews of Colorado, 1859–1959*, 283–87. Denver: U. of Denver, Hirschfield Press, 1960.

Congregation Hebrew Educational Alliance. *Dedication Brochure*. Denver: Feb. 1, 1953.

Denver Republican. "The Rise of the Jews." *PAJHS* 14 (1906): 208–10.

* Giese, James Richard. *Tuberculosis and the Growth of Denver's Eastern European Jewish Community: The Accommodation of an Immigrant Group to a Medium-Sized Western City, 1900–1920*. U. of Colorado, 1979.

Greengard, Roberta. "Occupation, Mobility and Jews: The Denver Story." *Rocky Mountain Jewish Historical Notes* 1 (Feb. 1978).

Hornbein, Marjorie. *Temple Emanu-El of Denver: A Centennial History*. Denver: Congregation Emanu-El, 1974. 194 pp.

Portnoy, Fern C. *A Community to Teen Service*. Denver: JWB Research Center in cooperation with Jewish Community Center of Denver, 1978?. 68 pp.

Reform Advocate. "The Story of the Jews of Denver." Oct. 1908.

Temple Emanu-El. *Dedication Booklet*. Denver: Jan. 27, 1899.

Denver: Education

Ehrmann, Eliezer, et al. *Status of Jewish Education in Denver*. N.Y.: AAJE, Oct. 1971.

Greenstone, Julius H. "Survey of Jewish Education in Denver." *Jew Ed* 7 (Oct.–Dec. 1935): 167–69.

———. *1937 Survey of Jewish Education in Denver*.

Hebrew Educational Alliance. *Tenth Anniversary Brochure*. 1943.

Hornbein, Marjorie. "Jewish Studies at the University of Denver: The Legacy of Rabbi Charles Eliezer Hillel Kauvar." *Rocky Mountain Jewish Historical Notes* 7–8 (Summer/Fall 1986).

Zion, Joel Y. *Sabbath Prayer Book for Young People*. Denver: Temple Emanu-El, 1953. 47 pp.

Denver: Press

Denver Jewish News. 1915–25.

Intermountain Jewish News. 1913–present.

Jewish Outlook. 1903–13.

Sanatorium. 1908–13.

Western Jewish Advocate. 1928–42.

CONNECTICUT

"Connecticut." In *Post*, 79–88.

Connecticut Jewish Ledger. Hartford, 1929–present. Weekly.

Connecticut Hebrew Record. Lynn, Mass., 1897–1933?. Semiweekly.

Hartford Jewish Ledger. 1929–33?. Monthly.

Jewish Digest. Bridgeport, 1955–86. Monthly.

Marcus, Jacob R. "Light on Early Connecticut Jewry." *Amer Jew Arc* 1 (Jan. 1949): 3–52.

New Haven Ledger. 1930–33?. Monthly.

Sloan, Sh. "כנוס המורים העברים במדינת קונקטיקוט" (Conference of Hebrew Teachers in the State of Connecticut). *Sh Hah* (H.) 8 (1948): 122–24.

Bridgeport: Education

Edidin, Ben M. *Jewish Education in Bridgeport—1946*. N.Y.: AAJE.

Ende, George, et al. *Assessment of Jewish Education*. N.Y.: AAJE, 1962.

Hartford

Davidson, Morris I. *Growing up in Hartford, Connecticut, 1908–1928*. Hartford: Andrew Mountain Press, 1987.

Feldman, Abraham J. *Remember the Days of Old: An Outline History of the Congregation Beth Israel, 1843–1943*. Hartford: Congregation Beth Israel, 1943.

Silverman, Morris. *Hartford Jews—1659–1970*. Hartford: 1970. 448 pp.

Greater Hartford Jewish Federation. *A Study of the Greater Hartford Jewish Population, 1982*. Hartford: 1983?. 118 pp.

Hartford: Education

Chanover, Hyman. Assessment of Teaching Personnel. N.Y.: AAJE, 1969.

PTA of the Emanuel Synagogue Religious School. "Model Constitution for a Parent Teacher Association." *Syn Sch* 11 (Sept. 1952): 30–32.

Pilch, Judah. *Survey of Jewish Education*. Hartford: JCC, 1945.

Rosen. Morton. "Hartford's Midrasha—A Community Hebrew High School." In *Teen*, 92–95.

Middletown

Henkin, A. Hillel. *Survey of Weekday and Weekend Programs of Congregation Adath Israel*. N.Y.: AAJE, 1969.

* Lindenthal, Jacob Jay. *Early History of the Jews of Middletown, Connecticut*. Yeshiva U., 1973.

New Haven

Antonovsky, Aaron. "Aspects of New Haven Jewry: A Sociological Study." *YA* 10 (1955): 128–64.

Davidson, Lawrence J. "The Jews in New Haven: A Study in Ethnic Group Cleavage." Unpublished senior thesis, Yale Department of Sociology.

Jews in New Haven. Vol. 4. Jewish Historical Society of New Haven, 1986. 110 pp.

Kisch, Guido. "Two American Jewish Pioneers of New Haven." *Historica Judaica* 4 (1942): 16–37.

Reznikoff, Charles. "New Haven: The Jewish Community." *Commentary* 4 (Nov. 1947): 465–77.

Sarna, Jonathan D., ed. *Jews in New Haven.* New Haven: Jewish Historical Society of New Haven, 1978. 148 pp.

Siskin, Edgar E., and Rolin G. Osterweiss, eds. *Congregation Mishkan Israel, 1840–1940.* New Haven: 1940.

New Haven: Education

BJE. *Course of Study for Three-Day Hebrew Schools*. New Haven.

———. *Prayer Outline for the Jewish School*. New Haven: 1949.

———. *Visual Guide for Jewish Schools*. New Haven: 1963.

Edidin, Ben M., and New Haven Study Committee. *Community Study of New Haven*. New Haven: NCJSW, NAJCW, and NCJE, 1943.

Heimowitz, Joseph. *Study of the New Haven Hebrew Day School and Ezra Academy in New Haven, Connecticut*. N.Y.: AAJE, 1978. 69 pp.

Henkin, Hillel. *Course of Studies Three-Day Hebrew School*. New Haven: BJE, 1960.

Levinson, Morris. Guide for the Musical Program of the Hebrew School. New Haven: BJE.

Schwartzman, Frances Zellick. *The Hebrew Nursery Holiday Book*. New Haven: BJE, 1954. 97 pp.

New London

Sulman, Esther, and Leonard J. Goldstein. *A Goodly Heritage: The Story of the Jewish

Community in New London, 1866–1955. New London: 1957. 81 pp.

Wessel, Bessie Bloom. "A Comparative Study of the Jewish Community of New London and Norwich, 1938." In *Pop,* 57–80.

Norwich

The Jews in Norwich, a Century of Jewish Life: In Commemoration of the Tercentenary of Jews in America. Norwich: 1956. 57 pp.

Waterbury: Education

Engelman, Uriah Z. *Jewish Education in Waterbury.* N.Y.: AAJE, Self-Study Committee on Jewish Education, 1952.

DELAWARE

Bluestone, Harry. *A Historical Review of a Century of Jewish Education in Delaware.* Wilmington: Jewish Historical Society of Delaware, 1976. 111 pp.

———. *A Historical Review of the Jewish Family Service of Delaware, 1899–1965.* Wilmington: 1969?. 49 pp.

"Delaware." In *Post,* 88–92.

Study of the Jewish Population in Northern Delaware, 1962. Wilmington: JCC Population Survey Committee, 1963. 96 pp.

Wilmington

Bluestone, Harry. *A Historical Review of the Jewish Community Center of Wilmington, Delaware, 1901–1965.* Wilmington: JCC, 1971.

Congregation Beth Emeth. *Reflections of the Past: A Few of the Memorable Highlights of Congregation Beth Emeth and its Sisterhood.* Wilmington: 1983. 34 pp.

Wilmington: Education

Engelman, Uriah Z. *Wilmington Jewish Community Survey: An Appraisal of the Educational Situation.* Wilmington: Jewish Federation, 1946.

Maliken, Esther. "Wilmington's Judaic Workshop" (program for the exceptional child). *Compass* 1 (Summer 1978): 20–21.

Rosen, Ben. *Survey of Jewish Education of Wilmington, Delaware.* N.Y.: Bureau of Jewish Social Research, 1929.

DISTRICT OF COLUMBIA

Altshuler, David, ed. *The Jews of Washington, D.C.: A Communal History Anthology* (articles from *Rec*). Washington D.C.: Jewish Historical Society of Greater Washington, 1985. 300 pp.

Bigman, Stanley. *The Jewish Population in Greater Washington in 1956.* Washington, D.C.: JCC of Greater Washington, May 1957.

Diamond, Luna Ereza. "History of the Sephardic Jews of Washington, D.C." Jan. 26, 1970.

"District of Columbia." In *Post,* 92–114.

* Fredman, Ruth Gruber. *Cosmopolitans at Home: An Anthropological View of the Sephardic Jews of Washington,* D.C Temple U., 1982

Goldberg, A. R. "Jewish Social Service in Washington, D.C., 1890–1940." *Rec* 4 (May 1969): 22–32.

Greenberg, Evelyn Levow. "Isaac Polock: Early Settler in Washington, D.C." *PAJHS* 48 (1958): 1–17.

Holland, Samuel H. "The First Jewish Child Born in Washington D.C., and the Mordecai Family." *Rec* 2 (Jan. 1967): 2–.

Johnson, George E. "Fabrangen: A Coming Together." In *Contemporary Judaic Fellowship in Theory and Practice,* edited by Jacob Neusner, 185–88. N.Y.: Ktav, 1972.

Marans, Hillel. *Jews in Greater Washington: A Panoramic History of Washington Jewry for the Years 1759–1960.* Washington, D.C.: 1961. 143 pp.

Moses, Nancy. "Jews of Georgetown, 1860–1900." In *The Jews of Washington, D.C: A Communal History Anthology,* edited by David Altshuler. Washington D.C.: Jewish Historical Society of Greater Washington, 1985.

**37
LOCAL
SOURCES
FOR JEWISH
EDUCATION

FLORIDA**

Nordlinger, Bernard J. *History of Washington Hebrew Congregation*. Washington, D.C.: 1956. See also *Rec* 4 (Nov. 1969).

Proctor, John Clagett. "Jews in Early Washington." *Washington Evening Star* (July 23, 1950).

Rec. "50 Years of Washington's UJA." 14 (July 1987).

———. "The First Jewish Settler in the District of Columbia." 1.

———. "The Humble Beginnings of the Washington Hebrew Congregation."

———. "Washington Jewry During the Civil War, 1861–1865." 1 (Mar. 1966): 2–.

Rosenblum, Edward. "Young Men's Hebrew Association, 1912–1923. Washington Jewish Community Center, 1923–1957: Fifty Years of Recollections." *Rec* 3 (Mar. 1968): 12–.

Rosenthal, Eric. "Jewish Intermarriage in Greater Washington." *AJYB* 64 (1963): 15–33.

Ruttkay, Paul, and Robert Agus. "Proposal for Fabrangen." In *Contemporary Judaic Fellowship in Theory and Practice*, edited by Jacob Neusner, 175–83. N.Y.: Ktav, 1972.

Shosteck, Robert. *The Jewish Community of Washington, D.C., during the Civil War*. Washington, D.C.: Jewish Historical Society of Greater Washington, 1967. Reprinted with supplementary materials from *AJHQ* (Mar. 1967): 319–47.

Simon, Abram. *A History of Washington Hebrew Congregation*. Washington, D.C.: 1905.

———. "Notes of Jewish Interest in the District of Columbia." *PAJHS* 26 (1918): 211–18.

Tobin, Gary A. *Executive Summary: A Demographic Study of the Jewish Community of Greater Washington, 1983*. Bethesda, Md.: UJA Federation of Greater Washington, 1984. 26 pp.

District of Columbia: Education

Brickman, William W., and George Pollak. *Evaluation of the Washington Day Schools at the Elementary and Secondary Levels*. N.Y.: AAJE, 1971.

Engelman, Uriah Z. *Comprehensive Quantitative Report on Jewish Education with Attitudinal Study*. N.Y.: AAJE, 1958.

Frank, Moshe. "אידישע דערציאונג אין וואשינגטאן" (Jewish Education in Washington). *School Journal* (Y.) (Apr. 1939): 15–16.

Frank, Rachel B., ed. *Forty-Six Award-Winning Projects in Jewish Classrooms*. Washington, D.C.: Curriculum Enrichment Program Committee, 1982. 64 pp.

Gelfar, L. "צוואנציק יאר קאמף פאר דער ארבעטער רינג שול" (20 Years of Struggle for the Workmen's Circle School). *School Journal* (Y.) (Apr. 1939): 10–11.

Golinkin, Noah, "F.J.T.A.—Maalah." (Recruiting teachers in Greater Washington D.C.). *Ed As* (1966): 32–33.

Kaganoff, Nathan M. "The Education of the Jewish Child in the District of Columbia, 1861–1915." Master's thesis, American U., 1958. Excerpts in *Jew Ed* 29 (Fall 1958): 39–49. See also *Rec* 2 (Jan. 1967) and 3 (Mar. 1968).

Rec. "Early Education of the Jewish Child in Washington was Parochial-Orthodox." 1 (Mar. 1966).

Rosen, Lester. "A History of Congregation and Talmud Torah B'nai Israel." *Rec* 3 (Mar. 1968).

Schlafer, Israel. "אקדמיה עברית בוושינגטון הבירה" (Hebrew Academy, Washington D.C.). *Sh Hah* (H.) 21 (Fall 1967): 61–62.

Teishoff, I. "אכט יאר ארבעטער רינג שול אין וואשינגטאן" (Eight Years of the WC School in Washington). *School Journal* (Y.) (Apr. 1939): 29–20.

District of Columbia Press and Periodicals

Washington Jewish Week. 1965–present. Weekly.

FLORIDA

Cowen, Elfrida D. "Moses Elias Levy's Agricultural Colony in Florida." *PAJHS* 25 (1917): 132–34.

"Florida." *In Post*, 114–22.

Green, Henry A. *Jewish Life in Florida*. Miami: U. of Miami, Judaic Studies Program, 1986.

Huhner, Leon. "David L. Yulee, Florida's First Senator." *PAJHS* 25 (1917): 1–29. See also Huhner's article in *Florida Historical Society Quarterly* 19 (1941): 319–45.

Proctor, Samuel. "Pioneers of Jewish Settlement in Florida, 1765–1900." In *Proceedings of the Conference on the Writing of Regional History of the South with Special Emphasis on Religious and Cultural Groups, convened by the University of Miami*, 81–115. 1956.

Fort Lauderdale

Jewish Journal. 1977–present. Weekly.

Jacksonville

Glickstein, Natalie H. *That Ye May Remember: Congregation Ahavath Chesed, 1882–1982.* Jacksonville: Congregation Ahavath Chesed, 1982. 127pp

Southern Jewish Weekly. 1924–present.

Miami

* Lehrman, Irving. *History of the Jews in Southern Florida.* JTS, 1957.

———. "The Jewish Community of Greater Miami, 1896–1935." In *Proceedings of the Conference on the Writing of Regional History of the South with Special Emphasis on Religious and Cultural Groups, convened by the University of Miami*, 116–30. 1956

Mehling, Harold. "Is Miami Beach Jewish?" In *The Most of Everything*, 129–44. N.Y.: Harcourt Brace and World, 1960.

Perlmutter, Nathan. "Bombing in Miami: Anti-Semitism and the Segregationists." *Commentary* 25 (June 1958): 498–503.

Rosen, Gladys. "The Rabbi in Miami—A Case History." In *"Turn to the South": Essays on Southern Jewry*, edited by Nathan M. Kaganoff and Melvin I. Urofsky, 33–43. Charlottesville: University Press of Virginia for the American Jewish Historical Society, 1979.

Shapiro, Manheim S. *The Bayville Survey of Jewish Attitudes* (Dade County, Florida). N.Y.: AJC, 1961. 106 pp.

Sheskin, Ira M. *Demographic Study of the Greater Miami Jewish Community: Summary Report.* Miami: Greater Miami Jewish Federation, 1984. 32 pp.

———. *Population of the Greater Miami Jewish Community.* Miami: Greater Miami Jewish Federation, 1983. 278 pp.

Simonhoff, Henry. "History of the Jewish Community in Miami." In *Under Strange Skies.* N.Y.: 1953.

Tebeau, Charlton W. *Synagogue in the Central City: Temple Israel of Greater Miami, 1922–1972.* Coral Gables: U. of Miami Press, 1972. 172 pp.

Miami: Education

BJE of Greater Miami. *Area of Subject Matter for Five Year Curriculum.* Miami: 1950. 4 pp.

Central Agency for Jewish Education. *Get Ready . . . Get Set . . . Play! A Manual of Early Childhood Readiness and Primary Grades.* Miami.

———. *Greater Miami Day School Survey.* Miami: 1976.

———. *Judaica High School: A Community Approach to Post Ban/Bat Mitzvah Education.* Miami.

Chanover, Hyman. *An Evaluation of the Judaica High School.* Prepared for the Planning Committee of the Greater Miami Jewish Federation. N.Y.: AAJE, April 1973.

Chipkin, Israel. *Suggested Plan for Coordination of Existing Afternoon Weekday Schools (Talmud Torah) in Greater Miami.* In *CA*, 221–23.

Eisenberg, Azriel, and Samuel Dinsky. *Study of the Community's Role in Jewish Education with Special Emphasis upon the Bureau, the YMHA and the Federation.* N.Y.: AAJE, 1967.

Engelman, Uriah Z. *Comprehensive Description of Schools, Bureau, and Facilities.* N.Y.: AAJE, 1957.

———. "Jewish Education in the U.S.: The Miami Report." *Jew Ed* 31 (Winter 1961): 47–54.

Friedl, Berthold C. *Principles and Techniques of Teaching Hebrew.* Miami: Greater Miami BJE, Hebrew Teachers' Association, Feb.–Mar. 1950. 24 pp.

Gannes, Abraham P. *Activities of the Bureau of Jewish Education of Greater Miami.* Miami: BJE, ca. 1945.

———. *Five Years of the Bureau of Jewish Education of Miami*. Phila.: 1950. 23 pp.

Gittelsohn, Abraham. "The Judaic High School Program of the Central Agency of Jewish Education of Greater Miami." *Ped Rep* 25 (Fall 1973): 3–7.

Goldstein, Richard K. "Greater Miami High School Quinmester Program in Israel." *Ped Rep* 26 (Fall 1974): 18–20.

Greenzweig, Gene, and Shimon Azalay. "The Miami Experience" (community high school program). *Jew Ed* 43 (Fall 1974): 56–58.

Herman, Dorothy C. *From Generation to Generation: An Experimental Approach to the Teaching of the Elderly in Our Community*. Miami: Central Agency for Jewish Education, 1985. See also *Ped Rep* (Jan. 1988): 26–28.

Horovitz, M. "Creative Approaches in Keeping Our Teenagers" (Yeshiva high school in Miami). *Jew Parent* 17 (Mar. 1966): 12–13.

Kipper, Lenore. *Aleph Bet of Jewish Life*. Miami: Beth Am Day School, 198?. 69 pp.

Lehrer, Deborah. "The Miami Program for Learning Disabled." *Ped Rep* 31 (Fall 1979).

National Center for the Evaluation of Educational Materials. *Survey of the Jewish Day Schools of Dade and Broward Counties* (11 day schools). Miami: Central Agency for Jewish Education, 1977. 70 pp.

Schwartzman, Louis, and Nathaniel Soroff. *Arakhim: Hebrew through Values* (H.). Miami: BJE, 1968.

WC, I. L. Peretz School. "א נייע הגדה של פסח„ (A New Haggadah for Passover) (Y.). 1964.

Miami: Press

Jewish Floridian Group. 1927–1990. Weekly.

Miami Jewish Tribune. 1986–present. Weekly.

Orlando

Greater Orlando Jewish Community Directory. Orlando: Jewish Community Center of Central Florida, 1984. 131 pp.

Palm Beach

Palm Beach Jewish World. 1982–present. Weekly.

Tampa

Wheeler, Ray. *A Social and Demographic Survey of the Jewish Community of Tampa, Florida*. Tampa: Tampa Jewish Federation, 1981. 88 pp.

GEORGIA

Atlanta Constitution. "The Hebrew in America" (1905, around Thanksgiving). *PAJHS* 14 (1906): 199–201.

"Georgia." In *Post*, 123–33.

Huhner, Leon. "The First Jew to Hold the Office of Governor of one of the United States." *PAJHS* 17 (1909): 187–95.

———. "The Jews of Georgia in Colonial Times." *PAJHS* 10 (1902): 65–95.

———. "The Jews of Georgia from the Outbreak of the Revolution to the Close of the 18th Century." *PAJHS* 17 (1909): 89–108.

Jones, Charles C. "The Settlement of the Jews in Georgia." *PAJHS* 1 (1893): 5–12.

Marcus, Jacob R. "Georgia, 1733–1783." In *EAJ*, 2:277–373.

Schmier, Louis. *Binding Ties: The Jews of Georgia*. Marietta: Georgia Pub. Co., 198?. 145 pp.

Southern Israelite. *One Hundred Years' Accomplishments of Southern Jewry*. Atlanta: Southern Newspaper Enterprises, 1964.

Atlanta

Abrams, Morris B. "Oral Interview." *AJH* 73 (Sept. 1983): 7–19.

Atlanta Jewish Federation. *Jews and Georgians: A Meeting of Cultures*. Atlanta: 1983.

———. *Metropolitan Jewish Population Study: Summary of Major Findings*. Atlanta: 1985. 16 pp.

Bauman, Mark K. "Centripetal and Centrifugal Forces Facing the People of Many Communities: Atlanta Jewry from the Frank Case to the General Depression." *Atlanta Historical J* 23 (Fall 1979): 25–54.

———. "The Emergence of Jewish Social Service Agencies in Atlanta." *Georgia Historical Quarterly* 49 (Winter 1985): 488–508.

———. "Role Theory and History: The Illustration of Ethnic Brokerage in the Atlanta Jewish Community in an Era of Transition and Conflict." *AJH* 73 (Sept. 1983): 71–95.

Beton, Sol, ed. *Sephardim: A History of Congregation Or Veshalom*. Atlanta: Congregation Or Veshalom, 1981. 256 pp.

Blumberg, Janice Rothschild. "The Bomb That Healed: A Personal Memoir of the Bombing of the Temple in Atlanta, 1958." *AJH* 73 (Sept. 1983): 20–38.

———. One Voice: Rabbi Jacob M. Rothschild and the Troubled South. Macon: Mercer U. Press, 1985. 239 pp.

Cameron, William. "The Leo Frank Case." Master's thesis, U. of Cincinnati, 1965.

Dinnerstein, Leonard. "Leo Frank and the American Jewish Community." *AJA* 20 (1968): 107–26.

* ———. *The Leo Frank Case*. Columbia U. 1966. Published by the Columbia U. Press in 1968. 240 pp.

Golden, Harry. *A Little Girl Is Dead*. Cleveland: World Pub., 1965.

Habif, Isaac N. "Or Veshalom: The Sephardic Congregation of Atlanta." *American Sephardi* 2 (1969).

Hertzberg, Steven. "The Jewish Community of Atlanta from the End of the Civil War Until the Eve of the Frank Case." *AJHQ* 62 (Mar. 1973): 250–85.

* ———. *The Jews of Atlanta, 1865–1915*. U. of Chicago, 1953.

———. "Making It in Atlanta: Economic Mobility in a Southern Jewish Community, 1870–1911." *YA* 17 (1978): 185–216.

———. *Strangers within the Gate City—The Jews of Atlanta, 1845–1915*. Phila.: JPS, 1978. 325 pp.

Kaganoff, Nathan M. "An Orthodox Rabbinate in the South: Tobias Geffen, 1870–1970." *AJH* 73 (Sept. 1983): 56–70.

Marx, David. "History of the Jews of Atlanta." *Reform Advocate* (Nov. 4, 1911): 9–72.

Rothschild, Janice O. *As but a Day: The First Hundred Years, 1867–1967*. Atlanta: Hebrew Benevolent Congregation, 1967. 148 pp.

Schmier, Louis. "For Him the 'Schwartzers' Couldn't Do Enough": A Jewish Peddler and His Black Customers Look at Each Other." *AJH* 73 (Sept. 1983): 49–55.

Shankman, Arnold. "Atlanta Jewry: 1900–1930." *Amer Jew Arc* 25 (Nov. 1973): 131–55.

Stein, Kenneth W. *A History of the Ahavath Achim Congregation, 1887–1977*. Atlanta: 1978. 89 pp. See also Stein's article in *Atlanta Historical J* 23 (Fall 1979): 107–18.

Sutker, Solomon. "The Jewish Organizational Elite of Atlanta, Georgia." In *JES*, 249–61.

* ———. *The Jews of Atlanta: Their Structure and Leadership Patterns*. U. of North Carolina, 1950.

———. "The Role of Social Clubs in the Atlanta Jewish Community." In *JES*, 262–70.

Atlanta: Education

Chipkin, Israel. *Tentative Proposals for a Community Program for Jewish Education*. N.Y.: AAJE, 1945.

Engelman, Uriah Z. *Evaluation of the School System and the Role of the Bureau*. N.Y.: AAJE, 1955.

Frankel, Ephraim. "The Hebrew Academy of Atlanta: An Assessment" (day school). *Ped Rep* 29 (Fall 1977).

Ped Rep. "Kollel Program: Yeshiva High School at Atlanta, Georgia." 35 (June 1984): 26–27.

WC. "דרום שטראלן„ (Southern Rays) (Y.). Student publication on the third graduation at the school, 1926. 64 pp.

Atlanta: Press

Atlanta Jewish Times (formerly *Southern Israelite*). 1925–present. Weekly.

Jewish Civic Press. 1965–present. Monthly.

Augusta

Occ. "Establishment in 1845 of a School of Religious Instruction in Augusta, Georgia" (11 children). Oct. 3, 1845.

Steinberg, Jack. *United for Worship and Charity: A History of Congregation Children of Israel*. Augusta: Phoenix Commercial Printers, 1983. 96 pp.

Brunswick

Temple Beth Tefillah, Seventy-Fifth Anniversary, 1886–1961. 1961. 34 pp.

Savannah

Levy, B. H. *Savannah's Old Jewish Cemeteries*. Macon, Ga.: Mercer U. Press, 1983. 191 pp.

Jewish Education. N.Y: AAJE, 1967.

Rubin, Saul Jacob. *Third to None: The Saga of Savannah Jewry, 1733–1983*. Savannah: Congregation Mikve Israel, 1983. 425 pp.

Stern, Malcolm H. "New Light On the Jewish Settlement of Savannah." *AJHQ* 52 (Mar. 1963): 166–99.

Savannah: Education

Engelman, Uriah Z. *Qualitative and Quantitative Analysis of Individual Schools*. N.Y.: AAJE, 1954.

Kulick, P. "The Self-Study of Jewish Education in Savannah, Georgia." *AJYB* 57 (1956): 209–19.

Margolis, Isidore, and Jacob Levin. *Community-Wide Audit of Savannah Jewish Council. Community Self-Study for Jewish Youth*. 1966.

Valdosta

Schmier, Louis. "The First Jews of Valdosta." *Georgia Historical Quarterly* 62 (Spring 1978): 32–49.

Waycross

Lebeau, James. "Profile of a Southern Jewish Community: Waycross, Georgia." *AJHQ* 58 (June 1969): 429–42.

HAWAII

Harris, Victor. "Honolulu Jewry in 1919." *WSJH* 11 (Apr. 1 1979): 279–82.

"Hawaii." In *Enc Jud*, 7:1495–96.

Levinson, Bernard H. "Jewish Population and Community Activities in Hawaii." *AJYB* 61 (1960): 170–71.

Nemoy, Leon. "Henry Obookaiah: The First Hawaiian Student of Hebrew." *PAJHS* 39 (1949): 190–93.

Young Judea Hawaii. *A Day in the Life of the Jewish Community of Hawaii*. Honolulu: 1986. 46 pp.

Zwerin, Kenneth C. "Jews and Judaism in the Hawaiian Islands in 1935." *WSJH* 12 (Apr. 1980): 206–8.

IDAHO

AJA. "Trailblazers . . ." 8 (Oct. 1956): 123–30.

"Idaho." In *Enc Jud*, 8:1223–24.

"Idaho." In *Post*, 133–37.

Schoenberg, Nancy. "The Jews of Southeastern Idaho." *WSJH* 18 (July 1986): 291–304.

Watters, Leon L. *The Pioneer Jews of Utah*. N.Y.: AJHS, 1952. 199 pp. (See index for items on Idaho.)

WSJH. "Idaho's First Jewish Congregation" (newspaper account). 8 (Oct. 1976): 124–25.

ILLINOIS

Eliassof, Herman. "The Jews in Illinois." *Reform Advocate* 21 (May 4, 1901).

"Illinois." In *Enc Jud*, 8:1254–56.

"Illinois." In *Post*, 138–61.

Champaign

Rubenstein, Asa. "Midwestern Jewish Commitment and Practical American Idealism: The Early History of Sinai Temple, Champaign, Illinois." *J of the Illinois State Historical Society* 75 (Summer 1982): 82–100.

Chicago

American Jews' Annual. "New Anshe Maariv Temple." (1890–91): 88.

Berent, Irwin M., and Joy Liljegren. *A Jewish-Chicago Record Survey: A Guide to the Records of the Jewish Community Institutions of West Rogers Park, Chicago, Illinois.* Chicago Jewish Archives, Spertus College of Judaica, 1984. 74 pp.

Bernheimer, Charles, ed. *The Russian Jew in the United States.* Phila.: J. C. Winston Co., 1905. (Contains several chapters on Jews in Chicago.)

Bregstone, Philip. *Chicago and Its Jews.* Chicago: Privately printed, 1933. 423 pp.

Cutler, Irving. "The Jews of Chicago: From Shtetl to Suburb." In *Ethnic Chicago,* 71:46–68, 69–108. Grand Rapids, Mich.: Eerdmans, 1984.

Eliassof, Leon H. "The Jews of Chicago." *PAJHS* 11 (1903): 117–30.

Felsenthal, Bernard. *The Beginnings of the Chicago Sinai Congregation.* Chicago: 1888.

———. "On the History of the Jews of Chicago." *PAJHS* 2 (1894): 21–27.

Felsenthal, Bernard, and Leon H. Eliassof. *History of Kehillath Anshe Ma'aariv.* Chicago: 1897.

Goldberg, W. A. *Jewish Population of Chicago, 1931, by Community Areas and Census Tracts.* Chicago: Jewish Social Service Bureau, July 1934.

Gutstein, Morris. *A Priceless Heritage: A Historical and Sociological Study of Chicago.* N.Y.: Bloch, 1953. 488 pp.

Heimowicz, Rachel Baron. *The Chicago Jewish Source Book.* Chicago: Follett, 1981. 336 pp.

Hutler, Albert. "The Story of Jewish Communal Life in Chicago." Chicago: Chicago Jewish Youth Assembly, 1942.

Jaffe, A. J. "A Study of Chicago Jewry (1930): Based on Death Certificates." In *Pop,* 131–51.

* Jaret, Charles L. *Residential Mobility and Local Jewish Community Organizations in Chicago.* U. of Chicago, 1977.

Jewish Federation of Metropolitan Chicago. *A Population Study: Metropolitan Chicago.* Chicago: 1985. 50 pp.

JNWA. „דער אידיש נאציאנאלער ארבעטער פארבאנד אין שיקאגא" (35 Years of the JNWA in Chicago) (Y. and E.). Chicago: 1949. 50 pp.

Krantz, Naphtali. „מאטעריאלן צו דער געשיכטע פון פערציק יאר יידישע קולטור-ארבעט אין שיקאגא" (Materials on the History of 40 Years of Jewish Cultural Life in Chicago). In *Shu P* (Y.), 538–80.

Krucoff, Carole. *Rodfei Zedek: The First Hundred Years.* Chicago: Congregation Rodfei Zedek, 1976. 218 pp.

Lebeson, Anita Libman. "Zionism Comes to Chicago." In *EHZA,* 155–90.

Levinson, Joseph. *120 Years: A History of K.A.M. Temple, 1847–1967.* Chicago. 8 pp.

Levitats, Isaac. "The Story of the Chicago Jewish Community." Chicago: BJE.

* Mazur, Edward H. *Minyans for a Prairie City: The Politics of Chicago Jewry, 1850–1950.* U. of Chicago, 1973.

Meites, Hyman L., ed. *History of the Jews of Chicago.* Chicago: Jewish Historical Society of Illinois, 1924. 854 pp.

Mishkin, Leah. „דפוסי שיקאגו-בעברית ובייידיש" (Hebrew and Yiddish Printing Presses in Chicago) (H.). In *Pinkas,* 79–122 (Hebrew section).

Rawidowicz, Simon, ed. *The Chicago Pinkas* (E. and H.). (Issued on the 25th Anniversary of the College of Jewish Studies.) Chicago: TCJS, 1952. 319 pp.

Rosenthal, Eric. "Acculturation without Assimilation: The Jewish Community of Chicago. "*American J of Sociology* 66 (Nov. 1960): 275–88.

* ———. *The Jewish Population of Chicago: Size and Distribution as Derived from Voters Lists.* U. of Chicago, 1948.

———. "Size and Distribution of the Jewish Population of Chicago." In *Pinkas,* 69–112.

———. "The Size of the Jewish Population of Chicago." *JSS* 7 (1945): 149.

———. "This Was North Lawndale: The Transplantation of a Jewish Community." *JSS* 22 (Apr. 1960): 67–82.

Rothblat, H. M. "העתונות העברית בשיקאגו" (The Hebrew Press in Chicago) (H.). In *Pinkas*, 36–68.

Seman, Philip L. *The Jewish Community Center: A Basic Program in Civic Education*. Chicago: 1925.

The Sentinel: The History of Chicago Jewry, 1911–1961. Chicago: Sentinel Pub. Co. 254 pp.

Shtarkman, Moshe. "עתונות יידיש בשיקאגו" (Yiddish Press in Chicago, 1877–1951) (H.). In *Pinkas*, 68–78.

Silver, Manuel, ed. *Guide to Jewish Chicago and Yearbook*. 4th ed. Chicago: American Jewish Congress, 1978. 48 pp.

Wirth, Louis. *The Ghetto* (1925). Chicago: U. of Chicago Press, 1975. 298 pp. (See pp. 153–291.)

Chicago: Education

Almond, David. *Hebrew Religious Education Treated Historically: Its American Antithesis and the Projected Remedy*. Chicago: Schulman Bros., 1922.

Bakal, M. "די מאדערנע קינדער ערציהונג" (The Modern Education of Children) (Y.). On the pedagogic systems of Fourier, Montessori, and Dewey. Chicago: 1917. 57 pp.

Blumenfeld, Samuel M. "חנוך הנוער בשיקאגו" (Jewish Youth Education in Chicago). *Ha-Hinukh* (H.) 2 (Kislev 1939): 209–12.

Horowitz, Jack. "Temple Isaiah's Beit Hayeled" (supplementary program as an alternative to the Jewish day school). *Compass* 4 (Spring 1981): 3–4, 26.

Unterman, Isaac Ben-Hayim. "אידישע און אלגעמיינע ערציהונג" (Jewish and General Education) (Y.). (How to educate Jewish children spiritually, morally, and socially.) Chicago: 1916. 115 pp.

Yaraslav, Z. "אן אנפאנג בוך פאר סיוויקס" (A Beginner's Book on Civics) (Y.). Chicago: 1921. 120 pp.

Chicago: Board of Jewish Education

Barkan, Irving. "The Board of Jewish Education of Metropolitan Chicago." *Jew Ed* 44 (Summer 1975): 9–13.

Board of Jewish Education. *Principles Governing the Policy of a Central Community Agency for Jewish Education*. Chicago: Nov. 1943. See also *CA*, 194–98.

Chicago BJE. "The Growth of the Board of Jewish Education." In *What Jewish Education Means to the Community*. 1936.

Dushkin, Alexander M. "Six Years of Jewish Educational Activity." *Jew Ed* 2 (Jan. 1930): 42–47.

———. "Report of the Jewish Education Committee." Chicago: BJE. (Files).

Honor, Leo L. "The Chicago Board of Jewish Education—Functions and Programs." Chicago: BJE, 1935.

Klinger, Maurice. *The Experience of Chicago Jewish Welfare Fund Ad Hoc Committee on Jewish Education* (June 1970). CJFWF, 1972. 6 pp.

Krug, Mark M. *The Development of the Community Approach to Jewish Education in Chicago*. Chicago: BJE, 1954.

Pilch, Judah. "Milestone in the History of Jewish Education in Chicago." *Jew Ed* 20 (Feb. 1949): 18–19.

Chicago Education: Administration

Braun, Isadore H. *Jewish School Building Manual*. 1954. 32 pp.

Chicago BJE. *Code of Personnel Practices for Sunday School Teachers*. 1952. 10 pp.

———. *Improving Jewish Education through Service Agreements*. 1979.

Edidin, Ben M. "Elimination in Chicago Schools." *Jew Ed* 1 (May 1929): 118–20.

* Small, Sarah. *Attitudes of Professional and Lay Leaders of Congregations in a Major Metropolitan Jewish Community, Chicago, toward the Employment of Women as Administrators of Congregational Schools*. U. of Missouri-Kansas City, 1983. 151 pp.

Chicago Education: Curriculum

Cedarbaum, David I. *Reform Adaptation of the Chicago Board of Jewish Education Curriculum*. Chicago: UAHC, 1950.

Chicago BJE. *Curriculum for Congregational Weekday Schools*. 1947. 4 pp.

———. *Five-Year Curriculum of the Herzliah Hebrew School*. 1936.

———. *Manual for the Nursery School and Kindergarten*.

Ginsberg, Marvelle. *Holidays in the Jewish Nursery School and Kindergarten*. Chicago: BJE, 1979.

Katzoff, Adina. "The Development of the Jewish Nursery in Chicago." Master's thesis, College of Jewish Studies, 1952.

———. *Holidays in the Jewish Nursery School*. Chicago: BJE.

Nudelman, Edward A. *Course of Study Outline for the Jewish Sunday School*. 1943, 1949. 136 pp.

———. "Outline of Curriculum of Chicago Jewish Sunday Schools." *Jew Ed* 6 (Apr–June 1934): 76–82.

Chicago Education: Arts in the Curriculum

Chicago BJE. *Artcraft Curriculum*. 1945–46.

———. *Sunday School Assembly Portfolio*.

Coopersmith, Harry. *Songs of My People*. Chicago: Anshe Emeth Synagogue, 1938. 248 pp.

Ehrmann, Eliezer L. *Visual Aids in Jewish Education*. Chicago: BJE.

Geller, Todres. *Artcraft Curriculum (Holidays)*. Chicago: BJE.

Greenberg, Samuel, and Maurice Yochim. *Arts and Crafts in the Jewish School*. Chicago: BJE, 1952. 51 pp.

Levin, Neil, ed. *Songs of the American Jewish Experience*. Chicago: BJE.

Reznick, H. *Song Sheets* (Holidays and General).

Vizonsky, Nathan. *Ten Jewish Folk Dances—A Manual for Teachers and Leaders*. Chicago: American Hebrew Theatrical League, 1942. 59 pp.

Wykell, Esther. *Creative Dramatics in the Jewish School*. 1962.

Chicago Education: Bible

Chicago BJE. *Bible and Festival Book*.

Honor, Leo L. *Biblical History Outlines*. 1928, 1946.

Maretz, Sylvia. *A Unit on Shepherd Life in Bible Times*. Chicago: BJE. 77 pp.

Chicago Education: Children's Magazines

Ha Ivri HaKatan. "העברי הקטן„ BJE and Midwest Hebrew Teachers Organization, 1938.

The Jewish Child. BJE.

Chicago Education: Hebrew

Cedarbaum, David, I., and Rose Shapiro. *Achievement Goals for Mid-Week Hebrew Classes*. 1953–54. 135 pp.

Kohn, Rebekah. *Language Teaching Devices: Suggestions to Teachers of Hebrew*. Chicago: BJE, 1949.

Marinoff, Shlomo, and Eliezer Schultz. "העברי„ *(Ha Ivri)* (H.). 3 beginning Hebrew textbooks. Chicago: 1943.

Nudelman, Edward A. *Readings in the Teaching of Hebrew Reading*. Chicago: BJE, 1964.

Romirowsky, Leah. *Teaching the Reading of Hebrew in the Early Grades*. Chicago: BJE, 1977?. 65 pp.

Chicago Education: History

Chicago BJE. *The Jewish Experience in America: Teacher Developed Units and Materials*. 2 vols. 1976.

Ehrmann, Eliezer L. *A Course of Study for Jewish History*. Chicago: BJE.

———. "מפתח להוראת תולדות ישראל„. (A Key to the Teaching of History) (H.). Chicago: BJE. 92 pp.

———. *Readings in Modern Jewish History: From the American Revolution to the Present*. N.Y.: Ktav for the BJE of Metropolitan Chicago, 1977. 491 pp.

Gurov, Jacob. "מיתודיקה להיסטוריה„ (Methodology for History) (H.). Guide for teaching history in the elementary schools. Chicago: 1943. 60 pp.

Honor, Leo L. *Survey of Jewish History: Directive Outlines and Bibliography*. Chicago: College of Jewish Studies, 1932. 64 pp.

Karlin, Miriam. *A Unit on Hebrew Life in Ancient Canaan*. Chicago: BJE, 1949. 88 pp.

37 LOCAL SOURCES FOR JEWISH EDUCATION — ILLINOIS

Chicago Education: Home and School

Chicago BJE. *Parent-Toddler Program.*

Maretz, Sylvia. *A Unit on the Jewish Home.* Construction and Artcraft by Todres Geller. Rev. ed. 1951. 56 pp.

Midwest Teachers Organization. "די עלטערן-לערער שטימע" (The Parents-Teachers Voice) (Y. and E.). 1937–39. Quarterly.

Samber, Moshe, ed. *Family Education Newsletter.* BJE.

Chicago Education: Jewish Life Cycle

Chicago BJE. *Prayer Course of Study for Congregational Hebrew School.*

———. *The Synagogue: A Guide for Teachers.* ca. 1972.

Cedarbaum, David I., ed. *The Teaching of God Concepts: Proceedings of a Sunday School Teachers' Conference, Nov. 16, 1958 and Dec. 6, 1959.* Chicago: BJE, 1960.

———. *The Teaching of Prayer: Proceedings of a Sunday School Teachers' Conference.* 1950. 75 pp.

Cedarbaum, David I., and Libbie Braverman. *Teach Me to Pray.* Chicago: BJE, 1955.

Ehrmann, Eliezer L. *Teaching Suggestions: Why We Celebrate Hannukah, and Jewish Life under Roman Rule.*

Glicenstein, Enrico, and Alexander M. Dushkin. *The Tree of Life: Sketches of Jewish Life of Yesterday and Today* (customs and ceremonies). Chicago: BJE, 1933. 112 pp.

Grishaver, Joel Lurie. *Shema Is for Real.* Teacher's guide. Chicago: UAHC.

Hershon, Jerome L. *Darkei Limud Hasidur* (H.). Chicago: College of Jewish Studies.

Kummel, S. B. *General Introduction to Teaching the Jewish Holidays in the Primary Grades.* Chicago: BJE.

Maretz, Sylvia. *The Synagogue.* Chicago BJE, 1948, 1951. 75 pp. Grade 2.

Marinoff, Shlomo. "עם ומועדיו" (A People and Their Festivals). Hebrew text for adult beginners. Chicago: College of Jewish Studies, 1934. 119 pp.

Stampfer, Nathaniel, et al. *Prayer Instruction in the Elementary Hebrew School.* Chicago: BJE, 1968.

Chicago Education: Pedagogy

Chicago BJE. *Manual of Suggestions to Teachers on the Use of the Individual Instruction Method.*

Golub, Jacob S. "Some Experiments in the Jewish Sunday Schools of Chicago." *Jew Ed* 1:1, (Jan. 1929): 34–43

Risinger, C. Frederick. *Developing an Instructional Unit.* Chicago: BJE, 1974.

Rosenberg, Pauline. "An Experiment in Creative Jewish Education." In *1948 Annual.* Chicago: College of Jewish Studies Student Organization, 1948.

Chicago: Secondary Education

Abramowitz, Aaron. *Midrash Va-Agadah.* Chicago: BJE, ca. 1948.

Bernstein, Sidney M. *The Jew in America: The Jewish Community and How It Came to Be.* Teacher's guide. 1966.

———. *The Jew in American Fiction.* 1962. 175 pp.

Bernstein, Sidney M., et al. *A Suggested Outline of Curriculum for the Jewish Secondary School.* 1964.

Goldman, Solomon. *Stories and Sketches by I. L. Peretz.* Hebrew reader for high school students with limited knowledge of the language. Chicago: BJE, ca. 1936.

Romirowsky, Leah. *Unit on Israel.* Resource text.

Rothblatt, Charles. *Anthology of Hebrew Literature.* Chicago: BJE, ca. 1938.

Silberman, Moshe. "בית הספר התיכון בשיקאגו והשפעתו" (The High School in Chicago and Its Influence). *Sh Hah* (H.) 12 (Sept. 1952): 214–17.

Chicago Education: Teachers and Professional Journals

Bita'on. "בטאון" (H.). Midwest Hebrew Teachers Organization, 1935–38?. Monthly.

Ha Gesher. "הגשר" (The Bridge) (H. and Y.). Teachers associated with the BJE, 1939. Quarterly.

Journal of Jewish Education. Associated Talmud Torahs and the Hebrew Theological College, 1953.

The Principal. Hebrew Principals Association of Chicago, 1963. Quarterly.

Rahash. "כנוס המורים העברים בשיקאגו" (Conference of Hebrew Teachers in Chicago). *Sh Hah* (H.) 5 (1945): 285–86.

Schub, Joseph Arye. "Today's Hebrew Teacher—A Chicago Profile." *Jew Ed* 38 (Mar. 1968): 47–50.

Teacher Bulletin. BJE. For Sunday school teachers.

Teurah. "תעורה" (Awakening) (H.). Organization of Midwest Hebrew Teachers and the Midwest Hebrew Organization, founded 1944–45. Quarterly.

Chicago Education: Surveys of Chicago Schools

Bricker, Harry. *Jewish Education in Chicago—Survey.* Chicago: Jewish Charities of Chicago, 1940.

Dushkin, Alexander M. *Survey of Jewish Education in Chicago.* Chicago: Jewish Charities of Chicago, 1923.

Hurwich, Louis. *Follow-up Survey of Ten Chicago Hebrew Schools, Part I.* Boston: BJE, 1922.

Kaplan, Louis. *Inventory of Educational Institutions in Chicago.* N.Y.: AAJE, 1954.

Pilch, Judah, et al. *Survey of Jewish Education in Chicago.* Chicago: AAJE, BJE, and JWF, 1966.

Chicago Education: Day Schools

Chicago Jewish Day School. "The Growth and Decline of a Jewish Day School, 1859–1874." In *JEUS*, 94–96.

Chicago Jewish Parochial School. "בית ספר תורה ודעת" *(Beit Sefer Torah Va-Daat).* On the school's 5th anniversary. 1931. 44 pp.

Chicago Education: Yiddish Schools

BenAaron. "צו דער געשיכטע פון דער שיקאגער יידיש וועלטלעכער שול באווענגונג" (On the History of the Chicago Yiddish Secular School Movement). In *Shu P* (Y.), 584–604.

David Pinski Folk School. "ערשטער יערלעכער שול זשורנאל" (First Annual School Journal) (Y.). 1950. 40 pp.

Farband Folk School–LZOA. Publication in Honor of the First Graduation of the I. L. Peretz and Yehoash Schools (Y.). 1928. 22 pp.

Feldman, M. (How Do We Fare in Chicago?). *Pro D* (Y.) (July–Aug. 1937): 20–21.

Goldberg. B. Z. "אידישע דערציאונג אין שיקאגא" (Jewish Education in Chicago). *Day* (Y.) (Mar. 28, 1950).

International Workers Orden. "אונדזער שול" (Our School) (Y.). 1937. 68 pp. On the 7th anniversary of the school.

Sholem Aleichem Folk School. "לידער זאמלונג און קאנטאטא" (Anthology of Songs—Cantata) (Y.). For Passover Concert. Chicago: SAFI. 14 pp.

———. "אפן שייד-וועג" (At the Cross Roads) (Y.) (anthology). Pomerantz and Provotiner, eds. Chicago: SAFI–Stein, 1937. 41 pp.

———. "זעכצן" (Sixteen) (Y.). A collection of compositions by elementary graduates. SAFI. 49 pp.

———. "יונג—אידיש" (Young Yiddish) (Y.). Written by students, Chicago: SAFI-Stein, 1935. 136 pp.

Tsiporin, Hyman. "די ערשטע נאציאנאל-ראדיקאלע שול אין שיקאגא" (The First National/Radical School in Chicago). Memoirs. *Oifn Shvel* (Y.) (Aug.–Oct. 1961): 6–9.

WC Schools. "אונזער ווינקל" (Our Corner) (Douglas Park School) (Y.). 1921. 31 pp.

———. "יונג לעבן" (Youth) (Y.). Anthology of student writings on the 15th Graduation. SAFI, 1942?. 74 pp.

Yiddish Radical School. "דער נייער דור" (The New Generation) (Y.). Marmor, Kalman, ed.

Yukelson, R. "די ערשטע אידישע קינדער שול אין שיקאגא" (The First Yiddish Elementary School in Chicago). *Morning Freiheit* (Y.) (June 27, 1957).

Chicago: Higher Education

Adelson, Saul. "Chicago's Hebrew Theological College." *Jew Life* (Dec. 1947): 43–48.

37 LOCAL SOURCES FOR JEWISH EDUCATION — ILLINOIS

Adler, Robert L. *Report on Higher Education in Chicago*. CJF, 1970, 1972. 5 pp.

Blumenfield, Samuel M. „המדרשה ללמודי היהודית בשיקאגו" (The College of Jewish Studies in Chicago). In *JB* (H.), 292–97.

———. "Twenty Years of the College of Jewish Studies, Chicago." *Rel Ed* 40 (Aug. 1945).

Fagin, Samuel I. „בית המדרש לתורה בשיקאגו" (The College for Torah in Chicago). In *JB* (H.), 280–91.

Fasman, Oscar Z. "The Hebrew Theological College." In *The Sentinel: The History of Chicago Jewry, 1911–1961*, 145–47. Chicago: Sentinel Pub. Co.

Hebrew Theological College, 30th Anniversary, 1922–1952. Chicago: Hebrew Theological College, 1952. 196 pp.

Katz, Morris Casriel. "Reminiscences of My Student Days in Chicago." In *The Jacob Dolnitzky Memorial Volume*, 22–30. Skokie, ill.: Hebrew Theological College, 1982.

Katzoff, Louis. "The Chicago College of Jewish Studies." *Jew Ed* 22 (Winter/Spring 1951): 29–32.

Rothblat, H. M. „המדרשה ללמודי היהדות בשיקאגו" (The College of Jewish Studies in Chicago). *Sh Hah* (H.) 10 (May 1950): 140–49.

Schoolman, Albert P. "The College of Jewish Studies in Chicago." *Jew Ed* 21 (Spring 1950): 9–10.

Chicago: History of Jewish Education

(For Chicago education published prior to 1900, see section on History of Jewish Education in the United States.)

Braun, Sarah Elkin. "The Board of Jewish Education and The College of Jewish Studies." In *The Sentinel: The History of Chicago Jewry, 1911–1961*, 148–50. Chicago: Sentinel Pub. Co.

Bregstone, Philip. "Religious Instruction and Jewish Education." *Chicago and Its Jews*, 62–65. Chicago: Privately Printed, 1933.

Gutstein, Morris A. "From the Melamed to the Sunday School," "From the Cheder to the Yeshiva," and "The Jewish Training School." *A Priceless Heritage*, 211–257. N.Y.: Bloch, 1953.

Hertz, Richard C. "Reform Jewish Education in Chicago—1871–1880." *Jew Ed* 20 (Feb. 1949): 34–35.

James, Edmund J. *The Immigrant Jew in America*. N.Y.: 1907. See pp. 176–78 for Jewish education in Chicago.

Korey, Harold. "The History of Jewish Education in Chicago." Master's thesis, U. of Chicago, 1942. 201 pp.

———. "The Story of Jewish Education in Chicago prior to 1923." *Jew Ed* 6 (Jan.–Mar. 1934): 37–47.

Lavin, Lottie. "Jewish Education in Chicago." Master's thesis, U. of Chicago, 1938. 86 pp.

Meites, Hyman L. "Religious, Cultural and Educational Organizations." *History of the Jews in Chicago*, 547–64. Chicago: Jewish Historical Society of Illinois, 1927.

Mishkin, Leonard C. "Associated Talmud Torahs." In *The Sentinel: The History of Chicago Jewry, 1911–1961*, 151–56. Chicago: Sentinel Pub. Co.

Rothblat, H. M. „ראשיתו של בית הספר התיכון בשיקאגו" (The Beginning of the Secondary School in Chicago). In „פכים קטנים" (Vignettes) (H.), 225–61. 1966.

Talmud Torah Yavneh. תלמוד תורה יבנה (E. and H.). On its 25th anniversary. Chicago: Globus, 1939. 128 pp.

Chicago: Student Publications

Anshe Emeth Schools. האור (*HaOr*) (The Light) (H.). 1937. Annual.

Beth HaMidrash LaTorah. המעין (The Fountain) (H. and E.). Published by the student organization, 1929–30. 38 pp.

College of Jewish Studies. עלון (*Alon*) (Bulletin) (H.). 1935. Monthly.

———. ספר השנה (Year Book) (H. and E.). Published by the student organization on the 10th anniversary of the school, 1935. 46 pp.

Hebrew High School. צפרירים (Zephyrs) (H.). Graduation annual. Printed in the Office of Hebrew Education, 1969. 64 pp.

Jewish Academy of Chicago. זכרונות (Memories) (H. and E.). 1948, 95 pp.

Chicago Newspapers and Journals (Selected Chronological List)

Israelitische Presse (Y.). 1877–80. Weekly.

Haykhal Ivriah (H.). 1877–? Weekly.

Jewish Advance (E. and G.). 1878–80?. Weekly.

Chicago Israelite. 1884–196?. Weekly.

Daily Jewish Courier (Y.). Daily until 1892, weekly from 1892 to 1945?

Der Bloomen Gortn (Y.). 1888–1905. Weekly.

Keren Or (H.) Hebrew Literary Association of Chicago. Two issues appeared. Monthly.

HaPisgah (H.). 1889–?. Weekly.

Reform Advocate. 1891–193?. Weekly.

The Sentinel. 1910–present. Weekly.

HaPardes (H.). 1913–195? Monthly.

Chicago Jewish Chronicle. 1918–195? Weekly, later biweekly.

Yiddishe Arbeiter Velt (Y.). 1908–17. Daily.

Yiddisher Kunst Friend (Y.). 1916. Ten issues. Weekly.

Proletarisher Gedank (Y.) LZOA, 1925–33. Weekly.

Chicago (Y.). Literary journal, 1930–39. Monthly.

Chicago Jewish Forum. 1942–196?. Quarterly.

Jewish Community News. 1945–present. Bi-monthly.

Chicago JUF News. Jewish Federation of Metropolitan Chicago, 1972–present. Monthly.

Jewish Chicago. 1982–86. Monthly.

East St. Louis

A Syllabus of Questions for Discussion on the Objectives of the Various Jewish School Subjects for Teachers and Parents. East St. Louis: Jewish Federation of Southern Illinois, ca. 1945.

Glencoe

Krumbein, Eliezer. *Family Worship Service*. Glencoe: North Shore Congregation Israel, 1951. 42 pp.

North Shore Congregation Israel. *The Sabbath: A Home Observance*. Glencoe: Parent Teacher Association, 1953. 42 pp.

Illinois–Iowa Jewish Community

* Fleishaker, Oscar. *The Illinois–Iowa Jewish Communnity on the Banks of the Mississippi River*. Yeshiva U., 1957.

Northbrook

Kessler, Harry. "The Sager Solomon Schechter Day School." *Ped Rep* 23 (Mar. 1972): 3.

Park Forest

Gans, Herbert J. "Park Forest: Birth of a Community." *Commentary* 11 (Apr. 1951): 330–39.

———. "The Origin and Growth of a Jewish Community in the Suburbs: A Study of the Jews of Park Forest." In *JES*, 205–48.

———. "Progress of a Suburban Jewish Community." *Commentary* 23 (Feb. 1957): 113–22.

Slesinger, Zalman. *Report on Survey of Jewish Education in Southern Illinois*. Jewish Federation of Southern Illinois, 1943.

Urbana

Mandelbaum, David G. "A Study of the Jews of Urbana." *JSSQ* 12 (1935): 230–.

INDIANA

"Indiana." In *Enc Jud*, 8:1360–62.

"Indiana." In *Post*, 161–70.

Indiana Jewish Historical Society. *More Indiana Jewish History*. Fort Wayne: 1985. 56 pp.

Columbus

Columbus Jewish History Project. *Community Survey*. Ohio Historical Society, 1975.

Kaminsky, Gladys. *History of the Jewish Community of Columbus, Indiana*. Fort Wayne: Indiana Jewish Historical Society, 1978. 53 pp.

37

LOCAL SOURCES FOR JEWISH EDUCATION

Fort Wayne

* Goldenholz, Gideon M. *The Emergence of a Jewish Community in Fort Wayne*. Hebrew Theological College, 1984. 150 pp.

Indiana Jewish Historical Society. *Indiana Jewish History*. Fort Wayne: 1986. 35 pp.

Highland

Illiana News. 1975–present. Ten times a year.

Indianapolis

Endelman, Judith E. *Jewish Community of Indianapolis, 1849 to the Present*. Bloomington: Indiana U. Press, 1984. 320 pp.

Furer, Max M. "Jewish Education Association—Indianapolis, Indiana." *Jew Ed* 44 (Summer 1975): 26–27.

Glazier, Jack. "The Indianapolis Sephardim—An Essay." *Shofar* 3 (Spring 1985): 27–34.

Grand, Samuel. *Survey of Jewish Education and Role of Jewish Education Association*. AAJE and JEA, 1965.

Honor, Leo L., and Herbert S. Greenwald. *A Survey of Jewish Education*. Indianapolis Association of Jewish Education, 1944.

Indiana Jewish Chronicle. 1921–197?. Weekly.

Indiana Jewish Post and Opinion. 1935–present. Weekly.

Muncie ("Middletown")

Belth, N. C. "The Jews in Muncie." In *JMW*, 310–15.

Gordon, Whitney H. *A Community in Stress*. 1964.

———. "Jews and Gentiles in Middletown 1961." *AJA* 18 (Apr. 1966): 41–70.

Hoover, Dwight W. "To Be a Jew in Middle-town: A Muncie Oral History Project." *Indiana Magazine of History* 81 (June 1985): 131–58.

Lipman, Eugene J., and Albert Vorspan. "Muncie Middle town in Slow Motion." In *Ten Cities*, 111–138.

St. Joseph County

JCC of St. Joseph County. *We See Ourselves: A Study of the Jewish Community of St. Joseph County*. South Bend: 1961.

South Bend

Temple Beth El: The First 75 Years, 1905–1980. South Bend: Temple Beth El, 1980.

Terre Haute

American Jews' Annual. "The First Temple in Terre Haute." (1892): 93, 100.

Vincennes

Solis-Cohen, J., Jr. "Jake Gimbel: A Hoosier Philanthropist." *PAJHS* 48 (June 1959): 256–61.

IOWA

AJA. "Trailblazers . . ." 8 (Oct. 1956).

Glazer, Simon. *The Jews of Iowa: A Complete History and Accurate Account of Their Religious, Social, Economical and Educational Progress in This State; A History of the Jews of Europe, North and South America in Modern Times; and a Brief History of Iowa*. Des Moines: Koch Bros. Printing Co., 1904. 359 pp.

"Iowa." In *Enc Jud*, 8:1437–39.

"Iowa." In *Post*, 171–77.

Rosenthal, Eric. "Studies of Jewish Intermarriage in the United States." *AJYB* 64 (1963). (For Iowa, see pp. 34–52).

Wolfe, Jack A. *A Century with Iowa Jewry: As Complete a History as Could Be Obtained of Iowa Jewry from 1833 thru 1940*. Des Moines: Iowa Printing Supply Co., 1941. 280 pp.

Davenport

Fleishaker, Oscar. "Zionism in the Upper Mississippi Valley." *HYB* 5 (1963): 211–19.

Des Moines

Bureau for Jewish Living. "A Holocaust Unit in a Public School." *Ped Rep* 35 (June 1984): 34–35.

Rosenthal, Frank. *The Jews of Des Moines: The First Century*. Des Moines: 1957. 280 pp.

The Iowa Jewish News. 1932–51. Weekly.

Zerin, Edward. *Curriculum in Jewish Living*. Des Moines: 1955.

Iowa City

M'Gdolim: The Jewish Quarterly. 1984–?.

Sioux City

Littlefield, Oscar, and Susan Marks Conner. *I Remember When . . .: Personal Recollections and Vignettes of the Sioux City Jewish Community, 1869–1984*. Sioux City: Jewish Federation of Sioux City, 1985. 108 pp.

Shuman, Bernard. *A History of the Sioux City Jewish Community, 1869–1969*. Sioux City: Sioux City Jewish Federation, 1969. 209 pp.

KANSAS

AJA. "Trailblazers . . ." 8 (Oct. 1956): 92–93.

"Kansas." In *Enc Jud*, 10:739–41.

"Kansas." In *Post*, 177–89.

Sapinsley, Elbert. "Jewish Agricultural Colonies in the West: The Kansas Example." *WSJH* 3 (Apr. 1971): 157–69.

WSJH. "The Beginnings of Organized Jewish Life in Kansas, 1858" (newspaper account). 12 (July 1980) (Apr. 1971): 304–5.

Beer Sheba

AJA. "A Colony in Kansas—1892" (diaries and letters of early settlers). 17 (Nov. 1965): 114–39.

Feld, Lipman G. "New Light on the Lost Jewish Colony of Beer Sheba, Kansas, 1882–1886." *AJHQ* 60 (Dec. 1970): 159–68.

Rudin, A. James. "Beersheba, Kansas: 'God's Pure Air on Government Land'." *Kansas Historical Quarterly* 34 (Autumn 1968): 282–98.

Kansas City

Congregation Ohev Shalom, 100th Anniversary, 1877–1977. Kansas City. 62 pp.

Topeka

Hymovitz, Kay S., ed. *The Spirit Unconsumed: A History of Topeka Jewish Community*. Topeka: Temple Beth Sholom, 1979. 86 pp.

KENTUCKY

Bernheimer, Isaac W. *History of the Settlement of Jews in Paducah and the Lower Ohio Valley*. Paducah: 1912. 78 pp.

Dembitz, Lewis N. "Jewish Beginnings in Kentucky." *PAJHS* 1 (1893): 99–101.

"Kentucky." In *Enc Jud* 10, 189–98.

Louisville

American Jewish Historical Society. *History of the Jews of Louisville*.

Dinsky, Samuel H. *Evaluation of the Bureau of Education, the Jewish Community Center, and the Federation*. N.Y.: AAJE, 1967.

Engelman, Uriah Z. "Survey of Louisville," in "Survey of Surveys." *Jew Ed* 17 (June 1946): 45–48.

Gamoran, Emanuel. *Survey of Jewish Education in Louisville, 1943*. AAJE.

Kentucky Jewish Post and Opinion. 1931–present. Weekly.

Landau, Herman. *Adath Louisville: The Story of a Jewish Community*. Louisville: Herman Landau and Associates, 1981.

Shapiro, Zipora. "A Comparative Study of Methods Teaching Arithmetic in the First Grade in Louisville Public Schools and in the Religious Schools, Haifa, Israel." Master's thesis, U. of Louisville, 1952.

Paducah

Bernheim, Isaac W. *History of the Settlement of Jews in Paducah and Lower Ohio Valley*. Paducah: Temple Israel, 1912.

LOUISIANA

Ashkenazi, Eliot. *The Business of Jews in Louisiana, 1840–1875*. University, Alabama: U. of Alabama Press, 1988. 219 pp.

37 LOCAL SOURCES FOR JEWISH EDUCATION

LOUISIANA

Dinnerstein, L., and Mary Dale Palsson. *Jews in the South*. Baton Rouge: Louisiana State U. Press, 1973. 392 pp.

"Louisiana." In *Enc Jud*, 11:517–20.

"Louisiana." In *Post*, 198–209.

Louisiana Historical Records Survey. *Inventory of the Church and Synagogue Archives of Louisiana*. Louisiana State U., 1941. 184 pp.

Kaplan, Benjamin. *The Eternal Stranger*. New York: Bookman Associates, 1957. See pp. 39–43.

* ———. *Selected Jewish Communities in Louisiana*. Louisiana State U., 1952.

Meyers, W. E. *The Israelites of Louisiana, Their Religious, Civic, Charitable and Patriotic Life*. New Orleans: W. E. Myers, 1904. 139 pp.

Nassatir, A. P., and Leo Shpall. "The Texel Affair." *AJHQ* 53 (Sept. 1963): 3–43.

Shpall, Leo. "The First Synagogue of Louisiana." *Louisiana Historical Quarterly* 21 (Apr. 1939): 518–31.

———. "A Jewish Agricultural Colony in Louisiana." *Louisiana Historical Quarterly* 20 (1937): 821–31.

———. *The Jews of Louisiana*. New Orleans: Steeg, 1936.

Nachitoches Parish

Goldman, Elliot. "The Jewish Community of Nachitoches Parish." Master's thesis, Northwestern State College of Louisiana, 1968.

New Orleans

* Feibelman, Julian B. *A Social and Economic Study of the New Orleans Jewish Community*. U. of Pennsylvania, 1939.

Fishman, Walda Katz, and Richard C. Zweigenhaft. "Jews and the New Orleans Economic Social Elites." *JSS* 44 (Summer/Fall 1962): 291–98.

Heller, Max. *Jubilee Souvenir of Temple Sinai, 1872–1922*. New Orleans: 1922. 154 pp.

Huhner, Leon. *The Life of Judah Touro, 1775–1854*. Phila.: JPS, 1946. 192 pp. Touro's will, pp. 129–42, includes many of the nation's educational institutions of the period.

Isaacson, Irma M. "A History of Jewish Philanthropy in New Orleans." Master's thesis, Tulane U., 1937.

Jewish Community Center. *Past to Present: Panorama of Jewish Collecting in New Orleans* (exhibit). New Orleans: 1967.

Korn, Bertram W. *The Early Years of New Orleans*. Waltham, Mass.: AJHS, 1969. 382 pp.

Nassatir, A. P., and J. R. Mills. *Commerce and Contraband in New Orleans during the French and Indian War*. Cincinnati: American Jewish Archives, 1968. 310 pp.

New Orleans' First Congregation. *An Act to Incorporate a Society of Israelites, in New Orleans, Mar. 25, 1828*. Includes school. In Schappes, 179–81.

New Orleans Temple Sinai. *Our First Hundred Years*. New Orleans: Temple Sinai, 1970.

Proctor, Samuel. "Jewish Life in New Orleans, 1718–1860." *Louisiana Historical Quarterly* 40 (Apr. 1957): 110–32.

Reissman, Leonard. "The New Orleans Jewish Community." *Jew J Soc* 4 (June 1962): 110–23.

Rosen, J. C. "A Study of Leadership in the New Orleans Jewish Community." Master's thesis, Tulane U., 1960.

Share, Nathaniel S. "Eighty-fifth Anniversary of Gates of Prayer." *Jewish Ledger* (Jan. 10, 1936).

Shpall, Leo. "Early Jewish Philanthropy in New Orleans." *Jewish Forum* 1:14, 3:52, 7:114.

Shteingart, Tzirl. „דער אידישער ישוב אין ניו ארלינס" (The Jewish Community in New Orleans). *For* (Y.) (Aug. 10, 17, 1984).

New Orleans: Education

JWF. *A Study of Jewish Adolescents*. New Orleans: 1966.

Reissman, Leonard. *Jewish Education in New Orleans: An Analysis of Findings*. New Orleans: JWF, 1963. 49 pp.

Schwartz, Larry, and Louis Schwartzman. *Survey of Elementary and Secondary Education in New Orleans*. New Orleans: AAJE and JWF, 1969.

Shpall, Aaron Shimon. „על חנוך העברי בניו אורליאנס" (On Jewish Education in New Orleans). *Sh Hah* (H.) 2 (1926): 64–67.

Shpall, Leo. *Jewish Religious Movements*. New Orleans: Press Steeg Pub. Co., c. 1975. 22 pp.

Silber, Mandel. *America in Hebrew Literature*. New Orleans: 1928.

New Orleans: Press

The Jewish Civic Press. 1965–present. Monthly.

Jewish Times. 1974–present. Biweekly.

Jewish Ledger. 1895–196?. Weekly.

Jewish Voice. 1989–present. Semiweekly.

Rapides Parish

Hinchin, Martin I. *Four Score and Eleven: A History of the Jews of Rapides Parish, 1828–1919*. Alexandria, La.: Congregation Gemiluth Chassodim, 1984. 363 pp.

Shreveport

Hewitt, Louise Matthews. *Days of Building: History of a Jewish Community*. Shreveport: Jewish Historical Commission, 1965. 184 pp.

Jewish Journal. 1937–195?. Weekly.

"Survey of Historical Records of Congregation Agudath Achim, Shreveport, 1890–1939." Unpublished (American Jewish Archives; copies from the Department of Archives, Louisiana State U.).

Sicily Island

Herscher, Uri D. "On Agricultural Colony at Sicily Island." In *JAUA*, 32–37.

MAINE

"Maine." In *Enc Jud*, 11:782–83.

"Maine." In *Post*, 207–9.

Lewiston-Auburn

Millgram, Abraham E. *Evaluation of the Hebrew School*. N.Y.: AAJE, 1972.

Manchester

Slesinger, Zalman. *A Partial and Preliminary Report on Survey of Jewish Education in Maine*. N.Y.: AAJE, 1944.

———. *Survey of Jewish Education in Manchester, Maine*. N.Y.: AAJE, 1950.

Portland

Band, Benjamin. *Portland Jewry: Its Growth and Development*. Portland: Jewish Historical Society, 1955. 117 pp.

Kohanski, Alexander S. *Survey of Jewish Education in Portland, Maine*. Portland: Jewish Federation, 1948.

Portland, Maine, Jewish Historical Society. *Portland Jewry: Supplement One*. Portland: 1961. 32 pp.

MARYLAND

Altfeld, E. Milton. *The Jew's Struggle for Religious and Civil Liberty in Maryland*. N.Y.: De Capo Press, 1970. 211 pp.

Barnett, George E. "The Jewish Population of Maryland." *AJYB* 4 (1902–3): 46–62.

Blau, Joseph L. "The Maryland Jew Bill." *Review of Religion* (1944): 227–39.

Brackenridge, H. M. *Speeches on the Jew Bill in the House of Delegates*. Phila.: J. Dobson, 1829. See pp. 59–156.

Eitches, Edward. "Maryland's 'Jew Bill'." *AJHQ* 60 (Mar. 1971): 258–78.

Generations. "Prominent Jewish Women and Women's Organizations in Early Maryland." 5 (June–July 1984).

Glushakow, A.D., ed. *A Pictorial History of Maryland Jewry*. Baltimore: Jewish Voice Pub. Co., 1955. 192 pp.

Goodman, Abraham V. "Blasphemy under the Calverts." In *American Overture*, 133–49. Phila.: JPS, 1947.

Hartogensis, Benjamin H. "Unequal Rights in Maryland since 1776." *PAJHS* 25 (1917): 93–107.

37 LOCAL SOURCES FOR JEWISH EDUCATION

MARYLAND

Hollander, J. H. "The Civil Status of the Jews in Maryland, 1634–1776." *PAJHS* 2 (1894): 33–44.

———. "Some Unpublished Materials Relating to Dr. Jacob Lumbardo of Maryland." *PAJHS* 1 (1892): 25–39.

"Maryland." In *Enc Jud*, 11:1076–77.

"Maryland." In *Post*, 209–19.

Skutch, Rachel Frank. *The Federation of Jewish Women's Organizations of Maryland, 1916–1961: A History*. Baltimore: 1961. 115 pp.

Baltimore

Associated Jewish Charities. *The Jewish Community of Greater Baltimore: A Population Study*. Baltimore: 1968. 107 pp.

Blum, Isadore. *The Jews of Baltimore: An Historical Summary of Their Progress and Status as Citizens of Baltimore from Early Days to the Year Nineteen Hundred and Ten*. Baltimore: Historical Review Pub. Co., 1910. 470 pp.

Cahn, Louis F. *The History of Oheb Shalom, 1853–1953*. Baltimore: Oheb Shalom Congregation, 1953.

Einhorn, David. "The Fate of Oheb Shalom Congregation in Baltimore." *Sinai* 4 (1859): 325–39.

Esterson, Rose. "History of the Young Men's and Young Women's Hebrew Association of Baltimore." In *YM–YWHA of Baltimore*, 31–40. 1930.

Fein, Isaac M. "Baltimore Jews during the Civil War." *AJHQ* 51 (1961): 76–96.

———. "Years of Dissension and Expansion, 1855–1880." In his *The Making of an American Jewish Community: The History of Baltimore Jewry from 1773 to 1920*, 81–137. Phila.: JPS, 1971.

Greenberg, Rose. *The Chronicle of Baltimore Hebrew Congregation, 1830–1975*. 1976. 115 pp.

Gutmacher, Adolf. *A History of the Baltimore Hebrew Congregation 1839–1905*. Baltimore: Lord Baltimore Press, 1905.

Hartogensis, Benjamin H. "Notes on the Early Jewish Settlers of Baltimore." *PAJHS* 22 (1914): 191–95.

———. "The Sephardic Congregation of Baltimore." *PAJHS* 23 (1915): 141–46.

Hashierg, Gertrude. *To Love Mercy: The Story of Chevra Ahavas Chesed of Baltimore* (congregation established in 1942 by refugees from Nazi Germany). Baltimore: Harrod, 1972.

Hendricks, Theodore W. "Baltimore's Growth: The Role of the Russian Jew." *Generations* 3 (June 1982).

Hollander, Jacob. *Forces and Tendencies of Jewish Charities*. Baltimore: 1910.

Kartman, Lauraine Levy. "The Jewish Board of Arbitration in Baltimore, the Early Years." *Maryland Historical Magazine* 79 (Winter 1984): 332–38.

Levin, Alexandra Lee. *The Szolds of Lombard Street: A Baltimore Jewish Family, 1853–1900*. Phila.: JPS, 1960. 418 pp.

Rosenwaike, Ira. "The Jews of Baltimore in 1810." *AJH* 64 (1975): 291–320.

———. "The Jews of Baltimore: 1810–1820." *AJH* 57 (1967): 101–24.

———. "The Jews of Baltimore: 1820 to 1830." *AJH* 57 (1967): 246–59.

Rubenstein, Charles A. *History of the Har Sinai Congregation in the City of Baltimore*. Baltimore: 1918.

Shusterman, Abraham. *The Legacy of a Liberal: A History of the Har Sinai Congregation of Baltimore, on the Occasion of Its 125th Anniversary*. Baltimore: 1967. 95pp

Sobeloff, Simon E. *Zionism in Baltimore*. Baltimore: 1967.

Tabak, Israel. "The Lloyd Street Synagogue of Baltimore: A National Shrine." *AJHQ* 61 (June 1972): 342–52.

Tobin, Gary A. *A Population Study of the Jewish Community of Greater Baltimore*. Baltimore: Associated Jewish Charities and Welfare Fund, 1986. 335 pp. See also *Summary Report*, 32 pp.

Baltimore: Education

Baltimore BJE. *Curriculum for Sunday Schools*. 1964.

———. *Parent Workshops*.

———. *Revised Course in Prayers*. 1929.

———. *Terms of Affiliation of Congregational Schools with the Board of Jewish Education of Baltimore.* In *CA*, 199–201.

"Baltimore Center for Jewish Education—A New Program Designed to Build Professional Jewish Leadership." *Ped Rep* 25 (Fall 1973): 31.

* Bloom, Raymond. *History of Jewish Education in Baltimore during the Nineteenth and Twentieth Centuries.* Dropsie U., 1972.

Bugatch, Simon. "Supervision through Testing in Baltimore." *Jew Ed* 21 (Spring 1950): 33–39.

Bureau of Jewish Social Research. *Survey of Jewish Education in Baltimore, 1926.* N.Y.: Bureau of Jewish Social Research and Council of Jewish Federations.

Chanover, Hyman. *Baltimore Jewish Education—Problems and Prospects.* Baltimore: BJE, January 1978. 101 pp.

———. "Coming to Grips with the Teacher Crisis: The Baltimore Story." *Jew Ed* 56 (Summer 1988): 4–14, (Fall 1988): 13–23, 46.

———, ed. *Family Guide for the High Holy Days.* Baltimore: BJE, ca. 1983.

Cohen, Gedaliah. "Notes from a Hebrew Teacher's Notebook." *Generations* 4 (Dec. 1983).

Fein, Isaac. See "Jewish Education" in contents (pp. xv–xvii) of *The Making of an American Jewish Community: The History of Baltimore Jewry from 1773 to 1920,* 81–137. Phila.: JPS, 1971.

Fraenkel, Mira, and David Schapiro. "The Role of the Teachers' Resource Center: A Holocaust Display for the Classroom." *Ped Rep* 33 (Mar. 1982): 18–20.

Greenstone, Julius H. *Statistical Data of the Jewish Religious Schools of Baltimore, Maryland, and Pittsburgh, Pennsylvania, for 1908–1909.* Phila.: Gratz College, 1909.

Hyman, H. Joseph. "Hebrew Education in Baltimore" (historical). *Jew Ed* 6 (Apr–June 1934): 109–10.

JESNA. *Baltimore: Evaluation of Two Education Programs.* N.Y.

Kaplan, Louis L. *Abridged Sabbath Service for Junior Congregations.* Baltimore: BJE, 1951. 72 pp.

———. *The Book of Genesis: An Outline and Interpretation of the Weekly Sedroth.* Baltimore: BJE, 1951.

———. *Introduction to the Teaching of the Torah by the Cycle Method.* Baltimore: BJE, 1942.

———. *A New Approach to the Teaching of Torah: A Guide for Teachers in Jewish Religious Schools.* 4 parts. Baltimore: BJE, 1942–55.

Kaplan, Louis L., and Hyman Saye. *Teaching the Bible in Jewish Religious Schools—Selected Readings on the Book of Joshua, the Book of Judges.* Baltimore: BJE, 1944.

———. *Teaching the Bible in Jewish Religious Schools—Selected Readings in the Book of Samuel (Books One and Two).* Baltimore: BJE, 1945.

Kargon, Marcia. *Selected Cooking Experiences for Jewish Pre-School.* Baltimore: BJE, 1975.

Kellman, Naomi. "Jewish Education in Baltimore, Dr. Samson Benderly." *Generations* 4 (Dec. 1983).

Lazaron, Morris S. *Religious Services for Jewish Youth: Designed for Use in the Assemblies of the High School Department of Jewish Religious and Sunday Schools.* Baltimore: 1927. 275 pp.

Levin, Alexandra Lee. "Henrietta Szold and the Russian Immigrant School." *Maryland Historical Magazine* 57 (Mar. 1962): 1–15.

Magida, Arthur J. "Jewish Education: Shield against Extinction." *Baltimore Jewish Times* (Oct. 12, 1984).

Rotenberg, Rena. "The Baltimore Experience." *Ped Rep* 31 (Spring 1980): 3–6.

Saye, Hymen. "Memories of the Talmud Torah." *Generations* 4 (Dec. 1983).

Schlafer, Israel. "נר ישראל„ (*Ner Israel*) (day school). *Sh Hah* (H.) 19 (Winter 1959): 64.

Schwartz, Benjamin. *Survey of Baltimore Talmud Torahs, 1921.*

Shapiro, Mannheim S. *The Baltimore Survey of Jewish Attitudes.* N.Y.: AJC, 1963. 124 pp.

Siegman, Sarah M., et al. *Classroom Ideas and Activities for Teaching Jewish History.* Baltimore: BJE, c. 1983. 198 pp. Intermediate grades.

Silverman, Rita. *Fun with Phonics*. Edited by S. M. Siegman. Baltimore: BJE, 1983. 36 pp.

Baltimore: Student Periodical

Hatzair (H.). Hebrew Education Society, 1912 (one issue). Monthly.

Baltimore: Higher Education

Rose, Robyn I. "The Beginnings of the Baltimore Hebrew College." *Generations* 4 (Dec. 1983).

Toshev, A. "הקאליג׳ העברי דבלטימור״ (The Hebrew College of Baltimore). In *JB* (H.), 305–7.

Baltimore: Newspapers and Periodicals (In Chronological Order)

Sinai (G.). 1856–62. Monthly.

Ha Pisgah (H.). 1890–92. Weekly.

Der Israelit (Y.). 1891–93. Weekly.

The Jewish Comment. 1895–1918. Weekly.

Der Vegvyazer (Y.). 1901–10. Weekly.

Baltimore Jewish Times. 1919–present. Weekly.

Silver Spring

American Jewish Journal. 1944–86. Quarterly.

MASSACHUSETTS

Broches, Samuel. „די געשיכטע פון דער ייִדישער פרעסע אין מאסאטשוזעטס" (The History of the Jewish Press in Massachusetts). *YA* (Y.) 2 (1938): 219–47.

———. *Jews in New England: Study of the Jews in Massachusetts, 1650–1750*. N.Y.: Bloch, 1942. 68 pp.

Friedman, Lee M. "Early Jewish Residents in Massachusetts." *PAJHS* 23 (1915): 79–90.

———. "Jewish Residents in Massachusetts before 1800." In *Early American Jews*, 3–21. Cambridge: Harvard U. Press, 1934.

Huhner, Leon. "The Jews of New England." *PAJHS* 11 (1903): 82–86.

Jewish Advocate. "New England Salute to American Jewish Tercentenary." January 27, 1955.

"Massachusetts." In *Enc Jud*, 11:1111–15.

"Massachusetts." In *Post*, 219–41.

Synagogue Directory of Massachusetts, 1989–5749. Newton Centre: Synagogue Council of Massachusetts, 1989. 51 pp. Also lists Jewish communal agencies and educational institutions.

Berkshire County

Horwitt, Pink, and Bertha Skole. *Jews in Berkshire County*. Williamstown, Mass.: Dor, 1972. 74 pp.

Boston

AJHS. *Jewish Boston: A Guide for Students and Newcomers, 5730 (1969–70)*. Waltham, Mass.: 1969.

Angoff, Charles. *When I Was a Boy in Boston*. Freeport, N.Y.: Books for Libraries Press, 1947.

Axelrod, Morris, Floyd Fowler, and Arnold Gurin. *A Community Survey for Long Range Planning: A Study of the Jewish Population of Greater Boston*. Boston: Combined Jewish Philanthropies of Greater Boston, 1967. 229 pp.

Broches, Samuel. "A Chapter in the History of the Jews of Boston." *YA* 9 (1954): 205–11.

———. "A History of Jewish Charity in Boston." *Jewish Advocate* (Nov. 10–17, 1939).

Cohen, A. K. "The First Welfare Federation in the United States." In *Fifty Years of Jewish Philanthropy in Greater Boston, 1895–1945*. Boston: 1945.

Combined Jewish Philanthropies of Boston.

Directory of Boston Jewish Community Services. Boston: 1984 (31 pp.), 1987 (172 pp.).

Ehrenfried, Albert A. *A Chronicle of Boston Jewry: From the Colonial Settlement to 1900*. Boston: Privately printed, 1963. 771 pp.

Fein, Isaac M. *Boston—Where It All Began: An Historical Perspective of the Boston Jewish Community*. Boston: Boston Jewish Bicentennial Committee, 1976.

———. *On Common Ground: The Boston Jewish Experience, 1649–1980*. Boston: AJHS, 1981.

Feldman, Steven, ed. *Genesis 2: Guide to Jewish Boston and New England*. Boston: 1986. 235 pp.

Fowler, Floyd J., Jr. *Community Survey: A Study of the Jewish Population of Greater Boston*. Boston: 1977.

Friedenberg, Albert M. "Early Jews in Boston." *PAJHS* 29 (1925): 153.

Friedman, Lee M. "A Beacon Hill Synagogue." In *Pilgrims in a New Land*, 145–50. Phila.: JPS, 1948.

———. "Boston in American Jewish History." *PAJHS* 42 (1953): 333–40.

———. "The Dedication of Massachusetts' First Synagogue." In *Jewish Pioneers and Patriots*, 116–29. Phila.: JPS, 1943.

———. "1854—Boston and Its Jews." In *Growth and Achievement of Temple Israel, 1854–1954*, edited by A. Mann, 14–24.

Green, Arthur. "Havurat Shalom: A Proposal." In *Contemporary Judaic Fellowship in Theory and Practice*, edited by Jacob Neusner, 149–55. N.Y.: Ktav, 1972.

———. "Some Liturgical Notes from Havurat Shalom." In *Contemporary Judaic Fellowship in Theory and Practice*, edited by Jacob Neusner, 155–60. N.Y.: Ktav, 1972.

Israel, Sherry. *Boston's Jewish Community: The 1985 CJP Demographic Study*. Boston: Combined Jewish Philanthropies of Greater Boston, 1987. 172 pp.

Lebowich, Joseph. "The Jews in Boston till 1875." *PAJHS* 12 (1904): 101–12.

Lipman, Eugene J., and Albert Vorspan. "Boston—Conflict along the Charles." In *Ten Cities*, 10–44.

Mostov, Stephen. "A Sociological Portrait of German Jewish Immigrants in Boston: 1845–1861." *American J Sociological Review* (1978): 142–47.

Neusner, Jacob. "The Impact of Immigration and Philanthropy upon the Boston Jewish Community, 1880–1914." *PAJHS* 46 (1956): 71–85.

———. "The Rise of the Jewish Community of Boston, 1880–1914." Master's thesis, Harvard U., 1953.

Reznikoff, Charles. "Boston's Jewish Community: Earlier Days." *Commentary* 15 (May 1953): 490–99.

Schindler, Solomon. *Israelites in Boston*. Boston: Barwick and Smith, 1890.

Segal, Robert. *The Early Years of the Jewish Community Council of Metropolitan Boston*. Boston: Jewish Community Relations Council of Greater Boston, 1985. 21 pp.

Solomon, Barbara Miller. *Pioneers in Service: The History of the Associated Jewish Philanthropies of Boston*. Boston: Associated Jewish Philanthropies, 1956. 197 pp.

Wieder, Arnold A. *The Early Jewish Community of Boston's North End: A Sociologically Oriented Study of an Eastern European Jewish Immigrant Community, 1870–1900*. Waltham, Mass.: Brandeis U., 1962. 100 pp.

Boston: Education

Ackerman, Walter I. "From Past to Present: Notes from the History of Jewish Education in Boston." *Jew Ed* 51 (Fall 1983): 16–26.

Band, Arnold J. "Trends in the Jewish School System—Boston: A Case Study." *JSS* 21 (1959): 7–14.

Boston BJE. *Curriculum for Five Day a Week Hebrew Schools*. 1964.

———. *Curriculum for the Talmud Torah of Boston*. Boston: BJE, 1951. 148 pp.

———. *Curriculum for Three Day a Week Hebrew Schools*. Boston: BJE, 1964.

Boston, Combined Jewish Philanthropies. *Report of the Study Committee on the Bureau of Jewish Education*. June 1973.

Broches, Samuel. "The History of One Hundred Years of Jewish Education in Boston." *Jewish Advocate* (Feb. 16, 1940).

Goldberg, Janet. *The Melton Research Center Torah Project: The Boston Experience*. Brandeis U., 1972.

Goldman, Emanuel. *Study Guide for Sabbath Prayers*. Boston: BJE, 1975.

37 LOCAL SOURCES FOR JEWISH EDUCATION

MASSACHUSETTS

Honor, Leo L., and Solomon Lowenstein. *A Survey of the Bureau of Jewish Education.* N.Y.: Bureau of Jewish Social Research, 1930.

Hurwich, Louis. "Jewish Education in Boston." *Jew Ed* 26 (Spring 1956): 22–34.

———. "למצב החנוך העברי בבוסטון". (On the Condition of Hebrew Education in Boston). *Sh Hah* (H.) 3 (1927): 59–65.

———. "Standard Examinations in the Greater Boston Hebrew Schools." *Jew Ed* 1 (May 1929): 114–18.

Hurwich, Louis, and Ben Rosen. *Survey of Jewish Education in Boston.* 1919.

Margolis, Daniel J. "The Evolution and Uniqueness of the Jewish Educational Structure of Greater Boston." In *Newman Festschrift*, 85–97. Boston: 1985.

Rosen, Ben. "Recent Surveys of Jewish Education." Jew; *Ed* 2 (1930): 87–89.

Shevach, Benjamin I. *How the Jewish Community in Metropolitan Boston is Organized for Jewish Education—A Report.* Boston; Jan. 15, 1959.

Shevitz, Susan R., ed. *Why Be Good: Sensitivities and Ethics in Rabbinic Literature.* Teacher's guide. Boston: BJE, 1977.

* Snow, Charles E. *Comparative Growth of Jewish and Non-Jewish Pupils in Greater Boston Public Schools.* Harvard U., 1938. 174 pp.

Wachstock, Eileen. "The Mechina Program of Yeshiva Program." *Ped Rep* 23 (Sept. 1971): 34.

Boston: Higher Education

Charif, L. "בית מדרש למורים דבוסטון". (Hebrew Teachers College of Boston). *Hadoar* (H.) 11 (Adar A 12, 1932).

Furie, William B. "Yavneh" (summer camp of Boston Hebrew Teachers College). *Jew Ed* 17 (June 1946): 28–30.

Hurwich, Louis. "בית המדרש בבוסטון". (The College in Boston). *Hadoar* (H.) 21 (Feb. 1932).

———. "לתולדות בית המדרש דמורים ד'בוסטון". (Concerning the History of the Hebrew Teachers' College in Boston). In *Sefer Touroff* (H.), edited by Silberschlag and Twersky, 104. 1938.

Margolis, Isidor. "Hebrew Teachers College of Boston." In *Jewish Teacher Training Schools*, 188–241. 1964.

Pollak, I. H. "בית המדרש למורים בבוסטון". (Boston Hebrew Teachers College). In *JB* (H.), 298–304.

———. "ד״ר טורוב בבוסטון". (Dr. Touroff in Boston). In *Sefer Touroff* (H.), edited by Silberschlag and Twersky.

Silberschlag, Eisig. "Postscript to Our Thirtieth Anniversary." *The Hebrew Teachers' College Bulletin* (1951).

Steiner, M. J. "Hebrew Teachers College of Boston (1921–1951)." *Jew Ed* 23 (Winter 1952): 30–35.

Newspapers and Periodicals (Selected Chronological List)

The Boston Hebrew Observer. 1883–96. Weekly.

The Jewish Chronicle. 1890–93. Weekly.

American Jewish History. 1893–present. Quarterly.

The Jewish Advocate. 1902–present. Weekly.

Der Vegvayzer (Y.). 1901–10. Weekly.

The New Word (Y.). 1914–32. Monthly.

Boston Jewish Times. 1945–present. Weekly.

Moment. 1975–present. Monthly.

Brookline

Engelman, Uriah Z., and Aaron Kessler. *Evaluation of Schools.* N.Y.: AAJE, 1947.

Nizel, Jeanette S., and Abraham E. Nizel. *Congregation Ohabei Shalom—Pioneers of the Boston Jewish Community: An Historical Perspective of the First One Hundred and Forty Years.* Brookline. 28 pp.

* Phillips, Bruce. *Acculturation, Group Service of the Jewish Community: History of the Jewish Community of Brookline, Massachusetts, 1915–1940.* Brandeis U., 1975.

Cambridge

Mann, Arthur, ed. *Growth and Achievement of Temple Israel, 1854–1954.* Cambridge: Temple Adath Israel, 1954.

Rischin, Moses. "Congregational Life: 1854–1954." In *Growth and Achievement of Temple Israel, 1854–1954*, edited by Arthur Mann. Cambridge: Temple Adath Israel, 1954.

Chelsea

Katzman, Jacob. "The Folk School in Chelsea" and "Influences of the School." In his *Commitment: The Labor Zionist Life-Style in America—A Personal Memoir*, 118–24. N.Y.: Labor Zionist Letters, 1975.

Chestnut Hill

Congregation Mishkan Tefila. Chestnut Hill. 28 pp.

Fall River

Friedman, Lee M. "Synagogues in Fall River." *PAJHS* 37 (1947): 421.

Framingham

Greater Framingham Federation. *100 Years of Jewish Settlement: Framingham's Past, Present and Future*. Framingham: 1985. 59 pp.

Jewish Reporter. 1970–present. Monthly.

Haverhill

Woodman, Bertha Shapiro. *From the Hill to Main Street: Jewish Life and Work in Haverhill, Massachusetts, 1880–1940*. Haverhill: Haverhill Public Library, 1987. 104 pp.

Lynn

Gannes, Abraham P., Samuel Grand, and Aaron Soviv. *Survey of Schools*. N.Y.: AAJE, 1967.

Malden

Klayman, Richard. *The First Jew: Prejudice and Politics in an American Community, 1900–1932*. Malden: Old Suffolk Square Press, 1985. 175 pp.

———. *A Generation of Hope, 1929–1941*. Malden: Old Suffolk Square Press, 1987. 210 pp.

Newburyport

The Jewish Community of Newburyport: A Photographic Exhibit. Newburyport: Congregation Ahavas Achim, 1986. 28 pp.

Newton and Newton Centre

Fleishman, Thelma. *Agudas Achim Anshei Sfard: The Adams Street Synagogue, Newton, Massachusetts. An Informal History Based on an Exhibition*. Newton: Jackson Homestead, 1986. 48 pp.

Jewish Cemetery Assocation of Massachusetts. *Guide to Jewish Cemeteries*. Newton Centre: 1985.

Temple Emanuel. *A History of Temple Emanuel, 1935–1985*. Newton: 1985. 36 pp.

Pittsfield

Newman, Robert G. *The History of Congregation Anshe Amonim*. Pittsfield: 1961. 13 pp.

Roxbury

Ha Kerem (H.). 1915 (three issues). Bimonthly.

Salem

The Journal of the North Shore Community Center. 1975–present. Biweekly.

Springfield

Gelin, James A. *Starting over: The Formation of the Jewish Community of Springfield, Massachusetts, 1840–1905*. Lanham, Md.: U. Press of America, 1984. 161 pp.

Goldstein, Sydney. *A Population Survey of the Greater Springfield Jewish Community*. Springfield: Jewish Community Council, 1968. 181 pp.

Jewish Weekly News. 1945–present. Weekly.

Springfield Hebrew Record. 1897–193?. Semiweekly.

Springfield Jewish Ledger. 1929–194?. Monthly.

Worcester

Jewish Civic Leader. 1923–?. Weekly.

Kaplan, Louis L. *A Study on Educational Objectives*. N.Y.: AAJE, 1964.

Tobin, Gary A., and Sylvia Barack Fishman. *A Population Study of the Greater Worcester Jewish Community: Summary Report*. Worcester: Worcester Jewish Federation, 1987. 191 pp.

MICHIGAN

* Elstein, Rochelle B. *Synagogue Architecture in Michigan and the Midwest: Material Culture and the Dynamics of Jewish Accommodation, 1865–1945*. Michigan State U., 1986.

Franklin, Leo M. "Jews in Michigan." *Michigan History Magazine* 23 (1939): 77–92.

Graff, George P. "Michigan's Early Settlers." *MJH* 10 (Jan. 1970): 10–14.

Heineman, David E. "Jewish Beginnings in Michigan before 1850." *PAJHS* 13 (1905): 47–70.

The Jewish News, Dec. 17, 1954. American Jewish Tercentenary Issue. Reports of the Jewish Tercentenary Committee and various articles on Jewish life in Michigan.

Katz, Irving I. "Jewish Pioneers in Michigan." *MJH* 1 (Mar. 1960): 4.

"Michigan." In *Enc Jud*, 11:1498–1500.

"Michigan." In *Post*, 241–53.

Michigan Jewish History. Jewish Historical Society of Michigan. 1960–present.

Warsen, Allen A. "Michigan Jews and the Jewish Legion." *MJH* 8 (June 1968): 3–6.

Ann Arbor

Aminoff, Helen. "The First Jews of Ann Arbor." *MJH* 23 (Jan. 1983): 3–14.

Vanek, Linda, and Rose Vainstein, eds. *Temple Beth Emeth: The First Fifteen Years, 1966–1981*. Ann Arbor: 1983. 102 pp.

Bad Axe

Applebaum, Emanuel. "The Palestine Colony—An Agricultural Endeavor." *MJH* 4 (May 1964): 14–17.

Davidson, Gabriel. "The Palestine Colony in Michigan: An Adventure in Colonization." *PAJHS* 29 (1925): 61–74

Herscher, Uri D. "Palestine, Michigan." In *JAUA*, 61–70.

Detroit

Alpert, Carl. *The Detroit Story: A History of the Detroit Chapter of the American Society for Technion Israel Institute of Technology*. Detroit: Detroit Chapter, American Society of Technion, 1989. 44 pp.

Boxerman, William I. "Detroit's Social Engineer Reminisces (Informal Chats with Fred M. Butzel)" *JSSQ* (Mar. and June 1941).

———. "Gentiles Preferred: Study of Employment Agencies in Detroit." *JSSQ* 16 (June 1940): 339–48.

———. "A Problem in Negro-Jewish Relations in Detroit." *Recon* (Oct. 27, 1939): 10–16.

Capeci, Dominic J., Jr. "Black-Jewish Relations in Wartime Detroit: The Marsh, Loving, Wolf Survey and the Race Riot of 1943." *JSS* 47 (Fall 1985): 221–42.

Fauman, S. Joseph. "Occupational Selection among Detroit Jews." In *JES*, 119–37.

Goldberg, David, and Harry Sharp. "Some Characteristics of Detroit Area Jewish and Non-Jewish Adults." In *JES*, 107–18.

JWF. *The Jewish Elderly of Metropolitan Detroit: A Socio-Demographic and Needs Assessment Study*. Detroit: 1984. 46 pp.

Lurie, Harry L. *General Summary of Survey of Detroit Jewish Community, 1923*. N.Y.: Bureau of Jewish Social Research, 1923.

Mayer, Albert J. *The Detroit Jewish Community—Geographic Mobility: 1963–1965, and Fertility—A Projection of Future Births*. Detroit: JWF, 1966, 27 pp.

———. *Income Characteristics of the Jewish Population in the Detroit Metropolitan Area, 1956*. Report No. 7. Detroit: JWF, 1960.

———. *Jewish Population Study: 1963*. Series II, No. 1. Detroit: JWF, Mar. 1964.

———. *Place of Birth-Educational Level of the Jewish Population of Metropolitan Detroit Area, 1956*. Reports 10 and 11. Detroit: JWF.

———. *Social and Economic Characteristics of the Jewish Community, 1963.* Detroit: JWF, 1964. 65 pp.

Meyer, Henry J. "The Economic Structure of the Jewish Community in Detroit." *JSS* 2 (1940): 127–48.

———. "The Position of the Jewish Community in Detroit in the Economy of Detroit." Proceedings of the Pacific Sociological Society (Research Studies of the State College of Washington) 8 (1940): 19–25.

* ———. *The Structure of the Jewish Community in the City of Detroit.* U. of Michigan, 1940.

———. "A Study of Detroit Jewry, 1935." In *Pop*, 109–30.

Detroit: Jewish Institutions and Organizations

Bercovich, Edith B. *Children under Care.* Detroit: JWF, 1940. 37 pp.

Boxerman, William I. "The Jewish Community Council of Detroit." *Recon* (Nov. 19, 1937): 11–14.

Chapin, Anna W. *History of the United Jewish Charities of Detroit (1899–1949). Story of the Jewish Welfare Federation (1926–1949).* 2 vols. Detroit: JWF. Unpublished.

Chapin, Mrs. Samuel. "Forty Years of the Detroit Jewish Welfare Federation." *MJH* 6 (June 1966): 2–8.

Crohn, Lawrence. "The Jewish Community Council of Detroit in Retrospect." *MJH* 7 (Nov. 1966): 3–5.

* Gurin, Arnold. *The Functions of a Sectarian Welfare Program in a Multigroup Society.* U. of Michigan, 1964.

Hurwitz, David S. "Study of the Problems of Administration in the Jewish Welfare Federation of Detroit." Master's thesis, Wayne U., 1948.

Jewish Chronicle. *The Jewish Community Bluebook.* Includes Jewish organizations and officers, a brief history of the Jewish community, the United Jewish Charities, the United Hebrew Schools, the Fresh Air Society, and the Young Women's Hebrew Association. Detroit: 1920. 216 pp.

Newmark, Louis. "Trends in Private Institutional Child Care: With a Study of Ten Years Intake of Jewish Children's Home of Detroit." Master's thesis, Wayne U., 1939.

Silver, Harold. "Jewish Child Placement Services in Detroit, 1933–1944." *MJH* 1 (Nov. 1960): 2–.

Sudran, Abe L. "The Detroit Experiment" (integration of Federation and Community Council). *JSSQ* (Mar. 1947): 336–38.

United Jewish Charities of Detroit. *In Observance of Our 60th Anniversary, 1899–1959.* Detroit: JWF, 1959. 24 pp.

Warsen, Allen A. *Jewish Communal Institutions in Detroit: 1952.* Detroit: 1952. 125 pp.

Weinberg, S. D. „אידישע אינסטיטוציעס און אנשטאלטן אין דעטראיט" (Jewish Institutions and Agencies in Detroit) (Y.). Detroit: JWF, 1940. 211 pp.

Weiner, Milton. "A Comparison of Theory and Practice of Psychiatric Consultation in Jewish Family and Children's Service of Detroit." Master's thesis, Wayne State U., 1959.

Detroit: History

Arlazaroff Branch No. 137, 10th Anniversary (Y. and E.). Detroit: JNWA, 1944. 38 pp.

Detroit Labor Zionist Organization. „25 יאריגער יובילעאום ... פועלי ציון" (Jubilee of the Jewish Socialist Workers Party, Poale Zion, 1905–1930) (Y.). Contains articles by national and local leaders. Detroit: LZOA, 1930. 88 pp.

Franklin, Leo M. *An Outline History of Congregation Beth El, Detroit, Michigan, 1850–1940.* Detroit: 1940. 80 pp.

Grad, Eli, and Bette Roth. *Congregation Shaarey Zedek, 1861–1981.* Southfield, Mich.: Congregation Shaarey Zedek, 1982. 192 pp.

* Grossberg, Sidney H. *Factors in Historical and Participation Identification of Detroit Area Jews.* Wayne State U., 1971.

Heineman, David E. "The Startling Experience of a Jewish Trader During Pontiac's Siege of Detroit in 1763." *PAJHS* 23 (1915): 31–35.

Katz, Irving I. *The Beth El Story, Detroit.* Detroit: Wayne State U. Press, 1953. 249 pp.

———. "Detroit's Jewish Community in 1867." *MJH* 4 (May 1964): 11–13.

———. "The Jewish Press in Detroit." *MJH* 14 (Jan. 1974): 18–22.

———. "Jews in Detroit prior to and Including 1850." *Bulletin of the Detroit Historical Society* 6 (Feb. 1950): 4–10.

———. "110 Years of Temple Beth El in Detroit, 1850–1960." Detroit: Temple Beth El, 1960, 1964.

———. "Temple Beth El, Detroit, 1850–1900." *Michigan History Magazine* 34 (Dec. 1950): 333–42.

Kohler, Kaufman. "A Call to Detroit." *AJA* 19 (Apr. 1967): 34–40.

Lederer, Phyllis. "A Study of Jewish Influences in Detroit (to 1914)." Master's thesis, Wayne U., 1947.

Michlin, Michael. "Some Memories of the Jewish Legion in Detroit." *MJH* 8 (June 1968): 7–.

* Miller, James A. *The Resident Yiddish Theater in Detroit from 1920 to 1937*. Wayne State U., 1966.

Moss, Leonard W., and Emanuel Applebaum. "Folklore among Detroit Jews." *MJH* 3 (June 1963): 2–10.

Rockaway, Robert A., "The Detroit Jewish Ghetto before World War I." *Michigan History Magazine* 52 (Spring 1968): 28–36.

———. "The Eastern European Jewish Community of Detroit, 1881–1914." *YA* 15 (1974): 82–105.

———. "Ethnic Conflict in an Urban Environment: The German and Russian Jew in Detroit, 1881–1914." *AJHQ* 60 (Dec. 1970): 133–50.

* ———. *From Americanization to Jewish Americanism: The Jews of Detroit, 1850–1914*. U. of Michigan, 1970.

———. *The Jews of Detroit, 1762–1914*. Detroit: Wayne State U. Press, 1986. 162 pp.

Tambor, Milton. "The Historical Development of the Detroit Jewish Community Center." *MJH* 3 (June 1963): 15–.

Temple Israel. *Temple Israel Dedication Volume*. Detroit: 1951.

Warsen, Allen A. "A Cultural Progress Report of the Greater Detroit Jewish Community." *MJH* 1 (Nov. 1960): 20–.

———. "The Detroit Jewish Community from the Founding of Beth El to the Founding of the Jewish Welfare Federation (1850–1926)." *MJH* 20 (June 1980): 11–23.

———. "Early Jewish Philanthropic Organizations in Detroit." *Michigan History Magazine* 34 (Dec. 1950): 343–45.

———. "Occupations and Organizational Affiliations of Detroit Jews Prior to 1920." *MJH* 6 (Nov. 1965): 14–15.

———. "The Survey of the Detroit Jewish Community" (1923). *MJH* 19 (June 1979): 811.

Weinberg, S. D. "דער אידישער קאמוניטי צענטער" (The Jewish Community Center in Detroit). In *Jewish Institutions and Agencies in Detroit* (Y.), 53–67. Detroit: JWF, 1940.

Detroit: Education

* Atzmon, Ezri. *The Impact of Educational Programs on the Acculturation of Adult Jewish Immigrants in Detroit (1949–1955)*. U. of Michigan, 1958. 264 pp..

Boxerman, William I. "A Problem in Consolidation of Jewish Educational Efforts." *Recon* (Mar. 1, 1941): 13–14.

Comay, Joseph, and Israel Drachler, eds. "אידישע פרויען לייענקרייזן אין דעטראיט" (Jewish Women's Reading Circles in Detroit) (Y.). On the 5th anniversary of the 26 Yiddish Reading Circles in Detroit. Includes greetings from Sh. Niger, H. Leivick, and Kadia Maladowski and a four-page account on the aims and activities of these groups. Detroit: Colonial Printing, 1939. 28 pp.

Crohn, Lawrence. "Detroit's Communal School System." *Recon* (Nov. 27, 1959): 22–27.

Detroit Jewish Community Council. *A Call to Jewish Parents: A Directory of Jewish Schools in Detroit*. Detroit: Culture Commission of the JCC, 1948, 1951. 14 pp.

Detroit Jewish News. "Community School: Solution to Education Problem" (editorial). Jan. 16, 1953.

* Donin, Hayim. *An Inquiry into the Value Presuppositions Underlying Jewish Education in Metropolitan Detroit*. Wayne State U. 1966, 242 pp.

Engelman, Uriah Z. *The Study of Jewish Education in Detroit*. N.Y.: Commission for the Study of Jewish Education in the United States. 32 pp.

Farber, Walter C. *Jewish Holidays, Cycle 1*. Detroit: Jewish Heritage Pub. House, ca. 1965. 71 pp.

Feinstein, Sara. *Federation Policy for Financing Jewish Education*. Detroit: JWF, 1979. 73 pp.

Garvett, Morris. "The Development of Jewish Education in Detroit." *MJH* 5 (May 1965): 4–10.

Isaacs, Bernard, and Aaron D. Markson. "מקרן זוית" (Out of a Corner) (H.). Detroit: 1921.

JWF. *Directory of Jewish Clubs and Societies*. Detroit: 1935. 120 pp.

———. *English Language Resource Center: Procedures and Results in Setting up a National Resource*. Detroit: 1979, 1981. CP, 31 pp.

Katz, Irving I. "Detroit's First Communal Talmud Torah." *MJH* 1 (Nov. 1960): 15–.

Kvutzah Ivrit. *Hed HaKvutzah* (An Echo of the Kvutzah) (H.). Detroit: Hebrew Society, 1941.

La Med, Louis. *A Community Accepts Responsibility for Jewish Education—Detroit*. Cleveland: East-Central Regional Council of Jewish Federations and Welfare Funds, Sept. 1954. 5 pp.

Markson, Aaron David. "החנוך בדטרויט" (Education in Detroit). *Hadoar* (H.) 4 (Mar. 6, 1925): 9–10.

———. "כתבי" (Writings) (H.). Edited by B. Isaacs and Daniel Persky. Detroit: Hebrew Society, 1938. 262 pp.

Rappoport, Israel B., and E. Picheny. *Summary of the Detroit Self Study of Cultural-Recreation-Education Resources and Needs of the Jewish Community, 1944–45*. Detroit: JWF. 33 pp.

Rosen, Ben. "Recent Surveys of Jewish Education—Detroit, Michigan, 1929." *Jew Ed* 2 (June 1930): 80–83.

Teller, Gerald A. "A Cooperative Effort between Formal and Informal Education Agencies" (United Hebrew Schools and the Fresh Air Society's camp). *Jew Ed* 49 (Fall 1981): 21–22. Also in *J Jew Com Ser* 58 (Spring 1982): 196–98.

Weine, Max. "Bernard Isaacs—A Memoir." In Morris Nobel, ed., *Sefer B. Isaacs*, 81–100. N.Y.: B. Isaacs Publication Committee, 1977.

Detroit: Congregational Schools

Baruch, Theodore H. *History of the Jews of the Middle Ages*. Detroit: Congregation Shaarey Zedeck Religious School, 1943. 108 pp.

Katz, Irving I. "Jewish Education at Temple Beth El, Detroit." *Michigan History Magazine* 52 (Fall 1968): 218–28.

———. "Jewish Education at Temple Beth El, Detroit, 1850–1871." *MJH* 8 (June 1968): 24–31.

Krohn, Samuel. "Lay Leadership of Education at the Shaarey Zedek." *Syn Sch* 17 (Sept. 1958).

Warsen, Allen L. *The Directors' Council of the Jewish Religious Schools of Metropolitan Detroit, 1953–1958*. Detroit: Directors' Council of the Jewish Religious Schools, 1958. 14 pp.

———. "The Story of Adas Shalom Religious School." *MJH* 6 (June 1966): 17–29.

Detroit United Hebrew Schools

Isaacs, Bernard. "The Dalton Plan in the United Hebrew Schools." *Jew Ed* 3 (Apr.–June 1931): 95–98.

———. "The History of the United Hebrew Schools of Detroit." *Jew Ed* 18 (Nov. 1956): 29–31.

Jew Ed. "Detroit's United Hebrew Schools." 1 (Mar. 1929): 129.

Marenof, Martha. *History through Literature: The Migrations of the Jewish People, from Its Earliest Times to Our Time*. Detroit: Dot Publications, 1960. 252 pp.

Mattis, I. M. "בתי הספר המאוחדים בדיטרויט" (The United Hebrew Schools in Detroit). *Sh Hah* (H.) 2 (1942): 61–68.

Michlin, Michael. "Memories of an Earlier Detroit." *MJH* 9 (Jan. 1969): 3–9.

Ror, M. *We Learn Hebrew*. Detroit: United Hebrew Schools, 1964.

Ruffman, Louis L., and Rebekah Kohn. *Evaluation of the United Hebrew Schools*. N.Y.: AAJE, 1968.

Teller, Gerald A. "What Has History Wrought—The United Hebrew Schools of Detroit." *Jew Ed* 53 (Fall 1985): 39–43.

United Hebrew Schools. *Tochnit Limudim* (program for high schools). Detroit: 1965.

Warsen, Allen L. "The United Hebrew Schools." *Michigan History Magazine* (Sept. 1951): 352–55.

Weinberg, S. D. "יוניייטעד היברו סקולס„" (The United Hebrew Schools). In *Jewish Institutions and Agencies in Detroit* (Y.), 151–61. Detroit: JWF, 1940.

Detroit: Yeshivah

Weinberg, S. D. "ישיבת בית יהודה„" (Yeshivath Beth Yehudah). In *Jewish Institutions and Agencies in Detroit* (Y.), 162–67. Detroit: JWF, 1940.

Detroit: Yiddish Schools

Biskin, Gabriel. "שול באוועגונג און קולטור דערגרייכונגען„" (The School Movement and Cultural Achievements). In *25th Jubilee of LZOA in Detroit, 1905–1930* (Y.), 8–15.

Farband Schools (LZOA). "יונג-לעבן„" (Young Life) (Y.). Collection of Student Writings.

Meyerowitz, Abraham. "די פאראייניקטע יידישע מיטלשול אין דעטראיט„" (The United Yiddish High School in Detroit). *Zuk* (Y.) (Mar. 1946): 224–.

Rosenshine, Jay. "History of the Sholem Aleichem Institute of Detroit." *MJH* 14 (June 1974): 9–20.

Segal, Samuel, and M. Blechman. "יובל-בוך פינף און צוואנציק יאר ארבעטער רינג שולן„" (Jubilee Book of 25 Years of WC Schools) (Y.). Detroit: WC Schools, 1944. 36 pp.

Shifris, Moshe. "די איצטיקע לאגע אין די דעטרויטער שולן„" (The Present Condition in the Detroit Schools). *Pro D* (Y.) (Feb. 1935): 19.

Weinberg, S. D. "די אידיש וועלטליכע שולען„" (The Yiddish Secular Schools). In *Jewish Institutions and Agencies in Detroit* (Y.), 168–81. Detroit: JWF, 1940.

Detroit: Newspapers

The Jewish American. Reform movement (as of Oct. 18, 1901), 1900–11. Weekly.

The Jewish Advocate. Young Men's Zion Association. 1904–?.

Detroit Jewish Chronicle. 1906–51 (later merged with *Detroit Jewish News*). Weekly.

Die Idishe Teglecher Presse (Y.). 1908–13. Daily. Also appeared in Cleveland.

Der Veg-Tageblat (Y.). Feb. 1919–Nov. 1920. Daily.

Detroit Jewish Guide (Y.). 1930–33. Weekly.

Detroit Jewish News. 1942–present. Weekly.

Flint

Mayer, Albert J. *Flint Jewish Population Study.* Flint: JCC, 1969.

Kalkaska County

Applebaum, Philip. "The Jews of Kalkaska County, Michigan." *MJH* 19 (Jan. 1979): 5–17.

Lansing

Jacobson, Daniel. "The Lansing Jewish Community: The Beginning." *MJH* 16 (Jan. 1976): 5–17.

Petoskey

Fryman, Zalman B. "Congregation B'nai Israel of Petoskey, Michigan." *MJH* 11 (July 1971): 4–12; 12 (Jan. 1972): 4–9.

Pontiac

Lapides, Abe. "History of the Jewish Community of Pontiac, Michigan." *MJH* 17 (July 1977): 3–10.

Sandusky

Leibowitz, Wendy. "Teaching Hebrew in Sandusky." *Moment* 10 (Dec. 1984): 48–51.

Southfield

Humanistic Judaism. 1986–present. Quarterly.

Traverse City

Stocker, Debra Steinberg, Bess Alper Deutsch, and Naomi Buchhalter Floch. "The History of the Traverse City Jewish Community." *MJH* 19 (June 1979): 13–33; and 20 (Jan. 1980): 4–19.

MINNESOTA

AJA. "Trailblazers . . ." 8 (Oct. 1956): 102–3.

"Minnesota." In *Post*, 253–59.

Plaut, W. Gunther. "How Zionism Came to Minnesota." *Herzl Yearbook* 5:221–35.

———. *The Jews in Minnesota*. AJHS, 1959. 347 pp.

———. "Teach Them Diligently." *The Jews in Minnesota*, 170–80. AJHS, 1959.

* Rapp, Michael G. *An Historical Overview of Anti-Semitism in Minnesota, 1920–1960*. U. of Minnesota, 1977

Sandler, P. „די געשיכטע פון דער יידישער געמיינדע אין מינעסאטא" (The History of the Jewish Community in Minnesota) (review of Plaut's *The Jews in Minnesota*). *CE* (Y.) 31 (Dec. 1967).

Schloff, Linda Mack. "Overcoming Geography: Jewish Religious Life in Four Market Towns." *Minnesota History* 51 (Spring 1988): 2–14.

Duluth

Eldot, Walter. "The Jews of Duluth, Minn." Unpublished (American Jewish Archives), 1955.

Engelman, Uriah Z. "Survey of Surveys—Duluth and Canton." *Jew Ed* (Nov. 1945): 31–33.

Gallin, Meyer. *Report and Recommendations on the Ida Cooke School*. N.Y.: AAJE, 1966.

Honor, Leo L., and Elias Picheny. *A Social, Recreational and Educational Survey of the Jewish Community of Duluth, 1944*. N.Y.: JWB and AAJE.

Papo, Joseph M. "A Study of the Jewish Community of Duluth." *JSSQ* 18 (Dec. 1941).

Minneapolis

American Jewish World. 1912–present. Weekly.

Cooper, Charles I. "The Jews of Minneapolis and Their Christian Neighbors." *JSS* 8 (1946): 33–38.

Danenbaum, Ruby. "A History of the Jews of Minneapolis." *Reform Advocate* (Nov. 16, 1907): 7–40.

* Gordon, Albert J. *The Jews of Minneapolis: A Study in Acculturation*. U. of Minnesota, 1948.

———. *Jews in Transition*. Minneapolis: U. of Minnesota, 1949.

Leventman, Seymour. "Zionism in Minneapolis." *Herzl Yearbook* 5 (1963): 237–46.

Lipman, Eugene J., and Albert Vorspan. "St. Paul and Minneapolis—Unlike Twins." In *Ten Cities*, 253–89.

Minda, Albert G. *The Story of Temple Israel, Minneapolis, Minnesota: A Personal Account*. Minneapolis: 1971. 138 pp.

Robison, Sophia M. "The Jewish Population of Minneapolis." In *Pop*, 152–59.

* Rutman, Herbert Samuel. *Defense and Development: A History of Minneapolis Jewry, 1930–1950*. U. of Minnesota, 1970.

Shabbosdige Post (Y., later E.). 1921–23.

Minneapolis: Education

Ben Tsemach, Sh. "דה גרשון יעקב גורדון ז״ל„ (Dr. Gershon Jacob Gordon). *Sh Hah* (H.) 5 (1945): 86–95.

Board of Directors of the Talmud Torah of Minneapolis, "A Tribute to the Memory of Dr. Gershon J. Gordon." *Jew Ed* 15 (Jan. 1944): 58.

Gelb, Sh. „על מוסדות החנוך העברײם במיניאפאליס" (On Jewish Educational Institutions in Minneapolis). *Sh Hah* (H.) 1 (1926): 83–85.

Kaiser, L. I. *Jewish Education in Minneapolis in 1944: A Survey*. Minneapolis: Talmud Torah, 1944.

———. "Minneapolis Is Different." *Jew Ed* 50 (Fall 1982): 34–38.

Minneapolis Talmud Torah. *Twenty-Five Years of Service to Jewish Youth*. 1938.

———. "סנסן„ (A Twig of a Palm Tree) (H.). 1923, 1926.

Pilch, Judah. "The Minneapolis Talmud Torah." *Jew Ed* 23 (Winter 1952): 6.

Ruffman, Louis L. *A Quantitative and Qualitative Analysis of Jewish Education in Minneapolis*. N.Y.: AAJE, 1957.

St. Paul

Chait, Marilyn J., and Chester Proshan. We Rolled up Our Sleeves: A History of the United Jewish Fund and Council and Its Beneficiary Agencies. St. Paul: United Jewish Fund and Council, 1985. 89 pp.

Frankel, Hiram D. "The Jews of St. Paul." *Reform Advocate* (Nov. 16, 1907): 41–53.

Gannes, Abraham P., Gene Greenzweig, and George Pollak. *A Study of Jewish Education in St. Paul, Minnesota, 1977–1978*. 150 pp.

Geer, Lois. *1981 Population Study of the St. Paul Jewish Community*. St. Paul: United Jewish Fund and Council, 198?.

Gordon, Yosi. "The Talmud Torah of St. Paul: A Picture of a Community School." *Ped Rep* 34 (Jan. 1988): 17–20.

Leibman, Morris. "Survey of Jewish Education in St. Paul." *Jew Ed* 7 (Apr.–June 1935): 98–100.

Lipman, Eugene J., and Albert Vorspan. "St. Paul and Minneapolis—Unlike Twins." In *Ten Cities*, 253–89.

Plaut, W. Gunther. *Mount Zion, 1856–1956*. St. Paul: Mt. Zion Congregation, 1956. 152 pp.

MISSISSIPPI

AJA. "Trailblazers . . ." 8 (Oct. 1956): 59–.

Braiterman, Marvin. "Mississippi Marrannos." *Mid* 10 (Sept. 1864): 30–35. Also in *JIS*, 351–59.

Brav, Stanley R. "Mississippi Incident." *Amer Jew Arc* 4 (1952): 59–65.

"Mississippi." In *Enc Jud*, 12:154–56.

"Mississippi." In *Post*, 260–67.

Turitz, Leo E., and Evelyn Turitz. *Jews in Early Mississippi*. Jackson: U. Press of Mississippi, 1983. 134 pp.

United States Works Project Administration, Mississippi Historical Records Survey Project. *Inventory of the Church and Synagogue Archives of Mississippi: Jewish Synagogues and Organization*. 1940.

Vicksburg

Brav, Stanley R. "Sampling Jewish Marriage Data." *JSS* 10 (1948): 71–72.

Phillipsborn, Gertrude. "The History of the Jewish Community of Vicksburg." 1969.

MISSOURI

AJA. "Trailblazers . . ." 8 (Oct. 1956): 61–67.

"Missouri." In *Enc Jud*, 12:156–58.

"Missouri." In *Post*, 267–81.

Kansas City

Adler, Frank J. *Roots in a Moving Stream: Congregation B'Nai Jehudah of Kansas City, 1870–1970*. Kansas City: Temple Congregation B'nai Jehudah, 1972. 466 pp.

Bell, William G. "The Kansas City Jewish Community, 1854–1954." Kansas City: Office of the Jewish Federation of Kansas City, 1954.

Beth Shalom Congregation. *Diamond Anniversary Book, 1878–1953*. Kansas City: 1953.

Feinman, Ethel R. "A History of the Jews of Kansas City." *Reform Advocate* (Mar. 28, 1908): 9–56.

Greater Kansas City Jewish Yearbook and Communal Register, 1921. Kansas City: United (Orthodox) Synagogues of Greater Kansas City, 1921.

Heiligman, Avron C. "The Demographic Perspective." In *Mid-America's Promise: A Profile of Kansas City Jewry*, edited by Joseph P. Schultz, 355–93. Kansas City: Jewish Community Foundation of Greater Kansas City and AJHS, 1982.

Guide to Jewish Life in Kansas City. Overland Park, Kans.: *Kansas City Jewish Chroncile*, 1987. 210 pp.

Kansas City Jewish Chronicle. 1920–present. Weekly.

Klausner, Carla L. "The Zionist Spectrum." In *Mid-America's Promise: A Profile of Kansas*

City Jewry, edited by Joseph P. Schultz, 81–145. Kansas City: Jewish Community Foundation of Greater Kansas City and AJHS, 1982.

Mayer, Albert. *A Study of Kansas City Jewry*. Kansas City: Jewish Federation of Kansas City, 1976.

Rosen, Michael J. "A History of the Religious Development of Kansas City Jewish Community." Master's thesis, U. of Oklahoma, 1968.

Sachs, Howard F. "Development of the Jewish Community of Kansas City, 1864–1908." *Missouri Historical Review* 60 (Apr. 1966): 350–60.

Schultz, Joseph P., ed. *Mid-America's Promise: A Profile of Kansas City Jewry*. Kansas City: Jewish Community Foundation of Greater Kansas City and AJHS, 1982. 405 pp.

Schultz, Joseph P., and J. Klausner. "Rabbi Simon Glazer and the Quest for Jewish Community in Kansas City, 1920–1923." *AJA* 35 (Apr. 1983): 13–26.

Shapiro, Mannheim S. *The Kansas City Survey of Jewish Attitudes*. N.Y.: AJC, 1967. 103 pp.

Tobin, Gary A. *A Demographic Survey of the Jewish Community of Greater Kansas City: Executive Summary*. Kansas City: Jewish Federation of Greater Kansas City, Summer 1986. 41 pp.

Kansas City: Education

Eisenberg, Yehuda, et al. *A Proposal for the Curriculum of the Hebrew Academy of Greater Kansas City* (H.). N.Y.: Department for Education and Culture, 1976. 19 pp.

Levitas, Irving. *Principles and Objectives of the Congregation B'nai Jehudah Religious School*. Kansas City: 1952.

Ruffman, Louis L. *Inquiry on the Need of a Central Educational Agency*. N.Y.: AAJE, 1962.

Schiff, Alvin I. *Audit of the Hebrew Program of the Hebrew Academy*. N.Y.: AAJE, 1969.

Schultz, Bella E. "Transmitting the Heritage: Jewish Education in Kansas City." In *Mid-America's Promise: A Profile of Kansas City Jewry*, edited by Joseph P. Schultz, 55–78. Kansas City: Jewish Community Foundation of Greater Kansas City and AJHS, 1982.

Kansas City: Educational Publications

Bikkurim (First Fruit) (H. and E.). Written by students of the Hebrew High School. First published 1927.

Glazer, Simon. *Guide of Judaism*. United Synagogue Schools (Orthodox).

———. *The Sabbath School Guide*. United Synagogue Schools (Orthodox), c. 1923.

St. Joseph

Levow, Mordecai. *Evaluation of the Community's Educational Program*. N.Y.: AAJE, 1969.

St. Louis

Bender, Avram B. "History of the Beth Ha-medrash Hagodol Congregation of St. Louis, 1879–1969." *Bulletin of the Missouri Historical Society* 17 (Oct. 1970): 64–89.

* Boxerman, Burton Alan. *Reaction of the St. Louis Jewish Community to Anti-Semitism*. St. Louis U., 1967.

———. "Rise of Antisemitism in St. Louis, 1933–1945." *YA* 14 (1969): 251–69.

Bronson, Rosalind Mael. *B'nai Amoona for All Generations*. St. Louis: Congregation B'Nai Amoona, 1982. 250 pp.

Ehrlich, Walter. "Jewish Historic Landmarks in St. Louis." *Gateway Heritage* 6 (Spring 1986): 2–15.

———. "Origins of the Jewish Community of St. Louis." *AJH* 77 (June 1988): 507–29.

Gorwitz, Kurt. "Jewish Mortality in St. Louis and St. Louis County." *JSS* 24 (Oct. 1962): 248–54.

Lang, Sheryl. "Fulfilling the American Dream: Jewish Life in St. Louis." *Gateway Heritage* 7 (Summer 1986): 10–17.

Makovsky, D. I. "Origin and Early History of United Hebrew Congregation of St. Louis, 1841–1859." Master's thesis, Washington U., 1958.

———. *The Phillipsons: The First Jewish Settlers in St. Louis, 1807–1858*. 1959.

"St. Louis." In *Enc Jud*, 14:662–66.

Tobin, Gary. *A Demographic and Attitudinal Study of the Jewish Community of St. Louis*. St. Louis: Jewish Federation, 1982. 239 pp.

———. "Jewish Population Movements in St. Louis." *Gateway Heritage* 7 (Fall 1986): 32–41.

St. Louis: Education

Dinin, Samuel, Walter Ackerman, Alvin I. Schiff, and Saul Spiro. *Report on the Status of Jewish Education in St. Louis.* N.Y.: AAJE, 1966. 72 pp.

Fish, Isidore, Louis Schwartzman, and Howard M. Graber. "Communal Jewish Education in St. Louis." *Jew Ed* 44 (Summer 1975): 22–25.

———. *Goals of the Study Program in Hebrew School.* St. Louis: BJE.

Honor, Leo L. *Preliminary Report on Associated Hebrew Schools.* St. Louis: Jewish Federation, 1939.

———. *Supplementary Report on Survey of Jewish Education: Distribution of Child Population.* St. Louis: Jewish Federation, 1943.

Modern View. "The Jewish Charitable and Educational Union in St. Louis." Apr. 5, 1907.

Kellner, Abraham H. "A Community School in St. Louis." *Jew Parent* 11 (Oct. 1959).

Rosenberg, Dan S. *Statistical Survey of Jewish Education.* St. Louis: Committee on Jewish Education, 1945.

Zack, B. G. „אידיש, אידישע דערציאונג און אונדזער חוב צו זיך אליין" (Yiddish, Yiddish Education and Our Obligation to Ourselves). *The Jewish Record* (Y.) (Sept. 13, 1947).

St. Louis: Educational Publications

Board of Jewish Education of Greater St. Louis. *Program Studies for Sunday Morning Sessions.* St. Louis: 1961. High school.

The Council News. Jewish Youth Council of St. Louis, first published Oct. 1933. Monthly.

Flexer, Jacob. *The Path to Judaism for School and Home.* St. Louis: 1927. 197 pp.

Silber, Mendel. *The Scripture Stories Retold for Young Israel.* St. Louis: Modern View Pub. Co., 1914. 80 pp.

Ury, Zalman F. *Curriculum of Rabbi H. I. Epstein Hebrew Academy of St. Louis* (H.). St. Louis: 1955–56. 37 pp. Day school.

St. Louis: Newspapers

The Jewish Voice. 1879–192?. Weekly.

Modern View. 1901–194?. Weekly.

The Jewish Record (Y. and E.). 1913–195?.

Jewish Tribune. 1943–195?. Monthly.

St. Louis Jewish Light. 1947–present. Semi-weekly.

Missouri Jewish Post. 1948–present. Weekly.

MONTANA

AJA. "Trailblazers . . ." 8 (Oct. 1956): 109–11.

Kelson, Benjamin. "The Jews of Montana." Master's thesis, Montana State U., 1950.

———. "The Jews of Montana." *WSJH* 3 (Jan. 1971): 113–20, (Apr. 1971): 170–89, (July 1971): 227–42; 4 (Oct. 1971): 35–49, (Jan. 1972): 101–12.

Levinson, Robert. "Julius Basinski: Pioneer Montana Merchant." *YA* 14 (1969): 219–33.

"Montana." In *Post*, 281–89.

Billings

Horowitz, Samuel. *History of Billings Jewish Community, 1954–1975.* Billings: 1974.

Helena

Coleman, Julie L. "Some Jews of Early Helena, Montana." *Rocky Mountain Jewish Historical Notes* 2 (Mar. 1979).

WSJH. "Jewish Beginnings in Helena, Montana" (1879) (newspaper account). 13 (Oct. 1980): 24–25.

Leaphart, Susan, ed. "Frieda and Belle Fligelman: A Frontier-City Girlhood in the 1890's." *Montana: The Magazine of Western History* 32 (Summer 1982): 85–92.

Stern, Norton B. "Helena, Montana Jewry Responds to a French Appeal in 1868" (the Mortara Case). *WSJH* 11 (Jan. 1979): 170–72.

NEBRASKA

AJA. "Trailblazers . . ." 8 (Oct. 1956): 111–21.

Pollak, Oliver B. "The Impact of Spiritual Identity on Communal Organization—Jews in Nebraska." *Nebraska Humanist* 6 (Fall 1983): 20–25.

"Nebraska." In *Enc Jud*, 12:911–12.

"Nebraska." In *Post*, 289–92.

Lincoln

Newmark, Maurice A. "Beginnings of the Pioneer Congregation of Lincoln, Nebraska." *WSJH* 14 (Oct. 1981): 45–49.

Omaha

Bernstein, Nathan. "The Story of Omaha Jews." *Reform Advocate* (May 2, 1908).

Bittner, David. "Hebraic Mortar: The Strength of a Community—A Short History of the Jewish Federation of Omaha, 1903–1983." *Nebraska Jewish Historical Society* 2 (Summer 1986).

University of Nebraska at Omaha Center for Applied Research. *Demographic Survey of the Omaha Jewish Community: Prepared for the Omaha Jewish Federation.* Omaha: 1976.

Dushkin, Alexander M. *Report of the Jewish Educational Situation in Omaha, Nebraska.* N.Y.: Bureau of Social Research, 1929.

Engelman, Uriah Z. *Evaluation of Enrollment, Programming, and Children's Attitudes in the Jewish Schools.* N.Y.: AAJE, 1957.

Gendler, Carol. "The First Synagogue in Nebraska: The Early History of the Congregation Israel of Omaha." *Nebraska History* 58 (Fall 1977): 323–41.

———. "A History of the Jews of Omaha." Master's thesis, U. of Omaha, 1967.

———. "The Jews of Omaha: The First Sixty Years." *WSJH* 5 (Apr. 1973): 205–24, (July 1973): 288–305; 6 (Oct. 1973): 58–71, (Jan. 1974): 141–54, (Apr. 1974): 222–33, (July 1974): 293–304.

Honor, Leo L. *Jewish Education in Omaha, Nebraska.* 1938.

Jewish Press. 1921–present. Weekly.

Pollak, Oliver B. "Communal Self Help and Capital Formation: Omaha's Jewish Loan Association, 1911–1979." *AJH* 78 (Sept. 1988): 20–35.

———. "The Jewish Peddlers of Omaha." *Nebraska History* 63 (Winter 1982): 474–501.

Rosenbaum, Jonathan. "Hebrew By-Laws of a Synagogue in Omaha, Nebraska" (1908). *Amer Jew Arc* 36 (Apr. 1984): 50–56.

Somberg, Suzanne Richards, and Sylvia Greene Roffman. *Consider the Years, 1871–1971: Congregation of Temple Israel, Omaha, Nebraska.* Omaha: 1971. 80 pp.

NEVADA

AJA. "Trailblazers . . ." 8 (Oct. 1956): 103–5.

Marschal, John P. "Jews in Nevada: 1850–1900." *J of the West* 23 (1984): 62–72.

"Nevada." In *Post*, 293–98.

Stern, Norton B. "The Jewish Community of a Nevada Mining Town." *WSJH* 15 (Oct. 1982): 45–78.

Stern, Norton B., and William M. Kramer. "An American Zion in Nevada: The Rise and Fall of An Agricultural Colony." *WSJH* 13 (Jan. 1981): 130–34.

Las Vegas

Jewish Reporter. 1976–present. Monthly.

Las Vegas Israelite. 1965–present. Biweekly.

NEW HAMPSHIRE

"New Hampshire." In *Enc Jud*, 12:1024–25.

"New Hampshire." In *Post*, 299–303.

NEW JERSEY

American Jews' Annual. "Jewish Colonies in New Jersey." (1893): 58, 87.

37 LOCAL SOURCES FOR JEWISH EDUCATION

NEW JERSEY

Bailey, Sidney, ed. *Yoval: A Symposium Upon the 50 years of the Jewish Farming Colonies of Alliance, Norm, and Brotmarville, New Jersey*. Phila.: 1932.

Brandes, George. *Immigrants to Freedom: Jewish Communities in Rural New Jersey since 1892*. Phila.: U. of Pennsylvania Press, 1971. 424 pp.

De Bella, Elliot R. *1951—An Analysis of Elementary Yeshiva School: Principals' and Faculties' Perceived Leadership Behavior and Organizational Climate in New Jersey and the New York City Burroughs of Brooklyn, Manhattan and Staten Island*. 1984.

* Douglas, Martin I. *Chronological Summary of Annotated Cards toward the History of the Jewish Agricultural Communities in South Jersey*. JTS, 1960.

Ducoff, Bernard. "Seventy Years of Jewish Schooling in New Jersey." *Jew Ed* 51 (Fall 1983): 27–30.

Federal Writers' Project, N.J. Ethnic Survey. "The Jews in New Jersey." Ms. 1940, N.J. State Archives.

Friedenberg, Albert M. "The Jews of New Jersey from the Earliest Times to 1850." *PAJHS* 17 (1909): 33–43.

Goldstein, P. R. *Social Aspects of the Jewish Colonies of South Jersey*. 1921.

Haberman, Joshua O. "The Jews in New Jersey, 1702–1953." Unpublished (American Jewish Archives).

Mounier, Louis. "Glimpses of Jewish Life in the Colonies of Southern New Jersey." *Vineland Historical Magazine* (Apr. 1956): 477–85.

"New Jersey." In *Enc Jud*, 12:1027–30.

"New Jersey." In *Post*, 303–29.

Patt, Ruth Marcus. *New Jersey Jewish History: A Bibliographical Guide*. New Brunswick: Jewish Historical Society of Central Jersey, 1984. 27 pp.

———. *New Jersey Jewish History: A Bibliographical Guide*. 2d ed. East Brunswick: Historical Society of Central Jersey, 1987. 31 pp.

Shtadlan, I. Z., and Batyah Shtadlan. „כנוס בניו-ג'ורסי" חנוכי (An Educational Conference in New Jersey). *Sh Hah* (H.) 18 (Spring 1958).

Stainsby, William. *The Jewish Colonies of South Jersey*. Trenton: Bureau of Statistics, 1901.

* Werb, Morris. *Jewish Suburbia—An Historical and Comparative Study of Jewish Communities in Three New Jersey Suburbs*. New York U., 1959.

Alliance

Herscher, Uri D. "Alliance" (agricultural colony). *In JAUA*, 73–83.

Levin, T. Harry. "History of Alliance, New Jersey, First Jewish Agricultural Settlement in the United States." *Vineland Historical Magazine* 54 (1978): 1–14.

Atlantic City

Jewish Record. 1939–present. Weekly.

National Jewish Ledger. 1927–193?. Weekly.

Beth Israel Congregation. "The Story of Beth Israel Congregation in Atlantic City, N.J., 1890–1951." American Jewish Archives. Unpublished.

Atlantic City

Benathen, Morris B. *Survey of Jewish Education in Atlantic County, New Jersey*. N.Y.: AAJE, 1966. 51 pp.

Bayonne

Eigns (Our Own) (Y.). 1935–194?. Bimonthly.

Engelman, Uriah Z. *Study of School System*. N.Y.: AAJE, 1949.

Jersey Voice (Y. and E.). 1926–193?. Weekly.

Schnitzer, Henry L. *The Goodly Tent: The First Fifty Years of Temple Emanu-El*. Bayonne: Temple Emanu-El, 1961. 88 pp.

Bergen County

Young Men's Hebrew Association of Bergen County. *A Survey of the Jewish Population of Bergen County*. Hackensack: 1963. 25 pp.

Camden

Engelman, Uriah Z. *Survey of Jewish Education in Camden, New Jersey*. N.Y.: AAJE, 1957.

Kaplan, Louis L. *Jewish Education in Camden, New Jersey*. N.Y.: AAJE, 1947.

Pollak, George, Martin Goldstein, Fannie Chipman, and Estelle Feldman. *Camden: Self-Study of Jewish Education*. N.Y.: AAJE, June 1971.

Rosen, Ben. *Survey of Jewish Education in Camden, New Jersey*. N.Y.: Bureau of Jewish Social Research, n.d.

Westoff, Charles F. *Population and Social Characteristics of the Jewish Community of the Camden Area*. Cherry Hill: Jewish Community of Camden County, 1965.

Cherry Hill

Jewish Community Voice. 1941–present. Biweekly.

East Orange

Journal of Jewish Communal Service. 1899–present. Quarterly.

Elizabeth

Gale, Joseph, ed. *Eastern Union: The Development of a Jewish Community*. Elizabeth: Jewish Culture Council of Eastern Union County, N.J., 1958. 122 pp.

Jewish Record. 1930–194?. Weekly.

Essex County

(See also Newark)

Jewish Education Association. *Curriculum for Congregational Schools*. Newark: 1945. 16 pp.

Engelman, Uriah Z. *Blueprint for Community-Directed Jewish Education*. N.Y.: AAJE, 1948.

Gelbart, Gerson, Sylvan H. Kohn, and David Rudavsky. *A History of the Jewish Community in Essex County, New Jersey* (text for religious schools). Newark: Jewish Education Association of Essex County, 1955. 76 pp.

Robison, Sophia M. *The Jewish Population of Essex County: Report of the Survey Committee on Jewish Education, Group Work and Jewish Population, Part I*. Newark: JCC.

Farmingdale

Dubrovsky, Gertrude W. "The Rural Experience of Jews in Farmingdale, N.J." In *New Jersey Ethnic Heritage*, 36–58. Trenton: Historical Commission, 1978.

Hackensack

Jewish Standard. 1931–present. Weekly.

Highland Park

Jewish Journal/Jewish Voice. 1956–86 (merged in 1985). Semimonthly.

Montclair

* Schnitzer, Jeshia. *A Human Relations Center in the Synagogue*. Columbia U., 1954.

Newark

(See also Essex County)

Bierman, Michael A. "A History of the Development of the Religious, Cultural and Community Institutions of Newark, New Jersey." Master's thesis, Brandeis U., 1972.

Bortniker, Elijah, et al. *Outline of Studies for the First Year of the Congregational Hebrew School*. Newark: Jewish Education Council, 1957. 44 pp.

Chipkin, Israel S. *Survey of Jewish Education in Newark*.

Jewish Chronicle. 1921–194?. Weekly.

Jewish Education Association of Newark. *Your Child*. First published 1952.

Jewish News. 1947–197?. Weekly.

Kussy, Nathan. "An Early History of the Jews of Newark." In *The Jewish Community Blue Book of Newark*. Newark: Jewish Community Blue Book Publishing Co., 1926.

———. "History of the Jews of Newark, New Jersey—Civil War to 1941." *Newark Jewish Chronicle* (June 20, 1941): 25–31, 44–45.

Kussy, Sarah. "Reminiscences of Jewish Life in Newark, N.J." *YA* 6 (1951): 177–86.

Newark, The Jewish Men's Club. *The Conditions of Jewish Education in Newark: An Investigation*. Newark: 1908.

Shapiro, Edward S. "Ethnicity and Employment: The Early Years of the Jewish Vocational Service of Newark, 1939–51." *New Jersey History* 106 (Spring/Summer 1988): 19–39.

Stavitsky, Michael A. "New Trends in Community Programs—Newark, New Jersey." *Jew Ed* 19 (Summer 1948): 17–22, 26.

New Brunswick

Colodner, Solomon. *Survey on Consolidation of Smaller Schools*. N.Y.: AAJE, 1959.

Ferman, Arlene, and Judy Kane, eds. *The Jewish Scene of New Jersey: A History and Activity Book*. New Brunswick: Jewish Historical Society of Central Jersey, 1984. 49 pp.

Paramus

Meier, Menachem. "The Mechina Program of the Frisch School" (day school). *Ped Rep* 23 (Mar. 1972): 7.

Passaic

Der Friend (Y.). 1910–195?. Monthly.

Jewish Tribune of Passaic. 1930–195?. Weekly.

Passaic Jewish Community Council. *Jewish Roots: A History of the Jewish Community of Passaic and Environs*. Tercentenary Committee of the JCC of Passaic, Clifton and Vicinity, 1959. 131 pp. See pp. 2–33 for Jewish education.

Robison, Sophia M. "The Jewish Population of Passaic, 1937." In *Pop*, 23–36.

Ruffman, Louis L. *Jewish Education in Passaic*. N.Y.: AAJE, 1946.

Paterson

Chipkin, Israel S., and Jack M. Horden. *Report of Survey of the Jewish Education Situation in Paterson*. N.Y; AAJE, 1943.

Engelman, Uriah Z. "Survey of Surveys: Paterson and Trenton." *Jew Ed* 18 (Summer 1947): 49–53.

Jewish Folk School. LZOA, "שול בוך„ (School Book) (Y.) (Student publication). Paterson: 1930–31. 29 pp.

Jewish Post. 1928–4?. Weekly.

Verbit, Marvin F. *Characteristics of a Jewish Community: The Demographic and Judaic Profiles of the Jews in the Area Served by the Jewish Federation of North Jersey*. Paterson: Jewish Federation of North Jersey, 1971. 115 pp.

Perth Amboy

Furer, Max. *Jewish Education in Perth Amboy*. AAJE, 1945.

Raritan Valley

Patt, Ruth Marcus. *The Jewish Scene in New Jersey's Raritan Valley, 1698–1948*. New Brunswick: Jewish Historical Society of Raritan Valley, 1978. 112 pp.

Rutgers

Patt, Ruth Marcus. *The Jewish Experience at Rutgers*. East Brunswick: Historical Society of Central Jersey, 1987. 108 pp.

Scotch Plains

Jewish Horizon. 1981–present. Weekly.

Teaneck

Applebaum, Jay Zacharia. *The History of the Jews in Teaneck*. Teaneck: JCC, 1977. 247 pp.

Bortniker, Elijah. *Study of the Jewish Community Center Religious Schools*. N.Y.: AAJE, 1969.

Trenton

Engelman, Uriah Z. "Survey of Surveys: Paterson and Trenton." *Jew Ed* 18 (Summer 1947): 49–53.

Goelman, Elazar. *Evaluation of the Day School*. N.Y.: AAJE, 1960.

Robison, Sophia M. "The Jewish Population of Trenton, 1937." In *Pop*, 10–21.

———. "Some Characteristics of Trenton and Passaic Jews." *JSS* 2 (1940): 249–54.

Rosen, Ben. "Recent Surveys of Jewish Education—Trenton." *Jew Ed* 2 (June 1930): 83–84.

Rudavsky, David. *Report on the Jewish Education Survey in Trenton*. N.Y.: AAJE, 1944.

Sterne, Richard S. *A Demographic Study of the Jewish Population of Trenton, New Jersey and Vicinity*. Trenton: Jewish Federation of Trenton, 1961.

Teicher, Paul. *Dr. Herzl Zion Hebrew School: 1883–1946, an Afternoon School; 1946–1965, a Day School*. Trenton: 1965.

Ventnor

Spotts, Leon H. *Survey of the Beth Judah Religious School.* N.Y.: AAJE, 1969.

Vineland

Centennial, 1861–1961. City of Vineland, 1961.

The Jewish Day School of Vineland, Yeshiva Yesod Hatorah, the Tenth Anniversary (E. and Y.). 1967.

Wayne

Stark, Rodney, and Stephen Steinberg. *It Did Happen Here: An Investigation of Political Anti-Semitism, Wayne, New Jersey, 1967.* N.Y.: ADL, 1967. 32 pp.

Westfield

Averick, Evelyn. *A Historic Narrative: The Story of Temple Emanu-El, 1950–1980.* Westfield, N.J.: 1981. 100 pp.

West Orange

Kramer, Sylvia. *Images of Metrowest, 1985.* West Orange: YM–YWHA of Metropolitan N.J., 1986.

Lowenstein, Amy. *One Hundred Years of the "Y," 1877–1977.* West Orange: 1977.

Woodbine

Herscher, Uri D. "Woodbine" (agricultural colony). In *JAUA*, 83–107.

Joseph, Samuel. "Woodbine." In *History of the Baron De Hirsch Fund: The Americanization of the Jewish Immigrant*, 48–115. Phila.: JPS, 1935.

NEW MEXICO

AJA. "Trailblazers . . ." 8 (Oct. 1956): 81–86.

Fierman, Floyd S. "Peddlers and Merchants on the Southwest Frontier 1850–1880." *Password* 8 (Summer 1963): 43–55.

———. "The Spiegelbergs: Pioneer Merchants and Bankers in the Southwest." *JSS* 56 (June 1967): 371–451.

Meketa, Jacqueline Dorgan. *Louis Felsenthal: Citizen-Soldier of Territorial New Mexico.* Albuquerque: U. of New Mexico, 1982. 152 pp.

"New Mexico." In *Enc Jud*, 12:1037–39.

"New Mexico." In *Post*, 330–39.

Parish, W. J. *The German Jew and the Commercial Revolution in Territorial New Mexico, 1850–1900.* 1960.

———. "The German Jew and the Commercial Revolution in Territorial New Mexico, 1850–1900." *New Mexico Historical Review* 35 (Jan. 1960): 1–29, (Apr. 1960): 129–50.

Albuquerque

WSJH. "First Synagogue at Albuquerque—1900" (newspaper account). 11 (Oct. 1978): 46–48.

Las Vegas

Livingstone, John. "The Jewish Community of Las Vegas, New Mexico, 1884–1889." *Rocky Mountain Historical Notes* 3 (Jan. 1981).

Stern, Norton B. "A Glimpse of Organized Jewry of Las Vegas, New Mexico, during Its Peak Years." *WSJH* 15 (Jan. 1983): 161–66.

Los Alamos

Shinedling, Abraham I. *History of the Los Alamos Jewish Center, 1944–1957.* Albuquerque: 1958. 68 pp.

Sperling, Paul. "Jews of Early Los Alamos: A Memoir." *WSJH* 18 (July 1986): 355–61.

NEW YORK

Huehner, Leon. "Naturalization of Jews in New York under the Act of 1740." *PAJHS* 13 (1905): 1–5.

Kohler, Max J. "Beginnings of New York Jewish History." *PAJHS* 1 (1893): 44–48.

———. "Civil Status of the Jews in Colonial New York." *PAJHS* 6 (1897): 83–106.

Marcus, Jacob R. "New Amsterdam—1654–1664." In *EAJ*, 1:24–33.

37 LOCAL SOURCES FOR JEWISH EDUCATION

NEW YORK

———. "New York—1664–1755." In *EAJ*, 1:34–72.

———. "New York—1755–1784." In *EAJ*, 1:73–101.

"New York." In *Post*, 339–346.

Phillips, N. Taylor. "Items Relating to the History of the Jews of New York." *PAJHS* 11 (1903): 149–61.

Postal, Bernard, and Lionel Koppman. *Jewish Landmarks in New York*. N.Y.: Hill and Wang, 1964. 277 pp.

Vaxer, Menassah. "Naturalization Roll of Jews of New York (1740–1759)." *PAJHS* 37 (1947): 369–89.

Albany

Albany Jewish World. 1965–present. Weekly.

Engelman, Uriah Z. *Jewish Communal Survey of Albany—Jewish Education*. N.Y.: AAJE and CJFWF, 1947.

Silver, Louis. "The Jews in Albany, New York, 1655–1914." *YA* 9 (1954): 213–46. First Published in *Yivo Annual* (Y.), edited by Shatzky and Mokdoni, 1:117–54.

Binghamton

Sussman, Lance J. *Beyond the Catskills: Jewish Life in Binghamton, New York, 1850–1975*. State U. of New York at Binghamton, 1989. 40 pp.

Buffalo

Adler, Delia Rubenstein. "Immigrants in Buffalo." *AJA* 18 (1966): 20.

Adler, Selig, and Thomas F. Connely. *From Ararat to Suburbia: The History of the Jewish Community of Buffalo*. Phila.: JPS, 1960. 498 pp.

Allen, Lewis T. "The Founding of the City of Ararat on Grand Island by Mordecai M. Noah." *Publications of the Buffalo Historical Society* 1 (1879): 305–28.

American Jews' Annual. "The New Temple." (1890–91): 105.

Arywitz, Annette F. *A Short History of the Jewish Community Service of Buffalo*. Master's thesis, U. of Buffalo, 1948.

Buffalo Jewish Review. 1918–present. Weekly.

Engelman, Uriah Z. "Demographic Note on Jewish Families in Buffalo." *JSS* (Oct. 1941): 399–408.

———. "The Jewish Population of Buffalo, 1938." In *Pop*, 37–50.

———. *A Study of the Size of Families in the Jewish Population of Buffalo*. U. of Buffalo Studies 16 (Nov. 1938): 64 pp.

Falk, Simon. "A History of the Israelites in Buffalo." *Publications of the Buffalo Historical Society* 1 (1879): 289–304.

Goldberg, Isaac. *Major Noah: American Jewish Pioneer*. Phila.: 1936. 316 pp.

Gordis, Robert. "Mordecai Manuel Noah: A Centenary Evaluation." *PAJHS* 41 (Sept. 1951): 1–26.

The Hebrew Standard (N.Y.C. weekly). "The Jewish Community of Buffalo." Nov. 16, 1906.

Sarna, Jonathan D. *Jacksonian Jew: The Two Worlds of Mordecai Noah*. N.Y.: Holmes and Meier, 1981. 233 pp.

Temple Beth El's First Century—Centennial Souvenir Book. Buffalo: Temple Beth El, 1947.

Warner, Eugene, et al. *Fiftieth Anniverary First Temple Beth Zion, 1865–1915; Twenty-Fifth Anniversary Present Temple, 1890–1915; Dedication of the Temple Centre, 1915*. Buffalo: Temple Beth Zion, 1915.

Weinryb, Bernard D. "Noah's Ararat Jewish State in its Historical Setting." *PAJHS* 43 (Mar. 1954): 170–91.

Buffalo: Education

Engelman, Uriah Z. *Distributional and Demographic Study of Jewish Education in Buffalo*. N.Y.: AAJE, 1957.

———. *Evaluation of the Role of the Bureau in Jewish Education*. N.Y.: AAJE, 1938.

———. "New Trends in Jewish Education in Buffalo." *Jew Ed* 16 (Sept. 1944): 39–42.

* Gitin, Louis. *The Development of a Reform Jewish Religious School, Buffalo, New York, 1864–1953*. State U. of New York at Buffalo, 1954. 133 pp.

Hurwich, Louis. *A Survey of Jewish Education in Buffalo*. N.Y.: Bureau of Jewish Social Research, 1929.

Klein, Aaron. "A History of Jewish Education in Buffalo." *Jew Ed* 14 (Apr.–June 1942): 28–32, 35.

———. "החנוך היהודי בבופאלו„ (Jewish Education in Buffalo). *Sh Hah* (H.) 2 (Spring 1942): 97–100, (June 1942): 203–9.

Plesur, Milton. "The Bureau of Jewish Education of Greater Buffalo, 1929–1979." *Jew Ed* 47 (Summer 1979): 41–45.

Pollak, George. "The Buffalo Population Study." *Jew Ed* 46 (Summer 1978): 16–22.

Resnik, Reuben. "Religious Education in Buffalo and Erie County." *Rel Ed* 56 (Sept.–Oct. 1961): 348–50.

Rosen, Ben. "Recent Surveys of Jewish Education—Buffalo." *Jew Ed* 2 (June 1930): 85–88.

———. *A Survey of Jewish Education in Buffalo, 1929*. N.Y.: Bureau of Jewish Social Research, 1929.

Silverman, Morris. *The Junior Congregation*. Buffalo: BJE, 1937.

Steinberg, Samuel. *Study of Post Elementary Jewish Educationi Buffalo*. N.Y.: AAJE, 1968.

Ithaca

* Sargent, Edward N. *Religious Knowledge of High School Seniors: Specific Facts Known Concerning Catholicism, Judaism, and Protestantism as Revealed by Tests in the Ithaca High School in the Year 1951–52*. Cornell U., 1954.

Mamaroneck

* Koslowe, I. *The Jewish Community of Mamaroneck*. Yeshiva U., 1962.

Massena

Friedman, Lee M. "The Murder at Massena." In *Pilgrims in a New Land*, 109–16. 1948.

Friedman, Saul S. *The Incident at Massena: The Blood Libel in America*. N.Y.: Stein and Day, 1978. 216 pp.

Newburgh

Kessler, Aaron. *Survey of Jewish Education in Newburgh, New York*. N.Y.: AAJE, 1947.

Rudavsky, David. *Report to Upgrade Instructional Content, to Establish Feasible Facilities, and to Develop Secondary Education*. N.Y.: AAJE, 1947.

NEW YORK CITY follows New York State.

Plainview

Lipman, Eugene J., and Albert Vorspan. "Plainview—From Potatoes to Rhubarb." In *Ten Cities*, 231–52. 1962.

Rochester

Jewish Community Council of Rochester. *The Jewish Population of Rochester, New York, 1961*. Rochester: JCC, 1964.

———. *The Jewish Population of Rochester, New York, 1980*. Rochester: Jewish Community Federation, 74 pp.

Jewish Ledger. 1924–present. Weekly.

Karp, Abraham J. "An East European Congregation on American Soil: Beth Israel, Rochester, New York, 1874–1886." In *A Bicentennial for Jacob Rader Marcus*, edited by B. W. Korn, 263–302. 1976.

———. "Simon Tuska Becomes a Rabbi." In *The Jewish Experience in America*, 2:316–34. Waltham, Mass.: AJHS, 1969.

McKelvey, Blake. "The Jews of Rochester: A Contribution to Their History during the Nineteenth Century." *PAJHS* 50 (Sept. 1950): 57–73.

Phillips, Sam. "The Jewish Population in Rochester, New York." Master's thesis, Western Reserve U., 1938.

* Rosenberg, Stuart E. *The Jewish Community in Rochester, 1843–1925*. Columbia U., 1954. (Published by Columbia U. Press.)

———. "Jewish Population Growth in Rochester, 1843–1938." *PAJHS* 49 (June 1955): 237–39.

Wile, Isaac. *The Jews of Rochester*. Rochester: 1938.

Rochester: Education

Diamond, Joseph. *Evaluation of Structure and Content of Jewish Education in Rochester*. N.Y.: 1945.

Elkins, Dov Peretz. *Clarifying Jewish Values.* Rochester: Growth Associates, 1977.

Engelman, Uriah Z. *Study of the Educational System in Rochester.* N.Y.: AAJE, 1955.

Fix, Elliot. "The Rochester Special Class Program." *Ped Rep* 31 (Fall 1979): 28–30.

NCSJW. *A Community Study of Rochester.* Jewish Education Section, 1944.

Pilch, Judah. "A Community Agency for Jewish Education—Five Years in Rochester." *Jew Ed* 16 (Jan. 1945): 23–28.

Rosen, Ben. *Survèy of Jewish Education in Rochester.* 1938.

Schiff, Alvin I., et al. *Rochester: A Design for Jewish Education.* N.Y.: AAJE, 1975.

Workmen's Circle School. *Jubilee Journal* (Y.). On the 3rd Year of the WC Mothers' Club (1926–29). Rochester: 1930.

Schenectady

BJE. *Developing a Curriculum for the Schools* (Sunday schools). Prepared by Ben Hurowitz. With teachers' manual. Rev. ed. Schenectady: 1957. 127 pp.

Dinsky, Samuel H. "The Schenectady Plan for Jewish Education." *Jew Ed* 23 (Winter 1952): 19–29.

Schenectady, N.Y. *Hebrew School Curriculum.* Schenectady: BJE, 1949. 5 pp.

Suffolk

Eisenberg, Yehuda, ed. *Curriculum Program—Hebrew Academy of Suffolk County* (H.). N.Y.: Greater N.Y. BJE, 1977. 76 pp.

* Ness, Levi. *Jewish Attitudes of the 1979 Graduates of Suffolk Conservative Afternoon Schools.* Yeshiva U., 1980. 260 pp.

Syracuse

Contemporary Jewish Record. "The Newport and Syracuse Celebrations." 3 (Jan.–Feb. 1940): 50–52.

Davis, Barbara Sheklin. *A History of the Jewish Community of Syracuse.* Syracuse: Jewish Federation, 1986.

Jewish Observer. 1978–present. Biweekly.

* Mesinger, Jonathan. *The Jewish Community in Syracuse, 1850–1880: The Growth and Structure of an Urban Ethnic Region.* Syracuse U., 1977.

Provol, William Lee. "Growing Up in Syracuse." *AJA* 1 (Apr. 1964): 22–40.

Rudolph, B. G. *From a Minyan to a Community: A History of the Jews of Syracuse.* Syracuse: Syracuse U., 1970. 314 pp.

Syracuse: Education

Engelman, Uriah Z. "Survey of Surveys—Louisville, Dallas, Syracuse." *Jew Ed* 17 (June 1946): 45–48.

Pilch, Judah. *Survey of Jewish Education—Syracuse.* Syracuse: JWF, 1945.

Rosen, Ben. *Jewish Education in Syracuse.* N.Y.: 1938.

Syracuse BJE. *Curriculum of the Syracuse Talmud Torah Department.* 1948. 6 pp.

Ulster County

Pool, David de Sola. "The Jewish Colony of Ulster County, New York, 1838." *PAJHS* 23 (1915): 178–79.

Utica

Jewish Community Council of Utica. *Jewish Community Self-Study of Utica, New York.* Utica: 1948.

Jewish Community Council of Utica. Utica: 1943.

Kohn, S. Joshua. *The Jewish Community of Utica, New York, 1847–1948.* N.Y.: AJHS, 1959. 221 pp.

Lipnick, Jerome. "Jewish Community of Utica." *Recon* 17 (Jan. 25, 1952): 17–21; 18 (May 2, 1952): 17–21.

Temple Beth El through 25 Years, 1919–1945. Utica: 1945.

Washington Heights

Lowenstein, Steven M. *Frankfurt on the Hudson—The German-Jewish Community of Washington Heights, 1933–1983: Its Structure and Culture.* Detroit: Wayne State U. Press, 1989. 347 pp.

———. "The German-Jewish Community of Washington Heights." *Leo Baeck Institute Yearbook* 30 (1985): 245–54.

Westchester

Arian, Philip. „סקירה על פעולות חיצוניות בבתי ספר העברי, בווסצעסטר קונטי" (A Survey on Extra Curricular Activities in Hebrew Schools in Westchester County) (H.). JTS, 1943.

Hurwitz, R. S. "The Westchester Experiment in the Jewish Education of Children." *Menorah J* 25 (Apr.–June 1937): 195–207.

Maurer, Herrymon. "The Yeshiva Comes to Westchester." *Commentary* 7 (Apr. 1949): 319–27.

White Plains

Kurzband, Toby. *Developing a Curriculum for a Jewish Religious School*. White Plains: JCC, 1958. 124 pp.

Lipman, H. T. *The White Plains Jewish Attitudes Survey*. N.Y.: 1958.

Woodbridge

Dinsky, Samuel. *Study of the Woodbridge Jewish Center*. N.Y.: AAJE, 1964.

Yonkers

Klausner, Abraham J. *A Child's Prayer Book for Rosh Hashanah and Yom Kippur*. Yonkers: Emanu-El Publications, ca. 1974. 82 pp.

New York City (NYC)

(See also New York State)

NYC: History

Abelow, Samuel P. *History of Brooklyn Jewry*. Brooklyn: Scheba Pub. Co., 1937. 344 pp.

AJYB. "Jewish Trade Unions in the City of New York." 31 (1929–30): 203–4.

Bercovici, Konrad. "Greatest Jewish City in the World." *The Nation* (Sept. 12, 1923): 259–61.

Bernard, Jacqueline. *The Children You Gave Us: A History of 150 Years of Service to Children* (New York City's orphanages). N.Y.: Jewish Child Care Association of New York, 1973. 186 pp.

* Berrol, Selma C. *Immigrants at School: New York City, 1898–1914*. City U. of New York, 1967.

———. "The Jewish West Side of New York City, 1920–1970." *J of Ethnic Studies* 13 (Winter 1986): 21–45.

Eisenstein, J. D. "The History of the First Russian-American Jewish Congregation." *PAJHS* 9 (1901): 63–74.

Federation of Jewish Philanthropies. *The Golden Heritage: A History from 1917 to 1967*. N.Y.: ca. 1969. 395 pp.

Fifth Avenue Synagogue, Silver Anniversary. N.Y.: Fifth Avenue Synagogue, 1983.

Fink, Reuben, and G. Richards. *Jewish Community Directory of Greater New York*. N.Y.: Jewish Information Bureau, 1947.

Friedman, Lee M. "The Coming of the Jews to New York." In *Early American Jews*, 49–112. Cambridge: Harvard U. Press, 1934.

Fuld, Stella F., Janer Stone, and M. Rose. *Central Synagogue, 140 Years: A Proud Tradition . . . A Vital Future*. 1979. 31 pp.

Glanz, Rudolf. "German Jews in New York City in the Nineteenth Century." *YA* 11 (1956–57): 9–38.

———. "The History of the Jewish Community in New York." *YA* 4 (1949): 34–50. Also in his *Studies in Judaica Americana*, 152–68. 1970.

Golden, Harry. *The Greatest Jewish City in the World*. Garden City, N.Y.: Doubleday, 1972. 236 pp.

Goldstein, Israel. *A Century of Judaism in New York: Congregation B'nai Jeshurun, 1825–1925*. N.Y.: Congregation B'nai Jeshurun, 1930. 460 pp.

Goldwasser, I. Edwin. "Federation for the Support of Jewish Philanthropic Societies of New York City." *AJYB* 20 (1918–19): 113–46.

* Grinstein, Hyman B. *The Rise of the Jewish Community of New York, 1654–1860*. Columbia U., 1945. (Published under same title, Phila.: JPS, 1946. 645 pp.)

* Gurock, Jeffrey S. "Harlem in Its Heyday." In *When Harlem Was Jewish, 1870–1930*, 58–113. N.Y.: Columbia U. Press, 1979.

——. *The History of the Jewish Community of Harlem, 1870–1930*. Columbia U., 1977.

Huhner, Leon. "A Noted Jewish Burgher of New Amsterdam" (Asher Levy). *PAJHS* 8 (1900): 9–23.

Israelowitz, Oscar. *Guide to Jewish New York City: A Guide for the Sophisticated Traveler*. Rev. ed. Brooklyn: Israelowitz Pub., 1990. 216 pp.

Jewish Social Service Association. *Fifty Years of Social Service: The History of the United Hebrew Charities of the City of New York, Now the United Jewish Social Service Association*. N.Y.: 1926. 110 pp.

Kaganoff, Nathan N. "The Jewish Landsmanshaften in the Period Preceding World War I." *AJH* 76 (Sept. 1986): 55–66.

——. *New York Jewry: A Reading List*. N.Y.: AJHS, 1964. 6 pp.

——. "Organized Jewish Welfare Activity in New York City (1846–1860)." *AJHQ* 56 (1966): 27–61.

* Kessner, Thomas. *The Golden Door: Immigrant Mobility in New York City, 1880–1915*. Columbia U., 1975.

——. *The Golden Door: Italian and Jewish Mobility in New York City, 1880–1915*. N.Y.: Oxford U. Press, 1977. 224 pp.

Kohler, Max J. "Phases of Jewish Life in New York Before 1800." *PAJHS* 2 (1894): 77–100.

Korn, Bertram W. "The Temple Emanu-El Theological Seminary of New York City." In *Ess*, 359–71.

Landesman, Alter F. *Brownsville*. N.Y.: Bloch, 1969. 418 pp.

Leiserson, William M. "History of the Jewish Labor Movement in New York City." Bachelor's thesis, U. of Wisconsin, 1908. (On deposit at Yivo library.)

Levine, Louis. *The Women's Garment Workers: A History of the International Ladies' Garment Workers' Union*. N.Y.: B. W. Huebsch, Inc., 1924.

Levitan, T. *Islands of Compassion: A History of the Jewish Hospitals in New York*. 1964.

Lipman, Eugene J., and Albert Vorspan. "New York City—The Falling Star." In *Ten Cities*, 166–203.

Mesivta Yeshiva Rabbi Chaim Berlin. *50 Years, 1936–1986: The Building of a Torah Citadel, an Historical Perspective*. Brooklyn: 1986.

Monsky, Jacob. *Within the Gates: A Religious, Social and Cultural History, 1837–1962*. N.Y.: Congregation Shaarey Zedek, 1964.

"New York City." In *Enc Jud*, 12:1062–1124.

Oppenheim, M. S. "The Early History of the Jews in New York, 1654–1664." *PAJHS* 18 (1909): 1–91.

Perilman, Nathan A., ed. *When Yesterday Becomes Tomorrow: 125th Celebration, 1845–1970*. N.Y.: Congregation Emanu-El, 1971. 205 pp.

Poll, Solomon. *The Hassidic Community of Williamsburg*. N.Y.: Free Press, 1962. 308 pp.

Reichel, Aaron I. *Back to the Past for Inspiration to the Future: West Side Synagogue Jubilee, 1937–1987*. N.Y.: West Side Institutional Synagogue, 1987. 24 pp.

Rischin, Moses. *The Promised City: New York's Jews, 1870–1914*. Cambridge: Harvard Un. Press, 1962. 342 pp.

Rodeph Sholom. *History of Congregation Rodeph Sholom, 1842–1892*. N.Y.: 1892.

Rontch, Isaac E., ed. „די אידישע לאנדסמאנשאפטען פון ניו יארק" (The Landsmanshaften of New York) (organizations whose members came to the United States from the same European community) (Y.). Prepared by the Yiddish Writers Group of the Federal Writers' Project. N.Y.: I. L. Peretz Writers' Union, 1938. 400 pp.

Rubin, Israel. *Satmar: An Island in the City*. N.Y.: Quadrangle, 1972. 272 pp.

Rubinow, Isaac Max. "The Jewish Question in New York City, 1902–1903." *PAJHS* 49 (1959): 90–136.

* Sobel, Ronald B. *A History of New York's Temple Emanu-El: The Second Half Century*. New York U., 1980. 508 pp.

Solomon, Elias L. *The Story of Shaarey Zedek: One Hundredth Anniversary of Congregation Shaarey Zedek*. N.Y.: Congregation Shaarey Zedek, 1937.

Special Committee of Seven. "Report of the Special Committee of Seven on Religious Educational Societies, made to the Organization

Committee of the Federation for the Support of Jewish Philanthropic Societies of New York City, Mar 12, 1917." In *CA*, 180–90. See also *JEUS*, 149–52.

Stern, Meyer. *The Rise and Progress of Reform Judaism, Embracing a History Made from the Official Records of Temple Emanu-El, of New York*. N.Y.: M. Stern, 1895.

Yaffe, James. *So Sue Me! The Story of a Community Court* (Jewish Conciliation Board). N.Y.: Saturday Review Press, 1972. 275 pp.

NYC: Sephardim

See also chapter 34

Campeas, Hyman. "A Bird's-Eye View of the Magen David Congregation." *The American Sephardi* (Dec. 1966): 9.

Erdberg, A. "The Sephardim of New York." *Yiddisher Tageblatt* (Y.) (Feb. 27, 1927).

Frank, Ben G. "Jews from Arab Lands: At Home in Brooklyn." *Cong M* 43 (Mar. 1976): 15–16.

Hacker, Louis M. "The Communal Life of Sephardic Jews in New York City." *JSSQ* 3 (Dec. 1926): 32–40.

Hartstein, Jacob I. "The Polonies Talmud Torah of New York." *PAJHS* 34 (1937): 123–41.

Hecht, A. D. "How the Sephardic Jews in New York Teach and Marry off Their Children." *The Morning Journal* (Y.) (Aug. 2, 1950).

Lieberman, Sidney Z. "Yeshibat Minhat Areb: The First Judaeo-Spanish Day School in America" (Shearith Israel). In *American Society of Sephardic Studies*, Series 1 (1968–69): 87–92.

Papo, Joseph M. "The Sephardic Jewish Community of New York." In *Studies in Sephardic Culture*, edited by Marc D. Angel, 65–94. N.Y.: David N. Barocas Memorial Volume, 1980.

Phillips, N. Taylor. "The Congregation Shearith Israel: An Historical Review." *PAJHS* 6 (1897): 123–40.

Plotnik, Leonard. "The Sephardim of New Lots." *Commentary* (Jan. 1958): 28–35.

Pool, David de Sola. "Descriptions of the Synagogues in New York 1776 and 1828." *PAJHS* 40 (1950): 187–89.

———. *Portraits Etched in Stone: Early Settlers, 1682–1831*. N.Y.: Columbia Un. Press, 1953. 543 pp.

Pool, David de Sola, and Tamar de Sola Pool. *An Old Faith in a New World: Shearith Israel, 1654–1954*. N.Y.: Columbia U. Press, 1955. 595 pp.

Sanua, Victor D. "The Social Adjustment of Sephardic Jews in the New York Metropolitan Area." *Jew J Soc* 9 (June 1967): 25–33.

The Sephardi. "United Sephardim of Brooklyn Report Progress." Sept. 1954.

Sisterhood of the Spanish Portuguese Synagogue. *Annual Reports* (1913–1950). (Also minutes.)

Sutton, Joseph A. D. "Youth and Education." In *Magic Carpet: Aleppo in Flatbush, the Story of a Unique Jewish Community*, 92–103. N.Y.: Thayer-Jacobs, 1979.

Zenner, Walter P. "Syrian Jews in New York Twenty Years Ago." In *Fields of Offerings: Studies in Honor of Raphael Patai*, 173–93. Rutherford, N.J.: Fairleigh Dickinson Press, 1983.

The "East Side"

Dawidowicz, Lucy S. "From Past to Present: Jewish East Europe to Jewish East Side." *Con Jud* 22 (Winter 1968): 19–27.

Fine, Jo Renee, and Gerard R. Wolfe. *The Synagogues of New York's Lower East Side*. New York U. Press, 1978.

Friedlander, Gertrude. "Need of Jewish Day Nurseries on Lower East Side." *Jewish Charity* 4 (Apr. 1915): 210.

Gartner, Lloyd P. "The Jews of New York's East Side, 1890–1930." *AJHQ* 53 (Mar. 1964): 264–84.

Hapgood, Hutchins. *The Spirit of the Ghetto*. Cambridge: Harvard U. Press, 1912, 1965. 300pp

Hindus, Milton, ed. *The Old East Side*. Phila.: JPS, 1969. 301 pp.

Israelowitz, Oscar. *The Lower East Side Guide*. 2d ed. N.Y.: 1987. 115 pp.

Menes, Abraham. "The East Side and the Jewish Labor Movement." In *Voices from the Yid-*

dish, edited by Irving Howe and Eliezer Greenberg, 202–18. N.Y.: Schocken, 1975.

Rischin, Moses. "The Lower East Side." In *The Promised City: New York's Jews, 1870–1914*, 76–94. Cambridge: Harvard Un. Press, 1962.

Sanders, Ronald. *The Downtown Jews*. N.Y.: Harper and Row, 1969. 477 pp.

Schoner, Allan, ed. *Portals to America: The Lower East Side, 1870–1925, Photographs and Chronicles*. N.Y.: Rinehart and Winston, 1967. 256 pp.

Yoffeh, Zalmen. "The Passing of the East Side." In *The Menorah Treasury*, edited by Schwarz, 528–42. 1964.

NYC: Demography and Social Welfare

* Arsenian, Seth. *Bilingualism and Mental Development: A Study of Intellectual and Social Background of Bilingual Children in New York City* (Italian and Jewish children). Columbia U. Teachers College, 1937. 164 pp.

Carp, J. "Jewish Youth and Jewish Identification: Problems and Programs." Presented at the Third Annual Conference of the City-Wide Teenage Supervisors Committee sponsored by the Metropolitan Section of the National Jewish Welfare Board, Oct. 1964.

* Cohen-Nusbacher, Ailene. *Responses to Secular Influences among Orthodox Jewish Women*. New York U., 1987.

Dushkin, Alexander M. "Jewish Population of New York City." In *Jewish Communal Register of New York City, 1917–1918*, 75–89.

Elinson, Jack, Paul W. Haberman, and C. Gell. *Ethnic and Educational Data on Adults in New York City*. N.Y.: Columbia U. School of Public Health and Administrative Medicine, 1967.

* Epstein, Shifra. *The Celebration of a Contemporary Purim in the Bobover Hasidic Community*. U. of Texas at Austin, 1979. 312 pp.

Federation of Jewish Philanthropies of New York, Commission on Synagogue Relations. *Intermarriage and the Future of the American Jew and the Psychological Implications of Intermarriage* (proceedings of a conference). N.Y.: 1965, 1966.

———. *The Jewish Population of Greater New York: Profiles, Counties, Boroughs and Areas*. N.Y.: 1985. 129 pp.

———. *The Staten Island Jewish Community in Perspective*. N.Y.: 1985. 57 pp.

Gans, Herbert J. "Negro-Jewish Conflict in New York City: A Sociological Evaluation." *Mid* (Mar. 1969): 3–15.

Glazer, Nathan, and Daniel P. Moynihan. *Beyond the Melting Pot: The Negroes, Puerto Ricans, Jews, Italians and Irish of New York City*. Cambridge: MIT Press, 1979. 360 pp.

* Goldberg, Jack Roy. *A Plan for Providing Resident Country Camp Services for the Jewish Population of Greater New York*. New York U., 1964. 258 pp.

Grinstein, Hyman B. "Flight from the Slums." In *Essays of Jewish Life and Thought*, edited by Joseph Blau, 285–97. 1959.

* Halpert, Max. *The Jews of Brownsville, 1880–1925*. Yeshiva U., 1958.

Harris, Louis, and Bert E. Swansen. *Black-Jewish Relations in New York City*. N.Y.: Praeger, 1970.

Horowitz, C. Morris, and Lawrence J. Kaplan. *The Estimated Population of the New York Area, 1900–1975*. N.Y.: Federation of Jewish Philanthropies.

* Joselit, Jenna W. *Dark Shadows: New York's Jews and Crime, 1900–1940*. Columbia U., 1981.

Klein, Ronald H. "Jewish Acculturation in New York City, 1880–1920." Master's thesis, Seton Hall U., 1967.

* Kranzler, George (Gershon). *The Jewish Community of Williamsburg: A Study of Factors and Patterns of Change in the Organization and Structure of a Community in Transition*. Columbia U., 1953. Published as *Williamsburg—A Jewish Community in Transition*. N.Y.: Phillip Feldheim, 1981. 310 pp.

———. *Williamsburg Memories*. Lakewood, N.J.: C.I.S. Publications, 1989. 219 pp.

Lazerwitz, B. "Jew—In and out of New York City." *Jew J of Soc* 56 (1961): 568–79.

Levin, Ezra. "The Jewish Suburban Movement in Metropolitan New York." *King's Crown Essays* (Spring 1955).

Levy, Stephen Jay, and Sheila B. Blume. *Addictions in the Jewish Community*. N.Y.: Commission on Synagogue Relations and Federation of Jewish Philanthropies of New York, 1986. 379 pp.

Maller, Julius B. "Juvenile Delinquency among the Jews in New York." *Social Forces* (May 1932).

* Markowitz, Francine S. *Knowledge, Sentiment, Socialization: The Unintended Community of Soviet Jewish Emigres*. (New York) U. of Michigan, 1987.

* Mayer, Egon. *The Boro Park Community Survey, 1982, 1983: A Report on the Demography and Human Service Needs of a Jewish Neighborhood in Brooklyn*. Brooklyn: Council of Jewish Organizations of Boro Park, 1984. 45 pp.

———. *From Suburb to Shtetl: The Jews of Boro Park*. Phila.: Temple U. Press, 1979.

———. *Modern Jewish Orthodoxy in Post-Modern America: A Case Study of the Jewish Community in Boro Park*. Rutgers U., 1975.

McGill, Nettie P. "Some Characteristics of Jewish Youth in New York City." In *JSSQ* 14 (1937): 251–72.

Mitchell, William E. *Mishpokhe: A Study of New York City Jewish Family Clubs*. The Hague, Paris, New York: Mouton Publishers, 1978.

* Moore, Debra D. *At Home in America: Second Generation New York Jews*. N.Y.: Columbia U. Press, 1981. 303 pp.

———. *The Emergence of Ethnicity: New York's Jews 1920–1940*. Columbia U., 1975.

Newmann, Tully Milton W. "The Jews in Crime in New York City: 1900–1904." Master's thesis, Yeshiva U., 1970.

Ritterbrand, Paul, and Steven M. Cohen. "The Social Characteristics of the New York Area Jewish Community, 1981." *AJYB* 84 (1984): 128–61.

Robison, Sophia M. "A Study of Delinquency among Jewish Children in New York City." In *JES*, 533–41.

* Scherzer, Kenneth A. *The Unbounded Community: Neighborhood Life and Social Structure in New York City, 1830–1875*. Harvard U., 1982.

* Schick, Sandor E. *Neighborhood Change in the Bronx, 1905–1960*. Harvard U., 1982.

Seligman, Ben B. "The Jewish Population of New York City: 1952." In *JES*, 94–106.

NYC: Selected Memoirs

Bernheimer, Charles S. *Half a Century in Community Service*. N.Y.: Associated Press, 1948. 146 pp.

Cahan, Abraham. "בלעטער פון מיין לעבען" (*Bieter fun Mein Leben*) (Pages from My Life) (Y.). 5 vols. N.Y.: Forverts Association, 1926–31. (Several volumes translated into English.)

———. *The Education of Abraham Cohan*. Autobiography translated from Yiddish by Leon Stein, Abraham P. Conin, and Lynn Dayison. Phila.: JPS, 1969. 450 pp.

Cohen, Morris Raphael. *A Dreamer's Journey, 1880–1947*. Boston: Beacon, 1949. 318 pp.

Drachman, Bernard. *The Unfailing Light: Memoirs of an American Rabbi*. N.Y.: Rabbinical Council of America, 1948. 456 pp.

Kobrin, L. L. *My Fifty Years in America* (Y.). N.Y.: 1946. (Yiddish writer and theater critic.)

Wald, Lillian. *Windows on Henry Street*. Boston: Little Brown, 1934. 348 pp.

Wise, Stephen S. *Challenging Years: The Autobiography of Stephen Wise*. N.Y.: Putnam's Sons, 1949. 323 pp.

NYC: The Arts

(*See also chapters 2 and 4*)

* Backalenick, Irene. *A History of the Jewish Repertory Theater*. City U. of New York, 1987.

Grossman, Samuel. "Five Years of the Yiddish Art Theatre." *Menorah J* (Aug. 1923).

Hapgood, Hutchins. "The Yiddish Theater." In *The Spirit of the Ghetto*, 118–75. Cambridge: Harvard U. Press, 1912, 1965.

———. "The Young Art and Its Exponents." In *The Spirit of the Ghetto*, 243–60. Cambridge: Harvard U. Press, 1912, 1965.

Halpern, Moyshe Leyb. *In New York: A Selection*. Translated from the Yiddish and edited by Kathryn Hellerstein. Phila.: JPS, Jewish Poetry Series, 1982.

37 LOCAL SOURCES FOR JEWISH EDUCATION NEW YORK

* Hellerstein, Kathryn A. *Moyshe Leyb Halpem's In New York.–A Modern Yiddish Verse Narrative*. Stanford U., 1981.

Howe, Irving. *World of Our Fathers*. N.Y.: Harcourt-Brace-Jovanovich, 1976. 714 pp.

* Kaufman, Rhoda H. *The Yiddish Theater in New York and the Immigrant Jewish Community: Theater as Secular Ritual*. U. of California-Berkeley, 1986.

Kayser, Stephen. *The Jewish Museum: Inaugural Exhibition*. N.Y.: JTS, 1944.

* Lifson, David S. *The History of the Yiddish Art Theater Movement in New York, 1918–1940*. New York U., 1962. Published as *The Yiddish Theater in America*. N.Y.: Yoseloff, 1964.

Politzer, Heinz. "Habima in New York." *Commentary* (July 1949): 152–56.

Sanders, Ronald. "Yiddish Theater." In *The Downtown Jews*, 236–77. N.Y.: Harper and Row, 1969.

* Seiger, Marvin. *A History of the Yiddish Theater in New York from 1882 to 1892*. U. of Indiana, 1960.

Werner, Alfred. "Ghetto Graduates." *American Art J* (Nov. 1973).

Zunser, Miriam Shomer. "The Jewish Literary Scene in New York at the Beginning of the Century." *YA* 7 (1952): 277–97.

NYC: The Jewish Press

AJYB. "List of Yiddish Dailies Published in New York City, 1885–1923." 26 (1924–25): 332.

Davis, Moshe. "הצופה בארץ החדשה,, (Ha Tsofeh in the new land) 1871–76). In *Alexander Marx Jubilee Volume* (H.) 115–41. 1950.

Margoshes, Samuel. "The Jewish Press of New York City." *Jewish Communal Register* (1917): 596–663.

Ravid, Zvulun. "היום—העתון העברי היומי הראשון באמריקה" (Ha-Yom—First Hebrew Daily in America) (1909) (H.). *JBA* 37 (1979–80): 71–77.

Sanders, Ronald. *"The Jewish Daily Forward."* Mid (Dec. 1962): 79–94. See also "The Founding of *The Jewish Daily Forward.*" In *The Downtown Jews*, 148–80. N.Y.: Harper and Row, 1969.

* Soltes, Mordecai. "List of Yiddish Dailies published in New York City, 1885–1923." In *The Yiddish Press: An Americanization Agency*, 182–83. N.Y.: Columbia U. Press, 1924, 1950. A major portion of the volume appeared in *AJYB* 26 (1924–25): 165–372.

NYC: History of Jewish Education

(*See also chapters 20, 21, 34*)

Abelow, S. P. "The Development of Education." In *History of Brooklyn Jewry*, 98–144. Brooklyn: Scheba Pub. Co., 1937.

* Baum, Eli H. *History and Development of the Orthodox Supplementary School of New York City*. N.Y.: Jewish Teachers Seminary, 1970.

* Berkson, Isaac B. "The Central Jewish Institute: A Community School." In *Theories of Americanization*, 177–223. Columbia U., 1920.

Berman, Jeremiah J. "יידישע דערציאונג אין ניו יארק" (Jewish Education in New York City, 1860–1890). *YB* (Y.) 38 (1954): 208–35. See also *YA* 9 (1954): 274–75.

Blacksin, Morris. "The History and Value of the Yeshiva in New York City." Master's thesis, Fordham U.. 1933.

Bloom, Samuel. "אנפאנג פון אידישער ערציהונג אין ניו יארק" (Beginning of Jewish Education in New York). *Morning Journal* (Y.) (Feb. 7, 1926).

Bokser, Ben Zion. "Jewish Education." In *The Golden Heritage: A History from 1917 to 1967*, 334–37. N.Y.: Federation of Jewish Philanthropies, ca. 1969.

* Dushkin, Alexander M. "History of Jewish Education in New York before 1881" and "History of Jewish Education in New York since 1881–1900." In *Jewish Education in New York City*. Columbia U., 1918. Published by New York BJE, 1918. See pp. 28–99.

Eisenstein, J. D. "Correspondence with Parents in Europe, on the Education of his Son" (1881–86). *AJHQ* 52 (Mar. 1963): 241–43. Also in *JEUS* 102–3.

Epstein, A. Joseph. "The Early History of the Central Jewish Institute." Master's thesis, Yeshiva U.

Erdberg, Sh. „צוואנציג יאהר פון אידישער דערציהונג אין ניו יארק" (Twenty Years of Jewish Education in New York). *Day* (Y.) (Nov. 4, 1934).

"Federation Plan For the Support of Jewish Educational Institutions" (report of the Committee of Twenty-Five Representing the Largest Jewish Educational Institutions in New York City). *Jewish Teacher* 1 (May 1917): 167–74.

Gannes, Abraham P. "Camping." In *The Golden Heritage: A History from 1917 to 1967*, 372–75. N.Y.: Federation of Jewish Philanthropies, ca. 1969.

Goldstein, Israel. "The B'nai Jeshurun Educational Institute." In *A Century of Judaism in New York: Congregation B'nai Jeshurun, 1825–1925*, 169–70. N.Y.: Congregation B'nai Jeshurun, 1930.

Grinstein, Hyman B. "An Early Parochial School" (Hebrew National School of Congregation Shaarey Zedek, 1852–55). *Jew Ed* 13 (Apr. 1941): 23–33.

———. "Education." In *The Rise of the Jewish Community of New York, 1654–1860*, 225–59. Phila.: JPS, 1946.

———. „לתולדות הוראת למודי החול בקרב היהודים בעיר ניו-יורק" (On the History of Secular Education among the Jews in New York) (colonial period). *Hagut* (H.) 3 (1974): 350–58.

———. "Studies in the History of Jewish Education in New York City, 1728–1864." *Jewish Review* 2 (Apr. 1944): 41–58, (July–Oct. 1944): 187–201.

* Harris, Zevi H. *A Study of Trends in Jewish Education for Girls in New York City*. Yeshiva U., 1956. 323 pp. See also his "The Growth of Jewish Education for Girls in New York." *Jew Ed* 29 (Fall 1958): 32–38, 64.

Hartstein, Jacob I. "Jewish Education in New York City before 1881." Master's thesis, City College of New York, 1933.

Jaffe, Philip. "The Reform Religious Schools of New York City, 1940–1950." *Jew Ed* 21 (Summer 1950): 25–31.

Kranzler, George. "The Educational Pattern." In *Williamsburg Memories*, 139–53. Lakewood, N.J.: C.I.S. Publications, 1989.

Lifshutz, Ezekiel. (The Minute-Book of a Hebrew Teachers' Organization in New York in the Beginning of the 20th Century). *YB* (Y.) 42 (1962): 284–89.

New York Council of Jewish Federations and Welfare Funds. *Community Organization for Jewish Education*. N.Y.: CJFWF, 1939. 44 pp.

* Rudavsky, David. *Jewish Education in New York City Since 1918*. New York U., 1945. 198 pp.

———. „טענדענצן אין דער אנטוויקלונג און אין וווקס פון די יידישע שולן אין ניו יארק" (Trends In Jewish School Organization and Enrollment in New York, 1917–50). *YB* (Y.) 39 181–215. See also *YA* 10 (1955): 45–81.

Rudens, S. P. "A Half Century of Community Service: The Story of the New York Educational Alliance." *AJYB* (1944–45): 73–85.

Sarna, Jonathan D. "Jewish Education in New York–1887." *Trad* 19 (Fall 1981).

Shmuelevitch, Sh. „ווי האלט עס מיט דער אידישער ערציהונג אין ניו יארק?" (How Does Jewish Education Fare in New York?). *For* (Y.) (Feb. 10, 1956).

Slavin, Simon. "Educational Alliance Has Served Two Generations of Jews." *Day* (Y.) (Mar. 9, 1958).

Tannenbaum, Samuel. "Brownsville's Age of Learning." *Commentary* 8 (Aug. 1949): 173–79.

New York's "Kehillah" and the Beginning of the Bureau of Jewish Education

AJYB. "The Jewish Community of New York City, 1909–1910." (1909–10): 4–54.

Benderly, Samson. "Aims and Activities of the Bureau of Education of the Jewish Community (Kehillah) of New York" (1912). Appears *in Jew Ed* 20 (Summer 1949): 92–109.

———. "The Jewish Community of New York City." N.Y.: Bureau of Education, Bulletin No. 1, 1910. Reprinted in *Jew Ed* 10 (Summer 1949): 110–12.

———. "The Present Status of Jewish Religious Education in New York City." *Jewish Communal Register of New York City* (1918).

———. "The Problem of Jewish Education in New York City." *American Hebrew* 88 (Mar. 1911).

37 LOCAL SOURCES FOR JEWISH EDUCATION

NEW YORK

———. "The Purpose and Work of the Bureau of Jewish Education." In *CA*, 202–10.

———. "Some of the Activities of the Bureau of Education." Sixth Annual Conference of the Kehillah, Apr. 24, 1915. Published by the Kehillah.

———. *A Survey of the Financial Status of the Jewish Religious Schools of New York City*. N.Y.: Bureau of Education, 1911.

Dushkin, Alexander M. "The Activities of The Bureau of Jewish Education." In *Jewish Education in New York City*, 100–128. N.Y.: BJE, 1918.

Friedlander, Israel. "The Problem of Jewish Education in America and the Bureau of Education of the Jewish Community of New York City." U.S. Commissioner of Education Report for the Year ended June 30, 1913, 1:365–93. Also in *JEUS*, 132–48.

Goldberg, David. "Attitudes toward the New York Kehillah in the Yiddish and Anglo Press of New York, 1908–1913." 2 vols. Master's thesis, Graduate School of Jewish Social Work, 1937.

Goren, Arthur A. "Education as a Communal Responsibility." In *New York Jews and the Quest for Community: The Kehillah Experiment, 1908–1922*, 86–109. N.Y.: Columbia U. Press, 1970.

———. "Education: Professionals and the Orthodox." In *New York Jews and the Quest for Community: The Kehillah Experiment, 1908–1922*, 110–33. N.Y.: Columbia U. Press, 1970.

* ———. *The New York Kehillah, 1908–1922*. Columbia U., 1966.

Gorenstein (Goren), Arthur. "The Commissioner and the Community: The Beginnings of the New York City 'Kehillah', 1908–1909." *YA* 13 (1965): 167–212.

The Jewish Communal Register of New York City, 1917–1918. 2d ed. N.Y.: Kehillah of New York City, 1918. 1597 pp.

Kaplan, Mordecai M., and Bernard Cronson. "First Community Survey of Jewish Education in New York City, 1909." Presented in 1910 at the First Annual Convention of the New York Kehillah. Appears in *Jew Ed* 20 (Summer 1949): 113–16, and in *JEUS*, 118–26.

Magnes, Judah L. "The Jewish Community of New York City." Address delivered at the Constituent Convention. N.Y.: Jewish Community Kehillah, 1915.

———. "Jewish Education and the Jewish Community." Excerpts from his *Reports*, 1914–18. *Jew Ed* 20 (Feb. 1949): 12, 17.

———. "Recent Progress in Religious Education—The Jewish Community of New York City." *CCAR* 24 (1914): 316–22.

———. "Reports a Loan for the Publication of Adequate Textbooks by the Board of Jewish Education of New York City" (Feb. 25, 1911). See Nathan Winter, *Jewish Education in a Pluralist Society: Samson Benderly and Jewish Education in the United States*, 69–70. N.Y.: New York U. Press, 1966.

New York Times. "How the Kehillah Worked an Educational Miracle." Jan. 25, 1914. (Interview with Samson Benderly.)

Rudavsky, David. "The Bureau of Jewish Education after 1918." *Jew Ed* 20 (Summer 1949): 38–52.

Bureau of Jewish Education and the Continuation of Central Educational Agencies

Chipkin, Israel L. "The Jewish Education Association of New York City." *Jew Ed* 12 (Jan. 1941): 136–45.

Eisenberg, Azriel. „ועד החינוך היהודי בניו יורק" (The Board of Jewish Education in New York) (H.). In *Scharfstein*, 138–45.

* Entin, Nathaniel A. *The Jewish Education Committee of New York, 1939–1965: A Critical History*. Dropsie U., 1972.

Gannes, Abraham P. "The Jewish Education Association in Retrospect, 1921–1939." *Jew Ed* 27 (Fall 1956): 29–34.

Jew Ed 53 (Winter 1985). Special issue celebrating the 75th anniversary of the BJE of Greater New York. Articles include:
  Berger, Zvi, "The Educational Resource Library," 32–33.
  Blum, Deborah Cardozo, "Resource Development for Jewish Education," 45–49.
  Casper, Deborah Shor, "BJE Survival through Education Drive," 50–53.
  Cohen, Floreva, and Ruth Musnikow, "The Jewish Early Childhood Educator: Coming of Age," 11–15, 27.

Daube, Rochelle Silbermintz, "Media Usage Modes in Jewish Education," 34–38.

Fisch-Aharoni, Linda, "Enhancing School Administration: BJE's Management Assistance Program," 42–44.

Glatzer, Shoshanah, "The Evolution of the BJE Teachers' Center," 16–19, 31.

Kaunfer, Neal, and Lali Ray, "The Principals' Center: A New Model for Educational Leadership Development," 24–27.

Lichter, Chani, "Keeping up with the Computer Age: BJE's Computer Resource Center," 39–41.

Preil, Joseph J., "IVN: In-Service Program for New Yeshiva Teachers," 20–23.

Schiff, Alvin I., "The Board of Jewish Education of Greater New York—Then and Now" (editorial comments), 2–3.

———. "New York's Central Agency for Jewish Education: Historical Perspectives," 7–10.

Schloss, Martin, "The BJE Special Education Center: Maximizing the Opportunties for Jewish Persons with Special Needs," 28–31.

Jewish Education Committee of New York. *Annual Report*. 1940. 20 pp.

Meckler, D. L. „ארגאניזירטער אידישער חינוך אין ניו יארק און איבערן לאנד" (Organized Jewish Education in New York and the Nation). *Day* (Y.) (Mar. 5, 1961).

Nardi, Noah. "ועד החינוך היהודי בניו יורק„ (The Jewish Education Committee of New York). In *JB* (H.), 314–37.

Penn, Ascher. „דער אידישער דערציאונגס קאמיטעט אין ניו יארק. זיין געשיכטע און זיינע אויפטוען" (The Jewish Education Committee in New York, Its History and Accomplishments). In *Penn*, 203–21.

Pilch, Judah. "Our Indebtedness to New York" (on the 50th anniversary of the N.Y. BJE). *Jew Ed* 30 (Winter 1960): 2, 16.

Rotenberg, Joshua. „דער אידישער דערציאונג קאמיטעט פון ניו יארק" (The Jewish Education Committee of New York) (on its 25th anniversary). *YK* (Y.) (Dec. 25, 1964).

Ruffman, Louis L. *Facts and Figures*. N.Y.: JEC, 1962.

———. "The JEC of New York: Profile of a Community Service Agency." *Jew Ed* 35 (Spring 1965): 148–65.

———. „הערות על מצב ההרשמה" (Observations on Enrollment in Jewish Schools) (1964–65). *Sh Hah* (H.) 26 (Winter 1966): 69–71.

———. „איבערבליק וועגן אידישן חינוך אין דער סטאט, ניו יארק" (Review of Jewish Education in New York) (Y.). Jewish World Congress, Jan. 1956.

Schiff, Alvin I. *Jewish School Enrollment in Greater New York* (annual reports). N.Y.: BJE of Greater New York, 1970–84.

Zemel, Bernard. „צען יאר ארבעט פאר אידישער דערציאונג" (Ten Years Work in Behalf of Jewish Education) (on the Jewish Education Association). *Day* (Y.) (Dec. 13. 1931).

NYC: Day Schools

(*See also chapters 20 and 21*)

Brill, Shraga. "ישיבת אור תורה„ (Manhattan Day School—Or Torah). *Sh Hah* (H.) 21 (Fall 1960): 59–60.

Charney, Bernard. „התפתחות הישיבה דסנטרל קווינס" (The Development of the Central Queens Yeshiva). *Sh Hah* (H.) 20 (Winter 1961): 96–101.

Derovan, David J. "Metropolitan New York Commission on Torah Education" (description of yeshiva high school seminar). *Ped Rep* 25 (Fall 1973).

* Feuerman, Chaim. *A Study of Views of the Principals in Elementary Orthodox Hebrew Day Schools in the New York City Area: Expectations Held by Principals and Their Lay Board Chairmen*. St. John's U., 1977. 175 pp.

* Goodside, Samuel. *A Social Studies Syllabus for Secular Teachers in Jewish All-Day Schools: A Companion Bulletin to the Social Studies Curriculum Bulletins of the Board of Education of the City of New York*. New York U., 1951. 304 pp.

* Heimowitz, Joseph. *A Study of the Graduates of the Yeshiva of Flatbush High School*. Yeshiva U., 1979.

* Himelstein, Samuel. *A Comparative Study of Teacher Satisfactions and Dissatisfactions between Teachers of Selected Day Schools and Orthodox Jewish Public School Teachers in New York City*. Columbia U. Teachers College, 1975. 319 pp.

37 LOCAL SOURCES FOR JEWISH EDUCATION

NEW YORK

Kamen, Robert Mark. *Growing up Hasidic: Education and Socialization in the Bobover Hasidic Community*. N.Y.: AMS Press, 1985. 139 pp.

Kaplan, Abraham. "Survey of Hebrew Parochial Schools of New York." Master's thesis, New York U., 1929.

Lookstein, Joseph H. *Course of Instruction in Judaic Studies* (for Ramaz High School). N.Y.: 1979.

* Pinsky, Irving. *A Follow-up Study of the Graduates of One of the Oldest Existing American Jewish Day Schools, the Rabbi Jacob Joseph School, 1898–1950*. Yeshiva U., 1961.

———. "History and Development of the Rabbi Jacob Joseph School, 1898–1950." Master's thesis, Yeshiva U.

Preil, Joseph J., and Lorraine K. Diamond. "The Greater New York Yeshiva High School Entrance Examination." *Jew Ed* 48 (Winter 1980): 28–36.

Ramaz School, Kehillath Jeshurin. "75 Years of Progress" *Jew Life* 15 (Oct. 1947).

Rosenfeld, Leonard. *The New York Story: Memorandum on Day-School Movement in New York City*. N.Y.: JEC, Nov. 1962.

———. *Report on the All-Day School Movement in New York City*. N.Y.: JEC, Nov. 1964.

Rudavsky, David. "The Brooklyn Jewish Center Academy." *Jew Ed* 20 (Nov. 1948): 5–9.

Sandler, F. „מוסטערהאפטע אידישע טאג-שול אין קווינס" (Outstanding Jewish Day School in Queens) (Solomon Schechter Day School). *Day* (Y.) (May 10, 1965).

Schiff, Alvin I. *Focus on the Jewish Day School*. N.Y.: JEC, 1964.

* Segal, Samuel M. *Jewish All-Day Schools in the City of New York, through 1948*. New York U., 1952. 644 pp.

Shudofsky, Noam. "The Senior Project of the Ramaz Upper School." *Ped Rep* 22 (June 1971): 28.

Shulamit School for Girls. *Suggested Curriculum Enrichment for the Hebrew Day School*. N.Y.: 1975.

Shurin, Aaron Ben Zvi. „חנוכת הבית פון 'שולמית'—די ערשטע מיידל שול אין אמעריקע" (Dedication of New School Building for "Shulamith"—the First School for Girls in America). *For* (Y.) (May 6, 1982).

———. „די ערשטע אידישע פאראקיעל סקול אויף דער איסט סאיד איז אלט געווארן 60 יאר" (First Jewish Day School on the East Side is 60 Years Old). *For* (Y.) (July 8, 1982).

Smolar, Boris. „מוסטער האפטע אידישע טאג-שול אין קווינס" (Model Jewish Day School in Queens). *For* (Y.) (May 16, 1983).

Steinback, Irene Bush. "The Progressive Center Academy." *Jew Ed* 16 (May 1945): 9–11; 20 (Feb. 1949): 40–44.

Taback, Ben Zion. „הישיבה דפלטבוש" (Yeshiva of Flatbush). *Sh Hah* (H.) 21 (Summer 1961): 246–47.

Yeshiva Department, JEC. *A Concise Memorandum Concerning the Day School Movement in New York City*. Nov. 1962.

NYC: Yiddish Schools

(*See also chapter 21*)

Baskin, I. „געדאנקען וועגן 20-יאריקן יובל פון די ארבעטער רינג שולן" (Thoughts on the 20th Jubillee of the WC Schools). In *WC Yearbook* (Y.) (1939): 5–8.

Chait, N. „די ארבעטער רינג שולן אין ניו יארק" (The WC Schools in New York City). In *S Alm* (Y.), 113–18.

———. „א יאר ארבעטער רינג שול טעטיקייטן אין ניו יארק" (A Year of Activities in the New York WC Schools). In *WC Yearbook* (Y.) (1939): 15–18.

Ginzberg, M. „דער שווערער קאמף פאר אידיש אין די ניו יארקער מיטעל-שולן" (The Struggle for Yiddish in the New York High Schools). *Canadian Eagle* (Y.) (Apr. 13, 1959).

Glantz, J. „פארוואס ניט אידיש אין די פאבליק סקולס?" (Why Not Yiddish in the Public Schools?). *Day* (Y.) (Feb. 13, 1930).

Grossfield, A. „די שולן אין ניו יארק" (The Schools in New York). *Pro D* (Y.) (Nov. 1935): 16–18.

Kaminetsky, N. „א יאר ארבעט אין די ניו יארקער שולן" (A Year of Work in the New York Schools). *Pro D* (Y.) (1938): 20.

Mark, Yudl. „די ארבעטער רינג שולן אין ניו יארק אין לערניאר 1939–1940" (The WC Schools in New York, 1939–1940). *YB* (Y.) 23 (1944): 416–19.

Meisl, A. "אין א שול אויף דער איסט-סייד" (In a School on the East Side). *Pro D* (Y.) (Aug. 1935): 21–22.

Ostrovsky, B. "די אורזאכען פון שול-קאמף אין ניו יארק" (The Reasons for the School Disputes in New York). *The Friend* (Y.) (Mar.–Apr. 1926) 7–9.

Penn, Ascher. "The First Quarter Century in the History the Sholem Aleichem Schools." In *OFFY*, 3–16.

Shapiro, Leib. "א יאר-ארדן שולן אין ניו יארק" (A Year the Orden School in New York). *Pro D* (Y.) (July/Aug. 1937): 20–21.

Spizman, L. "פראגרעסיווע טאג-שולען" (Progressive Day Schools) (on the founding of Kinnereth Day School in Brooklyn—Farband school). *Day* (Y.) (July 1947).

Unger, M. "וויפיל קינדער לערנען זיך אין די אידישע וועלטליכע שולן?" (How Many Children Attend the Yiddish Secular Schools?). *Day* (Y.) (Oct. 11, 1942).

Workmen's Circle Schools of New York. "ניו יארקער ארבעטער רינג יארבוך" (Yearbook of the WC Schools in New York) (Y.). N.Y.: Citywide School Board, 1941. 46pp.

Beth Ha Yeled—Experimental Hebrew Pre-School

Chipkin, Israel S. "The Beth Hayeled in New York." *Jew Ed* 16 (Jan. 1945): 18–20.

Dushkin, Alexander M. "The Educational Significance of the Beth Hayeled." *Jew Ed* 16 (Jan. 1945): 20–22.

Gelb, Leah S., and Miriam Heller. "Beth Ha Yeled—Pre-School for Jewish Children." *Jew Ed* 13 (Sept. 1941): 110–19.

Guttman, Miriam H. "The Emergence of Beth Ha Yeled." *Jew Ed* 27 (Fall 1956): 57–60.

Heller, Miriam. "The Beth Hayeled." *Jew Ed* 20 (Nov. 1948): 53–57.

Smolensky, Dvora, Peninah Linder, and Sue Schiff Mogilner. "Hebrew Experience in the Beth Hayeled of New York City." *Jew Ed* 24 (Spring 1953): 39–40, 64.

NYC: Hebrew in Public High Schools

Blumberg, Harry. "נסיון שהצליח" (An Experiment that Succeeded). In *Yesod* (H.), 218–35.

Chipkin, Israel S. "למוד הלשון העברית בבתי הספר הגבוהים" (Hebrew Language in High Schools of New York). *Hinuch* (H.) (Apr. 1935): 7–11.

Golub, Jacob S. "Hebrew in Public High Schools" (editorial). *Jew Ed* 11 (Apr. 1939): 3–4.

Hektin, Shalom. "עברית בבית הספר הצבורי" (Hebrew in the Public High School). *Hadoar* (H.) 34 (Oct. 14, 1955): 783, 791.

Kabakoff, Jacob. "נסיון שעלה יפה" (An Experiment That Fared Well). (Hebrew in the NYC public high schools) *Hadoar* (H.) 16 (11th of Sivan 1938).

Kessler, L. "דער לימוד העברעאיש אין די ניו יארקער הייסקול" (The Study of Hebrew in the New York High Schools). *YB* (Y.) 17 (1941): 277–79.

Lapson, Judah. "A Decade of Hebrew in the High Schools of New York City." *Jew Ed* 13 (Apr. 1941): 39–45.

———. "The Hebrew Culture Council and Two Decades of Hebrew in the Public High Schools." *Jew Ed* 21 (Summer 1950): 17–19, 59.

———. "Hebrew in the High Schools." *Day* (Apr. 4, 1960).

———. "Hebrew in the Public Schools." *Jew Fron* (Sept. 1953).

———. "הוראת העברית בבתי הספרי הגבוהים הצבוריים" (Hebrew Instruction in Public High Schools). *In JB* (H.), 206–20.

———. "New Challenges Facing Hebrew in the Public Schools+." *Jew Ed* 27 (Fall 1956): 38–42, 56.

———. "לעתידה של העברית בבית הספר הצבורי" (On the Future of Hebrew in the Public High School). *Hadoar* (H.) 36 (Feb. 22, 1957): 302–3.

Lewittes, Mordecai H. "Hebrew Enters New York High Schools." *Manorah J* 26 (Apr.–June 1938): 243–44.

NYC: Adult Education

Duker, Abraham G. *Adult Jewish Education in New York City, 1947*. N.Y.: JEC.

Feldheim, Eric. *The Beth El Chavurah Program*. N.Y.: UAHC, ca. 1974. 155 pp.

37 LOCAL SOURCES FOR JEWISH EDUCATION

NEW YORK

Mintz, Alan. "Along the Path to Religious Community." In *Contemporary Judaic Fellowship in Theory and Practice*, edited by Jacob Neusner, 167–74. N.Y.: Ktav, 1972.

Novak, Bill. "The Havurah in New York: Some Notes on the First Year." In *Contemporary Judaic Fellowship in Theory and Practice*, edited by Jacob Neusner, 161–66. N.Y.: Ktav, 1972.

Rabin, Florence. "Adult Jewish Educational Activities in Thirty-Seven Jewish Group Work Agencies in Metropolitan New York City." Master's thesis, Graduate School for Jewish Social Work, 1930.

Shtarkman, Moshe. „אידישע שולען פאר דערוואקסענע אין ניו יארק" (Jewish Schools for Adults in New York). *Day* (Y.) (Oct. 9, 1937).

UAHC. *Survey of Adult Education in the Reform Congregations of New York*. N.Y.: UAHC and JEC, 1963.

* Wadler, Nathan. *Adult Jewish Education in New York*. Columbia U., 1952. 219 pp.

NYC: Surveys of Jewish Education

Berkson, Isaac B. *The 1936 Jewish Education Study of New York City*. N.Y.: Friedsam Foundation. 193?. See also *Jew Ed* 10 (Oct.–Dec. 1938): 176–91.

Bloch, Joshua. *Survey of Jewish Religious School Conditions in Harlem*. Cincinnati: UAHC, 1921.

Chipkin, Israel S. *Survey of Jewish Education in New York City: Attitude Studies*. N.Y.: JEC, 1958.

———. *Survey of Jewish Education in Greater New York, 1951: Quantitative Studies, Findings and Recommendations*, edited by Louis L. Ruffman. N.Y.: JEC, 1957. 156 pp.

Jaffe, Philip, and Jacob R. Raphael. *Survey of High School Department of the Reform Religious Schools of Greater New York*. N.Y.: JEC, 1943.

JEC of New York. *Survey of Confirmation and Bar Mitzvah in the Reform Synagogues of New York*.

New York Board of Jewish Education. *Self Study Report: Conclusions and Recommendations*. N.Y.: BJE, 1972.

Penn, Ascher. „ניו יארקער אויספארשונג באשטעטיקט פון 80 ביז 85 פראצענט אידישע קינדער קריגן א אידישע דערציאונג" (New York Survey Confirms that 80–85 Percent of Jewish Children Receive Some Form of Jewish Education). In *Penn*, 251–81.

Rosen, Ben. *Jewish Communal Survey of Greater New York, Jewish Education Section*. N.Y.: Bureau of Jewish Social Research, 1928.

———. "Survey of Jewish Education in New York City." *Jew Ed* 1 (May 1929): 82–96.

Ruffman, Louis L. "The Survey of Jewish Education in New York City." *Jew Ed* 27 (Fall 1956): 10–26.

Survey Commission of the Bronx. *Survey of Religious Education*. N.Y.: Survey Commission of the Bronx, 1916

UAHC and JEC. *Survey of the Reform Religious Schools*. N.Y. 15 pp.

NYC: The Profession

Chipkin, Israel. "The Jewish Teacher in New York City and the Remuneration for His Services." *Jew Ed* 2 (Oct. 1930): 165–75. Also in *Hadoar* (H.) (11th, 25 of Tishri 1931).

Colodner, Solomon. *Classroom Management*. N.Y.: JEC, 1966. 70 pp.

Edan, M. „הכנוס למען החנוך היהודי בניו יורק" (A Conference on Jewish Education in New York). *Sh Hah* (H.) 12 (Spring 1952): 177–78.

* Edelstein, Menachem M. *The Status of the Professional Jewish Teacher in the Jewish Schools of America with Special Reference to New York City*. Dropsie U., 1951. 225 pp.

Eisenberg, Israel L. "The Jewish Principals Group of New York." *Jew Ed* 4 (Jan.–Mar. 1932): 54–55.

Glenn, Menahem G. „לתולדות אגודת המורים העברים בניו יורק" (On the History of the Jewish Teachers' Union in New York City). In *JB* (H.), 399–438.

Hebrew Principals Association of Greater New York. *Talmud Torahs*. (Jubilee journal, 1911–61). N.Y.: JEC, 1961.

Hebrew Teachers Union of New York and Vicinity. „חוקת אגודת המורים בניו יורק וסביבותיה" (Constitution of the Hebrew Teachers Union of New York and Vicinity). In *JB* (H.), 465–70. Excerpt in *JEUS*, 177–80.

Jaffe, Philip, and Jacob R. Raphael. "Study of Two Hundred Forty Teachers in New York City." *Jew Teach* 12 (Jan. 1944): 23–34.

JEC of New York. *Achievement Tests for the End of the Third Year in Weekday Afternoon Hebrew Schools.* 1961.

———. *Achievement Tests for Weekday Afternoon Congregational Schools* (The Jewish People, Jewish Life and Customs, and the Hebrew Language). Experimental ed. N.Y.: 1958.

———. "Code for Jewish Schools." *Jew Ed* 16 (Sept. 1944): 43–47.

———. *Code of Practice for Jewish Schools* (to regulate relations between teachers and schools). N.Y.: Mar. 1952.

———. *Functions and Procedures of the Board of License for Teachers and Principals in Hebrew Schools of Greater New York.* N.Y.: July 1949.

———. *Procedures of the Board of License for Teachers and Principals in Hebrew Schools of Greater New York.* N.Y.: July 1949.

———. *Readings in School Administration and Supervision.* N.Y.: c. 1958.

* Kaminetsky, Joseph. *A Plan for the Improvement of the Program of Religious Education in the Jewish Center Hebrew School.* Columbia U., 1944. 100 pp.

Konowitz, Israel. *A Brief Survey of Thirty-One Conferences Held by Talmud Torah Principals in New York City.* N.Y.: Bureau of Education, 1912.

New York Board of Review for Hebrew in Schools. "Code of Practice." *Jew Ed* 16 (Sept. 1944): 43–47.

New York City. "The First Conference of the Jewish Teachers Association." *Jewish Teacher* 5 (June 23–24, 1923): 1–11.

Queens Principals Council, United Synagogue Schools. *Course of Study, Years 1, 2, 3, and 4.* N.Y.: JEC and Queens Principals Council, United Synagogue Schools.

Roshan, A. „דין וחשבון של הכנוס הראשון של ניו יורק רבתי" (A Report on the First Conference by the BJE of Greater New York). *Sh Hah* (H.) 12 (Winter 1952): 124–27.

Rudavsky, David. "The Board of Review for Jewish Schools in New York City." *Jew Ed* 18 (Summer 1947): 38–45.

Ruffman, Louis L. "School Accreditation in Greater New York." *Jew Ed* 32 (Winter 1962): 85–95.

Scharfstein, Zevi, ed. „ספר היובל של אגודת המורים העברים בניו יורק" (Jubilee Book of the Hebrew Teachers Union of New York City and Vicinity) (H.). To commemorate the thirtieth year of its founding. N.Y.: 1944. 479 pp.

Sheviley Ha Hinukh (Second Conference of Teachers of Greater New York) (H.). *Sh Hah* 3 (1928): 322–26. See also *Sh Hah* 3 (1928): 417–21 and 4 (1929): 356–65.

Whiteman, Kalman. „אגודת המנהלים של בתי תלמודי התורה והישיבות בניו יורק וסביבותיה" (The Association of Principals of the Talmud Torahs and Yeshivot in Greater New York). In *JB* (H.), 337–39.

Yeshiva English Principals Association. *Proceedings of the 31st Annual Pedagogic Conference.* N.Y.: BJE, Nov. 12, 1972.

NYC: Viewpoints, Reports, and Questions

Azrieli, S. "Communal Responsibility for Jewish Education In New York City." *Jew Ed* 23 (Summer 1952): 5–8, 14.

Berger, Graenum. *The Jewish Community Center: A Fourth Force in America.* N.Y.: JEC Press, 1966. 34 pp.

Brayer, Menachem. "The Impact of the Creative Teaching Personality." In *Proceedings of the 17th Annual Pedagogic Conference* (Feb. 7–8, 1959), 14–16. N.Y.: JEC Press.

Cahan, Zevi. „אידישע ערציהונג אין ניו יארק" (Jewish Education in New York). *For* (Y.) (Mar. 6, 1961).

„איבער 145 טויזנט קינדער קריגן אידישע דערציאונג אין מעטראפאליטן ניו יארק" (Over 145 Thousand Children Receive a Jewish Education in Metropolitan New York). *Day* (Y.) (Dec. 24, 1964).

Dushkin, Alexander M. "Next Decade of Jewish Education in New York City." *Jew Ed* 12 (Sept. 1940): 65–78.

Edelstein, Menachem M. "Intensification of Jewish Education in New York City." *Jew Ed* (Nov. 1946): 43–48.

Eisenberg, Azriel. „אידישע דערציאונג אין ניו יארק" (How Does Jewish Education Fare in New York?). *Day* (Y.) (Jan. 2, 1959).

37 LOCAL SOURCES FOR JEWISH EDUCATION

NEW YORK

———. „ווי האלט עס טאקע מיט אידישער דערציאונג אין ניו יארק?" (Jewish Education in New York). *Day* (Y.) (Nov. 17, 1950).

Goldberg, Nathan. „יידישע דערציאונג אין די וולאדעק הײזער אין ניו יארק" (Jewish Education in the Vladek Homes in New York City). *YB* (Y.) 27 (Summer 1946): 380–87.

Goodman, Saul. „קהילה-אחריות פאר יידישער דערציאונג אין ניו יארק" (Communal Responsibility for Jewish Education in New York). *Zuk* (Y.) (Apr. 1954): 154–56.

———. „די פעדעראציע פון יידישע פילאנטראפיעס און די יידישע דערציאונג אין ניו יארק" (The Federation of Jewish Philanthropies and Jewish Education in NYC). *BYD* (Y.) (Spring 1962): 46–49.

Gordis, Robert. "Jewish Education in New York City: Its Chaos and a Possible Remedy." *Menorah J* 17 (Nov. 1929): 133–.

Hyat, Aaron. „וויפיל ניו יארקער אידישע קינדער באקומען א אידישע דערציאונג?" (How Many Jewish Children in New York City Receive a Jewish Education?). *Day* (Y.) (Sept. 3, 1945).

Landesman, Alter F. "Brownsville's Contribution to Jewish Survival." In *Brownsville*, 223–42. N.Y.: Bloch, 1969.

———. "The Hebrew Education Society of Brooklyn." In *Brownsville*, 170–200. N.Y.: Bloch, 1969.

Mathison, Zevi. „העליה והירידה בחינוך היהודי בניו יורק" (The Ups and Downs of Jewish Education in New York). *Hadoar* (H.) 50 (Mar. 19, 1971).

Penn, Ascher. „די בעסטע שול אין דער וועלט פאר טויב-שטומע" (Best School in the World for Deaf-Mutes). In *Penn* (Y.), 426–36.

———. „ברענגען ליכט" (Bringing Light) (on New York Guild for the Jewish Blind, whose members transcribe prayerbooks and other texts into Braille). In *Penn* (Y.), 413–25.

———. „חסידים און ישיבות אין ניו יארק" (Hasidim and Yeshivot in New York). In *Penn* (Y.), 603–71.

———. „אידישע הײסקול דערציאונג ..." (Jewish Secondary Education). In *Penn* (Y.), 481–89.

———. „פון אלע עקן וועלט קומען אידישע קינדער לערנען תורה אין ניו יארק" (Jews from Many Lands Come to Learn Torah in New York City). In *Penn* (Y.), 497–506.

———. „איבער 200 אידישע קינדערגארטנס אין ניו יארק און אומגעגנט" (Over 200 Jewish Kindergartens in Greater New York City). In *Penn* (Y.), 449–55.

Rudavsky, David. "A Study of the Jewish Families in the Vladek Houses." *Jew Ed* 16 (Mar. 1945): 47–51.

Schiff, Alvin I. "New York's Survival through Education Drive." *Jew Ed* 43 (Winter/Spring 1975): 14–25, 54.

Sharfstein, Chana and Albert Zachter. "Social Studies Conference Reports." *The Principal* (N.Y. BJE) (Oct. 1974): 9–11.

Siegel, Morton. "A Hebrew High School Grows in Brooklyn." *Un Syn Rev* 21 (Jan. 1969): 10–11.

Silverman, D. W. "Religious Education for the Handicapped: A Birthright." In *Proceedings of Fall Conference* (Sept. 1966). N.Y.: JEC, 1968.

Smolar, Boris. „די אידישע שול באוועגונג אין ניו יארק" (The Jewish School Movement in New York). *For* (Y.) (Oct. 31, 1976).

Steinbaum, Israel. „יידישקייט ביי צוואנציק יידישע משפחות אין ניו יארק" (A Study of Jewishness in Twenty Jewish New York Families—1940). *YB* (Y.) 31–32 (1948): 208–32. Also in *YA* 6 (1951): 232–55.

Whiteman, Kalman. „צו דערפראגע פון אידישער ערציהונג אין ניו יארק" (On the Question of Jewish Education in New York). *Day* (Y.) (Nov. 3, 1926).

NYC: Professional Periodicals

(*National journals published in New York City are listed in chapter 23*)

JEC Bulletin. 1943–77.

Darkenu. „דרכנו" (H.). Hebrew Teachers Union of New York City, 1938. Quarterly.

Pedagogic Bulletin, „פעדאגאגישער בולעטען" (Y.). Committee for Yiddish Schools and JEC of N.Y., 1941–66. 8 issues per year.

The Principal. „המנהל" (Hamenahel). Association of Yeshivah Day School Principals of General Studies (TU), BJE of Greater New York, 1954–present.

NYC: Curricula, Textbooks, and Special Materials

Edelstein, Menachem M. *Course of Study for Communal Talmud Torahs* (H.). Curriculum Committee of Principals Association and Jewish Education Committee, 1950. 51 pp.

——. (Special Classes) (H.) (children with special needs). N.Y.: BJE, 1943. 49 pp.

Hebrew Principals Association of New York. *Reshit Hokhmah* (Introduction to Wisdom) (H.) (prayers, blessings, and hymns). N.Y.: Hebrew Pub. Co, with Hebrew Principals Association and JEC, 1941. 76 pp.

——. *Talmud Torah Curriculum*. N.Y.: JEC, 1942. 121 pp.

Isseroff, Samson A. *Teachers Guide of Study for the Talmud Torah and Hebrew High School*. N.Y.: Metropolitan Council on Talmud Torah Education, JEC, 1970.

New York Curriculum Committee of the United Synagogue Schools. *Curriculum for Congregational Hebrew Schools*. N.Y.: JEC, 1944. 33 pp.

Queens Principals Council, United Synagogue Schools. *Course of Study, Years 1, 2, 3, and 4*. N.Y.: JEC.

Rudavsky, David. *Courses of Study Leading to Graduation*. N.Y.: BJE, 1930.

Stiskin, Hershel M. *A Curriculum Guide and Suggested Activities and Experience for Teachers of Children with Retarded Mental Development in Jewish Religious Schools*. N.Y.: JEC Press, Holiday Cycle.

——. *Religio-Ethnic Influences and Curriculum Planning within the Maimonides Institute*. N.Y.

Wasserman, Z. Z., and A. Tachrov. (Our Book) (H.). A Chrestomathy for Orthodox Schools-Lubawitch. Brooklyn: Center for Jewish Education, 1943.

Yeshiva of Flatbush. *Curriculum*. (H.). Brooklyn: 1957. 46 pp.

NYC: Curriculum: The Arts

Aronow, Sara Snyder. *Hava Nagilah* (H.). N.Y.: JEC, 1963.

Binder, A. W., and S. S. Grossman. *Bible in Song*. N.Y.: JEC.

Citron, Samuel J. "The Jewish Theatre for Children in New York—Twenty Creative Years." *Jew Ed* 37 (Winter 1967) 87–89, 95.

——. *Music for the Jewish School*. N.Y.: BJE.

——. *Teaching Aid and Song Curriculum for Hebrew Schools*. N.Y.: JEC Press, 1961.

Coopersmith, Harry. *Hebrew Songster for Kindergarten and Primary Grades*. N.Y.: JEC, 1948.

Dinin, Samuel. *School Assemblies*. N.Y.: BJE.

* Edelman, Marsha. *Music Education in the Jewish Schools of Metropolitan New York*. Columbia U., 1982.

Edidin, Ben M. *Clubs and Groups in Jewish Schools*. N.Y.: JEC, 1942, 1953. 138 pp.

Edidin, Ben M., and Louis L. Ruffman. *The School Assembly*. N.Y.: JEC, 1953. 41 pp.

* Eisenberg, Azriel Joseph. *Children and Radio Programs: A Study of More Than Three Thousand Children in the New York Metropolitan Area*. Columbia U. Teachers College, 1936.

Gezari, Temima. *Foot Prints and New Worlds: Experiences in Art with Child and Adult*. N.Y.: JEC, 1964. 170 pp.

——. "The Role of Art in My Life and in Jewish Education." *Jew Ed* 51 (Fall 1983): 31–36.

Grossman, Samuel S. *The Bible Story in Song Verses*. Music by S. E. Goldfarb. N.Y.: BJE, 1926. 31 pp.

Imber, Rebecca. *The Creative Audience*. N.Y.: JEC Press, 1962.

Lapson, Dvora. *Dances for Jewish Festivals*. N.Y.: JEC, 1941.

——. *Dances for Jewish Schools*. N.Y.: JEC.

——. *Folk Dances for Jewish Festivals*. N.Y.: BJE, 1981.

——. *Holiday Dances*. N.Y.: JEC.

——. *Jewish Dances the Year Round*. N.Y.: JEC, 1957. 58 pp.

Meyer, A. *Theatre and Education* (Y.) 1:17–18.

Neumann, Richard. *Jewish Music Guide for Teachers*. N.Y.: BJE.

37 LOCAL SOURCES FOR JEWISH EDUCATION NEW YORK

Penn, Ascher. 200 אין געלערנט טענץ „אידישע פון סקולס פאבליק אין און שולן אידישע יארק ניו" (Jewish dances are being taught in 200 Jewish schools and in the Public Schools of New York). In *Penn*, 464–72.

Riklis, L. I. "Hebrew School Assemblies in New York." Master's thesis, Columbia U., 1955.

Sofer, Tamar. "On Purple Cows and Pink Skies: An Interview with Temima Gezari." *Jew Ed* 53 (Winter 1985–86): 57–60.

Curriculum: Hebrew, Prayer, and Bible

Aronow, Sara Snyder. *A Hebrew Textbook for Small Children*. N.Y.: JEC, 1963. 83 pp.

Benari, Avivah. *Hebrew Roots and Fruits: A Guide to Jewish Concepts and Values through Hebrew Root Words*. N.Y.: BJE, 1983. 128 pp.

BJE. *Pupils Series: A Course in Hebrew for Sunday Schools*. N.Y.: BJE of the Kehillah, 1913.

———. *A Student Text in Hebrew*. 4 vols. N.Y.: 1922–27.

* Brayer, Menachem. *The Management of Achievement in the Hebrew High School of New York with Some Reference to Attitudes toward Judaism*. Yeshiva U., 1958.

Chomsky, William. "דרכי הוראה ולמידה„ (Methods for Instruction and Learning) (H.). N.Y.: JEC, 1969. 207 pp.

———. *Teaching Hebrew*. 3d ed. N.Y.: JEC, 1956. 151 pp.

Dinin, Samuel, and Azriel Eisenberg. *Bar Mitzvah Instruction*. N.Y.: JEC.

Edelstein, Menachem M., and Ben Zion Taback. "מדריך למורים„ (Guide for Teachers) (H.) (Hebrew for beginners). N.Y.: Curriculum Committee of Principals and JEC, 1950, 1952. 87 pp.

———. *Special Classes in Hebrew School* (H.). N.Y.: JEC, 1943.

Eisenberg, Israel L. (Azriel). *Accent on Hebrew: A Handbook for the Jewish School, Synagogue, Center, and Camp*. N.Y.: JEC Press. 294 pp.

———, ed. *Readings in the Teaching of Hebrew*. N.Y.: JEC, 1961. 298 pp.

———. "What Is Being Taught in the Leading Hebrew High Schools of New York?" *Jew Ed* 6 (Apr.–June 1934): 99–104.

* Goldstein, Martin. *A Study in the Degree of Prayer-Consciousness of Jewish Orthodox, Conservative and Reform Schools in New York City*. New York U., 1949. 193 pp.

Haramati, Shlomo. "גישה חדשה להוראת לשון„ (A New Approach to Language Teaching). N.Y.: JEC, 1967. 27 pp.

Haramati, Shlomo, and Asenath Rosenberg. *Hebrew in the Kindergarten*. N.Y.: JEC Press, 1971.

Isseroff, Shimshon A., and Abraham Etkin. *Humash, Sidrah Breishit*. N.Y.: Metropolitan Commission of Yeshivot in cooperation with the JEC, 1952. 60 pp.

———. *Targilim Lahumash, Sidrah Breishit*. N.Y.: Metropolitan Commission of Yeshivot in cooperation with the JEC, 1952. 61 pp.

JEC of New York. "תמונות עזר להוראת עברית„ (Pictorial Aids for the Study of Hebrew). N.Y.: JEC, 1948.

Klepper, Leah. *First Year Hebrew: Oral Instruction and Reading*.

———. *The Improvement of Hebrew Reading in the Preparation for Study of Siddur*. N.Y.: JEC, 1947.

———. *Preparing for the Study of Siddur: Case Studies in Classroom Teaching*. N.Y.: JEC, 1955. 28 pp.

———. *Teaching Elements of Hebrew Reading*. N.Y.: JEC, 1957.

Kohn, Rebecca. *A Practical Guide for Teaching Hebrew*. N.Y.: BJE, 1967. 271 pp.

Mosenkis, Rebekah Kohn. *A Practical Guide for Teaching Hebrew*. 2 vols. N.Y.: BJE, 1978–80.

Rubinstein, Simha, and Harry Kessler. (Elements of Hebrew) (H.). 2 vols. N.Y.: BJE, 1937.

Spiro, Pinchas. *Haftarah Chanting*. N.Y.: JEC Press, 1964.

Whiteman, Kalman. *Hadrakha B'Horaat Ha-humash* (A Guide for Teaching the Pentateuch) (H.). N.Y.: JEC, 1946.

Curriculum: History

Benderly, Samson, and Israel Goldberg. *Outline of Knowledge*. 3 vols. N.Y.: BJE, 1930.

BJE of New York. "Activities in the Day Schools" (seminars in integrated Jewish history and social studies). *The Principal* (Dec. 1974): 8, 10.

Eisenberg, Azriel, and Abraham Segal. *Teaching Jewish History*. N.Y.: JEC, 1954. 110 pp.

———. "The Subject of Jewish History: Aims, Viewpoints, and Special Difficulties in Teaching Jewish History." In *Teaching Jewish History*, 3–11. N.Y.: JEC, 1954.

———. *Readings in the Teaching of Jewish History*. N.Y.: JEC, 1956 (226 pp), 1961 (298 pp.).

Hartstein, Jacob J., and Benjamin Miller. *Jews in America: Heritage and History*. N.Y.: BJE of Greater New York, 1978. 304 pp.

Nadel, Max. *Case Studies in Classroom Teaching Jewish Social Studies in Religious School*. N.Y.: JEC, 1968.

———. "Lesson in Jewish History." *JEC Bulletin* 92 (1954). Also in *RTJH*, 171–82.

Pollack, Jacob B. "The Teaching of History in the Sunday Schools of Greater New York." *Jew Ed* 3 (Apr.–June 1931): 120–25.

Curriculum: Holidays and Jewish Life Cycle

Chanover, Hyman. *Teaching the Haggadah*. N.Y.: JEC, 1964. 226 pp.

Edidin, Ben M. *Syllabus on Children's Sabbath Services*. N.Y.: JEC, 1942.

———, ed. *Jewish Life and Customs: Unit Six—Passover*. N.Y.: JEC, 1944.

Feldman, Estelle. *Pesah and the Young Child*. N.Y.: JEC Press, 1968.

Heckelman, Dvorah. *Shabbat and the Young Child*. N.Y.: JEC Press, 1972.

JEC. *Holiday Songsters: Holiday Worksheets*. N.Y.: JEC.

———. *Jewish Life and Customs Series*. N.Y.: JEC, 1942, 1943, 1944.

———. *A Syllabus on the School Seder*. N.Y.: JEC.

Segal, Abraham. *The Jewish Congregation*. N.Y.: JEC, 1958. 44 pp.

———. *Teaching the Siddur*. N.Y.: JEC, 1954. 101 pp.

Curriculum: Holocaust

BJE of New York City. *The Holocaust: A Study of Genocide*. N.Y.: BJE Division of Curriculum and Instruction, 1979. 587 pp.

Feinstein, Sara. *Flame and Fury: Teaching of the Martyrdom of the Six Million*, edited by Yaakov Shihav. N.Y.: JEC.

Grama, Israel, Rebekah Mosenkis, and Yaakov Reshef. *We Who Survived*. Study guide by Shoshana Glatzer. N.Y.: BJE, 1977.

Curriculum: Israel

BJE of New York City. *The Place of Israel in Jewish Education in the United States*. (Proceedings of the Twenty-Ninth Annual Pedagogic Conference.) N.Y.: 1972.

Citron, Samuel J. *Israel: Dream and Fulfillment* (12 dramatizations). N.Y.: BJE, 1968. 259 pp.

Eisenberg, Azriel, ed. *Jerusalem Eternal*. N.Y.: JEC Press, 1972. 384 pp. Grades 6–7.

Indelman, Elchanan. *The Jewish State* (H.). N.Y.: JEC, 1948. 17 pp.

Segal, Abraham. *The Teaching of Israel*. N.Y.: JEC.

* Shapira, Rena N. *Patterns of Attitudes towards Israel among Jewish Adolescents in New York Jewish Schools*. Columbia U., 1965. 224 pp.

Curriculum: Literature

Aronin, Ben. *Helem: The City of Wise Men* (H.). N.Y.: JEC, 1963. 43 pp.

Belth, Norton, ed. *The First World Over Story Book: An Illustrated Anthology for Jewish Education for Youth*. N.Y.: JEC, 1952, 1970. 272 pp.

———, ed. *The Second World Over Story Book: From the Pages of* World Over *Magazine*. N.Y.: JEC, 1952, 1970. 168 pp.

Certner, Simon, ed. *101 Jewish Stories for Schools, Clubs and Camps*. N.Y.: JEC, 1961. 212 pp.

Eisenberg, Azriel, and Abraham Segal. *Presenting Bialik: A Study of His Life and Works*. N.Y.: JEC, 1956. 113 pp.

Eisenberg, Yehudah Moses. *Albert Einstein* (H.). N.Y.: JEC, 1963. 43 pp.

37 LOCAL SOURCES FOR JEWISH EDUCATION

NEW YORK

Friedland, H. A. *Dovedl* (H.). N.Y.: JEC, 1959.

Gamoran, Mamie. *Samson Benderly* (H.). Translated by E. Indelman. N.Y.: JEC, 1963. 44 pp.

Glen, Menahem G. *Henrietta Szold—A Mother in Israel* (H.). N.Y.: JEC, 1964. 34 pp.

Indelman, Eliezer. *Rambam—Maimonides* (H.). N.Y.: JEC and Histadruth Ivrith of America, 1954. 48 pp.

———. *Eliezer Ben Yehudah* (H.). N.Y.: JEC, 1959.

———, ed. *Selections from Hebrew Literature in America*. N.Y.: BJE, 1972. 88 pp.

JEC of New York. *Jewish Book and Author Quiz*. N.Y.

Nadel, Max. *American Jewish Literature for High School Grades*. N.Y.: BJE and Federation of Reform Synagogues, 1973. 152 pp.

Reichwald, Faye. *18 Lives* (for students of English as a second language). N.Y.: BJE, 1981. 249 pp.

Saretsky, Augusta, and Elias Schulman. *A Guide to Jewish Juvenile Literature*. N.Y.: JEC, 1968.

Shudofsky, Maurice. *Judah Touro* (H.). N.Y.: JEC, 1962. 42 pp.

Yarbloom, Moshe. *Hay im Weitzman* (H.). N.Y.: JEC, 1963. 45 pp.

Pedagogy

Chomsky, William. *Teaching and Learning: An Introduction to Jewish Education*. N.Y.: JEC Press, 1959. 213 pp.

Citron, Samuel. *Activity Programs for Jewish Schools*. N.Y.: JEC.

Feldman, Estelle, and Dvorah Heckelman. *Learning Experiences in the Jewish Foundation Schools*. N.Y.: BJE, 1971.

Fish, Nathaniel. *Teaching with JEC Filmstrips*. N.Y.: JEC.

Klepper, Leah. *Aspects of Classroom Management: Case Studies in Classroom Teaching*. N.Y.: JEC, 1954.

———. *Case Studies in Discipline*. N.Y.: JEC, 1954.

———. *The Importance of Motivation in Learning*. N.Y.: JEC, 1955.

———. *On Getting Acquainted: Exploring Their Apperceptive Mass*. N.Y.: JEC, 1954.

Krant, Jerome. "Experiences with Sex Education Programs in the Jewish Community Center at Staten Island." N.Y.: Federation of Jewish Philanthropies, 1968.

Levitan, Tina. *Viewpoints on Science and Judaism*. N.Y.: JEC. Ages 14–18.

Lieberman, J. *New Approaches to the Education of American Jewish Children*. N.Y.: JEC, 1942.

Mushnikow, Ruth A. *First Steps: Learning and Living for Young Jewish Children*. N.Y.: BJE, 1980.

Noskowitz, J. *A Manual for the Beginning Teacher*. Experimental ed. N.Y.: JEC, 1959.

School and Home

Gelbart, Gershon I. *Jewish Education in America: A Manual for Parents and School Board Members*. N.Y.: JEC, 1963. 132 pp.

JEC of New York. *Ten Commandments for the Jewish Parent*. N.Y.: JEC. 6 pp.

Jewish Education Association. *We and Our Children: Shall They Remain Jews?* N.Y.: 1924. 16 pp.

Perlman, Milton B. *The Congregational School Board in Action*. N.Y.: JEC, 1966.

Saretsky, Augusta. *Manual on Open School Week*. N.Y.: JEC.

———. *The PTA Manual*. N.Y.: JEC, 1958. 113 pp.

———. *PTAs in Action: Successful Programs and Activities*. N.Y.: JEC, 1968. 102 pp.

Stern, Jay E. *Know Your School*. N.Y.: JEC, 1961.

Curriculum: Values

Berman, Saul. "Jewish Value Perspective: Poverty, Sexuality, Family Life." In *Judaism and Mental Health*. N.Y.: BJE, 1978

Dushkin, Alexander M. *Personal Values in Education for Children under Care*. N.Y.: JEC, 1947. 36 pp.

Edidin, Ben M. *The Keren Ami Project—A Manual for Teachers and Leaders*. N.Y.: JEC, 1943. 264 pp.

Eisenberg, Azriel L. *Tzedakah and Federation: A Handbook for the Jewish School, Center, and Camp*. N.Y.: JEC, 1952. 78 pp.

Feinstein, Joseph. *I Am My Brother's Keeper*. N.Y.: JEC Press, 1970. 72 pp.

JEC. *Keren Ami Library Bulletin*. N.Y.

Jung, Leo. *Between Man and Man*. N.Y.: JEC Press, 1976. 254 pp.

———. *Human Relations in Jewish Law*. N.Y.: JEC, 1967. 173 pp.

Lister, Rebecca. *Instructional Units for Tzedakah and Federation*. N.Y.: JEC.

Rackman, Emanuel. *Jewish Values for Modern Man*. N.Y.: JEC Press, 1962. 134 pp.

Publications by and for Students

Beth Rachel of Satmar. *Annual* (Y.) Brooklyn: June 1970.

Merkos L'Yinyonei Chinuch. *Shmuesn mit Kinder un Yugnt* (Conversations with Children and Youth (Y.). 1951. Quarterly.

Sholem Aleichem Schools. *Commencement Journal* (Y.). June 2, 1926. 40 pp.

Shulamith Institute for Girls of Boro Park. *Graduation Folio* (H.). Brooklyn: 1936. 44 pp.

Workmen's Circle Schools, Bronx, New York. *Annual* (Y.). Central School Committee of WC, 1941 (36 pp.), 1945 (80 pp.).

———. *Student Ring* (Y.). Anthology of student writings from WC schools, Bronx. 1926. 32 pp.

———. *Workmen's Circle* (Y.). In honor of the elementary and secondary graduating classes. Dec. 1926. 64 pp.

Selected Early Newspapers and Periodicals

(In chronological order. Prior to 1900, see American Jewish History section)

Jewish Farmer (Y. and E.). 1891–92. Monthly.

Jewish American (Y.). 1900–195?. Weekly.

Jewish Morning Journal and Daily News (Y.). 1901–52. Daily (merged with *Day* in 1952).

Dos Neye Lebn (Y.). Literature and philosophy, 1908–14 and 1922–23. Monthly.

Der Groyser Kundes (The Big Prankster) (Y.). Humor and cartoons, 1908–27. Weekly.

Dos Yiddishe Folk (Y.). 1909–5?. Monthly.

Jewish Worker's Voice (Y. and E.). 1912–4?. Quarterly.

Ha-Toren (H.). 1913–25. First monthly, later weekly.

Der Tog (The Day) (Y.). 1914–53. Daily. Became *The Day-Jewish Journal* in 1953.

Menorah Journal. Literature, art, and current events, 1915–62. First, bimonthly, later quarterly.

Jewish Forum. 1917–6?. Monthly.

Insich (Y.). Literature, 1920–47?. Monthly.

Hadoar (H.). 1921–present. Daily, later weekly.

Na'Amat Woman (formerly *Pioneer Woman*) (E., Y, and H.). 1926–present. 5 times a year.

Jewish Frontier. 1934–present. Weekly, later monthly.

Horeb (H.). History and literature, 1934–60. Semi-annual, later annual.

Ramah (H.). Literature, 1937–39. Monthly.

Bitzaron (H.). 1939–present. Bimonthly.

Furrows (E. and H.). 1942–196?. Monthly.

Jewish Life. 1946–198?. Quarterly.

The Jewish Observer. 1963–present. Fortnightly.

Response. 1967–present. Quarterly.

NORTH CAROLINA

Evans, Eli K. *The Provincials: A Personal History of the Jews in the South*. Durham: Atheneum, 1973. 369 pp.

Golden, Harry. *Jewish Roots in the Carolinas: A Pattern of American Philo-Semitism*. Greensboro: 1955.

Hagedorn, Leah. *Syllabus: Jews in the American South, 1860–1965*. Chapel Hill: U. of North Carolina Department of History, 1987.

Henry, Jacob. "Jacob Henry's Speech, 1809, on the Petition to Vacate the Seat of Jacob Henry, North Carolina, in the House of Commons, 5th

December, 1809" (petition based on his being a Jew). In *JIS*, 43–46.

Huhner, Leon. "The Jews of Carolina Prior to 1800." *PAJHS* 29 (1925): 137–48.

———. "Jews in North Carolina in Colonial and Revolutionary Times." *PAJHS* 22 (1914): 183.

———. "The Struggle for Religious Liberty in North Carolina, with Special Reference to the Jews." *PAJHS* 16 (1907): 37–71.

Marcus, Jacob R. "North and South Carolina 1776–1790." In *EAJ*, 2:258–76.

"North Carolina." In *Post*, 476–84.

Rosenwaike, Ira. "Further Light on Jacob Henry." In *JIS*, 47–50.

Simonhoff, Henry. "Tolerance in Carolina in 1697." *Chicago Jewish Forum* 25 (Winter 1966–67): 144–51.

Task, Arnold. "The North Carolina-Virginia Junior High Experience." *Compass* 3:1 (Fall 1979): 8–9, 21.

Charlotte

American Jewish Times-Outlook. 1932–present. Monthly.

The Carolina Israelite. 1942–196?. Monthly.

Speizman, Morris A. *The Jews of Charlotte, North Carolina: A Chronicle with Commentary and Conjecture*. Charlotte: McNally and Lotin, 1978. 246 pp.

Greensboro and Winston-Salem

Zweigenhaft, Richard L. "The Jews of Greensboro: In or out of the Upper Class." *Contemporary Jewry* 4 (1978): 60–76.

———. "Two Cities in North Carolina: A Comparative Study of Jews in the Upper Class." *JSS* 41 (Summer/Fall 1979): 291–300.

Statesville

Adler, Hanna. *Congregation Emanuel, Statesville, North Carolina Centennial Celebration, 1881–1983*. Statesville. 119 pp.

Wilmington

Toplin, Robert Brent, ed. *A History of B'nai Israel Synagogue: In Celebration of the 81st Anniversary*. Wilmimgton: 194?.

NORTH DAKOTA

AJA. "Trailblazers . . ." (Oct. 1956): 105–9.

Fine, Henry, and Lea Fine. "North Dakota Memories." *WSJH* 9 (July 1977): 331–40.

Papermaster, Isadore. "A History of North Dakota Jewry and Their Frontier Rabbi." *WSJH* 10 (Oct. 1977): 74–89, (Jan. 1978): 170–84, (Apr. 1978): 266–83.

"North Dakota." In *Post*, 484–89.

Jewish Agricultural Colonies

Herscher, Uri D. "Painted Woods and Iola" and "Chananel." In *JAUA*, 70–72.

Plaut, W. Gunther. "Jewish Colonies at Painted Woods and Devils Lake." *North Dakota History* 32 (Oct. 1965): 96–106.

Schwarts, L. Fields. "Early Jewish Agricultural Colonies in North Dakota." *North Dakota History* 32 (Oct. 1965): 222–24.

OHIO

Chyet, Stanley F. "Ohio Valley Jewry during the Civil War." *Historical and Philosophical Society of Ohio Bulletin* 21 (July 1963): 179–87.

Jonas, Joseph. "The Jews in Ohio, Dec. 25, 1843." In *Schappes*, 223–35.

"Ohio." In *Post*, 489–510.

Philipson, David. "Are There Traces of the Ten Lost Tribes in Ohio." *PAJHS* 13 (1905): 37–46.

———. "The Jewish Pioneers of the Ohio Valley." *PAJHS* 8 (1900): 43–57.

Rappoport, Joseph. "The Relation of Jewish and General Institutional Development." In *Proceedings of the Conference on the Writing of Regional History*, 55–65. 1956.

Akron

BJE. *First Annual Report of the Executive Director of the Bureau of Jewish Education, Akron*. Akron: 1944. 72 pp.

Engelman, Uriah Z. *Evaluation of Educational System*. N.Y.: AAJE, 1955.

Halevi, Mordecai. *Survey of Jewish Education in Akron*. Akron: BJE, 1942.

* Kaplan, Helga E. *Century of Adjustment: Akron Jewish Community, 1865–1975*. Kent State U., 1978.

Canton

Engelman, Uriah Z. "Surveys of Surveys—Duluth and Canton, Ohio." *Jew Ed* 17 (Nov. 1945): 31–33.

Kaplan, Louis L. *Survey of Jewish Education—Canton, Ohio, 1944*. N.Y.: AAJE, 1944.

Stark Jewish News. 1920–present. Monthly.

Cincinnati

American Israelite. "The Jewish Institutions of Cincinnati." (Dec. 13, 1906).

AJA. "War on Lodge Street: Conflict between Reform and Orthodox Jews of Cincinnati, 1865." 18 (1966): 128.

Brav, Stanley R. *Temple Sholom 1954–1964, 10th Anniversary Souvenir: A Personal History*. Cincinnati: 1964. 19 pp.

* Brickner, Barnett R. *The Cincinnati Jewish Community, 1837–1933: An Historical and Descriptive Study*. U. of Cincinnati, 1935.

Ezekiel, H. C. "Notes on List of Names from Cincinnati Directory, 1825." *PAJHS* 9 (1901): 155.

Heller, James G. *As Yesterday When It Is Past: A History of the Isaac M. Wise Temple-K. K. B'nai Yeshurin of Cincinnati, 1842–1942*. 249 pp.

Marcus, Jacob R. "The Jews Come to Ohio—Memoirs of Joseph Jonas, the First Cincinnati Jew" (1855). In *Mem*, 1:203–15.

* Mostov, Stephen. *"Jerusalem" on the Ohio: The Social and Economic History of Cincinnati's Jewish Community, 1840–1875*. Brandeis U., 1980.

Philipson, David. "The Cincinnati Community in 1825." *PAJHS* 10 (1902): 97–99.

———. "The Oldest Jewish Congregation in the West." In *Souvenir of the 100th Anniversary of Congregation B'nai Israel of Cincinnati*. Cincinnati: 1924.

Roseman, Kenneth D. "Power in a Midwestern Jewish Community." *AJA* 21 (Apr. 1969): 57–83.

Rosenwaike, Ira. "The Utilization of Census Tract Data in the Study of American Jewish Population." *JSS* 25 (Jan. 1963): 42–56.

Seasongood, Emily. "Memories of a Middle-Class Cincinnati Jewish Childhood in the 1860s." In *Mem*, 3:60–62. Also in *JEUS*, 80–82.

Whiteman, Maxwell. "Notions, Dry Goods, and Clothing: An Introduction to the Study of the Cincinnati Peddler." *JQR* 53 (1963): 306.

Wise, Isaac M. *Reminiscences*. Translated and edited by David Philipson, 1901. Excerpts in *AJA* 6 (1954): 107–48.

Yerushalmi, Isaac. *Sephardic Life in Cincinnati, 1906–1976: A Synopsis*. Sephardic Beth Sholom Congregation. 28 pp.

Cincinnati: Education

(See also chapter 22)

Bortniker, Elijah, Philip Jaffe, and Alvin I. Schiff. *Report on the Status of Education in Cincinnati*. Cincinnati: Jewish Federation of Cincinnati and AAJE, 1968. 135 pp.

Brickner, Barnett R. "The History of Jewish Education in Cincinnati." *Jew Ed* 8 (Oct.–Dec. 1936): 115–26.

Chipkin, Israel. "החנוך העברי" (On Jewish Education in Cincinnati). *Hadoar* (H.) 19 (June 9, 1939): 522–23.

Congregation Bene Israel. *My Ethical Wills: Teenagers' Testimonials* (written by members of the 1958 confirmation class). Cincinnati: Congregation Bene Israel, 1958. 64 pp.

Eisenberg, Azriel. „נסיונותי בהנהלת הת״ת באבונדייל" (Experiences in Administration in the Avondale Talmud Torah). *Sh Hah* (H.) 2 (Oct. 1942): 268–75.

Feuer, Leon I. *Jewish Literature since the Bible*. Cincinnati: UAHC, 1937. 206 pp.

Frankel, Max. "Bureau of Jewish Education—Cincinnati, Ohio." *Jew Ed* 44 (Summer 1975): 19–21.

Gamoran, Emanuel. "Twenty-Five Years of the Cincinnati Bureau." *Jew Ed* 21 (Summer 1950): 8–9.

37 LOCAL SOURCES FOR JEWISH EDUCATION

OHIO

Heller, James G. "Jewish Education—Then and Now." In *As Yesterday When It Is Past: A History of the Isaac M. Wise Temple-K. K. B'nai Yeshurin of Cincinnati, 1842–1942*, 42–66.

* Lewis, David Trevor. *An Empirical Study of Jewish Identification: The Relationship between Home Life of Eighth-Grade Jewish Boys and Their Adjustment in the Public Schools of Cincinnati*. Ohio State U., 1960. 181 pp.

Perlow, P. "History of the Bureau of Jewish Education." Master's thesis, U. of Cincinnati, 1936.

Zalesky, Moses. *Education for Jewish Living: Messages to the Jewish Community of Cincinnati*. Cincinnati: Talmud Torah Association, 1949. 20 pp.

———. *Teacher's Kit No. 10—The Bulletin Board* (art). Cincinnati: BJE, 1950.

Zeligs, Dorothy. *A Child's History of the Jewish People*. Cincinnati: BJE, 1931. 157 pp.

Cincinnati: Periodicals

The American Israelite Weekly. 1854–present.

American Jewish Archives. 1947–present.

The Ark (formerly *Young Israel*). Juvenile, 1912–2?. Monthly.

B'nai B'rith Magazine. 1886–193?. Monthly.

Die Deborah (G.) (supplement to *American Israelite*). 1927–6?. Weekly.

Hebrew Review. Rabbinical Literary Association of America, 1881–82. Quarterly.

The Hebrew Sabbath School Visitor. 1874–93.

The Messenger. National Federation of Temple Youth–UAHC, 1944. Monthly.

Studies in Bibliography and Booklore. 1953–present.

The Youth Leader. DSSE, UAHC, 1932–?. Monthly.

Cleveland

Cleveland Jewish Centennial Committee. *The Jewish Community of Cleveland Historical Digest, 1837–1937*. Cleveland: 1937.

Gartner, Lloyd P. *History of the Jews of Cleveland*. Cleveland: Western Reserve Historical Society and JTS, 1978. 385 pp.

Goldhammer, Samuel. *Why Doncha Write a Book: A Half-Century in Jewish Communal Life*. Cleveland: 1963.

Green, H. W. *Jewish Families in Greater Cleveland*. 1939.

Gries, M. J. "The Jewish Community of Cleveland." In *A History of Cleveland*, edited by S. P. Orth, 380. 3 vols. Cleveland: 1910.

Herman, Jack J. "The Inner Life of the Jewish Community." In *Proceedings of the Conference on the Writing of Regional History with Special Emphasis on Religious and Ethnic Groups, Cleveland, Dec. 1, 1955*, 67–69. 1956.

Jewish Community Federation Population Research Committee. *Survey of Cleveland's Population, 1981*. Report 3. Cleveland: 1982. 5 pp.

Lipman, Eugene J., and Albert Vorspan. "Cleveland—City without Jews." In *Ten Cities*, 45–72.

Louis, Elmer. "A Study of the Organized Recreational Education, Leisure Time Activities Sponsored by the Jewish Community in the Mount Pleasant Area, Cleveland, Ohio, 1937." Master's thesis, Western Reserve U., 1950.

The Temple, 1850–1950. Cleveland: The Temple. 62 pp.

Weisenfeld, Leon. *Jewish Life in Cleveland in the 1920's and 1930's: The Memoirs of a Jewish Journalist*. Cleveland: Jewish Voice Pictorial, 1965. 145 pp.

Cleveland: Education

Berkson, Isaac B., and Ben Rosen. "The Jewish Education Survey of Cleveland." *Jew Ed* 9 (Jan.–Mar. 1937): 12–19.

———. "Social and Economic Change Reflected in Jewish School Enrollment." In *1936 Jewish Education Survey of Cleveland*. Cleveland: Jewish Welfare Fund, 1936. 82 pp. Excerpt in *JEUS*, 174–77.

Blumenfield, Samuel M. "The Role of Israel in the Jewish School." In *Second Annual Pedagogic Conference*, 32–39. Cleveland: Institute of Jewish Studies–BJE, Nov. 21, 1954.

Brilliant, Nathan. "Jewish Education for Youths and Adults in Cleveland." *Jew Ed* 22 (Summer 1951): 41–43.

Cleveland BJE. *The Cleveland Jewish Teacher*. Cleveland: 1980.

37 LOCAL SOURCES FOR JEWISH EDUCATION OHIO

Eisenberg, Azriel. "Jewish Education in Cleveland, 1945." *Jew Ed* 17 (Feb. 1946): 31–39.

———. *Teaching Biblical Literature*. Cleveland: BJE, 1940.

Feuer, Leon L. "The Religious Educational Program of the Temple Cleveland, Ohio." *Rel Ed* 27 (Sept. 1932): 629–34.

Friedland, A. H. "Report on the Jewish School Population of Cleveland." Cleveland: BJE, Jan. 24, 1935.

Gartner, Lloyd P. "Education and Culture." In *History of the Jews of Cleveland*, 186–208, 284–89. Cleveland: Western Reserve Historical Society and JTS, 1978.

Goldman, Sh., and A. H. Friedland. "השביל„ (The Pathway) (H.). Primer. Cleveland: 1926. 74 pp.

Goldstein, Michael. "נסיון חנוכי בקליבלנד„ (An Educational Experiment in Cleveland). *Sh Hah* (H.) 34 (1974): 33–37.

Intrater, Aaron. "The Bureau of Jewish Education—Cleveland, Ohio." *Jew Ed* 44 (Summer 1975): 14–18.

Intrater, Aaron, and Leon H. Spotts. *The Voice of Wisdom: A Guide to the Wisdom Literature of the Bible for Youth and Adults*. Teacher's guide by Leon H. Spotts. Cleveland: BJE, 1965. 204 pp. High school.

Janowsky, Oscar. "The Cleveland Bureau of Education: A Case Study 1924–1953." *AJHQ* 54 (Mar. 1965): 323–57.

Janowsky, Oscar, and Uriah Z. Engelman. *Jewish Education in Cleveland, 1953*. Supplementary report.

Jewish Community Federation of Cleveland. *Proposal Submitted to Task Force on Personnel in Jewish Education*. Jewish Community Federation of Cleveland, July 1987.

Levitin, Dov. "החנוך העברי בקליבלנד„ (Hebrew Education in Cleveland). *Hadoar* (H.) 32 (Feb. 6, 1953): 233–39.

Medini, Mordecai. "בית הספר הגבוה ובית המדרש למורים בקליבלנד„ (The High School and the Teachers' College in Cleveland). In *JB* (H.), 308–11.

Nahshon, Shmuel. "החנוך העברי התיכוני בקליבלנד„ (Secondary Education in Cleveland). *Sh Hah* (H.) 27 (Winter 1967): 85–91.

Palay, Sara, and Lillian Sugarman. *The Gateway to Prayer*. Cleveland: BJE, 1977. 77 pp.

Pilch, Judah. *Study of Secondary and Higher Jewish Education in Cleveland*. Cleveland: BJE, 1964. 56 pp.

Schreiber, Mordecai. "The Agnon School of Cleveland: The Unlikely Birth of a Day School." *CCAR J* (Apr. 1970): 67–70.

Sorin, Morris. "The Agnon School." *Ped Rep* 23 (Mar. 1972): 5.

Tannebaum, A. *What General Education Might Contribute to Jewish Education*. Cleveland: Cleveland College of Jewish Studies, 1968.

UAHC. "Jewish Education on the March" (UAHC workshop, Cleveland, Nov. 12–13, 1950). *Jew Teach* 19 (May 1950): 1–11.

Vincent, Sidney Z. "Summary of Jewish Education Study in Cleveland, Ohio." *AJYB* 57 (1956): 219–26.

Wertheim, Sally, and Barry Shrage. "The Need to Plan: A Cleveland Perspective." *Jew Ed* 53 (Spring 1985): 5–9.

Zeitlin, Aaron. "דער מוסר-השכל פון מעשה קליוולאנד ארום אידישער דערציאונג אין אמעריקע„ (The Moral of Cleveland—Jewish Education in America). *Day* (Y.) (July 12, 1955).

Cleveland: Curricula and Texts

Beth ha-Hinukh ha-Ivri Curriculum (H.). Cleveland: 1951. 20 pp.

BJE. *First Pedagogic Conference*. Nov. 28–29, 1953.

Braverman, Libby, and Nathan Brilliant. *Devices for Teaching Hebrew Prayer*. Cleveland: BJE.

Curriculum of the Talmud Torahs, 1949. Cleveland. 7 pp.

Dessler, N. *Suggested Curriculum for the Day School*. Cleveland: Hebrew Academy, 1972–73.

Eisenberg, Israel L. (Azriel). *Teaching Biblical Literature*. Cleveland: BJE, 1940. 16 pp.

———. *Teaching Jewish History*. Cleveland: BJE.

Friedland, A. H. "ספורים יפים„ (Sippurim Yafim). Cleveland: Hebrew School and Institute, 1936. Also published by BJE in 1950. 48 pp.

———. *Hebrew Literature Booklets for Use in Secondary Schools*. Cleveland: BJE, ca. 1935.

Helen Stein Institute. *Youth Speaks out on Jewish Education*. Cleveland: 1970. 21 pp.

Jewish Community Federation of Cleveland. *Facilitating the Adjustment of Adolescent Soviet Refugees*. Vol. 2, Nov. 26, 1980. Jewish Community Federation of Cleveland. 20 pp.

Levine, Samuel. *Manual for Teaching the Siddur* (H.). Cleveland: BJE, 1941. 40 pp.

Levitan, Miriam. *A Path to Scriptures* (for adults). Cleveland: BJE, 1967. 94 pp.

Nahshon, Samuel. *Torah Laws* (H.). Cleveland: BJE, 1964. 138 pp.

Spiro, Saul S. *The Ideal of Tzedakah. A Teacher's Manual*. Cleveland: BJE, 1965. 90 pp.

Spiro, Saul S., and Rena M. Spiro. *The Joy of Jewish Living: Jewish Holidays and Practices at Home and in the Synagogue*. Cleveland: BJE, 1965. 205 pp.

Tsafririm. "צפרירים„ (Zephyrs) (H.). Cleveland: Cleveland Hebrew Institute, 1924.

Cleveland: Periodicals

Cleveland Jewish News. 1964–present. Weekly.

Index to Jewish Periodicals. 1963–present. Semi-annual.

Jewish Independent. 1906–6?. Weekly.

Jewish Review and Observer. 1888–196?. Weekly.

Jewish Voice Periodical. 1938–6?. Semi-annual.

Jewish World (Y.). 1907–3?. Daily.

Columbus

JESNA. *Study of the Columbus Hebrew School*. N.Y.: 1983–84.

Kiner, Edward D., and Norman Shub. *Exploring American Judaism*. Columbus: Temple Israel, 1978. 146 pp. Junior and senior high school.

Levinger, Lee J. *Survey of Jewish Education in Columbus*. Columbus: Jewish Education Council, 1940.

Mayer, Albert J. *Columbus Jewish Population Study, 1969*. Columbus: JWF, 1970.

Ohio Jewish Chronicle. 1921–present. Weekly.

Pilch, Judah. *Study of the Columbus Hebrew School*. AAJE, 1960.

Rabin, Phillip Haskell. *A Study of American Jewish Community Backgrounds: A Description of Jewish Organizations and the Jewish Community Council in Columbus, Ohio, 1830–1942*. Ohio State U., unpublished (American Jewish Archives).

Raphael, Marc Lee. "The Early Jews of Columbus, Ohio: A Study in Economic Mobility, 1850–1880." In *Bicentennial Festschrift for Jacob Rader Marcus*, edited by Korn, 435–52.

———. "The Genesis of a Communal History: The Columbus Jewish History Project." *Amer Jew Arc* (Apr. 1977): 53–69.

———. *Jews and Judaism in a Midwestern Community: Columbus, Ohio, 1840–1975*. Columbus: Historical Society and Columbus Jewish Federation, 1979. 496 pp.

Wachs, Saul P. "The Impact of the Pilot Educational Project of the Melton Research Center on Congregation Tifereth Israel, 1960–1966." In *Studies in Jewish Education in Honor of Louis Newman*, edited by Alexander M. Shapiro and Burton I. Cohen, 57–83.

Dayton

Brilliant, Nathan. *Report on the Schools and the Curricula*. AAJE, 1948.

Chanover, Hyman. *Assessing the Reconstituting of a Communal School and Providing Services to the Community*. N.Y.: AAJE, 1965.

Dayton Jewish Chronicle. 1961–present. Weekly.

Engelman, Uriah Z. *Role of the Dayton Hebrew Institution*. AAJE, 1962.

Toledo

* Anderson, Elaine S. *The Jews of Toledo, 1845–1895*. U. of Toledo, 1974.

Dinsky, Samuel. *Supplement to Dr. Pilch's Report of 1963*. N.Y.: 1970.

Jewish Federation of Greater Toledo. *80th Anniversary: From Generation to Generation, 1907–1987*. Sylvania, Ohio: 1987.

Glazer, Simon. *Sabbath School: A Systematic Guide to the Instruction of Judaism Based upon the Bible and the Highest Rabbinical Authorities*. Toledo: 1907

Pilch, Judah. *Evaluation of General Educational Conditions*. N.Y.: AAJE, 1963.

Toledo Israelite. 1915–3?. Monthly.

Wickliffe

"יובל המאה של ישיבת טלז" (The Centenary of the Yeshivah Telz) (H.). 1981. 327 pp.

Youngstown

Intrater, Aaron, Henry Margolis, and Alan D. Bennett. *Comprehensive Appraisal of the Schools and Center and the Federation's Relation to Them*. N.Y.: AAJE, 1970.

Youngstown Jewish Times. 1935–present. Fortnightly.

OKLAHOMA

AJA. "Trailblazers. . ." 8 (Oct. 1956): 122–24.

Cooper, C. I. "Oklahoma—History." *Oklahoma Jewish Chronicle* (Dec. 1929 and Mar. 1930).

Levenson, Joseph. *The Story of Oklahoma Jewry, 1864–1953*. Unpublished (American Jewish Archives)

"Oklahoma." In *Post*, 510–17.

Tobias, Henry J. *The Jews in Oklahoma*. Norman: U. of Oklahoma Press, 1980. 78 pp.

Norman

Grossbard, Marilyn, ed. *Ha'Am—The People*. Norman: Members of the U. of Oklahoma Jewish Community, Dec. 1971. 4 pp.

Oklahoma City

Emanuel, 1904–1984:80 Years of Faith. Oklahoma City. 28 pp.

Southwest Jewish Chronicle. 1929–1991. Quarterly.

This Is Emanuel Synagogue. Oklahoma City: 1986. 12 pp.

Tulsa

B'nai Emunah, 1916–1966 (synagogue). 134 pp.

Tulsa Jewish Review. 1930–present. Monthly.

OREGON

Lowenstein, Steven. *The Jews of Oregon, 1850–1950*. Portland: Jewish Historical Society of Oregon, 1987. 236 pp.

"Oregon." In *Enc Jud*, 12:1451.

"Oregon." In *Post*, 517–23.

Jacksonville

Levinson, Robert E. "The Jews of Jacksonville, 1851–1880." Master's thesis, U. of Oregon, 1962.

New Odessa

Blummenthal, Helen E. "The New Odessa Colony of Oregon, 1882–1886." *WSJH* 14 (July 1982): 321–30.

Herscher, Uri D. "New Odessa, Oregon." In *JAUA*, 37–48.

Portland

American Hebrew News. 1892–1901. Weekly.

Cline, Scott. "Creation of an Ethnic Community: Portland Jewry, 1851–1866." *Pacific Northwest Quarterly* 76 (Apr. 1985): 52–60.

———. "The Jews of Portland, Oregon: A Statistical Dimension, 1860–1880." *Oregon Historical Quarterly* 88 (Spring 1987): 5–27.

Elzas, Barnett A. "The First Confirmation Ceremony in the American Synagogue." *The Jewish Tribune* (May 18, 1906).

Ettinger, Celia. "A Study of the Portland Hebrew School." Master's thesis, Reed College, 1962.

The Jewish Tribune. 1902–2?. Weekly.

Kohanski, Alexander S. *Survey of Jewish Education in Portland*. Portland: Jewish Federation, 1948.

The Observer. Ha-Tsofeh (E. and H.). Portland Hebrew School, 1930–39.

NCJSW and NCJE. *Community Study—Portland*. CJFWF, 1943.

Nodel, Julius J., and Alfred Apsler. *The Ties between: The History of Congregation Beth Israel, Portland, Oregon*. Portland: Temple Beth Israel, 1958. 194 pp.

Scribe. 1919–4?. Weekly.

Segal, Jack. "The Jews of Portland." Master's thesis, Oregon State U., 1965.

Stampfer, Joshua, ed. *The Sephardim: A Cultural Journey from Spain to the Pacific Coast*. Portland: Institute for Judaic Studies, 1987. 150 pp.

Stern, Norton B., and William M. Kramer. "Mayer May Pioneer Portland Rabbi." *WSJH* 21 (Jan. 1989): 103–13.

Toll, William. "American Jewish Families: The Occupational Basis of Adaptability in Portland, Oregon." *Jew J Soc* 19 (June 1977): 33–47.

———. "Fraternalism and Community Structure on the Urban Frontier: The Jews of Portland, Oregon—A Case Study." *Pacific Historical Review* 47 (Aug. 1978): 369–403.

———. *The Making of an Ethnic Middle Class—Portland, Oregon*. Albany: State U. of New York Press, 1982. 242 pp.

———. "Mobility, Fraternalism and Jewish Cultural Change." *AJH* (June 1979): 459–90.

AJA. "War on the Willamette" (newspaper account of an incident between a rabbi and one of his congregants, *Daily Standard and Daily Oregonian*, Oct. 2, 1880). *AJA* 19 (Oct. 1958): 121–24.

WSJH. "News from the Portland Jewish Community" (newspaper account–1885). 9 (Apr. 1977): 235–37.

PENNSYLVANIA

Feldman, Jacob S. *The Jewish Experience in Western Pennsylvania: A History, 1775–1945*. Pittsburgh: Historical Society of Western Pennsylvania, 1986. 331 pp.

Goodman, Abraham V. "Penn's Empire on the Delaware." In *American Overture*, 115–32. 1947.

Marcus, Jacob R. "Pennsylvania, 1734–1782." In *EAJ*, 2:3–164.

"Pennsylvania." In *Post*, 524–62.

Rosenbach, Abraham S. W. "Notes on the First Settlement of Jews in Pennsylvania." *PAJHS* 5 (1897): 191–98.

Samuel, John. "Some Cases in Pennsylvania Wherein Rights Claimed by Jews Are Affected." *PAJHS* 5 (1897): 35–37.

Aaronsburg

Fish, Sidney M. *Aaron Levy, Founder of Aaronsburg*. N.Y.: AJHS, 1950. 239 pp.

Lewis, Arthur H. *The Aaronsburg Story*. N.Y.: Vanguard, 1955. 253 pp.

Allentown

Pollak, George. *Evaluation of Community High School*. N.Y. AAJE, 1972.

Easton

Hart, Gustavus N. "Notes on Meyer Hart and Other Jews of Easton, Pennsylvania." *PAJHS* 8 (1900): 127–33.

Trachtenberg, Joshua. "An American Jewish Community: Easton, Pennsylvania, on Its Two Hundredth Anniversary." *PAJHS* 42 (Dec. 1952): 193–206.

———. *Consider the Years: The Story of the Jewish Community of Easton, 1752–1942*. Easton: Centennial Committee of Temple Brith Sholom, 1944. 327 pp.

Elkins Park

Congregation Adath Jeshurun. *To Commemorate 125 Years, 1858–1983*. Elkins Park: 1983. 36 pp.

Davis, Patricia Talbot. *Together They Built a Mountain*. Little, Pa.: Congregation Beth Shalom of Elkins Park, 1974. 179 pp.

Erie

Spiro, Saul S. *Assessment on Consolidating Educational Programs in the Community*. N.Y.: AAJE, 1970.

Harrisburg

Coleman, Michael B. *The Jews of Harrisburg: An Informal History by a Native Son*. Harrisburg: 1980. 141 pp.

Engelman, Uriah Z. *Self Study of Structure and Standards in Harrisburg, Pennsylvania*. N.Y.: AAJE, 1951.

Johnstown

Glosser, Larry. "After the Horse Died: A Cross-Generational Study of the Glosser Family of Johnstown, Pennsylvania." Master's thesis, HUC–JIR, 1977.

Winograd, Leonard. *The Horse Died at 'Windbar': A History of Johnstown Jewry*. HUC–JIR, 1967.

Lancaster

Brener, David. *The Jews of Lancaster, Pennsylvania: A Story with Two Beginnings*. Lancaster: Congregation Shaarai Shomayim, 1980. 200 pp.

Necarsulmer, Henry. "The Early Jewish Settlement at Lancaster." *PAJHS* 9 (1901): 29–44.

Rhodes, Irwin S. "Early Legal Records of Jews of Lancaster County, Pennsylvania." *AJA* 12 (1960): 96–108.

Merion

Jewish Quarterly Review. 1910–present.

Lorch, Steven C. "Louis Newman and the Idea of Akiba Hebrew Academy." In *Studies in Jewish Education in Honor of Louis Newman*, edited by Alexander M. Shapiro and Burton I. Cohen, 39–55.

Norristown

Norristown Jewish Community—Diamond Jubilee. Norristown: Jewish Community Center, 1970. 12 pp.

Philadelphia

Agran, Nathan. "The Problems of Philadelphia's Jews." *Congress Weekly* (Sept. 8, 1972): 8–12.

AJA. "Jewish Immigrant Life in Philadelphia." 9 (1957): 32–42.

American Jews' Annual. "Little Russia, the Russian Jewish Quarter in Philadelphia and its Denizens." (1890–91): 53.

Baltzell, E. Digby. "The Development of a Jewish Upper Class in Philadelphia, 1782–1940." In *JES*, 271–87. See also his *The Protestant Establishment* (1964).

Berkowitz, Henry. "Notes on the History of Earliest German-Jewish Congregation in America" (Rodeph Sholem). *PAJHS* 9 (1901): 123–27.

Davis, Edward. *The History of Rodeph Sholem Congregation, Philadelphia, 1802–1926*. Phila.: E. Stern and Co., 1926. 155 pp.

* Fish, Sidney M. *Bernard and Michael Gratz: Their Lives and Times*. Dropsie U., 1948.

* Fisher, Terry K. *Lending as Philanthropy: The Philadelphia Jewish Experience, 1847–1954*. Bryn Mawr College, 1987.

Freeman, Moses. „פופציג יאהר געשיכטע פון אידישען לעבן אין פילאדעלפיא" (Fifty Years of Jewish Life in Phila.) (Y.). Phila.: 1932.

Friedman, Murray, ed. *Jewish Life in Philadelphia, 1830–1940*. Phila.: Ishi Publications, 1983. 383 pp.

Geggel, E., and R. L. Schwartz. "Jewish Family Service of Philadelphia" (helping single mothers through the group process). *J Jew Com Ser* 50 (Spring 1974): 245–56.

Hecht, Lester S. *Reform Congregation Kenesseth Israel: Its First 100 Years, 1847–1947*. Phila.: 1950. 64 pp.

Jastrow, Morris, Jr. "The First Publication of a Jewish Character Printed in Philadelphia." *PAJHS* 1 (1893): 63–64.

———. "Notes on the Jews of Philadelphia from Published Annals." *PAJHS* 1 (1893): 49–61, 123.

Klein, Esther M. *A Guidebook to Jewish Philadelphia*. Phila.: Jewish Times Institute, 1965. 114 pp.

Langfield, William R. *The Young Men's Hebrew Association of Philadelphia—A Fifty Year Chronicle*. Phila.: E. Stern and Co., 1928.

Levitt, Joy D., ed. *A Guide to Jewish Philadelphia and Suburbs*. Phila.: Jewish Campus Activities Board, 1979. 103 pp.

37 LOCAL SOURCES FOR JEWISH EDUCATION

PENNSYLVANIA

Lipman, Eugene J., and Albert Vorspan. "Philadelphia—City of Brotherly Love." In *Ten Cities*, 204–32. 1962.

Morais, Henry Samuel. *The Jews of Philadelphia*. Phila.: Levytype Co., 1894. 576 pp.

Morais, Sabato. "Mikve Israel Congregation of Philadelphia." *PAJHS* 1 (1893): 13–24.

Philadelphia. *Annual Reports of the Jewish Community of Philadelphia*. Phila.: (1911–12) 1913; 1912–13 (1914); 1913–14 (1914); 1914–15 (1916).

"Philadelphia." In *Enc Jud*, 13:368–76.

Philadelphia Federation of Jewish Agencies of Greater Philadelphia. *A Study of the Jewish Population of Center City Philadelphia*. Phila.: 1966. 56 pp.

* Porter, Jack Nussan. *Differentiating Features of Orthodox, Conservative and Reform Jewish Groups in Metropolitan Philadelphia*. Temple U., 1958. 200 pp. Summarized in *JSS* 25 (July 1963): 186–94.

Rosenbach, Hyman Pollock. *The Jews of Philadelphia prior to 1800*. Phila.: E. Stern and Co., 1883. 43 pp.

Rosenbaum, Jeanette. "Hebrew-German Society Rodeph Sholem in the City and County of Philadelphia, 1880–1950." *PAJHS* 41 (Sept. 1951): 83–93.

Stern, Gail F., ed. *Traditions in Translation: Jewish Culture in Philadelphia, 1840–1940*. Phila.: Balch Institute for Ethnic Studies, 1989. 134 pp.

Sulzberger, David. "The Beginnings of Russo-Jewish Immigration to Philadelphia." *PAJHS* 19 (1910): 125–50.

Turkel, David Ber. „ביבליאגראפיע פון דער יידישער פרעסע אין פילאדעלפיע 1891–1928" (Bibliography of the Jewish Press in Philadelphia, 1891–1928). In *Pinkes: Studies in Historical Literature, Philology, and Bibliography* (Y.), 260–62. N.Y.: Yivo, 1928.

Whiteman, Maxwell. "Isaac Leeser and the Jews of Philadelphia: A Study in National Influence." *PAJHS* 48 (1959): 202–44.

———. "Philadelphia's Jewish Neighborhoods." In *The Peoples of Philadelphia: A History of Ethnic Groups and Lower Class Life, 1790–1940*, edited by A. F. Davis and M. Haller, 232–36. 1973.

———. "Zionism Comes to Philadelphia." In *EHZA*, 191–218.

Wolf, Edwin, 2d, and Maxwell Whiteman. *The History of the Jews of Philadelphia from Colonial Times to the Age of Jackson*. Phila.: JPS, 1957. 534 pp.

Yancey, William L., and Ira Goldstein. *The Jewish Population of the Greater Philadelphia Area*. Phila.: Federation of Jewish Agencies of Greater Philadelphia, 1985. 320 pp.

Philadelphia: History of Jewish Education

Adler, Cyrus. "Hebrew Instruction in Philadelphia, 1793" (newspaper account). *PAJHS* 35 (1939): 281.

Glenn, Menahem G. "Rabbi Sabato Morais' Report on the Hebrew Education Society of Philadelphia, 1889–1892." In *Ess*, 407–24.

Greenstone, Julius H. *Statistical Data of the Jewish Religious Schools of Philadelphia, 1906–1907*. Phila.: Gratz College, 1909.

Hebrew Education Society of Philadelphia. *Fifty Years Work of the Hebrew Education Society of Philadelphia*. Phila.: 1899. 194 pp.

James, Edwin J. "Jewish Education in Philadelphia." In *The Immigrant Jew in America*, 166–68. 1907.

King, Diana A. "Jewish Education in Philadelphia." In *Jewish Life in Philadelphia, 1830–1940*, edited by Murray Friedman, 235–52. Phila.: Ishi Publications, 1983.

Rosenbach, Abraham S. W. "The Hebrew Sunday School of Philadelphia, Founded by Rebecca Gratz." Gratz College Papers.

Sarner, Ruth Braude. *The Hebrew Sunday School Society of Philadelphia: Perspective and Promise*. Phila.: Hebrew Sunday School Society, 1964. 16 pp.

Temin, Annette. "The Hebrew Sunday School Society of Philadelphia." *Jew Ed* 7 (Apr.–June 1935): 66–70.

* Todes, David U. *History of Jewish Education in Philadelphia, 1782–1873*. Dropsie U., 1953. 159 pp.

Turkel, David Baer. „די געשיכטע פון ישיבת משכן ישראל וסענטראל תלמוד תורה" (The History of Yeshiva Mishkan Israel and Central Talmud Torah) (Y.). Phila.: 1934. 15 pp.

Philadelphia: Education

Bronstein, H. "החנוך העברי בפילדלפיה" (Hebrew Education in Philadelphia). *Hadoar* (H.) 3 (Tishri 25, 1925).

Chasen, Raphael. "The Special Preparation and Utilization of Public School Teachers for Positions in Jewish Education in the City of Philadelphia." *Ed As* (1966): 55–58.

Fachman, A. "מעג מען אנוועגדען קערפערליכע שטראף פאר אנגעהארכזאמע קינדער?" (May One Apply Corporal Punishment to Disobedient Children?). *Jewish World* (Y.) (June 6, 1926).

Gannes, Abraham P. *Director's Annual Report, April 1956*. Phila.: Council on Jewish Education, 1956. 12 pp.

———. "The Philadelphia Council on Jewish Education." *Jew Ed* 30 (Winter 1960): 17–34.

———. *Summary and Evaluation of the Council on Jewish Education—Philadelphia*. Phila.: 1956. 27 pp.

Gratz College. *Bulletin on Jewish Education in Philadelphia* (E. and H). Phila.: Gratz College, Division of Community Services.

Greifer, Julian E. "Realities in Jewish School and Jewish Center Cooperation." *Jew Ed* 23 (Summer 1952): 15–20, 24.

Halevi, Mordecai. "אחוד בתי הת"ת והישיבות בפילדלפיה" (Amalgamation of Talmud Torahs and Yeshivot in Philadelphia). *Sh Hah* (H.) 12 (Dec. 1951): 22–29.

Menachem, G. "מפעולות התרבות והחנוך בפילדלפיה" (Cultural and Educational Activities in Philadelphia). *Hadoar* (H.) 41 (July 27, 1962): 614.

Philadelphia. *Rules of the Jewish Educational Board of Philadelphia*. In *CA*, 191.

Philadelphia Council on Jewish Education. *Standardizing Qualifications of Teachers in the Jewish Congregational Schools of Philadelphia*. Phila.: 1927. 8 pp.

———. *Jewish Educational Systems in Philadelphia*. Phila.

Pitlick, Sh. "החנוך העברי בפילדלפיה" (Jewish Education in Philadelphia). *Hadoar* (H.) 13 (Heshvan 28, 1934).

Rockower, Jacob R. *Report on Continuing Adult Education—The Philadelphia Experience*. June 1972. 4 pp.

———. *Secondary Jewish Education—Large City Experience*. CJFWF, 1970. 11 pp.

Rosen, Ben. "The Extension High School in Philadelphia." *Jew Ed* 1 (Oct. 1929): 183–90.

Satinsky, Morris W. *Philadelphia's Planning for Jewish Education*. GA, 1962. 7 pp.

* Scheiner, Louis. *Interaction Analysis in Elementary Jewish Schools in the Philadelphia-Camden Area: A Study of One Hundred Twenty Classes*. Dropsie U., 1968.

Veret, Paul. *How to Conduct an Enrollment Campaign*. Phila.: Associated Talmud Torahs *Bulletin* #54, 1935. 61 pp.

Philadelphia: Curriculum-Courses of Study

Allied Jewish Appeal. *Course of Study*. Experimental ed. Phila.: 1943. 48 pp.

Lang, Leon S. *A Curriculum for the Congregational School*. Vol. 1. Phila.: BJE of the Philadelphia Branch of the USA, 1951. 240 pp.

Philadelphia. *Curriculum of the United Talmud Torahs and Yeshivas*. Phila.: 1948. 7 pp.

Philadelphia Associated Talmud Torahs. *Course of Study of the Philadelphia Associated Talmud Torahs*. Phila.: Associated Talmud Torahs *Bulletin* #63, Jan. 1936. 24 pp.

Philadelphia: Yiddish Schools

Glozman, Sholem. "אונדזערע ערשטע שולן אין פילאדעלפיא" (Our First Schools in Philadelphia). *Pro D* (Y.) (Jan. 1930): 30.

Orden Schools. "אונדזער שול אלמאנאך" (Our School Almanac—1937) (10 Years of Orden Schools).

Rivkin, B. "די אידישע פאלק-שולן פון נאציאנאלען ארבעטער פארבאנד אין פילאדעלפיא" (The Yiddish Folk Schools of the National Jewish Workers Alliance–LZOA). *Jewish World* (Y.) (Oct. 7, 1926).

Segal, H. "פופצן יאר ארבעטער רינג טעטיקייט אין פילאדעלפיא" (15 Years WC School Activity in Philadelphia). *S Alm* (Y.) (1935): 102–13.

Shapiro, Sh. "יום טוב העפטן פאר דער יידישער שול" (Holiday Workbooks for the Jewish

School) (Y.). Phila.: Central Committee Yiddish Folk Schools, 1944, 1945.

Wagner, N. „אונדזער שול-וועזן אין פילאדעלפיא" (Our Schools in Philadelphia). *Pro D* (Y.) (Mar. 1936): 20.

Workmen's Circle, I. L. Peretz School. „אונדזער יארבוך" (Our Annual) (Y.). 42nd Yearbook, May 1962. 99 pp.

Philadelphia: Surveys of Jewish Education (In Chronological Order)

Levitzky, Joseph. „סקירה על החנוך העברי בפילדלפיה" (A Survey of Hebrew Education in Philadelphia). *Sh Hah* (H.) 3 (1927): 155–58.

Samitz, Samuel. "Survey of Jewish Education in Philadelphia." Master's thesis, Temple U., 1928.

Segel, Alexander. "A Survey of One-Day-a-Week Jewish Education in Philadelphia." *Jew Ed* 4 (Apr.–June 1932): 116–18.

Rosen, Ben. *Jewish Education in Philadelphia, 1936.*

———. "Jewish Education in Philadelphia—1936." *Jew Ed* 9 (Apr.–June 1937): 61–73.

Philadelphia Council on Jewish Education. *Report of the Study Committee on Seven Jewish Educational Organizations, 1938–1939.* Phila.: 1940.

Honor, Leo L., and Morris Leibman. *Jewish Education in Philadelphia—A Survey.* Phila.: Federated Jewish Charities, Allied Jewish Appeal, Nov. 1943. 92 pp. Excerpt in *CA*, 218–20, "Proposal For the Establishment of a Central Educational Agency in Philadelphia."

Philadelphia Self-Study of Jewish Education. Nov. 1949. Gannes, Abraham P., Secretary, *Philadelphia's Self-Study of Jewish Education.* Phila.: 1951–52. 211 pp. + appendix. See also *Jewish Exponent* (Aug. 28; Sept. 4, 11, 28, 25; and Oct. 2, 1953).

Kaplan, Louis L., et al. *Assessment of the Community's Day Schools.* N.Y.: AAJE, 1965, 1968.

Ribner, Sol. *A Study of the Effects of Intensive Jewish Secondary Education on Adult Jewish Studies, Philadelphia, 1976–77.* Phila.: AAJE and Federation of Jewish Agencies of Greater Philadelphia.

Philadelphia: Pedagogy

Chomsky, William. *How to Teach in the Jewish School.* Phila.: Gratz College-Hebrew Education Society, 1948. 57 pp.

———. *The Story Method in Teaching Elementary Hebrew.* Phila.: Associated Talmud Torahs *Bulletin* #15, 1928. 28 pp.

Philadelphia Branch of the United Synagogues of America. "Providing Meaningful Experiences for Our Children." *Syn Sch* 14 (Nov. 1955): 3–30.

Rudavsky, David. *Suggestions for Teaching Jewish Current Events.* Phila.: Associated Talmud Torahs, 1934.

Segal, Abraham. *Methods of Teaching Pupils of the Bar Mitzvah-Bas Mitzvah Age.* Phila.: BJE, 1954.

Philadelphia: Educational Publications

Altman, Sholom. *The American Jewish Tercentenary Songbook.* Phila.: American Jewish Tercentenary Committee-Philadelphia Council on Jewish Education, 1954.

———. *Song Book for One Day a Week Schools.* Phila.: Council on Jewish Education, c. 1949.

Blumberg, Harry. *Outlines in Jewish Customs.* 2 vols. Phila.: Associated Talmud Torahs, 1931.

Chomsky, Zav (William). *Hebrew Achievement Tests.* 3 levels. Phila.: Council on Jewish Education.

———. „ספורי" (The Sippuri Series of Hebrew Textbooks) (H.). 3 vols. plus workbook. Phila.: Associated Talmud Torahs. 1937.

Edidin, Ben M. *Our Holidays and Customs.* Phila.: Associated Talmud Torahs, 1938.

King, Diane A., and Nancy Messinger. *Holidays and Practices: Instructional Objectives and Activities for Aleph, Bet and Gimel Grades.* Phila.: USA.

Kohn, Joshua, and Mrs. Joshua Kohn. *Outlines for Jewish Customs, Ceremonies and Institutions for Use in Hebrew High School Extension Department.* Teacher's manual. Phila.: Associated Talmud Torahs *Bulletin* #20, 1929. 98 pp.

Lurie, Rose G. *Assembly Programs for Jewish Schools.* Phila.: Associated Talmud Torahs.

Millgram, Abraham E. *An Anthology of Medieval Jewish Literature*. Phila.: Associated Talmud Torahs, 1935. 469 p.

Philadelphia Associated Talmud Torahs. *Jewish Community Life in America, Parts I and II*. Phila.: 1943.

Rosen, Ben, and William Chomsky. „ספריה לנוער" (A Library for Youth) (H.). Phila.: Associated Talmud Torahs, 1941. 80 pp.

Sussman, Samuel. *A Guide for Jewish Youth*. Phila.: USA, 1953. 175 pp.

Sussman, Samuel, and Samuel Grossman. *An Adventure in Jewish Living*. Phila.: Associated Talmud Torahs, 1930. 56 pp.

Unterman, Isaac. *Jewish Education*. Phila.: Federated Press, 1944. 110 pp.

Philadelphia: Educational Periodicals

Hebrew High School of the Associated Talmud Torahs, *The Jewish Youth*. First published Jan. 1924. Monthly.

Jewish Education. 1929–4?. 3 times a year.

Smodar. „סמדר" (Bud) (H.). United High School of Philadelphia's Talmud Torahs, 1923–24. Monthly.

Sussman, Samuel, ed. *Jewish Current Events*. Edited by Samuel Sussman. Associated Talmud Torahs. Weekly.

Philadelphia: Periodicals (Chronological Order)

Jewish Advocate. Edited by Isaac Leeser. 1840–43. See also *The Occident* (below).

The Occident and American Jewish Advocate. Edited by Isaac Leeser, 1843–68. Monthly, except for 1855, when it appeared weekly.

Jewish Record. 1874–87. Weekly.

Association Bulletin. YMHA, 1881–?. Bimonthly.

Jewish Exponent. 1887–present. Weekly.

Die Yiddishe Presse (Y.). Aug. 1892–Apr. 1894. Weekly.

Jewish Woman. Oct. 1892–Oct. 1893. Monthly.

Die Gegenwart (The Present) (Y.). 1895–190?. Weekly.

Jewish Morning Journal (formerly *Philadelphia Abend Post*) (Y.). 1899–191?. Daily.

The Review. YMHA, 1905–1?. 8 times per year.

The Jewish Chautauquan. 1908–1?. Monthly.

Jewish World (Y.). 1914–4?. Daily.

Jewish Times of the Greater Northeast. 1925–present. Weekly.

Jewish Current News. 1927–4?. Biweekly. *New Menorah*. 1979–present. Bimonthly.

Pittsburgh

Berzin, I. "Acculturation and Ethnic Maintenance: A Case Study of Pittsburgh Jews." Master's thesis, U. of Kentucky, 1972.

Cooper, Charles I. "The History of the Jews of Pittsburgh." *Jewish Criterion* (May 31, 1918).

Feldman, Jacob S. *The Early Migration of Jews to Pittsburgh, 1754–1894*. Pittsburgh: United Jewish Federation and Pittsburgh Council of B'nai B'rith, 1959. 92 pp.

Friedberg, Lillian. "Pittsburgh Jews Mark Bicentennial." *American Jewish Outlook* (June 26, 1939).

Goldman, M. R. "Hill District of Pittsburgh as I Knew It." *Western Pennsylvania Historical Magazine* (July 1968).

Jewish Community Center. *A Settlement Is a House Next Door to All the World*. Pittsburgh: 1988. 80 pp.

* Levinson, Burton E. *Jewish-Christian Relations in Pittsburgh*. U. of Pittsburgh, 1951.

Miller, Julia. "Jews Connected with the History of Pittsburgh, 1749–1865." Master's thesis, U. of Pittsburgh, 1910.

Pine, Kurt. "The Jews in the Hill District of Pittsburgh, 1910–1940: A Study of Trends." Master's thesis, U. of Pittsburgh, 1940.

National Council of Jewish Women, Pittsburgh Section. *By Myself I'm a Book: An Oral History of the Immigrant Jewish Experience in Pittsburgh*. Waltham, Mass.: AJHS, 1972. 166 pp.

Pittler, Arnold Z. "The Hill District of Pittsburgh." Master's thesis, U. of Pittsburgh, 1930.

* Selavan, Ida Cohen. *The Columbian Council of Pittsburgh, 1894–1909: A Case Study of*

37 LOCAL SOURCES FOR JEWISH EDUCATION

PENNSYLVANIA

Adult Immigrant Education. U. of Pittsburgh, 1976.

———. "Jewish Wage Earners in Pittsburgh, 1890–1930." *AJHQ* 65 (1976): 272–85.

———, ed. *My Voice Was Heard*. N.Y. Ktav, 1981

———. "The Yiddish Press in Pittsburgh: Agency for Americanization or Ethnic Identification?" *Yiddish* (Winter/Spring 1976): 49–53.

Shapiro, Charlotte Heller. "The Jewish Family Welfare Association of Pittsburgh." Master's thesis, U. of Pittsburgh, 1933.

Taylor, Maurice. *The Jewish Community of Pittsburgh*. Pittsburgh: Published by the author, 1941.

———. "A Sample Study of the Jewish Population of Pittsburgh, 1938." In *Pop*, 81–108.

United Jewish Federation of Pittsburgh. *The Jewish Community of Pittsburgh: A Population Study*. Pittsburgh: 1963. 47 pp.

———. *1986 Community Report: Jewish Population Study of Greater Pittsburgh*. Pittsburgh: 1986. 22 pp.

Pittsburgh: Education

Abrams, Israel A. *Curriculum of the Hebrew Institute High School and Teacher Training School*. Pittsburgh: Hebrew Institute, 1939. 5 pp.

———. *Six-Year Course of Hebrew Institute and Affiliated Hebrew Schools of Pittsburgh, Pennsylvania*. Pittsburgh: Hebrew Institute, 1929.

———. „בית המדרש למורים שעל יד המכון העברי בפיטסבורג" (The Teachers College of the Hebrew Institute in Pittsburgh). In *JB* (H.), 212–13.

Baradon, Eunice, and Aharon Kessler. *The Synagogue—A Social Unit for Primary Grades in One-Day-a-Week Schools*. Pittsburgh: Council on Jewish Education, 1956. 10 pp.

Educational News. "Pittsburgh: The Hebrew Institute." *Jew Ed* 1 (May 1929): 126–28.

Greenstone, Julius H. *Statistical Data of the Jewish Religious Schools of Baltimore and Pittsburgh for 1908–1909*. Phila.: Gratz College, 1909.

Kessler, Aharon, et al. *Teaching the Prayers—A Guide for Prayer*. Pittsburgh: Council on Jewish Education, 1956.

* Roseman, Shmuel D. *Jewish Education in Pittsburgh, Pennsylvania*. Pennsylvania State U., 1977. 254 pp.

Saffran, Elizabeth. *Bibliography for the Teaching and Learning of Dinim*. Pittsburgh: Congregation Poale Zedeck, 1979. 19 pp.

Selavan, Ida Cohen. "The Education of Jewish Immigrants in Pittsburgh, 1862–1932." *YA* 15 (1974): 126–44.

Pittsburgh: Surveys of Education

Abrams, Israel A. "A Study of Jewish Education in Pittsburgh." *American Jewish Outlook* (Mar. 8th, Apr 5th, 1939). See also Mar.–Apr. 1940.

Caplan, L., Solomon Freehof, E. Hailpern, J. Rosenbloom, and M. Taylor. *Survey of Jewish Education in Pittsburgh, 1940*.

Chipkin, Israel S. *Memorandum Concerning the Jewish Education Situation: Review of the Hebrew Institute and its Program*. N.Y.: 1940.

Chipkin, Israel S., et al. *Reports on Evaluation of Program of Hebrew Institute of Pittsburgh*. N.Y.: AAJE, NJWB, 1946.

Engelman, Uriah Z. *Jewish Education in Pittsburgh—1950*. N.Y.: AAJE, 1951.

Pittsburgh. *Jewish Education in Pittsburgh: A Self Study*. Pittsburgh: UJF of Pittsburgh, May 1951.

Toubin, Isaac, Director, and Abraham P. Gannes, Study Consultant. *Study and Recommendations for Secondary Jewish Education in Pittsburgh*. Pittsburgh: Jewish Federation of Pittsburgh, 1968. 21 pp.

Pittsburgh: Periodicals

Jewish Leader (Der Vegveiser) (Y. and E.). 1887–194?. Weekly.

Jewish Leader. 1889–197?. Monthly.

Jewish Criterion. 1892–196?. Weekly.

Der Volksfreund (*The People's Friend*) (Y. and H.). 1897–192?. Weekly.

The Jewish Post (Y.). 1903–1?. Weekly.

Jewish Chronicle of Pittsburgh. 1962–present. Weekly.

American Jewish Outlook. 1934–6?. Weekly.

Scranton

* Buch, Arthur T. *The Jewish Community of Scranton.* N.Y.: New School for Social Research, 1950.

Colodner, Solomon. *Relations of the Jewish Council to the Educational Agencies and Schools.* N.Y.: AAJE, 1970.

JESNA. *Study of the Community Hebrew School.* N.Y.: 1983–84.

Tower Hill, Schafferstown, Lebanon County

Mays, George. *The Jewish Colony at Tower Hill.* Phila.: Report Publishing Co., 1905. 20 pp.

Wilkes-Barre

Levitsky, Louis M. "Report of Adult Education Program in Wilkes Barre, Pennsylvania." *RA* (1933–38): 461–63.

Spitz, Jacob. "Length of Stay of Pupils in Religious Schools of Wilkes-Barre, Pennsylvania, as Related to Administration and Programming." Master's thesis, Yeshiva U., 1955.

RHODE ISLAND

Broches, S. "Jewish Merchants in Colonial Rhode Island." In *Jews in New England*, part 2. N.Y.: Bloch, 1942. 80 pp.

Dixon, Walter T., Jr. "The Jews in Colonial Rhode Island." *Jew Life* 18.

Egnal, Freda. "Bibliography of Materials Relating to Rhode Island Jews." *RIJHN* 4 (Nov. 1966): 305–6.

———. "A Catalogue of All Rhode Island Jews Mentioned in Materials Relating to the History of Jews in Rhode Island Depositories, 1678–1966." *RIJHN* (Nov. 1967): 7–80.

———. "A Guide to the More Important Materials Relating to Rhode Island Jews." *RIJHN* 4 (May 1963): 79–99.

Foster, Geraldine. *The Jews in Rhode Island: A Brief History.* Providence: Rhode Island Heritage Commission, 1985. 100 pp.

Marcus, Jacob R. "New England: Rhode Island." In *EAJ* 1:141–57.

Morris, Maxwell H. "Roger Williams and the Jews." *AJA* 3:24–27

"Rhode Island." In *Post*, 562–72.

Smith, S. L. "Jewish Education in Rhode Island during the Colonial Period." *Jew Ed* 47 (Winter 1979): 26–32.

Bristol

Culbertson, Steven. "A Study of the Emergence, Decline and Reestablishment of the Jewish Community of Bristol, Rhode Island" *RIJHN* 9 (Nov. 1986).

Newport

Chyet, Stanley F. "Synagogue in Newport." *AJA* 16 (1964): 41–50.

Guttstein, Morris A. *The Story of the Jews of Newport: Two and a Half Centuries of Judaism, 1658–1908.* N.Y.: Bloch, 1936. 393 pp.

———. *To Bigotry No Sanction: A Jewish Shrine in America, 1658–1958.* N.Y.: Bloch, 1958. 191 pp.

Kohler, Max J. "The Jews in Newport." *PAJHS* 6 (1897): 61–80.

Lewis, Theodore. "Touro Synagogue, Newport, Rhode Island, 1763–1963." *Newport Historical Society Bulletin* 3 (July 1963): 3–20.

Oppenheim, Samuel. "First Settlement of the Jews in Newport: Some New Matter on the Subject." *PAJHS* 34 (1931): 1–10.

Pool, David da Sola. "The Touro Synagogue: Aspects of the Missing Half Century of Its History." *PAJHS* 38 (1948–49): 57–76.

Rhodes, Irwin S. *References to Jews in* The Newport Mercury, *1756–1786.* Cincinnati: American Jewish Archives, 1961. 20 pp.

Shapiro, Chaim. "Touro Synagogue Past and Present." *Local Jewish Historical Society News* 1 (Fall 1987).

Society of Friends of Touro Synagogue. *Touro Synagogue of Congregation Jeshuat Israel, Newport, Rhode Island, Founded 1658, Dedi-*

37 LOCAL SOURCES FOR JEWISH EDUCATION

RHODE ISLAND

cated as National Historical Site, 1946. Newport: Remington Ward, 1950. 55 pp.

Solis, Elvira N. "Enterprise of the Early Jewish Settlers at Newport." *PAJHS* 9 (1910): 147–48.

Providence

Adelman, David C. "Congregation of the Sons of Israel and David (Temple Beth El): The Early Years." *RIJHN* 3 (May 1962).

———. "Early Days of the Providence Jewish Community" and "The Providence Jewish Community Unites." *RIJHN* 3 (Dec. 1960): 160–91.

———. "Population of the Jewish Community of Providence, 1877." *RIJHN* 1: 72–74

Goldman, Israel M. "The Early History of Temple Emanu-El." *RIJHN* 4 (May 1963): 3–46.

* Goldscheider, Calvin. *Trends and Differentials in Jewish Fertility: A Study of the Providence Metropolitan Area*. Brown U., 1964.

Goldstein, Sidney. *The Greater Providence Jewish Community: A Population Survey*. Providence: General Jewish Committee of Providence, 1964. 256 pp.

———. "The Providence Jewish Community after 125 Years of Development." *Rhode Island History* 25 (Apr. 1966): 51–58.

———. "A Social Profile of the Jewish Community of Greater Providence, 1963." *RIJHN A* (Nov. 1964).

Goldstein, Sidney, and Calvin Goldscheider. *Jewish Americans: Three Generations in a Jewish Community*. Englewood, N.J.: Prentice Hall, 1968. 274 pp.

Horvitz, David. *Temple Emanu-El: The First Fifty Years, 5684–5734*. Providence: 1974. 176 pp.

"Providence." In *Enc Jud*, 13:1276–79.

Rosen, B. "The Providence Conservative Synagogue, Temple Beth Israel." *RIJHN* (Nov. 1967): 81–99.

Segal, B. "Jewish Population of Providence, Rhode Island: Estimates and Studies over the Years." *RIJHN* 5 (Nov. 1970): 49–55.

Smith, Judith E. *Family Connections: A History of Italian and Jewish Immigrant Lives in Providence, Rhode Island, 1900–1940*. Albany: State U. of New York Press, 1985. 228 pp.

Temple Beth El. *Congregation of the Sons of Israel and David*. Providence: 198?.

Providence: Education

Cassola, Joel. "You Are There: In a Jewish History Class." Providence: BJE of Rhode Island, 1979.

Egozi, Akiva. "ישיבת פרובידנס„ (Yeshiva of Providence, Rhode Island). *Sh Hah* (H.) 21 (Spring 1961): 159–61.

Engelman, Uriah Z. *Jewish Education in Providence, Rhode Island*. Providence: General Jewish Community and AAJE, 1944.

———. *Study for Establishing a Day School*. AAJE, 1951.

Gannes, Abraham P., et al. *The Status of Jewish Education in Greater Providence*. N.Y.: AAJE, 1972.

Horvitz, Eleanor F. "The Providence Hebrew Day School." *RIJHN* 8 (Nov. 1982).

Schwartz, Elliot S. "Ethnic Heritage Program in Rhode Island." *Jew Ed* 43 (Fall 1974): 59–61.

———. *Organizing Classrooms for Jewish Special Children*. Providence: BJE and USCJE, 1979. 8 pp.

Segal, Beryl. "Jewish Schools and Teachers in Metropolitan Providence, the First Century." *RIJHN* 7 (Nov. 1972).

———. *Know Your Community: The Story of the Jewish Institutions and Agencies of Greater Providence—A Manual for School and Home*. Providence: BJE of Rhode Island, 1976. 67 pp.

Providence: Periodicals

Jewish Weekly (Y.). 1909–2?.

Jewish Review. 1920–3?. Weekly.

Rhode Island Herald. 1929–7?. Weekly.

Rhode Island Jewish Historical Notes. 1954–present.

Woonsocket

Horvitz, Eleanor F. "Jews of Woonsocket" and "The Chesterfield Community and Their Synagogue." *RIJHN* 9 (Nov. 1986).

SOUTH CAROLINA

Elzas, Barnett A. *The Jews of South Carolina: From the Earliest Times to the Present Day.* Phila.: J. B. Lippincott, 1905. 352 pp.

Golden, Harry. *Jewish Roots in the Carolinas: A Pattern of American Philo-Semitism.* Greensboro: 1955.

Goodman, Abraham V. "South Carolina from Shaftesbury to Salvador." In *American Overture*, 150–67. 1947. Also in *JIS*, 29–42.

Huhner, Leon. "The Jews of South Carolina from the Earliest Settlement to the End of the American Revolution." *PAJHS* 12 (1904): 49–61.

———. "Some Additional Notes on the History of the Jews of South Carolina." *PAJHS* 19 (1910): 151–56.

Marcus, Jacob R. "South Carolina, 1670–1776." In *EAJ*, 2:226–57.

"South Carolina." In *Post*, 573–79.

Charleston

Beth Elohim Synagogue. "The Petition of Forty-Seven Members of Beth Elohim Synagogue, 1824." In *Jews and Judaism in the United States: A Documentary History*, edited by Marc Lee Raphael, 186–92. N.Y.: Behrman, 1983.

Carolina Art Association and the Charleston Arrangement Committee. *American Jewish Art and History in the South, 1697–1900: An Exhibition.* Charleston: 1964. 11 pp.

Elzas, Barnett A. *The Old Jewish Cemeteries of Charleston, South Carolina.* 1903.

Engelman, Uriah Z. "Jewish Education in Charleston, South Carolina, during the Eighteenth and Nineteenth Centuries." *PAJHS* 42 (Sept. 1952): 43–70. See also *Sh Hah* (H.) 14 (Spring 1954): 175–79, 214–18.

———. "The Jewish Population of Charleston." *JSS* 13 (July 1959): 195–210.

———. "Jewish Social, Educational, and Religious Developments in Charleston, South Carolina, 1900–1950." *Recon* 18 (Mar. 21, 1952): 26–30.

Friedman, Lee M. "America's First Reform Jewish Congregation." In *Pilgrims in a New Land*, 151–62. 1948.

Kohler, Max J. "Isaac Harby, Jewish Religious Leader and Man of Letters." *PAJHS* 32 (1931): 35–53.

Morse, L. C. *Biography of Isaac Harby with an Account of the Reform Society of Israelites of Charleston, South Carolina, 1824–1833.* 1931. 145 pp.

Ped Rep. "The Aleph-bet Reading Readiness Program, Addleston Hebrew Academy, Charleston, South Carolina." 35 (June 1984): 4–5.

Reznikoff, Charles, and Uriah Z. Engelman. *The Jews of Charleston.* Phila.: JPS, 1950. 343 pp.

Tarshish, Allan. "The Charleston Organ Case." *AJHQ* 54 (June 1965): 411–49.

Tobias, Thomas J. "The Cemetery We Rededicate." *AJHQ* 53 (June 1964): 352–70.

———. *The Hebrew Benevolent Society of Charleston, South Carolina, Founded 1784, the Oldest Jewish Charitable Society in the United States—A Historical Sketch.* Charleston: Hebrew Benevolent Society, 1965.

———. *The Hebrew Orphan Society of Charleston, South Carolina, Founded in 1801: An Historical Sketch.* Privately published, 1957.

Columbia

Fischer, Susan Eleanor. *The Tree of Life Temple, 1896–1972.* Columbia: Tree of Life Congregation, 1972.

Hennig, H. *History of the Jews of Columbia, South Carolina.* 1940

SOUTH DAKOTA

AJA. "Trailblazers . . ." 8 (Oct. 1956): 195–99.

Colman, Blanche. "Early Jewish History of the Black Hills." Unpublished (American Jewish Archives).

Goering, Violet, and J. Orlando. "Jewish Farmers in South Dakota—The Am Olam." *South*

Dakota History 12 (Winter 1982): 232–47. An account of two Jewish agricultural colonies from 1882 to 1885.

———. "Jews of South Dakota: The Adaptation of a Unique Minority." *Heritage of the Great Plains* 16 (Spring 1983): 1–17.

Herscher, Uri D. "Bethlehem-Jehudah, South Dakota." In *JAUA*, 52.

———. "Cremieux, South Dakota." In *JAUA*, 48–52.

"South Dakota." In *Post*, 580–85.

TENNESSEE

Peck, Abraham J. "That Other 'Peculiar Institution': Jews and Judaism in the Nineteenth Century South." *Modern Judaism* 7 (Feb. 1987): 99–114.

"Tennessee." In *Enc Jud* 15, 1008–10.

"*Tennessee.*" In *Post*, 585–95.

Chattanooga

Chattanooga. *Congregation B'nai Zion—Diamond Jubilee, 1883–1963*. Chattanooga: 1964. 113 pp.

Memphis

Frankland, A. E. "Kronikals of the Times—Memphis 1862." *AJA* 9 (1957): 83–125.

Hebrew Watchman. 1925–present. Weekly.

Jewish Spectator. 1885–192?. Weekly.

Lee, Ernst, ed. *Our First Century, 1854–1954*. Memphis: Temple Israel, 1954.

Shankman, Sam. *Baron Hirsch Congregation: From Ur to Memphis*. Memphis: 1957. 153 pp.

Shapiro, Mannheim S. *The Southville (Memphis) Survey of Jewish Attitudes*. N.Y.: AJC, 1959.

Wax, James A. "The Jews of Memphis, 1860–1865." *The West Tennessee Historical Papers* 3 (1949): 39–89.

Nashville

Frank, Fedora. *Beginnings on Market Street: Nashville and Her Jewry, 1861–1901*. Nashville: Jewish Community of Nashville and Middle Tennessee, 1976.

———. *Five Families and Eight Young Men: Nashville and Her Jewry*. Nashville: Tennessee Book Co., 1962. 184 pp.

Hendrix, Nancy. *A Demographic Study of Nashville and Middle* Tennessee. Nashville: Jewish Federation of Nashville and Middle Tennessee, 1983. 37 pp.

Jewish Federation of Nashville and Middle Tennessee. *A Guide for Teaching the History of the Jews of Nashville, Tennessee*. Nashville: 1985. 22 pp.

Lipman, Eugene J., and Albert Vorspan. "Nashville—Athens with an Achilles Heel." In *Ten Cities*, 139–65. 1962.

Observer. 1934–present. Weekly.

Toby, Jackson. "Bombing in Nashville: A Jewish Center and the Desegregation Struggle." *Commentary* 25 (May 1958): 385–89.

TEXAS

* Adams, Bobby E. *Analysis of a Relationship: Jews and Southern Baptists*. Southwestern Baptist Theological Seminary, 1969.

AJA. "Trailblazers . . ." 8 (Oct. 1956): 71–79.

Cohen, Henry. "Henry Castro, Pioneer and Colonist." *PAJHS* 5 (1897): 39–43.

———. "The Jews in Texas." *PAJHS* 4 (1896): 9–19.

———. "Settlement of the Jews in Texas." *PAJHS* 2 (1893): 139–56.

Fierman, Floyd S. *Guts and Ruts: The Jewish Pioneer on the Trail in the American Southwest*. N.Y.: Ktav, 1985. 217 pp.

———. *Some Early Jewish Settlers on the Southwestern Frontier*. El Paso: Western Press, 1960. 60 pp.

Hecht, David. "Sunday Kibbutz in Texas." *Compass* 21 (1972–73).

Jewish Advisory Committee for the Texas Centennial Jewish Program. *One Hundred Years of Jews in Texas*. 1936.

"Texas." In *Post*, 596–608.

Viener, Saul. "Surgeon Moses Albert Levy: Letters of a Texas Patriot." *PAJHS* 46 (1956): 101–13, 49 (1960): 202–7. Also in *The Jewish Experience in America*, edited by A. J. Karp, 2:187–99.

WSJH. "Central Texas Jewry in 1875" (newspaper account). 13 (July 1981): 313–16.

* Weston, Joan Lavison. *School Directed and Non-School Directed Aspirations of Middle and Upper-Middle-Class Jewish High School Students in a Large Urban Jewish Texas Community.* North Texas State U., 1974. 155 pp.

Austin

Hertz-Lazorovitz, Rachel, and Reuben Hertz-Lazorovitz. "מי לומד עברית באוסטין, טקסס?" (Who Is Learning Hebrew in Austin, Texas?). *Sh Hah* (H.) 34 (1974): 214–18.

Dallas

AJC, Dallas Chapter. *The Treatment of Jewish History in World Civilization Textbooks: A Report to the Dallas Independent School District.* Dallas: 197?. 83 pp.

Congregation Shearith Israel. *The Golden Book of Shearith Israel Commemorating the Congregation's Fiftieth Anniversary, 1884–1934.* Dallas: ca. 1935. 120 pp.

Gamoran, Emanuel. *Survey of Jewish Education in Dallas.* Cincinnati: 1945.

Goldberg, Irving L. "The Changing Jewish Community of Dallas." *Amer Jew Arc* 11 (Apr. 1959): 82–97.

Hill, Marilyn Wood. "A History of the Jewish Involvement in the Dallas Community." Master's thesis, Southern Methodist U., 1968.

JESNA. *Evaluation of the Community's Two Jewish Day Schools, Akiba Academy and Solomon Schechter Academy.* N.Y.: 1983–84.

Jewish American. 1938–4?. Weekly.

Maynard, Betty I. *The Dallas Jewish Community.* Dallas: JWF, 1974. 176 pp.

Wolf, Kurt. "Traditionalists and Assimilationists: A Study of the Jewish Population in Dallas, Texas." *Studies in Sociology* (Southern Methodist U. Department of Sociology) 4 (1939–40): 1–2.

El Paso

Fierman, Floyd S. "Insights and Hindsights of Some El Paso Jewish Families." *El Paso Jewish Historical Review* 1 (Spring 1983).

Rosen, Evelyn Rosing. "Martin Zielonka, Rabbi and Civic Leader in El Paso." *El Paso Jewish Historical Review* 1 (Sept. 1982).

Fort Worth

Texas Israelite. 1908–1?. Monthly.

Texas Jewish Post. 1947–present. Weekly.

Galveston

Cohen, Henry. "The Galveston Movement: The First Year." *WSJH* 18 (Jan. 1986): 14–19. (From *B'nai B'rith Messenger* of Los Angeles, Mar. 26 and Apr. 16, 1909.)

Congregation B'nai Israel: The First Hundred Years. Galveston, 1970. 14 pp.

Dreyfus, A., ed. *Henry Cohen, Messenger of the Lord.* 1963.

Marinbach, Bernard. *Galveston: Ellis Island of the West.* N.Y.: State U. of New York Press, 1983. 240 pp.

* ———. *The Galveston Movement.* JTS, 1977.

Nathan, Anne, and Harry I. Cohen. *The Man Who Stayed in Texas: The Life of Rabbi Henry Cohen.* N.Y.: Whittlesy House, 1941.

Houston

Chanover, Hyman, Philip Jaffe, and Herbert Z. Berger. *Study of Elementary and Secondary Schools.* N.Y.: AAJE, 1969.

Cohen, Anne Nathan. *The Centenary History, Congregation Beth Israel, Houston, Texas, 1854–1954.* See especially "To Teach the Children the Mosaic Religion," pp. 13–16.

The Golden Book of Congregation Adath Yeshurin 1891–1941: Commemorating 50 Years of Service to the Jewish Community of Houston, Texas. 1942. 120 pp.

Graubart, Noel, and Morton L. Katz. "Jewish Education in Houston." *Jew Ed* 53 (Spring 1985): 10–11, 19.

JCC. *Report of the JCC of Metropolitan Houston for the Year 1937–38.* 1938–39.

Jewish Beacon. 1947–5?. Weekly.

Jewish Civic Press. 1971–1990. Monthly.

Jewish Digest. 1955–7?. Monthly.

Jewish Federation of Greater Houston. *Golden Jubilee: A Half Century of the Houston Jewish Federation, 1936–1986*. Houston: 1986. 61 pp.

Jewish Herald-Voice (formerly *Texas Jewish Herald*). 1908–present. Weekly.

Levitch, Sadie. "The Approach of One Central Agency" (camping program). *Ped Rep* 26 (Spring 1975): 11–15.

* Maas, Elaine. *The Jews of Houston: An Ethnographic Survey*. Rice U., 1975.

Ped Rep. "Learning Centers: Commission of Jewish Education, Houston, Texas." 35 (June 1984): 17.

Marshall

Kariel, Audrey Daniels. "The Jewish Story and Memories of Marshall, Texas." *WSJH* 14 (Apr. 1982): 195–206.

San Antonio

Jewish Journal of San Antonio. 1973–present. Monthly.

Jewish Record. 1924–3?. Biweekly. (Later *Texas Jewish Press*.)

Kallison, Frances. "100 Years of Jewry in San Antonio." Master's thesis, Trinity U., 1977.

Texas Jewish Press. 1933–5?. Monthly.

Tyler

Mann, Bridget C. *Temple Beth El, 1887–1987: Centennial Journal*. Tyler: 1987. 16 pp.

Waco

Podet, Mordecai. "Jacob de Cordova and the Origins of Waco." *Waco Heritage and History* 16 (Spring 1986): 1–7.

———. *Pioneer Jews of Waco*. Waco: 1986. 91 pp.

UTAH

AJA. "Trailblazers . . ." 8 (Oct. 1956): 98–101.

Brooks, Juanita. *History of the Jews in Utah and Idaho*. Salt Lake City: 1973. 252 pp.

Glanz, Rudolf. *Jew and Mormon: Historic Group Relations and Religious Outlook*. N.Y.: Walden Press, 1963. 379 pp.

Rudd, Hynda. "Congregation Kol Ami: Religious Merger in Salt Lake City." *WSJH* 10 (July 1978): 311–26.

Stern, Norton B. "The Founding of the Jewish Community in Utah." *WSJH* 8 (Oct. 1975): 65–69.

"Utah." In *Post*, 608–14.

Watters, Leon L. *The Pioneer Jews of Utah*. N.Y.: AJHS, 1952. 199 pp.

VERMONT

Feuer, Lewis S., and Marvyn W. Perrine. "Religion in a Northern Vermont Town: A Cross-Century Comparative Study." *J for the Scientific Study of Religion* 5 (Fall 1966): 367–82.

Friedman, Lee J. "Joshua Montefoire of St. Albans, Vermont." *PAJHS* 40 (1950): 119–34.

"Vermont." In *Post*, 615–19.

Burlington

JESNA. *Educational Needs Assessment of the Community's Conservative Synagogue*. N.Y.: 1983–84.

Samuelson, Myron. *The Story of the Jewish Community of Burlington, Vermont, from Early Times to 1946, with Much about the Jewish Community of the State*. Burlington: M. Samuelson, 1976. 187 pp.

VIRGINIA

Friedman, Murray. "Virginia Jewry and the School Crisis: Anti-Semitism and Desegregation." *Commentary* 27 (Jan. 1959): 17–22.

Ginsberg, Louis. *Chapters on the Jews of Virginia, 1658–1900*. Petersburg, Va.: Cavalier Press, 1969. 108 pp.

Huhner, Leon. "The Jews of Virginia from the Earliest Times to the Close of the Eighteenth

Century." *PAJHS* 20 (1911): 85–105. Also in *The Jewish Experience in America*, edited by A. J. Karp, 1:93–113.

Marcus, Jacob R. "Virginia, 1658–1879." In *EAJ*, 2:165–225.

Task, Arnold. "The North Carolina-Virginia Junior High Experience." *Compass* 3 (Fall 1979): 8–9, 21.

"Virginia." In *Post*, 619–32.

Albemarle County

Willner, Nancy E. "A Brief History of the Community in Charlottesville and Albemarle County." *Magazine of Albemarle County History* 40 (1982): 1–24.

Alexandria

Beth El Hebrew Congregation, 1859–1984. Alexandria: Beth El Hebrew Congregation, 1984. 62 pp.

Rosenberg, Maud, and Arthur Marmor. *Temple Beth El: A Centennial of Beth El Hebrew Congregation, Serving Northern Virginia since 1859*. Alexandria: 1962. 76 pp.

Fredericksburg

Friedman, Ruth. *A Portrait of Jewish Life, Fredericksburg, Virginia, 1860–1986*. Fredericksburg: Beth Sholom Temple, 1986. 100 pp.

Norfolk

(See also Tidewater, Virginia)

Stern, Malcolm H. "Some Notes on the History of the Organized Jewish Community of Norfolk, Virginia." *J of the Southern Jewish Historical Society* (Nov. 1963).

Petersburg

Ginsberg, Louis. *History of the Jews of Petersburg, 1789–1950*. Richmond: Williams Printing Co., 1954. 118 pp.

Portsmouth

Berent, Irwin M. "Jews of Portsmouth: 1786–1930." *Renewal: United Jewish Federation News* (Mar. 29, 1085): 46–50, 80–81.

Richmond

Berman, Myron. *Richmond's Jewry, 1769–1976*. Charlottesville: U. Press of Virginia, 1979. 450 pp.

Bernstein, David, and Adele Bernstein. "Slow Revolution in Richmond, Virginia: A New Pattern in the Making." *Commentary* 8 (Dec. 1949): 539–46. Also in JIS, 251–64.

Chyet, Stanley F. "Moses Jacob Ezekiel: A Childhood in Richmond." *PAJHS* 62 (1973): 286–94.

Congregation Beth Ahabah. *A History of Congregation "Beth Ahabah," Richmond, Virginia, from its Organization to its Sixtieth Anniversary, 1841–1901*. Richmond: 1926.

Eakin, Frank E. *Richmond Jewry: Fulfilling the Promise*. Richmond: Congregation Ahabah, Museum and Archives Trust, 1986. 16 pp.

Ezekiel, Herbert T., and Gaston Lichtenstein. *The History of the Jews of Richmond from 1769 to 1917*. Richmond: H. T. Ezekiel, 1917. 433 pp.

Ezekiel, Jacob. "The Jews of Richmond." *PAJHS A* (1896): 22–27.

Fischer, Anne. "A Study of the Problems of the Refugees in Richmond." Master's thesis, Richmond School of Social Work, College of William and Mary, 1944.

Friedman, Chaim. "How Torah Took Richmond." *Jew Parent* 20 (June 1969): 37.

Greenberg, Marilyn S. *Through the Years: A Study of the Richmond Jewish Community, 1870–1914*. Richmond: JCC Tercentenary Committee, 1955. 59 pp.

Jewish Community Federation of Richmond. *50 Years, 1935–1985:50th Anniversary Commemorative Journal*. Richmond: 1985. 55 pp.

Jewish Federation of Richmond. *Demographic Survey of the Jewish Community—Richmond*. Richmond: 1984. 56 pp.

Levinson, Selma. "A Study of the Richmond Jewish Community Council." Master's thesis, Richmond School of Social Work, College of William and Mary, 1946.

Lichtenstein, Gaston. "History of the Jews of Richmond: Their Progress and Prospects." *The Reform Advocate* (May 8, 1913): 3–12.

Silver, Helen. "Richmond." *Had Mag* (Apr. 1989): 28–31.

Southern Jewish Outlook. 1946–5?. Monthly.

Southern Jewish World. 1938–4?. Monthly.

Temple Beth El. *1931–1981, Our Jubilee Year: A Commemoration of the Founding and Growth of Temple Beth El, Richmond, Virginia.* 1981. 84 pp.

Tercentary Committee of the Richmond Jewish Community Council. *Through the Years: A Study of the Richmond Jewish Community.* 1955.

Viener, Saul, ed. *A Commemorative History of Congregation Beth Ahabah, 1844–1966.* Richmond: 1966. 24 pp.

Waddell, Alexander W. "Samuel Mordecai, Chronicler of Richmond, 1786–1865." *Virginia Magazine of History and Biography* 53 (1945): 265–87.

Roanoke

* Rothenberg, Tobias. *Jewish Educational Background of Roanoke Jews.* JTS, 1967.

Tidewater

(See also Norfolk, Virginia)

Berent, Irwin M. "A History of Tidewater Jewry." *Renewal: United Jewish Federation News* 3 (Feb. 20, 1987) and (May 15, 1987); 4 (Sept. 1987); 5 (Nov. 1987). See also *Renewal* (Apr. 1988): 50–61.

Ephross, Paul H., and Joan C. Weiss. *Analysis: Demographic Study of the Jewish Community of Tidewater, Virginia, 1982.* Norfolk: United Jewish Federation of Tidewater, 1982. 24 pp.

Ped Rep. "Teacher Recognition." 35 (June 1984): 27.

Renewal: United Jewish Federation News. 1959–present.

WASHINGTON

Levine, Raphael H., and Michael Robinson. "History of the Jews of the Pacific Northwest." Unpublished (American Jewish Archives).

"Washington." In *Post,* 632–38.

Seattle

Adatto, Albert. "Sephardim and the Seattle Sephardic Community." Master's thesis, U. of Washington, 1939.

Angel, Marc E. "History of Seattle's Sephardic Community." *WSJH* 7 (Oct. 1974): 22–30.

———. "*Progress:* Seattle's Sephardic Monthly, 1934–35." *American Sephardi* 5 (Autumn 1971): 91–95.

———. "The Sephardic Theatre of Seattle." *Amer Jew Arc* (Nov. 1973): 156–60.

Dash, Joan. "The Sephardim of Seattle." *Gourmet* 27 (Apr. 1967): 20–21, 56–60.

Dinin, Samuel, and Jacob M. Kartzinel. *Survey of Jewish Education in Seattle, Washington.* N.Y.: AAJE, 1949.

* Douglas, Martin. *The Jewish Community of Seattle, Washington.* JTSA, 1960.

Droker, Howard A. "Ohaveth Sholem: Seattle's First Jewish Congregation." *WSJH* 17 (Oct. 1984): 26–34.

Friedman, R. "American Jews of Seattle." *Chicago Jewish Forum* 11 (Spring 1953): 177–79.

Jewish Federation of Greater Seattle. *A Guide to Jewish Seattle.* 1979. 23 pp.

Jewish Transcript. 1924–present. Weekly.

McCann, James. *A Study of the Jewish Community in the Greater Seattle Area.* Seattle: Jewish Federation of Greater Seattle, 1979. 84 pp.

M'Godolim (H. and E.). 1979–1989. Quarterly.

Romey, David. "The Sephardim of Seattle." *Jew Life* 31 (May–June 1964): 47–55.

———. "Some Socio-Economic Comparisons of Six Seattle Jewish Congregations." *J of Human Relations* 2 (1954): 39–47.

Rosenbaum, Bella W. "In My Lifetime." (Immigrant from Russia who graduated in the first class of the U. of Washington Law School and who was the first woman to practice law in the state.) *AJA* 19 (Apr. 1967): 3–33.

Sones, Lenore. *Jewish Identity: A Teachers Guide.* Seattle: Jewish Education Council, 1983. 96 pp.

Spokane

Jewish Voice. 1928–3?. Weekly.

Tacoma

Kramer, William M., and Norton B. Stern. "The Beginning of the Organized Jewish Community of Tacoma, Washington." *WSJH* 17 (Oct. 1984): 48–51.

WEST VIRGINIA

Shinedling, Abraham I. *West Virginia: Origins and History, 1850–1958*. 3 vols. Phila.: 1963. For Jewish education see index pp. 1661, 1719.

"West Virginia." In *Post*, 639–43.

Beckley

Shinedling, A. I., and Manuel Pickus. *History of the Beckley Jewish Community*. Beckley: 1955. 205 pp.

Bluefield

Meodor, Michael M. "Faith, Knowledge and Practice: The Jews of Southern West Virginia." *Golden Seal* (Department of Culture and History, state of West Virginia) 2 (Summer 1985): 16–24.

Charleston

Jewish Population Committee. *11th Annual Report on the Jewish Population, Charleston, West Virginia: A Demographic Study*. Charleston: 1963 (8 pp.), 1969 (12 pp.).

Morgantown

Datan, N. "Bar Mitzvah in Morgantown, West Virginia." *Moment* 1 (Jan. 1976): 49–53.

WISCONSIN

"Wisconsin." In *Enc Jud*, 16:555–57.

"Wisconsin." In *Post*, 644–654.

Arpin

Rich, Adolph W. "The Story of the Founding and Progress of a Small Agricultural Settlement." *Wisconsin Jewish Chronicle* (Sept. 28, 1951).

Swichkow, Louis J. "The Jewish Agricultural Colony of Arpin." *AJHQ* 54 (1965): 82–91.

Fond Du Lac

Sumberg, Alfred D. "History of the Jews of Fond du Lac, Wisconsin, 1790–1954." Unpublished (American Jewish Archives).

Madison

Swarsensky, Manfred. *From Generation to Generation: The Story of the Madison Jewish Community, 1851–1955*. Madison: 1955. 115 pp.

Manitowoc

Sumberg, Alfred D. "History of the Jewish Community of Manitowoc, 1890–1954." Unpublished (American Jewish Archives).

Milwaukee

Congregation Beth El. *Centennial—Congregation Beth El, Milwaukee, Wisconsin, 1884–1985*. Milwaukee: 1986. 266 pp.

Der Zeitgeist (G.). 1880–83. (Also published in Chicago.)

Hecht, S. "The Jew and Judaism in Milwaukee." In *History of Milwaukee County from its First Settlement to the Year 1895*, edited by H. L. Conrad, 2:234.

Jewish Press and Milwaukee Wochenblat (Y. and E.). 1915–5?.

Mayer, Albert J. *Milwaukee Jewish Population Study: 1964–1965*. Milwaukee: JWF, 1966.

Milwaukee Jewish Voice (Y. and E.). 1930–3?.

Phillips, Bruce A., and Eve Weinberg. *The Milwaukee Jewish Population: Report of a Survey*. Policy Research Corporation, 1984.

* Polsky, Howard W. *The Great Defense: A Study of Jewish Orthodoxy in Milwaukee, Wisconsin*. U. of Wisconsin, 1957.

———. "A Study of Orthodoxy in Milwaukee: Social Characteristics, Beliefs, and Observances." In *JES*, 325–35.

Steren, Jody Sussman. *Yesterday's Jewish Milwaukee* (photos of early Milwaukee synagogues). Milwaukee: 1985.

Swichkow, Louis J. "A Century of B'nai B'rith in Milwaukee." In *A Century of Service*. Milwaukee: B'nai B'rith Centennial Committee, 1962.

*———. *A Dual Heritage: The Jewish Community of Milwaukee, 1900–1970*. Marquette U., 1973.

———. "The Jewish Community of Milwaukee, Wisconsin, 1860–1870." *PAJHS* 47 (Sept. 1957): 34–58.

Swichkow, Louis J., and Lloyd P. Gartner. *The History of the Jews in Milwaukee*. Phila.: JPS, 1963. 533 pp.

Wisconsin Jewish Chronicle. 1921–present. Weekly.

Wisconsin Jewish Publications Foundation. *Handbook of the Milwaukee Jewish Community, 5739*. Milwaukee: 1978. 160 pp.

Milwaukee: Education

"The Discipline of Our Sabbath Schools." In *JEUS*, 98–101.

Dushkin, Alexander M. *Report on the Educational Situation in Milwaukee*. N.Y.: Bureau of Social Research, 1929.

———. "Report on the Jewish Educational Situation in Milwaukee." In the *Milwaukee Jewish Community Survey*, 1923.

Golub, Jacob J. *Survey: Milwaukee*. 1948.

Kaplan, Louis L. *A Comprehensive Review of Jewish Education in Milwaukee*. N.Y.: AAJE, 1963.

Kessler, Aharon. *Evaluation of the Bureau of Jewish Education of Milwaukee, Wisconsin*. N.Y.: AAJE, 1950.

Levitats, Isaac. *The Story of the Milwaukee Jewish Community*. Milwaukee: Bureau of Jewish Education, 1954.

Rappoport, Israel B. *Report on a Preliminary Survey of Jewish Education in Milwaukee, Wisconsin, Submitted to the Milwaukee Jewish Welfare Fund, Aug 7, 1941*.

"Sunday School Curriculum." In *JEUS*, 97.

Weil, Herman. *The Wisconsin Society for Jewish Learning*. Milwaukee: 1963. 36 pp.

WYOMING

AJA. "Trailblazers . . ." 8 (Oct. 1956): 124–27.

Hallberg, Carl V. "Jews in Wyoming." *Annals of Wyoming* 61 (Spring 1989): 10–31.

Pearlstine, S. S. "Jewish Homesteaders in Wyoming, 1913." *WSJH* 12 (Oct. 1979): 31–32.

"Wyoming." In *Enc Jud*, 16:679–80.

"Wyoming." In *Post*, 655–58.

Cheyenne

Hallberg, Carl V. "Early Jews in Cheyenne." *Rocky Mountain Jewish Historical Notes* 8 (Winter/Spring 1987).

CRITERIA AND EVALUATION

PART IV | CRITERIA AND EVALUATION

CONTENTS

38 | THEOLOGY AND EDUCATION 521
  The Idea of God (Selected) 521
  Gleanings 522

39 | RELIGIOUS EDUCATION 524
  1900–1950 524
  Since 1950 526
  Texts, Readers, and Guides (Selected) 530
  Gleanings 530

40 | PHILOSOPHY OF JEWISH EDUCATION 533
  General (Selected) 537
  Gleanings 537

41 | GOALS OF JEWISH EDUCATION 539
  Prior to 1950 539
  Since 1950 540
  Gleanings 542

42 | RESEARCH IN JEWISH EDUCATION 545
  Call for Research 545
  Prior to 1950 545
  Since 1950 546
  Gleanings 547

43 | CHANGE IN JEWISH EDUCATION 551
  Prior to 1950 551
  Since 1950 552
  Gleanings 557

PART IV   CRITERIA AND EVALUATION

44 | THE SOCIAL SCIENCES AND JEWISH EDUCATION 559

Sociology and Related Fields (Selected) 559
Psychology and Social Psychology (Selected) 564
Identity (Selected) 566
Gleanings 570

45 | ASSESSMENT 573

Prior to 1950 573
Since 1950 576
America's Impact on Jewish Education prior to 1950 584
America's Impact on Jewish Education since 1950 584
Trends prior to 1950 586
Trends since 1950 586
Differences and Common Elements in Jewish Education prior to 1950 587
Differences and Common Elements in Jewish Education since 1950 587
Jewish Education and "Jewish Survival" prior to 1950 587
Jewish Education and "Jewish Survival" since 1950 588
Questions Old and New prior to 1950 (Selected) 588
Questions Old and New since 1950 (Selected) 589
Gleanings 590

46 | THE FUTURE OF JEWISH EDUCATION 597

Views prior to 1950 597
Views since 1950 597
Gleanings 598

47 | BIBLIOGRAPHIES OF JEWISH EDUCATION IN OTHER LANDS 600

General (Selected) 600
Textbooks (Selected) 601
Periodicals and Press (Selected) 601

48 | BIBLIOGRAPHIES OF JEWISH EDUCATION AND RELATED FIELDS IN THE UNITED STATES 603

Judaism and Jewish Life—General (Selected) 603
Education 604
Adult Education (Selected) 605
The Arts (Selected) 605
Audio-Visual Materials 606
The Bible and Hebrew 607
Camp 607
Day School 607
Early Childhood Education 607
Exceptional Children 607
History (Selected) 607
The Holocaust (Selected) 609
Home (Selected) 609
Israel (Selected) 609
Juvenile Literature 610

PART IV   CRITERIA AND EVALUATION

Magazines for Children and Youth 612
Mitzvot/Values (Selected) 612
Periodicals, Newspapers, and Annuals (Selected) 612
Prayer and Synagogue (Selected) 614
Religious Education 614
Sephardim 614
Social Sciences 615
Teachers 615
Teacher Training 615
Textbooks 615
Women (Selected) 616
Youth 616
Doctoral Dissertations and Master's Theses 616

38 | THEOLOGY AND EDUCATION

THE IDEA OF GOD (SELECTED)

Baeck, Leo. "Faith in Man: In Ourselves," "Faith in Man: In One's Fellow Men," and "Faith in Man: In Mankind." In *The Essence of Judaism*, 150–253. N.Y.: Schocken, 1948.

Bamberger, Bernard. *The Search for Jewish Theology*. N.Y.: Behrman, 1976. 112 pp.

Berkowitz, Eliezer. *Crisis and Faith*. N.Y.: Sanhedrin Press, 1976.

———. *God, Man and History: A Jewish Interpretation*. N.Y.: Jonathan David, 1959. 202 pp.

Birnbaum, Ruth. "The Man of Dialogue and the Man of Halakhah" (Buber and Soloveitchik). *Jud* 26 (Winter 1977): 52–62.

Borowitz, Eugene B. "The Idea of God." *CCAR* 67 (1957): 157–86.

* ———. *The Jewish Religion According to the Liberal Reform Tradition*. Columbia U., 1958. 218 pp.

———. *A New Jewish Theology in the Making*. Phila.: Westminster Press, 1968. 230 pp.

———. "Theological Problems in Teaching the Bible." *Jew Teach* 29 (Apr. 1961): 10–15.

———. "Theology and Jewish Education." *Rel Ed* (Sept.–Oct. 1958): 1–4.

———. "Toward a Theology of Reform Jewish Practice." *CCAR J* (Apr. 1960): 27–31.

———. *What We Believe*. N.Y.: UAHC, 1978.

Brickner, Barnett R. "The Modern God Idea." *Rel Ed* 26 (Dec. 1931): 851–57.

———. "Teaching the God Concept in the Light of the New Knowledge of Our Day." *CCAR* 40 (1930): 304–22.

Brusin, David. "The Chosenness of Israel: A Reconstructionist Perspective." *Ped Rep* 37 (Oct. 1986): 11–12.

Churgin, Pinchos. "חול וקודש בחנוכנו„" (The Secular and the Holy in Our Education). In *JB* (H.), 56–60.

Cohen, Arthur A. *The Natural and Supernatural Jew*. N.Y.: Pantheon, 1963. 326 pp.

Cohen, Henry. "The Idea of God in Jewish Education." *Jud* 12 (Spring 1963): 165–78.

Commentary. "The State of Jewish Belief" (symposium with 38 statements). 42 (Aug. 1966): 71–160.

Dimensions. "Fundamental Questions in Contemporary Jewish Theology" (symposium). Participants: Norman Lamm, Arnold J. Wolf, Mordecai M. Kaplan, and Samuel Atlas. 1 (Winter 1967): 5–31.

Eisen, Arnold. "Theology, Ideology: Jewish Thought in America, 1925–1955." *Modern Judaism* 2 (Feb. 1982): 91–103.

Eisenstein, Ira. "God, Israel and Torah." *Jew Ed* 31 (Winter 1961): 16–17.

Fackenheim, Emil. "An Outline of Modern Jewish Theology." *Jud* 3 (1954): 241–50

38 THEOLOGY AND EDUCATION

———. *Quest for Past and Future*. Bloomington: Indiana U. Press, 1968. 336 pp.

Greenberg, Irving. "From Modernity to Post-Modernity and the Revitalization of Traditional Religion." *Rel Ed* 73 (July–Aug. 1978): 449–69.

Heschel, Abraham J. *God in Search of Man: A Philosophy of Judaism*. N.Y.: Farrar, Straus and Cudahy, 1956. 437 pp.

Jud. "Jewish Law" (symposium with 18 perspectives). 29 (Winter 1980): 4–109.

Kaplan, Mordecai M. "Can Judaism Survive without Supernaturalism?" *Jew Ed* 27 (Winter 1956–57): 10–23.

———. "How Man Comes to Know God." *RA Proc* (1941–44): 256–71.

———. "The Judaic View of God." *Jud* 33 (Fall 1984): 402–15.

———. *The Meaning of God in Modern Jewish Religion*. N.Y.: Behrman, 1937. 368 pp.

Keeping Posted. *Jewish Views of God*. Mini-Course, no. 840720. Leader's edition, no. 840722.

Key, Andrew W. *The Theology of Isaac Mayer Wise*. Cincinnati: American Jewish Archives, 1962. 65 pp.

Lookstein, Joseph H. *Yesterday's Faith for Tomorrow*. N.Y.: Ktav, 1979. 89 pp.

Lopian, Eliyahu. "Zatzal" (Faith). Translated by Shraga Silverstein. In *BJC*, 191–220.

Neusner, Jacob. "Agenda for Religious Jewry." *Trad* 8 (Winter 1966): 65–77.

Olan, Levi A. "Current Trends in Jewish Theology." *Jew Teach* 33 (Apr. 1965): 25–32.

———. "God and the Modern Man." *Jew Teach* 33 (Apr. 1965): 21–24.

Petuchowsky, Jacob J. "The Question of Jewish Theology." *Jud* (1958): 49–55.

Rackman, Emanuel. "Israel and God: Reflections on Their Encounter." *Jud* 11 (1962): 233–41.

* Rosenak, Michael. *Tasks of Contemporary Jewish Theology in the Construction of Religious Educational Theory in the Diaspora*. Hebrew U. of Jerusalem, 1975.

Rothschild, Fritz A. *Between God and Man*. N.Y.: Free Press, 1965.

Schacter, Herschel. "Comments on Dr. Kaplan's Paper" (See "Can Judaism Survive without Supernaturalism?" above). *Jew Ed* 27 (Winter 1956): 24–28.

Schechter, Solomon. "The Law and Recent Criticism." In *Studies in Judaism*, 233–51. 1896.

Schulweis, Harold M. "American Influences on Jewish Religion." In *AJ*, 119–35.

Schwarzschild, Steven S. "The Lure of Immanence—The Crisis in Contemporary Religious Thought." *Trad* 9 (Spring/Summer 1967): 70–99.

Siegel, Seymour, and Elliot B. Gertel, eds. *God in the Teachings of Conservative Judaism*. N.Y.: Rabbinical Assembly-KTAV, 1985. 278 pp.

Silberman, Lou H. "Concerning Jewish Theology in North America: Some Notes on a Decade." *AJYB* 70 (1969): 37–58.

Soloveitchik, Joseph B. "Halakhic Man—His World View and His Life." In *Halakhic Man*, Translated from the Hebrew by Laurence Kaplan, 3–95. Phila.: JPS, 1983.

Tchernowitz, Chaim (Rav Tsair). „על הזרמים הדתיים של היהדות באמריקה" (On Religious Trends of American Judaism). *Sh Hah* (H.) 2 (1927): 1–16, 20–30.

GLEANINGS

Rabbinical Assembly, 27th Annual Conference (Proceedings), July 5–7, 1927.

> "We are the only group in Israel, who have a modern mind and a Jewish heart, prophetic passion and western science. It is because we have all these that we see Judaism so broadly. . . . And it is because we are alone in combining the two elements that we can make a rational religion, that we may rest convinced that, given due sacrifice and willingness on our part, the Judaism of the next generation will be saved by us. Certainly it cannot be saved by any other group. We have then before us both the highest of challenges and the greatest of opportunities."
>
> *RA*, 53. Quoted by Abraham J. Karp in *AJA* 35 (Nov. 1983), 255.

38 THEOLOGY AND EDUCATION

Kaplan, Mordecai M. (1934),

"Jewish education is inconceivable without reference to God. . . .

Religion is as much a progressive unlearning of false ideas concerning God as it is the learning of true ideas concerning God."

In his *Judaism as a Civilization*, 498, 505. 1957.

Heschel, Abraham J.,

"A critical reassessment of religion is necessitated by the very situation of our thinking. We cannot continue to employ our critical faculty in all our endeavors and at the same time abstain from raising questions in regard to religion. Our age is the age of criticism to which everything must be subjected. The sacredness of religion, and the authority of legislation, are by many regarded as grounds of exemption from the examination of this tribunal. But, if they are exempted, they become the subject of just suspicion, and cannot lay claim to sincere respect, which reason accords only to that which has stood the test of a free public examination."

Quoted in *Roads to Jewish Survival*, edited by M. Berger, et al., 85. 1967.

UAHC, Centenary Perspective of the CCAR (1976),

"Reform Judaism does more than tolerate diversity; it engenders it. In our uncertain historical situation we must expect to have far greater diversity than previous generations knew. . . . While we may differ in our interpretation and application of the ideas enunciated here, we accept such differences as precious and see in them Judaism's best hope for confronting whatever the future holds for us. Yet, in all our diversity we perceive a certain unity and we shall not allow our differences in some particulars to obscure what binds us together."

Quoted by Jonathan D. Sarna in *AJA* (Nov. 1983), 96.

Gurock, Jeffrey S.,

"Americanized Orthodoxy, too, has not been immune to . . . currents of change. Although a goodly proportion of the RCA membership has resisted to date either debate over or concession to women's goals, another smaller contingent has been searching, textually and sociologically, for the limits to which they can accommodate within the Orthodox reading of Jewish law that which is becoming part of the more liberal Jewish theological/sociological world. Accordingly, many Orthodox congregations now permit their women to serve on lay boards of trustees, and some even permit female membership on synagogue ritual committees."

"Resisters and Accommodators: Varieties of Orthodox Rabbis in America, 1886–1983." *AJA* 35 (Nov. 1983), 183.

39 | RELIGIOUS EDUCATION

(See also chapters 20 and 21)

For materials prior to 1900 see chapter 29

1900–1950

Almond, David. *Hebrew Religious Education Treated Historically: Its American Antithesis and the Projected Remedy*. Chicago: Schulman Bros., 1922.

Berkowitz, Henry. *The New Education in Religion: With Curriculum of Jewish Studies*. Phila.: Jewish Chautauqua Society, 1913. 128 pp.

Berkowitz, Henry, and Corrine B. Arnold. *Organization and Conduct of the Jewish Religious School*. Phila.: Jewish Chautauqua Society. 108 pp.

Brav, Stanley R. "Teaching the God Idea to Young Children." *Jew Ed* 11 (Apr. 1939): 40–44.

CCAR. "Catechism." 11 (1901): 77, 90; 13 (1903): 173.

CCAR. "How Can the Personal Side of Religion Be Cultivated in the Jewish Child?" (symposium). Participants: Henry Berkowitz, A. S. Isaacs, Abba Hillel Silver, Marcus Salzman, and B. West. 26 (1916): 224–46.

CCAR. "On Recent Progress in Religious Education" (symposium). Participants: Henry F. Cope (Religious Education Association), Judah L. Magnes (Jewish Community of New York City), Louis Grossman (HUC), George Zepin (CCAR), and William Rosenau (Chautauqua Society). 24 (1914): 312–38.

Charna, Shalom Y. "לשאלת החנוך הדתי„" (On the Question of Religious Education). *Sh Hah* (H.) 1 (1926): 7–15.

Chipkin, Israel S. "How Effective Is Religious Education in Meeting the Present Situation within the Jewish Group?" *Rel Ed* 31 (July 1936): 205–13.

Cohen, Samuel M. "The Objectives of Religious Education." In *The Progressive Jewish School*, 11–14. 1932.

Dinin, Samuel. "The Duty of the Religious School toward a Better Understanding of Judaism." *Jew Ed* 10 (Oct.–Dec. 1938): 157–61, 175.

———. "Nationalism and Religion in Jewish Education." *Jew Ed* 6 (Oct.–Dec. 1934): 143–50.

———. "Teaching the God-Idea to Children." *Jew Ed* 6 (Apr.–June 1934): 64–72.

———. "Teaching Religion in the Jewish School." *Jew Ed* 11 (Apr. 1939): 4–5.

Dushkin, Alexander M. "The Sources of Jewish Religious Teaching." *Recon* (May 14, 1948): 91–5.

———. "The Teaching of Religion in the American Jewish School." *Rel Ed* 43 (Mar.–Apr. 1948): 84–89.

Edidin, Ben M. *Projects about Religious Ideas and Customs*. Experimental ed. Cincinnati: CJE, UAHC, 1938. 54 pp.

Foster, Solomon. "The Aims of Religious Education." *CCAR* 30 (1920): 361–76.

Franzblau, Abraham N. "Jewish Religious Education: Desirable Character Objectives and Philosophy of Motivation." *Rel Ed* 25 (1930): 427–32.

———. "Towards the Reorientation of Jewish Religious Education." *CCAR* 46 (1936): 272–301. Excerpt in *JEUS*, 181–87.

Gittelsohn, Roland B. "Educating for Worship in Our Religious Schools." *Jew Teach* 12 (June 1942): 1–10.

———. "Further Reflections on the Teaching of God." *Jew Ed* 12 (Apr. 1940): 33–37.

Glazer, B. Benedict. "Jewish Religious Schools." *Child Study* 13 (1936): 144–45.

Golub, Jacob S. *The Jewish Religious School*. N.Y.: AAJE, 1944.

———. "A Study in Jewish Observance." *Recon* 11 (1945).

Greenberg, Simon. *The Conservative Movement in Judaism, an Introduction: Some Guiding Principles for a Conservative Approach to the Teaching of Judaism on God, Torah, and Israel*.

———. *Foundations of a Faith*. N.Y.: USCJE. 352 pp.

———. "Haelokim B'Hinukh Haivri" (God in Jewish Education) (H.). *RA* (1940): 361–75.

———. "The Religious Emphasis in Jewish Education." *Jew Ed* 13 (Jan. 1942): 187–93.

Greenstone, Julius H. *Methods of Teaching the Jewish Religion in Junior and Senior Grades* (correspondence school). Phila.: Jewish Chautauqua Society, 1915. 349 pp.

Grossman, Louis. "Does the Sunday School Make for Religious Consciousness?" *CCAR* 30 (1920): 294–308.

———. "Principles of Religious Education in Jewish Schools." In *Studies in Jewish Literature in Honor of Professor Kaufman Kohler*, 134–46. Berlin: 1913.

———. "The Scope of the Religious School." *CCAR* 19 (1909): 336–52.

Heller, Bernard. "The God Idea That Should Be Taught in the Jewish Religious School." *CCAR* 40 (1930): 323–57.

* Hertz, Richard C. *Religious Education among American Reform Congregations*. Northwestern U., 1949. 220 pp.

Hirsch, Emil. "Aim, Scope and Method of the Jewish Religious School." *Menorah* 34 (1903): 84–91, 166–77, 195–204.

Hurvitz, Shmarya Leib. ספר הדת והחינוך (Religion and Education) (H.). N.Y.: "Chinuch," 1927. 198 pp.

Jaffe, Samuel Z. "The Problem and Method of Making Religious Experience Meaningful in the Jewish Religious School." Master's thesis, HUC–JIR, 1948.

Jung, Leo. *Essentials of Judaism: A Guide to the Facts of Jewish Law and Life*. 6th ed. N.Y.: UOJCA, Yeshiva College. 31 pp.

Kallen, Horace M. "Religious Education in Democratic Society." *Jew Ed* 13 (Apr. 1941): 5–14.

Kaplan, Mordecai M. "The Belief in God and How to Teach It." *Jew Ed* 12 (Sept. 1940): 102–13.

———. "The Function of the Jewish Religious School." *Jewish Teacher* (Jan. 1916).

Katzoff, Louis. "Theological Climate of the Conservative School." In *Issues*, 125–34.

Kornfeld, Moshe. "הדת והחנוך העברי„ (Religion and Jewish Education). *Ha-Gesher* (H.) 1 (1939): 5–7.

Kurzband, Toby K. "Educating for Worship in the Jewish School." *Jew Teach* 1 (June 1933): 28–33.

Landman, Isaac. "Survival Values in Jewish Religious Education." *Rel Ed* 34 (July–Sept. 1939): 135–42.

Lang, Leon S. "Congregational School and Progressive Religious Education." *RA* (1932): 140–47.

Lefkowitz, David. "Religious Education and the Future of American Judaism." *CCAR* 29 (1919): 306–15.

* Levy, Beryl Harold. *Reform Judaism in America: A Study in Religious Education*. Columbia U., 1933.

Markowitz, Samuel H. "Experimenting in Jewish Worship." *Jew Teach* 7 (Nov. 1938): 15–22.

Mayer, Harry M. "The Jewish Religious School." *CCAR* 12 (1902): 187–201.

Newman, Louis I. "How Shall 'We Moderns' Teach Our Children Religion." *Rel Ed* 27 (Apr. 1932):311–17.

Persky, Daniel. "דת ולאומיות בחנוך העברי„ (Religion and Nationalism in Jewish Education). *Hadoar* (H.) 13 (17th of Heshvan 1935).

Piwosky, Abram P. "A Curriculum in Religion for the Elementary Department in Jewish Religious Schools" (grades 1–6). Master's thesis, Temple U., 1934. 84 pp.

Rosenman, Samuel I. "Buttressing Democracy through Religious Education." *Jew Ed* 11 (Jan. 1940): 173–77.

Scharfstein, Zevi. "היש צורך בלמוד הדת?„ (Is There a Need in the Teaching of Religion?). *Hadoar* (H.) 4 (28th of Tishri 1926).

———. "לחקר הפסיכולוגיה של הוראת הדת„ (Research in Psychology on the Teaching of Religion). *Sh Hah* (H.) 3 (1928): 228–35.

Schechter, Solomon. "The Problem of Religious Education." In Seminary Addresses, 105–17. 1915.

Schulman, Samuel. "Jewish Religious Education from the Reform Point of View." *Jewish Teacher* 1 (Jan. 1917): 76–84.

Scotford, J. R. "Judaism Lives by Religious Education." *International J of Religious Education* 8 (1932): 23–24.

Silverman, David M. "A Unit on Judaism." *Jew Teach* 15 (June 1947): 10–19.

Strouse, Edith M. "Notes on a Reform Religious School." *Jew Ed* 6 (Apr.–June 1934): 82–86.

Touroff, Nissan. "דת—שאלת הדת בחינוך היהודי„ (The Question of Religion in Jewish Education). In *Evaluations* (H.), 153–58. 1947.

Weglein, David E. *Methods of Teaching—Pedagogy Applied to Religious Instruction* (correspondence school). Phila.: Jewish Chautauqua Society, 1915. 114 pp.

Whiteman, Kalman. "איז מעגליך א רעליגיעזע אידישע ערציהונג הינט צו טאג?„ (Is a Jewish Religious Education Possible Today?). *Day* (Y.) (Feb. 3, 1929).

SINCE 1950

Ackerman, Walter I. *Jewish Religious Education*. N.Y.: ADL, 1963. 19 pp.

Alper, Janice P. "Creating Spiritual Space: Guidelines for the Religious School." *Compass* 10 (Fall 1987): 8, 24.

Bauman, Morton A. "The Teaching of God and the Bible." *Jew Teach* 27 (Jan. 1959): 5–7.

Ben-Horin, Meir. "Appointment with Education and Religion." *Rel Ed* 79 (Winter 1984): 5–7.

———. "Education as Religion." *Rel Ed* 71 (Sept–Oct. 1976): 509–18. See also *Recon* (Mar. 1981): 15–22

———. "The Proper Age for a Declaration of Faith." *Rel Ed* 58 (Sept.–Oct. 1963): 423–24.

Bernstein, M. M. "Teaching about God in the Classroom." *Ped Rep* 37 (Oct. 1986): 14–16.

* Birnbaum, Herbert A. *Attitudes, Beliefs, and Observances of Jewish Pupils with Varying Religious Educational Experiences*. U. of Maryland, 1963. 117 pp.

Bissell, Sherry H. "The Challenge of Teaching about God." In *JPH*, 87–96.

———. "God—The Struggle and the Dialogue: Curricular Approach to the Teaching of God and a Curriiculum for Junior High School." Analysis of basic curricular approaches to the subject of God, including a curriculum for junior high students that utilizes varied methodologies, culminating in a weekend experience. Master's project, HUC–JIR, 1976.

Borowitz, Eugene B. "Creating Commitment in Our Religious School." *Jew Teach* (Mar. 1956): 7–12. Also in *JJS*, 266–81.

———. "Jewish Education Is an Act of Faith." *Jew Teach* 31 (Apr. 1963): 21–22.

———. "On Dealing With Doubt." *Jew Teach* 33 (Dec. 1969): 15–18.

———. "Teaching the Knowledge of God." *Jew Teach* (Mar. 1959): 21–27.

Brickman, William. "The Education of American Jewish Children." *Rel Ed* 54 (Nov.–Dec. 1959). Also in JJS, 200–207.

Chanover, Hyman. "Educational Planning for Commitment." *Jew Ed* 45 (Fall/Winter 1976): 25–31.

Charry, E. "A Novel Experiment in Religious Education." *Con Jud* (Summer 1957): 20–33.

Chazan, Barry. "Indoctrination and Religious Education." In *LJE*, 57–76. Also in *Rel Ed* 67 (July–Aug. 1972).

———. "Is Jewish Education 'Religious' or 'Ethnic' Education?" In *Proceedings of the Philosophy of Education Society*. Edwardsville, Ill.: Philosophy of Education Society, 1975.

———. "Moral and Religious Education." In *LJE*, 77–94.

Clair, Richard P. "The Whole School Teaches God." *Jew Teach* 28 (Oct. 1959): 10–11.

Cohen, Jack J. "Teaching Religion in the Jewish School." *Syn Sch* 12 (Apr. 1954): 3–6.

Cohen, Steven H. "The Impact of Jewish Education on Religious Identification and Practice." *JSS* 36 (July–Oct. 1974): 316–26.

Colodner, Solomon. "What Is Religious Education and Where Do You Get It." *Impact* 35 (Summer 1977): 15–17.

Compass. "What's New!: Suggested Activities for Teaching Spirituality." 10 (Oct. 1987): 14–15.

Con Jud. "Religiously Oriented Schools in the United States." (Sept. 1964): 1–14.

Cronbach, Abraham. "Spirituality among Jewish Children." *Rel Ed* (Mar. 1956): 11–115.

Diskind, Zalman. "Views on Judaism and Religious Education by American Orthodox Jewish Leaders." *Rel Ed* 63 (Jan.–Feb. 1968): 63–66.

Ed As. "Symposium: "Developing a Religious Personality." In *NICD*, 71–107.

Ed As. "Teaching Conservative Judaism: Curricular Implications" (symposium). Participants: Gerson D. Cohen, Shimon Frost, Simon Greenberg, and Samuel Schafler. (1979).

Elias, J. "The Three Publics of Religious Educators." *Rel Ed* 77 (Nov.–Dec.1982): 615–27.

Ende, George. "On Developing a Religious Personality." *Syn Sch* 18 (Mar. 1960): 6–12.

Fein, Elliot. *Three Paths to One God: Reform, Conservative and Orthodox Ideology for High School Students*. A nine-lesson unit of study. L.A.: HUC–JIR, Tartak Learning Center, 1986.

Fenster, Myron. "On Teaching Religion in the Conservative School." *Syn Sch* 18 (Sept. 1959): 15–18.

Fram, Leon. "The Conference and Jewish Religious Education." In *Retrospect and Prospect, CCAR, 1899–1964*, 181–98.

Freehof, Solomon B. "Jewish Learning and Religious Education." *Jew Teach* 33 (Dec. 1964): 10–12.

Friedman, Maurice S. "Martin Buber and Religious Education." *Rel Ed* 54 (Jan.–Feb. 1959): 5–17.

Fuchs-Kreiner, Nancy. "Challenge to Jewish Religious Educators." *Rel Ed* 78 (Fall 1983): 483–87.

Geller, Joshua. "The Impact of Jewish Education on Student Religious Attitudes." *Syn Sch* 25 (Winter 1967): 9–14.

* ———. *A Study of Early Adolescent Attitudes toward Ethnic and Democratic Beliefs as Related to Attendance in the Public and Jewish Schools*. U. of Michigan, 1968. 252 pp.

Gerard, Bert. "The Hidden Agenda in Religious Education." *Rel Ed* 69 (Mar.–Apr. 1974).

Gerstle, Brad. *Quest for God*. A ten-lesson unit for high school students. L.A.: HUC–JIR, Tartak Learning Center, 1988.

Gilbert, Arthur. "Symposium: The Proper Age for a Declaration of Faith." *Rel Ed* 58 (Sept.–Oct. 1963): 429–30.

Gittelsohn, Roland B. "The Challenge of Teaching Theology." *Jew Teach* 29 (Apr. 1961): 3–6.

Glasser, Harry A. "Guides and Goals in Teaching Comparative Religion." *Jew Teach* 32 (Oct 1963): 15–17.

Gordon, H. "Religious Education as Expressed in the Hasidic Stories of Martin Buber." *Rel Ed* 72 (Jan.–Feb. 1977): 61–73.

Graubart, Alexander. "Teaching about God—A Critique." *Syn Sch* 24 (Fall 1965).

39 RELIGIOUS EDUCATION

Greenberg, Simon. "Lifetime Education as Conceived and Practiced in the Jewish Tradition." *Rel Ed* 68 (June 1973): 339–47.

———. "הוראת דת בארצות הגולה„ (Teaching of Religion in the Diaspora). In *Ed Enc* (H.), 2:372–75.

Harr, Sheldon. *Church, State, and the Schools: A Jewish Perspective*. HUC–JIR, 1973.

Hertzberg, Arthur. "Jewish Education Must Be Religious Education." *Commentary* (May 1953): 448–53.

Heschel, Abraham J. "Jewish Education." In *Insecurity of Freedom*, 223–41. 1966.

———. "The Spirit of Jewish Education." *Jew Ed* 24 (Fall 1953): 9–19, 62. Also in *Readings in Jewish Educational Philosophy*, edited by Judah Pilch, 18–24. N.Y.: NCRI and AAJE, 1962.

———. "Teaching Jewish Theology in the Solomon Schechter School." *Syn Sch* 28 (Fall 1969): 4–33.

Hofmann, Justin. "Religion, Ethics and Moral Education in Judaism." *Rel Ed* 77 (Jan.–Feb. 1982): 57–68.

Holtz, David K. "The Book of Miracles: An Interview with Lawrence Kushner." *Compass* 10 (Oct. 1987): 3–4.

Israel, Richard J. "Providing Religious Models for Students." *Rel Ed* 63 (Jan.–Feb. 1968): 52–58.

Jacob, W. "Education" *Rel Ed* 79 (Winter 1984): 75–78.

* Jaffe, Bernette K. *The Evolution of Jewish Religious Education in America in the Twentieth Century*. Case Western U., 1980. 291 pp. Abstracted in *Rel Ed* 77 (July–Aug. 1982): 442–43.

Jaffe, Samuel Z. "The Problem and Method of Making Religious Experiences Meaningful in the Jewish Religious School." Master's thesis, HUC–JIR, 1948.

Joseph, Samuel K. "The Teacher as Spiritual Role Model." *Compass* 10 (Oct. 1987): 12, 26.

Kane, Gerald M. "4 Ways to Make Worship Work." *Compass* 10 (Fall 1987): 9.

Keeping Posted. "Youth in Search of God." 17 (Jan. 1972). Teacher's edition.

Klein, Joseph. "Traditional Elements In Reform Jewish Education." *CCAR* 66 (1956): 145–.

Knoff, Howard M., and Corrine R. Smith. "The Relationship of Student Attitude toward Religious Education and a Parent Involvement Program at a Jewish Supplementary School." *Jew Ed* 48 (Spring 1980): 27–34.

Kripke, Dorothy K., and Meyer Levin. *God and the Story of Judaism*. N.Y.: Behrman, 1962. 191 pp. Ages 10–13.

Kurzweil, Zvi E. "Fundamental Principles of Jewish Education in the Light of Halachah." *Jud* 16 (1967): 176–85.

Kushner, Lawrence S. "The Idea of God in the Jewish Classroom." *Recon* 50 (Oct.–Nov. 1984): 9–12.

* Levine, Betty Carrol. *Religious Commitment and Integration into the Jewish Community*. Purdue U., 1979. 265 pp.

* Levine, Shlomo D. *A Study of the Effects of Group Counseling on Religious Attitudes and Verbal Behaviors of Members of a Conservative Synagogue*. College of William and Mary, 1974. 143 pp.

Levinson, B. M. "Problems of Jewish Religious Youth." *Genetic Psychology*, Monograph 60 (1959): 309–48.

Lewis, Albert M. "In the Field of Religious Education." *CCAR J* (Oct. 1956): 51–54; (Jan. 1958): 47–50.

Lipman, Matthew. "Thinking Skills in Religious Education." *Ped Rep* 34 (Mar. 1984): 26–29.

* Lipnick, Bernard. *A Description and Analysis of an Innovative Program in Jewish Religious Education*. Washington U., 1972. 327 pp.

———. *An Experiment that Works in Teenage Religious Education*. N.Y.: Bloch, 1976. 234 pp.

Lookstein, Joseph H. "Strategies for Making Adequate Provisions for Religious Education for All Our Young." *Rel Ed* (Mar.–Apr. 1954): 98–.

* Margolis, Daniel J. *Covenant: A Religious Entry into Curricular Design for Jewish Education in America*. Columbia U. Teachers College, 1975. 262 pp.

Marx, Robert J. "Religious Education and Our Technological Society." *Rel Ed* 63 (Sept.–Oct. 1968): 384–87.

Meyers, Lawrence. "Teaching about God in the Religious School." Master's thesis, HUC–JIR, 1960.

Mirel, James. "A Deveopmental Approach to Religious Education." Master's thesis, HUC–JIR, 1974.

Mizrahi, Nina. "The Spiritual Choice of Jews-by-Choice: A Protest." *Compass* 10 (Oct. 1987): 10, 24.

Moscowitz, Nachama Skolnik. "Kedushah: A Model for Teacher Training." *Compass* 10 (Oct, 1987): 13, 23.

* Newman, Max. *Basic Principles of American Reform Judaism and Their Reflection in the Movement's Program of Religious Education from 1848 to the Present*. HUC–JIR, 1965.

Olitzky, Kerry M. "The Language of Holiness." *Compass* 10 (Fall 1987): 5, 22.

———. "Teaching Torah in Our Schools." *Ped Rep* 37 (Oct. 1986): 13–14.

Orkand, Robert J. "Finding Religion in Our Religious Schools." *Compass* 10 (Fall 1987): 10, 22.

Ped Rep. "Denominational or Interdenominational Judaism—Which Shall the School Teach?" 10 (Jan. 1959).

Pilch, Judah. "The Proper Age for a Declaration of Faith." *Rel Ed* 58 (Sept.–Oct. 1963): 417–18.

Pilchik, Eli. "Teaching Love of God to Children." *CCAR J* (Oct. 1966): 27–30.

Rackman, Emanuel. "Israel: Three Principles of Faith." *Jew Ed* 42 (Spring 1973): 34–40.

Reimer, Joseph. "The Moral Component of Religious Education: Theories of Character Development and Their Relation to Jewish Education." Master's thesis, Brandeis U., 1970.

Rosenak, Michael. "A Theory of Religious Education" (4 chapters). In *Commandments and Concerns: Jewish Religious Education in Secular Society*, 191–269. Phila.: JPS, 1987.

Rosenberg, Stuart E. "The Proper Age for a Declaration of Faith." *Rel Ed* 58 (Sept.–Oct. 1963): 290–.

———. "Should We Teach Tots about God?" *Recon* (May 2, 1952): 22–26.

Rosenthal, Ira. "What Should Religious School Be *Like*?" *Jew Teach* 19 (Nov. 1950): 36–39.

Rossel, Seymour. *Judaism*. N.Y.: Watts, 1976. 61 pp.

Roswaski, C, and A. R. Miaston. "The Relationship of the Label, Orthodox, to the Acceptance of Jewish Religious Concepts of Children." *Jew Ed* 33 (Summer 1963): 226–30.

Rothschild, F. A. "The Concept of God in Jewish Education." *Con Jud* 24 (Sept.–Oct. 1970): 2–20. See also *RA* (1965).

Rudavsky, David. "Jewish Education and the Religious Revival." *YA* 13 (1965): 95–124.

Schanin, Norman, et al. "Developing a Religious Personality" (symposium). In *NICD*, 72–107.

Schiff, AJvin I. "Religion in Education: A Jewish Perspective." *Rel Ed* 64 (Nov.–Dec. 1969): 485–91.

Schimmel, Sol. "Michael Rosenak's Commandments and Concerns: Jewish Education in Secular Society." *Jew Ed* 56 (Summer 1988): 18–28.

Schindler, Alexander M. "Jewish Religious Education." In *An Introduction to Christian Education*, 373–80. 1966.

Schmidt, H. D. "Jewish Religious Education and the Challenge of Modernism." *Jud* 7 (Winter 1958): 42–48.

Schnaidman, Mordecai. "Teaching Basic Concepts in an Orthodox School." *Ped Rep* 37 (Oct. 1986): 7–9.

Schwab, Joseph J. "The Religiously Oriented School in the United States: A Memorandum of Policy." *Con Jud* 18 (Spring 1964): 1–14.

Schwartzman, Sylvan D. "Religious Rout or Resistance." *Rel Ed* 66 (Apr.–May 1966): 91–93.

Shapiro, Howard M., and Arnold Dashefsky. "Religious Education and Ethnic Identification: Implications for Ethnic Pluralism." *Review of Religious Research* 15 (Winter 1974): 93–102.

Shapiro, Sanford. "Teaching Theological Concepts to Young People." *CCAR J* (Apr. 1961): 45–49.

Shire, Michael J. "Faith Development and Jewish Education." *Compass* 10 (Oct. 1987): 17–18, 24–25.

———. "Teaching Adolescents about God." Master's thesis, HUC–JIR, 1983.

Siegel, Morton. "On Teaching God." *Ped Rep* 37 (Oct. 1986): 9–10.

Silverman, David W. "On Teaching the Jewish Religion in Conservative Congregational Schools." *Syn Sch* 23 (Spring 1965): 4–10.

Simon, Ted, and Morris Glazer. "How the Knowledge of God Is Taught in the Religious School." Cincinnati: HUC College of the School of Education, 1958. 10 pp.

Spotts, Leon. "Creative Teaching of Jewish Life and Religious Practice." *Syn Sch* 25 (Spring 1967).

* Syme, Daniel B. *Prescriptive and Non-Prescriptive Teacher Language in Intermediate Grade Classes about God in Reform Jewish Religious Schools*. Columbia U. Teachers College, 1980. 136 pp. See also *Rel Ed* 77 (July–Aug. 1982): 446.

Umen, Samuel. "A Call for Religious Education." *Jew Teach* 29 (Dec. 1960): 3.

Wachs, Saul. "The Impact of a Pilot Project in Religious Education upon a Midwestern Conservative Jewish Congregation." Master's thesis, Ohio State U., 1966.

Wax, James, and Alvin Rubin. *How Do We Teach Children to Be Religious?* N.Y.: UAHC. 8 pp.

TEXTS, READERS, AND GUIDES (SELECTED)

Bissell, Sherry H. *God: The Eternal Challenge*. Denver: ARE, 1980. Grades 8–11.

Blume, Judy. *Are You There God? It's Me, Margaret*. Scarsdale, N.Y.: Bradbury Press, 1970.

Bogot, Howard, and Daniel Syme. *I Learn about God*. N.Y.: UAHC. 32 pp. Grades 1–3.

Brichto, Mira. *The God around Us: A Child's Garden of Prayer*. N.Y.: UAHC, 1958.

Cone, Molly. *About God*. N.Y.: UAHC, 1958.

Feuer, Leon L., and Benedict Glazer. *The Jew and His Religion*. N.Y.: Bloch, 1947.

Finkelstein, Louis. *The Beliefs and Practices of Judaism*. Teacher's guide. N.Y.: Devin Adair Co., 1952.

Kipper, Morris, and Lenore Kipper. *God's Wonderful World*. Shengold, 1968.

Klaperman, Libby H. *Jeremy Learns about God*. N.Y.: Behrman, 1957.

Klein, Isaac. *A Guide to Jewish Religious Practice*. N.Y.: JTS/Ktav, 1979. 588 pp.

Kripke, Dorothy K. *Let's Talk about God*. N.Y.: Behrman, 1957. 32 pp.

——— and Meyer Levin. *God and the Story of Judaism*. Workbook by Toby K. Kurzband, teacher's guide by W. J. Daunhauser. N.Y.: Behrman.

Kushner, Lawrence. *The Book of Miracles: A Young Person's Guide to Jewish Spirituality*. N.Y.: UAHC, 1987.

Schwartzman, Sylvan. *The Story of Reform Judaism*. Cincinnati: UAHC, 1953.

Sonsino, Rifat, and Daniel B. Syme. *Finding God: Ten Jewish Responses*. N.Y.: UAHC, 1986. For adolescents.

GLEANINGS

Kaplan, Mordecai M.,
"Despite the progress that has been achieved in educational theory, as a whole, the religious phase of it has by no means kept pace. Nearly all educational writers either avoid the subject or content themselves with a few unanalyzed commonplaces, to which they think their respective creeds commit them. . . . The security of American institutions need not and should not be made to depend upon the suppression of the open discussion of religious problems."
Jewish Teacher 1 (Jan. 1916), 6.

CJE–UAHC,
"The aim of Jewish education is to enable the young to participate fully and loyally in Jewish life by bringing home to them the feeling of God in their lives, in nature,

and in history. It is to make them understand that God demands as His service, the sanctification of life. It is to imbue them with the idea of holiness (the Biblical word for what we today call moral perfection), in short, to teach them the life which Judaism inculcates. It is to make the young feel that God and holiness, or the ideal of moral and spiritual life, have been made known through Israel, as a great historic community."

Quoted by Jacob B. Pollak in *NCJSS Proceedings* (1926), 284.

Cohen, Samuel M.,

"The problem of living in a non-Jewish and often anti-Jewish environment is a peculiarly difficult one. It cannot be met by creating a sense of self-sufficiency and superiority. This would only lead to the destruction of the Jewish ideal of Human Brotherhood in which the value of every citizen of the kingdom of God is unique and incomparable. The best approach seems to be to live out in one's own life the Jewish ideal of peace and good will. The aspiration of being a brother to all mankind is accordingly emphasized as a part of Israel's mission or as a function of a Jewish national group. Without ignoring or belittling the actual injustice or wickedness in the world, the child is made to sense his membership in the human race by contact and cooperation with children of other races and creeds and by contact and cooperation with civic institutions and their officers."

The Progressive Jewish School, 1–18. N.Y.: United Synagogue of America, 1932.

Brav, Stanley R.,

"The parent must be in no extreme haste in bringing the child the consciousness of God. The mother must refrain from thrusting prayers, however simple, down the throat of the child. There must be a clear understanding that religion is no mere belief that is added to the thoughts of the child. Religion must grow out of the child's inner feelings and wishes, and dare not be imposed upon them. It is only of value to the child when it satisfies his needs, desires and feelings. God must be a part of the child's actual experience in order to be meaningful to him. . . . Under all circumstances wait until his imagination and curiosity begin to show themselves in questions concerning the whys and wherefores, and then satisfy the divine inquisitiveness that is evinced with all the intelligence and sympathy you can bring to bear."

"Teaching the God Idea to Young Children." *Jew Ed* 11 (Apr. 1939), 43.

Borowitz, Eugene B.,

"If we are devoted to Jewish religious education it is because we have faith in Him and His purposes, because we know we want to help Him—as difficult and unlikely as that seems—because working with Him, we cannot fail. From the calculating, the hardheaded, the realist point of view, Jewish religious education cannot succeed. From the standpoint of faith it cannot fail. Commitment then is not only the goal, it is the means, the motive, and the source of hope as well."

"Creating Commitment in Our Religious Schools." *Jew Teach* 24 (Mar. 1956), 12.

CJE–USA,

"The Curriculum should be constructed in accordance with the following goals:

1. To imbue the child with a love of God and trust in His goodness. Every phase of the school program and every member of the faculty should reflect this objective. It should find direct expression in the pupils' experiences of prayer, Sabbath and holiday observances, the performances of the Mitzvot, and in instruction in the principles and practices of Judaism.

2. To provide opportunities for the child to develop spiritual and ethical sensitivity through curricular and co-curricular experiences which call for spiritual and ethical action.

3. To develop a desire and convey the skills to practice the Mitzvot and the traditions of Jewish life in the synagogue and in the home through joyous and meaningful religious observances in school and at home."

Objectives and Standards for the Congregational School, 7. 1958.

Scharfstein, Zevi,

"We must find forthright ways of teaching

which will bring the student to appreciate Judaism and its commandments, even when he should find in the Bible ordinances and views that have become obsolete."

Quoted by Meir Ben-Horin, *Jew Ed* 30 (Spring 1960), 8.

Dinin, Samuel,

"Teachers will have to come to grips with the nature and essence of Judaism. If Judaism is religious ethnic in nature, they will have to develop a religious philosophy which has meaning and credibility and which they can conscientiously and in all honesty transmit to the children in their charge. Very few things can be taught without commitment, even language, but certainly religion in a Jewish school cannot be taught neutrally."

Jew Ed 32 (Fall 1961), 33.

Schwab, Joseph,

"The component of the curriculum which bears the main burden of supplying lineage, peerage and linkage would have the following parts and functions:

1. Teaching the lineal language and literature.

2. Imparting, through a history of heroes and heroic events, personified models of the style of life which constitute the lineage.

3. Imparting through a further history of national vicissitudes, suffering and surmounting, a sense of community which will lay a basis for peerage, as well as contribute further to lineage.

4. Constructing a pattern of daily actions—both ritual and end-oriented in which children and adults will each have their reciprocal roles (linkage).

5. Constructing a pattern of collaboration and uniform action in which the children will work and play in interaction with one another (peerage).

6. Constructing a pattern of collaboration and adult education through which the parents of its children are encouraged and enabled to make their contribution to the above, especially to number 1, 4 and 5."

"The Religiously Oriented School in the United States: Memorandum on Policy." *Con Jud* 18 (Spring 1964), 8.

National Commission on Torah Education

"1. To design a program which enables Talmud Torah education to meet the religious needs and interests of our students for the last quarter of the Twentieth Century and well beyond.

2. To engender in our students love, reverence, and appreciation of the Torah, halakha, and teachings which have enabled Judaism to survive, despite many adversities throughout the centuries—and despite many opportunities to assimilate to the majority culture and lose its identity."

Curriculum Guide for Afternoon Religious Schools, edited by Eli Baum, 2. 1979.

Rosenak, Michael,

"If a theory of religious Jewish education will help us to discover some unsuspected affinities between 'religious' and 'nonreligious' Jews, it will not create artificial harmony; at times, it will accentuate principled distinctions and disagreements. Yet, one must place at the top of any agenda for educational deliberation the question of how we can learn from those with whom we disagree and live with those from whom we do not particularly desire to learn anything, while yet maintaining our principles and testifying to our truth as we have experienced it."

Commandments and Concerns: Jewish Religious Education in Secular Society, 272. Phila.: JPS, 1987.

40 | PHILOSOPHY OF JEWISH EDUCATION

GENERAL (SELECTED)

* Abramowitz, Mordecai. *Toward a Philosophy of Jewish Education for Conservative Congregations.* U. of Chicago, 1960.

Ackerman, Walter I. "Chosenness." In *Stu*, 195–209.

Adler, Morris. "The Jewish View of Education." *Congress Weekly* (Jan. 20, 1958): 5–6.

Agus, B. Jacob. "Toward a Conservative Philosophy of Jewish Education." *Syn Sch* 19 (Mar. 1961). Also in *JJS*, 228–41.

Alexander, H. A. "The Inward Turn in Jewish Educational Thought." *Jew Ed* (Fall 1985): 23–32.

———. "Jewish Studies, Liberal Learning and Education." *Jew Ed* 55 (Spring 1987): 9–17.

Alper, Michael. "Guiding Principles and Selective Criteria for American Jewish Education." In *Reconstructing Jewish Education*, 43–62. 1959.

Aron, Isa, and David Ellinson. "The Dilemma of Jewish Education: To Learn and to Do." *Jud* 33 (Spring 1984): 212–20.

Arzt, Raphael B. "Jewish Education: A Perspective on Strategies and Tactics." In *Stu*, 139–67.

* ———. *Towards an Existential Model for Jewish Education.* Columbia U., 1973.

Barylko, H. "Jewish Education and Thought." *WZO* 51/52 (Spring/Summer 1984): 17–19.

Belkin, Samuel. *In His Image: The Jewish Philosophy of Man as Expressed in Rabbinic Tradition.* N.Y.: Abelard-Schuman, 1960.

Ben-Horin, Meir. "Jewish Education: The Challenge." *Jew Spec* (Sept. 1959). See also *Phil*, 64–66.

———. "The Role of Educational Philosophy in the Jewish School Is Sovereign, Equal and Subordinate." *Rel Ed* 58 (Sept.–Oct. 1963): 470–73.

———. "Six Theses on Jewish Education." *Recon* (Jan. 1, 1954): 17–21.

———. "עיונים בפילוסופיה של החנוך" (Studies in Educational Philosophy). *Sh Hah* (H.) 37 (June 1978): 216–21.

———. "Theses on Democracy, Judaism and Jewish Education." In *Lown*, 62–69.

Berkson, Isaac B. "A Community Philosophy of Jewish Education." In *Phil*, 33–37.

———. "Education and the Jewish Renaissance." *Jew Ed* 33 (Summer 1963): 198–208.

Blau, Joseph L. "Problems of Modern Jewish Thought: Tensions between Particularism and Universalism." *RJ* 25 (Fall 1978): 47–62.

———. "Scholarly Works on Jewish Philosophy and Religion." *JBA* 25 (1967–68): 148–54.

Borowitz, Eugene B. "Education is Not I-Thou." *Rel Ed* 66 (Sept.–Oct. 1971): 326–30.

———. "Existentialism's Meaning for Jewish Education." *Commentary* 28 (Nov. 1959): 414–20.

———. "Problems Facing Jewish Educational Philosophy in the Sixties." *AJYB* 62 (1961): 145–53.

Brickman, William W. "Education for Eternal Existence: The Philosophy of Jewish Education." *School and Society* (May 15, 1943). See also *JJS*, 200–207.

Buber, Martin. "Education." In *Between Man and Man*. 1947.

Chazan, Barry. "Contemporary Philosophy of Jewish Education." In *LJE*, 20–36.

———. "The Crisis in Contemporary Philosophy of Jewish Education." *Jew Ed* 42 (Summer 1973): 21–28.

———. "The Nature of Contemporary Philosophy of Jewish Education." In *Proceedings of the Philosophy of Education Society*. Edwardsville, Ill.: Philosophy of Education Society, 1975.

———. "Tradition and Autonomy: The Paradox of Contemporary Jewish Education." *Con Jud* 35 (Spring 1982): 55–65.

Chein, Isidor. "The Challenge of Individual Needs and Aspirations for Jewish Education." In *Phil*, 38–47.

Chomsky, William. "Agenda for American Jewish Education." *Recon* 28 (Feb. 23, 1962): 11–16.

———. "This I Believe." *Jew Ed* 39 (Jan. 1969): 6–17.

Churgin, Gershon A. „הזרמים בפילוסופית החנוך באמריקה" (Currents in the Philosophy of Education in America). *Sh Hah* (H.) 14 (Spring 1954): 147–54.

———. „תגובתנו ההיסטורית" (Our Historic Response). *Sh Hah* (H.) 8 (Aug. 1948): 67–72.

———. „החנוך הפרוגרסיבי ומתנגדיו" (Progressive Education and Its Critics). *Sh Hah* (H.) 20 (Winter 1960).

Cohen, Jack J. "New Emphases in Jewish Education." *Jew Ed* 26 (Summer 1955): 14–21. See also "The Search for the Philosophy of Jewish Education" in *Phil*, 29–32.

Cohen, Nathaniel. „הוראה או חינוך מה עדיף?" (Instruction or Education—Which Is Preferable?). *Hadoar* (H.) 60 (Aug. 21, 1981).

Dinin, Samuel. "Materialism and Idealism in Jewish Education." *Jew Ed* 8 (Apr. 1936): 67–72, 78.

———. "My Educational Credo." In *JJS*, 318–22.

———. "Recent Trends in Educational Philosophy." *Jew Ed* 37 (Spring 1967): 104–12.

———. "Some Current Issues in American Jewish Educational Philosophy." *Jew Teach* 30 (Apr. 1962): 29–31.

———. „אחדותיות" (Unity). In *JB* (H.), 61–69.

Dushkin, Alexander M. "Guiding Principles in My Life." *Jew Ed* 41 (Summer/Fall 1971): 9–12.

———. "Personal Values in Jewish Education." *JSSQ* 23 (Mar. 1947).

Efros, Israel. „ארבעה עגולים" (Four Spheres). *Hadoar* (H.) 11 (28th of Heshvan 1934).

Essrig, Harry. "Thesis for a Working Philosophy." *CCAR J* (Apr. 1963): 72–76. See also *JJS*, 323–28.

Feldman, M. "Educated Observance, Not Indoctrination." *Nat Jew M* 88 (Feb. 1974): 34.

Finkel, Elliott. "Philosophy of Education in Selected Judaic Sources and Values in Four Secular Philosophers." Master's thesis, Loyola U. of Chicago, 1971.

Fox, Seymour. "Prolegomenon to a Philosophy of Jewish Education." In *Essays in Education Presented to Akiva Ernst Simon* (H.). Jerusalem: 1968.

———. "Toward a General Theory of Jewish Education." In *FJCA*, 260–70. See also *Jewish Education and Jewish Identity: Determining the Goals of Jewish Education*, 1–11. N.Y.: AJC, 1977.

Gamoran, Emanuel. "Philosophy and Principles of the Union Curriculum." *CCAR J* (Apr. 1957): 13–20.

* Goldman, Lee Y. *Jewish Philosophy of Education*. Wayne State U., 1957. 300 pp.

Golomb, Abraham. „דער פעדאגאגישער געדאנק ביי יידן" (Educational Thought among Jews). In *Shu P* (Y.), 119–32.

———. „די ארעמקייט פון פעדאגאגישן געדאנק ביי יידן" (The Poverty of Pedagogic

Theory among Jews). In *Our Course among Nations* (Y.), 269–82. 1961.

Goodman, Ruth. "Dialogue and Hasidism: Elements of Buber's Philosophy of Education." *Rel Ed* 73 (Jan.–Feb. 1978): 69–79.

Gordis, Robert. "Toward a Liberal Jewish Education." *Hadassah Newsletter* (Oct. 1960). Also in *Phil*, 67.

Gordon, Haim. "Existential Education as Expressed in the Hasidic Stories of Martin Buber." *Rel Ed* 69 (Sept.–Oct. 1974): 579–92.

Greenberg, Simon. "The Concept of Man Underlying the Biblical Rabbinic Philosophy of Education." *Jew Ed* 39 (Jan. 1969): 18–35.

——. *A Jewish Philosophy and Pattern of Life*. N.Y.: JTSA, 1981.

——. "The Role of the Concept of K'lal Yisrael in Jewish Education." *Jew Ed* 32 (Spring 1962): 137–46.

——. "The Tangibles of Jewish Education." *Jew Ed* 31 (Winter 1961): 5–11. Also in *Phil*, 71–76.

* Hachen, David A. *A Guiding Philosophy for Reform Jewish Education*. Columbia U., 1961.

Halevi, Mordecai. "החינוך העברי והפרוגרסיבי" (Jewish Education and the Progressive). *Sh Hah* (H.) 12 (June 1952): 160–65.

* Handelman, Sholom. *Progressive Education and Its Influence on Jewish Education in the United States, 1900–1965*. Dropsie U., 1969.

Heschel, Abraham J. "Jewish Education." In *The Insecurity of Freedom*, 233–41. 1966.

——. "The Spirit of Jewish Education." *Jew Ed* 24 (Fall 1953): 9–19. See also *Phil*, 18–24.

Jew Fron. "American Jewish Education: 1963." 30 (Nov. 1963): 7–18.

Joseph, Samuel K. "Curriculum Philosophy of Education and the Jewish Religious School." *Rel Ed* 78 (Spring 1983): 193–200.

Kadushin, Max. *Organic Thinking: A Study in Rabbinic Thought*. N.Y.: JTSA, 1938. 366 pp.

Kaplan, Louis L. "Challenges Confronting Jewish Education Today." In *Phil*, 93–99.

——. "For Our Time: A Philosophy of Jewish Education." *NATE* (15th Annual Convention, 1969): 3–24.

Kaplan, Mordecai M. "American Approaches to Jewish Education." *Jew Rev* 1 (May 1943): 5–12.

——. התפתחותו של התהליך החינוכי (The Evolution of the Educational Process) (H.). Jerusalem: Hebrew U. Press, 1938. 22 pp.

——. "The Jewish Conception of Education." *Jew Ed* 14 (Sept.–Dec. 1942): 71–76, 84.

——. "The Meaning of Jewish Education in America." In *Readings in Jewish Educational Philosophy*, edited by Judah Pilch, 59–63. N.Y.: NCRI and AAJE, 1962.

Katz, Shlomo. "Of Jewish Education." *Mid* 15 (Oct. 1969).

Katzoff, Louis. "Formulating a Philosophy of Jewish Education for the Conservative Congregational School." *Syn Sch* 22 (Winter 1964): 27–35.

——. *Issues in Jewish Education: A Study of the Philosophy of the Conservative Congregational School*. N.Y.: Bloch, 1949. 192 pp.

* ——. *The Structure and Philosophy of the Curricula of the Conservative Congregational Hebrew School*. U. of Pennsylvania, 1948.

Kaufman, Yehudah. "החינוך החברתי" (Social Education). *Sh Hah* (H.) 1 (1926): 9–15, 22–27.

Kerdeman, Debby. "The Dialectic Of Jewish Education." A discussion of the dialectic between schooling and learning as it manifests itself in contemporary Jewish education. Master's project, HUC–JIR, 1981.

* Keuer, Edward John. *A Comparison: Educational Theory and Practice in the Elementary Schools of Contemporary American Judaism, Catholicism and Lutheranism*. U. of Texas, 1963. 525 pp.

* Kiner, Edward D. *The Existentialism of Martin Buber and Implications for Education*. Ohio State U., 1967–68.

Kohanski, Alexander S. "Origin and Functions of Modern Tenets in Jewish Education." *Jew Ed* 36 (Spring/Summer 1966): 143–54.

Lehrer, Leibush. "באמערקונגען וועגן דער פילאזאפיע פון טראדיציאנאלען חינוך ביי ייִדן" (Observations on the Philosophy of Traditional Education among Jews). In *Wiseman* (Y.), 229–44.

———. "Reflections on Traditional Education." *Jew Ed* 28 (Winter 1958): 7–12.

———. "The Secular and the Sacred in Jewish Education" In *OFFY*, 97–101.

* Lerman, Herbert K. *The Educational Philosophy of Conservative Judaism and the Curriculum of its Elementary Schools*. Dropsie U., 1964.

Levine, Etan. "Educational Implications of Reconstructionism." *Recon* 46 (Mar. 1980): 7–11.

Levine, Joel Lawrence. "Teacher's Syllabus for an Introduction to the Philosophy of Reform Judaism for the Intermediate Grades." Master's thesis, HUC–JIR, 1973.

Lewis, Justin Harley. *Vision of Redemption: The Educational Philosophy of Rabbi Abraham Isaac Kook in Historical Perspective*. New Haven, Conn.: Four Quarters Pub. Co., 1979.

Mark, Yudel. "On the Intangibility of Tangibles." *Jew Ed* 31 (Winter 1961): 23–24.

NATE. "A Philosophy of Jewish Education." (15th Annual Convention, 1969). 70 pp.

Niger, Shmuel. "Theses on Jewish Education." In *Proceedings of the First National Conference on Jewish Education*. N.Y.: AAJE, 1951. See also *JJS*, 195–98.

Petuchowski, Jakob. "The Limits of People-Centered Judaism." *Commentary* 27 (May 1959): 387–94.

Pilch, Judah. "Jewish Educational Philosophies." *Jewish Cultural Affairs* (July 1957). Also in *JJS*.

———. "לבירור יסודות החינוך היהודי באמריקה" (On Clarifying the Principles of Jewish Education in America). In *Sefer Ha-doar* (H.), 26–28. N.Y.: *Hadoar* and DEC, 1957.

———, ed. *Readings in Jewish Educational Philosophy*. N.Y.: NCRI and AAJE, 1962. 99 pp.

Rackman, Emanuel. *One Man's Judaism*. Tel Aviv: Greenfield Ltd.

Ravid, Zvulun. "עקרים בחנוך העברי באמריקה" (Principles of Jewish Education in America). *Sh Hah* (H.) 22 (Fall 1961): 12–17.

Rawidowicz, Simon. "On Jewish Learning." In *Studies in Jewish Thought*, edited by N. N. Glatzer, 387–404. 1974.

Recon. "Wanted—A Philosophy for Jewish Education" (editorial). (Jan. 10, 1947): 5–7.

Rosenak, Michael. "The Tasks of Jewish Religious Educational Philosophy." *Rel Ed* 73 (Sept.–Oct. 1978): 513–28.

Rosenzweig, Franz. *On Jewish Learning*. Edited by N. N. Glatzer. N.Y.: Schocken, 1955. 128 pp.

Scharfstein, Zevi, ed. יסודות החנוך היהודי באמריקה (Principles of Jewish Education in America) (H.). N.Y.: Teachers Institute of the JTS, 1947. 235 pp.

———. "לבחינת הפילוסופיות של החינוך היהודי בתפוצות" (Toward an Examination of Jewish Educational Philosophies in the Diaspora). *Ha Hinnukh* (H.) (10th of Kislev 1966): 76–86.

Schiff, Alvin I. "The Centrist Torah Educator Faces Critical Ideological and Communal Challenges." *Trad* 19 (Winter 1981): 275–89.

Shoham, Gilbert L. "Should Doctrine Be Central to Jewish Schooling?" *Jew Ed* 51 (Winter 1983): 46–48.

Silberschlag, Eisig. "My Educational Credo." *Jew Ed* 39 (Dec. 1969): 7–13.

Slesinger, Zalmen. "In Quest for a Philosophy of Jewish Education for Our Times." *Recon* 39 (June 1973): 13–24.

———. "Towards a Philosophy of Jewish Education—Some Basic Considerations." *Ped Rep* 12 (Jan. 1961): 10–11, 23.

Soloff, Mordecai I. "A Philosophy of Education for Today and Tomorrow." *Jew Teach* 28 (May 1960): 3–4.

Spiro, Jack D. "A Dialogue between Plato and Rabbah on the Nature and Purpose of Education." *Rel Ed* 67 (Nov.–Dec. 1972): 449–56.

———. "Existentialism and Jewish Education." *Jew Ed* 39 (Apr. 1969): 13–18.

———. "Jewish Education and the Quest for Meaning." *Ped Rep* 20 (Dec. 1968): 11–13.

———. *To Learn and to Teach: A Philosophy of Jewish Education*. N.Y.: Philosophical Library, 1983. 128 pp.

Stern, Jay B. "Building a Working Philosophy for the Conservative School." *Syn Sch* 22 (Winter 1964).

* Teller, Gerald A. *Humanistic Education: A Clarification of its Meaning for Jewish Education*. Wayne State U., 1976. 188 pp.

Touroff, Nissan. "פילוסופיה של החנוך העברי" (Philosophy of Hebrew Education). In *JB* (H.), 9–48.

Weisberg, Harold. "Ideologies of American Jews." In *Jan 2*, 339–59.

Wollman, Benjamin. "הנחות לפילוסופיה חנוכית עברית" (Theses on Hebrew Educational Philosophies). *Sh Hah* (H.) 15 (Summer 1955): 215–27.

GLEANINGS

Felsenthal, Bernard (1822–1908, Chicago),
"'Judaism' and 'Jewish religion' are not synonomous terms. 'Judaism' is more comprehensive than 'Jewish religion,' for 'Jewish religion' is only a part of 'Judaism.' Judaism is the composite of the collected thoughts, sentiments and efforts of the Jewish people. In other words, Judaism is the sum total of all the manifestations of the distictively Jewish national spirit. The Jewish religion is, then only a part of Judaism, though by far its most important part. Among no other people on earth has religion occupied so large, so significant a place in the spiritual life as it has among the Jews. But besides religion there were and still are, other elements in Judaism."
Quoted in AJA 35 (Nov. 1983), 285.

Dinin, Samuel,
"By making nationalism and not religion the integrating factor in Jewish life, we widen the base upon which all Jews can get together, we re-establish once more the basis for a common group life. The important thing now is not so much to see Jewish life as holy—but to see it as whole."
Jew Ed 6 (Oct.–Dec. 1934), 150.

Buber, Martin (1936),
"For the adolescent who is frightened and disappointed by an unreliable world, confidence means the liberating insight that there is human truth, the truth of human existence. When the pupil's confidence has been won his resistance against being educated gives way to a singular happening; he accepts the educator as a person. He feels that he may trust this man, that this man is not making a business out of him but is taking part in his life, accepting him before desiring to influence him. And so he learns to ask."
Quoted in *MTJE*, 232.

Hartstein, Jacob I.,
"To the traditionalist, the Jewish life and the Jewish religion are inseparable. The raison d'etre for Jewish education as far as he is concerned is the Jewish religious life. He sees no reason for the perpetuation of Jewish culture or the furtherance of Jewish nationalism, if it is separated from the Jewish religious life. He draws no line of demarcation between ideals and commandments, between theory and practice. Indeed, all his philosophical concentration is directed at practice "לשמור, לעשות, ולקיים" (to observe, to perform, and to fulfill)."
Jew Ed 17 (Feb. 1946), 40.

Berkson, Isaac B.,
"Jewish education may be defined as a process of transformation. It is the process of transforming a person who happens to have been born a Jew—in itself a physical event—into a person who remains a Jew consciously by reason of his appreciation of the cutltural and spiritual values in his heritage, and by reason of his recognition of his responsibilities as a participant in the life and destiny of the community. It involves the transformation of an accidental connection into a loyalty."
Jew Ed 24 (Fall 1953), 36.

Borowitz, Eugene B.,
"The preoccupation with technique is in large part a flight from the real issues of Jewish life in America, a defense against facing the problems which only a stubborn faith can solve. Most educators feel more comfortable with practical or technical questions. They are less than comfortable examining the faith that keeps them consecrated to their calling and that they need to arouse in others."

"Problems Facing Jewish Educational Philosophy." *AJYB* 62 (1961), 153.

Ben-Horin, Meir,

"The challenge of the requirement of Jewish survival under freedom is the liberation and cultivation of Jewish creative intelligence and creative love to the end that we may find and define our innermost essence and to the end that we may produce our greatest works. After all, the greatest source of the Jewish people is not this or that literary 'source' but the source called our inquiring minds and other source called our compassionate hearts, our capacity to grasp the essentials of the events before us and our capacity to perform the unprecedented. The Jewish people's greatest resource is—the Jewish people's men, women and children."

In *Lown*, 67.

Ackerman, Walter I.,

"There is little in the theory and method of modern Jewish education that is not derivative and while that may be one of the root causes of the failure of Jewish schooling, the fact is that until Jews succeed in developing a powerful and generative theory of education which is drawn from our tradition and responsive to our needs and purposes we shall be dependent on the work of others."

"The Present Moment in Jewish Education." *Mid* (Dec. 1972), 8.

Engel, David, and John F. Rothman,

"In our view,... religious belief and practice comprise but one aspect of a total Jewish civilization. Jewish history, the Hebrew language, Jewish literature, Jewish religion and philosophy, and Jewish artistic expression—these are the five basic elements which go on to make up the Jewish civilization. Jewish education must expose the student to all of these, and most important of all, it must make clear to him that they are all intimately linked to one another."

Recon 39 (Oct. 1973), 8–9.

Fox, Seymour,

"Jewish education can have a significant impact on the future of Jewish life in the United States only if it is prepared to establish, through serious deliberation, philosophies of education to guide the creation of new programs and pratices. These programs must be based on sound analysis of both the reality and the potential of Jewish life."

In *FJCA*, 269.

Chazan, Barry,

"The literature of contemporary Jewish educational philosophy is characterized by practical educational concerns to the exclusion of educational depth or sophistication. Sometimes, philosophic, sometimes Jewish, and always passionately concerned with the day-to-day functioning of Jewish schools, the literature has lacked the educational rigor and depth necessary to make a substantive contribution to thoughtful change."

In *LJE*, 36.

Kronish, Ronald,

"Previous generations of Jewish educators were able to give lip service to Dewey and accept some general aspects of his philosophic and social world view, but they were unable to substantively translate his concepts into practice in schools. This is because they were Jewish survivalists first and progressivists second. People like Dushkin, Berkson, and Gamoran believed in the primacy of Torah and Jewish tradition; although they espoused liberal, secular, humanist points of view, they believed in the history and cultural continuity of the Jewish Tradition and the Jewish People.... If we have learned anything from Dewey, it is the need for a sense of balance and a refusal to create and live by false dichotomies. The need for intelligent, proportioned, critical thinking, which Dewey instilled in his followers, is more than ever a need and ideal that we should cherish and preserve."

"The Influence of John Dewey upon Jewish Education in America." In *Stu*, 2:120–21.

41 | GOALS OF JEWISH EDUCATION

PRIOR TO 1950

Assaf, Simha. "מטרות ומגמות בחינוך העברי" (Goals and Objectives in Jewish Education). In *JED* (H.), 20–24.

Berman, Morton. "Jewish Education as Jewish Experience." *CCAR* 44 (1934): 276–77.

Brill, Mordecai L. "Education for Jewish Morale." *Recon* (June 1, 1945): 19–22.

Dinin, Samuel. "The Purposes of Jewish Education in a Democracy." *Recon* (Feb. 7, 1941): 5–10.

Dushkin, Alexander M. "מטרות ומגמות בחינוך העברי בתפוצות" (Aims and Objectives in Jewish Education in the Diaspora) (H.). (At World Conference on Jewish Education, Jerusalem, July 30, 1947). *Jew Ed* 19 (Fall 1947): 6–13. Also in *Sh Hah* (H.) 7 (Oct. 1947): 187–95 and in *JED* (H.), 11–20.

———. "Education for Jewish Living." *The Torch* 4 (May 1945). See also *RTJS*, 189–93.

Gamoran, Emanuel. "The Aim of Jewish Education in America." In *Principles of the Jewish Curriculum in America*, Part 2 of *Changing Conceptions in Jewish Education*, 24–54. 1924.

Golub, Jacob S. "Some Principles of Jewish Education." *Jew Ed* 9 (Oct.–Dec. 1937): 119–24.

———. "מה מטרת החנוך העברי?" (What is the Goal of Jewish Education?). *Sh Hah* (H.) 2 (1942): 11–19.

Greenberg, Simon. "Basic Premises and a Proposed Structure for Jewish Education in America." *Con Jud* (Feb. 1947): 5–13.

Kaplan, Mordecai M. "The Aim of American Jewish Education." In *FAJ*, 429–46.

———. "Aims of Jewish Education in America." *Opinion* (June 30, 1932).

———. "The Function of the Jewish Religious School." *Jewish Teacher* (Jan. 1916).

———. "מטרת החנוך היהודי באמריקה" (Goal of Jewish Education in America). In *Yesod* (H.), 9–28.

Katzoff, Louis. "Objectives of Instruction in Jewish Education." In *Issues*, 115–24.

Kohn, Eugene. "The Objectives of Jewish Education in America." *RA* (1938): 3–29.

Kook, Abraham Isaac. "מטרת החנוך" (Educational Goal). *Sh Hah* (H.) 5 (Oct. 1944): 3–4.

Levine, D. "מטרות ומגמות בחינוך העברי בתפוצות" (Goals and Objectives in Jewish Education in the Diaspora). In *JED* (H.), 25–36.

Millgram, Abraham E. "The Objectives of Jewish Education." *Jew Ed* 18 (Feb.–Mar. 1947): 23–26.

Philipson, David. "Aims of the Jewish Religious School." *Jew Teach* 1 (Nov. 1932).

Scharfstein, Zevi. "תורת מלים או תורת חיים" (The Study of Words or the Study of Life). *Sh Hah* (H.) 4 (1928): 125–30.

41 GOALS OF JEWISH EDUCATION

Shetzer, Simon. "The Function of Jewish Education in America." *Jew Ed* 15 (Sept. 1943): 7–9, 20.

Sh Hah (H.). „המועט והמרבה בחנוך העברי באמריקה" (The Minimum and Maximum in Hebrew Education in America) (symposium). Participants: Sh. Ginzberg, Menahem Ribalow, Zevi Scharfstein, M. Feinstein, Emanuel Gamoran, Pinchos Churgin, Shimon Halkin, Abraham N. Franzblau, Sh. Kushtai, M. Click, Israel Konowitz, Bernard Isaacs, and A. Goldstein. 3 (1928): 345–99.

Touroff, Nissan. „דרישותינו המינימלית" (Our Minimal Requirements). *Sh Hah* (H.) 2 (1927): 4–10.

———. „דרישותינו בנוגע לתכנית ורוח של בית-הספר העברי" (Our Requirements Pertaining to Program and Spirit of the Jewish School). *Sh Hah* (H.) 3 (1928): 255–65.

Usishkin, M. „רעיון הגאולה במרכז החנוך" (The Idea of Redemption in the Center of Education). *Sh Hah* (H.) 2 (1942): 164–72.

Waxman, Meyer. „אידיאלים חנוכיים" (Educational Ideals). *Sh Hah* (H.) 2 (1927): 17–26.

SINCE 1950

AJC. *Determining the Goals of Jewish Education: Jewish Education and Jewish Identity*. N.Y.: *Colloquium Papers*, 1977. 37 pp.

American Council for Jewish Education. *Education in Judaism*. N.Y.: 1965.

Baron, Salo W. „דאס דערציען קינדער אין אידישן גייסט איז שטענדיק געווען די גרעסטע מצוה ביי אידן" (The Education of Children within the Spirit of Judaism Has Always Been Paramount among Jews) (interview). In *Penn* (Y.), 141–51.

Bemporad, Jack. "Framing the Question." *Ped Rep* 19 (Dec. 1967): 24–25.

Ben-Horin, Meir. "Education for Jewish Living." *Congress Weekly* (Nov. 7, 1955): 10–11.

* Berger, Julius. *Fundamental Jewish Educational Ideals*. U. of Ottawa, 1950. 100 pp.

CCAR J. "The Goals of Jewish Religious Education" (symposium). 11 (Apr. 1963).

Chazan, Barry. "Goals and Jewish Education." In *LJE*, 43–56.

Chomsky, William. "Jewish Education—For What?" *Recon* (Oct. 6, 1961): 13–19.

———. "What Do We Teach For?" *Ped Rep* 4 (Jan. 1953).

Colodner, Sol. "Are We Achieving Our Jewish Educational Goals?" *Syn Sch* 30 (Summer 1972): 5–10.

Dinin, Samuel. "Goals for Jewish Education." In *The Goals of Jewish Education* (Dropsie College symposium). Phila.: Dropsie College, 1957.

———. "The Goals of Jewish Education." *Recon* (Oct. 20, 1957): 7–13.

Diskind, Zalman. "The Rationale for Jewish Education as Expressed in *Jewish Education* Magazine, 1929–1955." *Jew Ed* 30 (Spring 1960): 16–21, 32.

Dropsie College. *The Goals of Jewish Education* (Dropsie College symposium). Papers by: Samuel Dinin, Horace M. Kallen, Philip Klutznick, Joseph Lookstein, and Emanuel Neuman. Phila.: 1957. 62 pp.

Efron, Mordecai V. "Formulating Aims for American Jewish Education." *Jew Ed* 25 (Winter 1958): 22–29.

Eisenberg, Azriel. "Mainspring of Jewish Education." *Congress Biweekly* (June 14, 1965): 7–8.

Essrig, Harry. "The Goals of Reform Religious Education." *CCAR* 68 (1959): 151–52.

———. "Realistic Goals in Liberal Jewish Education." *Jew Teach* (Mar. 1957): 3–7.

Fierman, Morton C. "Aims and Objectives for Liberal Jewish Education." *CCAR J* (Jan. 1962): 32–38.

Forse, C. "Search for Jewish Self-Fulfillment." *Un Syn Rev* 28 (Winter 1976): 5–7.

Franzblau, Abraham N. "New Goals in Jewish Religious Education." *CCAR* 63 (1953): 43–160.

Goldfarb, William B. "The Goals of Jewish Education—A Layman's Point of View." *Jew Ed* 34 (Summer 1964): 230–37.

Halevi, Mordecai. "Divergent Formulations of Objectives in American Jewish Education." *Jew Ed* 25 (Winter 1955): 11–21, 64.

Hertz, Richard C. "What Really Is Jewish Education." In *The Education of the Jewish Child: A Study of 200 Reform Jewish Religious Schools*, 15–24. N.Y.: UAHC, 1953.

Hoffman, Justin. "The Ends of Jewish Education." *Jew Ed* 50 (Spring 1982): 10–15, 21.

Honor, Leo L. „גישות שונות בקביעת מטרות החנוך היהודי בארצות הברית" (Different Approaches in the Determination of Jewish Educational Goals in the United States). *Sh Hah* (H.) 15 (1955): 75–83.

Kallen, Horace M. "Goals for Jewish Education." In *The Goals of Jewish Education* (Dropsie College symposium). Phila.: Dropsie College, 1957. See also *JJS*, 171–77.

Kaplan, Louis L. "Beyond the Four Walls." *Jew Ed* 32 (Spring 1962): 155–63.

Kessler, Aharon. "Reconsidering the Terminal Objectives of Jewish Education." In *Intrater*, 9–14.

Kipper, M. A. "Maximalist Education." *Jew Spec* 37 (May 1972): 20–22.

Klutznick, Philip M. "Goals for Jewish Education." In *The Goals of Jewish Education* (Dropsie College symposium). Phila.: Dropsie College, 1957.

Lamm, Norman. "An Orthodox Prospective on Jewish Education and Jewish Identity." In *Determining the Goals of Jewish Education*, 25–27. N.Y.: AJC *Colloquium Papers*, 1977.

Leiman, Harold I. "Ends and Means in Jewish Education." *Jew Obs* (May 1965).

Levine, T. "Primacy of Jewish Education." *Un Syn Rev* 20 (Jan. (1968): 5–7.

Lieber, David. "Goals for the Conservative Jewish School." In *Determining the Goals of Jewish Education*, 28–33. N.Y.: AJC *Colloquium Papers*, 1977.

Lookstein, Joseph. "Goals for Jewish Education." In *The Goals of Jewish Education* (Dropsie College symposium). Phila.: Dropsie College, 1957. See also *JJS*, 213–19 and *Trad* 3 (Fall 1960): 34–43.

Margoshes, Samuel. „מאקסימום אידישקייט" (Maximum Jewishness). *Day* (Y.) (June 16, 1956).

Markowitz, Samuel H. "The Goals of Jewish Religious Education." *CCAR J* (Apr. 1963): 76–80.

Martin, Bernard. "The Goals of Jewish Religious Education" (in symposium, "The Adult I Want My Children to Become"). *CCAR J* 11 (Apr. 1963): 98–.

Mervis, Leonard J. "Principles, Goals and Policy." *Jew Teach* 27 (Jan. 1960): 9–11.

Neumann, Emanuel. "Goals For Jewish Education." In *The Goals of Jewish Education* (Dropsie College symposium). Phila.: Dropsie College, 1957.

Neusner, Jacob. "City, Society and Self: Goals for Jewish Education." *CCAR J* (Apr. 1962): 52–55. See also *Rel Ed* (Sept.–Oct. 1962): 363–66.

Pilch, Judah. "The Aim: Intensive Jewish Education." *Congress Weekly* 26 (May 25, 1959): 10–11.

———. *Analysis of Study of the Assessment of Priorities on Specific Goals in Jewish Education*. N.Y.: AAJE-National Curriculum Research Institute. 35 pp.

* Prystowsky, Seymour. *The Purpose and Direction of Contemporary Reform Religious Schools in the United States and Canada*. Dropsie U., 1974.

* Rosenblatt, Howard B. *The Social Purposes of Jewish Education in the United States*. Case Western Reserve, 1977. 311 pp.

Rosenberg, Martin. "A Perspective on Reform Religious Education." In *Determining the Goals of Jewish Education*, 34–37. N.Y.: AJC *Colloquium Papers*, 1977.

Schaalman, Herman, ed. "The Goals of Jewish Religious Education" (introduction). *CCAR J* (Apr. 1963): 68–.

Shurin, Aaron Ben-Zvi. „דער צוועק פון בילדונג" (The Purpose of Education). *For* (Y.) (Oct. 7, 1983).

Silberman, Charles. "Goals and Practice in Jewish Education: A Personal Perspective." In *Jewish Education and Jewish Identity*. N.Y.: AJC, 1977.

Skolnick, Irving H. *A Guide to the Determination of Objectives in the Jewish School*. Chicago: College of Jewish Studies, 1957.

UAHC, CCAR, and CJE. *Goals of Reform Jewish Education*. N.Y.: 1975.

Ulman, Sh. B. "החינוך היהודי ומטרותיו„ (Jewish Education and Its Goals). *Sh Hah* (H.) 18 (Summer 1958): 197–212.

Urbach, Ephraim. "האידיאל החינוכי בתפיסת היהדות" (The Educational Ideal in Jewish Perception). In *MJET* (H.), 46–55.

USA. *A Guide to Congregational Standards*. N.Y.: 1977.

USCJE. *Objectives and Standards for the Congregational School*. N.Y.: 1958. 29 pp.

Weiss-Rosmarin, Trude. "What Should We Teach?" *Jew Spec* 27 (Mar. 1962): 3–5.

Weistrop, J. "Teaching to Be Different." *Jew Spec* 31 (Winter 1955).

Zuckerman, Herbert. "The Implementation of Goals." *Jew Ed* 25 (Winter 1955): 29–32.

GLEANINGS

Kaplan, Mordecai M.,
"To create within the child a sense of exultation in those experiences of his people which have constituted for the race the very footprints of God, and to implant within him a high ambition to contribute his share towards the perpetuation and enrichment of its spirit."
Jewish Teacher (Jan. 1916). Quoted by Alter F. Landesman in *A Curriculum for Religious Schools*, 1.

Dushkin, Alexander M.,
"Jewish education is essentially the process of integrating the young growing Jew into the Jewish fellowship, and of preparing him to share in the destinies of that fellowship and to contribute to its welfare and development."
Jew Ed 1 (May 1929), 69.

Golub, Jacob S., and Leo L. Honor.
"We should like the Jewish child to feel that membership in the Jewish people is like membership in his family, conditioned altogether by birth and in no wise by choice or by any overt act of affiliation."
Jew Ed 4 (Oct.–Dec. 1932), 154.

Rappoport, Israel B.,
"The primary aim of this [elementary] school should be the integration of the personality of the Jewish child, which integration may be best accomplished by providing the child with joyous experiences so that he will consider his Jewishness as something worthwhile."
Jew Ed 5 (Apr.–June 1933), 88.

Kaplan, Mordecai M. (1934),
"The only raison d'etre for Jewish education is the assumption that without it the Jew cannot possibly know what to make of his status as a Jew. . . .
Primary is the objective of developing in the rising generation a desire and capacity to participate in Jewish life."
In his *Judaism as a Civilization*, 479, 483. 1957.

Dushkin, Alexander M.,
"Jewish education, like all other systems of education, must educate the human being for complete living; that is, giving him understanding of the world in which he lives, ability to order his life toward the achievement of freedom and happiness, and the will to be the partner of the Almighty in the betterment of the world."
Jew Ed 19 (Fall 1947), 6.

Kallen, Horace M.,
"To be complete, education in the Jewish being must embrace studying, knowing, understanding sympathetically and judging objectively not one set of values affirmed by one sect or party but all the values of all the sects and all the parties and their interaction."
Jew Ed 19 (Summer 1948), 15.

First National Conference on Jewish Education (1951), Charter of the Rights of the Jewish Child,
"A continuing education which will provide the Jewish child with accurate knowledge and sympathetic understanding of the life, the labors, the ideals, and the struggles and achievements of the Jewish people from the beginnings of their history to the present day; and which will provide him with the opportunity to express his own personality in the perpetuation and development of the

Jewish religio-cultural heritage."
Jew Ed 22 (Summer 1951), 76.

Heschel, Abraham J.,
"I would like to suggest as a goal of Jewish education that every Jew become a representative of the Jewish spirit, that every Jew become aware that Judaism is an answer to the ultimate problem of human existence and not merely a way of handling observances."
Jew Ed 24 (1953), 15.

Neusner, Jacob,
"The central problem facing American Jewry is whether it will find a way to engage all who by birth belong to it, but by choice do not. We must try to reach out to the other half, to stem the hemorrhage that deprives us of our sustenance, to try—at least, to try to hold our people....
Study of the Torah is, therefore, the foundation of all Jewish enterprise and the one certain way—a way proved certain by our history—to assure our future. It should stand, at the head of the agenda of every Jewish group simply because every Jewish enterprise is ultimately dependent on the study of the Torah for its very existence."
Syn Sch 25 (Winter 1967), 14, 17.

UAHC,
"To translate conviction into action: worship, righteous living, character development (hopefulness, courage faith); to teach appreciation of Jewish art, music, literature."
Quoted by A. M. Dushkin and U. Z. Engelman in *Jewish Education in the United States*, 35. 1959.

UOJCA,
"To teach the application of Torah ideals to the one hundred and one tasks of daily life; to make clear the interrelation between practice and ideals. The purpose of the teaching of the Torah is divine guidance to worth-whileness, peace and happiness."
Quoted by A. M. Dushkin and U. Z. Engelman in *Jewish Education in the United States*, 35. 1959.

USA,
"To provide opportunities for the child to develop keen spiritual and ethical sensitivity through curricula and extra curricula experiences."
Quoted by A. M. Dushkin and U. Z. Engelman in *Jewish Education in the United States*, 35. 1959.

Greenberg, Simon,
"The uniqueness of each people is reflected in the uniqueness of the tangibles through which its peoplehood expressed itself. As for the Jews, I believe that their peoplehood is most fully embodied and concretized in three primary tangibles, each one of which is equally indispensable to it, not only at this particular juncture in its history, but for all the humanly foreseeable future. They are Erets Yisrael, the Hebrew language, and the Synagogue, particularly as a Beth Tefilah. These tangibles of Jewish peoplehood are and should be the tangibles of Jewish education in the United States."
Jew Ed 31 (Winter 1961), 7.

Kaplan, Mordecai M.,
"The child should experience belonging prior to believing as Jews."
Dimensions 1 (Winter 1967), 18.

Donin, Hayim H.,
"[The purpose of Jewish education] is to help parents raise their children to become affirmatively aware of themselves as Jews, to be happy with their Judaism, and to be prepared to find meaning and purpose in their Jewish identities and tradition."
In his *To Raise a Jewish Child*, xv. 1977. Quoted by Steven Strolman in *Recon* 44 (Feb. 1978): 27.

UAHC and CCAR,
Goals of Reform Jewish Education
"1. Jews who affirm their Jewish identity and bind themselves inseparably to their people by word and deed.
2. Jews who bear witness to the brit (the covenant between God and the Jewish People) through the practice of mitzvot (commandments) as studied in Torah and the classic Jewish literature it has generated, and interpreted in light of historic development and contemporary liberal thought.
3. Jews who affirm their historic bond

to Eretz Yisrael, the land of Israel.

4. Jews who cherish and study Hebrew, the language of the Jewish People.

5. Jews who value and practice tefilah (prayer).

6. Jews who further the causes of justice, freedom and peace by pursuing tsedek (righteousness), mishpot (justice), and chesed (loving deeds).

7. Jews who celebrate Shabbat and the festivals and observe the Jewish ceremonies marking the significant occasions in their lives.

8. Jews who esteem their own person and the person of others; their own family and the family of others; their own community and the community of others.

9. Jews who express kinship with K'lal Yisrael by actively seeking the welfare of Jews throughout the world.

10. Jews who support and participate in the life of the synagogue.

To See the World through Jewish Eyes (UAHCWolliamandSchusterCurriculum). 4 vols. Quoted in *RJ* (Spring 1985), 22.

42 RESEARCH IN JEWISH EDUCATION

(See also chapters 23 and 44)
Surveys of cities are by states and cities.

CALL FOR RESEARCH

Baron, Salo W. "Communal Responsibility for Jewish Social Research." *JSS* 7 (July 1955): 242–55.

Chazan, Barry. "Introduction: Research and Education." In *Stu*, 1:9–19.

Cohen, Morris R. "The Need for Research in Jewish Life." *Jew Ed* 9 (Jan.–Mar. 1937): 3–4.

Engelman, Uriah Z. "Jewish Education and Social Research." *JSSQ* (Summer 1952): 353.

Fishman, Joshua A. "American Jewry as a Field of Social Science Research." *YA* 12 (1958–59): 70–102.

Golub, Jacob S. "Some Needed Research in Jewish Education." *Jew Ed* 12 (Sept. 1940): 89–96.

Kaplan, Hyman. "Jewish Social Research in the United States." *AJYB* 22 (1920–21): 31–52.

Kuselevitz, David. "מדע ומחקר בחנוך העברי„ (Science and Research in Jewish Education). *Sh Hah* (H.) 1 (1941): 30–36.

Lehrer, Leibush. "פארשפראבלעמען פון ייִדישער דערציאונג„ (Research Problems in Jewish Education) *YB* (Y.) 16 (Nov.–Dec. 1940): 97–104.

Lurie, Harry, and Max Weinreich, eds. "Jewish Social Research in America: Status and Prospects" (symposium with 59 social scientists). *YA* 4 (1949): 147–312.

Mailer, Julius B. "Needed Investigation in Jewish Education." *Jew Ed* 1 (May 1929): 97–109.

Resnick, David A. "Toward an Agenda for Research in Jewish Education." *Jew Ed* 50 (Summer 1982): 24–28. Also in *Understanding American Jewry*, edited by Marshall Sklare, 125–40. New Brunswick, N.J.: Transaction Books, 1982.

Slesinger, Zalmen. "Research—The Missing Ingredient in Jewish Education." *Ped Rep* 14 (May 1963): 6–9.

PRIOR TO 1950

Dushkin, Alexander M. "Two Decades of Progress in Jewish Education—A Survey." *Jew Ed* 4 (Jan.–Mar. 1932): 3–13.

Engelman, Uriah Z. "Survey of 14 schools in 14 cities outside of New York." Information Bulletin no. 10. N.Y.: AAJE, 1947.

Gamoran, Emanuel. "השואה בין ילדים עברים ובין ילדים איטלקים„ (Comparison between

Jewish and Italian Children in the Public Schools). *Sh Hah* (H.) 2 (1927): 18–19.

———. *A Survey of 125 Religious Schools*. N.Y.: UAHC, 1925. 50 pp.

Jaffe, Philip, and Sylvia Goldman. "Survey of Thirty-six Reform Religious Schools." *Jew Teach* 11 (June 1943): 1–12.

Kadushin, Evelyn Garfiel. "A Note on the Use of Statistics in Jewish Education." *Jew Ed* 2 (Jan. 1930): 48–52.

Nardi, Noah. "Studies in Attitudes towards the Hebrew School." *J of Educational Research* 42 (1948): 37–46.

Rosen, Ben. "Recent Surveys of Jewish Education." *Jew Ed* 2: 78–89.

SINCE 1950

Arzt, Raphael. "Jewish Education: A Perspective on Strategies and Tactics." In *Stu*, 139–67.

Bennett, Alan D. "Curriculum Research in Reform Jewish Education." *Rel Ed* (Jan.–Feb. 1963): 44–48.

———. "Some Implications of the NATE Curriculum Survey." *Jew Teach* 32 (Apr. 1964): 3–6.

Chanover, Hyman. "National Curriculum Research Institute of the AAJE." *Ped Rep* 23 (Sept. 1971): 5.

Congress Weekly. "Studies on Jewish Education." (Mar. 22, 1954): 18–19.

Cook, S., ed. *Research Plans Formulated at the Research Planning on Religious and Character Education*. N.Y.: Religious Education Association, 1961. 310 pp.

Cutter, William. "Affect and Cognition in Jewish Education—Some Comments on the Promise of a Project." *Jew Ed* 46 (Spring 1978): 22–32, 53.

Dushkin, Alexander M., and Uriah Z. Engelman. *Jewish Education in the United States: Report of the Commission for the Study of Jewish Education in the United States*. N.Y.: AAJE, 1959. 265 pp. Summary report of the commission appears in *Jew Ed* 30 (Fall 1959): 14–23, 33.

Engel, R. C. "Curriculum Practice or Research, Which Is Ahead?" *Ped Rep* 20 (Dec. 1968): 3–6.

Engelman, Uriah Z. "The First National Study of Jewish Education." *Jew Ed* 29 (Fall 1958): 3–9.

Fromer, Seymour. "The First Survey of Jewish Education." *Congress Biweekly* (May 25, 1959).

Gannes, Abraham P. "Surveys and Studies of Jewish Education" (extensive list of surveys, indicating year, sponsor, and location). *CA*, 170–72.

Gertman, Stuart A. *And You Shall Teach Them Diligently: A Study of the State of Religious Education in the Reform Movement*. N.Y.: NATE and UAHC Department of Education, 1977. 96 pp.

Greenberg, Irving. "Research on Religious Development: A Comprehensive Handbook." *Rel Ed* 66 (Sept.–Oct. 1971): 390–93.

Greenberg, Simon. "The Samuel Melton Research Center in American Jewish Education." *Syn Sch* 23 (Fall 1964).

Himmelfarb, Harold S. "The Non-Linear Impact of Schooling: Comparing Different Types and Amounts of Jewish Education." *Sociology of Education* 50 (Apr. 1977): 114–32.

Janowsky, Oscar I. *Prospectus for a Comprehensive Study of Jewish Education in the United States*. N.Y.: Dec. 1953.

* **Kastenbaum, Jerome.** *The Melton Research Center in American Education*. Vanderbilt U., 1970. 76 pp.

Krumbein, Eliezer. "Research for Evaluating Jewish Learning." *Ped Rep* 7 (Sept. 1966).

Landesman, Jacob. „סיכום מחקר בעניני נוער יהודי" (A Summary of Research on Jewish Youth). *Sh Hah* (H.) (Tishri 1969).

Lang, Gerhard. "Instruments for Determining Reactions of Students, Parents, and Teachers to the Program of a Regional Hebrew High School." *Jew Ed* 42 (Summer 1973): 34–37.

———. "Perceptions of Jewish Education." *Ped Rep* 35 (Oct. 1984): 22–23.

Passow, A. Harry. "Research on Jewish Education in the Diaspora." *Jew Ed* 53 (Fall 1984): 4–9.

Pollak, George, and Gerhard Lang. *Perceptions of Jewish Education*. JESNA Research and Information Bulletin no. 55. July 1983. 50 pp.

Resnick, David A. "The Current State of Research in Jewish Education." In *Stu*, 3:11–22.

Roseman, Yehuda. "Research on the Jewish Family and Jewish Education." *J Jew Com Ser* (Spring 1984).

Rothman, J. "Construction of an Instrument for Measuring Minority Group Identification among Adolescents: An Exploratory Attempt." *J Jew Com Ser* 34 (1957): 84–94.

Schanin, Norman. "Research in Jewish Education." *Jew Ed* 36 (Fall 1965): 28–29.

———. "A Review of American Pedagogic Literature Relevant to Jewish Education." *Jew Ed* 33 (Winter 1963): 97–113; 34 (Winter 1964): 108–17; 35 (Winter 1965): 112–23; 36 (Winter 1966): 112–20.

Scharfstein, Zevi. „עם מסקר החנוך היהודי בארצות הברית" (A National Survey of Jewish Education in the United States). *Hadoar* (H.) 39 (Feb. 26, 1960): 291–92; (Mar. 4, 1960): 311–12.

Schiff, Alvin I., and Chaim Y. Botwinick. "The Relevance of the Recommendations of Major National Studies on Education to Jewish Schooling." *Jew Ed* 52 (Summer 1984): 7–18.

Schoolman, Albert P. "Jewish Education Surveyed" (editorial). *Jew Ed* 24 (Spring 1953): 2–4.

———. "The 1959 Study of Jewish Education in the United States." *J Jew Com Ser* 36 (Fall 1960). Also in *Jew Ed* 31 (Winter 1961): 41–46, 54, and in *JJS*, 177–81.

Spotts, Leon H. "Current Research in Jewish Education—Description and Evaluation." *Jew Ed* 36 (Fall 1965): 30–37.

Stone, Gerald C, and Neil Newman. "Investigation of Goals in a Jewish Religious School." *Jew Ed* 43 (Winter/Spring 1975): 46–54.

Syn Sch. "Pilot Schools of the Melton Research Center." 22 (Spring 1964): 3–5.

Weisel, Alfred. "Our National Research Program." *Syn Sch* 20 (1962).

Wolfson, Ronald G., and Stuart Kelman. "Research in Jewish Religious Education: An Addendum to the Annual Review of Research in Religious Education." *Rel Ed* 75 (Nov–Dec. 1980): 692–97.

World Jewish Congress-American Section. *A Survey of Current Jewish Research*. N.Y.: July 1979. 33 pp.

GLEANINGS

Finkelstein, Louis (1940),
"There are probably a hundred people, and more, whose profession is to discover all that can be known about the Jews in Jerusalem in the first century; there does not seem to be one who has the same duty for the Jews of New York in the twentieth century."
Quoted by Marshall Sklare in *The Jew in American Society*, 3. 1974.

Lewin, Kurt,
"Democracy and Judaism have nothing to fear from truth and fact finding, but they have much to gain by them. The love of Torah and research is old in Israel. It can and should be made a living force to link its organizations closer with the facts of reality and in this way help to make Jewish life more normal and strong."
Jew Ed 15 (May 1944), 137.

Olan, Levi,
"Much of our cultural program still endeavors to live off the creativity of a once thriving civilization which is now a matter of history, not of life. The time has come for the emergence of an American Jewish Cultural Pattern. . . . It is penny wise and dollar foolish to continue the present neglect of the cultural demands of the American Jew."
Liberal Judaism (Feb. 1949), 8.

Niger, Shmuel (Charney),
"So long as the Jews in America, as a group, will not emancipate themselves from the utilitarian outlook in the realm of culture, the conditions will not be pro-

pitious for Jewish social research, unless a miracle takes place and such research undertaking will no longer require public support."

YA 4 (1949), 202.

Kohs, Samuel S.,
"Jews in the United States stand out for their remarkable progress in Jewish community organization and for their unexampled generosity in meeting local, national, and overseas Jewish needs. On one important item, however, they have maintained an unconscionable and unexplicable blindness and immaturity. That shortcoming is in the field of social research."

YA 4 (1949), 233–34.

Pinson, Kopel S.,
"What American Jewry has not yet learned, however, is that even utilitarian and pragmatic ends are best served in the long run only if there is sufficient encouragement to adequate impersonal, objective, and purely scholarly research in the community."

YA 4 (1949), 239–40.

Duker, Abraham G.,
"The realities of Jewish life in this country have produced a situation whereby the needs of communal agencies are usually judged by criteria other than scholarly achievement, criteria that depend greatly on the institution's capacity for interpretation. Jewish social research will have to adjust to these realities or will continue to be neglected in the future as it has been in the past."

YA 4 (1949), 270.

Fishman, Joshua A., on M. E. Spiro, "Acculturation of American Ethnic Groups" (*American Anthropologist* 57 [1955], 1240–52),
"Spiro mentions many famous American anthropologists—some by name and some by implication, but nearly all of them Jewish who have travelled to distant corners of the world in order to become expert in the manifold problems of culture and personality—but who have ignored (and continue to ignore) the world's greatest laboratory for such studies in their own back yard."

Jew Ed 28 (Winter 1957), 52.

Slesinger, Zalmen,
"It is important to recognize that the present program of the Jewish school is, by no means, an outgrowth of cumulative successful experiences. It is founded more upon faith and enthusiasm than upon experimental data. It lacks social validation, be it creative survival, or commitment to Jewish values. It is the momentum of tradition rather than the evidence of research that guides our school policies and generates our educational activities. We have little empirical data to justify the contents of our curricula, the selection, scope and sequence of the various subjects that we teach, the respective emphasis we place on them, the age levels at which they are introduced in the school, etc. . ."

"Research—The Missing Ingredient in Jewish Education." *Ped Rep* (May 1963). Quoted in *Jew Ed* 36 (Fall 1965): 28–29.

Schanin, Norman,
"The American Jew looks to Jewish education for many perplexing and serious problems. The struggle against assimilation and intermarriage, the need for developing a relevant philosophy and program for Jewish life in America, the effort to build a real two way bridge with Israel, and the task of recruiting new leadership and developing creative talent for the very survival of the American Jewish community, are all being focused on the Jewish school.

Society, the general community and the Jewish community, are demanding better answers to some very old questions. Influenced greatly by the results of living in a scientific age and from the knowledge explosion which has revolutionized life in the second half of the twentieth century, people are rejecting as inadequate the authoritative pronouncements of status leadership, individuals and learned societies, which cannot be substantiated by objective fact or duplicated or evaluated and tested by the scientific method. Research has become the accepted way by which the knowledgeable leadership deals with ideas and problems."

"Research in Jewish Education." *Jew Ed* 36 (Fall 1965), 28.

Spotts, Leon H.,
"The matter of the content of Jewish education research, however, is only one aspect of an appraisal of its adequacy. One must also evaluate the efficacy of its methodology. To be sure, a detailed evaluation of the methodological adequacy of current research must await the publication of these studies. At the same time, some overall generalizations are possible. An examination of the titles and general character of these studies indicates, for example, that out of the 51 projects, 28 or a full 55% appear to draw their data largely, if not exclusively, from published source material rather than from classroom experimentation or from original questionnaire or interview studies. Only 14 of the 51 projects appear to use the questionnaire or interview techniques of data collection, while a mere 9 investigations employ actual classroom experimentation of some sort. And even of these 9 not one is what could be called a truly scientific experiment, in which all variables, except the one tested for are held constant and the effect of varying one factor is assessed against a control group in which that factor is not varied."

"Current Research in Jewish Education—Description and Evaluation." *Jew Ed* 36 (Fall 1965), 36.

Fox, Seymour,
"We will have to invest a good deal of money and energy in social science research to accompany our investigation of goals and content of Jewish education. I do not pretend to know whether ample psychological and sociological research has been undertaken concerning the Jewish community. However, almost no information concerning the attitudes, reactions, and commitments of students in Jewish schools is available to the educator. We know even less about parents and the family as related to Jewish education."

The Future of the Jewish Community in America, Edited by David Sidorsky, 266–67. 1973.

Resnick, David A.,
"Some educators have altogether despaired of educational research as well as research in Jewish education. . . . Nonetheless, countless educational decisions and innovations are made daily. There must be some reflective stock-taking of these decisions and their effects, else education proceeds willy-nilly and loses one of its defining characteristics—purposiveness. Empirical research need not be the sum total of the required evaluation and analysis, but neither can such analysis long endure without an underpinning of empirical research. It is certainly time to begin."

"Toward an Agenda for Research in Jewish Education." Planning Conference for Modern Studies, Brandeis U. Oct. 21–24, 1979.

Wolfson, Ronald G., and Stuart Kelman,
"One of the reasons for the paucity of research in Jewish education is the lack of perceived need for such studies among the leaders of the Jewish community, including many Jewish educators. Most of the money and energy expended in the field goes toward the attempt to keep the ship afloat and, perhaps, to generate a few new action solutions to old problems. However, if Jewish educators are to ever systematically approach the improvement of their field, the case for research funds must be made to the leaders of the Jewish community. At the same time the practitioners of Jewish education must themselves fully accept the commitment to include a research component in any important program or approach."

"Research in Jewish Religious Education." *Rel Ed* 17 (Nov.–Dec. 1980), 692–98.

Ackerman, Walter,
"There is no end of materials that describe what is wrong with Jewish schools. On the other hand, I do not know of a single study, based upon recognized research procedure, which describes a good Jewish school and what makes it so. There is almost a total absence of any appreciation of the role of research in Jewish education."

Quoted by Elliot Schwartz in *Jew Ed* 51 (Winter 1983), 14.

Passow, Harry A.,
"Jewish education in the diaspora, like general education, has a long history and

has operated on tradition rather than on research and evaluation. Yet, in the 1980s it seems hardly necessary to argue that the myriad of educational policies and decisions are better made when they are informed by research and theory. Just as general/secular education in the United States is always described as being in a state of crisis, Jewish education of all types faces critical problems. Just the demographic data, incomplete and spotty as they are, let alone the outcome data, should be enough to spur those who are interested in the future of Judaism in the diaspora to grapple more intelligently and effectively with the issues and problems of Jewish education. Nor is it clear that the Orthodox day school as it presently functions is the model that will preserve Judaism in the diaspora. All aspects of Jewish education in the diaspora need to be studied because it comes in a tremendous variety of shapes and forms, of goals and purposes, of structures and operations."

"Research on Jewish Education In the Diaspora: Some Reflections." *Jew Ed* 53 (Fall 1984), 8.

43 CHANGE IN JEWISH EDUCATION

(See also chapters 20 and 21)

PRIOR TO 1950

Barack, Nathan. "Vitalize Jewish Education." *Recon* (Nov. 29, 1946): 16–19.

Brennan, Alice M. "Problems of a Progressive Jewish School." *Jew Ed* 6 (Oct.–Dec.1934): 162–67.

Brickner, Barnett R. "Changing Conceptions in Sunday School Work." *Jewish Teacher* 2 (Apr. 1918): 26–33.

———. "The Project Method." In *The Project Method in the Jewish School*, edited by Emanuel Gamoran. 1927.

Chipkin, Israel S. "Proposals for the Study, Evaluation and Reconstruction of the Jewish Educational System in America." *Jew Ed* 16 (Jan. 1945): 34–36.

Chomsky, William. "On 'Vitalizing the Jewish Curriculum': A Reply to Rabbi Barack." *Recon* (Mar. 21, 1947): 9–11.

Comins, Harry L. "An Experiment with an Activity Program." *Jew Ed* 3 (Jan.–Mar. 1931): 39–49.

———. "An Integrated Curriculum for the Jewish School." *Jew Ed* 4 (Apr.–June 1932): 93–102.

———. "Recent Contributions to Jewish Education." *CCAR* 43 (1933): 205–41.

* Dinin, Samuel. "Jewish Education in a Changing Civilization." In *Judaism in a Changing Civilization*, 183–212. Columbia U., 1933.

———. "בית-הספר העברי והסדר החדש" (The Jewish School and the New Agenda). *Hadoar* (H.) 13 (4th of Sivan 1934).

Gamoran, Emanuel. "The Changing Jewish Curriculum." In *Principles of the Jewish Curriculum in America*, Book II, *Changing Conceptions in Jewish Education*, 1–11. 1924.

———. "An Experiment in Jewish Education." *Jew Teach* 11 (June 1943): 17–21.

———. "Experimenting in Jewish Education." *Rel Ed* 42 (July 1947): 193–98.

———. "A New Platform." *Hebrew Union College Monthly* (May 1935). See also *Gamoran*, 110–15.

———, ed. *The Project Method in the Jewish School*. Cincinnati; DSSE and UAHC, 1921. See *CCAR* 36 (1926): 322–36.

———. "Recent Tendencies in Education and Their Application to the Jewish School." *CCAR* 33 (1923): 314–27.

———. "The Reconstruction of the Curriculum." In *Principles of the Jewish Curriculum in America*, Book II, *Changing Conceptions in Jewish Education*, 140–73. 1924.

———. "Some of the Difficulties of the Project Method Discussed" (symposium on the project method in the Jewish school). Cincinnati: DSSCH, 1926.

Ginsburg, Morris B. "Creative Teaching: Opportunities for Creative Teaching and Learning in Our Religious School." *Jew Teach* 3 (June 1935): 34–37.

Golub, Jacob S. "An Experiment with a Full-Time Sunday School Teacher." *Jew Ed* 18 (Summer 1947): 22–26.

———. "Individuality and the System." *Jew Ed* 1 (Oct. 1929): 165–72.

———. "השיטה האינדיבידואלית„ (The Individualized Teaching Method). *Sh Hah* (H.) 4 (1928): 27–33.

———. "Raising the Status of Education." *Liberal Judaism* (Mar. 1946): 33–39.

———. "Reconstructionism and Jewish Education." *Recon* 11 (Feb. 23, 1945): 38–43.

Gordon, Hirsch L. "השיטה הפרוייקטיבית בחנוך„ (The Project Method in Education). *Sh Hah* (H.) 1:1 (1925): 13–20; 1:2 (1925): 14–19; 1:3 (1926): 18–34.

———. "The Project Method in Jewish Religious Education." Master's thesis, Columbia U. Teachers College, 1926.

Grossman, Louis. "The New Jewish Pedagogy." *Jewish Teacher* 1 (May 1917): 131–60.

Isserman, Ruth. "Experimenting in Our School." *Jew Teach* (Nov. 1938): 1–14.

———. "Religious Schools and the New Education." *Jew Teach* 5 (Nov. 1936): 1–6.

Kandel, Isaac L. "The Vitalizing of Jewish Education." *Menorah J* 7 (June 1921).

Klausner, Gustave. "Changing Requirements of the Jewish Educational Program in American Communities." *Jew Ed* 13 (Apr. 1941): 14–16.

Nudelman, Edward A. "Improving the Work of Our Schools." *Jew Ed* 10 (Apr.–June 1938): 91–96.

Pool, D. de Sola. "An Experiment in Jewish Education." *Jew Ed* 10 (Apr.–June 1938): 82–84, 90.

Powers, Helen F. "The Full-Time Experiment." *Jew Teach* 15 (Nov. 1946): 1–14.

Rappoport, Israel B., and Edward A. Nudelman. "An American Jewish School—A Proposal." *Jew Ed* 11 (Sept. 1939): 105–20.

Rosenberg, Pauline. "An Experiment in Creative Jewish Education." In *1948 Annual*. Chicago: College of Jewish Studies Student Organization, 1948.

Scharfstein, Zevi. "התביעות של 'אמריקניות' ופרוגרסיביות' בחנוך העברי בארצות הברית„ (The Demands of 'Americanism' and 'Progressivism' upon Jewish Education in the U.S.). *Sh Hah* (H.) 1 (1940): 3–22. Also in *ES* (H.), 43–70.

———. "הזרמים החדשים בחנוך„ (New Currents in Education). *Hadoar* (H.) 7 (20th of Sivan 1928).

———. "אפקים חדשים לחנוך העברי באמריקה„ (New Horizons for Jewish Education in America). *Hadoar* (H.) 25 (Dec. 28, 1945).

Touroff, Nissan. "לתקנת החנוך העברי„ (Toward the Improvement of Jewish Education). *Sh Hah* (H.) 1 (1926): 1–14; 2:1 (1926): 19–24; 2:2 (1926): 16–22.

SINCE 1950

AAJE. "A Charter of the Rights of the Jewish Child." *Ped Rep* 3 (Mar. 1952). See also *Jew Ed* 22 (Summer 1951): 77.

AAJE. *Education and the Creative Life*. Addresses by: Philip Lown, Buell Gallagher, Milton R. Konvitz, and Horace M. Kallen. N.Y.: AAJE, Aug. 5, 1957. 31 pp.

AAJE. *Individualizing Instruction*. N.Y.: 1972.

AAJE. "Towards the Open Classroom and the Individualization of Instruction." *Ped Rep* 23 (Dec. 1971): 7.

AJC. *Jewish Education for Modern Needs*. This Is Our Home Series, vol. 13. N.Y.: 1955. 15 pp.

* Alper, Michael. "Tradition and Change in Jewish Education." In *Reconstructionism and Jewish Education: The Implications of Reconstructionism for Jewish Education in the United States*, 92–110. Columbia U., 1954.

Altman, Shalom. "Creativity in the Classroom." *Jew Teach* 34 (Apr. 1966): 38–39.

Auspitz, Gabriella. "Individualizing Instruction and the Congregational School." *Jew Ed* 42 (Summer 1973): 38–44.

Barish, Shirley. "Enrichment Programs." In *JPH*, 337–43.

Ben-Horin, Meir. "Jewish Education in an Age of Science." *Jud* 9 (1960): 339–45.

———. "Redesigning Jewish Education." *Recon* 29 (Dec. 27, 1963): 6–12.

Bennett, Alan D. "Jewish Education in a Time of Change: Response and Reaction." *J Jew Com Ser* 56 (Winter 1979–80): 146–48.

Blaser, Elissa. "Experimental Education in the Jewish Setting: A Rational and Pragmatic Example." Master's thesis, HUC–JIR, 1974.

Bogot, Howard I. "Foundations for Change: Perspectives on Process." *RJ* (Spring 1982): 69–73.

Bortniker, Elijah. "Needed—Radical Action." *Syn Sch* 19 (Oct. 1960): 12–19.

Botwinick, Moshe L. "Jewish Education in a Technological Age." *Ped Rep* 35 (Jan. 1984): 5–7.

Braver, Joseph, and Shimon Frost. "New Directions in the Jewish School Curriculum." In *Ed As 1972 Yearbook*. N.Y.: Ed As, 1973.

Brichto, Mira. "Creative Thinking in the Classroom." *Jew Teach* 28 (May 1960): 18–19.

Chanover, Hyman, and Fradle Freidenreich, eds. *Opening the School and Individualizing Instruction*. N.Y.: AAJE, c. 1975. 95 pp.

———. *To Everything There Is a Time* (open classroom). N.Y.: AAJE, 1975.

Chomsky, William. „התמורות בחנוך היהודי האמריקני בדור האחרון" (The Changes in American Jewish Education during the Last Generation). *Sh Hah* (H.) 36 (Summer 1966): 176–284.

Cohen, Burton. "New Educational Responsibilities for the Conservative Synagogue." *MJ* 14 (Spring 1982): 4, 20, 24.

Cohen, Burton, and Joseph Lukinsky. "The Evaluator as Change Agent: A Practical Approach in a Limited Time Frame." *Jew Ed* 49 (Spring 1981): 4–9.

Cohen, Jack J. "New Emphases in Jewish Education." *Recon* (Jan. 13, 1956): 23–30. Also in *Jew Ed* 26 (Summer 1955): 14–21, and *JJS*, 312–18.

———. "New Trends in Jewish Education." In *AJHE*, 201–23.

Cohn-Sherbok, L. "Jewish Education: A New Approach." *Jew Spec* 47 (Sept. 1982): 33–35.

Congress Biweekly. "New Directions in American Jewish Education" (special issue). Includes articles by: Horace M. Kallen, Alexander M. Dushkin, Hyman Chanover, Judah Pilch, and Seymour Fromer. (May 25, 1959).

Cutter, William. "Affect and Cognition in Jewish Education: Some Comments on the Promise of a Project." *Jew Ed* 46 (Spring 1978): 12–32, 53.

Cutter, William, and Jack Dauber. "Confluent Education." *Ped Rep* 23 (June 1972): 14.

Dauber, Jack, and William Cutter. "Confluent Education in the Jewish Setting." *J Jew Com Ser* 49 (Fall 1972): 58–65.

* Dorph, Sheldon A. *A Model for Jewish Education in America: Guidelines for the Restructuring of Conservative Congregational Education*. Columbia U. Teachers College, 1976. 570 pp.

Dorph, Sheldon A. *A New Focus For Jewish Education in America*. 1978. 19 pp.

Ducoff, Bernard. "New Programs in Jewish Education." N.Y.: CJFWF, July 1971. CP. 3 pp.

Eisenstein, Ira. "New Directions in Jewish Education." *Recon* 21 (Feb. 18, 1955): 50–54.

———. "New Directions in Jewish Education." In *Creative Judaism*, 160–71. N.Y.: Jewish Reconstructionist Foundation, 1953.

Engel, David, and John F. Rothman. "Jewish Education—A New Direction." *Recon* 39 (Oct. 1973): 7–15.

* Epstein, Sandra S. *A Needs Assessment Approach to Curriculum Development in Jewish Education*. U. of Pennsylvania, 1983.

Essrig, Harry. "The Next Steps in Liberal Jewish Education." *CCAR J* (Jan. 1961): 20–28.

Euster, Sandra D. "Piaget Goes to Sunday School." *Compass* 4 (Spring 1981): 8–9.

43 CHANGE IN JEWISH EDUCATION

Fein, Leonard. "Suggestions Toward the Reform of Jewish Education in America." *Mid* 18 (Feb. 1972): 41–50.

Fein, Leonard, and Bernard Reisman, et al. *Reform Is a Verb*. N.Y.: UAHC.

Fireman, Theodore. "Jewish Education in a Changing World." *Rel Ed* (May–June 1961). See also *JJS*, 241–48.

Fox, Seymour. "Education for the Twentieth Century Jew: A Pilot Program." *Had Mag* 48 (Sept. 1966).

———. "Seeking the Opportunity—Confronting the Challenge." *Ed As* (1966): 8–13.

Friedman, Audrey. *The Temple Micah Conference Plan*. UAHC, 1969.

Friedman, Theodore. "Jewish Education in a Changing World." In *JJS*, 241–48. See also *Rel Ed* 56 (May–June 1961): 191–97.

Gamoran, Emanuel. "Jewish Education in a Changing Community." *Jew Ed* 34 (Winter 1964): 87–95.

———. "Progress and Prospects in Jewish Education." *Jew Teach* (Mar. 1950).

Gannes, Abraham P. "Restructuring Jewish Education?" *Congress Weekly* (June 1977): 15–17.

———, ed. *Revitalization of the Jewish School*. Contributors: Meir Ben-Horin, Hyman Chanover, Azriel Eisenberg, Shimon Frost, Eli Grad, Henry Margolis, Rebekah Mosenkis, Matthew Mosenkis, Judah Pilch, Zalmen Slesinger, and I. Witty. (Workshop at International Conference of Jewish Communal Service, Aug. 1975. N.Y.: DEC, World Zionist Organization, American Section. 42 pp.

Gertman, Stuart A., ed. *Individualized Learning Unit*. N.Y.: UAHC, c. 1974. Includes:
  (1) Bennett, Alan D, "Post-Biblical Personalities."
  (2) Cooper, Roberta, "The Jewish Life Cycle."
  (3) Fine, Helen, "Israel in Our Lives."
  (4) Gamoran, Mamie G., "Biblical Issues and Personalities."
  (5) Morin, Cynthia, and Richard Morin, "Jewish Social Values."

Glasner, Samuel. "Radical Proposals for the Religious School." *Ped Rep* 19 (June 1968): 10–12.

Goldberg, Mark F. "Jewish Education: Change and Responsibility." *Ped Rep* 24 (Spring 1973): 1, 31; (Winter 1980): 17.

Grad, Eli. "The Role of the Professional in the Process of Change in Jewish Education." *Jew Ed* 48 (Fall 1980): 40–43.

Grand, Samuel. "The Role of NATE in the Experimental Program of the UAHC." *Jew Teach* (Mar. 1958): 15–17.

Green, Kathy. "Inter-Generational Jewish Education." *MJ* 17 (Winter 1980): 9–10, 24.

* Greenberg, Meyer. *Changing Observances of Traditional Jewish Practice: A Study of Generations*. U. of Maryland, 1958.

Greenberg, Simon. "New Approaches to Jewish Education." *Jew Ed* 37 (Winter 1967): 162–68.

Hachen, David S. "Old-New Frontiers in Education." *Jew Teach* 33 (Oct. 1964): 1–2.

Hakimian, Leah. "Changing Hebrew Schools?" *Ped Rep* 33 (Mar. 1982): 30–31.

Hass, Alizah. „נסיון הוראה בכתות פתוחות בביה״ס העברי של אחה״צ" (An Experiment in Open Classrooms within the Framework of an Afternoon School). *Sh Hah* (H.) 36 (1976): 109–23.

Hollander, Ben. "The Soft Revolution and the Jewish School." *Response* 5 (Fall 1971): 58–66.

Holtz, Barry W., and Eduardo Rauch. "Education for Change: Toward a Model of Jewish Teacher Education." In *Stu*, 3:62–90.

Honor, Leo L. "Changing Approaches to Curriculum Development in Supplemental Jewish Week Day Schools." *Jew Ed* 24 (Spring 1954): 12–21.

Horowitz, Jack. "Temple Isaiah's Beit Hayeled: A Supplementary Program—An Alternative to the Jewish Day School." *Compass* 4 (Spring 1981): 3–4, 26.

Hurwich, Louis. „שני בתי-ספר למופת" (Two Schools as Models). *Sh Hah* (H.) 16 (Summer 1956): 195–212.

Intrater, Aaron. "Emerging Changes in Planning for Jewish Education." *Jew Ed* 34 (Fall 1963): 23–28.

JESNA. *Revitalizing Supplementary Schooling*. In *Proceedings of the Jesna Board Institute, Apr. 13–14, 1983*. N.Y.

Jewish Education Newsletter (AAJE). Nov. 1971. (Reports on change.)

Klein, Bernard, and Judah Pilch. *New Developments in Jewish School Curriculum.* N.Y.: NCRI. 53 pp. See also *Reg*, 44–48.

Koller, C. "A Time for Joy: The Open Classroom and the Jewish School." *Response* 5 (Winter 1971–72): 43–50.

Krug, Mark. „שנויים אין לעבן פון דער אידישער קהילה אין אמעריקע און זייער וויכטיקער בייטראג פאר אידישער דערציאונג" (Changes in the Life of the American Jewish Community and Their Significant Contribution to Jewish Education) (Y.). N.Y.: Jewish World Congress, Oct. 1956.

Lappin, Robert I. "The Need to Restructure Jewish Educators to Preserve American Jewish Continuity." *Ped Rep* 22 (Dec. 1970): 15–16.

Levine, Etan. "Educational Implications of Reconstructionism." *Recon* 46 (Mar. 1980): 7–11.

Lipschultz, Karen. "Alternative Educational Systems." Participants: Joanne Glaser, Ronald Wolfson, Sima Lessor, and Judith Bin-Nun. In *NATE* (23rd Annual Conference, Dec. 1977): 23–28.

Mandelbaum, D. G. "Change and Continuity in Jewish Life." In *JES*, 509–19.

Marcus, Audrey Friedman. "The Conference Plan: Eight Years Later." *Ped Rep* 26 (Spring 1975): 3–5. (See also Friedman, Audrey.)

———. "Six Exciting Happenings in Jewish Education." *Compass* 1 (Spring 1978): 5–7.

Margoshes, Samuel. "Five Years of Jewish Schooling—Revolution in Jewish Education." *Day* (Feb. 5, 1961).

Markowitz, Samuel H. "Reforming Reform Jewish Education." *CCAR J* (Apr. 1954): 47–51.

Mass, Ronald S., ed. *What's Happening: Tried and True Ideas for the Jewish Classroom and Home.* N.Y.: UAHC. 28 pp.

Moment. "Old Problems, New Appetites: A Conversation with Practitioners." 3 (Oct. 1978): 25–26.

Moroz, Sh. „דרכים ודרך בחינוך" (Directions and Direction in Education). *Hadoar* (H.) 59 (Nov. 23, 1979).

Nardi, Noah. "Jewish Education in the United States: Changes and Prospects." *In the Dispersion* (Winter 1962): 22–42.

Olitzky, Kerry M. "The Beth Israel Mini-Mester Program: An Approach to Individualized Instruction." *Compass* 6 (Summer 1983): 16–19.

Olshansky, B. "Jewish Education in a Time of Change." *J Jew Com Ser* 55 (Summer 1979): 323–28.

Ped Rep. "Open School Project Launched by NCRI." 24 (Winter 1973): 13

Ped Rep. "Annual Roundup of New Programs in Jewish Education." 24 (Spring 1973); 25 (Winter 1974); 26 (Winter 1974–75); 27 (Winter 1976); 28 (Winter 1977). From 1978 to 1984, *Roundup* appeared as a separate publication.

Phillips, Bruce, and Jerry Dash. "Experiments in Jewish Education: The 'Rishonim' Project of Temple Isaiah." *AM* (Spring 1975): 6–12.

Pilch, Judah. "Changing Patterns in Jewish Education." *JSS* 21 (Apr. 1959): 91–117.

———. "Jewish Education in a Changing World." *Jew Spec* (Apr. 1961): 9–12.

———. "Some New Developments in the Jewish School Curriculum." *Rel Ed* 56 (July–Aug. 1961): 256–60.

———. "Towards a Revised Jewish School Curriculum." *Rel Ed* 61 (May–June 1966): 181–83.

Polish, David. "A Radical Departure: A Plan for a Second Congregational Board to Devote Its Time to Education." *Compass* 2 (Spring 1979): 5–6.

Pollak, George. "Back to the Basics." *Jew Ed* 45 (Winter 1977): 5–9, 48.

Pomerantz, George. "The Revitalization of the Talmud Torah." *Jew Ed* 21 (Summer 1950): 20–24.

Rauchwerger, Diane. "Orientation Innovation." *Compass* 2 (Summer 1979): 10–11.

Ravid, Zvulun. „תכנון הלמודים בעולם משתנה" (Planning the Curriculum in a Changing World). *Sh Hah* (H.) 24 (Fall 1963): 15–19.

Recon. "Reconstructionism and Jewish Education." 29 (Oct. 18, 1963): 17–22; (Nov.

43 CHANGE IN JEWISH EDUCATION

1963): 16–21. See also *Ped Rep* 15 (Dec. 1963) (condensed).

Recon. "Reinstating Jewish Education" (editorial). (Jan. 26, 1951): 3–5.

Recon. "Striving for Excellence" (editorial). 32 (Apr. 1966): 3–5.

Reich, P. "Realistic Experiment in Jewish Education." *Recon* 31 (June 21, 1966): 23–25.

Reimer, Joseph. "If I Had Power to Change Jewish Education." *Un Syn Rev* 28 (Fall 1975): 8–9.

Rudavsky, David. "A Shift in Emphasis in the Curriculum of the Weekday Afternoon Jewish Schools." *Jew Ed* 24 (Spring 1953): 13–18, 63.

Schachter, S. J. "An Experiment That Failed." *Syn Sch* 26 (1968).

Schafler, Samuel. "From Alternatives to Excellence." *Jew Ed* 51 (Summer 1983): 9–11.

Scharfstein, Zevi. „השינויים בחינוך היהודי באמריקה" (The Changes in Jewish Education in America). In *Hadoar Jubilee Volume* (H.), 36–42. 1952.

Schein, Jeffrey. "Changes in the Reform Curriculum: An Educational Mirror to the Relationship between Reform Judaism and Reconstructionism." *RJ* (Spring 1982): 58–68.

———. "The Open Classroom." In *JPH*, 353–62.

Schiff, Alvin I. *In Search of Educational Excellence*. N.Y.: BJE, 1970. 12 pp.

———. "The Jewish Supplementary School—A System in Need of Change." *Jew Ed* 55 (Winter 1988): 4–8.

——— (study director). *Jewish Supplementary Schooling: An Educational System in Need of Change*. N.Y.: BJE of Greater New York, 1988. 160 pp.

———. "The Reconstruction of Jewish Education." *Jew Ed* 39 (Apr. 1969): 19–24.

Schiff, Alvin I. and Chaim Y. Botwinick. "The Relevance of the Recommendations of Major National Studies on Education to Jewish Schooling." *Jew Ed* 52 (Summer 1984): 7–18.

Schindler, Alexander M. "The American Jew: Retrospect and Prospect—A New Curriculum for a New Community." *Jew Teach* 34 (Apr. 1966).

———. "Toward a New Curriculum." *Jew Teach* 34 (Dec. 1965).

Schoem, David. "Improving School Climate in an Afternoon School." *Ped Rep* 35 (Oct. 1984): 20–21.

Schwartz, Elliott. "Team Teaching: Applications and Implications in Jewish Education." *Syn Sch* 21 (Feb. 1963): 3–10.

Schwartz, Sidney H. "Reconstructionism In Our Hebrew Schools." *Recon* 47 (Oct. 1981): 27.

Schwartzman, Sylvan D. "Some New Approaches to Reform Religious Education." *Jew Teach* 20 (May 1952): 10–12.

———. *Toward a New Curriculum for the One-Day-a-Week Reform Religious School*. Cincinnati: HUC, 1955. 35 pp.

Segal, Abraham. "Encouraging Teacher Creativity." *Jew Teach* 24 (Apr. 1966): 36–37. See also *Ped Rep* 18 (Sept. 1966).

Seidenfeld, Morton A. "Meeting Individual Needs through Jewish Education." *Jew Teach* 25 (May 1957): 3–6.

Seltzer, Sanford. "Reform Judaism and the Lesson of Progressive Education." *CCAR J* (Oct. 1962): 28–29.

Shapiro, Jack. "Bureau Personnel as Agents for Change." *Jew Ed* 48 (Summer 1980): 47–49.

Sherwin, Byron. "Restructuring Jewish Education." *Congress Weekly* 43 (Nov. 1976): 10–13.

Skolnik, Nachama. "Micah-Rachel: A Conclave Approach for the Intermediate Grades." A new approach to the conclave structure for Jewish education. Master's project, HUC–JIR, 1977.

Sleeper, James A. "A Radical View of Jewish Culture: Why Modern Jewish Education Must Begin outside the Tradition." In *FJCA*, 230–59.

Slesinger, Zalmen. "Assessing and Redesigning Jewish Education in the United States—A Task for the 70's." *Ped Rep* 22 (Sept. 1970).

———. "Dare the Schools Stand Still in a World of Change?" *Ped Rep* 11 (May 1960). See also *JJS*, 181–86.

———. "New Perspectives on Jewish Education." *Jew Fron* (Aug.–Sept. 1976): 20–25.

———. "Providing for Individual Differences." *Ped Rep* (May 1958).

———. "Reducing the Educational Lag in the Jewish School." *Ped Rep* 13 (May 1962): 12–14, 30.

Spertus, Byron. "Restructuring Jewish Education." *Congress Weekly* (Nov. 1976): 10–13.

Spiro, Jack D. "Focus on Alternatives." *Ped Rep* 22 (Mar. 1971): 13.

Teller, Gerald A. "A New Model for Jewish Education." *Impact* 35 (Summer 1977): 4–14. See also *Rel Ed* 72 (May–June 1977): 293–305.

Toubin, Isaac. "A Shift in Educational Focus." *Con Jud* 24 (Fall 1969): 59–61.

Troy, Dov. "Team Teaching: A Personal Experience." *Syn Sch* 21 (Feb. 1063): 11–20.

UAHC. *Ideabook*. 3 vols. N.Y.: 1977–80.

Wachs, Saul P. "Back to the Basics: A Cautionary Reaction." *Jew Ed* 46 (Summer 1978): 36–42.

Warschauer, Heinz. "New Approaches in Reform Jewish Education." Address delivered at Canadian Council of Reform Congregations, Nov. 1964. 8 pp.

Wittstein, Joel, and Ailene Avner. "Planning An Open Classroom? Read This First." *NATE News* 20 (Apr. 1977): 1–2.

* Zeldin, Michael. *Change in Jewish Education: The Development of a Comprehensive Theory*. U. of Southern California, 1979. 245 pp.

———. "A Framework for Understanding Change in Jewish Education." In *Stu*, 2:175–89.

———. "Implementing Change." In *JPH*, 13–19.

GLEANINGS

Piexotto, Dr. D. L. M., proposing a modern Jewish school before the Society for the Education of the Poor Children and the Relief of Indigent Persons of the Jewish Persuasion (1830),
"1. The first [proposal] is the formation of a school on principles similar to those of Pestalozzi.... I would direct that one of the first objects to be taught the pupil should be a knowledge of the Hebrew language."
In *JDH*, 2:437–38.

Benderly, Samson,
"We need to shift the emphasis in our schools from the children of the ages 7 to 13 to the ages of 10 to 17.... The adolescent and pre-adolescent periods are the ideal periods for giving our pupils an interpretation of Jewish life and Judaism which will best adapt them to Jewish life of today and orient them Jewishly in a non-Jewish environment."
Quoted in *Jew Ed* 32 (Fall 1961), 19.

Slesinger, Zalmen,
"A comparative analysis of the program of the Jewish school of today with that of a half century ago would lead one to assume that our world is at standstill. To be sure, there have been some changes during this time in the quality of our programs, instructional materials, co-curricular activities, teaching personnel, school facilities and equipment, etc. But there is hardly any indication of basic curricular reorganization reflecting recent achievements of science in related areas, especially in child development; the phenomenon of social change; the spirit of human interdependence, as well as the social changes which transpired in Jewish life during this period."
"Dare the School Stand Still in a World of Change?" In *JJS*, 184. Also in *Ped Rep* (May 1960).

Freidenreich, Fradle,
"There are no universal answers in education. It takes careful judgment and dedicated and creative work to relate, modify, and adapt to one school that which is meaningful to another. Such service cannot be rendered long distance. We felt, therefore, that the time has come for key people involved to discuss together the issues and problems underlying innovative efforts in Jewish education, to share materials and to evaluate, by way of media, some of the present classroom procedures. In short, we viewed this conference as initiating a dialogue on the most basic level."

43 CHANGE IN JEWISH EDUCATION

To Everything There Is a Time, 1. N.Y.: AAJE, 1975.

Frost, Shimon,

"Non-fixedness-education, like growth, is an ever-evolving task. It is a process. So is curriculum content, so is curriculum organization of the school; so is the evolving tradition. The dictum, mesorat avoteinu b'yadeinu was not meant to fossilize tradition but only to give a sense of direction. This attitude of non-fixedness applies to both levels: emunot v'deiot and mitzvot ma'asiyot. Our task is to make Judaism challenging in terms of the former and meaningful in terms of the latter."

Con Jud 33 (Spring 1980), 75.

Zeldin, Michael,

"In sum, assessing the success or failure of a change project in a Jewish school requires both in looking at the impact on the school and at the effects on students and teachers. Understanding what led to the outcomes requires looking at the awareness of the need for change, the impetus of the change, and the relationship among these elements."

"A Framework for Understanding Change in Jewish Education." In *Stu*, 2:189.

BJE of Greater New York,

"This study ends as it began, with the fervent hope that it will be instrumental in helping to initiate the necessary change in the Jewish supplementary school—a system in need of change. It concludes with a set of four recommendations designed to respond to the four overall challenges that derive from the findings:

(1) changing the focus and structure of synagogue schooling;

(2) increasing the exposure and quality of supplementary education via the integration of formal and informal learning strategies;

(3) training professionals for effective performance; and

(4) developing appropriate career opportunities for educational personnel.

Jewish Supplementary Schooling: An Educational System in Need of Change, 140. Alvin I. Schiff, study director. N.Y.: BJE of Greater New York, 1988.

44 | THE SOCIAL SCIENCES AND JEWISH EDUCATION

(See also chapter 31 and "America's Impact on Jewish Education" in chapter 45)

SOCIOLOGY AND RELATED FIELDS (SELECTED)

Alt, H. "Jewish Education and Social Adjustment." *JSSQ* 23 (1947): 276–84.

* Berkson, Isaac B. *Theories of Americanization: A Critical Study with Special Reference to the Jewish Group.* Columbia U. Teachers College, 1920. 226 pp.

* Berman, Barbara Ann Portnoy. *Environmental Impact on the Ideology of a Social Movement Organization:* The Jewish Daily Forward, *1897–1966.* U. of Michigan, 1972.

* Berman, Myron. *The Attitude of American Jewry towards East European Jewish Immigration, 1881–1914.* Columbia U., 1963.

Blumenfeld, Samuel M. "American Jewry—Reflections on Social, Communal and Spiritual Trends." In *Essays on Jewish Life and Thought*, edited by Joseph L. Blau, 123–38. N.Y.: Columbia U. Press, 1959. Also in *Thou Shalt Teach*, edited by Judah Pilch, 99–117. 1973.

* Bock, Geoffry Ephraim. *The Jewish Schooling of American Jews: A Study of Non-Cognitive Educational Effects.* Harvard U., 1976. 316 pp.

———. *The Social Context of Jewish Education: A Literature Review.* Jewish Education and Jewish Identity Series. N.Y.: AJC, 1976. 39 pp.

* Bressler, Marvin. *Jewish Behavior Patterns as Exemplified by W. I. Thomas' Unfinished Study of the Bintel Brief* (advice column in *The Forward*). U. of Pennsylvania, 1952.

Brotz, Howard. "The Negro-Jewish Community and the Contemporary Race Crisis." *JSS* 27 (1965): 10–17.

Chein, Isidor. "Basic Issues in Jewish Education and Group Work." N.Y.: Commission on Community Relations. Reprinted by Department of Adult Education, JEC of N.Y., 1958.

Cohen, Bernard. "Changing Jewish Education." In *Sociological Changes in American Jewish Life as Reflected in Selected Literature*, 154–72. Rutherford, N.J.: Fairleigh Dickinson U. Press, 1972.

* ———. *Social and Cultural Change in American Jewish Life as Reflected in Selected Jewish Literature.* U. of Southern California, 1957.

Cohen, Jack J. "Our Schools and Our Society." *Jew Ed* 31 (Fall 1960): 4–18.

* Cohn, Werner. *Sources of American Jewish Liberalism: A Study of the Political Alignments of American Jews.* New School for Social Research, 1956.

Dean, John P. "Patterns of Socialization and Association between Jews and Non-Jews." *JSS* 17 (July 1955): 247–68.

* Dershowitz, Zachary. *Influences of Cultural Patterns on the Thinking of Children in Certain Ethnic Groups: A Study of the Effect of Jewish Subculture on the Field Dependence-Independence Dimension of Cognition*. New York, 1966.

Diamond, Jack. "A Reader in the Demography of American Jews." *AJYB* 77 (1977): 251–317.

Dinin, Samuel. "The Socio-Dynamics of Jewish Education." *Jew Ed* 32 (Fall 1961): 27–33.

Drachsler, Julius. *Democracy and Assimilation*. N.Y.: Macmillan, 1920.

Duker, Abraham G. "Emerging Patterns in American Jewish Life." *AJHS* 39 (June 1950): 351–88. Reprinted by JEC, 1950. 40 pp. With a leader's discussion guide by Abraham Segal, 1953.

———. *Jewish Attitude to Child Adoption: A Study of Adoption Practices*. Edited by M. Shapiro. N.Y.: Child Welfare League of America, 1956.

———. "Notes on the Culture of American Jewry." *Jew J Soc* 2 (June 1960): 98–102.

———. "On Religious Trends in American Jewish Life." *YA* 4 (1949): 51–63.

Dushkin, Alexander M. "The Social Basis of Jewish Education in America." *Jewish Teacher* 2 (Apr. 1918): 9–20.

* Edson, C. H. *Immigrant Perspectives on Work and Schooling: Eastern European Jews and Southern Italians, 1880–1920*. Stanford U., 1979. 287 pp.

Fishman, Joshua A. "Social Science Research Relevant to American Jewish Education." *Jew Ed* 28 (Winter 1957–58): 49–60; 29 (Winter 1959): 64–71; 30 (Winter 1960): 35–45.

* Fishman, Morris. *Jewish Reactions to Anti-Semitism*. New School for Social Research, 1959.

Frank, Herman. „ייִדישע דעמאָגראַפֿיע אין די פֿאַראייניקטע שטאַטן (אירע פּראָבלעמען מעטאָדן און רעזולטאַטן)" (Jewish Demography in the United States: Its Problems, Methodology and Results). *Yivo Annual* (Y.) (American Branch) 1 (1938): 153–84.

Friedman, Norman L. "Religion's Sub-System: Toward a Sociology of Jewish Education." *Sociology of Education* 42 (Winter 1969): 104–13.

Gans, Herbert J. "The Origin and Growth of a Jewish Community in the Suburbs." In *JES*, 205–48.

Ginzberg, Eli. "Jews in the Changing Urban Emvironment." *Con Jud* 27 (Summer 1973).

Gittler, Joseph B. "Towards a Definition of a Jew and Implications of a General Systems Theory for the Study of Jewish Life." In *Jewish Life in the United States: Perspectives from the Social Sciences*, edited by Joseph B. Gittler, 1–29. New York U. Press, 1981.

Glasner, Samuel. *A Self-Survey of a Congregation's Social Attitudes*. N.Y.: UAHC.

Glazer, Nathan. *American Judaism*. Chicago: U. of Chicago Press, 1957. 176 pp.

———. "The Jewish Revival in America: A Sociologist Reports." *Commentary* (Dec. 1955): 493–99.

———. "Social Characteristics of American Jews, 1654–1954." *AJYB* 56 (1955): 3–41. See also *Jews*, 2:1694–1735, and *The Characteristics of American Jews*, 11–55. N.Y.: JEC Press, 1965.

———. "What Sociology Knows about American Jews." *Commentary* 9 (Mar. 1950): 275–84.

Goldberg, Nathan. "Demographic Characteristics of American Jews." In *JMW*, 2:638–717.

Goldscheider, Calvin. *Jewish Continuity and Change: Emerging Patterns in America*. Bloomington: Indiana U. Press, 1985.

———. "Socio-Economic Status and Jewish Fertility." *Jew J Soc* 7 (Dec. 1965): 228–33.

Goldstein, Sidney. "American Jewry, 1970: A Demographic Profile." In *JAS*, 93–162.

———. "The Changing Socio-Demographic Structure of an American Jewish Community." *Jew J Soc* 8 (June 1966): 11–30.

———. "Jews in the United States: Perspectives from Demography." In *JLUS*, 31–102. Also in *AJYB* 81 (1981): 3–59.

———. "Population Movement and Redistribution among American Jews." *Jew J Soc* 24 (June 1982): 5–23.

Gordon, Albert I. "Aspects of Jewish Education in Suburbia." *Syn Sch* 19 (Mar. 1961): 16–20.

———. *Jews in Suburbia.* Boston: Beacon Press, 1959. 264 pp.

———. *Jews in Transition.* Minneapolis: U. of Minnesota Press, 1949.

———. "The Problems and Promises of Suburban Life." *RA* (1960): 49–55.

Gordon, Milton M. *Assimilation in American Life: The Role of Race, Religion, and National Origin.* N.Y.: Oxford U. Press, 1964. 276 pp.

Gould, J. "American Jewry: Some Social Trends." *Jew J Soc* 3 (1961): 55–75.

Graeber, Isacque, and Stuart Henderson Britt, eds. *Jews in a Gentile World.* N.Y.: Macmillan, 1942.

Grand, Samuel. "The Study of Cultural Factors in Jewish Social Service." *Jew Ed* 20 (Feb. 1949): 24–28.

* Grossfield, Avery J. *Some Jewish Juvenile Delinquents: A Study of Three Hundred Cases.* HUC–JIR, 1950. Summarized in *Rel Ed* 46 (1951): 171–72.

Halpern, Ben. "A Problem in Jewish Education: Alienation." *Jew Fron* (June 1964): 13–18.

Handlin, Oscar. "Changing Patterns in Group Life in America and Their Implication for the American Jewish Community." *J Jew Com Ser* 34 (1958): 347–53.

Hansen, M. L. "The Third Generation in America" (classic essay in American immigrant history). *Commentary* 14 (Nov. 1952): 492–500.

Harris, A., and G. Watson. "Are Jewish or Gentile Children More Clannish?" *Social Psychology* 24 (1946): 171–72.

Heilman, Samuel E. "Inner and Outer Identities: Sociological Ambivalence among Orthodox Jews." *JSS* 39 (Summer 1977): 227–40.

———. *Inside the Jewish School: A Study of the Cultural Setting for Jewish Education* N.Y.: AJC, 1983. 50 pp.

———. "The Sociology of American Jewry: The Last Ten Years." *Amer Rev of Soc* 8 (1982): 135–60.

———. *Synagogue Life: A Study in Symbolic Interaction.* Chicago: U. of Chicago Press, 1976.

Herberg, Will. "Religious Trends in American Jewry." *Jud* 3 (Summer 1954): 229–40.

———. "The 'Triple Melting Pot': The Third Generation from Ethnic to Religious Diversity." *Commentary* 20 (Aug. 1955): 101–8.

Himmelfarb, Harold S. "Fertility Trends and Their Effects on Jewish Education." *Analysis* 60 (Nov.–Dec. 1976).

———. "The Interaction Effects of Parents, Spouse and Schooling: Comparing the Impact of Jewish and Catholic Schools." *Sociological Quarterly* 18 (Autumn 1977): 464–77.

Himmelfarb, Milton. *The Jews of Modernity.* N.Y.: Basic Books, 1973. 369 pp.

Hochbaum, Jerry. "The Changing Socio-Religious Profile of American Orthodoxy." *Trad* 9 (Spring–Summer 1967): 138–46.

———. "The Orthodox Community and the Urban Crisis." *Trad* 10 (Spring 1969): 41–48.

———. "Who Is a Jew: A Sociological Perspective." *Trad* 13 (Spring-Summer 1973): 35–41.

Honor, Leo L. "Forces Shaping Jewish Culture." *Jew Ed* 18 (Summer 1947): 17–22.

Horowitz, C. Morris. *Demographic Techniques and Jewish Education.* N.Y.: AAJE, 1955. See also *Jew Ed* 26 (Fall 1955): 17–23.

Hurvitz, Nathan. "Sources of Motivation and Achievement of American Jews." *JSS* 23 (Oct. 1961): 217–34.

———. "Understanding the Self-Hate of Jewish Young Adults." *Recon* (Dec. 14, 1952): 18–24.

JSS. "Tercentenary Conference on American Jewish Sociology." (July 1955): 155–285.

Jung, Leo. "Judaism and the New World Order." *American J of Economics and Sociology* 4 (1944–45): 385–93.

Koenig, Samuel. "Methods of Studying Jewish Life in America." *YA* 2–3 (1947–48): 282–94. See also *YB* (Y.) (1942).

Kramer, Judith R., and Seymour Leventman. *Children of the Gilded Ghetto.* New Haven: Yale U. Press, 1961. 228 pp.

Kranzler, Gerson. "The Changing Orthodox Jewish Community." *Trad* 16 (Fall 1976).

Liebman, Charles S. *The Ambivalent American Jew*. Phila.: JPS, 1973. 215 pp.

———. "Changing Social Characteristics of Orthodox, Conservative, and Reform Jews." *Sociological Analysis* 27 (Winter 1966): 210–21.

———. "A Sociological Analysis of Orthodox, Conservative, and Reform Jews." *Jud* 13 (Summer 1964): 285–384.

Lipset, Seymour M. "Jewish Sociologists and Sociology of the Jews." *JSS* 17 (1955): 177–78.

———. "The Study of Jewish Communities in a Comparative Context." *Jew J Soc* 5 (1963): 157–66.

Maier, J., and W. Spinrad. "Comparison of Religious Beliefs and Practices of Jewish, Catholic, and Protestant Students." *Phylon* 18 (1958): 355–60.

Mailer, Julius B. "The Young Jewish Delinquent." *JSSQ* (Sept. 1930).

Mandelbaum, David G. "Change and Continuity in Jewish Life." In *JES*, 509–19.

Mayer, Egon, and Chaim Waxman. "Modern Jewish Orthodoxy in America: Towards the Year 2000." *Trad* 16 (Spring 1977).

Neusner, Jacob. *American Judaism: Adventure in Modernity*. Englewood Cliffs, N.J.: Prentice Hall, 1972.

NFTB. *Findings of NFTB's Survey of Laymen's Attitudes*. N.Y.: 1953.

Pilch, Judah. *The Demographic Status of the Jewish People*. Rochester, N.Y.: AAJE.

Porter, Jack N., ed. *The Sociology of American Jews: A Critical Anthology*. Rev. ed. Washington D.C.: U. Press of America, 1980. 330 pp.

* Rappaport, Joseph. *Jewish Immigrants and World War I: A Study of American Yiddish Press Reaction*. Columbia U., 1951.

Ravich, Jesse. "Relative Rate of Change in Attitude among First, Second and Third Generation Jews." Master's thesis, Columbia U., 1926.

Rose, Arnold M. "America Is Changing the Mutual Images of Jews and Catholics." *Social Order* 13 (Feb. 1963): 19–33.

Rose, Peter Isaac, ed. *The Ghetto and Beyond: Essays on Jewish Life in America*. N.Y.: Random House, 1969.

* ———. *Strangers in Their Midst: A Sociological Study of the Small Town Jew and His Neighbor*. Cornell U., 1959. See also *Jew J Soc* 3 (Dec. 1961): 174–79.

Rosen, B. "Race, Ethnicity and the Achievement Syndrome." *American Sociological Review* 24 (1959): 47–48.

Rosen, Bernard C. "Minority Group in Transition: A Study of Adolescent Religious Conviction and Conduct." In *JES*, 336–46.

Rosenak, Michael. "The Jewish Types: Responses and Educational Options." *Jew Ed* 52 (Summer 1984): 19–29.

Rudavsky, David. „דער כאראקטער אין דעם רעליגיעזן אויפלעב און זיין ווירקונג אויף דער אידישער שול" (The Character of the Religious Revival and Its Effect upon the Jewish School) (Y.). N.Y.: Jewish World Congress, Apr. 1957. See also YA 13 (1965): 95–124.

———. "Religion and Religiosity in American Jewish Life." *J Ed Soc* 33 (1960): 314–20.

Sanua, Victor D. "A Review of Social Science Studies on Jews and Jewish Life in the United States." *Journal for the Scientific Study of Religion* 4 (Fall 1964): 71–83.

———. "Social Science Examines the Jews." *Jew Digest* 2 (1966): 1–13.

———. "Social Science Research Relevant to American Jewish Education." *Jew Ed* 32 (Winter 1962): 99–114; 33 (Spring 1963): 162–75; 34 (Spring 1964): 187–202; 35 (Summer 1965): 238–56.

Schafler, Samuel. "The Demographic Crisis and Jewish Education." *Jew Ed* 45 (Winter 1977): 13–15.

Schmelz, U. O. "Demographic Background to Diaspora Education." In *Stu*, 3:137–49.

———. "Jewish Survival: The Demographic Factors." *AJYB* 81 (1981): 61–117.

Schmidt, Nancy J. "An Orthodox Jewish Community in the United States: A Minority within a Minority." *Jew J Soc* 7 (Dec. 1965): 176–206.

Schneider, Dorothee. "Aufbau—Reconstruction and the Americanization of German-Jewish Immigrants, 1934–1944." Master's thesis, U. of Massachusetts, 1975.

* Schoem, David. *Ethnic Survival in America: An Ethnography of a Jewish Afternoon School*. U. of California-Berkeley, 1979. 279 pp.

Schwartz, Lita S., and Natalie Isser. "Attitudes towards the Jewish Minority in Public Education." *Jew Ed* (Summer/Fall 1977): 33–39.

Seidenfeld, Morton. "Raising a Jewish Child in a Non-Jewish Community." *Recon* (June 16, 1950): 22–27.

Seligman, Ben B., and Aaron Antonovsky. "The Demographic Crisis in Jewish Education." In *JES*, 45–93.

* Shapiro, Howard Martin. *Marginality, Familial Interaction, and Intellectuality: The Shaping of Perspective in a Jewish Community*. U. of Minnesota, 1969.

Shapiro, Mannheim S. "The Sociology of Jewish Life. In *Meet the American Jews*, edited by B. Menkus. N.Y.: Broadman Books, 1963.

Sherman, C. Bezalel. "Demographic and Social Aspects." In *Jan 2*, 27–51.

———. "Emerging Patterns and Attitudes in American Jewish Life." *Jew J Soc* 5 (June 1963): 47–54.

———. *The Jew within American Society: A Study in Ethnic Individuality*. Detroit: Wayne State U. Press, 1961.

Sidorsky, David, ed. *The Future of the Jewish Community in America*. N.Y.: Institute of Human Relations Press/Basic Books, 1973.

* Siegel, Morris. *Social Class and Jewish Participation*. Brandeis U., 1966.

Simon, E. "Suburbia, Its Effect on the American Jewish Teenager." *J of Educational Sociology* 36 (1962): 124–33.

Singer, David. "The Jewish Gangster: Crime as 'Unser Shtik'." *Jud* 23 (1974).

Sklare, Marshall. "The Conversion of Jews." *Commentary* 56 (Sept. 1973): 44–53.

———. *Not Quite at Home: How the American Jewish Community Lives with Itself and Its Neighbors*. N.Y.: AJC, 1969. 85 pp.

———. "The Social Background of American Jewish Education: A Commentary." In *The Social Context of Jewish Identity*, 12–26. N.Y.: AJC, 1972.

———. "Some Socio-Psychological Aspects of the Jew in America." In *CPA*, 9–24.

Sklare, Marshall, and Joseph Greenbaum. "The Lakeville Jews Look to the Next Generation." In *JI*, 291–320.

Sklare, Marshall, and Marc Vosk. *The Riverton Study: How Jews Look at Themselves and Their Neighbors*. N.Y.: AJC, 1957. 48 pp.

Steinberg, Bernard. "Jewish Education in the United States: A Study in Religio-Ethnic Response." *Jew J Soc* 21 (June 1979): 5–31.

Steinberg, Milton, and Moshe Davis. "Contemporary Social Problems in the Light of Jewish Tradition." *Jew Ed* 13 (Jan. 1942): 197–98.

Stember, Charles, et al. *Jews in the Mind of America*. N.Y.: AJC Institute of Human Relations and Basic Books, 1966. 413 pp.

Syme, Daniel. "A Forum on 'Assimilation'." *Jew Digest* 29 (Nov.–Dec. 1983): 59–61.

Teller, Judd. "The Changing Status of American Jewry." *Mid* 3 (Summer 1957): 5–15.

Theus, Kathryn T. "From Orthodoxy to Reform: Assimilation and the Jewish-English Press of Mid-Nineteenth Century America." Master's thesis, U. of Maryland, 1982.

Trachtenberg, Joshua. "Religious Background of Anti-Semitism." *JSS* 17 (July 1955): 219–28.

Tribuch, Baruch. "The Attitude of the Early *Jewish Daily Forward* toward Selected Aspects of American Judaism." Master's thesis, Yeshiva U., 1974.

Warner, W. Lloyd, and Leo Srole. "Assimilation or Survival: A Crisis in the Jewish Community of Yankee City." In *JES*, 347–56.

* Weinberg, A. I. *Judaism in America: The Influence of America as a New World Frontier upon Judaism of Tradition*. U. of Texas, 1953.

Wolfe, George. "The 'Bintel Brief [advice column of the *Jewish Daily Forward*] as an Immigrant Institution and a Research Source." Master's thesis, Graduate School for Jewish Social Work, 1933.

Wurtzel, Yehuda. "Towards an Applied Anthropology of Jewish Education." In *Stu*, 1:23–25.

PSYCHOLOGY AND SOCIAL PSYCHOLOGY (SELECTED)

Adelson, J. "A Study of Minority Group Authoritarianism." In *JES*, 475–92.

Adler, M. "A Study of the Effects of Ethnic Origin on Giftedness." *Gifted Child Quarterly* 7 (1963): 98–101.

Arlow, J. A. "Jewish Tradition and Psychological Integration." In *CPA*, 85–95.

Baggaley, A. R. "Comparison of Temperament Scores of Jewish and Gentile Male Students." *Psychological Reports* 13 (1963): 598.

Baron, R. R. V. "The Measurement of Religious Observances among Jews." *Jewish Journal of Sociology* 6 (1964): 81–90.

Bemporad, Jack. "A Religious Program in a Residential Treatment Center." *News and Views* (Sept.–Oct. 1962).

Berman, I., and Georgene Seward. "A Little Boy under Pressure of Orthodoxy." In *Clinical Studies in Culture and Conflict*, edited by Georgene Seward, 455–77. N.Y.: Ronald Press, 1958.

Bettelheim, Bruno. "How to Arm Our Children against Anti-Semitism." In *Securing Our Children against Prejudice*. N.Y.: National Association for Mental Health. 31 pp.

Biber, Barbara. "Effective Learning and Healthy Personality." *Ped Rep* 13 (Mar. 1962).

Boehm, L. "The Development of Conscience: A Comparison of Upper-Middle Class Academically Gifted Children Attending Catholic and Jewish Parochial Schools." *J of Social Psychology* 59 (1963): 101–10.

Brayer, Menachem. „הבעיות הפסיכולוגיות בחנוך הילדים הפליטים" (Psychological Problems in the Education of D.P. [Displaced Persons] Children." *Sh Hah* (H.) 13 (1953): 226–33.

Brill, Moshe. "Comparative Psychological Studies of Jews and Non-Jews and Their Implications for Jewish Education." *Jew Ed* 8 (Apr.–June 1936): 73–78.

Brown, F. A. "A Note on the Stability and Maturity of Jewish and Non-Jewish Boys." *J of Social Psychology* 12 (1940): 171–75.

Chein, Isidor. "The Challenge of Individual Needs and Aspirations in Jewish Education." In *JER*, 32–53.

———. "Education and Knowledge." *Jew Teach* 21 (Nov. 1952): 5–8.

———. "Jewish Adjustment: A Diagnosis and an Outline of a Program." In *CPA*, 39–50.

Chein, Isidor, and J. Hurwitz. *A Study of Minority Group Membership: The Reaction of Jewish Boys to Various Aspects of Being Jewish*. N.Y.: Jewish Center Division of the NJWB, 1950.

Clark, E. "Motivation of Jewish Students." *J of Social Psychology* 29 (1949): 113–17.

Cohen, I. L. *Intelligence of Jews as Compared with Non-Jews*. Ohio State U. Contributions to Psychology, no. 8.

Copeland, Steven. "Bibliotherapy in a Jewish Educational Perspective." In *Stu*, 1:214–35.

* Dlugacz, Irving. *A Psychological View of the American Jews and its Significance for the Psychological Approach to Case-Work*. Columbia U., 1961.

Duker, Abraham G. "Socio-Psychological Trends in American Jewish Life since 1900." *YA* 9 (1954): 166–78. See also *YB* (Y.) 38 (1954): 134–55.

Elkin, Harry. "Jewish Education and Individual Security." *Jew Ed*. 21 (Summer 1950): 32–36.

Elkind, D. "The Child's Conception of His Religious Denomination—The Jewish Child." *J of Genetic Psychology* 71 (1970): 101–21.

Falk, G. F. "Psychology and Our Educational Program." *Jew Teach* 14 (June 1946): 12–17.

* Fishman, Joshua A. "Childhood Indoctrination for Minority-Group Membership." *Daedalus* 90 (1961): 329–49.

———. *Negative Stereotypes Concerning Americans among American-Born Children Receiving Various Types of Minority Group Education*. Columbia U., 1953. 123 pp.

Flowerman, S. H. "Psychological Effects upon Pupils of Religious Instruction in Schools." *Jew Ed* 23 (Fall 1952): 29–33, 40.

Fromm, Eric. "The Nature of Symbolic Language." *Jew Teach* 34 (Oct. 1955): 3–7.

Frumkin, H. M. "The Jewish Intellectual and His Jewishness: A Social Psychological Analysis." *Ethos* 3 (1958): 7–9.

Gittelsohn, Roland. "Judaism and Mental Health." *Jud* 8 (Fall 1959): 323–25.

Glasner, S. "Judaism and Its Therapeutic Application." *Annals of Psychotherapy* 1 (1959): 40–46.

Goldberg, G. "די אינטעליגענץ פון יידישע און אנדערע קינדער" (The Intelligence of Jewish and Other Children). *CE* (Y.) 11 (Dec. 1941).

Golovensky, D. I. "Marginal Man Concept: An Analysis and Critique." *Social Forces* 30 (1952): 333–39.

* Gordon, Whitney H. *Stress and the Jewish Community of Middletown*. Purdue U., 1962.

Gross, Morris B. "Jewish Ethics and Self-psychology." *Trad* 1 (Spring 1959): 184–92.

* Henoch, C. *Dynamics of Anxiety in Two Culturally Different Groups*. Yeshiva U., 1961.

Hollander, Arthur S. "Some Applications of Positive Mental Hygiene in the Congregational School." *Syn Sch* 22 (Winter 1964): 48–56.

Imber, Rebbecca. "The School Psychologist in a Synagogue School." *Jew Ed* 30 (Spring 1960): 33–38.

Kahn, Alfred J. "Jewish Elements in the Development of the Child." *Jew Ed* 18 (Summer 1947): 12–17.

Krieger, L. H. "Aiding the Unpopular Student." *Jew Teach* 32 (Oct. 1963): 8–9.

Lehrer, Leibush. "קינדער און יידישע קינדער אין מלחמה צייט" (Children and Jewish Children during the War). *Jew Rev* (Y. section) (May 1943): 31–50.

———. "די אינטעליגענץ פון אמעריקאנער יידישע קינדער" (The Intelligence of American Jewish Children). *YB* (Y.) (1936): 217–36.

———. "דאס 'יידישע' אין דער פסיכיק פון אמעריקאנער יידישן קינד" (The "Jewish" Element in the Mental Health of the American Jewish Child). *YB* (Y.) 4 (Dec. 1932): 330–53. See also *YA* 1 (1946): 195–216.

———. "די יידישקייט פון צווייטן דור וועלטלעכע" (The Jewishness of Second Generation Secularist Jews). *YB* (Y.) 42 (1962): 167–80. Also in *YA* 13 (1965): 79–94.

———. פסיכאלאגיע און דערציאונג (Psychology and Education) (Y.). N.Y.: Farlag Matones, 1937. 488 pp.

Levinson, B. M. "A Comparative Study of the Verbal Performance of Monolingual and Bilingual Children of Traditional Parentage." *J of Clinical Psychology* 97 (1960): 93–112.

———. "Comparison of the Performance of Bilingual and Mono-lingual Native-Born Jewish Pre-school Children of Traditional Parentage on Four Intelligence Tests." *J of Clinical Psychology* 15 (1959): 74–76.

———. "Psychology: Its Practice and Teaching in a Jewish College" (Yeshiva U.). *Jew Ed* 31 (Spring 1961): 46–53.

———. "Some Research Findings with Jewish Subjects of Traditional Backgrounds." *Mental Hygiene* 47 (1963): 129–34.

Lewin, Kurt. "דאס גרופ-אנגעהעריקייט און די יידישע קינד אין די פאראייניקטע שטאטן" (Group Belongingness and the Jewish Child in the United States). In *DER* (Y.), 2:285–304.

———. "Psychological Problems in Jewish Education." *JSSQ* 23 (1947): 291–96.

———. *Resolving Social Conflicts*. Edited by Gertrude Weiss Lewin. N.Y.: Harper and Bros., 1948. 230 pp.

———. "Self-Hatred among Jews." *Contemporary Jewish Record* 4 (June 1941): 219–32.

Lewin, Mrs. Kurt. "Group Belongingness and Jewish Education." *Jew Ed* 18 (Feb.–Mar. 1947): 14–17.

Lewitt, D. W., "Minority Group Belonging, Social Preference, and the Marginal Personality." *J of Abnormal and Social Psychology* 59 (1959): 357–62.

Mailer, Julius B. "The Maladjusted Jewish Child." *JSSQ* 9 (1933): 285–95.

———. "Personality Adjustment of the Jewish Child." *Jew Ed* 5 (Apr.–June 1933): 109–14.

———. "Studies in the Intelligence of Young Jews." *Jew Ed* 3 (Jan.–Mar. 1931): 29–39.

Maron, Neil, and Martin H. Rock. "Jewish Belief, Observance and Ego Development." *Jew Ed* 52 (1984–85): 35–40.

Matzner-Bekerman, Shoshana. *The Jewish Child: Halakhic Perspective*. N.Y.: Ktav, 1984. 314 pp.

Moshowitz, I. "Psychology of the Jew in the Light of Traditional Jewish Religious, Cultural, and Folk Patterns." In *CPA*, 25–38.

M'ron, M. "L'heker Ishiut Hayeled Hay'hudi B'artsot Habrit" (Research on the Personality of the Jewish Child in the United States). *Ha Hinukh* (H.) 25 (1952–53): 25–43.

Nardi, Noah. "Applying Kurt Lewin's Method to Jewish Education." *Recon* 14 (June 25, 1948): 13–19.

———. "Group Dynamics in Jewish Education." *Jew Ed* 18 (Feb.–Mar. 1947): 7–14.

———. "הפסיכולוגיה של הלמידה" (The Psychology of Learning). *Sh Hah* (H.) 9 (1949): 72–84.

———. "הפסיכולוגיה של למוד הקריאה" (The Psychology of Study of Reading). *Sh Hah* (H.) 8 (1948): 73–90.

———. "Some Applications of Kurt Lewin's Social Dynamics." *Recon* (June 11, 1948): 915.

———. "Studies in Intelligence of Jewish Children." *Jew Ed* 19 (1948): 41–50.

Noveck, Simon, ed. *Judaism and Psychiatry*. N.Y.: NAAJS of the USA, 1955.

Perlmutter, Elsie K. "The Role of the Case Worker in the Jewish School." *Jew Ed* 28 (Winter 1957–58): 38–41.

Revitch, Eugene. *The Mental Hygiene Value of Jewish Education for Parents*. N.Y.: USCJE, 1954. 8 pp.

Rinken, M. M. "Today's Judaism: A Social-Psychological Evaluation." *Perspectives* (Harvard U. B'nai B'rith Hillel Foundation) (May 1953).

* Sanua, Victor D. *Differences in Personality Adjustment among Different Generations of Jews and Non-Jews as Reflected in Objective and Projective Tests of Personality*. Michigan State U., 1956. See also *Culture and Mental Health*, edited by M. K. Opler, 443–36. 1959.

———. "Minority Status and Psychological Adjustment." *Jew J Soc* 4 (1962): 241–53.

Schneierson, Fishl. "העצבניות ותורת האדם" (The Study of Mankind). *Sh Hah* (H.) 3 (1928): 175–83; 4 (1928–29): 10–18, 73–78, 318–25, 512–19.

Schoem, David. "Inside the Classroom: Reflections of a Troubled People." *Jew Ed* 48 (Spring 1980): 35–41.

* Segelman, Ralph. *A Test of the Lewinian Hypothesis on Self-Hatred among the Jews*. New York U., 1966. 562 pp.

Seward, G., and J. Marmor. "Jews between Two Worlds." In *Psychotherapy and Culture Conflict*, 248–83. N.Y.: Ronald Press, 1956.

Shuey, A. M. "Differences in Performance of Jewish and Non-Jewish Children on the American Council Psychological Examination." *J of Social Psychology* 15 (1942): 221–43.

Soloff, Rav A., Howard M. Newburger, and Sidney A. Cohlan. "Course in Psychology for Religious Schools." *CCAR J* 16 (1969): 65–72.

Spector, S. I. "The Talmud and the Search for Security." *Trad* 8 (Fall 1966): 40–46.

Stein, K. E. "Emotional Conditioning." *Jew Teach* (Oct. 1963): 3–5.

Sukov, May, and E. G. Williamson. "Personality Traits and Attitudes of Jewish and Non-Jewish Students." *J of Applied Psychology* 22 (Oct. 1938): 487–92.

Touroff, Nissan. "הפסיכולוגיה החדשה והחנוך" (The New Psychology and Education). *Sh Hah* (H.) (May–June 1939): 3–27.

———. "יסודות פסיכולוגיים לחינוך לאומי" (Psychological Principles for National Education). In *Evaluations* (H.), 3–140. N.Y.: Teachers' Organization of America and Hebrew Organization of America, 1947.

Zucker, Arnold. "A Psychiatrist's View of the Jewish School." *Your Child* 4 (Winter 1970): 19–23.

IDENTITY (SELECTED)

* Adelson, Joseph B. *A Research in Jewish Group Identification*. U. of California, 1950.

Adler, J. R. "Jewish Students Profess Identity, Discard Belief." *Rel Ed* 55 (1960): 34–37.

Agus, Jacob B. *Jewish Identity in an Age of Ideologies: An Inquiry into the Jewish Self-Image*. N.Y.: 1979.

AJC. *Papers from Colloquium on Jewish Education and Jewish Identity, 1976–1977*.
The Social Context of Jewish Education: A Literature Review. 39 pp.

The Social Context of Jewish Identity. 26 pp.
Summary Report and Recommendations. 31 pp.
Issues in Jewish Identity. 66 pp.

* Antonovsky, Aaron. *The Ideologies of American Jews: A Study of a Marginal Situation.* Yale U.: 1955.

———. "Toward a Refinement of the Marginal Man Concept." *Social Forces* 35 (1956): 57–62.

Applebaum, Harold. "What Does Identity Really Mean?" *Recon* 37 (May 7, 1971): 25–29.

* Ausabel-Danzig, Rivka. *Marginality: On the Jewish Students in Social Work.* Yeshiva U., 1981.

Beck, E. T. "'No More Masks': Anti-Semitism as Jew-Hating." *Women's Studies Quarterly* 11 (Fall 1983): 11–14.

Beck, Yoram, ed. *Jewish Identity Today.* Jerusalem: World Zionist Organization Department of Information, 1979. 111 pp.

Bell, Daniel. "A Parable of Alienation." *Jew Fron* 13 (Nov. 1946): 12–19.

———. "Reflections on Jewish Identity." *Commentary* (June 1961): 471–78. Also in *The Ghetto and Beyond: Essays on Jewish Life in America*, edited by Peter I. Rose, 465–76. N.Y.: Random House, 1969.

Bennett, Alan D. "Marketing Jewish Identity: Services to Congregational Supplementary Schools." *J Jew Com Ser* (Winter 1986).

* Berg, Bruce L. *Jewish Identity: Subjective Declarations or Objective Styles.* Syracuse U., 1983.

Bernik, Herman C. "Jewish Identification." *Syn Sch* 26 (Fall 1967): 17–20.

Blum, Irving. "Jewish Identity—Recommendations for Action" (GA Paper, Nov. 1971). CP, 1972. 10 pp.

Borowitz, Eugene B. "The Rise of the Modern Marrano." In *The Masks Jews Wear: The Self-Deceptions of American Jewry*, 26–41. N.Y.: Simon and Schuster, 1973.

* Brenner, Leon Oscar. *Hostility and Jewish Group Identification.* Boston U., 1961.

Brodsky, Irving. "Jewish Identity and Jewish Identification." *J Jew Com Ser* 44 (Spring 1968): 254–59.

Cahnman, Werner J. "Suspended Alienation and Apathetic Identification." *JSS* 17 (July 1955): 223–28.

Chazan, Barry. "Jewish National Identity and Jewish Education." *WZO* 51–52 (Spring/Summer 1984): 1–14.

Chein, Isidor. "The Problem of Jewish Identification." *JSS* 17 (1955): 219–22.

* Cohen, Eli. *On the Nature of Jewish Identification: A Methodological Approach.* Indiana U., 1977. 142 pp.

Cohen, Gerson D. "Jewish Identity and Jewish Collective Will in America from an Historical Perspective." *Con Jud* 28 (Summer 1974): 61–77.

Cohen, Henry. *Why Judaism? A Search for Meaning in Jewish Identity.* N.Y.: UAHC, 1973. 171 pp.

Cohen, Steven M. *American Modernity and Jewish Identity.* N.Y.: Tavistock, 1983. 210 pp.

———. "The Impact of Jewish Education on Religious Identification and Practice." *JSS* 36 (July–Oct. 1974): 316–26.

Commentary. "Jewishness and the Younger Intellectuals—A Symposium." 31 (1961).

Contemporary Jewish Record. "A Symposium on American Literature and the Younger Generation of American Jews." 7 (Feb. 1944): 3–36.

CJFWF. *Task Force on Jewish Identity.* 1971.

Dashefsky, Arnold, and Howard Shapiro. *Ethnic Identification among American Jews: Socialization and Social Structure.* Lexington, Mass.: Lexington Books, 1974.

Dawidowicz, Lucy S. "Jewish Identity: A Matter of Fate, a Matter of Choice." In *The Jewish Presence—Essays on Identity and History*, 3–31. N.Y.: Holt, Rinehart and Winston, 1977.

Dawidowicz, Lucy S., and Milton Himmelfarb, eds. *Conference on Jewish Identity.* N.Y.: AJC, 1967.

Fear, Frank A. "How Jews Collectively Respond to Felt Jewish Identity in a Small-Town Milieu." Master's thesis, West Virginia U., 1972.

Fein, Leonard J. "Dilemma of Jewish Identity on the College Campus." *Jud* 17 (Winter 1968): 10–21.

———. *Studying Jewish Identity: Observations*. N.Y.: Commission on Jewish Affairs of the American Jewish Congress, 1966. 48 pp.

Fishman, Joshua A. "Patterns of American Self-identification among Children of a Minority Group." *YA* 10 (1955): 212–66.

Frost, Shimon. „דרכים חנוכיים לזהות יהודית בחברה פתוחה" (Educational Paths to Jewish Identity in an Open Society). *Sh Hah* (H.) 34 (1975): 152–58.

* Furman, Frida Kerner. *The Construction of American Jewish Identity: A Case Study*. U. of Southern California, 1980.

Geismar, Ludwig. "A Scale for the Measurement of Ethnic Identification." *JSS* 16 (1954): 33–60.

Gliner, Robert Victor. "Marginality: The Jewish Fraternity." Master's thesis, U. of Minnesota, 1966–67.

Goldberg, A. „אסימילאציע און אינטעגראציע אין אמעריקע" (Assimilation and Integration in America). *Yiddish Culture* (Y.) (June-July 1970): 18–22.

Golub, Jacob S. "Factors in Jewish Adjustment." *Hebrew Union College Monthly* (Jan. 1932).

Gordon, Milton J. "Marginality and the Jewish Intellectual." In *The Ghetto and Beyond: Essays on Jewish Life in America*, edited by Peter I. Rose, 477–91. N.Y.: Random House, 1969.

Halpern, Ben. "Letters to an Intellectual." *Jew Fron* 13 (Dec. 1946): 13–20.

———. "Jewish Education and Thought: Structures of Jewish Self-Identification." *WZO* 51–52 (Spring/Summer 1984): 46–48.

Harman, A. "Jewish National Identity: Discussion." *WZO* 53 (Fall 1984): 6–8.

Herberg, Will. "Judaism as Personal Decision." In *Tradition and Contemporary Experience*, edited by Alfred Jospe, 77–90. 1970.

Herman, Simon N. "The Components of Jewish Identity: A Social Psychological Analysis." In *Issues in Jewish identity*, 28–38. N.Y.: AJC, 1977.

———. *Jewish Identity*. N.Y.: Herzl Press, 1977.

———. *Jewish Identity: A Social Psychological Perspective*. Beverly Hills, Calif.: Sage Publications, 1977.

Hertzberg, Arthur. "Jewish Identification after the Six Day War." *JSS* 31 (1969): 267–71.

———. "The Jewish Intelligentsia and Their Jewishness/'Mt, 30 (Nov. 1984): 35–39.

Hoenig, Sidney B. "Jewish Identity in a Changing World." *Jew Ed* 45 (Winter 1977): 39–48.

* Hudson, Alan J. *Language Attitudes in Relation to Varieties of Jewish Identification*. Yeshiva U., 1977.

Israel, Richard J. "The Challenge of Outreach: Turning on Turned-off Jews." *J Jew Com Ser* 56 (Summer 1980).

Jud. "My Jewish Affirmation." 21 Statements. 10 (1961).

Juran, Richard. "The Formation of Jewish Identity: Extrapolations from the Theories of Erikson, Piaget and Kegan." Master's thesis, Hebrew U. of Jerusalem, 1984. 135 pp.

Kahn, Benjamin M. "Freedom and Identity: The Challenge of Modernity." In *Tradition and Contemporary Experience*, edited by Alfred Jospe, 7–19. 1970.

Kahn, Charlotte. "I Am That I Am: Toward a Psychology of Jewish Identity." *Rel Ed* 75 (May–June 1980): 354–75.

Kaplan, Mordecai M. "Comments on a Parable of Alienation." *Jew Fron* 13 (Dec. 1946): 10–12.

Karff, Samuel E. "Marginality and Authoritarianism in Jewish Adolescents." *Recon* (Jan. 23, 1953): 7–11.

Kelman, Herbert C. "The Place of Jewish Identity in the Development of Personal Identity." In *Issues in Jewish Identity*, 1–27. N.Y.: AJC, 1977.

Koppman, Lionel. "An Adventure in Jewish Identity in Our School System." *Ped Rep* 23 (Dec. 1971).

Kriegel, A. "Jewish National Identity: Diaspora and Nation: The Contemporary Scene." *WZO* 50 (Winter 1983–84): 18–21.

Lamm, Norman. "An Orthodox Perspective on Jewish Education and Jewish Identity." In *Determining the Goals of Jewish Education*, 25–27. N.Y.: AJC, 1977.

Lang, Judith. "Jewish Identity and the Family Children's Agency." *J Jew Com Ser* 60 (Winter 1983): 138–41.

Lasson, Moshe. "Alienation among Yeshiva Youth." *Jew Obs* (Oct. 1969): 9–11. See also *Jew Obs* 6 (July 1970): 12–15.

Lazerwitz, Bernard. "Religious Identification and Its Ethnic Correlates: A Multivariate Model." *Social Forces* 52 (Dec. 1973): 204–20.

———. "Some Factors in Jewish Identification." *JSS* 15 (Jan. 1953): 3–24.

Lear, Elmer. "Providing Meaningful Experiences through Developing Identification with the American Jewish Community." *Syn Sch* 14 (Nov. 1955): 19–22.

Lehrer, Leibush. „די יידישע אנגעהעריקייט פון דער יוגנט ביי יידן" (The Jewish Belongingness of Jewish Youth). *YB* (Y.) 38 (1954): 78–105. Also in *YA* 9 (1954): 137–65.

———. "Retention of Jewish Identity." *JSS* 17 (July 1955): 229–31.

Levine, Gene N. "An Adventure in Curing Alienation." *Jew Ed* 41 (Fall 1972): 10–18.

Liebman, Charles S. "American Jewry: Identity and Affiliation." In *FJCA*, 127–52.

Lor, A. "The Quest for Jewish Identity in a Changing Social Milieu." *Rel Ed* 74 (Mar.–Apr. 1979): 73–180.

Mann, Theodore R. "Jewish Identity and Jewish Community Relations." *Cong M* (May 1977): 5–10

Margoshes, Samuel. „אידענטיפיקאציע" (Identification). *Day* (Y.) (Feb. 24, 1956).

Massarick, Fred. *Jewish Identity: Facts for Planning*. N.Y.: CJFWF, 1974.

Miller, C. "Jewish Identity and Agency Function." *J Jew Com Ser* 60 (Fall 1983): 23–33. Comment by B. Reisman, pp. 34–36

Mirsky, Norman B. "Constructing A Reform Jewish Identity." *RJ* 31 (Spring 1984): 3–19.

———. "Yavneh vs. Massada: Conscious and Unconscious Uses of Historical Legend in the Formation of American Jewish Identity." In *Marcus*, 377–400.

Neger, A. "Jewish Education and Thought: Structures of Jewish Self-Identification: A Survey." *WZO* 51–52 (Spring/Summer 1984): 38–43.

Nussbaum, Max. "Integration without Assimilation." *A Jud* (Fall 1962): 12–13, 53.

Oppenheim, Michael. "A 'Fieldguide' to the Study of Modern Jewish Identity." *JSS* 46 (Summer/Fall 1984): 215–32.

Ostow, Mortimer. "The Determinants of Jewish Identity: A Maturational Approach." In *Issues in Jewish Identity*, 39–66. N.Y.: AJC, 1977.

* Phipps, James Ronald. *Critical Observations about Identity Rhetoric in Representative Strategies of the American Jewish Community*. Ohio State U., 1975. 204 pp.

Podhoretz, Norman, ed. "Jewishness and the Younger Intellectuals." *Commentary* 31 (1961): 306–59.

Poppel, Stephen M. "Jewish Identity and the Modern Jew." *Mid* 14 (Nov. 1968): 65–69.

Radke, Marian. *Group Belonging of Jewish Children in Relation to Their Age*. N.Y.: American Jewish Congress, Commission on Community Relations.

Raphael, Marc Lee. "Denominational Jewish Confirmation and Jewish Identity." *Rel Ed* 73 (Nov.–Dec. 1978): 6–60.

Reisman, Bernard. *Experiential Workshop on Jewish Identity*. N.Y.: CJFWF, 1974.

Rivkin, Ellis. "The Crisis of Identity in the Dynamics of Jewish Life." *Jew Ed* 45 (Fall/Winter 1976): 4–16, 31.

Rose, Arnold M. "Cultural Values and Identification." *Jud* 10 (1961): 338–40.

Rosenak, Michael. "Education for Jewish Identification." *Forum* 28 (Winter 1978): 118–29.

———. "Identity." *Rel Ed* (Nov.–Dec. 1978).

Rosenberg, Stuart E. "The Jew in the Non-Jewish World." *RA* (1967): 70–83.

———. *The Search for Jewish Identity in America*. Garden City, N.Y.: Doubleday, 1965. 300 pp.

Rosenman, Yehuda. "Jewish Education and Jewish Identity." Plenary Session of the AJC, 71st Annual Meeting, May 1972.

Rotenstreich, Nathan. "Expressions of Jewish National Identity in the United States." *WZO* 48 (Spring 1983): 41–46.

Rothman, Jack. "Construction of an Instrument for Measuring Minority Group Identification among Adolescents: An Exploratory Attempt." *J Jew Com Ser* 34 (1957): 84–94.

*———. *Minority Group Identification and Intergroup Relations.* Columbia U., 1965.

Russler, Gwynn. "Jewish Identity and Contact with Israel." Master's thesis, HUC–JIR, 1978.

Rutchik, Allen. "Self Esteem and Jewish Identification." *Jew Ed* 38 (Mar. 1968): 40–46.

Sanua, Victor D. "The Relationship between Jewish Education and Jewish Identification." *Jew Ed* 35 (Fall 1964): 37–50.

———. "Social Science Research Relative to Patterns of Identification with the Jewish Community in the United States." *Jew J Soc* 6 (1964): 190–212.

Scheffler, T. "How Can a Jewish Self-Consciousness Be Developed?" In *A Symposium: The Study of Jewish Identity—Issues and Approaches,* edited by S. N. Herman. Jerusalem: Institute of Contemporary Jewry, 1971.

Schiff, Alvin I. "On Responding to the Challenge of the Alienated and Indifferent Jew in America." *J Jew Com Ser* (Spring 1984): 193–203.

* Schoenfeld, Eugene. *Small-Town Jews: A Study in Identity and Integration.* Southern Illinois U., 1967.

Schulweiss, Harold M. "Achieveing Jewish Self-Esteem." *Jew Spec* (Mar. 1971): 8–11.

Schwartz, Charles. "A Study of Determining the Effects of Religious Education upon Jewish Identification." Master's thesis, Yeshiva U., 1961.

Schweid, E. "Jewish Education and Thought: Structure of Jewish Self-Identification: A Survey." *WZO* 51–52 (Spring/Summer 1984): 32–38.

Segalman, Ralph. "Jewish Identity Scales." *JSS* 29 (Jan. 1967).

Shapiro, Mannheim S. "The Role of Jewish Communal Agencies in Maintaining Jewish Identity." *J Jew Com Ser* 41 (Spring 1965).

Sidorsky, David. "Jewish Education and Thought: Contemporary Theoretical Structures of Jewish Self-Identification—A Survey." *WZO* 51–52 (Spring/Summer 1984): 26–31.

———. *Summary Report and Recommendations.* N.Y.: AJC, 1976. 31 pp.

Sklare, Marshall, and Joseph Greenblum. *Jewish Identity on the Suburban Frontier.* N.Y.: AJC-Basic Books, 1967. 362 pp.

Sklare, Marshall, et al. "Forms and Expressions of Jewish Identification." *JSS* 17 (1955): 205–18.

Slawson, John. *Toward a Community Program for Jewish Identity.* N.Y.: AJC, 1966.

Slesinger, Zalmen. "Education and the Crisis of Jewish Identity." *Ped Rep* 20 (Sept. 1962): 7–10.

———. "Education for Jewish Identity and Jewish Continuity in the Open Society." *Jud* 28 (Spring 1979): 225–35.

Soviv, Aaron. "Self-Acceptance of Jewishness by Young People." *Jew Ed* 26 (Summer 1955): 22–31.

Steg, A. "Jewish National Identity: Jewish Community and its Environments" (symposium, part 4). *WZO* 53 (Fall 1984): 12–14.

Verbit, M. F. "Jewish Identity and the Israel-Diaspora Dialogue." *WZO* 48 (Spring 1983): 63–74.

Wachs, Saul P. "The Congregational School Crisis of Identity." *Impact* 35 (Winter 1976–77): 37–46.

Wachstock, David. "Fostering Self-Esteem." *Ped Rep* 32 (Fall 1980): 14–16.

Weider, Leland. "A Teaching Strategy on 'Jewish Identity' through Tzedakah." Master's thesis, HUC–JIR, 1973.

Wiesel, Eli. "On Teaching Jewish Identity." *Jew Ed* 43 (Winter/Spring 1975): 8–13.

———. "To Be a Jew." In *A Jew Today,* 3–13. N.Y.: Random House, 1979.

Zisenwine, David, and Joel Walters. "Jewish Identity, Israel and the American Adolescent." *Forum* 45 (Summer 1982): 79–85.

GLEANINGS

Lewin, Kurt, (1940),
"Strong and well-organized groups, far from being fully homogeneous, are bound to contain a variety of different subgroups and individuals. It is not sim-

ilarity or dissimilarity that decides whether two individuals belong to the same or to different groups, but social interaction or other types of interdependence. A group is best defined as a dynamic whole based on interdependence rather than on similarity. . . .

Parents should not be afraid of so-called 'double-allegiance.' Belonging to more than one overlapping group is natural and necessary for everyone. The real danger lies in standing 'nowhere,' in being a 'marginal man,' an 'eternal adolescent.'"

Resolving Social Conflicts, edited by Gertrude Weiss Lewin, 184, 185. N.Y.: Harper and Bros., 1948.

Bettelheim, Bruno,
"Inescapably, the question of how best to prepare our child to face anti-Semitism rests on our answer to a proper question: how do we prepare ourselves to face up to and struggle against the actual anti-Semitism that still remains in our American society, with inner security and without fear. One wonders how long it will be before American Jews are ready for this larger question, not merely 'for the children', but for themselves and including the children."

Securing Our Children against Anti-Semitism, 18. N.Y.: Community Relations Service. See also *Commentary* (Sept. 1951), 209.

Lipset, Seymour,
"One of the most interesting problems for any discussion of Jewish sociology is to discover why there are so many Jewish sociologists and so few sociologists of the Jews."

JSS 17 (July 1955), 177.

Kaplan, Benjamin,
"The Jews still find themselves far from constituting fullfledged members of the general community and their position remains one of ambivalence."

From *The Eternal Stranger: A Study of Jewish Life in the Small Community*. 1957. Quoted by Murray Pollner in *Rabbi: The American Experience*. N.Y. Holt, Rinehart and Winston, 1979. 580.

Herman, Simon N.,
"It becomes the task of a Jewish education to provide a clear and realistic understanding of the relationship between the Jewish minority and the non-Jewish majority group—of what they have in common and in what they differ. In this context it is also necessary to deal with the confusion which exists around the question of anti-Semitism. Our studies of American Jewish students show that there are those among them who attribute a portion of the blame for anti-Semitism to Jewish 'behavior' or characteristics."

Jewish Education and Jewish Identity, 32. 1972.

Sleeper, James S.,
"It is possible to dismiss the hostility to the Jewish community that some . . . young [Jewish] people exhibit as a function of pathology or adolescent trauma. But the fact remains that many young Jews today simply turn their backs on Jewishness neither in the spirit of spite nor out of personal difficulty. In the wake of the old community's collapse they have almost no memories, no association with even the glimmer of a viable, organic Jewish community in which Jewish language, symbols, and values were compellingly operative during their early years. Nothing recognizably Jewish has shaped their lives. Why, then should they recognize themselves as Jews? . . . Hence, any discussion of Jewish education must begin with a discussion of the fundamentally non-Jewish context in which our students have developed as human beings. The would-be Jewish educator must know the world in which his students move if he is to address them uncompromisingly with the riches of Jewish tradition, and if he is truly to become a meeting point of student and tradition."

FJCA, 240–41.

Sklare, Marshall,
"Suburbanization brought with it the problem of the maintenance of Jewish identity—and it was to the synagogue that the new Jewish suburbanite tended to look for identity maintenance. The result was that the synagogue emerged in

the 1950's and 1960's as the crucial institution in Jewish life. And Conservatism exemplified the tupe of synagogue that was most appealing to the suburban Jew."

Quoted by S. P. Wachs in *Impact* 35 (Winter 1976–77), 39.

Colloquium Papers,
"A. The Colloquium recommends that it be a Jewish communal responsibility to make possible, in plural and diverse ways, educational opportunities and environments at a high level of excellence for persons of high school age.

B. The Colloquium recommends that there be a communal effort of the highest priority to establish, augment and enhance Jewish educational opportunities, both formal and informal for college students.

C. The Colloquium recommends as a priority communal responsibility the intensification of efforts in Jewish family education."

Colloquium Papers from AJC Colloquium on Jewish Education and Jewish Identity, 1976–1977: Summary Report and Recommendations, 23–29.

45 | ASSESSMENT

PRIOR TO 1950

Adler, Morris. "Jewish Education in Wartime." *Jew Ed* 14 (Sept.–Dec. 1942): 102–6.

Benderly, Samson. "The Fundamental Element in the Solution of the Problem of Jewish Education in America." *Jewish Teacher* 1 (1916).

———. "Jewish Education in America." *Jewish Exponent* (Jan. 17, 1908). Also in *Jew Ed* 20 (Summer 1949): 80–86.

———. "Jewish Education in the United States." *Jew Ed* 7 (Jan.–Mar. 1935): 5–8, 33.

———. "The Jewish Educational Problem." *Jewish Comment* (June 12, 1902). Also in *Maccabean* 5 (1903): 16–20.

———. "The Problem of Jewish Education" (address given Nov. 26, 1910). See *JEUS*, 127–31.

———. "The Schoolman's Viewpoint" (1927). *Jew Ed* 20 (Summer 1949). Also in *JJS*, 33–42.

Berkson, Isaac B. "Jewish Education—Achievements and Needs." In *Jan 1*, 56–91.

Blau, Joel. "The Case of Jewish Education." *Menorah J* 11 (Feb. 1925): 1–13.

Blumenfield, Samuel M. "Facing Realities in Jewish Education." *Recon* (Aug. 11, 1939).

———. "Jewish Education in the Postwar World." *J of Educational Sociology* 18 (1945): 262–67.

———. "A Mid-Century of Jewish Education: Retrospect and Prospect." *Jew Spec* 16 (1950).

———. "A Study of the Correlation between Elementary Jewish Education and Interest in Jewish Life and Problems." *Jew Ed* 9 (Oct–Dec. 1937): 143–47.

Boraisha, Menachem. „א דור איז פון אונדז אוועק—וואס זאלען מיר טאן פאר'ן נייעם דור?" (We Have Lost a Generation—What Shall We Do for the Next Generation?). *Day* (Y.) (Jan. 18, 1948).

Brilliant, Nathan. "The Progressive Reform School" (Sunday plus 3 days Hebrew language). *Jew Ed* 7 (Oct.–Dec. 1935): 178–86.

Bronstein, H. „למצב החנוך העברי באמריקה" (On the Condition of Jewish Education in America). *Hadoar* (H.) 3 (8th of Ab 1924).

Chipkin, Israel S. „המשבר בחנוך העברי" (The Crisis in Jewish Education). *Hadoar* (H.) 13 (Nov. 17. 1933): 54–55.

———. „החנוך העברי בארצות הברית" (Jewish Education in the United States). In *Sefer HaShanah* (H.) (1931): 291–308.

Chomsky, William. "Realities and Illusions in Jewish Education." *Recon* (Jan. 8, 1943).

———. "Toward a Real Jewish Education." *Recon* (Jan. 23, 1943): 12–17.

45 ASSESSMENT

Churgin, Pinchos. "חנוך ותכלית„ (Education and Practical Application). *Sh Hah* (H.) 6 (1929): 198–201.

Cohen, Beryl. "Impulse and Direction in Jewish Education." *Education* 59 (1939): 289–90.

Cohen, Morris R. "די וויכטיקייט פון אידישער דערציאונג„ (The Importance of Jewish Education). *Day* (Y.) (Sept. 21, 1947).

Dinin, Samuel. "The Jewish School." *Recon* (July 1, 1938): 10–16.

Dushkin, Alexander M. "The Character of Jewish Education" (editorial). *Jew Ed* 1 (May 1929): 69–70.

———. "The Jewish Educational System—A Plea for Organic Unity." *Jew Ed* 4 (Apr.–June 1932): 76–80.

Efros, Israel. "The School and World Jewry." *Jew Ed* 5 (Oct.–Dec. 1933): 152–55.

Eisenberg, Azriel. "הצבור והחנוך בערי השדה„ (The Community and Education in Suburbia). *Hadoar* (H.) 21 (Apr. 17, 1942): 344.

———. "The Extent of Jewish Education in the United States." *JSSQ* 18 (1941).

Eisner, Mark. "A Layman's View of Jewish Education." *Jew Ed* 15 (Sept. 1943): 4–6, 16.

Enelow, Hyman G. "The Jewish Sunday School." *Jewish Teacher* 1 (Jan. 1916): 35–40.

Engelman, Uriah Z. "Developments in Jewish Education." *Day* (Oct. 20, 1946).

———. "Education and Culture." *AJYB* 48 (1946–47): 136–56.

———. "Educational and Cultural Activities." *AJYB* 47 (1945–46): 228–54.

———. "Jewish Education." *AJYB* 49 (1947): 154–75; 50 (1948–49): 148–62; 51 (1950): 157–67.

Federbush, Simon. "New Horizons for Jewish Traditional Education." *Jew Ed* 16 (May 1945): 16–19, 29.

Feldman, Abraham J. "Our Religious School." *Jew Teach* 6 (Nov. 1937): 22–24.

Fineberg, Solomon A. "A Critical Evaluation of the Reform Religious School." *CCAR* 39 (1929): 439–63.

Frankel, Aaron. "העם והחנוך„ (The People and Education). *Hadoar* (H.) 4 (Jan. 16, 1925): 3–6.

Friedenwald, Harry. "The Problem of Jewish Education." *Jewish Teacher* 1 (Jan. 1916): 13–27.

Friedland, A. H. "The Current Year in Jewish Education." *Jew Ed* 6 (Oct.–Dec. 1934): 137–42.

Gamoran, Emanuel. "Concerning the Sunday School Society." *Jew Ed* 8 (Jan.–Mar. 1936): 29–32.

———. "The General Situation in the Jewish Sunday School." *Jew Ed* 1 (June 1929): 25–33.

———. "Realities and Limitations." *Jew Teach* 8 (Jan. 1940): 10–14.

———. "The Union's Contribution to Jewish Education." *Jewish Layman* (Feb. 1946).

———. *Week-Day Jewish Instruction*. Cincinnati: DSSE, 1928.

Gingold, Pinchos. "אידישע דערציאונג און דער היינטיקער תקופה„ (Jewish Education in the Present Era). *YK* (Y.) (Jan. 27, 1950): 27–28.

Goldberg, I. "Education and Culture." *AJYB* 43 (1942): 33–58.

Goldman, Israel. "Let Us Search Our Ways." *Con Jud* 3 (Feb. 1947).

Golub, Jacob S. "Jewish and Hebraic Education." *Recon* (Dec. 1941): 6–10.

———. "The Jewish Religious School." In *What Is Jewish Education?*, 10–17. N.Y.: AAJE, 1944.

Goodblatt, Morris. "Basic Premises and a Proposed Structure for Jewish Education in America." *Con Jud* (Feb. 1947): 5–13.

———. "Elementary Education." *RA* (1940): 38–41.

———. "Report on Commission on Jewish Education." *RA* (1940): 253–55.

Gordon, H. L. "סיג להוראה„ (A Limit to Instruction). *Hadoar* (H.) 7 (Kislev 8 and 15, 1928).

Hays, Mortimer. "The Need for Jewish Education Today." *Jew Ed* 12 (Jan. 1941): 154–64.

Honor, Leo L. "Jewish Education—Problems and Solutions." *Reform Advocate* (Oct. 30, 1936).

———. "Maturing Into Jewish Life." *Jew Ed* 10 (Oct.–Dec. 1938): 162–66, 191.

Hurwitz, Henry. "*Menorah*'s Contribution to Jewish Education." *NCJSS Proceedings* (1926): 274–80.

Joseph, Robert. "Sunday School Instruction Update." *Jew Teach* 6 (Jan. 1938): 25–27.

Kallen, Horace M. "Critical Problems in Jewish Education." *Jew Ed* 19 (Summer 1948): 11–16.

———. "Education of Jews in Our Time." *Jew Ed* 11 (Sept. 1939): 84–89.

Kandel, Isaac L. "Two Views of Jewish Education." *Menorah J* 6 (Apr. 1920): 109–15.

Katzoff, Louis. "Strengths and Weaknesses of the Conservative School." In *Issues*, 143–54.

Konowitz, Israel. "פתדונים„ (Solutions). *Hadoar* (H.) 6 (1927–28).

———. "מצב החנוך העברי באמריקה„ (Status of Hebrew Education in America). *Luach Ahiever* (H.) (1918): 39–62.

Krantzler, Gershon. "Double Standards in Jewish Education." *Jew Spec* (July–Aug. 1948): 23–34.

Lehrer, Leibush. "דערציאונג נאך דער מלחמה„ (Education after the War). *CE* (Y.) (Mar. 1941): 8–10.

Lewin, Kurt. *Jewish Education and Reality*. N.Y.: AAJE, 1940. See also *Jew Ed* 15 (May 1944): 125–29, 137.

Marcson, Simon. "The Role of Voluntary Segregated Education in an Ethnic Group." Master's thesis, U. of Chicago, 1941.

Marshall, James. "Jewish Education in the Light of Tradition." *Jew Ed* 8 (Jan.–Mar. 1936): 9–11.

Medini, Mordecai. "רצון ויכלת בחנוך„ (Will and Ability in Education). *Sh Hah* (H.) 2 (Oct. 1942): 239–46.

Millgram, Abraham E. "Intensive Jewish Education in the Congregational School." *Con Jud* 5 (June 1949).

———. "A Practical Approach to Jewish Education." *The Torch* (Oct. 1948). See also *RTJS*, 194–200.

———. "United Synagogue Commission Report." *RA* (1948): 48.

Nardi, Noah. "עשרים וחמש שנות חנוך עברי באמריקה„ (Twenty-five Years of Jewish Education in America). *Hadoar* (H.) 26 (May 23, 1947): 722–26.

NCJW. *Jewish Education in the United States: A Symposium and Guide for the Study of the Status, Aims and Prospects of Jewish Education*. N.Y.: 1935, 43 pp. Includes:

> Benderly, Samson, "Jewish Education in the U.S.";
> Friedland, A. H., "The Current Year in Jewish Education";
> Golub, Jacob S., "Toward an American Jewish School";
> Kaplan, Mordecai M., "Aims of Jewish Education in the U.S."

Pilch, Yehudah (Judah). "נחפשה דרכינו„ (Let Us Examine Our Ways). *Hadoar* (H.) 11 (12th of Adar 1932).

Pollak, Jacob B. "The Union of American Hebrew Congregations and the Problems of Jewish Education." *NCJSS Proceedings* (1926): 280–93.

Pool, David de Sola. "The Challenge to Jewish Education." In *Judaism in a Changing World*, edited by Leo Jung, 53–65. 1939.

Rabinowitz, Zenah. "המלחמה והחנוך העברי„ (The War and Jewish Education). *Hadoar* (H.) 21 (Feb. 5, 1941): 213–19.

Rosen, Ben. "Education." *AJYB* 44 (1942–43): 111–23; 45 (1943–44): 150–65; 46 (1944–45): 100–108.

———. "Preface to a Program for Jewish Education." *National Jewish Monthly* (Jan. 1945).

Rosenman, Samuel I. "Jewish Education and the Jewish Way of Life." *Jew Ed* 10 (Oct.–Dec. 1938): 134–38.

Scharfstein, Zevi. "החנוך העברי על פרשת דרכים„ (Jewish Education at the Crossroads). *RA* (1941–44): 107–15.

———. "על החנוך העברי באמריקה„ (On Jewish Education in America). *Hadoar* (H.) (Oct. 3, 1930): 749–51.

———. "בעיות החנוך היהודי בארצות הברית„ (Problems of Jewish Education in the United States). In *JED* (H.), 63–69.

———. "שאלות ותשובות„ (Questions and Answers). *Hadoar* (H.) 28 (Oct. 14, 1949): 1093–94.

———. "Rebuilding Jewish Education After the War." *Jew Ed* 16 (Jan. 1945): 6–10.

———. "המצב בחינוך העברי באריקה" (The Status of Jewish Education in America). *Hadoar* 22 (Apr. 16, 1942): 391–92; (Apr. 23, 1942): 416–18.

Schoolman, Albert P. "The Yeshivah and the Talmud Torah—An Evaluation." *Jew Ed* 16 (May 1945): 26–29.

Shetzer, Simon. "The Function of Jewish Education in America." *Jew Ed* 15 (Sept. 1943): 7–9, 20.

Silver, Abba Hillel. "The Answer Today Must Be Judaism." *Jew Ed* 1 (Jan.–Mar. 1943): 130–33.

Soltes, Mordecai. "Nation-Wide Observance of Jewish Education Week." *Jew Ed* 9 (Apr.–June 1937): 95–97.

Tabak, I. "The Need for Jewish Missionaries." *Jew Life* 14 (June 1947).

Tarshish, Allan. "A Four-Day-A-Week School." *Jew Teach* 7 (Apr. 1939): 17–21.

Touroff, Nisson. "ברוכים הבונים" (Blessed Are the Builders). *Sh Hah* (H.) 3 (1928): 170–74.

———. "דברים כהויתם" (Matters as They Are). *Sh Hah* (H.) 1 (1925): 3–5.

———. "שלשה דברים" (Three Issues). *Hadoar* (H.) 15 (16th of Iyyar 1936).

Whiteman, Kaiman. "מצב החנוך בשעה זו" (The Present Condition of Education). *Hadoar* (H.) (Oct. 3, 1930): 751–53.

———. "מציאות וחזון בחינוך" (Reality and Vision in Education). *Hadoar* (H.) 22 (10th of Elul 1943).

Wolf, Horace J. "A Remedy for the Sunday School." *Menorah J* 3 (Feb. 1917): 31–36.

Wolfson, Harry A. "Escaping Judaism." *Menorah J* (June–Aug. 1921).

———. "The Need of Jewish Scholarship in America." *Menorah J* 7 (Feb. 1921): 28–35.

Zalesky, Moshe. "בעיות החנוך היהודי באמריקה" (Problems in American Jewish Education). *Hadoar* (H.) 28 (Oct. 14, 1949): 1090–91.

SINCE 1950

AAJE. *A Mid-Century of Jewish Education: Retrospect and Prospect*. N.Y.: 1950.

Ackerman, Walter I. *Forms of Jewish Education*. Jerusalem: World Leadership Conference for Jewish Education, 1984.

———. "Jewish Education." In *Movements and Issues in American Judaism: An Analysis and Sourcebook of Developments since 1945*, edited by Bernard Martin, 184–205. Westport, Conn.: Greenwood Press, 1978.

———. "Jewish Education—Today." *AJYB* 80 (1980): 130–48.

———. "The Jewish School System in the United States." In *FJCA*, 176–210.

———. "On the Making of Jews." *Jud* 30 (1981).

———. "The Present Moment in Jewish Education." *Mid* (Dec. 1972): 3–24.

———. "Some Uses of Justification in Jewish Education." In *Association for Jewish Studies*, Vol. 2, 1977.

AJC. "Educational System" (task force report). In *FJCA*, 39–59.

Alpert, David B. "Frills in Jewish Education." *Jew Teach* 18 (Jan. 1950): 25–26.

Arian, Philip. *"Needed: Emotional Relevance in Jewish Education."* Con Jud 23 (Fall 1968): 46–52.

———. "Realities and Challenge Facing Jewish Education in the 70's: Challenge and Promise." *Ed As* (1970): 3–11.

Avital, Moshe. "התועים בדרכי החינוך היהודי" (The Strayings on the Paths of Jewish Education). *Hadoar* (H.) 51 (Aug. 18, 1972).

Banki, Judith. "Jewish Perspective." *Rel Ed* 74 (Sept.–Oct. 1979): 451–56.

Bardin, Shlomo. "Meaningful Jewish Education." *Jew Spec* 37 (Jan. 1972) 16–17.

Bass, Hyman. "Some Problems of Jewish Education." In *JJS*, 187–91.

Ben-Horin, Meir. "Jewish Education's First Requirement." *Rel Ed* 76 (Jan.–Feb. 1981): 70–76.

———. "Priorities in Jewish Education." *Jew Ed* 43 (Fall 1973): 11–16.

Bennett, Alan D. "The Bandwagon and the Jewish Problem." *Ped Rep* 24 (Fall 1972): 18.

———. "Challenge and Crisis." *Jew Teach* 33 (Apr. 1965): 3–7.

Berkovitz, Eliezer. "Jewish Education in a World Adrift." *Trad* 11 (Fall 1970): 5–12.

Berkson, Isaac B. "Education and the Jewish Renaissance." *Jew Ed* 30 (Summer 1963): 198–208.

Birnbaum, David. "The Quantification of Jewish Education: A Strategic Error." *Mid* 29 (Dec. 1983): 40–42.

Blond, Leo. "Is It Good for the Jews? Some Observations on the Rise of Ethnic Studies in Public Schools." *Ped Rep* 23 (June 1972): 5.

Blumenfield, Samuel M. "הישגים וסיכויים בחינוך היהודי" (Achievements and Expectations in Jewish Education). In *S Ed* (H.), 92–98. See also *Hadoar* (H.) 34 (Nov. 19, 1954): 45–46.

———. "החינוך העברי לאור המציאות באמריקה" (Jewish Education in Light of American Reality). In *FPDE* (H.), 53–58.

———. "The Present Status of Jewish Education in America." In *Proceedings of the First American Zionist Assembly*, 98–106. N.Y.: 1954.

Bock, Geoffrey Ephraim. "Does Jewish Education Matter?" In *Jewish Education and Jewish Identity*. N.Y.: AJC, 1977.

———. "The Functions of Jewish Schooling In America." In *Stu*, 2:233–54.

Bokser, Ben Zion. "Communication, Language and Tradition." *Jew Ed* 33 (Summer 1963): 209–18.

Braver, Joseph, ed. "United Synagogue Commission on Jewish Education." *Ped Rep* 25 (Fall 1973): 19–22.

Braverman, Joel. "על תקנת חינוך" (On Improving Education). *Hadoar* (H.) 36 (Aug. 9, 1957): 618.

Brickman, William. "The State of the Jewish School in America." *Jew Life* 27 (Dec. 1959): 32–45.

Chamiel, Haim. "Diaspora Education Today." *Mid* (May 1980): 36–39.

Chazan, Raphael. "The Failure of Jewish Education." In *LJE*, 13–18.

Chazan, Raphael, and Abraham Martan. "עת לדבר—נקודת משבר בחינוך העברי" (A Time to Speak—the Focal Point of the Crisis in Jewish Education). *Hadoar* (H.) (Mar. 7, 1975): 66.

Chomsky, William. "American Jewish Life and Education—in Retrospect and Prospect." *Jew Ed* 40 (Spring 1971): 20–25.

———. "Jewish Education in America." *Gratz College Annual of Jewish Studies* 6 (1977): 5–23.

Cohen, Gerson. "כיוונים בחינוך יהודי בארצות הברית" (Directions in Jewish Education in the United States) (H.). *Ed As* (1972): 86–92.

Cohen, Howard M. "Who Are Our Children? An Informal Questionnaire." *Ped Rep* 32 (Sept. 1981): 31–33.

Colodner, Solomon. "Blueprint for Jewish Education." *Jew Spec* 35 (Nov. 1970): 15–17.

Cutter, William. "Present Status of Jewish Education." *CCAR* 83 (1973): 167–73.

Decter, Midge. "The Fruits of Modern Jewish Education." *Commentary* (Oct. 1951): 324–29.

Derby, Josiah. "The Present Status of Jewish Education in the Conservative Movement." *RA Proc* (1955): 191–98.

Dingol, S. "דער נייער שול-זמן" (The New School Year). *Day* (Y.) (Sept. 29, 1956).

Dinin, Samuel. "An Analysis and Critique of Jewish Education in America." *Jew Ed* 26 (Fall 1955): 6–16.

———. "Content and Discontent in Jewish Education" (editorial). *Jew Ed* 36 (Summer 1966): 131–32.

———. "Issues Facing the Jewish School." *Jew Ed* 26 (Spring 1956): 18–21, 50.

Diskind, Zalman. *Can We Neglect the Talmud Torah?* 8 pp. Also in *Jew Life* 30 (Oct. 1962).

Duker, Abraham. "A Time of Crisis." *Jew Ed* 39 (Dec. 1969): 24–32.

Dushkin, Alexander M. "A Mile Wide and an Inch Deep." *Hadassah Letter* (Dec. 1959): 2.

———. "The National Image of Jewish Education." *Congress Weekly* 26 (May 25, 1959): 5–7.

45
ASSESSMENT

Edelstein, Menachem. "מקומו של בית התה"ת בחינוך היהודי באמריקה" (The Place of the Talmud Torah in American Jewish Education). *Sh Hah* (H.) 15 (Fall/Winter 1955): 31–33.

Ehrlich, Abraham J. "Elementary Jewish Education." *RA* (1973): 80–84.

Eisenberg, Azriel. "אורות וצללים בחינוך" (Lights and Shadows in Jewish Education). *Gesher* (H.) (1954).

Elovitz, Mark H. "The Failure of Jewish Education." *Jew Spec* 35 (Oct. 1970): 30.

Engelman, Uriah Z. "Educating the Jewish Child." In *JMW*, 2:436–81.

———. "Jewish Education." *AJYB* 52 (1951): 97–110; 53 (1952): 165–78; 54 (1953): 109–23; 57 (1956): 205–8; 59 (1958): 124–39; 61 (1960): 127–49; 64 (1963): 151–66.

Fein, Leonard. "Half Full—Half Empty." *Moment* 3 (Oct. 1978): 11–13.

Feldman, M. "Educated Observance, Not Indoctrination." *National Jewish Monthly* 88 (Feb. 1974): 34.

Fisch, Dov, and Linda Yellin Fisch. "Problems of Jewish Education." *Mid* (May 1980): 39–43.

Fishman, Sylvia Barack. *Learning about Learning: Insights on Contemporary Jewish Education from Jewish Population Studies.* Waltham, Mass.: Cohen Center for Modern Jewish Studies, Brandeis U., 1987. 73 pp.

Fishweicher, Israel. "A Study of Two Types of Private Hebraic Educational Systems: The Yeshiva-Hebrew Day School and talmud Torah-Afternoon School." Master's thesis, Jersey City State College, 1970.

Fox, Seymour. "Education for the Twentieth Century Jew: A Pilot Program." *Had Mag* (Sept. 1966).

———. "Seeking the Opportunity—Confronting the Challenge." *Ed As* (1966): 8–13.

Frankel, Theodore. "Suburban Jewish Sunday School." *Commentary* (June 1958): 481–91.

Friedman, Norman L. "On the 'Non Effects' of Jewish Education on Most Students: A Critique." *Jew Ed* 52 (Summer 1984): 30–32, 48.

Frost, Shimon. "Crucial Challenges to the Non-Orthodox School." *Jew Ed* 51 (Spring 1983): 25–26, 37.

———. "New Educational Realities in Light of New General Conditions." *Jew Ed* 50 (Summer 1982): 14–17, 28.

———. "Schools Can Be for Learning Too." *Jew Ed* 51 (Winter 1983): 8–10.

Furie, William B. "Jewish Education in the United States." In *Jewish Life in America*, edited by Friedman and Gordis, 227–45. 1955.

Gamoran, Emanuel. "After Thirty-Five Years—Report by the Director of Education." *CCAR* 68 (1958).

———. "The Commission on Jewish Education." *Jew Teach* (Nov. 1952).

———. "Reform Jewish Education: The Backward and the Forward Look." *Jew Teach* 33 (Dec. 1964): 24–27.

———. "Reform Jewish Education: Its Strengths and Its Weaknesses." *Jew Teach* 23 (Mar. 1955): 3–6.

Gannes, Abraham P. "Needs in Jewish Education as Reflected in Recent Community Studies." *Jew Ed* 44 (Summer 1975): 42–49, 59.

Gartner, Lloyd P. "Jewish Education in the United States." In *JCA*, 221–48.

Gittelsohn, Roland B. "The Larger Context." *Jew Teach* 34 (Apr. 1966): 13–16.

Glicksman, William. "One Man's Opinion Concerning the Place of the Yiddish Secular school in America Today." *Jew Ed* 39 (July 1969): 17–22.

Goldrich, G. "Operation Headstart Jewish Style." *Had Mag* 52 (Sept. 1970): 12–13.

Golomb, Abraham. "פאלשע דערציאונג„ (False Education). *YK* (Y.) (Nov. 18, 1966): 6–7.

———. "Looking at Our Education and at Education among other Nations." *Sh Hah* (H.) 32 (1972): 160–73.

Gordis, Robert. "Open Forum: On Judaism and Jewish Learning." *Con Jud* 35 (Winter 1982): 47–55.

Grad, Eli. "Issues of Quality in Jewish Education." *Jew Ed* 46 (Autumn 1978): 10–15.

Graeber, I. "Jewish Educational Jungle." *Jew Life* 31 (Sept.–Oct. 1963): 33–45.

Greenberg, Irving. "Jews or Zombies: A Hard Look at Jewish Education." *Jewish Advocate* (Sept. 20, 1966).

Greenstein, R. R. "Toward a Reassessment of Jewish Education." *Recon* 40 (Nov. 1979): 18–20.

Hachen, David S. "Old-New Frontiers in Education." *Jew Teach* 3 (Oct. 1964).

Hakimian, Leah. "Schools Are Accountable." *Ped Rep* 36 (Sept. 985): 18–20.

Halkin, Abraham S. "American Judaism—A Balance Sheet." *Jud* 2 (Spring 1954).

Halpern, Ben. "A Problem in Jewish Education." *Jew Fron* (June 1964): 13–19.

* Hamburger, Lewis D. *A Study of the Failures and Dilemmas of Part-Time American Jewish Education and Implications of Elements from Talmudic Schools and Educational Camping.* U. of Maryland, 1971. 215 pp.

* Hartman, Eliyahu E. *A Follow-up Study of Graduates of Selected Hebrew Elementary Educational Institutions.* Memphis State U., 1976. 183 pp.

* Himmelfarb, Harold S. *The Impact of Religious Schooling: The Effects of Jewish Education upon Adult Religious Involvement.* U. of Chicago, 1974. 100 pp.

———. "The Impact of Religious Schooling: A Synopsis." In *Stu*, 2:225–86.

———. "Jewish Education for Naught: Educating the Culturally Deprived Jewish Child." *Analysis* 51 (Sept. 1975). 12 pp.

———. "The Non-Linear Impact of Schooling: Comparing Different Types of Jewish Education." *Sociology of Education* 50 (Apr. 1977): 114–32.

Hirsch, B. "Dilemmas on the Education Front." *Jew Life* 16 (Apr. 1949).

Hollander, Benjamin. "Brain Drain or New Opportunities." *Con Jud* 25 (Winter 1971): 63–67.

Horowitz, Jack. "Why We Have Failed the Jewish Child." *Jew Teach* 33 (Dec. 1964): 21–23.

Isaacman, Daniel. "Jewish Education in America—1971: An Analysis." In *Gratz College Anniversary Volume, 1895–1970*, 147–64.

* Jacobs, Herman. *Jewish Education: A Perspective for Modern Times.* Wayne State U., 1952. 354 pp.

Jacobs, Y. "The Bankruptcy of Jewish Education." *Jew Obs* (Apr. 1966): 3–5.

Janowsky, Oscar. "Jewish Education: Achievements, Problems and Needs." In *Jan 2*, 123–72.

Jew Ed. "Progress and Prospects in Jewish Education" (symposium). Participants: I. Margolis (Mizrachi), Abraham E. Millgram (USA), Joseph Kaminetsky (TU), and Emanuel Gamoran (UAHC). 21 (Spring 1950).

Jew Fron. "American Jewish Education, 1963." (Nov. 1963): 7–18.

Jew Life. "Jewish Education in the Spotlight" (editorial). 18 (Feb. 1951).

Jew Obs. "Education: Better Deal for Children—Strong Helping the Weak." 24 (May 30, 1975).

Jick, Leon A. "Can Minimal Jewish Education Be Made Viable?" In *Jan 3*, 311–15.

Kaplan, Mordecai M. "The Problem of Jewish Education." *Recon* 28 (Oct. 5, 1962).

Katz, S. K. et al. "A Lay Professional Forum on Jewish Education." *B'nai B'rith International Jewish Monthly* 51 (Summer 1963): 3–19.

Kaufman, Jay. "The Child Is Father to the Man." *Jew Teach* 33 (Apr. 1965): 18–25.

Kimel, Meyer. „הירידה בחינוך העברי באמריקה" (The Decline in Jewish Education in America). *Sh Hah* (H.) 11 (Dec. 1950): 22–27.

Kiner, Edward D. "Judaism Is for Real." *CCAR J* 22 (Winter 1975). See also *AM* (Winter 1976).

Kittner, Susan. "Major Concerns of Jewish Education in the 1960's. A collection of twenty-two articles that reflect the issues facing Jewish education in the 1960s." Master's project, HUC–JIR, 1980.

Kodesh, Shlomo. „החינוך היהודי בארה"ב בעיני מחנך ישראלי" (Jewish Education in the U.S. as Seen by an Israeli Educator). *Hadoar* (H.) 51 (June 2, 1972).

Konvitz, Milton. "Jewish Education—Higher and Deeper." *Jew Ed* 27 (Spring 1957): 35–36.

Korn, I. "Jews without Judaism." *Jew Fron* 44 (Jan. 1977): 11–15.

Kuselewitz, David, ed. and trans. *Jewish Education in Response to the Challenge of Our Times.* N.Y.: DEC, 1957. 96 pp.

45 ASSESSMENT

Lakritz, William B. "Implications of the National Survey of Jewish Education for Conservative Schools." *Syn Sch* 19 (Mar. 1961).

Lander, Leon. „אידישע דערציאונג אין אמעריקע" (Jewish Education in America). In *Jewish Life in America* (Y.), 129–79. 1964.

Lang, Gerhard. "Jewish Education." *AJYB* 69 (1968): 370–83.

———. "Perceptions of Jewish Education." *Ped Rep* 35 (Oct. 1984): 22–23.

Lauer, H. Chaim. "Perspective on Jewish Education." *J Jew Com Ser* 61 (Winter 1984): 144–49.

Lehrer, Leibush. „אידישע דערציאונג אין אמעריקע" (Jewish Education in America). *YK* (Y.) (Mar. 12, 1954): 2–6. See also *YK* (Y.) (June 26, 1959).

Levine, Etan. "Some Reconstructionist Views on Jewish Education." *Jew Ed* 47 (Winter 1979): 13–16.

Levine, T. "Primacy of Jewish Education." *Un Syn Rev* 20 (Jan. 1968): 5–7.

Lieber, David. "The Conservative Congregational School: Prospects for the Future." *Ed As* (1972): 11–20.

Lieberman, Chaim. *A House on Fire: A Plea for Intensive Jewish Education*. N.Y.: Chaim Lieberman Foundation, 1965. 256 pp.

Lookstein, Joseph H. „הנוער העברי וחינוכו לאזרחיות" (Jewish Youth and Education for Citizenship). *Hadoar* (H.) 41 (Dec. 30, 1961): 129–40.

Lubinsky, M. "Jewish Education in the '80's." *Rel Ed* 75 (Nov.–Dec. 1980): 654–58.

Margoshes, Samuel. "Jewish Education." *Day* (June 14, 1955).

———. "Worry about Jewish Education." *Day* (May 10, 1965).

Mark, Yudel. "Unbalanced Schools." In *JJS*, 191–95. From *CE*, (Y.) 34 (Jan. 1964).

Meckler, H. L. „דערפאלגן און דירכפאלן פון אידישן חינוך אין אמעריקע" (Successes and Failures in American Jewish Education). *Day* (Y.) (Mar. 20, 1955).

Meyers, Eric M. "The Jewish Student Today: Patterns and Prospects." *Jew Ed* 38 (June 1968): 30–35.

Meyers, Lawrence. "Some Thoughts on Education." *Ped Rep* 23 (Sept. 1971): 24.

Mirsky, Samuel K. „הרהורים על המשבר בבתי הספר באמריקה" (Reflections on the Crisis in Jewish Education in America). *Hadoar* (H.) 39 (Mar. 11, 1960): 311–12.

Nadel, Max. "What We Can Learn from General Education." *Ped Rep* 35 (Mar. 1984): 1–3.

National Commission on Torah Education. *The Jewish Educational Scene—A Critical Appraisal*. N.Y.: 1966.

Neusner, Jacob. "Jewish Education: Aspirin? Penicillin?" *Jewish Advocate* (Mar. 20, 1975).

———. "Jewish Learning in America." *CCAR J* 23 (Winter 1976): 1–11.

Newman, L. "Jewish Education." *AJYB* 65 (1964): 84–92.

Orlan, Chaim. „לתקון החנוך העברי באמריקה" (On Improving Jewish Education in America). *Hadoar* (H.) (Sept. 11, 1962): 668.

Pearl, C. "American Jewish Education: An English View." *Jew J Soc* 3 (1961): 76–87.

Pekarsky, Maurice. "The Challenge to Our Students." *Hadassah Newsletter* (Nov. 1955).

Pilch, Judah. „החנוך היהודי בארצות הברית על פרשת דרכים" (American Jewish Education at the Cross Roads). *Hagut* (H.) 3 (1974): 329–42.

———. "Basic Problems in American Jewish Education." *The Dispersion* (Winter 1964–65): 39–47.

———. "Discussions on Jewish Education." *Jew Fron* 42 (Apr. 1975): 19–26.

———. "The Intellectual as Layman in Jewish Education." *Recon* (May 28, 1965).

———. "Jewish Education in America." *Jew Teach* 28 (Mar. 1960): 7–10.

———. "The Status of Jewish Education." *Congress Weekly* 21 (Mar. 22, 1954): 3–5.

———. "What Can We Learn from the National Study of Jewish Education?" *Jew Teach* 28 (Mar. 1960): 7–10.

———. „מה נעשה לחנוך בנינו" (What to Do for the Education of Our Children). *Sh Hah* (H.) 11 (June 1951): 125–29.

Pollak, George. "Afternoon Jewish Schools." *Jew Spec* 29 (Dec. 1964): 22–23.

———. "The Carnegie Report and Jewish Education." *Ped Rep* 35 (Mar. 1984): 3–7.

———. "For a Jewish Coleman Report." *Jew Ed* 51 (Fall 1983): 43–44, 48.

———. "Issues in Education." *Jew Ed* 51 (Winter 1983): 38–42, 45.

———. "Needed: An Educational Elite." *Jew Spec* 30 (Mar.–Apr. 1965): 38–39.

Pollak, George, and Gerhard Lang. *Perceptions of Jewish Education*. N.Y.: JESNA Department of Research and Information, 1983. 58 pp.

Popkin, R. "Dedication and Education." *Had Mag* 66 (Dec. 1984): 4.

Rabinowitz, Stanley. "Converting the Sunday School into a Hebrew School." *Syn Sch* 9 (Jan. 1951): 3–7.

Resnikoff, Bernard. "On Producing Healthy Rebels." *Syn Sch* 21 (Fall 1962).

Rosenak, Michael. "Jewish Education: A Reappraisal Seminar." *WZO* 44 (Sept. 1982): 1–15.

Rossel, Seymour. "Can We Make Jewish Education Better?" *Present Tense* (Winter 1980): 23–24.

Rotenberg, Joshua. „וועגן אידישער דערציאונג אין אמעריקע" (Concerning Jewish Education in America). *YK* (Y.) (Jan. 10, 1964); 4–5.

Rubinstein, Robert E. "Raising Standards in Hebrew School." *Ped Rep* 30 (Spring 1979).

Rudin, Jacob P. "The Mood of Reform Jewish Education." *Ped Rep* 21 (Sept. 1969): 20–23.

Sandrow, Edward T. "Our Educational Dilemma Today." *Ed As* (1970): 12–22. See also *Syn Sch* 31 (Winter 1973): 4–15.

Schafler, Samuel. "From Alternatives to Excellence." *Jew Ed* 51 (Summer 1983): 9–11.

Schanin, Norman. "The Interrelationship between Formal and Informal Education." *Jew Ed* 37 (1967): 135–39.

———. "Jewish Education Today." *Ed As* (1966): 91–98.

Scharfstein, Zevi. „על פרשת תקופות—החינוך היהודי בארצות הברית בחצי המאה" (At the Crossroads of Eras—Jewish Education in the United States at the Midcentury). In *M. M. Kaplan Jubilee Volume*, edited by Davis, 249–59. 1953.

———. „עליות וירידות בחינוך העברי" (Ups and Downs in Jewish Education). *Hadoar* (H.) 37 (Oct. 3 1958): 747–48, 753.

Schiff, Alvin I. "Challenges in Jewish Education." *Jew Ed* 39 (Dec. 1969): 3.

———. *Contemporary Jewish Education—Issachar American Style: Essays on Jewish Educational Issues*. Dallas: Rossell Books, 1988. 318 pp.

———. "In Search of Educational Excellence." In *Intrater*, 15–19.

———. "Jewish Education in America: Achievement and Challenge." *Jew Ed* 45 (Spring 1977): 12–22.

———. *Jewish Education at the Crossroads: The State of Jewish Education*. N.Y.: BJE, Mar. 1983. 13 pp.

———. "Jewish Education in Light of Peace." *Jew Ed* 47 (Fall 1979): 8–10.

———. "Jewish Education: Problems, Prospects and the Challenges." *Jew Ed* 49 (Winter 1981): 2–8.

———. "On the Status of the Jewish Supplementary School." *Jew Ed* 50 (Winter 1982): 2–4.

———. *A Profile of Jewish Education in the United States*. N.Y.: BJE. 12 pp.

———. "Public Education and the Jewish Schools." *J Jew Com Ser* 61 (Summer 1985): 305–11.

———. "Role of the National Commission on Torah Education." *Ped Rep* 21 (June 1970): 24.

Schindler, Alexander M. "The Assembly Speaks toward Standards of Reform Religious Education." *Jew Teach* 32 (Feb. 1964): 2.

———. "Disciplined Cooperation: A Vital Need for Education Programs." *A Jud* 14 (Fall 1964): 28.

Schlussel, Mark E. "Jewish Education in Transition—A Layman's View." *Jew Ed* 50 (Spring 1982): 22–27, 36.

Schneider, Susan Weidman. "Women and Jewish Education." *Women's American ORT Reporter* (Sept.–Oct. 1979): 13–14.

Schoem, David. "Exploring Jewish Student Failure." *Anthropology and Education Quarterly* (Winter 1982). See also *Ped Rep* 35 (Oct. 1984).

———. "What the Afternoon School Does Best." *Jew Ed* 51 (Winter 1983): 11–18.

Schoolman, Albert P. "National Progress in Jewish Education." *Jew Ed* 25 (Summer 1954): 6–8.

———. *Selected Essays on Various Aspects of Jewish Education in the United States*. N.Y.: 1953. 62 pp.

Schulweis, Harold. "A Call for Holy Discontent." *Un Syn Rev* 26 (Winter 1974): 28–29.

———. "The Public and Private Agenda in Jewish Education." *Ped Rep* 30 (Fall 1978): 2–6.

Schwartz, Simon. "The Current State of the Supplementary School." *Ped Rep* 35 (Jan. 1984): 31–32.

Schwartzman, Sylvan D. "The Break-Down in Reform Jewish Education—Why and What to Do about It?" *CCAR J* (Jan. 1954): 13–18.

———. "Lost Horizons for the Reform Jewish Educator." In *JJS*, 295–305.

Segal, B. "Priorities: Education at Home, Israel, Abroad." *Un Syn Rev* 22 (Winter 1970): 8–9.

Shapiro, David S. "Secular Studies and Judaism." *Trad* (Summer 1966): 15–30.

Shereshevsky, Esra. "Hebrew Alone Is Not Enough." *Ped Rep* 17 (June 1966).

———. "Reflections on Jewish Education." *Jew Spec* 26 (Dec. 1964): 17–18.

Sherman, J. "Jewish Education Today Must Meet Today's Needs." *National Jewish Monthly* 84 (Nov. 1969): 30.

* Shevitz, Susan R. *The Deterioration of Jewish Supplementary School Teaching: An Analysis of the Effects of Communal Myths on Policy and Program*. Harvard U. Graduate School of Education, 1983.

———. "Sexism in Jewish Education." *Response* 18 (Summer 1973): 107–13.

Shmueli, Eliezer. "Repairing the Educational Imbalance." *Cong M* 53 (Apr. 1986): 16–17.

Shudofsky, Maurice M. "Minimalist Infection in Jewish Education." *Recon* (June 15, 1951).

———. "My People Are Destroyed by Lack of Knowledge." *Jew Fron* (Apr. 1951): 6–7.

———. "Neither Jewish nor Education." *Congress Weekly* (Oct. 26, 1953): 7–8.

Shurin, Ben Zion. „די ירידה פון אידישן חינוך אין אמעריקע" (The Decline of Jewish Education in America). *For* (Y.) (July 13, 1984): 13, 28.

———. „אויף דער שוועל פון נייעם אידישן לערן-יאר" (On the Threshold of the New Jewish School Year). *For* (Y.) (Sept. 21, 1984).

Siegel, Morton. "In Defense of the Afternoon School." *Un Syn Rev* 24 (Spring 1971): 10–11.

Silberman, Charles E. "Crisis in the Classroom: A Jewish Perspective." *Ed As* (1972): 21–29.

Silver, Abba Hillel. "Jewish Education—Supreme Task." *Day* (June 15, 1959).

Sleeper, James A. "Authenticity and Responsiveness in Jewish Education." In *The New Jews*, edited by Sleeper and Mintz, 121–42. 1971.

Slesinger, Zalmen. "Jewish Education in a Pluralistic Community—Building Unity in Diversity." *Ped Rep* 21 (Dec. 1969): 9–12.

———. "New Perspectives on Jewish Education." *Jew Fron* (Aug.–Sept. 1976): 20–25.

———. "Reducing the Educational Lag in the Jewish School." *Ped Rep* 13 (May 1962): 12–14, 30.

———. "Re-examining Our Assumptions on Jewish Education." *Ped Rep* 20 (June 1969): 21–24.

———. "Toward a More Realistic Conception of the Capabilities of the School." *Ped Rep* 17 (Sept. 1965).

Smolar, Boris. „געמיינדע זארגן וועגן אידישער קולטור אין אמעריקע" (Communal Concerns about Jewish Culture in America). *For* (Y.) (Oct. 10, 1976).

———. „דער צושטאנד פון אידישער דערציאונג" (The Condition of Jewish Education). *For* (Y.) (Jan. 13, 1980).

———. „צושטאנד פון דער אידישער שול סיסטעם אין לאנד" (The Condition of the Jewish School System in the Nation). *For* (Y.) (Jan. 24, 1982).

———. "איצטיקער אידישער שול סעזאן" (The Current Jewish School Season). *For* (Y.) (Oct. 24, 1976).

———. "אידישע דערציאונג אין אמעריקע" (Jewish Education in America). *For* (Y.) (Nov. 2, 1975).

———. "דער אידישער שול סעזאן" (The Jewish School Season). *For* (Y.) (Sept. 21, 1983). See also *For* (Nov. 23, 1984).

———. "דער אידישער שול סעזאן אין אמעריקע" (The Jewish School Year in America). *For* (Y.) (Sept. 26, 1977, Oct. 8, 1978).

———. "דער נייער אידישער שול סעזאן" (The New Jewish School Season). *For* (Y.) (Sept. 28, 1980).

———. "דאס נייע אידישע שול-יאר אין אמעריקע" (The New Jewish School Year in America). *Day* (Y.) (Sept. 27, 1967).

Spizman, L. "ליכט און שאטן אין אידישן חינוך" (Light and Shadow in Jewish Education). *Day* (Y.) (Nov. 3, 1956).

Spiro, Jack D. "The Value of Jewish Supplementary Education." *Ped Rep* 23 (Sept. 1971): 21–23; *Jew Ed* 47 (Fall 1979): 19–21, 35.

Steinbach, Alexander A. "Raising Standards of Achievement in Religious Schools." *Jew Teach* 24 (Mar. 1956): 3–6.

Steinberg, Bernard. "Macro and Micro Perspectives on Jewish Schooling." *Jew Ed* (Winter 1988): 12–19.

———. "The Present Era in Jewish Education: A Global Comparative Perspective." *Jew J Soc* 26 (Dec. 1984): 93–109.

Stern, Jay. "The Afternoon Jewish School." *Jew Spec* (Spring 1975).

———. "Looking Back at What Succeeded." *Ped Rep* 33 (Oct. 1983): 18–20.

Tabachinsky, Y. "Jewish Education." *Day* (Sept. 15, 1964).

Tannenbaum, A. *What General Education Might Contribute to Jewish Education*. Cleveland: Cleveland College of Jewish Studies, 1968.

Tenenbaum, Joseph. "The Perennial Problem: Jewish Education." *Day* (Oct. 18, 1961).

Teplitz, Saul I. "The Heart of Education." *Congress Weekly* (Oct. 30, 1961): 9–11.

Toubin, Isaac. "The Means of Transmitting Jewishness in the United States." *Congress Weekly* 37 (Apr. 3, 1970): 49–51.

———. "The Right Hand's Cunning." *Jew Ed* 42 (Spring 1973): 44–47.

———. "There is a Task, There is a Place, Give Us the Tools, Let Us Do the Job." *Ped Rep* 22 (Sept. 1970).

———. "A Time for Reassessment." *Ped Rep* 29 (Fall 1977).

Unger, M. "What They Learn in Our Jewish Schools." *Day* (Y.) (Sept. 29, 1957).

USCJE. *On Issues Which Present Themselves to the Commission for the Next Three Years* (position paper). 16 pp.

Vishny, Paul, Theodore Bikel, and Julius Schatz. "Where We Stand on Jewish Education." *Congress Weekly* (Apr. 17, 1970).

Warzburger, Walter S. "The Need for More Balance in Jewish Education." *Jew Ed* 46 (Autumn 1978): 28–29.

Waskaw, Arthur I. "Watering the Seed of Abraham and Sarah." *CCAR J* (Summer 1974): 19–2?.

Weinberg, Julius. "The 'Greening' of Jewish Education." *Jud* 34 (Spring 1985): 180–96.

Weinberger, B. "The Space Age Cult of Practibility." *Jew Life* 29 (Apr. 1962).

Weinberger, Paul. "The Effects of Jewish Education." *AJYB* 72 (1971): 230–49.

Weiss-Rosmarin, Trude. "The Failure of Jewish Education" (editorial). *Jew Spec* 35 (Mar. 1970). Responses to this editorial were made by Samuel Dinin, Azriel Eisenberg, Pesach Schindler, Morton Siegel, and Max Zeldner. See *Jew Spec* 35 (June 1970).

———. "Jewish Education." *Jew Spec* (Sept. 1964): 4–6.

———. "Jewish Education in a Vacuum." *Jew Spec* (Apr. 1961): 3–6.

Weistrop, J. "Teaching to be Different." *Jew Spec* 31 (Mar. 1966).

Winer, Gershon. "Eliminating the Sunday School." *Syn Sch* 9 (Jan. 1951): 12–15.

45 ASSESSMENT

Winter, Nathan A. "The Shift in Emphasis in the Structure of Jewish Education." *Syn Sch* 28 (Spring 1970): 12–16.

Wollman, Benjamin. „תכנית היסוד והחנוך העברי בארצות הברית" (A Basic Program and Jewish Education in the United States). *Sh Hah* (H.) 14 (Fall 1954): 3–18.

Woocher, Jonathan. *Sacred Survival: The Civil Religion of American Jews*. Bloomington: Indiana U. Press, 1986.

Zaiman, Joel H. "On Educating Our Children." *Con Jud* 31 (Winter 1977): 80–81.

Zeitlin, Solomon. "Jewish Learning in America." *JQR* 45 (Apr. 1955): 582–616.

Zohar, C. "One Million Get No Education." *Jew Obs* 25 (Sept. 24, 1976): 31.

AMERICA'S IMPACT ON JEWISH EDUCATION PRIOR TO 1950

Berkson, Isaac B. "Democracy and Jewish Culture." *Jew Ed* 9 (Oct.–Dec. 1937): 125–27.

Boraisha, Menachem. "Cultural Pluralism and the School." *Congress Weekly* (Mar. 21, 1947).

―――. „א סביבה פאר דער שול—דער אידישער שול פראבלעם אין אמעריקע" (An Environment for the School—The Jewish School Problem in America). *Day* (Y.) (May 14, 1948).

Chipkin, Israel. "Planning for American Jewish Education." *Jew Ed* 17 (Feb. 1946): 7–16.

Dinin, Samuel. „זרמים בחנוך האמריקני" (Currents in American Education). *Sh Hah* 1 (Fall 1940): 14–19.

―――. „חנוך המכין לחיים באמריקה" (Education that Prepares for Life in America). *Sh Hah* (H.) (May–June 1939): 65–70.

Dushkin, Alexander M. "Democracy and Jewish Education." *Jew Ed* 14 (Sept.–Dec. 1942): 94–100.

―――. „השפעת החנוך האמריקני על החנוך היהודי" (The Influence of American Education upon Jewish Education). In *JB* (H.), 99–113.

―――. "Towards an American Jewish Education." *Jew Ed* 13 (Apr. 1941): 17.

―――. "What Is American Jewish Education?" *Education* 6 (May 1944). Also in pamphlet published by AAJE, 1944, pp. 3–9.

Edidin, Ben M. "Teaching Democracy in the Jewish School." *Jew Ed* (Jan.–Mar. 1943): 155–60.

Epstein, A. „הילד העברי באמריקה" (The Jewish Child in America). *Sh Hah* (H.) 3 (1927): 9–16, 119–25.

Feibelman, Julius B. "Jewish Education Confronts American Reality." *CCAR* 45 (1935): 419–31.

Gamoran, Emanuel. "The Role of Jewish Education in Developing a Creative Jewish Center in America." *Jew Ed* 19 (Fall 1947): 24–30.

Golub, Jacob S. "We Have No Jewish School for America." *Opinion* (June 13, 1932).

Honor, Leo L. "Jewish Education and Democracy." *Jewish Forum* 1 (1942). Also in pamphlet published by AAJE, 1944, pp. 3–9.

Kallen, Horace M. "Jewish Education in the American Scene." *Jew Ed* 21 (Winter 1949): 25–31, 63.

Kaplan, Mordecai M. "American Approaches to Jewish Education." *Jew Rev* 1 (May 1943): 5–12.

―――. "Jewish Education for Democracy." *Recon* (Nov. 24, 1939): 11–16.

―――. "Judaism's Contribution to Education for Democracy." In *FAJ*, 480–522.

―――. "The Meaning of Jewish Education in America." In *Judaism as a Civilization*, 479–508. 1959. Also in *JJS*, 328–36.

Rappoport, Israel B. *Education for Living as American Jews*. N.Y.: AJC, 1946. 56 pp.

AMERICA'S IMPACT ON JEWISH EDUCATION SINCE 1950

Ackerman, Walter I. "The Americanization of Jewish Education." *Jud* 24 (Fall 1975): 416–35.

Adelsberg, David. „די אמעריקאניזירונג פון אידישן חינוך" (The Americanization of Jewish Education). *Day* (Y.) (July 7, 1961).

45 ASSESSMENT

Adler, Morris. "Jewish Education in a Free Society." *Pio Woman* 38 (Nov. 1963): 7–8.

Ben-Horin, Meir. "Agenda for American Jewish Education." *Recon* (Feb. 23, 1962): 11–16.

———. "Reschooling American Jewry." *J Jew Com Ser* 52 (Spring 1976): 278–80.

Blumenfield, Samuel M. "Changes in the American Jewish Scene." *Jew Ed* 23 (Winter 1952): 12–18.

———. "Jewish Education in America." *Day* (Jan. 4, 1950).

———. "החינוך העברי באמריקה" (Jewish Education in America). In *S Ed* (H.), 75–80.

———. "החינוך היהודי בתמורות הסביבה האמריקאית" (Jewish Education in the Changing American Scene). In *S Ed* (H.), 99–104.

———. "החינוך היהודי בארצות הברית" (Jewish Education in the United States). In *S Ed* (H.), 81–91.

Chipkin, Israel S. "Comments on Samuel Dinin's Democracy and Education." *Recon* 20 (Mar. 12, 1954).

Chomsky, William. "Why Jewish Education in a Democratic Society." In *Teaching and Learning*. N.Y.: JEC Press, 1959. See also *JJS*, 51–60.

Cohen, Jack J. "Our Schools and Our Society." *Jew Ed* 31 (Fall 1960): 4–18.

Congress Weekly. "The Current Scene in American Jewish Education" (special issue). Includes articles by Michael Alper, Israel Chipkin, L. A. Feldman, Abraham Katsh, Judah Pilch, David Rudavsky, and Louis Ruffman. (Mar. 22, 1954).

Dinin, Samuel. "American Influences on Jewish Education." In *AJ*, 94–118.

———. "The Contribution of Jewish Education to the Development of the American Jewish Personality." *Jew Ed* 22 (Summer 1951): 19–23.

———. "Democracy and Jewish Education." *Recon* 19 (Jan. 29, 1954): 7–20.

Drachler, Norman. "American Education Today." *Jew Teach* 27 (Mar. 1959): 27–30.

———. "The Ferment in the Public Schools and Its Implications for the Religious School." *Jew Teach* 31 (Apr. 1963): 7–10.

Duker, Abraham G. "Impact of American Jewish Life on Jewish Tradition." In *CPA*, 67–84.

———. "Some Limits on Jewish Education in American Society." *Jew Ed* 31 (Fall 1960): 18–24.

Fox, Marvin. "Jewish Education in a Pluralistic Community." *RA* (1966): 31–40.

Glueck, Nelson. "מיר מוזן פאנגען די הערצער פון אונדזערע קינדער מיט אמעריקאנער אידישקייט" (We Must Capture the Hearts of Our Children with American Judaism) (interview). In *Penn* (Y.), 54–63.

Goodman, Saul. "דאס פנים פון יידישע חינוך אין אמעריקע" (The Face of Jewish Education in America). *Zuk* (Y.) (Sept. 1960): 313–16.

Gottschalk, Shimon. "The Protestantization of Jewish Education." *Jew Teach* 32 (Dec. 1963): 11–12.

Greenberg, Simon. "Jewish Pluralism and Jewish Education." *Jew Ed* 45 (Spring 1977): 23–28, 40.

Had Mag. "Assimilation: Can the Jews Survive Their Encounter with America?" (a dialogue). 65 (Aug.–Sept. 1983): 16–19.

Honor, Leo L. "The Impact of American Environment and American Ideas on Jewish Education in the United States." *JQR* 45 (tercentenary issue) (Apr. 1955): 451–96.

Kallen, Horace M. "Jewish Education for American Jews." *Congress Weekly* (Jan. 8, 1951): 2–4.

Karff, Samuel E., Ely E. Pilchik, Frederick C. Schwartz, and Daniel J. Silver. *Judaism In a Secular Age*. UAHC, Nov. 1977. 32 pp.

Konvitz, Milton. "Thoughts on Jewish Education." In *Jewish Education in the United States*, edited by Dushkin and Engelman, vii–xi. 1959. See also *JSS*, 99–103.

Kranush, Leonard. "Secularization of Jewish Education." *Compass* 2 (Winter 1979): 12–13.

Kronish, Ronald. "Adjusting Jewish Education to America." *Rel Ed* 74 (July–Aug. 1979): 381–95.

Levin, Nora. "The Cultural Integration of the Jewish Community into the Body of American Society." *Ped Rep* 28 (Fall 1976): 5–19.

Martin, Bernard. "The Americanization of Reform Judaism." *RJ* 27 (Winter 1980): 35–58.

45 ASSESSMENT

Nemzoff, Samuel A. "Relating Learning to Living: The Challenge of the American Environment." *Jew Teach* 31 (Apr. 1963): 3.

Sachar, Howard M. *The Impact of America on American Jews*. CJF, March 1976. 8 pp.

Schindler, Alexander M. "Jewish Education in a Pluralistic Community." *RA* (1966): 40–46.

Shahar, Michael. "חינוך יהודי בחברה הפתוחה„ (Jewish Education in an Open Society). *Hadoar* (H.) 53 (Nov. 2, 1973).

Shapiro, Yehudah. "װעגן יידישער דערציאונג אין אמעריקע„ (On Jewish Education in America). *Zuk* (Y.) (Apr. 1960): 186–90.

Sh Hah (H.). (Symposium on Education for Jewish Continuity in an Open Society). Participants: Jack J. Cohen, Elazar Goelman, Abraham P. Gannes, and Aryeh Ben-Yosef. 43 (Summer 1984): 200–208.

Slesinger, Zalmen. "חינוך לזהות יהודית ולהמשכיות יהדות בחברה הפתוחה„ (Education for Jewish Identity and Jewish Continuity in the Open Society). *Sh Hah* (H.) 43 (Winter 1983–84): 76–85.

* Solomon, Sidney. *The Conservative Congregational School as a Response to the American Scene*. Ann Arbor, Mich.: U. Microfilms International, 1983. 256 pp.

Spotts, Leon H. "Jewish Education and the Public Schools—The Debt and the Danger." *Jew Ed* 37 (1967): 122–34.

Zeitlin, Aaron. "אידישע דערציאוג אין אנגלא-זאקסישער קולטור„ (Jewish Education in Anglo-Saxon Culture). *Day* (Y.) (July 31, 1952).

Zeldin, Michael. "Jewish Schools and American Society: Patterns of Action and Reaction." *Rel Ed* 78 (Spring 1983): 182–92.

TRENDS PRIOR TO 1950

Dinin, Samuel. "General Trends in Jewish Education." *Jew Ed* 18 (Nov. 1946): 7–20.

Dushkin, Alezander M. "The Threefold Trend in American Jewish Education." *Jew Ed* 19 (Spring 1948): 14–19.

Gamoran, Emanuel. "Recent Trends in Jewish Education." *Jew Ed* 11 (Jan. 1940): 213–17, 244.

———. "Tendencies in Jewish Education." *Jew Ed* 1 (Oct. 1929): 149–53.

Golub, Jacob S. "Some Trends in Jewish Education." *Jew Ed* 14 (Apr.–June 1942): 36–39, 52.

———. "Transition in Jewish Education." *Jew Ed* 3 (Apr.–June 1931): 67–76.

Greenberg, Simon. "Trends in Jewish Education." *Contemporary Jewish Record* 5 (Apr. 1942): 162–70.

Rosen, Ben. "Trends in Jewish Education as Reflected in Recent Surveys." *Jew Ed* 12 (Apr. 1940): 14–20.

TRENDS SINCE 1950

Ben-Horin, Meir. "Some Recent Trends in Jewish Educational Thought." *AJYB* 60 (1959): 100–108. Also in *Reg* (1959).

Dinin, Samuel. "Trends in Jewish Education." *Rel Ed* 53 (Jan.–Feb. 1958).

Hochberg, Hillel. "Trends and Developments in Jewish Education." *AJYB* 73 (1972): 194–235.

Honor, Leo L. "Trends in Jewish Education." *Rel Ed* 47 (Jan.–Feb. 1953): 18.

Massarik, Fred. "Trends in United States Jewish Education—National Jewish Populations Study Findings." *AJYB* (1977): 240–50.

Mosenkis, Matthew. "החנוך העברי לאור הזרמים החדשים„ (New Trends in Jewish Education). *Sh Hah* (H.) 23 (Spring 1963).

Rosenak, Michael. "Trends and Problems in Current Jewish Educational Scholarship." In *Stu*, 2:9–18.

Ruffman, Louis L. "Trends in Elementary Education." *Congress Weekly* (Mar. 22, 1954): 8–10.

———. "Trends and Recent Developments in the Field of Jewish Education." *JSSQ* 29 (Fall 1952): 29–37. Also in *Trends and Issues in Jewish Social Welfare in the United States,*

1897–1958, edited by Morris and Freund, 559–73.

Silverman, William B. "The Emerging Patterns of Reform Jewish Education." *Jew Teach* 27 (Mar. 1959): 17–21.

DIFFERENCES AND COMMON ELEMENTS IN JEWISH EDUCATION PRIOR TO 1950

Dushkin, Alexander M. "Common Elements in Jewish Education." *Jew Ed* 17 (Nov. 1945): 5–13.

———. „פירוד און אחדות אין אידישער דערציאונג" (Differences and Unity in Jewish Education). *Zuk* (Y.) (Mar. 1946): 172–74. Also in *Yesod* (H.), 157–64.

Edelstein, Menachem M. „לשאלת הידיאלוגיה בחנוך העברי" (On the Question of Ideology in Jewish Education). *Sh Hah* (H.) 6 (Sept. 1946): 268–73.

Gamoran, Emanuel. "Liberal Jewish Education in America." *The Liberal Jewish Monthly* (Pentecost 1949).

———. "Nationalism and Religion in Jewish Education." *Jew Ed* 7 (Jan.–Mar. 1935): 9–20.

Golub, Jacob S. "Our Common Burden." *Jew Ed* 9 (Oct.–Dec. 1936): 104–14.

Greenberg, Simon. "Some Universal Aspects of Jewish Education in America." *Jew Ed* 14 (Apr.–June 1942): 5–10.

Hartstein, Jacob L., and Yudel Mark. "Common Elements in Jewish Education" (symposium). *Jew Ed* 17 (Feb. 1946): 40–43.

Lehrer, Leibush. „נאציאנאלער כאראקטער" (National Character). *YB* (Y.) 31/32 (1948): 293–351.

Niger, Sh. „קאנען אלע אידן האבן איין שול פאר זייערע קינדער?" (Can All Jews Have One School for Their Children?). *Day* (Y.) (Feb. 6, 1926).

Rudavsky, David. „מחלקות רגילות ומיוחדות בבתי ספרנו" (Regular and Particular Classes in Our Schools). *Sh Hah* (H.) 8 (Oct. 1948): 154–60.

Stavitsky, Michael. „אלע אידישע שולען אין אמעריקע האלטן זיך בא פאראייניקן" (All Jew-ish Schools im America are Close to Uniting). *Day* (Y.) (Sept. 21, 1948).

Touroff, Nissan. „הדת והלאומיות בחינוך" (Religion and Nationalism in Education). *Miklat* (H.) 5 (1930). 160 pp.

DIFFERENCES AND COMMON ELEMENTS IN JEWISH EDUCATION SINCE 1950

Allon, Yigal. "Education: The Key to Unity." *World Jewry* 13 (Jan.–Feb. 1970): 12.

Ben-Horin, Meir. "Loyalties in Jewish Education." *Recon* (May 23, 1956): 17–21.

Duker, Abraham G. "The Problem of Coordination and Unity." In *Jan 2*, 323–38.

Freehof, Solomon B. "The Contribution of Reform Judaism to Jewish Education." *Jew Ed* 34 (Winter 1964): 84–86.

Greenberg, Simon. „חנוך הבנים בתנועת השמרנית" (Education of Children in the Conservative Movement). *Sh Hah* (H.) 22 (Fall 1962): 4–11.

Hertzberg, Arthur. "Community and Nation: Basis for Jewish Commitment." *Jew Ed* 45 (Fall–Winter 1976): 17–24.

Klein, Joseph. "Traditional Elements in Reform Religious Education." *CCAR Yearbook* 66 (1956).

Konvitz, Milton. "Unity for Jewish Education." *Congress Weekly* (Feb. 5, 1951): 8–10.

Lamm, Norman. "The Unity Theme and Its Implications for Moderns." *Trad* 4 (Fall 1961): 44–63.

Schindler, Alexander M. *Jewish Unity and Jewish Education*. UAHC, May 18, 1966. 5 pp.

Schein, Jeff. "Unity within Diversity in Jewish Education." *Recon* 41 (June 1975): 13–19.

JEWISH EDUCATION AND "JEWISH SURVIVAL" PRIOR TO 1950

Blumenfield, Samuel M. "Jewish Education and the War for Survival." *Jew Ed* 14 (Sept.–Dec. 1942): 87–93.

45 ASSESSMENT

Dinin, Samuel. "The Role of Jewish Education in the Present Crisis." *Jew Ed* 11 (Sept. 1939): 101–4.

Golomb, Abraham. "קיום און דערציאונג„ (Survival and Education). *Zuk* (Y.) 53 (Sept. 1948): 518–21.

Greenstein, Harry L. "Our Survival as Jews." *Jew Ed* 14 (Sept.–Dec. 1942): 85–86, 105.

Kallen, Horace M. "Judaism as Disaster." *Jew Ed* 13 (Sept. 1942): 82–91.

Levinthal, Louis E. "Jewish Education, the Path to Creative Survival." *Jew Ed* (Oct.–Dec. 1938): 144–47.

Scharfstein, Zevi. "המשבר בחינוך העברי באמריקה„ (The Crisis in Jewish Education in America). *Hadoar* (H.) 23 (Apr. 16, 30, 1944).

Wirth, Louis. "Education for Survival: The Jews." *American J of Sociology* 48 (1943): 682–91.

JEWISH EDUCATION AND "JEWISH SURVIVAL" SINCE 1950

Gordis, Robert. *Jewish Learning and Jewish Existence—Retrospect and Prospect*. Leo Baeck Institute, 1963. 34 pp.

———. "A Strategy for Jewish Survival." *Congress Biweekly* 38 (Sept. 17, 1971): 8, 13, 20.

Hertzberg, Arthur. "Jewish Education—and Brute Survival." *Mid* (May 1980): 32–36.

Jung, Leo. "דער רוף פון הרב לעא יאונג צו ראטעווען קינדער פון קיינעם לאנד„ (The Call by Rabbi Leo Jung to Save the Children in 'No Man's Land') (interview). In *Penn* (Y.), 119–25.

Kallen, Horace M. "Education for Jewish Survival." *Congress Weekly* (May 25, 1959): 3–4.

———. "Jewish Education and Jewish Survival." *Jew Ed* 34 (Summer 1964): 223–29.

Lewis, Frieda S. "Survival through Education." *Had Mag* (Mar. 1984): 4.

Morgan, T. B. "The Vanishing American Jew." *Look Magazine* (May 1964).

Sanua, Victor D. "Jewish Survival and Jewish Education: A Review of Empirical Studies." *Orot* (H.) (1965).

Schiff, Alvin I. "Jewish Continuity through Jewish Education: A Human Resource Imperative." *Jew Ed* 48 (Summer 1980): 5–11, 33.

———. "Responding to Threats to Jewish Survival" (editorial). *Jew Ed* 43 (Winter/Spring 1975): 3–5.

Schoem, David. "Jewish Schooling and Jewish Survival in the Suburban American Community." In *Stu*, 2:52–64.

Spector, S. I. "Jewish Survival: A Cultural Paradox." *J of Educational Sociology* 30 (1956): 200–208.

QUESTIONS OLD AND NEW PRIOR TO 1950 (SELECTED)

Cohen, Mortimer. "Are We Reaching the Soul of the Jewish Child?" *The Torch* (Jan. 1949). See also *RTJS*, 201–4.

Gamoran, Emanuel. "What Do We Mean by Jewish Education?" (address and discussion). In *NCJSS Proceedings* (1925): 249–88.

Honor, Leo L. "To Whom Shall We Entrust Our Children?" *Day* (May 3, 1940).

Niger, Shmuel. "איז גענוג פאר אונדז די פאבליק סקול?„ (Is the Public School Sufficient for Us?). *Day* (Y.) (Sept. 17, 19, 1926).

Pilch, Judah. "Is the Talmud Torah Doomed?" *Jew Ed* 18 (Nov. 1946): 21–28.

Rappoport, Israel B. "The Elementary Jewish School of Tomorrow—Linguistic or Experiential." *Jew Ed* 5 (Apr.–June 1933): 89–95.

Rosen, Ben. "Some Mooted Questions In Jewish Eduucation." *Jew Ed* 2 (Oct. 1930): 124–32.

Rubinstein, Simha. "למוד או חנוך„ (Learning or Education?). *Hadoar* (H.) 13 (17th of Heshvan 1935).

Scharfstein, Zevi. "היש ירידה בחנוך העברי?„ (Is There a Decline in Jewish Education?). *Hadoar* (H.) 6 (13th of Kislev 1937).

———. "היש תקוה?„ (Is There Hope?). *Hadoar* (H.) 4 (1st of Kislev 1925).

Taback, Ben Zion. "היש סכוי לתקון החנוך?" (Is There a Prospect to Improve Education?). *Sh Hah* (H.) 4 (Mar. 1944): 142–45.

Touroff, Nissan. "חנוך יהודי לשעה או לדורות?" (Jewish Education for the Present or for the Ages?). *Sh Hah* (H.) 6 (Mar. 1946): 99–104. See also *JJS*, 118–23.

QUESTIONS OLD AND NEW SINCE 1950 (SELECTED)

Ackerman, Walter I. "Jewish Education for What?" *AJYB* 70 (1969): 3–36.

Arian, Shraga. "An Agenda of Questions for Jewish Education." *Syn Sch* 30 (Fall 1971). See also *Ed As* (1972): 3–10.

Bernstein, Eliezer Z. "החנוך העברי לאן?" (Whither Jewish Education?). *Hadoar* (H.) 52 (Sept. 7, 1973).

Chazan, Raphael. "חינוך יהודי—לשם מה?" (Jewish Education—For What?). *Hadoar* (H.) 52 (Feb. 2, 1973).

Chipkin, Israel S. "Why Should I Be Interested in Jewish Learning?" *Detroit Jewish News* (Oct. 7, 1952).

Chomsky, William. "What Is a Good Jewish Education?" *Recon* 26 (Mar. 4, 1960): 24–29.

Cohen, Howard M. "Who Are Our Children?: An Informal Questionnaire." *Ped Rep* 32 (Sept. 1981): 31–33.

Dashefsky, Arnold. "Jewish Education—For What and for Whom?" *Jew Ed* (Fall 1985): 44–47.

Diskind, Zalman. "Can We Neglect the Talmud Torah?" *Jew Life* 30 (Oct. 1962). Also printed by UOJCA, 8 pp.

Eisenberg, Azriel. "Jewish Education—For What?" (editorial). *Jew Ed* 40 (Summer 1970): 4–5.

Eliach, David. "האם יש עתיד לחינוך היהודי בארצות הברית?" (Is There a Future for Jewish Education in the United States?). *Sh Hah* (H.) 43 (Winter 1983–84): 69–75.

Frost, Shimon. "Is Jewish Education a Discipline?" *Ped Rep* 36 (Sept. 1985): 27.

———. "Is There a Future in Jewish Education?" (interview by Phil Baum). *Cong M* (Jan. 1982): 11–12.

Gittelsohn, Roland B. "Why Jewish Education?" In *Modern Jewish Problems* (1964): 178–94. High school.

Goodman, Y. "For Whom Do I Labor?" *Syn Sch* 26 (Summer 1968): 26–30.

Gorr, Alan. "What Sort of Jew Have We Produced?" *Syn Sch* 30 (Fall 1971): 5–17.

Greenberg, Blu. "Will there be Orthodox Women Rabbis?" *Jud* 33 (Winter 1984): 23–33.

Grossman, R. "על שאלה ה'לאן' בחינוך העברי" (On the Question 'Whither' in Jewish Education?). *Hadoar* (H.) (Nov. 24, 1972).

Hertz, Richard C. "What Really is Jewish Education?" *Jew Ed* 22 (Summer 1952): 33–36.

Hoffman, J. "Are We Teaching Our Values?" *Jew Life* 22 (Apr. 1955).

Jew Fron. "A Questioned Education" (editorial). (June–July 1979): 3, 29.

Levine, Y. "Jewish Education to What End?" *Congress Biweekly* (Dec. 27, 1965): 21–23.

Lipton, Ann Lynn. "Who Is Accountable for What, and to Whom?" *Ped Rep* 36 (Sept. 1985): 16–18.

Mahler, Raphael. "החנוך היהודי בגולה—לאן?" (Jewish Education in the Diaspora—Whither?). *BaTefoozoht Ha Golah* (H.) (Oct. 1959).

Margoshes, Samuel. "אידישע דערציאונג וואוהין?" (Jewish Education—Whither?). *Day* (Y.) (Oct. 28, 1961).

Millgram, Abraham E. "What Kind of Jewish Education Do Our Children Need?" *Syn Sch* 12 (Nov. 1953): 3–9.

Rabinowitz, Dorothy. "Are Jewish Students Different?" *Change* (Summer 1971): 47–50.

Rosenthal, Ira A. "What Should Religious School Be Like?" *Jew Teach* 19 (Nov. 1950): 36–39.

Schiff, Alvin I. "Who Speaks for Jewish Education?" *Jew Ed* 46 (Summer 1978): 9–15. See also *For* (Sept. 1979) (E. section).

Sigal, P. "Whither Diaspora Judaism?" *Con Jud* 14 (Summer 1960): 35–45.

45
ASSESSMENT

Silberman, Charles. "Where Are Our Children?" *Moment* 1 (Jan. 1976): 7–12.

Spiro, Jack D. "Are Our Religious Schools Obsolete?" *Dimensions* (Winter 1968): 34–36.

Steinberg, Paul M. "On the Horizon—What Is Ahead for Reform Jewish Education in the Religious School?" *Jew Teach* 28 (Mar. 1959): 30–31.

Todes, David. "מחנך עברי—מהמלילי?„ (Jewish Educator—What of the Night?). *Sh Hah* (H.) 32 (1972): 174–76.

Waxman, Meyer. "Is Jewish Education Necessary?" *Congress Weekly* (Jan. 8, 1951): 7–10.

Weiss, Avraham. "Is There An Alternative to the Decline of the Jewish Supplementary School?" *Jew Ed* 49 (Summer 1981): 8–17.

Weiss-Rosmarin, Trude. "What Should We Teach?" *Jew Spec* (Mar. 1962): 3–5.

Werb, Morris R. "What Are We Teaching Our Children?" *Jew Ed* 22 (Summer 1951): 29–30.

GLEANINGS

Weinberger, Moses (1887),

"There is nothing in the way of schooling here for the young men of Israel. Our faithful Orthodox brethren, who pride themselves on not seeking reforms, and revel in their own piety and righteousness, unhesitatingly allow their sons to grow up without Torah or faith. They don't mind that their children, while still babes, run after lucre, a life of pleasure, and all human gratifications—forgetting altogether their faith, Torah, and holy roots. Instead of training their sons to follow in their ways, they spend their time inspecting cantors, parnasim, sextons, and other synagogue officials. They heed not the march of time as it rages, billows, and slowly destroys the best part of Jewry."

Jews and Judaism in New York (H.) (1887). Translated and edited by Jonathan D. Sarna as *People Walk on Their Heads*, 51. N.Y.: Holmes and Meier, 1981. See Sarna's introduction, pp. 4–29.

Benderly, Samson (1909),

"I must . . . say that the 40,000 boys who attend the Chedarim are worse off than the 90,000 boys who attend no school."

"Jewish Education in America." *Jew Ed* 20 (Summer 1949), 83.

Revel, Bernard,

"It is evident to every impartial observer of conditions in our communal and congregational schools that these schools have not fully met their responsibility as the bearers of the spirit of Judaism, the conscience of Universal Israel, to our youth. Until recently many of these schools have concentrated upon the national aspect of Judaism, to the neglect of its high religious ideals and values; of the spiritual and moral verities of Israel, and of the character-molding values of religious practice. The center of gravity of Jewish education, its spirit and goal, in many of our schools has shifted from the Torah and Jewish ideals of life to abstract nationalism, from a spiritual to a linguistic education, ignoring the spiritual interpretation of Jewish history and destiny."

"The Day School and the Yeshiva in Jewish Education." *NCJSS Proceedings* (1926), 294.

Golub, Jacob S., and Leo L. Honor,

"The effectiveness of our schools . . . should be judged by the degree which they lead to creative adjustment, growing out of our own group experience as well as the experience of other Jewries. In light of these criteria, the inadequacy of the existing Jewish schools become evident. Neither the Talmud Torah, nor the congregational daily school, nor the Sunday School are institutions for creative adaptation."

Jew Ed 4 (Oct.–Dec. 1932), 152.

Friedland, A. H.,

"I make bold to assert that if we concentrate Jewish education around, let us say, the concept of Palestine with all of its implications, the Jewish teaching profession would receive a new lease of life."

Jew Ed 6 (Jan.–Mar. 1934), 13.

Rappoport, Israel B., and Edward A. Nudelman,

"There is no Jewish educational institution in America that may properly be considered the American Jewish School or even the basis for such a school."
Jew Ed 11 (1939), 105.

Berkson, Isaac B.,
"During the last thirty years, there has been a great change in the character of Jewish education. While the proportion of children in regular attendance has not increased, a larger number now attend organized schools. The teachers are better trained, several well-directed teachers' training schools have been developed. The American-born teacher now has a competent knowledge of Hebrew, Jewish literature and history; the foreign-born teachers, who still are superior in Jewish knowledge, include men of excellent general education and pedagogical ability. Text books have been greatly improved; in some cases these are as good as those used in the public schools. The courses of study have been broadened to include history, current problems, singing, celebration of holidays and various extra-curricular activities, as well, as a much more systematic teaching of Hebrew."
Jan 1, 66–67.

Blumenfield, Samuel M.,
"There is common agreement that the early twenties constituted the golden age in Jewish educational aspirations and endeavors in America.... The Russian Revolution of 1917, the Balfour Declaration, the Treaty of Versailles and its provisions for minority rights; all these brought about a heightened mood of optimism in all spheres of Jewish life, including education....

In America, for the first time in the history of the Jewish diaspora, society and government, instead of seeking to disparage the Jewish cultural and religious heritage or to convert its followers to another creed, are favoring the Jewish group to remain loyal to its faith and traditions. This new positive influence of the American environment should contribute to the strengthening of the Jewish school."
Jew Ed 21 (Winter 1949), 44, 48.

Konvitz, Milton R.,
"A tradition must be won and won over. The process by which one takes it is not possession, but repossession."
Jud 1 (1952), 18.

Dushkin, Alexander M.,
"If we conceive of Jewish living as consisting of four levels (madregot) of being, the last generation of American Jews has succeeded in establishing rather firmly the two lower ones: the biological level of identification and belonging, and the social level of fellowship and participation. During the coming years the struggle will be to raise Jewish living to the two higher madregot: the cultural level of study and knowledge of source materials, and the ethical level of integrating Jewish culture into personality and behavior."
Jew Ed 30 (Fall 1959), 77–78.

Ben-Horin, Meir,
"Jewish education in the first half of the twentieth century was made more attractive, more pertinent, more meaningful. Physical conditions of Jewish schools became aesthetically more satisfying. Textbooks appealing to the eye as well as the mind replaced older models or European imports. Activities came into the life of the school. Clubs, arts, crafts, congregations junior version, were introduced in accordance with Dewey's insistence that better learning requires better doing instead of mere absorbing. Newer forms of educational structure were developed, such as foundation schools and summer camps. Teacher education programs reflected emphasis on learners' needs, interests, differences, capacities. We may think of these results of Dewey's impact on Jewish education as a managerial revolution, an industrial, technological revolution affecting the life of the school just as applied science affects the life of society as a whole."
Quoted by Ronald Kronish in *Stu*, 1:188, from *Recon* (Oct. 30, 1959).

Dushkin, Alexander M., and Uriah Z. Engelman,
"The over-all 'finding' of the Study confirms the general opinion that much progress has been made during the past decades (a) toward interesting parents and community leaders in the Jewish education of their children, (b) toward increas-

45 ASSESSMENT

ing enrollment in the Jewish schools, and (c) toward promoting in the children the sense of Jewish identification and of satisfying fellowship; but that, (d) little has been accomplished toward teaching our children the literary-historic culture of their people. Consequently American Jewish schooling is like a shallow river, 'a mile wide and an inch deep.'

During the coming decades combined cooperative efforts need to be made to deepen the stream of Jewish education....

Congregations should be encouraged to limit one-day schooling attendance only to the primary grades (ages 5–7) and require all children thereafter to attend weekday afternoon schools."

Jewish Education in the United States: Report of the Commission for the Study of Jewish Education in the United States, 222, 234. 1959.

Cohen, Jack J.,
"Jewish education has nothing to fear from a confrontation with the often-harsh reality surrounding the Jewish school; it has everything to fear from a continuation of the present ostrichlike burying of the head in the sands of denominational confines."

In *JEDS*, 77.

Mark, Yudl, on "unbalanced schools,"
"There is nowhere a well-rounded Jewishness, only one's particular version of Judaism.... Are the children of the orthodox schools told of the strong conservative movement and its schools? Are reform Jews studied in conservative schools? And in all these religious schools—are the secular Jews and their culture discussed there?.... The demand is not cease what you are. The demand is only: do not persuade yourselves and do not persuade your children that you are the only 'true' Jews in this country. Tolerance ... must not begin with adults. It must be present already in the school atmosphere. Is it? Among us it is easier to get acceptance that all men are men, than to get acceptance of the survival-ensuring principle that all Jews are Jews. ... Granted the 'versions', but there must be some balance between 'version' and the entire community."

In *JJS*, 194.

Janowsky, Oscar I.,
"This survey of trends has outlined areas in which considerable progress has been made in Jewish education. Enrollments have multiplied; school facilities and methods have been modernized; efforts have been made to advance the professional status of teachers; and community-wide coordinating services have been furnished to many of the schools. Especially noteworthy has been the increasing acceptance of Jewish education by parents, children, and the general community. However, Jewish education is beset by serious problems which hamper the realization of the school's objectives. The efforts of Jewish educators have not yielded commensurate pupil achievement."

In *Jan 2*, 152.

Weisberg, Harold,
"Throughout Jewish history, creeds, beliefs, 'positions' and theologies were never enough. Significant Jewish ideologies require institutional embodiments and forms of communal identification. Jewish ideologies which are predominately expressions of dissatisfaction with Judaism and the Jewish community, or are largely positions emphasizing the anxiety of the age and the perils of existence will not be significant alternatives to the dominant direction of American Jewish ideology without the institutionalization and communal identification characteristic of the best in traditional and modern (not contemporary) Jewish ideologies."

In *Jan 2*, 358.

Schindler, Alexander M.,
"There is much that we can do to deepen the devotion of our children to the larger community, to extend their reach of heart and mind to encompass all of Israel.... We can begin by teaching Judaism in our schools, teaching it, moreover, not as some kind of denominational possession, but as a shared possession to which variant interpretations have a vital relation. And when we speak of our differences as they really are, we can approach them, examine them—teacher and student both—in an atmosphere of respectful in-

quiry. We can bring our children into contact with one another crossing denominational barriers for communal programs of education and for united activity arising to advance our common cause. Surely more than ideas are involved in our problem. People are involved. The sense of communion is sustained by encounter."

Remarks before the RA 66th Annual Convention, May 18, 1966.

Lisitzky, Ephraim E.,
"Whatever the reason for the failure of Jewish education in America, in no way is the child himself to be blamed for it. I had ample opportunity to get to know this child well during my years of teaching. He is excellent human material, free from the dross ghetto life used to deposit in his counterpart across the ocean. What is more, through the public school he comes into possession of the American culture which potentially is a blessing to Jewish education, for he is thus better prepared to absorb the highest that Jewish culture has to offer."

Quoted by Blumenfield in *Lown*, 86.

Alter, Robert,
"I would contend that we have little prospect for surviving as a distinctive community unless there are appreciable number of Jews—however strong their linguistic loyalty to English—who are capable of reading the Bible in its original language, who understand the Hebrew of the prayerbook and of rabbinic law and legend, and for whom the reborn language of Israel, if not fully intelligible, is at least not a foreign tongue. We are, by general standards, a highly educated community, but in regard to knowledge of Jewish culture, rank ignorance prevails, as much among Jewish Ph.D's as among Jewish cab-drivers."

Commentary 46 (July 1968), 62.

Elazar, Daniel J.,
"If the implications of the community studies for Jewish education were to be summarized in a single sentence, it would be that Jewish education can be blamed for many deficiencies but that it is not to blame for the present condition of American Jewry. The word 'blame' is used here advisedly, even though the situation is more mixed than the word might indicate. If this article is generally pessimistic, it should not obscure the curious and at times surprising opportunities for educating Jews present in today's American Jewish community, either."

"What the Community Studies Tell Us." *Ped Rep* (Mar. 1970), 3.

Blumenfield, Samuel M.,
"The sad reality remains that except for the arduous labors in the Orthodox sector in behalf of the Jewish Day School, one can hardly point to a single new Jewish education enterprise, within the last forty years, of enduring value or importance."

Jew Ed 40 (Spring 1971), 48.

Weinberger, Paul,
"While American Jewry has enthusiastically seized on secular education as an appropriate vehicle to further career aspirations and facilitate upward social mobility, Jewish education has remained a peripheral enterprise for most American Jews. Preoccupation with secular education, to the exclusion of all else, was understandable for immigrants and first-generation Jews, whose primary goals were to make a decent living and to become integrated into American society. Although these goals have now been fully achieved, Jewish education continues to remain peripheral."

"The Effects of Jewish Education." *AJYB* 72 (1971), 246.

Sklare, Marshall,
"The constant dunning of the Jewish community, the restless urging that it do more and more, is not simply the voice of a few miscontents. This criticism is sensitive to the changing tides of history, it reflects an awareness, however unarticulated, of the awesome responsibilities which have befallen American Jewry, and as often as not, it is directed at encouraging actions which help to assure the survival of Jewish life."

In *JCA*, 16.

Stern, Jay,
"The average Hebrew afternoon school pupils, by Bar/Bat Mitzvah, have spent—if they attend a good Jewish school—the

Rackman, Emanuel,
"The young who get turned off by Jewish education are not doing it because they are rejecting the subject matter. They are rejecting the models."
Jew Ed 45 (Summer/Fall 1977), 11.

Slesinger, Zalmen,
"If Jewish education is to become a creative force in guiding and shaping the future destiny of the Jewish community, it must undergo a fundamental reconstruction. We need a new vision and a fresh design of Jewish education that is reflective of the spirit of our age and the demands of our time; that is receptive to the critical challenges confronting the Jew in the open society; that is receptive to disciplined change, and is concerned with the building and strengthening of Jewish identity within the open society. No piecemeal educational reforms will mend the erosion threatening the fabric of Jewish life."
Jud 28 (Spring 1979), 230.

Margolis, Daniel J. (1975),
"Progressivism was adopted by Jewish educators naively and with all good intentions. They wanted to provide a modern sound educational approach and had not the slightest desire to diminish intrinsic Jewish values. Yet, they seemed to have no notion of what might happen if they adopted a mode of educational thought and practice geared specifically to the American lifestyle and system of values. A strange ideological amalgamation resulted in which the slogans of progressive education—themselves well on the way to thorough misinterpretation by Dewey's students—were transvaluated to accommodate Jewish interests and needs."
Quoted by Ronald Kronish in *Stu*, 1:185.

Schiff, Alvin I.,
"The history of Jewish education in America is marked by many positive accomplishments, including the development of the Jewish day school as a major mode of Jewish schooling; the introduction of modern instructional strategies; the establishment of dynamic teacher center programs; the creative use of media in instruction; the convening of exciting educational conferences, workshops and seminars; the development of central agencies for Jewish education; the building of impressive Jewish educational facilities; the emergence of many outstanding professional leaders in administration and teaching; and especially the development of a wide variety of Israel-American programs such as teenage and family tours, summer and year long study in Israeli educational institutions, teacher education projects and cooperative curriculum activities. . . .

However, despite all the progress that has taken place in Jewish education, the Jewish community in America may soon lose this instrumentality as an effective method for transmitting Jewish heritage and Jewish values. It may lose the institution most needed for Jewish continuity. Now, as never before, Jewish education holds out much promise for assuring the creative continuity of Jewish life and the Jewish people."
Jewish Education at the Crossroads: The State of Jewish Education, 1. N.Y.: BJE, Mar. 1983.

JESNA,
"9. Lastly, the Jewish community must understand that no educational institution will succeed without parental involvement and support. The respondents clearly understood that the disinterest of parents is not only a fact, but a symptom that parents do not really care much and that their expectations are not too high. Therefore, one of the major tests before the community is to deal with the disinterest of parents, which is not a purely a educational, but a communal issue."
Perceptions of Jewish Education, 38. 1983.

Bock, Geoffrey E.,
"Jewish schooling affects Jewish identification to some extent. But the relative effects of school experiences, compared to the relative impact of other factors affecting socialization, depend on the form of identification in question. Jewish school-

ing has relatively greater impact on public Jewishness than Jewishness of family background, all other factors being equal. Jewishness of family background has a relatively greater impact on personal Jewishness than schooling, all other factors being equal. One suspects that public behaviors of being Jewishly identified—such as contributing to a Jewish organization or attending synagogue services—are most easily taught in the formal curricula of Jewish schools than personal practices, attitudes, and beliefs. It comes as little surprise that home environment has the greatest effect on personal Jewishness, as feeling good about being Jewish or having Jewish friends, or practicing Judaism in one's daily life are more private kinds of concerns, which one learns primarily from one's family.... A certain minimum amount of Jewish schooling is necessary before school experiences begin to affect identification. I estimate this critical threshold at 1,000 hours for public Jewishness and 500 hours for personal Jewishness. That is, roughly 8. 2 years of one-day Hebrew school, 3 years of afternoon Hebrew school, and 1.5 years of day school. 1,000 hours is perhaps the more crucial threshold."

"The Functions of Jewish Schooling in America." In *Stu*, 2:252–54.

Weinberg, Julius,

"Recent studies in education demonstrate clearly that the educational enterprise of any society—its techniques, goals and values—cannot be divorced from the greater society from which it is derived. Similarly, the fate of Jewish education rests ultimately on the ideology of the American-Jewish community, what priorities it sets for itself and with what skills and intensity of purpose these goals are pursued. To date, from the late nineteenth century to the present, Jewish education has been of only marginal concern to the organized Jewish community—in terms of funding, personnel, institutional arrangements, and pedagogic technique.... We are at a point where the continuity of the American-Jewish community is too critical a matter to be left to educators alone. The priorities that American-Jewry sets for itself are more than a mirror of its ideology, they are at the same time, a prognostication of its future."

"The 'Greening' of Jewish Education." *Jud* 34 (Spring 1985), 196.

Siegel, Morton,

"A. To begin with, the need for reemphasis on teaching Judaism is 'ethic' rather than 'ethnic.' Ethnicity, which stresses identity ('Jewishness is in the blood') is no substitute for ethicity which stresses that 'Jewishness is in the doing.' Put otherwise, the rehabilitation of elementary Jewish education as a discipline of sense and reason, not primarily sensation and feeling, is essential. Hence the reemphasis on theology and ideology—yedah rather than regesh....

C. Methodologically, elementary education must move away from 'viewing' to 'reading-studying.' The penchant to imitate secular educational enterprises which accentuate teaching the child to look at things rather than to read and understand these things require redress. Put otherwise, children are now being trained to 'find answers' rather than to think through answers. The computer, which simulates reason to facilitate finding a solution, with its popularity has become a basic tool for Jewish education—and prototypes a tendency to teach to response rather than to thought....

E. It is necessary to halt the excess Israelization of the elementary educational process. Jewish elementary education should mediate Jewishness/Judaism as a matter how one lives rather than where one lives. Without in any way questioning the self-evident significance of Israel to the Jew, the advocacy of Israel as the cornerstone of Jewishness, rather than recognizing life style as the cornerstone must be reversed. Israel is to be presented as part of Jewishness, and not, as is done today, Jewishness as part of Israel."

"The Afternoon School." *Jud* 36 (Spring 1987), 218–19.

Schiff, Alvin I. (study director),

1. Transform the Educational Thrust of the Synagogue from Supplementary Schooling for Pupils to Jewish Family Ed-

ucation.

a) Change the education focus of the synagogue from schooling of the young to education of all members of the family.

b) Change the structure of the synagogue to accomplish the above. In the new structure, all synagogue professionals, including the rabbi, principal, teachers, youth leader and cantor, will become members of a family educator team, with the rabbi assuming the role of Judaic content leader.

c) Sensitize and reeducate synagogue lay leadership regarding the family focus of synagogue education and the changing roles of synagogue professionals.

d) Educate parents regarding the family focus of synagogue education.

e) Orient rabbis to the family focus of synagogue education and their potential involvement in family education programs.

f) Encourage rabbinic seminaries and educator training institutes to incorporate Jewish family education components in the pre-service training of rabbis and educators.

g) Involve Jewish knowledgeable workers with expertise in family education and group work in planning and implementing Jewish family education programs. Involve schools of social work in the process of retraining synagogue professionals as Jewish family educators."

Jewish Supplementary Schooling: An Educational System in Need of Change, 133–34. N.Y.: BJE, 1988.

46 | THE FUTURE OF JEWISH EDUCATION

VIEWS PRIOR TO 1950

Benderly, Samson. "The Next Decade in Jewish Education." *Jew Ed* 4 (Jan.–Mar. 1932): 14–17, 62.

Chipkin, Israel S. "Ten Years of Jewish Education—Era of Progress, Pattern for the Future." *Day* (June 15, 1949).

Davis, J. "The Future of American Jewish Education." *NCJSS Proceedings* (1926): 272–73.

Dinin, Samuel. "Jewish Education Faces the Future." *Recon* 13 (Feb. 6, 1948): 11–18.

Gamoran, Emanuel. "The Curriculum of the Future Jewish Sunday School." *Jew Ed* 5 (Jan.–Mar. 1933): 31–39.

Isaacs, Nathan. "The Future of the Jewish Student in America." *Jewish Forum* 5 (1922): 131–41.

Kaminetsky, Joseph. "The Talmud Torah Looks to the Future." *Jew Life* 14 (Dec. 1946).

Lefkowitz, David. "Religious Education and the Future of American Judaism." *CCAR* 29 (1919): 306–15.

Neumann, Abraham A. "The Future of Torah in America." In *Landmarks and Goals*, 321–32. 1948.

Touroff, Nissan. "Jewish Education for the Moment or for the Future?" *Jew Ed* 16 (May 1945): 30–37.

———. "הוה ועתיד בחנוך העברי" (The Present and Future in Jewish Education). *Bitzaron* (H.) 6 (Apr. 1943): 11–17.

———. "שלשה דברים" (Three Issues). *Hadoar* (H.) 15 (16th of Iyyar 1936).

VIEWS SINCE 1950

Arian, Philip. "1989: The New Hebrew School." *Ed As* (1968): 71–76.

Azneer, J. L. "Community Education and the Future of the Synagogue." *Syn Sch* 8 (Feb. 1950).

Baron, Salo W. "Future of American Jewry." *Day* (Sept. 21, 1964).

Blumenfield, Samuel M. "Toward a World Jewish Education Assembly." *Recon* (Oct. 6, 1961): 10–12.

Borowitz, Eugene. "Facing the Future of Jewish Education." *Jew Ed* 45 (Spring 1977): 33–40.

Braver, Joseph. "Jewish Education: A Backward Look—September 2078." *Jew Ed* 46 (Autumn 1978): 37–39.

Chomsky, William. "American Jewish Life and Education in Retrospect and Prospect." *Jew Ed* 40 (Spring 1971): 20–23.

Cohen, Jack J. "The Future of the Congregational School." In *JEDS*, 277–99.

———. "The Future of the Hebrew Teacher." *Jew Ed* 21 (Spring 1957): 18–22.

Dinin, Samuel. "The Future of Hebrew in America." *Congress Weekly* (Oct. 1961): 7–10.

———. "The Future of Hebrew Teacher Education." *Jew Ed* 34 (Fall 1963): 29–35.

———. "The Future of the Jewish Teaching Profession." *Jew Ed* 35 (Fall 1964): 3.

———. "The Future of the Profession of Jewish Education." *Jew Ed* 15 (Jan. 1944): 79–84.

Eisenberg, Azriel. "The NCJE Faces the Future." *Jew Ed* 32 (Fall 1961): 43–44.

Freehof, Solomon B. "American Jewish Education in the Future." *CCAR* 64 (1954): 175–85.

Frost, Shimon. "Any Change Will Be for the Better: On the Future of Supplementary Schooling." *Jew Ed* 56 (Summer 1988): 32–33.

Gillette, Robert H. "Our Educational Future." *NATE* (24th Annual Conference, Dec. 1978): 13–16.

Goldman, Solomon. "The Jewish Supplementary School in 1990—What Will It Be Like?" *Jew Ed* 51 (Summer 1983): 25–26.

Goodman, Saul. "The Future of the Jewish Secular School." *Recon* (May 29, 1964): 7–13.

Mayer, Egon. *Future—A National Study in Summary*. N.Y.: AJC, 1979.

Millgram, Abraham E. "The Future of Jewish Education in America." *The Torch* (Winter 1956). See also *RTJS*, 205–13.

NATE. *Shaping Our Destiny: The New Temple Educator*. (24th Annual Conference, Dec. 1978). 81 pp.

Schafler, Samuel. "The Future of Congregational Schools." *Jew Ed* 46 (Fall 1978): 16–18, 25.

Scharfstein, Zevi. „עתידו של 'תלמוד התורה' בארצות הברית" (The Future of the Talmud Torah in the United States). *Hadoar* (H.) 30 (Shevat 19, 1951).

Schiff, Alvin I. "Looking Towards the 21st Century: Who Needs Hebrew Teachers in Our Supplementary Schools?" (editorial). *Jew Ed* 5 (Winter 1983): 3–7.

Schindler, Alexander. "The Future of the Synagogue." *NATE* (18th Annual Conference, Dec. 1972): 1–16.

Sherman, Bezalel C. „די צוקונפטיקע אידישע קהילה אין אמעריקע" (The Jewish Community of the Future in America). *YK* (Y.) (Sept. 1, 1950): 6–9.

Shulman, Charles E. *Jewish Education Looks Ahead*. N.Y.: AAJE, 1952. 8 pp.

Siegel, Morton. "The Future Curriculum of the Jewish School." In *New Directions in the Jewish School Curriculum*, edited by Braver and Frost, 30–39. Ed As, 1972.

———. "Toward a Decade of Promise." *Ed As* (1970): 23–28.

Slesinger, Zalmen. "Educational Policy for an Emerging Age." *Ped Rep* 14 (Nov. 1962): 7–10, 22.

Sobel, Z. "The Future of the Reform Synagogue." *Dimensions* 3 (Summer 1969): 14–16.

Spiro, Jack D. "Jewish Education—Today and Tomorrow." *CCAR* 78 (1968): 200–214.

Stein, J. "Design for the Future." *Un Syn Rev* 22 (Winter 1970).

Tannenbaum, Marc H. "Religious Education in the Future Tense." *Rel Ed* 68 (Mar.–Apr. 1973): 157–69.

GLEANINGS

Neuman, Abraham A. (1945),
"Will American Jewry meet the requirements to assure a future for Torah in America? There are hopeful signs. On the lower elementary level there is a growing awareness of the need of intensifying Jewish education. The drive for increased enrollment is giving way to the more urgent need of improving the content and quality of the existing educational program. Hours of instruction are being increased in all systems from the Sunday School to the weekly Talmud Torah. Most significant is the starting of Hebraically con-

ducted summer school camps and the all-day Jewish School."
Landmarks and Goals, 329. 1953.

Baron, Salo W.,
"When we speak about the future of the Jews in America, quality is at least as important as quantity. If I were assured today that a generation hence we shall have 100 first-rate Jewish scholars, 100 first-rate rabbis, 100 first-rate teachers, 100 first-rate communal leaders and 100 first-rate writers, publicists and artists, their total number would amount to only 500, which in a population of some five million would be just one-hundredth of one per cent. Nevertheless, I should feel assured of a great future for the Jews in this country."
Jew Ed 19 (Spring 1948), 13.

Arendt, Hannah,
"What the future of Jewish spiritual life in this country seems to need more than anything else is the development and education of independent individual scholars, who by the very excellency of their work can set the standards for the organized research work which will be carried out by the great organizations anyhow."
YA 4 (1949), 292.

Honor, Leo L.,
"The Jewish school of tomorrow is to be seen dimly on the horizon. In that school Jewish youth will be afforded the opportunity to engage in satisfying Jewish experiences which will lead many of them to try to master the Hebrew language, the key to the treasure house of Jewish spiritual values, and, through the imbibing of these values, to develop for themselves patterns of Jewish living in which these values have been imbedded."
JQR 45 (1955), 496.

Millgram, Abraham E.,
"When God chose Abraham to be the leader of our people, He justified that choice by saying: "For I am certain that he (Abraham) will instruct his children and his household after him that they keep the way of the Lord to do righteousness and justice." I cannot speak with the same certainty. I must add to my prophecy a number of "ifs." If the leaders of Conservative Judaism in America will be thoroughly imbued with the conviction that Jewish education must at all times receive first priority in all congregational activities, then I am certain that the people and the households of our communities will instruct their children to keep the way of the Lord. Our efforts will in time transform the climate for Jewish education in our communities and in the children's homes. A new generation of willing students, devoted teachers, and an adequate school program will be the blessings of American Jewish life."
"The Future of Jewish Education in America." *The Torch* (Winter 1956.) Also in *RJTS*, 213.

47 BIBLIOGRAPHIES OF JEWISH EDUCATION IN OTHER LANDS

GENERAL (SELECTED)

Abbink, Jon. "A Bibliography on the Ethiopian Jews, 1958–1984." *Studies in Jewish Bibliography and Booklore* 16 (1986): 37–48.

BJE, Toronto. *Pedagogic Bibliography*. 1954. 27 pp.

Bloch, Joshua. *Jewish Life in Oriental Societies: A List of Books and Manuscripts Exhibited at the New York Public Library, March 30th thru December 31, 1926* (general list with some educational items). N.Y.: New York Public Library, 1927. 15 pp.

Buckley, J. J. "Janus Korczak Bibliography." *Studies in Bibliography and Booklore* 9 (Winter 1975–76): 85–92.

Engelman, Uriah Z. *Jewish Education in Europe, 1914–1962* (annotated bibliography). Jerusalem: Institute of Contemporary Jewry of Department of Jewish Education in the Diaspora, 1965. 430 pp.

Halevi, Meshullam, ed. „מדריך ביבליוגרפי לספרות פדגוגית [בעברית] ולאמצעי עזר בהוראה" (Bibliographic Guide to Hebrew Pedagogic Literature and Instructional Aids) (H.). 4 vols. Jerusalem: Ministry of Education and Culture, 1963–64.

Lehmann, Ruth P. *Nova Bibliotheca Anglo-Judaica: A Bibliographical Guide to Anglo-Jewish History, 1937–1960*. London: Jewish Historical Society of England, 1961. 232 pp.

Liebman, Seymour B. *A Guide to Jewish References in the Mexican Colonial Era, 1521–1821*. Phila.: U. of Pennsylvania Press, 1964. 134 pp.

Mishkin, L. Y. "Festschriften of Jewish Educational Institutions" (lists publications from 1834 to 1961). *Studies in Bibliography and Booklore* 5 (June 1961): 92–101.

Ormian, Hayim Yosef. „ביבליוגראפיה פדגוגית יהודית" (A Bibliography of Jewish Pedagogy). In *Ed Enc* (H.), 1:819–26.

Poops, M. „דערציאונג ... ביי יידן" (Jewish Education and Pedagogy) (Y.). *Bibliographic Annuals of Yivo* (1928): 105–17. 375 entries.

Roth, Cecil. *Magna Bibliotheca Anglo-Judaica: A Bibliographical Guide to Anglo-Jewish History*. London: Jewish Historical Society of England, 1937. 463 pp.

Shmeruk, Kh., ed., and Yosef Yizhak Cohen, comp. „פרסומים יהקדיים בברית-המועצות" (Bibliography of Jewish Publications in the Soviet Union, 1917–1960) (H. and Y.). 2 vols. Jerusalem: Historical Society of Israel, 1961. 502 pp. See "Education and Texts" (H.), pp. 33–37, item nos. 290–309, and p. 409, item nos. 3930–31; "Education and Texts" (Y.), pp. 263–311, item nos. 2744–3272, and 415–16, item nos. 3985–92; "Education and Texts" (Russian), pp. 11–235, item nos. 1–1399.

Shunami, Shlomo. „מפתח המפתחות" (Bibliography of Jewish Bibliographies) (H.). References are in language written and are international. Jerusalem: Magnes Press, Hebrew U., 1969. 997 pp. See "Education," pp. 275–90, item nos. 1568–1644.

TEXTBOOKS (SELECTED)

Anilowicz, J. „הוספות צו דער ביבליאגראפיע ייִדישע לערנביכער און פּעדאגאגיק" "1900–1933 (Supplement to Yiddish Textbooks and Pedagogy, 1931–1933). *Studies in Psychology and Education* (Y.) 2 (1940): 330–37.

———. „ייִדישע לערנביכער און פּעדאגאגיק" "1939–1934 (Yiddish Texts and Pedagogy, 1934–1939). *Studies in Psychology and Education* (Y.) 2 (1940): 293–329. 705 entries.

———, and M. Yoffe. „ייִדישע לערנביכער און פּעדאגאגיק" (Yiddish Textbooks and Pedagogy, 1900–1930). *Studies in Psychology and Education* (Y.) 1 (1933): 465–528. Includes texts in general studies, such as math, nature, and so forth. 893 entries. See also "Yiddish Textbooks and Pedagogy, 1931–1933." *YB* (Y.) 7 (1934): 165–88 (item nos. 1–325).

Assaf, Simha. „ספרי למוד במשך הדורות בארצות שונות" (Textbooks That Have Been Published through the Generations in Various Countries). In his מקורות לתולדות „החינוך בישראל" (Sources for the History of Jewish Education) (H.), 4:254–328. Jerusalem: Rabbi Kook Publishing House. 348 entries prior to 1840.

Engelman, Uriah Z. "Textbooks, Other Materials, and Student Publications." In his *Jewish Education in Europe, 1914–1962*, 328–78. 165 entries.

Gudemann, M. *Quellenschriften* (Sources on the History of Instruction and Education of German Jewry until Mendelssohn) (G.). Berlin: A. Hofmann and Co., 1891. 324 pp. Includes index of textbooks in German and Hebrew.

Scharfstein, Zevi. „ספרי לימוד וזרמים חברתיים" (Textbooks and Social Currents) (19th-century Hebrew textbooks in Europe from Mapu to Fichman). In *Sefer Hashanah* (H.) (1929): 260–75. Also in his *ES* (H.), 115–40.

Shatzky, Jacob. „א ביבליאגראפיע פון ייִדישע שולביכער אין קאנגרעס־פּוילן פון די יארן

1864–1817" (A Bibliography of Yiddish Textbooks Written from 1817 to 1864.) In *Jewish Educational Policies in Poland from 1806 to 1866* (Y.), 224–28. N.Y.: Yivo, 1943. 34 entries.

Strassburger, Baruch. "Bibliography on Jewish Pedagogy in Chronological Sequence, 1200 C.E.–1882." In his *History of Jewish Education and Instruction* (G.), 273–318. Stuttgart: 1885.

PERIODICALS AND PRESS (SELECTED)

Berlin, Charles. "Jewish Bibliographic Journals" *JBA* (1971–72): 22–38.

Cukier, G. *Canadian Jewish Periodicals: A Preliminary Listing*. Montreal: Jewish Public Library, 1939. 30 pp.

Enc Jud. "Press." 13:1023–56. Arranged by countries, with extensive bibliograhy on p. 1056.

Fraenkel, Josef. *The Jewish Press of the World*. London: World Jewish Congress, ca. 1961. 104 pp., 933 entries.

„קרית ספר" (*Kiryat Sefer*) (H.) (bibliographical quarterly of the Jewish National and University Library). Jerusalem. 1924–present. Includes section on education and periodicals in Israel and other countries.

Kosover, Mordecai. „געשיכטע פון דער העברעישער פּרעסע" (History of the Hebrew Press). In *Algemeine Encyclopedia* (Y.), 3:284–350. 38 entries.

Ormian, Hayim Yosef. „כתבי־עת יהודיים" (Jewish Educational Periodicals). In *Ed Enc* (H.), 1:844–49.

Poops, M., comp. „ביבליאגראפישע יארביכער פון ייִוואָ" (Worldwide Bibliography of Yiddish Journals and Newspapers in 1926). In *Yearbook of Yiddish Bibliography* (Y.), 102–19 (item nos. 1694–2186). Warsaw: Kulturliga Pub. Co., 1928.

Reisin, Zalmen. „ייִדישע פּעריאדישע אויסגאבן" "(1913–1686) (Yiddish Periodicals, 1686–1913). In his *Lexicon of the Yiddish Literature and Press* (Y.), 661–742. Warsaw: 1914. Annotated.

47 BIBLIOGRAPHIES OF JEWISH EDUCATION IN OTHER LANDS

Schwab, Moise. *Index of Articles Relative to Jewish History and Literature Published in Periodicals from 1665 to 1900*. N.Y.: Ktav, 1971. 613 pp.

Shatzky, Jacob. „געשיכטע פון דער יידישער פרעסע" (History of the Yiddish Press). In *Algemeine Encyclopedia* (Y.), 3:201–84.

Shayn, Israel. „מאטעריאלן צו א ביבליאגראפיע פון יידישער פעריאדיקע אין פוילן 1918-1939" (Materials for a Bibliography of Jewish Periodicals in Independent Poland). In *Studies on Polish Jewry, 1919–1939* (Y. and Polish), edited by Joshua A. Fishman, 422–83. N.Y.: Yivo, 1974.

Shulman, V. „פרעטע ביי יידן אין אנדעדע שפראכן" (Jewish Press in Other Languages). In *Algemeine Encyclopedia* (Y.), 3:354–68.

Shunami, Shlomo. "Periodicals" (listed by language). In *Shunami*, 94–128 (item nos. 515–723).

48 | BIBLIOGRAPHIES OF JEWISH EDUCATION AND RELATED FIELDS IN THE UNITED STATES

JUDAISM AND JEWISH LIFE—GENERAL (SELECTED)

ADL. *Jews in American Life: A Selected Bibliography*. N.Y.

ADL. *Teaching about Jews and Judaism: Bibliographic and Audio-Visual Aids*. N.Y.: 15 pp.

AJC. *Media Information Bulletin*. N.Y.: Commission on Jewish Life and Culture.

Berlin, Charles, ed. *Index to Festschriften in Jewish Studies*. N.Y.: Ktav, 1971.

Bloch, Joshua, comp. *The People and the Book: The Background of 300 Years of Jewish Life in America* (annotated list of illuminated manuscripts, rare books, authentic documents, and related materials.) N.Y.: New York Public Library, 1954. 134 pp.

Brickman, William W. *The Jewish Community in America: An Annotated and Classified Bibliographical Guide*. N.Y.: Burt Franklin, 1977. 396 pp. See "Education," pp. 147–65.

Brisman, Shimeon. *A History and Guide to Judaic Bibliography*. 2 vols. Cincinnati: HUC Press and Ktav, 1977, 1989.

Con Jud. "A Selective Bibliography on Conservative Judaism." 1 (Jan. 1945).

Cutter, Charles, and Micha Falk Oppenheim. *Jewish Reference Sources: A Selective, Annotated Bibliographic Guide*. N.Y.: Garland Publishing, 1982. 180 pp.

Deinard, Ephraim. *Koheleth America* (H.). Includes an annotated bibliography of Hebrew books published in America, 1735–1926. St. Louis: Moinester, 1926.

Efron, Benjamin, comp., and Lionel Koppman. *Multi-Media Resources on the Jewish Community: A Selected, Annotated and Graded Listing of Materials for Teaching Jewish Civics*. NCRI, Spring 1973. 98 pp.

Endelman, Judith E. "Judaica Americana." *AJHQ* 64 (1974): 55–68; 64 (1974–75): 149–60, 245–57, 344–57. (See also Kaganoff, Nathan.)

Goodman, Hannah Grad. *Aspects of Jewish Life: A Selected and Annotated Bibliography of Books and Multimedia Materials*. N.Y.: JBC, 1974. 111 pp.

Hadassah. *Recommended Books of Jewish Interest*. N.Y.: 1968.

JWB Jewish Book Council. *Jewish Book Annual* (1942–present). Includes annually newly published books, fiction and nonfiction, in English, Hebrew and Yiddish.

———. *Jewish Reference Books: A Selected List*. N.Y.: 1970, 16 pp.

Kaganoff, Nathan M. "Judaica Americana: An Annotated Bibliography of Monographic and Periodical Literature Published since 1960 and Received in the Library of the American Jewish Historical Society." General Works: Bibliogra-

48 BIBLIOGRAPHIES OF JEWISH EDUCATION AND RELATED FIELDS IN THE UNITED STATES

phy, Historiography, Local History, Periodicals. Special Studies: Biography, Cultural Life, Education, Geneology, Relations with Non-Jews, Relations Overseas, Sociology, Synagogue History, Zionism. *AJHQ* 52 (1962–63): 58–66, 152–58, 244–51, 320–55; 53 (1963–64): 179–87, 396–403; 54 (1964–65): 202–9, 450–59; 55 (1965): 235–44, 521–29; 56 (1966–67): 232–40, 457–65; 57 (1967–68): 254–62, 573–81; 58 (1968–69): 278–86, 507–14; 59 (1969–70): 215–22, 523–31; 60 (1970–71): 185–94, 383–92; 61 (1971–72): 157–66, 353–60; 62 (1972–73): 171–79, 401–13; 65 (1975): 163–74, 353–67.

Linzer, Norman, ed. *Jewish Communal Services in the United States, 1900–1970: A Selective Bibliography.* N.Y.: Federation of Jewish Philanthropies, 1972.

Lubetski, Edith, and Meir Lubetski. *Building a Judaica Library Collection and Resource Guide.* Littleton, Colo.: Libraries Unlimited Inc.

Marcus, Jacob R. *An Index to Jewish Festschriften 1937.* Reprint ed. N.Y.: Kraus Reprint, 1970. See pp. 36, 37, and 119.

———. *An Index to Scientific Articles on American Jewish History.* N.Y.: American Jewish Archives and Ktav, 1971. See "Education," pp. 61–64.

Oppenheim, Micha F. *The Study and Practice of Judaism: A Selected Annotated List.* N.Y.: Published by Torah Resources, 1979. 78 pp.

Patai, Raphael, ed. "Education." In *Current Jewish Social Research*, 26–31. N.Y.: Theodor Herzl Foundation, 1958.

Rossoff, Don. "Reform Judaism—An Annotated Bibliography of Learning Materials." A listing of the books and other media that can be of use for the study of Reform Judaism. Master's project, HUC–JIR, 1979.

Rothenberg, Joshua, comp. *Judaica Reference Materials—A Selective and Annotated Bibliography.* Waltham, Mass.: Brandeis U., 1971. 87 pp.

Schneider, Ilene. "Where Can I Find . . .?: Resources for Jewish Education." *Recon* 54 (Dec. 1988): 29–31.

Schwartz, Berbie G., ed. *The ATID Bibliography: A Resource for the Questioning Jew.* N.Y.:

USA Department of Youth Activities, 1977. 153 pp.

Segall, Aryeh, ed. *Guide to Jewish Archives* (lists 60 Jewish archival centers, research institutes, and organizations that preserve Jewish archival materials in the United States, Canada, Israel, Australia, and Europe). N.Y.: National Foundation for Jewish Culture, 1981.

Warburg, Ronnie F. "A Bibliographic Guide to Mishpot Ivri" (Jewish law books and articles in English). *National Jewish Law Review* 1 (1986): 61–135.

ייװא—ביבליאגראפיע (Bibliography of Yivo Publications, 1925–1950) (Y.). 2 vols. Vilna and N.Y.: Yivo, 1943, 1955. For pedagogy, see 1:132–35 (item nos. 1616–57), 1:186–87 (item nos. 2376–79), 1:196 (item nos. 2472–74), 2:99–102 (item nos. 3679–720), 2:151 (item nos. 4393–97).

Zafran, Herbert C. "Jewish Reference Books: A Select List." *JBA* 20 (1962–63): 57–69; 28 (1970–71): 56–71.

EDUCATION

Ben-Horin, Meir. "Major Writings in American Jewish Education." *Jew Ed* 30 (Spring 1960): 4–15.

Blumenfield, Samuel M. "Books on the History and Philosophy of Jewish Education." *JBA* 25 (1967–68): 155–64.

Brickman, William W. "Selected Bibliography of Jewish Education in Historical and International Perspective." *Jew Ed* 41 (Fall 1972): 46–51.

Buber, Martin M., and Haim Y. Ormian, eds. "אנציקלופדיה חינוכית" (Educational Encyclopedia: Thesaurus of Jewish and General Education) (H.). 5 vols. Jerusalem: Ministry of Education and Culture and Bialik Institute, 1961–69. Includes Jewish education in the United States and other lands and extensive bibliographies in the language of the original publications.

Edelstein, Menachem M. "ספרות חנוכית" (Educational Literature) (H.). *JBA* (1943–45): 39–

43 (H. section). See also *JBA* (1946–47): 41–43 (H. section).

Gamoran, Emanuel. "Selected Bibliography." In *Changing Conceptions in Jewish Education*, Part 1, 213–28; Part 2, 177–84. N.Y.: Macmillan, 1924.

Golub, Jacob S. "A Bibliography on Jewish Education." *JBA* 2 (1943–44): 31–40.

Jeshurin, Ephim H. "ביבליאגרפישע רשימה פון ארטיקלען וואס זיינען דערשינען אין דער 'צוקונפט' אין משך פון 50 יאר וועגן דער וועלטלעכער שול, יידישען יוגנט, און קינדער דערציאונג" (Bibliography of Articles that Appeared in the *Zukunft* over a period of 50 years [1892–1942] on the Secular School. Jewish Youth, and Education for Children). *CE* (Y.) 12 (1942): 19–20.

———. "ביבליאגרפיע וועגן שול-באוועגונג און דערציאונגס פראבלעמען" (Bibliography of the School Movement and Educational Problems) (Yiddish secular schools). In *One Hundred Years of Modern Yiddish Literature* (Y.), 260–541. N.Y.: WC Education Committee, 1965. See "Education," Part 2, for more than 4,000 entries from Yiddish periodicals and newspapers in the United States and other lands.

JESNA. *Jewish Curriculum for the Armed Forces Part II: Resource Guide Update, 1982–83*. Miami: JESNA and CAJE. 91 pp.

JESNA. *Jewish Curriculum for the Armed Forces Part II: Resource Guide Update, 1984*. Miami: JESNA and CAJE, 1984.

JESNA. *Materials-Resource Guide for Jewish Education*. Miami: JESNA and CAJE, 1980. 336 pp.

Malachi, Eliezer R. "אישים בחנוך" (Educators). In *JB* (H.), 363–64. 34 entries

———. "ספרות החנוך העברית באמריקה" (Literature on Hebrew Education in America). In *JB* (H.), 361–96. 729 annotated entries.

———. "מקורות לתולדות החינוך העברי באמריקה" (Source Materials on Jewish Education in America). *Sh Hah* (H.) 38 (1979): 156–61, 217–22; 39 (1980): 57–60, 111–14.

Ped Rep. "Co-Curricular Materials for the Jewish School: A Bibliography." 4 (May 1953).

Rubin, George. *An Annotated Bibliography of Individualized Instruction in Jewish Schools: A Listing with Description of Programs of Individual Instruction*. Includes several articles that evaluate the quality of contemporary education. Master's thesis, HUC–JIR, 1975.

Targan, Judith. "Bibliography for the Educated and the Educator." In *Cat 2*, 201–7.

USCJE. *Bibliography of Reference and Methodological Materials for the Jewish Teacher*. N.Y.: 1973.

WZO. *Jewish Education in the Diaspora: A Selected Bibliography*. Jerusalem: World Zionist Organization, 1962. 64 pp.

ADULT EDUCATION (SELECTED)

Feinstein, Morley. *Resources for Aging: An Annotated Bibliography for Synagogue Programming*. Designed for teachers, this cumulative bibliography has been created to aid those in synagogue settings who work with older people. Master's project, HUC–JIR, 1979.

Fischler, Ben-Zion. *A Bibliography in Teaching Hebrew to Adults*. N.Y.: Dec. 1964.

JBC. *A Booklist for the Jewish Adult*. N.Y.: 1970. 20 pp.

Singer, Jacob, comp. "Adult Education and Judaism." *CCAR* 38 (1938): 361–71.

Soltes, Mordecai. "Materials for Jewish Extension Education for Youth and Adults." *The Jewish Center* 5 (1927): 23–25. 95 entries.

THE ARTS (SELECTED)

AJYB. "A List of Works by Jewish Artists In the United States, Aug. 1906–July 1907." (1907–8): 467–73.

Berk, Fred. *Bibliography of Israeli and Jewish Folk Dances*. N.Y.: Jewish Agency, Youth and Hechalutz Department, 1960.

Goldberg, Ira S., comp. *Bibliography of Instrumental Music of Jewish Interest*. N.Y.: National Jewish Music Council, 1970.

Goldman, Bertram. "Bibliography." In *The Sacred Portal: A Primary Symbol in Ancient Judaic Art*, 191–206. Detroit: Wayne State U. Press, 1966.

Goodman, Hannah Grad. *An Annotated and Selected Bibliography of Dramatic Scripts on American Jewish Themes*. N.Y.: JBC of JWB, 1975.

Gutmann, Joseph. "Jewish Ceremonial Art: A Basic Bibliography." In *Studies in Jewish Bibliography in Honor of I. Edward Kiev*, edited by Berlin, 161–65. 1971.

Heskes, Irene. "Jewish Music Literature." *JBA* 23 (1965): 31–41.

Jewish Music: A Guide and Bibliography. N.Y.: ADL.

Kampf, Avram. "Select Bibliography." In *Jewish Experience in the Art of the Twentieth Century*, 220–23. Granby, Mass.: Bergin and Garvey, 1984.

Landsberger, Franz. "Bibliography." In *A History of Jewish Art*, 341–53. Cincinnati: 1956.

Mayer, Leo A. *Bibliography of Jewish Art*, edited by Otto Kurz. Jerusalem: Magnes Press, 1967. 374 pp.

National Jewish Music Council. *Bibliography of Articles and Books on Jewish Music*. N.Y.: 1947. 6 pp.

Ped Rep. "Jewish Music Materials for the Teacher and Group Leader: A Bibliography." 4 (Jan. 1953).

Rubin, Ruth. "Literature on Jewish Music." *JBA* 6 (1947–48): 64–70.

Sendry, Fred. *Bibliography of Jewish Music*. N.Y.: Columbia U. Press, 1951. 404 pp., 10,682 entries.

Shunami, Shlomo. "Music." In *Shunami*, 193–99. 44 entries.

Starkoff, Bernard, ed. *250 Selected Plays of Jewish Interest—An Index*. Cincinnati: UAHC, 1945.

Weisser, Albert. *Bibliography of Publications and Other Resources on Jewish Music*. Rev. ed. N.Y.: National Jewish Music Council, 1969. 117 pp.

Werner, Eric. "Books on Jewish Art." *JBA* 13 (1955–56): 20–28.

———, ed. *Reviews of Selected Recordings of Jewish Music*. N.Y.: National Jewish Music Council, 1953.

———. "Writings of Jewish Artists." *JBA* 18 (1960–61): 69–75.

Wischnitzer, Rachel Bernstein. "Bibliography." In *Gestalten und Symbolen Der Judischen Kunst* (Forms and Symbols in Jewish Art) (G.), 143–51. Berlin: 1953.

———. "Books on Jewish Art." *JBA* 5 (1946–47): 64–69.

———. "Jewish Art Books and Albums." *JBA* 11 (1952–53): 129–35.

———. "Judische Kunstgeschichtsschreibung. Bibliographische Skizze" (Historical Writings on Jewish Art. Bibliographical Outline). In *Festschrift in Honor of Simon Dybnow's 70th Birthday* (G.), 129–35. Berlin: 1930.

AUDIO-VISUAL MATERIALS

AAJE. *Films and Filmstrips for the Jewish School*. N.Y.

AAJE. *Jewish Audio-Visual Review* (films and filmstrips with description and evaluation). N.Y.

ADL. *ADL of B'nai B'rith Catalog*. N.Y.

Baum, Eli, ed. *Curriculum Guide for Afternoon Religious Schools*. N.Y.: National Commission on Torah Education, 1979. Has extensive audiovisual bibliography.

B'nai B'rith Hillel Foundation. *Film Programs*.

Gellert, Charles Lawrence. *A Guide to Motion Pictures on Jewish History in the National Archives of the United States*. Washington, D.C.: 1984. 123 pp.

Golub, Jacob, and Zalmen Slesinger. *List of Recommended Films and Filmstrips*. N.Y.: AAJE, 1949.

NJWB. *Catalogue of Audio-Visual Materials*. N.Y.

TU. "Filmstrips, Visual Aid Charts and Related Materials." In *TU Catalog, 1985*, 18–62. N.Y.: 1985.

Yeshiva U. *Filmstrips and Films of Jewish Interest*. N.Y.

Schwartz, Shirley, ed. *Traveling Exhibitions: Perspectives on the Jewish Experience*. N.Y.: National Foundation for Jewish Culture, 1984. 104 pp.

Slesinger, Zalmen. *Films and Filmstrips of Jewish Interest*. Series 1–6. N.Y.: National Council on Jewish Audio-Visual Service.

THE BIBLE AND HEBREW

Hadassah Education Department. *Leaders' Guides* (for the books of the Bible).

Malachi, Eliezer R. "מיתודיקה„ (Methodology). In *JB* (H.), 375–79.

Orlinsky, Harry M. "Recent Selected Books on Biblical History and Archaeology." *JBA* 18 (1960): 38–43. See also *JBA* 25 (1967): 176–83.

Ped Rep. "Audio-Visual Aids in the Teaching of Bible: A Bibliography." 9 (Jan. 1958); 10 (Nov. 19, 1958).

Scharfstein, Zevi. "ביבליוגרפיה קצרה בהוראת הלשון העברית„ (A Brief Bibliography on Teaching Hebrew: Books and Articles). In *Methods of Teaching Hebrew* (H.), 387–403. 1940.

———. דרכי למוד התנ"ך (Methods of Teaching the Bible) (H.). 1934. See bibliography, pp. 346–48.

Zeldner, Max A. *Bible Teaching: A Bibliography of Materials, Methods, and Model Lessons*. N.Y.: 1959–60.

———. *A Bibliography of Methods and Materials of Teaching Hebrew in the Light of Modern Language Methodology*. N.Y.: JEC, 1953. 117 pp., 1,400 entries.

CAMP

Golub, Jacob S. "Bibliography on Jewish Camping." *Jew Ed* 17 (June 1946): 36–44.

DAY SCHOOL

Schiff, Alvin I. "Bibliography." In *Jewish Day School in America*, 273–84. N.Y.: JEC Press, 1966.

Schiff, Alvin I., and Benjamin Miller. "Selected Bibliography on the Jewish Day School." *Ped Rep* 29 (Fall 1977).

EARLY CHILDHOOD EDUCATION

Ped Rep. "Nursery and Kindergarten Education: A Bibliography." 3 (Mar. 1952).

EXCEPTIONAL CHILDREN

AAJE. *Bibliography of Jewish Special Education*. N.Y.: 1969.

Greenberg, Barbara. *Bibliography of Resources on Jewish Special Education*. N.Y; USCJE, 1973.

Jewish Braille Institute of America. 1962. *Catalogue of the Jewish Braille Library*. N.Y.

HISTORY (SELECTED)

AJA. *Manuscript Catalog of the American Jewish Archives*. 4 vols. Boston: G. K. Hall, 1971.

AJC. *Writings on Jewish History*. N.Y.: 1970. 32 pp. Annotated list for grades 5–12

AJHS. *Index to the Publications of the American Jewish Historical Society Numbers 1 to 20*. 1914. 600 pp.

AJHS. *Manuscript Collections in the American Jewish Historical Society: Cataloged Jan. 1968–June 1969*. Waltham, Mass.: 1969.

Cohen, Iva. "American Jewish Bibliography 1942–43." *AJYB* 45 (1943–44): 431–46.

ERC. *The American Jewish Experience: A Graded, Annotated Bibliography for Grades 7–12, Part Two*. Cleveland: 1972. 27 pp.

ERC. *World Jewish History, Religion, and Culture: A Graded, Annotated Bibliography for Grades 7–12, Part One*. Cleveland: ERC and AAJE, 1972. 24 pp.

Glanz, Rudolf. *The German Jew in America: An Annotated Bibliography Including Books, Pamphlets, and Articles of Special Interest*. Cincinnati: HUC Press and Ktav Publishing House, 1969.

Glenn, Menachem G. „ביבליוגרפיה עברית קצרה של דברי ימי היהודים באמריקה" (Selected Hebrew Bibliography on American Jewish History) (H.). *JBA* (1953–55): 51–59.

Gurock, Jeffrey. *American Jewish History—A Bibliographical Guide*. N.Y.: ADL, 1983. 195 pp.

Hartstein, Jacob I., ed. *The Jews in American History: A Resource Book for Teachers of Social Studies and American History*. N.Y.: National Program Division of the ADL and the Yeshiva U. School of Education and Community Administration, 1955. Has extensive bibliography on books, films, holidays, etc.,

JBC. *Historical Fiction on Jewish Themes*. N.Y.: JWB–JBC.

Kaganoff, Nathan M. "Selected Books on American Jewish Biography." *JBA* 33 (1975–78): 64–71.

———. "Selected Books on American Jewish History." *JBA* 33 (1975–78): 51–63.

———. "Supplement III: Judaica Americana Printed before 1851." In *Studies in Jewish Bibliography in Honor of I. Edward Kiev*, edited by Berlin, 177–209. 1971.

Kohn, Gary J. *The Jewish Experience: A Guide to Manuscript Sources in the Library of Congress*. N.Y.: Ktav, 1986.

Kripke, Dorothy K. *Children's Books and Stories about American Jewish Life and History: A Bibliography*. N.Y.: AJHS, 1962. 11 pp.

Levine, Allan E. *An American Jewish Bibliography: A List of Books and Pamphlets by Jews or Relating to Them Printed in the U.S. from 1851–1875, Which Are in the Possession of the HUC–JIR Library in Cincinnati*. Cincinnati: American Jewish Archives Monograph, No. 2, 1959. 100 pp.

Lifschutz, E. *Bibliography of American and Canadian Jewish Memoirs and Autobiographies* (Y., H., and E.). N.Y.: Yivo, 1970. 76 pp.

Lubetski, Edith, comp. *Writings on Jewish History: A Selected Annotated Bibliography*. N.Y.: AJC, 1970. 31 pp.

Malachi, Eliezer R. „תולדות החנוך והמוסדות באמריקה" (History of Education and Institutions in America). In *JB* (H.), 386–95. 159 entries.

Marcus, Jacob R. "A Brief Bibliography of American Jewish History." *JBA* 2 (1943–44): 23–30.

———. *A Brief Introduction to the Bibliography of Modern Jewish History (Selected and Annotated), 1650 to Modern Times*. Cincinnati: HUC, 1935. 170 pp.

———. *Jewish Americana: A Catalogue of Books and Articles by Jews or Relating to Them in the United States from the Earliest Days to 1850*. Cincinnati: American Jewish Archives, 1954. 115 pp.

———. "A Selected Bibliography of American Jewish History." *AJHQ* 51 (Dec. 1961): 97–134. Annotated.

Meyer, Isidore S. *American-Jewish Biography—An Introductory List*. N.Y.: AJHS and NJWB, 1950. 9 pp. (Reprinted from *JBA* 8 [1949–50]: 77–96.)

Miller, Benjamin. "A Selected Annotated and Graded List of Print/Non-Print Materials for Teaching Jewish History and Social Studies." *Ped Rep* 29 (Winter 1978).

Nudelman, Edward A., and Zalmen Slesinger. *The Jew in America: A Syllabus for Teachers, Two Parts*. Issued in observance of the American Jewish Tercentenary. N.Y.: 1954. See extensive bibliography, pp. 127–69.

Rischin, Moses. *An Inventory of American Jewish History*. Cambridge: Harvard U. Press, 1954. 66 pp.

Rosenbach, A. S. W. *An American Jewish Bibliography: Being a List of Books and Pamphlets by Jews or Relating to Them, Printed in the United States from the Establishment of the Press in the Colonies until 1850*. N.Y.: AJHS, 1926. 486 pp.

Shpall, Leo. *Selected Items of American Jewish Interest in the Yiddish Periodicals of Russia and Poland, 1862–1940*. Cincinnati: American Jewish Archives, 1966. 38 pp.

Wolf, Edwin, 2d. "Some Unrecorded American Judaica Printed before 1851." In *Ess*, 187–245.

THE HOLOCAUST (SELECTED)

Bas, David. *Bibliography of Yiddish Books on the Catastrophe and Heroism* (Y.). N.Y.: Yivo and Yad Vashem, ca. 1972.

Freidenreich, Fradle. "Materials for Teaching the Holocaust" (annotated bibliography). *Ped Rep* 33 (Mar. 1982): 26–29. See also *Materials-Resource Guide for Jewish Education*, 48–75. Miami: JESNA and CAJE, 1980. 336 pp.

Friedman, Philip. "The Bibliography of the Warsaw Ghetto." *JBA* 11 (1952–53): 121–28.

———. „דער גורל פון יידישן קינד און פון דער יידישער יוגנט אונטער נאצי-רעזשים" (The Fate of the Jewish Child and of Jewish Youth under the Nazi Regime) (selected and annotated). *BYD* (Y.) 2 (1949): 78–85; 3 (1950) 80–92.

———. „100 ביכער אין יידיש וועגן חורבן און גבורה" (100 Yiddish Books on Destruction and Resistance during the Holocaust) (Y.). *JBA* (Y. section) 8 (1949–50) 122–32; 9 (1950–51): 80–92.

Gar, Joseph, and Philip Friedman. „ביבליאגראפיע פון יידישע ביכער וועגן חורבן און גבורה" (Bibliography of Yiddish Books about Destruction and Resistance) (Y.). N.Y.: Yivo and Yad Vashem, 1962. 361 pp., 1,762 entries.

Halpern, Irving. *Selected Bibliography on the Jewish Holocaust*. N.Y.: JBC.

Jewish National Fund. *Suggested Background Materials on the Teaching of Martyrdom and Heroism: The Warsaw Ghetto Uprising*. N.Y.: Jewish National Fund Youth and Education Department.

Muffs, Judith Herschlag. *The Holocaust in Books and Films: A Selected, Annotated List*. N.Y.: ADL Center for Studies on the Holocaust, 1982. 67 pp.

Reiss, Asher. "A Quarter Century of Books on the Warsaw Ghetto Battle." *JBA* 26 (1968–69): 23–33.

Robinson, Jacob, and Philip Friedman. *Guide to Jewish History under Nazi Impact*. N.Y.: Yivo and Yad Vashem, 1960. 27–69, 3, 634 entries.

Spiro, Jack D. "A Partial Survey of Holocaust Literature." *CCAR J* (Jan. 1969): 84–88.

Szonyi, David M. *The Holocaust: An Annotated Bibliography and Resource Guide*. Hoboken, N.J.: Ktav, 1985. 396 pp.

HOME (SELECTED)

Grayzel, Solomon. *Jewish Books for Your Home*. N.Y.: JBA and NJWB, 1950. 16 pp. Reprinted from *The Torch*.

Oblath, Sunny R. *An Annotated Bibliography Concerning the Family and Family Programming*. Covers such areas as camping, chavurah, family-life education, synagogue programs, and Jewish family Service Agencies. Master's project, HUC–JIR, 1975.

Schlesinger, Benjamin. *The Jewish Family: A Survey and Annotated Bibliography*. U. of Toronto, 1971. 175 pp.

Schwarts, Mrs. Charles. "Bibliography for Parents." *Syn Sch* 29 (Fall 1979): 40–63.

Singer, David. *Focus on the American Jewish Family: A Select Annotated Bibliography*. N.Y.: AJC, 1982. 27 pp.

ISRAEL (SELECTED)

Cohen, Iva, comp. *Israel: A Bibliography*. N.Y.: ADL. More than 100 titles listed. 70 pp.

ERC. *Jews in Israel and in Other Lands Abroad: A Graded, Annotated Bibliography for Grades 7–12*. Cleveland: ERC and AAJE, 1972. 17 pp.

Fine, Morris. *Israel-Diaspora Relations: A Selected Bibliography, 1973–1983*. N.Y.: AJC,

**48
BIBLIOGRA-
PHIES OF
JEWISH
EDUCATION
AND
RELATED
FIELDS
IN THE
UNITED
STATES**

Institute on American Jewish-Israeli Relations, 1983. 45 pp.

Hessel, Carolyn Starman. "Israel: Selected Readings." *Ped Rep* 39 (Apr. 1988): 43–47.

Katzir, I., ed. *A Selection of Articles on Jewish Education Prepared for the Educators from the Diaspora and Israel.* Jerusalem: DEC, WZO, Conference of Jewish Organizations, July 1974.

Kersten, Solomon. "American Books on Israel and Zionism 1956–1957." *JBA* 15:109–11.

Koplewitz, Batya. *Eretz Yisrael and State of Israel in the Writings of Conservative Judaism: A Selected Bibiliography.* Jerusalem: World Council of Synagogues, 1962. 24 pp.

Malachi, Eliezer R. „החנוך בארץ ישראל ובתפוצות" (Education in Israel and the Diaspora). In *JB* (H.), 365–67. 31 entries. (See sections on "Israel" and "Teaching Israel.")

———. „ארץ ישראל והחנוך" (Israel and Education). In *JB* (H.), 364–65. 28 entries.

Popper, William. "One Hundred Available Books in English on Palestine." *AJYB* 7 (1905–6): 153–62.

Skirball, Hank. "70 Books about Israel." In *Cat 3*, 384–87.

Tuchman, Hyman. *The Selected Bibliography of Books on Israel.* N.Y.: DEC.

Yaari, Abraham. "Educational Books and Books for Children that Were Published in Israel, 1890–1928." In *Jubilee Volume—Teachers Organization* (H.), edited by Kimhi, 338–69. Jerusalem: 1929.

JUVENILE LITERATURE

Bloch, Joshua. *Of Making Many Books: An Annotated List of the Books Issued by the Jewish Publication Society of America, 1890–1952.* Phila.: JPS, 1953. 329 pp.

Davis, Enid. *A Comprehensive Guide to Children's Literature with a Jewish Theme.* N.Y.: Schocken Books, 1981. 177 pp.

Frischer, R. "New Books for Jewish Children." *Moment* 4 (Nov. 1979): 43–51.

———. "Our Shelves Runneth Over." *Moment* 5 (Nov. 1980): 34–40.

Green, Kathy. "An Annotated Reading List." *MJ* 14 (Spring 1982): 6, 27.

———. "Jewish Books for Children" *MJ* 14 (Spring 1982): 5, 16.

Inglehart, Babette F., and Anthony R. Mangione. "Literature Dealing with the Jewish-American Experience." In *The Image of Pluralism in American Literature: An Annotated Bibliography on the American Experience of European Ethnic Groups*, 32–45. N.Y.: AJC, 1974.

Jewish Book Annual:

JBA 1 (1942):
  Lifshitz, Ch., "Hebrew Books for Youth and Adults" (H.), 34–36.
  ———, "List of Children's Books" (H.), 37–39.

JBA 5 (1946–47)
  Goldstein, Fanny, "The Jewish Child in Bookland," 84–100.

JBA 9 (1950–51)
  Golub, Jacob S., "American Jewish Juvenile Books," 27–29.

JBA 10 (1951–52)
  Saretsky, Augusta, "American Jewish Juvenile Books," 19–22.

JBA 11 (1952–53)
  Goldstein, Fanny, "American Jewish Juvenile Books," 27–31.

JBA 12 (1953–55)
  Goldstein, Fanny, "American Jewish Juvenile Books," 114–19.

JBA 13 (1956)
  Goldstein, Fanny, "American Jewish Juvenile Books," 89–92.

JBA 14 (1956–57)
  Goldstein, Fanny, "American Jewish Juvenile Books," 101–4.

JBA 15 (1957–58)
  Goldstein, Fanny, "American Jewish Juvenile Books," 116–19.

JBA 16 (1958–59)
  Goldstein, Fanny, "American Jewish Juvenile Books," 131–35.

JBA 17 (1959–60)
    Leikind, Miriam, "American Jewish Juvenile Books," 111–14.

JBA 18 (1960–61)
    Kripke, Dorothy K., "American Jewish Juvenile Books," 162–65.

JBA 19 (1961–62)
    Kripke, Dorothy K., "American Jewish Juvenile Books," 152–56.

JBA 20 (1962–63)
    Cedarbaum, Sophia N., "American Jewish Juvenile Books," 164–67.

JBA 21 (1963–64)
    Cedarbaum, Sophia N., "American Jewish Juvenile Books," 166–69.

JBA 22 (1964–65)
    Cedarbaum, Sophia N., "American Jewish Juvenile Books," 151–54.

JBA 23 (1965–66)
    Cedarbaum, Sophia N., "American Jewish Juvenile Books," 159–62.

JBA 24 (1966–67)
    Cedarbaum, Sophia N., "American Jewish Juvenile Books," 141–44.

JBA 25 (1967–68)
    Cedarbaum, Sophia N., "American Jewish Juvenile Books," 290–94.
    ———. "American Jewish Juvenile Literature during the Past Twenty-Five Years," 192–203.

JBA 26 (1968–69)
    Cedarbaum, Sophia N., "American Jewish Juvenile Books," 171–76.

JBA 27 (1969–70)
    Kanner, Ruth C., "American Jewish Juvenile Books," 148–54.

JBA 28 (1970–71)
    Kanner, Ruth C., "American Jewish Juvenile Books," 195–200.

JBA 29 (1971–72)
    Wagner, Hilda B., "American Jewish Juvenile Books," 142–46.

JBA 30 (1972–73)
    Wagner, Hilda B., "American Jewish Juvenile Books," 127–32.

JBA 31 (1973–74)
    Chipman, Fannie, "American Jewish Juvenile Books," 137–40.

JBA 32 (1974–75)
    Brodie, Deborah, "American Jewish Juvenile Books," 118–21.

JBA 33 (1975–76)
    Brodie, Deborah, "American Jewish Juvenile Books," 194–99.
    ———. "Selected Juvenile Books on American Jewish Life," 80–84.

JBA 34 (1976–77)
    Brodie, Deborah, "American Jewish Juvenile Books," 143–48.

JBA 35 (1977–78)
    Frishman, Nettie, and Marcia Posner, "American Jewish Juvenile Books," 192–200.
    ———, "Jewish Juvenile Book Awards: Survey and Evaluation," 76–91.

JBA 36 (1978–79)
    Frishman, Nettie, "American Jewish Juvenile Books," 163–68.

JBA 37 (1979–80)
    Frishman, Nettie, "American Jewish Juvenile Books," 196–204.

JBA 38 (1980–81)
    Frishman, Nettie, "American Jewish Juvenile Books," 192–97.

JBA 39 (1981–82)
    Frishman, Nettie, "American Jewish Juvenile Books," 202–8.

JBA 40 (1982–83)
    Frishman, Nettie, "American Jewish Juvenile Books," 209–19.

JBA 41 (1983–84)
    Frishman, Nettie, "American Jewish Juvenile Books," 225–32.

JBA 42 (1984–85)
    Frishman, Nettie, "American Jewish Juvenile Books," 250–57.

JBA 43 (1985–86)
    Miller, Inabeth, "American Jewish Children's Literature: Narrow Perspectives and Mixed Messages," 92–105.
    Posner, Marcia W., "American Jewish Juvenile Books," 236–42.

JBA 44 (1986–87)
    Posner, Marcia W., "American Jewish Juvenile Books," 244–50.

JBA 45 (1987–88)
    Posner, Marcia W., "American Jewish Juvenile Books," 229–37.

JBA 46 (1988–89)
　　Posner, Marcia W., "American Jewish Juvenile Books," 268–76.

Koltun, Liz. "Children's Books." In *Cat 1*, 242–47.

Lieberman, Morris. *The Use of Fiction in Jewish Religious Education* (annotated bibliography). Cincinnati: Department of Jewish Religious Education, 1935. 108 pp.

Malachi, Eliezer R. "ספרות-ילדים„ (Children's Literature). In *JB* (H.), 381.

Persky, Daniel. "ספרותנו החדשה באמריקה„ (Our New Literature in America). *Hadoar* (H.) (1927): 341–46.

Ribalow, Harold U. *120 American Jewish Novels: Annotated and Classified*. N.Y.: JEC Press, 1962. 29 pp.

———. *Selected Books of American Jewish Fiction*. N.Y.: JBC.

Rosen, E. "The Year That Was: Jewish Children's Books, 1978." *Moment* 4 (Dec. 1978): 40–46.

Saretsky, Augusta, and Elias Schulman. *A Guide to Jewish Juvenile Literature*. N.Y.: JEC, 1968.

Segal, Judith. *An Annotated Bibliography of General Juvenile Literature to be Used within the Jewish Educational Curriculum*. N.Y.: Melton Research Center.

MAGAZINES FOR CHILDREN AND YOUTH

Gewirtz, Eliezer, and Gitty Lebovitz, comps. *A Thirty Year Index of Themes and Personalities in* Olmeinu—Our World. N.Y.: TU Publications, 1980. 34 pp.

MITZVOT/VALUES (SELECTED)

AAJE. "Selected List of Audio-Visual Materials for Teaching Brotherhood." *Ped Rep* 5 (Nov. 1953).

ADL. *A Bibliography on Judaism and Jewish-Christian Relations*. N.Y.: ADL, 1965. 62 pp., 1,300 entries.

ADL. *Human Relations Materials for the School, Church, and Community*. N.Y.: 62 pp.

AJC. *Children of One Father*. N.Y.: 1966. 29 pp.

AJC. *A Selected Bibliography of Books, Pamphlets, and Articles on Negro-Jewish Relations*. N.Y.: 1971. 18 pp.

AJC. *The Pen Is Mightier: A Bibliography of Publications on Intercultural Relations*. N.Y.: 1954.

Celnik, Max, and Isaac Celnik. *Bibliography on Judaism and Jewish-Christian Relations*. N.Y.: ADL. 72 pp.

CSS–UAHC. *Bibliography*. N.Y.: UAHC Commission on Social Action of Reform Judaism, 1971. 20 pp.

Davis, Lenwood G. *Black-Jewish Relations in the United States, 1752–1984: A Selected Bibliography*. Westport, Conn.: Greenwood Press, 1984. 130 pp.

Nahshon, Nadav, ed. *Jewish Values and the Jewish Tradition—Part 1: An Annotated Guide to Educational Media*. Jerusalem: Hebrew U. Centre for Jewish Education in the Diaspora, DEC and WZO, 1983. 56 pp.

Oppenheim, Micha Falk. "Resources for Teaching Mitzvot." *Ped Rep* 34 (Oct. 1983): 27–30.

Singerman, Robert. *Anti-Semitic Propaganda: An Annotated Bibliography and Research Guide*. N.Y.: Garland Publishing, 1982.

Vorspan, Albert. *Jewish Values and Social Crisis* (bibliographies of Jewish primary sources, contemporary articles, books, and audio-visual aids follow each chapter). N.Y.: UAHC, 1968. 306 pp.

PERIODICALS, NEWSPAPERS, AND ANNUALS (SELECTED)

AJYB, edited by David Singer, (lists current periodicals annually).

AJYB. "Jewish Periodicals Appearing in the United States, 1900–1931." 33 (1931): 256–60.

AJYB Index, Vols. 1–50, 1899–1949, compiled by Elfrida Solis-Cohen. N.Y.: Ktav, 1967. *AJYB* 71 (1970) contains index of special articles in vols. 51–70.

Alternative Magazine Index, Vols. 1–8, 1970–1978 by Micha F. Oppenheim.

American Jewish Periodical Center. *Jewish Newspapers and Periodicals on Microfilm Available at the American Jewish Periodical Center*. Cincinnati: 1957. 56 pp. Augmented ed., 1984. 158 pp.

Berlin, Charles. "Jewish Bibliographic Journals." *JBA* (1971–72): 22–38.

Brody, Fannie M. "The Hebrew Periodical Press in America." *PAJHS* 33 (1934): 127–70.

CCAR J Index, 1953–1978, compiled by Marsha Bernstein, Chava Pollack, and Elliot L. Stevens.

CCAR Year Book Index, Volumes 1–50. 1941. 108 pp.

Con Jud Index, Vols. 1–17, 1945–1963, compiled by Doris Noveck. N.Y.: RA, 1963. *Con Jud* 31 (Summer 1977) has index to vols. 18–30 (1963–77).

Freidus, Abraham S. "A List of Jewish Periodicals Published in the United States." *AJYB* 1 (1899): 271–82.

Gladstone, Jacob, Sh. Niger, and Harry Rogoff, eds. "List of Yiddish Periodicals." In *75 Years of Yiddish Press in America, 1870–1945* (Y.), 49–54. N.Y.: I. L. Peretz Writers Union, 1945.

Gottheil, Richard, and William Popper. "Periodicals." In *The Jewish Encyclopedia*, 9:601–39. 1905.

Hadoar Index, 1921–1963, compiled by Leo Shpall.

Jacobs, Joseph. *Directory of the Jewish Press in America*. N.Y.: Joseph Jacobs Organization, 1970.

JBC. *The Jewish Press: A Selected Listing*. 1971. 6 pp.

Jew Ed Index, Vols. 1–25 (Jan. 1929–Winter 1954–55), compiled by Zalmen Slesinger. Supplement to *Jew Ed* 25:79–120.

Jew Ed Index, Vols. 26–30 (Summer 1955–Spring 1960), compiled by Zalmen Slesinger. *Jew Ed* 30:56–66.

Jew Ed Index, Vols. 31–43 (Summer 1960–Winter 1974), compiled by Alvin I. Schiff and Elias Schulman. *Jew Ed* 44 (Spring 1975): 5–30.

Jew Ed Index, Vols. 44–53 (Summer 1975–Winter 1985), compiled by Stanley Fischman. *Jew Ed* 54 (Spring 1986): 3–36.

Jew Life Index, 1946–1965, compiled by Micha F. Oppenheim.

JSS Cumulative Index, 1939–1964, Vols. 1–25, compiled by Max M. Rothschild. N.Y.: Conference of Jewish Studies. 1967.

JSS. *Preliminary List and Subject Index of JSS, 1964–1978*, compiled by Tobey B. Gitele. 41 (Winter 1979).

Judaism. *Twenty Years Cumulative Index, 1952–1971*. N.Y.: American Jewish Congress, 1972

Leikind, Miriam, ed. *Index to Jewish Periodicals*. Cleveland Heights, Ohio: College of Jewish Studies Press.

Liberal Judaism, Cumulative Index, 1943–1948. N.Y.: UAHC.

Malachi, Eliezer R. „דער באגינען פון דער ייִדישער פרעסע און אמעריקע" (The Beginning of the Yiddish Press in America). In *Pinkes for the Research of the Yiddish Literature and Press* (Y.), 2:253–93. N.Y.: Congress for Jewish Culture, 1972.

———. "Bibliography of the Hebrew Press in America." *Hadoar* (H.) (Aug. 26, 1932): 515; (Sept. 9, 1932): 533; (Sept. 23, 1932): 584; (Nov. 18, 1932): 44; (Dec. 1932): 76; (Jan. 1933): 140.

———. „א קורצע געשיכטע פון דער העברעאישער פרעסע אין אמעריקע" (A Brief History of the Hebrew Press in America, 1870–1945) (Y.). In *75 Years of Yiddish Press in America*, (Y.), 100–107.

———. „עתונים פדגוגיים". (Educational Periodicals). In *JB* (H.), 362–63.

———. „שבעים וחמש שנה לעתונות העברית באמריקה" (Seventy-five Years of Hebrew Press in America) (H.). In *Sefer ha-Shanah Le-Yehude Amerikah*, 662–76. August 9, 1946.

Menorah Journal Third of a Century Index, 1915–1948. *Menorah J* 36 (Summer 1948).

Minkin, Jacob S. "Survey of the Jewish Press in America." *JBA* (1944–45): 53–58.

"*Pedagogic Reporter* Index, Vols. 1–30 (Oct. 1949–Spring 1979)." *Ped Rep* 31 (Feb. 1980): 32–37.

Prager, Leonard, and A. A. Greenbaum. *Yiddish Literary and Linguistic Periodicals and Miscellanies: Publication for the Study of Jewish Languages*. Darby, Pa., and Haifa: Norwood Editions, 1982. 271 pp.

RA. *Index to the Proceedings of the Rabbinical Assembly, 1927–1968*. 45 pp.

Ravid, Zvulun. "Jewish Pedagogic Literature." *Sh Hah* (H.) 26 (1965–66): 225–37.

Sh Hah. שבילי החנוך compiled by Zalmen Slesinger and Akibah Ben-Ezra. "Index to *Sh Hah* Vols. 1–5, Series I (1925–1939) and Vols. 1–18, Series II (1940–1958)." 19 (Autumn 1959). See also *Sh Hah* 30:1, pp. 4–36.

Shtarkman, Moshe. „קוועלן־ליטעראטור צו דער געשיכטע פון דער יידישער פרעסע אין אמעריקע(1870–1900)" (1900–1870) (Literary Sources on the History of the Yiddish Press in America, 1870–1920). *Pinkes* (Y.) 1 (1937–38): 312–20.

———. „געקליבענע מקורים צו דער געשיכטע פון דער יידישער פרעסע אין אמעריקע" (Selected Bibliography on Yiddish Press in America) (Y., H., and E. sources). *JBA* (1944–45): 22–25 (Y. section).

Singerman, Robert. "The American Jewish Press, 1823–1983." *AJH* 73 (June 1984): 422–44.

"*Syn Sch* Index, Vols. 18–31." See *Syn Sch* (Mar. 1960–Summer 1973).

Trad Index, Vols. 1–10 (1958–1969), compiled by Micha F. Oppenheim. N.Y.: RCA, 1970.

Un Syn Rev Index, 1957–1978, compiled by Stuart Wise. N.Y.: USA, 1978.

Weine, Mae. *A Basic Periodical List for the Small Jewish Library*. Rev. ed. N.Y.: Association of Jewish Libraries, 1978.

Yiddish Scientific Insitutute. "Yiddish Periodicals in North America, 1926–27" (includes daily newspapers, periodicals, and literary, professional, and trade journals in Yiddish) (Y.). In *Yearbook of Yiddish Bibliography* (Y.), 17–24. Warsaw: Kulturliga Pub. Co., 1928.

Yivo Annual of Jewish Social Science Cumulative Author-Title Index and Table of Contents, 1946–1974 (E.). N.Y.: Yivo, 1974.

PRAYER AND SYNAGOGUE (SELECTED)

Korros, Alexandra Shecket, and Jonathan D. Sarna. *American Synagogue History: A Bibliography and State-of-the-Field Survey*. 1988. 200 pp.

Landau, Diane Fishman. "An Annotated Bibliography on Liturgy Curriculum and Related Materials." A descriptive listing of educational materials dealing with prayer. Master's project, HUC–JIR, 1982.

RELIGIOUS EDUCATION

Bissel, Sherry H. "To Answer Questions about God—An Annotated Bibliography." Contains various materials available for children and young adults about God. Arranged by age-appropriateness, including general as well as Jewish references. Master's project, HUC–JIR, 1975.

SEPHARDIM

Angel, Marc D. "Bibliography." In *La America*, 209–12. Phila.: JPS, 1982.

———. "A Topical Bibliography in the Appendix to *The Sephardim of the United States: An Exploratory Study*." *AJYB* 74 (1973): 136–38.

Benardete, Mair Jose. "Bibliography." In *Hispanic Culture and Character of the Sephardic Jews*, 173–86. N.Y.: 1952, 1982.

Bunuis, David M. *Sephardic Studies: A Research Bibliography*. N.Y.: Garland Publishing, 1981.

Gaon, Moshe David. *A Bibliography of the Judeo-Spanish (Ladino) Press* (lists Ladino newspapers in the Western Hemisphere). Jerusalem: Ben-Zvi Institute, Hebrew U., 1965. 143 pp.

Kittner, Susan. "An Annotated Multi-Resource List of Materials for Teaching Sephardi Jewry." A listing of fifty-two resources of value when studying Sephardi Jewry. Master's project, HUC–JIR, 1980.

Liebman, Seymour B., comp. *A Guide to Jewish Reference in the Mexican Colonial Era, 1521–1821*. Phila.: Univ. of Pennsylvania Press, 1964. 134 pp.

Papo, Joseph M. "Bibliography." In *Sephardim in Twentieth Century America: In Search of Unity*, 423–33. San Jose and Berkeley, Calif.: Pele Yoetz Books and Judah L. Magnes Memorial Museum, 1987.

Pool, David de Sola, and Tamar Pool. "Reading List" and "Bibliography." In *An Old Faith in the New World*, 547–53, 555–62.

SOCIAL SCIENCES

Baron, Salo W. *Bibliography of Jewish Social Studies, 1938–39*. N.Y.: Conference on Jewish Relations, 1941. 291 pp.

Fein, Leonard J. *Bibliographies on Jewish Identity*. N.Y.: American Jewish Congress. 36 pp.

Katz, David. "Essays for the Ba'al Teshuvah: An Annotated Bibliography of 21 Articles for the Jew Whose Identity is Becoming More Important to Him." A bibliography of articles to help clarify the thoughts and alleviate the anxiety often caused by the reconsideration of values and beliefs. Master's project, HUC–JIR, 1979.

Malachi, Eliezer R. "החנוך והחברה„ (Education and Society). In *JB* (H.), 368–75. 158 entries.

———. "פדגוגיה ופסיכולוגיה„ (Pedagogy and Psychology). In *JB* (H.), 381–83. 40 entries.

Wollman, Benjamin. "The Jewish Adolescent: A Bibliographical Review of Current Psychological and Educational Literature in the United States and Israel." *JSS* 13 (Oct. 1951): 333–44. Also in *Sh Hah* (H.) 12 (Dec. 1951): 3–16.

TEACHERS

Birnbaum, David. "מדריך ביבליוגרפי למורה ולתלמיד„ (A Bibliographical Guide for Teacher and Student) (H.). N.Y.: Keren Beth HaNosee Vaad Hachinukh, 1968. 228 pp.

Jeshurin, Ephim H. "ביבליאגראפיע פון ארטיקלען אויף די טעמעס פון לערע, לערנען און פעדאגאגיק„ (Bibliographical List of Articles on Teachers, Teaching and Pedagogy). *CE* (Y.) 27 (May 1957): 33–37.

Malachi, Eliezer R. "מצב המורה„ (The Status of the Teacher) (H.). In *JB* (H.), 379–81. 36 entries.

TEACHER TRAINING

Berk, Aliza Wallin. "Annotated Bibliography on In-Service Training: An Update." An update (May 1975) focusing primarily on programs within Jewish education. Master's project, HUC–JIR, 1978.

Gamoran, Emanuel. "Bibliography." In his *Teacher-Training for Jewish Schools*, 37–66. 1924.

Mayo, Maxine. "Annotated Bibliography: In-Service Training." Areas examined include philosophical determinants, interpersonal relations, psychology, administration, specific educational in-put, and assessment of students. Articles are summarized and evaluated. Master's project, HUC–JIR, 1975.

TEXTBOOKS

Anilovitch, I. "די יידישע ביכער-פראדוקציע אין צפון אמעריקע פאר די יארן 1926–1931„ (Yiddish Books in North America, Education and Culture, 1926–1931). *YB* (Y.) 5 (Feb. 1933): 178–89; (Mar-May 1933): 409–13. 291 entries.

JESNA. *Materials-Resource Guide for Jewish Education*. Miami: JESNA and CAJE, 1980.

336 pp. See "Textbooks" in table of contents. Extensive and annotated lists for children, young adults, and adults.

Kaunfer, Marcia. *An Annotated Bibliography of Jewish Textbooks*. N.Y.: Melton Research Center, 1975.

WOMEN (SELECTED)

Cantor, Avivah. *The Jewish Woman: 1900–1980*. 2d ed. Fresh Meadows, N.Y.: Biblio Press, 1982. 88 pp.

Goldstein, Fanny. "Bibliographic Material on the Jewish Woman." In *The Jewish Woman*, edited by Leo Jung, 475–502. N.Y.: 1934.

Greenberg, Blu. "Recent Literature on Jewish Women." *JBA* 35 (1977–78): 97–107.

Hamelsdorf, Ora, and Sandra Adelsberg. *Jewish Women and Law: A Bibliography*. Fresh Meadows, N.Y.: Biblio Press, 1981.

Korman, Ezra. "Biographies and Bibliographies of Yiddish Poets." In his ייִדישע דיכטערינס (Anthology of Yiddish Women Poets) (Y.), 337–74. Chicago: 1928.

Marcus, Jacob R. "Bibliographical Note." In *The American Jewish Woman, 1654–1980*, 189–218. N.Y. and Cincinnati: Ktav and American Jewish Archives, 1981.

Ruud, Inger Marie. *Women and Judaism: A Select Annotated Bibliography*. N.Y.: Garland Publishing, 1988. 232 pp.

Shunami, Shlomo. "Women." In *Shunami*, 298–300 (item nos. 1691–1706).

Steinschneider, Moritz. "The Jewish Woman and Jewish Literature." In his *Hebrew Bibliography* (G.). 1879. 23 entries.

Yiddish Scientific Institute. „פרויענפראגע" (Issues Concerning Women) (articles that appeared in Yiddish periodicals world-wide during 1926). In *Yearbook of Yiddish Bibliography* (Y.), 119–20 (item nos. 2217–39). Warsaw: Kulturliga Pub. Co., 1928.

Young, Susan Winter. "An Annotated Bibliography of Books and Articles on the Jewish Marriage Contract." Master's thesis, on file at the Women's Research Center, New York.

Zuckoff, Avivah Cantor, and Leora Fishman. "A Guide to Jewish Women's Activities." In *Cat 1*, 258–61.

YOUTH

Porter, Nussan, comp. *Jews and the Cults: Bibliography* (annotated). Fresh Meadows, N.Y.: Biblio Press, 1981. 49 pp.

Rosenfeld, Geraldine. *What We Know about Young American Jews: An Annotated Bibliography*. N.Y.: AJC, 1970. 19 pp.

DOCTORAL DISSERTATIONS AND MASTERS' THESES

Dinsky, Samuel H. "A Summary of Doctoral Dissertations on Jewish Education." *Jew Ed* 34 (Summer 1964): 267–69.

Disenhouse, Phyllis, and Witta Ravid, eds. *American Doctoral Dissertations and Masters Theses on Jewish Subjects: 8 Monographs, 1963–1975*. N.Y.: Yivo Institute For Jewish Research.

Eels, Walter C. "American Graduate Dissertations on Jewish Education Outside the United States." *Jew Ed* 28 (Winter 1958): 61–63.

Graeber, Isaque A. "Jewish Themes in American Doctoral Dissertations, 1933–1962." *YA* 13 (1965): 279–304.

Parker, Franklin, and Judah Pilch. "Doctoral Dissertations in Jewish Education and Related Areas." *Jew Ed* 31 (Apr. 1961): 60–62.

Pollak, George, comp. *Doctoral Dissertations in Jewish Education, 1975–1982*. N.Y.: JESNA Research and Information Bulletin No. 53, Jan. 1983.

———. "A Review of Doctoral Dissertations in Jewish Education." *Jew Ed* 47 (Spring 1979): 35–43.

Raphael, Marc Lee. "American Jewish Studies." *AJH* 69 (1980): 401–4; 70 (1980–81):

223–25, 493–95; 71 (1982): 381–85; 72 (1982–83): 124–26, 399–401; 73 (1983–84): 97–98, 327–30; 74 (1984–85): 73–75, 308–11; 75 (1985–86): 86–88, 341–44; 76 (1986–87): 78–80, 354–57; 77 (1987): 155–58; 78 (1988–89): 109–12, 425–27; 79 (1989): 111–17.

Rosenthal, Frank. "Bibliography of Doctoral and Master's Dissertations." *Reg* (1965): 49–53.

Rosenthal, Frank, and Judah Pilch. *Abstracts of Doctoral and Masters Dissertations in Jewish Education and Related Areas*. U. of Judaism, JTSA, and NCRI, AAJE. Dec. 1964. 137 pp. Annotated.

Soltes, Mordecai. "Doctoral Dissertations and Master's Theses on Jewish Education." *Jew Ed* 7 (Apr.–June 1935): 112–113; 11 (Jan. 1940): 188–96.

48 BIBLIOGRAPHIES OF JEWISH EDUCATION AND RELATED FIELDS IN THE UNITED STATES

SUPPLEMENT

CURRICULUM

Curriculum Development and Assessment

Abraham, Joel. "Together We Stand: Curricular Reform and the Logic of Inclusion—the Case for Jewish Studies." *Response*, 58 (Spring 1991): 23–25.

Bogot, Howard I. "The Reform Curriculum Resource Center." *Compass*, 16:1 (Fall 1993): 26.

Goldflam, Dov. "Towards a New Approach to Curriculum Design in Jewish Education." *Jew Ed* 59:3 (Winter 1992): 37–38.

Grossman, Judith E. "Curriculum and Ideology: Indoctrination as an Approach to Conservative Jewish Education." *Jew Ed* 57:2, 3, 4 (Summer/Winter 1989): 39–41.

Jacobson, Shira. "An Integrated Curriculum." Department of Education, Jewish Theological Seminary, M.A. Thesis, 1990.

PEDAGOGY

Pedagogic Projects, Methods and Concerns—Old and New

Ackerman, Walter I. *The Structure of Jewish Education*. N.Y.: Commission on Jewish Education in North America, 1990, 16pp.

Bayer, Sue. "Creative Caregivers." *Ped Rep*, 40:1 (Fall 1990): 10–11.

Bogot, Howard I. "One Hour of Jewish Education." *Ped Rep*, 40:4 (April 1990): 15.

Bretton-Granatoor, Gary M. "Peer-Guided Study." *Ped Rep*, 40:3 (January 1990): 12–14.

Folpe, Joan. "The Discovery Room." *Ped Rep* 41:1, (Fall 1990): 16–17.

Glatzer, Shoshana. "Classroom Management Clinic." *Ped Rep* (40:1) (Fall 1990): p. 22.

Heilpern, Minna. "Learning Styles." *Ped Rep* 40:1 (Fall 1990): 22–23.

Holtz, Barry W. "What We Should Know about Tests and Testing." A Review-Essay. *MJ* 24 (Spring 1991): 27, 29.

Isaacs, Leora W. *A Blueprint for School Improvement: A Step-by-Step Workbook Guide for Jewish Schools*. N.Y.: JESNA, 1988. 64pp.

Isaacs, Mel. "Inspiring a Lifelong Quest." *Ped Rep* 40:4 (April 1990): pp. 23–24.

Jacobs, Charles. "Interpreting the Media for our Students." *Ten Da'at* 4:2 (Spring 1990): 13–17.

Loebl, Judy Silberg. "Jewish Reading Program." *Ped Rep* 41:1, (Fall 1990): 31.

Lubetski, Meir. "Enriching Jewish Education through Media." *Ten Da'at* 5:2 (Spring 1991): 43–45.

Mandell, Ronni S. "An Activity-Oriented School." *Ped Rep* 40:4 (April 1990); 28–30.

48 PEDAGOGY

* Rosoff, Barbara L. *Student Motivation to Learn in the Conservative Jewish Supplemental School.* Rutgers U. 1990.

Schlanger, Sandy. "Conference on Teaching and Learning." *Ped Rep*, 40:1 (Fall 1990): 23–24.

Schneck, Michelle. "Professional Day." *Ped Rep* 40:1 (Fall 1990): 24–25.

Schwartz, Lillian. "LAP (Learning and Parents)." *Ped Rep* 40:1 (Fall 1990): p. 30.

Shapiro, Jane S. "Communities of Learners." *Ped Rep* 40:3 (January 1990): p. 34.

Silverman, Jerry. "Eighteen Classroom Techniques." *Ped Rep* 40:4 (April 1990): 41–45.

Skelker, Philip. "Developing Jewish Individuality." *L'Eylah* 29 (April 1990): 15–19.

Solovy, Delores Kohl, and Marilyn Finesilver. "Evaluation Techniques for the Jewish Classroom." *Ped Rep* 36 (September 1985).

Soltes, Ori Z. "The Use of Video in the Classroom." *Ped Rep* 40:3 (January 1990): 39.

UAHC, Department for Religious Education. *The 1990 Idea Book.* N.Y.: UAHC, 1990.

Yasgur, Benjamin S. "Learning Styles." *Ped Rep* 40:1 (Fall 1990): 22–23.

Judaic Sources—Teaching the Texts

Abrams, Judith Z. *The Talmud for Beginners.* Vol. I: Prayer. Northvale, N.J.: Jason Aronson, 1991, 202p Vol. 2: *Text*, 1992.

Goldin, Barbara Diamond. *A Child's Book of Midrash.* Northvale, N.J.: Jason Aronson, 1990, 125pp. Folio size.

Goldin, Grace. *Come under the Wings: A Midrash on Ruth.* Introduction by Maurice Samuels. Phila.: JPS, n.d. 80pp.

Goldin, Judah. *The Living Talmud.* Chicago: U. of Chicago Press, 1957. 244pp.

———. *Studies in Midrash and Related Literature.* Edited by Barry L. Eichler and Jeffrey H. Tigay. Phila.: JPS, 1988. 419pp.

Holtz, Barry W. ed. *Back to the Sources, Reading the Classic Jewish Texts.* N.Y.: Summit Books, 1984. 448pp. Authors and topics follow:
  Fine, Lawrence. "Kabbalistic Texts." Pp. 305–359.
  Goldenberg, Robert. "Talmud." Pp. 129–175.
  Green, Arthur. "Teachings of the Hasidic Masters." Pp. 361–401.
  Greenstein, Edward L. "Biblical Law." Pp. 83–103.
  ———. "Medieval Bible Commentaries." Pp. 213–259.
  Holtz, Barry W. "Introduction." Pp. 11–29.
  ———. "Midrash." Pp. 177–211.
  Lichtenstein, Murray H. "Biblical Poetry." Pp. 105–127.
  Mintz, Alan. "Prayer and the Prayerbook." Pp. 403–429.
  Rosenberg, Joel. "Biblical Narrative." Pp. 31–81.
  Samuelson, Norbert M. "Medieval Jewish Philosophy." Pp. 261–303.

Kravitz, Leonard, and Kerry M. Olitzky. *Pirke Avot: A Modern Commentary on Jewish Ethics.* Introduction by W. Gunther Plaut. N.Y.: UAHC Press, 1990.

Roth, Amy E. "Can Rabbinics Be Taught Without Teaching Jewish Values? A Study of Behrman House and Taura Aura Rabbinics Curricula," Department of Education, JTSA, M.A. Thesis, 1990.

Segal, Benjamin J. "Midrash: The Search For A Contemporary Past, *Purim,*" *Shofar* 7:6 (March 1990).

Silberman, Shoshana. *The Whole Megillah (Almost).* Illustrated by Katherine Janus Kahn. Kar-Ben Inc., 1991.

Singer, Ellen, with Bernard M. Zlotowitz. *Our Sacred Texts.* N.Y.: UAHC Press, 1992. Ages 11–13.

Steinsaltz, Adin. *The Essential Talmud.* Translated from the Hebrew by Chaya Galai. N.Y.: Basic Books, 1976. 296pp.

———. *The Talmud—The Steinsaltz Edition, A Reference Guide.* Translator and editor, Israel V. Berman. N.Y.: Random House, 1989. 323pp. Folio size.

Zimand, Esther. "Inivitation to Talmud." *Ped Rep.* 40:1 (Fall 1990): 3–i.

Games

Isaacs, Ronald H. *The Jewish Instructional Games Book.* N.Y.: Board of Jewish Education of Greater New York, c. 1989. 141pp.

Moskowitz, Nachama Skolnik. *Games, Games, and More Games for the Jewish Classroom*. N.Y.: UAHC Press, 1993. Ages 9–12.

Sex Education and the School

Freestone, Julie. "Educators Confront How to Teach AIDS in Jewish Classrooms." *The Northern California Jewish Bulletin*, June 5, 1992, p. 30.

Freund, Richard A. "Some Aspects of Jewish Sexual Ethics and Hellenism." *Journal of Reform Judaism* 36:4 (Fall 1989): 55–69.

Gittleson, Roland B. *How Do I Decide? Jewish Morality in an Age of Sexual Revolution*. West Orange, N.J.: Behrman House, 1990. Ages 13–16.

Herman, Agnes G., Ed. *Tikvah. A Publication of the UAHC-CCAR Committee on AIDS.* 1:6 (Fall 1993): 4pp.

Merians, Mel. "Battling AIDS." *Tikvah*. N.Y.: UAHC-CCAR Committee on AIDS (Fall 1992): 4pp.

Education for New Immigrants

Rosenblum, Eileen. "Educating Russian Children." *Ped Rep* 40:1 (Fall 1990): p. 33.

Cults, Drinking, Suicide and Youth

Anonymous [sic]. "Breaking the Chains of Mind Control." *Moment* 18:4 (August 1993): 32–33, 64.

Bardin, David and Livia. "Hanging by a Thread." *Moment* 18:4 (August 1993): 28–29, 56.

Buchwald, Ephraim. "The Outreach Program: A Revolution Gaining Momentum." *Jew Ed* 56:3 (Fall 1988): 24–28.

Gordon, Sol. "Teen and Drugs: Why Just Saying "No" Isn't Enough." *Compass* 13:1 (Fall 1990).

Hoffmann, Yvonne. "Suicide and Its Impact on Grief." *CAJE*, (Autumn 1987): 7–8.

Markowitz, Arnold. "Jews in Cults—Why We're Vulnerable and How They Snare Our Children." *Moment* 18:4 (August 1993): 22–27.

Olitzky, Kerry M., and Stuart M. Copans. *Twelve Jewish Steps to Recovery*. Woodstock, Vt: Jewish Lights Publishing, c. 1992. 136pp.

———, and Aaron Z. [sic]. *Daily Twelve Step Recovery Meditations Based on the Bible*. Woodstock, Vt.: Jewish Lights Publishing, c. 1992. 2 volumes, 224pp. and 280pp.

———. *100 Blessings Every Day: Daily Twelve Step Recovery Affirmations and Exercises for Personal Growth and Renewal Reflecting Seasons of the Jewish Year*. Woodstock, Vt.: Jewish Lights Publishing, c. 1992. 416pp.

Polish, Daniel P., Daniel B. Syme, and Bernard M. Zlotowitz. *Drugs, Sex, and Integrity: What Does Judaism Say?* Illustrated by, Jose Diaz. N.Y.: UAHC Press, 1992.

Schiff, Alvin I. "The Drug Culture and the Jewish School." *Jew Ed* 56:3 (Fall 1988): 2.

Seltzer, Sanford, ed. *Derech* 1:2 (Fall 1993): Brookline, MA: UAHC, 4pp.

Simon, Linda. "Synanon: A Game Gone Sour." *Moment* 18:4 (August 1993): 30–31, 57–58.

Computers in the School

Holtzberg, Carol S. "Electronic Haftarah, Torah, and Tefillah Tutors." *CAJE* (Summer 1990): 6–7.

Matanky, Leonard A. "The State of Jewish Educational Software." *Ten Da'at* 111:3 (Spring 1989): 42–13.

———. "Bits of Bytes." A Guide to Hebrew/English Word Processing. *Ten Da'at* IV: 1 (Fall 1989): 43–45.

———. "Whatever Happened to the Computer Revolution?" *Compass* 13:3 (Spring/Summer 1991): 17–19.

Solow, M. *An Overview of the Relationship Between Computers and Jewish Education: A Solution in Jewish Education*. Report to the L.A. Pincus Jewish Education Fund for the Diaspora, Joint Program for Jewish Education, Jerusalem, 1985.

Marriage, Divorce, and Intermarriage

Alper, Sherri. "Reconsidering Conversion." *Compass* 14:1 (Fall 1991): 10.

Brenner, Reeve Robert. "Intra-marriage, Mitzva-marriage, Mixed-marriage, Inter-marriage and the Family: Toward Reworking Definitions." *Response* 16:4, (Winter 1990): 11–16.

Finkle, Arthur L. "A Jewish View of Love, Sex and Marriage." *Ped Rep* 40:1 (Fall 1990): p. 19.

Gittelsohn, Roland B. *Love In Your Life, A Jewish View of Teenage Sexuality*. N.Y.: UAHC Press, 1991, 110pp.

Goldscheider, Calvin. "American Jewish Marriage: Erosion or Transformation." *Studies In Contemporary Jewry*, Vol. 5, 1989, Jerusalem: Institute of Contemporary Jewry, The Hebrew U. N.Y.: UAHC Press, 1992.

Mailer, Allen S. "Jewish Educators vs. Mixed Marriages." *Jew Ed* 57:2/3/4 (Summer/Winter 1989): 77–79.

Mayer, Egon. "Why Not Judaism," *Moment* 16:5 (October 1991): 28–42.

Pergola, Sergio Delia and Schmelz, Uziel O. "Demographic Transformation of American Jewry: Marriage and Mixed Marriage in the 1980's." *Studies In Contemporary Jewry*, Vol. 5, 1989. Jerusalem: Institute of Contemporary Jewry, The Hebrew U.

Polish, Daniel F., Daniel B. Syme, and Zlotowitz, Bernard M. "Intermarriage: Why Does It Upset Jews?" *Compass* 14:1 (Fall 1991): 7–8.

Romanoff, Lena with Lisa Hostein. *Your People, My People: Finding Acceptance and Fulfillment As A Jew By Choice*. Phila: JPS (1990): 200pp.

Schrag, Carl. "Like Abraham and Ruth." *Had Mag* 21:8 (April 1990): 24–27.

Seltzer, Robert M. "Intermarriage, Outreach & Conversion in American Jewry." *Cong M*, 57:4 (May/June 1990): 10–12.

Syme, Daniel B. *The Jewish Wedding Book, A Keepsake for Your Special Day*. N.Y.: UAHC Press, 1992.

Tobin, Gary A. "From Alarms to Open Arms," (Interfaith Marriage) *Had Mag* 73:4 (December 1991): 22–25.

Bereavement

Brener, Anne. *Mourning & Mitzvah: A Guided Journal for Walking the Mourner's Path through Grief to Healing*. Woodstock, Vt.: Jewish Lights Publishing, 1993. 288pp.

Feld, Edward. *The Spirit of Renewal: Crisis and Response in Jewish Life*. Woodstock, Vt.: Jewish Lights Publishing, 1993. 216pp.

Podell, Craig and Vicki Rosentreich. "Broken Parenthood: The Death of a Child." *Compass* 13:2 (Winter 1991): 11–12.

Rabinowitz, Tzvi. *A Guide to Life: Jewish Laws and Customs of Mourning*. Northvale, N.J.: Jason Aronson, 1989. 242pp.

Silverman, William B., and Kenneth B. Cinnamon. *When Mourning Comes: A Book of Comfort for the Grieving*. Northvale, N.J.: Jason Aronson, 1990. 145pp.

Sonsino, Rifat and Daniel B. Syme. *What Happens After I Die?: Jewish Views of Life After Death*. N.Y.: UAHC, 1990.

Techner, David, and Judith Hirt Mannheimer. *A Candle For Grandpa, A Guide to the Jewish Funeral for Children and Parents*. Illustrated by Joel Iskowitz. N.Y.: UAHC Press, 1993. Ages 5–8.

THE ARTS

General

Epstein, Saundra Starling. "Jewish Arts Festival." *Ped Rep* 40:1, (Fall 1990): 7–8.

Frazier, Nancy. *Jewish Museums of North America: A Guide to Artifacts and Memorabilia*. N.Y.: John Wiley & Sons, 1991.

Seldin, Ruth R. "American Jewish Museums: Trends and Issues." *AJYB* 91 (1991): 71–117.

Art in the Jewish School

Brinn, Ruth Essrig. *Let's Celebrate 57 Jewish Holiday Crafts For Young Children*. Rockville, M.D.: Kar-Ben Copies, n.d.

Magnus, Joann, with Howard I. Bogot. *An Artist You Don't Have To Be*. N.Y.: UAHC Press, 1990.

Mermelstein, Shoshana and Chava Shapiro. *Arts & Crafts Around The Jewish Calendar*. Vols. I and II. N.Y.: Torah Umesorah, 1988.

Music

Mlotek, Eleanor Gordon & Joseph Mlotek, compilers. *Pearls of Yiddish Song*, (Y & E). Illustrated by Tsirl Waletzky. Texts and Music.

N.Y.: Education Department of the Workmen's Circle, 1989. 286pp.

North American Federation of Temple Youth. *NFTYs Fifty Songbook.* N.Y.: Transcontinental Music Publications, n.d.

Richards, Stephen, Editor. *Manginot, 201 Songs for Jewish Schools.* N.Y.: Transcontinental Music Publications, a Division of UAHC, n.d.

Robinovitch, Sid. *Mosaic of Jewish Folksongs.* N.Y.: Transcontinental Music Publications, n.d.

Dance

Rauch, Eduardo. "Dancing, Dancing Metaphors: Teaching as Religious Search and Experience." "A Review-Essay of *Teaching and Religious Imagination.* San Francisco: Harper & Row, 1987." *MJ* 23 (Spring 1990): 24–25.

BAR/BAT MITZVAH

Bronstein, Herbert. "UAHC Resolution on Bar/Bat Mitzvah." *Compass* 16:1 (Fall 1993): 19.

Cohen, Aharon. "Bat Mitzvah: A Challenge for Religious Education." *Ten Da'at* 111:3 (Spring 1989): 31–32.

Glatzer, Shoshana. *Coming of Age as a Jew—Bar/Bat Mitzvah.* Teacher's Guide and Student Workbook. N.Y.: BJE, 1988. 155pp. & 180pp. A curriculum guide for Grades 6 & 7.

Hyman, Paula. "The Introduction of Bat Mitzvah in Conservative Judaism in Postwar America." *YA* 19, 1990. Ed. Deborah Dash Moore. 133–146.

Marder, Janet. "When Bar/Bat Mitzvah Loses Meaning." *RJ* 21:2 (Winter 1992): 4–8, 13, 69.

Paterson, Moira, Editor. *The Bar Mitzvah Book.* N.Y.: Praeger, 1975.

Rosenfield, Bea and Jerry Rosenfield. A review of Nachman Cohen's *Bar/Bat Mitzvah and Beyond.* Ten Da'at 111:3 (Spring 1989): 35–37.

Rosman, Steven M. "Reclaiming the Bar/Bat Mitzvah." *Compass* 16:1 (Fall 1993): 14–15.

Salkin, Jeffrey K. *Putting God on The Guest List.* Woodstock, Vt.: Jewish Lights Publishing, c. 1991. 184pp.

Schiff, AJvin I. Editorial, "A Jerusalem Diaspora Bar Mitzvah." *Jew Ed* 58:1/2 (Spring/Summer 1990): 2.

Segal, Danny. "Bar/Bat Mitzvah Heroes." *RJ* 21:2 (Winter 1992): 10–12.

Tomberg, Robert F. "Bar/Bat Mitzvah: A Bit of Theory and a Practical Response." *Compass* 16:1 (Fall 1993): 16–17.

Wolff, Ferida. *Pink Slippers, Bat Mitzvah Blues.* Phila.: JPS, 1989. 137pp.

THE BIBLE

The Bible General

Curzon, David, Editor and Introduction. *Modern Poems on the Bible.* Phila.: JPS, 1993. 416pp.

Friedman, Richard. *Who Wrote the Bible?* N.Y.: Harper & Row, 1989.

Leibowitz, Nehama. *Studies in the Book of Genesis . . . Deuteronomy.* Jerusalem: World Zionist Organization, 1981. 6 vols.

The JPS Torah Commentary. "The Traditional Hebrew Text with the New JPS Translation." Phila., N.Y., Jerusalem (All volumes Folio size):
   Sarna, Nahum M. *Commentary*, Genesis. Phila: JPSA, 1989. 414pp.
   ———. *Commentary*, Exodus. Phila.: JPSA, 1991. 278pp.
   Levine, Baruch A. *Commentary*, Leviticus. Phila.: JPSA, 1989. 284pp.
   Milgrom, Jacob. *Commentary*, Numbers. Phila.: JPSA, 1990. 520pp.

Teaching the Bible

Alter, Robert, and Frank Kermode, Ed. *The Literary Guide to the Bible.* Cambridge, Mass. Harvard U. Press, 1987. 688pp.

———. "Interpreting The Bible." *Commentary* 89:3 (March 1990): 52–59.

Beiner, Stan J. *Bible Scenes: Joshua to Solomon.* Denver, Colo.: ARE, 1988. 235pp.

Berson, Mark. "Teaching Bible: The Goals of Teaching Text." Department of Education, JTSA, M.A. Thesis, 1990.

Burstein, Chaya M. *The Hebrew Prophets: A Story Workbook*. Illustrations by the author. N.Y.: UAHC Press, 1990. 80pp.

Cassaway, Esta, writer and illustrator. *The Five Books of Moses for Young People*. Northvale, N.J.: Jason Aronson, 1992. All ages.

Chubara, Yona. *Torah Talk: An Early Childhood Teaching Guide*. Denver, Colo.: ARE, 1989. 270pp.

Fields, Harvey J. *A Torah Commentary for Our Times*. Volume I, *Genesis;* Vol. II, *Exodus and Leviticus;* Vol. HI, *Numbers and Deuteronomy*. N.Y.: UAHC Press, 1990, 1992, 1993. Ages 9–12.

Greenstein, Edward L. "On Ways of Reading the Torah." (A Review of Michael Walzer's *Exodus and Revolution*), N.Y.: Basic Books, 1985. 29pp.

Grishaver, Joel Lurie, author and illustrator. *Learning Torah*. A Self-Guided Journey Through the Layers of Jewish Learning. N.Y.: UAH Press, c. 1990.

Gurvis, Laura Kizner. *Learn and Do Bible Book*. Illustrated by Jana Ben-Moshe, West Orange, N.J.: Behrman House, 1993. K–2.

Karkowaky, Nancy. *The Ten Commandments, A Text and Activity Book*. West Orange, N.J.: Behrman House, 1988. 95pp.

Levy, B. Barry. "The Bible Laboratory." *Ten Da'at* IV:1 (Fall 1989): 30–32.

Miller, Lori. *The Book Of Joshua*. N.Y.: Board of Jewish Education of Greater New York, 1990. 58pp. Ages 12–15.

Nachshoni, Yehuda. *Studies in the Weekly Parashah: The Classical Interpretations of Major Topics and Themes in the Torah*. Brooklyn, N.Y.: Mesorah Publications/Artscroll, 1988. 319pp.

Rose, Shirley. *Let's Discover The Bible*. Illustrated by Lane Yerkes. West Orange, N.J.: Behrman House, 1993. 2 Sets and T. Ed. K–2.

Rosenbaum, Alan B. "Tanakh Programs for Computers." *Ten Da'at* 5:1 (Fall 1990): 22–23.

Rosman, Steven M. *Sidrah Stories: A Torah Companion*. N.Y.: UAHC Press, 1989. 185pp.

Rossel, Seymour. *A Child's Bible: Lessons from the Torah*. West Orange, N.J.: Behrman House, 1988. 160pp.

Steinbock, Steven E. *Torah, The Growing Gift*. Illustrated by Timothy Granger Smith. Also Teacher's Guide. N.Y.: UAHC Press, 1993. Ages 9–12.

Waskow, Arthur I. *Before There Was a Before*. N.Y.: Adama Books, 1984. 85pp.

EARLY CHILDHOOD EDUCATION

Articles, Manuals, and Books

Borok, Bernice S. "Nursery School Assistants." *Ped Rep* 40:1 (Fall 1990): 9–10.

Chanover, Hyman. "Reactions to the Current Academic Twist in Childhood Education." *Jew Ed* 59:1 (Spring/Summer 1991): 6–12.

* Feinberg, Miriam P. *Placement of Sectarian Content for Jewish Religious Nursery Schools and Kindergartens in the United States*. U. of Maryland, 1988.

Ginsberg, Marvell. "Whither Early Childhood Education?" *Ped Rep* 40:2 (October 1989): 1620.

Gittelson, Abraham J. "Early Childhood Hebrew Readiness Program." *Ped Rep* 40:1 (Fall 1990): p. 12.

———. "Early Childhood Hebrew Readiness Program." *Ped Rep* 41:1 (Fall 1991): 2.

Kleinman, Susan. "The First School Decision." *Had Mag* 72:10 (June/July 1991): 32–34.

Shub, Phyllis. "Early Childhood Drama." *Ped RepW.l* (Fall 1990): 11.

Wolf, Sandy Furfine and Nancy Cohen Nowak. *Jewish Preschool Teacher's Book*. (Revised) Denver, Colo.: ARE Publishing Inc., 1991. 189pp.

EXCEPTIONAL CHILDREN

Special Education

David, Avi. "Pitfalls in Early Placement for Bright Children." *Jew Obs* 24:7 (October 1991): 36.

Jacobs, Betty S. "Teach Your Children—All Your Children." *Moment* 15:1 (February 1990): 34–39, 57.

Katz, David A. "Gregory's Bar Mitzvah." *Compass* 16:1 (Fall 1993): 17–18 (A Bar Mitvah for a special child).

Levine-Stern, Carol. "Committee for Special Education." *Ped Rep* 41:1 (Fall 1990): 35.

Lipson, Norman B. "Bat-Bar Mitzvah for Special People." *Ped Rep* 41:1 (Fall 1990): 5.

Nissenfeld, Betty. "Volunteers for Special Education." *Ped Rep* 40:1 (Fall 1990): 34–35.

Schanzer, Sharon. "Tips for Teaching Children with Special Needs." *The Lehiyot Connection* 5:1 (Fall 1991): 6.

Schwartz, Carole. *A Manual for the Teacher of Parents of Jewish Special Children*. N.Y.: USCJE, 1981. 90pp.

Stern-Levine, Carol. "Committee for Special Education." *Ped Rep* 40:1 (Fall 1990): 35.

Werk, Susan E. "Developing Learning Disabled Programs in the Afternoon Hebrew Schools." Department of Education, JTSA, M.A. Thesis, 1990.

GUIDANCE

In the School

Brier, Rosemary S. "Occupations." *Ped Rep* 41:1 (Fall 1990): 15.

HEBREW

Hebrew in Jewish Life and Early America

Gliner, Lewis. *The Joys of Hebrew*. N.Y.: Oxford U. Press, 1992. 292pp.

Goldman, Shalom. "Biblical Hebrew in Colonial America: The Case of Dartmouth." *AJH* 89:2 (Winter 1989–1990): 173–180.

———. "Hebrew at the Early Colleges: Orations at Harvard, Dartmouth and Columbia." *Amer Jew Arc* 42:1 (Spring/Summer 1990): 23–26.

Gross, Michael. "Why Hebrew?" *Recon* 55:3 (January/February 1990): 19–20, 24.

Mintz, Alan, Editor. *Hebrew in America*. Detroit: Wayne State U. Press, 1992. 288pp.

———. "Hebrew in America." *Commentary* 96:1 (July 1993): 42–46.

Methodology and Teaching Aids

Bar-Lev, Zev. "Glyphs: A Shortcut to Reading Hebrew." *Ped Rep* 40:4 (April 1990): 38–40.

Bayar, Ilene. "Using the Resource Room for Hebrew Instruction." *Ped Rep* 40:1 (Fall 1990): 13–14.

Board of Jewish Education of Greater New York. *Hebrew Roots and Fruits, A Guide to Jewish Concepts and Values through Root Words*. Teacher's Guide and Student Text. N.Y.: BJE, 1987. 136pp.

Bogot, Howard I. *My First 100 Hebrew Words: A Young Person's Dictionary of Judaism*. Illustrated by Giora Carmi. N.Y.: UAHC Press, 1993. Ages 5–9.

Borodkin, Thelma L., and Adina Ofek. "Intervention Techniques: Teaching the Learner to Learn." *MJ* 24 (Spring 1991): 23.

Brettler, Marc. "Classical Hebrew in the Modern Hebrew Curriculum." *MJ* 24 (Spring 1991): 25–26.

Burstein, Chaya. *The Jewish Kids' Hebrew-English Workbook*. Phila.: JPS, 1993. 40pp. Ages 7 and up.

Cohen, David. "Using the Resource Room for Hebrew Instruction." *Ped Red* 40:1 (Fall 1990): 13–14.

Cohen, Leo M. *From Generation to Generation: The Hebrew Alphabet*. Santa Cruz: Kol Yisrael Pub. Co., 1989.

Ganz, Yaffa. *Alef to Tav*. Brooklyn, N.Y.: Messorah Pub., 1989. 21pp.

Golinkin, Noah. "You Can Learn to Read Hebrew in One Day." *Moment* 15:4 (August 1990): 25–27.

Herson, Benjamin. *Secret of the Pyramid, The Syllable Key to Hebrew Reading*. A primer for teachers and independent learners. N.Y.: Remark Book. Service, Inc., c. 1993.

Kaminetsky, Alex. *Syllable by Syllable and Siddur Ot L'Ot, Teaching Hebrew Phonetically*. Remark Book. Service, Inc., c. 1993.

Kasakove, David P., and Kerry M. Olitzky. *Hebrew, Holidays & Heroes: The Jewish Fun Book*. Cartoons by Mark Lerer. N.Y.: UAHC Press, c. 1992. Ages 9–12.

Levinson, Julie. "Using the Resource Room for Hebrew Instruction." *Ped Rep* 40:1 (Fall 1990): 13–14.

Naymark, Soryl. "Language Study Integration." *Ped Rep* 41:1 (Fall 1990): 38–39.

Rossel, Seymour. *20 Tips for Classroom Management with the New Siddur Program for Hebrew and Heritage*. West Orange, N.J.: Behrman House, 1993.

Silverman, Jerry. "Using the Resource Room for Hebrew Instruction." *Ped Rep* 40:1 (Fall 1990): 13–14.

———. "Hebrew Advertisements." *Ped Rep* 41:1 (Fall 1990): 14–15.

HISTORY

General

Dawidowicz, Lucy. *What is the Use of Jewish History*. Edited and with an Introduction by Neal Kozodoy. N.Y.: Schocken, c. 1992. 278pp.

Evyater, Friesel. *Atlas of Modern Jewish History*. N.Y.: Oxford U., 1990. 159pp. Folio size.

Role and Goal

Blank, Paul J. "Teaching Jewish History: Panorama of Jewish History." Department of Education, JTS, MA Thesis, 1990.

Cohen, Steven M. "Uses and Misuses of Jewish History." *Cong M* 57:3 (March/April 1990): 23–25.

Goldblum, Henry. "Uses for Jewish History: Functional Jewish-Historical Education." *L'Eylah* 32 (September 1991): 32–36.

Social Studies

Hurwitz, Ann Ricki and Sue Hurwitz. *Klal Israel: Our Jewish Community*. West Orange, N.J.: Behrman House, c. 1990.

Tobesman, Rachmiel. *Jewish Social Studies*. N.Y.: Coalition for the Advancement of Jewish Education, Spring 1991. 13pp.

Texts and Readers

Leiman, Sondra. *The Jewish Experience*. Consulting Editor, Jonathan D. Sarna. N.Y.: UAHC Press, 1993. Also a teacher's guide by author. Ages 9–12.

Muggamin, Howard. *The Jewish Americans*. N.Y.: Chelsea House Publishers, 1988. Ages 11–14.

Rosenblum, Richard, author and illustrator. *Journey to the Golden Land*. Phila.: JPS, n.d. 32pp. Ages 5–9.

THE HOLOCAUST

Teaching and Commemoration

Alexander, Edward. "What the Holocaust Does Not Teach." *Commentary* 95:2 (February 1993): 32–36.

Bar-On, Dan. *Legacy of Silence. Encounters with Children of the Third Reich*. Cambridge, Mass.: Harvard U. Press, 1989. 384pp.

Berenbaum, Michael. "Issues in Teaching the Holocaust." in *After Tragedy and Triumph: Essays in Modern Jewish Thought and the American Experience*. Cambridge: Cambridge U. Press, (1990): 61–67.

Blume, Harvey. "The Holocaust as a Teaching Tool." *For* (E.) (August 28, 1992): 12.

Brothers, Eric. "On Teaching the Holocaust and Jewish Resistance." *Jew Ed* 59:3 (Winter 1992): 29–32.

Bunting, Eve. *Terrible Things: An Allegory of the Holocaust*. Phila.: JPS, 1989. 32pp.

Commission on Social Action, UAHC. *The Miracle of Denmark: Saying Thank You 8,000 Times, A Letter-writing Campaign to the Queen of Denmark*. N.Y.: CSA, UAHC, 1993. 27pp.

Dawidowicz, Lucy S. "How They Teach the Holocaust." *Commentary* 90:6 (December 1990): 25–32.

Flender, Harold. *Rescue in Denmark: How Occupied Denmark Rose as a Nation to Save the Danish Jews From Nazi Extermination.* N.Y.: Simon & Schuster, 1963.

* Frampton, Wilson. *A Descriptive Study to Ascertain Curriculum Guidelines for Holocaust Education as Provided by State Departments of Education.* Temple U. 1990.

———. "Holocaust Education and the Need For Consistency." *Jew Ed* 59:1 (Spring/Summer 1991): 81–35.

Gamoran, Hillel. *The Righteous among the Nations: A Six Lesson Unit for Grades 5–7.* N.Y.: Reform Curriculum Resource Center, UAHC, c. 1991. 27pp.

———. "Honoring the Righteous Among the Nations." *Compass* 14:2 (Winter 1992): 14.

Garber, Zev, Alan L. Berger, and Richard Libowitz, eds. *Methodology in the Academic Teaching Of The Holocaust.* Lanham, Md. U. Press of America and Studies in Judaism, 1988. 364pp.

Gilbert, Martin. *The Holocaust: A History of the Jews of Europe during the Second World War.* N.Y.: Holt. Rinehart and Winston, 1986. 959pp.

Glick, Michael. "The March of the Living." *Shofar* (April 1991): 6–9.

Goldfarb, Jack. "The Legend of Dr. Korczak." *Shofar* 7:8 (May 1990): 16–18.

Helmreich, William B. "The Impact of Holocaust Survivors on American Society: A Socio-Cultural Portrait." *Jud* 39:1 (Winter 1990): 14–27.

Hershan, Stella K. "A Memoir of Nazi Austria and the Jewish Refugee Experience in America." *AJA* 43:2 (Fall/Winter 1991): 181–206.

Holin, Elliot J. "Dealing with Desecration—A Communal Response." *Compass* 14:2 (Winter 1992): 18–20.

Huerta, Carlos C. "Sephardim and the Shoah." A review. *Midstream* 39:7 (October 1993): 41.

Jacobs, Steven L., Editor. *Contemporary Jewish Religious Responses to the Shoah.* Lanham, Md.: U. Press of America, 1993. Vol. V, 264pp.

———. *Contemporary Christian Religious Responses to the Shoah.* Lanham, Md.: U. Press of America, 1993. Vol. VI, 336pp.

Kohn, Rachael. "Commemorating the Holocaust: An Educational Imperative." *Generation* 2:2 (April 1991): 34–35.

Lauer, H. Chaim. "The Auschwitz Moment." *Jew Ed* 59:1 (Spring/Summer 1991): 36–38.

Levy, Isaac Jack, translator and editor. *And the World Stood Silent: Sephardic Poetry of the Holocaust.* Urbana and Chicago: U. of Illinois Press, 1989.

Lipson, Alfred. "The Overlooked Holocaust: Sephardim in Europe." *Midstream* 39:7 (October 1993): 25–28.

Margolis, P. "A Guide to Teaching about Anti-Semitism and the Holocaust." *Compass* 14:2 (Winter 1992): 15–17.

Nir, Yehuda. *The Lost Childhood: A Memoir.* N.Y.: Harcourt Brace Jovanovich, c. 1990. 256pp.

Oliner, Samuel P., and Pearl M. Oliner. *The Altruistic Personality: Rescuers of Jews in Nazi Europe.* N.Y.: The Free Press, 1992.

Reform Judaism. "What Is the Meaning and Purpose of the United States Holocaust Memorial Museum?" 22:2 (Winter 1993). Articles follow:
    Hatch, Orrin. Pp. 17–18.
    Kunin, Madeleine M. Pp. 20 and 68.
    Rifkin, Jeremy. Pp. 68–69.
    Rosensaft, Menachem Z. Pp. 18–20.

Riley, Karen. "The Holocaust And Values Education." *Jew Ed* 58:1 2 (Spring/Summer 1990): 33–35.

Robinson, Colin. *Toward A Curriculum for Teaching The Holocaust in an Elementary Jewish School in the Diaspora.* Jerusalem: Hebrew U., Melton Centre for Jewish Education, 1991.

Rock, Andrea White. "The Jewish Adolescents: Toward A Personal Understanding of Collective Tragedy." *MJ* 24 (Spring 1991): 21–22.

Roskies, David G. *Against the Apocalypse: Responses to Catastrophe in Modern Jewish Culture.* Harvard U. Press, n.d. 352pp.

———. *The Literature of Destruction: Jewish Responses to Catastrophe.* Phila.: JPS, n.d. 650pp.

Schwartz, Elliot. "Holocaust Instruction in Public Schools." *Ped Rep* 40:1 (Fall 1990): 30–21.

Shapiro, Edward S. "The Holocaust & American Jewish Consciousness." *Cong M.* 57:7 (November/December 1990): 18–19. A Review Essay.

Shawn, Karen. "Goals for Helping Young Adolescents Learn About The Shoah." *Ten Da'at*. 5:2 (Spring 1991): 7–11.

Sicher, Efraim. "The Burden of Remembrance: Second Generation Literature." *JBA* 48 (1990–1991): 26–41.

Spiegelman, Art. *Maus: A Survivor's Tale*. A cartoon history of the Shoah. N.Y.: Pantheon Books, 1986.

Tory, Avraham. *Surviving the Holocaust: The Kovno Ghetto Diary*. Edited by Martin Gilbert. Translated by Jerzy Michalowicz. Cambridge: Harvard U. Press, 1990. 554pp.

Wieseltier, Leon. "After Memory: Reflections on the Holocaust Memorial Museum on the Mall, and the reasons for it." *New Republic* (May 3, 1993): 16–21 and 24–26.

Yankelovich, Daniel, Lipstadt, Deborah and Peters, C. Brooks. Articles on "The Holocaust and the American Media." *Dimensions* 4:3 (1989): N.Y.: International Center for Holocaust Studies, ADL of B'nai B'rith.

Texts and Literature

Adler, David. *The Number on My Grandfather's Arm*. N.Y.: UAHC Press, 1987. 28pp. Ages 7–8.

———. *We Remember The Holocaust*. N.Y.: H. Holt, 1988. 147pp.

Linnea, Sharon. *Raoul Wallenberg, the Man Who Stopped Death*. Phila.: JPS, 1992. 168pp. Ages 12 and up.

Meltzer, Milton. *Rescue: The Story of How Gentiles Saved Jews in the Holocaust*. N.Y.: Harper, 1988. 168pp.

Neimark, Anne E. *One Man's Valor: Leo Baeck and the Holocaust*. N.Y.: Lodestar Books, 1986. Ages 11–14.

SCHOOL LIBRARY

Hart, Merrily F. *Creating a Collection: A Resource Booklist for a Beginning Judaic Library*. N.Y.: Association of Jewish Libraries, 1989. 16pp.

LIFE CYCLE OF A JEW

General

Elbogen, Ismar. *Jewish Liturgy—A Comprehensive History*. Translated by Raymond P. Scheindlin. Phila.: JPS and JTSA, 1993. 500pp.

Synagogue and Prayer in the Classroom

Bogot, Howard I., and Orkand, Robert and Joyce. *Gates of Wonder*. Illustrated by Neil Waldman. N.Y.: CCAR Press, 1991. 48pp.

———. *Gates of AWE*. Holy Day Prayers for Very Young Children. Illustrated by Neil Waldman. CCAR Press, 1991. 64pp.

Garfiel, Evelyn. *Service of the Heart: A Guide to the Jewish Prayer Book*. Northvale, N.J.: Jason Aronson, 1989. 251pp.

Gillman, Neil. "Why You Can't Pray and What You Can Do About It." *Moment* 15:5 (October 1990): 48–19, 52–55.

Gross, David C. *How to Be Jewish*. N.Y.: Hippocrene Books, 1989. 198pp.

Moskowitz, Nachama Skolnik. *A Bridge to Prayer*. Vol 2, "The Amidah, Torah Service, and Concluding Prayers." N.Y.: UAHC Press, c. 1990.

Reimer, Jack. *The Synagogue as a Context for Jewish Education*. Cleveland: Mandel Associated Foundations, 1990.

Sagarin, James. *Oseh Shalom*. N.Y.: UAHC Press, 1990. 21pp.

Segal, Benjamin J. "Teaching Prayer: Considerations." *Jew Ed* 57:2/3/4 (Summer/Winter 1989): 72–75.

Shanks, Hershel. "Bless Your Children An Entry into Prayer." *Moment* 15:5 (October 1990): 52.

Slobin, Mark. "Engendering the Cantorate." *YA* 19, 1990. Ed. Deborah Dash Moore, 147–167.

Spiro, Jack. "Formative Process in Jewish Tradition." *Rel Ed* 82:4 (Fall 1987): 547–54.

Wasser, Eric L. "Issues in the Teaching of Prayer: A Curriculum Guide." Department of Education, JTSA, M.A. Thesis, 1990.

Wolf, Alfred. "A Few Thoughts on Inter-religious Worship." *Compass* 13:2 (Winter 1991): 11–12.

Yedwab, Paul Michael. *The Aleph-Bet of Blessing.* N.Y.: UAHC Press, 1990. 72pp.

Holidays—Ceremonies—Customs

Black, Naomi, Editor. *Celebration—The Book of Jewish Festivals.* N.Y.: Jonathan David, 1989.

Buxbaum, Yitzhak. *Jewish Spiritual Practices.* Northvale, N.J.: Jason Aronson, Inc., 1990. 757pp.

Chaikin, Miriam. *Sound the Shofar: The Story and Meaning of Rosh HaShanah and Yom Kippur.* N.Y.: Clarion Books, n.d. 90pp.

Cohen, Floreva G. *Before Shabbat Begins.* N.Y.: Board of Jewish Education, 1985. 31pp.

Ehrlich, Amy. *The Story of Hanukkah.* N.Y.: Dial Books, 1989. 22pp.

Einstein, Stephen J. *Judaism—Customs and Practices.* N.Y.: UAHC Press, 1989. 195pp.

Eisenberg, Robin L. "Celebrating the Jewish Life Cycle." *Compass* 14:1 (Fall 1991): 14.

Fisher, Adam, Editor and Author. *Seder Tu Bishvat, The Festival of Trees.* N.Y.: CCAR, 1990. 112pp.

———. *My Jewish Year, Celebrating Our Holidays.* West Orange, N.J.: Behrman House, Inc., 1992. 32pp.

Greenberg, Irving. *The Jewish Way: Living the Holidays.* N.Y.: Summit Books, 1988. 463pp.

Kuskin, Karla. *A Great Miracle Happened There—A Chanukah Story.* Illustrated by Robert Andrew Parker. N.Y.: Harper-Collins, Willa-Perlman Books, c. 1992. 32pp.

Labovitz, Annette. *Time for My Soul: A Treasury of Jewish Stories for Our Holy Days.* Northvale, N.J.: Jason Aronson, 1987. 427pp.

Levy, Eugene. "How We Celebrate." *Compass* 13:2 (Winter 1991): 9–10.

Olomeinu. "Passover." 44:7 (March/April 1990).

Peli, Pinchas. *Shabbat Shalom: A Renewed Encounter with the Sabbath.* Washington D.C.: B'nai B'rith Books, 1988. 179pp.

Raphael, Chaim. *History of Jewish Celebrations.* N.Y.: Grove-Weidenfeld, 1990. 160pp.

Reimer, Jack, Editor. *The World of the High Holidays.* Anthology . . . on the High Holiday Prayerbook. Miami, Fla.: 1990. 550pp.

Silverman, Maida. *Festival of Esther: The Story of Purim.* N.Y.: Simon & Schuster, 1989. 24pp.

Strassfeld, Michael. *The Jewish Holidays: A Guide and Commentary.* N.Y.: Harper & Row, 1985.

Wachs, S.P. "Jewish Education: Erev Shabbat or New Year's Eve?" In S. Katz, Ed., *Jewish Concepts in Today's World.* New York: KTAV and B'nai B'rith, 1992.

Young Judea. The Zionist Youth Movement. *Tu B'Shevat: A Resource.* N.Y.: 1990. 3 pamphlets.

Juvenile Literature

Backman, Aidel, author and illustrator. *One Night, One Hanukkah Night.* Phila.: JPS, n.d. 32pp. Ages 3–7.

Baum, Roberta Osser. *Shabbat Shalom.* Illustrated by Jana Paiss. West Orange, N.J.: Behrman House, c. 1991.

Bin-Nun, Judy with Franne Einhorn. *Rosh Hashanah: A Holiday Funtext.* Drawings by Heidi Steinberger. N.Y.: UAHC Press, c. 1990. Ages 5–8.

Burstein, Chaya. *The UAHC Kids Catalog.* N.Y.: UAHC Press, 1993. Ages 9–12.

De Paola, Tomie. *My First Chanukah.* N.Y.: G.P. Putnam's Sons, 1989. 12pp.

Gantz, David, Author and Illustrator. *Davey's Hanukkah Golem.* Phila.: JPS, n.d. 32pp. Ages 5–8.

Greenberg, Melanie Hope. *Celebrations: Our Jewish Holidays.* Phila.: JPS, n.d. 32pp. Ages 3–6.

Manushkin, Fran. *Latkes and Applesauce.* Illustrated by Robin Spavart. N.Y.: Scholastic, 1990. 32pp. Hanukkah story. Ages 4–8.

Rosenblum, Richard, Author and Illustrator. *The Old Synagogue.* Phila.: JPS, 1989. 32pp. Ages 5–8.

Sperling, Jerry. *The Little Menorah Who Forgot Chanukah*. Story and music. Illustrated by Glora Carmi. N.Y.: UAHC Press, 1993. A book and cassette set.

Zwerin, Raymond A. *Like a Maccabee*. N.Y.: UAHC Press, 1991. 26pp.

LITERATURE

Bresnick-Perry, Roslyn. *Leaving for America*. Illustrated by Mira Reisberg. Children's Book Press, 1992.

Frankel, Ellen. "Struggling for Meaningful Values in Children's Literature." (A Review of Barbara Cohen's *The Secret Grove*. N.Y.: UAHC, 1985; and David Rosoffs *Growing Up: A Bar Mitzvah Story*. N.Y.: Feldheim, 1984): *MJ* 23 (Spring 1990): 26.

Posner, Marcia W. "Jewish Juvenile Books—1990." *JBA* 49 (1990–1991): 210–19.

———. "Fifty Years of Jewish Children's Books." *JBA* 50 (1992–1993): 81–98.

Rauch, Eduardo. "On the Renewal of Teaching and Storytelling." *MJ* 26 (Autumn 1992): 32.

Sadeh, Pinhas, selected and retold by. *Jewish Folktales*. Translated from the Hebrew by Hillel Halkin. N.Y.: Doubleday, 1989. 443pp.

Sarna, Jonathan D. "From *K'tonton*, to the Torah." *Moment* 15:5 (October 1990): 44–47.

Schwartz, Howard and Barbara Rush. *The Diamond Tree: Jewish Tales From Around the World*. Illustrated by Luri Shulevitz. N.Y.: Harper Collins Publishers, 1991.

———. Selected and Retold by. *Lilith's Cave: Jewish Tales of the Supernatural*. N.Y.: Oxford U. Press, 1990. 306pp.

Schwartz, Lillian. "Literary Lights." *Ped Rep* 40:1 (Fall 1990): 30–31.

Weinreich, Beatrice Silverman. *Yiddish Folktales*. Translated by Leonard Wolff. N.Y.: Pantheon, c. 1989. 413pp.

Juvenile Literature

Carmi, Gloria, Author and Illustrator. *And Shira Imagined*. Phila.: JPS, n.d. 32pp. Ages 3–7.

Patterson, Jose. *Angels, Prophets, Rabbis and Kings: From the Stories of the Jewish People*. Illustrated by Claire Bushe and Edward Ripley. Phila.: JPS, n.d. 144pp. Ages 10 and up.

Roseman, Kenneth D. *West of the Hudson*. N.Y.: UAHC Press, 1993. Ages 9–12.

Ross, Lillian Hammer. *Buba Leah and Her Paper Children*. Illustrated by Mary Morgan. Phila.: JPS, n.d. 32pp. Ages 5–8.

Sasso, Sandy Eisenberg. *God's Paintbrush*. Illustrated by Annette Compton. Woodstock, Vt: Jewish Lights, 1992. Ages 4–8.

Schwartz, Amy, Author and Illustrator. *Mrs. Moskowitz and the Sabbath Candles*. Phila.: JPS, n.d. 32pp. Ages 5–9.

Schwartz, Amy. *Yossel Zissell and the Wisdom of Chelm*. Phila.: JPS, 1986. Ages 8–11.

Shevrin, Aliza, Selected and translated by. *Around the Table: Family Stories of Sholom Aleichem*. N.Y.: C. Scribner's Sons, 1991. Ages 10–1.

Snyder, Carol. *God Must Like Cookies, Too*. Illustrated by Beth Glick. Phila.: JPS, 1992. 32pp.

MITZVOT/VALUES AND CONTEMPORARY ISSUES

Transmitting Values in the Classroom

Alper, Sherri. "Confronting Stereotypes: A Workshop for Teens." *Compass* 14:2 (Winter 1992): 21–23.

Artson, Bradley Sharit. *Love Peace and Pursue Peace: A Jewish Response to War and Nuclear Annihilation*. N.Y.: USCJE, 1988. 276pp.

———. "Teaching Contemporary Jewish Values." *MJ* 24 (Spring 1991): 24, 30.

Bennett, Alan D., Ed. *Journey through Judaism: The Best of Keeping Posted*. N.Y.: UAHC Press, 1992.

Bettman, Batia. "Tzedakathon." *Ped Rep* 40:1 (Fall 1990) pp. 36–37.

Bogot, Howard I., and Albert Vorspan. "Teaching Social Action." *Compass* 13:1 (Fall 1989): 3–4 and 30.

Bretton-Granatoor, Gary M. "Understanding Others Reinforces Our Own Identity." *Compass* 13:2 (Winter 1991): 15–16.

———. "Twenty-six Years that Changed Two Thousand: The Jewish Community and the Catholic Church in Dialogue." *Compass* 14:2 (Winter 1992): 10–11.

Brickner, Balfour and Albert Vorspan. "Jewish Views on Peace and War: What Does Tradition Say?" *Compass* 13:3 (Spring/Summer 1991): 8–9.

Cohen, Shlomo. "The Force of Jewish Values." *Cong M* 57:3 (March/April 1990): 27–29.

Fishkoff, Sue. "Hate on the Campus." *RJ* 22:1 (Fall 1993): 28–32, 44.

Friedman, Jerry. "New Approaches to Jewish Moral Education." *Jew Ed* 56:3 (Fall 1988): 312.

Gittelsohn, Ronald Bertram. *How Do I Decide: A Contemporary Jewish Approach to What's Right and What's Wrong*. West Orange, N.J.: Behrman, c. 1990. 170pp.

Goldstein, Gabriel. "Integrating Jewish Values Within the Curriculum." *L'Eylah* 30 (September 1990): 16–20.

Goodman, Roberta L. "Lawrence Kohlberg's Theory of Moral Development: Implications for Jewish Education." *Compass* 12:1 (Fall 1989): 21–23.

Goor, Donald. "Jewish/Catholic Dialogue." *Compass* 13:2 (Winter 1991): 12–13.

Green, K. "Toward Teaching Menschlichkeit." *MJ* 19 (1985): 30–32.

Holtz, Barry W. *Finding Our Way: Jewish Texts and the Lives We Lead Today*. N.Y.: Schocken, 1990. 257pp. (*See* Bibliographies).

Indianapolis Hebrew Congregation. *The Jewish Literacy Handbook. Compass* 15:2 (Winter 1993): 22pp.

Kadden, Barbara Binder and Bruce Kadden. *Teaching Mitzvot: Concepts Values and Activities*. Denver, Colo.: ARE, 1988. 175pp.

Kelman, Vicky. *Windows: Together 2*. N.Y.: The Melton Center for Jewish Education, JTSA, 1990.

Konvitz, Milton R., Editor. *Judaism and Human Rights*. N.Y.: WW Norton & Co., 1972. 315pp. Articles below:

Bokser, Ben-Zion. "Democratic Aspirations in Talmudic Judaism." Pp. 145–55.
Finkelstein, Louis. "Foundations of Democracy in the Scriptures and Talmud." Pp. 140–44.
Frankfort, Henri. "Kingship under the Judgment of God." Pp. 92–98.
Gordis, Robert. "The Right of Dissent and Intellectual Liberty." Pp. 190–211.
———. "The Vision of Micah." Pp. 278–87.
Hirsch, Richard. "There Shall Be No Poor." Pp. 234–46.
Irwin, William A. "A Common Humanity under One God." Pp. 55–74.
———. "The Rule of a Higher Law." Pp. 99–114.
Konvitz, Milton R. "Man's Dignity in God's World." Pp. 27–32.
———. "Many Are Called and Many Are Chosen." Pp. 74–84.
———. "Judaism and the Democratic Ideal." Pp. 119–39.
———. "Conscience and Civil Disobedience in the Jewish Tradition." Pp. 161–78.
———. "The Good Life." Pp. 216–24.
Lamm, Norman. "The Right of Privacy." Pp. 225–33.
Lord Acton. "The Bible and the Rule of Law." Pp. 89–91.
Mendelssohn, Moses. "Freedom of Religion—Absolute and Inalienable." Pp. 179–89.
Rackman, Emanuel. "Judaism and Equality." Pp. 33–54.

Knobel, Oeter S. "Anti-Semitism and Prejudice: Rabbinic Perspectives." *Compass* 14:2 (Winter 1992): 5–6.

Kushner, Lawrence S. *Honey from the Rock: Visions of Jewish Mystical Renewal*. Woodstock, Vt: Jewish Lights Publishing, 1990. 151pp.

———. *The Book of Letters: A Mystical Hebrew Alef-Bait*. Woodstock, Vt: Jewish Lights Publishing, 1990. 80pp.

———. *The Book of Words*. Woodstock, Vt: Jewish Lights Publishing, 1993. 152pp.

Lamm, Maurice. *Becoming a Jew*. N.Y.: Jonathan David, 1991. 463pp.

Meier, Levi, Editor. *Jewish Values in Health and Medicine*. Lanham, Md.: U. Press of America, 1991. 220pp.

Moment. "Why Be Jewish?" Symposium participants: Samuel Heilman, Jennifer M. Green, David Epstein, Ruth Calderon Ben-Shahar, Lawrence Kushner, Yosef J. Abramowitz, Hershel Shanks, Irving Greenberg, and Hillel Halkin. *Moment* 17:6 (December 1992): 36–51.

Neusner, Jacob. *The Way of Torah: An Introduction to Judaism.* Belmont, Calif.: Wadsworth Publishing, 1988.

Novak, David. *Jewish Social Ethics.* N.Y.: Oxford, 1992. 264pp.

Olitzky, Kerry M. "The Elderly among Us." *Compass* 14:1 (Fall 1991): 17–18.

Rubenstein, Jeffrey. "Ethics and the Liturgy of Conservative Judaism." *Jud* 40:1 (Winter 1991): 95–114.

Sandel, Lenore. "The Language of Prejudice." *Compass* 14:2 (Winter 1992): 24.

Schulweis, Harold M. "If I Am Only for Myself." *RJ* 21:3 (Spring 1993): 14–17.

Schwartz, Earl. *Moral Development: A Practical Guide for Jewish Teachers.* Denver: ARE, 1983.

Sherwin, Byron L. *In Partnership with God: Contemporary Jewish Law and Ethics.* Syracuse, N.Y.: Syracuse U. Press, 1990. 290pp.

Silverman, William B. *The Sages Speak: Rabbinic Wisdom and Jewish Values.* Northvale, N.J.: Jason Aronson, Inc., 1989. 251pp.

Smith, Tom W. *Jewish Attitudes toward Blacks and Race Relations.* N.Y.: AJC, 1990. 44pp.

Stern, Kenneth S. "Beyond Hate: Teaching for Tomorrow." *Compass* 14:2 (Winter 1992): 3–1.

Syme, Deborah Shayne. *Partners.* N.Y.: UAHC Press, 1990. 26pp.

Tsedek V'Shalom. "Social Justice in the Religious School." Newsletter of the Commission on Social Action of Reform Judaism, (Formerly "Briefings") N.Y.: UAHC, (1993): 12.

Vorspan, Albert and David Saperstein. "Jews and Blacks: After Crown Heights." *Compass* 14:2 (Winter 1992): 7–9.

Wasser, Amy Katz. "Teaching Mitzvot in an Informal Educational Setting." Department of Education, JTSA, M.A. Thesis, 1990.

Zlotowitz, Bernard M. "The Biblical and Rabbinic Attitude toward Non-Jews," *Compass* 13:2 (Winter 1991): 5.

Textbooks, Juvenile Literature and Teacher Guides

Pasachoff, Naomi. *Basic Judaism For Young People.* Vol. I, *Israel* (Grades 4–5); Vol. II, *Torah* (Grades 5–6); Vol. III. *God* (Grades 6–7). *Teacher's Guides and Student Activity Books:* Cynthia F. Reich; Lois Miller Cohn; Lesley Silverstone. West Orange, N.J.: Behrman House, c. 1992.

Thum, Robert and Susan Dworski. *My Jewish World: An Introduction to Judaism.* West Orange, N.J.: Behrman House, c. 1991. 159pp. Ages 8–10.

Judaism and Ecology: A New Topic Based on Ancient Sources

Amerling, Suzanne and Josh Saltzman. "Project Tikkun Olam." *Compass* 12:1 (Fall 1989): 17–19.

Bernstein, Ellen. "Judaism and Ecology." *Compass* 13:1 (Fall 1990): 23–26.

Biere, Matthew. "Teaching the Environment through Torah." *Compass* 13:1 (Fall 1990): 26.

Cohen, Jordan D. "Jewish Environmental Programming." *Compass* 13:1 (Fall 1990): 14–16.

Dresner, Samuel H. "Jewish Birds." A Meditation and a Parable. *MJ* 23 (Spring 1990): 16.

Ganz, Yaffa. *The Wonderful World We Live In: A Youthful Introduction to Tehillim—#104.* N.Y.: Mesorah Pub. 1989. 29pp.

Gendler, Everett. "Our Environment: Jewish Study and Action." *Compass* 13:1 (Fall 1990): 11–12.

Gordis, Robert. "Judaism and the Environment." *Cong M* 57:6 (September/October 1990): 7–10.

Konvitz, Milton R., Editor. *Judaism and Human Rights.* N.Y.: WW. Norton & Co., 1972. 315pp. Articles:
    Belkin, Samuel. "Man as Temporary Tenant." Pp. 251–58.
    Freudenstein, Eric G. "Ecology and the Jewish Tradition." Pp. 265–74.
    Hirsch, Samson Raphael. "Do Not Destroy." Pp. 259–64.

Konvitz, Milton R. "The Earth Is the Lord's." Pp. 249–50.

Tucker, JaAnne and Susan Freeman. "A Dance Midrash Activity: Protecting Trees During War." *Compass* 13:1 (Fall 1990): 22–23.

Waskow, Arthur. "The Greening of Judaism." *Moment* 17:3 (June 1992): 45–47, 52.

Judaism and Ecology—Our Earth and Our Tradition

In *The Melton Journal*, part I, 24 (Spring 1991). Articles:
Aronson, Robin. "Animal Life in Light of Jewish and Christian Traditions." (Review of books by Elijah Judah Schochet, *Animal Life in Jewish Tradition: Attitudes and Relationships*. N.Y.: Ktav, 1984; Andrew Lindsey, *Christianity and the Rights of Animals*; and Andrew Lindsey and Tom Regan, *Animals and Christianity: A Book of Readings*. Both by Crossroad, N.Y.: 1989, 1988). Pp. 8, 10.
"Editoral." P. 2.
Eisenberg, Freda. "The Diaspora of the Diaspora. Jews in Rural New England as a Model for Jewish Renewal." Pp. 15, 19.
Fink, Dan, "From a High School Curriculum on Judaism and Ecology: On Becoming *Shomrei Adamah*—Keepers of the Earth," by Ellen Bernstein, director of Shomrei Adamah, Wyncote, Pa. Pp. 18–19.
Green, Arthur. "God, World, Person:, A Jewish Theology of Creation, Part I." Pp. 4, 6, 7.
Katz, Eric. "Are We the World's Keepers? Toward an Ecological Ethic for Our Home Planet." Pp. 3, 11.
Posnick, Michael. "Trace Memories." (Review of *Illuminations: A Bestiary*, by Rosamund Wolff. Purcell & Stephen J. Gould. N.Y.: WW. Norton, 1986. 120pp; *As Dead As A Dodo*. Illustrated by Shawn Rice. Text by Paul Rice & Peter Mayle. Boston: David O. Goodine Pub. 1981, Un-paginated; *The Painter and the Wild Swans*, by Claude Clement. Pictures by Frederic Clement. N.Y.: Dial Books, 1986. Pp. 16, 19.
Rauch, Eduardo. Review-Essay, *The Journey Without Is about the Journey Within. (The Home Planet*, conceived and edited by Kevin W. Kelley for the Association of Space Explorers: Foreword by Jacques-Yves Cousteau. Addison-Wesley, 1988). P. 17.
Rotenberg, Memorah Lebowitz. "Reflections of an Almost Failed, May Yet Fail, Kosher Vegetarian Wife and Mother." Pp. 9–10.
Schorsch, Ismar. "Tending to Our Cosmic Oasis." P. 2.
Wyschograd, Michael. "Judaism and the Sanctification of Nature." Pp. 5, 7.

Towards a Jewish Ecological Paradigm: Essays and Explorations, Part II

The Melton Journal 25 (Spring, 1992):
Fink, Dan. "From a High School Curriculum On Judaism and Ecology: On Becoming *Shomrei Adamah*—Keepers of the Earth," by Ellen Bernstein, director of Shomrei Adamah, Wyncote, Pa. Pp. 18–19.
Gendler, Everett. "Woodchucks in the Garden, Beavers in the Stream and Messiah Nowhere in Sight." Pp. 16–17.
Green, Arthur. "God, World, Person: A Jewish Theology of Creation, Part II." Pp. 4–5.
Kissileff, Harry R. "Starting a Hug (Choog) Tevah (Nature Circle) in Your Community." P. 26.
Kushner, Lawrence, "I is the Lord your God. The SELF of the Universe," (Section of Kushner's book, *God Was in This Place & I. Did Not Know*, Woodstock, Vt.: Jewish Lights Publishing, 1991.) Pp. 8–11.
Rauch, Eduardo, "Redeeming the Wilderness from a Dangerous Exile." A Review-Essay of Gary Snyder's *The Practice of the Wild*. Pp. 27–30.
Schorsch, Ismar. "Trees for Life." Pp. 3, 6.

Judaism and the Focus on the Environment

Reform Judaism 19:1 (1990):
Bernstein, Ellen. "Our Sacred Legacy." Pp. 18–20.
"Cain the Slayer." (Excerpt from *Seder Tu Bishvat: The Festival of Trees*, CCAR, Press). P. 23.
Fink, Dan. "Honi the Sleeper." P. 22.
Heschel, Abraham Joshua. "The Shabbat Solution." P. 21.

"Living Lightly on the Earth." (Excerpts from *50 Simple Things You Can Do to Save the Earth*, Earthworks Press and Earth Day, 1990). Pp. 26–28.
"The ABC of Pollution." P. 24.

TEXTBOOKS

Benderly, Samson. "The Solution of the Problem." *The Jewish Teacher* 1:1 (Jan. 1916).

Hessel, Carolyn Starman. "Textbooks in Jewish Education." *JBA* 48 (1990–1991): 156–168.

Rosenbach, A.S.W. "Early American Jewish Schoolbooks." *98th Annual Report*, The Hebrew Sunday School Society, Phila.: 1927.

Walter, Gabrielle, and Brichta, Lisa. *Textbook Idea Exchange*. N.Y.: Reform Curriculum Resource Center, UAHC, n.d. 44pp.

THE HIGH SCHOOL

* Amsel, Norman A. *A High School Judaic Values Curriculum Using Media as Motivation*. N.Y.: Yeshiva University, 1988.

Bleiweiss, Robert. "Bardin's Model High School." *Jew Spec* 55:4 (Spring 1991): 3–1.

Brier, Evelyn F. "Russian Teen Goodie Bag." *Ped Rep* 40:1 (Fall 1990): 32–33.

* Jaret, Beth Gerstel. *Factors Related to Religiosity in Jewish Adolescents*. Hofstra U., 1989.

Krieger, Shelley G. "Merkaz: The Community High School for Jewish Studies." *Ped Rep* 40:2 (October 1989): 21–24.

Michaeli, Moshe. "Hebrew Curriculum for High Schools." *Ped Rep* 40:1 (Fall 1990): 13.

AMERICAN JEWRY AND THE LAND OF ISRAEL

Amsel, Norman. "The Israel Experience: A Closer Look from Israel." *Ten Da'at* 5:1 (Fall 1990): 34–36.

Ariel, Yakov. "Kaufmann Kohler and His Attitude towards Zionism: A Reexamination." *AJA* 43:2 (Fall/Winter 1991): 207–23.

Auerbach, Jerold S. "American Jews & Israel: Are We One?" *Cong M* 58:5 (August 1991): 11–14.

Bell, Roselyn. "Are We One or Two?" *Had Mag* 73:3 (November 1991): 22–27.

Cohen, Steven M. *Israel and the Diaspora: Jews—United States—Attitudes towards Israel*. Tel Aviv: Israel-Diaspora Institute, 1990. 108pp.

Congress Monthly. "The Jewish State and Jewish Identity: Divergence and Convergence." *Cong M* 573 (March/April 1990): 30–35.

Conservative/Masorti Movement. *Deepening The Commitment: Zionism and the Conservative/Masorti Movement: Papers from a Conference of Conservative/Masorti Movement Leadership*. Held September 7–8, 1988, at the JTSA. JTSA, 1990. 199pp.

Davids, Stanley M. "God, Reform Judaism and Zion." N.Y.: ARZA: *The Journal of Reform Zionism*. 1:1, pp. 4–5.

Davis, Moshe and Yehoshua Ben Arieh, Editors. *With Eyes Toward Zion III: Western Society and the Holy Land*. N.Y.: Aeger, 1991. 275pp.

Eisen, Arnold M. *Galut: Modern Jewish Reflections on Homelessness and Homecoming*. Bloomington, Ind.: Indiana U. Press, 1986. 233pp.

Fackenheim, Emil L. "Pillars of Zionism." *Mid* 38:9 (December 1992): 13–15.

Fenyvesi, Charles. "U.S. Jewry's Response to the Intafada." In *Survey of Jewish Affairs 1989*. Edited by William Frankel. Cambridge, Mass.: 1989, pp. 108–117.

Friedlander, Dov. *The One-Year Program in Israel: An Evaluation*. N.Y.: AJC, Institute On American Jewish-Israeli Relations, 1991, 40pp.

Gal, Allon. "The Zionist Influence on American Jewish Life." *AJA* 41:2 (Fall/Winter 1989): 173–84.

Ganz, Yaffa. "Focus on Israel." *Jewish Action* 52:1 (Winter 1991): 35–36.

Gordon, Uri. "Israeli-Diaspora Relations at a Fateful Crossroads." *The Forum*, A Publication of the North American Jewish Forum. (Autumn 1989): 14–15.

Greenspan, Ellen A. *The Reform Movement and Israel: A Philosophical Approach and the Educational Implications*. Jerusalem: Hebrew U. The Melton Center for Jewish Education in the Diaspora, 1991. 28pp.

Halevi, Ben Israel. *A Modern Guide to the Jewish Holy Places*. Photography by David Posner. Foreword by Louis I. Rabinowitz. N.Y.: Remark Book Service, Inc., c. 1992.

Hirsch, Richard G. "Reform Zionism's Task Today." N.Y.: ARZA: *The Journal of Reform Zionism*. 1:1 (1993): 22–32.

Kasakove, David P. "Covenant People, Covenant Land." *Compass* 10:2 (Winter 1988): 3–4, 23.

Kimelman, Reuven. "Israel-Diaspora Relations in the Wake of the *Who Is A Jew* Question." *The Forum*, A Publication of the North American Jewish Forum, pp. 13–18.

Konvitz, Milton R. "America and the Holy Land." *Mid* 38:9 (December 1992): 40–41.

Kronish, Amy W. "Equal Rights for Women: Is Israel Different?" *MJ* 23 (Spring 1990): 9–10.

Kronish, Ronald, Editor. *Towards the Twenty-first Century: Judaism and the Jewish People in Israel and America. Essays in Honor of Rabbi Leon Kronish on the Occasion of His Seventieth Birthday*. Hoboken, N.J.: KTAV, 1988. 341pp.

Livni, Michael. "Reform Judaism and Reform Zionism in Israel." *Journal of Reform Judaism* 38:2 (Spring 1991): 49–57.

Mallow, Jeffry V. "Rethinking the Jerusalem Program." *Jew Fron* 57:5 (September/October 1990): 1–7.

Marmur, Dow. "Reform Zionism in the Postmodern Age." N.Y.: ARZA: *The Journal of Reform Zionism* 1:1 (June/July 1993): 14–19.

Rotenstreich, Nathan. "Can There Be a Revival of Zionist Ideology?" *Mid* 36:4 (May 1990): 7–10.

St. John, Robert. *Ben Gurion: Builder of Israel*. Washington D.C.: B'nai B'rith Books, 1986.

Shimoni, Gideon. "How Central Is Israel?" *Moment* 16:5 (October 1991): 24–27.

Ukeles, Jacob B. *American Jewish Leaders and Israel: A Survey of Attitudes*. N.Y.: AJC, Institute on American Jewish-Israeli Relations, 1991. 32pp.

Umansky, Ellen M. "Zionism and Reform Judaism: A Theological Reassessment." N.Y.: ARZA: *The Journal of Reform Zionism* 1:1 (1993): pp. 44–19.

Israel in the Classroom

Artson, Bradley S. "The Gulf (War) in Jewish Education." *Jew Ed* 59:3 (Winter 1992): 39–11.

Breakstone, David. "The Challenge to Teach Israel." *Jew Ed* 57:1 (Spring 1989): 22–27.

Burstein, Chaya. *A Kid's Catalog of Israel*. Phila.: JPS, 1988.

Danan, Julie Hilton. *Israel Education*. N.Y.: Coalition for the Advancement of Jewish Education, Spring 1991, 13pp.

Gaizband, Cynthia. "Yom Ha-Atzmaut." *Ped Rep* 40:1 (Fall 1990): 29.

Gingold, Barbara. "In Search of Ecology: A Sukkot Pilgrimage in Israel." *The Melton Journal* 25 (Spring 1992): 12–14.

Glatzer, Shoshana. "Teaching Israel at the B.J.E. Teachers' Center." *Ten Da'at* 4:2 (Spring 1990): 36–38.

Goldman, Joel. "Israel and the Gulf War: A New Sense of Realism." *Jew Ed* 59:3 (Winter 1992): 44–45.

Goldman, Solomon. "Zionist Education: The Essential Conflict." *Mid* 39:4 (May 1993): 25–28.

Haim, Aviva. "The Ulpan Experience." *Ped Rep* 40:3 (January 1990): 15–16.

Ingwer, Carmela. "Jewish Education and the Intifada." *Jew Spec* 55:4 (Spring 1990): 14–17.

Jacobson, Burt. "The Exodus Story and the Israeli-Palestinian Conflict." *Response* 16:3 (Winter 1989): 3–14.

Korn, Lila M. "Planting the Seeds: On Teaching Zionism and the Birth of the Jewish State." *Ten Da'at* 4:2 (Spring 1990): 23–24.

Kraut, Penina Besdin. "Israel and the Palestinians." (curriculum) *Ten Da'at* 4:2 (Spring 1990): 22.

Levitin, Sonia. *The Return*. N.Y.: Atheneum, 1987. Ages 12 and up. Concerns ". . . The return of Ethiopian Jews to Eretz Yisrael."

Matanky, Leonard A. "Where in Israel . . . A Review of Israel Software." *Ten Da'at* 4:2 (Spring 1990): 25–26.

Natelson, Nina B. "The Treatment of Animals in Israel." *The Melton Journal* 25 (Spring 1992): 18, 20.

Odenheimer, Micha. "Retrieving the Garden of Eden." Environmental Organizations in Israel. *The Melton Journal* Part I: 24 (Spring 1991): 12–14, 20.

Schiff, Alvin I. "Jewish Zionist Education Revisited." Editorial. *Jew Ed* 59:3 (Winter 1992): 2–3.

Segal, Benjamin J. *Returning: The Land of Israel as Focus in Jewish History*. Jerusalem: DEC, WZO, 1987. 320pp.

Segal, Harriet. "Israel: We Are One People." *Ped Rep* 40:1 (Fall 1990): 28–29.

Shofar. "Israel's 43 Year Quest: Peace." *Shofar* 9:4 (January 1992): 2–5.

Soffin, Joel E. "Jews and Arabs: Fighting Stereotypes." *Compass* 14:2 (Winter 1992): 12–13.

Spotts, Leon H. "Persian Gulf War and the Jewish School." *Jew Ed* 59:3 (Winter 1992): 42–43.

Stracuzzi, Malanie R. "Mission to Israel." *Ped Rep* 40:1 (Fall 1990): 27–28.

Yoffie, Eric H. "Teaching Israel: The New Reality." *Compass* 13:3 (Spring/Summer 1991): 3–7.

Juvenile Books on Israel

Gurko, Miriam. *Theodor Herzl: The Road to Israel*. Illustrated by Erika Weihs. Phila.: JPS, c. 1992. 96pp. Ages 8 to 12.

Schur, Maxine. *Hannah Szenes: A Song of Light*. Illustrated by Donna Ruff. Phila.: JPS, c. 1991. 106pp. Ages 8 to 12.

Segal, Sheila F. *Joshua's Dream: A Journey to the Land of Israel*. Illustrated by Joel Iskowitz. N.Y.: UAHC Press, 1993. Ages 5–8.

DAY SCHOOL

Growth and Development

Leiman, Shnayer Z. "Yeshivat Or Ha-Hayyim: The First Talmudical Academy in America." *Trad* 25:2 (Winter 1990): 77–89.

Shurin, Aaron Ben Zion. "Torah Umesorah—Rise of Day Schools in America." *For* (Y.) (February 8, 1991): 14, 23.

———. "Two Day Schools—95 Years Ago—Today—560." *For* (Y.) (May 22, 1992): 12, 21.

———. "On Jewish Education in the Past." *For* (Y.) (October 30, 1992): 13.

Curriculum and Pedagogy

Amsel, Norman. "Teaching Students to Cheat or Not to Cheat." *Ten Da'at* IV:1 (Fall 1989): 19–21.

Armon, Naomi. "Methodology of Teaching Tanakh: What Does a Teacher Do After Reaching the Radical Conclusion, That One Can't Just Walk into a Class, Read Pasuk after Pasuk, Perush after Perush, and Consider One's Job Well Done." *Ten Daat* 2:2 (Winter 1988): 13–15.

Bernstein, David I. *Two Approaches to the Teaching of Jewish History in Orthodox Yeshiva High Schools*. Ann Arbor, Mich.: U.M.I., Dissertation Information Service, 1987. 219pp.

Freestone, Julie. "Day Schools Scurry to Keep up with Trends, Growth." *The Northern California Jewish Bulletin* (August 21, 1992): 18.

* Friedman, Jerome. *A Comparison of Moral Reasoning Stage among Jewish Day School and among Public School Students*. Harvard U., 1987.

* Goldflam, Dov. *Survey of Current Practices and Attitudes of Jewish History Teachers in the High Jewish Day Schools in the United States*. U. of Miami, 1989.

Goldmintz, Jay. "The Post-High School Yeshiva Experience in Israel: Goals and Benefits." *Ten Da'at* 5:2 (Spring 1991): 32–36.

Grossman, Heshy. "Teaching Moral Sensitivity—and Truth." *Jew Obs* 23:9 (December 1990): 17–26.

* Grysman, Charles O. *A Halakhah Curriculum for Nonobservant Students in an Orthodox School*. Yeshiva U., 1989.

———. "The Orthodox Day School and Its Non-Observant Population." *Jew Ed* 57:2, 3, 4 (Summer/Winter 1989): 32–38.

Katzin, Arye. "Designing a Curriculum." *Jew Obs* 23:5 (Summer 1990): 42.

* Kaunfer, Alvan. *Teaching Midrash in the Conservative Day School: A Rationale and Curriculum Proposal*, Ann Arbor, Mich.: University Microfilms, 1990.

Leiman, Sondra. *A New Integrated Social Studies Curriculum For Yeshiva-Day Schools Grades 2–6*. N.Y.: S-A-R Academy, 1987. 251pp.

Myers, Michael. "Teaching Tehillim to Jewish Adolescents." *Ten Da'at* IV:1 (Fall 1989): 14–16.

Rabinowitz, Yosef B. "Extra-Curricular Programs: Asset or Liability." *Ten Da'at* IV: 1 (Fall 1989): 17–18.

Schulman, Robert H. and Susan. "A Plea for Exercise in Yeshiva Programs." *Jew Obs* 24:4 (May 1991): 21–24.

Schweid, Lawrence R. "Testing: The First Ten Points." *Ten Da'at* IV:1 (Fall 1989): 22–23.

* Smiley, Mark S. *Adopting New Means in Education: A Case Study of Computer Applications in a Rabbinics Curriculum in a Jewish Day School*, JTSA, 1988.

Wolowelsky, Joel B. "Reducing Grades as a Means of Imposing Discipline." *Ten Da'at* IV:1 (Fall 1989): 24–25.

Organization and Administration

Bennett, Daniel W. "A Community Day School Network." *Ped Rep* 39:1 (January 1988): 13–16.

Elkin, Joshua. "Lay-Professional in the Jewish Day School." In Daniel Margolis and E.S. Schoenberg (Eds.), *Curriculum, Community and Commitment: Views on the American Jewish Day School in memory of Bennett I. Solomon*, 1990.

* Elmaleh, Haim. *Causal Factors for Termination of Jewish Day School Principals*. Yeshiva U., 1988.

Friedman, Esther. *Day School Principals*. N.Y.: Coalition for the Advancement of Jewish Education, Spring 1991. 15pp.

Greenberg, Yisroel. "And Who Will Do the Teaching?" *Jew Obs* 23:5 (Summer 1990): 42–43.

Grossman, Yosef. "And Who Will Do the Teaching?" *Jew Obs* 23:5 (Summer 1990): 42–13.

Warmer, Moshe. "And Who Will Do the Teaching?" *Jew Obs* 23:5 (Summer 1990): 42–13.

Parents and Jewish Day School

* Cohen, Helen K. *Caught in Between: When Jewish Home and Jewish School Tell the Child a Different Story*. Harvard U., 1990.

* Gans, Murray Z. *Parents and Educator Ratings of Goals of Jewish Day School*, U. of Colorado at Boulder, 1987.

Assessment

Abramson, Robert. "Kedushah: One Focus in the Vision of Our Day Schools." *MJ* 23 (Spring 1990): 32 (ends on p. 31).

Bieler, Jack. "The Day School: A Modern Orthodox Jewish Community's Reflection Or Guiding Light?" *Ten Da'at* 5:1 (Fall 1990): 27–29.

Egozi, R. "Historical Perspective on Funding Torah Education." *Jew Obs* 23:3 (April 1990): 41–42.

Gurock, Jefrey S., Editor. *Ramaz: School, Community, Scholarship and Orthodoxy*, Hoboken, N.J.: Ktav, 1989. 203pp.

Kipper, Lenore C. "Why Should Reform Judaism Support Day Schools?" In *Progress* 1:1 (1992): 4–6.

Lamm, Norman. "Torah Education at the Crossroads." *Ten Da'at* IV:1 (Fall 1989): 3–7.

Moses, Avi. "Funding Torah Education—Anatomy of a Crisis." *Jew Obs* 22:10: 36–42.

Rothman, Sholom Dov. "Other Roads to Cover Educational Costs." *Jew Obs* 23:3 (April 1990): 42–43.

* Schoenburg, Harry D. *The Practical Knowledge of Jewish Day School Teachers*. U. of California—LA, 1989.

Shurin, Aaron Ben Zion. "Three Types of Yeshivoth in America." *For* (Y.) (August 21, 1992).

———. "Many Potential Day-School Students Are Unable to Enroll Due to Tuition Costs." *For* (Y.) (November 6, 1992): p. 13.

———. "Educational Problems at the 37th Yeshiva Conference." *For* (Y.) (June 11, 1993): 13.

Sourkes, Tzvi. "What Kind of School" *Jew Obs* 23:5 (Summer 1990): 40–41.

Stahler, Moshe. "What Kind of School?" *Jew Obs* 23:5 (Summer 1990): 40–41.

Stolovitsky, Mark. "The Role of Hebrew Language in the Day School." *Jew Ed* 57:2, 3, 4, pp. 27–31.

Syme, Daniel. "Statement on PARDeS, Progressive Association of Reform Jewish Day Schools." In *Progress* 1:1 (1992): 1–2.

Tannenbaum, Abraham J. "Nostalgic Notes On My Day School Years." *Jew Ed* 60:1 (Spring 1993): 35–13.

UAHC, Department for Religious Education, *The Reform Jewish Day School: Visions of Excellence*. Essay by Alexander M. Schindler and interviews with leaders of the Reform Jewish Day School Movement. N.Y.: UAHC, c. 1991.

Zeldin, M. *In Yesterday's Shadow: Case Study of the Development of a Jewish Day School*. Presented at the Fourth Annual Conference of the Network for Research in Jewish Education. N.Y.: June 1990.

YIDDISH SECULAR SCHOOLS

Fishman, Joshua A. *Yiddish: Turning to Life*. Describes the evolution of the Yiddish language. Amsterdam, Holland: 1991. 522pp.

Goldsmith, Emanuel S. *Modern Yiddish Culture: The Story of the Yiddish Language Movement*. N.Y.: Shapolsky Publishers and The Workmen's Circle Educational Department, 1987. 309pp.

HIGHER EDUCATION

Jewish Institutions of Higher Learning

Breslauer, S. Daniel. "From Curiosity to Commitment: Religion and Modern Higher Education." *Recon* 57:1 (Autumn 1991): 18–20.

Cardin, Nina Beth, and David Wolf Silverman, ed. *The Seminary at 100*. N.Y.: The Rabbinical Assembly and The Jewish Theological Seminary of America, JTS, 1987. 475pp.

Cooperman, Bernard D. "Jewish Studies in the University." In *Jewish Identity in America*. Los Angeles: U. of Judaism, pp. 195–206. D. H. Gordis, Editor.

Dicker, Herman. *Of Learning and Libraries: The Seminary Library at One Hundred*. N.Y.: JTS, 1988. 130pp.

Eisen, Arnold M. "Jews, Jewish Studies, and The American Humanities." *Tikkun* 4:5 (September/October 1989): 23–33.

Fierstein, Robert E. *A Different Spirit: The Jewish Theological Seminary of America, 1886–1902*. N.Y.: JTS, 1990. 146pp.

Garber, Zev, Editor. *Methodology in the Academic Teaching of Judaism*. Lanham, M.: U. Press of America and Studies in Judaism, 1986. 308pp.

Gurock, Jeffrey S. *The Men and Women of Yeshiva: Higher Education, Orthodoxy and American Judaism*. N.Y.: Columbia U. Press, 1988. 302pp.

Sherwin, Byron L. *Contexts and Content: Higher Jewish Education in the United States: Spertus College of Judaica*. A Case Study. Chicago: Spertus College of Judaica Press, 1987. 632pp.

———. "Jewish Studies at American Colleges and Universities." *Shofar* 7:4 (Summer 1989): 48–56.

Sh'ma. "Jewish Studies." 20:383 (December 8, 1989).

———. "Jewish Life on Campus." 20:393 (April 27, 1990).

Shimoff, Sandra R. "Judaic Studies: An Interdisciplinary Model." *Jew Ed* 57:2, 3, 4, pp. 13–16.

Starin, Carol Oseran. *New! CAJE College Program*. N.Y.: Coalition for the Advancement of Jewish Education, Spring 1991. 29pp.

Symposium, "Jewish Studies and the Canon." *Response* 17:2 (Spring 1991): 7–32. Participants: Abraham, Joel; Bean, Lisa; Braiterman, Zachary; Brettschneider, Marla; Graff, Bennett; Kamil, Seth; Kaufman, David; Kianovsky, Nahum; Lerner, Paul; Magder, Ruth; Svonkin, Stuart.

Wechsler, Harold S. "Anti-Semitism in the Academy: Jewish Learning in American Universities, 1914–1939." *AJA* 42:1 (Spring/Summer 1990): 8–21.

Younger, David. "New Talmud Course in Cooperation with University of Minnesota." *Ped Rep* 40:1 (Fall 1990): 18–19.

ADMINISTRATION

Pedagogic Issues

Ackerman, David. "School Improvement." *Ped Rep* 40:4 (April 1990): 16–17.

Flexner, P. "The Goals of Staff Development: An Overview." *Ped Rep* 39 (1989): 3–5.

Lewis, Hilary. *Resource Center Network Provides Something for Everyone*. N.Y.: Coalition for the Advancement of Jewish Education, Spring 1991. 20pp.

Rosenblum, Eileen. "Teaching Learning Center." *Ped Rep* 40:1 (Fall 1990): 25–26.

Rothbard, Madelyn. "Creating Learning Centers." *Ped Rep* 41:2 (Winter/Spring 1991): 32–34.

The Principal

Dr. Sue. "Confessions of a Supplementary School Principal." *Jew Ed* 57:1 (Spring 1989): 39–40.

UAHC, Department for Religious Education, *Educational Management Guide*, for UAHC Congregational Education Committees, c. 1989.

In-Service Training

Halpern, Jacob I., and Jay Shotel. "Two Teacher Training Models." *Jew Ed* 59:1 (Spring/Summer 1991): 13–20.

Ingall, Carol K. "Teaching Teachers: One Community's Experience." *Jew Ed* 58:1, 2 (Spring/Summer 1990): 23–25.

Schremer, Oded. "A Call For Policy Discussion On Teacher Training Programs." *Jew Ed* 57:2, 3, 4 (Summer/Winter 1989): 17–25.

Schwartz, Elliot S. "A Multi-Faceted Approach to Teacher Training." *Ped Rep* 40:2 (October 1989): 35–37.

Zeldin, Michael. "Creating In-Service That Make a Difference." Rhea Hirsch School of Education, HUC–JIR, *Newsletter* (Spring 1993): 7–8.

The Teacher Shortage

Aron, Isa. "Where Have All the Teachers Gone? And How Do We Find New Ones?" Rhea Hirsch School of Education, HUC–JIR, *Newsletter* (Spring 1993): 1–3.

Evaluation

Collins, Larry. "What Parents Think of Our Schools." *Education and Culture Review* 14:1, pp. 13–16.

Siegel, Danny. "Final Exams: Pavlov's Dogs, Pinball Machines, and the Jews." *Ped Rep* 40:3 (January 1990): 45–17.

THE TEACHER

Bettman, Batia. "The Teacher as Decision Maker: A Follow-Up." *Ped Rep* 40:1 (Fall 1990): 22.

Ben-Peretz, Miriam. *The Teacher-Curriculum Encounter*. Foreword by Lee S. Shulman. Albany, N.Y.: State U. of New York, 1990. 152pp.

Cutter, William. "Creating A Climate For Positive Educational Experience." Rhea Hirsch School of Education, HUC–JIR, *Newsletter* (Spring 1993): 4.

Ingall, Michael. "A Teacher Remembered." *MJ* 23 (Spring 1990): 19.

Joseph, Samuel K. "Musar Study and Teacher Growth." *Compass* 12:1 (Fall 1989): 21, 30.

Moskowitz, Gertrude and Saul Wachs. "Enhancing Perceptions of Future Teachers Towards Jews and Judaism." *Jew Ed* 56:3 (Fall 1988): 31–14.

* Ofek, Adina A. *Peer Supervision from Theory to Practice: An Exploratory Study in the Field of Jewish Education*, Ann Arbor, Mich.: U. Microfilm International, 1986. VI, 161pp.

Schiff, Alvin I. "Teachers and Principals." *Jew Ed* 57:1 (Spring 1989): 2–11.

Symposium—The Jewish School Teacher Today and Tomorrow. Jew Ed 55:1 (Spring 1987): Opening Essay, Alvin I. Schiff, p. 5.

Alexander, Hanan A.,	8
Aron, Isa and Adrienne Bank,	10
Braverman, Jay,	14
Chazan, Barry,	16
Chinitz, Benjamin,	20
Ducoff, Bernard,	21
Flexner, Paul A.,	23
Grad, Eli,	25
Grishaver, Joel,	26
Handel, Yitzchak,	30
Himmelfarb, Harold S.,	32
Joseph, Samuel,	34
Katz, Betty,	37
Korman, Michael,	40
Lee, Sara S.,	42
Olitzky, Kerry M.,	45
Reimer, Joseph,	47
Sherwin, Byron L.,	49
Sturm, Ephraim H.,	52
Tornberg, Robert E.,	54
Ury, Zalman F.,	56
Woocher, Jonathan,	59

Wasserman, Joy and Rob Weinberg. "Nurturing Students into Teachers: Personal Reflections." Rhea Hirsch School of Education, HUC–JIR, *Newsletter* (Spring 1993): 5–7.

Israelis Teaching in American Jewish Schools

* Stern, Raymond. *Israelis Teaching in American Jewish Schools: Job-related Variables.* Yeshiva U., 1988.

THE RABBI AND JEWISH EDUCATION

General (Selected)

Friedenberg, Robert V. *Hear, 0 Israel: The History of American Jewish Preaching.* Tuscaloosa, Ala.: The U. of Alabama Press, 1990. 177pp.

Nadell, Pamela S. "Developing an American Judaism: Conservative Rabbis as Ethnic Leaders." *Jud* 39:3 (1990): 345–65.

Robinson, Ira. "The Education of an American Orthodox Rabbi: Mayer Joshua Rosenberg Comes to Holyoke, Massachusetts." *Jud* 40:4 (Fall 1991): 543–51.

Sh'ma. *The Problem of Being A Rabbi Today.* 20/386 (January 19, 1990). (Whole Issue)

———. "The Special Tensions of Being "The Rabbi," No. 200 (March 16, 1990).

Staub, Jacob J. "The Rabbi: Past Images. Future Vision." *Recon* 55:4 (March–April 1990): 9–12.

CONFERENCES IN JEWISH EDUCATION

1990

Spotts, Leon H. "Educators' Symposium in Israel." *Ped Rep* 40:1 (Fall 1990): 27.

1992

Kontorovich, E.V. "Educators to Tackle Tough, Timely Issues." (CAJE Conference) *For* (E) (August 14, 1992): 1, 12.

MEN AND WOMEN WHO INFLUENCED JEWISH EDUCATION

Brinner, William M., and Moses Rischin, Editors. *Like All the Nations? The Life and Legacy of Judah I. Magnes.* Albany: State U. of New York Press, 1987. 241pp.

Bronstein, Rose. "Eli Grad—In Memoriam." *Jew Ed* 60:1 (Spring 1993): 4.

Etkes, Immanuel. *Rabbi Israel Salanter and the Mussar Movement: Seeking the Torah of Truth.* Phila.: JPS, 1993. 400pp.

Goelman, Elazar. "Avraham Hayim Friedland—On the 50th Anniversary of His Death." *Jew Ed* 57:2, 3, 4 (Summer/Winter 1989): 4–6.

Goldman, Solomon. "Shimon Frost—In Memoriam." *Jew Ed* 60:1 (Spring 1993): 3.

Goldsmith, Emanuel, Mel Scult, and Richard M. Seltzer, Editors. *The American Judaism of*

Mordecai Kaplan. N.Y.: New York U. 1990. 460pp.

Katzoff, Adina A., Ed. *Louis Katzoff—An American Jewish Educator: Collected Essays and Studies*. Jerusalem: B.A.L. 1989. 207pp.

Lerner, Israel. "Alex Kaminetsky—In Memoriam." *Jew Ed* 60:1 (Spring 1993): 5.

Pasachoff, Naomi. *Great Jewish Thinkers, Their Lives and Work*. West Orange, N.J.: Behrman House, 1992. 192pp. Teacher's Supplement for Grades 8–12.

* Prager, Elliot H. *The Work of Max Kadushin and Its Implications for Jewish Education*. Columbia U. 1988. 307pp.

Sarna, Jonathan D. "Cyrus Adler and the Development of American Jewish Culture: The 'Scholar-Doer' as a Jewish Communal Leader." *AJH* 78:3 (March 1989): 382–94.

Schiff, Alvin I. "Samuel Schafler—In Memoriam." *Jew Ed* 59:1 (Spring/Summer 1991): 5.

———. "Jacob Hartstein—In Memoriam." *Jew Ed* 59:3 (Winter 1992): 4.

———. "Jacob M. Horden—In Memoriam." *Jew Ed* 60:1 (Spring 1993): 4–5.

Seltzer, Robert M. "On Rereading Hayim Greenberg." *Cong M* 59:1 (January 1992): 13–15.

Veerman, Philip E. "In the Shadow of Janusz Korczak—The Story of Stefania Wilczynska." *MJ* 23 (Spring 1990): 8, 15.

HISTORICAL BACKGROUND OF JEWISH EDUCATION

Ancient Period

Shurin, Aaron Ben Zion. "Ancient Jewish Education." On goals of education in the Talmud. *For* Y. (October 30. 1992): 13.

The Middle Ages

Jacobs, Yaakov. "Let Them Play Chess: A Bohemian Rabbi Speaks About Hinukh (Education)." *Ten Da'at* IV:1 (Fall, 1989): 26–29. (On the educational writings of Rabbi Loew of Prague).

Kanarfogel, Ephraim. *Jewish Education and Society in the High Middle Ages*. Detroit: Wayne State U. Press, 1990. 160pp.

Modern Israel Education Prior to 1948

Shapiro, David H. "The First Hebrew Kindergarten in Mia." *Ariel* No. 81 (1990): 33–53.

Modern Israel—Education Since 1948

Abramovitch, Stanley. *Programmatic Renewal and Budgetary Reconstruction: A Progress Report*. Jerusalem: The Education-Religious-Cultural Affairs Program in Israel, 1989. 35pp.

Dinitz, Simcha. "Report on The Jerusalem Fellows Program for Leadership in Jewish Education in the Diaspora." Jerusalem: The Jewish Agency for Israel, *Annual Report, 1990/91*. pp. 179–201.

Elazar, Daniel J., Editor. *Two Peoples . . . One Land: Federal Solutions for Israel, the Palestinians, and Jordan*. Lanham, Md.: U. Press of America and the Jerusalem Center for Public Affairs, 1991. 216pp.

Gutman, Renana. "Report on the Program for Overseas Students." Jerusalem: The Jewish Agency for Israel, *Annual Report, 1989/90*. pp. 183–187.

The Ministry of Education and Culture. *Lifelong Learning in Israel: Values and Practices*. Jerusalem: 1989. 256pp.

Swirski, Shlomo. "Grass-Roots Organizing for Better Education in Mizrahi Communities in Israel." *MJ* 26 (Autumn 1992): 25.

HISTORY OF JEWISH EDUCATION IN THE UNITED STATES

Jewish Education in the United States

Dinin, Samuel. "These Things I Remember." *Jew Ed* 60:1 (Spring 1993): 16–13.

Dushkin, Alexander M. "Fifty Years of American Jewish Education: Retrospect and Prospect." (Address in July 1966) *Jew Ed* 60:1 (Spring 1993): 44–54.

Grad, Eli. "Reflections on a Career in Jewish Education." *Jew Ed* 60:1 (Spring 1993): 14–17.

Pollak, George. "Vignettes from the Life of a Jewish Educator." *Jew Ed* 60:1 (Spring 1993): 21–28.

Rosenberg, Asenath. "A Lifetime Serving the Jewish Child." *Jew Ed* 60:1 (Spring 1993): 29–31.

Schiff, Alvin I. "Wisdom At Sixty." *Jew Ed* 60:1 (Spring 1993): 32–34.

Schwartz, Elliot. "Jewish Education—Then and Now." *Jew Ed* 60:1 (Spring 1993): 32–34.

History of American Jewry

Cohen, Naomi W. *Jews in Christian America: The Pursuit of Religious Equality*. N.Y.: Oxford U. Press, 1992. 300pp.

Cowan, Neil M., and Ruth Schwartz Cowan. *Our Parents' Lives: The Americanization of Eastern European Jews*. N.Y.: Basic Books, 1989. 305pp.

Diner, Hasia R. *A Time for Gathering: The Second Migration, 1820–1880*. Baltimore: The Johns Hopkins U. Press, Second printing, 1992. 313pp. A Series, The Jewish People in America, Sponsored by AJHS.

Faber, Eli. *A Time For Planting: The First Migration, 1654–1820*. Baltimore: The Johns Hopkins U. Press, Second printing, 1992. 188pp. A Series, The Jewish People in America, Sponsored by AJHS.

Feingold, Henry L. *A Time for Searching*. Entering the Mainstream, 1920–1945. Baltimore: The Johns Hopkins U. Press, Second printing, 1992. 338pp. A Series, The Jewish People in America, Sponsored by AJHS.

Frischer, Rita Berman. *To a Golden Land: Ellis Island and Beyond*. N.Y.: Jewish Book Council, 1989.

Goldenberg, David M., Editor. *To Bigotry No Sanction: Documents in American Jewish History*. Phila.: Annenberg Research Institute, 1988. 107pp.

Hertzberg, Arthur. *The Jews in America: Four Centuries of an Uneasy Encounter: A History*. N.Y.: Simon & Schuster, 1989. 428pp.

Peck, Abraham J., Editor. "The German-Jewish Legacy in America, 1938–1988, A Symposium." *AJA* 40:2 (November 1988). Articles follow:

Ascher, Carol, Renate Bridenthal, Marion Kaplan and Atina Grossmann. "Fragments of a German-Jewish Heritage in Four 'Americans'." Pp. 365–84.

Aschheim, Steven E. "The German-Jewish Legacy Beyond America: A South African Example." Pp. 359–64.

Feingold, Henry L. "Bildung: Was It Good for the Jews?" Pp. 243–17.

Freudenheim, Tom L. "Thoughts About My German-Jewish Legacy." Pp. 331–41.

Gay, Peter. "The German-Jewish Legacy—and I: Some Personal Reflections." Pp. 203–10.

Gottschalk, Alfred. "The German-Jewish Legacy: A Question of Fate." Pp. 267–72.

Hallo, William W. "A German Jewish Past, an American Jewish Future." Pp. 343–45.

Heilbut, Anthony. "My German-Jewish Legacy and Theirs." Pp. 385–91.

Henry, Frances. "Reflections on the German-Jewish Legacy: North American Style." Pp. 397–400.

Herscher, Uri D. "Bildung: An Agenda of the Soul." Pp. 393–95.

Holdheim, Wolfgang. "The Less Than Total Break." Pp. 261–65.

Huttenbach, Henry R. "Le Deracine: Finding New Roots in Exile." Pp. 313–20.

Iggers, George G. "An Autobiographical Approach to the German-Jewish Legacy." Pp. 221–26.

Jacob, Walter. "The German Jew in America: The Last Wave of Immigrants." Pp. 351–53.

Jonas, Manfred. "A German-Jewish Legacy." Pp. 237–42.

Juergensen, Hans. "The German-Jewish Heritage: A View from 1988." Pp. 307–311.

Liberies, Robert. "The German-Jewish Legacy in America: A Process of Continuity and Completion." Pp. 401–1.

Lowenstein, Steven M. "The German-Jewish Legacy: A Past with No Future." Pp. 405–7.

Maier, Joseph B. "A Precious Legacy." Pp. 281–87.

Meyer, Henry. "The German-Jewish Legacy: One Man's Dilemma and Solution." Pp. 347–19.

Meyer, Michael A. "A Heritage Freighted Across the Abyss." Pp. 297–301.

Mosse, George L. "The End Is Not Yet: A Personal Memoir of the German-Jewish

Legacy in America." Pp. 197–202.
Neier, Aryeh. "Engagement and the German-Jewish Legacy." Pp. 303–6.
Niers, Gert. "A Non-Jewish German Looks at the German-Jewish Legacy." Pp. 409–11.
Peck, Abraham J. "Introduction."
Plaut, W. Gunther. "The Elusive German-Jewish Heritage in America." Pp. 273–79.
Secher, Herbert Pierre. "Bildung and the Dilemma of Hyphenation." Pp. 249–56.
Silberman, Curt C. "Reflections on the *Kristallnacht* and the End German Jewry: Some Transcendant Thoughts." Pp. 257–60.
Spielmann, Diane R., and Lee A. Spielmann. "Fifty Years after Kristallnacht: Another Second-Generation Perspective." Pp. 413–18.
Steinitz, Hans J. "Thoughts about the German-Jewish Legacy in the United States by a Man from *Aufbau*." Pp. 327–30.
Steinitz, Lucy Y. "The German-Jewish Legacy in America: A Second-Generation Perspective." Pp. 355–58.
Stern, Guy, "German Culture, Jewish Ethics." Pp. 211–19.
Strauss, Herbert A. "Emancipation and Post-Emancipation Identities Reflections on On-Going Research." Pp. 289–96.
Weinberg, Werner. "Fifty Years After Crystal Night and Forty in America." Pp. 321–25.
Wertheimer, Jack. "The German-Jewish Experience: Toward a Usable Past." Pp. 419–424.
Wiener, Theodore. "The German-Jewish Legacy: An Overstated Ideal." Pp. 337–41.
Wollheim, Norbert. "The German-Jewish Legacy After Auschwitz." Pp. 233–35.
Zohn, Harry. "German Jewry as Spirit and Legacy." Pp. 227–31.

Perlman, Robert. *Bridging Three Worlds: Hungarian—Jewish Americans, 1848–1914*, Amherst, Mass.: U. of Massachusetts Press, 1991. 302pp.

Sarna, Jonathan D. "American Jewish History." *Modern Judaism* 10:3 (October 1990): 343–65.

Shapiro, Edward S. *A Time For Healing*, American Jewry since World War II. Baltimore: The Johns Hopkins U. Press, Second printing, 1992. 313pp. A Series, The Jewish People In America, Sponsored by AJHS.

Sorin, Gerald. *A Time For Building, The Third Migration, 1880–1920*. Baltimore: The Johns Hopkins U. Press, Second printing, 1992. 306pp. A Series, The Jewish People In America, Sponsored by AJHS.

Young, Mel. *Where They Lie*. Lanham: Md.: U. Press of America, 1991. 2971pp. "Concerns... the role Jews played in the American Civil War. ..."

Jewish Religious, Organizational and Cultural Life

Berger, David. "Modern Orthodoxy in the United States: A Review Essay." *Modern Judaism* 11:2 (May 1991): 261–72.

Bulka, Reuven P. *Dimensions of Orthodox Judaism*. Hoboken, N.J.: Ktav Publishing House, 1983.

Chazan, Robert. "The Study of Judaism and the Jews: The American Perspective." *Shofar* Purdue U., 7:2 (Winter 1989): 48–56.

Cohen, Naomi W. "American Jews: Fusing Two Cultures." *Cong M* 60:1 (January 1993): 17–19.

Cohen, Steven M. *Content or Continuity?: Alternative Bases for Commitment*. N.Y.: AJC, 1991.

Goldstein, Sidney. "Profile of American Jewry: Insights from the 1990 National Jewish Population Survey." *AJYB* 92 (1992): 77–172.

Meyer, Michael A. *Response to Modernity: A History of the Reform Movement in Judaism*. N.Y.: Oxford U. Press, 1990. 494pp.

Nadell, Pamela S. *Conservative Judaism in America: A Biographical Dictionary and Sourcebook*. New York, Westport, London: Greenwood Press, 1988. 409pp.

Olitzky, Kerry M. Sussman, Lance, and Stern, Malcolm, Eds. *Reform Judaism in America: A Biographical Dictionary and Sourcebook*. Westport. Conn.: Greenwood Publishers Group, Inc., 1993.

Snyder, Herman Eliot. "The American Synagogue World of Yesterday, 1901–1925: Rethinking the American Jewish Experience." *AJA* 42:1 (Spring/Summer 1990): 71–78.

Wertheimer, Jack, Editor. *The American Synagogue: A Sanctuary Transformed.* N.Y.: Cambridge U. Press, 1987. 433pp.

THE AMERICAN JEWISH COMMUNITY

Introduction

Wertheimer, Jack. *A People Divided: Judaism in Contemporary America.* N.Y.: Basic Books, c. 1992. 267pp.

The Community and Jewish Education

Council of Jewish Federations. *1990 National Jewish Population Study.* New York, 1991.

Jordan, Cecile B. "How Should the Community Serve the Non-Day School Population." *Jew Ed* 58:3, 4 (Fall/Winter 1990): 42–44.

Schwartz, Sidney H. "Training American-Jewish Leadership for the 21st Century." *Ped Rep* 41:2 (Winter/Spring 1991): 19–22.

The Jewish Center

Appelman, Harlene Winnick. "Mission Mish-pacha: A Continental Agenda for Jewish Community Centers." *Circle* 48:3 (October 1991): 8–13.

Chazan, B. and Y. Poupko. *Guide to Jewish Knowledge for the Center Professional.* Jewish Community Centers Association, 1989.

———. "A Jewish Educational Philosophy for JCCs." *J Jew Com Ser* 63:3 (Spring 1987).

———. *The JCC Israel Seminar: A Preparation Guide.* N.Y.: JWB and World Confederation of Jewish Community Centers, 1990. 235pp.

Frank, S. *A New Phenomenon at JCCs: Jewish Education Professional Specialists.* Jewish Welfare Board Circle 47:1 (1990).

Kimelman, Reuven. "Jewish Centers as Jewish Environment Centers." *J Jew Com Ser* 69:1 (Fall 1992): 75–79.

Reisman, Bernard. *Informal Jewish Education in North America: A Report Submitted to the Commission on Jewish Education in North America.* Cleveland, Ohio, 1990.

———. *Social Change and Response—Assessing Efforts to Maximize Jewish Educational Effectiveness in Jewish Community Centers in North America.* N.Y.: Jewish Community Centers Association. 1991. 107pp.

Solender, Stephen D. "Pursuing Excellence in Jewish Communal Policy, Program, and Professional Practice in Times of Change." *J Jew Com Ser* 69:1 (Fall 1992): 35–42.

The Synagogue and Jewish Education

Communal Support For Congregational Schools: Current Approaches. N.Y.: JESNA, 1988.

Lippmann, Ellen. "Single Jews and the Synagogue." *Compass* 12:2 (Fall 1991). (Whole Issue)

Snyder, Herman Eliot. "The American Synagogue World of Yesterday 1901–1925." *AJA* 42:1 (Spring/Summer 1990): 71–80.

UAHC Task Force on Soviet Jewry. *Am Echad: Congregations Reaching Out to Soviet Jewry in Our Community.* N.Y.: UAHC, c. 1989.

Financial Support for Jewish Education

Horn, Susan. "Communal Funding as a Qualitative Educational Tool." *Jew Ed* 55:2 (Summer 1987): 27–35.

Stern, Jay. "A Voucher Plan for Federation Funding of Jewish Schooling." *Jew Ed* 59:3 (Winter 1992): 9–11.

Assessing Central Educational Agencies and New Needs

Abrams, Sylvia F. "Coordinating Inservice Education: Bureau and College Partnership." *Ped Rep* 40:4 (April 1990): 36–37.

Abramson, Robert. "Bureaus and Movements—Towards Cooperation and Synergism." *Jew Ed* 58:3, 4 (Fall/Winter 1990): 28–29.

Ackerman, Walter I. "Protecting the Past or Facing the Future." *Jew Ed* 58:3, 4 (Fall/Winter 1990): 4–8.

Bennett, Alan D. "The Vanishing Magic Wand." *Jew Ed* 58:3, 4 (Fall/Winter 1990): 39–10.

Bogot, Howard I. "Central Agency Renewal and Educational Goal Setting." *Jew Ed* 58:3, 4 (Fall/Winter 1990): 9–31.

Elazar, Daniel I. "The Future of Central Agents." *Jew Ed* 58:3, 4 (Fall/Winter 1990): 8–10.

Fishman, Joshua. "The Bureau and the Denominations." *Jew Ed* 58:3, 4 (Fall/Winter 1990): 32.

Graff, Gil. "Bureaus of Jewish Education and the Supplementary School." *Jew Ed* 59:3 (Winter 1992): 12–14.

Grishaver, Joel Lurie. "The Best Possible Future for the Central Agency." *Jew Ed* 58:3, 4 (Fall/Winter 1990): 22–25.

Hyfler, Robert. "A Planner's Observations on Serving the Non-Day School Family." *Jew Ed* 58:3, 4 (Fall/Winter 1990): 25–37.

Ingall, Carol K. "Insuring the Future of Central Agencies." *Jew Ed* 58:3, 4 (Fall/Winter 1990): 40–42.

Lauer, Chaim. "Planning for the Future." *Jew Ed* 58:3, 4 (Fall/Winter 1990): 36–39.

Lee, Sara S. "Future Directions for the Central Agency." *Jew Ed* 58:3, 4 (Fall/Winter 1990): 11–14.

Raben, Harvey A. "A Small Bureau's Point of View." *Jew Ed* 58:3, 4 (Fall/Winter 1990): 44–45.

Schacter, Lifsa Block. "Coordination—Inservice Education: Bureau and College Partnership." *Ped Rep* 40:4 (April 1990): 36–37.

Schafler, S. "Voluntary and Professional Leadership for More Effective Jewish Education." *J Jew Com Ser* 137 (Winter 1987).

———. "Bureaus of Jewish Education: Yesterday's Vision Will Not Do." *Jew Ed* 58:3, 4 (Fall/Winter 1990): 14–16.

Schiff, Alvin I., Editorial. "The Central Agency for Jewish Education Looks in the Mirror." *Jew Ed* 58:3, 4 (Fall/Winter 1990): 1–3.

———. "Selected Characteristics of Bureau Executives." *Jew Ed* 58:3, 4 (Fall/Winter 1990): 57–65.

Schnaidman, Mordecai. "On the Role of Central Agencies." *Jew Ed* 58:3, 4 (Fall/Winter 1990): 33–35.

Shluker, David. "Changes and Challenges in Central Agency/Federation Relationships in Planning for Jewish Education." *Jew Ed* 58:3, 4 (Fall/Winter 1990): 17–21.

Showstack, G. "Lay-Professional Relations in Jewish Communal Institutions." *J Jew Com Ser* 70 (Winter 1989).

Spotts, Leon H. "Needed: Communal Planning and Better Funding." *Jew Ed* 58:3, 4 (Fall/Winter 1990): 45–47.

Steinberg, Barbara. "Redefining Bureau Effectiveness." *Jew Ed* 58:3, 4 (Fall/Winter 1990): 47–49.

Teller, Gerald. "The Changing Role of the Central Agencies." *Jew Ed* 58:3, 4 (Fall/Winter 1990): 49–50.

Weissberg, Leon. "The Real Mission of the Bureau." *Jew Ed* 58:3, 4 (Fall/Winter 1990): 50–52.

Witty, Irwin S. "The Bureau—Valuable Today and Even More So Tomorrow." *Jew Ed* 58:3, 4 (Fall/Winter 1990): 52–56.

Women and the Jewish Community

Goldstein, Alice. "Jewish Women's Involvement in the Community's Organizational Structure." *Contemporary Jewry* 11:1 (1990): 49–76.

Women and the Rabbinate in the Community

Davidson, Jessica R. "When the Rabbi Is a Woman." *Cong M* 56:6 (September/October 1991): 10–13.

Changing Jewish Communities—Implications for Jewish Education

Bayme, Steven. "A New Agenda For Tomorrow's Jewish Community." *J Jew Com Ser* 65:4 (Summer 1989): 268–78.

Dubin, David. "Communal Considerations in Jewish Education." *J Jew Com Ser* 65:4 (Summer 1989): 279–84.

Grossman, Lawrence. "Jewish Communal Affairs." *AJYB* 89 (1989): 212–32.

Reisman, Bernard. "The Ideologies of Post-Modern American Jews." *J Jew Com Ser* 65:4 (Summer 1989).

THE HOME AND JEWISH EDUCATION

Aft, Bruce D. "The Family Living Room." *Ped Rep* 40:1 (Fall 1990): 4–5.

Alper, Janice P. "Reaching and Teaching the Jewish Family." *Compass* 13:2 (Winter 1991): 13–15.

———. "Celebrating The Jewish Holidays With Your Family." *Compass* 16:1 (Fall 1993): 11–13.

Appelman, Horlene Winnick. "Family Education Can Lead Us Out of Our Jewish Morass." *Detroit Jewish News*, November 13, 1992.

———. "Learning Together: Parents and Children Find Judaism Works." *Moment* 18:4 (August 1993): 48–47.

———. "The Family Living Room." *Ped Rep* 40:1 (Fall 1990): 4–5.

ARE. *Learning Together: A Sourcebook on Jewish Family Education*. Denver, Colo.: 1987. 477pp.

Balin, Carole B. "Fitness Is Not New for Jews: The Rabbinic Perspective on the Body and Health." *Compass* 13:12 (Fall 1990): 3–4.

———. "Challenging Traditional Myths: The Historical Reality of the Jewish Home." *Compass* 14:1 (Fall 1991): 5–6.

Bell, Roselyn, Editor. *Hadassah Magazine Jewish Parenting Book*. N.Y.: Free Press/Macmillan, c. 1989. 416pp.

Berger, Marilyn Shlachter. "Children and Divorce." *Had Mag* 71:9 (May 1990): 40–41.

Bernard, S. E. "Family Jewishness and Family Education." *J Jew Com Ser* 67:4 (1990): 290–99.

Blumberg, Sherry H. "Your Jewish Home Library." *Compass* 14:1 (Fall 1991) 22–23.

Bogot, Howard I. "Judaism at Home Ideas for Jewish Living and Learning." *Compass* 14:1 (Fall 1991): 11–14.

Brodmann, Aliana. *The Gift*. (A Hanukkah story). Illustrated by Anthony Carnabuci. N.Y.: Simon & Schuster Children's Books. 40pp.

Brownstein, Solomon N. "The Contemporary Jewish Family." *Jew Fron* 57:1 (January/February 1990): 32–35.

Bubis, Gerald B. "Strengthening of the Jewish Family as an Instrument of Jewish Community." *J Jew Com Ser* (Spring 1982): 306–17.

Cohen, Mark. "The Family Living Room." *Ped Rep* 40:1 (Fall 1990): 4–5.

Cohen, Steven M. *Alternative Families in the Jewish Community: Singles, Single Parents, Childless Couples, and Mixed-Marriages*. N.Y.: AJC, 1989. 39pp.

Compass. "Jewish Family Education." *Compass* 14:1 (Fall 1991) (Entire Issue).

Diamant, Anita and Howard Cooper. *Living a Jewish Life: Jewish Customs, Traditions, and Values for Today's Family*. N.Y.: Harper Collins, 1991.

Donin, Hayim H. *To Raise a Jewish Child: A Guide for Parents*. N.Y.: Basic Books, 1990.

Dunkelman, David M. "Why a Jewish Home?" *J Jew Com Ser* 69:1 (Fall 1992): 43–51.

Ephrose, Joan and Rena Rotenberg. "In the Beginning . . . The Jewish Lamaze Program." *Compass* 13:2 (Winter 1991): 9–10.

Fisher, Ofra. "The Family Living Room." *Ped Rep* 40:1 (Fall 1990): 4–5.

Fishman, Sylvia Barack. "The Changing Jewish Family in the 80's." *Contemporary Jewry* 9:2 (Fall 1988): 1–33.

———. *Jewish Households, Jewish Homes: Serving American Jews in the 1990s*. Waltham, Mass.: Brandeis U., 1990.

Friedman, Dayle A. "L'Dor Va-Dor: Living the Chain of Tradition Through Intergenerational Programs." *Compass* 13:2 (Winter 1991): 6–7.

Frishman, Elyse D., Ed. *Haneirot Halalu. These Lights are Holy*. Illustrated by Leonard Baskin. A Home Celebration of Chanuka. N.Y.: CCAR, 1989. 54pp.

Geffen, Rela M., Ed. *Celebration and Renewal: Rites of Passage in Judaism*. Phila.: JPS, 1993. 288pp.

Gittelson, Abraham J. "Adult and Family." *Ped Rep* 41:1 (Fall 1990): 3.

Greenwood, Dru. "Bringing Interreligious Dialogue Home." *Compass* 13:2 (Winter 1991): 6–8.

Halper, Sharon. *Mishpaha: A Sampler of Family Education Programs*. N.Y.: Coalition for the Advancement of Jewish Education, 1991. 36pp.

Handelman, Susan. "Family: A Religiously Mandated Deal." *J Jew Com Ser* (1988): 238–42.

Jewish Educator. The "Parents/Symposium." 3 (February 1990): 9–11.

Kane, Gerald M. Moving From Dropping Off To Jumping In: How to Encourage Parent Involvement in Supplementary Jewish Education. *Compass* 16:1 (Fall 1993): 9–11.

Kelman, Vicky. *Scaffolds vs. Lifesupports: A Theory of Jewish Family Education.* Paper presented at Conference on Research in Jewish Education, 1989.

———. *Jewish Family Retreats: A Handbook.* N.Y.: The Melton Research Center For Jewish Education and Whizin Institute for Jewish Family Life at the U. of Judaism, 1993. 260pp.

King, Andrea. *If I'm Jewish and You're Christian, What Are The Kids? A Parenting Guide for Interfaith Families.* Foreword by Alexander M. Schindler. N.Y.: UAHC Press, c. 1992.

Klein, Abigail. "The Generation Gap: Religious Children, Assimilated Grandparents." *Jewish Action* 50:2 (Spring 1990): 70–76.

Kraemer, David, Editor. *The Jewish Family: Metaphor and Memory.* N.Y.: Oxford U. Press, 1988. 248pp.

Levin, Sunie. "Keeping The Lines Open." *Had Mag* 74:10 (June/July 1993): 26–27.

Levine, Harriet. *Family Education.* N.Y.: Coalition for the Advancement of Jewish Education, Spring 1991. 12pp.

Levine, Shlomo D. *The Singular Problems of the Single Jewish Parent.* N.Y.: USCJE, 1981. 39pp.

Lichtig, Judith G. "Parents as Partners." *Ped Rep* (November 1988): 4–6.

Linzer, Norman. "A Perspective On Jewish Family Education." *Jew Ed* 58:1, 2 (Spring/Summer 1990): 26–30.

———. "Translating Conceptions of Jewish Family Education into Practice." *Jew Ed* 59:3 (Winter 1992): 5–8.

Morton, Sharon. "The Family Treasure Chest." *Compass* 16:1 (Fall 1993): 13.

Orchant, Glenda. "School, Family and Synagogue." *Ped Rep* 40:3 (January 1990): 31–32.

Pearl, Jonathan and Judith Pearl. "All In The (Jewish) Family," Understanding, Utilizing, and Enhancing Images of Intermarriage and Other Jewish Family Relationships on Popular Television. *J Jew Com Ser* 69:2/3 (Winter/Spring): 1993: 24–38.

Reshotko, Deborah. *Parents Are Teachers Too: The Patt Program Parent Activity Guide.* N.Y.: The National Federation of Temple Sisterhoods, 1985. 73pp.

* Robbins, Richard C. *A Curricular Model for the American Jewish Family.* Temple U., 1988.

Rosenblatt, Gary. "Starting from Aleph: Baltimore Tries a New Approach to Revitalize Family Education." *Baltimore Jewish Times*, November 11, 1992.

Schiff, Alvin I. "The Jewish Family in Socio-educational Perspective." *Jew Ed* 57; 2, 3, 4 (Summer/Winter 1989): 42–44, 52.

Schulweis, Harold M. "Where Education Begins." *Had Mag* (August/September 1991): 35'37.

Seltzer, Sanford. "The Evolving Jewish Home." *Compass* 14:1 (Fall 1991): 3–4.

Schindler, Alexander M. "The Covenant of the Generations." *Compass* 13:2 (Winter 1991): 5.

Syme, Daniel B. *The Jewish Home: A Guide to Jewish Living.* Northvale, N.J.: Jason Aronson, c. 1989.

Wohl, Renee. "The Family Living Room." *Ped Rep* 40:1 (Fall 1990): 4–5.

Wolfson, Don. *Art of Jewish Living, The Shabbat Seder.* Los Angeles: Federation of Jewish Men's Clubs and the U. of Judaism, 1985. 256pp.

Yad Tikvah. "Aging and Family Concerns." Vol. 3 (Fall 1989). N.Y.: UAHC.

Zachary, Lois J., and Roberta L. Goodman. "A Learner-Centered Approach to Family Life Education Programming: The B'nai Mitzvah Experience." *Jew Ed* 59:1 (Spring/Summer 1991): 25–30.

Zlotowitz, Bernard M. "The Ideal Jewish Family." *Compass* 12:2 (Winter 1990): 3, and 26.

ADULT EDUCATION

General

Abrams, Ruth. *The Educational Needs of Soviet Jews: A First Hand Account.* N.Y.: Coalition for the Advancement of Jewish Education, Winter 1991. 35pp.

Blustain, Sara. "A Hebrew School for Adults." (NYC 92nd Street Y) *For* (E.) (August 1992): 12, 14.

Bogot, Howard I., and Paul M. Yedwab. *Learn Hebrew Today: Alef-Bet for Adults*. N.Y.: UAHC Press, 1992.

——— and Jonathan A. Stein. *To See the World through Jewish Eyes—Guideline for Adult Jewish Study*. N.Y.: UAHC, 1992. 26pp. *Compass*. "Coming of Age: Adult Bat Mitzvah." (Review) *Compass* 12:3 (Spring/Summer 1990): 21.

Epstein, Jerome M. *The Home Study Group: An Adult Education Cluster Program: What It Is. How to Plan. What to Do*. N.Y.: USCJE, 1983. 16pp.

Frankel, P. "Building Self-Esteem through New Approaches to Adult Jewish Education." *J Jew Com Ser* 66:2 (Winter 1989): 161–71.

Goodman Roberta Louis. "The Neglected Learner: The Adult in Our Reform Community." *Compass* 16:1 (Fall 1993): 20–22.

Goldberg, Simcha R. "Jewish Acculturation and the Soviet Immigrant." *J Jew Com Ser* (Winter 1980–1981).

Jacobs, Louis. *Jewish Personal and Social Ethics*. West Orange, N.J.: Behrman House, c. 1990.

Katz, Betsy Dolgin. "Diversity in Adult Jewish Education." *Ped Rep* 40:3 (January 1990): 5–7.

———. "Models of Successful Practice: The Florence Melton Adult Mini-School." *Jew Ed* 58:1, 2 (Spring/Summer 1990): 31–32.

Lipstadt, D. *The Debate on Quality of American Jewish Life: Policy Implications for Adult Jewish Learning*. N.Y.: AJC, February 1988.

Malinow, Peter. "Jewish Acculturation and the Older Soviet Jewish Adult." *Jew Ed* 57:2, 3, 4 (Summer/Winter 1989): 69–71.

Matanky, Leonard S. "Computers and Adult Jewish Learning." *Ped Rep* 40:3 (January 1990): 22–24.

Olitzky, Kerry M. "Renewing Jewish Education For Older Adults." *Compass* 16:1 (Fall 1993): 23–25.

Orbach, Alexander. "The Jewishness of Soviet Culture: Historical Considerations." *J Jew Com Ser* (Winter 1980–1981).

Pedagogic Reporter. "Adult Jewish Education." *Ped Rep* 41:3 (January 1990).

Prell, Riv-Ellen. *Prayer and Community: The Havurah in American Judaism*. Detroit, Mich.: Wayne State U. Press, 1989. 335pp.

Reimer, Joseph. "Toward a Theory of Adult Jewish Education." *Ped Rep* 40:3 (January 1990): 22–24.

Rosen, Gladys. "Raising the Level of Adult Jewish Learning." *Ped Rep* 40:3 (January 1990): 8–11.

Rossel, Seymour. "Lifelong Learning: The Art of Being Jewish." *Compass* 16:1 (Fall 1993): 3–6.

Samuel, Edith. *Your Jewish Lexicon*. N.Y.: UAHC, 1982. 171pp.

———. *A Teacher's Guide to Our Sacred Texts*. N.Y.: UAHC Press c. 1992.

UAHC, Department for Religious Education. *To See the World through Jewish Eyes: Guidelines for Adult Jewish Study*. N.Y.: UAHC, 1988. 362pp.

———. *Directions for Adult Jewish Education: Raising Competency, Commitment, and Involvement*, A review of current opinions about how to improve Adult Jewish Education. N.Y.: UAHC Press, c. 1990.

———. Department of Interreligious Affairs, the Presbyterian Church's Working Group on Interfaith Relations and the National Council of Churches. *Thinking and Working Together: "Study and Action Suggestions for Jewish and Christian Congregations."* N.Y.: UAHC Dept. of Interreligious Affairs, c. 1992.

Vorspan, Albert and David Saperstein. *Tough Choices: Jewish Perspectives on Social Justice*. N.Y.: UAHC Press, 1993.

Weiss, Andrea and Gary M. Bretton-Granatoor, Editors. *Shalom Salaam: Jewish-Muslim Dialogue Resource Guide*. N.Y.: UAHC Press, 1993.

Weissler, Chava. "Making Davening Meaningful: Worship in the Havura Movement." *YA* 19 (1990): 255–82. Ed. Deborah Dash Moore.

Woocher, Jonathan. "Planning for Adult Jewish Education." *Ped Rep* 40:3 (Fall 1990): 27–28.

THE WOMAN'S ROLE AND JEWISH EDUCATION

Abramson, Ellen M. "Listening to a Different Voice: Jewish Women and Adult Education." Department of Education, Jewish Theological Seminary, M.A. Thesis, 1990.

Adelman, Penina. *Miriam's Well: Rituals for Jewish Women around the Year*. Fresh Meadows, N.Y.: Biblio Press, 1990.

Aschkenasy, Nehama. "Women Reacting to Oppression." A Story From Our Biblical Tradition. (From her book, *Eve's Journey*, U. of Pennsylvania Press, 1986) *MJ* 23 (Spring 1990): 11–12.

Baskin, Judith R., Editor. *Jewish Women in Historical Perspective*. Detroit: Wayne State U. Press, 1991.

Berkovitz, Eliezer. *Jewish Women in Time and Torah*. Hoboken, N.J.: Ktav, 1990. 143pp.

Bieler, Jack. "Issues Concerning Torah Education for Women." *Ten Da'at* 111:3 (Spring 1989): 19–21.

Billet, Renee Rookie. "Women Administrators: A Survey." *Ten Da'at* 111:3 (Spring 1989): 24–28.

Bletter, Diana. Interviews, Photographs by Lori Grinker. *The Invisible Thread: A Portrait of Jewish American Women*. Phila.: JPS, 1989. 224pp.

Blumfield, Hanita. "Jewish Feminism in the 1990s." *Cong M* (September/October 1992): 12–15.

Bodoff, Lippman. "Kabbalistic Feminism in Agnon's *Betrothed*." *Jud* 42:4 (Fall 1993): 423–37.

Bronner, Leila Leah. "From Veil to Wig: Jewish Women's Hair Covering." *Jud* 42:4 (Fall, 1993): 465–77.

Fishbane, Simcha. "In Any Case There Are No Sinful Thoughts: The Status of Women in Jewish Law as Expressed in the *Arukh Hashulhan*," *Jud* 42:4 (Fall 1993): 492–503.

Goldstein, Alice. "New Roles, New Commitments? Jewish Women's Involvement in the Community's Structure." *Contemporary Jewry* (1990): 49–76.

Lerner, Eleanor. "Jewish Involvement in the New York City Woman Suffrage Movement." *AJHS* 70:4 (June 1981): 442–61.

Lichtenstein, Aharon. "Torah Study for Women." *Ten Da'at* 111:3 (Spring 1989): 7–8.

Lubitch, Rivkah. "A Feminist's Look at Esther." *Jud* 42:4 (Fall 1993): 438–46.

Magnus, Shulamit. "'Out of the Ghetto': Integrating the Study of Jewish Women into the Study of 'The Jews'." *Jud* 39:1 (Winter 1990): 28–36.

Minkoff, Harvey & Evelyn B. Melamed. "Was the First Feminist Bible in Yiddish?" *Moment* 16:3 (June 1991): 28–33, 52.

* Morris, Bonnie J. *Women of Valor: Female Religious Activism and Identity in the Lubavitcher Community of Brooklyn, 1955–1987*. SUNY at Binghamton, 1990.

Ochs, Vanessa L. *Words on Fire: One Woman's Journey into the Sacred*. N.Y.: Harcourt Brace, 1991. 328pp.

Plaskow, Judith. *Standing Again at Sinai: Judaism from A Feminist Perspective*. San Francisco: Harper & Row, 1990. 283pp.

———. "It Is Not In Heaven. Feminism and Jewish Authority." *Tikkun* 5:2 (March/April 1990): 39–40.

Prell, Riv Ellen. "The Begetting of America's Jews." "Seeds of American Jewish Identity in the Representations of American Jewish Women." *J Jew Com Ser* 69:2/3 (Winter/Spring 1993): 4–23.

Response. "Judaism and Gender: A New Look." No. 61 (Fall 1993). Articles follow:

    Braiterman, Zak. "Rashi and Phyllis Trible: And Never the 'Twain Shall Meet." Pp. 10–17.

    Brettschneider, Marla. "Feminist Judaism: Providing Models for Continuity through Multiculturalism." Pp. 18–21.

    Ciolkowski, Laura E. "A Question of Identity: Jewish-Feminist Politics in the 1990s." Pp. 42–15.

    Feinhor, Noam. "Writing On The Wall: Tisha B'Av." Pp. 39–41.

    Hyman, Miriam. "Renewing Ritual: The Brit Mikvah." Pp. 22–31.

    Weinthal, Edith C. "The Image of the City in E. M. Broner's *A Weave of Women*." Pp. 46–52.

Rogow, Faith. *Gone to Another Meeting: The National Council of Jewish Women, 1893–1993*. With a Foreword by Joan Bronk. Tuscaloosa, Ala.: U. of Alabama Press, 1993. 264pp.

Ross, Tamar. "Can the Demand for Change in the Status of Women Be Halakhically Legitimated." *Jud* 42:4 (Fall 1993): 478–91.

* Schonfeld, Bella. *Orthodox Jewish Professional Women who Return to School for Professional Degrees During Their Middle Years*. Columbia U., 1989.

Simon, Rita James. "Teachers, Preachers, and Feminists in America: Women Rabbis." *Shofar* 10:1 (Fall 1991): 2–10.

Straus, Barrie Ruth Waldman. "Ideological Agendas and Images of Women in Jewish Literature." *JBA* 47 (1989–1990): 27–39.

Toll, William. "A Quiet Revolution: Jewish Women's Clubs and the Widening Female Sphere, 1870–1920." *AJA* 41:1 (Spring/Summer 1989): 7–26.

Weinberg, Sydney Stahl. *The World of Our Mothers: The Lives of Jewish Immigrant Women*. N.Y.: Schocken Books, 1988. 325pp.

———. "Longing to Learn: The Education of Jewish Immigrant Women in New York City, 1900–1934." *Journal of American Ethnic History* 8:2 (Spring 1989): 108–126.

Weissman, Deborah. "The Education of Jewish Women." *Bat Kol* (Fall 1987): 10–15.

Yuter, Alan J. "The Feminist Challenge to Judaism." *Mid* 38:2 (February/March 1992): 14–16.

Women and Prayer

Caedin, Nina Beth. Editor and Translator. *Out of the Depths I Call You: A Book of Prayers for the Married Jewish Woman*. Northvale, N.J.: Jason Aronson, Inc., 1992.

Falk, Marcia. "Notes on Composing New Blessings: Toward a Feminist-Jewish Reconstruction of Prayer." *Recon* 53:3 (December 1987): 10–15.

Judaism. "Further on Women as Prayer Leaders and Their Role in Communal Prayer: An Exchange." *Jud* 42:4 (Fall 1993). (See below).
    Broyde, Michael J. "Communal Prayer and Women." Pp. 387–394.
    Hauptman, Judith. "Some Thoughts on the Nature of Halakhic Adjudication: Women and Minyan." Pp. 396–413.
    Wolowelsky, Joel B. (Reaction to Hauptman's article). Pp. 394–95.

Klirs, Tracy Guren, Compiler and Introduction. *The Merit of Our Mothers: A Bilingual Anthology of Jewish Women's Prayers*. Cincinnati: Hebrew Union College Press, 1992.

Wegner, Judith Romney. *Shattel or Person? The Status of Women in the Mishnah*. N.Y. & Oxford: Oxford U. Press, 1988.

Weiss, Avraham. *Women at Prayer: A Halakhic Analysis of Women's Prayer Groups*. Hoboken, N.J.: KTAV, 1990. 147pp.

Zakutinsky, Rivka. *Techinas: A Voice from the Heart: A Collection of Jewish Women's Prayers*, "As Only A Woman Can Pray." Brooklyn, N.Y.: Aura Press Inc., 1992.

SEPHARDIM AND JEWISH EDUCATION

General

Alexy, Trudi. *The Mezuzah in the Madonna's Foot*. "Oral Histories Exploring 500 Years in the Parodoxical Relationship of Spain and the Jews." N.Y.: Simon & Schuster, c. 1993. 316pp.

Amateau, Albert J. "The Sephardic Immigrant from Bulgaria: A Personal Profile of Moise Gadol." *Amer Jew Arc* 42:1 (Spring/Summer 1990): 57–70.

Angel, Marc D. "After the Expulsion: Aspects of the Sephardic Spirit." *Cong M* 59:7 (November/December 1992): 12–15.

———. *The Rythms of Jewish Living: A Sephardic Approach*. N.Y.: Sepher-Hermon Press, 1986. 199pp.

———. "The Sephardic Spirit." *RJ* 19:2 (1990): 30–31. Interviewed by Hirt-Manheimer.

———. *Voices in Exile: A Study in Sephardic Intellectual History*. Hoboken, N.J.: Ktav Publishing House in association with Sephardic House, 1991.

Canelo, David Augusto. *Last Crypto-Jews of Portugal*. Portland, Ore.: n.p., 1990. 185pp.

Carlebach, Elisheva. "Rabbinic Circles as Messianic Pathways in the Post-Expulsion Era." *Jud* 41:3 (Summer 1992): 208–16.

Cohen, Marsha B. "Images of Spanish Jewry." *RJ* 19:2 (1990): 22–25.

Dan, Joseph. "The Epic of a Millenium: Judeo-Spanish Culture's Confrontations." *Jud* 41:2 (Spring 1992): 115–29.

Elazar, Daniel. "Can Sephardic Judaism Be Reconstructed." *Jud* 41:3 (Summer 1992): 217–28.

Elkin, Judith Laikin. "Jews and the Encounter with the New World 1492–1992." *MJH* 33 (Winter 1992): 2–5.

Esses, Dianne O. "A Hunger For Syrian 'Exotica'." *MJ* 26 (Autumn 1992): 12–13.

Finkelstein, Norman H. *The Other 1492: Jewish Settlement in the New World*. N.Y.: Charles Scribner's Sons, 1989. 100pp. (Written for juveniles.)

Fromm, Annette B. "Food Traditions Tell Rich Stories." (Balkan Jews in America) *MJ* 26 (Autumn 1992): 19.

Gampel, Benjamin R. *The Last Jews on Iberian Soil: Navarrese Jewry 1479/1498*. Los Angeles: U. of California Press, 1989.

Gerber, Jane S. *The Jews of Spain: A History of the Sephardic Experience*. N.Y.: The Free Press, 1992. 333pp.

Goldberg, Harvey E. "What's in a Name? Sephardi Jews in their Own Terms." *MJ* 26 (Autumn 1992): 3–4.

Goldman, Frederick. "The 'Other' 1492." *Mid* 38:1 (January 1992): 9–13.

Gross, Abraham. "The Expulsion and the Search for the Ten Tribes." *Jud* 41:2 (Spring 1992): 130–47.

Gruen, George E. "Israel's Sephardim: Myth and Reality." *RJ* 19:2 (1990): 26–29.

Gubbay, Lucien and Abraham Levy. *Sephardim: Their Glorious Tradition from the Babylonian Exile to the Present Day*. Phila.: JPS, n.d. 224pp.

Haragaal, Ya'aqov Halevi. "Back to Spain: Full Circle." *Mid* 38:6 (August/September 1992): 36–38.

Herculano, Alexandre. *History of the Origin and Establishment of the Inquisition in Portugal*. N.Y.: Ktav Pub. House, 1972. 504pp.

Ingall, Carol K. "Nancy Drew with a Sephardic Twist, A Review of *Out of Many Waters*, by Jacqueline Dembar Greene." *MJ* 26 (Autumn 1992): 28–29.

Kaplan, Yosef. "The Jewish Profile of the Spanish-Portuguese Community of London During the Seventeenth Century." *Jud* 41:3 (Summer 1992): 229–40.

Lacave, Jose Luis. "The Final Disposition of the Synagogues and Other Jewish Communal Property After the Expulsion." *Jud* 41:3 (Summer 1992): 241–47.

Lasker, Daniel J. "Jewish-Christian Polemics in Light of the Expulsion from Spain." *Jud* 41:2 (Spring 1992): 148–55.

Mark, Jonathan, and Tzvi Blanchard. "Sephardic Spirituality." *MJ* 26 (Autumn 1992): 9–10.

Matza, Diane. "Sephardi Beginnings in America." *Mid* 33:3 (March 1987): 34–36.

———. "Sephardic Jews Transmitting Culture Across Three Generations." *AJH* 79:3 (Spring 1990): 336–54.

———. "Self-Perception Among American Sephardim." *MJ* 26 (Autumn 1992): 11, 12.

Melamed, Renee Levine. "Women in (Post–1942) Spanish Crypto-Jewish Society." *Jud* 41:2 (Spring 1992): 156–68.

Nahon, Gerard. "The Impact of the Expulsion from Spain on the Jewish Community of the Pre-Revolutionary France, 1550–1781." *Jud* 41:2 (Spring 1992): 169–79.

Papo, Joseph M. "Nissim Behar—Sephardic Innovater." *Mid* 33:3 (March 1987): 44–16.

Perera, Victor. "The Cross and the Pear Tree." *MJ* 26 (Autumn 1992): 3, 6.

Popkin, Richard A. "Jewish Christians and Christian Jews in Spain." *Jud* 41:3 (Summer 1992): 248–67.

Raphael, Chaim. "Sepharad '92." *Commentary* 93:3 (March 1992): 44–45.

Ravid, Benjamin. "An Introduction to the Economic History of the Iberian Diaspora in the Mediterranean." *Jud* 41:3 (Summer 1992): 268–85.

Rejwan, Nissim. "The Sephardic Mystique." *Mid* 39:2 (February/March 1993): 28–30.

Rodrigue, Aron. *French Jews, Turkish Jews: The Alliance Israelite Universalle and the Politics of Jewish Schooling in Turkey, 1860–1905*. Bloomington: Indiana U. 1990. 256pp.

———. *The Teachers of the Alliance Israelite Universelle, 1860–1939*. Seattle, Wash.: U. of Washington Press, c. 1992.

Roth, Cecil. *Dona Gracia, of The House of Nasi*. Phila.: JPS, n.d. 232pp.

———. *The Duke of Naxos, of The House of Nasi*. Phila.: JPS, 1947–48. 270pp.

Sanua, Marianne. "Sephardi Pride and Plaint." *Cong M* 57:5 (July/August 1990): 10–12.

Sarna, Jonathan D. "Columbus & the Jews." *Commentary* 94:5 (November 1992): 38–41.

Schacter, Jacob J. "Echoes of the Spanish Expulsion in Eighteenth Century Germany: The Baer Thesis Revisited." *Jud* 41:2 (Spring 1992): 180–89.

Scheindlin, Raymond P. "Judah Abravanel to His Son." *Jud* 41:2 (Spring 1992): 190–99.

Seltzer, Robert M. "Philosophy, Demography and History: Several Recent Books on Sephardic Jewry." *MJ* 26 (Autumn 1992): 27, 30.

Shelemay, Kay Kaufman. "Remembering the Past, Creating a Future: The Sephardic Tradition in Song." *MJ* 26 (Autumn 1992): 87–8.

Stillman, Norman A. *The Jews of Arab Lands in Modern Times*. Phila.: JPS, 1991. 624pp.

Stow, Kenneth R. "Ethnic Rivalry or Melting Pot: The 'Edot' in the Roman Ghetto." *Jud* 41:3 (Summer 1992): 286–96.

Sutton, Joseph A.D. *Aleppo Chronicles: The Story of the Unique Sephardeem of the Ancient Near East—in Their Own Words*. Introduction by Raphael Patai. N.Y.: Thayer-Jacoby, c. 1989. 576pp.

Swissa, Albert. "Escaping the Cauldron Unscathed." *MJ* 26 (Autumn 1992): 14–15.

Wald, Alexandra. "Return to Toledo." *Cong M* 159:6 (September/October 1992): 6–9.

Whitman, Pearl. "Letter from Madrid." *Mid* 38:1 (January 1992): 14–16.

American Jewish Archives. "Sephardim in the Americas." Martin A. Cohen, Guest Editor. Cincinnati, Ohio: *AJA* 44:1 (Spring/Summer 1992): 500pp. Articles:

    Armistead, Samuel G. "Judeo-Spanish Traditional Poetry in the United States." Pp. 357–77.

    Cohen, Martin A. "The Sephardic Phenomenon: A Reappraisal." Pp. 1–7.

    Hernandez, Frances. "The Secret Jews of the Southwest." Pp. 411–54.

    Katz, Israel J. "The Sacred and Secular Musical Traditions of the Sephardic Jews in the United States." Pp. 331–56.

    Lida, Denah. "Language of the Sephardim in Anglo America." Pp. 309–29.

    Levy, Emma Fidanque. "The Fidanques: Symbols of the Continuity of the Sephardic Tradition in America." Pp. 179–207.

    Matza, Diane. "Tradition and History: Sephardic Contributions to American Literature." Pp. 379–109.

    Metz, Allan. "Those of the Hebrew Nation . . . The Sephardic Experience in Colonial Latin America." Pp. 209–33.

    Mirelman, Victor C. "Sephardim in Latin America after Independence." Pp. 235–65.

    Papo, Joseph M. "The Sephardim in North America in the Twentieth Century." Pp. 267–308.

    Stern, Malcolm H. "Portuguese Sephardim in America." Pp. 141–78.

    Weinstein, Rochelle. "Stones of Memory: Revelations from a Cemetery in Curacao." Pp. 81–140.

Education

CAJE. "Special Focus: Sephardic and Oriental Jewry." In *CAJE* (Summer 1990). (Entire Issue).

Holtz, Barry W. "Teaching Spanish Jewry: New Curriculum Materials." *MJ* 26 (Autumn 1992): 26, 30.

The Melton Journal. Editorial. *MJ* 26 (Autumn 1992): 2, 24.

Rauch, Eduardo. "The Drama of Sephardic Jewry—On How to Tell the Story to Our Children." *MJ* 26 (Autumn 1992): 28.

Resnick, Martha Ezor. *Jewish History through Primary Texts: An Approach To Teaching The Golden Age of Spain To High School Students*. N.Y.: New York BJE, 1991. 52pp.

Schwartz, Howard and Barbara Rush (Retold). "The Sabbath Lion: A Jewish Folktale from Algeria." *MJ* 26 (Autumn 1992): 16–17.

LOCAL SOURCES FOR JEWISH EDUCATION

YOUTH AND JEWISH EDUCATION

Goldberg, Ari Y. "Youth Empowerment: An Insurance Policy for the Future." Department of Education, Jewish Theological Seminary, M.A. Thesis, 1990.

Samlan, Arnold. "Youth Leadership Institute." *Ped Rep* 40:1 (Fall 1990): 15–16.

CAMP

Camping Programs and Jewish Education

American Zionist Youth and Young Judaica. *Jewish Identity: Junior Camp Theme*. Ages 12–14. N.Y.: 1990. 53pp.

Bardin, Livia. "Are Jewish Camps Educational Stepchildren?" *Moment* 17:1 (February 1992): 22–25.

Davidson, Jessica. "Summer Time and the Living Is Jewish, Jewish Camps and Jewish Identity." *Moment* 18:1 (February 1993): 56–60. (This issue also includes a Guide to Jewish Camps, pp. 60–77.)

Ettenberg, Sylvia C, and Geraldine Rosenfield, Eds. *The Ramah Experience: Community and Commitment*. N.Y.: JTSA, 1989. 228pp.

Melzer, Asher. "Reflections on Fifty Years in Jewish Camping—A Labor of Love." *Jew Ed* 60:1 (Spring 1993): 18.

Shulsinger, Shlomo, Editor. *Kovetz Massad: Hebrew Camping in North America*, Vol. II, (Hebrew). Jerusalem: Irgun Machanot "Massad" B'Israel and Alumni of Massad Camps in U.S.A., 1989.

Smith, Allan L. "The Challenge of Informal Education." *Compass* 16:1 (Fall 1993): 7–8.

ALABAMA

Birmingham

Cowett, Mark. *Birmingham's Rabbi: Morris Newfield and Alabama, 1895–1940*. Tuscaloosa, Ala.: U. of Alabama Press, 1986. 240pp.

Tuscaloosa

Stritikus, George R. "Stepping into the Past: The Story of the Battle-Friedman Garden." *Alabama Heritage* 5 (Summer 1987): 30–47.

ALASKA

Eisenberg, Matthew J. "The Last Frontier: Jewish Pioneers in Alaska." Part I. *WSJH* 24:1 (October 1991): 51–73.

———. "The Last Frontier: Jewish Pioneers in Alaska." Part II. *WSJH* 24:2 (January 1992): 119–35.

ARIZONA

Phoenix

Greater Phoenix Jewish News. *Jewish Living in the Valley of the Sun*. Phoenix: 1989–1990. 96pp.

Lamb, Blaine P. "Frontiersmen in Broadcloth: Jews in Early Phoenix 1870–1920." *WSJH* 25:1 (October 1992): 3–21.

CALIFORNIA

Kramer, William M. "Kaspar Cohn: A Man Who Helped Make Southern California—Part I."

WSJH 23:3 (April 1991): 195–211; Part II. WSJH 23:4 (July 1991): 324–43.

Labau, Henry J. "The Jews in California Commerce—1856." *WSJH* 24:1 (October 1991): 34–36.

Stern, Norton B. "The Early History Which Preceded the Establishment of Jewish Farm Colonies." *WSJH* 23:3 (April 1991): 223–30.

Butte County

Levenson, Rosaline. "Jewish Community of Butte County," part 5. In Butte County Historical Society. *Diggin's* 33:2 (Summer 1989): 27–53.

———. "Jews in the Gold Rush: Thirty-Seven Years of Jewish Shopkeepers and Postmasters in Butte County, California." *WSJH* 25:3 (April 1993): 227–12.

Long Beach

"Long Beach, California Jewry Viewed in 1930 and 1968." *WSJH* 23:2 (January 1991): 168–72.

Los Angeles

General

Ben-Zvi, Hava and Sandra R. Bernstein. *Los Angeles Jewry—A Salute!* Los Angeles Jewish Community Library, 1981. 153pp.

Goldman, May W. "The Federation of Jewish Charities of Los Angeles in 1923." *WSJH* 23:1 (October 1990): 22–25.

Kronzek, Lynn C. "Fairfax... A Home, A Community, A Way of Life." *Legacy* 1:4 (Spring 1990): Los Angeles: Southern California Jewish Historical Society.

Los Angeles, *City of Los Angeles Cultural Affairs Department Folk Arts Program*. Treasures of Fairfax: A Salute to Jewish Cultural Traditions. Los Angeles, 1988. 8pp.

Maidenberg, Harry F. "An 1890s Arrival in Los Angeles from the Ukraine." *WSJH* 24:1 (October 1991): 40–47.

Moore, Deborah Dash. "Jewish Migration and Community in Postwar Los Angeles." *YA* 19 (1990): 17–36.

Pratt, Norma Fain. "Women's Moving Forward: Dreamers, Builders, Leaders: A History of Jewish Women in Southern California." *Legacy* 1:3 (Spring 1989): Los Angeles: Southern California Jewish Historical Society.

Rubin, Susan E. "The Jewish Response to the Los Angeles Riots." *WSJH* 25:3 (April 1993): 195–210.

Tugend, Tom. "Los Angeles." *Had Mag* 74:10 (June/July 1993): 30–33.

Education

Aron, I., and Philips B. *Findings of the Los Angeles Bureau of Jewish Education's Jewish Teacher Census.* Paper presented at the Fourth Annual Conference on Research in Jewish Education. New York City, 1990.

Kopulsky, Andrew. *The Story of Jewish Los Angeles: A Teacher's Guide for the Fourth Grade Jewish Day School.* Los Angeles, 1980.

Oroville

Levenson, Rosaline. "Oroville's Jewish Cemetery: Enduring Legacy of the Gold Rush." *WSJH* 23:1 (October 1990): 3–14.

Petaluma

Naftaly, Phillip. "Jewish Chicken Farmers in Petaluma, California, 1904–1975." *WSJH* 23:3 (April 1991): 231–17.

Sacramento

Kaplan, Bernard M. "An Historical Outline of the Jews of Sacramento in the Nineteenth Century." *WSJH*, 23:3 (April 1991): 256–67.

"The Blue Laws Debate: A Sacramento Shopkeeper's Story." *WSJH*, 25:3 (April 1993): 211–24.

San Diego

Schwartz, Henry. "The Silver Shirts: Anti-Semitism in San Diego, 1930–1940." *WSJH* 25:1 (October 1992): 52–60.

San Francisco

Gold, Steven J. "Patterns of Interaction and Adjustment Among Soviet Jewish Refugees: Findings from an Ethnography in the San Francisco Bay Area." *Contemporary Jewry* 9:2 (Fall 1988). N.Y.: Association for the Social Scientific Study of Jewry.

Jacobs, Monty. "The San Francisco Jewish Community in 1955," *WSJH* 24:1 (October 1991): 28–31.

Jenicot, Michel. "The Weissbein Brothers of Grass Valley and San Francisco: Banking, Mining and Real Estate." *WSJH* 22:3 (April 1990): 223–25.

Levy, Harold L. "Julius Friedman, Benefactor of the Jewish Home for the Aged, San Francisco." *WSJH* 23:2 (January 1991): 99–105.

Olcott, Sylvia G. "My Father, Richard Gutstadt of B'nai B'rith: A Memoir." *WSJH* 25:1 (October 1992): 61–76.

Stern, Norton B. "The First Western Jewish Newspaper and Its Probable Describer," *WSJH* 23:4 (July 1991): 320–23.

COLORADO

Denver

Abrams, Jeanne. *"For a Child's Sake": The Denver Sheltering Home for Jewish Children in the Progressive Era AJH* 89:2 (Winter 1989–90): 181–202.

CONNECTICUT

Hamden

Wenger, Beth S. *Congregation and Community: The Evolution of Jewish Life at Congregation Mishkan Israel, 1840–1990*. Hamden, CT: Congregation Mishkan Israel, 1990. 68pp. Illus.

New Haven

Jews in New Haven. Vol. 5, 1988. New Haven: The Jewish Historical Society of New Haven.

Stamford

Koenig, Samuel. *An American Jewish Community: 50 Years of History, 1889–1939*. Stamford, CT: Stamford Historical Society, 1991. 175pp.

DISTRICT OF COLUMBIA

Diner, Hasia. *Fifty Years of Jewish Self-Governance: The Jewish Community of Greater Washington, 1938–1988*. Washington D.C.: The Jewish Community Council of Greater Washington, 1989. 150pp.

FLORIDA

Florida Jewish Demography, 1:1, March 31, 1988. "Miami: Judaic Studies Program," Un. of Miami. 2:1 December 1, 1988.

Miami

General

Nagler, Richard, and Isaac Bashevis Singer. *My Love Affair With Miami Beach*. N.Y.: Simon Schuster, 1991. 118pp.

Education

Ross, Lillian, ed. *The Jewish Experience in America*. Miami: Central Agency for Jewish Education, 1987. 152pp.

Sheskin, I. *The Miami Jewish Educator Study*. Miami: Central Agency for Jewish Education, 1988.

West Palm Beach County

Sheskin, Ira M. "In the Community: Estimating the Number of Jews in the Service Area of the Jewish Federation of West Palm Beach County." *Contemporary Jewry* 10:2 (Fall 1989). N.Y.: Association for the Social Scientific Study of the Jews.

GEORGIA

Schmier, Louis. "The New Canaan: The Jewish Experience in Georgia." Part I. *The Georgia Historical Quarterly* 73:2 (Summer 1989): 349–63.

Atlanta

Atlanta Jewish Times. *Guide to Atlanta Jewish Life*. Atlanta: 1989. 67pp.

Bauman, Mark. "Rabbi Harry H. Epstein and the Adaptation of Second-Generation East European Jews in Atlanta." *AJA* 42:2 (Fall/Winter 1990): 133–45.

ILLINOIS

Chicago

Gleicher, David. "The Origins and Early Years of Chicago's Hebrew Theological College." *Trad* 27:2 (Winter 1993): 56–68.

Kaplan, Nathan. "Twenty Questions on Local Jewish History." *Chicago Jewish History* 12:4 (June 1989). Chicago Jewish Historical Society.

Mallow, Jeffry V. "The Jews of Chicago." *Jew Fron* (January/February 1990): 19–21.

Roth, Walter. "An Unsettling Look at the Jewish Experience in America." *Chicago Jewish History* 13:4 (Summer 1990). Chicago Jewish Historical Society.

Sandler, Bernard I. "How Unhappy Migrants to Chicago Established a Colony in Palestine." *Chicago Jewish History* 13:4 (Summer 1990). Chicago Jewish Historical Society.

Zenner, Walter P. "Chicago's Unknown Jews: Story of Local Sephardim." *Chicago Jewish History* 12:3 (March 1989). Chicago: Chicago Jewish Historical Society.

———. "Chicago's Sephardim: A Historical Exploration." *AJHS* 79:2 (Winter 1989/1990): 221–11.

INDIANA

Indianapolis

Glazier, J. "Stigma, Identity and Sephardic-Ashkenazic Relations in Indianapolis." In Walter P. Zenner, ed., *Persistence and Flexibility*. Albany, N.Y., 1988, pp. 41–62.

Indiana Jewish Historical Society. *Indiana Jewish History*. Fort Wayne, 1990, 32pp.

KENTUCKY

Weissbach, Lee Shai. "Stability and Mobility in the Small Jewish Community: Examples from Kentucky History." *AJH* 79:3 (Spring 1990): 355–75.

MAINE

Goodwin, George M. *Sketches of the Lawrence Jewish Community*. Andover, MA: Temple Emanuel, 1990. 101pp.

MASSACHUSETTS

Boston

* Braverman, William A. *The Ascent of Boston's Jews, 1630–1918*. Dissertation. Cambridge: Harvard U. 1990.

Combined Jewish Philanthropies of Greater Boston. *Shalom Boston: A Directory of Greater Boston Jewish Community Services*. Boston, 1989.

Education

Kaye, J.S. *Jewish Family Life Through Jewish Family Education*. Boston: Bureau of Jewish Education of Greater Boston, 1989.

Waltham

Lazaroff, Tovah. "The Jewish Community." *Waltham Rediscovered: An Ethnic History of Waltham, Massachusetts*. Portsmouth, NH: Peter E. Rendall, 1988, pp. 313–401.

Pollak, Oliver. "The City Directory: A Tool in Researching Jewish History." *Local Jewish Historical Society News* 1:4 (Fall 1988). Waltham, MA.

MICHIGAN

Detroit

Bolkosky, Sidney M. *Harmony and Dissonance: Voices of Jewish Identity in Detroit, 1914–1967*. Detroit: Wayne State U. Press, 1991. 464pp.

———. "The New Immigrants." *Michigan Jewish History* 31 (November 1990): 28–34.

Cantor, Judith Levin, comp. "The Sephardic Community of Greater Detroit: A Rich Heritage." *MJH* 33 (Winter 1992): 6–7.

Cohen, Annabel. "Sephardic Treats." *MJH* 33 (Winter 1992): 8.

Goldman, Mrs. Bernard (Norma). "David E. Heineman." *Michigan Jewish History* 30 (October 1989): 16–17.

Goode, Selma. "Some Jewish Contributions to the Michigan Trade Union Movement." *Michigan Jewish History* (October 1989): 26–28.

Kaufman, Dorothy. "100 Years of Service: National Council of Jewish Women, Greater Detroit Section." *Michigan Jewish History* (Winter 1991): 18–23.

Raimi, Ralph A. *The Philomathic Debating Club, 1898–1950: A History*. Published by the author, 46 Glen Ellyn Way, Rochester, N.Y.: 146–18, 1991, 153pp. A history of a Jewish debating club in Central High School, Detroit. Includes topics debated over the years.

———. "The Philomathic Debating Club." *Michigan Jewish History* 31 (November 1990): 10–27.

Rockaway, Robert. "Philip Slomovitz: Jewish Journalist." *Michigan Jewish History* 32 (Winter 1991): 13–17.

Midland

Grosberg, Julius. "The History of the Jewish Midland Community." *The Midland Log*. Midland County Historical Society, Midland, MI. Winter 1987. Pp. 1–11.

Muskegon

Devlin, Dennis S. *Muskegon's Jewish Community: A Centennial History, 1888–1988*. Muskegon, MI: Congregation B'nai Israel, 1988. 90pp.

Pontiac

Barnett, Sidney. "Pontiac's First Jewish Residents, Joseph and Rachel Barnett." *Michigan Jewish History* 31 (November 1990): pp. 3–7.

MINNESOTA

American Jewish World. *The Cycles of Life: A Minnesota Guide to Jewish Living*. Minneapolis, 1989. 100pp.

Minneapolis

City and Education

Gordon, Theodore H. "George J. Gordon and the Minneapolis Talmud Torah." *Jew Ed* 55:1 (Spring 1987): 36–11.

Lewin, Rhoda G. *Temple Israel: A Brief History, 1878–1987*. Minneapolis: Temple Israel, 1987. 31pp.

MISSISSIPPI

Hadda, Janet. "Ashkenaz on the Mississippi." *YA* 19 (1990): 93–103. Ed. Deborah Dash Moore.

MISSOURI

St. Louis

St. Louis Jewish Light. Guide to Jewish Life in St. Louis. St. Louis, 1990. 64pp.

NEBRASKA

Memories of the Jewish Midwest. Vol. 5. Omaha: Nebraska Jewish Historical Society, Fall 1989.

NEW JERSEY

* Eisenberg, Ellen M. *Jewish Agricultural Colonies in Southern New Jersey: The Processes of Migration, Settlement and Adaptation.* Dissertation. U. of Pennsylvania, 1989.

Metro-West Jewish News. *Metrosource: A Guide to Jewish Living 1990–1991.* East Orange, NJ, 1990. 128pp.

Meyers, Allen. *Southern New Jersey Synagogues: A Social History, Highlighted by Stories of Jewish Life in the 1880's–1980's.* Sewell, NJ, 1990. 338pp.

Farmingdale

Dubrovsky, Gertrude W. *The Land Was Theirs: Jewish Farmers in the Garden State.* Tuscaloosa, AL: The U. of Alabama Press, 1992. 272pp.

Newark

Shapiro, Edward S. "Ethnicity and Employment: The Early Years of the Jewish Vocational Service of Newark, 1939–1952." *New Jersey History* 106:1–2 (Spring/Summer 1988): 19–39.

NEW MEXICO

Hordes, Stanley M. "The Inquisition and the Crypto-Jewish Community in Colonial New Spain and New Mexico." *WSJH* 24:2 (January 1992): 106–118.

New Mexico Jewish Historical Society. "Stones of Remembrance: The Historic Jewish Cemetery in Las Vegas, New Mexico." Photos by Cary Herz. Santa Fe, 1990. 20pp.

Rubin, Nan. "The Hidden Jews of New Mexico." *MJ* 26 (Autumn 1992): 5.

Tobias, Henry J. *A History of the Jews in New Mexico.* Albuquerque: U. of Mexico Press, 1990. 294pp.

NEW YORK STATE

New York City
General

Boyarin, Jonathan. "Observant Participation: Ethnography of Jews on the Lower East Side." *YA* 19 (1990): 233. Ed. Deborah Dash Moore.

Ehrlich, Evelyn. *A History of the Hebrew Tabernacle Congregation of Washington Heights, A German-Jewish Community in New York City.* N.Y.: Hebrew Tabernacle Congregation, 1985, 59pp.

Gribetz, Edith R. "Little Known Places of Jewish Interest in New York City." *Ten Da'at* 111:3 (Spring 1989): 40–41.

Horowitz, Irving Louis. *Daydreams and Nightmares: Reflections of a Harlem Childhood.* Jackson: U. Press of Mississippi, 1990, 104pp.

Israelowitz, Oscar. *Flatbush Guide.* Brooklyn: Israelowitz Pub., 1990. 111pp.

———. *Guide to New York City: A Guide for the Sophisticated Traveler.* Brooklyn: Israelowitz Pub., 1990. 216pp.

Joselit, Jenna Weissman. *New York's Jewish Jews: The Orthodox Community in the Inter-war Years.* Bloomington, IN: Indiana U. Press, 1990. 208pp.

K'hal Adath Jeshurun. *The Living Hirschian Legacy: Essays on "Torah and Derech Eretz" and the Contemporary Hirschian Kehilla.* N.Y.: Phillip Feldheim, 1988. viii + 210 + 92pp.

Kugelmass, Jack. "Green Bagels: An Essay on Food, Nostalgia, and the Carnivalesque." *YA* 19 (1990): 57–80. Ed. Deborah Dash Moore.

Marx, Jeffrey A. "Give My Childhood Again": The Grand Street Boys Association, 1915–1945. *AJA* 43:2 (Fall/Winter 1991): 115–33.

Sorin, Gerald. *The Nurturing Neighborhood: The Brownsville Boys Club and Jewish Community in Urban America, 1940–1990.* N.Y.: New York U. Press, 1990. 255pp.

———. "Street Corner Jews: The Boys of Brownsville." *YA* 19 (1990): 37–52.

Wisse, Ruth R. *A Little Love in Big Manhattan: Talented Yiddish Poets on the Lower East Side*. Cambridge, MA, 1988. 179pp.

Education

Ackerman, Walter I. "Community and Education." *AJHS* 60:2 (Winter 1990–91): 175–82.

Bellow, Adam. *The Educational Alliance: A Centennial Celebration*. N.Y.: The Educational Alliance 1990. 261pp.

Brumberg, Stephan F. "An Education for Life in Two Communities. Reflections on Arthur Goren's *New York's Jews and the Quest for Community*." *AJHS* 80:2 (Winter 1990–91): 164–74.

Schiff, Alvin I. "Beyond the New York Jewish Supplementary School Study." *Ped Rep* 40:4 (April 1990): 3–4.

Sephardim in New York City

* Dahbany-Miraglia, D. *An Analysis of Ethnic identity among Yemenite Jews in the Greater New York Area*. Dissertation. Columbia U. 1983.

Sanua, Marianne. "From the Pages of the *Victory Bulletin:* The Syria Jews in Brooklyn during World War II." *YA* 19 (1990): 283–330. Ed. Deborah Dash Moore.

NORTH DAKOTA

Chananel

Herscher, Uri D. "Chananel, North Dakota." *WSJH* 25:3 (April 1993): 225–26.

OHIO

Ornstein-Galicia, Jacob L. "An American Jewish Family's Farm Odyssey." *Amer Jew Arc* 41:1 (Spring/Summer 1989): 53–76.

Cincinnati

Kraut, Benny. *German-Jewish Orthodox in an Immigrant Synagogue: Cincinnati's New Hope Congregation and the Ambiguities of Ethnic Religion*. N.Y.: Markus Wiener, 1988. 303pp.

Peck, Abraham J., and Uri D. Herscher. *Queen City Refuge: An Oral History of Cincinnati's Jewish Refugees from Nazi Germany*. West Orange, N.J.: Behrman House, 1989.

Sarna, Jonathan D., and Nancy H. Klein. *The Jews of Cincinnati*. Cincinnati: Center for the Study of the American Jewish Experience, 1989. 190pp.

Winkler, Henry R. "Between Uniqueness and Commanality: Reflections on the Cincinnati Jewish Experience." *AJA* 42:2 (Fall/Winter 1990): 155–66.

Cleveland

Education

Cleveland Bureau of Jewish Education. *From Generation To Generation [KIT]: History Through Images: An Examination of Jewish Continuity in Cleveland, Ohio, 1989.*

Columbus

Ohio Jewish Chronicle. "Guide to the Columbus Jewish Community." in *New Year Edition 1990–1991*. Pp. 112–128.

OKLAHOMA

Apache

Lovett, John R. "The Levites of Apache, Oklahoma." *WSJH* 24:4 (July 1992): 299–307.

OREGON

Jacksonville

"The Jacksonville, Oregon Jewish Cemetery." *WSJH* 23:2 (January 1991): 106–111.

Portland

Miranda, Gary. *Following a River: Portland's Congregation Neveh Shalom, 1869–1989.*

Congregation Neveh Shalom, 1989. 160pp. Illus.

PENNSYLVANIA

Pittsburgh

Burstin, Barbara Stern. *After the Holocaust: The Migration of Polish Jews and Christians to Pittsburgh*. Pittsburgh: U. of Pittsburgh Press, 1989. 219pp.

Silverman, Myrna. *Strategies for Social Mobility: Family, Kinship and Ethnicity within Jewish Families in Pittsburgh*. N.Y.: AMS Press, 1989. 215pp.

RHODE ISLAND

Brown, Edwin C. "Workmen's Circles and Jewish Labor Unions." *Rhode Island Jewish Historical Notes* 10:2 (November 1988).

Buhle, Paul M. "Jews in Rhode Island Labor: An Introductory Investigation." *Rhode Island Jewish Historical Notes* 10:2 (November 1988).

Goldscheider, Calvin, and Sidney Goldstein. *The Jewish Community of Rhode Island: A Social and Demographic Study, 1987*. Providence: Jewish Federation of Rhode Island, 1988. 412pp.

Goldstein, Sidney, Calvin Goldscheider, and Alice Goldstein. "A Quarter Century of Change: Rhode Island Jewry, 1963–1987." *Rhode Island Jewish Historical Notes* 10:2 (November 1988).

Stern, Malcolm H. "Ashkenazim vs. Sephardim in the Colonial Era." *Rhode Island Jewish Historical Notes* 10:2 (November 1988).

SOUTH CAROLINA

Charleston

Hagy, James William. *This Happy Land: The Jews of Colonial and Antebellum Charleston*. Tuscaloosa, AL: The U. of Alabama Press, 1993. 440pp.

TENNESSEE

Knoxville

Silver, Helen S. "Yiddish with a Southern Accent: Growing Up Jewish in Knoxville, Tennessee." *Southern Jewish Heritage* 3:2 (May 1990). Memphis: Jewish Historical Society of Memphis and the Mid-South.

Nashville

Feintuch, Burt. "West End Synagogue Schools, Nashville, Tennessee." In *Ethnic Heritage and Language Schools in America*. Washington: Library of Congress, 1988, Pp. 265–83.

TEXAS

Ornish, Natalie. *Pioneer Jewish Texans: Their Impact on Texas and American History for Four Hundred Years, 1590–1990*. Dallas: Texas Heritage Press, 1989. 323pp.

Winegarten, Ruthe, and Cathy Schechter. *Deep in the Heart: The Lives and Legends of Texas Jews. A Photographic History*. Rabbi Jimmy Kessler, Consulting Editor. Austin, TX: Eakin Press, 1990. 253pp.

Amarillo

Raffkind, Myrna G., and Jean M. Low. *Jewish Identification: A Survey of the Jewish Community in Amarillo, Texas*. Department of Behavioral Sciences, West Texas U., Canyon, Texas. Article in *JJew Com Ser* 69:1 (Fall 1992): 63–74.

Dallas

General

Orodsky, Ruth S. "How Dallas Sees the Holocaust." *Jew Fron* 59:2 (March/April 1992): 20–21.

Jewish Community Center of Dallas. *1989–1990 Jewish Community Yearbook*. Dallas, 1989. 115pp.

Education

Jacobs, Liner Chesnik. *The Levin Years: A Golden Era—1929–1951, Dallas, Texas: Hebrew School of Dallas and Its Extended Activities, A Special Tribute to Jacob Levin*. Dallas, 1989. 11pp.

Gonzales

Salinger, Gerhard. "Southeast Texas Picture Story." *WSJH* 24:2 (January 1992): 157–59.

Luling

Salinger, Gerhard. "The Luling, Texas Jewish Cemetery." *WSJH* 23:4 (July 1991): 314–16.

UTAH

Clarion

Goldberg, Robert Alan. *Back to the Soil: The Jewish Farmers of Clarion, Utah, and Their World*. Salt Lake City: U. of Utah Press, 1986. 196pp.

VIRGINIA

Richmond

Baron, Juhn H. "A Brief History of Reform Jewish Music." *Generations* 2:1 (September 1989). Congregation Beth Ahaba Museum and Archives Trust.

Joel, Jane Milstein. "Growing Up Jewish: Edith Lindeman Calisch." *Generations* 3:1 (October 1990). Congregation Beth Ahaba Museum and Archives Trust.

Richmond, VA, Congregation Beth Ahaba Museum and Archives Trust. *Customs and Ritual in Jewish Ceremonial Life*. Richmond, 1990. 27pp. Illus.

Rosenbaum, Claire Millhiser. *Universal and Particular Obligations*. Richmond, VA: Congregation Beth Ahaba Museum and Archives Trust. 1988. 64pp.

Tidewater

Berent, Irwin. "History of Tidewater Jewry." Part XI and Part XII. In *Renewal* (Jewish Federation of Tidewater) 6:1 (September 1990), 6:3 (April 1990), and September 1990.

Ruberg, Miriam Brunn. "Tidewater Summer Institute." *Ped Rep* 40:1 (Fall 1990): 25.

WASHINGTON

Jewish Transcript. *Sixth Annual Guide to Jewish Washington*. Seattle, 1990. 80pp.

Seattle

Buttnick, Meta. "Herzl-Ner Tamid Conservative Congregation of Seattle: The Beginning Years, Part I." *WSJH* 25:3 (April 1993): 243–66; "Part II." *WSJH* 25:4 (July 1993): 326–35.

Spokane

"Spokane Jewry in 1897." *WSJH* 22:3 (April 1990): 218–22.

WYOMING

Blanc, Esther Silverstein. *Berchick*. A children's story about a Jewish homesteading family in Wyoming at the beginning of the 20th century. Volcano, CA: Volcano Press, 1989.

Cheyenne

Elliott, Mark, and Marie Still. *Lest We Forget: Remembrances of Cheyenne's Jews*. Cheyenne: Aaron Mountain Publishing, 1990. 196pp.

THEOLOGY AND EDUCATION

The Idea of God

Blumberg, Sherry H. "What Does God Require of Us?" (Symposium.) *Reform Judaism* 22:1 (Fall 1993): 70 and 71.

Borowitz, Eugene B., ed. *Ehad: The Many Meanings of God Is One*. N.Y.: Sh'ma, 1988. 102pp.

———. *Renewing the Covenant: A Theology for the Postmodern Jew*. Phila.: JPS, n.d. 320pp.

Breslauer, S. Daniel. *Covenant and Community in Modern Judaism*. N.Y.: Greenwood Press, 1989. 126pp.

Cohen, Gerson D. *Studies in the Variety of Rabbinic Cultures*. Phila.: JPS, c. 1990. 344pp.

Danziger, Murray Herbert. *Returning To Tradition: The Contemporary Revival of Orthodox Judaism*. New Haven, CT: Yale U. Press, 1989. 374pp.

Dorff, Elliot S. "The Concept of God in the Conservative Movement." *Jud* 40:4 (Fall 1991): 429–41.

Eisen, Arnold. *The Chosen People in America*. Bloomington: Indiana U. Press, 1983.

Eisen, Arnold. "Jewish Theology in North America: Notes on Two Decades." *AJYB* 91 (1991): 3–33.

Eisenstein, Ira. *Reconstructing Judaism*. N.Y.: Reconstructionist Press, 1986. 242pp.

Fackenheim, Emil. "What Does God Require of Us?" (Symposium.) *Reform Judaism* 22:1 (Fall 1993): 18 and 20.

Ferris, Helene. "What Does God Require of Us?" (Symposium.) *Reform Judaism* 22:1 (Fall 1993): 21 and 70.

Gillman, Neil. *Sacred Fragments: Recovering Theology for the Modern Jew*. Phila.: JPS, c. 1990. 296pp.

———. *Conservative Judaism: The New Century*. West Orange, N.J.: Behrman House, c. 1992. 240pp.

Gittelsohn, Roland. "What Does God Require of Us?" (Symposium.) *Reform Judaism* 22:1 (Fall 1993): 10–11.

Glaser, Joseph B., ed. *Tanu Rabbanan: Our Rabbis Taught*. N.Y.: CCAR, 1990. 155pp.

Goldy, Robert G. *The Emergence of Jewish Theology in America*. Bloomington: Indiana U. Press, 1990. 149pp.

Gordis, Robert, ed. *Emet y'Emunah: Statement of Principles of Conservative Judaism*. N.Y.: JTSA, USA, Women's League for Conservative Judaism, Federation of Jewish Men's Clubs, 1988. 57pp.

———. *The Dynamics of Judaism: A Study of Jewish Law*. Bloomington: Indiana U. Press, 1990. 244pp.

Green, Arthur. "Rethinking Theology: Language, Experience and Reality." *Recon* (September 1988).

———. "Where We Stand: Theory and Practice of Contemporary Reconstructionsm." *Recon* 56:1 (Autumn 1990): 12–17.

Herman, Floyd. "What Does God Require of Us?" (Symposium.) *Reform Judaism* 22:1 (Fall 1993): 70.

Hertzberg, Arthur. "What Does God Require of Us?" (Symposium.) *Reform Judaism* 22:1 (Fall 1993): 14 and 16.

Hoffman, Lawrence. "What Does God Require of Us?" (Symposium.) *Reform Judaism* 22:1 (Fall 1993): 9–10.

Jacobs, Louis. *Principles of the Jewish Faith*. Northvale, NJ: Jason Aronson, 1988. 474pp.

Kamin, Ben. "What Does God Require of Us?" (Symposium.) *Reform Judaism* 22:1 (Fall 1993): 20 and 21.

Katz, Jacob. *The Shabbes Goy: A Study in Halakhic Flexibility*. Trans. Yoel Lerner. Phila.: JPS, 1989. 253pp.

Kushner, Harold. *Who Needs God*. N.Y.: Summit, c. 1992.

Kushner, Lawrence. *The River of Light: Spirituality, Judaism, Consciousness*. Woodstock, VT: Jewish Lights Publishing, 1990. 153pp.

Neusner, Jacob. *Foundations of Judaism*. Phila.: Fortress Press, 1989. 126pp.

Plaut, Gunther W. "What Does God Require of Us?" (Symposium.) *Reform Judaism* 22:1 (Fall 1993): 16 and 18.

Schechter, Daniel S. "What Does God Require of Us?" (Symposium.) *Reform Judaism* 22:1 (Fall 1993): 71.

Schechter, Solomon. *Aspects of Rabbinic Theology*. Introduction by Neil Gillman. Woodstock, VT: Jewish Lights Publishing, 1993. 410pp.

Shuman, Barbara K. "What Does God Require of Us?" (Symposium.) *Reform Judaism* 22:1 (Fall 1993): 12 and 14.

Syme, Daniel B. "What Does God Require of Us?" (Symposium.) *Reform Judaism* 22:1 (Fall 1993): 11–12.

Winston, Diane. "Searching for Spirituality—Reform Judaism Responds." *Moment* 17:3 (June 1992): 28–29, 31–35.

RELIGIOUS EDUCATION

Compass. "Interreligious Education." 13:2 (Winter 1991).

Dukakis, Andrea. "Emigre Teens Learn Old-Time Religion." *For* (E), August 24, 1992, 13–14.

Heller, David. *The Children's God*. Chicago: U. of Chicago Press, 1989. 165pp.

Kushner, Lawrence. *The Book of Miracles: A Young Person's Guide to Jewish Spirituality*. Ill. by Devis Grebu. N.Y.: UAHC, c. 1990. Ages 9–12.

Levitz, Irving N. "Education for Two Worlds." *Ten Da'at* 5:1 (Fall 1990): 3–7.

Sasso, Sandy Eisenberg. *God's Paintbrush*. Ill. by Annette Compton. Woodstock, VT: Jewish Lights Publishing, 1993. 32pp.

Schafler, Samuel. "God and the Jewish School. *Jew Ed* 57:1 (Spring 1989): 41–14.

Telushkin, Joseph. *Jewish Literacy."* N.Y.: William Morrow, 1991.

———. "Jewish Literacy." *Had Mag* 73:8 (April 1991): 24–26.

Textbooks and Teacher Guides

Olitzky, Kerry. *I Am a Reform Jew: A Workbook Diary for Explaining Reform Judaism*. West Orange, N.J.: Behrman House, 1987. 90pp.

PHILOSOPHY OF JEWISH EDUCATION

General

Blumenfield, Yisrael. "An Educator's Credo." *Jew Obs* 23:9 (December 1990): 6–9.

Birnbaum, David. *God and Evil*. Hoboken, N.J.: Ktav, c. 1989.

Goodman, L.E. *On Justice:* An Essay in Jewish Philosophy. New Haven, CT: Yale U. Press, 1990. 296pp.

Korn, Eugene. "Tradition Meets Modernity: On the Conflict of Halakha and Political Liberty." *Trad* 25:4 (Summer 1991): 30–17.

Samuelson, Norbert Max. *An Introduction to Modern Jewish Philosophy*. Albany, N.Y.: State U. of New York Press, 1989. 320pp.

GOALS OF JEWISH EDUCATION

Rosenak, Michael. *Building Jewish Culture in the Diaspora: Diaspora–Israel Partnership in Strengthening Jewish Education*. Jerusalem: Study Circle on World Jewry, 1987. 41pp.

RESEARCH IN JEWISH EDUCATION

Aron, Isa. "Instruction and Enculturation in Jewish Education." Paper presented to the Conference on Research in Jewish Education. N.Y., 1987.

Chervin, Steven. "The Role of Organizational Growth Phases in Consulting." *Jew Ed*. 58:1, 2 (Spring/Summer 1990): 19–22, 25.

Fishman, Sylvia Barack, and Alice Goldstein. *When They Are Grown They Will Not Depart: Jewish Education and the Jewish Behavior of American Adults*. Waltham, MA: Cohen Center for Modern Jewish Studies, Brandeis U., and JESNA. CMJS Research Report 8, March 1993. 18pp. + tables, 10pp.

Kelman, Stuart L., ed. *What We Know about Jewish Education*. A handbook of today's research for tomorrow's Jewish education. Los Angeles, CA: Torah Aura Productions, 1992. 346pp. Chapters:

    Ackerman, Walter I. "What We Know about... Schools." Pp. 21–32.
    Alexander, H. A. "What We Know about ... Understanding Jewish Educational

Research: A Guide for Decision Makers." Pp. 13–19.

Alexander, H.A., and Ian Russ. "What We Know about . . . Youth Programming." Pp. 89–96.

Aron, Isa. "What We Know about. . . Jewish Teachers." Pp. 35–42.

Botwinick, Moshe L. "What We Know about . . . Jewish Video and Television." Pp. 271–77.

Chazan, Barry, and Richard Juran. "What We Know about. . . Jewish Education in the Jewish Community Centers." Pp. 169–76.

———. "What We Know about . . . the Teaching of Israel." Pp. 241–52.

Cohen, Steven M. "What We Know about . . . the Marginally Affiliated." Pp. 115–27.

Dashefsky, Arnold. "What We Know about . . . The Effects of Jewish Education on Jewish Identification." Pp. 103–114.

Dori, Rivka. "What We Know about . . . Hebrew Language Education." Pp. 261–69.

Feiman-Nemser. "What We Know about . . . Learning to Teach." Pp 51–57.

Feldman, Ruth Pinkenson. "What We Know about . . . Early Childhood Education." Pp. 81–87.

Galperin, Misha and Patricia Cipora Harte. "What We Know about. . . Jewish Education for New Americans." pp. 137–45. (Written prior to the break-up of the Soviet Union.)

Goodman, Roberta Louis. "What We Know about . . . Faith Development" Pp. 129–35.

Isaacs, Leora W. "What We Know about . . . Enrollment." Pp. 61–70.

Katz, Betsy Dolgin. "What We Know about. . . Adult Education." Pp. 97–102.

Kelman, Stuart L. "What We Know about . . . Parent Motivation." Pp. 187–95.

Lauer, Chaim. "What We Know about. . . Communal Planning for Jewish Education." Pp. 197–204.

Matanky, Leonard A "What We Know about . . . Computers in Jewish Education." Pp. 279–90.

Monson, Rela Gedffen. "What We Know about. . . Women and Jewish Education." Pp. 43–50.

Reimer, Joseph. "What We Know about . . . Jewish Family Education." Pp. 177–82.

Reisman, Bernard. "What We Know about . . . The Role of Lay People." Pp. 221–29.

Reynolds, Ron. "What We Know about. . . Evaluation." Pp. 291–300.

Schein, Jeffrey. "What We Know about. . . Moral Education." Pp. 253–59.

Schiff, Alvin I., "What We Know about. . . The Jewish Day School." Pp. 149–61.

Schoem, David, What We Know about. . . the Jewish Supplementary School. Pp. 163–68.

Shevitz, Susan L. "What We Know about . . . Changing Jewish Schools, or Surf, Don't Pitch!" Pp. 205–20.

Tobin, Gary A., "What We Know about. . . Demography." 71–80.

Winter, J. Alan. "What We Know about . . . The Costs of Jewish Education," 231–37.

Shapiro, Sara S. and Ruth Ravid. "Student Team Learning in Jewish Schools." A Research Project. *Jew Ed* 57:1 (Spring 1989): 11–14, 34.

CHANGE IN JEWISH EDUCATION

Eisenberg, Robin L. "Growth." *Ped Rep* 40:4 (April 1990): 21–22.

Holtz, Barry W. "Prospects for Innovation in Jewish Education." *The Melton Journal* 25 (Spring 1992): 21, 24.

Lubliner, Shira. "The Transformation of a Congregational School: A Case Study." *Ped Rep* 40:4 (April 1990): 25–27.

Newman, Mordecai. "An Anchor for Growth." *Had Mag* 72:5 (January 1991): 24–27.

Rosman, Steven M. "New Directions in Religious Education—An Interview with Gabriel Moran." *Compass* 13:2 (Winter 1991): 3–4.

Rossel, Seymour. "A New Vision for Reform Jewish Education." *RJ* 21:4 (Summer 1993): 24–26.

Schiff, Alvin Irwin. "Transforming Jewish Education." *Moment* 16:1 (February 1991): 49–50.

THE SOCIAL SCIENCES AND JEWISH EDUCATION

Sociology and Related Fields

Friedman, Peter B., and Mark Zober. "In the Community: Current Jewish Population Studies." *Contemporary Jewry* 10:1 (Spring 1989). N.Y.: Association for the Social Scientific Study of the Jews.

Gallup, George Jr. "Gallup Looks at American Jews." *Moment* 15:3 (June 1990): 34–35.

Goldscheider, Calvin, and Frances Goldscheider. *The Transition to Jewish Adulthood: Education, Marriage and Fertility*. Jerusalem: Paper presented at the Tenth World Congress of Jewish Studies, 1989.

Goldstein, Sidney. "Jews On The Move: Implications for American Jewry and for Local Communities." *Jew J Soc* 32:1 (June 1990): 5–30.

Liebman, Charles S., and Steven M. Cohen. *Two Worlds of Judaism: The Israeli and American Experience*. New Haven, CT: Yale U. Press, 1991.

Monson, Rela Geffen. "The Sociology of the American Jewish Community." *Modern Judaism* 11:1 (February 1991): 147–56.

Phillips, Bruce A. "Sociological Analysis of Jewish Identity." In *Jewish Identity in America*, D.H. Gordis, ed. Los Angeles: U. of Judaism, 1991, 3–25.

Schall, David J. *The Jewish Agenda: Essays in Contemporary Jewish Life*. Praeger, 1987. 186pp.

Waxman, Chaim I. "The Emancipation, the Enlightenment and the Demography of American Jewry." *Jud* 38:4 (Fall 1989): 488–501.

* Williams, Nancy R. *A Retrospective Examination of Differentiation, Parentification and Identity: A Comparison of Jewish Intermarried and Homogamously Married Couples*. Florida State U., 1989.

Winter, J. Alan. "Income, Identity, and Involvement in the Jewish Community: A Test of an Estimate of the Affordability of Living Jewishly." *J Jew Com Ser* 66:2 (Winter 1889): 149–56.

Psychology and Social Psychology

Bulka, Reuven P. *Critical Psychological Judaic Perspectives*. 1992, 162pp.

London, Perry. "The Psychology of Identity Formation." In *Jewish Identity in America*. D.H. Gordis, ed. Los Angeles: U. of Judaism, 1991. pp. 31–50.

London, Perry and Barry Chazan. *Psychology and Jewish Identity Education*. N.Y.: AJC, 1990.

Identity

Chernow, Arlene Sarah. "Who Am I—How Do I Fit In?" *Compass* 14:1 (Fall 1991): 9–10.

Cohen, Stephen P. "Diaspora Identity: A Primer for Israelis and North American Jews," *The Forum*. A Publication of the North American Jewish Forum. Winter 1990; pp. 5–10.

Cohen, Steven M. "Israel in the Jewish Identity of American Jews: A Study in Dualities and Contrasts." In *Jewish Identity in America*, D.H. Gordis, ed., Los Angeles: U. of Judaism, 1991, pp. 119–35.

Cooney, Terry A. "New York Intellectuals and the Question of Jewish Identity" *AJH* 80:3 (Spring 1991): 344–60.

Cooperman, Bernard D. "Jewish Studies and Jewish Identity: Some Implications of Secularizing Torah." *Jud* 42:2 (Spring 1993): 229–42.

Fein, Leonard J. *Where Are We? The Inner Life of America's Jews*. N.Y.: Harper & Row, 1988.

Feingold, Henry. "The American Component of Jewish Identity." In *Jewish Identity in America*, D.H. Gordis, ed. Los Angeles: U. of Judaism, 1991. pp. 69–80.

Furman, Frida Kerner. *Beyond Yiddishkeit: The Struggle for Jewish Identity in a Reform Synagogue*. Albany: State U. of New York Press, 1987.

Goodman, Martin. "Identity and Authority in Ancient Judaism." *Jud* 39:2 (Spring 1990): 192–201.

Hadef, Helen B. "The Jewish Education of Adolescents: Implications for Identity Development." M.A. Thesis. Department of Education, Jewish Theological Seminary, 1990.

Herman, Simon N. "Jewish Education and Jewish Identity." *Ped Rep* 41:2 (Winter/Spring 1991): 6–7.

Lipset, Seymour Martin, ed. *American Pluralism and the Jewish Community*. New Brunswick: Transaction Publishers, 1990. 281pp.

Lipstadt, Deborah E. "Rediscovering the True Meaning of Jewish Identity." *The Forum*. A Publication of the North American Jewish Forum. Spring/Summer 1989, pp. 3–4.

Medding, Peter Y., Gary A. Tobin, Sylvia Barack Fishman, and Mordechai Rimor. "Jewish Identity in Conversionary and Mixed Marriages." *AJYB* 92 (1992): 3–76.

Meyer, Michael. *Jewish Identity in the Modern World*. Seattle, WA: U. of Washington, 1990. 110pp.

* Miller, Bennett F. *Reform Jewish Identity: Developing a Program of Ministry to Guide the New Member of a Reform Synagogue to Mature Jewish Living*. Princeton Theological Seminary, 1988.

Schulweis, Harold M. "The Role of the Synagogue in Jewish Identity." In *Jewish Identity in America*, D.H. Gordis, ed. Los Angeles: U. of Judaism, 1991. pp. 159–65.

Shapiro, Edward S. "Jewishness and the New York Intellectuals." *Jud* 38:3 (Summer 1989): 282–92.

———. "The Crisis of American Jewish Identity." *Cong M* 59:7 (November/December 1992): 5–7.

* Shapiro, Zvi. *From Generation to Generation: Does Jewish Schooling Affect Jewish Identification?* New York U., 1988.

Steinmetz, Daniel. "An Agenda for the Study of Jewish Identity and Denomination among Children." In *Jewish Identity in America*, D.H. Gordis, ed. Los Angeles: U. of Judaism, 1991, pp. 181–93.

Tannenbaum, Avraham J. "Jewish Texts, Education and Identity: Inseparable," *Jew Ed* 57: 2/3/4, pp. 7–12, 26.

Wasserman, Michael. "Jewish Identity and Adulthood—A Family-Systems Approach to Adult Jewish Education." In *Jewish Identity in America*, D.H. Gordis, ed. Los Angeles: U. of Judaism, 1991, pp. 52–82.

ASSESSMENT

Abramowitz, Yosef I. "In Search of Continuity." *The Reporter*, Women's American Ort 43:1 (Spring 1993): 14–16.

Abramson, Robert. "The Conservative Synagogue School." *Ped Rep* 40:4 (April 1990): 810.

Ackerman, Walter I. "Graduation: Motifs and Meanings." *Shofar* 10:1 (Fall 1991): 72–64.

Bank, Emily. "The Ivriah: A Joint Congregational School." *Ped Rep* 40:4 (April 1990): 18–20.

Chazan, Barry I. *The State of Jewish Education*. N.Y.: JESNA, 1988. 22pp.

Chervin, Steven. "The Role of Organizational Growth Phases in Consulting." *Jew Ed* 58:1, 2 (Spring/Summer 1990): 19–22.

Elazar, Daniel J. "The National Cultural Movement in Hebrew Education in the Mississippi Valley." In *Hebrew in America*, Alan Mintz, Ed. Detroit: Wayne State U. Press, 1992. Pp. 129–54.

———. "The State of American Jewry: Is Momentum Enough?" *Cong M* 59:2 (February 1992): 18–19.

Fishman, Sylvia Barack. *Learning About Learning: Insights on Contemporary Jewish Education From Jewish Population Studies*. Waltham, MA: Center for Modern Jewish Studies, Brandeis U., 1987. 67pp.

Goldman, Solomon. "The March of the Living in Retrospect." *Jew Ed* 59:3 (Winter 1992): 33–36.

Haberman, Joshua O. "The New Exodus Out of Judaism." *Moment* 17:4 (August 1992): 34–37, 51–52.

Hoffman, Paul. "Summing Up." *Cong M* 58:3 (March/April 1991): 22.

Isaacs, Leora W. "A Look Back and A Look Ahead: Four Decades of Jewish Education." *Ped Rep* 40:2 (October 1989): 3–12.

Kosmin, Barry. "The Permeable Boundaries of Being Jewish in America." *Moment* 17:4 (August 1992): 30–33, 51–52.

Kronish, Ronald. "Jewish Education: Schools and Society." *Rel Ed* 82:1 (Winter 1987): 30–38.

Marder, Janet. "The Trouble With Jewish Education." *RJ* 21:4 (Summer 1993): 19–23, 66–67.

Price, Marilyn. "There's No Business Like School Business." *Recon* 56:2 (Winter 1991): 19–20.

Rothchild, Sylvia. "The Sixtees Meet the Ninetees." *Had Mag*, 74:10 (June/July 1993): 24–25.

Schafler, Samuel. "From Rhetoric to Reality." *Ped Rep* 40:3 (January 1990): 43–44.

Schein, Jeffrey L. "Whither the Supplementary School: A Reconstructionist Perspective." *Ped Rep* 40:4 (April 1990): 11–14.

Schiff, Alvin I. *Contemporary Jewish Education: Issachar American Style*. Dallas: Rossel Books, 1988. 318pp. Distributed by Behrman House.

———. "Educational Readiness for 1992." Editorial. *Jew Ed* 59:1 (Spring/Summer 1991): 2–4.

———. *Divrei Ish: Selected Addresses and Essays On Jewish Life and Jewish Education*. Published on the Occasion of the 80th Anniversary of the Board of Jewish Education of Greater New York. Foreword by Elie Wiesel. N.Y.: Board of Jewish Education of Greater New York, 1992. 288pp.

Schnaidman, Mordecai. "The Orthodox Community and the Supplementary School." *Ped Rep* 40:4 (April 1990): 5–7.

Wexler, Dorothy. "Personal Expressions," *Ped Rep* 40:4 (April 1990): 32–35.

A Time To Act, The Report of The Commission on Jewish Education in North America. Convened by the Mandel Associated Foundations, The Jewish Community Center (formerly JWB), The Jewish Education Service of North America, and The Council of Jewish Federations. San Francisco, November 1990. Lanham, New York: U. Press of America, 1991. 97pp.

Symposium on *A Time To Act*, *Jew Ed* 59:2 (Fall 1991):
    Elazar, Daniel. "A Report On What Is Known." Pp. 12–14.
    Executive Summary, "A Time To Act." Pp. 4–5.
    Gannes, Abraham P. "Needed More Serious Questions and Responses." Pp. 15–16.
    Gelberd, Howard, "The Challenge of Bureaus of Jewish Education." Pp. 19–20.
    Hochstein, Annette and Seymour Fox. "Responses." Pp. 35–40.
    Passow, A. Harry. "A Hopeful Blueprint for the Future." Pp. 6–7.
    Poupko, Yehiel E. "Needed: Standards for Jewish Education," Pp. 29–31.
    Raab, Menachem, "And Money Answereth All Things (Ecclesiastes 10, 19)." Pp. 21–23.
    Schiff, Alvin I. "It Is a Time to Act." p. 2.
    Schoenfeld, Stuart. "A Research Perspective." pp. 10–11.
    Schnaidman, Mordecai. "An Inspiration to Educators and Lay Leaders." Pp. 24–26.
    Shevitz, Susan L. "Trailblazers of Educational Change." Pp. 8–9.
    Steinberg, Barbara. "Building Blocks and Firm Foundations." Pp. 27–28.
    Steinmetz, Ira J. "Communal Realities Must Be Major Focus." pp. 17–18.
    Wische, Jerry. "A Jewish Community Center Response." Pp. 32–34.

Cohen, Debra Nussmaum. "2–Year Jewish Education Study Urges Overhaul." *Jewish Bulletin* (San Francisco), November 16, 1990, pp. 1 &42.

Pedagogic Reporter. "Mandel Associated Foundations. The Commission on Jewish Education in North America." *Ped Rep* 40:3 (January 1990): 3–4.

Weinberg, Michael A. "Commission on Jewish Education: *A Time to Act*." N.Y.: Coalition for the Advancement of Jewish Education, Spring 1991. 2pp.

America's Impact on Jewish Education

Feldman, Egal. *The Jewish Encounter with Protestant America*. Urbana: U. of Illinois Press, 1990. 268pp.

Jordan, Cecile. "The Quest for Excellence in Public Education Affects Jewish Education." *Jew Ed* 59:1 (Spring/Summer 1991): 23–24, 35.

O'Malley, Charles J. "The Impact of 'The Quest' for Excellence—Private Education." *Jew Ed* 58:1, 2 (Spring/Summer 1990): 45–47.

Sarna, Jonathan. *The Americanization of Jewish Culture, 1888–1988*. History of the Jewish Publication Society. Phila.: JPS, 1989. 430pp.

Trends

Schmelz, Uziel O., and Sergio Delia Pergola. *Trends in American Jewish Demography*. Jewish Demography Papers. N.Y.: AJC, 1988.

Wertheimer, Jack. "Recent Trends in American Judaism." *AJYB* 89 (1989): 63–162.

Jewish Education and "Jewish Survival"

Eisen, Arnold. "An All Volunteer Jewry." *Had Mag* 74:10 (June/July 1993): 18–20.

Kazzaz, David S. "Coping Mechanisms for Survival: A Jewish Perspective." *Jew Ed* 59:3 (Winter 1992): 15–24.

Lipstadt, Deborah. "Benefits of Belonging." *Had Mag* 74:10 (June/July 1993): 14–17.

Schoem, David. *Ethnic Survival in America: An Ethnography of a Jewish Afternoon School*. Atlanta, Georgia: Scholars Press, 1989. 157pp.

Woocher, Jonathan. "Jewish Survival Tactics." *Had Mag* 74:10 (June/July 1993): 10–13.

Questions—Old and New

Education and Culture Review. "Should Jewish Supplementary Religious Schools Be Like the Public Schools?" 15:4 (June/July 1991): 5–9.

Elish, Barbara. "Should Jewish Supplementary Religious Schools Be Like The Public Schools?" *Jew Ed* 57:2/3/4 (Summer/Winter 1989): 45–51.

Tobin, Gary A. "Will the Synagogue Survive?" *Moment* 15:4 (August 1990): 44–47.

THE FUTURE OF JEWISH EDUCATION

Aviv, Aviva. "Jewish Education and the Future." *Humanistic Judaism* 19:1 (Winter 1991): 50–52.

Bayme, Steven, ed. *Facing the Future: Essays on Contemporary Jewish Life in Memory of Yehuda Rosenman*. Hoboken, NJ: KTAV Publishing House 1989. 234pp.

Bleiweiss, Robert. "An Education Agenda for the Next Century." *Jew Spec* 56:2 (Fall 1991): 3–4.

Braverman, Jay. "The Jewish School Teacher—Today and Tomorrow." *Jew Ed* 55:4 (Winter 1988): 38–40.

Education and Culture Review. "Future Models for Jewish Education." 15:2 (February/March 1991): 8–11.

Elkins, Dov Peretz. "Giving Form to Our Imagination: The Synagogue School in the 21st Century." *Jew Ed* 59:1 (Spring/Summer 1991): 21–22.

Feldman, Ruth Duskin. "Jewish Education and the Future." *Humanistic Judaism* 19:1 (Winter 1991): 52–56.

Lewittes, Mordecai. "Whither Supplementary Schools?" *Ped Rep* 40:4 (April 1990): 2.

Lorch, Steven C. "The Community School as a Visionary Institution." *Generation* 1:2 (February 1990): 3–4.

Price, Roger. "The Future of Reconstructionism: A Symposium—Understanding Our Mission." *Recon* 56:3 (Spring 1991): 8–9.

Schein, Jeffrey L. "Reconstructionist Education: Present and Future." *Recon* 55:6 (July–August 1990): 14–17.

Schiff, Alvin I. "Toward the Year 2000—Condition of Jewish Life: Implications for Jewish Education." *Jew Ed* 58:1, 2, (Spring/Summer 1990): 3–10. Discussion of Dr. Schiff's paper, "Toward the Year 2000":

    Goldman, Emanuel, pp. 11–12.
    Lauer, Chaim, pp. 13–16.
    Monson, Rela Geffen, pp. 17–18.

Zwiebel, David. "Reflections on the 'America 2000 Excellence in Education Act,'" *Jew Ed* 59:3 (Winter 1992): 25–28.

BIBLIOGRAPHIES OF JEWISH EDUCATION

General

Holtz, Barry W. *Finding Our Way: Jewish Texts and the Lives We Lead Today*. N.Y.: Schocken,

1990. 257pp. Authors and topics follow:
> Diamond, Eliezer. "The World of the Talmud." Pp. 47–69.
> Elwell, Sue Levy. "Jewish Women Studies." Pp. 228–13.
> Fox, Everett. "The Bible and Its World." Pp. 28–46.
> Frischer, Rita Berman. "The Bar/Mitzvah Book." Pp. 303–28.
> Ginsburg, Elliot K. "Jewish Mysticism." Pp. 164–202.
> Holtz, Barry W. "Introduction." Pp. 3–8.
> Kushner, Lawrence Square. "Ports of Entry: Introductory Jewish Books." Pp. 927.
> Lipstadt, Deborah E. "The Holocaust." Pp. 128–48.
> Marcus, Ivan G. "The Jewish Middle Ages." Pp. 70–91.
> Mintz, Alan. "Hebrew Literature." Pp. 244–58.
> Paley, Michael, and Jacob J. Staub. "Jewish Philosophy: Medieval and Modern." Pp. 203–27.
> Roskies, David G. "Yiddish Literature." Pp. 259–73.
> Sarna, Jonathan D. "The American Jewish Experience." Pp. 108–27.
> Shechner, Mark. "The Jewish Novelist in America." Pp. 274–302.
> Stanislawski, Michael. "The European Experience: Jews Confront Modernity." Pp. 92–107.
> Twersky, David. "Israel and Zionism." pp. 149–63.

The Arts

Edelman, Marsha Bryan. *A Bibliography of Jewish Music: Resource Materials for Educators*. N.Y.: Hebrew Arts School, 1988. 15pp.

Freudenheim, Tom W. "Books on Art and the Jewish Tradition: 1980–1990." *JBA* 48 (1990–1991): 106–19.

Jewish Museum. National Jewish Archives of Broadcasting. *An Annotated Catalogue of Selected Holdings*. N.Y.: The Jewish Museum, 1989. 355pp.

Bar/Bat Mitzvah

Nussbaum, Esther. "On the Bat Mitzvah Celebration: An Annotated Bibliography." *Ten Da'at* 111:3 (Spring 1989): 33–34.

Holocaust

Wollheim, William. *The Holocaust: An Annotated Bibliography*. ". . . includes fiction, non-fiction books for younger readers." N.Y.: Jewish Book Council, 1991.

School Library

Posner, Marcia W. *Twelve Steps to Starting a Judaica Library*. N.Y.: Jewish Book Council, 1992.

Standards Review Committee of the Association of Jewish Libraries. *Guide to Excellence: Standards for Schools, Synagogues and Jewish Community Center Libraries*. N.Y.: Jewish Book Council, 1990.

Life Cycle

Ben Zvi, Hava. *Days of Awe: A Selected Bibliography for Teachers*, Parents and Children. N.Y.: Jewish Book Council, 1993.

Posner, Marcia W. *Haggadot for Young Readers*. "An annotated list . . . for children with suggested age levels." N.Y.: Jewish Book Council, 1990.

———. *The Jewish Calendar: A Family Resource Guide*. "Books for parents and children to mark the many Jewish holidays around the year." N.Y.: Jewish Book Council, 1993.

Literature

Posner, Marcia W. "Jewish Juvenile Books, 1988–1989." *JBA* 47 (1989–1990): 227–37.

———. "Juvenile Books, 1989–1990," *JBA* 48 (1990–1991): 244–55.

———. *Notable Books for Jewish Children*. "A list of 'must have' Jewish children's books . . ." N.Y.: Jewish Book Council, c. 1992.

———. *Selected Fiction and Non-Fiction for Jewish Teens*. N.Y.: Jewish Book Council, 1990.

Judaism

Breslauer, S. Daniel. *Contemporary Jewish Ethics: A Bibliographic Survey; Modern Jewish Morality: A Bibliographical Survey*. Westport, CT: Greenwood Press, 1986.

Karkhanis, Sharad. *Jewish Heritage in America: An Annotated Bibliography*. N.Y.: Garland, 1988. 434pp.

Posner, Marcia W. *Save Our Earth: A Selected Bibliography*. "An annotated bibliography on ecology and Jewish values." N.Y.: Jewish Book Council, 1991.

Selavan, Ida Cohen. "A Survey of Bibliographies of Jewish Interest, 1980–1990." *JBA* (1990–1991): 89–105.

American Jewry and the Land of Israel

Jick, Leon A., and Mark A. Raider. "A Selected and Annotated Bibliography of Reform Judaism and Zionism." N.Y.: ARZA: *The Journal of Reform Zionism* 1993 1:1: 63–83.

Higher Education

Wechsler, Harold. "Jewish Seminaries." In *Religious Seminaries in America: A Selected Bibliography*. N.Y.: Garland, 1989. Pp. 128–39.

History of American Jewry

Posner, Marcia W. *American Jewish History: A Selected Bibliography for Teens*. N.Y.: Jewish Book Council, 1992.

Singerman, Robert. *Judaica Americana: A Bibliography of Publications to 1900*. N.Y.: Greenwood Press, 1990. 2 volumes.

Home and Family

Wollheim, William. *Building Your Home Jewish Library: A Beginner's List*. N.Y.: Jewish Book Council, 1990.

Women and Education

Posner, Marcia W. *Organizing a Jewish Woman's Library*. N.Y.: Jewish Book Council, 1988.

Sephardim

Congregation Shearith Israel, New York. *A Preliminary Guide to the Archives of Congregation Shearith Israel, the Spanish and Portuguese Synagogue in the City of New York*. N.Y.: 1990. ii + 1911pp.

Local Sources for Jewish Education by State and City

California

Kramer, William M., and Norton B. Stern. "A Guide To California Jewish History." Part One. *WSJH* 24:4 (July 1992): 377–83; Part II, *WSJH* 25:4 (July 1993): 369–76.

San Diego

Schwartz, Henry. "A Bibliography of San Diego Jewish History." *WSJH*, 26:1, October 1993, pp. 49–52.

Rhode Island

Frost, Carol J. "An Annotated Bibliography of Materials Relating to the History of Jews in Rhode Island. Located in Rhode Island Depositories (1967–1989)." *Rhode Island Jewish Historical Notes* 10:3, Part A (November 1989).

Miscellaneous

Posner, Marcia W. *The Key to Jewish Knowledge: A Selected List of Reference Books*. Jewish Book Council, 1993.

Western States Jewish History. "The Jews and American Indians: A Bibliographical Record." *WSJH* 23:2 (January 1991): 162–67.

INDEX

Note: The author has listed the citations in the text as they appeared in the original or secondary sources used to compile this bibliography. Whenever it appeared appropriate, entries listed under different variations in spelling or form of the name of the same individual have been combined into a single index entry. Entries having no author are listed by sponsor organization or publication in this index.

Aaron, Ruth S., 60
Aaroni, Abraham, 76
Abbink, Jon, 600
Abeles, Herbert R., 355
Abelow, Samuel P., 475, 480
Abelson, Estelle, 104
Abner, Ira, 30
Aboff, Samuel E., 194
Abraham, Joel, 619
Abrahams, Edith, 31
Abrahams, Israel, 304, 320
Abram, L., 321
Abramovitch, Stanley, 641
Abramovitz, Hayim, 54
Abramovitz, Hirsch, 290, 310
Abramowicz, Dina, 204
Abramowitch, Stanley, 322
Abramowitz, Aaron, 444
Abramowitz, Hayim, 60
Abramowitz, Mordecai, 533
Abramowitz, Naomi Ruth, 385
Abramowitz, Tammy Rubin, 119
Abramowitz, Yosef I., 666
Abrams, A. A., 351
Abrams, Arthur I., 72
Abrams, Beverly, 129
Abrams, Israel A., 506; literature on, 287
Abrams, Jeanne, 432, 433, 655
Abrams, Judith Z., 620
Abrams, Morris B., 438
Abrams, N. B., 232

Abrams, Percy, 367
Abrams, Ruth, 647
Abrams, Sol, 287
Abrams, Solomon, 129, 185
Abrams, Sylvia F., 41, 644
Abrams, William, 360, 390
Abramson, Charlotte, 76
Abramson, Ellen M., 649
Abramson, Lillian S., 110, 115
Abramson, Robert, 637, 644, 666
Achtenberg, Minnie R., 104
Ackerman, Andrew S., 31
Ackerman, David, 639
Ackerman, K. L., 98
Ackerman, Nathan W., 124
Ackerman, Walter I., 9, 12, 14, 47, 72, 88, 91, 129, 140, 164, 176, 180, 233, 247, 265, 285, 299, 300, 309, 327, 355, 380, 417, 455, 466, 526, 533, 538, 549, 576, 584, 589, 619, 644, 659, 663, 666
Acton, Lord, 631
Adams, Bobby E., 510
Adams, Hannah, 338
Adams, Louise L., 188
Adams, Theodore L., 271
Adar, Zvi, 45, 47, 124, 164, 327
Adatto, Albert, 514
Addison, Robert, 35, 99
Adelman, David C., 508
Adelman, Hannah B., 245

Adelman, Martin D., 18
Adelman, Penina, 649
Adelman, Philip J., 245
Adelsberg, David, 410, 584
Adelsberg, Sandra, 616
Adelson, Joseph B., 564, 566
Adelson, Saul, 445
Adini, Uziel, 76, 129, 295, 299
Adiv, Ellen, 72, 180
Adler, Andrew B., 286
Adler, Cyrus, 159, 235, 305, 308, 502
Adler, David, 57, 628
Adler, Della Rubinstein, 472
Adler, Frank J., 464
Adler, Hanna, 494
Adler, I. N., 278
Adler, J. R., 566
Adler, Lillian W., 81
Adler, M., 564
Adler, Morris, 263, 272, 373, 410, 533, 573, 585
Adler, Robert L., 446
Adler, Ruth, 398
Adler, Samuel, 342
Adler, Selig, 472
Adri, Battya, 263
Adult Jewish Education, 394
Aft, Bruce D., 645
Aft, Martha, 380, 388
Ages, Arnold, 164
Agran, Nathan, 501

INDEX

Agrillo, Anita Bach, 413
Agris, Aryeh, 265
Agudath Israel of America, 188
Aguilar, Grace, 342, 343
Agus, Abraham, 180
Agus, Irving A., 92, 307
Agus, Jacob B., 124, 301, 305, 390, 533, 566
Agus, Robert, 436
Ahad Ha-Am, 326; literature on, 287
Ahyloni (Sh. Niger), 279, 312, 321, 349, 398, 587, 613
Ain-Globe, Leah, 172
Akibah, Rabbi, 144
Akselrad, Sanford D., 99
Akselrad, Sidney, 311
Al-Agha, Reyad Fahmi, 327
Albany Jewish World, 472
Albert, Burton, 259
Albright, William F., 45, 52
Alcalay, Isaac, 407
Aleichem, Sholem. *See* Sholem Aleichem
Alexander, Chanan, 256, 417
Alexander, Edward, 626
Alexander, Hanan A. (Chanan, Henry A.), 256, 429, 533, 640, 663–64
Alexy, Trudi, 650
Alifaz, Abner, 296
Alk, Jeremy David. 97, 147
Alkalay, Judith, 327
Alkin, Abraham, 190
Allen, Lewis I., 159, 472
Allied Jewish Federation of Denver, Colo., 433
Alton, Yigal, 164, 587
Allouche, Edith K., 77
Allport, Gordon W., 124
All Your Children (Kol Banaikh), 253
Almazov, Sh., 219
Almond, David, 442, 524
Alofsin, Dorothy, 91, 368

Alper, Janice, 60, 110, 386, 526, 646
Alper, Michael, 49, 278, 288, 300, 355, 363, 533, 552; literature on, 287
Alper, Robert A., 108
Alper, Sherri, 621, 630
Alperson, M., 410
Alpert, Carl, 458
Alpert, David B., 576
Alpert, Sumner, 163
Al-Sa'ad, Farouk F., 327
Alt, H., 559
Alter, Robert, 233, 593, 623
Alternatives in Religious Education (ARE), 32, 33, 133, 134, 253
Altfeld, E. Milton, 451
Altman, Addie R., 49
Altman, Barry Martin, 149
Altman, Hal, 430
Altman, M., 216
Altman, Shalom, 33, 37, 504; literature on, 287
Altmann, Alexander, 305
Altschuler, Joanne, 386
Altshul, William, 129
Altshuler, David, 435
Altshuler, David A., 101
Altusky, Zev W., 194
Amateau, Albert J., 650
Ament, Susan G., 101
America, La, 407
American Association for Jewish Education (AAJE), 33, 80, 99, 165, 167, 174, 197, 245, 248, 253, 255, 258, 263, 265, 278, 280, 281, 283, 284, 300, 359. 361–65, 367, 369, 375, 393, 417, 552, 576, 606, 607, 612. *See also* Jewish Education Service of North America (JESNA); National Commission on the Teaching of Zion and Israel

American Council for Jewish Education, 540
American Council for Judaism, 7, 161
American Hebrew, 8, 344, 351
American Hebrew College of the City of New York, 343
American Hebrew Congregations, 240
American Hebrew News, 499
American Israelite Weekly, 495, 496
American Jewess, 346
American Jewish Archives (AJA), 337–38, 415, 423, 424, 432, 440, 448, 449, 463, 464, 466–68, 471, 494–96, 499–501, 509. 510. 512, 516, 607, 652
American Jewish Committee (AJC), 99. 125, 127, 158, 355, 370, 386, 400, 410, 511, 540, 552, 566, 572, 576, 603, 607, 612
American Jewish Historical Quarterly (AJHQ), 237
American Jewish Historical Society (AJHS), 337–38, 345, 449, 454, 607
American Jewish History (AJH), 162, 456
American Jewish Journal, 454
American Jewish Outlook, 507
American Jewish Periodical Center, 613
American Jewish Tercentenary Committee, 369
American Jewish Times-Outlook, 494
American Jewish World, 463, 657
American Jewish Year Book (AJYB), 30, 235, 288–99, 301–6, 309–12, 347, 475, 480, 481, 605, 612–13
American Jews' Annual, 441, 448, 467, 472, 501

Key to Index

7–9: *Types of Jewish Schools* | 10–17: *Curriculum* | 18–29: *Pedagogy* | 30–40: *The Arts* | 41–44: *Bar/Bat Mitzvah* | 45–53: *The Bible* | 54–59: *Early Childhood Education* | 60–65: *Exceptional Children* | 66–68: *Guidance* | 69–85: *Hebrew* | 86–96: *History* | 97–103: *The Holocaust* | 104–6: *School Library* | 107–18: *Life Cycle of a Jew* | 119–22: *Literature* | 123–42: *Mitzvot/Values and Contemporary Issues* | 143–46: *Textbooks* | 147–58: *The High School* | 159–75: *American Jewry and the Land of Israel* | 176–203: *Day School* | 204–31: *Yiddish Secular Schools* | 232–42: *Higher Education* | 245–62: *Administration* | 263–69: *The Teacher* | 270–73: *The Rabbi and Jewish Education* | 274–86: *Conferences in Jewish Education, 1890–1988* | 287–312: *Men and Women Who Influenced Jewish Education* | 317–34: *Historical Background of Jewish Education* | 335–52: *History of Jewish Education in the United States* | 353–78: *The American Jewish Community* | 379–89: *The Home and Jewish Education* | 390–97: *Adult Education* | 398–404: *The Woman's Role and Jewish Education* | 405–8: *Sephardim and Jewish Education* | 409–16: *Youth and Jewish Education* | 417–21: *Camp* | 422–516: *Local Sources for Jewish Education* | 521–23: *Theology and Jewish Education* | 524–32: *Religious Education* | 533–38: *Philosophy of Jewish Education* | 539–44: *Goals of Jewish Education* | 545–50: *Research in Jewish Education* | 551–58: *Change in Jewish Education* | 559–72: *The Social Sciences and Jewish Education* | 573–96: *Assessment* | 597–99: *The Future of Jewish Education* | 600–602: *Bibliographies of Jewish Education in Other Lands* | 603–17: *Bibliographies of Jewish Education and Related Fields in the United States* | 619–70: *Supplement*

INDEX

American Sephardi Federation, 405
American Student Zionist Federation, 159
American Zionist Youth Commission, 164, 653
Amerling, Suzanne, 632
Amidon, Edmund, 60
Aminoff, Helen, 458
Amir, Abraham, 317
Amirom, P., 80, 120
Amitzer, N., 303
Amsel, Norman A., 634, 636
Anderson, Elaine S., 498
Andrews, Joseph, 380
Andrews, Violet, 380
Andron, Sandy, 25
Angel, Marc D., 108, 271, 405, 407, 408, 514, 614, 650
Angoff, Charles, 348, 454
Anilowicz, J., 601, 615
Anisfeld, M. M., 72, 153
Anshe Emeth Schools, 446
Anspacher, Abraham S., 46
Anti-Defamation League of B'nai B'rith (ADL), 33, 99, 115, 603, 606, 612
Antonovsky, Aaron, 434, 563, 567
Aphek, Edna, 47, 72
Appel, Gershon (George), 124, 190, 305, 394
Appelman, Harlene Winnick, 644, 646
Applebaum, Emanuel, 458, 460
Applebaum, Harold, 567
Applebaum, Jay Zacharia, 470
Applebaum, Morton, 112
Applebaum, Philip, 462
Apsler, Alfred, 500
Aptchik, T., 398
Aptowitzer, Avigdor, 307
Arendt, Hannah, 599
Arfa, Milton, 306
Arffa, Elaine, 390
Arffa, Gerald, 390
Ariam, Sima, 328
Arian, Meri Lovenger, 37
Arian, Philip (Shraga), 37, 66, 67, 99, 108, 129, 148, 150, 365, 417, 475, 576, 589, 597; literature on, 287
Ariav, Tamar, 12, 164
Arieh, Yehoshua Ben, 634
Ariel, 30
Ariel, Yakov, 634
Arizona Post, 423
Ark, The, 496
Arlow, J. A., 564
Armistead, Samuel G., 652

Armon, Naomi, 636
Arnold, Corrine B., 524
Aroestry, Ruth M., 72
Aron, Isa, 31, 129, 253, 390, 429, 533, 639, 640, 654, 663, 664
Aronin, Ben, 491
Aronow, Sara Snyder, 489, 490
Aronson, David, 41, 112, 271, 390
Aronson, L. J., 367
Aronson, Robin, 633
Arrane, Z., 328
Arrowood, C. F, 318
Arsenian, Seth, 478
Artson, Bradley Sharit, 630, 635
Artzt, Edya, 380
Arywitz, Annette F., 472
Arzt, Max, 108, 124, 317, 359, 372
Arzt, Morris, 70, 77
Arzt, Raphael, 84, 129, 410, 417, 546, 533
Aschheim, Steven E., 642
Aschkenasy, Nehama, 402, 649
Asheri, Michael, 107
Ashkenazi, Eliot, 449
Ashkenazi, Ellen, 380
Ashkenazi, T., 326
Ashton, Eliyahu, 405
Askowith, Dora, 237
Asmonean, The, 341, 403
Assaf, Simha, 320, 539, 601
Assembly of the Jewish Theological Seminary, 362
Associated Jewish Charities (Baltimore, Md.), 452
Association of Jewish Libraries, 104, 669
Atkin, Abraham, 197, 322, 398
Atkins, W. A., 317
Atlanta (Ga.) *Constitution,* 438
Atlanta (Ga.) Jewish Federation, 438
Atlanta (Ga.) *Jewish Times,* 439, 656
Atzmon, Ezri, 390, 460
Auerbach, Ephraim, 164, 222, 225, 278–79, 281
Auerbach, Jerold S., 634
Aufrecht, L., 343
Ausabel-Danzig, Rivka. 567
Auspitz, Gabriella, 553
Averbach, Moshe, 54, 317
Averick, Evelyn, 471
Avgar, Amy, 402
Aviad, Janet, 417
Avidor, M., 282, 328
Avigal, Moshe, 328, 330
Avironi, Israel, 279
Avital, Moshe, 164, 166, 172, 291, 302, 322, 576

Aviv, Aviva, 668
Avner, Ailene, 58, 557
Avner, Sylvia, 104
Avrunin, William, 355
AvRutick, A. N., 390
Axelrod, Herman C., 9, 72, 135, 179–81, 185, 194
Axelrod, Morris, 454
Axelroth, Dorothy, 61, 66, 68, 78, 92, 164, 248, 380
Azalay, Shimon, 438
Azneer, J. L., 597
Azriel, Elyce, 31, 413
Azrieli, Shlomo. *See* Chipkin, Israel S.
Azrieli, Yehuda, 328
Azulary, Shimon. 164

Baba Bathra, 332
Bachelis, Faith G., 189
Bachrach, Kalman, 81
Backalenick, Irene, 479
Backman, Aidel, 629
Bacon, Brenda, 129
Badanes, Ida, 212
Baeck, Leo, 123, 138, 521
Baer, Yitzhak, 405
Bagali, Yona, 24
Baggaley, A. R., 564
Bahn, Charles, 129
Bailey, Sidney, 468
Bakal, M., 442
Baker, Shimon, 217
Bakst, Joshua S., 100
Balgur, Raphael, 77
Balin, Carole B., 646
Balin, Harry, 112
Ballonof, Martin, 390
Balswick, Jack, 386
Baltimore (Md.) Center for Jewish Education, 453
Baltimore (Md.) *Jewish Times,* 454
Baltzell, E. Digby, 501
Bamberger, Bernard J., 47, 270, 273, 294, 521
Bamberger, David, 108, 110
Bamberger, Gabriel, 345
Bamberger, Henry B., 129
Banchefsky, Howard S., 367
Band, Arnold J., 237, 238, 241, 455
Band, Benjamin, 451
Band, Orah, 81
Bank, Adrianne. 253, 256, 356, 428, 640
Bank, Emily, 666
Banki, Judith, 576

INDEX

Bannan, Rosemary Shamborsky, 124
Barack, Nathan, 551
Baradon, Eunice, 506
Baradon, Howard S., 129
Barakin-Melamdavitch, Feigl, 296
Barash, Y., 181
Bardin, David, 621
Bardin, Livia, 621, 653
Bardin, Shlomo H., 326, 417, 427, 576; literature on, 288
Bardis, P. D., 386
Bargad, W., 72
Bar-Ilan, Meir. *See* Berlin, Meyer
Barish, Louis, 69
Barish, Shirley, 129, 553
Barkan, H., 211, 215, 225, 227
Barkan, Irving, 7, 360, 442
Bar-Lev, Zev, 625
Barnett, George E., 451
Barnett, Richard, 405
Barnett, Sara, 55, 59
Barnett, Sidney, 657
Baron, A., 277
Baron, Charlotte, 150
Bar-On, Dan, 626
Baron, Jeanette M., 159
Baron, John H., 661
Baron, Leora, 135
Baron, R. R. V., 564
Baron, Salo W., 86, 97, 159, 161, 270, 320, 322, 347, 354, 356, 397, 540, 545, 597, 599, 615
Barrington, Joanne, 112
Barron, Harry, 359
Barryte, Marcia Aron, 425
Barthold, Judith Bin-Nun, 181. *See also* Bin-Nun, Judith
Baruch, Theodore H., 461
Barwell, B., 380
Barylko, H., 533
Barzilay, Isaac, 307
Bas, David, 609
Baskett, Charles, 181
Baskin, L, 484

Baskin, Judith R., 649
Bass, Hyman, 7, 205, 208, 210, 212, 215, 216, 219, 222, 227–29, 279, 335, 576; literature on, 288
Bauer, Yehuda, 97
Baum, Charlotte, 400
Baum, Eli, 14, 17, 33, 66, 248, 407, 480, 606
Baum, Emanuel, 380
Baum, Roberta Osser, 629
Bauman, Mark K., 438–39, 656
Bauman, Morton, 148
Bauman, Morton A., 153, 428, 526
Baumblatt, Lori B., 23
Baumel, Morris, 317
Baumgard, Herbert M., 107, 264
Bausel, R. Barker, 379
Bavli, Hillel, 163, 310; literature on, 288
Baxt, Roland, 66
Bayar, Ilene, 625
Bayar, Steven, 245, 251
Bayer, Sue, 619
Baylinson, David, 90
Baylor, Ruth M., 129
Bayme, Steven, 356, 645, 668
Bay Psalm Book, 338
Bearman, Jane, 57
Beck, E. T, 567
Beck, Yoram, 567
Becker, Charles S., 163
Beckerman, Avi, 72
Beckerman, Marvin, 390
Beckerman, Solomon, 41
Behar, Rivka, 55
Behrman, Nicolas L., 248
Beilin, Harry, 130
Beiner, Stan J., 623
Beizer, Ruth, 254
Bekerman, Zvi, 417
Bekritsky, Morris, 194
Belkin, Louis, 36

Belkin, Samuel, 533, 632; literature on, 288
Bell, Daniel, 567
Bell, Roselyn, 285, 634, 646
Bell, William G., 464
Beilin, H., 47
Beilin, L. E., 124, 353
Bellow, Adam, 659
Belsky, Meir, 177, 190
Belsky, Yisrael, 190
Belth, Nathan C, 124, 448
Belth, Norton, 491
Bemnion, Adam Samuel, 46
Bemporad, Jack, 60, 107, 124, 130, 135, 540, 564
Ben Aaron, 445
Benardete, Mair Jose, 405, 614
Benari, Avivah, 490
Ben Ari, Raikin, 35
Benathan, Morris, 7, 76, 233, 291, 468; literature on, 288
Bender, Avram B., 465
Bender, Daniel, 41, 417
Benderly, Samson, 69, 70, 91, 144, 199, 235, 267, 289, 305, 335, 351, 354, 362, 399, 417, 481–82, 490, 557, 573, 575, 590, 597, 634; literature on, 288
Benderly, Shlomo, 33
Ben-Ezra, Akivah, 308, 310
Ben Gurion, David, 130
Ben ha-Dor, 121
Ben-Haim, Meir, 185
Ben-Horin, Mei[e]r, 72, 124, 130, 237, 270, 288, 291, 300, 306, 308, 309, 328, 335, 365, 377, 390, 526, 533, 537, 540, 553, 576–77, 585–87, 591, 604; literature on, 288
Ben-Israel, M., 278
Ben-Jacob, J., 328
Benjamin, I. I., 343, 399, 430
Ben Levi, Joshua, 335
Ben-Mayer, M. Sh., 219

Key to Index

7–9: *Types of Jewish Schools* | 10–17: *Curriculum* | 18–29: *Pedagogy* | 30–40: *The Arts* | 41–44: *Bar/Bat Mitzvah* | 45–53: *The Bible* | 54–59: *Early Childhood Education* | 60–65: *Exceptional Children* | 66–68: *Guidance* | 69–85: *Hebrew* | 86–96: *History* | 97–103: *The Holocaust* | 104–6: *School Library* | 107–18: *Life Cycle of a Jew* | 119–22: *Literature* | 123–42: *Mitzvot/Values and Contemporary Issues* | 143–46: *Textbooks* | 147–58: *The High School* | 159–75: *American Jewry and the Land of Israel* | 176–203: *Day School* | 204–31: *Yiddish Secular Schools* | 232–42: *Higher Education* | 245–62: *Administration* | 263–69: *The Teacher* | 270–73: *The Rabbi and Jewish Education* | 274–86: *Conferences in Jewish Education, 1890–1988* | 287–312: *Men and Women Who Influenced Jewish Education* | 317–34: *Historical Background of Jewish Education* | 335–52: *History of Jewish Education in the United States* | 353–78: *The American Jewish Community* | 379–89: *The Home and Jewish Education* | 390–97: *Adult Education* | 398–404: *The Woman's Role and Jewish Education* | 405–8: *Sephardim and Jewish Education* | 409–16: *Youth and Jewish Education* | 417–21: *Camp* | 422–516: *Local Sources for Jewish Education* | 521–23: *Theology and Jewish Education* | 524–32: *Religious Education* | 533–38: *Philosophy of Jewish Education* | 539–44: *Goals of Jewish Education* | 545–50: *Research in Jewish Education* | 551–58: *Change in Jewish Education* | 559–72: *The Social Sciences and Jewish Education* | 573–96: *Assessment* | 597–99: *The Future of Jewish Education* | 600–602: *Bibliographies of Jewish Education in Other Lands* | 603–17: *Bibliographies of Jewish Education and Related Fields in the United States* | 619–70: *Supplement*

INDEX

Bennett, Alan D., 16, 88, 99, 145, 152, 164, 171, 172, 251, 245, 248, 262, 299, 356, 365, 369, 499, 546, 553, 567, 577, 630, 644
Bennett, Daniel W., 356, 637
Bennett, James M., 130
Bennett, Mrs. Leon, 108
Benor, J., 328
Benov, Ethel, 189
Ben-Peretz, Miriam, 639
Ben Ra-Shalom, Avrael, 345
Ben-Sasson, H. H., 86
Ben-Shoham, Hannah, 18, 247
Benson, Paulette, 7, 25–26, 386
Ben-Sorek, Esor, 143, 145
Ben-Tsemach, Sh., 296, 463
Bentwich, Joseph S., 328
Bentwich, Norman, 304, 308, 326
Ben-Vered, Tamar, 328
Ben-Yehudah, Baruch, 164, 326, 328
Ben-Yosef, I. A., 289
Ben-Zvi, Hava, 428, 429, 654, 669
Bercovich, Edith B., 459
Bercovich, Shloime, 205, 219
Bercovici, Konrad, 220, 475
Berdichevsky, Zalman: literature on, 288
Berdugo, Yehuda, 181
Berenbaum, Michael, 626
Berent, Irwin M., 441, 513, 514, 661
Berg, Bruce L., 567
Berg, Esther L., 33
Berg, Jacob, 205
Berger, Alan L., 627
Berger, David, 643
Berger, Elmer, 159, 161
Berger, Felix, 187
Berger, Graenum, 367, 487
Berger, Helene, 153
Berger, Herbert Z., 511
Berger, Herschel, 181
Berger, Isaiah, 235
Berger, Julius, 317, 540
Berger, Kenneth R., 41
Berger, Marilyn Shlachter, 646
Berger, Mira, 300, 322
Berger, Philmore, 77
Berger, Zvi, 482
Bergman, A., 220, 227
Bergman, Bella, 81
Bergman, Robert, 328
Bergman, Shlomo, 128
Berk, Aliza Wallin, 148, 615
Berk, Fred, 34–35, 605
Berk, Phyllis L., 186
Berkey, Jane, 357

Berkovitz, Eliezer, 203, 521, 577, 649
Berkowitz, A. L., 214
Berkowitz, Alice J., 72
Berkowitz, Gila, 400
Berkowitz, Henry, 159, 232, 501, 524
Berkson, Isaac B., 139, 164, 201, 257, 290, 291, 295, 298, 326, 353, 356, 359, 368, 369, 373, 399, 403, 417, 480, 486, 496, 533, 537, 559, 573, 577, 584, 591; literature on, 288–89
Berkson, Mrs. Isaac B., 399; literature on, 289
Berlin, Charles, 349, 601, 603, 613
Berlin, Donald B., 150
Berlin, Lewis L., 317
Berlin, Meyer: literature on, 289
Berlin, Naphtali Levi Judah: literature on, 289
Berman, Barbara Ann Portnoy, 559
Berman, Bonnie, 115
Berman, I., 564
Berman, J. M., 166
Berman, Jack, 190
Berman, Jeanne, 128
Berman, Jeremiah J., 179, 480
Berman, Margot S., 104
Berman, Morton, 539
Berman, Myron, 24, 148, 386, 513, 559
Berman, Nancy, 31
Berman, Saul, 190, 202, 400, 492
Bernal, A. I. H., 341
Bernard, Jacqueline, 475
Bernard, S. E., 646
Bernards, Solomon S., 130
Bernheim, Isaac W., 449
Bernheimer, Charles, 441
Bernheimer, Charles S., 348, 479
Bernik, Herman C., 567
Bernstein, Adele, 513
Bernstein, Bennie, 55
Bernstein, David, 513
Bernstein, David I., 181, 636
Bernstein, Dorothy, 190
Bernstein, Eliezer Z., 72, 589
Bernstein, Ellen, 632, 633
Bernstein, Elliot M., 356
Bernstein, I., 212
Bernstein, Louis, 164, 417
Bernstein, Mashey M., 130, 526
Bernstein, Mendel, 179
Bernstein, Nathan, 467
Bernstein, Philip, 270, 279, 310, 311, 356, 360

Bernstein, Rachel. *See* Wischnitzer, Rachel
Bernstein, S., 237, 348
Bernstein, Sandra R., 428, 654
Bernstein, Sidney M., 444
Bernstein, Simon, 306
Berrol, Selma C., 475
Berson, Mark, 623
Bertisch, Felix P., 88
Berzin, I., 505
Besdin, Abraham, 395
Bessler, Helen, 58
Beth Arieh, David, 164
Beth El Hebrew Congregation (Alexandria, Va.), 513
Beth Elohim Synagogue (Charleston, S.C.), 509
Beth ha-Hinukh ha-Ivri, 497
Beth HaMedrash HaGadol, 433
Beth HaMidrash LaTorah, 446
Beth Israel Congregation (Atlantic City, N.J.), 468
Beth Rachel of Satmar, 198, 493
Beth Shalom Congregation (Kansas City, Mo.), 464
Beton, Sol, 439
Bets, Johanna, 212
Bettan, Israel, 41, 107
Bettelheim, Bruno, 98, 301, 564, 571
Bettman, Batia, 12, 630, 639
Beyer, Arthur, 164
Beyer, Jimmie Lee, 317
Bial, Morrison David, 115, 380
Biale, Rachel, 400
Bialik, M. L., 21
Bialostotzky, B. J., 205, 210, 220
Biber, Barbara, 55, 564
Biberfield, Marcee, 60
Biblia Hebraica, 338
Bick, A., 289
Bickel, Shlomo, 177, 219, 222, 297, 311, 312
Biederman, I. M., 215
Bieler, Jack, 185, 637, 649
Biere, Matthew, 632
Bierman, Michael A., 469
Bigman, Stanley, 435
Bikel, Theodore, 583
Bikkurim, 465
Bildersee, Adele, 49, 91
Bilik, Dorothy S., 97
Billet, Renee Rookie, 649
Binder, Abraham W., 37, 489
Bin-Nun, David, 425
Bin-Nun, Judith, 57, 112, 181, 190, 629. *See also* Barthold, Judith Bin-Nun
Biographical Dictionary of Modern Yiddish Literature,

675

288, 290, 302, 303, 305, 311, 312
Birmingham, Stephen, 405
Birnbaum, David, 77, 577, 615, 663
Birnbaum, Herbert A., 200, 526
Birnbaum, I., 321
Birnbaum, Paltiel, 108
Birnbaum, Philip, 110, 123
Birnbaum, Ruth, 289, 309, 405, 521
Birner, Louis, 60
Biskar, Herbert Morris, 425
Biskin, Gabriel, 462
Bissel, Sherry, 25–27, 148. *See also* Blumberg, Sherry Bissel
Bissel, Sherry H., 152, 526, 530, 614, 646, 661
Bitaon, 310, 444
Bittner, David, 467
Bitzaron, 310, 493
Black, Naomi, 629
Blackman, Murray, 335
Blacksin, Morris, 480
Blackstone, T., 328
Blanc, Esther Silverstein, 661
Blanchard, Tzvi, 651
Blank, Irwin, 112, 153
Blank, Paul J., 626
Blank, Sheldon, 47
Blaser, Elissa, 23, 380, 553
Blass, Jerome Harold, 66
Blatt, Gloria T., 120
Blatter, Janet, 31
Blau, Joel, 573
Blau, Joseph L., 177, 238, 347, 349, 451, 533
Blau, Yoseph, 190
Blau, Zina Smith, 386
Blaushtein, M., 216
Blechman, M., 462
Bleiberg, James S., 177
Bleich, David J., 130
Bleiweiss, Robert, 634, 668

Bleter far Yiddisher Dertsiung, 217, 226, 278
Bletter, Diana, 649
Blinder, Robert, 390
Blitstein, Sheldon, 41
Bloch, Abraham P., 112
Bloch, Joshua, 486, 600, 603, 610
Bloch, Sam E., 169
Block, Asher, 379
Block, C., 399
Blond, Leo, 577
Bloom, Bernard H., 348
Bloom, D. I., 248
Bloom, David I., 36, 60, 245
Bloom, Jessie S., 423
Bloom, Mrs. Joel, 108
Bloom, Raymond, 453
Bloom, Samuel, 480
Bloom, Sh. Z., 209
Bloomberg, Jon, 99
Bloomen Gortn, Der, 447
Bloomstone-Korb, Deena, 41
Bloore, John Stephen, 120
Bluestone, Harry, 435
Blum, Deborah Cardozo, 24, 482
Blum, Irving, 567
Blum, Isadore, 452
Blumberg, Harry, 72, 80, 81, 119, 485, 504
Blumberg, Herman J., 99
Blumberg, Janice Rothschild, 439
Blumberg, Sherry Bissel, 380. *See also* Bissel, Sherry H.
Blumberg, Zevi, 70
Blume, Harvey, 626
Blume, Judy, 530
Blume, Sheila B., 479
Blumenfield, Samuel M., 22, 69, 124, 161, 164–65, 232, 233, 236, 250, 264, 279, 287, 289, 291, 293, 294, 296, 297, 300, 301, 303, 304, 307, 310, 317, 320, 335, 352, 354, 368, 370, 390, 394, 409, 417, 442, 446, 496, 559, 573, 577, 585, 587, 591, 593, 597, 604
Blumenfield, Yisrael, 663
Blumenthal, Aaron, 41, 155, 400
Blumenthal, Louis, 427, 430
Blumenthal, Y. C., 197
Blumfield Hanita, 649
Blummenthal, Helen E., 499
Blustain, Sara, 648
B'nai B'rith, 33. *See also* Anti-Defamation League of B'nai B'rith
B'nai B'rith Hillel Foundation, 410, 606
B'nai B'rith Magazine, 496
B'nai B'rith Messenger, 429
B'nai B'rith Vocational Service, 66
B'nai Emunah (synagogue), 499
B'nei Akiva of America, 198
Bnei Akiva of North America, 118
Board of Jewish Education of Greater New York, 625
Board of Jewish Education of Greater St. Louis, 466
Bobrowsky, Ida, 258
Bock, Geoffrey E., 559, 577, 594
Bodoff, Lippman, 649
Boehm, L., 564
Bogart, Leo, 97
Bogot, Howard I., 12, 18, 31, 47, 55, 57, 60, 88, 130, 136, 369, 380, 530, 553, 619, 622, 625, 628, 630, 644, 646, 648
Bokser, Ben Zion, 115, 124, 161, 176, 185, 301, 304, 480, 577, 631
Bolkosky, Sidney M., 657
Bomzer, Herbert W., 237
Bonder, David, 410
Bonder, Evelyn D., 112
Boraisha, Menachem, 204, 409, 573, 584
Borgersen, Richard, 61
Borodkin, Thelma L., 77, 625

Key to Index

7–9: *Types of Jewish Schools* | 10–17: *Curriculum* | 18–29: *Pedagogy* | 30–40: *The Arts* | 41–44: *Bar/Bat Mitzvah* | 45–53: *The Bible* | 54–59: *Early Childhood Education* | 60–65: *Exceptional Children* | 66–68: *Guidance* | 69–85: *Hebrew* | 86–96: *History* | 97–103: *The Holocaust* | 104–6: *School Library* | 107–18: *Life Cycle of a Jew* | 119–22: *Literature* | 123–42: *Mitzvot/Values and Contemporary Issues* | 143–46: *Textbooks* | 147–58: *The High School* | 159–75: *American Jewry and the Land of Israel* | 176–203: *Day School* | 204–31: *Yiddish Secular Schools* | 232–42: *Higher Education* | 245–62: *Administration* | 263–69: *The Teacher* | 270–73: *The Rabbi and Jewish Education* | 274–86: *Conferences in Jewish Education, 1890–1988* | 287–312: *Men and Women Who Influenced Jewish Education* | 317–34: *Historical Background of Jewish Education* | 335–52: *History of Jewish Education in the United States* | 353–78: *The American Jewish Community* | 379–89: *The Home and Jewish Education* | 390–97: *Adult Education* | 398–404: *The Woman's Role and Jewish Education* | 405–8: *Sephardim and Jewish Education* | 409–16: *Youth and Jewish Education* | 417–21: *Camp* | 422–516: *Local Sources for Jewish Education* | 521–23: *Theology and Jewish Education* | 524–32: *Religious Education* | 533–38: *Philosophy of Jewish Education* | 539–44: *Goals of Jewish Education* | 545–50: *Research in Jewish Education* | 551–58: *Change in Jewish Education* | 559–72: *The Social Sciences and Jewish Education* | 573–96: *Assessment* | 597–99: *The Future of Jewish Education* | 600–602: *Bibliographies of Jewish Education in Other Lands* | 603–17: *Bibliographies of Jewish Education and Related Fields in the United States* | 619–70: *Supplement*

Boroff, D., 386
Boroff, David, 153, 410
Borok, Bernice S., 624
Borovetz, Fran, 18
Borowitz, Eugene B., 14, 24, 41, 47, 111, 112, 116, 124, 135, 297, 322, 360, 410, 521, 526, 531, 533–34, 537, 567, 597, 662
Borowsky, Alice, 112
Borowsky, Samuel I., 279, 282; literature on, 289
Bortniker, Elijah, 72, 77, 165, 251, 278–80, 289, 306, 308, 320, 322–23, 328, 365, 469, 470, 495, 553
Bos del Pueblo, La, 407, 408
Boston Hebrew Observer, 456
Boston Jewish Community Services, 454
Boston Jewish Times, 456
Botwinick, Chaim Y., 360, 547, 556
Botwinick, Moshe L., 18, 553, 664
Botwinik, B., 220
Boxerman, Burton Alan, 465
Boxerman, Nahoma, 181
Boxerman, William I., 458–60
Boyarin, Jonathan, 658
Boyle, Kay, 97
Brackenridge, H. M., 451
Brademus, John, 328
Brafman, Aaron, 190
Brafman, M., 190
Bragin, Joseph: literature on, 289
Bragman, Louis J., 33
Bragman, Rae, 31, 33
Braiterman, Marvin, 464
Braiterman, Zak, 649
Brandeis, Louis D., 159
Brandes, George, 468
Brandt, Doray, 88, 181
Branscomb, Harvie, 238
Braude, A., 400
Braun, Barbara, 394
Braun, Isadore H., 442
Braun, Sarah Elkin, 446
Brauner, Ronald A., 47
Brav, Stanley R., 256, 386, 464, 495, 524, 531
Braver, Haim, 288
Braver, Joseph, 12, 154, 248, 380, 553, 577, 597
Braverman, Jay, 181, 185, 186, 248, 640, 668
Braverman, Joel, 577
Braverman, Libbie L., 18, 22, 35–37, 70, 72, 78, 104, 110–12, 171, 247, 289, 294, 379, 380, 497

Braverman, William A., 656
Brawer, Chaim Isaac, 328
Brayer, Menachem, 398, 487, 490, 564
Breakstone, David, 161, 168, 172, 635
Breck, Allen D., 432, 433
Bregman, Alan, 380, 390
Bregstone, Philip, 441, 446
Brener, Anne, 622
Brener, David, 501
Brennan, Alice M., 18, 551
Brenner, Anton, 18
Brenner, Leon Oscar, 567
Brenner, Reeve Robert, 621
Breslau, David, 161, 410, 417
Breslauer, S. Daniel, 297, 638, 662, 669
Breslavner, S. N., 181, 190
Bresnick-Perry, Roslyn, 630
Bressler, G., 212
Bressler, Marvin, 386, 559
Brettler, Marc, 625
Bretton-Granatoor, Gary M., 619, 631, 648
Brettschneider, Marla, 649
Breuer, Isaac, 298
Breuer, Jacob, 190
Breuer, Mordecai, 298
Breuer, Stephen E., 417
Brevis, Anna Bear, 385
Brevis, Harry J., 60
Brichta, Lisa, 634
Brichto, Mira, 18, 57, 530, 553
Bricker, Harry, 445
Brickman, Benjamin, 185
Brickman, S., 184
Brickman, William, 527, 577
Brickman, William B., 306
Brickman, William W., 165, 176, 179, 190, 194, 196, 237, 264, 317, 328, 436, 534, 603, 604; literature on, 289
Brickner, Balfour, 25, 125, 136, 150, 165, 172, 353, 631
Brickner, Barnett R., 8, 237, 359, 495, 521, 551; literature on, 289
Bridenthal, Renate, 642
Bridger, David, 12, 35, 72, 76–79, 190, 201, 208, 209, 212, 216, 220, 227, 427, 428
Bridger, Hyman, 212
Brier, Evelyn F., 634
Brier, Rosemary S., 625
Brill, Mordecai L., 539
Brill, Moshe, 564
Brill, Shraga, 47, 483

Brilliant, Nathan, 18, 22, 35–37, 110, 112, 247, 276, 379, 380, 496–98, 573; literature on, 289
Brinn, Ruth Essrig, 32, 622
Brinner, William M., 640
Brisman, Shimeon, 603
Britt, Stuart Henderson, 561
Broches, Samuel, 454, 455, 507
Brodie, Deborah, 611
Brodkin, Arthur, 417
Brodmann, Aliana, 646
Brodsky, Edith, 390
Brodsky, Irving, 567
Brody, Arthur, 356
Brody, Fannie M., 69, 613
Brody, H., 256
Bronner, Leila Leah, 649
Bronson, Rosalind Mael, 465
Bronstein, H., 503, 573
Bronstein, Herbert, 88, 171, 623
Bronstein, Rose, 640
Bronznick, Norman, 99
Brooks, Juanita, 512
Brooks, Mildred, 148
Bror, Chaim, 165
Brothers, Eric, 626
Brotz, Howard, 559
Brown, Alexander, 310
Brown, Edwin C., 660
Brown, F. A., 153, 564
Brown, Joni Bass, 60
Brown, Leonard N., 380
Brown, Meyer, 295
Brown, Michael Gary, 349
Brown, Samuel Wolfe, 47
Brown, Sheldon S., 18, 55, 66, 76, 108
Brown, Stephen Ira, 185
Brown, Steven M., 12, 18, 111
Brownstein, Solomon N., 646
Brownstone, Nathan, 92
Broyde, Michael J., 650
Bruckerman, Yigal, 173
Brumberg, Stephan F., 659
Brusilov, Nathan, 214
Brusin, David, 521
Bryan, Marsha, 38
Buber, Martin, 123, 390, 534, 537, 604; literature on, 289–90
Bubis, Gerald, 367, 386
Bubis, Gerald B., 55, 394, 646
Buch, Arthur T., 507
Buchover, E., 219
Buchwald, Ephraim, 621
Buckley, J. J., 301, 600
Budick, Isadore, 410
Budoff, Lippman, 196
Buffalo (N.Y.) *Jewish Review,* 472
Bugatch, Samuel, 37

INDEX

Bugatch, Simon, 10, 80, 256, 453
Buhle, Paul M., 660
Bulka, Reuven P., 643, 665
Buller, Rochelle, 32
Bulletin (SAFI), 226
Bulman, Nachman, 190, 194
Bundt, Barbara A. K., 112
Bunting, Eve, 626
Bunuis, David M., 614
Burack, Solomon, 181
Bureau for Jewish Living (Des Moines, Ia.), 448
Bureau of Jewish Education (BJE), 257; of Akron, Oh., 494; of Baltimore, 452–53; of Boston, 455; of Chicago, 442–44; of Cleveland, 496, 497; of Los Angeles, 428–29; of Greater Miami, 437; of New Haven, 434; of Greater New York, 558; of New York City, 486, 490, 491; of San Francisco, 431; of Schenectady, N.Y., 474; of Syracuse, N.Y., 474; of Toronto, 600
Bureau of Jewish Social Research, 453
Burnstein, Steven, 256
Burstein, Chaya, 624, 625, 629, 635
Burstin, Barbara Stern, 660
Bush, Isidor, 198, 342
Bush, Lawrence, 136
Buttenweiser, M., 45, 123
Buttnick, Meta, 661
Butwin, Frances, 92
Buxbaum, Yitzhak, 629

Caedin, Nina Beth, 650
Cagan, Jack, 233
Cahan, Abraham, 479
Cahan, Zevi, 487
Cahen, G. M., 343
Cahn, L. M., 354
Cahn, Louis F., 452

Cahn, Steven M., 264
Cahnman, Werner, 128, 410, 567
Cain, Seymour, 97
CAIE Jewish Education News, 253
California Jewish Bulletin and Directory, 429
California Jewish Voice, 429
Calisch, Edith L., 49, 57
Calisch, Edward, 86, 346
Cameron, William, 439
Campbell, Kenneth James, 390
Campeas, Hyman, 130, 248, 380, 405, 476
Canelo, David Augusto, 650
Canter, I., 130
Cantor, Avivah, 616
Cantor, Judith Levin, 657
Capeci, Dominic J., Jr., 458
Caplan, L., 506
Cardin, Nina Beth, 638
Cardin, Shoshana, 378
Cardozo, Arlene Rossen, 386
Cardozo, D. A. J., 405
Carlebach, Elisheva, 651
Carlebach, Joseph, 321
Carlebach, Shmuel, 328
Carlson, E. Leslie, 318
Carmi, Gloria, 630
Carmon, A., 99
Carolina Art Association, 509
Carolina Israelite, 494
Carp, Bernard, 37
Carp, Joel M., 154, 478
Carpenter, James Walter, 318
Carroll, Andrew Silow, 286
Carroll, Maureen, 246
Carsch, Judith, 104
Carvalho, E. N., 338
Carvalho, Solomon Nunes, 342, 424
Casper, Deborah Shor, 482
Cassaway, Esta, 624
Cassola, Joel, 508
Castberg, C., 81

Cedarbaum, David, 39, 111, 256, 362, 391, 442–44
Cedarbaum, Sophia M., 57, 104, 115, 611
Celnick, Isaac, 612
Celnik, Max, 104, 612
Central Agency for Jewish Education (Miami, Fla.), 437
Central Conference of American Rabbis (CCAR), 37, 41, 59, 110, 112, 138–39, 143, 153, 178, 252, 274–84, 346, 376, 415, 524, 540, 541, 543, 613. *See also* Commission on Jewish Education; Commission on Jewish Education of UAHC and CCAR; Union of American Hebrew Congregations
Certner, Simon, 491
Chaikes, E., 213
Chaikin, J., 205
Chaikin, Miriam, 629
Chaikind, H. K., 104
Chait, Marilyn J., 464
Chait, N., 484
Chamiel, Haim, 165, 577
Chammou, Eliezer, 425
Chanin, Nathan, 205, 213, 214, 216, 220, 222, 229, 277; literature on, 290
Chankin, Beatrice, 55
Chanover, Alice, 57
Chanover, Hyman, 55, 57–59, 110, 111, 116, 136, 172, 237, 253, 255, 264–66, 353, 356, 357, 365, 380, 434, 437, 453, 491, 498, 511, 527, 546, 553, 624
Chapin, Anna W., 459
Charak, Gail, 165
Charif, L., 456
Charish, Sharon, 18, 187
Charles, Fred, 57
Charleston Arrangement Committee, 509

Key to Index

7–9: *Types of Jewish Schools* | 10–17: *Curriculum* | 18–29: *Pedagogy* | 30–40: *The Arts* | 41–44: *Bar/Bat Mitzvah* | 45–53: *The Bible* | 54–59: *Early Childhood Education* | 60–65: *Exceptional Children* | 66–68: *Guidance* | 69–85: *Hebrew* | 86–96: *History* | 97–103: *The Holocaust* | 104–6: *School Library* | 107–18: *Life Cycle of a Jew* | 119–22: *Literature* | 123–42: *Mitzvot/Values and Contemporary Issues* | 143–46: *Textbooks* | 147–58: *The High School* | 159–75: *American Jewry and the Land of Israel* | 176–203: *Day School* | 204–31: *Yiddish Secular Schools* | 232–42: *Higher Education* | 245–62: *Administration* | 263–69: *The Teacher* | 270–73: *The Rabbi and Jewish Education* | 274–86: *Conferences in Jewish Education, 1890–1988* | 287–312: *Men and Women Who Influenced Jewish Education* | 317–34: *Historical Background of Jewish Education* | 335–52: *History of Jewish Education in the United States* | 353–78: *The American Jewish Community* | 379–89: *The Home and Jewish Education* | 390–97: *Adult Education* | 398–404: *The Woman's Role and Jewish Education* | 405–8: *Sephardim and Jewish Education* | 409–16: *Youth and Jewish Education* | 417–21: *Camp* | 422–516: *Local Sources for Jewish Education* | 521–23: *Theology and Jewish Education* | 524–32: *Religious Education* | 533–38: *Philosophy of Jewish Education* | 539–44: *Goals of Jewish Education* | 545–50: *Research in Jewish Education* | 551–58: *Change in Jewish Education* | 559–72: *The Social Sciences and Jewish Education* | 573–96: *Assessment* | 597–99: *The Future of Jewish Education* | 600–602: *Bibliographies of Jewish Education in Other Lands* | 603–17: *Bibliographies of Jewish Education and Related Fields in the United States* | 619–70: *Supplement*

Charna, Shalom Yonah, 293, 297, 318, 524; literature on, 290
Chamer, M., 181
Charney, Baruch (Bernard) 185, 483
Charney, Israel W., 99
Charry, Dana, 400
Charry, Elias, 92, 128, 360, 381, 527
Chasen, Raphael, 503
Chasen, Simon, 72
Chazan, Barry (Baruch), 18, 125, 130, 163, 165, 169, 265, 418, 527, 534, 538, 540, 545, 567, 640, 664–66
Chazan, Raphael, 577, 589
Chazan, Robert, 92, 155, 643
Chefitz, Mitchel, 396
Cheil, Arthur, 111
Chein, Isidor, 248, 534, 559, 564, 567
Chernoff, Shulamith S., 55
Chernow, Arlene Sarah, 665
Chertoff, Esther, 328
Chertoff, Mordecai, 161
Chertoff, Sheraga, 318
Chervin, Steven, 663, 666
Chesler, Evan, 24
Chicago (journal), 447
Chicago Board of Jewish Education, 442
Chicago Israelite, 447
Chicago Jewish Chronicle, 447
Chicago Jewish Day School, 445
Chicago Jewish Forum, 447
Chicago Jewish Parochial School, 445
Chicago JUF News, 447
Chinitz, Benjamin, 640
Chinsky, Bloome, 220
Chipkin, Israel S. (Shlomo Azrieli), 7, 32, 54, 55, 80, 123, 125, 165, 251, 253, 256, 258, 263, 264, 272, 278, 280, 288, 292, 296, 300, 326, 335, 356, 361, 363, 391, 409, 437, 439, 469, 470, 482, 485, 486, 506, 524, 551, 573, 584, 585, 589, 597; literature on, 290
Chipman, Fannie, 381, 469, 611
Chochem, Corrine, 34, 428
Chomsky, Elsie, 112; literature on, 290
Chomsky, William (Zav), 10, 18, 46, 47, 69–73, 76–80, 84, 88, 165, 233, 264, 292, 297, 298, 307, 335, 354, 356, 391, 410, 490, 492, 504, 505, 534, 540, 551, 553, 573, 577, 585, 597; literature on, 290–91

Chorowsky, Joshua, 12, 45, 112, 349
Choynski, I. N., 344
Christopherson, V. A., 386
Chubara, Yona, 624
Churgin, Gershon A., 130, 290, 306, 534; literature on, 291
Churgin, Pinchos, 232, 307, 311, 521, 574; literature on, 291
Chwat, Sheldon, 181
Chyet, Stanley F., 494, 507, 513
Cinnamon, Kenneth B., 622
Ciolkowski, Laura E., 649
Citron, Paul, 120
Citron, Samuel J., 33, 35, 489, 491, 492; literature on, 291
Clair, Richard P., 527
Clar, Reva, 426
Clare, Rosa, 432
Clark, E., 564
Clark, Matthew, 251, 253
Cleveland Bureau of Jewish Education, 659
Cleveland Hebrew Institute, 498
Cleveland Jewish Centennial Committee, 496
Cleveland Jewish News, 498
Clinchy, Everett R., 123
Cline, Scott, 499
Coalition for Alternatives in Jewish Education, 252
Coalition for the Advancement of Jewish Education (CAJE), 285, 286, 652. See also *CAJE Jewish Education News;* North American Jewish Student [network]
Coen, R. N., 32
Cogan, Sarah G., 424, 425, 430
Cohen, A., 86, 290
Cohen, A. K., 454
Cohen, Adir, 290, 301
Cohen, Aharon, 623
Cohen, Alfred, 181
Cohen, Annabel, 657
Cohen, Anne Nathan, 511. *See also* Nathan, Anne
Cohen, Arthur, 97, 521
Cohen, Benjamin L., 425
Cohen, Bernard, 559
Cohen, Beryl, 574
Cohen, Beryl D., 264, 394
Cohen, Boaz, 30, 294
Cohen, Burton, 18, 165, 256, 553
Cohen, Burton I., 130, 306, 361, 418
Cohen, Carl, 78
Cohen, David, 60, 190, 195, 625
Cohen, David S., 134

Cohen, David Sanford, 190
Cohen, Debra Nussmaum, 667
Cohen, Edward M., 35, 407
Cohen, Elaine Shizgal, 367, 400
Cohen, Eli, 567
Cohen, Esther, 54
Cohen, Floreva, 55, 482, 629
Cohen, Frances L., 104
Cohen, Gedaliah, 453
Cohen, Gerson D., 88, 238, 241, 300, 367, 388, 567, 577, 662
Cohen, H. Hirsch, 55
Cohen, Harry I., 511
Cohen, Helen K., 637
Cohen, Henry, 510, 511
Cohen, Henry, 60, 125, 155, 521, 567
Cohen, Howard M., 577, 589
Cohen, I. L., 564
Cohen, Irving B., 123
Cohen, Isabel E., 346
Cohen, Israel M., 396
Cohen, Iva, 607, 609
Cohen, Jack J., 17, 18, 22, 28, 32, 42, 47, 73, 88, 107, 108, 112, 120, 125, 130, 161, 165, 172, 178, 190, 237, 247, 264, 268, 296, 356, 391, 392, 397, 527, 534, 553, 559, 585, 592, 598
Cohen, Jeffrey, 112
Cohen, Jessica Lynn, 386
Cohen, Joan Freeman, 36, 40
Cohen, Joel, 130
Cohen, Jonathan, 130
Cohen, Jordan D., 632
Cohen, Joseph, 463
Cohen, Joseph L., 410
Cohen, Judy R., 47
Cohen, Lauren Marshall, 381
Cohen, Lenore, 49
Cohen, Leo M., 625
Cohen, M., 340
Cohen, Mark, 646
Cohen, Marsha B., 651
Cohen, Martin A., 136, 652
Cohen, Michael, 190
Cohen, Miles B., 73, 81, 82, 85
Cohen, Mimi, 18
Cohen, Montague N. A., 153
Cohen, Morris R., 86, 335, 545, 574
Cohen, Morris Raphael, 479
Cohen, Mortimer J., 49, 588
Cohen, Naomi, 159, 161, 348
Cohen, Naomi W., 642, 643
Cohen, Nathaniel, 311, 534
Cohen, Reba, 36
Cohen, S. I., 339
Cohen, Samuel, 11, 41, 104, 108, 344

Cohen, Samuel J., 391, 394, 397
Cohen, Samuel M., 66, 137, 379, 409, 524, 531
Cohen, Samuel S., 237
Cohen, Sarah B., 35
Cohen, Shlomo, 631
Cohen, Stephen P., 665
Cohen, Steven H., 527
Cohen, Steven M., 165, 400, 479, 567, 626, 634, 643, 646, 664, 665
Cohen, Steven Martin, 386, 410
Cohen, Yehuda, 181, 190
Cohen, Yosef Yizhak, 600
Cohen-Keiner, Andrea, 356
Cohen-Nusbacher, Ailene, 478
Cohlan, Sidney A., 566
Cohn, Edward L., 130
Cohn, Haim H., 125
Cohn, Hillel, 271, 381
Cohn, J., 328
Cohn, Morton J., 36
Cohn, S., 321
Cohn, Werner, 559
Cohn-Levine, Debra, 108
Cohn-Schechter, A., 70
Cohn-Sherbok, D., 400, 553
Cohon, Beryl D., 107, 409
Cohon, S. S., 123
Cohon, Samuel M., 301
Cohon, Samuel S., 159
Colandra, Alexander, 181
Colbert, Scott E., 73
Cole, Bruce K., 47
Cole, Melanie Joy, 381
Coleman, Julie L., 466
Coleman, Michael B., 501
Coles, R., 99
College of Jewish Studies, 446
Collegiate Zionist League, 159
Collins, Larry, 639
Colman, Blanche, 509
Colodner, Samuel, 323
Colodner, Solomon, 22, 47, 110, 120, 248, 335, 369, 470, 486, 507, 527, 540, 577; literature on, 291
Colton, Lawrence M., 55
Columbus (Ind.) Jewish History Project, 447
Comay, Joseph, 399, 460
Combined Jewish Philanthropies of Greater Boston, 656
Comer, Gerald, 381
Comet, Theodor, 361
Comins, Harry L., 10, 32, 49, 54, 91, 143, 551
Commentary, 521, 567
Commission for Jewish Education (CJE), 8, 16, 34, 59, 171, 197, 252, 278, 376, 530, 531, 541. See also *Jewish Education*
Commission for the Study of Jewish Education in the United States, 16, 373
Commission on Jewish Education, 11, 15, 43, 142, 252. *See also* Union of American Hebrew Congregations
Commission on Jewish Education in North America, 667
Commission on Jewish Education of UAHC and CCAR, 14
Commission on Reform Jewish Outreach, 26
Committee of Twenty-Five (NYC), 481
Community Sephardic Bulletin, 407
Compass, 171, 253, 381, 527, 646, 663
Cone, Molly, 49, 57, 530
Conference of Jewish Educator Organizations, 251
Congregation Adath Jeshurun (Elkins Park, Pa.), 500
Congregation Adath Yeshurin (Houston, Tex.), 511
Congregation Agudath Achim (Shreveport, La.), 451
Congregation Ahavas Achim (Newburyport, Mass.), 457
Congregation Bene Israel (Cincinnati, O.), 495
Congregation Beth Ahabah (Richmond, Va.), 513, 661
Congregation Beth El (Milwaukee, Wis.), 515
Congregation Beth Emeth (Wilmington, Del.), 435
Congregation Beth Israel (San Francisco, Calif.), 345
Congregation B'nai Israel (Galveston, Tex.), 511
Congregation B'nai Zion (Chattanooga, Tenn.), 510
Congregation Emanu-El (San Francisco, Calif.), 343
Congregation Mishkan Tefila (Chestnut Hill, Mass.), 457
Congregation Neveh Shalom (Portland, Ore.), 660
Congregation Ohev Shalom (Kansas City, Kans.), 449
Congregation Rodeph Sholom (NYC), 476
Congregation Shearith Israel (Dallas, Tex.), 511
Congress, U.S., 161
Congress Bi-Weekly, 98, 125, 553
Congress Monthly (Cong M), 162, 405, 634
Congress Weekly, 163, 253, 546, 585
Connecticut Hebrew Record, 433
Connecticut Jewish Ledger, 433
Connely, Thomas F., 472
Conner, Susan Marks, 449
Conovitz, Michael, 368
Conservative Judaism (Con Jud), 13, 61, 161, 237, 270, 527, 603, 613

Key to Index

7–9: *Types of Jewish Schools* | 10–17: *Curriculum* | 18–29: *Pedagogy* | 30–40: *The Arts* | 41–44: *Bar/Bat Mitzvah* | 45–53: *The Bible* | 54–59: *Early Childhood Education* | 60–65: *Exceptional Children* | 66–68: *Guidance* | 69–85: *Hebrew* | 86–96: *History* | 97–103: *The Holocaust* | 104–6: *School Library* | 107–18: *Life Cycle of a Jew* | 119–22: *Literature* | 123–42: *Mitzvot/Values and Contemporary Issues* | 143–46: *Textbooks* | 147–58: *The High School* | 159–75: *American Jewry and the Land of Israel* | 176–203: *Day School* | 204–31: *Yiddish Secular Schools* | 232–42: *Higher Education* | 245–62: *Administration* | 263–69: *The Teacher* | 270–73: *The Rabbi and Jewish Education* | 274–86: *Conferences in Jewish Education, 1890–1988* | 287–312: *Men and Women Who Influenced Jewish Education* | 317–34: *Historical Background of Jewish Education* | 335–52: *History of Jewish Education in the United States* | 353–78: *The American Jewish Community* | 379–89: *The Home and Jewish Education* | 390–97: *Adult Education* | 398–404: *The Woman's Role and Jewish Education* | 405–8: *Sephardim and Jewish Education* | 409–16: *Youth and Jewish Education* | 417–21: *Camp* | 422–516: *Local Sources for Jewish Education* | 521–23: *Theology and Jewish Education* | 524–32: *Religious Education* | 533–38: *Philosophy of Jewish Education* | 539–44: *Goals of Jewish Education* | 545–50: *Research in Jewish Education* | 551–58: *Change in Jewish Education* | 559–72: *The Social Sciences and Jewish Education* | 573–96: *Assessment* | 597–99: *The Future of Jewish Education* | 600–602: *Bibliographies of Jewish Education in Other Lands* | 603–17: *Bibliographies of Jewish Education and Related Fields in the United States* | 619–70: *Supplement*

INDEX

Contemporary Jewish Record, 474, 567
Cook, Julian I., 22
Cook, Ray M., 38
Cook, S., 546
Cooke, Bridget Litherland, 77
Cooney, Terry A., 665
Cooper, Charles I., 463, 499, 505
Cooper, Howard, 646
Cooper, Nancy, 57
Cooperman, Bernard D., 638, 665
Coopersmith, Ethel, 379
Coopersmith, Harry, 38, 39, 379, 443, 489
Cooperstein, L., 323
Copans, Stuart M., 621
Copeland, Steven R., 77, 564
Cornill, Carl, 318
Corre, A. D., 24
Corseri, Richard Alan, 256
Cottle, Thomas, 26, 44
Coun, Ronald, 251
Council for Jewish Education (*Sheviley Hahinuch [Sh Hahj]*), 272, 278, 283, 290, 292, 308, 310, 414, 540, 614
Council News (St. Louis [Mo.] publication), 466
Council of Educators for the Jewish National Fund in the United States, 167
Council of Jewish Federations (CJF), 196, 359, 364, 644
Council of Jewish Federations and Welfare Funds (CJFWF), 162, 197, 250, 356, 410, 481, 567
Council of Jewish Women, 107
Council Publication (of CJF), 24
Covich, Edith S., 112
Cowan, Neil M., 642
Cowan, Ruth Schwartz, 642
Cowen, Elfrida D., 436
Cowen, Ida G., 86
Cowett, Mark, 653
Crohn, Lawrence, 459, 460
Cronbach, Abraham, 45, 123, 128, 527
Cronson, Bernard, 482
CSS (UAHC), 612
Cubberley, Ellwood P., 318
Cukier, G., 601
Culbertson, Steven, 507
Culture and Education (*CE*), 206, 219, 226, 311
Curtis, Jerome M., 356
Curzon, David, 623
Cutler, Irving, 441
Cutler, Charles, 603

Cutter, William, 19, 28, 97, 192, 233, 381, 546, 553, 577, 639
Cytron, Barry D., 125

Dagani, E., 104
Daggett, Emerson, 430
Dahbany-Miraglia, D., 659
Daiches, David, 45
Daily Jewish Courier, 447
Dalin, David G., 430
Dan, Joseph, 651
Danan, Julie Hilton, 635
Danenbaum, Ruby, 463
Daniels, Abraham G., 346
Daniels, Leona, 120
Danzig, Jerry M., 108, 391
Danzig, Yehuda, 253
Danziger, Gustav Adolf, 430
Danziger, Harry K., 12
Danziger, Murray Herbert, 662
Darkenu, 488
Dash, Jerry, 555
Dash, Joan, 514
Dashefsky, Arnold, 529, 567, 589, 664
Dashevsky, Arieh, 359
Datan, N., 515
Daube, Rochelle Silbermintz, 483
Dauber, Jack, 19, 28, 553
Daum, Annette, 25, 247, 366
David, Avi, 184, 624
David, L., 237
David Pinski Folk School, 445
Davids, Stanley M., 634
Davidson, B., 218
Davidson, C., 37
Davidson, Gabriel, 458
Davidson, Israel, 119, 305
Davidson, Jerome K., 110, 410
Davidson, Jessica, 653
Davidson, Jessica R., 645
Davidson, Joan L., 130
Davidson, Lawrence J., 434
Davidson, Morris I., 434
Davis, Barbara Sheklin, 474
Davis, David, 394
Davis, Edward, 501
Davis, Eli, 32
Davis, Elise, 32
Davis, Enid, 120, 122, 610
Davis, J., 597
Davis, Lenwood G., 612
Davis, Maurice, 153, 411
Davis, Minna, 98
Davis, Moshe, 19, 110, 124, 153, 165, 236, 237, 253, 272, 289, 292, 302, 349, 354, 480, 563, 634; literature on, 291–92
Davis, Patricia Talbot, 500

Davis, Perry, 185
Davis, Stuart E., 248
Dawidowicz, Lucy S., 97, 222, 231, 305, 347, 477, 567, 626
Dawidowicz, Moshe, 30
Dawidowitch, Sh., 223
Day, 179, 197, 205, 217, 280, 487
Dayan, S. I., 411
Day-Jewish Journal, 493
Dayton Jewish Chronicle, 498
Dean, John P., 560
De Bella, Elliot R., 468
Deborah, Die, 496
DEC. *See* Jewish Agency
Decker, Peter R., 430
Decter, Midge, 577
Deinard, Amos, 196
Deinard, Ephraim, 603
Deinard, Samuel N., 123
Deitcher, Howard, 181
Deitchman, Emily, 70
Dekel, Aviva L., 237
De Koven, Ralph, 111
Delakova, K., 34–35
Delia Pergola, Sergio, 258, 622, 668
Delores Kohl Educational Foundation, 173
Delouya, Achiah, 407
Dembicer, P., 189
Dembitz, Lewis N., 449
Dembo, Myron, 247
Demsky, A., 318
De Nola, D., 411
Denver Jewish News, 433
Denver Republican, 433
De Paola, Tomie, 629
Derby, Josiah, 179, 191, 577
Derby, Lavey, 148
Derovan, David J., 483
Dershowitz, Zachary, 560
De Solla, J. Mendes, 343, 344
Des Press, Terrence, 97
Dessel, Susan, 400
Dessler, N. W., 198, 497
Dessor, Julius Heinreich, 342
Detroit Jewish Chronicle, 462
Detroit Jewish Community Council, 460
Detroit Jewish Guide, 462
Detroit Jewish News, 460, 462
Detroit Labor Zionist Organization, 459
Deutch, S., 165
Deutch, Samuel, 253
Deutsch, Bess Alper, 462
Deutsch, Emanuel, 346
Deutsch, Solomon, 343
Devlin, Dennis S., 657

681

Dewey, John: literature on, 291
Diamant, Anita, 646
Diamond, Eliezer, 669
Diamond, Jack, 560
Diamond, Joseph, 178, 185, 289, 356, 473
Diamond, L. A., 391
Diamond, Lorraine K., 484
Diamond, Luna Ereza, 435
Diamond, Stanley C., 191
D.I.B., 288
Dick, Judah, 196
Dicker, Herman, 638
Dickman, Marci, 127, 418
Dimensions, 386, 411, 521
Dinburg, Ben Zion, 232, 323
Diner, Hasia R., 642, 655
Diner, Loisan, 181
Dinerman, M., 153
Dingol, S., 577
Dinin, Samuel, 10, 13, 163, 165, 178, 196, 199, 232, 234, 236, 251, 265, 269, 276, 283, 288, 291, 295, 298, 302, 354–56, 365, 367, 388, 391, 397, 428, 429, 466, 489, 490, 514, 524, 532, 534, 537, 539, 540, 551, 560, 574, 577, 584–86, 588, 597, 598, 641; literature on, 292
Dinitz, Simcha, 641
Dinnerstein, Leonard, 439, 450
Dinning, Pat, 73
Dinsky, Samuel, 148, 357, 422, 437, 475, 498
Dinsky, Samuel H., 150, 280, 281, 304, 365, 449, 474; literature on, 292
Dinur, Ben Zion, 162, 165, 312
Disenhouse, Phyllis, 616
Diskind, Zalman, 7, 176, 251, 527, 540, 577, 589
D'Israel, L. S., 341
Divinsky, Oscar, 47, 367
Dixon, Walter T, Jr., 507

Dlugacz, Irving, 564
Dobinsky, P. S., 154
Dobrinsky, Herbert C., 405
Dobroszycki, Lusjan, 97
Dolgin, S. A., 181
Dolins, Joseph Lehman, 181
Domb, Cyril, 191
Doniger, A., 159
Doniger, S., 409
Donin, Hayim H., 107, 125, 364, 460, 543, 646
Dorff, Elliot, 19, 125, 130, 136, 662
Dori, Rivka, 73, 77, 148, 664
Doroshkin, I., 205
Doroshkin, Milton, 204, 349
Dorph, Gail, 113, 429
Dorph, Gail Zaiman, 29, 111, 115, 118, 181
Dorph, Isaac, 427
Dorph, Sheldon, 428
Dorph, Sheldon A., 19, 553
Dotan, Beth Seldin, 113
Douglas, Martin, 514
Douglas, Martin I., 468
Dove, Y., 195
Dover, Amy, 418
Downing, William L., 46
Drachler, Israel, 219, 399, 460
Drachler, Norman, 247, 251, 585
Drachman, Bernard, 123, 345, 479
Drachsler, Julius, 560
Drasin, Mrs. Samuel, 55
Drazin, Nathan, 318, 323
Dresner, Ruth Rapp, 400
Dresner, Samuel H., 113, 130, 136, 297, 632
Drew, David E., 411
Dreyfus, A., 511
Dreyfus, A. Stanley, 381
Dreyfus, Miriam W., 86
Droker, Howard A., 514
Dropsie College, 540
Dror-Elboim, Rachel, 328

Dubb, Allie A., 245, 258
Dubin, Bernard, 264
Dubin, C., 153
Dubin, David, 367, 645
Dubnow, Shimon, 227
Dubnow, Simon, 86, 93, 323
Dubrovsky, Gertrude W., 469, 658
Duckat, Walter, 66, 67, 400
Ducoff, Bernard, 357, 359, 431, 468, 553, 640
Duggan, Stephen, 318
Dukakis, Andrea, 663
Duker, Abraham G., 130, 162, 353, 357, 361, 396, 485, 548, 560, 564, 577, 585, 587
Dunkelman, David M., 646
Dunsky, Shimon, 211, 212, 215
Dunsky, Shimshon, 211, 311
Durant, Will, 45
Dushkin, Alexander M., 10, 16, 22, 128, 162, 163, 165–66, 174, 176, 177, 191, 196, 234, 251, 260, 264, 266, 271, 277, 288, 289, 291, 292, 300, 303–5, 307, 309–11, 326, 328, 335–36, 353, 355, 357, 359, 363, 368, 372, 391, 409, 428, 442, 444, 445, 467, 478, 480, 482, 485, 487, 492, 516, 524, 534, 539, 542, 545, 546, 560, 574, 577, 584, 586, 587, 591, 641; literature on, 292
Dushkin, Julia Aronson: literature on, 292
Dworski, Susan, 632
Dwyer, Alexander, 339

Eakin, Frank E., 513
East Bay Echo, 430
Eban, Abba, 92, 328–29
Ebner, Eliezer, 318
Eby, Frederick, 318
Eckardt, A. Roy, 125
Eckstein, Simon L., 270
Edan, M., 486

Key to Index

7–9: *Types of Jewish Schools* | 10–17: *Curriculum* | 18–29: *Pedagogy* | 30–40: *The Arts* | 41–44: *Bar/Bat Mitzvah* | 45–53: *The Bible* | 54–59: *Early Childhood Education* | 60–65: *Exceptional Children* | 66–68: *Guidance* | 69–85: *Hebrew* | 86–96: *History* | 97–103: *The Holocaust* | 104–6: *School Library* | 107–18: *Life Cycle of a Jew* | 119–22: *Literature* | 123–42: *Mitzvot/Values and Contemporary Issues* | 143–46: *Textbooks* | 147–58: *The High School* | 159–75: *American Jewry and the Land of Israel* | 176–203: *Day School* | 204–31: *Yiddish Secular Schools* | 232–42: *Higher Education* | 245–62: *Administration* | 263–69: *The Teacher* | 270–73: *The Rabbi and Jewish Education* | 274–86: *Conferences in Jewish Education, 1890–1988* | 287–312: *Men and Women Who Influenced Jewish Education* | 317–34: *Historical Background of Jewish Education* | 335–52: *History of Jewish Education in the United States* | 353–78: *The American Jewish Community* | 379–89: *The Home and Jewish Education* | 390–97: *Adult Education* | 398–404: *The Woman's Role and Jewish Education* | 405–8: *Sephardim and Jewish Education* | 409–16: *Youth and Jewish Education* | 417–21: *Camp* | 422–516: *Local Sources for Jewish Education* | 521–23: *Theology and Jewish Education* | 524–32: *Religious Education* | 533–38: *Philosophy of Jewish Education* | 539–44: *Goals of Jewish Education* | 545–50: *Research in Jewish Education* | 551–58: *Change in Jewish Education* | 559–72: *The Social Sciences and Jewish Education* | 573–96: *Assessment* | 597–99: *The Future of Jewish Education* | 600–602: *Bibliographies of Jewish Education in Other Lands* | 603–17: *Bibliographies of Jewish Education and Related Fields in the United States* | 619–70: *Supplement*

Edel, Abraham, 125
Edelman, Lily, 116, 125, 391, 393, 394, 396
Edelman, Marsha, 489, 669
Edelstein, Menachem M., 10, 47, 70, 81, 111, 251, 264, 265, 277, 278, 295, 310, 311, 486, 487, 489, 490, 578, 587, 604, 669; literature on, 292
Edelstein, Rosalind, 182
Eden, 121
Edidin, Ben, 78, 308
Edidin, Benjamin M., 147, 163, 171
Edidin, Ben M., 10, 22, 36, 91, 113, 135, 275–77, 302, 367–69, 394, 410, 434, 442, 489, 491, 492, 504, 525, 584; literature on, 292
Edson, C. H., 560
Educational Encyclopedia (*Ed Enc*), 318, 329
Educational News (Pittsburgh, Pa.), 506
Educational Research Council of America (ERC), 608, 609
Education and Culture Review, 668
Educators Assembly of the USA (Ed As), 278, 280, 283–85, 527
Educators Council of America, 285
Edwards, B., 82
Eels, Walter C., 616
Efron, Ben, 381
Efron, Benjamin, 24, 42, 50, 73, 90, 111, 369, 370, 603
Efron, Mordecai V., 540
Efros, Israel, 69, 70, 534, 574; literature on, 292
Egelson, Louis I., 152, 355
Egnal, Freda, 507
Egozi, Akivah, 99, 182, 187, 185, 191, 248, 301, 427, 428, 508
Egozi, R., 637
Ehrenfried, Albert A., 454
Ehrlich, Abraham J., 84, 111, 578
Ehrlich, Amy, 629
Ehrlich, Evelyn, 658
Ehrlich, Irvin S., 88, 234
Ehrlich, Rae, 104
Ehrlich, Walter, 465
Ehrmann, Eliezer, 33, 73, 90, 94, 104, 150, 306, 433, 443, 444
Eichenbaum, Rose, 427
Eichenbaum, Sharon, 58
Eichhorn, Jonathan, 394
Eichold, Samuel, 422
Eidlin, Harold, 347

Eigns, 468
Einhorn, David, 342, 343, 411, 452
Einhorn, Franne, 57, 112, 629
Einsider, Harold, 110
Einstein, Stephen J., 394, 629
Eisemann, Meir, 191
Eisen, Arnold, 521, 662, 668
Eisen, Arnold M., 634, 638
Eisen, Sylvia, 104
Eisenberg, Ann, 380
Eisenberg, Azriel (I. L. Eisenberg; Israel L. Eisenberg), 10, 14, 19, 33, 42, 46, 49, 70, 73, 77, 80, 86, 92, 101, 107, 108, 116, 119, 120, 135, 136, 148, 166, 170–72, 178, 233, 248, 251, 256, 258, 259, 264, 267, 272, 276, 288, 291, 295, 302, 305–7, 361, 369, 370, 379, 381, 437, 482, 486–91, 493, 495, 497, 540, 574, 578, 589, 598; literature on, 292–93
Eisenberg, Dov, 400
Eisenberg, Ellen M., 658
Eisenberg, Freda, 633
Eisenberg, I. L. *See* Eisenberg, Azriel
Eisenberg, Israel. *See* Eisenberg, Azriel
Eisenberg, Matthew J., 653
Eisenberg, Robin L., 381, 629, 664
Eisenberg, Yehuda, 108, 427, 465, 474
Eisenberg, Yehudah Moses, 491
Eisendrath, Maurice N., 411
Eisenpreis, B., 60
Eisenstein, Ira, 36, 38, 113, 123, 125, 148, 156, 159, 279, 288, 292, 300, 336, 357, 521, 553, 662
Eisenstein, J. D., 345, 475, 480
Eisenstein, Judith K., 30, 36–38
Eisenstein, Miriam, 323
Eisner, Mark, 361, 574
Eitches, Edward, 451
Ekrony, A., 328
Elazar, Albert, 357
Elazar, Daniel J., 148, 166, 203, 237, 270, 347, 348, 353, 361, 362, 370, 377, 400, 405, 593, 641, 645, 651, 666, 667
Elbaz, Nissim Maxim, 248
Elbe, Leon, 205, 225, 227
Elbogen, Ismar, 628
Eldot, Walter, 463
Elefant, William L., 304
Elfenbaum, Esther, 361, 429

Eliach, David, 182, 191, 202, 589
Eliakim, Isaac C., 333
Elias, J., 527
Elias, Joseph, 185, 195
Elias, Marcus, 298
Eliassof, Leon H. (Herman), 440, 441
Elijah Ben Solomon Zalman: literature on, 293
Elinson, Jack, 478
Elish, Barbara, 668
Elishav, Mordecai, 296
Elkin, Harry, 19, 70, 166, 280, 290, 298, 357, 391, 396, 397, 564; literature on, 293
Elkin, Joshua, 182, 195, 637
Elkin, Joshua Charles, 27
Elkin, Judith Laikin, 651
Elkind, Alan, 182
Elkind, D., 564
Elkins, Dov Peretz, 130, 134, 172, 381, 474, 668
Elkins, Marilyn, 156
Ellinson, David, 129, 533
Elliott, Mark, 661
Elliott, Roberta, 196
Ellman, Eugene B., 411
Elmaleh, Haim, 637
Elon, Amos, 172
Elovitz, Mark H., 422, 578
Elstein, Rochelle B., 458
Elwell, Sue Levi (Ellen), 156, 348, 367, 400, 669
Elzas, Barnett A., 499, 509
Emanu-El (San Francisco temple publication), 432
Emanuel, Itzhak, 431
Emanuel Synagogue (Oklahoma City), 499
Emanuel Synagogue Religious School (Hartford, Conn.), 434
Emil, Charles, 10, 86
Encyclopaedia Judaica (*Enc Jud*), 30, 34, 35, 37, 120, 288–99, 301–3, 305–7, 309–12, 422–24, 440, 447–52, 454, 458, 464–68, 471, 476, 499, 502, 508, 510, 515, 516, 601
Ende, George, 13, 125, 150, 248, 434, 527
Endelman, Judith E., 448, 603
Enelow, Hyman G., 391, 574
Engel, Alvin David, 33
Engel, David, 73, 77, 427, 538, 553
Engel, David E., 130
Engel, G., 411
Engel, Gerald, 270
Engel, R. C., 166, 546

Engel, Sophie B., 403
Engelman, Uriah Z., 16, 69, 70, 78, 79, 179, 196, 220, 257, 258, 260, 264, 267, 273, 290, 357, 360, 361, 363, 370, 375, 388, 427, 435–37, 439, 440, 449, 456, 460, 463, 467–70, 472, 474, 495, 497, 498, 501, 506, 508, 509, 545, 546, 574, 578, 591, 600, 601; literature on, 293
Englander, Henry, 302
Engman, Suzy, 120
Entin, Joel, 205–7, 210, 214, 216, 218, 220, 223, 227, 228, 293
Entin, Nathaniel A., 33, 75, 81, 166, 482
Ephraim, Miriam R., 153, 411, 418
Ephrose, Joan, 646
Ephross, Paul H., 514
Epoca de New York, La, 407, 408
Eppstein, E., 343
Epstein, A., 10, 584
Epstein, A. Joseph, 480
Epstein, David, 386
Epstein, David H., 245
Epstein, Helen, 99
Epstein, I., 301
Epstein, Ita, 198
Epstein, Izhac: literature on, 293
Epstein, Jerome M., 648
Epstein, Jerome Michael, 391
Epstein, Judith G., 159
Epstein, Kyla, 99
Epstein, Melech, 312, 348
Epstein, Morris, 116, 120
Epstein, Sandra S., 553
Epstein, Saundra Starling, 622
Epstein, Seymour, 33, 88
Epstein, Shifra, 478
Erdberg, Sh., 481
Erdberger, A., 407
Esses, Dianne O., 651

Essrig, Harry (Chaim), 22, 78, 152, 157, 172, 232, 360, 391, 396, 409, 534, 540, 553
Esterson, Rose, 452
Etan, Israel, 46
Etkes, Emanuel, 308, 640
Etkin, Abraham, 490
Etscovitz, L., 290
Ettenberg, Sylvia C., 166, 234, 271, 653
Ettinger, Celia, 499
Etzioni, A., 411
Euster, Sandra D., 19, 553
Evans, Beth J., 27
Evans, Eli K., 493
Even-Shmuel (Kaufman), Judah, 295
Evyater, Friesel, 626
Ezekiel, H. C., 495
Ezekiel, Herbert T., 513
Ezekiel, Jacob, 513
Ezrachi, Elan, 329
Ezrat Nashim, 400
Ezring, Sheldon, 150

Faber, Eli, 642
Fachman, A., 503
Fackenheim, Emil, 97, 103, 126, 152, 156, 521–22, 634, 662
Fagin, Samuel I., 446
Falk, G. F., 564
Falk, Marcia, 650
Falk, Randall M., 290
Falk, Simon, 472
Falkenan, Jacob J. M., 340
Farago, Uri, 418
Farband, 281
Farband Folk Schools, 275, 277, 445, 462
Farber, Sh., 214
Farber, Walter C., 461
Fargell, Harris C., 60
Fasman, Oscar Z., 191, 446
Fass, David E., 116
Fastenau, Maureen K., 400

Fauman, S. Joseph, 458
Faur, Jose, 237, 406, 408
Fear, Frank A., 567
Feder, Chaim, 173
Feder, Sarah, 223
Feder, Shirley Sloan, 191
Federal Writers' Project, 468
Federation of Jewish Philanthropies of New York, 475, 478
Federation of Reconstructionist Congregations and Fellowships, 282
Federbush, S., 290
Federbush, Simon, 307, 574
Federman, Allan, 364
Fefferman, Michael, 150
Feibelman, Julian B., 450
Feibelman, Julius B., 584
Feierstein, Francine, 75
Feierstein, Milton, 302
Feifer, Richard, 19
Feigin, Samuel I., 289; literature on, 293
Feiman-Nemser, 664
Fein, Elliot, 527
Fein, Eve Melman, 166, 429
Fein, Isaac M., 452, 453, 454–55
Fein, Leonard, 554, 567–68, 578, 615, 665
Feinberg, Charles K., 236
Feinberg, Miriam, 55, 381, 624
Feinberg, N. S., 81
Feinberg, Paul, 391
Feinberg, Paul R., 418
Feingold, Henry, 665
Feingold, Henry L., 162, 347, 411, 642
Feinhor, Noam, 649
Feinman, Ethel R., 464
Feinstein, Jerome Tov, 108
Feinstein, Joseph H., 13, 73, 381, 493
Feinstein, M., 294
Feinstein, Marvin, 159

Key to Index

7–9: *Types of Jewish Schools* | 10–17: *Curriculum* | 18–29: *Pedagogy* | 30–40: *The Arts* | 41–44: *Bar/Bat Mitzvah* | 45–53: *The Bible* | 54–59: *Early Childhood Education* | 60–65: *Exceptional Children* | 66–68: *Guidance* | 69–85: *Hebrew* | 86–96: *History* | 97–103: *The Holocaust* | 104–6: *School Library* | 107–18: *Life Cycle of a Jew* | 119–22: *Literature* | 123–42: *Mitzvot/Values and Contemporary Issues* | 143–46: *Textbooks* | 147–58: *The High School* | 159–75: *American Jewry and the Land of Israel* | 176–203: *Day School* | 204–31: *Yiddish Secular Schools* | 232–42: *Higher Education* | 245–62: *Administration* | 263–69: *The Teacher* | 270–73: *The Rabbi and Jewish Education* | 274–86: *Conferences in Jewish Education, 1890–1988* | 287–312: *Men and Women Who Influenced Jewish Education* | 317–34: *Historical Background of Jewish Education* | 335–52: *History of Jewish Education in the United States* | 353–78: *The American Jewish Community* | 379–89: *The Home and Jewish Education* | 390–97: *Adult Education* | 398–404: *The Woman's Role and Jewish Education* | 405–8: *Sephardim and Jewish Education* | 409–16: *Youth and Jewish Education* | 417–21: *Camp* | 422–516: *Local Sources for Jewish Education* | 521–23: *Theology and Jewish Education* | 524–32: *Religious Education* | 533–38: *Philosophy of Jewish Education* | 539–44: *Goals of Jewish Education* | 545–50: *Research in Jewish Education* | 551–58: *Change in Jewish Education* | 559–72: *The Social Sciences and Jewish Education* | 573–96: *Assessment* | 597–99: *The Future of Jewish Education* | 600–602: *Bibliographies of Jewish Education in Other Lands* | 603–17: *Bibliographies of Jewish Education and Related Fields in the United States* | 619–70: *Supplement*

INDEX

Feinstein, Morley, 23, 391, 605
Feinstein, Moses, 86, 232; literature on, 293
Feinstein, Moshe, 182
Feinstein, Sara, 100, 172, 173, 245, 357, 391, 400, 461, 491
Feintech, Vivian, 381
Feintuch, Burt, 660
Feitman, Yaakov, 189
Feld, Edward, 622
Feld, Lipman G., 449
Feldheim, Eric, 19, 248, 485
Feldman, Abraham J., 33, 128, 152, 270, 360, 434, 574
Feldman, David M., 113, 400
Feldman, Egal, 88, 667
Feldman, Emanuel, 191, 237
Feldman, Estelle, 55, 469, 491, 492
Feldman, Esther, 215, 218
Feldman, Irving, 196
Feldman, Jacob S., 500, 505
Feldman, Leon A., 391, 396, 411
Feldman, Lisa, 267
Feldman, M., 445, 534, 578
Feldman, Moshe, 227
Feldman, Patricia Shirley, 391
Feldman, Ruth Duskin, 668
Feldman, Ruth Pinkenson, 664
Feldman, Sadie, 369
Feldman, Sara, 411
Feldman, Steven, 455
Fellus, Gail Teicher, 120
Fell-Yellin, Sarah, 218
Felsenthal, Bernhard (Baruch), 199, 343, 345, 441, 537; literature on, 293
Felsenthal, Emma, 293
Felsenthal, Julia I., 346
Fendel, Meyer, 191
Fenster, M. M., 125
Fenster, Myron, 527
Fenyvesi, Charles, 634
Ferman, Arlene, 470
Ferris, Helene, 662
Feuer, Avraham C., 189
Feuer, Leon L., 42, 113, 119, 152, 495, 497, 530
Feuer, Lewis S., 512
Feuerman, Chaim, 191, 483
Feuerstein, Samuel C.: literature on, 294
Feuerstein, Samuel L., 176
Fidanque, E. Alvin, 406
Field, Ben, 223
Fields, Harvey J., 19, 111, 624
Fierman, Floyd S., 336, 423, 471, 510, 511
Fierman, Morton, 113, 297
Fierman, Morton C., 540
Fierstein, Robert E., 236, 638
Fifth Avenue Synagogue (NYC), 475
Fifth National Conference on Jewish Education, 283
Fine, Alvin, 115
Fine, Helen, 116, 136, 171
Fine, Henry, 494
Fine, Irene, 237
Fine, Jeanne, 19
Fine, Jo Renee, 477
Fine, Lawrence, 620
Fine, Lea, 494
Fine, Morris, 609
Fineberg, Solomon A., 46, 86, 163, 256, 574
Finell, David, 185
Fineman, I., 310
Fineschreiber, William, 86
Finesilver, Marilyn, 620
Finger, Seymour, 97
Fink, Dan, 633
Fink, Reuben, 475
Finkel, Elliott, 534
Finkel, Nisson Z., 195
Finkelstein, Eleanor, 191
Finkelstein, Hayim, 166, 361
Finkelstein, Louis, 123, 125, 236, 237, 263, 295, 304, 321, 530, 547, 631
Finkelstein, Milton, 88
Finkelstein, Norman H., 651
Finkle, Arthur L., 622
Finnel, David B., 369
Finstenberg, Rochelle, 329
Fireman, Theodore, 554
Firer, Ruth, 329
First National Conference on Jewish Education, 279
First World Conference for Hebrew Education in Diaspora, 173
Fisch, Dov, 578
Fisch, Linda Y., 400
Fisch, Linda Yellin, 578
Fisch-Aharoni, Linda, 483
Fischbach, Suzanne, 113
Fischer, Anne, 513
Fischer, Susan Eleanor, 509
Fischer, Wilhelm, 343
Fischler, Ben-Zion, 605
Fischman, Joyce, 32, 50
Fischman, M. E., 428
Fischman, Stanley, 613
Fish, Isidore, 466
Fish, Nathan, 33, 492
Fish, Nathan M., 36
Fish, Sidney M., 237, 500, 501
Fishbane, Simcha, 649
Fisher, Adam, 629
Fisher, Eugene J., 125
Fisher, Gershon, 391
Fisher, Leon D., 25
Fisher, Ofra, 646
Fisher, Phyllis J., 23
Fisher, Terry K., 501
Fishkoff, Sue, 631
Fishman, Hertzel, 381
Fishman, I., 323
Fishman, Joshua A. (Shikl), 19, 47, 51, 79, 84, 204, 209, 220, 256, 304, 361, 370, 386, 411, 545, 548, 560, 564, 568, 638, 645
Fishman, Joyce, 58
Fishman, L. J., 307
Fishman, Leora, 400–401, 616
Fishman, Morris, 560
Fishman, Priscilla, 111, 394
Fishman, Sylvia Barack, 458, 578, 646, 663, 666
Fishman, Walda Katz, 450
Fishman, Yehudah, 166, 411
Fishweicher, Israel, 578
Fix, Elliot, 474
Flam, Alan C., 166
Flatto, Zehava, 187
Flaxman, Leslie L., 410
Fleischmann, Rienne, 60
Fleishaker, Oscar, 447, 448
Fleishman, Thelma, 457
Flander, Harold, 627
Flexer, Jacob, 466
Flexner, Paul A., 639, 640
Flinker, Moshe, 101
Floch, Naomi Buchhalter, 462
Flowerman, S. H., 564
Fogelman, L., 225
Fogelson, George, 432
Fohrman, Nadine, 429
Folkman, Jerome D., 54, 147, 259, 379
Folks Zeitung, 429
Folpe, Joan, 619
Forse, C., 540
Forward, The (For), 225, 346
Foster, Geraldine, 507
Foster, Solomon, 123, 525
Fowler, Floyd, 454, 455
Fox, Brian, 150
Fox, Cherie Koller, 42
Fox, Ethel, 49
Fox, Everett, 669
Fox, Frank, 418
Fox, J. S., 336
Fox, Karen L., 367
Fox, Maier B., 159

685

Fox, Marcia, 156
Fox, Marvin, 125, 130, 141, 178, 191, 195, 200, 237, 585
Fox, Seymour, 13, 125, 166, 234, 329, 534, 538, 549, 554, 578, 667
Fraenkel, Josef, 601
Frankel, Mira, 47, 453
Fram, Leon, 147, 159, 391, 394, 527
Frampton, Wilson, 627
Franck, Isaac, 19, 99, 125, 370
Frank, Anne, 101
Frank, Avraham, 166
Frank, Ben G., 407, 477
Frank, Bernard S., 150
Frank, Beryl, 73
Frank, Evelyn W., 54
Frank, Fedora, 510
Frank, H. P., 73
Frank, Herman, 560
Frank, Ivan Cecil, 329
Frank, L. H., 344
Frank, Moshe, 436
Frank, Rachel B., 436
Frank, Ruth S., 104
Frank, S., 644
Frankel, A. H., 326
Frankel, Aaron, 574
Frankel, Edwin R., 25, 177
Frankel, Ellen, 630
Frankel, Ephraim, 100, 259, 439
Frankel, Hertz, 50
Frankel, Hiram D., 464
Frankel, J., 188
Frankel, Max, 172, 251, 265, 495
Frankel, P., 391, 648
Frankel, Reuben, 38
Frankel, Theodore, 578
Frankfort, Henri, 631
Frankland, A. E., 510
Franklin, Leo, 318
Franklin, Leo L., 147
Franklin, Leo M., 458, 459

Franzblau, Abraham, 11, 73, 86, 113, 119, 128, 147, 232, 245, 248, 260, 386, 525, 540; literature on, 294
Frazier, Nancy, 622
Frazin, Lester A., 125
Fredman, Ruth Gruber, 435
Freedman, Joseph L., 411
Freehof, Florence, 35
Freehof, Lillian S., 50, 116, 136
Freehof, Solomon B., 49, 50, 95, 107, 108, 111, 159, 336, 506, 527, 587, 598; literature on, 294
Freeman, Elayne, 99
Freeman, Grace, 111
Freeman, Julian, 357
Freeman, Moses, 501
Freeman, Mrs. Edward M., 381
Freeman, Samuel D., 162, 368, 391
Freeman, Susan, 633
Freestone, Julie, 621, 636
Freid, Jacob, 61
Freidenreich, Fradle, 13, 55, 90, 99, 125, 148, 166, 185, 251, 256, 310, 361, 381, 418, 553, 557, 609
Freidman, Reena Sigman, 367
Freidus, Abraham S., 613
Freie Arbeiter Shtimme, 347
Frenkel, L., 309
Freudenberg, I. G., 329
Freudenheim, Tom L., 642
Freudenheim, Tom W., 669
Freudenstein, Eric G., 632
Freund, Charles J., 123
Freund, Iser L., 32
Freund, Michael, 348
Freund, Richard A., 621
Frey, J. S. C. F., 339
Frickles, Anita A., 19
Fridkus, Ari Lloyd, 267
Fried, Haya Rachel Greenberg, 318

Fried, Irving, 179, 183, 189
Fried, Jacob, 178, 353, 411
Friedberg, Lillian, 505
Friedenberg, Albert M., 455, 468
Friedenberg, Robert V., 640
Friedenwald, Harry, 574
Friedl, Berthold C., 437
Friedland, Abraham, 81, 265, 497–98, 574, 575; literature on, 294
Friedland, H. A., 492
Friedland, I., 424
Friedlander, Albert H. (Henry), 97, 99, 101
Friedlander, Dov, 182, 634
Friedlander, Gertrude, 477
Friedlander, Israel, 287, 351, 482; literature on, 294
Friedlander, Saul, 97
Friedman, Alfred, 88
Friedman, Armin, 323
Friedman, Audrey, 58, 554. *See* Marcus, Audrey Friedman
Friedman, Barry Roger, 26
Friedman, Chaim, 513
Friedman, Dayle A., 646
Friedman, Esther, 637
Friedman, Florence B., 33
Friedman, Hillel, 191
Friedman, Jerome, 130, 631, 636
Friedman, L., 198
Friedman, Lee J., 512
Friedman, Lee M., 336, 454, 455, 457, 473, 475, 509
Friedman, Leslie, 270
Friedman, Maurice, 290, 527
Friedman, Murray, 501, 512
Friedman, Murray J., 179, 182, 195, 201
Friedman, Natalie, 26
Friedman, Norman L., 256, 560, 578
Friedman, Peter B., 665
Friedman, Philip, 97, 306, 609
Friedman, R., 185, 514

Key to Index

7–9: *Types of Jewish Schools* | 10–17: *Curriculum* | 18–29: *Pedagogy* | 30–40: *The Arts* | 41–44: *Bar/Bat Mitzvah* | 45–53: *The Bible* | 54–59: *Early Childhood Education* | 60–65: *Exceptional Children* | 66–68: *Guidance* | 69–85: *Hebrew* | 86–96: *History* | 97–103: *The Holocaust* | 104–6: *School Library* | 107–18: *Life Cycle of a Jew* | 119–22: *Literature* | 123–42: *Mitzvot/Values and Contemporary Issues* | 143–46: *Textbooks* | 147–58: *The High School* | 159–75: *American Jewry and the Land of Israel* | 176–203: *Day School* | 204–31: *Yiddish Secular Schools* | 232–42: *Higher Education* | 245–62: *Administration* | 263–69: *The Teacher* | 270–73: *The Rabbi and Jewish Education* | 274–86: *Conferences in Jewish Education, 1890–1988* | 287–312: *Men and Women Who Influenced Jewish Education* | 317–34: *Historical Background of Jewish Education* | 335–52: *History of Jewish Education in the United States* | 353–78: *The American Jewish Community* | 379–89: *The Home and Jewish Education* | 390–97: *Adult Education* | 398–404: *The Woman's Role and Jewish Education* | 405–8: *Sephardim and Jewish Education* | 409–16: *Youth and Jewish Education* | 417–21: *Camp* | 422–516: *Local Sources for Jewish Education* | 521–23: *Theology and Jewish Education* | 524–32: *Religious Education* | 533–38: *Philosophy of Jewish Education* | 539–44: *Goals of Jewish Education* | 545–50: *Research in Jewish Education* | 551–58: *Change in Jewish Education* | 559–72: *The Social Sciences and Jewish Education* | 573–96: *Assessment* | 597–99: *The Future of Jewish Education* | 600–602: *Bibliographies of Jewish Education in Other Lands* | 603–17: *Bibliographies of Jewish Education and Related Fields in the United States* | 619–70: *Supplement*

Friedman, Reena Seegman, 401
Friedman, Richard, 623
Friedman, Rivka, 79
Friedman, Ruth, 513
Friedman, S. S., 99
Friedman, Saul S., 473
Friedman, Seymour I., 130
Friedman, Theodore, 391, 411
Friend (periodical), 347
Friend, Der (Passaic [N.J.] publication), 470
Friesel, Evyatar, 162
Frimer, Norman E., 125
Frisch, Daniel: literature on, 294
Frisch, Ephraim, 46
Frischer, Rita Berman, 120, 610, 642, 669
Frishberg, I. Z. (Israel), 12, 15, 49, 70, 311; literature on, 294
Frishberg, Mrs. Leo, 163
Frishman, Elyse D., 646
Frishman, Nettie, 611
Fromer, Morris, 348
Fromer, Seymour, 258, 336, 411, 546
Fromm, Annette B., 651
Fromm, Eric, 564
Frost, Carol J., 670
Frost, Shimon, 12, 13, 47, 61, 73, 79, 100, 148, 166, 177, 185, 187, 191, 201, 203, 247, 301, 358, 361, 553, 558, 568, 578, 589, 598
Froug, Charles, 357
Frumkin, Norman, 125, 565
Fryman, Zalman B., 462
Fuchs, Jay Levi, 195
Fuchs-Kreiner, Nancy, 527
Fuld, Stella F., 475
Furer, Max, 470
Furer, Max M., 312, 448
Furfine, Sandy S., 59
Furie, William, 323
Furie, William B., 321, 456, 578
Furman, Frida Kerner, 568, 665
Furman, Phyllis, 411
Furrows, 493
Futorian, Naomi, 298

Gabriel, Michelle, 36
Gafni, Y., 318
Gaines, Marlene S., 430
Gaizband, Cynthia, 635
Gal, Allon, 162, 634
Gale, Joseph, 469
Galin, Meyer, 296
Gallin, Meyer, 463
Gallup, George, Jr., 665
Galperin, Misha, 664

Galupkin, Esther, 198
Gamoran, Emanuel, 7, 10, 12, 14, 46, 47, 49, 51, 54, 70, 81, 83, 86, 88, 105, 113, 119, 128, 150, 178, 232, 250, 263, 265, 289, 290, 294, 295, 298, 301, 304, 310, 321, 326, 329, 336, 360, 363, 370, 379, 392, 397, 449, 495, 511, 534, 539, 545–46, 551–52, 554, 574, 578, 584, 586–88, 597, 605, 615; literature on, 295
Gamoran, Hillel, 73, 79, 295, 627
Gamoran, Mamie, 49, 92, 116, 166, 265, 292, 295, 492
Gampel, Benjamin R., 651
Gands, Solomon, 318
Gannes, Abraham P., 69, 79, 90, 120, 166, 169, 245, 284, 288, 289, 291–93, 297, 298, 302, 306, 308, 309, 329, 357, 365, 368, 376, 418, 437–38, 457, 464, 481, 482, 503, 504, 506, 508, 546, 554, 578, 667
Gans, Herbert J., 370, 447, 478, 560
Gans, Manfred, 182
Gans, Murray Z., 637
Gantz, David, 629
Gantzfried, Solomon, 321
Ganz, Yaffa, 625, 632, 634
Gaon, Moshe David, 614
Gar, Joseph, 609
Garber, Zev, 627, 638
Garfiel, Evelyn, 394, 628
Garfinkel, Helen, 182
Garfinkel, Joseph I., 304
Garfinkel, Marvin H., 135
Garfinkle, Harry, 204
Garte, Sumner H., 411
Gartner, Lloyd P., 336, 376, 427, 477, 496, 497, 516, 578
Garvett, Morris, 357, 461
Garvey, Robert, 58, 116
Garvine, H., 88
Gaster, Theodor H., 42, 43, 113
Gates, Edith B., 113
Gates, Gunther G., 431
Gattman, Eric, 253, 255
Gay, Peter, 642
Gay, Ruth, 92
Geer, Lois, 464
Geffen, Peter A., 148
Geffen, Rela M., 646
Gegenwart, Die, 505
Geggel, E., 501
Geismar, Ludwig, 568
Gelb, Leah S., 485
Gelb, Sh., 463

Gelbart, Frances S., 55
Gelbart, Frances Spitzer: literature on, 295
Gelbart, Gershon, 7, 469, 492; literature on, 295
Gelbart, Michael, 213
Gelberd, Howard, 667
Gelfand, Mitchell, 426
Gelfand, Sidney, 105
Gelfar, L., 436
Gelin, James A., 457
Gell, C., 478
Geller, Bonnie S., 61
Geller, Joshua, 131, 140, 527
Geller, Todres, 443
Geller, Victor B., 188
Gellert, Charles Lawrence, 33, 606
Gellman, Leo, 159
Gelman, Reuben, 191
Gendler, Carol, 467
Gendler, E. E., 125
Gendler, Everett, 632, 633
Generations (periodical), 451
Gennert, Pamela, 61
Genser, Moshe, 73
Gentile, Michael, 131
Gerard, Bert, 527
Gerard, Bert S., 153
Gerber, Jane S., 651
German, Joseph, 22
Gerson-Kiwi, E., 37
Gersh, Harry, 116
Gershenzon, R., 99
Gersten, Leon, 131
Gerstle, Brad, 527
Gertel, E. B., 120
Gertel, Eliot B., 131
Gertel, Elliot B., 401, 522
Gertman, Stuart A., 13, 27, 28, 47, 55, 145, 546, 554
Gevirtz, Stanley, 47
Gewirtz, Eliezer, 612
Gewirtz, Max, 247
Gewirtz, Shimon, 36
Gezari, Temima, 32, 39, 58, 59, 379, 489
Giese, James Richard, 433
Gifter, Mordecai, 191, 195
Gilbert, Arthur, 61, 527
Gilbert, Martin, 101, 627
Gilbreath, Stuart H., 270
Gillette, Robert H., 598
Gillman, Neil, 154, 628, 662
Gillman, Neil G., 418
Gingold, Barbara, 635
Gingold, Pinchos, 207, 208, 210, 212, 216, 217, 219, 220, 223, 574; literature on, 295

INDEX

Ginsberg, Louis, 512, 513
Ginsberg, Marvell, 55, 443, 624
Ginsberg, Morris B., 36, 552
Ginsberg, Ruth, 32
Ginsberg, Sara, 429
Ginsburg, Elliot K., 669
Ginsburg, Lenore, 47
Ginsburgh, Stanley, 409
Ginsburgh, Sylvan J., 259, 329
Ginzberg, Eli, 372, 560
Ginzberg, Louis, 293, 308, 322, 334, 397; literature on, 295
Ginzberg, M., 484
Ginzberg, Sh., 363
Gitele, Tobey B., 613
Githon, Naftali, 330
Gitin, Louis, 472
Gittelsohn, Roland B. (Ronald), 26, 108, 126, 128, 131, 147, 152, 156, 248, 294, 401, 411, 525, 527, 565, 578, 589, 621, 622, 631, 662
Gittelson, Abraham J., 88, 182, 185, 287, 418, 438, 624, 646
Gittleman, Sol, 386
Gittler, Joseph B., 125, 560
Gladstein, Laura, 115
Gladstein, Sally S., 191
Gladstone, Jacob, 98, 205, 217, 220, 293, 297, 349, 411, 613
Glantz, A., 205, 484
Glantz-Leyelis, A., 205
Glanz, Aaron, 283
Glanz, Rudolph, 423, 424, 430, 475, 512, 608
Glaser, Joseph B., 662
Glasman, Naftali, 248
Glasner, S., 565
Glasner, Samuel, 10, 13, 19, 73, 79, 152, 178, 245, 392, 554, 560
Glass, Charlotte, 265
Glasser, Benis, 42
Glasser, Harry A., 131, 247, 527
Glassman, Barbara, 73

Glassman, Leo M., 159
Glassman, Naftaly, 329
Glatstein, Harry N., 10
Glatstein, Jacob. *See* Gladstone, Jacob
Glatstein, Zevi, 279, 282
Glatzer, Nahum N., 308
Glatzer, Shoshana, 166, 265, 483, 619, 623, 635
Glazer, B. Benedict, 124, 152, 525, 530
Glazer, Morris, 530
Glazer, Nathan, 478, 560
Glazer, Simon, 448, 465, 499
Glazier, Jack, 448, 656
Glazman, Sh., 223
Gleaner, The (San Francisco publication), 432
Gleicher, David, 656
Glenn, Menahem G., 291, 303, 306, 307, 308, 310, 486, 492, 502, 608; literature on, 295
Glicenstein, Enrico, 444
Glick, M., 263
Glick, Michael, 627
Glick, Seymour, 195
Glickman, Carl D., 245
Glickman, Jacob, 267
Glickman, Leah, 187
Glicksberg, Abraham A., 22, 195, 323
Glicksberg, Charles I., 411
Glicksman, David, 407
Glicksman, William, 99, 207, 212, 578
Glickstein, Natalie H., 437
Gliner, Lewis, 625
Gliner, Robert Victor, 568
Glinert, Joan, 32
Glinert, Lewis, 32
Globe, Leah A., 42
Glosser, Joanne Katz, 113, 131
Glosser, Larry, 501
Glozman, Sholem, 503
Gluck, Peggy Isaak, 286

Glueck, Nelson, 585
Glueckl von Hamil, 323
Glushakov, A. D., 451
Glustrom, Simon, 156, 381, 386
Glustron, S., 125
Godshaw, Alfred T., 153
Goelman, Elazar, 73, 100, 234, 237, 267, 284, 288, 290–92, 302, 306, 336, 470, 640; literature on, 295
Goelman, Eliezer, 119
Goering, Violet, 509–10
Goff, Ronald H., 150
Goichberg, I., 209, 225
Goitein, Sh. D., 47, 321, 323
Golant, M., 391
Gold, Abraham, 91
Gold, Charles H., 36
Gold, H., 225
Gold, I., 205
Gold, Manuel, 47, 250
Gold, Milton J., 182
Gold, P. K., 24
Gold, Steven J., 654
Goldberg, A., 212, 220, 276, 568
Goldberg, A. R., 435
Goldberg, Ari Y., 653
Goldberg, Ben Zion, 178, 205, 220, 326, 349, 409, 445
Goldberg, David, 458, 482
Goldberg, G., 213, 565
Goldberg, Hannah L., 166
Goldberg, Harvey E., 651
Goldberg, Henry R., 148, 177, 178, 234, 249, 259, 361; literature on, 296
Goldberg, Hillel, 237, 298
Goldberg, I., 204, 574
Goldberg, Ira S., 605
Goldberg, Irving L., 511
Goldberg, Isaac, 423, 472
Goldberg, Israel, 91, 490
Goldberg, Jack Roy, 478
Goldberg, Janet, 455
Goldberg, Mark F., 554

Key to Index

7–9: *Types of Jewish Schools* | 10–17: *Curriculum* | 18–29: *Pedagogy* | 30–40: *The Arts* | 41–44: *Bar/Bat Mitzvah* | 45–53: *The Bible* | 54–59: *Early Childhood Education* | 60–65: *Exceptional Children* | 66–68: *Guidance* | 69–85: *Hebrew* | 86–96: *History* | 97–103: *The Holocaust* | 104–6: *School Library* | 107–18: *Life Cycle of a Jew* | 119–22: *Literature* | 123–42: *Mitzvot/Values and Contemporary Issues* | 143–46: *Textbooks* | 147–58: *The High School* | 159–75: *American Jewry and the Land of Israel* | 176–203: Day School* | 204–31: *Yiddish Secular Schools* | 232–42: *Higher Education* | 245–62: *Administration* | 263–69: *The Teacher* | 270–73: *The Rabbi and Jewish Education* | 274–86: *Conferences in Jewish Education, 1890–1988* | 287–312: *Men and Women Who Influenced Jewish Education* | 317–34: *Historical Background of Jewish Education* | 335–52: *History of Jewish Education in the United States* | 353–78: *The American Jewish Community* | 379–89: *The Home and Jewish Education* | 390–97: *Adult Education* | 398–404: *The Woman's Role and Jewish Education* | 405–8: *Sephardim and Jewish Education* | 409–16: *Youth and Jewish Education* | 417–21: *Camp* | 422–516: *Local Sources for Jewish Education* | 521–23: *Theology and Jewish Education* | 524–32: *Religious Education* | 533–38: *Philosophy of Jewish Education* | 539–44: *Goals of Jewish Education* | 545–50: *Research in Jewish Education* | 551–58: *Change in Jewish Education* | 559–72: *The Social Sciences and Jewish Education* | 573–96: *Assessment* | 597–99: *The Future of Jewish Education* | 600–602: *Bibliographies of Jewish Education in Other Lands* | 603–17: *Bibliographies of Jewish Education and Related Fields in the United States* | 619–70: *Supplement*

INDEX

Goldberg, Martin, 176, 336
Goldberg, Nathan, 326, 409, 488, 560
Goldberg, Robert Alan, 661
Goldberg, S. P., 353
Goldberg, Simcha R., 648
Goldberg, Stella, 386
Goldberg, W. A., 441
Goldberger, A., 227
Goldblath, Maurice, 379
Goldblatt, Charles Israel, 160
Goldblum, Chaim, 427
Goldblum, Henry, 626
Goldburg, Norman M., 178
Golden, Harry, 125, 439, 475, 493, 509
Golden, Hyman, 81
Golden, Patti, 113, 381
Goldenberg, Bernard, 179, 191, 196
Goldenberg, David M., 642
Goldenberg, Robert, 620
Goldenberg, Rose L., 381
Goldenholz, Gideon M., 448
Goldfarb, I., 37
Goldfarb, Jack, 627
Goldfarb, Samuel E., 37, 38
Goldfarb, William B., 370, 540
Goldflam, Dov, 619, 636
Goldgraber, Elizabeth, 329
Goldhammer, Douglas, 61
Goldhammer, Samuel, 496
Goldin, Alice, 58
Goldin, Barbara Diamond, 620
Goldin, Grace, 620
Goldin, Hyman, 116
Goldin, I. E., 234
Goldin, Judah, 13, 234, 270, 620
Goldman, Bertram, 606
Goldman, Elliot, 450
Goldman, Emanuel, 73, 245, 311, 455, 668
Goldman, Frederick, 651
Goldman, Henry, 66
Goldman, Israel, 10, 574
Goldman, Israel M., 251, 392, 394, 508
Goldman, Joel, 635
Goldman, Lee Y., 534
Goldman, Lucille W., 10
Goldman, M. R., 505
Goldman, Mark N., 150
Goldman, Maurice, 428
Goldman, May W., 654
Goldman, Mrs. Bernard (Norma), 657
Goldman, Nahum, 162, 282, 297
Goldman, Norman Saul, 24
Goldman, Robert, 73, 413

Goldman, Sh., 497
Goldman, Shalom, 625
Goldman, Solomon, 45, 52, 99, 166–67, 251, 323, 444, 598, 635, 640, 666; literature on, 296
Goldman, Sylvia, 36, 70, 361, 546
Goldman, Yehuda, 11, 22, 110
Goldmann, Jack B., 424
Goldmeier, Harold, 381
Goldmintz, Jay, 636
Goldoftas, M., 211
Goldreich, G., 61
Goldreich, Gloria, 120
Goldress, Leslie, 108
Goldrich, G., 578
Goldscheider, Calvin, 508, 560, 622, 660, 665
Goldscheider, Frances, 665
Goldschmidt, J., 329
Goldsmith, Bernard, 394
Goldsmith, Emanuel, 640
Goldsmith, Emanuel S., 204, 312, 638
Goldsmith, Harry, 340
Goldstein, Albert E., 114, 257
Goldstein, Alice, 645, 649, 660, 663
Goldstein, Belle J., 160
Goldstein, David A., 271
Goldstein, Fabian, 259
Goldstein, Fanny, 610, 616
Goldstein, Gabriel, 631
Goldstein, I., 107
Goldstein, Ira, 502
Goldstein, Israel, 292, 357, 475, 481
Goldstein, Leonard J., 434
Goldstein, Mark, 250
Goldstein, Martin, 61, 131, 150, 153, 217, 381, 469, 490
Goldstein, Michael, 497
Goldstein, P. R., 468
Goldstein, Richard K., 438
Goldstein, Rose B., 38
Goldstein, Sh., 220
Goldstein, Sheldon, 108
Goldstein, Sidney, 457, 508, 560, 643, 660, 665
Goldstein, Sidney I., 131
Goldstein, Stephen K., 347
Goldwasser, I. Edwin, 475
Goldy, Robert G., 662
Golinkin, Noah, 42, 105, 436, 625
Gollancz, Herman, 318
Golomb, Abraham, 167, 178, 207, 208, 210, 211, 215, 217, 218, 220, 223, 300, 323, 329, 534, 578, 588; literature on, 296

Golomb, Deborah Grand, 399
Golovensky, David I., 195
Golovensky, D. I., 565
Golub, Ellen, 120
Golub, Jacob J., 516
Golub, Jacob S., 10–12, 19, 27, 34, 54, 87, 88, 91, 94, 105, 113, 120, 245, 255, 263, 271, 293–95, 301, 302, 305, 363, 409, 418, 444, 485, 525, 539, 542, 545, 552, 568, 574, 575, 584, 586, 587, 590, 605–7, 610; literature on, 296
Golub, Rose L., 116, 379
Goobkin, I., 211, 214, 228, 295
Goodblatt, Morris, 574
Goode, Selma, 657
Goodelman, Israel, 227
Goodis, Karen-Lipshutz, 135
Goodis, Sally, 131
Goodman, Abram V., 11, 119, 347, 451, 500, 509
Goodman, Hannah Grad, 26, 50, 92, 603, 606
Goodman, Isaac M., 411
Goodman, Jerry, 25
Goodman, L. E., 663
Goodman, Martin, 665
Goodman, Mrs. Abram V., 11, 119
Goodman, Nathaniel, 67, 357
Goodman, Philip, 26, 91, 113, 279, 392, 394, 418
Goodman, Robert, 105, 109, 116, 167, 173
Goodman, Roberta L., 631, 647, 648, 664
Goodman, Ruth, 535
Goodman, Saul, 205, 207, 213–15, 218, 220, 223, 279, 302, 305, 412, 488, 585, 598
Goodman, Y., 589
Goodnick, Benjamin, 80
Goodnick, Bernard, 256
Goodside, Samuel, 182, 185–86, 483
Goodwin, George M., 656
Goor, Donald, 631
Gopstein, Alizah, 79, 288
Gordis, Robert, 30, 45, 52, 107, 113, 125–26, 177, 178, 191, 367, 381, 472, 488, 535, 578, 588, 631, 632, 662
Gordon, Abba, 220
Gordon, Aharon David, 296
Gordon, Albert I., 379, 409, 463, 561
Gordon, Cyrus H., 45
Gordon, George J.: literature on, 296

689

Gordon, Haim, 527, 535
Gordon, Hirsch L., 552, 574
Gordon, Joel, 73
Gordon, Louis: literature on, 296
Gordon, Macy Aaron, 321
Gordon, Milton J., 568
Gordon, Milton M., 561
Gordon, Miriam, 46, 381
Gordon, Samuel, 357
Gordon, Sh. L., 46
Gordon, Sol, 25, 621
Gordon, Susan, 148, 256, 259
Gordon, Theodore H., 412, 657
Gordon, Uri, 634
Gordon, Whitney H., 448, 565
Gordon, Yosi, 73, 464
Goren, Arthur A., 304, 482
Goren, B., 35
Gorenstein (Goren), Arthur, 482
Gorin, Paul, 13
Gorodetzer, Philip, 19, 412
Gorr, A., 250
Gorr, Alan, 589
Gorwitz, Kurt, 465
Gottfried, Z., 430
Gottheil, Richard, 613
Gottheil, Richard J. H., 160
Gottlieb, Albert S., 245
Gottlieb, Lynn, 61
Gottlieb, Malke, 215
Gottschalk, Alfred, 270, 287, 642
Gottschalk, Shimon, 585
Gould, J., 561
Graber, Howard M., 131, 466
Grabla-Valetsky, Tzirl, 213
Grad, Edna, 80
Grad, Eli, 153, 154, 245, 255, 258, 267, 361, 382, 459, 554, 578, 640, 641
Grade, Chaim, 122, 323
Graeber, I., 578
Graeber, Isacque, 561
Graeber, Isaque A., 616
Graetz, Heinrich, 86
Graf, Gil, 429

Graff, George P., 458
Graff, Gil, 645
Grama, Israel, 491
Grand, Samuel, 32, 34, 73, 79, 91, 92, 160, 162, 163, 172, 247, 251, 280, 295, 336, 368, 379, 448, 457, 554, 561
Grand, Tamar, 32, 58, 73, 116, 172
Grant, Arnold, 67
Grant, Ch., 210
Grant, Hyman, 227
Gratz, Rebecca, 340; literature on, 296–97
Gratz College, 503
Graubart, Alexander, 527
Graubart, Judah L., 412
Graubart, Noel, 511
Graubert, David, 401
Grayzel, Solomon, 89, 92, 94, 156, 236, 298, 353, 386, 609
Graziani, Bernice, 348
Greater Framingham Federation, 457
Greater Hartford Jewish Federation, 434
Greater Phoenix Jewish News, 423, 653
Greeley, Andrew M., 125
Green, A. S., 382
Green, Alan S., 87, 113, 382, 392
Green, Arthur, 107, 126, 401, 455, 620, 633, 662
Green, Barry H., 113
Green, Gerald, 98
Green, H. W., 496
Green, Henry A., 436
Green, Kathy, 19, 32, 55, 59, 385, 554, 610, 631
Green, P. G., 126
Green, Roberta M., 61
Greenbaum, A. A., 614
Greenbaum, Joseph, 563
Greenberg, B. D., 379
Greenberg, Barbara, 58, 61, 607

Greenberg, Blu, 98, 382, 401, 403, 589, 616
Greenberg, Cheryl, 143
Greenberg, Evelyn Levow, 435
Greenberg, Harold S., 100
Greenberg, Hayim, 167, 174, 223; literature on, 297
Greenberg, Herbert, 58, 61
Greenberg, Irving, 126, 238, 412, 415, 522, 546, 578, 629; literature on, 297
Greenberg, Louis S., 303
Greenberg, M., 182, 195, 412
Greenberg, Marilyn S., 513
Greenberg, Melanie Hope, 629
Greenberg, Menachem, 186
Greenberg, Meyer, 409, 412, 554
Greenberg, Moshe, 45, 48, 52
Greenberg, Rose, 452
Greenberg, Samuel, 443
Greenberg, Shlomo, 48, 272
Greenberg, Sidney, 42
Greenberg, Sidney J., 87
Greenberg, Simon, 7, 11, 69, 70, 81, 107, 109, 126, 153, 167, 177, 186, 191, 234, 270, 272, 273, 321, 336, 357, 360, 367, 392, 394, 525, 528, 535, 539, 543, 546, 554, 585–57; literature on, 297
Greenberg, Sydney J., 427, 431
Greenberg, Yisrael, 637
Greenblum, Joseph, 570
Greene, Walter Martin, 181
Greenfield, Howard, 42
Greenfield, M., 182
Greenfield, Marcus, 109
Greenfield, William P., 379
Greenfield, Yeshayahu, 187
Greengard, Roberta, 433
Greenspan, Ellen A., 635
Greenspan, Jay Seth, 32
Greenspon, Bennett H., 329
Greenstein, Edward L., 620, 624
Greenstein, Harry, 128, 588

Key to Index

7–9: *Types of Jewish Schools* | 10–17: *Curriculum* | 18–29: *Pedagogy* | 30–40: *The Arts* | 41–44: *Bar/Bat Mitzvah* | 45–53: *The Bible* | 54–59: *Early Childhood Education* | 60–65: *Exceptional Children* | 66–68: *Guidance* | 69–85: *Hebrew* | 86–96: *History* | 97–103: *The Holocaust* | 104–6: *School Library* | 107–18: *Life Cycle of a Jew* | 119–22: *Literature* | 123–42: *Mitzvot/Values and Contemporary Issues* | 143–46: *Textbooks* | 147–58: *The High School* | 159–75: *American Jewry and the Land of Israel* | 176–203: *Day School* | 204–31: *Yiddish Secular Schools* | 232–42: *Higher Education* | 245–62: *Administration* | 263–69: *The Teacher* | 270–73: *The Rabbi and Jewish Education* | 274–86: *Conferences in Jewish Education, 1890–1988* | 287–312: *Men and Women Who Influenced Jewish Education* | 317–34: *Historical Background of Jewish Education* | 335–52: *History of Jewish Education in the United States* | 353–78: *The American Jewish Community* | 379–89: *The Home and Jewish Education* | 390–97: *Adult Education* | 398–404: *The Woman's Role and Jewish Education* | 405–8: *Sephardim and Jewish Education* | 409–16: *Youth and Jewish Education* | 417–21: *Camp* | 422–516: *Local Sources for Jewish Education* | 521–23: *Theology and Jewish Education* | 524–32: *Religious Education* | 533–38: *Philosophy of Jewish Education* | 539–44: *Goals of Jewish Education* | 545–50: *Research in Jewish Education* | 551–58: *Change in Jewish Education* | 559–72: *The Social Sciences and Jewish Education* | 573–96: *Assessment* | 597–99: *The Future of Jewish Education* | 600–602: *Bibliographies of Jewish Education in Other Lands* | 603–17: *Bibliographies of Jewish Education and Related Fields in the United States* | 619–70: *Supplement*

INDEX

Greenstein, R. R., 579
Greenstone, Joseph, 34
Greenstone, Julius H., 7, 113, 117, 147, 233, 267, 293, 336, 360, 433, 453, 502, 506, 525; literature on, 297
Greenwald, Eli B., 270
Greenwald, Herbert S., 448
Greenwood, Dru, 646
Greenzweig, Gene, 438, 464
Greifer, Julian, 367, 368, 503
Gribetz, Edith R., 658
Gribitz, Beverly, 89
Gries, M. J., 496
Griffel, Rhina, 382
Griffen, William L., 131
Gringardas, Nordchajus, 287
Grinstein, Hyman B., 160, 176, 234, 336, 475, 478, 481; literature on, 297
Grishaver, Joel, 22, 116, 382, 640
Grishaver, Joel Lurie, 23, 109, 111, 247, 265, 444, 624, 645
Grob, Paul, 191
Grollman, Earl A., 23, 26, 27, 143, 145, 382
Grosberg, Julius, 657
Gross, Abraham, 651
Gross, Alexander, 191, 305
Gross, Barbara, 382
Gross, David C., 628
Gross, Maurice B., 182, 191
Gross, Michael, 625
Gross, Morris B., 19, 56, 67, 565
Gross, Naphtali, 225
Gross, Rita M., 401
Gross, Sukey, 198
Gross, Ted, 253
Gross, Victor, 248
Grossbard, Marilyn, 499
Grossberg, Sidney H., 459
Grossfield, A., 220, 484
Grossfield, Avery J., 561
Grossman, Atina, 642
Grossman, Barney, 48
Grossman, Cheryl S., 120
Grossman, Hanna, 71
Grossman, Henry, 25
Grossman, Herman E., 382
Grossman, Heshy, 636
Grossman, Jacob B., 110
Grossman, Jacob D., 81
Grossman, Judith E., 619
Grossman, Lawrence, 645
Grossman, Louis, 19, 232, 323, 346, 525, 552
Grossman, Mordecai, 178, 199
Grossman, R., 589
Grossman, Reuben, 38
Grossman, Samuel, 479, 505
Grossman, Samuel S., 489
Grossman, Yosef, 637
Grossman-Sherman, Hannah, 394
Grover, Judy, 120
Groyser Kundes, Der, 493
Gruber, Ruth, 248
Gruen, George E., 651
Gruenberg, Sandra S., 182
Gruenwald, Uri, 323
Gruesser, M. Jeanne, 126
Grunfeld, I., 298
Grunfeld-Rosenbaum, Judith, 309
Grunwald, Emily, 56
Grusd, Edward E., 348
Grysman, Charles O., 637
Gubbay, Lucien, 651
Gudemann, Moritz, 321, 324, 601
Gumbiner, Abigail, 394
Gumbiner, Joseph A., 92
Gundersheimer, Ernest M., 298
Gup, Eva, 105
Gurim, Sara, 100
Gurin, Arnold, 357, 454, 459
Gurko, Miriam, 636
Gurock, Jeffrey S., 270, 475–76, 523, 608, 637, 638
Gurov, Jacob, 427, 443
Gursky, Samuel, 23
Gurvis, Laura Kizner, 624
Gutheim, J. K., 341
Gutmacher, Adolf, 452
Gutman, Jacob, 256
Gutman, Joseph, 30, 107, 606
Gutman, Renana, 641
Gutstein, Morris, 441, 446
Guttman, Julius, 298
Guttman, Miriam H., 485
Guttman, Nahum, 167
Guttstein, Morris A., 507

Haber, Leo, 81
Haberman, Joshua O., 468, 666
Haberman, Paul W, 478
Habif, Isaac N., 439
Hachen, David S., 19, 153, 178, 394, 535, 554, 579
Hacker, Louis M., 477
Hacohen, Devora, 407
Hacohen, Menahem, 407
Hadassah, 603, 607
Hadassah Magazine (Had Mag), 585
Hadda, Janet, 657
Haddad, Heskel M., 407
Hadef, Helen B., 665
Hadoar, 150, 162, 207, 264, 427, 493
HaDoar la No'ar, 121
Hagedorn, Leah, 493
HaGesher, 445
Haggadah, 341
Hagy, James William, 660
HaHinukh, 253
Hailperin, H., 307
Hailperin, Harriet, 150
Hailpern, E., 506
Haim, Aviva, 635
Halvri, 346
Halvri HaKatan, 443
HaKerem, 457
Hakimian, Leah, 113, 167, 256, 382, 554, 579
Haklai, Michael, 329
Halberstam, Chaim, 195
Halel's, Shlomo, 233
Halevi, Abraham Zvi, 288
Halevi, Ben Israel, 635
Halevi, Menachem, 296
Halevi, Meshullam, 600
Halevi, Mordecai, 48, 71, 73, 277, 287, 288, 290, 292–95, 298, 299, 307, 311, 312, 379, 495, 503, 535, 540; literature on, 297
Halevi-Levin, I., 329
Halevy, Zvi, 323
Halkin, A. Sh., 293
Halkin, Abraham S., 69, 79, 83, 305, 392, 579
Halkin, Abraham Sh., 87
Halkin, Simon, 69, 120
Hall, G. Stanley, 236
Hallberg, Carl V., 516
Hallo, William, 238
Hallo, William W., 642
Hallowicz, George, 176
Halper, Jeffrey Lewis, 329
Halper, Sharon, 646
Halperin, Moses P., 30
Halperin, Samuel, 162
Halpern, Ben, 160, 162, 297, 561, 568, 579
Halpern, Harry, 179
Halpern, I., 131
Halpern, Irving, 609
Halpern, Jacob I., 639
Halpern, Moyshe Leyb, 479
Halpert, Max, 478
Halpert, Mrs. A., 136, 198
Halporn, Roberta, 105
Halzel, Michael, 186
Hamburger, Lewis D., 418, 579
Hamelsdorf, Ora, 616
Hammer, Reuven, 61
Hammer, Robert A., 77
Hammer, Robert Alan, 48
Hammer, Zevulun, 167

INDEX

Hanan, Rubin Morris, 422
Hanapolski, M. B., 71
Handel, Yitzchak, 189, 382, 640
Handelman, Sholom, 535
Handelman, Susan, 646
Handler, Zevi, 251
Handlin, Mary F., 347
Handlin, Oscar, 347, 370, 561
Hanhala Artzit-B'nei Akiva of North America, 112
Hannover, Nathan Note, 333
Hansen, M. L., 561
HaPardes, 447
Hapgood, Hutchins, 399, 477, 479
HaPisgah, 447, 454
Haragaal, Ya'aqov Halevi, 651
Haramati, Amnon, 61
Haramati, Shlomo, 73, 77, 81, 84, 294, 396, 490
Harap, Louis, 120
Harari, Raymond, 407
Harlow, Jules, 92, 109
Harman, A., 568
Harper, Sheila Zarb, 386
Harr, Sheldon, 528
Harris, A., 561
Harris, Hannah, 56, 58
Harris, Louis, 478
Harris, R., 346
Harris, S. W., 153
Harris, Sarah, 342
Harris, Victor, 440
Harris, Zevi H., 481
Hart, Elizabeth J., 54
Hart, Gustavus N., 500
Hart, H., 341
Hart, Merrily F., 628
Harte, Patricia Cipora, 664
Hartford Jewish Ledger, 433
Hartman, David, 126, 386
Hartman, Eliyahu E., 256, 579
Hartman, Emanuel, 167
Hartman, Geoffrey, 238
Hartmann, Sidney A., 425

Hartogensis, Benjamin H., 451, 452
Hartstein, Jacob, 233
Hartstein, Jacob I., 92, 197, 236, 288, 355, 361, 477, 481, 491, 537, 608
Hartstein, Jacob L., 587
Hashierg, Gertrude, 452
Hass, Alizah, 554
Hassan, Aron, 426
Hatch, Orrin, 627
Ha-Toren, 493
Ha-Tsofeh, 344
Hatzair, 454
Hauptman, Judith, 401, 650
Hauslich, A., 329
Hausner, Gideon, 98
Havivi, Mrs. Moshe, 56
Hayim of Volozhin: literature on, 297
Haykhal Ivriah, 447
Hays, Mortimer, 574
Hazan, Bertha, 330
Heavenrich, Elaine, 61
Hebrew, The, 432
Hebrew Educational Alliance, 433
Hebrew Education Society of Philadelphia, 351, 502
Hebrew High School (Chicago), 446
Hebrew Leader, 342
Hebrew Observer, 432
Hebrew Principals' Association, 12
Hebrew Principals Association of Greater New York, 486
Hebrew Principals Association of New York, 489
Hebrew Review, 496
Hebrew Sabbath School Visitor, 496
Hebrew Standard, 399, 472
Hebrew Teachers Union of New York and Vicinity, 486
Hebrew Theological College, 446

Hebrew University, 169, 329
Hebrew Watchman, 510
Hechalutz Organization of America, 160
Hecht, A. D., 477
Hecht, Abraham B., 182
Hecht, David, 510
Hecht, Emanuel, 343
Hecht, Lester S., 501
Hecht, S., 346, 515
Hecht, Sigmund, 346
Hecht, Simon, 344
Heckelman, Dvorah, 491, 492
Heckelman, Tziporah, 105
Hefterman, A., 259, 318
Heilbraun, Judith, 61
Heilbraun, Regina, 109
Heilbut, Anthony, 642
Heiligman, Avron C., 464
Heilman, Samuel C., 392
Heilman, Samuel E., 561
Heilpern, Jehiel: literature on, 297
Heilpern, Minna, 619
Heimowicz, Rachel Baron, 441
Heimowitz, Joseph, 158, 191, 434, 483
Heine, Heinrich, 50
Heineman, David E., 458, 459
Hektin, Shalom, 485
Helen Stein Institute, 498
Heller, Bernard, 128, 525
Heller, David, 663
Heller, James G., 311, 495, 496
Heller, Max, 298, 450
Heller, Miriam, 485
Heller, Robert I., 357
Hellerstein, Kathryn A., 480
Heilman, Peter, 98
Helmreich, William B., 195, 238, 293, 301, 627
Hendricks, Theodore W., 452
Hendrix, Nancy, 510
Hendry, Charles E., 124
Henkin, Alan, 61

Key to Index

7–9: *Types of Jewish Schools* | 10–17: *Curriculum* | 18–29: *Pedagogy* | 30–40: *The Arts* | 41–44: *Bar/Bat Mitzvah* | 45–53: *The Bible* | 54–59: *Early Childhood Education* | 60–65: *Exceptional Children* | 66–68: *Guidance* | 69–85: *Hebrew* | 86–96: *History* | 97–103: *The Holocaust* | 104–6: *School Library* | 107–18: *Life Cycle of a Jew* | 119–22: *Literature* | 123–42: *Mitzvot/Values and Contemporary Issues* | 143–46: *Textbooks* | 147–58: *The High School* | 159–75: *American Jewry and the Land of Israel* | 176–203: *Day School* | 204–31: *Yiddish Secular Schools* | 232–42: *Higher Education* | 245–62: *Administration* | 263–69: *The Teacher* | 270–73: *The Rabbi and Jewish Education* | 274–86: *Conferences in Jewish Education, 1890–1988* | 287–312: *Men and Women Who Influenced Jewish Education* | 317–34: *Historical Background of Jewish Education* | 335–52: *History of Jewish Education in the United States* | 353–78: *The American Jewish Community* | 379–89: *The Home and Jewish Education* | 390–97: *Adult Education* | 398–404: *The Woman's Role and Jewish Education* | 405–8: *Sephardim and Jewish Education* | 409–16: *Youth and Jewish Education* | 417–21: *Camp* | 422–516: *Local Sources for Jewish Education* | 521–23: *Theology and Jewish Education* | 524–32: *Religious Education* | 533–38: *Philosophy of Jewish Education* | 539–44: *Goals of Jewish Education* | 545–50: *Research in Jewish Education* | 551–58: *Change in Jewish Education* | 559–72: *The Social Sciences and Jewish Education* | 573–96: *Assessment* | 597–99: *The Future of Jewish Education* | 600–602: *Bibliographies of Jewish Education in Other Lands* | 603–17: *Bibliographies of Jewish Education and Related Fields in the United States* | 619–70: *Supplement*

INDEX

Henkin, Anne D., 19, 48
Henkin, Hillel, 256, 434
Hennig, H., 509
Hennig, Helen Kohn, 152
Henoch, C., 565
Henry, Abraham A., 342, 343
Henry, Frances, 642
Henry, H. A., 341
Henry, Jacob, 493
Herberg, Will, 126, 348, 561, 568
Herculano, Alexandre, 651
Heritage-Southwest Jewish Press, 429, 430
Herman, Agnes G., 621
Herman, Dorothy C., 167, 173, 394, 438
Herman, Floyd, 662
Herman, Floyd L., 61
Herman, Jack J., 496
Herman, Menahem, 48, 167
Herman, Simon N., 167, 568, 571, 666
Hernandez, Frances, 652
Herscher, Uri D., 347, 433, 451, 458, 468, 471, 494, 510, 642, 659
Hershan, Stella K., 627
Hershfield, Nathan, 303
Hershinow, Sheldon Jay, 120
Hershman, Morris M., 150
Hershon, Jerome L., 265, 444
Herson, Benjamin, 167, 625
Herstein, Isabell Smith, 32
Hertz, Frankel, 117
Hertz, J. B., 205
Hertz, Joseph H., 45, 111
Hertz, Richard C., 15, 446, 525, 541, 589
Hertzberg, Arthur, 162, 174, 270, 336, 352, 353, 528, 587, 588, 642, 662
Hertzberg, Nat, 423
Hertzberg, Steven, 439
Hertz-Lazorovitz, Rachel, 511
Hertz-Lazorovitz, Reuben, 511
Herxheimer, S., 341
Herzog, Chaim, 329
Herzog, E., 322
Heschel, Abraham, 382
Heschel, Abraham J., 30, 40, 45, 98, 107, 113, 131, 140, 268, 522, 523, 528, 535, 543, 633; literature on, 297–98
Heschel, Susannah, 401
Heskes, Irene, 37, 38, 606
Hessel, Carolyn Starman, 13, 90, 167, 407, 610, 634
Hewitt, Louise Matthews, 451
Hilberg, Raul, 98

Hill, Marilyn Wood, 511
Hillelsohn, Michael J., 257
Hillman, Andy, 382
Himelstein, Schmuel, 248
Himmelfarb, Harold S., 258, 382, 546, 561, 579, 640
Himmelfarb, Milton, 191, 412, 561, 567
Himmelstein, Samuel A., 187, 483
Hinchin, Martin I., 451
Hindus, Milton, 477
Hirsch, B., 189, 191, 579
Hirsch, Ben, 167
Hirsch, Emil, 525
Hirsch, Richard G., 126, 131, 139, 162, 167, 631, 635
Hirsch, Samson Raphael, 117, 124, 318, 323, 333, 388, 632; literature on, 298
Hirschfield, Burt, 172
Hirschowitz, Abraham E., 399
Hirsh, Marilyn, 58
Hirt, Robert S., 255
Hirt-Manheimer, Aron, 382, 396, 412
Hirt-Manheimer, Judith, 382
Histadruth Ivrith of America, 69
Hitch, Norma Schier, 432
Hochbaum, Jerry, 561
Hochberg, Hillel, 80, 154, 157, 265, 586
Hochman, Judith Whitman, 401
Hochstein, Annette, 667
Hochstein, Joshua, 407
Hodes, Phyllis, 209
Hoenig, Martin A., 270
Hoenig, Sidney B. (Steven, Simcha), 186, 233, 291, 307, 394, 401, 568; literature on, 298
Hoffman, B. *See* Tsivion
Hoffman, Carl, 60
Hoffman, Judy, 101, 172
Hoffman, Lawrence, 662
Hoffman, M. N. H., 71
Hoffman, Meinrod L., 46
Hoffman, Paul, 666
Hoffman, Rae D., 73, 77
Hoffmann, Justin, 131, 238, 318, 412, 528, 541, 589
Hoffmann, Yvonne, 621
Hoffnet, N., 182
Hoffseyer, Benjamin, 310
Hofman, Shlomo, 38
Hofstein, Saul, 387
Holdheim, Wolfgang, 642
Holin, Elliot, 382
Holin, Elliot J., 627

Holland, Samuel H., 435
Hollander, Arthur S., 253, 259, 565
Hollander, B., 191
Hollander, Ben, 24, 554
Hollander, Benjamin, 579
Hollander, Carl, 36
Hollander, J., 191
Hollander, J. H., 452
Hollander, Jacob, 452
Hollander, Vicki Lee, 401
Hollender, Betty Rosett, 50
Hollender, C. T., 238
Holtz, Avraham, 177
Holtz, Barry, 107
Holtz, Barry W., 22, 113, 181, 186, 235, 241, 554, 619, 620, 631, 652, 664, 668, 669
Holtz, David K., 528
Holtzberg, Carol S., 621
Home and Education, 226
Honan, Bernard W., 238
Honor, Jennie J., 58
Honor, Leo L., 9, 11, 13, 16, 27, 45, 87, 94, 131, 163, 199, 233, 234, 251, 255, 264, 265, 267, 268, 288, 290, 294, 318, 336, 355, 365, 372–73, 392, 431, 442, 443, 448, 456, 463, 466, 467, 504, 541, 542, 554, 561, 574, 584–86, 588, 590, 599; literature on, 298–99
Hook, Sidney, 300
Hoover, Dwight W., 448
Hopfinger, Jana, 131
Horden, Jack M., 470
Hordes, Stanley M., 658
Horeb, 493
Horn, David, 394
Horn, Ronnie M., 118, 392
Horn, Susan, 357, 644
Hornbein, Marjorie, 433
Hornstein, Shmuel, 329
Horovitz, Moshe, 195, 438
Horowitz, A. L., 233, 365
Horowitz, Bethanie, 329
Horowitz, C. Morris, 255, 258, 363, 478, 561
Horowitz, Cyma, 401
Horowitz, David, 155, 179, 412
Horowitz, David A., 182
Horowitz, I., 382
Horowitz, Irving Louis, 658
Horowitz, Jack, 167, 442, 554, 579
Horowitz, Samuel, 466
Horowitz, Stanley B., 167
Horvitz, David, 508
Horwitt, Pink, 454

Hostein, Lisa, 622
Houston, W. Robert, 247
Howe, Irving, 120, 204, 480
Howitz, Eleanor F., 508
Huberman, S., 353
Huberman, Steven, 426
Hudson, Alan J., 568
Huehner, Leon, 471
Huerta, Carlos C., 627
Huhner, Leon, 399, 437, 438, 450, 454, 476, 494, 509, 512
Humanistic Judaism, 462
Hurvitz, Aharon, 155
Hurvitz, Liane, 329
Hurvitz, Mark, 412
Hurvitz, Nathan, 412, 561
Hurvitz, Shmarya Leib, 525
Hurwich, Louis, 23, 71, 76, 234, 310, 336, 445, 456, 472, 554; literature on, 299
Hurwitz, Ann Ricki, 626
Hurwitz, David S., 459
Hurwitz, Henry, 236, 575
Hurwitz, Hyman, 341
Hurwitz, J., 564
Hurwitz, Joseph Zatzal, 195
Hurwitz, Marc, 323
Hurwitz, Maximilian, 205, 348
Hurwitz, R. S., 475
Hurwitz, Sh., 220, 227, 323
Hurwitz, Solomon, 176
Hurwitz, Sue, 626
Hutler, Albert, 441
Hutner, Yitzchak, 177
Huttenbach, Henry R., 642
Huttler, Rubin, 238
Hyamson, B., 281
Hyamson, D., 221
Hyat, Aaron, 488
Hyfler, Robert, 645
Hyman, Frieda Clark, 89, 92
Hyman, H. Joseph, 355, 453
Hyman, Miriam, 649
Hyman, Paula, 400, 401, 623
Hyman, Paula E., 386

Hyman, Philip, 120
Hyman, Robert S., 358
Hyman, Ruth Salinger, 105
Hyman, Sh., 204
Hymovitz, Kay S., 449
Hymovitz, Leon, 99

I. L. Peretz School, 438
Iddishes Tageblatt, 345
Idelsohn, Abraham Z., 37, 38, 107, 114
Idishe Tegleche Presse, Die, 462
Illiana News, 448
Imber, Naphtali Herz, 346
Imber, Rebbecca, 565
Imber, Rebecca, 392, 489
Impact, 253
Inbar, Efraim, 191
Indelman, A., 213
Indelman, E., 81
Indelman, Elchanan, 120, 306, 491
Indelman, Eliezer, 492
Indelman, Ruchla L., 379
Indiana Jewish Chronicle, 448
Indiana Jewish Historical Society, 447, 448, 656
Indiana Jewish Post and Opinion, 448
Indianapolis Hebrew Congregation, 631
Ingall, Carol K., 19, 42, 89, 116, 392, 639, 645, 651
Ingall, Michael, 639
Inglehart, Babette F., 610
Ingwer, Carmela, 635
Inkling, The, 253
Insich, 493
Institute for Jewish Life, 56, 461, 382
Intermountain Jewish News, 433
International Workers Orden (IWO), 204, 276, 445
Intrater, Aaron, 344, 371, 497, 499, 554; literature on, 299

Iowa Jewish News, 448
Iram, Jacob, 73
Iram, Yaakov, 290, 292
Irlen, Barbara, 382
Irwin, William A., 631
Isaac, F., 189
Isaac, Mel, 42
Isaac Elchanan Yeshiva, 233
Isaacman, Daniel, 223, 282, 284, 418, 420, 579; literature on, 299
Isaacs, Benjamin, 197
Isaacs, Bernard, 294, 461; literature on, 299
Isaacs, David L., 311
Isaacs, Jacob, 198
Isaacs, Leora W., 619, 664, 666
Isaacs, Mel, 619
Isaacs, Nathan, 597
Isaacs, Ronald H., 23, 620
Isaacs, Samuel M., 340
Isaacson, Irma M., 450
Iser, Alexander, 424
Ish Kishor, Judith, 171
Ish-Kishor, Sulamith, 49, 91
Isorov, A., 263
Israel, A. B., 343
Israel, Eric, 99
Israel, Raymond, 107
Israel, Richard J., 23, 126, 189, 358, 412, 528, 568
Israel, Sherry, 19, 131, 455
Israel, state of, 641
Israeli, Eitan, 392, 396
Israeli, Eytan, 267
Israelit, Der, 454
Israelitische Presse, 447
Israel Meir Ha-Kohen: literature on, 299
Israelowitz, Oscar, 476, 477, 658
Israel's Herald, 341
Isser, Natalie, 563
Isser, Stanley, 369
Isserman, Ruth, 114, 257, 552

Key to Index

7–9: *Types of Jewish Schools* I 10–17: *Curriculum* I 18–29: *Pedagogy* I 30–40: *The Arts* I 41–44: *Bar/Bat Mitzvah* I 45–53: *The Bible* I 54–59: *Early Childhood Education* I 60–65: *Exceptional Children* I 66–68: *Guidance* I 69–85: *Hebrew* I 86–96: *History* I 97–103: *The Holocaust* I 104–6: *School Library* I 107–18: *Life Cycle of a Jew* I 119–22: *Literature* I 123–42: *Mitzvot/Values and Contemporary Issues* I 143–46: *Textbooks* I 147–58: *The High School* I 159–75: *American Jewry and the Land of Israel* I 176–203: *Day School* I 204–31: *Yiddish Secular Schools* I 232–42: *Higher Education* I 245–62: *Administration* I 263–69: *The Teacher* I 270–73: *The Rabbi and Jewish Education* I 274–86: *Conferences in Jewish Education, 1890–1988* I 287–312: *Men and Women Who Influenced Jewish Education* I 317–34: *Historical Background of Jewish Education* I 335–52: *History of Jewish Education in the United States* I 353–78: *The American Jewish Community* I 379–89: *The Home and Jewish Education* I 390–97: *Adult Education* I 398–404: *The Woman's Role and Jewish Education* I 405–8: *Sephardim and Jewish Education* I 409–16: *Youth and Jewish Education* I 417–21: *Camp* I 422–516: *Local Sources for Jewish Education* I 521–23: *Theology and Jewish Education* I 524–32: *Religious Education* I 533–38: *Philosophy of Jewish Education* I 539–44: *Goals of Jewish Education* I 545–50: *Research in Jewish Education* I 551–58: *Change in Jewish Education* I 559–72: *The Social Sciences and Jewish Education* I 573–96: *Assessment* I 597–99: *The Future of Jewish Education* I 600–602: *Bibliographies of Jewish Education in Other Lands* I 603–17: *Bibliographies of Jewish Education and Related Fields in the United States* I 619–70: *Supplement*

INDEX

Isseroff, Sampson A. (Shimshon), 19, 48, 74, 150, 167, 247, 489, 490
Itkin, W., 131
Itzkowitz, Benjamin, 326
Ivri, I., 281
Izban, Sh., 217

Jabotinsky, Ze'ev (Vladimir), 76, 418
Jacob, Walter, 99, 294, 528, 642
Jacobs, Betty S., 625
Jacobs, Charles, 619
Jacobs, Ella, 54, 58
Jacobs, Herman, 368, 579
Jacobs, Joseph, 51, 613
Jacobs, Liner Chesnik, 661
Jacobs, Louis, 136, 156, 648, 662
Jacobs, Monty, 655
Jacobs, N. L., 382
Jacobs, Solomon, 342
Jacobs, Steven, 131
Jacobs, Steven Bennet, 89
Jacobs, Steven L., 627
Jacobs, Y., 579
Jacobs, Yaakov, 641
Jacobson, Burt, 107, 109, 148, 635
Jacobson, Daniel, 462
Jacobson, David, 321
Jacobson, Isaac W., 191
Jacobson, Shira, 619
Jacoby, Emil, 133, 167, 428, 429
Jaffa, Herbert, 34
Jaffe, A. J., 441
Jaffe, Bernadette, 172, 528
Jaffe, Philip, 336, 481, 486, 487, 495, 511, 546
Jaffe, Reuven Ralph Martin, 394, 425
Jaffe, Samuel Z., 525, 528
Jakabov, B., 213
Jakobovitz, Immanuel, 126, 178, 192
James, Edmund J. (Edwin), 446, 502
James, Muriel Marshall, 318
Janicot, Michel, 429
Janowsky, Oscar I., 74, 234, 281, 303, 353, 357, 368, 374, 396, 497, 546, 579, 592
Jaret, Beth Gerstel, 634
Jaret, Charles L., 441
Jaskoll, Ira L., 24, 67
Jastrow, Morris, Jr., 160, 501
JEC Bulletin, 488
Jelenko, Edward W., 298
Jenicot, Michel, 655

Jeshurin, Ephim H., 293, 605, 615
Jew, The (periodical), 339
Jewish Academy of Chicago, 446
Jewish Advance, 447
Jewish Advisory Committee for the Texas Centennial Jewish Program, 510
Jewish Advocate, 454, 456, 462, 505
Jewish Agency, 179, 280
Jewish American, 462, 493, 511
Jewish Audio-Visual Review, 253
Jewish Beacon, 511
Jewish Book Council (JBC), 105, 605, 608, 613
Jewish Braille Institute of America, 607
Jewish Braille Review, 61
Jewish Bulletin of the East Bay, 430
Jewish Cemetery Association of Massachusetts, 457
Jewish Chautauquan, 505
Jewish Chautauqua Society, 336
Jewish Chicago, 447
Jewish Child, 121, 443
Jewish Chronicle, 456, 459, 469
Jewish Chronicle of Pittsburgh, 507
Jewish Civic Leader, 457
Jewish Civic Press, 439, 451, 512
Jewish Comment, 454
Jewish Community Center of Central Florida, 438
Jewish Community Center of Dallas, Tex., 661
Jewish Community Center of Metropolitan Houston, Tex., 511
Jewish Community Center of Pittsburgh, 505
Jewish Community Center of St. Joseph County, Ind., 448
Jewish Community Council of Rochester, N.Y., 473
Jewish Community Council of Utica, N.Y., 474
Jewish Community Federation of Cleveland, Ohio, 496–98
Jewish Community Federation of Richmond, Va., 513
Jewish Community News, 447
Jewish Community Press, 429
Jewish Community Voice, 469
Jewish Criterion, 506
Jewish Current Events, 121
Jewish Current News, 505
Jewish Daily Forward, 406

Jewish Day School of Vineland, N.J., 471
Jewish Digest, 61, 433, 512
Jewish Education, 7, 71, 138, 167, 234, 251, 253, 263, 264, 276, 277, 281, 282, 284, 288, 290, 298, 308, 329–30, 355, 357, 361, 365, 368, 428, 440, 461, 482, 505, 543, 579. *See also* Adult Jewish Education; Jewish Education in the United States
Jewish Educational Board of Philadelphia, 503
Jewish Education Association, 469, 492
Jewish Education Association of Newark, N.J., 469
Jewish Education Committee of Greater New York (JEC), 483, 484, 486, 487, 490–93
Jewish Education in the United States (JEUS), 516
Jewish Education News, 281
Jewish Education Newsletter, 555
Jewish Education Service of North America (JESNA), 171, 175, 252, 253, 255, 360, 364, 365, 377, 382, 423, 453, 498, 507, 511, 512, 554, 594, 605, 615, 644. *See also* American Association for Jewish Education; National Board of License
Jewish Education Society of Chicago, 156, 344
Jewish Educator, 647
Jewish Educators Assembly, 252, 253
Jewish Exponent, 505
Jewish Farmer, 493
Jewish Federation Council of Greater Los Angeles, 426
Jewish Federation of Greater Houston, 512
Jewish Federation of Greater Phoenix, 423
Jewish Federation of Greater Seattle, 514
Jewish Federation of Greater Toledo, 498
Jewish Federation of Metropolitan Chicago, 441
Jewish Federation of Nashville and Middle Tennessee, 510
Jewish Federation of Southern Illinois, 447
Jewish Floridian Group, 438
Jewish Folk School (Paterson, N.J.), 470

695

Jewish Folk Schools of America, 208
Jewish Forum, 493
Jewish Frontier, 179, 493, 535, 579, 589
Jewish Herald-Voice, 512
Jewish Historical Society of Michigan, 458
Jewish Historical Society of New Haven, Conn., 434, 655
Jewish Historical Society of Portland, Maine, 451
Jewish Horizon, 470
Jewish Independent, 498
Jewish Journal: Los Angeles, 429; San Francisco, 432; Fort Lauderdale, 437; Shreveport, 451; Highland Park, N.J., 469
Jewish Journal of San Antonio, 512
Jewish Labor Committee, 101
Jewish Leader, 506
Jewish Ledger, 422, 451, 473
Jewish Life, 192, 193, 493, 579
Jewish Media Service, 401
Jewish Messenger, 342, 344
Jewish Messenger of the Pacific, 432
Jewish Monitor, 422
Jewish Morning Journal, 505
Jewish Morning Journal and Daily News, 493
Jewish Museum, 669
Jewish National and University Library, 601
Jewish National Fund (JNF), 101, 165, 609
Jewish National Fund for America, 160
Jewish National Workers Alliance (JNWA), 278, 441, 459. See also Labor Zionist Alliance; Labor Zionist Organization of America
Jewish News, 458, 469
Jewish Observer, 167, 474, 493, 579
Jewish Observer of the East Bay, 430
Jewish Outlook, 433
Jewish Parent, 253
Jewish Population Committee (Charleston, W.Va.), 515
Jewish Post, 470, 506
Jewish Press, 467
Jewish Press and Milwaukee (Wis.) Wochenblat, 515
Jewish Progress, 432
Jewish Publication Society of America (JPS), 37
Jewish Quarterly Review (JQR), 501
Jewish Radical, 425
Jewish Record, 466, 468, 469, 505, 512
Jewish Reporter, 457, 467
Jewish Review, 508
Jewish Review and Observer, 498
Jewish School and Democracy (JSD), 109, 128, 135, 263, 379
Jewish Social Service Association, 476
Jewish Social Service Quarterly (JSSQ), 355
Jewish Social Studies (JSS), 127
Jewish Society for the Deaf, 61
Jewish Spectator, 432, 510
Jewish Standard, 469
Jewish Star, 432
Jewish Teacher, 251. See also Compass
Jewish Teachers Association (NYC), 487
Jewish Teachers Seminary and People's University, 218
Jewish Theological Seminary of America (JTSA), 240, 252, 382, 634. See also Assembly of the Jewish Theological Seminary; Melton Research Center
Jewish Times, 343, 432, 451
Jewish Times and Observer, 432
Jewish Times–Die Zeit, 429
Jewish Times of the Greater Northeast, 505
Jewish Transcript, 514, 661
Jewish Tribune, 432, 466, 499
Jewish Tribune of Passaic, N.J., 470
Jewish Voice, 432, 451. 466, 468, 469, 514
Jewish Voice Periodical, 498
Jewish Weekly, 508
Jewish Weekly News, 457
Jewish Welfare Board (JWB). See National Jewish Welfare Board
Jewish Welfare Federation of Detroit (JWF), 450, 458, 461
Jewish Woman, 505
Jewish Women's Congress, 403
Jewish Worker's Voice, 493
Jewish World, 498, 505
Jewish Youth, 121
Jewish Youth Magazine, 121
Jick, Leon A., 107, 234, 238, 579, 670
Jochnowitz, Cindy, 172
Jochnowitz, George, 406
Jochsberger, Tziporah, 38
Joel, Jane Milstein, 661
Johnson, George E., 435
Johnson, S. Y., 131
Jonas, Joseph, 494
Jonas, Manfred, 642
Jones, Charles C., 438
Jordan, Cecile, 667
Jordan, Cecile B., 24, 644
Jordan, Cecille Blank, 187, 250
Joselit, Jenna W., 478
Joselit, Jenna Weissman, 658
Joseloff, Samuel H., 120, 156
Joseph, A. B., 406
Joseph, Aaron, 361
Joseph, Michael, 131
Joseph, Morris, 346

Key to Index

7–9: *Types of Jewish Schools* | 10–17: *Curriculum* | 18–29: *Pedagogy* | 30–40: *The Arts* | 41–44: *Bar/Bat Mitzvah* | 45–53: *The Bible* | 54–59: *Early Childhood Education* | 60–65: *Exceptional Children* | 66–68: *Guidance* | 69–85: *Hebrew* | 86–96: *History* | 97–103: *The Holocaust* | 104–6: *School Library* | 107–18: *Life Cycle of a Jew* | 119–22: *Literature* | 123–42: *Mitzvot/Values and Contemporary Issues* | 143–46: *Textbooks* | 147–58: *The High School* | 159–75: *American Jewry and the Land of Israel* | 176–203: *Day School* | 204–31: *Yiddish Secular Schools* | 232–42: *Higher Education* | 245–62: *Administration* | 263–69: *The Teacher* | 270–73: *The Rabbi and Jewish Education* | 274–86: *Conferences in Jewish Education, 1890–1988* | 287–312: *Men and Women Who Influenced Jewish Education* | 317–34: *Historical Background of Jewish Education* | 335–52: *History of Jewish Education in the United States* | 353–78: *The American Jewish Community* | 379–89: *The Home and Jewish Education* | 390–97: *Adult Education* | 398–404: *The Woman's Role and Jewish Education* | 405–8: *Sephardim and Jewish Education* | 409–16: *Youth and Jewish Education* | 417–21: *Camp* | 422–516: *Local Sources for Jewish Education* | 521–23: *Theology and Jewish Education* | 524–32: *Religious Education* | 533–38: *Philosophy of Jewish Education* | 539–44: *Goals of Jewish Education* | 545–50: *Research in Jewish Education* | 551–58: *Change in Jewish Education* | 559–72: *The Social Sciences and Jewish Education* | 573–96: *Assessment* | 597–99: *The Future of Jewish Education* | 600–602: *Bibliographies of Jewish Education in Other Lands* | 603–17: *Bibliographies of Jewish Education and Related Fields in the United States* | 619–70: *Supplement*

INDEX

Joseph, Robert, 575
Joseph, Samuel, 471, 640
Joseph, Samuel K., 19, 24, 27, 93, 131, 167, 248, 250, 257, 262, 265, 301, 358, 528, 535, 639
Josephus, Flavius, 338
Josephy, Marcia R., 387
Jospe, Alfred, 238, 305, 412
Jospe, Erwin, 38
Journal of Jewish Communal Service, 289, 310, 469
Journal of Jewish Education, 445
Journal of the North Shore Community Center (Salem, Mass.), 457
Judah Loew Ben Bezalel: literature on, 299
Judaism (Jud) (periodical), 126, 290, 401, 522, 568, 613, 650
Judaisme Sephardi, Le, 408
Juergensen, Hans, 642
Jung, Leo, 12, 126, 143, 289, 307, 493, 525, 561, 588
Jung, Leo L., 144
Jung, M., 387
Juran, Richard, 568, 664
Justman, Joseph, 251

Kabakoff, Jacob, 69, 114, 160, 299, 347, 349, 485
Kadden, Barbara Binder, 50, 56, 89, 93, 631
Kadden, Bruce, 26, 135, 631
Kadison, Elaine F., 114
Kadosh, Mary Anne, 150
Kadushin, Evelyn Garfiel, 546
Kadushin, Max, 108, 128, 138, 412, 415, 535; literature on, 299
Kagan, Henry E., 19, 387
Kagan, I. M., 195
Kagan, Joan, 172
Kagan, Shaul, 302
Kaganoff, Nathan M., 436, 439, 476, 603, 608
Kahan, Linda S., 370
Kahane, Sh. Z., 323
Kahn, Alfred J., 128, 565
Kahn, Benjamin M., 568
Kahn, Benjamin N., 412
Kahn, Blanche, 185
Kahn, Charlotte, 568
Kahn, Edgar, 430
Kahn, Edward M., 358
Kahn, Eugene, 287
Kahn, Juliette B., 326
Kahn, L., 120
Kahn, Max, 185
Kahn, Paul, 195

Kahn, Robert I., 87, 323
Kahn, Ruby, 105
Kahn, S., 214
Kahnstam, Aharon: literature on, 300
Kaiman, Arnold G., 61, 79, 89
Kaiser, Alois, 344
Kaiser, L. I., 463
Kaitz, Abraham, 323
Kalband, Regina, 74
Kalisch, Isidor, 341, 342
Kalisher, Betty, 91
Kallen, Horace M., 105, 124, 126, 178, 279, 352, 355, 361, 392, 525, 541, 542, 575, 584, 585, 588; literature on, 300
Kallison, Frances, 512
Kamen, Robert Mark, 484
Karni, Ben, 662
Kamin, Benjamin A., 89
Kamin, Ira, 286
Kaminetsky, Alex, 74, 626
Kaminetsky, Joseph, 7, 12, 67, 176, 177, 179, 182, 187, 189, 192, 195, 201, 238, 305, 330, 487, 597; literature on, 300
Kaminetsky, N., 484
Kaminetzky, Edward, 61
Kaminetzky, Yaacov, 177
Kaminker, H., 427
Kaminker, Samuel: literature on, 300
Kaminsky, Gladys, 447
Kaminsky, I., 225, 227
Kampf, Avram, 30, 606
Kamrat, Mordecai, 392, 394
Kanarfogel, Ephraim, 641
Kandel, Isaac L., 552, 575
Kane, Gerald M., 528, 647
Kane, Judy, 470
Kane, Rhoda H., 38
Kane, W., 318
Kaniel, Shoshana, 330
Kann, Kenneth, 430
Kansas City Jewish Chronicle, 464
Kantor, M., 207, 223
Kantor, Nathan C., 150
Kanver, Ruth C., 611
Kapel, David E., 79, 182, 189
Kapel, Marilyn B., 182
Kaplan, A. S., 25
Kaplan, Abraham, 484
Kaplan, Aryeh, 111
Kaplan, Benjamin, 450, 571
Kaplan, Bernard M., 654
Kaplan, Deborah B., 259
Kaplan, Felisa Berman, 396
Kaplan, Harry, 24, 128, 412

Kaplan, Helga E., 495
Kaplan, Hyman, 545
Kaplan, I. K., 321
Kaplan, Lawrence J., 478
Kaplan, Louis, 300, 445
Kaplan, Louis L., 46, 114, 238, 253, 255, 336, 358, 453, 457, 468, 495, 504, 516, 535, 541
Kaplan, Marion, 642
Kaplan, Mordecai M., 39, 46, 52, 83, 109, 111, 124, 126, 128, 160, 162, 233, 238, 270, 272, 288, 289, 290, 297, 299, 354, 372, 388, 392, 396, 399, 403, 482, 522, 523, 525, 530, 535, 539, 542, 543, 568, 575, 579, 584; literature on, 300
Kaplan, Nathan, 656
Kaplan, Rivkah, 213
Kaplan, Yosef, 651
Kaplovitz, Abbey P., 401
Kapp, Lisa, 120
Karan, Val Elliot, 131
Karbal, Albert, 89
Karbal, Harold, 255
Karff, Samuel E., 178, 349, 568, 585
Kargon, Marcia, 453
Kariel, Audrey Daniels, 512
Karigal, Haim Isaac, 338
Karkhanis, Sharad, 669
Karkowaky, Nancy, 624
Karlin, Meyer, 182
Karlin, Miriam, 443
Karp, Abraham, 156, 303
Karp, Abraham J., 162, 271, 272, 347, 349, 382, 385, 473
Karp, B. I., 382
Karp, Deborah, 92
Karp, Hazel, 105
Karp, Renee, 382
Karpf, Maurice J., 236, 354
Karner, Alvin, 56
Karni, Leon J.: literature on, 301
Karpeles, Gustav, 346
Karten, Esther, 19, 77, 257
Kartman, Lauraine Levy, 452
Kartzinel, Jacob M., 514
Kasakove, David P., 626, 635
Kass, Alvin, 92
Kassof, Marvin, 56
Kastelianski, N., 323
Kastenbaum, Jerome, 546
Kastle, Harold D., 382
Kates, Eileen, 99
Katsh, Abraham I., 42, 81, 236, 238, 409
Katz, Betsy, 390
Katz, Betsy Dolgin, 265, 648, 664

INDEX

Katz, Betty, 56, 115, 640
Katz, David, 36, 382, 615, 625
Katz, Dina, 89, 250
Katz, Eric, 633
Katz, F., 401
Katz, Harold E., 32
Katz, I. E., 238
Katz, Irving I., 458–61
Katz, Israel J., 652
Katz, Israel Joseph, 406
Katz, Jacob, 662
Katz, Morris Casriel, 446
Katz, Morton L., 511
Katz, Moshe, 210, 212, 218, 221
Katz, Nancy H., 347
Katz, Robert, 271
Katz, S. K., 579
Katz, Sally Klein, 247, 255
Katz, Shlomo, 535
Katzin, Arye, 637
Katzir, I., 610
Katzir, Isoschar, 427
Katzman, Jacob, 231, 457
Katzoff, Adina, 56, 360, 443
Katzoff, Adina A., 641
Katzoff, Louis, 109, 153, 163, 254, 272, 336, 360, 372, 446, 525, 535, 539, 575
Kaufman, Dorothy, 657
Kaufman, Jay, 125, 167, 178, 295, 579
Kaufman, Judah. *See* Even-Shmuel, Judah
Kaufman, Kopl Leib, 217
Kaufman, Rhoda H., 480
Kaufman, Yehezkel, 45; literature on, 301
Kaufman, Yehudah, 535
Kaunfer, Alvan, 22, 637
Kaunfer, Marcia, 23, 114, 116, 616
Kaunfer, Neal, 100, 483
Kaunfer, Neil, 150, 158, 234, 269
Kauvar, C. E. Hillel, 432
Kavaler, Vigdor W., 294

Kay, J., 382
Kaye, Gerard W. (George), 100, 418
Kaye, J. S., 656
Kayser, Stephen S., 30, 39, 480
Kazdan, Ch. Sh., 210, 213, 214, 223, 228, 322, 323
Kazzaz, David S., 668
Keeping Posted (*KP*), 24–27, 35, 50, 100, 121, 126, 132, 135, 156, 172, 173, 382, 387, 401, 522, 528
Kehillah of New York City, 482
Kellman, Beth, 431
Kellman, Naomi, 453
Kellner, Abraham H., 466
Kellner, Menachem M., 126
Kelman, Herbert C., 568
Kelman, Joseph H., 61–62, 64
Kelman, Naamith, 62
Kelman, Stuart, 109, 192, 251, 547, 549
Kelman, Stuart L., 189, 663, 664
Kelman, Victoria Koltun, 29, 111, 113, 118, 181, 631, 647
Kelman, W., 358
Kelson, Benjamin, 392, 466
Kentucky Jewish Post and Opinion, 449
Kerdeman, Debby, 535
Kerdeman, Deborah, 148
Keren Or, 447
Kermode, Frank, 623
Kersht, I. M., 214
Kersten, Solomon, 610
Kerzner, Jerome, 132
Kessler, A. A., 330
Kessler, Aaron, 456, 473
Kessler, Aharon, 23, 251, 267, 506, 516, 541
Kessler, Harry, 36, 81, 182, 447, 490
Kessler, Harry L., 71
Kessler, L., 485
Kessner, Thomas, 476

Keuer, Edward John, 535
Key, Andrew W., 522
Keyserling, Meyer, 398
K'hal, Adath Jeshurun, 658
Khodosh, Rinna, 382
Kiddushin, 332
Kieffer, Sam, 116
Kiell, Norman, 37, 38
Kiev, I. Edward, 236
Kieval, Herman, 396
Kilstein, Sandra, 418
Kimelman, Reuven, 635, 644
Kimmel, Eric A., 120
Kimmel, Meyer, 233, 382, 579
Kinder Journal, 226
Kinderland, 226
Kinderwelt-Olam haYalodim, 226
Kinder Zeitung, 226
Kiner, Edward D., 290, 382, 498, 535, 579
King, Andrea, 647
King, Diane A., 77, 236, 502, 504
King, Marian, 171
Kinsey, Stephen D., 432
Kipper, Lenore C., 136, 438, 530, 637
Kipper, M. A., 541
Kipper, Morris, 530
Kipper, Morris A., 132
Kipust, P. J., 132
Kirk, F., 218
Kirschenbaum, Aaron, 19, 22
Kisch, Guido, 434
Kissileff, Harry R., 633
Kitov, A. E., 383
Kittner, Susan, 579, 615
Klaperman, Gilbert, 92, 238
Klaperman, Libby, 92
Klaperman, Libby L., 58, 530
Klarberg, Fred, 77
Klarberg, Manfred, 324
Klausner, Abraham J., 475
Klausner, Bertram, 383
Klausner, Carla L., 464
Klausner, Gustave, 552

Key to Index

7–9: *Types of Jewish Schools* | 10–17: *Curriculum* | 18–29: *Pedagogy* | 30–40: *The Arts* | 41–44: *Bar/Bat Mitzvah* | 45–53: *The Bible* | 54–59: *Early Childhood Education* | 60–65: *Exceptional Children* | 66–68: *Guidance* | 69–85: *Hebrew* | 86–96: *History* | 97–103: *The Holocaust* | 104–6: *School Library* | 107–18: *Life Cycle of a Jew* | 119–22: *Literature* | 123–42: *Mitzvot/Values and Contemporary Issues* | 143–46: *Textbooks* | 147–58: *The High School* | 159–75: *American Jewry and the Land of Israel* | 176–203: *Day School* | 204–31: *Yiddish Secular Schools* | 232–42: *Higher Education* | 245–62: *Administration* | 263–69: *The Teacher* | 270–73: *The Rabbi and Jewish Education* | 274–86: *Conferences in Jewish Education, 1890–1988* | 287–312: *Men and Women Who Influenced Jewish Education* | 317–34: *Historical Background of Jewish Education* | 335–52: *History of Jewish Education in the United States* | 353–78: *The American Jewish Community* | 379–89: *The Home and Jewish Education* | 390–97: *Adult Education* | 398–404: *The Woman's Role and Jewish Education* | 405–8: *Sephardim and Jewish Education* | 409–16: *Youth and Jewish Education* | 417–21: *Camp* | 422–516: *Local Sources for Jewish Education* | 521–23: *Theology and Jewish Education* | 524–32: *Religious Education* | 533–38: *Philosophy of Jewish Education* | 539–44: *Goals of Jewish Education* | 545–50: *Research in Jewish Education* | 551–58: *Change in Jewish Education* | 559–72: *The Social Sciences and Jewish Education* | 573–96: *Assessment* | 597–99: *The Future of Jewish Education* | 600–602: *Bibliographies of Jewish Education in Other Lands* | 603–17: *Bibliographies of Jewish Education and Related Fields in the United States* | 619–70: *Supplement*

Klausner, J., 326, 465
Klaw, Rose, 74
Klayman, Richard, 457
Kleiman, Blanche, 71
Klein, Aaron, 143, 258, 265, 366, 392, 401, 418, 473
Klein, Abigail, 647
Klein, Adaire, 426
Klein, Bernard, 555
Klein, Betty Dolgin, 248
Klein, Debra L., 152
Klein, Debra Lynn, 162
Klein, Edward E., 126
Klein, Esther M., 501
Klein, Hilda, 59
Klein, Isaac, 177, 178, 272, 530
Klein, Jenny Machlowitz, 167, 396
Klein, Joseph, 74, 79, 528, 587
Klein, Joyce, 36
Klein, Nancy H., 659
Klein, Ronald H., 478
Klein, Stephen, 192
Kleinberger, A. F., 330
Kleinberger, Alex Fritz, 299
Kleinhaus, Rosalie, 189
Kleinman, Susan, 624
Klepper, Jeff, 38
Klepper, Leah, 490, 492
Klepper, Leah H., 81
Kligfield, B., 26
Kligfield, Bernard, 135
Kline, Alexander S., 30
Kline, David, 394
Kling, S., 255
Kling, Simcha, 132
Klinger, Maurice, 442
Klirs, Tracy Guren, 650
Klotz, Miriam, 251
Klotz, Ronald, 418
Klughaupt, Sol, 177
Klutznick, Philip, 373
Klutznick, Philip M., 264, 541
Knee, Stuart E., 160
Kneller, Herbert Samuel, 330
Knikhon, Abraham, 321
Knobel, Oeter S., 631
Knoff, H. M., 383, 528
Knox, Israel, 98, 205, 207, 217, 218, 223, 311, 312, 409
Kobernick, Gerald, 358
Koblenz, Maxine L., 383
Kobrin, L. L., 479
Kobrin, Lawrence A., 187
Kochvi, I. B., 267
Kodesh, Shlomo, 167, 265, 267, 289, 579
Koehn, Ilse, 101
Koenig, Benjamin, 38

Koenig, S., 354
Koenig, Samuel, 561, 655
Kohanski, A. S., 279
Kohanski, Alexander S., 19–20, 358, 370, 431, 451, 499, 535
Kohansky, Mendel, 35
Kohl Jewish Teacher Center, 25
Kohler, Kaufman, 460
Kohler, Kaufmann, 114, 236, 324, 345, 398; literature on, 301
Kohler, Max J., 160, 471, 476, 507, 509
Kohn, Eugene, 46, 49, 108, 111, 124, 128, 143, 192, 245, 355, 539
Kohn, Fannie, 219
Kohn, Gary J., 608
Kohn, Harriet Korach, 38
Kohn, Jacob, 294, 383, 387
Kohn, Joshua, 504
Kohn, Mrs. Joshua, 504
Kohn, Rachael, 627
Kohn, Rebekah J., 59, 71, 74, 81, 182, 443, 461, 490
Kohn, S. Joshua, 474
Kohn, Sylvan H., 62, 469
Kohn, Theresa, 168
Kohn, Therese, 32, 87, 379
Kohs, Samuel C., 354, 426
Kohs, Samuel K., 427, 548
Kohut, George A., 346, 424
Kohut, Rebecca B., 346, 399, 430; literature on, 301
Kokhba, Moshe, 326
Kol, Moshe, 168, 330
Kolatch, Arthur, 34
Kolatch, Mollie, 116
Koller, C., 555
Kollin, Gilbert, 20
Kolodner, Anna, 25
Kolodner, Milton A., 168
Kolodner, S., 223
Koltun, Elizabeth, 401
Koltun, Judy, 32
Koltun, Liz, 612
Konowitz, Israel, 78, 81, 245, 248, 326, 336, 487, 575; literature on, 301
Kontorovich, E. V., 640
Konvitz, Milton, 108, 300, 579, 585, 587
Konvitz, Milton, R., 126, 347, 591, 631–33, 635
Kook, Abraham Isaac, 539; literature on, 301
Koolak, Bayle, 77
Koolik, Murry W., 168
Koolyk, Shirley, 126
Kopin, Rita, 23, 32

Kopinski, Ruth, 332
Koplewitz, Batya, 610
Koppman, L., 192
Koppman, Lionel, 369, 422–24, 432, 433, 435, 436, 438, 440, 447–52, 454, 458, 463, 464, 466–68, 471, 472, 494, 499, 500, 507, 509, 510, 512–16, 568, 603.
Kopulsky, Andrew, 654
Korczak, Janusz: literature on, 301
Kordimon, Sh., 232
Korenblit, Ari, 114
Korey, Harold, 446
Korin, Uri, 100, 255
Korman, Ezra, 400, 616
Korman, M., 250
Korman, Michael, 58, 74, 132, 168, 173, 272, 273, 640
Korn, Bertram W., 302, 336, 347, 422, 450, 476
Korn, Eugene, 663
Korn, I., 579
Korn, Lila M., 635
Korn, Rachel, 311
Kornblum, Sholem, 418
Kornfeld, Joseph S., 46
Kornfeld, Moshe, 525
Korros, Alexandra Shecket, 614
Kosberg, J. Livingston, 358
Koslowe, I., 473
Kosmin, Barry, 666
Kosover, Mordecai, 601
Kostman, Samuel, 248
Kotler, Aaron, 241; literature on, 301–2
Kozberg, Cary, 383
Kozlowski, Ida Glazer, 225
Kozodoy, Ruth, 116
Kraemer, David, 647
Kraemer, David C., 22
Kraft, Louis, 368; literature on, 302
Krakower, Isidore E., 155
Kramer, Bernard M., 124
Kramer, Daniel J., 176, 192
Kramer, Judith R., 561
Kramer, N., 77, 379
Kramer, Selma, 129
Kramer, Sylvia, 471
Kramer, William M., 423, 424–26, 429, 430, 467, 500, 515, 653, 670
Kramish, Len, 102
Kramish, Leonard, 248
Krant, Jerome, 492
Krantz, Naphtali, 441
Krantzler, Gershon, 182–83, 575

Krantzler, Harold, 38, 394
Krantzler, Harold I., 383
Kranush, Leonard, 585
Kranzler, David H., 324
Kranzler, George (Gershon), 478, 481
Kranzler, Gerson, 561
Kranzler, Moses N., 183
Krasner, Norman, 412
Krass, Nathan, 128
Kraus, William H., 150
Krause, Allen S., 126
Krause, Sherri, 56
Krauskopf, Joseph, 345
Krauss, Simcha, 183
Kraut, Benny, 93, 659
Kraut, Penina Besdin, 635
Kravitz, Leonard, 620
Kravitz, Leonard S., 89, 108
Kreinan, Fannie, 183
Kresel, G., 238
Kretzman, Paul E., 319
Kriegel, A., 568
Krieger, Leslie H., 20, 565
Krieger, Shelley G., 634
Krinsky, M., 81
Kripke, Dorothy K., 136, 528, 530, 608, 611
Kripke, Mrs. Myer S., 383
Krochmal, Nahman, 27
Krohn, Risa Rosenbaum, 182
Krohn, Samuel, 461
Kroloff, Theresa Klausner, 120
Kroman, Nathan, 13
Kronish, Amy, 23
Kronish, Amy W., 34
Kronish, Leon, 109, 129
Kronish, Ronald, 168, 272, 291–92, 300, 330, 370, 412, 538, 585, 635, 667
Kronzek, Lynn C., 654
Krucoff, Carole, 441
Krug, Mark M., 13, 168, 245, 249, 259, 279, 360, 371, 442, 555
Kruger, Laurie, 412

Krumbein, Eliezer, 132, 447, 546
Krupnick, Lillian, 189
Kubie, Nora Benjamin, 172
Kudan, Harold L., 13
Kugelmass, Jack, 658
Kuk, Abraham Isaac. *See* Kook, Abraham Isaac
Kukoff, Lydia, 26, 394
Kulick, P., 440
Kummel, S. B., 444
Kunin, Madeleine M., 627
Kupinsky, Bonnie Zwebner, 56, 77
Kurland, Mildred, 105
Kurtz, Shoshana, 186
Kurtz, V., 383
Kurzband, Toby K., 11, 13, 32, 87, 109, 111, 116, 129, 148, 152, 249, 255, 361, 369, 379, 383, 475, 525
Kurzweil, Zvi, 290
Kurzweil, Zvi E., 132, 139, 296, 298, 301, 308, 309, 311, 528
Kurzweil, Zvi F., 398
Kurzweil, Zvi H., 330
Kuselewitz, David, 155, 168, 173, 278, 394, 545, 579; literature on, 302
Kushner, Harold, 64, 662
Kushner, Lawrence S., 528, 530, 631, 633, 662, 663
Kushner, Lawrence Square, 669
Kushtai, Sh., 129, 263
Kuskin, Karla, 629
Kussy, Nathan, 469
Kussy, Sarah, 469
Kutcher, Carol B., 160
Kutner, Joel, 330
Kutzin, Margaret, 183
Kuzmack, Linda Gorden, 401
Kvutzah Ivrit, 461

L. L., 326
Labau, Henry J., 654

Labor Zionist Alliance, 225. *See also* Jewish National Workers Alliance; Labor Zionist Organization of America
Labor Zionist-Farband, 208
Labor Zionist Organization of America (LZOA), 178, 179, 200, 275, 277, 278, 281, 283, 445. *See also Jewish Frontier;* Jewish National Workers Alliance; Labor Zionist Alliance
Labovitz, Annette, 629
Lacave, Jose Luis, 651
Ladd, E. C., Jr., 239
Lakritz, Isaac, 150
Lakritz, William B., 13, 20, 89, 155, 187, 299, 580
Lamb, Blaine P., 423, 653
Lambert, W. E., 72, 153
La Med, Louis, 461
Lamm, Maurice, 27, 631
Lamm, Norman, 24, 26, 100, 126, 189, 241, 266, 412, 541, 568, 587, 631, 637
Lamont, Marian S., 423
Lampert, S., 100
Lampner, Carl, 153, 155, 412
Landau, Diane Fishman, 383, 614
Landau, Herman, 449
Landau, S., 394
Lander, Adele, 412
Lander, Dov Ber, 291
Lander, Harry, 74
Lander, Leon, 580
Landes, Morris A., 124
Landes, Ruth, 387
Landes, Sora, 135, 383
Landesman, Alter F., 12, 46, 105, 106, 153, 336, 476, 488
Landesman, Jacob, 546
Landis, J. C., 204
Landman, Eva, 58
Landman, Isaac, 49, 129, 246, 392, 525
Landman, R. H., 25

Key to Index

7–9: *Types of Jewish Schools* | 10–17: *Curriculum* | 18–29: *Pedagogy* | 30–40: *The Arts* | 41–44: *Bar/Bat Mitzvah* | 45–53: *The Bible* | 54–59: *Early Childhood Education* | 60–65: *Exceptional Children* | 66–68: *Guidance* | 69–85: *Hebrew* | 86–96: *History* | 97–103: *The Holocaust* | 104–6: *School Library* | 107–18: *Life Cycle of a Jew* | 119–22: *Literature* | 123–42: *Mitzvot/Values and Contemporary Issues* | 143–46: *Textbooks* | 147–58: *The High School* | 159–75: *American Jewry and the Land of Israel* | 176–203: *Day School* | 204–31: *Yiddish Secular Schools* | 232–42: *Higher Education* | 245–62: *Administration* | 263–69: *The Teacher* | 270–73: *The Rabbi and Jewish Education* | 274–86: *Conferences in Jewish Education, 1890–1988* | 287–312: *Men and Women Who Influenced Jewish Education* | 317–34: *Historical Background of Jewish Education* | 335–52: *History of Jewish Education in the United States* | 353–78: *The American Jewish Community* | 379–89: *The Home and Jewish Education* | 390–97: *Adult Education* | 398–404: *The Woman's Role and Jewish Education* | 405–8: *Sephardim and Jewish Education* | 409–16: *Youth and Jewish Education* | 417–21: *Camp* | 422–516: *Local Sources for Jewish Education* | 521–23: *Theology and Jewish Education* | 524–32: *Religious Education* | 533–38: *Philosophy of Jewish Education* | 539–44: *Goals of Jewish Education* | 545–50: *Research in Jewish Education* | 551–58: *Change in Jewish Education* | 559–72: *The Social Sciences and Jewish Education* | 573–96: *Assessment* | 597–99: *The Future of Jewish Education* | 600–602: *Bibliographies of Jewish Education in Other Lands* | 603–17: *Bibliographies of Jewish Education and Related Fields in the United States* | 619–70: *Supplement*

INDEX

Landsberg, Z., 62
Landsberger, Franz, 30, 606
Lang, Gerhard, 15, 67, 68, 90, 135, 143, 146, 154, 155, 157, 171, 187, 197, 246, 258, 265, 546, 547, 580, 581
Lang, Judith, 387, 568
Lang, Leon S., 13, 20, 129, 147, 152, 387, 392, 394, 503, 525; literature on, 302
Lang, Sheryl, 465
Langer, Hajnalka, 114
Langer, Michael, 168
Langfield, William R., 501
Langh, Philip A., 394
Lapides, Abe, 462
Lappin, Robert I., 555
Lapson, Dvorah, 35, 39, 489; literature on, 302
Lapson, Judah, 81, 238, 276, 277, 485; literature on, 302
Laquer, Walter, 162
Large City Budgeting Conference, 364
Lasker, Arnold A., 27, 114, 383
Lasker, Daniel J., 651
Lasker, R., 343
Lasson, Morris (Moshe), 195, 569
Las Vegas (Nev.) *Israelite,* 467
Lateef, Nasir Abed, 330
Latham, L., 257
Latham, Luisa, 183, 186
Lauer, Chaim, 358, 645, 664, 668
Lauer, H. Chaim, 580, 627
Laufman, Larry, 114
Lauterbach, Jacob Z., 319
Lavender, A. D., 412
Lavender, Abraham D., 126
Lavender, Bernard, 406
Laver, H. C., 366
Lavin, Lottie, 446
Lawson, Martin S., 62
Layman, Jonah, 26
Layman, Robert, 62
Lazar, Jeffrey B., 109
Lazar, Meyer, 192
Lazar, Moshe, 406
Lazaroff, Tovah, 656
Lazaron, Morris S., 110, 147, 453
Lazarson, I., 207, 214, 217, 223
Lazarus, Emma, 343
Lazarus, Mrs. Louis, 74
Lazerwitz, Bernard, 478, 569
Lazowski, Philip, 108
Leaf, Hayim, 288, 291
Leaf, R., 32
Leaphart, Susan, 466
Lear, Elmer, 132, 370, 569
Lear, Elmer N., 20, 74, 392

Learsi, Rufus, 347
Leary, Carolyn Frances, 177
Lebeau, James, 440
Lebeson, Anita L., 347
Lebeson, Anita Libman, 401, 441
Lebovitz, George, 187
Lebovitz, Gitty, 612
Lebow, Karen, 407
Lebowich, Joseph, 455
Lederberg, J., 126
Lederer, Phyllis, 460
Lee, Barton, 114
Lee, Ernst, 510
Lee, Joseph, 152
Lee, Sara S., 20, 168, 249, 250, 640, 645
Leeman, S., 45
Leeser, Isaac, 8, 144, 240, 339–42, 350, 403; literature on, 302
Leeson, Jerrold I, 412
Leff, Barbara, 105, 106
Lefkovitz, Lori, 402
Lefkowitz, David, 525, 597
Leftwich, I., 296
Lehiyot Connection, 253
Lehman, Emil, 168, 172, 360
Lehman, Eugene H., 12, 49, 129
Lehman, Herbert H., 304
Lehmann, Ruth P., 600
Lehrer, Deborah, 438
Lehrer, Leepe, 205, 210
Lehrer, Leibush, 26, 114, 204, 206, 207, 212–15, 217, 219, 221, 223, 230, 293, 297, 303, 312, 322, 380, 409, 412, 420, 535–36, 545, 565, 569, 575, 580, 587; literature on, 302
Lehrman, Irving, 319, 437
Leib, Mani, 225
Leibman, Morris, 87, 250, 257, 259, 429, 464, 504; literature on, 302
Leibman, Moshe, 11, 109
Leibovutz, Harry H.: literature on, 302
Leibowitz, A. H., 195
Leibowitz, Nehama, 623
Leibowitz, Shmaya: literature on, 302
Leibowitz, Wendy, 462
Leibowitz, Yeshia, 132
Leibson, Howard, 246
Leiderman, Lillian, 58, 110
Leigh, Ruth, 127
Leikind, Miriam, 105, 611, 613
Leiman, Harold I., 541
Leiman, Sandra, 418, 637
Leiman, Shnayer Z., 192, 412, 636

Leiman, Sondra, 626
Leinow, Benjamin J., 418
Leinwohl, Debi M., 100
Leipziger, Emil William, 319
Leipziger, Henry M., 319
Leiser, Jacob, 240
Leiserson, William M., 476
Leivick, H., 207, 210, 221
Lelyveld, Arthur J., 127, 415
Le Master, Carolyn Gray, 424
Lenchner, Orna, 77
Lenn, Theodore I., 271
Lennard, Henry L., 410
Leos, Irving, 20
Lerer, Deborah, 62
Lerit, Alan, 394
Lerman, H. K., 280
Lerman, Herbert K., 536
Lerner, Anne Lapidus, 127, 367, 401
Lerner, Barry Dov, 109
Lerner, Benjamin, 183
Lerner, Eleanor, 649
Lerner, Israel, 100, 310, 641
Lerner, Israel D., 127, 132, 393
Lerner, Jack, 62
Lerner, Stephen C., 418, 421
Leslau, Wolf, 25
Lesser, Anna, 129
Lesser, Charles B., 114
Lesser, Sim, 177, 192
Lestchinsky, Jacob, 258, 324
Leven. L. T., 341
Levenberg, A., 330
Levenberg, M., 406
Levenson, Edward R., 400
Levenson, Jacob, 233
Levenson, Joseph, 499
Levenson, Rosaline, 654
Leventman, Seymour, 463, 561
Levi, A. R., 347
Levi, Charles S., 123, 150
Levi, David, 338
Levi, Jossef, 187
Levi, Linda, 183
Levi, Miriam, 185
Levi, S. Gershon, 273
Leviant, D., 62
Levies, Caspar, 160
Levin, Alan J., 25
Levin, Alexandra Lee, 452, 453
Levin, Ezra, 478
Levin, Herschel, 160
Levin, Irene S., 121
Levin, Jacob, 440
Levin, Kay L., 387
Levin, Leo, 239
Levin, Marlin, 401
Levin, Meyer, 111, 116, 136, 160, 528

701

INDEX

Levin, Mildred, 11
Levin, Nancy Prager, 48, 247, 255
Levin, Nehemia, 330
Levin, Neil, 443
Levin, Nora, 98, 585
Levin, Shalom Dober, 349
Levin, Sunie, 647
Levin, T. Harry, 468
Levinas, Emanuel, 308
Levine, A., 380, 400
Levine, Aaron, 195
Levine, Abraham, 147
Levine, Allan E., 337–38, 608
Levine, Allan Marshall, 267
Levine, Baruch A., 56, 238, 623
Levine, Betty Carrol, 528
Levine, D., 539
Levine, Eric, 358
Levine, Etan, 162, 168, 536, 555, 580
Levine, Etan B., 22, 234
Levine, Gene N., 419, 569
Levine, Goldie S., 124
Levine, Hadassah, 116
Levine, Harriet, 647
Levine, Hillel, 413
Levine, Jacob, 206, 207, 209, 211, 213, 214, 218, 221, 223, 227
Levine, Jacqueline, 402
Levine, Joel Lawrence, 536
Levine, Louis, 476
Levine, Raphael H., 514
Levine, Ronald A., 155
Levine, Samuel, 498
Levine, Samuel H., 160
Levine, Shlomo, 168
Levine, Shlomo D., 528, 647
Levine, T., 541, 580
Levine, Y., 589
Levine, Yaacov: literature on, 303
Levine-Stern, Carol, 625
Levinger, Elma Ehrlich, 36, 50, 91, 92, 111, 116, 152, 400
Levinger, Lee J., 67, 91, 498

Levinsohn, Isaac Baer: literature on, 303
Levinson, B. M., 62, 67, 132, 183, 187, 192, 413, 528, 565
Levinson, Bernard H., 440
Levinson, Burton E., 505
Levinson, D., 26
Levinson, Howard, 361
Levinson, I., 277
Levinson, Jay H., 74
Levinson, Joseph, 441
Levinson, Julie, 626
Levinson, Maria H., 26
Levinson, Morris, 434
Levinson, Robert E., 424, 466, 499
Levinson, Rosaline, 425
Levinson, Selma, 513
Levinson, William B., 113
Levinson-Lavi, M., 263
Levinthal, L., 71, 254
Levinthal, L. L., 380
Levinthal, Louis E., 588
Levitan, Miriam, 498
Levitan, Ruth, 225
Levitan, Sar, 380
Levitan, T., 476
Levitan, Tina, 407, 492
Levitas, Irving, 89, 160, 465
Levitats, Isaac, 41, 42, 74, 132, 155, 246, 266, 292, 324, 361, 365, 366, 369, 401, 441, 516
Levitch, Sadie, 512
Levitin, Bernard, 289
Levitin, Dov, 497
Levitin, Miriam, 50
Levitin, Sonia, 636
Leviton, Elsie, 105
Levitsky, J., 264
Levitsky, Louis M., 149, 272, 507
Levitt, Joy D., 501
Levitz, Irving N., 663
Levitz, J., 227
Levitz, Jacob, 324
Levitzky, Joseph, 504

Levow, Mordecai, 234, 250, 419, 465
Levy, Abraham, 651
Levy, Albert J., 407
Levy, B. Barry, 624
Levy, B. H., 440
Levy, Beryl Harold, 525
Levy, Beverly, 358
Levy, Charles S., 354
Levy, D., 32
Levy, Deborah, 20, 59, 116
Levy, Emma Fidanque, 652
Levy, Eugene, 629
Levy, Ezekiel, 37
Levy, Harold L., 655
Levy, Henry W., 413
Levy, Isaac Jack, 627
Levy, Louis, 74
Levy, Louis N., 406
Levy, M., 62
Levy, Maria, 38
Levy, Phyllis S., 250, 257
Levy, R. N., 413
Levy, Stephen Jay, 479
Lewbin, Hyman J., 30
Lewin, Kurt, 124, 385, 547, 565, 570, 575; literature on, 303
Lewin, Mrs. Kurt, 565
Lewin, Rhoda G., 657
Lewis, Adele, 89
Lewis, Albert L., 154, 155
Lewis, Albert M., 528
Lewis, Arthur H., 500
Lewis, David Trevor, 496
Lewis, Frieda S., 588
Lewis, Hilary, 639
Lewis, Judith S., 100
Lewis, Justin, 89, 151, 183
Lewis, Justin Harley, 536
Lewis, Schnayer, 179
Lewis, Stuart Arthur, 121
Lewis, Theodore, 507
Lewis, Theodor N., 400
Lewisohn, Ludwig, 42
Lewitt, D. W, 565

Key to Index

7–9: *Types of Jewish Schools* | 10–17: *Curriculum* | 18–29: *Pedagogy* | 30–40: *The Arts* | 41–44: *Bar/Bat Mitzvah* | 45–53: *The Bible* | 54–59: *Early Childhood Education* | 60–65: *Exceptional Children* | 66–68: *Guidance* | 69–85: *Hebrew* | 86–96: *History* | 97–103: *The Holocaust* | 104–6: *School Library* | 107–18: *Life Cycle of a Jew* | 119–22: *Literature* | 123–42: *Mitzvot/Values and Contemporary Issues* | 143–46: *Textbooks* | 147–58: *The High School* | 159–75: *American Jewry and the Land of Israel* | 176–203: *Day School* | 204–31: *Yiddish Secular Schools* | 232–42: *Higher Education* | 245–62: *Administration* | 263–69: *The Teacher* | 270–73: *The Rabbi and Jewish Education* | 274–86: *Conferences in Jewish Education, 1890–1988* | 287–312: *Men and Women Who Influenced Jewish Education* | 317–34: *Historical Background of Jewish Education* | 335–52: *History of Jewish Education in the United States* | 353–78: *The American Jewish Community* | 379–89: *The Home and Jewish Education* | 390–97: *Adult Education* | 398–404: *The Woman's Role and Jewish Education* | 405–8: *Sephardim and Jewish Education* | 409–16: *Youth and Jewish Education* | 417–21: *Camp* | 422–516: *Local Sources for Jewish Education* | 521–23: *Theology and Jewish Education* | 524–32: *Religious Education* | 533–38: *Philosophy of Jewish Education* | 539–44: *Goals of Jewish Education* | 545–50: *Research in Jewish Education* | 551–58: *Change in Jewish Education* | 559–72: *The Social Sciences and Jewish Education* | 573–96: *Assessment* | 597–99: *The Future of Jewish Education* | 600–602: *Bibliographies of Jewish Education in Other Lands* | 603–17: *Bibliographies of Jewish Education and Related Fields in the United States* | 619–70: *Supplement*

INDEX

Lewitter, Sidney R., 239
Lewittes, Mordecai, 92, 119, 668
Lewittes, Mordecai H., 22, 48, 50, 68, 81, 90, 151, 168, 183, 485
Libby, Claire, 105
Libenson, Michael A., 419
Liber, Maurice, 307
Liberal Judaism, 613
Liberies, Robert, 642
Libman, Melvin L., 249
Libowitz, Richard, 627
Licht, Jacob, 45
Lichtblau, Amy P., 189
Lichtenstein, Aharon, 127, 132, 309, 649
Lichtenstein, Gaston, 513
Lichtenstein, Isaac, 30
Lichtenstein, Murray H., 620
Lichter, Chani, 483
Lichtig, Judith, 383, 647
Lichtman, J., 125
Lichtman, William, 62
Lida, Denah, 652
Lieb, David S., 114
Lieber, David, 127, 132, 301, 360, 541, 580
Lieberman, Herman (Chaim), 221, 580
Lieberman, J., 492
Lieberman, Morris, 119, 271, 612
Lieberman, Phyllis, 134
Lieberman, Sidney, 186
Lieberman, Sidney Z., 477
Liebert, Sarah, 227
Liebert, Sarah L., 50
Liebman, Charles S., 162, 300, 349, 413, 562, 569, 665
Liebman, Leslie, 246
Liebman, Melvin S., 254
Liebman, Moshe, 287
Liebman, Seymour B., 600, 615
Lifschutz, E., 608
Lifshitz, A. M., 322
Lifshitz, Ch., 610
Lifshitz, I., 212
Lifshitz, I. I., 198
Lifshutz, Ezekiel, 481
Lifson, David S., 480
Liheyot, 64
Lilienthal, Max, 341, 342, 344; literature on, 303
Lilith: The Jewish Woman's Magazine, 401
Liljegren, Joy, 441
Lilker, Martin, 155
Lindenthal, Jacob Jay, 434
Linder, Peninah, 485
Linfield, Harry S., 354
Linick, Samuel, 246

Linn, Louis, 401
Linnea, Sharon, 628
Linzer, Lila, 56
Linzer, Norman, 105, 132, 368, 383, 387, 604, 647
Lipchutz, Karen S., 383
Lipkin, Bela, 36
Lipman, Eugene J., 127, 137, 149, 426, 448, 455, 463, 464, 473, 476, 496, 502, 510
Lipman, H. T., 475
Lipman, Matthew, 20, 528
Lipman, Steve, 152, 155
Lipnick, Bernard, 154, 366, 370, 528
Lipnick, Jerome, 474
Lippman, Froma, 26, 27, 383
Lippmann, Ellen, 644
Lipschultz, Karen, 555
Lipschutz, Karen S., 27
Lipset, Harry, 324
Lipset, Seymour M., 127, 239, 562, 571
Lipset, Seymour Martin, 666
Lipskin, Lee, 186
Lipsky, Louis, 160
Lipson, Alfred, 627
Lipson, Norman B., 625
Lipson, Norman S., 259
Lipstadt, D., 648
Lipstadt, Deborah, 628, 666, 668, 669
Lipton, Ann Lynn, 589
Liptzin, Sol, 296
Lisitzky, Ephraim E., 593; literature on, 303
Lissek, Gail Porter, 181
Lister, Louis, 20, 23, 36, 62, 74, 121, 247, 259, 361
Lister, Rebecca, 14, 23, 62, 74, 77, 93, 121, 259, 361, 370, 493
Lithuanian Council on Advanced Study, 333
Littlefield, Oscar, 449
Litvak, A., 217
Livingstone, John, 471
Livingstone, Nancy, 56, 368, 383
Livni, Michael, 635
Lobel, Eve, 387
Lobman, Frances W., 20, 183
Locke, Shaun, 392
Loeb, Henri, 340
Loeb, Sorel Goldberg, 50, 93
Loebl, Judy Silberg, 619
Lomner, Nathan Perek, 198
London, Perry, 665
Lookstein, Haskel, 98, 192
Lookstein, Joseph, 186, 541

Lookstein, Joseph H., 7, 178, 183, 236, 298, 303, 413, 484, 522, 528, 580
Lopez, Moses, 338
Lopian, Eliyahu, 522
Lor, A., 569
Lorch, Steven C., 192, 501, 668
Lorch, Steven Charles, 37
Loren, Morris J., 239
Los Angeles, Calif., 426, 654
Los Angeles Yiddish Writers Society of YKUF, 424
Louis, Elmer, 496
Louis, Minnie D., 346
Louis, Roberta L., 383
Louisiana Historical Records Survey, 450
Lovett, John R., 659
Low, Jean M., 660
Lowe, William T., 89
Lowenstein, Amy, 471
Lowenstein, Steven, 499
Lowenstein, Steven M., 474–75, 642
Lowi, Theodore, 422
Lown, Jacob S., 303
Lown, Philip W., 254; literature on, 303–4
Lown, P. W., 361
Lowth, Robert, 339
Lozowick, Louis, 30
Lubavitch Educational Foundation for Jewish Marriage Enrichment, 401
Lubetski, Edith, 105, 604, 608
Lubetski, Meir, 105, 604, 619
Lubinsky, M., 580
Lubinsky, Menachem, 67
Lubitch, Rivkah, 649
Lubliner, Shira, 664
Lucas, Alice, 345
Lucia, Sister, 46
Luckens, Reuben, 419
Lucks, Alvin S., 87
Ludlow, Victor L., 293
Lujiken, Marianne, 149
Lukinsky, Joseph, 13, 20, 114, 121, 132, 149, 185, 186, 192, 234, 256, 553
Lukinsky, Joseph Sender, 266
Luria, Max Aaron, 406
Lurie, Harry, 545
Lurie, Harry L., 348, 458
Lurie, Rose G., 20, 36, 76, 91, 93, 419, 504
Lustig, Shane, 192
Lutz, Barry, 156
Luz, La, 407
Luzatto, Moses Hayyim, 137

703

Lyon, George, 340
Lyons, L. L., 340

M. A., 330
Maas, Elaine, 512
Machlis, Leon, 179
MacIver, R. M., 354
Mackmann, Beverly C., 62
Magida, Arthur J., 453
Magil, Joseph, 49
Magnes, Judah L., 83, 294, 355, 371, 482; literature on, 304
Magnus, Joann, 622
Magnus, Shulamit, 649
Mahler, Raphael, 312, 589
Mahler, Yehudah, 129
Mahrer, Lawrence M., 152
Maidenberg, Harry F., 654
Maier, J., 132, 562
Maier, Joseph B., 642
Mailbaum, Matthew, 413
Maimon, Solomon, 322, 333
Maimonides, Moses, 332; literature on, 304
Maimoodes, I., 427
Maisl, N., 401
Maislin, Simeon J., 114
Makovsky, D. I., 465
Makovsky, Nancy, 257
Malachi, Eliezer R., 236, 308, 310, 312, 336, 349, 605, 607, 608, 610, 612, 613, 615; literature on, 304
Maladowsky, Kadya, 227, 295
Malamut, 424, 426, 427
Malev, Milton, 402
Maliken, Esther, 435
Malin, Harry, 258, 366
Malin, Penina C., 151
Malinow, Peter, 648
Mallay, Ruth, 387
Maller, Allan S., 100
Maller, Allen S., 24, 26, 178, 387, 622
Maller, Julius, 233

Maller, Julius B., 80, 129, 257, 319, 324, 333, 410, 479, 545, 562, 565
Mallow, Jeffry V., 635, 656
Malofsky, Lyn, 50
Maltz, Saul, 215, 223
Malzberg, Amy S., 177
Mandel, Irving Aaron, 347
Mandelbaum, Bernard, 132
Mandelbaum, David G., 447, 555, 562
Mandelbaum, Naomi, 132
Mandell, Ronni S., 619
Mangione, Anthony R., 610
Mann, Arthur, 456
Mann, Bridget C., 512
Mann, David, 297, 366
Mann, Louis L., 124
Mann, Mendl, 296
Mann, Theodore R., 569
Mannenberg, Eliezer, 324
Mannheimer, Judith Hirt, 622
Mannheimer, Sigmund, 344
Manoz, S. R., 153
Mansoor, Menahem, 82, 239
Mantinband, Anna K., 271
Manushkin, Fran, 629
Marans, Hillel, 435
Marcson, Simon, 575
Marcus, Audrey Friedman, 20, 23, 27, 42, 58, 59, 93, 102, 116, 117, 132, 135, 246, 249, 250, 266, 383, 392, 555
Marcus, Charles, 192
Marcus, Eliezer, 114, 117
Marcus, Fred, 132, 255
Marcus, George, 419
Marcus, Ivan G., 669
Marcus, Jacob R., 95, 114, 271, 296, 302, 321, 336, 347, 402, 406, 433, 438, 471–72, 494, 495, 500, 507, 509, 513, 604, 608, 616
Marcuson, Isaac E., 20
Marder, Janet, 623, 667

Marenof, Martha, 74, 370, 461
Marenoff, M., 81
Maretz, Sylvia, 109, 443, 444
Marev, 429
Margolis, Daniel J., 456, 528, 594
Margolis, Henry, 77, 168, 254, 283, 299, 499
Margolis, Henry M., 364
Margolis, Isidor, 7, 116, 234, 456; literature on, 304
Margolis, Isidore, 440
Margolis, M. J., 45
Margolis, P., 627
Margoshes, Samuel, 13, 74, 98, 149, 162, 168, 178, 180, 207, 233, 246, 281, 283, 324, 337, 355, 413, 480, 541, 555, 569, 580, 589; literature on, 304
Marguleas, Anton, 192
Marinbach, Bernard, 511
Marinoff, Shlomo, 319, 443, 444
Mark, Jonathan, 651
Mark, Yud[e]l, 1, 7, 8, 76, 79, 83, 132, 180, 206–11, 215, 216, 218, 221, 223, 226–30, 277, 283, 296, 303, 358, 372, 395, 484, 536, 580, 587, 592; literature on, 304–5
Markowich, Mrs. Sh., 136
Markowitz, Arnold, 621
Markowitz, Francine S., 479
Markowitz, Mrs. Sh., 198
Markowitz, S. L., 116
Markowitz, Samuel H., 11, 117, 380, 392, 526, 541, 555
Marks, Cara Goldberg, 31
Markson, Aaron David, 461
Marmor, Arthur, 513
Marmor, J., 566
Marmor, Kalman, 218
Marmur, Dow, 635
Maron, Neil, 565
Marrow, Alfred, 124, 303
Mars, Alvin, 186, 187, 308
Marschal, John P., 467

Key to Index

7–9: *Types of Jewish Schools* | 10–17: *Curriculum* | 18–29: *Pedagogy* | 30–40: *The Arts* | 41–44: *Bar/Bat Mitzvah* | 45–53: *The Bible* | 54–59: *Early Childhood Education* | 60–65: *Exceptional Children* | 66–68: *Guidance* | 69–85: *Hebrew* | 86–96: *History* | 97–103: *The Holocaust* | 104–6: *School Library* | 107–18: *Life Cycle of a Jew* | 119–22: *Literature* | 123–42: *Mitzvot/Values and Contemporary Issues* | 143–46: *Textbooks* | 147–58: *The High School* | 159–75: *American Jewry and the Land of Israel* | 176–203: *Day School* | 204–31: *Yiddish Secular Schools* | 232–42: *Higher Education* | 245–62: *Administration* | 263–69: *The Teacher* | 270–73: *The Rabbi and Jewish Education* | 274–86: *Conferences in Jewish Education, 1890–1988* | 287–312: *Men and Women Who Influenced Jewish Education* | 317–34: *Historical Background of Jewish Education* | 335–52: *History of Jewish Education in the United States* | 353–78: *The American Jewish Community* | 379–89: *The Home and Jewish Education* | 390–97: *Adult Education* | 398–404: *The Woman's Role and Jewish Education* | 405–8: *Sephardim and Jewish Education* | 409–16: *Youth and Jewish Education* | 417–21: *Camp* | 422–516: *Local Sources for Jewish Education* | 521–23: *Theology and Jewish Education* | 524–32: *Religious Education* | 533–38: *Philosophy of Jewish Education* | 539–44: *Goals of Jewish Education* | 545–50: *Research in Jewish Education* | 551–58: *Change in Jewish Education* | 559–72: *The Social Sciences and Jewish Education* | 573–96: *Assessment* | 597–99: *The Future of Jewish Education* | 600–602: *Bibliographies of Jewish Education in Other Lands* | 603–17: *Bibliographies of Jewish Education and Related Fields in the United States* | 619–70: *Supplement*

INDEX

Marsh, Leon, 319
Marshall, James, 304, 575
Marshall, Louis, 236, 371;
   literature on, 305
Martan, Abraham, 577
Martin, Alon, 192
Martin, Bernard, 41, 108, 541, 585
Marx, Alexander, 294, 295, 304, 307, 308; literature on, 305
Marx, Betty Furth, 54
Marx, David, 439
Marx, Jeffrey A., 658
Marx, R. J., 131
Marx, Robert J., 127, 529
Mascatel, Cynthia Thal, 381
Mashewitzky, M., 295
Maslin, Simeon J., 117
Maslow, Will, 354
Mason, Patrice Goldstein, 151
Mason, Patricia Goldsmith, 111
Mass, Ronald S., 555
Massar, Rita, 89
Massarik, Fred, 425, 429, 430, 569, 586
Matanky, Leonard A., 24, 132, 151, 621, 636, 648, 664
Matek, Ord, 20
Mathews, Carole, 402
Mathison, Zevi, 488
Matt, H. J., 109
Matt, Hershel, 48
Matt, Hershel J., 24
Matteoni, Louis, 100
Mattis, I. M., 461
Matz, Marcia S., 393, 396
Matza, Diane, 406, 651, 652
Matzner-Bekerman, Shoshana, 192, 565
Maurer, Herrymon, 475
Maximon, Sh. B., 287
Mayefsky, Isaac, 195
Mayer, Albert J., 458–59, 462, 465, 498, 515
Mayer, Egon, 26, 387, 479, 562, 598, 622
Mayer, Harry M., 526
Mayer, Isaac, 342, 344
Mayer, Leo A., 606
Maynard, Betty I., 511
Maynard, John A., 319
Mayo, Maxine, 74, 615
Mays, George, 507
Mazur, Edward H., 441
McAllister, Joy T., 426
McCann, James, 514
McDonald (*New Yorker* writer), 306
McGill, Nettie P., 479
McKelvey, Blake, 473
Meckler, D. L., 218, 383, 483, 580
Medding, Peter Y., 666
Medini, Mordecai, 74, 497, 575
Mehler, Judith, 71
Mehling, Harold, 437
Mehlman, Israel, 168, 324
Meier, Levi, 631
Meier, Menachem, 470
Meir, Shlomo, 168
Meiselman, Moshe, 402
Meisels, Stanley, 100
Meisl, A., 485
Meisl, Nachman, 218
Meites, Hyman L., 441, 446
Meitlis, J., 305
Meketa, Jacqueline Dorgan, 471
Melamed, Evelyn B., 649
Melamed, Israel, 132
Melamed, Joseph, 383
Melamed, Renee Levine, 651
Melamed, Samuel M., 160
Melconian, Vartin, 46, 319
Melkman, Joseph, 168
Melton, Samuel Mendel:
   literature on, 305
Melton Journal (MJ), 253, 305, 402, 633, 652
Melton Research Center (MRC), 13, 17, 42, 252, 383. *See also* Jewish Theological Seminary of America
Melton Research Center Newsletter (MRCN), 109
Meltz, Jacob J., 426
Meltzer, Milton, 93, 101, 628
Melzer, Asher, 653
Memorial Foundation for Jewish Culture, 100
Menachem, G., 503
Menachowski, M., 62, 210, 213, 296
Mendelsohn, Ezra, 324
Mendelsohn, Moses, 631;
   literature on, 305
Mendelsohn, Phyllis, 168
Mendelsohn, Sh., 217, 221
Mendelson, I., 293
Mendes, Frederick de Sola, 345
Mendes, Henry Periera, 236;
   literature on, 305
Mendlowitz, Shraga Feivel:
   literature on, 305
Menes, Abraham, 138, 212, 218, 324, 383, 413, 477
Menes, G., 226
Menitoff, Michael N., 132
Menitoff, Paul J., 151
Menorah, The, 430
Menorah Journal, 30, 493, 613
Menuhin, Moshe, 326, 431
Meodor, Michael M., 515
Merel, Sheldon F., 247
Merians, Mel, 621
Merkos L'Inyonei Chinuch, 12, 188, 197, 493
Mermelstein, Jacob, 183, 187, 189
Mermelstein, Shoshana, 622
Merowitz, Morton, 289, 303
Mersky, David, 27
Mervis, Leonard, 117
Mervis, Leonard J., 127, 541
Mesinger, Jonathan, 474
Mesivta Yeshiva Rabbi Chaim Berlin, 476
Mesivta Yeshiva Rabbi Chaim Berlin Rabbinical Academy, 188
Messenger, Howard, 183
Messenger, The (Cincinnati), 496
Messenger, The (Los Angeles), 429
Messing, A. J., 422
Messing, Aaron, 346
Messing, Aron, 345
Messinger, Nancy, 504
Metro-West Jewish News, 658
Metz, Allan, 652
Meyer, A., 489
Meyer, Eric M., 413
Meyer, Gerard P., 93
Meyer, H. Jack, 361
Meyer, Henry, 642
Meyer, Henry J., 459
Meyer, Isidore S., 347, 608
Meyer, Isidor S., 160
Meyer, L., 32
Meyer, Martin A., 424
Meyer, Michael, 89, 666
Meyer, Michael A., 642, 643
Meyer, Michael M., 239
Meyerowitz, Abraham, 211, 462
Meyers, Allen, 658
Meyers, E. M., 345
Meyers, Eric M., 580
Meyers, I. H., 343
Meyers, Jack, 357
Meyers, Larry, 255
Meyers, Lawrence, 20, 529, 580
Meyers, M. H., 343
Meyers, Myron T., 433
Meyers, W. E., 450
Meyouhas, J., 330
M'Gdolin: The Jewish Quarterly, 449, 514
Miami, University of, 655
Miami (Fla.) *Jewish Tribune*, 438
Miaston, A. R., 529
Michael, Robert, 98

INDEX

Michaeli, Moshe, 634
Michel, Sonya, 400
Michelson, Mrs. Julius, 105
Michlin, Michael, 11, 460, 461
Midwest Teachers Organization, 444
Mihaly, Eugene, 304
Mikliszanski, I. K., 321
Mikliszanski, J. K., 121
Mikliszanski, Jacques K., 69
Milbauer, I., 206
Milch, Robert, 383
Milgram, Josephine, 62
Milgram, Rebecca, 62
Milgram, Roberta, 132
Milgram, Roberta M., 247
Milgrom, I., 24
Milgrom, Jacob, 623
Millburn, Ronald R., 48
Miller, Benjamin, 491, 607, 608
Miller, Bennett F., 666
Miller, C., 569
Miller, Deborah D., 114
Miller, Deborah Uchill, 58
Miller, Donald H., 348
Miller, Inabeth, 611
Miller, Israel, 168
Miller, James A., 460
Miller, Julia, 505
Miller, Lillian, 36
Miller, Linda R.: literature on, 305
Miller, Lori, 624
Miller, Milton G., 136, 151
Miller, Miriam, 104
Miller, Norman, 361
Miller, Paul A., 189
Miller, Philip, 121
Miller, Richard, 74
Miller, Sh., 427
Miller, Yisroel, 402
Millgram, Abraham E., 7, 20, 42, 71, 108, 110, 114, 149, 187, 246, 254, 264, 268, 272, 293, 360, 383, 385, 451, 505, 539, 575, 589, 599; literature on, 305
Millner, Achitob, 77
Mills, J. R., 450
Millstone, Mark, 224
Milman, Henry Hart, 339
Milstein, M., 221, 223
Milton, Sybil, 31
Milwaukee Jewish Voice, 515
Minda, Albert G., 463
Mindel, Nissan, 111, 183, 198
Minkin, Jacob S., 304, 614
Minkoff, Harvey, 649
Minkovich, A., 330
Minneapolis (Minn.) Talmud Torah, 463
Mintz, Alan, 486
Mintz, Charles D., 395
Mir, Donia, 183
Miranda, Gary, 659
Mirel, Ida, 70
Mirel, James, 529
Mirel, Joan, 59
Mirelman, Victor C., 652
Mirsky, David, 69
Mirsky, Norman, 271
Mirsky, Norman B., 569
Mirsky, Samuel K., 22, 192, 319, 324, 580; literature on, 305–6
Mishaan, Marc, 168
Mishiah, Igal, 186
Mishkin, L. Y., 600
Mishkin, Leah, 441
Mishkin, Leonard C., 311, 446
Mishkin, Madelyn, 407
Missouri Jewish Post, 466
Missri, M. A., 197
Mitchell, William E., 479
Mittleman, Jacob, 11
Mizberg, I. D., 355
Mizrachi, Sh., 277
Mizrachi Teachers Institute, 12
Mizrahi, Nina, 529
Mlotek, Chane, 215
Mlotek, Eleanor Gordon, 213, 622
Mlotek, Joseph, 206, 210, 213, 217, 218, 224, 227, 230, 622
Modern View, 466
Mogilner, Sue Schiff, 485
Mokdoni, A., 36, 218, 295
Moladowsky, Kadia, 102
Moment, Samuel, 430
Moment, 456, 555, 621, 632
Monis, A. Judah, 338
Monsky, Arthur, 13
Monsky, Henry, 355
Monsky, Jacob, 476
Monson, Rela Geffen, 270, 370, 400, 413, 419, 664, 665, 668
Montenette, Marcia, 324
Moore, Deborah Dash, 239, 479, 654
Morais, Henry Samuel, 346, 502
Morais, Sabato, 297, 502
Mordecai, Rosa, 346
Morgan, T. B., 588
Morgenlander, Frances, 20
Moriel, Yehuda, 319
Morin, Cynthia, 132
Morin, Richard, 132
Moroz, Sh., 285, 555
Morris, Bonnie J., 649
Morris, Elaine, 266
Morris, F. S., 181
Morris, Herbert, 151
Morris, Maxwell H., 507
Morris, Nathan, 319, 321; literature on, 306
Morris, Robert, 348
Morse, Arthur D., 98
Morse, L. C., 509
Morton, Laurence, 39
Morton, Sharon, 647
Moscowitz, Nachama Skolnik, 529
Mosenkis, Matthew, 284, 285, 291, 293, 295, 306, 586
Mosenkis, Rebekkah K., 15, 74, 490, 491
Mosenson, Israel, 129

Key to Index

7–9: *Types of Jewish Schools* | 10–17: *Curriculum* | 18–29: *Pedagogy* | 30–40: *The Arts* | 41–44: *Bar/Bat Mitzvah* | 45–53: *The Bible* | 54–59: *Early Childhood Education* | 60–65: *Exceptional Children* | 66–68: *Guidance* | 69–85: *Hebrew* | 86–96: *History* | 97–103: *The Holocaust* | 104–6: *School Library* | 107–18: *Life Cycle of a Jew* | 119–22: *Literature* | 123–42: *Mitzvot/Values and Contemporary Issues* | 143–46: *Textbooks* | 147–58: *The High School* | 159–75: *American Jewry and the Land of Israel* | 176–203: *Day School* | 204–31: *Yiddish Secular Schools* | 232–42: *Higher Education* | 245–62: *Administration* | 263–69: *The Teacher* | 270–73: *The Rabbi and Jewish Education* | 274–86: *Conferences in Jewish Education, 1890–1988* | 287–312: *Men and Women Who Influenced Jewish Education* | 317–34: *Historical Background of Jewish Education* | 335–52: *History of Jewish Education in the United States* | 353–78: *The American Jewish Community* | 379–89: *The Home and Jewish Education* | 390–97: *Adult Education* | 398–404: *The Woman's Role and Jewish Education* | 405–8: *Sephardim and Jewish Education* | 409–16: *Youth and Jewish Education* | 417–21: *Camp* | 422–516: *Local Sources for Jewish Education* | 521–23: *Theology and Jewish Education* | 524–32: *Religious Education* | 533–38: *Philosophy of Jewish Education* | 539–44: *Goals of Jewish Education* | 545–50: *Research in Jewish Education* | 551–58: *Change in Jewish Education* | 559–72: *The Social Sciences and Jewish Education* | 573–96: *Assessment* | 597–99: *The Future of Jewish Education* | 600–602: *Bibliographies of Jewish Education in Other Lands* | 603–17: *Bibliographies of Jewish Education and Related Fields in the United States* | 619–70: *Supplement*

INDEX

Moses, Alfred G., 422
Moses, Avi, 637
Moses, Isaac S., 345, 346
Moses, Isidor R., 319
Moses, Nancy, 435
Moshowitz, I., 566
Moskowitz, Aron, 324
Moskowitz, Gertrude, 639
Moskowitz, Henry, 346
Moskowitz, Nachama Skolnik, 111, 249, 259, 621, 628
Moskowitz, Sarah, 56
Moss, Leonard W., 460
Moss, Penrod, 90
Mosse, George L., 642
Mossinsohn, Ben Zion, 326
Mostov, Stephen, 455, 495
Mounier, Louis, 468
Moynihan, Daniel P., 478
M'ron, M., 566
Muffs, Judith Herschlag, 609
Muggamin, Howard, 626
Mumford, Lewis, 31, 326
Muschel, Nahum, 185
Musella, Donald, 257
Musher, Ruth Weiss, 362
Musnikow, Ruth, 55, 56, 482, 492
Myers, Michael, 637
Mykoff, David, 195

Naamani, Israel, 424; literature on, 306
Na'Amat Woman, 493
Nachshoni, Yehuda, 624
Nadel, Max, 20, 24, 34, 74, 87, 90, 93, 100, 132, 156, 168, 186, 246, 370, 491, 492, 580
Nadell, Pamela S., 640, 643
Nadich, Judah, 106, 393
Nadler, Meir, 309
Naftaly, Phillip, 654
Nagler, Richard, 655
Nahir, Moshe, 74
Nahon, Gerard, 651
Nahshon, Nadav, 612
Nahshon, Samuel (Shmuel), 76, 77, 168, 497, 498
Naman, P., 275
Nanus, Susan, 36, 117
Napaha, Shraga, 326
Nardi, Noah, 7, 11, 20, 78, 80, 113, 163, 168, 180, 183, 249, 281, 303, 326–27, 330, 380, 483, 546, 555, 566, 575; literature on, 306
Narell, Irena, 430
Narkiss, Bezalel, 31
Narot, Joseph B., 383
Narot, Joseph R., 272

Nassatir, A. P., 450
Natelson, Herman, 7
Natelson, Nina B., 636
Nateman, Evelyn, 35
Nathan, Anne, 511. *See also* Cohen, Anne Nathan
Nathan, Marvin, 410
Nathan, Moses N., 340
National Academy for Adult Jewish Studies (NAAJS), 393, 395
National Association of Hebrew Teachers and Principals of America, 275
National Association of Temple Educators of the UAHC (NATE), 100, 131, 149, 252, 255, 261, 280–86, 536, 598
National Board of License for Teachers and Principals in American and Canadian Jewish Schools, 235, 251, 261
National Center for the Evaluation of Educational Materials, 438
National Commission on Communal Services, 354
National Commission on the Teaching of Zionism and Israel, 171, 198
National Commission on Torah Education (NCTE), 13, 25, 158, 169, 184, 532, 580
National Committee for Teacher Education and Welfare, 235
National Committee on Leadership Development of CJF and JESNA, 246
National Community Relations Advisory Council, 139
National Conference of Jewish Social Service (NCJSS), 275
National Conference of Jewish Social Workers (NCJSW), 474, 500
National Conference of Synagogue Youth, 37, 115
National Council for Jewish Education (NCJE), 178, 200, 277–79, 282, 285, 366, 500
National Council of Jewish Women (NCJW), 274, 505, 575
National Council on Adult Jewish Education, 393
National Council on Jewish Audio-Visual Materials, 34
National Federation of Temple Brotherhoods (NFTB), 396, 562
National Federation of Temple Sisterhoods (NETS), 348, 383

National Federation of Temple Youth, 125
National Jewish Community Relations Advisory Council (NJCRAC), 141, 348, 354
National Jewish Ledger, 468
National Jewish Music Council, 606
National Jewish Welfare Board (NJWB, JWB), 25, 33, 34, 361, 367, 393, 418, 419, 603, 606
National Religious Jewish Students Association Yavne, 198
National Women's League of the USA, 348
Natkin, Fred A., 151
Nattiv, Rachel, 48
Naumoff, I. Sh., 426
Naymark, Soryl, 626
Nebraska, University of, 467
Nebraska Jewish Historical Society, 657
Necarsulmer, Henry, 501
Neeley, Charlene, 249
Neger, A., 569
Neibert, Aimee, 169
Neida, Fanny, 343
Neier, Aryeh, 643
Neiman, David, 169
Neimark, Anne E., 628
Nelson, Harry, 149
Nemoy, Leon, 440
Nemzoff, Samuel, 133
Nemzoff, Samuel E., 62, 362, 586
Nemzoff, Samuel L., 14, 152, 337
Ness, Levi, 474
Netter, Esther, 109
Neulander, Arthur H., 108, 393
Neuman, Abraham, 239, 321, 597
Neuman, Abraham A., 95, 299, 598
Neuman, L., 194
Neuman, Tillie, 105
Neumann, Emanuel, 541
Neumann, Fannie R., 192
Neumann, J. H., 163
Neumann, Richard, 32, 39, 489
Neusner, Jacob, 22, 136, 189, 237–39, 358, 375, 393, 395, 455, 522, 541, 543, 562, 580, 632, 662
Newark (N.J.) Jewish Men's Club, 469
Newbauer, N., 188
Newburger, Howard M., 566
Newfield, Morris, 422
New Haven Ledger, 434
New Haven (Conn.) Study Committee, 434

707

INDEX

Newman, A., 192, 330
Newman, Aryeh, 307
Newman, I. M., 300
Newman, L., 149, 192, 580
Newman, Louis, 154; literature on, 306
Newman, Louis I., 236, 526
Newman, Max, 529
Newman, Mordecai, 36, 664
Newman, Neil, 547
Newman, Robert G., 457
Newman, Shirley, 48, 50, 56
Newmann, Tully Milton W., 479
Newmark, Harris, 424
Newmark, Louis, 459
Newmark, Maurice A., 467
New Menorah, 505
New Mexico Jewish Historical Society, 658
New Orleans (La.) First Congregation, 350
New Orleans (La.) Jewish Community Center, 450
New Orleans (La.) Temple Sinai, 450
New Word, 456
New York Board of Review for Hebrew in Schools, 487
New York Council of Jewish Federations and Welfare Funds, 481
New York Hebrew Times (Iddishe Tseitung), 343
New York Times, 482
Neye Lebn, Dos, 493
Niebuhr, Reinhold, 125, 127
Niers, Gert, 643
Niger, Sh. *See* Ahyloni
Niger, Shmuel, 204, 206–8, 210, 213, 215, 216, 218, 219, 221, 224. 536, 547, 588
Nir, Amos, 330
Nir, Yehuda, 627
Nissenfeld, Betty, 625
Nizel, Abraham E., 456

Nizel, Jeanette S., 456
Noah, J. J., 137, 344
Noah, Mordecai Manuel, 160, 339, 340
Noar, Gertrude, 127, 133
No'ar, 121
Noble, Moshe, 299; literature on, 306
Noble, Shlomo, 160, 192, 322, 324, 395, 398
Nodel, Julius J., 500
Nordheimer, Isaac, 340
Nordlinger, Bernard J., 436
Norman, Jean Schiffer, 330
Norov, Jacob, 89
Norristown (Pa.) Jewish Community Center, 501
North American Federation of Temple Youth (NFTY), 623
North American Jewish Student [network], 285. *See also* Coalition for the Advancement of Jewish Education
Northern California Jewish Bulletin, 432
North Shore Congregation Israel (Glencoe, Ill.), 447
Noskowitz, I., 224
Noskowitz, J. A., 492
Notik, D., 398
Novadaska, Rose, 218
Novak, Bill, 169, 413, 486
Novak, David, 632
Novak, H., 210, 214
Novak, William, 419
Noveck, H., 206, 221, 312
Noveck, Simon, 287, 296, 393, 395, 396, 566
Nowak, Nancy Cohen, 56, 59, 624
Nudelman, Edward A., 36, 71, 74, 76, 79, 80, 89–91, 93, 183, 254, 443, 552, 590, 608; literature on, 306
Nudelman, Ludwig, 109
Nudelman, William A., 265

Nulman, Louis, 183, 189, 195
Nussbaum, Aaron M., 89, 186, 192
Nussbaum, Esther, 669
Nussbaum, Max, 426, 569

Oakland (Calif.) Jewish Welfare Federation, 429
Obasi, I., 147
Oberstein, Elchonon, 192
Oberstein, Leonard, 149
Oblath, Sunny Romer, 384, 609
Observer (Nashville, Tenn.), 510
Observer, The (Portland, Ore.), 500
Occident, The (Occ), 340, 341, 439
Occident and American Jewish Advocate, 505
Ochs, Vanessa L., 649
Odenheimer, Micha, 636
Oder, Irwin, 160
Ofek, Edina, 77, 625, 639
Ohana, Samuel, 192
Ohel, Chaim, 77
Ohio Jewish Chronicle, 498, 659
Olam Hadash, 121
Olan, Levi, 547
Olan, Levi A., 89, 522
Olcott, Sylvia G., 655
Olgin, Moshe, 217
Oliansky, Carol, 62
Oliker, Lilyan G., 249
Oliner, Pearl M., 627
Oliner, Samuel P., 627
Olitzky, Kerry M., 26, 62, 117, 149, 154, 295, 337, 384, 392, 395, 413, 529, 555, 620, 621, 626, 632, 640, 643, 648, 663
Olitzky, Matis, 215, 224, 227
Olomeinu, 121, 629
Olshansky, Bernard, 358, 555
Olson, Sallie D., 62
O'Malley, Charles J., 668
Omer-Man, Jonathan, 29

Key to Index

7–9: *Types of Jewish Schools* | 10–17: *Curriculum* | 18–29: *Pedagogy* | 30–40: *The Arts* | 41–44: *Bar/Bat Mitzvah* | 45–53: *The Bible* | 54–59: *Early Childhood Education* | 60–65: *Exceptional Children* | 66–68: *Guidance* | 69–85: *Hebrew* | 86–96: *History* | 97–103: *The Holocaust* | 104–6: *School Library* | 107–18: *Life Cycle of a Jew* | 119–22: *Literature* | 123–42: *Mitzvot/Values and Contemporary Issues* | 143–46: *Textbooks* | 147–58: *The High School* | 159–75: *American Jewry and the Land of Israel* | 176–203: *Day School* | 204–31: *Yiddish Secular Schools* | 232–42: *Higher Education* | 245–62: *Administration* | 263–69: *The Teacher* | 270–73: *The Rabbi and Jewish Education* | 274–86: *Conferences in Jewish Education, 1890–1988* | 287–312: *Men and Women Who Influenced Jewish Education* | 317–34: *Historical Background of Jewish Education* | 335–52: *History of Jewish Education in the United States* | 353–78: *The American Jewish Community* | 379–89: *The Home and Jewish Education* | 390–97: *Adult Education* | 398–404: *The Woman's Role and Jewish Education* | 405–8: *Sephardim and Jewish Education* | 409–16: *Youth and Jewish Education* | 417–21: *Camp* | 422–516: *Local Sources for Jewish Education* | 521–23: *Theology and Jewish Education* | 524–32: *Religious Education* | 533–38: *Philosophy of Jewish Education* | 539–44: *Goals of Jewish Education* | 545–50: *Research in Jewish Education* | 551–58: *Change in Jewish Education* | 559–72: *The Social Sciences and Jewish Education* | 573–96: *Assessment* | 597–99: *The Future of Jewish Education* | 600–602: *Bibliographies of Jewish Education in Other Lands* | 603–17: *Bibliographies of Jewish Education and Related Fields in the United States* | 619–70: *Supplement*

Opatoshu, Joseph, 226
Opender, Barry T., 193
Oppenheim, M. S., 476
Oppenheim, Michael, 569
Oppenheim, Micha Falk, 603, 604, 612, 613
Oppenheim, Samuel, 507
Orbach, Alexander, 648
Orbach, Harold, 39, 169
Orchant, Glenda, 647
Orden Schools, 94, 503
Orenstein, Walter, 50, 117
Orentlicher, Edward, 337
Orkand, Joyce, 628
Orkand, Robert, 271, 628
Orkand, Robert J., 529
Orlan, Chaim, 580
Orlan, Hayim, 294
Orlando, J., 509–10
Orlant, A. Sh., 224
Orleans, Ilo, 50
Orlinsky, Harry W., 45, 607
Orlow, Eva D. K., 193
Ormian, Hayim, 324, 330, 337, 600, 601, 604
Orner, G., 319
Ornish, Natalie, 660
Ornstein, Daniel, 133
Ornstein-Galicia, Jacob L., 659
Orodsky, Ruth S., 660
ORT Reporter, 179
Osherowitz, H., 226
Osterweis, R., 297
Osterweiss, Rolin G., 434
Ostow, Mortimer, 402, 413, 569
Ostrich, David E., 89
Ostrowsky, B., 213, 227, 485
Our Age (Dorenu), 122
Our School, 226
Owen, Tom, 426
Ozer, Charles, 324
Ozick, Cynthia, 402

Packscher, Hazel G., 105, 114
Page, Fred G., 259
Palay, Sara, 497
Paley, Michael, 669
Pallay, Eva, 62
Palm Beach Jewish World, 438
Palnick, Elijah E., 424
Palsson, Mary Dale, 450
Panich, Avigdor, 189
Panoff, Mark J., 151
Panoff, Susan R., 109
Panzer, Mitchell E., 239
Papermaster, Isadore, 494
Papo, Joseph M., 406–8, 463, 477, 615, 651, 652
Parelis, Mrs. Maurice, 56

Parish, W. J., 471
Parker, Franklin, 616
Parker, Sandra, 208, 224
Parks, Miriam Ben-Hayne, 74
Parnes, Hannah, 189
Parr, Jordan, 74
Parsons, Sanford Bernard, 305
Parzen, Herbert, 149, 157, 160, 294, 298, 309
Pasachoff, Naomi, 632, 641
Pasific, 429
Paskind, Judy, 183
Passaic (N.J.) Jewish Community Council, 470
Passamaneck, Stephen, 127
Passow, A. Harry, 62, 547, 549, 667
Pat, Emanuel, 207
Pat, Jacob, 210, 258, 281, 295
Patai, Raphael, 121, 160, 162, 604
Paterson, Moira, 623
Patt, Ruth Marcus, 468, 470
Patterson, Jose, 630
Patz, Naomi, 121
Paul, Simon M., 89
Pearce, C. S., 319
Pearl, C., 580
Pearl, Jonathan, 647
Pearl, Judith, 647
Pearlman, David W., 11, 147
Pearlman, Ezekiel, 358, 366
Pearlstein, Mitchell B., 127
Pearlstine, S. S., 516
Peck, Abraham J., 98, 271, 510, 642, 643, 659
Pedagogic Bulletin, 211, 212, 217, 226
Pedagogic Reporter, 14, 25, 33, 56, 61, 67, 90, 100, 134, 148, 167, 185, 186, 249, 253, 254, 310, 330, 366, 384, 407, 419, 439, 448, 509, 512, 514, 529, 555, 605–7, 614, 648, 667
Peikus, Annette, 58
Peixotto, Daniel M., 339, 350, 557
Peixotto, Simha C., 342, 344
Pekarsky, Maurice, 20, 580
Pelavin, Michael, 400
Pelcovitz, Ralph, 180
Peli, Pinchas, 109, 629
Penn, Ascher, 8, 39, 62, 149, 169, 180, 206, 218, 224, 239, 302, 309, 310, 362, 483, 485, 486, 488, 490
Perera, Victor, 651
Peretz, David J. H., 183
Peretz, I. L., 94
Peretz, Josephine, 89
Peri, Chaim, 20, 169, 172, 186

Perilman, Nathan A., 410, 476
Perkal, Ezra: literature on, 306
Perl, Joseph: literature on, 306
Perla, Shoshana, 169
Perlman, Milton, 249
Perlman, Milton B., 492
Perlman, Robert, 643
Perlmutter, Elsie, 358, 566
Perlmutter, Fishel A., 367
Perlmutter, Nathan, 437
Perlmutter, Philip, 133
Perlow, P., 496
Perr, Yechiel, 193, 239
Perrine, Marvyn W., 512
Perry-Marx, Jeffrey A., 20
Persky, Daniel, 69, 294, 337, 526, 612; literature on, 306
Persky, Elias, 82, 111, 136
Peskind, Steven J., 14
Pesselnick, Ruth, 48
Pessin, Deborah (Dorothy), 58, 59, 89, 91, 93, 95
Petagorsky, David W., 279
Peters, C. Brooks, 628
Peterson, J. L., 154
Petuchowsky, Jakob J., 98, 108, 324, 522, 536
Pfeffercorn, Eli, 98
Pfeifer, Paula, 402
Pheley, Gordon E., 327
Philadelphia Abend Post. See *Jewish Morning Journal*
Philadelphia Associated Talmud Torahs, 503, 505
Philadelphia Council on Jewish Education, 503, 504
Philadelphia Federation of Jewish Agencies of Greater Philadelphia, 502
Philips, Bruce A., 426, 456, 515, 555, 654, 665
Philipson, David, 236, 297, 303, 345, 494, 495, 539
Phillips, Jonas B., 341
Phillips, N. Taylor, 472, 477
Phillips, Sam, 473
Phillipsborn, Gertrude, 464
Phipps, James Ronald, 569
Picheny, Elias, 368, 461, 463
Pick, Manfred, 183
Picker, Chaim, 287
Pickett, Winston, 258
Pickus, Manuel, 515
Pike, Samuel, 338
Pilch, Judah (Yehuda[h]), 13, 71, 78, 80, 100–103, 133, 149, 155, 156, 169, 173, 178, 252, 254, 256, 264, 282, 284, 285, 287, 289, 290, 292, 293, 299, 304,

INDEX

307–9, 322, 337, 352, 360, 362, 364, 384, 396, 434, 442, 445, 463, 474, 483, 497–99, 529, 536, 541, 555, 562, 575, 580, 585, 588, 616, 617; literature on, 306
Pilchik, Eli, 529
Pilchik, Ely, 169, 294
Pilchik, Ely E., 585
Pine, Kurt, 505
Pinkenson, Ruth S., 56
Pinkos, The, 430
Pins, Arnulf M., 114, 249, 358, 384
Pins, Margot C., 14
Pinski, David, 221
Pinsky, Irving, 484
Pinson, Kopel S., 548
Pinto, Isaac, 338
Pioneer Woman. See *Na'Amat Woman*
Pitlick, Samuel (Sh.), 21, 23, 307, 310, 503; literature on, 307
Pittler, Arnold Z., 505
Piwosky, Abram P., 526
Plaskow, Judith, 402, 649
Plaut, Gunther W., 662
Plaut, W. G. Gunther, 46
Plaut, W. Gunther, 114, 271, 325, 463, 464, 494, 643
Plaut, Walter H., 149, 152
Plavin, Irving, 80
Plesur, Milton, 89, 160, 473
Plontovski, Noah, 325
Plotnik, Leonard, 477
Podell, Craig, 622
Podet, Allen H., 114
Podet, Mordecai, 512
Podhoretz, Norman, 569
Podolsky, Judy, 249
Podwal, Mark, 31
Poisson, Joseph A., 62, 257
Polak, I., 49, 81
Polans, Hymen, 344
Polatnick, Samuel, 133

Polish, Daniel P., 621, 622
Polish, David, 246, 271, 555
Politzer, Heinz, 480
Poll, Samuel, 204, 476
Pollak, George, 13, 15, 25, 48, 62, 114, 143, 146, 154, 155, 169, 171, 187, 193, 197, 246, 249, 252, 254, 258, 264–66, 358, 364, 366, 370, 393, 436, 464, 469, 473, 500, 547, 555, 580–81, 616, 642
Pollak, I. H., 456
Pollak, I. Sh., 11
Pollak, Jacob B., 87, 147, 233, 246, 257, 337, 491, 575
Pollak, Oliver, 656
Pollak, Oliver B., 467
Pollock, Shimon, 233, 264, 266, 267; literature on, 307
Polner, Murray, 271, 406
Polonies Talmud Torah, 350
Polsky, Howard W., 515
Polzin, Robert M., 319
Pomerantz, Frederic S., 151
Pomerantz, George, 555
Pomerantz, Hyman, 56, 250, 256, 267
Pomerantz, I. Chaim, 205, 216, 217, 221, 229
Pomerantz, N., 221
Pool, David de Sola, 87, 108, 111, 160, 305, 337, 347, 406, 474, 477, 507, 552, 575, 615
Pool, Tamar de Sola, 477, 615
Poops, M., 600, 601
Popkin, R., 581
Popkin, Richard A., 651
Popkin, Richard H., 126
Popkin, Zelda, 413
Poppel, Stephen M., 569
Popper, William, 160, 610, 613
Porath, Gerald, 24
Porath, Jonathan D., 25, 93
Porter, Jack Nussan, 399, 413, 502, 562, 616

Portnoy, Fern C., 433
Portnoy, Joseph, 424
Portnoy, Joseph L., 39, 133
Portowicz, David J., 330
Posner, Marcia W., 121, 611–12, 630, 669
Posnick, Michael, 633
Post, Albert, 100
Post, Lillian, 58
Post. See Koppman, Lionel; Postal, Bernard
Postal, Bernard, 422–24, 432, 433, 435, 436, 438, 440, 447–52, 454, 458, 463, 464, 466–68, 471, 472, 494, 499, 500, 507, 509, 510, 512–16, 568, 603
Potok, Chaim, 413
Poupko, Bernard A., 395
Poupko, Yehiel E., 644, 667
Powell, B., 288
Powell, David R., 90
Powers, Helen F., 552
Pozner, Marcia W, 670
Prager, Elliot H., 641
Prager, Leonard, 614
Prager, Moshe, 309
Pratt, Charles Lynn, 319
Pratt, Norma Fain, 400, 654
Pray, Lewis G., 341
Preil, Joseph J., 254, 483, 484
Preisand, Sally, 151, 402
Preiss, Madeline, 56
Prell, Riv-Ellen, 648, 649
Prensky, Frieda, 38
Preshl, T., 306
Press, Judith A., 133
Press, Judith Ann, 257
Preston, David, 66
Preston, Shari Ann, 39
Price, Marilyn, 667
Price, Roger, 668
Principal, The (Chicago), 445
Principal, The (NYC). 488
Proctor, John Clagett, 436

Key to Index

7–9: Types of Jewish Schools | *10–17: Curriculum* | *18–29: Pedagogy* | *30–40: The Arts* | *41–44: Bar/Bat Mitzvah* | *45–53: The Bible* | *54–59: Early Childhood Education* | *60–65: Exceptional Children* | *66–68: Guidance* | *69–85: Hebrew* | *86–96: History* | *97–103: The Holocaust* | *104–6: School Library* | *107–18: Life Cycle of a Jew* | *119–22: Literature* | *123–42: Mitzvot/Values and Contemporary Issues* | *143–46: Textbooks* | *147–58: The High School* | *159–75: American Jewry and the Land of Israel* | *176–203: Day School* | *204–31: Yiddish Secular Schools* | *232–42: Higher Education* | *245–62: Administration* | *263–69: The Teacher* | *270–73: The Rabbi and Jewish Education* | *274–86: Conferences in Jewish Education, 1890–1988* | *287–312: Men and Women Who Influenced Jewish Education* | *317–34: Historical Background of Jewish Education* | *335–52: History of Jewish Education in the United States* | *353–78: The American Jewish Community* | *379–89: The Home and Jewish Education* | *390–97: Adult Education* | *398–404: The Woman's Role and Jewish Education* | *405–8: Sephardim and Jewish Education* | *409–16: Youth and Jewish Education* | *417–21: Camp* | *422–516: Local Sources for Jewish Education* | *521–23: Theology and Jewish Education* | *524–32: Religious Education* | *533–38: Philosophy of Jewish Education* | *539–44: Goals of Jewish Education* | *545–50: Research in Jewish Education* | *551–58: Change in Jewish Education* | *559–72: The Social Sciences and Jewish Education* | *573–96: Assessment* | *597–99: The Future of Jewish Education* | *600–602: Bibliographies of Jewish Education in Other Lands* | *603–17: Bibliographies of Jewish Education and Related Fields in the United States* | *619–70: Supplement*

INDEX

Proctor, Samuel, 437, 450
Progress, The, 432
Progresso, El, 408
Proletarian Education, 226
Proletarisher Gedank, 447
Proshan, Chester, 464
Provol, William Lee, 474
Prystowsky, S., 13
Prystowksy, Seymour, 541
Pryzant, Nancy, 15
Publications of the American Jewish Historical Society (PAJHS), 350
Pyke, C., 343
Pyke, E., 343

Quarterly Pedagogic School Journal, 226
Quarterly Theological Magazine, 82
Queens (NYC) Principals Council, 487, 489

Raab, David, 303
Raab, Earl, 431
Raab, Menachem, 197, 667
Rabbi Isaac Elchanan Theological Seminary, 240, 284
Rabbinical Assembly (RA), 124, 138, 275–77, 279, 280, 282–84, 393, 395, 522, 614
Rabbinical Council of America (RCA), 284
Raben, Harvey A., 645
Rabin, A. I., 330
Rabin, Chaim, 74
Rabin, Florence, 486
Rabin, Phillip Haskell, 498
Rabinowitch, 211, 217
Rabinowitch, Israel, 37
Rabinowitz, Benjamin, 348
Rabinowitz, C. D., 198
Rabinowitz, Dorothy, 102, 330, 413, 589
Rabinowitz, I., 210, 411
Rabinowitz, J., 235
Rabinowitz, Stanley, 26, 581
Rabinowitz, Tzvi, 622
Rabinowitz, Yosef B., 637
Rabinowitz, Zina, 79, 215, 266, 575
Rachlis, A., 290
Rackman, Bennett M., 62
Rackman, Emanuel, 108, 133, 141, 169, 239, 352, 367, 493, 522, 529, 536, 594, 631
Radin, H., 226
Radin, Hayim, 427
Radke, Marian, 569

Radke, Marion, 413
Radzik, Abraham, 133
Radzik, Avraham, 48
Rafael, Ruth Kelson, 424, 431
Raffkind, Myrna G., 660
Raider, Mark A., 670
Raik, Jerome, 384
Raimi, Ralph A., 657
Raisin, J. S., 303
Raiskin, Max, 136
Raizin, Abraham, 221, 226
Ramah, 493
Rambam. *See* Maimonides, Moses
Rand, Baruch, 358, 366
Ranson, Marius, 11, 249
Rapchinski, B., 296
Raphael, Ahi Shimshun, 413
Raphael, Chaim, 406, 629, 651
Raphael, Jacob, 169
Raphael, Jacob R., 486
Raphael, Marc Lee, 92, 347, 349, 354, 498, 569, 616
Raphael, Ruth, 183
Raphaeli, Ruth, 74, 78, 81, 82
Raphaels, Rose, 56
Raphall, Morris Jacov, 341, 342
Rapoport, I., 296
Rapoport, Israel S., 355
Rapoport, Solomon Judah Loeb: literature on, 307
Rapp, Michael G., 463
Rappaport, David, 76, 78
Rappaport, Joseph, 562
Rappaport, Julius, 123
Rappoport, Israel B., 11, 71, 81, 246, 461, 516, 542, 552, 584, 588, 590
Rappoport, Joseph, 494
Rashi: literature on, 307
Raskin, Aliza, 105
Raskin, Saul, 31
Ratner, Sidney, 300
Rauch, Eduardo, 121, 193, 235, 241, 250, 337, 384, 389, 402, 554, 623, 630, 633, 652
Rauch, Max, 330
Rauchwanger, Diane, 249, 555
Ravich, Jesse, 562
Ravid, Benjamin, 651
Ravid, Moshe, 155
Ravid, Ruth, 56, 80, 664
Ravid, Witta, 616
Ravid, Zvulun, 264, 288, 289, 291, 293, 299, 303, 304, 306, 308, 311, 393, 480, 536, 555, 614
Ravin, Noach, 193
Rawidowicz, Shimon, 304
Rawidowicz, Simon, 305, 441, 536

Ray, Lali, 483
Ray, Natalie, 48, 56, 384
Recess, Asher, 98
Reconstructionist, The, 162, 358, 393, 426, 436, 536, 555–56
Reed, Judith, 330
Reeder, Joseph, 236
Reform Advocate (Chicago), 447
Reform Advocate (Denver), 433
Reformed Society of Israelites, 339
Reform Judaism, 627, 633
Regelson, Abraham, 39
Reich, Cindy, 156
Reich, Nathan, 311
Reich, P., 556
Reich, Zvi, 419
Reichel, Aaron I., 476
Reichert, Irving F., 114
Reichert, Max, 78
Reichert, Victor E., 199
Reichwald, Faye, 25, 55, 492
Reifenberg, R. J., 31
Reifman, Toby Fishbein, 402
Reikes, Vicki, 23, 60
Reimer, Jack, 628, 629
Reimer, Joseph, 114, 133, 252, 529, 556, 640, 648, 664
Reines, Ch. Z., 398
Reines, Chaim Wolf, 321
Reines, Isaac Jacob: literature on, 307
Reingold, Harold A., 67
Reinhold, H., 169
Reisin, Zalmen, 601
Reisman, Bernard, 136, 169, 254, 387, 389, 395, 396, 554, 569, 644, 645, 664
Reisman, Diana, 74
Reisner, Neil, 426
Reiss, Asher, 609
Reissman, Leonard, 450
Reiter-Zedek, Miriam, 121
Reizenstein, Jennie, 49
Rejwan, Nissim, 652
Religious Action Center, 145
Relkin, Stanley T., 151
Rembrandt, Elaine, 117
Rembrandt, Esther, 36
Reneh, H., 384
Renewal: United Jewish Federation News, 514
Rephun, Sholom, 183
Reshef, Yaakov, 491
Reshotko, Deborah, 647
Resnick, David, 169, 249
Resnick, David A., 545, 547, 549
Resnick, Hyman, 39
Resnick, Martha, 89, 235, 652

711

Resnick, Miriam Roher, 21
Resnik, Reuben, 13, 283, 473
Resnikoff, Bernard, 581
Resnikoff, M. Bernard, 419
Resnikoff, Moses B., 319
Response, 108, 493, 649
Reuben, Steven, 257
Revel, Bernard, 178, 199, 236, 240, 590; literature on, 307
Review, The (Philadelphia), 505
Revitch, Eugene, 48, 51, 385, 566
Reynolds, Ronald Lewis, 246, 257, 664
Reznick, Anita, 117
Reznick, H., 443
Reznik, Reuben, 283, 291, 337
Reznikoff, Charles, 305, 434, 455, 509
Rhode Island Herald, 508
Rhode Island Jewish Historical Notes, 508
Rhodes, Irwin S., 501, 507
Ribalow, Harold U., 189, 612
Ribalow, Menachem, 74, 83, 162, 279, 294; literature on, 307
Ribicoff, P., 42
Ribner, I., 368
Ribner, Israel, 74, 135, 252
Ribner, R., 56
Ribner, Sol, 393, 504
Ribowsky, H., 185
Rich, Adolph, 515
Rich, S. Esther, 169
Richards, Bernard, 160
Richards, Bernard G., 354
Richards, G., 475
Richards, Stephen, 623
Richman, Julia, 129, 347
Richman, Milton, 109, 118
Richman, Thelma, 139
Richmond (Va.) Jewish Community Council, 514
Rieger, Eliezer, 74, 327; literature on, 307–8
Rieger, Eliezer L., 76

Riemer, Jack, 27, 108, 133
Rifkin, Jeremy, 627
Riklis, L. I., 490
Riley, Karen, 627
Rimon, Pinchas, 33
Rimor, Mordechai, 666
Rinder, Irwin D., 127
Rinder, Reuben, 37
Rinegrad, N., 277
Ringelbaum, Emmanuel, 98
Ringer, Benjamin B., 163
Rinken, M. M., 566
Ripinsky, Sol, 423
Rips, Mrs. A. S., 54
Rischall, Joseph, 184
Rischin, Moses, 161, 424, 457, 476, 478, 608, 640
Risinger, C. Frederick, 444
Riskin, Steven, 193
Rittenband, Ruth, 186
Ritterbrand, Paul, 479
Rittner, Stephen, 42
Rivkin, B., 221, 503
Rivkin, Ellis, 125, 569
Rivkin, Mrs. Nacha, 198
Rivkin, Sholom, 127
Rivkind, Isaac, 41
Robbins, Edward, 368
Robbins, Richard C., 647
Robbins, Ruth Honor, 298
Roberts, Daniel A., 396
Roberts, Dorothy, 433
Robin, Robert, 75
Robin, Stanley, 75
Robinovitch, Sid, 623
Robinson, Colin, 627
Robinson, Ira, 640
Robinson, Jacob, 609
Robinson, Jessie, 116
Robinson, Michael, 514
Robison, Sophia M., 463, 469, 470, 479
Rochlin, Fred, 423
Rochlin, Harriet, 423
Rock, Andrea White, 627

Rock, Martin H., 565
Rockaway, Robert A., 460, 657
Rockland, Mae Shaffer, 31
Rockovsky, Boris, 413
Rockower, Jacob R., 503
Rocky Mountain Curriculum Planning Workshop, 15
Rodrigue, Aron, 652
Roffman, Sylvia Greene, 467
Rogers, Theresa F., 26
Rogoff, Harry, 349, 613
Rogow, Faith, 650
Rogow, Sally, 62
Rohn, Aryeh, 325
Rojanski, Samuel, 210
Rokeach, M., 184
Rolnick, Don, 162
Romanoff, Lena, 622
Romey, David, 514
Romirowsky, Leah, 443, 444
Romm, Diane, 47
Romm, J. Leonard, 109
Ron, Lazer, 296
Ronch, I. A., 217, 219
Ronen, Chanan, 331
Ronen, D., 169
Rontch, Isaac E., 476
Roos, Roberta M., 172
Ror, M., 461
Rose, Arnold M., 562, 569
Rose, Ernestine, 399
Rose, Herbert H., 296
Rose, Isaac B., 395
Rose, M., 475
Rose, Marvin, 143, 145
Rose, Nathan H., 387
Rose. O. L., 371
Rose, Peter Isaac, 562
Rose, Robyn I., 454
Rose, Ruth W., 149, 266
Rose, Shirley, 624
Roseman, Kenneth D., 90, 495, 630
Roseman, Saul, 358
Roseman, Shmuel D., 506

Key to Index

7–9: *Types of Jewish Schools* | 10–17: *Curriculum* | 18–29: *Pedagogy* | 30–40: *The Arts* | 41–44: *Bar/Bat Mitzvah* | 45–53: *The Bible* | 54–59: *Early Childhood Education* | 60–65: *Exceptional Children* | 66–68: *Guidance* | 69–85: *Hebrew* | 86–96: *History* | 97–103: *The Holocaust* | 104–6: *School Library* | 107–18: *Life Cycle of a Jew* | 119–22: *Literature* | 123–42: *Mitzvot/Values and Contemporary Issues* | 143–46: *Textbooks* | 147–58: *The High School* | 159–75: *American Jewry and the Land of Israel* | 176–203: *Day School* | 204–31: *Yiddish Secular Schools* | 232–42: *Higher Education* | 245–62: *Administration* | 263–69: *The Teacher* | 270–73: *The Rabbi and Jewish Education* | 274–86: *Conferences in Jewish Education, 1890–1988* | 287–312: *Men and Women Who Influenced Jewish Education* | 317–34: *Historical Background of Jewish Education* | 335–52: *History of Jewish Education in the United States* | 353–78: *The American Jewish Community* | 379–89: *The Home and Jewish Education* | 390–97: *Adult Education* | 398–404: *The Woman's Role and Jewish Education* | 405–8: *Sephardim and Jewish Education* | 409–16: *Youth and Jewish Education* | 417–21: *Camp* | 422–516: *Local Sources for Jewish Education* | 521–23: *Theology and Jewish Education* | 524–32: *Religious Education* | 533–38: *Philosophy of Jewish Education* | 539–44: *Goals of Jewish Education* | 545–50: *Research in Jewish Education* | 551–58: *Change in Jewish Education* | 559–72: *The Social Sciences and Jewish Education* | 573–96: *Assessment* | 597–99: *The Future of Jewish Education* | 600–602: *Bibliographies of Jewish Education in Other Lands* | 603–17: *Bibliographies of Jewish Education and Related Fields in the United States* | 619–70: *Supplement*

INDEX

Roseman, Yehuda, 547
Rosen, B., 508, 562
Rosen, Ben, 71, 78, 246, 257, 355, 359, 362, 363, 365, 435, 456, 461, 469, 470, 473, 474, 486, 496, 503–5, 546, 575, 586, 588; literature on, 308
Rosen, Bernard Carl, 154, 562
Rosen, E., 612
Rosen, Ellen, 55, 245
Rosen, Evelyn Rosing, 511
Rosen, Gladys, 21, 93, 261, 366, 387, 402, 437, 648
Rosen, H., 67, 414
Rosen, Harry J., 79
Rosen, J. C., 450
Rosen, Leah, 305
Rosen, Lester, 436
Rosen, M., 110
Rosen, Michael J., 465
Rosen, Morton, 193, 434
Rosenak, Michael, 169, 173, 522, 529, 532, 536, 562, 569, 581, 586, 663
Rosenau, William, 237
Rosenbach, Abraham S. W., 500, 502, 608, 634
Rosenbach, Hyman Pollock, 502
Rosenbaum, Alan, 24, 624
Rosenbaum, Bella W., 514
Rosenbaum, Claire Millhiser, 661
Rosenbaum, Fred, 429, 431
Rosenbaum, Jeanette, 502
Rosenbaum, Jonathan, 252, 364, 467
Rosenberg, Amye, 117, 136
Rosenberg, Ariah, 71
Rosenberg, Asenath, 490, 642
Rosenberg, Benjamin B., 254
Rosenberg, Chaim, 266
Rosenberg, Dan S., 466
Rosenberg, Harold, 31
Rosenberg, Joel, 620
Rosenberg, Martin, 541
Rosenberg, Maud, 513
Rosenberg, Meyer J., 319
Rosenberg, Pauline, 444, 552
Rosenberg, Samuel, 169
Rosenberg, Stanley, 188
Rosenberg, Stuart C., 180
Rosenberg, Stuart E., 42, 271, 272, 388, 473, 529, 569
Rosenberger, Mrs. Sh., 136, 198
Rosenblatt, Dona, 34
Rosenblatt, Gary, 285, 647
Rosenblatt, Howard B., 21, 186, 541
Rosenblatt, Samuel, 237
Rosenbloom, J., 506
Rosenbloom, J. R., 154
Rosenbloom, Joseph R., 297, 399
Rosenbloom, Milton, 149
Rosenbloom, Noah H., 98, 298
Rosenblum, Edward, 436
Rosenblum, Eileen, 621, 639
Rosenblum, Jerome, 113
Rosenblum, Paul C., 184
Rosenblum, Richard, 626, 629
Rosenblum, William, 193
Rosenfeld, David, 133
Rosenfeld, Geraldine, 616
Rosenfeld, H., 98
Rosenfeld, Israel, 22, 189, 198
Rosenfeld, Leonard, 484
Rosenfield, Bea, 623
Rosenfield, Geraldine, 13, 284, 653
Rosenfield, Jerry, 623
Rosenkrantz, Samuel, 133, 178
Rosenkranz, Samuel, 23, 62
Rosenman, Samuel I., 526, 575
Rosenman, Yehuda, 569
Rosenman, Yehudah, 387
Rosenmond, A., 235
Rosensaft, Menachem Z., 627
Rosenshine, Jay, 462
Rosenstock, E. D., 178
Rosenstock, Morton, 305
Rosenthal, Eric, 436, 441, 448
Rosenthal, Frank, 152, 413, 448, 617
Rosenthal, Gilbert S., 136, 156
Rosenthal, Henry W., 393
Rosenthal, Ira, 21, 26, 87, 369, 384, 529
Rosenthal, Ira A., 46, 589
Rosenthal, Judah, 311
Rosenthal, Lester H., 235
Rosenthal, Norma, 100
Rosenthal, Stephen, 188, 193
Rosentreich, Vicki, 622
Rosenwaike, Ira, 452, 494, 495
Rosenwasser, Rose K., 62, 105
Rosenzweig, Ephraim, 58
Rosenzweig, Franz, 51, 325, 334, 536; literature on, 308
Rosenzweig, Linda W., 89, 133
Rosenzweig, Marion J., 58
Rosewater, Adeline R., 39, 54, 114
Roshal, Margit, 109
Roshan, A., 487
Rosin, Avivah, 75
Roskies, David G., 627, 669
Roskies, Diana K., 46, 322
Roskies, Diane, 100
Roskin, Laurie, 413
Rosman, Steven M., 21, 114, 319, 384, 623, 624, 664
Rosoff, Barbara, 255, 266
Rosoff, Barbara L., 620
Rosoff, Dan, 382
Ross, Lillian, 655
Ross, Lillian Hammer, 630
Ross, Tamar, 650
Rossel, Karen Trager, 54, 111, 255
Rossel, Seymour, 93, 102, III, 133, 134, 136, 172, 266, 285, 387, 529, 581, 624, 626, 648, 664
Rossoff, Don, 22, 604
Roswaski, C., 529
Rotenberg, I., 221, 282
Rotenberg, Joshua, 227, 581
Rotenberg, Memorah Lebowitz, 633
Rotenberg, Rena, 56–57, 453, 646
Rotenstreich, Nathan, 296, 298, 301, 305, 331, 569, 635
Roth, Alvin S., 319
Roth, Amy E., 620
Roth, Bette, 459
Roth, Cecil, 31, 42, 91, 398, 406, 600, 652
Roth, H. I., 327
Roth, L., 304
Roth, Norman, 127
Roth, Shana, 26, 156
Roth, Walter, 656
Rothbard, Dvorah, 161
Rothbard, Madelyn, 639
Rothberg, Abraham, 42
Rothblatt, Ch. M., 311, 442, 444, 446
Rothchild, Sylvia, 667
Rothenberg, Joshua, 172, 483, 604
Rothenberg, Tobias, 514
Rothenheim, W., 342
Rothkoff, Aaron, 193, 307
Rothman, Eugene, 193
Rothman, Iris, 23, 35, 75
Rothman, Irving N., 21
Rothman, Jack, 303, 547, 569–70
Rothman, John F., 427, 538, 553
Rothman, R. C., 331
Rothman, Sholom Dov, 637
Rothschild, Fritz, 52, 298, 522, 529
Rothschild, Janice O., 439
Rothschild, Max M., 613
Rothschild, William Lee, 100
Rothstein, Ann, 413
Rothstein, Arnold, 37
Rothstein, D. G., 393
Routtenberg, Max, 193
Routtenberg, Max J., 42, 395

Rubee, Lillie, 20, 75
Rubenowitz, Mignon L., 31
Rubenstein, Asa, 440
Rubenstein, Charles A., 452
Rubenstein, Frank J., 237
Rubenstein, Jeffrey, 632
Rubenstein, L., 282
Rubenstein, Richard L., 98, 271
Rubenstein, Sandra, 402
Ruberg, Miriam Brunn, 661
Rubin, Alvan D., 42
Rubin, Alvin, 530
Rubin, George, 384, 605
Rubin, Israel, 202, 476
Rubin, Leonard, 99
Rubin, Nan, 658
Rubin, Ph., 254
Rubin, Philip, 178
Rubin, Ruth, 37, 606
Rubin, Saul Jacob, 440
Rubin, Susan E., 654
Rubinow, Isaac Max, 476
Rubinstein, I., 216
Rubinstein, L., 295
Rubinstein, Robert E., 581
Rubinstein, Simha, 81, 171, 266, 490, 588
Rubinsztejn, Zionna, 266
Ruby, Hemdah, 79
Rudai, Pinchos, 227
Rudavsky, David, 121, 147, 154, 155, 157, 169, 239, 277, 306, 309, 337, 349, 366, 410, 469, 470, 473, 481, 482, 484, 487–89, 504, 529, 556, 562, 587
Rudd, Hynda, 512
Rudens, S. P., 481
Ruderman, Jerome L., 93
Rudin, A. James, 449
Rudin, Jacob, 169
Rudin, Jacob P., 581
Rudin, Marcia R., 371
Rudman, S., 224
Rudolph, B. G., 474

Ruffman, Louis L., 12, 13, 15, 36, 57, 246, 249, 256, 257, 259, 279, 299, 300, 431, 461, 463, 465, 470, 483, 486, 487, 489, 586; literature on, 308
Rugoff, Kathy, 98
Rush, Barbara, 114, 117, 630, 653
Russ, Ian, 664
Russler, Gwynn, 570
Rustin, Bayard, 127
Rutchik, Allen, 413, 570
Ruthen, Marlene Lobell, 42
Rutman, Herbert Samuel, 463
Ruttkay, Paul, 436
Ruud, Inger Marie, 616
Rypins, Isaac L., 123

Sabar, Naama, 100
Sachar, Abraham L., 129, 237
Sachar, Howard M., 86, 162, 169, 586
Sacher, Byron, 13
Sachs, Howard F., 465
Sachs, Moses B., 259
Sachs, Moshe, 42, 169
Sachs, Nellie, 98
Sacks, Maxwell L., 319
Sadeh, Pinhas, 630
Sadker, David Miller, 121
Sadker, Myra Pollock, 121
Saffran, Elizabeth, 506
Sagarin, James, 628
Sager, Steven R., 152
Saint John, Robert, 635
Saint Louis (Mo.) *Jewish Light,* 466, 657
Saks, Honan, 214
Saks, Robert J., 413
Salanter, Israel Lipkin, 308
Salczer, David, 184
Salinger, Gerhard, 661
Salinger, Rosemarie D., 57
Salkin, Jeffrey K., 623
Salkowitz, Selig, 26
Salpeter, H., 31

Saltzman, Elly, 235
Saltzman, Josh, 632
Saltzman, Manuel, 149
Salvay, Betty, 57
Samber, Moshe, 366, 444
Samlan, Arnold D., 169, 653
Samler, Joseph, 67
Sampter, Jessie E., 117, 171, 327
Samuel, Edith, 648
Samuel, John, 500
Samuel, Maurice, 161, 205
Samuels, Robert, 331
Samuels, Ruth, 93
Samuelson, Myron, 512
Samuelson, Norbert M., 620, 663
Sanatorium (Denver [Colo.] publication), 433
Sandberg, Jeanne Glazer, 75
Sandberg, Neil C., 426
Sandberg, Ruth, 272
Sandel, Lenore, 632
Sanders, Ira E., 424
Sanders, Ronald, 478, 480
Sandler, Bernard I., 656
Sandler, F., 484
Sandler, P., 206, 432, 463
Sandler, Ron, 100
Sandmel, Samuel, 238, 320
Sandrow, Edward T., 581
Sanua, Marianne, 652, 659
Sanua, Victor D., 154, 387, 413, 477, 562, 566, 570, 588
Saperstein, David, 632, 648
Saperstein, Jeffrey, 121
Saperstein, Marc E., 413
Saphire, Shelley R., 180
Sapinsley, Elbert, 449
Saposnik, Tamar Lubin, 78
Saretsky, Augusta, 362, 384, 388, 492, 610, 612
Sargent, Edward N., 473
Sarna, Jonathan D., 93, 271, 347, 349, 434, 472, 481, 614, 630, 641, 643, 652, 659, 668, 669
Sarna, Nahum M., 50, 238, 623

Key to Index

7–9: *Types of Jewish Schools* | 10–17: *Curriculum* | 18–29: *Pedagogy* | 30–40: *The Arts* | 41–44: *Bar/Bat Mitzvah* | 45–53: *The Bible* | 54–59: *Early Childhood Education* | 60–65: *Exceptional Children* | 66–68: *Guidance* | 69–85: *Hebrew* | 86–96: *History* | 97–103: *The Holocaust* | 104–6: *School Library* | 107–18: *Life Cycle of a Jew* | 119–22: *Literature* | 123–42: *Mitzvot/Values and Contemporary Issues* | 143–46: *Textbooks* | 147–58: *The High School* | 159–75: *American Jewry and the Land of Israel* | 176–203: *Day School* | 204–31: *Yiddish Secular Schools* | 232–42: *Higher Education* | 245–62: *Administration* | 263–69: *The Teacher* | 270–73: *The Rabbi and Jewish Education* | 274–86: *Conferences in Jewish Education, 1890–1988* | 287–312: *Men and Women Who Influenced Jewish Education* | 317–34: *Historical Background of Jewish Education* | 335–52: *History of Jewish Education in the United States* | 353–78: *The American Jewish Community* | 379–89: *The Home and Jewish Education* | 390–97: *Adult Education* | 398–404: *The Woman's Role and Jewish Education* | 405–8: *Sephardim and Jewish Education* | 409–16: *Youth and Jewish Education* | 417–21: *Camp* | 422–516: *Local Sources for Jewish Education* | 521–23: *Theology and Jewish Education* | 524–32: *Religious Education* | 533–38: *Philosophy of Jewish Education* | 539–44: *Goals of Jewish Education* | 545–50: *Research in Jewish Education* | 551–58: *Change in Jewish Education* | 559–72: *The Social Sciences and Jewish Education* | 573–96: *Assessment* | 597–99: *The Future of Jewish Education* | 600–602: *Bibliographies of Jewish Education in Other Lands* | 603–17: *Bibliographies of Jewish Education and Related Fields in the United States* | 619–70: *Supplement*

INDEX

Sarner, Ruth Braude, 502
Sasek, M., 172
Sass, Stephen J., 426
Sasso, Sandy Eisenberg, 156, 367, 630, 663
Sassoon, Solomon David, 407
Satinsky, Morris W., 503
Satlowe, Lewis, 54
Satt, Flora Jane, 433
Savan, Isaac, 264
Sawdayee, Maurice M., 320
Saye, Hyman, 453
SCA, 395
Schaalman, H. E., 396
Schaalman, Herman, 541
Schachter, Lifsa, 21, 75, 169, 188, 193, 235, 645
Schachter, Stanley J., 246, 556
Schacter, Herschel, 522
Schacter, Jacob J., 652
Schaefer, Alice L., 119
Schaefer, Molly A., 75
Schaffler, Israel, 75
Schaffler, Lawrence D., 239
Schaffzin, Linda K., 89
Schaffzin, Stephen, 89
Schafler, S., 645
Schafler, Samuel, 57, 133, 306, 337, 366, 376, 384, 395, 556, 562, 581, 598, 663, 667
Schaktman, Peter B., 169
Schall, David J., 665
Schanin, Norman, 14, 21, 112, 133, 151, 169, 249, 413, 529, 547, 548, 581
Schanzer, Sharon, 625
Schanzer, Sharon Stern, 75
Schapiro, David, 453
Schappes, 338, 341
Schappes, Morris U., 348
Scharfstein, Sol, 82, 111, 112, 117, 172
Scharfstein, Zevi, 21, 41, 46, 49, 69, 71, 76, 79, 81, 87, 91, 117, 119, 170, 171, 264, 277, 288–90, 292–94, 297, 299–301, 306, 308–12, 320, 322, 325, 327, 331, 337, 358, 363, 366, 384, 398, 487, 526, 531, 536, 539, 547, 552, 556, 575–76, 581, 588, 598, 601, 607; literature on, 308
Schatz, Boris, 327
Schatz, Julius, 583
Schatz, Shirley, 23, 266
Schauss, Hayyim, 114, 211, 215, 227
Schechner, Mark, 669
Schechter, Cathy, 660

Schechter, Daniel S., 662
Schechter, Jay, 81, 101
Schechter, Joseph, 211
Schechter, Solomon, 46, 51, 82, 118, 144, 293, 346, 398, 522, 526, 662; literature on, 308–9
Schechtman, Aaron, 47
Scheffler, T., 570
Schefler, Sh., 193
Schein, Jeffrey L., 21, 133, 272, 556, 587, 664, 667, 668
Scheindler, Ronny, 79
Scheindlin, Raymond P., 652
Scheindling, Lawrence, 384
Scheiner, Louis, 503
Scheirer, Elinor, 249
Schenirer, Sarah, 398; literature on, 309
Schenker, Avraham, 170, 419
Scherer, Allan, 152
Scherman, N., 272
Scherman, Nosson, 112
Scherzer, Kenneth A., 479
Schichman, V., 209
Schichman, Z., 295
Schick, Sandor E., 479
Schickler, Rolf W., 370
Schiff, Alvin I., 8, 21, 26, 79, 127, 133, 140, 170, 176, 178, 180, 193, 201–3, 235, 246, 249, 252, 254, 258, 262, 264, 266, 268, 284, 286, 288, 298, 303, 325, 358, 360, 362, 364, 377, 429, 465, 466, 474, 483, 484, 488, 495, 529, 536, 547, 556, 570, 581, 588, 589, 594, 595, 598, 607, 613, 621, 623, 636, 640–42, 645, 647, 659, 664, 667, 668
Schiff, Alvin Irwin, 664
Schiff, Gary, 358
Schiff, Gary S., 331
Schiff, Harold, 87
Schiftan, Harriet Kaplowitz, 431
Schimmel, Sol, 529
Schimmel, Solomon, 133, 247
Schindler, Alexander M., 15, 149, 163, 360, 370, 375, 529, 556, 581, 586, 587, 592, 598, 647
Schindler, Pesach, 155, 188, 193, 360
Schindler, Solomon, 345, 455
Schlafer, Israel, 436, 453
Schlaffman, Helene, 255
Schlager, Milton J., 109
Schlanger, Sandy, 620
Schlein, Miriam, 58
Schlesinger, Benjamin, 609
Schlessinger, June Hirsch, 413

Schloff, Linda Mack, 463
Schloss, Martin, 483
Schlossberg, David, 193
Schlosser, Sonya, 384
Schlossel, J. L., 184
Schlossel, Mark E., 362, 581
Schmeltzer, Menahem H., 349
Schmelz, Uziel O., 562, 622, 668
Schmida, Mirjam, 331
Schmidt, H., 87
Schmidt, H. D., 529
Schmidt, Nancy J., 562
Schmidt, Sarah L., 163, 300
Schmier, Louis, 438–40, 655
Schmuckler, Miriam, 109
Schnaiderman, Sh. L., 101
Schnaidman, Mordecai, 63, 134, 186, 193, 195, 529, 645, 667
Schneck, Michelle, 620
Schneerson, Isaac Joseph: literature on, 309
Schneerson, Menachem M.: literature on, 309
Schneider, Dorothee, 562
Schneider, Ilene, 604
Schneider, Louis, 87
Schneider, Paul David, 249
Schneider, Susan Weidman, 247, 366–67, 402, 404, 581
Schneierson, Fishel, 295
Schneierson, Fishl, 566
Schnitzer, Henry L., 468
Schnitzer, Jeshia, 469
Schoem, David, 21, 266, 556, 563, 566, 582, 588, 664, 668
Schoenberg, Elliot S., 27, 42, 154
Schoenberg, Nancy, 440
Schoenburg, Harry D., 637
Schoenfeld, Eugene, 570
Schoner, Allan, 478
Schonfeld, Bella, 650
School and Home, 226
School and Society, 179
School and Teacher, 226
School Bulletin, 226
School Center for Yiddish Culture, 215
Schoolman, Albert P., 235, 254, 265, 295, 299, 355, 363, 419, 446, 547, 576, 582; literature on, 309
Schorsch, Ismar, 633
Schottland, Charles I., 371
Schrag, Carl, 622
Schram, Peninah, 57, 121
Schreiber, Emanuel, 345
Schreiber, Max, 246
Schreiber, Mordecai, 497
Schremer, Oded, 14, 75, 639

Schub, Joseph Arye, 445
Schulman, Elias, 325, 334, 492, 612, 613
Schulman, Robert H., 637
Schulman, Samuel, 526
Schulman, Susan, 637
Schultz, Bella E., 465
Schultz, Eliezer, 443
Schultz, Joseph P., 465
Schultz, L., 81
Schulweiss, Harold M., 101, 127, 358, 387, 522, 570, 582, 632, 647, 666
Schur, Maxine, 636
Schussheim, Morris, 294
Schwab, Joseph J., 529, 532
Schwab, Moise, 602
Schwarcz, Ernest, 188, 193
Schwardelson, Susan J., 36
Schwarts, L. Fields, 494
Schwarts, Mrs. Charles, 609
Schwarts, Sidney Howard, 349
Schwartz, Amy, 630
Schwartz, Arnold, 26
Schwartz, Benjamin, 453
Schwartz, Berbie G., 604
Schwartz, Carole, 625
Schwartz, Celia, 27
Schwartz, Charles, 570
Schwartz, Dannel I., 395
Schwartz, David, 31
Schwartz, E., 42, 89
Schwartz, Earl, 134, 136, 632
Schwartz, Elkhanan, 189, 193, 195, 362
Schwartz, Elliot S., 63, 110, 149, 246, 247, 252, 255, 360, 366, 508, 556, 627, 639, 642
Schwartz, Frederick C., 294, 585
Schwartz, Gedalia, 196
Schwartz, Henry, 430, 670
Schwartz, Howard, 121, 122, 414, 630, 653
Schwartz, I. I., 211
Schwartz, Jacob D., 91

Schwartz, Larry, 63, 450
Schwartz, Lawrence W., 11, 410
Schwartz, Lillian, 620, 630
Schwartz, Lita Linzer, 25, 414
Schwartz, Lita S., 563
Schwartz, M. G., 105
Schwartz, R. L., 501
Schwartz, Shirley, 31, 607
Schwartz, Shuley Rubin, 419
Schwartz, Shuly Rubin, 90, 95
Schwartz, Sidney H., 271, 556, 644
Schwartz, Simon, 582
Schwartz, Z., 277
Schwartzman, Frances Zellick, 434
Schwartzman, Louis, 57, 136, 178, 257, 359, 438, 450, 466
Schwartzman, M., 211, 219
Schwartzman, Sylvan D., 14–16, 50, 82, 114, 117, 136, 152, 156, 178, 235, 246, 266, 272, 384, 529, 530, 556, 582
Schwarz, J. D., 171
Schwarz, Joseph, 341
Schwarz, Karl, 31
Schwarzschild, Steven, 298
Schwarzschild, Steven S., 522
Schweid, E., 331, 570
Schweid, Lawrence R., 637
Schweitzer, Ira H., 247, 266
Scotford, J. R., 526
Scribe (Portland, Ore.), 500
Scribe, The (Los Angeles), 429
Scult, Mel, 235, 640
Seasongood, Emily, 495
Secher, Herbert Pierre, 643
Segal, Abraham, 14, 21, 23, 36, 41–43, 76, 87, 92, 93, 117, 134–36, 170, 172, 235, 249, 385, 393, 491, 504, 556; literature on, 309
Segal, Benjamin J., 170, 620, 628, 636
Segal, Berl, 226

Segal, Bernard, 254
Segal, Beryl, 508, 582
Segal, Danny, 623
Segal, H., 503
Segal, Harriet, 636
Segal, J. J., 226
Segal, Jack, 414, 500
Segal, Jacob, 179
Segal, Judith, 106, 612
Segal, Leon, 293
Segal, Louis, 161, 311
Segal, Robert, 455
Segal, Samuel, 462
Segal, Samuel M., 194, 484
Segal, Sheila, 172, 636
Segall, Aryeh, 604
Segalman, Ralph, 570
Segel, Alexander, 325, 504
Segel, Kenneth I., 134, 414
Segelman, Ralph, 566
Seglin, Joyce, 247
Seidel, Julius, 71
Seidenfeld, Morton, 563
Seidenfeld, Morton A., 21, 556
Seidler-Feller, Chaim, 367
Seidman, Aaron B., 185
Seidman, Hillel, 305
Seiger, Marvin, 480
Seixas, James, 339
Seixes, Gershon, 338
Selavan, Ida Cohen, 163, 505–6, 670
Seldin, Ruth, 173
Seldin, Ruth R., 622
Selekman, Ben M., 371
Selig, Sidney, 134, 249, 250, 259
Seligman, Ben B., 479, 563
Seligman, Ralph, 303
Seligson, Isaac, 359
Seller, Maxine Schwartz, 161, 302
Sellinger, Benjamin, 369
Seltzer, Richard M., 640
Seltzer, Robert M., 622, 641, 652
Seltzer, S., 414

Key to Index

7–9: *Types of Jewish Schools* | 10–17: *Curriculum* | 18–29: *Pedagogy* | 30–40: *The Arts* | 41–44: *Bar/Bat Mitzvah* | 45–53: *The Bible* | 54–59: *Early Childhood Education* | 60–65: *Exceptional Children* | 66–68: *Guidance* | 69–85: *Hebrew* | 86–96: *History* | 97–103: *The Holocaust* | 104–6: *School Library* | 107–18: *Life Cycle of a Jew* | 119–22: *Literature* | 123–42: *Mitzvot/Values and Contemporary Issues* | 143–46: *Textbooks* | 147–58: *The High School* | 159–75: *American Jewry and the Land of Israel* | 176–203: *Day School* | 204–31: *Yiddish Secular Schools* | 232–42: *Higher Education* | 245–62: *Administration* | 263–69: *The Teacher* | 270–73: *The Rabbi and Jewish Education* | 274–86: *Conferences in Jewish Education, 1890–1988* | 287–312: *Men and Women Who Influenced Jewish Education* | 317–34: *Historical Background of Jewish Education* | 335–52: *History of Jewish Education in the United States* | 353–78: *The American Jewish Community* | 379–89: *The Home and Jewish Education* | 390–97: *Adult Education* | 398–404: *The Woman's Role and Jewish Education* | 405–8: *Sephardim and Jewish Education* | 409–16: *Youth and Jewish Education* | 417–21: *Camp* | 422–516: *Local Sources for Jewish Education* | 521–23: *Theology and Jewish Education* | 524–32: *Religious Education* | 533–38: *Philosophy of Jewish Education* | 539–44: *Goals of Jewish Education* | 545–50: *Research in Jewish Education* | 551–58: *Change in Jewish Education* | 559–72: *The Social Sciences and Jewish Education* | 573–96: *Assessment* | 597–99: *The Future of Jewish Education* | 600–602: *Bibliographies of Jewish Education in Other Lands* | 603–17: *Bibliographies of Jewish Education and Related Fields in the United States* | 619–70: *Supplement*

INDEX

Seltzer, Sanford, 27, 556, 621, 647
Seman, Philip, 362
Seman, Philip L., 442
Semel, Bernard, 279; literature on, 309
Sendry, Fred, 606
Sentinel, The, 442, 447
Sephardi, The, 406, 408, 477
Sephardic Bulletin, 408
Sephardic Home News, 408
Sephardi World, 407, 408
Serels, Mitchell, 407
Serotta, Isaac, 156
Setleis, Lloyd, 368
Seward, G., 566
Seward, Georgene, 564
Sewell, Stephen, 338
Seybolt, R. F., 337
Shabatay, Y., 362, 384
Shabatay, Yehuda, 414
Shabbosdige Post, 463
Shahar, Michael, 586
Shahar, Yonai, 151
Shaharut, 122
Shain, Samson A., 424
Shamah, Lind, 407
Shandler, Jeffrey, 32
Shane, Paul, 266
Shangold, Benjamin, 395
Shankman, Arnold, 439
Shankman, Jacob K., 271
Shankman, Sam, 510
Shanks, Hershel, 628
Shapero, Sanford M., 152
Shapira, Meir: literature on, 309
Shapira, Rina, 170, 491
Shapiro, Alexander M., 306
Shapiro, B. M., 63
Shapiro, Chaim, 507
Shapiro, Charlotte Heller, 506
Shapiro, Chava, 622
Shapiro, David H., 641
Shapiro, David S., 582
Shapiro, D. S., 380
Shapiro, E., 63, 185
Shapiro, Edward S., 469, 628, 643, 658, 666
Shapiro, Ezra, 170
Shapiro, Harvey, 154, 419
Shapiro, Helen, 63
Shapiro, Howard M., 529, 567
Shapiro, Howard Martin, 563
Shapiro, Isaac, 209, 212, 213, 228
Shapiro, Israel, 320
Shapiro, J., 63
Shapiro, Jack, 366, 556
Shapiro, Jane S., 620
Shapiro, Jonathan Z., 257
Shapiro, Joseph, 320
Shapiro, Judah, 124, 348
Shapiro, Judah S., 348
Shapiro, Leib, 485
Shapiro, M. S., 24
Shapiro, Mannheim S., 117, 124, 135, 354, 437, 453, 465, 510, 563, 570
Shapiro, Max A., 75, 143, 359
Shapiro, Miriam Klein, 170, 249, 367
Shapiro, Roni, 39
Shapiro, Rose, 443
Shapiro, S. S., 131
Shapiro, Sanford, 529
Shapiro, Sara S., 100, 250, 664
Shapiro, Sh., 295, 503
Shapiro, Solomon, 206, 213, 224, 228; literature on, 309
Shapiro, Yehudah, 207, 586
Shapiro, Zipora, 331, 449
Shapiro, Zvi, 666
Share, Nathaniel S., 450
Sharfman, I. Harold, 425
Sharfstein, Chana, 488
Shargel, Baila Round, 294
Sharon, Ruth, 32
Sharp, Harry, 458
Shaskolsky, Rinah Lipis, 127
Shatzky, Jacob, 325, 398, 601, 602
Shawn, Karen, 628
Shayn, Israel, 602
Shazar, Zalman, 297
Shearith Israel Congregation (NYC), 350, 670
Shefner, B., 224, 303
Sheier, Ira Jay, 331
Sheinkopf, David J., 186
Sheinman, Hildy L., 115
Sheintuch, I., 331
Sheinzon, I. D., 39, 78
Shelemay, Kay Kaufman, 652
Shemen, N., 399
Sheniak, Mazal, 70
Sherer, Moshe, 197
Shereshevsky, Ezra, 79, 180, 307, 384, 582
Sherith Israel Congregation (San Francisco), 342, 344
Sherman, Bernard A., 121
Sherman, Bezalel C, 161, 163, 224, 279, 302, 354, 563, 598
Sherman, Frank, 110
Sherman, J., 582
Sherman, Robert, 21, 109, 184
Sherwin, Byron L., 101, 102, 136, 239, 414, 556, 632, 638, 640
Sherwood, John M., 393
Sheskin, Ira M., 437, 655
Shetzer, Simon, 540, 576
Shevach, Benjamin: literature on, 309
Shevach, Benjamin I., 456
Sheviley Hahinuch (Sh Hah). See Council for Jewish Education
Shevitz, Susan L., 664, 667
Shevitz, Susan R., 134, 151, 367, 456, 582
Shevitz, Susan Rosenblum, 254
Shevrin, Aliza, 630
Shifman, M., 48
Shifman, Pinchos, 320
Shifris, Moshe, 226, 228, 462
Shiloh Publishing Company, 112
Shiloni, Nathan Ariah, 247
Shimoff, Sandra R., 638
Shimoni, Gideon, 635
Shinedling, Abraham I., 471, 515
Shipton, Clifford K., 348
Shirazi, Helen, 406
Shire, Michael J., 530
Shirpser, Sol, 423
Shkedi, Asher, 127
Shlavin, Benjamin, 296
Shloush, Rita, 266
Shluker, David, 80, 246, 257, 645
Sh'ma, 638, 640
Shmeruk, Kh., 600
Shmueli, Eliezer, 582
Shmueli, Ephraim, 75, 299
Shmulevitch, I., 312, 481
Shneider, Sh., 267
Shoah (journal), 253
Shofar, 122, 636
Shoham, Gilbert L., 134, 536
Shoham, Joseph, 254
Shohamy, Elana, 12, 75, 80
Sholem Aleichem, 226
Sholem Aleichem Folk Institute (SAFI), 205, 207, 208, 219, 225, 228, 230, 231, 302. See also *Bulletin* (SAFI)
Sholem Aleichem Folk School, 445
Shoob, E., 293
Shook, Mark L., 115
Shoolblat, 226
Shoop, Simon H., 143
Shosteck, Robert, 259, 414, 436
Shotel, Jay, 639
Shoub, M., 402
Shoulson, Bruce D., 362
Showstack, G., 645
Shpall, Aaron Shimon, 451
Shpall, Leo, 303, 450, 451, 609, 613
Shpan, Shlomo, 78

717

Shraga, Sh. Z., 331
Shrage, Barry, 497
Shreiber, Ben Zion, 419
Shrire, T., 31
Shtadlan, Batyah, 468
Shtadlan, I. Z., 468
Shtarkman, Moshe, 296, 349, 442, 486, 614
Shteingart, Tzirl, 450
Shtern, I., 208, 209, 211
Shtern, Yekhiel, 322
Shtrigler, Mordecai, 22
Shuart, Adele Kronick, 63
Shub, Norman, 498
Shub, Phyllis, 624
Shubow, Joseph Sh., 161, 170
Shuchatowitz, Joseph, L., 184
Shudofsky, Adele A., 90
Shudofsky, Chanuch, 135, 149, 184
Shudofsky, Maurice, 492
Shudofsky, Maurice M., 582
Shudofsky, Noam, 184, 484
Shuey, A. M., 566
Shulamith Institute for Girls of Boro Park, 493
Shulamit School for Girls, 184, 484
Shulman, A., 224
Shulman, Avi, 180, 184, 188, 194, 198
Shulman, Charles E., 297, 598
Shulman, Elias, 293
Shulman, Lee S., 257
Shulman, M., 117
Shulman, Moses L., 233
Shulman, S. N., 188
Shulman, V., 602
Shulsinger, Shlomo, 419, 653
Shuman, Barbara K., 662
Shuman, Bernard, 449
Shumsky, Abraham, 75, 82, 136, 331
Shumsky, Adaia, 136
Shumsky, Adina, 82

Shunami, Shlomo, 600, 602, 606, 616
Shunk, William R., 320
Shurin, Aaron Ben-Zion, 63, 177, 194, 309, 399, 484, 541, 582, 636–38, 641
Shurin, Zvi H., 284
Shusterman, Abraham, 24, 452
Shvadron, Benjamin, 327
Sicher, Efraim, 628
Sidorsky, David, 127, 563, 570
Siegel, Berl, 153
Siegel, Daniel, 58
Siegel, Danny, 22, 90, 134, 135, 639
Siegel, Ernst, 63
Siegel, Gertrude, 170
Siegel, Jonathan R, 34
Siegel, Judith C., 31
Siegel, Max, 384
Siegel, Morris, 563
Siegel, Morton, 8, 15, 21, 34, 63, 80, 135, 155, 170, 173, 177, 180, 186, 194, 254, 360, 384, 395, 488, 530, 582, 595, 598
Siegel, Seymour, 112, 127, 402, 522
Siegman, Sarah M., 23, 32, 453
Sierad, Jack, 419
Sigal, P., 589
Sigal, Philip, 402
Sigalowski, M., 219
Sigel, Gerald, 25
Silber, Mandel, 451
Silber, Mendel, 466
Silber, Theresa K., 82
Silberberg, Yaffa, 186
Silberman, Charles, 541, 590
Silberman, Charles E., 582
Silberman, Curt C., 643
Silberman, Lou H., 238, 522
Silberman, Melvin, 247
Silberman, Morris, 112
Silberman, Moshe, 444

Silberman, Shoshana (Rosalind), 48, 249, 620
Silberschlag, Eisig, 121, 170, 235, 254, 279, 303, 310, 337, 456, 536
Silver, A. M., 184, 402
Silver, Abba Hillel, 161, 268, 359, 363, 576, 582
Silver, Cheri Ellowitz, 384
Silver, Daniel, 63
Silver, Daniel J., 127, 585
Silver, Daniel Jeremy, 239, 241
Silver, David L., 194
Silver, Harold, 459
Silver, Helen, 514
Silver, Helen S., 660
Silver, Jeremy, 149
Silver, L., 206, 219, 228
Silver, Louis, 472
Silver, Manuel, 442
Silver, Menachem, 255
Silver, Sam, 115
Silver, Sheri Ellowitz, 156
Silverberg, David, 101, 239
Silverman, A. O., 379
Silverman, Althea, 50
Silverman, Charles, 127
Silverman, D. W., 488
Silverman, David M., 526
Silverman, David W., 149, 530, 638
Silverman, Hillel, 249, 362
Silverman, Jerry, 21, 620, 626
Silverman, Maida, 629
Silverman, Marc R., 172
Silverman, Morris, 434, 473
Silverman, Myrna, 660
Silverman, Rita, 454
Silverman, S., 194, 196
Silverman, S. S., 414
Silverman, Simon G., 196
Silverman, William B., 71, 136, 137, 156, 587, 622, 632
Silverstein, Philip, 39
Silverstein, Ruth, 32

Key to Index

7–9: *Types of Jewish Schools* | 10–17: *Curriculum* | 18–29: *Pedagogy* | 30–40: *The Arts* | 41–44: *Bar/Bat Mitzvah* | 45–53: *The Bible* | 54–59: *Early Childhood Education* | 60–65: *Exceptional Children* | 66–68: *Guidance* | 69–85: *Hebrew* | 86–96: *History* | 97–103: *The Holocaust* | 104–6: *School Library* | 107–18: *Life Cycle of a Jew* | 119–22: *Literature* | 123–42: *Mitzvot/Values and Contemporary Issues* | 143–46: *Textbooks* | 147–58: *The High School* | 159–75: *American Jewry and the Land of Israel* | 176–203: *Day School* | 204–31: *Yiddish Secular Schools* | 232–42: *Higher Education* | 245–62: *Administration* | 263–69: *The Teacher* | 270–73: *The Rabbi and Jewish Education* | 274–86: *Conferences in Jewish Education, 1890–1988* | 287–312: *Men and Women Who Influenced Jewish Education* | 317–34: *Historical Background of Jewish Education* | 335–52: *History of Jewish Education in the United States* | 353–78: *The American Jewish Community* | 379–89: *The Home and Jewish Education* | 390–97: *Adult Education* | 398–404: *The Woman's Role and Jewish Education* | 405–8: *Sephardim and Jewish Education* | 409–16: *Youth and Jewish Education* | 417–21: *Camp* | 422–516: *Local Sources for Jewish Education* | 521–23: *Theology and Jewish Education* | 524–32: *Religious Education* | 533–38: *Philosophy of Jewish Education* | 539–44: *Goals of Jewish Education* | 545–50: *Research in Jewish Education* | 551–58: *Change in Jewish Education* | 559–72: *The Social Sciences and Jewish Education* | 573–96: *Assessment* | 597–99: *The Future of Jewish Education* | 600–602: *Bibliographies of Jewish Education in Other Lands* | 603–17: *Bibliographies of Jewish Education and Related Fields in the United States* | 619–70: *Supplement*

INDEX

Silverstone, Leslie, 47
Simmons, L. M., 346
Simms, Laura, 50, 137
Simon, Abram, 263, 320, 436
Simon, E., 154, 371, 563
Simon, Ernst, 170, 308, 327
Simon, Joseph, 320
Simon, Leon, 287
Simon, Linda, 621
Simon, Norma, 58, 117
Simon, Ralph, 72
Simon, Rita James, 650
Simon, Sara, 63
Simon, Shirley, 117
Simon, Sidney, 124
Simon, Solomon, 206, 211, 215, 221, 224, 226, 295, 312
Simon, Ted, 530
Simonhoff, Henry, 437, 494
Sinai, 454
Singer, A., 263
Singer, Aaron, 272
Singer, David, 177, 180, 239, 563, 609
Singer, Ellen, 620
Singer, Herman, 173
Singer, Howard, 112, 134, 156, 189
Singer, Isaac Bashevis, 655
Singer, Jacob, 393, 605
Singer, Mrs. M. M., 155
Singer, Richard, 49
Singer, Richard E., 134
Singer, Sh. D., 224
Singerman, Robert, 612, 614, 670
Sinkoff, Nancy B., 400
Siskin, Edgar E., 42, 434
Sisterhood of the Spanish Portuguese Synagogue, 477
Sivan, Tamar, 184
Skaist, Solomon N., 22, 180, 188
Skaist, Solomon W., 186
Skelker, Philip, 620
Skiddell, Elliot, 271
Skirball, Haim, 170
Skirball, Hank, 610
Skirball, Henry F., 289
Sklar, Samuel, 57, 109
Sklare, Marshall, 163, 201, 202, 237, 238, 271, 352, 354, 384, 563, 570, 571, 593
Skoble, Rose, 54
Skoff, Benson, 364
Skole, Bertha, 454
Skolnick, Irving A., 80
Skolnick, Irving H., 14, 75, 134, 186, 366, 541
Skolnik, Nachama, 23, 419, 556
Skooler, Chaim, 219

Skutch, Rachel Frank, 452
Skydell, A., 179, 194
Slade, Irving L., 414
Slavin, Simon, 481
Slavitt-Moore, Bonnie, 267
Slawson, John, 570
Sleeper, James A., 414, 556, 571, 582
Slesinger, Zalmen, 14, 21, 34, 48, 63, 80, 90, 93, 101, 106, 134, 154, 158, 170, 194, 202, 246, 249, 252, 254, 257, 259, 264, 359, 362, 364, 370, 374, 380, 384, 393, 419, 447, 451, 536, 545, 548, 556–57, 570, 582, 586, 594, 598, 606–8, 613; literature on, 309
Sloan, Jacob, 163
Sloan, Sh., 434
Slobin, Mark, 628
Slominsky, Henry, 109
Slominsky, J. D., 11
Slonimsky, David, 384
Slonimsky, David T., 115
Slouschz, Nahum, 119
Small, Sarah L., 246, 442
Smilansky, Moshe, 331
Smiley, Mark S., 637
Smith, Allan L., 653
Smith, Corrine R., 383, 528
Smith, Judith E., 508
Smith, S. L., 507
Smith, Tom W., 632
Smodar, 505
Smolar, Boris, 286, 349, 359, 364, 384, 393, 419, 484, 488, 582–83
Smolar, Leivy, 151
Smolar, Levi, 291
Smolensky, Dvora, 485
Snarey, John R., 331
Sneh, Shlomo, 331
Snitow, Virginia, 402
Snitzer, Lee H., 32, 127
Snow, Charles E., 456
Snyder, Carol, 630
Snyder, Herman E., 42
Snyder, Herman Eliot, 643, 644
Snyder, Wolf, 212, 213, 228
Sobel, Karen A., 152
Sobel, Louis, 67
Sobel, Ronald B., 476
Sobel, Z., 598
Sobeloff, Simon, 374, 452
Sochen, June, 402
Sochen, Mordecai, 75, 80, 337
Society for the Education of Poor Children and Relief of Indigent Persons of the Jewish Persuasion, 340

Society of Friends of Touro Synagogue, 507
Sodden, Jesse, 134
Sofer, B., 239
Sofer, Tamar, 490
Soffer, Abraham, 184, 186
Soffin, Joel E., 636
Soifer, Maralyn, 63
Sokobin, Alan M., 90
Sokol, Moshe Z., 190
Sokolow, Judy, 246
Solender, Sanford, 371
Solender, Stephen D., 359, 644
Solis, Jacob S., 339
Solis-Cohen, E., 115
Solis-Cohen, Elfrida, 613
Solis-Cohen, J., Jr., 448
Soloff, Mordecai I., 87, 91, 93, 115, 536
Soloff, Rav A., 566
Solomon, Barbara Miller, 455
Solomon, Bennett I., 186–87
Solomon, Elias L., 476
Solomon, George, 12, 401
Solomon, Louis, 340
Solomon, Sidney, 586
Solomon ben Isaac. *See* Rashi
Soloshin, Etta, 358
Soloveichik, A., 24
Soloveichik, Aaron, 194
Soloveitchik, Aaron, 196, 402
Soloveitchik, Joseph B., 415, 522; literature on, 309
Solovy, D. K., 184
Solovy, Delores Kohl, 115, 620
Solow, M., 621
Soltes, Avraham, 161
Soltes, M., 22
Soltes, Mordecai, 117, 367, 368, 480, 576, 605, 617; literature on, 310
Soltes, Ori Z., 620
Somberg, Suzanne Richards, 467
Sondheim, Uri, 196
Sone, J. Jacques, 115
Sones, Lenore, 514
Sonne, I., 320
Sonneschein, Solomon H., 344
Sonsino, Rifat, 530, 622
Soref, Irwin I., 21, 34, 90, 170, 250, 300, 426, 428, 429
Sorin, Gerald, 643, 658
Sorin, Morris, 246, 497
Sorkin, Nachman, 182
Soroff, Nathaniel, 136, 438
Sosevsky, Morris, 151
Soshuk, Levi, 170, 173, 418, 419
Sosovsky, Moshe Chaim, 134
Sourkes, Tzvi, 638

719

INDEX

Southern Israelite, 438
Southern Jewish Outlook, 514
Southern Jewish Weekly, 437
Southern Jewish World, 514
Southwest Jewish Chronicle, 499
Soviv, Aaron, 75, 119, 246, 281, 293, 325, 354, 457, 570
Sparks, Jack L., 252
Special Committee of Seven (NYC), 476
Spector, Noya, 78
Spector, S. I., 566, 588
Speizman, Morris A., 494
Sperber, Matthew, 23
Sperling, Jerry, 630
Sperling, Paul, 471
Spero, Robert, 180
Spertus, Byron, 557
Spicehandler, Arnold, 101
Spicehandler, Ezra, 75
Spiegel, Elliot D., 170
Spiegel, M., 426
Spiegel, Shalom, 70, 83, 327
Spiegelman, Art, 628
Spiegelman, Marvin J., 101
Spiegler, S., 24, 154, 364
Spielmann, Diane R., 643
Spielmann, Lee A., 643
Spiers, B., 320
Spinrad, W., 132, 562
Spiro, Jack, 50, 135, 628
Spiro, Jack D., 21, 42–43, 48, 98, 149, 153, 170, 259, 298, 360, 384, 536, 557, 583, 590, 598, 609
Spiro, Joseph, 179
Spiro, Pinchas, 490
Spiro, Rena M., 498
Spiro, S., 134
Spiro, Saul, 137, 161, 466
Spiro, Saul S., 425, 498, 500
Spitz, Jacob, 507
Spitzer, Frances, 90
Spitzer, Julie, 134
Spivack, Harold, 75

Spizman, L., 161, 214, 224–25, 279, 325, 485, 583
Spolsky, Bernard, 70
Spotts, Leon H., 14, 21, 25, 48, 63, 76, 80, 110, 121, 154, 155, 170, 188, 249, 255, 284, 358, 363, 364, 366, 414, 463, 471, 497, 530, 547, 549, 586, 636, 640, 645
Springer, Josephine, 32
Springfield Hebrew Record, 457
Springfield Jewish Ledger, 457
Srole, Leo, 563
Stadtler, Bea, 63, 101, 102, 117
Stahler, Moshe, 638
Stainsby, William, 468
Stampfer, Joshua, 500
Stampfer, Nathaniel, 100, 444
Stampfer, Nathaniel I., 110
Stampfer, Shaul, 322
Stanislawski, Michael, 669
Starin, Carol Oseran, 638
Stark, Rodney, 471
Stark Jewish News, 495
Starkoff, Bernard, 606
Starr, Arthur F., 151
Starr, Earl S., 384
Starr, Harry, 279
Starr, Janice, 61
Starr, Joshua, 87
Starr, Raymond, 61
Staub, Jacob J., 21, 640, 669
Staub, Sholom, 406
Stavitsky, Michael, 587
Stavitsky, Michael A., 279, 469
Stavsky, David, 414
Steckel, Charles W., 98
Steg, A., 354, 570
Stein, Adele, 115
Stein, Gisela, 135
Stein, Gizela, 170
Stein, J., 598
Stein, Jacob, 367, 402
Stein, Jonathan, 395
Stein, Jonathan A., 648

Stein, Kenneth E., 21, 134, 566
Stein, Kenneth W., 439
Stein, Louise S., 362
Stein, Regina, 298
Steinbach, Alexander A., 134, 153, 246, 583
Steinback, Irene Bush, 484
Steinbaum, Israel, 209, 213, 215, 216, 218, 221, 228, 488
Steinberg, Arthur, 190
Steinberg, Barbara, 184, 645, 667
Steinberg, Barbara Summers, 249
Steinberg, Bernard, 563, 583
Steinberg, Gerald D., 151
Steinberg, Harriet P., 257
Steinberg, Jack, 440
Steinberg, Milton, 88, 124, 161, 563
Steinberg, Paul, 134, 170
Steinberg, Paul M., 127, 590
Steinberg, Samuel, 75, 473
Steinberg, Stephen, 471
Steinberg, Theodore, 109, 299
Steinberg, Yehudah, 226
Steinberger, Heidi, 32
Steinbock, Steven E., 624
Steiner, C., 128
Steiner, George, 126
Steiner, M. J., 456
Steinhorn, Sharon, 384
Steinitz, Hans J., 643
Steinmetz, Daniel, 666
Steinmetz, Ira J., 667
Steinsaltz, Adin, 620
Steinschneider, Moritz, 616
Stember, Charles, 563
Steren, Jody Sussman, 515
Stern, Carolyn H., 115
Stern, Chaim, 112, 136, 385
Stern, Gail F., 502
Stern, Guy, 643
Stern, Heidi, 170
Stern, Ian, 25
Stern, Jack, 41
Stern, Jack, Jr., 414

Key to Index

7–9: *Types of Jewish Schools* | 10–17: *Curriculum* | 18–29: *Pedagogy* | 30–40: *The Arts* | 41–44: *Bar/Bat Mitzvah* | 45–53: *The Bible* | 54–59: *Early Childhood Education* | 60–65: *Exceptional Children* | 66–68: *Guidance* | 69–85: *Hebrew* | 86–96: *History* | 97–103: *The Holocaust* | 104–6: *School Library* | 107–18: *Life Cycle of a Jew* | 119–22: *Literature* | 123–42: *Mitzvot/Values and Contemporary Issues* | 143–46: *Textbooks* | 147–58: *The High School* | 159–75: *American Jewry and the Land of Israel* | 176–203: *Day School* | 204–31: *Yiddish Secular Schools* | 232–42: *Higher Education* | 245–62: *Administration* | 263–69: *The Teacher* | 270–73: *The Rabbi and Jewish Education* | 274–86: *Conferences in Jewish Education, 1890–1988* | 287–312: *Men and Women Who Influenced Jewish Education* | 317–34: *Historical Background of Jewish Education* | 335–52: *History of Jewish Education in the United States* | 353–78: *The American Jewish Community* | 379–89: *The Home and Jewish Education* | 390–97: *Adult Education* | 398–404: *The Woman's Role and Jewish Education* | 405–8: *Sephardim and Jewish Education* | 409–16: *Youth and Jewish Education* | 417–21: *Camp* | 422–516: *Local Sources for Jewish Education* | 521–23: *Theology and Jewish Education* | 524–32: *Religious Education* | 533–38: *Philosophy of Jewish Education* | 539–44: *Goals of Jewish Education* | 545–50: *Research in Jewish Education* | 551–58: *Change in Jewish Education* | 559–72: *The Social Sciences and Jewish Education* | 573–96: *Assessment* | 597–99: *The Future of Jewish Education* | 600–602: *Bibliographies of Jewish Education in Other Lands* | 603–17: *Bibliographies of Jewish Education and Related Fields in the United States* | 619–70: *Supplement*

Stern, Jay B., 14, 15, 78, 247, 250, 254, 256, 266, 337, 385, 492, 536, 583, 593, 644
Stern, Kenneth E., 266
Stern, Kenneth S., 632
Stern, Leonard W., 134
Stern, Malcolm, 643
Stern, Malcolm H., 440, 513, 652, 660
Stern, Meyer, 477
Stern, Nathan, 246, 325
Stern, Norton B., 153, 423, 425, 426, 430, 432, 466, 467, 471, 500, 512, 515, 654, 655, 670
Stern, Raymond, 640
Stern, Shirley, 93, 112
Stern, Stephen, 426
Stern, Suzanne C., 21
Sterne, Richard S., 470
Sternfeld, Ruth, 57
Stern-Levine, Carol, 625
Sternstein, Joseph P., 161
Steven, Reuben, 250
Stewart, Eliyahu, 197
Still, Marie, 661
Stillman, Norman A., 652
Stillpass, Leo J., 41
Stiskin, Herschel M., 63, 185, 489
Stitskin, Leon, 288
Stocker, Debra Steinberg, 462
Stocker, Joseph, 423
Stolovitsky, Mark, 638
Stolper, Pinchas, 414
Stolz, Joseph, 88, 293
Stone, Anne, 11
Stone, Gerald C., 547
Stone, Irving, 197
Stone, Janer, 475
Stone, Selma Weiss, 106
Stow, Kenneth R., 652
Stracuzzi, Malanie R., 636
Strassburger, Baruch, 325, 601
Strassfeld, Michael, 629
Strassfield, Michael, 108
Strassfield, Sharon, 108, 385
Straus, Barrie Ruth Waldman, 650
Straus, Livia, 170
Strauss, Herbert A., 643
Strauss, Herschel Ira, 419
Strauss, Ruby G., 34, 135
Stright, H. L., 164
Stritikus, George R., 653
Strober, Gerald S., 144
Strodtbeck, Fred L., 387
Stroll, Milton, 90
Strouse, Edith M., 11, 526
Stuart, Moses, 339
Studies in Bibliography and Booklore, 496

Studner, Mrs. David K., 380
Sturm, Ephraim H., 640
Stutman, Suzanne, 386
Suchoff, Libbie. *See* Berkson, Mrs. Isaac B.
Sud, Ira, 78
Sudran, Abe L., 459
Sue, Doctor, 639
Sugar, Robert, 93, 407
Sugarman, Allan, 58
Sugarman, Alvin Marx, 14
Sugarman, Joan, 106
Sugarman, Joan G., 111
Sugarman, Lillian, 36, 72, 497
Sukov, May, 566
Sulkes, Zena W., 63
Sulman, Esther, 434
Sulzberger, David, 502
Sulzberger, Mayer, 302, 345
Sumberg, Alfred D., 515
Summer, Morton J., 197
Summers, Barbara F., 135, 414
Sundheim, Frank, 395
Survey Commission of the Bronx, 486
Suskowitz, Meir, 190
Sussman, A., 117
Sussman, Eva, 34
Sussman, Eva W., 57
Sussman, Lance, 643
Sussman, Lance J., 302, 472
Sussman, Leonard R., 15
Sussman, Samuel, 36, 88, 505
Sutker, Solomon, 439
Sutton, Joseph A. D., 477, 652
Swansen, Bert E., 478
Swarsensky, Manfred, 515
Swartz, Michael, 43
Swerdloff, S., 67, 414
Swerling, Norman P., 419
Swichkow, Louis J., 515, 516
Swift, Fletcher Harper, 320
Swift, Isaac L., 184, 196
Swirski, Shlomo, 641
Swirsky, Michael, 148
Swissa, Albert, 652
Switkin, Linda R., 402
Syden, Martin, 63
Syme, Daniel B., 27, 34, 57, 176, 180, 194, 239, 261, 385, 530, 563, 621, 622, 638, 647, 663
Syme, Deborah Shayne, 58, 632
Synagogue Council of America (SCA), 179, 395
Synagogue Directory of Massachusetts, 454
Synagogue School, 23, 41, 42, 56, 78, 106, 109, 110, 113, 114, 128, 154, 155, 167, 178, 247,
257, 282, 284, 385, 419, 547, 614. See also *Impact*
Syrkin, Marie, 98, 101, 119, 297
Szajkowski, Zosa, 325
Szold, Benjamin, 343, 344
Szold, Henrietta, 346, 399; literature on, 310
Szonyi, David M., 385, 609

Tabachinsky, Y., 583
Taback, Ben Zion, 177, 194, 292, 484, 490, 589
Taback, Samuel, 287
Tabak, I., 576
Tabak, Israel, 452
Tachrov, A., 489
Tadmor, Shlomo, 331
Talmach, Regina Entin, 206
Talmud Torah Yavneh, 446
Tambor, Milton, 460
Tanenbaum, Roy, 149
Tanenzapf, Sol, 298
Tanhuma Bar Abba, 137
Tannenbaum, A., 21, 497, 583
Tannenbaum, Abraham J., 638
Tannenbaum, Avraham J., 666
Tannenbaum, Marc H., 598
Tannenbaum, Samuel, 481
Tarant, Devorah, 214
Tarant, Dvorah, 228
Tarasow, Morris, 57, 63, 80, 250
Targan, Judith, 247
Targan, Judith L., 24
Tarnor, Mrs. Norman, 34
Tarnor, Norman, 135, 155
Tarnor, Pearl G., 78, 90
Tarshish, Allan, 348, 509, 576
Tartakover, Arieh, 282, 325
Taschman, Dershon, 180
Tashrak, 226
Task, Arnold, 494, 513
Taube, Herman, 399
Tauben, Carol, 31
Taylor, Maurice, 506
Tcherikover, E. M., 88
Tchernowitz, Chaim (Rav Tsair), 522; literature on, 310
Teacher Bulletin (Chicago BJE), 445
Teachers of Greater New York, 487
Tebeau, Charlton W., 437
Techner, David, 622
Teicher, Paul, 470
Teishoff, I., 436
Teitelbaum, Eli, 184
Teitelbaum, Joel: literature on, 310
Teitelbaum, Samuel, 414

INDEX

Teitelbaum, Simcha, 188, 194
Teitz, Pinchas M., 194, 370
Tekumah, 253
Teller, Gerald A., 63, 134, 151, 266, 359, 371, 420, 461, 462, 537, 557, 645
Teller, I. L., 410
Teller, Judd, 563
Teller, Judd L., 161, 163
Telsner, David, 171
Telushkin, Joseph, 663
Temin, Annette, 502
Temkin, Sefton D., 311, 350
Temko, Allan, 431
Temple, The (Cleveland), 496
Temple Beth El (Buffalo, N.Y.), 472
Temple Beth El (Providence, R.I.), 508
Temple Beth El (Richmond, Va.), 514
Temple Beth El (South Bend, Ind.), 448
Temple Beth El (Utica, N.Y.), 474
Temple Beth Israel (Phoenix, Ariz.), 423
Temple Beth Tefillah (Brunswick, Ga.), 440
Temple Emanu-El (Birmingham, Ala.), 422
Temple Emanu-El (Denver, Colo.), 433
Temple Emanuel (Newton, Mass.), 457
Temple Emanu-El (NYC), 344
Temple Emanu-El (San Jose, Calif.), 432
Temple Emanu-El (Tucson, Ariz.), 423
Temple Israel (Detroit, Mich.), 460
Tendler, M. D., 63
Tendler, Moses D., 184
Tenenbaum, Joseph, 583
Teplitz, Saul I., 154, 583
Teurah, 445
Teutch, Betsy Plotkin, 187
Texas Israelite, 511
Texas Jewish Herald. See *Jewish Herald-Voice*
Texas Jewish Post, 511
Texas Jewish Press, 512
Thal, Linda, 115
Theus, Kathryn T., 563
Thiemann, F., 109
Third National Conference on Jewish Education, 280
Thum, Robert, 632
Tibbon, Ibn, 106
Tikkun, 430
Tishkoff, Larry, 171
Tobesman, Rachmiel, 626
Tobias, Henry J., 499, 658
Tobias, Thomas J., 509
Tobin, Gary A., 436, 452, 458, 465–66, 622, 664, 666, 668
Tobin, Herbert, 271
Toby, Jackson, 510
Todes, David, 264, 267, 590
Todes, David U., 302, 502
Tofield, Aaron, 402
Tofield, Sanders A., 154
Tog, Der, 493
Tokayer, Shmuel, 184
Toledo Israelite, 499
Tolidano, J. M., 402
Toll, William, 500, 650
Tollier, A., 431
Tomberg, Robert F., 623
Tomrov, M. M., 91
Tonger, Judith, 255
Toplin, Robert Brent, 494
Torah Umesorah Day Schools (TU), 33, 36, 176, 179–82, 184, 187, 188, 196–98, 281, 284, 606
Torcyk, D., 277
Tornberg, Robert, 109
Tornberg, Robert E., 250, 640
Tornheim, William, 425
Tory, Avraham, 628
Toshev, A., 454
Touber, Rosalyn, 135
Toubin, Isaac, 14, 101, 180, 196, 197, 250, 292, 359, 385, 506, 557, 583; literature on, 310
Touroff, Nissan, 11, 21, 54, 72, 164, 263, 337, 380, 526, 537, 540, 552, 566, 576, 587, 589, 597; literature on, 310
Trachtenberg, Joshua, 325, 500, 563
Trachtenberg, Martin, 98
Tradition, 126, 614
Trainin, Isaac N., 135
Tranin, Donald, 359
Trepp, Leo, 115, 156, 308
Tribuch, Baruch, 563
Tropp, E., 368
Tropper, Daniel, 171, 331
Tropper, S., 402
Troupp, Leonard B., 23, 414
Troy, Dov, 250, 557
Trunk, I., 98
Tsamriyon, Tsemach, 331
Tsanin, M., 331
Tsedek V'Shalom, 632
Tseitman, Chanan, 331
Tsiporin, Hyman, 445
Tsivion, 206
Tuchman, Hyman, 610; literature on, 310
Tuchman, Maurice S., 106
Tucker, JaAnne, 633
Tugend, Tom, 654
Tulin, David P., 171
Tulsa Jewish Review, 499
Turitz, Evelyn, 464
Turitz, Leo E., 464
Turk, Samuel D., 194
Turkel, David Ber, 502
Turkow, Y., 301
Turner, Justin G., 427
Turner, Pearl G., 75
Twerski, Abraham, 196

Key to Index

7–9: *Types of Jewish Schools* | 10–17: *Curriculum* | 18–29: *Pedagogy* | 30–40: *The Arts* | 41–44: *Bar/Bat Mitzvah* | 45–53: *The Bible* | 54–59: *Early Childhood Education* | 60–65: *Exceptional Children* | 66–68: *Guidance* | 69–85: *Hebrew* | 86–96: *History* | 97–103: *The Holocaust* | 104–6: *School Library* | 107–18: *Life Cycle of a Jew* | 119–22: *Literature* | 123–42: *Mitzvot/Values and Contemporary Issues* | 143–46: *Textbooks* | 147–58: *The High School* | 159–75: *American Jewry and the Land of Israel* | 176–203: *Day School* | 204–31: *Yiddish Secular Schools* | 232–42: *Higher Education* | 245–62: *Administration* | 263–69: *The Teacher* | 270–73: *The Rabbi and Jewish Education* | 274–86: *Conferences in Jewish Education, 1890–1988* | 287–312: *Men and Women Who Influenced Jewish Education* | 317–34: *Historical Background of Jewish Education* | 335–52: *History of Jewish Education in the United States* | 353–78: *The American Jewish Community* | 379–89: *The Home and Jewish Education* | 390–97: *Adult Education* | 398–404: *The Woman's Role and Jewish Education* | 405–8: *Sephardim and Jewish Education* | 409–16: *Youth and Jewish Education* | 417–21: *Camp* | 422–516: *Local Sources for Jewish Education* | 521–23: *Theology and Jewish Education* | 524–32: *Religious Education* | 533–38: *Philosophy of Jewish Education* | 539–44: *Goals of Jewish Education* | 545–50: *Research in Jewish Education* | 551–58: *Change in Jewish Education* | 559–72: *The Social Sciences and Jewish Education* | 573–96: *Assessment* | 597–99: *The Future of Jewish Education* | 600–602: *Bibliographies of Jewish Education in Other Lands* | 603–17: *Bibliographies of Jewish Education and Related Fields in the United States* | 619–70: *Supplement*

INDEX

Twerski, Michael, 190
Twersky, David, 190, 669
Twersky, Y., 310
Twersky, Yochanan, 265, 304
Tzemnon, Tsemach, 367, 402
Tzipkin, Samuel, 88

Uchill, Ida L., 432
Udin, Sophie A., 161
Ukeles, Jacob B., 635
Ulanovsky, Lev, 25
Ulich, Robert, 320
Ullman, Solomon Baruch, 134, 542; literature on, 310
Umansky, Ellen, 402
Umansky, Ellen M., 635
Umen, Samuel, 530
Unger, M., 180, 217, 221, 282, 485, 583
Ungerfeld, M., 301
Union of American Hebrew Congregations (UAHC), 8, 11, 15, 25, 26, 30, 59, 84, 119, 128, 151, 171, 252, 286, 345, 360, 383, 385, 395, 414, 486, 497, 523, 530, 541, 543, 557, 612, 620, 626, 638, 639, 644, 648. *See also* Central Conference of American Rabbis; Commission on Jewish Education; *Compass; Jewish Teacher; Keeping Posted;* National Association of Temple Educators; National Federation of Temple Brotherhoods; National Federation of Temple Sisterhoods
Union of Orthodox Jewish Congregations of America (UOJCA), 23, 51, 94, 115, 141, 173, 188, 285, 414, 543. *See also* National Conference of Synagogue Youth
United Federation of Teachers, 101
United Hebrew Beneficent Society of Philadelphia, 339
United Hebrew Schools (Detroit, Mich.), 462
United Jewish Charities of Detroit, 459
United Jewish Federation of Pittsburgh, 506
United Synagogue Commission on Jewish Education (USCJE), 59, 62, 83, 95, 118, 139, 149, 151, 177, 200, 250, 277–80, 365, 385, 542, 583, 605

United Synagogue Review, 178, 614
United Synagogue Schools, 489
United Synagogues of America (USA), 13, 154, 157, 179, 197, 252, 279, 281, 284, 373, 396, 504, 531, 542, 543. *See also* Commission for Jewish Education; Jewish Educators Assembly; *Synagogue School*
United (Orthodox) Synagogues of Greater Kansas City, 464
United Synagogue Youth, 414
United Talmud Torahs and Yeshivas, 503
Unterman, Isaac, 117, 505
Unterman, Isaac Ben-Hayim, 442
Unzer Zeitung, 226
Urbach, Ephraim, 542
Urial, Akivah, 331
Urofsky, Melvin J., 161, 162, 163
Ury, Zalman F., 101, 128, 134, 184, 187, 194, 196, 198, 254, 308, 428–29, 466, 640
Ury, Zalmen, 101
Ury, Zalmen F., 100, 428, 429
Usishkin, M., 540

Vaad Haharedi, 12
Vainstein, Jacob, 115
Vainstein, Rose, 458
Vanek, Julie, 115
Vanek, Linda, 458
Vanek, Zdenek, 257
Vara, La, 407, 408
Varon, Isaac M., 427
Vaxer, Menassah, 472
Vayer, Geraldine T., 186
Veerman, Philip E., 641
Veg-Tageblat, Der, 462
Vegvayzer, Der, 454, 456
Velder, Eli, 325
Ventura, Moise, 407
Verbit, Mervin, 414
Verbit, Mervin F., 387, 470, 570
Veret, Paul, 503; literature on, 310
Vernon, Lisa, 35, 385
Vidaver, Falk, 345
Viener, Saul, 511, 514
Vignola, Susan L., 402
Vilna, Gaon of. *See* Elijah Ben Solomon Zalman
Vincent, Sidney Z., 359, 497
Vineland, N.J., 471
Vishny, Paul, 583
Vizonsky, Nathan, 35, 443
Vladovsky, M., 215
Vogel, H., 124

Vogelstein, Ilene, 63
Voice of Israel, 432
Volksfreund, Der, 506
Voorsanger, Jacob, 431
Vorspan, Albert, 125, 127, 128, 134, 136, 137, 140, 426, 448, 455, 463, 464, 473, 476, 496, 502, 510, 612, 630–32, 648
Vorspan, Max, 376, 427
Vosk, Marc, 563
Votheek, K., 380

Wachs, Saul P., 15, 109–10, 134, 146, 151, 155, 196, 235, 259, 266, 360, 414, 498, 530, 557, 570, 629, 639
Wachsman, Celia, 88
Wachstock, David, 67, 570
Wachstock, Eileen, 456
Waddell, Alexander W., 514
Wadler, Nathan, 194, 486
Wagner, Hilda B., 611
Wagner, Hilman, 21
Wagner, Joseph, 152
Wagner, N., 504
Wahl, A. Z., 37
Wahl, Amiel, 21
Wahlberg, Jeffrey A., 254
Wald, Alexandra, 652
Wald, Lillian, 479
Waldenberg, Shelley Michael, 385
Waldman, Elliot D., 320
Waldman, Leon, 151
Waldman, Mark, 320
Waldman-Lewin, Alisa, 99
Waldridge, Earle E., 300
Waldstein, A. Sh., 88, 91
Walkomitz, Simha Hayyim: literature on, 310–11
Wall, Susan, 385
Wallace, Herrice P., 154
Wallenrod, Reuben, 72
Walter, Gabrielle, 634
Walters, J., 386
Walters, Joel, 331, 570
Warburg, Ronnie F, 604
Ward, Nahum, 420
Warkow, Seymour, 73
Warmer, Moshe, 637
Warner, Eugene, 472
Warner, Paul, 255
Warner, W. Lloyd, 563
Warschauer, Heinz, 171, 557
Warsen, Allen A., 458–60, 461, 462
Warshal, Bruce, 151, 395
Warshaw, Ephraim, 151, 154, 155, 370
Warzburger, Walter S., 583

INDEX

Washington (D.C.) *Jewish Week,* 436
Waskow, Arthur, 115, 583, 624, 633
Wasser, Amy Katz, 632
Wasser, Eric L., 629
Wasserman, Henry W., 394
Wasserman, Howard, 23
Wasserman, Joy Beth, 254, 640
Wasserman, Michael, 666
Wasserman, Z. Z., 489
Watson, G., 149, 561
Watters, Leon L., 440, 512
Wax, James, 530
Wax, James A., 128, 510
Waxman, Chaim, 387, 562, 665
Waxman, Meyer, 70, 121, 232, 233, 293, 307, 540, 590; literature on, 311
Waxman, Robert, 115
Waxman, Shirley T., 35
Webb, Arnold Henry, 320
Wechman, Robert J., 295
Wechsler, Harold, 670
Wechsler, Harold S., 240, 425, 639
Weglein, David E., 526
Wegner, Judith Romney, 650
Weider, Leland, 570
Weil, Herman, 516
Weilerstein, Sadie Rose, 48, 58, 93, 117, 172
Weinbaum, Joseph, 267
Weinberg, A. I., 563
Weinberg, Debora, 27
Weinberg, Dudley, 108
Weinberg, E., 101
Weinberg, Eve, 515
Weinberg, Jacob S., 196
Weinberg, Julius, 583, 595
Weinberg, Michael A., 667
Weinberg, Rob, 640
Weinberg, S. D., 459, 460, 462
Weinberg, Sydney Stahl, 650
Weinberg, Werner, 36, 643

Weinberger, Bernard, 271, 583
Weinberger, Moses, 345, 590
Weinberger, Paul, 583, 593
Weine, Mae, 105, 106, 614
Weine, Max, 299, 385, 461
Weiner, Lazar, 215
Weiner, Leo, 347
Weiner, Milton, 459
Weingarten, I., 49, 81, 88, 90, 212, 214
Weinlez, I., 306
Weinreich, Beatrice Silverman, 630
Weinreich, Max, 98, 545
Weinreich, Uriel, 209
Weinryb, Bernard D., 144, 325, 472
Weinryb, D., 218
Weinsbank, Annette B., 257
Weinsberg, Edgar James, 100
Weinstein, B., 226
Weinstein, David, 75, 76, 78, 272
Weinstein, Deborah, 117
Weinstein, Jacob J., 46, 124
Weinstein, Joshua, 247, 304; literature on, 311
Weinstein, Marvin, 247
Weinstein, Rochelle, 652
Weinstone, Mrs. Howard. 32
Weinthal, Edith C., 649
Weintraub, Ruth G., 124
Weintraub, Simkha, 23, 48
Weisband, Howard, 360
Weisbard, M., 214, 222
Weisberg, Harold, 537, 592
Weisberg, Phyllis G., 63
Weisberg, Stephen E., 171
Weisel, Alfred, 547
Weisenfeld, Leon, 496
Weisfogel, Alex, 196
Weisl, Naphtali. *See* Wessely, Naphtali Herz
Weisman, Deborah, 332
Weiss, Andrea, 648
Weiss, Avraham, 590, 650

Weiss, Benjamin, 184
Weiss, Carole, 171
Weiss, Dean Clifford, 152
Weiss, Ernest Yehudah, 325
Weiss, Fannie, 72
Weiss, Gabriele, 385
Weiss, Isaac, 325
Weiss, Joan C., 514
Weiss, S. R., 393
Weiss, Samuel, 428
Weiss, Samuel Abraham, 134, 190
Weissbach, Lee Shai, 656
Weissberg, Leon, 645
Weissberg, Victor, 110
Weisser, Albert, 606
Weisser, Michael, 112
Weissler, Chava, 648
Weissman, Debbie, 403, 650
Weissman, Herman L., 161
Weissman, Jackie, 39
Weiss-Rosmarin, Trude, 101, 179, 271, 287, 387, 393, 399, 402, 542, 583, 590
Weistrop, J., 542, 583
Weitz, Emil, 93
Weitz, Martin M., 153, 369
Weitzman, Alan G., 14
Weitzman, Laura, 184
Well, Harvey A., 197, 362
Welt, Mildred G., 348
Wenger, Beth S., 655
Wengeroff, Pauline, 399
Werb, Morris, 468
Werb, Morris R., 590
Werb, Sherry, 48
Werbe, Z., 143
Werber, Bracha, 420
Werk, Susan E., 625
Werner, Alfred, 31, 98, 480
Werner, Anita, 105
Werner, Eric, 606
Wertheim, David, 161
Wertheim, David H., 277
Wertheim, Sally, 497
Wertheimer, Jack, 643, 644, 668

Key to Index

7–9: *Types of Jewish Schools* | 10–17: *Curriculum* | 18–29: *Pedagogy* | 30–40: *The Arts* | 41–44: *Bar/Bat Mitzvah* | 45–53: *The Bible* | 54–59: *Early Childhood Education* | 60–65: *Exceptional Children* | 66–68: *Guidance* | 69–85: *Hebrew* | 86–96: *History* | 97–103: *The Holocaust* | 104–6: *School Library* | 107–18: *Life Cycle of a Jew* | 119–22: *Literature* | 123–42: *Mitzvot/Values and Contemporary Issues* | 143–46: *Textbooks* | 147–58: *The High School* | 159–75: *American Jewry and the Land of Israel* | 176–203: *Day School* | 204–31: *Yiddish Secular Schools* | 232–42: *Higher Education* | 245–62: *Administration* | 263–69: *The Teacher* | 270–73: *The Rabbi and Jewish Education* | 274–86: *Conferences in Jewish Education, 1890–1988* | 287–312: *Men and Women Who Influenced Jewish Education* | 317–34: *Historical Background of Jewish Education* | 335–52: *History of Jewish Education in the United States* | 353–78: *The American Jewish Community* | 379–89: *The Home and Jewish Education* | 390–97: *Adult Education* | 398–404: *The Woman's Role and Jewish Education* | 405–8: *Sephardim and Jewish Education* | 409–16: *Youth and Jewish Education* | 417–21: *Camp* | 422–516: *Local Sources for Jewish Education* | 521–23: *Theology and Jewish Education* | 524–32: *Religious Education* | 533–38: *Philosophy of Jewish Education* | 539–44: *Goals of Jewish Education* | 545–50: *Research in Jewish Education* | 551–58: *Change in Jewish Education* | 559–72: *The Social Sciences and Jewish Education* | 573–96: *Assessment* | 597–99: *The Future of Jewish Education* | 600–602: *Bibliographies of Jewish Education in Other Lands* | 603–17: *Bibliographies of Jewish Education and Related Fields in the United States* | 619–70: *Supplement*

INDEX

Wertstein, Irving, 102
Wessel, Bessie Bloom, 387, 435
Wessel, Harvey A., 147, 157
Wessely, Naphtali, 325, 344
Wessely (Weisl), Naphtali Herz: literature on, 311
West, C. T., 25
West, J., 12
West, Jane Dora, 134
Western Jewish Advocate, 433
Western States Jewish Historical Quarterly (WSJH), 432, 440, 449, 466, 471, 500, 511, 654, 659, 661, 670
Westoff, Charles F., 469
Weston, Joan Lavison, 511
Wexler, Dorothy, 667
Whartman, Eliezer, 163
Wheeler, Ray, 438
Whiman, David A., 90
White, Martha, 393
Whiteman, Kaiman, 7, 47, 49, 54, 72, 177, 222, 254, 265, 487, 488, 490, 526, 576; literature on, 311
Whiteman, Maxwell, 495, 502
Whitman, Pearl, 652
Wice, David H., 161
Widom, R., 135
Wieder, Arnold A., 455
Wieder, Leland E., 135
Wiener, C. L., 431
Wiener, Marvin S., 396
Wiener, Theodore, 643
Wiesel, Eli, 570
Wiesel, Elie, 98, 102, 126, 128
Wieseltier, Leon, 628
Wigoder, Geoffrey, 31, 291
Wikler, Meir, 27
Wilchesky, Nachman, 194
Wile, Isaac, 473
Willensky, Marjory Koch, 403
Williams, Dorothy S., 115
Williams, Nancy R., 665
Williamson, E. G., 566
Willner, Eric, 63, 75, 184, 190, 196, 385
Willner, Nancy E., 513
Wilson, Don W., 423, 425
Winegarten, Ruthe, 660
Winer, Gershon, 214, 218, 332, 583
Winer, Toby, 403
Wineshenker, I., 225
Winkler, Henry R., 659
Winograd, Leonard, 501
Winston, Diane, 663
Winter, Herman, 196
Winter, J. Alan, 664, 665
Winter, Magda, 75
Winter, Nathan, 235, 310
Winter, Nathan H., 155, 288, 365, 584
Winters, Alton, 320
Wirth, Louis, 387, 442, 588
Wische, Jerry, 667
Wischnitzer, Rachel, 31, 606
Wisconsin Jewish Chronicle, 516
Wisconsin Jewish Publications Foundation, 516
Wise, Aaron M., 80
Wise, Isaac Mayer, 342–44, 495; literature on, 311
Wise, Stephen S., 479; literature on, 311
Wise, Syd, 33
Wiseman, Shlomo (Shloime), 207, 208, 214, 215, 228; literature on, 311
Wisnia, Eric B., 152
Wisse, Ruth R., 659
Witkin, Sharon G., 19
Wittstein, Ailene, 385
Wittstein, Joel, 58, 91, 135, 385, 557
Witty, Irwin, 463
Witty, Irwin S., 645
Witty, Y., 64
Wohl, A. Z., 48
Wohl, Harry: literature on, 311
Wohl, I. Z., 280
Wohl, Joseph, 215
Wohl, Renee, 647
Wohlberg, Max, 43
Wohlgemuth, Isaiah, 194
Wohlman, L., 301
Wolf, A., 393
Wolf, Alfred, 629
Wolf, Edwin, II, 362, 502, 609
Wolf, Ernest M., 11
Wolf, Horace J., 576
Wolf, Kurt, 511
Wolf, Larry M., 362
Wolf, M., 93
Wolf, Michael, 187, 385
Wolf, Sandy Furfine, 624
Wolf, Simon, 302
Wolf, Sylvia, 75
Wolfe, Arnold Jacob, 153
Wolfe, George, 563
Wolfe, Gerard R., 477
Wolfe, Horace J., 123
Wolfe, Jack A., 448
Wolfenstein, M., 387
Wolff, Ferida, 623
Wolfson, Don, 647
Wolfson, Harry A., 576
Wolfson, Ron, 134
Wolfson, Ronald, 257, 429
Wolfson, Ronald G., 171, 370, 547, 549
Wolk, Asher, 250, 264
Woll, A. Z., 301
Wollenberg, Charles M., 423
Wollheim, Norbert, 643
Wollheim, William, 104, 669, 670
Wollman, Benjamin, 14, 154, 171, 327, 332, 537, 584, 615
Wolowelsky, Joel B., 27, 152, 637, 650
Wolpin, Nissan, 194, 197
Woocher, Jonathan, 171, 252, 359, 362, 584, 640, 648, 668
Woodman, Bertha Shapiro, 457
Woods, Sheila, 25
Worenklein, Abe, 64
Workmen's Circle Education Committee, 215
Workmen's Circle Schools (WC), 174, 208, 222, 225, 229, 275–77, 282, 438, 439, 445, 474, 493, 504
Workmen's Circle Schools of New York, 485
Works Project Administration (WPA), 464
World Bureau for Yiddish and Jewish Culture, 285
World Conference of Yiddish Schools, 283
World Conference on Hebrew Education in the Diaspora, 277
World Conference on Jewish Education, 281
World Congress for Yiddish Culture, 225
World Jewish Congress, 98, 204, 281, 547
World Leadership Conference for Jewish Education, 286
World Over, 122
World Yiddish Culture Congress, 276
World Zionist Organization (WZO), 113, 175, 284, 605. *See also* National Commission on the Teaching of Zion and Israel
Wortman, David A., 320
Wortman, Ruth, 55, 245
Wunsch, Lee R., 414
Wurtzburger, Walter S., 297
Wurtzel, Yehuda, 563
Wyenn, Than R., 36, 429
Wykell, Esther, 443
Wyman, David, 98
Wyschograd, Michael, 98, 633
Wyschogrod, Michael, 98

INDEX

Yaari, Abraham, 327, 610
Yad Tikvah, 647
Yaffe, James, 476
Yaget, Moshe, 196
Yamen, Ben, 214
Yancey, William L., 502
Yankelovich, Daniel, 628
Yanover, Abraham, 75, 78
Yapko, Benjamin L., 337, 359, 368
Yaraslav, Z., 442
Yarbloom, Moshe, 492
Yari, Hava, 75
Yaron, Zvi, 301
Yasgur, Benjamin S., 620
Yashuv, Shlomo Shulsinger-Shear, 337
Yasser, Joseph, 37
Yavne, 414. *See also* National Religious Jewish Students Association
YD. *See* Central Committee of Jewish Folk Schools (*Yiddishe Dertsiung*)
Ydit, Meir, 391
Yedwab, Myra, 43
Yedwab, Paul M., 648
Yedwab, Paul Michael, 629
Yefroikin, Zalman, 9, 206, 208, 209, 215, 216, 219, 222, 225, 227–28, 279, 283, 290, 337; literature on, 311–12
Yeger, Dvorah, 171
Yehoash, 211
Yehudah, R., 380
Yellin, David, 304; literature on, 312
Yenish, Joseph, 75
Yerushalmi, Isaac, 495
Yerushalmi, Yosef Hayim, 95, 320
Yerushalmi, Yoseph H., 406
Yeshiva and Mesivta Arugath Habasem of Williamsburg, 198
Yeshiva Education, 62

Yeshiva English Principals Association, 487
Yeshiva Etz Chaim, 183
Yeshiva of Flatbush, 489
Yeshiva University, 33, 36, 607, *See also* Rabbi Isaac Elchanan Theological Seminary
Yiddishe Arbeiter Velt, 447
Yiddishe Dertsiung, 226
Yiddishe Folk, Dos, 493
Yiddishe Kind, Dos, 226
Yiddishe Presse, Die (Los Angeles), 429
Yiddishe Presse, Die (Philadelphia), 505
Yiddisher Biznessman, Der, 429
Yiddisher Kinder Journal, 226
Yiddisher Kunst Friend, 447
Yiddish Radical School, 445
Yiddish Scientific Institute, 614, 616
Yidn, 204
Yihiel, B., 233
Yivo Publications, 604, 614
Yizhar, Michael, 272
YMHA Bulletin (Philadelphia), 505
Yochim, Maurice, 443
Yodfat, Aryeh, 325
Yoffe, M., 601
Yoffeh, Zalmen, 478
Yoffie, Eric H., 636
Yoshor, M. M., 299
Young, Mel, 643
Young, Moshe L., 184
Young, Susan Winter, 616
Younger, David, 639
Young Israel. See Ark, The
Young Judaica, 653
Young Judea Hawaii, 440
Young Judean, 122
Young Men's Hebrew Association of Bergen County, N.J., 468
Youngstown Jewish Times, 499
Youth (Yungvarg), 226

Youth Leader, 496
Yudkin, Marjorie S., 403
Yukelson, R., 445
Yuter, Alan J., 650

Zabell, Emil M., 64
Zachary, Lois J., 647
Zachter, Albert, 488
Zack, B. G., 466
Zafran, Estelle, 57
Zafran, Herbert C., 604
Zahn, Jane C., 396
Zaiman, Joel H., 385, 584
Zai, Rav. *See* Tchernowitz, Chaim
Zak, Ita, 163
Zakutinsky, Rivka, 650
Zalenitz, Alan N., 187
Zalesky, Jacob, 75
Zalesky, Mrs. Jacob, 90
Zalesky, Moses, 496; literature on, 312
Zalesky, Moshe, 576
Zaltsman, R., 208, 222
Zaltz, F., 216, 311
Zaltzman, R., 211
Zamichow, Abraham, 101, 184
Zarchin, Michael M., 431
Zaretski, Samuel, 49
Zatkin, Joseph, 430
Zborowski, Mark, 322, 387
Zederbaum, A. D., 72, 258
Zeidman, Hillel, 240
Zeitgeist, Der, 515
Zeitlin, Aaron, 258, 308, 414, 497, 586
Zeitlin, Joseph, 271
Zeitlin, Solomon, 307, 584
Zeldin, Michael, 179, 180, 187, 194, 420, 557, 558, 586, 638, 639
Zeldner, Max, 48, 80, 607
Zelenitz, Alan N., 48
Zeligs, Dorothy F., 37, 48, 49, 51, 88, 91, 93, 117, 171, 172, 263, 496

Key to Index

7–9: *Types of Jewish Schools* | 10–17: *Curriculum* | 18–29: *Pedagogy* | 30–40: *The Arts* | 41–44: *Bar/Bat Mitzvah* | 45–53: *The Bible* | 54–59: *Early Childhood Education* | 60–65: *Exceptional Children* | 66–68: *Guidance* | 69–85: *Hebrew* | 86–96: *History* | 97–103: *The Holocaust* | 104–6: *School Library* | 107–18: *Life Cycle of a Jew* | 119–22: *Literature* | 123–42: *Mitzvot/Values and Contemporary Issues* | 143–46: *Textbooks* | 147–58: *The High School* | 159–75: *American Jewry and the Land of Israel* | 176–203: *Day School* | 204–31: *Yiddish Secular Schools* | 232–42: *Higher Education* | 245–62: *Administration* | 263–69: *The Teacher* | 270–73: *The Rabbi and Jewish Education* | 274–86: *Conferences in Jewish Education, 1890–1988* | 287–312: *Men and Women Who Influenced Jewish Education* | 317–34: *Historical Background of Jewish Education* | 335–52: *History of Jewish Education in the United States* | 353–78: *The American Jewish Community* | 379–89: *The Home and Jewish Education* | 390–97: *Adult Education* | 398–404: *The Woman's Role and Jewish Education* | 405–8: *Sephardim and Jewish Education* | 409–16: *Youth and Jewish Education* | 417–21: *Camp* | 422–516: *Local Sources for Jewish Education* | 521–23: *Theology and Jewish Education* | 524–32: *Religious Education* | 533–38: *Philosophy of Jewish Education* | 539–44: *Goals of Jewish Education* | 545–50: *Research in Jewish Education* | 551–58: *Change in Jewish Education* | 559–72: *The Social Sciences and Jewish Education* | 573–96: *Assessment* | 597–99: *The Future of Jewish Education* | 600–602: *Bibliographies of Jewish Education in Other Lands* | 603–17: *Bibliographies of Jewish Education and Related Fields in the United States* | 619–70: *Supplement*

INDEX

Zeligs, Rose, 129
Zelizer, Gerald L., 403
Zeltzer, George M., 359
Zemel, Bernard, 483
Zenner, Walter P., 477, 656
Zenofsky, B., 63
Zerin, Edward, 152, 272, 414, 449
Zevin, Jack, 136
Zhitlowsky, Chaim (Hayyim), 51, 205, 410; literature on, 312
Zibbell, Charles, 359, 360, 371, 374
Zielenger, Ruth, 49, 50, 52, 53
Zigmond, Maurice L., 415
Zilberberg, Israel, 211, 212, 228, 283, 302
Zill, N., 154
Zimand, Esther, 620
Zimmer, Alex, 39
Zion, Joel, 46, 105
Zion, Joel Y., 433
Zionist Organization of America (ZOA), 161
Zionist Youth Council, 163
Zionist Youth Movement, 629
Zipper, I., 216, 225
Zipper, J., 211
Ziprin, Nathan, 194, 385
Zirndorf, Henry, 399
Zisenwine, David, 12, 14, 21, 332, 570
Zlatin, Edward, 397
Zlotowitz, Bernard, 171, 385
Zlotowitz, Bernard M., 620–22, 632, 647
Zlowe, Pauline, 11
Zober, Mark, 665
Zohar, C., 584
Zohn, Harry, 643
Zola, Gary P., 149, 367, 395
Zolotkoff, Leon, 70
Zoreff, Ephraim, 34
Zubin, Joseph, 67
Zucker, Arnold, 566
Zucker, David J., 27
Zuckerman, Baruch, 296
Zuckerman, Ben, 428
Zuckerman, Helen, 33
Zuckerman, Herbert, 90, 250, 542
Zuckerman, I. J., 110
Zuckoff, Aviva, 401, 403, 616
Zukunft, Die, 98, 162, 346
Zumoff, Nachum, 228
Zunland, 429
Zunser, Miriam Shomer, 480
Zuroff, Abraham N., 194
Zussman, Mrs. Morris, 57, 78, 110, 111
Zuto, A., 279
Zweigenhaft, Richard C., 450, 494
Zwerin, Kenneth C., 440
Zwerin, Raymond A., 27, 58, 93, 102, 117, 135, 249, 370, 630
Zwiebel, David, 668
Zyskind, Howard B., 110

www.ingramcontent.com/pod-product-compliance
Lightning Source LLC
Chambersburg PA
CBHW081025240426
43661CB00074B/2799